Bisk Education

CPA REVIEW™

AMERICA'S  71

GET READY TO PASS THE CPA EXAM

SAVE HUNDREDS OF DOLLARS!

See coupons at back of book for special offers on VIDEO and ONLINE exam reviews.

WITH BISK'S ONLINE CPA REVIEW

HUNDREDS OF SIMULATIONS

STEP 4
RELY ON OUR EXPERT GUIDANCE

Bisk Instructor-Led CPA Review Online allows you to interact with professors and fellow exam candidates via email, message boards and chat rooms. With both our instructor-led and self-directed online review, you get direct access to our editorial and technical support staffs. Plus, customer service personnel will be standing by to help with any other questions you might have!

STEP 5
FIRE UP THE CPA EXAM TEST ENGINE

The CPA Exam Test Engine allows you to practice taking an unlimited number of final exams (formatted just like the real thing) before you sit. Multiple-choice questions feature instant on-screen grading – helping track your study performance from start to finish and ensuring your success on the CPA Exam.

ENHANCE YOUR CPA REVIEW WITH:

SIMULATION STRATEGIES VIDEO SERIES

Designed to aid candidates in their final preparation for the exam.

- Available by section or as a full set
- Focuses on simulation drills
- Will help to remove any concerns candidates may have regarding simulation questions

HOT • SPOT DVDs

Choose from topic-specific videos to help with specific areas of difficulty. These DVDs focus on the toughest, most challenging and most frequently tested topics. Each is packed with valuable tips, plus a viewer guide so you can follow along.

CPA REVIEW e-BOOKS

Available now at www.CPAexam.com

CALL NOW 888-CPA-BISK

CPA

Comprehensive Exam Review

Financial Accounting & Reporting

Nathan M. Bisk, JD, CPA

ACKNOWLEDGMENTS

CONTRIBUTING EDITORS

J. Ralph Byington
PhD, CPA
Coastal Carolina University

Anne Keaty
JD
University of Louisiana at Lafayette

Robert L. Monette
JD, CPA
Philadelphia CPA Review

Paul Munter
PhD, CPA
KPMG

Thomas A. Ratcliffe
PhD, CPA
Warren Averett, LLC

C. William Thomas
MBA, PhD, CPA
Baylor University

Mark A. Turner
DBA, CPA, CMA
Texas State University

We wish to thank the **American Institute of Certified Public Accountants** and other accounting organizations for permission to reprint or adapt the following copyrighted © materials:

1. Uniform CPA Examination Questions and Unofficial Answers, Copyright by American Institute of Certified Public Accountants, Inc. All rights reserved. Reprinted with permission.
2. Audit and Accounting Guides, Auditing Procedure Studies, Risk Alerts, Statements of Position, and Code of Professional Conduct, Copyright by American Institute of Certified Public Accountants, Inc. All rights reserved. Reprinted with permission.
3. *The FASB Accounting Standards Codification*™ and Statements of Financial Accounting Concepts, Copyright by the Financial Accounting Standards Board, 401 Merrit 7, P.O. Box 5116, Norwalk, CT 06856, are reprinted with permission.
4. Governmental Accounting Standards Board (GASB) Codification of Governmental Accounting and Financial Reporting Standards, GASB Statements, GASB Concepts Statements, and GASB Interpretations – Copyright by the Governmental Accounting Standards Board, 401 Merritt 7, Norwalk CT 06856-5116. All rights reserved.
5. Statements on Auditing Standards, Statements on Standards for Consulting Services, Statements on Responsibilities in Personal Financial Planning Practice, Statements on Standards for Accounting and Review Services, Statements on Quality Control Standards, Statements on Standards for Attestation Engagements, and Statements on Responsibilities in Tax Practice, Copyright by American Institute of Certified Public Accountants, Inc. All rights reserved. Reprinted with permission.
6. IASB International Accounting Standards Board (IASB) International Reporting Standards (IFRS), International Accounting Standards (IAS) and Interpretations – Copyright © 2010 International Standards Committee Foundation. All rights reserved.

PREFACE

Our texts provide comprehensive, complete coverage of <u>all</u> the topics tested on all <u>four</u> sections of the CPA Examination, including **Financial Accounting & Reporting, Auditing & Attestation, Regulation,** and **Business Environment & Concepts.** Used effectively, our materials will enable you to achieve maximum preparedness for the Uniform CPA Examination. Here is a brief summary of the **features** and **benefits** that our texts will provide for you:

1. **Unique Objective Question Coverage and Unofficial Answers Updated**...We explain ***why*** the multiple-choice alternatives are either right or wrong. Plus, we update the Unofficial Answers to correctly reflect current business and tax laws and AICPA, IAASB, IASB, FASB, GASB, and other authoritative pronouncements.

2. **Complete Coverage**...No extra materials are required to be purchased. We discuss and explain all important AICPA, IAASB, IASB, FASB, GASB, PCAOB, and SEC pronouncements as well as the current tax code and UCC. Our coverage is based on the most recent **AICPA Content Specification Outlines for the Uniform CPA Exam.**

3. **Thousands of Pages of Text**...Including a selection of thousands of recent CPA Examination and exclusive Bisk Education multiple-choice questions, simulations, and written communications with Unofficial Answers from past CPA exams. Solving these questions under test conditions with immediate verification of results instills confidence and reinforces our **SOLUTIONS APPROACH**™ to solving exam questions.

4. **Separate Volumes**...Each volume includes text, multiple-choice questions, and either task-based simulations or written communications with solutions for an entire exam section. There is no need to refer to any other volume.

5. **Detailed Summaries**...We set forth the significant testable concepts in each CPA exam topic. These highly readable summaries are written in complete sentences using an outline format to facilitate rapid and complete comprehension. The summaries isolate and emphasize topics historically tested by the CPA examiners.

6. **Emphasis on "How to Answer Questions" and "How to Take the Exam"**...We teach you to solve free-response and simulations using our unique and famous **SOLUTIONS APPROACH**™.

7. **Discussion and Development of**...AICPA grading procedures, grader orientation strategies, examination confidence, and examination success.

8. **Information on the Computer-Based Exam**...The Uniform CPA Examination is administered at secure testing centers on computers. See Appendix B for a full discussion of this issue. This edition contains up-to-date coverage, including complete coverage of all exam changes.

9. **Research and Writing Skills**...Each volume contains a section to help you brush up on either your research or writing skills for the related section of the CPA exam.

10. **Indexes**...We have included a comprehensively compiled index for easy topic reference in all four sections.

11. **Cross References**...If you do decide to use our other materials, the software uses the same chapter numbering system as the book to allow for easy synchronization between the two formats. Our video programs also are referenced to these same chapters (page B-2).

12. **Practice Examination to Test Your Preparedness**...We include a **Practice Exam** to test your exam preparedness under actual exam conditions. These testing materials are designed to help you identify for concentrated study any exam topic areas in which you remain dangerously deficient after reviewing each of the chapters.

Our materials are designed for the candidate who previously has studied accounting. Therefore, the rate at which a candidate studies and learns (not merely reads) our material will depend on a candidate's background and aptitude. Candidates who have been out of school for a period of years might need more time to study than recent graduates. The point to remember is that <u>all</u> the material you will need to know to pass the exam is here, except for the professional databases available for free through www.aicpa.org to candidates with a *Notice to Schedule.* All you need to do is apply yourself and learn this material at a rate that is appropriate to your situation. **As a final thought,** keep in mind that test confidence gained through disciplined preparation equals success.

OUR EDITORIAL BOARD INCLUDES THE NATION'S LEADING CPAs, ATTORNEYS AND EDUCATORS!

The Only CPA Review Texts Developed By Full-Time Experts.

Publisher and Editor-in-Chief
NATHAN M. BISK, JD, CPA (FL), is both an attorney and certified public accountant in the State of Florida. He is a graduate of Franklin and Marshall College and the University of Florida College of Law. He is a member of the AICPA, Florida Institute of Certified Public Accountants, American Association of Attorney-CPAs, Florida Bar, American Bar Association, and American Business Law Association. His background includes public accounting experience at both Ernst & Young and Arthur Andersen & Co. He is a graduate of the two-year JET program of Merrill Lynch, Pierce, Fenner & Smith, Inc. Mr. Bisk has written and taught accounting, auditing, taxation, and business law programs since 1970.

Contributing Editor
ROBERT L. MONETTE, JD, CPA (PA), is a specialist in continuing professional education and nationally recognized as an expert on the CPA exam. He is an entrepreneur with extensive experience in business acquisitions. His background includes experience in statistical sampling, EDP auditing, financial statement analysis, and taxation. Mr. Monette also has taught CPA Review in Boston, New York, New Jersey, and Philadelphia, where he has helped tens of thousands of candidates become CPAs. He is one of the expert instructors on Bisk Education's CPA Review video series and has appeared as an expert commentator in several Bisk Education CPE programs. Mr. Monette earned an undergraduate degree from Bentley College and a law degree from Villanova University.

Contributing Editor
PAUL MUNTER, PhD, CPA, is currently a partner in the Department of Professional Practice—Audit with KPMG. Previously, he served as KPMG Professor and Chairman of the Department of Accounting at the University of Miami in Coral Gables, Florida. Dr. Munter also served as the Academic Fellow in the Office of the Chief Accountant at the U.S. Securities and Exchange Commission from 2002-2003 where he worked on many of the Commission's Sarbanes-Oxley initiatives and rule-making activities.

Consulting Editor
MORTIMER M. CAPLIN, LLB, JSD, LLD, is a Senior Partner with the Washington, D.C. law firm of Caplin & Drysdale. He is a former IRS Commissioner, and served as a member of the President's Task Force on Taxation. He is a recipient of the Alexander Hamilton Award (the highest award conferred by the Secretary of the Treasury) "for outstanding and unusual leadership during service as U.S. Commissioner of Internal Revenue." For more than 30 years, Mr. Caplin has been in private practice with his present law firm, and has served as Adjunct Professor for the University of Virginia Law School. He is a nationally acclaimed author of numerous articles on tax and corporate matters.

YOU WILL LEARN FROM OUR OUTSTANDING EXPERTS... WITHOUT LEAVING YOUR HOME OR OFFICE.

Consulting Editor
RICHARD M. FELDHEIM, MBA, JD, LLM, CPA (NY), is a New York CPA as well as an attorney in New York and Arizona. He holds a Master's in Tax Law from New York University Law School. Mr. Feldheim is a member of the AICPA, New York State Society of CPAs, American Bar Association, New York State Bar Association, and Association of the Bar of the City of New York. His background includes practice as both a CPA with Price Waterhouse & Co. and as a Senior Partner with the Arizona law firm of Wentworth & Lundin. He has lectured for the AICPA, the Practising Law Institute, Seton Hall University, and the University of Arizona.

Consulting Editor
WILLIAM J. MEURER, CPA (FL), is former Managing Partner for both the overall operations in Central Florida and the Florida Audit and Business Advisory Services sector of Arthur Andersen LLP. During his 35-year career with the firm, Mr. Meurer developed expertise in several industries, including high technology, financial services, real estate, retailing/distribution, manufacturing, hospitality, professional services, and cable television. A graduate of Regis University, Mr. Meurer is a member of both the American Institute of CPAs and the Florida Society of CPAs.

Consulting Editor
THOMAS A. RATCLIFFE, PhD, CPA (TX), serves as the senior accounting and auditing technical advisor for Warren Averett, LLC, as well as advising and consulting for six different associations of CPA firms throughout the country. Dr. Ratcliffe has served as a member of the Auditing Standards Board (ASB) during the development of the clarified and converged auditing and quality control standards. He also has served on the Audit Issues Task Force, the AICPA Council, AICPA Accounting and Review Services Committee, and the Private Company Financial Reporting Committee. Dr. Ratcliffe is the primary contributing author to the AICPA Guide for Compilation and Review Engagements. He is a member of the Auditing Panel for The Journal of Accountancy. Dr. Ratcliffe has received numerous research and teaching awards throughout his career, including the Alabama Society of CPAs Outstanding Professional Educator award, which since was renamed in his honor.

Consulting Editor
C. WILLIAM THOMAS, MBA, PhD, CPA (TX), is J.E. Bush Professor and former chairman of the Department of Accounting and Business Law at Baylor University. He is a member of the AICPA, the Texas Society of CPAs, the Central Texas Chapter of CPAs, and the American Accounting Association, where he is past Chairperson for the Southwestern Regional Audit Section. In addition, he has received recognition for special Audit Education and Curriculum projects he developed for Coopers & Lybrand. His background includes public accounting experience with KPMG Peat Marwick.

FASB CHANGE ALERTS

ASU No. 2012-02, ***Intangibles-Goodwill and Other (Topic 350): Testing Indefinite-Lived Intangible Assets for Impairment —An Amendment of the FASB Accounting Standards Codification*** **(Issued 7/12)**

The amendments in this Update provide that an entity will have the option not to calculate annually the fair value of an indefinite-lived intangible asset if the entity determines (by assessing qualitative factors) that it is not more likely than not (defined as having a likelihood of more than 50 percent) that the asset is impaired. This new guidance improves consistency in impairment testing among long-lived asset categories.

The amendments are effective for annual and interim impairment tests performed for fiscal years beginning after September 15, 2012. Early adoption is permitted. The material in this update is eligible to be tested beginning in the **April-May 2013** exam window.

ASU No. 2012-01, ***Health Care Entities (Topic 954): Continuing Care Retirement Communities—Refundable Advance Fees*** **(Issued 7/12)**

The amendments in this Update clarify that an entity should classify an advance fee as deferred revenue when a continuing care retirement community has a resident contract that provides for payment of the refundable advance fee upon reoccupancy by a subsequent resident, which is limited to the proceeds of reoccupancy. Refundable advance fees that are contingent upon reoccupancy by a subsequent resident but are not limited to the proceeds of reoccupancy should be accounted for and reported as a liability.

For public entities (including conduit bond obligors), the amendments in this Update are effective for fiscal periods beginning after December 15, 2012. For nonpublic entities, the amendments in this Update are effective for fiscal periods beginning after December 15, 2013. Early adoption is permitted. The material in this update is eligible to be tested beginning in the **July-August 2013** exam window.

ASU No. 2011-12, ***Comprehensive Income (Topic 220): Deferral of the Effective Date for Amendments to the Presentation of Reclassifications of Items Out of Accumulated Other Comprehensive Income in ASU Update No. 2011-05—An Amendment of the FASB Accounting Standards Codification*** **(Issued 12/11)**

Stakeholders raised concerns that the new presentation requirements about reclassifications of items out of accumulated other comprehensive income would be difficult for preparers and may add unnecessary complexity to financial statements. In addition it is difficult for some stakeholders to change systems in time to gather the information for the new presentation requirements by the effective date of Update 2011-05.

In order to defer only those changes in Update 2011-05 that relate to the presentation of reclassification adjustments, the paragraphs in this Update supersede certain pending paragraphs in Update 2011-05. The amendments are being made to allow the Board time to redeliberate whether to present on the face of the financial statements the effects of reclassifications out of accumulated other comprehensive income on the components of net income and other comprehensive income for all periods presented. While the Board is considering, entities should continue to report reclassifications out of accumulated other comprehensive income consistent with the presentation requirements in effect before Update 2011-05.

All other requirements in Update 2011-05 are not affected by this Update, including the requirement to report comprehensive income either in a single continuous financial statement or in two separate but consecutive financial statements. Public entities should apply these requirements for fiscal years, and interim periods within those years, beginning after December 15, 2011. Nonpublic entities should begin applying these requirements for fiscal years ending after December 15, 2012, and interim and annual periods thereafter. The material in this update is eligible to be tested beginning in the **July-August 2012** exam window.

ASU No. 2011-11, *Balance Sheet (Topic 210): Disclosures about Offsetting Assets and Liabilities—An Amendment of the FASB Accounting Standards Codification* (Issued 12/11)

An entity is required to apply the amendments for annual reporting periods beginning on or after January 1, 2013, and interim periods within those annual periods. An entity should provide the disclosures required by those amendments retrospectively for all comparative periods presented. The material in this update is eligible to be tested beginning in the **July-August 2013** exam window.

The differences in the offsetting requirements in U.S. GAAP and IFRS account for a significant difference in the amounts presented in statements of financial position prepared in accordance with U.S. GAAP and in the amounts presented in those statements prepared in accordance with IFRS for certain institutions. This Update is the result of a joint project conducted by the FASB and the IASB to enhance disclosures and provide converged disclosures about financial instruments and derivative instruments that are either offset on the statement of financial position or subject to an enforceable master netting arrangement or similar agreement, irrespective of whether they are offset on the statement of financial position. Entities are required to provide both net and gross information for these assets and liabilities in order to enhance comparability between those entities that prepare their financial statements on the basis of U.S. GAAP and those entities that prepare their financial statements on the basis of IFRS.

ASU No. 2011-10, *Property, Plant and Equipment (Topic 360): Derecognition of in Substance Real Estate—A Scope Clarification—An Amendment of the FASB Accounting Standards Codification* (Issued 12/11)

For public entities, the amendments in this Update are effective for fiscal years, and interim periods within those years, beginning on or after June 15, 2012. For nonpublic entities, the amendments are effective for fiscal years ending after December 15, 2013, and interim and annual periods thereafter. Early adoption is permitted. The material in this update is eligible to be tested beginning in the **July-August 2012** exam window.

Under the amendments in this Update, when a parent (reporting entity) ceases to have a controlling financial interest in a subsidiary that is in substance real estate as a result of default on the subsidiary's nonrecourse debt, the reporting entity should apply the guidance in Subtopic 360-20 to determine whether it should derecognize the in substance real estate. Generally, a reporting entity would not satisfy the requirements to derecognize the in substance real estate before the legal transfer of the real estate to the lender and the extinguishment of the related nonrecourse indebtedness.

The amendments in this Update do not eliminate the existing differences in accounting and reporting between U.S. GAAP and IFRS. IFRS guidance on accounting for decreases in ownership of subsidiaries may apply to all subsidiaries, even those that involve in substance real estate.

ASU No. 2011-09, *Compensation—Retirement Benefits—Multiemployer Plans (Topic 715-80): Disclosures about an Employer's Participation in a Multiemployer Plan—An Amendment of the FASB Accounting Standards Codification* (Issued 09/11)

For public entities, the amendments in this Update are effective for annual periods for fiscal years ending after December 15, 2011, with early adoption permitted. For nonpublic entities, the amendments are effective for annual periods for fiscal years ending after December 15, 2012, with early adoption permitted. The amendments should be applied retrospectively for all prior periods presented. The material in this update was eligible to be tested beginning in the **April-May 2012** exam window.

The amendments create greater transparency in financial reporting by requiring additional disclosures about an employer's participation in a multiemployer pension plan. The additional disclosures will increase awareness about the commitments that an employer has made to a multiemployer pension plan and the potential future cash flow implications of an employer's participation in the plan.

Currently, U.S. GAAP differs from IFRS in the recognition and measurement guidance for an employer's participation in multiemployer plans for both plans that provide pension benefits and plans that provide other postretirement benefits. The IASB issued amendments to IAS 19, *Employee Benefits,* on June 16, 2011, which should be retrospectively applied in annual periods beginning on or after January 1, 2013. Among other provisions, the IASB's amendments enhance the disclosures about an employer's participation in a multiemployer plan. The FASB's amendments in this Update are similar, but not identical, to the IASB's disclosure guidance.

ASU No. 2011-08, *Intangibles—Goodwill and Other (Topic 350)—Testing Goodwill for Impairment—An Amendment of the FASB Accounting Standards Codification* (Issued 09/11)

The amendments in this Update are effective for annual and interim goodwill impairment tests performed for fiscal years beginning after December 15, 2011. Early adoption is permitted. The material in this update was eligible to be tested beginning in the **April-May 2012** exam window.

The objective of this Update is to simplify how entities, both public and nonpublic, test goodwill for impairment. The amendments permit an entity to first assess qualitative factors to determine whether it is more likely than not that the fair value of a reporting unit is less than its carrying amount as a basis for determining whether it is necessary to perform the two-step goodwill impairment test described in Topic 350. The more-likely-than-not threshold is defined as having a likelihood of more than 50 percent. An entity is not required to calculate the fair value of a reporting unit unless the entity determines that it is more likely than not that its fair value is less than its carrying amount.

International Accounting Standard 36, *Impairment of Assets,* requires an entity to test goodwill for impairment using a single-step quantitative test performed at the level of a cash-generating unit or group of cash-generating units. The test must be performed at least annually and between annual tests whenever there is an indication of impairment. The Board recognizes that this Update does not advance the convergence of Topic 350 and IAS 36. The Board concluded that such an effort is beyond the scope of this Update and should be done more broadly, by comprehensively addressing these and other differences in impairment guidance between U.S. GAAP and IFRS.

GASB CHANGE ALERTS

GASB 68, *Accounting and Financial Reporting for Pensions,* (Issued 06/12)

The provisions in this statement are effective for fiscal years beginning after June 15, 2014. Earlier application is encouraged. The material in this Update is eligible to be tested beginning in the **January-February 2013** exam window.

Statement 68 replaces the requirements of Statement No. 27, *Accounting for Pensions by State and Local Governmental Employers* and Statement No. 50, *Pension Disclosures,* as they relate to governments that provide pensions through pension plans administered as trusts or similar arrangements that meet certain criteria. Statement 68 requires governments providing defined benefit pensions to recognize their long-term obligation for pension benefits as a liability for the first time, and to more comprehensively and comparably measure the annual costs of pension benefits. The Statement also enhances accountability and transparency through revised and new note disclosures and required supplementary information (RSI).

GASB 67, *Financial Reporting for Pension Plans* (Issued 06/12)

The provisions in this statement are effective for financial statements for periods beginning after June 15, 2013. Earlier application is encouraged. The material in this Update is eligible to be tested beginning in the **January-February 2013** exam window.

This Statement replaces the requirements of Statement No. 25, *Financial Reporting for Defined Benefit Pension Plans and Note Disclosures for Defined Contribution Plans* and Statement 50 as they relate to pension plans that are administered through trusts or similar arrangements meeting certain criteria. The Statement builds upon the existing framework for financial reports of defined benefit pension plans, which includes a statement of fiduciary net position (the amount held in a trust for paying retirement benefits) and a statement of changes in fiduciary net position. Statement 67 enhances note disclosures and RSI for both defined benefit and defined contribution pension plans. Statement 67 also requires the presentation of new information about annual money-weighted rates of return in the notes to the financial statements and in 10-year RSI schedules.

GASB 66, *Technical Corrections-2012—an amendment of GASB Statements No. 10 and No. 62* (Issued 03/12)

The provisions of this Statement are effective for financial statements for periods beginning after December 15, 2012. Earlier application is encouraged. The material in this Update is eligible to be tested beginning in the **October-November 2012** exam window.

This Statement amends Statement No. 10, *Accounting and Financial Reporting for Risk Financing and Related Insurance Issues,* by removing the provision that limits fund-based reporting of an entity's risk financing activities to the general fund and the internal service fund type. As a result, governments should base their decisions about fund type classification on the nature of the activity to be reported, as required in Statement No. 54 and Statement No. 34. This Statement also amends Statement No. 62 by modifying the specific guidance on accounting for (1) operating lease payments that vary from a straight-line basis, (2) the difference between the initial investment (purchase price) and the principal amount of a purchased loan or group of loans, and (3) servicing fees related to mortgage loans that are sold when the stated service fee rate differs significantly from a current (normal) servicing fee rate. These changes clarify how to apply Statement No. 13, and result in guidance that is consistent with the requirements in Statement No. 48, respectively.

GASB 65, *Items Previously Reported as Assets and Liabilities* (Issued 03/12)

The provisions of this Statement are effective for financial statements for periods beginning after December 15, 2012. Earlier application is encouraged. The material in this Update is eligible to be tested beginning in the **October-November 2012** exam window.

This Statement establishes accounting and financial reporting standards that reclassify, as deferred outflows of resources or deferred inflows of resources, certain items that were previously reported as assets and liabilities and recognizes, as outflows of resources or inflows of resources, certain items that were previously reported as assets and liabilities. This Statement amends the financial statement element classification of certain items previously reported as assets and liabilities to be consistent with the definitions in Concepts Statement 4. This Statement also provides other financial reporting guidance related to the impact of the financial statement elements deferred outflows of resources and deferred inflows of resources, such as changes in the determination of the major fund calculations and limiting the use of the term *deferred* in financial statement presentations.

FINANCIAL ACCOUNTING & REPORTING

VOLUME I of IV

TABLE OF CONTENTS

The editors recommend that candidates remain cognizant of the depth of coverage of a topic and their proficiency with it when studying for the exam. Ensure you review the AICPA Content Specification Outline and make informed decisions about your study plan by reading the information in the **Getting Started** and **Exam Preparation Tips** sections of this volume.

QUICK TEXT REFERENCE

The editors strongly recommend that candidates read the entire "Foreword: Getting Started," "Appendix B: Exam Preparation Tips," and "Appendix C: Research Skills" sections of this volume. The references on this page are intended only for conveniently relocating selected parts of the volume. Add items to this list that you find yourself revisiting frequently.

FOREWORD: GETTING STARTED

Step One: Read Section One of the Exam Preparation Tips Appendix

Section One of the **Exam Preparation Tips** material (Appendix B) is designed to familiarize you with the CPA examination. Included in **Exam Preparation Tips** are general comments about the exam, a schedule of exam dates, contact information, attributes required for exam success, and other valuable information.

Step Two: Estimate Your Strengths and Weaknesses in Exam Topics

An "average" candidate is finishing or recently has finished academic training, attended a school in the United States that has a solid accounting curriculum, and received above average grades in accounting and other business courses. An "average" candidate has completed or is completing an "extra" year of accounting classes beyond a bachelor's degree (required in most states). Further, an "average" candidate's native language is English.

Consider your education and work experience and how they differ from the "average" CPA candidate. For instance, if you specialized in tax issues while earning your accounting degree, you probably are exceptionally strong in tax topics, but not so strong in auditing and attestation topics. If you work in the A&A practice of a CPA firm, you probably are particularly strong in many auditing and attestation topics. If you work with corporate governance issues at a public company, you probably are particularly strong in corporate governance topics.

NOTE: If you already have taken one or more CPA exam sections, also analyze your performance on these sections to help you determine how to refine your efforts for the remaining sections.

Step Three: Develop a Personalized Review Plan

Based on your initial estimate of strengths and weaknesses, develop your personalized review plan. The sample review plan on page F-7 has a minimum of 20 hours per week. This level of intensity should increase during the final weeks of your review and peak the final week before the exam. Obviously, if you review for fewer hours per week, your review will take more weeks. Remember, "average" is merely a benchmark. Many candidates are not "average," so adjust your plan accordingly.

A few weeks after you implement your review plan, evaluate how realistic it is. Make adjustments accordingly.

How to Find 20 Hours a Week to Review

The typical CPA candidate is a very busy individual. He or she goes to school and/or works full or part time. Some candidates have additional responsibilities such as a spouse, children, a house to take care of—the list can go on and on. Consequently, your first reaction may be, "I don't have 20 hours a week to devote to review for the CPA exam." We will show you how to find the time that you need to develop your review schedule. Prepare a chart with each column as a day of the week and each line as an hour (or half-hour) of the day.

1. Keeping in mind what you would consider to be a typical week, first mark the time that you know you won't be able to review. For example, mark an "X" in each block which represents time that you normally sleep, have a class, work, or have some other type of commitment. Be realistic.

2. Next, put a "C" in each block that represents commute time, an "M" in each block that represents when you normally eat, and an "E" in each block that represents when you exercise.

3. Now pick one hour each day to relax and give your mind a break. Write "B" in one block for each day. Do not skip this step. By taking a break, you will review more efficiently and effectively.

4. Write "R" in the remaining blocks. Count the "R" blocks. Are there 20? If not, count your "C", "M", and "E" blocks; if needed, these blocks of time can be used to gain additional review time by using Bisk Education CPA Review video programs. For example, watch video lectures a second time when eating or exercising and gain valuable review time each week.

5. If you do not have 20 "R" blocks, you still are able to pass the exam. You have several options: (1) repri-oritize and make a block that has an "X" in it available review time; (2) concentrate on fewer exam sections; or (3) review for more weeks, but fewer hours per week. Many candidates find that the Bisk Education CPA Review video programs make their study time more effective, requiring fewer hours than without these valuable study aids.

How to Allocate Your Weeks

Develop your overall review plan. Starting on page F-7, we outline a sample review plan for one exam section alone. On our web-site (www.cpaexam.com) under the support menu, we also have plans for two concurrent exam sections. The time allocated to each topic is based on the length of the chapter, the difficulty of the material, and how heavily the topic is tested on the exam (refer to the exam content specifications found in the Exam Preparation Tips section). Keep in mind that this plan is for the "average" CPA candidate. You should customize one of these plans based on your comfort with the exam and an estimated level of knowledge in each area tested. Warning: When reviewing, be careful not to fall into the trap of spending too much time on an area that is tested lightly.

The following are number of weeks from the Bisk Education one-exam-section-at-a-time review plans.

Financial Accounting & Reporting (FAR)	8	Regulation (REG)	6
Auditing & Attestation (AUD)	7	Business Environment & Concepts (BEC)	4

Exam Scheduling Strategies

Most candidates likely will split the exam between two or more windows. Sitting for all four exam sections during one exam window is preferable only for candidates who want to pass quickly or who travel far to take the exam. Sitting for one exam section during one exam window is the best means of ensuring a passing score; however it does take a long time.

Sitting for two exam sections during one exam window halves the number of exam windows and takes advantage of the synergy resulting from reviewing more than one exam section in close proximity. By scheduling one exam toward the beginning of a window and the second toward the end of a window, several weeks may separate the two exam sections. Given the AICPA examiner's stated intent to make the BEC exam section integrative, the editors strongly recommend that candidates plan to sit for the BEC section last.

Bear in mind, the sample review plans are rigorous schedules that assume the candidate recently has graduated from a school with a strong accounting program, etc. You may want to sit for only one section during your first window to get a realistic idea of the preparation involved for your circumstances. Alternatively, you could plan to sit for two exam sections during your first window, but have a contingency to cut back if needed. Once you have the experience of one exam section behind you, sitting for two or even three exam sections in the next window will be facilitated by the review habits that you will have developed.

Step Four: Read or Skim the Rest of the Exam Preparation Tips Appendix

In Section Two of the **Exam Preparation Tips** material, we discuss examination strategies. Later sections familiarize you with how the CPA examination is graded and our Solutions Approach™, an approach that helps you to maximize your score. In the last section, we provide the AICPA exam content specifications with corresponding coverage percentages.

Step Five: Integrate Your Review Materials

Optimize the effectiveness of your review plan. Find and read the section that corresponds to the materials that you purchased. (To facilitate easy reference to guidance pertaining to your materials, you may want to strike through the sections corresponding to other materials.)

NOTE: If you purchase software, you also will want to go through all of the software tutorials prior to beginning intensive review. They are each only a few minutes long, but they are loaded with valuable information. There simply is no better way to get the most from the software.

Videos

The Hot•Spot™ and Simulation Strategies video programs are designed to supplement all of the other review materials. FYI: The Hot•Spot™ and Simulation Strategies videos have similar content as the Online and Classic video lectures, but they rarely are exactly the same.

Each of the Hot•Spot™ videos concentrates on a few topics. Use them to help you review the areas that are most troubling for you.

Designed to round out your review program, each of our Simulation Strategies video series concentrates on simulation-answering and exam-taking techniques as opposed to focusing on content.

These videos also contain CPA exam tips and techniques that will help you to learn the material needed to pass the exam. The video titles are listed on page B-2. Also see the video study tips in Step Six.

Online Review or Classic Review

Our most comprehensive review package, the Online Review provides the discipline and learning experience of a classroom setting with the convenience of self-study. Access to the class site lasts for about four months—through the end of the exam window. The Online Review also provides personal attention from a faculty advisor for about seven weeks. The Online Review includes video lectures, weekly assignments, a full set of comprehensive CPA review textbooks, and powerful software review tools not available elsewhere in the market. The Classic Review is similar to the Online Review; obviously, it is without a web-site and live faculty advisor.

These packages are intended for those candidates who want to make sure that they pass the exam the **first** time. By using one of these packages, you are eligible to qualify for Bisk Education's money-back guarantee. Contact a customer representative for details on these packages' components.

Information about integrating materials is available on the web-site for the Online Review and in the materials that ship with the Classic Review. If you have questions after viewing this information, then contact your faculty advisor. (The editors strongly recommend that candidates working full-time take a maximum of two sections of the Online Review or Classic Review concurrently.) The review plans included with these packages generally work better for candidates with this material than the review plans designed for candidates without this material (such as the review plan outlined in this foreword).

Books & CPA Review Software

This self-study review combination is designed expressly for the serious CPA candidate. It is intended for those candidates who want to make sure that they pass the exam the **first** time (or *this* time, if you already have attempted the exam). By using the software, you are eligible to qualify for Bisk Education's money-back guarantee.

How to Use This Material:

In chapters where you are strong:

1. Answer the multiple-choice questions using the Bisk CPA Review Software.

2. Read the subsections of the chapter that correspond to your weak areas.

3. Using the Bisk CPA Review Software, answer the multiple-choice questions that you previously answered incorrectly. If you answer 70% or more correctly, you are ready to move on to the next chapter. If you answer less than 70% correctly, this chapter counts as one in which you are weak.

4. Answer at least one simulation or written communication (if there are any).

In chapters where you are weak:

1. Read the chapter in the book.

2. Using the Bisk CPA Review Software answer the multiple-choice questions for this chapter. If you answer 70% or more of the questions correctly, you are ready to move to the next chapter. (Your weekly review should suffice to raise you to a passing score.) If you get less than 70% of the questions correct, review the subtopics where you are weak. Then answer the questions that you previously answered incorrectly. Allocate more time than you originally budgeted, if necessary.

3. Answer at least one simulation or written communication (if there are any).

Printed Books Alone

This route is available for the candidate who has a strong preference for hard copy; bear in mind, the exam is administered only on computer.

How to Use This Material:

In chapters where you are strong:

1. Answer the multiple-choice questions for that chapter. Using the performance-by-subtopic worksheet provided, analyze your strong and weak areas. This worksheet is after the multiple-choice answers.

2. Read the subsections of the chapter that correspond to your weak subtopics.

3. Answer the multiple-choice questions that you previously answered incorrectly. If you answer 70% or more correctly, you are ready to move on to the next chapter. If you answer less than 70% correctly, this chapter counts as one in which you are weak.

4. Answer at least one simulation or written communication (if there are any).

In chapters where you are weak:

1. Read the chapter in the book.

2. Re-read the subsections of the chapter that correspond to your weak subtopics, if any.

3. Answer the multiple-choice questions and score yourself using the worksheet provided. If you answer 70% or more of the questions correctly, you are ready to move to the next chapter. (Your weekly review should suffice to raise you to a passing score.) If you answer less than 70% of the questions correctly, review the subtopics that are still giving you trouble. Then answer the questions that you previously answered incorrectly. Allocate more time than you originally budgeted, if necessary.

4. Answer at least one simulation or written communication (if there are any).

Step Six: Use These Helpful Hints as You Review

- SKIM THROUGH THE EXAM PREPARATION TIPS.

  Avoid wasting time due to misconceptions by becoming familiar with the exam.

- VISIT THE EXAMINER'S WEB SITE.

  A half-hour each viewing the tutorial and navigating the sample exam can be very valuable. Access to these resources is not available at the physical exam sites.

- INTEGRATE YOUR REVIEW MATERIALS.

  Intersperse reading text, answering questions, and watching video programs to suit your particular learning style as well as your strengths and weaknesses.

- SPEND YOUR WEEKLY REVIEW TIME EFFECTIVELY. DURING EACH WEEKLY REVIEW:

  Answer the multiple-choice questions that you previously answered incorrectly or merely guessed correctly. Remember, you moved on to the next chapter with a score that might be as low as 70%. You need to increase that score to a **minimum** of 75% during your weekly review activities to expect to pass the exam. How high do you need to increase it? A cushion to assure that you pass the exam is preferable. The size of that cushion depends on your personal tolerance for risk.

  Go through your flashcards or notes.

  Answer at least one written communication (BEC) or one research simulation and one other type of simulation (FAR, AUD, and REG). Do not wait until the end of your review to attempt a research simulation, another type of simulation, or a written communication.

- DO NOT MARK THE ANSWERS IN THE BOOK OR VIEWER GUIDES.

  Do not circle the answer to questions in the book. You should work every multiple-choice question at least twice and you do not want to influence later answers by knowing how you previously answered.

  If you are at all weak in a topic, avoid marking the answer to questions in the viewer guide.

  Date your answer sheets to facilitate tracking your progress.

- NOTE QUESTIONS THAT YOU ANSWER INCORRECTLY OR GUESS CORRECTLY.

  This way you know to answer these questions again at a later time.

- MAKE FLASHCARDS OR TAKE NOTES AS YOU REVIEW

  Make flashcards for topics that are tested heavily on the exam or that are giving you trouble. By making your own flashcards, you learn during their creation plus you can tailor them to your individual learning style and problem areas. You will find these very useful for weekly reviews and your final review. Replace flashcards of information you know with new material as you progress through your review plan. Keep flashcards handy and review them when you are waiting in line or on hold. This will turn nonproductive time into valuable review time. Review your complete set during the last two weeks before the exam.

  Make notes and/or highlight when you read the chapters in the book. When possible, make notes as you listen to the lectures. You will find these notes useful for weekly reviews and your final review.

- EFFECTIVELY USE THE VIDEO LECTURES

  Watch video lectures in an environment without distractions—especially the first time. Be prepared to take notes and answer questions just as if you were attending a live class. Frequently, the instructors will have you stop the program to work a question on your own. This means a 2-hour program may take 2½ hours or more to view.

  Consider playing select lectures or portions of lectures repeatedly when you are exercising, getting ready for school or work, folding laundry, etc. Repetition will help you to memorize and retain key concepts. It also will reinforce your reading and question drill. The more times that you hear a lecture, the more familiar you will become with the material and the easier it will be for you to recall it during the exam.

Step Seven: Implement Your Review Plan

This is it! You are primed and ready. You have decided which tools will work best for you and you know how to use them. As you implement your personalized review plan, keep yourself focused. Your goal is to obtain a score of 75 or better on each section and, thus, pass the CPA exam. Therefore, you should concentrate on learning new material and reviewing old material only to the extent that it helps you reach this goal. Also, keep in mind that now is not the time to hone your procrastination skills. Utilize the personalized review plan that you developed in step three so that you do not fall behind schedule. Adjust it when necessary if you need more time in one chapter or less time in another. Refer to the AICPA content specification outlines to make sure that the adjustment is warranted. Above all else, remember that passing the exam is an **attainable** goal. Good luck!

The editors strongly recommend that candidates develop personalized training plans. The following training plan is outlined for candidates to modify. The time allocated to each topic was based on the length of the chapter, the difficulty of the material, and percentages the topic is tested on the exam (refer to the exam content specifications found in Appendix B). You should **customize this plan** based on your prior level of knowledge in each area.

FAR Sample Training Plan (1 exam section)

		Hours
Week 1:	Read *Getting Started* and *Exam Preparation Tips* sections	1
	Chapter 1—U.S. GAAP Concepts & Framework	7
	Chapter 2—Cash, Receivables & Investments	8
	Chapter 3—Inventory	4
Week 2:	Chapter 4—Property, Plant & Equipment	5
	Chapter 5—Intangibles, R&D, Software & Other Assets	4
	Chapter 6—Bonds	5
	Chapter 7—Liabilities	6
Week 3:	Weekly review of weeks 1 - 2	2
	Chapter 8—Leases	5
	Chapter 9—Postemployment Benefits	5
	Chapter 10—Owners' Equity	8
Week 4:	Weekly review of weeks 1 - 3	2
	Chapter 11—Revenue & Expense Recognition	6
	Chapter 12—Reporting the Results of Operations	8
	Chapter 13—Reporting: Special Areas	4
Week 5:	Weekly review of weeks 1 - 4	2
	Chapter 13—Reporting: Special Areas	2
	Chapter 14—Accounting for Income Taxes	7
	Chapter 15—Statement of Cash Flows	5
	Chapter 16—Business Combinations and Consolidations	4
Week 6:	Weekly review of weeks 1 - 5	2
	Chapter 16—Business Combinations and Consolidations	4
	Chapter 17—IFRS & SEC Reporting	8
	Chapter 18—Government Funds & Transactions	6
Week 7:	Weekly review of weeks 1 - 6	4
	Chapter 19—Governmental Financial Reporting	8
	Chapter 20—Nonprofit Accounting	8
Week 8:	Review areas in which you still feel weakest	8
	Take Practice Exam under exam conditions (see page A-1)	4
	Appendix D Research Simulations (see page D-1)	3
	Do final review and check for an updating supplement	5

Updating Supplements

Bisk Education's updating supplements are small publications available from either customer representatives or our CPA Review website (http://www.cpaexam.com/content/support.asp).

The editors recommend checking the website for new supplements a month and again a week before your exam.

Version 42 (and higher) updating supplements are appropriate for candidates with the 42nd edition. Information from earlier supplements (for instance, Version 41.2) is incorporated into this edition.

Supplements are issued no more frequently than every three months. Supplements are not necessarily issued every three months; supplements are issued only as information appropriate for supplements becomes available.

CHAPTER 1

U.S. GAAP CONCEPTS & FRAMEWORK

CHAPTER 1

U.S. GAAP CONCEPTS & FRAMEWORK

I. Accounting Environment

A. Financial Accounting

The American Institute of Certified Public Accountants (AICPA) defines accountancy as "the art of recording, classifying, and summarizing in a significant manner and in terms of money, transactions and events which are, in part at least, of financial character, and interpreting the results thereof."

External users such as shareholders and creditors need to assess the amount, timing, and uncertainty of future net cash inflows to the entity in order to form opinions about the returns that they expect from an investment. Since most external users cannot require entities to provide information directly to them, they must rely upon general purpose financial statements. To be considered useful for decision making, financial information must be both relevant and faithfully representational. The usefulness is further enhanced if it is also comparable, verifiable, timely, and understandable.

Financial accounting reports and statements are usually created for a specific period of time, and are generally historical in nature. These statements have predictive value to those who wish to make financial decisions or investments in a company, and include the reporting requirements of profitability, liquidity, solvency and stability. Managerial accounting reports are prepared exclusively for managers within the organization. Examples of managerial reports include: sales forecasts; budget analysis; feasibility studies; and detailed product information. These reports are often not in monetary form.

B. Underlying Environmental Assumptions

Accounting operates in an environment almost as varied as the many types of entities which accounting serves. To provide a basis for comparison, it has been necessary to formulate certain underlying environmental assumptions on which financial accounting theory is based. The most important of these assumptions are as follows:

1. **Economic Entity** In order to properly report those economic events affecting an entity, the specific economic entity must be defined and separated from other entities. A distinction is also made between a business concern and its owners.

2. **Going Concern** The business is not expected to liquidate in the near future. Where there is a reasonable expectation of an upcoming liquidation, the going concern assumption is abandoned. Liquidation accounting, characterized by the use of net realizable values rather than historical costs, is then employed.

3. **Unit-of-Measure** Monetary units are used for the measurement and reporting of economic activity. Costs incurred at different points in time are intermingled in the accounts and, thus, it must be assumed that the purchasing power of the dollar remains constant over time. Inflation makes this assumption questionable. Enterprises are encouraged to issue voluntary supplementary reports based on current costs and dollars of constant purchasing power. This information is furnished in addition to the usual historical cost financial statements.

4. **Periodicity** This assumption recognizes the necessity of providing financial accounting information on a periodic, timely basis, so that it is useful in decision making.

C. Basic Accounting Principles

Based upon these underlying environmental assumptions, a set of basic accounting principles has evolved.

1. **Measurement** Assets acquired, as well as liabilities incurred by an enterprise, are recorded at cost. Cost is generally defined as the cash equivalent amount that would be paid in an arm's-length transaction. When costs benefit more than one period, they are apportioned among the periods benefited through depreciation or amortization. Acquisition cost is considered a reliable basis upon which to account for assets and liabilities of a company. Historical cost has an advantage over other valuations—it is thought to be reliable. However, fair value information may be more useful than historical cost for certain types of assets and liabilities and in certain industries.

2. **Revenue Recognition** Revenue is generally recognized when both of the following conditions are met:

   a. The earnings process is complete or virtually complete.

   b. An exchange has taken place. This implies that revenues are usually recognized at the point of sale. Under certain conditions, however, revenue recognition takes place on a different basis, such as a percentage of completion, production, installment, or cost recovery basis.

3. **Matching** For income to be stated fairly, all expenses incurred in generating the revenues for a period must be recognized in that same period.

4. **Objectivity** Accounting data should be both (a) objectively determined and (b) verifiable. While this does not preclude the use of estimates, they must be verifiable in the sense that an independent, knowledgeable person would find such estimates reasonable.

5. **Materiality** The relative importance of data, the cost-benefit relationship of additional accuracy, and the possible confusion resulting from the use of too much detail are considerations that must be weighed in determining the materiality of accounting information. When an item is immaterial, good accounting theory can be abandoned.

6. **Consistency** The usefulness of accounting information is enhanced when the information is presented in a manner consistent with that used in prior periods. This provides for interperiod comparability and the identification of trends. Consistency in the application of accounting principles also prevents income manipulation by management.

7. **Full Disclosure** Financial statements should be presented in a manner that will reasonably assure complete and understandable communication of all relevant accounting information useful for decision making. When the nature of relevant information is such that it cannot appear in the accounts, this principle dictates that such relevant information be included in the accompanying notes to the financial statements.

8. **Conservatism** Where use of the most appropriate accounting treatment is uncertain, when making estimates or when data conflicts, the favored accounting treatment should be that which understates rather than overstates income or net assets. Conservatism, however, should not be used in place of a more conceptually sound approach when the difference in results is of a material nature.

D. **Accounting Model**
The aforementioned principles and assumptions are implemented through the use of the basic accounting model, upon which the accounting for most profit-oriented entities is based. This model is composed of three main sub-models, each focusing on a different aspect of the economic activities of an enterprise.

1. **Financial Position** Assets = Liabilities + Owners' equity. The financial position sub-model purports to present the economic resources, the economic obligations, and the resulting residual interest in the assets of the entity to its owners. This information is reported by means of a balance sheet.

2. **Results of Operations** Revenues – Expenses = Net income. The purpose of the results of operations sub-model is to report on the relative success of the profit-directed activities of an entity. The revenues obtained through the sale of goods and services are compared to the expenses incurred in providing those goods and services. The resulting difference is the operating income or loss for the period. To arrive at net income, gains, losses, and the effect of accounting changes must be incorporated into the sub-model. The results of operations sub-model is formally represented by the income statement and the statement of changes in comprehensive income.

3. **Statement of Cash Flows** Cash flows from operating activities +(–) Cash flows from investing activities +(–) Cash flows from financing activities = Change in cash. The objective of this sub-model is to provide information about the cash receipts and cash payments of an entity during the period. The statement of cash flows reports the net cash provided or used by operating, investing, and financing activities, and the aggregate effect of those flows on cash during the period.

E. **Accounting Policies**
All significant accounting policies followed by an enterprise should be disclosed in its financial statements. No specific disclosure format is required. A separate note, or a summary preceding the notes entitled *Summary of Significant Accounting Policies* is preferred. The accounting policy disclosures should identify and describe the principles and methods that materially affect the financial position and operations. Prospective financial statements should not only include a summary of significant policies, but they should also include a summary of significant assumptions.

1. **Policy Choices** Disclosure should include policies involving a choice of alternative acceptable policies, policies peculiar to that particular industry, and unusual applications of acceptable principles.

2. **Examples** Examples of disclosure requirements include: criteria for determining which investments are treated as cash equivalent; basis of accounting for loans and trade receivables; method used in determining the lower-of-cost for fair value of nonmortgage loans held for sale; the method of recognizing interest income on loan and trade receivables; depreciation methods; methods of pricing inventory; methods of recognizing profit on long-term construction contracts; and basis of consolidation.

3. **No Duplication of Information** Financial statement disclosure of accounting policies should **not** duplicate details presented elsewhere as part of the financial statements, such as composition of inventories or plant assets, depreciation expense, and maturity dates of long-term debt.

F. **Responsibility for Financial Statements**
Financial statements are the responsibility of an organization's management. An organization's board of directors and senior management generally set the code of conduct for the organization. This code of conduct is often referred to as the company's "ethic." This ethic is the standard by which all other employees tend to conduct themselves.

1. **Entity's Objectives** An entity's objectives and the way they are achieved are based on preferences, value judgments and management styles. Those preferences and value judgments, which are translated into standards of behavior, reflect management's integrity and its commitment to ethical values.

2. **Integrity** Integrity is a prerequisite for ethical behavior in all aspects of an entity's activities. The National Commission on Fraudulent Financial Reporting, called the Treadway Commission (the Commission) undertook a study to identify causal factors that can lead to fraudulent financial reporting and to develop recommendations to reduce its incidence. As the Treadway Commission reported, "A strong corporate ethical climate at all levels is vital to the well-being of the corporation, all of its constituencies, and the public at large. Such a climate contributes importantly to the effectiveness of company policies and control systems, and helps influence behavior that is not subject to even the most elaborate system of controls."

3. **Establishing Ethical Values** Establishing ethical values is often difficult because of the need to consider the concerns of several parties. Top management's values must balance the concerns of the enterprise, its employees, suppliers, customers, competitors, and the public. Balancing those concerns can be a complex and frustrating effort because interests are often at odds. Managers of well-run enterprises have increasingly accepted the view that "ethics pays" (i.e. that ethical behavior is good business). Positive and negative examples abound. The well-publicized handling by a pharmaceutical company of a crisis involving tampering with one of its major products was both sound ethics and good business. The impact on customer relations and stock prices of slowly leaked bad news, such as profit shortfalls or illegal acts, generally is worse than if full disclosures are made as quickly as possible.

4. **Corporate Culture** Ethical behavior and management integrity are a product of the "corporate culture." Corporate culture includes ethical and behavioral standards, how they are communicated and how they are reinforced in practice. Official policies specify what management wants to happen. Corporate culture determines what actually happens, and which roles are obeyed, bent or ignored. Top management—starting with the CEO—plays a key role in determining the corporate culture. The CEO usually is the dominant personality in the organization, and individually often sets its ethical tone.

II. Statement of Financial Position—Balance Sheet

A. Description

The balance sheet presents the assets, liabilities, and owners' equity of an entity at a specific point in time, measured in conformity with generally accepted accounting principles (GAAP).

B. Format

The formats most commonly used are the account format and the report format.

Exhibit 1 ▸ Balance Sheet Formats (assumed amounts)

Account Format		Report Format	
Assets	Liabilities	Assets	$50,000
$50,000	$35,000		
		Liabilities	$35,000
	Owners' equity		
	$15,000	Owners' equity	$15,000

1. **Assets** Assets are probable future economic benefits obtained or controlled by a particular entity as a result of past transactions or events. Assets are classified in their order of liquidity and intended use.

   a. Current assets are assets or resources that are reasonably expected to be converted into cash, sold or consumed during the normal operating cycle of the business or one year, whichever is longer. An operating cycle is the average time intervening between the acquisition of materials or services and the final cash realization.

   b. Investments are assets held for control, appreciation, regular income, or a combination of these. Examples include stocks, bonds, subsidiaries, land held as a future plant site, and the cash surrender value of life insurance. Also included are special purpose funds such as bond sinking funds and plant expansion funds.

   c. Operational assets are assets that are directly used by the enterprise in generating revenues.

   d. Valuation accounts are reductions or increases in an asset account to reflect adjustments beyond the historical cost or carrying amount of the asset. Valuation accounts are part of the related asset; they are neither assets nor liabilities in their own right.

2. **Liabilities** Liabilities are probable future sacrifices of economic benefits arising from present obligations of a particular entity to transfer assets or provide services to other entities in the future as a result of past transactions or events. Liabilities are classified according to their due date as either current or long-term.

   a. Current liabilities are obligations whose liquidation is expected to require the use of existing current assets or the creation of other current liabilities.

   b. Long-term liabilities are obligations not requiring the use of existing current assets or the creation of current liabilities for their extinguishment.

   c. Valuation accounts may increase or decrease the carrying amount of a liability. Examples include the premium or discount on outstanding bonds payable. Valuation accounts are part of the related liability; they are neither assets nor liabilities in their own right.

3. **Owners' Equity** Owners' equity is the residual interest in the assets of an entity that remains after deducting its liabilities.

   a. An equity interest derives its value from being a potential source of distribution of cash or other assets to its owner. In case of liquidation, all liabilities must be satisfied first.

      (1) Equity is originally created by the initial investment of the enterprise owners. Subsequent investments by the owners, or the admission of new owners, increase equity, while distributions to owners decrease it.

      (2) Equity is also changed as a result of the operating activities of the enterprise and other events and circumstances affecting it. This combined effect constitutes comprehensive income.

   b. Proprietorship's equity consists of a single proprietor's equity account.

   c. Partnership's equity consists of one capital account for each partner. Each individual partner's capital account records her/his investment and subsequent allocations of income and withdrawals.

d. Corporation's equity consists of several accounts that are segregated according to source.

(1) Par or stated value represents minimum legal required capital as determined by articles of incorporation and state law. Additional paid-in capital reflects the amount received in excess of the par or stated value of the stock at the time of issuance.

(2) Retained earnings are accumulated earnings less losses and dividends. They represent resources retained by the entity for use in expansion and growth.

(3) Comprehensive income is defined as the change in equity (net assets) of a business entity during a period from transactions and other events and circumstances from non-owner sources. It includes all changes in equity during a period except those resulting from investments by owners and distributions to owners. Other comprehensive income includes revenues, expenses, gains, and losses that under GAAP are included in comprehensive income but excluded from net income.

Accumulated other comprehensive income (OCI) must be adjusted for unrealized gains and losses on available-for-sale securities. Also, certain foreign currency translation adjustments and adjustments from recognizing certain additional pension liabilities must be reported in OCI.

e. The net assets of a nonprofit organization represent a residual, but are not an ownership interest.

4. **Off-Balance-Sheet Risk** Off-balance-sheet risk is the risk of accounting loss from a financial instrument that exceeds the amount recognized for the instrument in the balance sheet. Examples include standby loan commitments written, options, letters of credit, and noncancelable operating leases with future minimum lease commitments.

Recent pronouncements attempt to eliminate off-balance-sheet risk by requiring that more risks are reflected within the balance sheet. Where not directly reflected on the balance sheet, there are increased disclosure (note) requirements. In addition, companies are now required to provide off-balance-sheet related information in their management discussion and analysis sections. As such they must disclose all contractual agreements in a tabular format and all contingent liabilities and commitments in either a textual or tabular format.

C. Valuation

1. Assets

a. Historical cost is the acquisition cost less depreciation or amortization to date. While this method of valuation is both verifiable and systematic, it often fails to reflect either the current value of the asset or changes due to the purchasing power of the dollar.

b. Market value is the price that would be received to sell an asset or paid to transfer a liability in an orderly transaction between market participants at the measurement date.

c. Replacement cost attempts to value assets on the basis of their current replacement cost. Current replacement cost is defined as the price of a new, similar item after allowance for use and depreciation. It is the amount of cash or its equivalent that would have to be paid if the same or equivalent assets were acquired currently. This method is used in the primary financial statements only in certain cases where the utility of inventory items has diminished.

d. Price-level adjusted historical cost adjusted to reflect changes in the general purchasing power of the dollar.

e. Discounted cash flows value assets in terms of the present value of the future benefits associated with the ownership of the asset. Notes receivable and bond investments are valued at present value upon acquisition.

2. **Liabilities** Liabilities are valued at their current debt equivalent. For long-term liabilities this implies discounting to their present value the future sums required to satisfy the liability. Due to materiality considerations, short-term liabilities are usually presented at their face amount.

3. **Owners' Equity** The valuation of owners' equity depends on the amounts presented for assets and liabilities.

D. Fair Value Measurements

1. **Background** Historical cost has been the primary basis for recording assets and liabilities for many years. Its advantage over other measurement methods was objectivity. However, recent standards have been developed that require periodic impairment assessment of value when evidence indicates that an item's current cost might be less than its historical cost.

2. **Fair Value Measurement** SFAS No. 157 was issued in 2006 and has been amended several times since being codified as Topic 820 in the *FASB Accounting Standards Codification.* ASU 2011-04: *Fair Value Measurement* (Topic 820) was issued in May 2011 as a result of the work of the FASB and IASB to align their guidance with respect to fair value measurements and disclosures. (The IASB issued IFRS 13, *Fair Value Measurement.*) These standards do not require additional fair value measurements and are not intended to establish valuation standards or affect valuation practices outside of financial reporting.

3. **Definition** Fair value is a market-based (not an entity-based) measurement. Observable market transactions or market information may or may not be available; however, the objective is the same: to estimate the price that would be received to sell an asset or paid to transfer a liability in an orderly transaction between market participants at the measurement date (that is, an *exit* price at the measurement date from the perspective of a market participant that holds the asset or owes the liability). The term "orderly transaction" assumes that the item has been exposed to the marketplace prior to the measurement date for a reasonable period of time. In other words, it is not a forced transaction.

   The principal (or most advantageous) market is determined from the standpoint of the entity that holds the asset or liability, and requires the entity to consider the market in which it conducts its highest volume or level of activity. If a price for an identical asset or liability is not observable, fair value can be measured using another valuation technique that maximizes the use of relevant observable inputs and minimizes the use of unobservable inputs. An entity's intention to hold an asset or to settle a liability is not relevant when measuring fair value.

4. **Initial Measurement** When as asset is acquired or a liability assumed, the transaction price is the price paid to acquire the asset or received to assume the liability (an entry price). The fair value of the asset or liability is the price that would be received to sell the asset or paid to transfer the liability (an exit price). In many cases, the transaction price will equal the fair value. When determining whether the transaction price equals the fair value, an entity shall consider factors specific to the transaction and to the asset or liability. For example, the transaction price might not represent fair value if the transaction is between related parties, takes place under duress, the transaction did not occur in the principal (i.e., most advantageous) market, etc. In *determining* the most advantageous market, transaction costs must be netted against the price of the asset; however, the fair value price itself is **not** adjusted for transaction costs.

5. **The Transaction** It is assumed that the asset or liability is exchanged in an orderly transaction between market participants under current market conditions. Additionally, it is assumed that the transaction takes place in either the principal market or in the most advantageous market if a principal market does not exist. In the absence of evidence to the contrary, the market in which the entity would normally enter into for all transactions is deemed to be the principal market. The price in that market is the fair value measurement of the asset or liability.

   When measuring the fair value of an asset or liability, an entity must use the same assumptions that other market participants would use. When defining that group of participants, an entity shall identify characteristics that distinguish the participants, considering factors specific to all of the following: the asset or liability; the principal market; and market participants with whom the entity would enter into a transaction in that principal market. Market participants are: independent of each other; knowledgeable and sufficiently informed about the asset or liability and the transaction; and able and willing (not forced) to enter into a transaction for the asset or liability.

6. **Highest and Best Use** A fair value measurement of a nonfinancial asset only considers the ability to generate economic benefits by using the asset in its highest and best use; the use of the asset that is physically possible, legally permissible, and financially feasible at the measurement date. Current use is assumed to be the highest and best use unless market or other factors suggest that a different use by market participants would maximize the value of the asset. (The concepts of highest and best use and valuation premise concepts are not relevant when measuring the fair value of financial assets or financial liabilities.)

   a. **Application to Nonfinancial Assets** The highest and best use of a nonfinancial asset established the valuation premise used to measure fair value of an asset, as follows.

      (1) If the highest and best use is in combination with other assets or with other assets and liabilities, then the fair value is the price what would be received to sell the asset assuming that the asset would be used with other assets or with other assets and liabilities.

      (2) If the highest and best use is to use it on a standalone basis, the fair value is the price that would be received to sell the asset to market participants that would use the asset on a standalone basis.

   b. **Application to Liabilities and Instruments Included Within Shareholders' Equity**

      (1) A fair value measurement assumes that a financial or nonfinancial liability or an instrument classified in shareholders' equity is transferred to a market participant at the measurement date and, and assumes that a liability or an instrument classified in a reporting entity's shareholders' equity would remain outstanding and would not be settled, cancelled or otherwise extinguished on the measurement date.

      (2) Nonperformance risk (i.e., the risk that an entity will not fulfill an obligation) includes, but is not limited to, the entity's own credit risk. Fair value of a liability reflects the effect of nonperformance, which is assumed to be the same before and after the transfer of the liability.

(3) The effect of a restriction that prevents the transfer of a liability or an instrument classified in a reporting entity's shareholders' equity is either implicitly or explicitly included in the other inputs to the fair value measurement, and an entity shall not include a separate component to adjust for this restriction when measuring fair value.

c. Application to Financial Assets and Financial Liabilities With Offsetting Positions If a reporting entity manages a group of financial assets or financial liabilities on the basis of its net exposure to either market risks that are substantially the same (i.e., interest rate risk, currency risk, or other price risk) or counterparty credit risks, then the entity may apply an exception to the requirements of Topic 820, and is allowed to measure fair values for such groups of financial assets and financial liabilities using a price that would be received or paid to sell or transfer the net position of the groups in an orderly transaction between market participants at the measurement date under current market conditions (i.e., on the basis of the reporting entity's net risk of exposure, not gross risk).

7. Valuation Techniques The technique(s) used shall be the most appropriate in the circumstance and for which sufficient data are available to measure fair value, maximize the use of relevant observable inputs and minimize the use of unobservable inputs. A single valuation may be appropriate in some cases. For other situations, a weighted, multiple valuation technique might be more appropriate.

The valuation techniques used to measure fair value shall be consistently applied. A change in a valuation technique may be reasonable if any of the following events occur: new markets develop; new information becomes available; information previously used is no longer available; valuation techniques improve; and/or market conditions change. Revisions resulting from a change in the valuation technique shall be accounted for as a *change in accounting estimate*.

a. Inputs

(1) Valuation techniques shall maximize the use of relevant observable inputs and minimize the use of unobservable inputs. Markets with observable inputs include: exchange markets, dealer markets, brokered markets, and principal-to-principal markets. If there is a quoted price in an active market (i.e., a Level 1 input) for an asset or liability, an entity shall use that quoted price without adjustment when measuring fair value. Premiums or discounts may be applied in a fair value measurement to the extent that they are consistent with the unit of account and market participants would consider them in a transaction for the asset or liability. However, adjustments commonly referred to as blockage factors are prohibited to all three levels of the fair value hierarchy.

(2) If an asset or liability has a bid price and an ask price, the price within the bid-ask spread that is most representative of fair value in the circumstances shall be used to measure fair value regardless of where the input is categorized within the fair value hierarchy. This does not preclude the use of mid-market pricing or other pricing conventions as a practical expedient for fair value measurement in a bid-ask spread.

b. **Valuation Technique Approaches**

(1) **Market Approach** The market approach uses prices and other relevant information generated by market transactions involving identical or comparable assets or liabilities.

(2) **Income Approach** The income approach uses valuation techniques to convert future amounts to a single present amount. The measurement is based on the value indicated by current market expectations about those future amounts. Valuation techniques include: present value; option-pricing models (such as Black-Scholes-Merton); and the multiperiod excess earnings method.

(3) **Cost Approach** The cost approach is based on the amount that currently would be required to replace the service capacity of an asset, often referred to as the current replacement cost. From the perspective of a market seller, the price that would be received for the asset is based on the cost to a market buyer to acquire or construct a substitute asset of comparable use, adjusted for obsolescence. (A buyer would not pay more for an asset than it would cost to replace the service capacity of that asset.) Oftentimes, the current replacement cost method is used to estimate fair value.

c. **Fair Value Hierarchy** Inputs to valuation technique are categorized into three levels. Highest priority is given to quoted prices (unadjusted) in active markets for identical assets or liabilities (Level 1 inputs) and the lowest priority to unobservable inputs (Level 3 inputs). Valuation techniques used need to maximize the use of observable inputs and minimize the use of unobservable inputs.

(1) **Level 1 Inputs** Are quoted prices (unadjusted) in active markets for identical assets or liabilities that can be accessed on the measurement date by the reporting entity. A quoted active market price provides the most reliable evidence of fair value and shall be used without adjustment, except for certain circumstances.

(2) **Level 2 Inputs** Are inputs other than quoted prices included within Level 1 that are observable for the asset or liability, either directly or indirectly. Level 2 inputs include: quoted prices for similar (not identical) assets or liabilities in active markets; quoted prices for identical or similar assets or liabilities in nonactive markets; interest rates and yield curves observable at commonly quoted intervals; implied volatilities; and credit spreads. Adjustments to Level 2 inputs depend on the condition and location of the asset; the extent to which inputs relate to items that are comparable to the asset or liability; and the volume or level of activity in the market within which the inputs are observed.

(3) **Level 3 Inputs** Are unobservable inputs for the asset or liability. These are most often used where there is little, if any, market activity for the asset or liability at the measurement date. An entity needs to develop unobservable inputs using the best information available, which might include using the entity's own data. That data should be adjusted if other market participants would use different data or if there is something unique in the entities' data not available to other market participants. An entity is required to disclose quantitative information about the unobserved inputs used in the measurements.

8. **Disclosures** Reporting entities are required to expand the disclosures for fair value to provide information related to which assets and/or liabilities are measured at fair value, the methods and assumptions used in measuring fair values, and the effect of fair value measurements on reported income. Within the fair value hierarchy, the farther down the chain reporting entities go to determine fair value measurements, the higher up the chain they go for the disclosures required in the financial statement notes. There is an element of fluidity that progresses as the FASB continues to modify and raise-the-bar with required disclosures.

A reporting entity shall disclose information that helps users of its financial statements to assess assets and liabilities that are measured at fair value on a recurring or nonrecurring basis, the valuation techniques and the inputs used to develop those measurements.

a. **Additional Considerations** For recurring fair value measurements using significant unobservable inputs (Level 3), the effect of the measurements on earnings (or change in net assets) or other comprehensive income for the period. An entity shall consider all of the following:

(1) The level of detail necessary to satisfy the disclosure requirements

(2) How much emphasis to place on each of the various requirements

(3) How much aggregation or disaggregation to undertake

(4) Whether users of financial statements need additional information to evaluate the quantitative information disclosed.

b. **Minimum Disclosures** A reporting entity shall disclose, at a minimum, the following:

(1) For recurring and nonrecurring fair value measurements: the fair value measurement at the end of the reporting period, and for nonrecurring fair value measurements, the reasons for the measurement; and the level of the fair value hierarchy within which the fair value measurements are categorized in their entirety.

(2) For assets and liabilities held at the end of the reporting period that are measured at fair value on a recurring basis, the amounts of any transfers between Level 1 and Level 2 of the fair value hierarchy, the reasons for those transfers, and the reporting entity's policy for determining when transfers between levels are deemed to have occurred. Transfers into each level shall be disclosed and discussed separately from transfers out of each level.

(3) For recurring and nonrecurring Level 2 and Level 3 fair value measurements, a description of the valuation technique(s) and the inputs used in the fair value measurement. If there has been a change in valuation technique (for example, changing from a market approach to an income approach), the reporting entity shall disclose that change and the reason(s) for making it.

(4) For Level 3 fair value measurements: a description of the valuation processes used by the reporting entity; a qualitative narrative description of the sensitivity of the fair value measurement to changes in unobservable inputs and the interrelationships between those unobservable inputs, if any; and quantitative information about significant unobservable inputs used for all Level 3 measurements.

(5) For recurring Level 3 fair value measurements, a reconciliation from the opening balances to the closing balances, disclosing separately changes during the period attributable to the following:

(a) Total gains or losses for the period in earnings (or changes in net assets) and the line item(s) in the statement of income (or activities) in which those gains or losses are recognized

(b) Total gains or losses for the period recognized in other comprehensive income, and the line item(s) in other comprehensive income in which those gains or losses are recognized

(c) Purchases, sales, issues, and settlements (each of those types of changes disclosed separately)

(d) The amounts of any transfers into or out of Level 3 of the fair value hierarchy, the reasons for those transfers, and the reporting entity's policy for determining when transfers between levels are deemed to have occurred. Transfers into Level 3 shall be disclosed and discussed separately from significant transfers out of Level 3.

(6) For recurring Level 3 fair value measurements: the amount of the total gains or losses for the period included in earnings (or changes in net assets) that is attributable to the change in unrealized gains or losses relating to those assets and liabilities still held at the end of the reporting period, and the line item(s) in the statement of income (or activities) in which those unrealized gains or losses are recognized; and a narrative description of the sensitivity of the fair value measurement to changes in unobservable inputs if a change in those inputs to a different amount might result in a significantly higher or lower fair value measurement. If there are interrelationships between those inputs and other unobservable inputs used in the fair value measurement, a reporting entity shall also provide a description of those interrelationships and of how they might magnify or mitigate the effect of changes in the unobservable inputs on the fair value measurement.

(7) For recurring and nonrecurring fair value measurements, if the highest and best use of a nonfinancial asset differs from its current use, a reporting entity shall disclose that fact and why the nonfinancial asset is being used in a manner that differs from its highest and best use.

c. **Classes** A reporting entity shall determine appropriate classes of assets and liabilities on the basis of the nature, characteristics, and risks of the asset or liability. The level of the fair value hierarchy within which the fair value measurement is categorized is also a consideration. The number of classes may need to be greater for fair value measurements categorized within Level 3 of the fair value hierarchy because those measurements have a greater degree of uncertainty and subjectivity.

A class of assets and liabilities will often require greater disaggregation than the line items presented in the statement of financial position. However, a reporting entity shall provide information sufficient to permit reconciliation to the line items presented in the statement of financial position.

E. Fair Value Option

Entities are permitted to measure many financial instruments and certain other assets and liabilities at fair value on an instrument-by-instrument basis under a fair value option (FVO) available under FASB ASC 825, *Financial Instruments*.

1. **Eligible Items** The FVO applies primarily to financial assets and financial liabilities. In addition to certain commonly recognized financial assets and financial liabilities, such as loans receivable and payable, the following items qualify for the FVO under FASB ASC 825:

   a. A recognized financial asset and financial liability, except any listed in paragraph 2.

      (1) Cash, evidence of ownership interest in an entity, or a contract that conveys to one entity a right to (a) receive cash or another financial instrument, or (b) exchange other financial instruments on potentially favorable terms with the second entity.

      (2) A contract that imposes on one entity an obligation to (a) deliver cash or another financial instrument to a second entity, or (b) exchange other financial instruments on potentially unfavorable terms with the second entity.

   b. A firm commitment that would otherwise not be recognized at inception and only involves financial instruments; or a written loan commitment.

   c. The rights and obligations under an insurance contract or warranty that is not a financial instrument but permits the insurer or warrantor to settle by paying a third party to provide goods or services.

   d. Resulting from the separation of an embedded nonfinancial instrument from a nonfinancial hybrid instrument.

2. **Financial Instruments Not Eligible** No entity may elect the fair value option for the following financial assets and financial liabilities:

   a. An investment in a subsidiary or interest in a variable interest entity that the entity is required to consolidate.

   b. Employers' and plans' obligations for pension benefits, other postretirement benefits, post employment benefits, employee stock option and stock purchase plans, and other forms of deferred compensation.

   c. Financial instruments recognized under leases.

   d. Deposit liabilities, withdrawable on demand, of banks, savings and loan associations, credit unions, and other similar depository institutions.

   e. Financial instruments that are classified by the issuer as a component of shareholder's equity.

3. **Method of Electing FVO** Entities are permitted to choose the FVO on an instrument-by-instrument basis. An entity can elect the FVO for certain loans, individual shares, or participations, but not for others. If the FVO is not elected for all eligible instruments within a group of similar instruments, the entity is required to disclose the reasons for its partial election, and disclose the amounts to which it applied the FVO and the amounts to which it did not apply the FVO within that group.

   The FVO does not need to be elected for all instruments issued or acquired in a single transaction. For example, an investor in a bond offering may apply the FVO to a portion of the bonds acquired in a single transaction; however, entities are required to disclose the reasons for partial election and disclose the amounts to which it applied the FVO and the amounts to which it did not apply the FVO within that group. A financial instrument that represents a single contract may not be further separated into parts for purposes of electing the FVO. Exceptions to the instrument-by-instrument election exist for the following:

   a. If multiple advances are made to one borrower under a single instrument (such as a line of credit or construction loan) and the individual advances lose their identity and become part of the larger loan balance, the FVO may only be applied to the larger loan balance and not the individual advances.

   b. If an investment would otherwise be accounted for under the equity method of accounting pursuant to FASB ASC 323, the election of the fair value option must be applied to all of the investor's financial interests (equity and debt, including guarantees) in that investee that would qualify for the FVO, rather than on an instrument-by-instrument basis.

   c. The FVO must be applied to all claims and obligations under the eligible insurance or reinsurance contract.

   d. If the FVO is elected for insurance contracts containing integrated or non-integrated contract features or coverages, the FVO cannot be elected for only the non-integrated contract features or coverages even though those features and coverages are accounted for separately under FASB ASC 944, *Financial Services—Insurance*.

4. **Election Dates** An entity may choose to elect the fair value option only on the date that one of the following occurs:

   a. The entity first recognizes the eligible item; or enters into an eligible firm commitment.

   b. Financial assets that, because of specialized accounting principles, have been reported at fair value with unrealized gains and losses included in earnings cease to qualify for fair value measurement.

   c. The accounting treatment for an investment in another entity changes because the investment becomes subject to the equity method of accounting; or the investor ceases to consolidate a subsidiary or variable interest entity but retains an interest.

   d. An event that requires an eligible item to be measured at fair value at the time of the event but does not require fair value measurement at each reporting date after that.

5. **Reporting** A business entity shall report unrealized gains and losses on items for which the fair value option has been elected in earnings at each subsequent reporting date. Upfront costs and fees related to items for which the fair value option is elected shall be recognized as incurred and not deferred. The remeasurement to fair value at adoption is reported as a cumulative-effect adjustment to the opening balance of retained earnings.

6. **Presentation** Entities shall report assets and liabilities that are measured using the fair value option separately from similar assets and liabilities measured differently on the balance sheet. An entity may either present the aggregate fair value and non-fair-value on the same line item and parenthetically disclose the amount measured at fair value or present two separate line items to display the fair value and non-fair-value amounts.

7. **Disclosures** The objectives of the disclosures are to facilitate comparisons between entities that choose different measurement attributes for similar assets and liabilities and also facilitate comparisons between assets and liabilities in the financial statements of an entity that selects different measurement methods for similar assets and liabilities.

   a. **Balance Sheet** As of each date for which a statement of financial position is presented, entities shall disclose the following:

      (1) Management's reasons for electing a fair value option for each eligible item or group of similar eligible items

      (2) If the fair value option is elected for some but not all eligible items within a group of similar eligible items; (a) a description of those similar items and the reasons for partial election, and (b) information to enable users to understand how the group of similar items relates to individual line items on the statement of financial position

      (3) For each line item in the statement of financial position that includes an item or items for which the fair value option has been elected; (a) information to enable users to understand how each line item relates to major categories of assets and liabilities presented in accordance with fair value disclosure requirements, and (b) the aggregate carrying amount of items included in each line item that are not eligible for the fair value option, if any

      (4) The difference between the aggregate fair value and the aggregate unpaid principal balance of loans, long-term receivables, and long-term debt instruments that have contractual principal amounts and for which the fair value option has been elected

      (5) For loans held as assets for which the fair value option has been elected; (a) the aggregate fair value of loans that are 90 days or more past due and of loans in nonaccrual status (if the policy is to recognize interest income separately from other changes in fair value), and (b) the difference between the aggregate fair value and the aggregate unpaid principal balance for loans that are 90 days or more past due, in nonaccrual status, or both

      (6) The information required for investments that would have been accounted for under the equity method if the entity had not chosen to apply the fair value option.

   b. **Income Statement** For each period for which an income statement is presented, entities shall disclose the following about items for which the fair value option has been elected:

      (1) For each line item in the statement of financial position, the amounts of gains and losses from fair value changes included in earnings during the period and in which line in the income statement those gains and losses are reported

      (2) A description of how interest and dividends are measured and where they are reported in the income statement

(3) For loans and other receivables held as assets; (a) the estimated amount of gains and losses included in earnings during the period attributable to changes in instruments-specific credit risk, and (b) how the gains or losses attributable to changes in instrument-specific credit risk were determined

(4) For liabilities with fair values that have been significantly affected during the reporting period by changes in the instrument-specific credit risk; (a) the estimated amount of gains and losses from fair value changes included in earnings that are attributable to changes in the instrument-specific credit risk, (b) qualitative information about the reasons for those changes, and (c) how the gains or losses attributable to changes in instrument-specific credit risk were determined

III. Reporting of Operations—Income Statement

A. Description

The income statement for a period presents the revenues, expenses, gains, losses, and net income (net loss) recognized during the period and thereby presents an indication, in conformity with GAAP, of the results of the enterprise's profit-directed activities during the period. Information in the income statement helps users do the following:

1. Evaluate past performance of the company

2. Provide a basis for predicting future performance of the company

B. Format

Two basic formats are used to present the income statement.

1. **Single-Step Format** Focuses on two classifications of items: revenues and expenses. All revenues are added together to arrive at a total revenue figure. The sum of all expenses is subtracted from this figure. The resultant amount is "Income Before Extraordinary Items."

2. **Multiple-Step Format** Focuses on multiple classifications of revenue and expense items. This format is characterized by several intermediate subtotals, such as gross margin and operating income, which together produce "Income Before Extraordinary Items."

Exhibit 2 ▸ Income Statement Formats (assumed amounts)

Single-Step Format		
Revenues:		
Sales revenue	$500,000	
Other revenues, gains	20,000	
Total revenues		$520,000
Expenses:		
CGS	350,000	
Selling	80,000	
Administrative	30,000	
Other expenses, losses	10,000	
Income taxes	5,000	
Total expenses		475,000
Income from continuing operations		45,000
Extraordinary gain, net of $1,200 applicable taxes		7,000
Net income		$ 52,000

Multiple-Step Format		
Net sales	$500,000	
Less CGS	350,000	
Gross margin		$150,000
Less operating exp.		
Selling	80,000	
Administrative	30,000	
Total operating exp.		110,000
Operating income		40,000
Other revenues, gain	20,000	
Other exp., losses	10,000	10,000
Income from continuing operations before taxes		50,000
Income taxes		5,000
Income from continuing operations		45,000
Extraordinary gain, net of $1,200 applicable taxes		7,000
Net income		$ 52,000

C. Elements

1. **Revenues** Revenues are inflows or other enhancements of assets of an entity or settlements of its liabilities (or a combination of both) during a period from delivering or producing goods, rendering services, or other activities that constitute the entity's ongoing major or central operations.

   a. Revenues represent actual or expected cash inflows (or equivalents) resulting from the entity's major or central operations.

   b. Revenues are usually recognized at the point of sale, in conformity with the basic accounting principle of revenue realization. Several exceptions to this principle are permitted under very specific circumstances.

2. **Expenses** Expenses are outflows or other use of assets or incurrence of liabilities (or a combination of both) from delivering or producing goods, rendering services, or carrying out other activities that constitute the entity's ongoing major or central operations during a period. Expenses represent actual or expected cash outflows (or equivalents) resulting from the entity's major or central operations. Expenses generally are recognized in accordance with one of three principles.

   a. Some costs are presumed to be directly related to specific revenues. Examples are cost of goods sold and sales commissions.

   b. If a direct association between costs and revenues is not apparent, costs must be allocated on a systematic and rational basis among the periods benefited. Depreciation of fixed assets, amortization of intangible assets, and allocation of prepaid rent and insurance are applications of this principle.

   c. Costs that are deemed to provide no discernible future benefits are expensed in the current period. Likewise, costs recorded as assets in prior periods that no longer have discernible benefits are expensed in the current period.

3. **Gains and Losses** Gains and losses are defined as increases (or decreases) in equity—i.e., net assets—from peripheral or incidental transactions of an entity and from all other transactions and other events and circumstances affecting the entity during a period, except those that result from revenues (expenses) or investments (withdrawals) by owners.

   a. Gains and losses related to the business enterprise's central operations (e.g., write-down of inventory to lower of cost or market) are classified as operating.

   b. Gains and losses not attributable to operations are classified as nonoperating.

D. Statement of Retained Earnings

This statement is presented as a supplement to the income statement and serves as a link between beginning and ending retained earnings.

Exhibit 3 ▸ Statement of Retained Earnings

Beginning balance, as reported	$ XXX
+/– Prior period adjustments, net of $______ tax	XXX
Beginning balance, as adjusted	XXX
+ Net income (– Net loss)	XXX
– Dividends	(XXX)
Ending balance	$ XXX

IV. Financial Analysis

A. Purpose

Financial statement analysis is an attempt to evaluate a business entity for financial and managerial decision-making purposes. In order to draw valid conclusions about the financial health of an entity, it is essential to analyze and compare specific types and sources of financial information. This analysis would include (1) a review of the firm's accounting policies, (2) an examination of recent auditors' reports, (3) analysis of footnotes and other supplemental information accompanying the financial statements, and (4) the examination of various relationships among items presented in financial statements (i.e., ratio analysis).

Financial ratios measure elements of the firm's operating performance and financial position so that internal as well as industry-wide comparisons can be made on a consistent basis. Ratio analysis provides an indication of the firm's financial strengths and weaknesses and generally should be used in conjunction with other evaluation techniques. Ratio analysis is used primarily to draw conclusions about the solvency, operational efficiency, and profitability of a firm.

B. Factors

When computing a ratio, consider the following:

1. Net or gross amounts (e.g., receivables)
2. Average for the period or year-end amounts (e.g., receivables, inventories, common shares outstanding)
3. Adjustments to income (e.g., interest, income taxes, preferred dividends)

C. Solvency

1. **Short-Term Solvency** Short-term solvency is the ability of a firm to meet its current obligations as they mature. The following ratios may be of primary interest to short-term creditors.

Exhibit 4 ▸ Working Capital

Current Assets – Current Liabilities

Comments: Represents the liquid portion of resources or enterprise capital. The greater the amount of working capital, the greater the cushion of protection available to short-term creditors, and the greater assurance that short-term debts will be paid when due.

Exhibit 5 ▸ Current Ratio

$$\frac{\textit{Current Assets}}{\textit{Current Liabilities}}$$

Comments: This is a primary test of the overall solvency of the enterprise and its ability to meet current obligations from current assets. When the current ratio exceeds 1.0 to 1.0, an equal increase in current assets and current liabilities decreases the ratio. When the current ratio is less than 1.0 to 1.0, an equal increase in current assets and current liabilities increases the ratio.

Exhibit 6 ▸ Acid-Test or Quick Ratio

$$\frac{\textit{Cash + Marketable Securities + Net Receivables}}{\textit{Current Liabilities}}$$

Comments: This ratio provides a more severe test of immediate solvency by eliminating inventories and prepaid expenses (current assets that are not quickly converted into cash).

Exhibit 7 ▸ Defensive-Interval Ratio

$$\frac{\text{Cash + Marketable Securities + Net Receivables}}{\text{Average Daily Cash Expenditures}}$$

Comments: This ratio estimates the number of days that the company can meet its basic operational costs. The average daily cash expenditures can be approximated by reducing total expenses for the year by noncash charges (e.g., depreciation, amortization of intangibles) and dividing this amount by 365.

2. **Long-Term Solvency** Long-term solvency is the ability to meet interest payments, preferred dividends, and other fixed charges. Similarly, long-term solvency is a required precondition for the repayment of principal.

Exhibit 8 ▸ Debt to Equity

$$\frac{\text{Total Liabilities}}{\text{Owners' Equity}}$$

Comments: This ratio provides a measure of the relative amounts of resources provided by creditors and owners.

Exhibit 9 ▸ Times Interest Earned

$$\frac{\text{Income Before Income Taxes and Interest Charges}}{\text{Interest Charges}}$$

Comments: Measures the ability of the firm to meet its interest payments. Income taxes are *added* back to net income because the ability to pay interest is not dependent on the amount of income taxes to be paid, since interest is tax deductible.

Exhibit 10 ▸ Times Preferred Dividends Earned

$$\frac{\text{Net Income}}{\text{Annual Preferred Dividend Requirement}}$$

Comments: Measures the adequacy of current earnings for the payment of preferred dividends.

D. Operational Efficiency

Operational efficiency is the ability of the business entity to generate income as well as its efficiency and effectiveness in using the assets employed.

Exhibit 11 ▸ Total Asset Turnover

$$\frac{\text{Total Sales (Revenue)}}{\text{Average Total Assets}}$$

Comments: This ratio is useful to determine the amount of sales that are generated from each dollar of assets. Average total assets is generally determined by adding the beginning and ending total assets and dividing by two.

Exhibit 12 ▸ Accounts Receivable Turnover

$$\frac{\textit{Net Credit Sales}}{\textit{Average Net Receivables}}$$

Comments: This ratio provides an indication of the efficiency of credit policies and collection procedures, and of the quality of the receivables. Average net receivables include trade notes receivable. Average net receivables is generally determined by adding the beginning and ending net receivables balances and dividing by two.

Exhibit 13 ▸ Number of Days' Sales in Average Receivables

$$\frac{\textit{360}}{\textit{Receivables Turnover}}$$

Comments: Tests the average number of days required to collect receivables. Some analysts prefer to use 365, 300, or 250 as the number of business days in the year.

Exhibit 14 ▸ Inventory Turnover

$$\frac{\textit{Cost of Goods Sold}}{\textit{Average Inventory}}$$

Comments: Indicates the number of times inventory was acquired and sold (or used in production) during the period. It can be used to detect inventory obsolescence or pricing problems. Average inventory is generally determined by adding the beginning and ending inventories and dividing by two.

Exhibit 15 ▸ Number of Days' Supply in Average Inventory

$$\frac{\textit{360}}{\textit{Inventory Turnover}} \quad \text{or} \quad \frac{\textit{Average (Ending) Inventory}}{\textit{Average Daily Cost of Goods Sold}}$$

Comments: Indicates the number of days inventory is held before it is sold. Some analysts prefer to use 365, 300, or 250 as the number of business days in the year. Average daily cost of goods sold is determined by dividing cost of goods sold by the number of business days.

Exhibit 16 ▸ Length of Operating Cycle

Number of days' sales in average receivables + *Number of days' supply in average inventory*

Comments: Measures the average length of time from the purchase of inventory to the collection of cash from its sale.

E. Profitability

Profitability ratios are measures of the success or failure of an entity over a period of time.

Exhibit 17 ▸ Book Value Per Common Share

$$\frac{\textit{Common Stockholders' Equity}}{\textit{Number of Common Shares Outstanding}}$$

This ratio measures the amount that common shareholders would receive if all assets were sold at their carrying amounts and if all creditors were paid. To determine common stockholders' equity, preferred stock is subtracted from total stockholders' equity at the greater of its liquidation, par or stated value. Cumulative preferred stock dividends in *arrears* are also similarly subtracted. Treasury stock affects the denominator as the number of common shares outstanding is *reduced.*

Exhibit 18 ▸ Book Value Per Preferred Share

$$\frac{\textit{Preferred Stockholders' Equity}}{\textit{Number of Preferred Shares Outstanding}}$$

This ratio measures the amount that preferred shareholders would receive if the company were liquidated on the basis of the amounts reported on the balance sheet. Preferred stockholders' equity is comprised of (a) preferred stock at the greater of its liquidation, par or stated value and (b) cumulative preferred stock dividends in arrears.

Exhibit 19 ▸ Return on Total Assets

$$\frac{\textit{Net Income + Interest Expense (Net of Tax)}}{\textit{Average Total Assets}}$$

This ratio provides a measure of the degree of efficiency with which resources (total assets) are used to generate earnings.

Exhibit 20 ▸ Return on Common Stockholders' Equity

$$\frac{\textit{Net Income – Preferred Dividends}}{\textit{Average Common Stockholders' Equity}}$$

Comments: Measures the rate of earnings on resources provided by common stockholders. Common stockholders' equity is measured as indicated in Exhibit 14. Average common stockholders' equity is generally determined by adding beginning and ending common stockholders' equity and dividing by two.

Successful use of *leverage* is where a company earns more by the use of borrowed money than it costs to use the borrowed funds. When compared to the return on total assets, the return on common stockholders' equity measures the extent to which leverage is being employed for or against the common stockholders. When the return on common stockholders' equity is greater than the return on total assets, leverage is positive and common stockholders benefit.

Exhibit 21 ▸ Return on Stockholders' Equity

$$\frac{\textit{Net Income}}{\textit{Average Stockholders' Equity}}$$

Comments: Measures the rate of earnings on resources provided by all stockholders (i.e., common and preferred). Average stockholders' equity is generally determined by adding beginning and ending stockholders' equity and dividing by two.

Exhibit 22 ▸ Earnings Per Share (EPS)

$$\frac{\textit{Net Income} - \textit{Preferred Dividends}}{\textit{Average Number of Common Shares Outstanding}}$$

Comments: Measures the ability to pay dividends to common stockholders by measuring profit earned per share of common stock. (EPS is discussed more thoroughly later in this chapter.)

Exhibit 23 ▸ Price Earnings Ratio

$$\frac{\textit{Market Price Per Common Share}}{\textit{Earnings Per Common Share}}$$

Comments: A measure of whether a stock is relatively cheap or relatively expensive based on its present earnings.

Exhibit 24 ▸ Dividend Payout Ratio

$$\frac{\textit{Cash Dividend Per Common Share}}{\textit{Earnings Per Common Share}}$$

Comments: This ratio represents the percentage of earnings per share distributed to common stockholders in cash dividends. A low ratio would probably indicate the reinvestment of profits by a growth-oriented firm.

Exhibit 25 ▸ Yield on Common Stock

$$\frac{\textit{Dividend Per Common Share}}{\textit{Market Price Per Common Share}}$$

Comments: Measures cash flow return on common stock investment.

V. Statement of Comprehensive Income

A. Description

Comprehensive income is the change in equity of a business enterprise during a period from transactions and other events and circumstances from nonowner sources. Comprehensive income is to be displayed prominently within a financial statement in a full set of general-purpose financial statements. It must be shown on the face of a statement, not just in the notes to the statements.

1. Comprehensive income includes all changes in equity during a period except those resulting from investments by owners and distributions to owners.

2. Over the life of the business, comprehensive income equals the net difference between cash receipts and outlays, excluding cash investments by owners and cash distributions to owners, regardless of whether cash or accrual accounting is used.

3. Comprehensive income is divided into the components of net income and other comprehensive income.

4. Other comprehensive income (OCI) refers to revenues, expenses, gains, and losses that are included in comprehensive income, but excluded from net income.

B. Format

There are two acceptable means of reporting comprehensive income: a statement of income and comprehensive income, or a statement of income and a separate statement of comprehensive income.

1. **Classification** Comprehensive income is comprised of two components, net income and other comprehensive income. An entity must classify items of other comprehensive income by their nature: foreign currency items, pension adjustments, unrealized gains and losses on certain investments in debt and equity securities, and certain gains and losses on hedging activities.

2. **Accumulated Balance of OCI** An entity must also display the accumulated balance of other comprehensive income separately from retained earnings and additional paid-in capital in the equity section of a statement of financial position. An entity must disclose accumulated balances for each classification in that separate component of equity on the face of the statement of financial position, in the statement of changes in equity, or in the notes to the financial statements.

Exhibit 26 ▸ Comprehensive Income Reporting (Separate Statement)

Net Income			$XXX
Foreign currency adjustments, net of tax of $XXX		$XXX	
Unrealized holding gain/loss arising during period, net of tax of $XX	$XX		
Reclassification adjustment, net of tax of $XX, for gain/loss included in net income	XX		
Unrealized Gain/Loss on Marketable Securities		XXX	
Pension adjustment, net of tax of $XX		XXX	
Other Comprehensive Income			XXX
Comprehensive Income			$XXX

VI. Statement of Cash Flows

A. Description

A statement of cash flows must be issued whenever a balance sheet and an income statement are issued. This financial statement provides relevant information about the cash receipts and cash payments of an enterprise during a period.

1. **Classification** The statement of cash flows classifies cash receipts and cash payments resulting from operating, investing, and financing activities.

2. **Noncash Investing and Financing Transactions** Noncash investing and financing transactions are not reported in the statement of cash flows because the statement reports only the effects of operating, investing, and financing activities that directly affect cash flows. If significant, noncash investing and financing transactions are reported in related disclosures.

B. Format

Net cash from operating activities can be determined under either the direct or indirect method. Under the direct approach, operating cash payments are deducted from operating cash receipts, effectively resulting in a cash basis income statement. The indirect approach converts net income to net cash flow from operating activities by adding back noncash charges in the income statement to net income and subtracting noncash credits from net income.

VII. Statements of Financial Accounting Concepts

A. Objectives

The FASB has issued pronouncements called Statements of Financial Accounting Concepts (SFACs) in a series designed to constitute a foundation of financial accounting standards. The framework is designed to prescribe the nature, function, and limits of financial accounting and to be used as a guideline that will lead to consistent standards of accounting and reporting.

SFACs do **not** establish standards prescribing accounting procedures or disclosures, nor supersede, amend, or otherwise modify GAAP. They are not enforceable under the Rules of Conduct of the Code of Professional Ethics. SFACs are **not** considered authoritative pronouncements, but they have been a constant, although limited, source of CPA exam questions.

B. *Objectives of Financial Reporting by Nonbusiness Organizations* (SFAC 4)

SFAC 4 established the objectives of general purpose external financial reporting by nonbusiness organizations. Those objectives, together with the objectives set forth in FASB Concepts Statement No. 8 (which supersedes SFAC No. 1), serve as the foundation of the conceptual framework the FASB developed for financial accounting and reporting. Its goal was to develop an integrated conceptual framework that has relevance to all entities and that provides appropriate consideration of any different reporting objectives and concepts that may apply to only certain types of entities.

This Statement focuses on organizations that have predominantly nonbusiness characteristics that heavily influence the operations of the organization. The objectives stem primarily from the needs of external users who generally cannot prescribe the information they want from an organization.

1. **Objectives** The objectives in this Statement apply to general purpose external financial reporting by nonbusiness organizations. The objectives of financial reporting are affected by the economic, legal, political, and social environment in which financial reporting takes place.

   a. The operating environments of nonbusiness organizations and business enterprises are similar in many ways. Both nonbusiness organizations and business enterprises produce and distribute goods and services and use scarce resources in doing so.

   b. Differences between nonbusiness organizations and business enterprises arise in the ways they obtain resources. Noneconomic reasons are commonly factors in decisions to provide resources to particular nonbusiness organizations. The objectives also are affected by the characteristics and limitations of the kind of information that financial reporting can provide.

   c. Financial reporting by nonbusiness organizations should provide information that includes explanations and interpretations to help users understand the financial information, and that is:

      (1) Useful to present and potential resource providers and other users in making rational decisions about the allocation of resources to those organizations

      (2) Helpful to present and potential resource providers and other users in assessing the services that a nonbusiness organization provides and its ability to continue to provide those services

      (3) Useful to present and potential resource providers and other users in assessing how managers of a nonbusiness organization have discharged their stewardship responsibilities and about other aspects of their performance

      (4) About the economic resources, obligations, and net resources of an organization, and the effects of transactions, events, and circumstances that change resources and interests in those resources

(5) About the performance of an organization during a period. Periodic measurement of the changes in the amount and nature of the net resources of a nonbusiness organization and information about the service efforts and accomplishments of an organization together represent the information most useful in assessing its performance

(6) About how an organization obtains and spends cash or other liquid resources, about its borrowing and repayment of borrowing, and about other factors that may affect an organization's liquidity

2. **Nonbusiness Characteristics** The line between nonbusiness organizations and business enterprises is not always sharp since the incidence and relative importance of those characteristics in any organization are different. For purposes of developing financial reporting objectives, a spectrum of organizations exists ranging from those with clearly dominant nonbusiness characteristics to those with wholly business characteristics. The major distinguishing characteristics of nonbusiness organizations include:

   a. Receipts of significant amounts of resources from resource providers who do not expect to receive either repayment or economic benefits proportionate to resources provided.

   b. Operating purposes that are primarily other than to provide goods or services at a profit or profit equivalent.

   c. Absence of defined ownership interests that can be sold, transferred, or redeemed, or that convey entitlement to a share of a residual distribution of resources in the event of liquidation of the organization

3. **Transactions** These characteristics result in certain types of transactions that are infrequent in business enterprises, such as contributions and grants, and in the absence of transactions with owners.

4. **Examples** Examples of organizations that clearly fall within the focus of this Statement include most human service organizations, churches, foundations, and some other organizations, such as those private nonprofit hospitals and nonprofit schools that receive a significant portion of their financial resources from sources other than the sale of goods and services.

5. **Exclusions** Examples of organizations that clearly fall outside the focus of this Statement include all investor-owned enterprises and other types of organizations, such as mutual insurance companies and other mutual cooperative entities that provide dividends, lower costs, or other economic benefits directly and proportionately to their owners, members, or participants.

C. *Recognition & Measurement in Financial Statements of Business Enterprises* (SFAC 5)
Some information is provided better by financial statements, and some is provided better or can only be disclosed in notes to financial statements, parenthetically, or by supplementary information or other means of financial reporting. The scope of SFAC 5 is limited to recognition and measurement in financial statements.

1. **Completeness** A full set of financial statements provides information that is necessary to satisfy the broad purposes of financial reporting. A full set of financial statements includes information (some of which may be combined in a single statement) showing the financial position at the end of the period, earnings (net income) for the period, comprehensive income (total nonowner changes in equity) for the period, cash flows during the period, and investments by and distributions to owners during the period.

2. **Maintenance Concepts** The full set of articulated financial statements discussed in SFAC 5 is based on the concept of financial capital maintenance. The main difference between the two concepts involves the effect of price changes during the period. Under the financial capital concept, if the effects of price changes are recognized, they are reported as holding gains or losses, (i.e., included in income). Under the physical capital concept, such changes are considered adjustments to equity.

   a. Under the financial concept, a return on financial capital results only if the financial (money) amount of an enterprise's net assets at the end of a period exceeds the corresponding amount at the beginning of the period, after excluding the effects of transactions with owners. The financial capital concept is the traditional view and is the capital maintenance concept in present financial statements and comprehensive income.

   b. Under the physical concept, a return on physical capital results only if the physical productive capacity of the enterprise at the end of the period exceeds its capacity at the beginning. Thus, the physical capital concept can be implemented only if the enterprise's productive assets, inventory, etc., are measured by their current cost.

3. **Recognition** The process of formally recording or incorporating an item into the financial statements of an entity as an asset, liability, revenue, expense, or the like. An item and information about it must meet four fundamental recognition criteria to be recognized, subject to cost-benefit and materiality considerations.

   a. The item meets the definition of an element of financial statements.

   b. The item has a relevant attribute measurable with sufficient reliability.

   c. The information may make a difference in user decisions.

   d. The information is representationally faithful, verifiable, and neutral.

4. **Revenues and Gains** Revenues and gains are recognized when they are both realized and earned.

   a. Revenues and gains generally are not recognized until realized or realizable.

   b. Revenues are not recognized until earned. For gains, being earned is generally less significant than being realized or realizable, since gains commonly involve no "earning process."

5. **Expenses and Losses** Expenses and losses are recognized based on the following:

   a. Consumption of economic benefits may be recognized either directly or by relating them to revenues recognized during the period.

   b. Expenses or losses are recognized if it becomes evident that previously recognized future economic benefits of assets have been reduced or eliminated, or that liabilities have been incurred or increased, without associated economic benefits.

D. ***Elements of Financial Statements*** **(SFAC 6)**

1. **Elements** SFAC 6 identifies ten elements of financial statements. Seven elements of financial statements of both business enterprises and not-for-profit organizations—assets, liabilities, equity (business enterprises) or net assets (not-for-profit organizations), revenues, expenses, gains, and losses. Three elements of business enterprises only—investment by owners, distributions to owners, and comprehensive income.

2. **Accrual Accounting** Accrual accounting attempts to record the financial effects on an entity of transactions and other events and circumstances that have cash consequences for the entity in the periods in which those transactions, events, and circumstances occur, rather than only in the periods in which cash is received or paid by the entity. Accrual accounting is characterized by the use of accruals, deferrals, allocations, and amortizations.

   a. Accrual is the accounting process of recognizing assets or liabilities and the related liabilities, assets, revenues, expenses, gains, or losses for amounts expected to be received or paid, usually in cash, in the future.

   b. Deferral is the accounting process of recognizing a liability resulting from a current cash receipt or an asset resulting from a current cash payment with deferred recognition of revenues, expenses, gains, or losses.

   c. Allocation is the accounting process of assigning or distributing an amount according to a plan or a formula.

   d. Amortization is the accounting process of reducing an amount by periodic payments or write-downs. It is an allocation process for accounting for prepayments and deferrals by reducing a liability or an asset and recognizing a revenue or an expense.

3. **Realization and Recognition**

   a. Realization is the process of converting noncash resources and rights into money. This term is most precisely used in accounting and financial reporting to refer to sales of assets for cash or claims to cash. The related terms realized and unrealized, therefore, identify revenues or gains or losses on assets sold and unsold, respectively.

   b. Recognition is the process of formally recording or incorporating an item in the financial statements of an entity. Thus, an asset, liability, revenue, expense, gain, or loss may be recognized (recorded) or unrecognized (unrecorded).

4. **Matching** Combined or simultaneous recognition of the revenues and expenses that result directly and jointly from the same transactions and other events.

   a. Period costs cannot be directly related to particular revenues, yet result in benefits that are exhausted in the same period in which the cost was incurred. These costs are usually recognized as expenses in the period in which incurred. Examples: administrative salaries, store utilities, etc.

   b. Other costs yield their benefits over two or more periods of time. These costs are usually allocated to the periods benefited through a systematic and rational cost allocation method (e.g., depreciation and amortization).

E. ***Using Cash Flow Information & Present Value in Accounting Measurements* (SFAC 7)**

SFAC 7 presents the FASB's conclusions about the use and approach to making interest computations in financial reporting. It is limited to measurement issues and does not address recognition.

1. **Present Value Measurement of Assets and Liabilities** Most accounting measurements use an observable marketplace-determined amount, such as cash exchanged, current cost, or current market value. However, in other instances, estimates of future cash flows must be used as the basis for measuring an asset or a liability. SFAC 7 provides a framework for using future cash flows as the basis for accounting measurements at initial recognition or fresh-start measurements as well as for the interest method of amortization. Additionally, it provides general principles that govern the use of present value computations, particularly when the amount and/or timing of future cash flows are uncertain.

2. **Present Value as Surrogate for Market Value** In order to provide more relevant information (a primary qualitative characteristic of financial reporting), present value must represent some observable measurement attribute of assets or liabilities. In the absence of observed transaction prices, accounting measurements at initial recognition and fresh-start measurements should attempt to capture the elements that taken together would comprise a market price if one existed (fair value). While the expectations of management are often useful and informative, ultimately, it is the market that dictates market price when exchanges occur. However, for certain assets or liabilities, management's estimates may be the only information available on which to value the asset or liability. In that case, the use of present value can be seen as a surrogate for market value.

3. **Uncertainties** An accounting measurement that uses present value should reflect the uncertainties inherent in the estimated cash flows. This means that risk should be specifically incorporated into the computation. SFAC 7 provides guidance on how to incorporate risk into the analysis, including its effect on both the timing and amount of future cash flows.

4. **Projection of Future Cash Flows** In the past, present value computations have relied on a single estimate of cash flows and a single interest rate. SFAC 7 calls for the use of expected cash flows, which incorporates uncertainty, use of ranges, and probabilistic computations in the projection of future cash flows.

5. **Measuring Liabilities** In measuring liabilities, the SFAC 7 indicates that there are different issues at hand. Nonetheless, the ultimate objective remains the same—to reflect fair value. SFAC 7 provides additional guidance for measuring liabilities.

6. **Credit Risk** Credit risk can affect a variety of components in the present value computation and should be incorporated in the present value computation. Additionally, in measuring liabilities, the entity's credit standing should always be incorporated into that measurement.

F. ***Conceptual Framework for Financial Reporting* (SFAC 8)**

This Concepts Statement includes two chapters of the new conceptual framework resulting from a joint project between the FASB and the IASB designed to improve and converge each organization's conceptual framework. FASB Concepts Statement No. 1, *Objectives of Financial Reporting by Business Enterprises*, and No. 2, *Qualitative Characteristics of Accounting Information*, have been superseded by SFAC 8. As the FASB and IASB complete additional phases of their joint project, new chapters will be added to SFAC 8, and other Concepts Statements will be superseded.

1. **Chapter 1: The Objective of General Purpose Financial Reporting** The objective of general purpose financial reporting forms the foundation of the Conceptual Framework. The other aspects of the Conceptual Framework, including: a reporting entity concept; the qualitative characteristics of, and the constraints on, useful financial information; elements of financial statements; recognition, measurement; presentation; and disclosure all derive from that initial objective.

   a. **Usefulness and Limitations** Users need to assess the amount, timing, and uncertainty of future net cash inflows to the entity in order to form opinions about the returns that they expect from an investment. Specifically, users need information about the resources of an entity, claims against the entity, and how efficiently and effectively the entity's management and governing board have discharged their responsibilities to use the entity's resources. Since most external users cannot require entities to provide information directly to them, they must rely upon general purpose financial statements. As such, these external users are the primary users to whom general purpose financial reports are directed.

      General purpose financial statements are not intended to show the value of a reporting entity. They do not and cannot provide all the information that existing and potential users need. Users should also consider relevant and useful information from other sources, such as general economic conditions and expectations, political events and political climate, and industry and company outlooks.

      To a large extent, financial reports are based on estimates, judgments, and models rather than exact depictions. It is the intention of the Boards that the Conceptual Framework establish the concepts that underlie those estimates, judgments and models.

   b. **Economic Resources, Claims, and Changes in Resources and Claims**

      (1) A reporting entity's financial strengths and weaknesses can be identified through information about the nature and amount of a reporting entity's economic resources available for use in a reporting entity's operations. Users need to know not only the nature and amount of resources available for use in an entity's operations, but they also need to know the different *types* of resources. Some future cash flows derive directly from existing economic resources (such as accounts receivable); while other cash flows result from using several resources in combination to produce and market goods or services to customers.

      (2) Changes in resources and claims result from the entity's financial performance and other transactions, such as issuing debt or equity instruments. Users need to be able to distinguish between both of these changes in order to properly assess the prospects of future cash flows from the entity.

      (3) Financial performance information helps users to evaluate the return that the entity has produced. This information also helps users assess how well management has discharged its responsibilities to make efficient and effective use of the entity's resources; in assessing the uncertainty of future cash flows; and in predicting the entity's future returns on its economic resources.

(a) Accrual accounting records the effects of transactions on an entity's economic resources and claims in the periods in which those effects occur; not based on the cash receipts and payments that occurred during that period. Accrual accounting results in information that provides a better basis for assessing the entity's past and future performance than cash based accounting. Information about *changes* in an entity's economic resources and claims other than by obtaining additional resources directly from investors and creditors is useful in assessing the entity's past and future ability to generate net cash flows.

(b) Information about how an entity obtains and spends cash, including borrowing and repayment of debt information, cash dividends or other cash distributions to investors, helps users assess the entity's ability to generate future net cash flows, evaluate its financing and investing activities, assess its liquidity or solvency, and interpret other information about financial performance.

(c) Nonfinancial reasons, such as issuing additional ownership shares, may result in changes to an entity's economic resources and claims. Users need a complete understanding of why the reporting entity's economic resources and claims have changed and the implications of those changes for its future financial performance.

2. **Chapter 3: Qualitative Characteristics of Useful Financial Information** Financial reports provide information about a reporting entity's economic resources, claims against the reporting entity, and the effects of transactions and other events and conditions that change those resources and claims (this is referred to as *economic phenomena*). Some financial reports also include nonfinancial information about management's expectations and strategies and other types of forward-looking data. The qualitative characteristics of useful financial information apply to financial information provided in financial statements and in other ways. The constraint of cost applies similarly.

Useful financial information must be both relevant and faithfully representational. The usefulness is further enhanced if it is also comparable, verifiable, timely, and understandable.

a. **Fundamental Qualitative Characteristics** Relevance and faithful representation are *fundamental* qualitative characteristics.

(1) **Relevance** Information is relevant if it is capable of making a difference in a decision by helping users to form predictions about the outcomes of past, present, and future events or to confirm or correct prior expectations. Predictive, or confirmatory, value is the trait that allows financial information to make a difference. Information has *predictive value* if it can be useful in predicting future outcomes by users. *Confirmatory value* provides feedback (confirms or changes) about previous assessments.

Information is *material* if omitting it or misstating it could influence decisions that users make on the basis of the financial information of a specific reporting entity. Materiality is different for each entity.

(2) **Faithful Representation** A perfectly faithful representation would have three characteristics. It would be: complete, neutral and free from error.

(a) Complete information includes all the information necessary for a user to understand the economic phenomena being reported, including all necessary descriptions and explanations. This may include data about the quality and nature of the item, factors and circumstances that might affect the quality and nature of the item, and the process used to determine the numerical quantity.

(b) Neutral information is without bias in the selection or presentation of financial information.

(c) Free of error means there are no errors or omissions in the description or preparation of the information reporting on the phenomenon

b. **Applying the Fundamental Qualitative Characteristics** First, identify any economic phenomenon that can be useful to users. Second, identify the type of information about the phenomenon that would be most relevant if it is available and can be faithfully represented. Third, if the information is available and faithfully representational, the process of satisfying the fundamental qualitative characteristics ends at this point. If not, repeat the process with the next most relevant information.

c. **Enhancing Qualitative Characteristics** These characteristics enhance the usefulness of information that is relevant and faithfully represented. They can also help in determining which of two ways should be used to depict a phenomenon if both are considered equally relevant and faithfully represented.

(1) **Comparability** Information is more useful if it helps users to choose between alternative decisions (i.e., buy or sell an investment) by comparing similar information about other entities. It aids users in identifying and understanding similarities and differences among items.

Consistency is related to comparability, and refers to the use of the *same* method for making comparisons across entities or periods of time. Consistency helps to achieve comparability.

(2) **Verifiability** When a large number of independent observers derive similar results using the same measurement methods, information is verifiable. It can be direct or indirect. If information cannot be verified (i.e., projections), it would be helpful to disclose the underlying assumptions, methods of compiling the information, and other factors and circumstances that support the information.

(3) **Timeliness** Information is timely if it is available to a decision maker before it loses its capacity to influence decisions. Older information is generally less useful than newer information, but older information can assist in identifying and assessing trends.

(4) **Understandability** Classifying, characterizing, and presenting information clearly and concisely makes it understandable. Complex information should not be omitted in an attempt to make financial statements easy to understand. Users of financial statements are assumed to possess a reasonable knowledge of business and economic activities.

d. **Applying the Enhancing Qualitative Characteristics** These characteristics should be maximized to the extent possible, but the underlying information must first be relevant and faithfully represented in order to be useful.

e. **Cost Constraint on Useful Financial Reporting** Cost is a pervasive constraint, and must be balanced with the benefits of providing that information. Different assessments of costs and benefits may be reasonable given the different sizes of entities, ways of raising capital (publicly or privately), different users' needs, or other factors.

VIII. Authority of Pronouncements

A. Accounting Standard-Setting Bodies & Their Pronouncements

1. **Committee on Cooperation With Stock Exchanges (1932–1934)** The American Institute of Accountants (known today as the American Institute of Certified Public Accountants, or AICPA) created in 1932 a Committee on Cooperation With Stock Exchanges. The Committee made a series of recommendations, which later were adopted by the AICPA.

2. **Committee on Accounting Procedure (1939–1959)** In 1939, the Institute formed a second committee, the Committee on Accounting Procedures (CAP), with the objective of narrowing the areas of differences and inconsistencies in the practice of accounting. During its existence, CAP issued 51 pronouncements, known as Accounting Research Bulletins (ARBs). ARB No. 43 consisted of a rewrite of the prior 42 pronouncements.

3. **Accounting Principles Board (1959–1973)** CAP was replaced in 1959 by the Accounting Principles Board (APB). From 1959 through 1973, the APB promulgated 31 pronouncements known as Opinions. In addition, the Board issued four Statements. Unlike Opinions, APB Statements were simply recommendations, not requirements.

4. **Financial Accounting Standards Board (1973–Present)** The APB was substituted in 1973 by the Financial Accounting Standards Board (FASB), an independent private-sector body composed of seven full-time members and a 35 member Advisory Council. The first promulgations issued by the FASB had the same authority as the prior APB Opinions and were known as Statements of Financial Accounting Standards (SFASs). In addition, the FASB also issued FASB Interpretations, Staff Positions, Technical Bulletins, and Emerging Issues Task Force (EITF) Consensuses. The FASB did a major restructuring of accounting and reporting standards into the *FASB Accounting Standards Codification.* The Codification superseded all accounting standards in existing FASB, EITF, AICPA, and related standards.

B. FASB Accounting Standards Codification

On July 1, 2009, the *FASB Accounting Standards Codification* became the single official source of authoritative, nongovernmental U.S. generally accepted accounting principles (GAAP), superseding existing FASB, AICPA, EITF, and related literature. The Codification does not change GAAP; it presents it in an organized and easily accessible new structure. It reorganizes the thousands of U.S. GAAP pronouncements into approximately 90 accounting topics. Also included is relevant SEC guidance that follows the same topical structure.

1. **GAAP Hierarchy** With the Codification, only two levels of U.S. GAAP exist: (1) authoritative represented by the Codification, and (2) nonauthoritative represented by all other literature. For reference by public companies, the Codification also includes Securities and Exchange Commission (SEC) content (displayed separately below the related topical content).

2. **Content** The Codification includes all previous level A–D GAAP issued by a standard setter, including pronouncements issued by the FASB, EITF, the Accounting Standards Executive Committee (AcSEC), the APB, etc. The source of material used by the Codification is from the as-amended versions of accounting standards, and as such, the Codification does not identify any documents that only amended other standards. The Codification will contain content from new standards not yet fully effective for all entities. This content will be labeled as such and appear specially marked.

3. **Exclusions** The Codification does not include guidance for non-GAAP matters such as Other Comprehensive Basis of Accounting (OCBOA), Cash Basis, Income Tax Basis, and Regulatory Accounting Principles (RAP). The Codification also does not include governmental accounting standards.

4. **Topics** Topics represent a collection of related guidance. For example, "Leases" is a Topic. The Topics correlate very closely to standards issued by the International Accounting Standards Board. The Topics reside in four main areas as follows:

   a. These Topics relate only to presentation matters and do not address recognition, measurement, and derecognition matters. Topics include Income Statement, Balance Sheet, Earnings per Share, and so forth.

   b. The Codification organizes Topics in a financial statement order including Assets, Liabilities, Equity, Revenue, and Expenses. Topics include Receivables, Revenue Recognition, Inventory, and so forth.

   c. These Topics relate to multiple financial statement accounts and are generally transaction-oriented. Topics include Business Combinations, Derivatives, Nonmonetary Transactions, and so forth.

   d. These Topics relate to accounting that is unique to an industry or type of activity. Topics include Airlines, Software, Real Estate, and so forth.

5. **Subtopics** Subtopics represent subsets of a Topic and are generally distinguished by type or by scope. For example, Operating Leases and Capital Leases are two Subtopics of the Leases Topic. Each Topic contains an Overall Subtopic representing pervasive guidance for the Topic. Each additional Subtopic represents incremental or unique guidance not contained in the Overall Subtopic. In some cases, the Overall Subtopic represents overall guidance. In other cases, Topics may not contain overall guidance, but instead may represent miscellaneous content that does not fit into another Subtopic.

6. **Sections** Sections represent the nature of the content in a Subtopic such as Recognition, Measurement, Disclosure, and so forth. Every Subtopic uses the same Sections, unless there is no content for a particular Section. Similar to Topics, Sections correlate very closely with Sections of individual International Accounting Standards.

Exhibit 27 ▸FASB Codification Sections

XXX-YY-ZZ *where XXX = Topic, YY = Subtopic, ZZ = Section*
XXX-YY-00 Status
XXX-YY-05 Overview and Background
XXX-YY-10 Objectives
XXX-YY-15 Scope and Scope Exceptions
XXX-YY-20 Topical Definitions—Glossary
XXX-YY-25 Recognition
XXX-YY-30 Initial Measurement
XXX-YY-35 Subsequent Measurement
XXX-YY-40 Derecognition
XXX-YY-45 Other Presentation Matters
XXX-YY-50 Disclosure
XXX-YY-55 Implementation Guidance and Illustrations
XXX-YY-60 Relationships
XXX-YY-65 Transition and Open Effective Date Information
XXX-YY-70 Links to Grandfathered Material
XXX-YY-75 XBRL Definitions

C. New Standards

The FASB no longer considers new standards as authoritative in their own right. Instead, the new standards serve only to update the Codification and provide the basis for conclusions for the standard. New standards are composed of two items: the standard (similar to existing standards including the Basis for Conclusions) and an appendix containing Codification Update instructions. The title of the combined set of standard and instructions is "Accounting Standards Update YYYY-XX," where YYYY is the year and XX is the sequential number for each Update. For example, the combined numbers would be 2010-301, 2010-302, etc.

Content Specification Outline (CSO)

The Financial Accounting and Reporting section of the Uniform CPA Examination tests knowledge and understanding of the financial reporting framework used by business enterprises, not-for-profit organizations, and governmental entities. Exam content is specified in the Content and Skill Specification Outlines (CSOs/SSOs). In addition to demonstrating knowledge and understanding of accounting principles, candidates must also demonstrate the skills required to *apply* that knowledge in performing financial reporting and other tasks as CPAs.

Two new testing areas have been added to the CSO content: International Financial Reporting Standards and U.S. Securities and Exchange Commission Reporting requirements. This content is eligible for testing beginning with the January-February 2011 exam window.

Candidates will be expected to:

- Illustrate their understanding of the process by which standards are set and the roles of the U.S. Securities and Exchange Commission (SEC) and International Accounting Standards Board (IASB).
- Identify and understand the differences between financial statements prepared on the basis of accounting principles generally accepted in the United States (U.S. GAAP) and International Financial Reporting Standards (IRFS).
- Demonstrate the knowledge and skills necessary to comply with SEC reporting requirements (e.g., Form 10-Q, 10-K, Annual Report).
- Demonstrate their proficiency in first-time adoption of IFRS reporting requirements.

CHAPTER 1—U.S. GAAP CONCEPTS & FRAMEWORK

Problem 1-1 MULTIPLE-CHOICE QUESTIONS

1. Which of the following is true regarding the comparison of managerial to financial accounting?
   a. Managerial accounting is generally more precise.
   b. Managerial accounting has a past focus and financial accounting has a future focus.
   c. The emphasis on managerial accounting is relevance and the emphasis on financial accounting is timeliness.
   d. Managerial accounting need not follow generally accepted accounting principles (GAAP) while financial accounting must follow them. (R/07, FAR, #5, 8326)

2. Which of the following assumptions means that money is the common denominator of economic activity and provides an appropriate basis for accounting measurement and analysis?
   a. Going concern
   b. Periodicity
   c. Monetary unit
   d. Economic entity (R/06, FAR, #47, 8114)

3. Ande Co. estimates uncollectible accounts expense using the ratio of past actual losses from uncollectible accounts to past net credit sales, adjusted for anticipated conditions. The practice follows the accounting concept of
   a. Consistency
   b. Going concern
   c. Matching
   d. Substance over form (R/10, FAR, #1, 9301)

4. What is the purpose of information presented in notes to the financial statements?
   a. To provide disclosures required by generally accepted accounting principles
   b. To correct improper presentation in the financial statements
   c. To provide recognition of amounts not included in the totals of the financial statements
   d. To present management's responses to auditor comments (5/94, FAR, #6, 4821)

5. Which of the following is a generally accepted accounting principle that illustrates the practice of conservatism during a particular reporting period?
   a. Capitalization of research and development costs
   b. Accrual of a contingency deemed to be reasonably possible
   c. Reporting investments with appreciated market values, at market value
   d. Reporting inventory at the lower of cost or market value (R/07, FAR, #19, 8340)

6. Which of the following must be included in a company's summary of significant accounting policies in the notes to the financial statements?
   a. Description of current year equity transactions
   b. Summary of long-term debt outstanding
   c. Schedule of fixed assets
   d. Revenue recognition policies (R/06, FAR, #23, 8090)

7. Which of the following statements regarding basic accounting principles is false?
   a. Assets acquired, as well as liabilities incurred, by an enterprise are recorded at fair value.
   b. For income to be stated fairly, all expenses incurred in generating the revenues for a period must be recognized in that same period.
   c. The relative importance of data, the cost-benefit relationship of additional accuracy, and the possible confusion resulting from the use of too much detail are considerations that must be weighed in determining the materiality of accounting information.
   d. The usefulness of accounting information is enhanced when the information is presented in a manner consistent with that used in prior periods. (Editor, 6187)

8. The accounting model is divided into sub-models. The purpose of the results of operations sub-model is to report on the relative success of the profit-directed activities of an entity and is defined as which of the following?
   a. Assets = Liabilities + Owners' equity
   b. Revenues – Expenses = Net income
   c. Cash flows from operating activities +(–) Cash flows from investing activities +(–) Cash flows from financing activities = Change in cash
   d. All of the above (Editor, 6610)

9. Which of the following should be disclosed in a summary of significant accounting policies?
   a. Basis of profit recognition on long-term construction contracts
   b. Future minimum lease payments in the aggregate and for each of the five succeeding fiscal years
   c. Depreciation expense
   d. Composition of sales by segment (R/06, FAR, #1, 8068)

10. Which of the following is correct concerning financial statement disclosure of accounting policies?
    a. Disclosures should be limited to principles and methods peculiar to the industry in which the company operates.
    b. Disclosure of accounting policies is an integral part of the financial statements.
    c. The format and location of accounting policy disclosures are fixed by generally accepted accounting principles.
    d. Disclosures should duplicate details disclosed elsewhere in the financial statements. (R/06, FAR, #27, 8094)

11. Which of the following is true regarding a business enterprise that prepares its financial statements in U.S. dollars and in conformity with U.S. generally accepted accounting principles?
    a. The entity is required to disclose the effects of changing prices in the body of the financial statements.
    b. The entity is required to disclose supplementary information on the effects of changing prices.
    c. The entity is prohibited from disclosing changing prices information.
    d. The entity is encouraged, though not required, to disclose supplementary information on the effects of changing prices. (Editor, 89576)

12. According to the FASB's conceptual framework, asset valuation accounts are
    a. Assets
    b. Neither assets **nor** liabilities
    c. Part of stockholders' equity
    d. Liabilities (11/88, Theory, #1, 9001)

13. Bake Co.'s trial balance included the following at December 31, year 3:

Accounts payable	$ 80,000
Bonds payable, due 2004	300,000
Discount on bonds payable	15,000
Deferred income tax liability	25,000

The deferred income tax liability is not related to an asset for financial accounting purposes and is expected to reverse in year 4. What amount should be included in the current liability section of Bake's December 31, year 3, balance sheet?

a. $365,000
b. $390,000
c. $395,000
d. $420,000 (R/07, FAR, #35, 8356)

14. According to the FASB conceptual framework, certain assets are reported in financial statements at the amount of cash or its equivalent that would have to be paid if the same or equivalent assets were acquired currently. What is the name of the reporting concept?

a. Replacement cost
b. Current market value
c. Historical cost
d. Net realizable value (R/08, FAR, #1, 8556)

15. Which of the following is the market with the greatest volume and level of activity for an orderly transaction to occur for an asset or liability?

a. Perfect market
b. Principle market
c. Common market
d. Most advantageous market (Editors, 8516)

16. Which of the following is not considered in evaluating the highest and best use of an asset by market participants at the measurement date?

a. Physically possible
b. Legally permissible
c. Readily accessible
d. Financially feasible (Editors, 8517)

17. Which of the following is not a valuation technique used to measure fair value?

a. Market approach
b. Income approach
c. Cost approach
d. Sales approach (Editors, 8518)

18. What priority is given to unobservable inputs in the fair value hierarchy for inputs to valuation techniques used to measure fair value?

a. Level 1
b. Level 2
c. Level 3
d. Level 4 (Editors, 8519)

19. Which of the following items are not eligible to be measured at fair value using the fair value option?
    a. Financial instruments that are classified by the user as a component of shareholder's equity
    b. A firm commitment that would otherwise not be recognized at inception and only involves financial instruments
    c. The rights and obligations under a warranty that is not a financial instrument but permits the warrantor to settle by paying a third party to provide goods or services
    d. A host financial instrument resulting from the separation of an embedded nonfinancial instrument from a nonfinancial hybrid instrument (Editors, 8520)

20. According to the FASB conceptual framework, which of the following is an essential characteristic of an asset?
    a. The claims to an asset's benefit are legally enforceable.
    b. An asset is tangible.
    c. An asset is obtained at a cost.
    d. An asset provides future benefits. (5/92, Theory, #2, 2694)

21. Which of the following statements regarding fair value is false?
    a. Fair value is defined as the price that would be received to sell an asset or paid to transfer a liability in an orderly transaction between market participants at the measurement date.
    b. The definition of fair value is based on an exit price (for an asset, the price at which it would be sold), regardless of whether the entity plans to hold or sell the asset.
    c. The definition of fair value is based on an entry price (for an asset, the price at which it would be bought), regardless of whether the entity plans to hold or sell the asset.
    d. Fair value is market based rather than entity specific. (Editor, 89569)

22. In the FASB's fair value hierarchy, Level ______ estimates should be determined using quoted prices for identical assets or liabilities in active reference markets, if available.
    a. 1
    b. 2
    c. 3
    d. 4 (Editor, 89571)

23. Which of the following is not a characteristic of market participants when measuring fair value?
    a. They are independent of each other.
    b. They are knowledgeable and sufficiently informed about the transaction.
    c. They are related parties.
    d. They are willing and able to enter into the transaction. (Editor, 89430)

24. In its December 31 balance sheet, Butler Co. reported trade accounts receivable of $250,000 and related allowance for uncollectible accounts of $20,000. What is the total amount of risk of accounting loss related to Butler's trade accounts receivable, and what amount of that risk is off-balance sheet risk?

	Risk of accounting loss	Off-balance sheet risk
a.	$0	$0
b.	$230,000	$0
c.	$230,000	$20,000
d.	$250,000	$20,000

(R/99, FAR #6, 6775)

25. According to the FASB conceptual framework, an entity's revenue may result from
    a. A decrease in an asset from primary operations
    b. An increase in an asset from incidental transactions
    c. An increase in a liability from incidental transactions
    d. A decrease in a liability from primary operations (11/92, Theory, #3, 3436)

26. According to the FASB conceptual framework, comprehensive income includes which of the following?

	Loss on discontinued operations	Investments by owners	
a.	Yes	Yes	
b.	Yes	No	
c.	No	Yes	
d.	No	No	(6604)

27. Which of the following items is **not** classified as "other comprehensive income"?
    a. Extraordinary gains from extinguishment of debt
    b. Foreign currency translation adjustments
    c. Minimum pension liability equity adjustment for a defined-benefit pension plan
    d. Unrealized gains for the year on available-for-sale marketable securities (R/08, FAR, #3, 8558)

28. A business entity would not be in compliance with FASB ASC 220, *Reporting Comprehensive Income*, if the entity does which of the following?
    a. Reports comprehensive income by preparing a statement of income and a separate statement of comprehensive income
    b. Classifies items of other comprehensive income by their nature, such as foreign currency items or minimum pension liability adjustments
    c. Adds the accumulated balance of other comprehensive income to the retained earnings account balance, and describes the combined total as the retained earnings balance
    d. None of the above (Editor, 6612)

29. The information provided in a statement of cash flows does not help investors, creditors, and others to assess which of the following?
    a. The enterprise's financial position
    b. The enterprise's ability to generate positive future net cash flows
    c. The enterprise's ability to meet its obligations, its ability to pay dividends, and its needs for external financing
    d. The reasons for differences between net income and associated cash receipts and payments. (Editor, 89585)

30. Under the _____________ method, enterprises are encouraged to report major classes of gross cash receipts and gross cash payments and their arithmetic sum – the net cash flow from operating activities.
    a. Direct
    b. Indirect
    c. Asset and liability
    d. Cash operating (Editor, 89587)

31. In analyzing a company's financial statements, which financial statement would a potential investor primarily use to assess the company's liquidity and financial flexibility?
    a. Balance sheet
    b. Income statement
    c. Statement of retained earnings
    d. Statement of cash flows (11/94, FAR, #5, 5270)

32. A company's year-end balance sheet is shown below:

Assets	
Cash	$ 300,000
Accounts receivable	350,000
Inventory	600,000
Property, plant and equipment (net)	2,000,000
	$3,250,000
Liabilities and shareholder equity	
Current liabilities	$ 700,000
Long-term liabilities	600,000
Common stock	800,000
Retained earnings	1,150,000
	$3,250,000

What is the current ratio as of December 31?

a. 1.79
b. 0.93
c. 0.67
d. 0.43 (R/08, FAR, #4, 8559)

33. What effect would the sale of a company's trading securities at their carrying amounts for cash have on each of the following ratios?

	Current ratio	Quick ratio
a.	No effect	No effect
b.	Increase	Increase
c.	No effect	Increase
d.	Increase	No effect

(11/95, FAR, #58, 6140)

34. At December 30 of the current year, Vida Co. had cash of $200,000, a current ratio of 1.5:1 and a quick ratio of .5:1. On December 31, all cash was used to reduce accounts payable. How did these cash payments affect the ratios?

	Current ratio	Quick ratio
a.	Increased	Decreased
b.	Increased	No effect
c.	Decreased	Increased
d.	Decreased	No effect

(5/94, FAR, #60, amended, 4875)

35. North Bank is analyzing Belle Corp.'s financial statements for a possible extension of credit. Belle's quick ratio is significantly better than the industry average. Which of the following factors should North consider as a possible limitation of using this ratio when evaluating Belle's creditworthiness?

a. Fluctuating market prices of short-term investments may adversely affect the ratio.
b. Increasing market prices for Belle's inventory may adversely affect the ratio.
c. Belle may need to sell its available-for-sale investments to meet its current obligations.
d. Belle may need to liquidate its inventory to meet its long-term obligations. (R/99, FAR, #4, 6773)

36. Redwood Co.'s financial statements had the following information at year end:

Cash	$ 60,000
Accounts receivable	180,000
Allowance for uncollectible accounts	8,000
Inventory	240,000
Short-term marketable securities	90,000
Prepaid rent	18,000
Current liabilities	400,000
Long-term debt	220,000

What was Redwood's quick ratio?

a. 0.81 to 1
b. 0.83 to 1
c. 0.94 to 1
d. 1.46 to 1 (R/08, FAR, #29, 8584)

37. At December 31 of the current year, Curry Co. had the following balances in selected asset accounts:

	Current year	Increase over previous year
Cash	$ 300	$100
Accounts receivable, net	1,200	400
Inventory	500	200
Prepaid expenses	100	40
Other assets	400	150
Total assets	$2,500	$890

Curry also had current liabilities of $1,000 at December 31 and net credit sales of $7,200 for the year. What is Curry's acid-test ratio at December 31 of the current year?

a. 1.5
b. 1.6
c. 2.0
d. 2.1 (5/93, PII, #15, amended, 4123)

38. Are the following ratios useful in assessing the liquidity position of a company?

	Defensive-interval ratio	Return on stockholders' equity
a.	Yes	Yes
b.	Yes	No
c.	No	Yes
d.	No	No

(11/90, Theory, #10, 1755)

39. The following information pertains to Ali Corp. as of and for the current year ended December 31:

Liabilities	$ 60,000
Stockholders' equity	500,000
Shares of common stock issued and outstanding	10,000
Net income	30,000

During the year, Ali's officers exercised stock options for 1,000 shares of stock at an option price of $8 per share. What was the effect of exercising the stock options?

a. Debt-to-equity ratio decreased to 12%
b. Earnings per share increased by $0.33
c. Asset turnover increased to 5.4%
d. No ratios were affected (5/92, PII, #17, amended, 2649)

40. Barr Co. has total debt of $420,000 and stockholders' equity of $700,000. Barr is seeking capital to fund an expansion. Barr is planning to issue an additional $300,000 in common stock and is negotiating with a bank to borrow additional funds. The bank is requiring a debt-to-equity ratio of .75. What is the maximum additional amount Barr will be able to borrow?

    a. $225,000
    b. $330,000
    c. $525,000
    d. $750,000 (11/95, FAR, #59, 6141)

Items 41 and 42 are based on the following:

The following selected financial data pertains to Alex Corporation for the current year ended December 31:

Operating income	$ 900,000
Interest expense	(100,000)
Income before income tax	800,000
Income tax expense	(320,000)
Net income	480,000
Preferred stock dividends	(200,000)
Net income available to common stockholders	$ 280,000

41. The times interest earned ratio is

    a. 2.8 to 1
    b. 4.8 to 1
    c. 8.0 to 1
    d. 9.0 to 1 (11/86, PI, #56, amended, 9039)

42. The times preferred dividend earned ratio is

    a. 1.4 to 1
    b. 1.7 to 1
    c. 2.4 to 1
    d. 4.0 to 1 (11/86, PI, #57, amended, 1263)

43. Stent Co. had total assets of $760,000, capital stock of $150,000, and retained earnings of $215,000. What was Stent's debt-to-equity ratio?

    a. 2.63
    b. 1.08
    c. 0.52
    d. 0.48 (R/07, FAR, #17, 8338)

44. The following financial ratios and calculations were based on information from Kohl Co.'s financial statements for the current year:

    Accounts receivable turnover
    10 times during the year

    Total assets turnover
    2 times during the year

    Average receivables during the year
    $200,000

    What was Kohl's average total assets for the year?

    a. $2,000,000
    b. $1,000,000
    c. $ 400,000
    d. $ 200,000 (R/05, FAR, #16, 7760)

45. The controller of Peabody, Inc. has been asked to present an analysis of accounts receivable collections at the upcoming staff meeting. The following information is used:

	12/31, year 2	12/31, year 1
Accounts receivable	$100,000	$130,000
Allowance, doubtful accounts	(20,000)	(40,000)
Sales	400,000	200,000
Cost of goods sold	350,000	170,000

What is the receivables turnover ratio as of December 31, year 2?

a. 5.0
b. 4.7
c. 3.5
d. 0.6 (R/07, FAR, #46, 8367)

46. TGR Enterprises provided the following information from its statement of financial position for the year ended December 31, year 1:

	January 1	December 31
Cash	$ 10,000	$ 50,000
Accounts receivable	120,000	100,000
Inventories	200,000	160,000
Prepaid expenses	20,000	10,000
Accounts payable	175,000	120,000
Accrued liabilities	25,000	30,000

TGR's sales and cost of sales for year 1 were $1,400,000 and $840,000, respectively. What is the accounts receivable turnover, in days?

a. 26.1
b. 28.7
c. 31.3
d. 41.7 (R/08, FAR, #5, 8560)

47. Kline Co. had the following sales and accounts receivable balances at the end of the current year:

Cash sales	$1,000,000
Net credit sales	3,000,000
Net accounts receivable, 1/1	100,000
Net accounts receivable, 12/31	400,000

What is Kline's average collection period for its accounts receivable?

a. 48.0 days
b. 30.0 days
c. 22.5 days
d. 12.0 days (R/02, FAR #3, 7058)

48. Selected data pertaining to Lore Co. for the calendar year is as follows:

Net cash sales	$ 3,000
Cost of goods sold	18,000
Inventory at beginning of year	6,000
Purchases	24,000
Accounts receivable at beginning of year	20,000
Accounts receivable at end of year	22,000

What was the inventory turnover for the year?

a. 1.2 times
b. 1.5 times
c. 2.0 times
d. 3.0 times (5/95, FAR, #59, 5595)

49. Selected information from the accounting records of Dalton Manufacturing Company is as follows:

Net sales for the current year	$1,800,000
Cost of goods sold for the current year	1,200,000
Inventories at December 31, previous year	336,000
Inventories at December 31, current year	288,000

Assuming there are 300 working days per year, what is the number of days' sales in average inventories for the current year?

a. 78
b. 72
c. 52
d. 48

(11/83, PI, #18, amended, 9162)

50. The following computations were made from Clay Co.'s current year end books:

Number of days' sales in inventory	61
Number of days' sales in trade accounts receivable	33

What was the number of days in Clay's current year operating cycle?

a. 33
b. 47
c. 61
d. 94

(5/92, PII, #16, amended, 2648)

51. Hoyt Corp.'s current balance sheet reports the following stockholders' equity:

5% cumulative preferred stock, par value $100 per share; 2,500 shares issued and outstanding	$250,000
Common stock, par value $3.50 per share; 100,000 shares issued and outstanding	350,000
Additional paid-in capital in excess of par value of common stock	125,000
Retained earnings	300,000

Dividends in arrears on the preferred stock amount to $25,000. If Hoyt were to be liquidated, the preferred stockholders would receive par value plus a premium of $50,000. The book value per share of common stock is

a. $7.75
b. $7.50
c. $7.25
d. $7.00

(11/91, PII, #3, 2451)

52. The following is the stockholders' equity section of Harbor Co.'s balance sheet at December 31:

Common stock $10 par, 100,000 shares authorized, 50,000 shares issued of which 5,000 have been reacquired, and are held in treasury	$ 450,000
Additional paid-in capital common stock	1,100,000
Retained earnings	800,000
Subtotal	2,350,000
Less treasury stock	(150,000)
Total stockholders' equity	$2,200,000

Harbor has insignificant amounts of convertible securities, stock warrants, and stock options. What is the book value per share of Harbor's common stock?

a. $31
b. $44
c. $46
d. $49

(R/08, FAR, #38, 8593)

53. The following data pertain to Cowl Inc. for the current year ended December 31:

Net sales	$ 600,000
Net income	150,000
Total assets, January 1	2,000,000
Total assets, December 31	3,000,000

What was Cowl's rate of return on assets?

a. 5%
b. 6%
c. 20%
d. 24% (11/95, FAR, #60, amended, 6142)

54. On December 31 of the previous and current year, Taft Corporation had 100,000 shares of common stock and 50,000 shares of noncumulative and nonconvertible preferred stock issued and outstanding. Additional information for the current year follows:

Stockholder's equity at 12/31	$4,500,000
Net income year ended 12/31	1,200,000
Dividends on preferred stock year ended 12/31	300,000
Market price per share of common stock at 12/31	72

The price-earnings ratio on common stock at December 31 was

a. 5 to 1
b. 6 to 1
c. 8 to 1
d. 9 to 1 (11/87, PI, #60, amended, 1259)

55. The following data pertain to Thorne Corp. for the current calendar year:

Net income	$240,000
Dividends paid on common stock	120,000
Common stock outstanding (unchanged during year)	300,000 shares

The market price per share of Thorne's common stock at December 31 was $12. The price-earnings ratio at December 31 was

a. 9.6 to 1
b. 10.0 to 1
c. 15.0 to 1
d. 30.0 to 1 (11/89, PI, #57, amended, 1255)

56. How are dividends per share for common stock used in the calculation of the following?

	Dividend per share payout ratio	Earnings per share
a.	Numerator	Numerator
b.	Numerator	Not used
c.	Denominator	Not used
d.	Denominator	Denominator

(5/87, Theory, #40, 9040)

57. What are the Statements of Financial Accounting Concepts intended to establish?

a. Generally accepted accounting principles in financial reporting by business enterprises
b. The meaning of "Present fairly in accordance with generally accepted accounting principles"
c. The objectives and concepts for use in developing standards of financial accounting and reporting
d. The hierarchy of sources of generally accepted accounting principles (5/94, FAR, #2, 4817)

58. During a period when an enterprise is under the direction of a particular management, its financial statements will directly provide information about

    a. Both enterprise performance and management performance
    b. Management performance but **not** directly provide information about enterprise performance
    c. Enterprise performance but **not** directly provide information about management performance
    d. Neither enterprise performance nor management performance (5/94, FAR, #4, 4819)

59. According to Statements of Financial Accounting Concepts, neutrality is an ingredient of

	Faithful Representation	Relevance
a.	Yes	Yes
b.	Yes	No
c.	No	Yes
d.	No	No

(5/11, amended, FAR, #1, 5266)

60. According to the FASB conceptual framework, which of the following correctly pairs a fundamental qualitative characteristic of accounting information with one of its components?

    a. Relevance and free from error
    b. Faithful representation and confirmatory value
    c. Relevance and predictive value
    d. Faithful representation and materiality (5/11, amended, FAR, #26, 9326)

61. Which of the following is a false statement?

    a. Information is material if omitting it or misstating it could influence decisions that users make.
    b. Comparability and consistency are the same thing.
    c. Classifying, characterizing, and presenting information clearly and concisely makes it understandable.
    d. If financial information is to be useful, it must be relevant and faithfully represent what it purports to represent. (5/11, amended, 5537)

62. According to the FASB conceptual framework, the usefulness of providing information in financial statements is subject to the constraint of

    a. Consistency
    b. Cost-benefit
    c. Reliability
    d. Representational faithfulness (11/94, FAR, #2, 6084)

63. FASB's conceptual framework explains both financial and physical capital maintenance concepts. Which capital maintenance concept is applied to currently reported net income, and which is applied to comprehensive income?

	Currently reported net income	Comprehensive income
a.	Financial capital	Physical capital
b.	Physical capital	Physical capital
c.	Financial capital	Financial capital
d.	Physical capital	Financial capital

(11/91, Theory, #1, 2509)

64. Which of the following statements best describes an operating procedure for issuing a new Financial Accounting Standards Board (FASB) Standard?

    a. The emerging issues task force must approve a discussion memorandum before it is disseminated to the public.
    b. The exposure draft is modified per public opinion before issuing the discussion memorandum.
    c. A new Standard is issued only after a majority vote by the members of the FASB.
    d. A new Standard can be rescinded by a majority vote of the AICPA membership.

(R/06, FAR, #48, 8115)

65. In the hierarchy of generally accepted accounting principles, there are how many levels of authoritative GAAP?
    a. 1
    b. 2
    c. 3
    d. 4 (Editors, 8943)

66. Guidance for which of the following is included in the FASB Accounting Standards Codification?
    a. Governmental Accounting Standards (GAS)
    b. Regulatory Accounting Principles (RAP)
    c. Securities and Exchange Commission (SEC) content
    d. Other Comprehensive Basis of Accounting (OCBOA) (Editors, 8944)

67. Which of the following statements regarding Statements of Financial Accounting Concepts (SFACs) is true?
    a. The SFACs are designed to constitute a foundation of financial accounting standards.
    b. These conceptual statements establish account standards and disclosure practices for particular items.
    c. These conceptual statements are enforceable under the Rules of Conduct of the Code of Professional Ethics.
    d. All of the above (Editor, 89526)

68. Which of the following is not included in the FASB Accounting Standards Codification?
    a. FASB Statements and Interpretations
    b. FASB Technical Bulletins
    c. AICPA Accounting Interpretations
    d. FASB Statements of Financial Accounting Concepts (Editor, 89527)

Problem 1-2 SIMULATION: Ratio Analysis

Daley Inc. is consistently profitable. Daley's normal financial statement relationships are as follows:

I.	Current Ratio	3 to 1
II.	Inventory turnover	4 times
III.	Total debt/total assets ratio	0.5 to 1

For each event in the table below, determine whether each transaction or event Increased, Decreased, or had No effect on each of the ratios for the year.

Event	Current Ratio	Inventory Turnover	Total debt/ Total assets
Daley issued a stock dividend.			
Daley declared, but did not pay, a cash dividend.			
Customers returned invoiced goods for which they had not paid.			
Accounts payable were paid on December 31.			
Daley recorded both a receivable from an insurance company and a loss from fire damage to a factory building.			
Early in the year, Daley increased the selling price of one of its products that had a demand in excess of capacity. The number of units sold was the same as the previous year.			

(Editor, 9016)

Problem 1-3 SIMULATION: Research

Question: A business enterprise that prepares its financial statements in U.S. dollars and in accordance with U.S. generally accepted accounting principles is encouraged, but not required, to disclose supplementary information on the effects of what?

FASB ASC: [ ] - [ ] - [ ] - [ ]

(9102)

Solution 1-1 MULTIPLE-CHOICE ANSWERS

Accounting Environment

1. (d) Financial and managerial accounting both provide information useful for decision making. Besides differences in primary user, external for financial and internal for managerial, financial accounting must follow generally accepted accounting principles (GAAP), whereas managerial accounting does not. Managerial accounting is not necessarily more precise. Managerial and financial accounting are not distinguished by temporal focus. Relevance and timeliness are important in both managerial and financial accounting. (8326)

2. (c) Accounting operates in an environment almost as varied as the many types of entities which accounting serves. To provide a basis for comparison, it has been necessary to formulate certain underlying environmental assumptions on which financial accounting theory is based. The monetary unit (unit-of-measure) assumption is used for the measurement and reporting of economic activity. The going concern assumption is that the business is not expected to liquidate in the near future. The periodicity assumption recognizes the necessity of providing financial accounting information on a periodic, timely basis, so that it is useful in decision making. The economic entity assumption states in order to properly report those economic events affecting an entity, the specific economic entity must be defined and separated from other entities. (8114)

3. (c) This practice follows the accounting concept of matching. The matching concept is a basic accounting principle that believes for income to be stated fairly, all expenses incurred in generating revenues for a period must be recognized in that same period. Consistency provides for interperiod comparability and the identification of trends. Going concern is an underlying environmental assumption that the business is not expected to liquidate in the near future. The concept of substance over form means that the financial statements reflect the financial reality of the entity (the economic substance) rather than the underlying legal form of transactions or events. (9301)

4. (a) The notes to the financial statements provide disclosures required by generally accepted accounting principles. The notes may be used to amplify or explain items presented in the main body of the financial statements but not to correct errors or omissions in the statements. Management's responses to auditor comments would normally be reported in a separate letter to the auditors and not as part of the financial statements. (4821)

5. (d) Conservatism is using the accounting treatment which understates rather than overstates income or net assets. Reporting inventory at the lower of cost or market is a generally accepted accounting principle that illustrates conservatism. Future economic benefits deriving from research and development activities, if any, are uncertain in their amount and timing. Due to these uncertainties GAAP requires most research and development costs to be expensed and not capitalized. Contingent liabilities arise from events or circumstances occurring before the balance sheet date, the resolution of which is contingent upon a future event or circumstance. Contingent losses deemed to be reasonably possible are not accrued unless the amount also can be reasonably estimated. Contingent gains are disclosed but not recognized in income. Reporting investments with appreciated market values at market value clearly is not a choice that understates rather than overstates net assets. (8340)

6. (d) The summary of significant accounting policies should disclose policies involving a choice of alternative acceptable polices, policies peculiar to that particular industry, and unusual applications of acceptable principles. This includes revenue recognition policies. Financial statement disclosure of accounting policies should not duplicate details presented elsewhere as part of the financial statements. Descriptions of transactions, summaries of debt, and schedules of assets are not policies and are located elsewhere in the financial statements. (8090)

7. (a) Assets acquired, as well as liabilities incurred, by an enterprise are recorded at cost, not at fair value. All other choices are true statements. (6187)

8. (b) The purpose of the results of operations sub-model is to report on the relative success of the profit-directed activities of an entity. The revenues obtained through the sale of goods and services are compared to the expenses incurred in providing those goods and services. Revenues – Expenses = Net income is the results of operations sub-model. Cash flows from operating activities +(–) Cash flows from investing activities +(–) Cash flows from financing activities = Change in cash is a sub-model of the statement of cash flows. Assets = Liabilities + Owners' equity is the financial position sub-model. (6610)

9. (a) The summary of significant accounting policies should disclose policies involving a choice of alternative acceptable polices, policies peculiar to that particular industry, and unusual applications of acceptable principles. This includes methods of profit recognition on long-term construction contracts. Financial statement disclosure of accounting policies should not duplicate details presented elsewhere as part of the financial statements. Future minimum lease payments in the aggregate and for each of the five succeeding fiscal years generally are presented in the notes to the financial statements, but not with the summary of significant accounting policies. Depreciation expense and composition of sales by segment are presented on the face of the financial statements. (8068)

10. (b) Disclosure of all significant accounting policies in an enterprise's financial statements is required. Thus, disclosure of accounting policies is an integral part of the financial statements. Disclosures should not be limited to principles and methods peculiar to the industry in which it operates, but instead include policies involving a choice of alternative acceptable polices, policies peculiar to that particular industry, and unusual applications of acceptable principles. There is no specific required format and location of accounting policy disclosures. Financial statement disclosure of accounting policies should not duplicate details presented elsewhere as part of the financial statements. (8094)

11. (d) A business enterprise that prepares its financial statements in U.S. dollars and in conformity with U.S. GAAP is encouraged, though not required, to disclose supplementary information on the effects of changing prices. (89576)

Balance Sheet & Fair Value

12. (b) A separate item that reduces or increases the carrying amount of an asset is sometimes found in financial statements. For example, an estimate of uncollectible amounts reduces receivables to the amount expected to be collected, or a premium on a bond receivable increases the receivable to its cost or present value. Those 'valuation accounts' are part of the related asset or liability and do not stand on their own. (9001)

13. (b) Current liabilities are obligations whose liquidation is expected to require the use of existing current assets or the creation of other current liabilities. The accounts payable and bonds payable are expected to require the use of existing current assets. The discount on bonds payable is a valuation account that reflects a reduction in bonds payable to $285,000 ($300,000 – $15,000). The deferred income tax liability is a current liability in that it will reverse in the following year. The amount included in the current liability section of the balance sheet would be $390,000 ($80,000 + $285,000 + $25,000). (8356)

14. (a) This reporting concept is replacement cost. It is defined as the price of a new, similar item after allowance for use and depreciation. Current market value is the hypothetical selling price that could be obtained in an arm's-length transaction. Historical cost is the acquisition cost less depreciation or amortization to date. Net realizable value is the net amount expected to be received in cash. (8556)

15. (b) The principle market is the market with the greatest volume and level of activity for an orderly transaction to occur for an asset or liability. A perfect market is where individuals have perfect information and there is perfect competition. A financial market is where entities can easily buy and sell financial securities. Accounting standards make no reference to perfect or financial markets. A most advantageous market is the market with the price that maximizes the amount that would be received for an asset or minimizes the amount that would be paid to transfer a liability. (8516)

16. (c) An asset being readily accessible is not considered in evaluating an asset for fair value measurement. The highest and best use of an asset establishes the valuation premise used to measure the fair value of an asset. The highest and best use of the asset is applied considering the use of the asset that is physically possible, legally permissible, and financially feasible at the measurement date. (8517)

17. (d) The sales approach is not a valuation technique used to measure fair value. Valuation techniques consistent with the market approach, income approach, and/or cost approach shall be used to measure fair value. The technique(s) used shall be the best appropriate in the circumstance and for which sufficient data is available. (8518)

18. (c) The lowest priority, Level 3, is given to unobservable inputs. The highest level, Level 1, is given to quoted prices in active markets for identical assets or liabilities. Level 2 inputs are other than quoted prices included within Level 1 that are observable for the asset or liability, either directly or indirectly. There is no Level 4 in the fair value hierarchy. (8519)

19. (a) Financial instruments that are classified by the user as a component of shareholder's equity are not eligible to be measured at fair value using the fair value option. Certain commitments, rights and obligations, and a host financial instrument resulting from the separation of an embedded nonfinancial instrument from a nonfinancial hybrid instrument are eligible to be measured using the fair value option. (8520)

20. (d) An asset has three essential characteristics: (1) it embodies a probable future benefit that involves a capacity, singly or in combination with other assets, to contribute directly or indirectly to future net cash inflows, (2) a particular entity can obtain the benefit and control others' access to it, and (3) the transaction or other event giving rise to the entity's right to or control of the benefit has already occurred. The legal enforceability of a claim to a benefit is not a prerequisite for a benefit to qualify as an asset if the entity has the ability to obtain and control the benefit in other ways. Assets may be intangible and acquired without cost. (2694)

21. (c) The definition of fair value is based on an exit price (for an asset, the price at which it would be sold) rather than an entry price (for an asset, the price at which it would be bought), regardless of whether the entity plans to hold or sell the asset. All other statements are true. (89569)

22. (a) Level 1 estimates should be determined using quoted prices for identical assets or liabilities in active reference markets, if available. Level 2 estimates should be determined using quoted prices for similar assets or liabilities in active markets, adjusted as appropriate for differences. Level 3 estimates should be determined based on the results of multiple valuation techniques whenever the information necessary to apply those techniques is available. There is no Level 4 in the fair value hierarchy. (89571)

23. (c) Market participants are buyers and sellers in the market for the asset or liability that are independent of the reporting entity, knowledgeable, willing and able to transact for the asset or liability (not forced). (89430)

24. (b) The total risk of accounting loss is the amount of potential loss the entity would suffer if all parties to the financial instruments failed completely to perform and the amounts due proved to be of no value to the entity. Butler Co. had already recorded an allowance for uncollectible accounts of $20,000 on its trade accounts receivable of $250,000, so the net of $230,000 is the risk of accounting loss. The entire amount is shown on the balance sheet, thus there is no off-balance sheet risk involved. (6775)

Other Financial Statements

25. (d) Revenues are inflows or other enhancements of assets or settlements of liabilities from activities that constitute the entity's major or central operations. An expense would result from an outflow or other using up of assets from activities that constitute the entity's major or central operations. Gains and losses result from changes in net assets from an entity's peripheral or incidental transactions. (3436)

26. (b) Comprehensive income includes all changes in equity during a period except those resulting from investments by owners and distributions to owners. Loss on discontinued operations is part of comprehensive income. (6604)

27. (a) Extraordinary gains from extinguishment of debt is not classified as other comprehensive income. Foreign currency translation adjustments, pension liability adjustments for a defined benefit pension plan, and unrealized gains on available-for-sale marketable securities are all classified as other comprehensive income. (8558)

28. (c) An entity must display the accumulated balance of other comprehensive income separately from retained earnings and additional paid-in capital, in the equity section of a statement of financial position. One of the acceptable ways that an entity can report comprehensive income is to prepare a statement of income and a separate statement of comprehensive income. An entity must classify items of other comprehensive income by their nature. Some examples of classifications of comprehensive income include foreign currency items and minimum pension liability adjustments. (6612)

29. (a) The information provided in a statement of cash flows helps investors, creditors, and others to assess the reasons for differences between net income and associated cash receipts and payments, not financial position. The information provided in a statement of financial position (balance sheet) helps investors, creditors, and others to assess the enterprise's financial position. (89585)

30. (a) Under the direct method, enterprises are encouraged to report major classes of gross cash receipts and gross cash payments and their arithmetic sum – the net cash flow from operating activities. The indirect method calculates the net cash flow from operating activities by adjusting net income to reconcile it to net cash flow from operating activities. (89587)

Financial Analysis—Solvency

31. (a) The balance sheet is the financial statement that should be primarily used to assess a company's liquidity and financial flexibility. The balance sheet, however, provides an incomplete picture of either a company's liquidity or financial flexibility, unless it is used in conjunction with at least a cash flow statement. (5270)

32. (a) The current ratio is a primary test of the overall solvency of the enterprise and its ability to meet current obligations from current assets. It is derived by dividing the current assets by the current liabilities. Current assets include the $300,000 in cash, $350,000 in accounts receivable, and $600,000 in inventory for a total of $1,250,000. The current liabilities are given as $700,000. [$1,250,000 / $700,000 = 1.79] (8559)

33. (a) The sale of a company's trading securities at their carrying amounts for cash has no effect on either ratio. Both the trading securities and cash are current assets, thus the current asset amount does not change in the current ratio (current assets divided by current liabilities). The numerator of the quick ratio is cash plus marketable securities plus net receivables; so cash increases for the same amount that marketable securities decreases. (6140)

34. (a) When the current ratio is greater than 1:1, any decrease in current liabilities, even when accompanied by a decrease in current assets by an equal amount, will cause an increase in the current ratio. When the quick ratio is less than 1:1, any decrease in quick assets, even when accompanied by a decrease in current liabilities by an equal amount, will cause a decrease in the quick ratio. (4875)

35. (a) The quick ratio is calculated by dividing the total of cash, marketable securities, and net receivables by current liabilities. Fluctuating market prices may cause the marketable securities in the numerator to decrease, thus creating an adverse effect on the quick ratio. Because inventory is not included in the quick ratio, increasing inventory market prices would have no effect on the quick ratio. The quick ratio provides a measure to help North evaluate if Belle has sufficient liquid assets, such as available-for-sale investments, to meet its current obligations. The quick ratio does not include inventory or long-term obligations. (6773)

36. (a) The quick ratio, also known as the acid-test ratio, provides a test of immediate solvency. It is derived by dividing the sum of cash, marketable securities, and net receivables by the current liabilities. [($60,000 + $90,000 + ($180,000 – $8,000)) / $400,000 = 0.805] Rounding the 0.805 to two decimal places gets the quick ratio of 0.81 to 1. (8584)

37. (a) The acid-test ratio is computed by dividing cash, short-term marketable securities, and net receivables by current liabilities.

$$\text{Acid-test ratio} = \frac{\text{Cash + Marketable securities + Net receivables}}{\text{Current liabilities}}$$

$$= (\$300 + \$0 + \$1{,}200) / \$1{,}000 = 1.5$$

(4123)

38. (b) The defensive-interval ratio is a liquidity ratio and the return on stockholders' equity is a profitability (performance) ratio. The defensive-interval ratio is computed by dividing defensive assets (cash, marketable securities, and net receivables) by projected daily expenditures from operations. Projected daily expenditures are computed by dividing cost of goods sold plus selling and administrative expenses and other ordinary cash expenses by 365 days. This ratio measures the time span a firm can operate on present liquid assets without resorting to revenues from a future period. (1755)

39. (a) During the year the exercise of the stock options increased Ali's total assets and total stockholders' equity by $8,000 (i.e., 1,000 × $8). The debt-to-equity ratio is computed by dividing total liabilities by total stockholders' equity. Therefore, the exercise of the stock options decreased the debt-to-equity ratio to 12% (i.e., $60,000 / $500,000) because it increased total stockholders' equity, the denominator of the ratio, but did not affect total liabilities, the numerator of the ratio. Earnings per share (EPS) is computed by dividing net income to common stockholders by the weighted-average number of common shares outstanding. The exercise of the stock options increased the weighted-average number of common shares outstanding, the denominator of the earnings per share ratio, but did not affect net income to common stockholders, the numerator of the ratio, thereby decreasing EPS. Asset turnover is computed by dividing sales by average total assets. Since the exercise of the stock options increased total assets, Ali's asset turnover would decrease as a result. (2649)

40. (b)

Current stockholders' equity	$ 700,000
Anticipated sales of stock	300,000
Total projected stockholders' equity	$ 1,000,000

Maximum debt-to-equity ratio: MD / $1,000,000 = .75

Maximum debt ($1,000,000 × .75)	$ 750,000
Less: Current debt	(420,000)
Additional maximum Barr may borrow	$ 330,000

(6141)

41. (d) The times-interest-earned (TIE) ratio measures an entity's ability to meet its interest payments. Income taxes are not subtracted from operating income because interest is tax deductible.

$$\text{TIE Ratio} = \frac{\text{Income before interest \& taxes}}{\text{Interest expense}} = \frac{\$900{,}000}{\$100{,}000} = 9.0 \text{ to } 1$$

(9039)

42. (c) The times-preferred-dividend-earned (TPDE) ratio measures an entity's ability to meet preferred dividend payments. Because dividends are not tax deductible, this ratio is computed on the basis of net income (i.e., after income taxes).

$$\text{TPDE Ratio} = \frac{\text{Net income}}{\text{Preferred dividends}} = \frac{\$480{,}000}{\$200{,}000} = 2.4 \text{ to } 1$$

(1263)

43. (b) The debt-to-equity ratio provides a measure of the relative amounts of resources provided by creditors and owners and is computed by dividing total liabilities by owners' equity. The owners' equity consists of the $150,000 capital stock and $215,000 retained earnings for a total of $365,000. Since assets = liabilities + owners' equity, total liabilities equals $395,000. Then $395,000 / $365,000 = 1.08 debt-to-equity ratio. (8338)

Financial Analysis—Operational Efficiency

44. (b)

Net credit sales / average net receivables = accounts receivable turnover
Net credit sales / $200,000 = 10
Net credit sales = $2,000,000

Total assets turnover = total sales (net credit sales in this case) / average total assets
2 = 2,000,000 / average total assets
Average total assets = $2,000,000 / 2
Average total assets = $1,000,000 (7760)

45. (b) The receivables turnover ratio is calculated by dividing net credit sales by the average net receivables. An average generally is determined by adding the beginning and ending balances and dividing by two. The beginning net receivables balance of $90,000 ($130,000 A/R – $40,000 doubtful allowance) plus ending net receivables balance of $80,000 ($100,000 A/R – $20,000 doubtful) equals $170,000; dividing this by two results in $85,000 average net receivables. The sales of $400,000 divided by the $85,000 equates into a 4.7 receivables turnover ratio. (8367)

46. (b) The accounts receivable turnover in days tests the average number of days to collect receivables and is computed by taking the number of business days used in a year over the accounts receivable turnover. The accounts receivable turnover is the net credit sales over the average net accounts receivable. The number 360 is commonly used as the number of business days in a year because it is easily divisible by 12 to get a monthly number. Some analysts prefer to use 365, 300, or 250 as the number of business days in the year. The net credit sales of $1,400,000 over the average net receivables of $110,000 equals approximately 12.72. Using 365 days divided by 12.72 equals approximately 28.7. This question is an example of how you may have to try the different number of business days used to get to one of the answer choices. (8560)

47. (b) Receivables Turnover:

$$\frac{\text{Net Credit Sales}}{\text{Average Net Receivables}} = \frac{\$3{,}000{,}000}{(\$100{,}000 + \$400{,}000)\,/\,2} = 12$$

$$\text{Number of Day's Sales in Average Receivables:} = \frac{360}{\text{Receivables Turnover}}$$

$$= \frac{360}{12} = 30\text{ days}$$

(7058)

48. (c) To compute the inventory turnover for the year, the inventory at the end of the year must first be determined. Inventory turnover equals cost of goods sold divided by average inventory.

Inventory, 1/1	$ 6,000
Plus: Purchases	24,000
Goods available for sale	30,000
Less: Cost of goods sold	(18,000)
Inventory, 12/31	$ 12,000

$$\text{Inventory turnover} = \frac{\$18{,}000}{(\$6{,}000 + \$12{,}000)\,/\,2} = 2.0\text{ times}$$ (5595)

49. (a) Number of days sales in average inventories = average inventory / cost of goods sold / 300 business days.

$$\frac{(\$336{,}000 + \$288{,}000)\,/\,2}{\$1{,}200{,}000\,/\,300} = \frac{\$312{,}000}{\$4{,}000} = 78\text{ days}$$ (9162)

50. (d) The operating cycle is the average length of time that it takes to sell an inventory item and to collect the cash from the sale.

Number of days' sales in inventory	61
Number of days' sales in trade accounts receivable	33
Number of days in Clay's operating cycle	94

(2648)

Financial Analysis—Profitability

51. (d) The book value per common share is calculated as total stockholders' equity less preferred stockholders' equity, divided by the number of common shares outstanding. The liquidating value of the preferred stock of $300,000 ($250,000 par value + $50,000 premium) is used to determine preferred stockholders' equity because that amount exceeds the par value of the preferred stock. The cumulative preferred stock dividends in arrears of $25,000 is also used in determining preferred stockholders' equity because they must be paid before any dividends can be paid on the common shares.

$$\text{Book value per common share} = \frac{\text{Stockholders' equity} - \text{Preferred stockholders' equity}}{\text{Common shares outstanding}}$$

$$= \frac{\$1{,}025{,}000^{*} - (\$300{,}000 + \$25{,}000)}{100{,}000} = \$7.00$$

* $250,000 + $350,000 + $125,000 + $300,000 (2451)

52. (d) Book value per common share is used to measure the amount that common stockholders would receive if all assets were sold at their carrying values and all creditors were paid. It is derived by dividing the common stockholders' equity by the number of common shares outstanding. The number of common shares outstanding is the 50,000 shares issued less the 5,000 shares that have been reacquired and are held in treasury. Thus, $2,200,000 / 45,000 = $48.89 book value per share of common, rounded to the nearest dollar is $49. (8593)

53. (b) Rate of Return on Assets = Net Income / Average Total Assets

$$\frac{\$150{,}000}{(\$2{,}000{,}000 + \$3{,}000{,}000) / 2} = \$150{,}000 / \$2{,}500{,}000 = 6\%$$

(6142)

54. (c) To determine the price-earnings ratio on common stock, the current year earnings per share must first be computed, as follows:

EPS = Net income to common stockholders / Weighted average common shares = (Net income – Preferred dividend requirement) / Weighted average common shares = ($1,200,000 – $300,000) / 100,000 shares = $9.00

Price earnings ratio = Market price per share / EPS = $72 / $9.00 = 8 to 1. (1259)

55. (c) To determine the price-earnings ratio on common stock, the earnings per share must first be computed.

$$\text{Earnings per share} = \frac{\text{Net income – Preferred dividend requirement}}{\text{Weighted average common shares}} = \frac{\$240{,}000 - \$0}{300{,}000}$$

$$\text{Price earnings ratio} = \frac{\text{Market price per share}}{\text{Earnings per share}} = \frac{\$12.00}{\$0.80} = 15.0 \text{ to } 1$$

(1255)

56. (b) Dividends per share for common stock are used in the numerator of the dividend per share payout ratio, but are not used in computing earnings per share.

$$\text{Dividend per share payout ratio} = \frac{\text{Cash dividends per common share}}{\text{Earnings per share}}$$

$$\text{Earnings per share} = \frac{\text{Net income to common stockholders}}{\text{Weighted average common shares outstanding}}$$

(9040)

Concept Statements

57. (c) The Statements of Financial Accounting Concepts are intended by the FASB to set forth objectives and fundamentals that will be the basis for future development of financial accounting and reporting standards. SFACs do not establish standards prescribing accounting procedures or disclosures, nor supersede, amend, or otherwise modify present GAAP. (4817)

58. (c) Financial statements provide information about an enterprise's economic resources, obligations, and owner's equity. In addition, they should provide information concerning financial performance, earnings, how the entity spends and receives cash, and how it distributes dividends. The objective of financial reporting is to aid investors, creditors, and others in making sound economic decisions. Information regarding management performance is also part of financial reporting. Since management is responsible for the earnings of an enterprise, management performance can be closely correlated to increases or decreases in earnings. However, this information is not *directly* provided for, but rather inferred from the financial data contained in the financial statements. (4819)

59. (b) Information faithfully represents what it purports to represent. Faithful representation must be complete, neutral, and free from error. Information is relevant if it has the capacity to make a difference in a decision by helping users form predictions about the outcomes of past, present, and future events or confirm or correct prior expectations. For information to be relevant, it must have either predictive or confirmatory value, or both. (5266)

60. (c) Information is relevant if it is capable of making a difference in a decision by helping users to form predictions about the outcomes of past, present, and future events or to confirm or correct prior expectations. Components of relevance are predictive value or confirmatory value or both. Information must faithfully represent what it purports to represent. It must be complete, neutral, and free from error. (9326)

61. (b) Comparability and consistency are related but not the same. Comparability enables users to identify and understand similarities in, and differences among, items. Consistency refers to the use of the same methods for the same items, either from period to period within an entity or in a single period across entities. (5537)

62. (b) A specific constraint in terms of the usefulness of information in financial statements pertains to the cost-benefit relationship. In determining the kind and amount of information to be provided, the cost of obtaining the information must be considered. Information is valuable only to the extent that the cost of procuring and analyzing it is less than the benefits derived from its use. While consistency, reliability, and representational faithfulness are important aspects of financial information, they are not associated with constraints. (6084)

63. (c) The financial capital maintenance concept defines income as the change in net resources other than from owner transactions. It is the capital maintenance concept used in present financial statements and comprehensive income. In contrast, under the physical capital maintenance concept, a return on physical capital results only if the physical productive capacity of the enterprise at the end of the period exceeds its capacity at the beginning of the period, also after excluding the effects of transactions with owners. The physical capital maintenance concept can be implemented only if inventories and property, plant, and equipment are measured by their current costs. (2509)

Authority of Pronouncements

64. (c) A new Financial Accounting Standards Board (FASB) Standard is issued only after a majority vote by the FASB board members. The emerging issues task force assists the FASB in improving financial reporting through the timely identification, discussion, and resolution of financial accounting issues within the framework of existing authoritative literature. It does not approve a discussion memorandum before it is disseminated to the public. A discussion memorandum is prepared before any deliberations on a new major project and, thus, before any exposure draft. FASB standards are not rescinded by the AICPA member's votes. (8115)

65. (a) There are two levels of U.S. GAAP, but only one level is authoritative. The authoritative level is represented by the FASB Accounting Standards Codification. The second level is nonauthoritative and represented by all other literature. (8943)

66. (c) The Codification includes Securities and Exchange Commission (SEC) content for reference by public companies. It does not include guidance for Other Comprehensive Basis of Accounting (OCBOA), Regulatory Accounting Principles (RAP) or governmental accounting standards. (8944)

67. (a) The SFACs are designed to constitute a foundation of financial accounting standards. The framework is designed to prescribe the nature, function, and limits of financial accounting and to be used as a guideline that will lead to consistent standards. They are not enforceable under the Rules of Conduct of the Code of Professional Ethics, and they do not establish account standards and disclosure practices for particular items. (89526)

68. (d) FASB Statements of Financial Accounting Concepts are not part of the FASB Accounting Standards Codification. FASB Statements and Interpretations, FASB Technical Bulletins, and AICPA Accounting Interpretations are part of the FASB Accounting Standards Codification. (89527)

PERFORMANCE BY SUBTOPICS

Each category below parallels a subtopic covered in Chapter 1. Record the number and percentage of questions you correctly answered in each subtopic area.

Accounting Environment

Question #	Correct √
1	
2	
3	
4	
5	
6	
7	
8	
9	
10	
11	
# Questions	11
# Correct	______
% Correct	______

Balance Sheet & Fair Value

Question #	Correct √
12	
13	
14	
15	
16	
17	
18	
19	
20	
21	
22	
23	
24	
# Questions	13
# Correct	______
% Correct	______

Other Financial Statements

Question #	Correct √
25	
26	
27	
28	
29	
30	
# Questions	6
# Correct	______
% Correct	______

Financial Analysis—Solvency

Question #	Correct √
31	
32	
33	
34	
35	
36	
37	
38	
39	
40	
41	
42	
43	
# Questions	13
# Correct	______
% Correct	______

Financial Analysis—Operational Efficiency

Question #	Correct √
44	
45	
46	
47	
48	
49	
50	
# Questions	7
# Correct	______
% Correct	______

Financial Analysis—Profitability

Question #	Correct √
51	
52	
53	
54	
55	
56	
# Questions	6
# Correct	______
% Correct	______

Concept Statements

Question #	Correct √
57	
58	
59	
60	
61	
62	
63	
# Questions	7
# Correct	______
% Correct	______

Authority of Pronouncements

Question #	Correct √
64	
65	
66	
67	
68	
# Questions	5
# Correct	______
% Correct	______

Solution 1-2 SIMULATION ANSWER: Ratio Analysis

Event	Current Ratio	Inventory Turnover	Total debt/ Total assets
Daley issued a stock dividend.	[1] NE	[2] NE	[3] NE
Daley declared, but did not pay, a cash dividend.	[4] DEC	[5] NE	[6] INC
Customers returned invoiced goods for which they had not paid.	[7] DEC	[8] DEC	[9] INC
Accounts payable were paid on December 31.	[10] INC	[11] NE	[12] DEC
Daley recorded both a receivable from an insurance company and a loss from fire damage to a factory building.	[13] INC	[14] NE	[15] INC
Early in the year, Daley increased the selling price of one of its products that had a demand in excess of capacity. The number of units sold was the same as the previous year.	[16] INC	[17] NE	[18] DEC

[1] Since the issuance of the stock dividend was recorded entirely within Daley's stockholders' equity accounts, it had **no effect** on the amount of Daley's current assets, current liabilities, or the current ratio.

[2] Since the issuance of the stock dividend was recorded entirely within Daley's stockholders' equity accounts, it had **no effect** on the amount of Daley's cost of goods sold, average inventory, or the inventory turnover ratio.

[3] Since the issuance of the stock dividend was recorded entirely within Daley's stockholders' equity accounts, it had **no effect** on the amount of Daley's total assets, total liabilities, or the total debt/total assets ratio.

[4] The declaration of the cash dividend increased current liabilities, the denominator of the current ratio. Therefore, Daley's current ratio **decreased** as a result of the declaration of the cash dividend.

[5] Since the declaration of the cash dividend had **no effect** on the amount of Daley's cost of goods sold, average inventory, or inventory turnover ratio.

[6] The declaration of the cash dividend increased total debt, the numerator of the ratio. Therefore, Daley's total debt/total assets ratio **increased** as a result of the declaration of the cash dividend.

[7] Assuming that the goods had been sold at a profit, the customer returns decreased current assets—the numerator of the current ratio—because the amount of the decrease to accounts receivable exceeded the amount of the increase to merchandise inventory. Therefore, Daley's current ratio **decreased** as a result of the customer returns.

[8] The customer returns decreased cost of goods sold (the numerator of the ratio) and increased average inventory (the denominator of the ratio). Therefore, Daley's inventory turnover ratio **decreased** as a result of the customer returns.

[9] Assuming that the goods had been sold at a profit, the customer returns decreased total assets—the denominator of the ratio—because the amount of the decrease to accounts receivable exceeded the amount of the increase to merchandise inventory. Therefore, Daley's total debt/total assets ratio **increased** as a result of the customer returns.

[10] The payment of the accounts payable decreased current liabilities and current assets by an equal amount; therefore, since Daley's current ratio was greater than 1:1 (i.e., 3.0 to 1), Daley's current ratio **increased** as a result of the payment of the accounts payable.

[11] Since the payment of the accounts payable had no effect on the amount of Daley's cost of goods sold or average inventory, it also had **no effect** on Daley's inventory turnover ratio.

[12] The payment of the accounts payable decreased total debt and total assets by an equal amount; therefore, since the total debt/total assets ratio was less than 1:1 (i.e., 0.5 to 1), the ratio **decreased** as a result of the payment of the accounts payable.

[13] The recording of the receivable from the insurance company increased current assets, the numerator of the current ratio. Therefore, Daley's current ratio **increased** as a result of the recording of the receivable from the insurance company.

[14] Since the recording of the receivable from the insurance company and the loss from fire damage to the factory building had no effect on the amount of Daley's cost of goods sold or average inventory, they also had **no effect** on Daley's inventory turnover ratio.

[15] Daley recorded a loss from the fire damage to the factory building. Therefore, the amount of the receivable recorded from the insurance company was less than the carrying amount of the building (or portion thereof) removed from the accounts. This decreased total assets, the denominator of the ratio. Therefore, Daley's total debt/total assets ratio **increased** as a result of these events.

[16] Daley increased the selling price of a product that had a demand in excess of capacity. The number of units of the product sold in 20X1 and 20X2 was the same. Therefore, Daley was more profitable in 20X2 than 20X1. The increased profits increased retained earnings, which in turn increased total stockholders' equity; therefore, since the increase in the selling price of the product had no effect on total liabilities, total assets must have increased. Since noncurrent assets would not be affected by the increase in the product's selling price, current assets—the numerator of the current ratio—must have increased. Therefore, Daley's current ratio **increased** as a result of the increase in the selling price of the product.

[17] Since the increase in the selling price of the product had no effect on the amount of Daley's cost of goods sold or average inventory, it also had **no effect** on Daley's inventory turnover ratio.

[18] Daley increased the selling price of one of its products that had a demand in excess of capacity. The number of units sold in 20X1 and 20X2 was the same. Therefore, Daley was more profitable in 20X2 than 20X1. The increased profits increased retained earnings, which in turn increased total stockholders' equity. Since the increase in the selling price of the product increased total stockholders' equity while having no effect on total liabilities, it also increased total assets, the denominator of the ratio. Therefore, Daley's total debt/total assets ratio **decreased** as a result of the increase in the selling price of the product. (9016)

Solution 1-3 SIMULATION ANSWER: Research

FASB ASC: 255 - 10 - 50 - 1

(9102)

Using Videos to Study

Actively watch video lectures, taking notes and answering questions as if it were a live class. If the lecturer recommends you to work an example as the video plays, write the information in the viewer guide, rather than merely following along. If the lecturer instructs you to stop the video to answer questions, stop the video. If the lecturer advises you to take notes, personalize your copy of the viewer guide. The lecturers provide these instructions with the insight gained from years of CPA review experience.

Each of the Hot•Spot™ videos concentrates on a few topics. Use them to help you study the areas that are most troubling for you. If you are strong in a topic, watching the video and answering the questions may be sufficient review. If your strength is moderate in a topic, you probably should read the related text before watching the video. If you are weak in a topic, one successful strategy is to watch the video (including following all of the lecturer's instructions), read the book, and then watch the video again.

CHAPTER 2

CASH, RECEIVABLES & INVESTMENTS

CHAPTER 2

CASH, RECEIVABLES & INVESTMENTS

I. Current Assets

A. Definition

Current assets are economic benefits owned by a firm that are reasonably expected to be converted into cash or consumed during the entity's operating cycle or one year, whichever is longer.

B. Examples

Current assets include: cash available for current operations; temporary investments in marketable securities; trade accounts and notes receivable, receivables from officers, employees, affiliates, and others, if collectible in the ordinary course of business within a year; inventories; most prepaid expenses; and property held for resale.

C. Cash & Cash Equivalents

Cash is by definition the most liquid asset of an enterprise; thus, it is usually the first item presented in the current assets section of the balance sheet. The following are components of cash.

1. Coin and currency on hand, including petty cash funds

2. Negotiable paper (i.e., transferable by endorsement). Examples include claims to cash such as bank checks, money orders, traveler's checks, bank drafts, and cashier's checks

3. Money market funds

4. Passbook savings accounts (although banks have the legal right to demand notice before withdrawal, they seldom exercise this right)

5. Deposits held as compensating balances against borrowing arrangements with a lending institution that are not legally restricted

6. Checks written by the enterprise, but not mailed until after the financial statement date, should be *added back* to the cash balance

7. Time certificates of deposit with original maturities of three months or less

D. Exclusions

1. **Certain Time Certificates of Deposit** Time certificates of deposit with original maturities of longer than three months are classified as either temporary or long-term investments depending upon maturity dates and managerial intent.

2. **Compensating Balances** Legally restricted deposits held as compensating balances against borrowing arrangements with a lending institution are classified as follows:

    a. If held as a compensating balance against a short-term borrowing arrangement, the restricted deposit is classified as a current asset but segregated from unrestricted cash.

    b. If held as a compensating balance against a long-term borrowing arrangement, the restricted deposit is classified as a noncurrent asset in either the investments or other assets section and should be disclosed in the financial statements.

3. **Restricted Cash** Restricted cash is classified based upon the date of availability or disbursement.

   a. If restricted for a current asset or current liability, the restricted cash is classified as a current asset, but segregated from unrestricted cash.

   b. If restricted for a noncurrent asset or noncurrent liability (e.g., cash to be used for plant expansion or the retirement of long-term debt), the restricted cash is classified as a noncurrent asset in either the investments or other assets section regardless of whether the cash is expected to be disbursed within one year of the financial statement date. This accounting policy should be disclosed in the financial statements.

4. **Overdrafts** Overdrafts in accounts with no available cash in another account at the same bank to offset are classified as current liabilities.

5. **Certain Deposits** Deposits in banks under receivership or in foreign banks that are restricted as to conversion into dollars and/or transfer are segregated from unrestricted cash and are classified as current or noncurrent assets depending upon expected dates of availability.

6. **Postdated Checks** Postdated checks received from customers are classified as receivables.

7. **IOUs** IOUs from officers or employees are classified as receivables.

8. **Postage** Postage stamps are classified as supplies or prepaid expenses.

E. Bank Reconciliation

1. **Periodic Reconciliation**

   a. Errors can be uncovered and corrected on a timely basis.

   b. Appropriate amounts are provided for entries in books.

2. **Reasons for Differences**

   a. Items in books and not in bank statement: Deposits in transit and cash on hand should be added to the bank balance. Outstanding checks should be subtracted from the bank balance.

   b. Items in bank statement and not in books: Interest earned and collections by the bank should be added to the book balance. Bank service charges, returned checks (i.e., NSF checks), and payments by the bank should be subtracted from the book balance.

   c. Errors: Differences may also result from errors in books or bank statement.

   d. Certified and cashier's checks: As both the bank and the enterprise have deducted the amounts of these checks from the enterprise's account, they do not represent reconciling items.

3. **Format** A common format of the bank reconciliation statement is to reconcile both book and bank balances to a common amount known as the "true balance." This approach has the advantage of providing the cash figure to be reported in the balance sheet. Furthermore, journal entries necessary to adjust the books can be taken directly from the "book balance" section of the reconciliation.

Example 1 ▸ Bank Reconciliation

On July 31 of the current year, The Company's bank statement showed a balance of $4,056, whereas the book balance was $4,706. Deposits in transit and cash on hand amounted to $588 and $456, respectively. During July, the bank collected a $215 note for The Company and charged the account $15 for service fees; neither of these transactions had been recorded by The Company. In addition, a check for $110 received from a customer and deposited by The Company was returned on July 31 for lack of funds. The following checks were outstanding at the end of July:

#320	$ 24.00
#321	$235.00
#325	$ 45.00

Required: Reconcile both balances to the true cash amount at July 31.

Solution:

BANK			BOOKS		
7/31 balance per bank		$4,056	7/31 balance per books		$4,706
Deposit in transit	$588		Note collected by bank	$215	
Cash on hand	456		Add		215
Add		1,044	Subtotal		4,921
Subtotal		5,100			
Outstanding checks:			Bank service charge	15	
#320	24		Returned NSF check	110	
#321	235		Less		(125)
#325	45				
Less		(304)	True cash		$4,796
True cash		$4,796			

Entries to adjust the books are taken directly from the reconciliation:

Cash	215	
Notes Receivable		215
Bank Service Charge Expense	15	
Cash		15
Special Receivable—NSF Check	110	
Cash		110

II. Accounts Receivable

A. Definition

Accounts receivable is used for claims arising from the sale of goods or the performance of services. Receivables not arising from normal operations, such as amounts due from stockholders, officers, or employees, should be reported separately from trade accounts receivable.

B. Valuation

Accounts receivable should be reported at their net realizable value—the net amount expected to be received in cash. This raises two major problems: (1) determining the amount due, and (2) estimating the extent to which receivables will not be collected.

1. Determining the Amount Due

a. Discounts for prompt payment: Conceptually, sales and receivables should be recorded net of any discounts for prompt payment. Failure by the purchaser to take advantage of the discount offered should not be regarded as additional consideration received for the goods or services provided. These additional amounts should be considered as interest revenue. If receivables are recorded at gross, such discounts should be anticipated at year-end and deducted from the accounts receivable.

b. Trade and quantity discounts: Sales and accounts receivable should be recorded net of any trade or quantity discounts. The actual consideration agreed upon should be the amount recorded for the transaction. Sometimes the list price of a product is subject to several trade discounts. When more than one discount is given, each discount is applied to the declining balance successively. If a product has a list price of $100 and is subject to trade discounts of 20% and 10%, the actual amount recorded for the sale would be: $100 – 20%($100) = $80; $80 – 10%($80) = $72.

c. Sales returns and allowances: Future returns and allowances associated with accounts receivable outstanding at the balance sheet date should be anticipated. An allowance account should be credited for the estimated amount. The offsetting debit is to a special inventory account to reflect the expected net realizable value of returned items and the balance is charged to the sales return expense account (a "plug" amount).

d. Freight charges: The treatment of freight charges depends on the terms of the sale. If they are to be borne by the seller, an expense account is charged; however, if the seller pays the freight but the amount is ultimately charged to the customer, the freight charges are included in the receivable.

   (1) FOB shipping point: When goods are shipped FOB shipping point, the buyer is responsible for paying the freight charges.

   (2) FOB destination: When goods are shipped FOB destination, the seller is responsible for paying the freight charges.

2. **Estimating Uncollectible Receivables** There are basically two generally accepted allowance methods of recognizing the amount of uncollectible receivables and the related bad debt expense.

   a. Percentage-of-sales method: Under this approach, bad debt expense is calculated as a percentage of credit sales for a period. This percentage is determined on the basis of the company's overall experience with credit sales over a period of time and is then adjusted for any relevant conditions. The amount thus estimated is charged to *Bad Debt Expense* and credited to the *Allowance for Uncollectible Accounts,* a contra-account to *Accounts Receivable.* Any previous balance in the allowance account is **not** considered in determining the amount of bad debt expense recognized for the period. The percentage-of-sales method is income statement oriented because it attempts to match bad debt expense with the revenues generated by the credit sales in the same period.

   b. Percentage-of-outstanding-receivables method: This approach is based on the balance in the trade receivables accounts and attempts to value the accounts receivable at their future collectible amounts. A percentage of uncollectible accounts in the gross accounts receivable is determined based on the company's overall experience with uncollectible accounts over a period of time, and is then adjusted for any relevant conditions. This percentage is applied to the ending balance of the gross accounts receivable to obtain the desired ending balance of the allowance for uncollectible accounts. The amount of bad debt expense recognized is the difference between the *existing* balance in the allowance account and the *desired* ending balance. A more refined version of this method entails the *aging* of the gross accounts receivable. Under this approach, gross accounts receivable are classified by age intervals and a different percentage is applied to each age group. After the desired ending balance of the allowance group is determined, the amount of bad debt expense recognized is determined in exactly the same manner as when only one percentage is used—the amount of bad debt expense recognized is the difference between the *existing* balance in the allowance account and the *desired* ending balance. The percentage-of-outstanding-receivables method is balance sheet oriented because it attempts to achieve a proper carrying amount for the accounts receivable at the end of a period because they are reported at their net realizable value.

c. Interim: Some companies estimate bad debt expense during the year using the percentage-of-sales method and then age their accounts receivable at the end of the year to determine the desired ending balance of the allowance for uncollectible accounts. In this situation, the total amount of bad debt expense recognized for the year is the amount of bad debt expense recognized during the year **plus** the amount recognized at the end of the year to adjust the existing balance in the allowance account to its desired ending balance.

Example 2 ▸ Estimating Uncollectible Receivables

Beginning balances:

Accounts receivable	$10,000
Allowance for uncollectible accounts	(750)
Accounts receivable, net	$ 9,250

During the period, there were credit sales of $60,000 and collections on credit sales of $55,000. Also, accounts receivable amounting to $1,000 were written off as uncollectible, bringing the allowance for uncollectible accounts to a $250 debit balance.

Aging of AR, Year-End:

		Days Outstanding			
	Total	0-30	31-60	61-90	Over 90
Accounts receivable*	$14,000	$9,000	$3,000	$1,000	$1,000
Est. % uncollectible		× 2%	× 6%	× 20%	× 50%
Est. amount uncollectible	$ 1,060	$ 180	$ 180	$ 200	$ 500

* [$10,000 + ($60,000 – $55,000 – $1,000) = $14,000]

Required: Estimate uncollectible receivables using the following methods.

a. Percentage-of-Sales: 3% of credit sales is the estimated bad debt expense.

b. Simple Percentage-of-Outstanding-Receivables: 6% of outstanding accounts receivable is estimated to be uncollectible.

c. Aged Percentage-of-Outstanding-Receivables

Solution:

a. Percentage-of-Sales Method: The balance of the allowance for uncollectible accounts would be $1,550 ($1,800 – $250) at the end of the period.

	Debit	Credit
Bad Debt Expense (3% × $60,000)	1,800	
Allowance for Uncollectible Accounts		1,800

b. Percentage-of-Outstanding-Receivables Method—Simple Percentage

Desired balance in allowance, credit (6% × $14,000)	$ 840
Present balance, debit	250
Bad debt expense to be recognized	$1,090

	Debit	Credit
Bad Debt Expense	1,090	
Allowance for Uncollectible Accounts		1,090

c. Percentage-of-Outstanding-Receivables Method—Aged Accounts Receivable

Desired balance, credit [total column of aging]	$1,060
Present balance, debit	250
Bad debt expense to be recognized	$1,310

	Debit	Credit
Bad Debt Expense	1,310	
Allowance for Uncollectible Accounts		1,310

3. Recording Valuation Adjustments

a. Recording bad debt expense: Regardless of the allowance method used, the same entry is used to record bad debt expense (see Example 2). NOTE: This entry decreases net income, net accounts receivable, current assets, and working capital.

b. Recording accounts written off: Regardless of the allowance method used to estimate uncollectible receivables, the following journal entry should be made to record accounts written off during the period. NOTE: This entry has no effect on net income, net accounts receivable, current assets, or working capital.

Allowance for Uncollectible Accounts	XX	
Accounts Receivable—Joe Doe		XX

c. Recording subsequent collections: Journal entries to record the collection of an account previously written off as uncollectible are as follows. These entries have no net effect on net income, current assets, or working capital.

Accounts Receivable—Joe Doe	XX	
Allowance for Uncollectible Accounts		XX
Cash	XX	
Accounts Receivable—Joe Doe		XX

d. Direct write-off method: The direct write-off method of recognizing bad debt expense requires the identification of specific balances that are deemed to be uncollectible before any bad debt expense is recognized. At the time that a specific account is deemed uncollectible, the account is removed from accounts receivable and a corresponding amount of bad debt expense is recognized. Since the direct write-off method does not recognize bad debt expense until a specific amount is deemed uncollectible, it does not match the cost of making a credit sale with the revenues generated by the sale, and it does not achieve a proper carrying amount for the accounts receivable at the end of a period because they are reported at more than their net realizable value.

III. Notes Receivable

A. Definition

Notes receivable are claims usually not arising from sales in the ordinary course of business. Legally, the claim is evidenced by a note representing an unconditional promise to pay. Typically, notes receivable result from the following transactions.

1. Sale of property other than in the ordinary course of business—for instance, disposition of operating assets

2. Special arrangements concerning overdue accounts receivable

3. Loans to stockholders, employees, and affiliates

B. Types

Notes can be classified as either *interest-bearing,* in which case the maker of the note pays an interest amount in addition to the face amount of the note, or *noninterest-bearing,* in which case the interest is included in the face amount.

C. Valuation

The recording of notes receivable is generally required at their present value.

1. **Interest-Bearing Notes** For interest-bearing notes calling for the prevailing rate of interest at the time of issuance, the present value of the note is the same as the face amount of the note.

2. **Exchanged for Cash** Where a note is exchanged *solely* for cash and no other rights or privileges are exchanged, it is presumed to have a present value at issuance equal to the cash proceeds exchanged. When a note is exchanged for cash and a promise to provide merchandise at a discount from market price, the issuer records the note at present value.

3. **Noninterest-Bearing or Other Notes** For noninterest-bearing notes and those with an unrealistic stated rate of interest, the receivable must be reported at its present value or the fair value of the property, good, or service exchanged, whichever is more clearly determinable. If material, the resultant discount or premium should be amortized over the life of the note by use of the *interest method.* Under this method, interest is calculated by applying the prevailing rate at the time of issuance to the carrying amount of the note at the beginning of the period. The prevailing rate of interest is usually defined as the cost of borrowing for a specific debtor.

4. **Loan Origination Fees** Loan origination fees are deferred and amortized over the life of the loan as an adjustment to interest income. Such amounts, if material, are amortized using the interest method.

Example 3 ▸ Recording Notes Receivable, Interest Method

On January 1, year 1, Company X received a $10,000 note in exchange for equipment sold. The stated rate of interest was 5%, payable yearly on December 31. The prevailing interest rate at the time of the exchange was determined to be 8%. The note matures on December 31, year 5.

Required: Compute the discount and interest income. Prepare the journal entries required to record the sale, the discount amortization, and the collection of the note, assuming no gain or loss on the sale of equipment.

Solution:

Determine the present value (PV) of the note at the time of acquisition.

Obtaining the interest factors from the tables in Appendix D, the calculation is:

PV = $10,000 (0.681)* + $500 (3.993)** = $8,807

* The present value of $1 for 5 periods at 8%.
** The present value of an annuity of $1 in arrears for 5 periods at 8%.

NOTE: Interest factors are provided in the CPA examination. Memorizing the present value interest factor and annuity interest factor formulas is not necessary. The ability to select the correct interest factor is necessary.

Construct a discount amortization table. ($8 difference due to rounding.)

1	2	3	4	5
Date	Interest Income (8% × Col. 5)	Interest Payment (5% × $10,000)	Discount Amortiz. (2 – 3)	Present Value (PV + 4)
1/1, year 1	—	—	—	$ 8,807
12/31, year 1	$705	$500	$205	9,012
12/31, year 2	721	500	221	9,233
12/31, year 3	739	500	239	9,472
12/31, year 4	758	500	258	9,730
12/31, year 5	770	500	270	$10,000

Provide the entries required to record the sale of the equipment, the discount amortization, and the collection of the note.

		Debit	Credit
1/1, year 1	Notes Receivable	10,000	
	Discount on Note Receivable		1,193
	Equipment		8,807
	To record the exchange of the equipment for the note receivable.		
12/31, year 1	Cash	500	
	Discount on Note Receivable	205	
	Interest Income		705
	To record the receipt of a $500 nominal interest payment and amortize the discount on the note. (This entry would be repeated at the end of each year until maturity, using the amounts from the amortization table.)		
12/31, year 5	Cash	500	
	Discount on Note Receivable	270	
	Interest Income		770
	To record receipt of interest and amortization (as before).		
12/31, year 5	Cash	10,000	
	Notes Receivable		10,000
	To record the receipt of the $10,000 principal.		

D. Impairment

A creditor considers a loan to be impaired when, "based on current information and events, it is probable that the creditor will be unable to collect all amounts due according to the contractual terms of the loan agreement."

1. Initial Recognition

a. The creditor measures the impaired loan using one of three methods.

(1) Present value method: The present value of future principal and interest cash inflows, net of discounted disposal costs, all discounted at the loan's effective interest rate

(2) Market price method: The loan's observable market price

(3) Fair value of collateral method: The fair value of collateral pledged, if the loan is collateral-dependent; if foreclosure is probable, this method is to be used.

b. If the measure of the impaired loan is less than the recorded investment in the loan (excluding any existing valuation allowance, but including accrued interest and net deferred loan fees/costs and unamortized premium or discount), the creditor creates or adjusts an existing valuation allowance account (Allowance for Impaired Loan) with a corresponding charge or debit to the bad debt expense account.

c. The loan's net carrying amount shall not exceed the loan's recorded investment at any time.

Example 4 ▸ Initial Recognition of Impairment

On January 1, year 1, Risky Developers Inc. borrowed $100,000 from Easymoney Corp. The promissory note called for 10% interest, payable annually on Dec. 31, with a maturity date of December 31, year 3. Risky made the first interest payment on time but, due to financial difficulties, defaulted on the payment due Dec. 31, year 2. On July 1, year 3, Risky and Easymoney reached an agreement to reduce the principal amount to $60,000, and the interest rate to 6%, with the payment of principal and interest due December 31, year 5. The discounted present value of the principal and interest is $54,000, net of discounted related costs, and discounted at the loan's effective interest rate.

Required: Provide the journal entry to record the initial recognition of impairment on the creditor's (Easymoney's) books.

Solution:

		Debit	Credit
7/1, year 3	Bad Debt Expense	61,500	
	Allowance for Impaired Loan		61,500

Principal		$100,000
12/31, year 2 ($100,000 × 10%)	$10,000	
6/30, year 3 ($100,000 + $10,000)(10%)(1/2)	5,500	
Accrued interest		15,500
Investment in loan		115,500
PV of principal and interest		(54,000)
Allowance for impaired loan		$ 61,500

2. **Subsequent Recognition of Income or Expense**

   a. If the initial impairment was measured by the discounted future cash flows method, use any of the following three methods:

      (1) An *increase* in present value attributable to *time passage* is reported as interest income accrued on the net carrying amount of the loan, using the same effective interest rate used in discounting the future cash flows.

      (2) The entire change in the present value in amounts or timing of future cash flows is reported as an increase or reduction in bad debt expense.

      (3) A cost recovery basis of accounting may be used for income recognition purposes. Thus, an impaired loan on which no amounts of cash are collected would result in no income recognition. Use of the cost recovery method does not, of course, alter the total income recognized on the loan; it merely delays the timing of the income recognition.

   b. If the initial impairment was measured by the observable market price of the impaired loan, or by the fair value of the collateral:

      (1) A decrease in the measure of the impaired loan is an addition to the bad debt expense.

      (2) An increase in the measure of the impaired loan is a reduction of the bad debt expense.

Example 5 ▸ Subsequent Recognition of Income or Expense

Refer to Example 4, and add the following information: At December 31, year 3, based upon the effective rate of interest, income to be recognized on creditor's books is $2,700.

Required: Provide the journal entry to record the recognition of income at December 31, year 3.

Solution:

Allowance for Impaired Loan	2,700	
Interest Income (or Bad Debt Expense)		2,700

3. **Subsequent Change** If there is a subsequent material change in the future cash flows' amounts or timing, or in the loan's market price or the collateral's fair value, the creditor should remeasure the impairment amount, and adjust accordingly the valuation allowance and the bad debt expense accounts.

Example 6 ▸ Subsequent Material Change in Cash Flows

Refer to Examples 4 and 5, and add the following information: At July 1, year 4, there is a further change to extend the term to June 30, year 6. The new discounted future cash flows is $53,000.

Required: Provide the journal entry to record the revised recognition of impairment on creditor's books.

Solution: ($115,500 – $61,500 + $2,700) – $53,000 = $3,700

Bad Debt Expense	3,700	
Allowance for Impaired Loan		3,700

4. **Disclosures**

   a. The total receivable, differentiating between the receivables with related allowances and receivables without allowances, must be disclosed. The amounts of the related allowances must also be disclosed. The reconciliation of the allowance account must be disclosed, because of the possibility of additional changes from cash flows charged against the allowance or direct write-offs.

   b. How the interest income was recognized must be disclosed; whether all in bad debt or broken into an interest income component and a bad debt component. The company's policy for recognizing income on impaired loans must also be disclosed.

   c. The amount of cash received for the period and how the cash was recognized must be disclosed.

IV. Receivables as Immediate Sources of Cash

A. Overview

It may become desirable for the holder of receivables to immediately convert them into cash. This can be accomplished by any of four methods discussed below: discounting, assignment, factoring, and pledging. If the holder surrenders control over those receivables, the transaction is accounted for as a sale. If not, the transfer is accounted for as a secured borrowing with pledge of collateral.

B. Discounting

Discounting refers to the sale of a note to a third party, usually a bank or other financial institution. These sales are usually on a "with recourse" basis, which means that upon default of the debtor, the seller of the note becomes liable for its maturity value. The contingent liability assumed by the seller of a note "with recourse" must be disclosed. Either a footnote disclosure or a "contra asset" to notes receivable is used. Two calculations are necessary prior to discounting.

1. **Interest** Interest accrued prior to discounting must be determined

2. **Proceeds** The proceeds to be received from discounting must be calculated

Example 7 ▸ Discounting

Y Company has a $4,000, 90-day, 8% interest-bearing note; 30 days after acquiring the note, Y Company decides to discount it at a bank that charges a 10% discount rate.

Required: Determine the accrued interest income for the 30 days that Y Company held the note. Determine the proceeds Y Company received from the bank.

Solution: Accrued interest income: $4,000 × 8% × 1/12 = $26.67

Face amount	$4,000
Interest ($4,000 × 8% × 3/12)	80
Maturity value	4,080
Discount charged by bank ($4,080 × 10% × 2/12)	(68)
Proceeds from discounting the note receivable	$4,012

Example 8 ▸ Contingent Liability

The note in Example 7 was discounted with recourse.

Required: Provide the entries to record the discounting, and the repayment or default, for each of the two approaches.

Solution:

	Footnote disclosure		Contra asset	
	Dr.	Cr.	Dr.	Cr.
a. *Discounting of N/R*				
Cash	4,012.00		4,012.00	
Interest Expense*	14.67		14.67	
Interest Income*		26.67		26.67
N/R		4,000.00		—
N/R Discounted		—		4,000.00
b. *Repayment of note by maker*				
N/R Discounted	(no entry)		4,000.00	
N/R				4,000.00
c. *Default by maker on note discounted "with recourse"*				
N/R Overdue	4,080.00		4,080.00	
Cash		4,080.00		4,080.00
N/R Discounted	(no entry)		4,000.00	
N/R				4,000.00

* For greater disclosure, interest income and expense are recorded separately, rather than as a net amount.

C. Assignment

The assignment of accounts receivable represents a formal arrangement whereby the rights to accounts receivable are assigned to a financial institution in exchange for cash. Recording the transaction involves the transfer of the receivables to a special account, *Accounts Receivable Assigned.* At the same time, a liability is entered for the amount of cash received from the financial institution. Assignment usually includes "with recourse" and "non-notification" clauses. "With recourse" means that the assignor remains liable for the collection of the receivables. "Non-notification" means that the debtors are not notified of the assignment, and, therefore, continue making their payments to the seller. These payments are forwarded by the seller to the financial institution, thus reducing the original liability. At any point, the seller's equity in the receivables is represented as the difference between the accounts assigned and the related liability.

Example 9 ▸ Assignment of Accounts Receivable

Retro Co. assigns accounts receivable having a net carrying amount of $10,000 to Finn Inc. in exchange for $7,000 cash. Interest of 1% per month is charged on the outstanding balance of the obligation. Collections on accounts receivable are to be remitted to Finn Inc. on a monthly basis; $2,000 is collected during the first month.

Required: Record these transactions in Retro Co.'s books.

Solution:

Account	Debit	Credit
Accounts Receivable Assigned	10,000	
Accounts Receivable		10,000
Cash	7,000	
Note Payable—Finn Inc.		7,000
Cash	2,000	
Accounts Receivable Assigned		2,000
Note Payable—Finn Inc.	1,930	
Interest Expense	70	
Cash		2,000

Following these transactions, Retro Company would present accounts receivable in its balance sheet as follows:

A/R assigned (net) ($10,000 – $2,000)	$ 8,000
Less: N/P on A/R assigned ($7,000 – $1,930)	(5,070)
Equity in A/R assigned	$ 2,930

D. Factoring

Factoring is similar to a sale of receivables because it is generally without recourse (i.e., the financing institution or "factor" assumes the risk of collectivity) and the factor generally handles the billing and collection function. A transfer of receivables to a factor without recourse is accounted for as any other sale of an asset: debit cash, credit the receivables, and record a gain or loss for the difference. If the factoring is *with recourse,* it may be accounted for as a sale of the receivables or as secured borrowing, depending on whether certain criteria are met.

E. Pledging

Receivables may be pledged as security for loans. Collections on the receivables are usually required to be applied to a reduction of the loan. Where receivables are pledged, adequate disclosure must be made in the financial statements.

Exhibit 1 ▶ Sale of Receivables

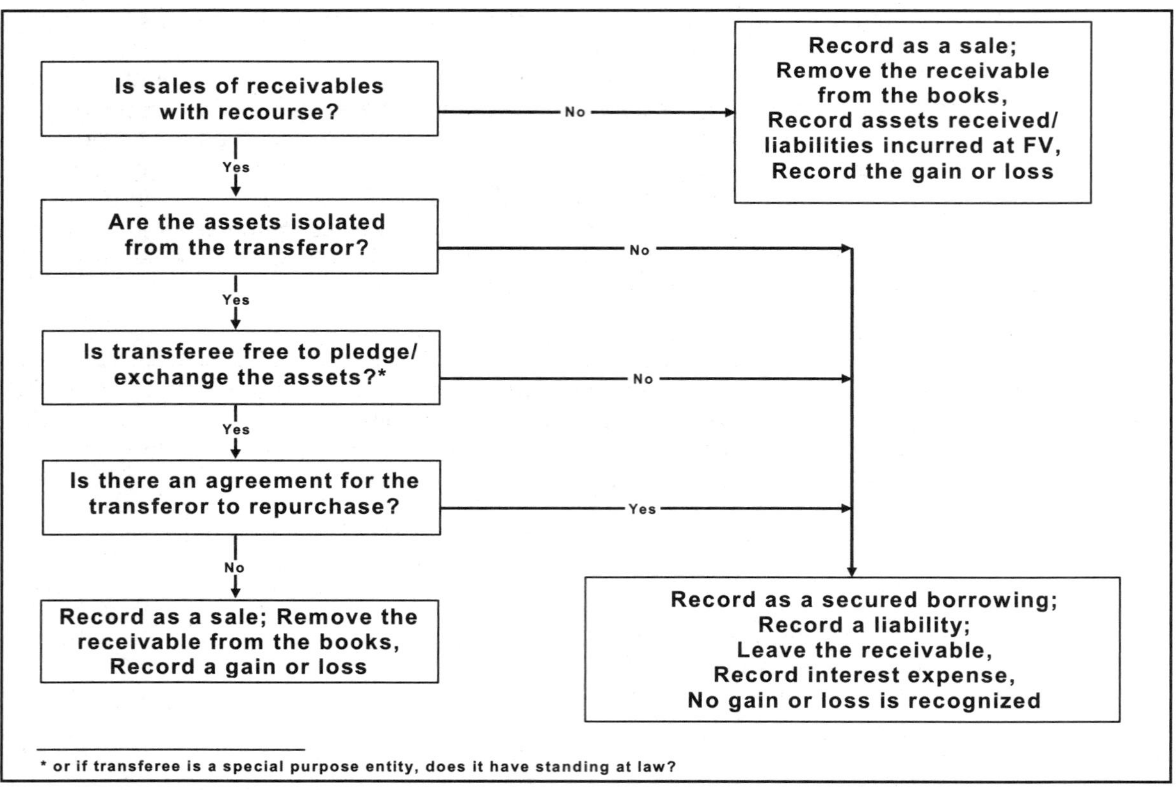

F. Disclosures About Credit Quality

1. **Definition** A financing receivable is defined as a contractual right to receive money on demand or on fixed or determinable dates. Those rights are recognized as assets in statements of financial position. Financing receivables include, but are not be limited to, loans, certain trade accounts receivable, notes receivable, credit card receivables, and receivables under leases other than operating leases. Financing receivables would not include debt securities, unconditional promises to give, and/or acquired beneficial interests or transferor beneficial interests in securitized financial assets.

2. **Scope** In July 2010, the FASB issued Accounting Standards Update [ASU] 2010-20, *Disclosures about the Credit Quality of Financing Receivables and the Allowance for Credit Losses*. The guidance incorporates required additional robust and disaggregated disclosures about the credit quality of financing receivables and the allowance for credit losses reflected in statements of financial position of reporting entities. The fundamental objective associated with enhancing the disclosures is to provide additional information so that end-users of financial statements will have an enhanced understanding of the nature of credit risk associated with financing activities, along with assessments made by reporting entities about risks associated with estimating the allowance for credit losses, to include changes in the allowance and the reason that those changes were determined to be needed.

   Any financing receivables held by public or private companies fall within the scope of the new disclosure requirements, with exceptions related to short-term trade accounts receivable or receivables measured at fair value, with changes at fair value recorded in earnings, or lower-of-cost for fair value. As such, the disclosures would be applicable to lessor entities and reporting entities that have financing subsidiaries.

3. **Objective** Reporting entities need to provide disclosures that facilitate financial statement user evaluation of the following:

   a. The nature of credit risk inherent in financing receivable portfolios

   b. How that risk is analyzed and assessed in arriving at the allowance for credit losses

   c. The changes, and reasons for those changes, in the allowance for credit losses

4. **Disaggregated Basis** In order to achieve the disclosure objective, reporting entities need to provide disclosures on two levels of disaggregation: portfolio segment and class of financing receivable. A portfolio segment is defined as the level used by the entity in developing and documenting a systematic method for determining the allowance for credit losses. Classes of financing receivables generally represent a disaggregation of a portfolio segment. At a minimum, classes of financing receivables first need to be segregated on the basis of the measurement attribute (e.g., amortized cost and present value of amounts to be received, etc.) and then disaggregated to the level used by the entity in assessing and monitoring the risk and performance of the portfolio (to include assessments by the reporting entity of the risk characteristics of the financing receivables).

5. **Enhanced Disclosures** The enhanced disclosures about credit quality of financing receivables and the allowance for credit losses should be helpful in providing additional information needed by end-users in making evaluations related to information in the financial statements. Reporting entities are required to provide the following disclosures about financing receivables on a disaggregated basis:

   a. A roll-forward schedule of the allowance for credit losses from the beginning of the reporting period to the end of the reporting period on a portfolio segment basis, with the ending balance further disaggregated on the basis of the impairment method

   b. For each disaggregated ending balance, the recorded investment in financing receivables

   c. The nonaccrual status of financing receivables by class of financing receivables

   d. Impaired financing receivables by class of financing receivables

6. **Additional Disclosures** Additional disclosures about financing receivables include the following:

   a. Credit quality indicators of financing receivables at the end of the reporting period by class of financing receivables

   b. The aging of past-due receivables at the end of the reporting period by class of financing receivables

   c. The nature and extent of troubled debt restructuring that occurred during the reporting period by class of financing receivables and their effect on the allowance for credit losses

   d. The nature and extent of financing receivables as modified troubled debt restructurings within the previous 12 months that defaulted during the reporting period by class of financing receivables and their effect on the allowance for credit losses

   e. Significant purchases and sales of financing receivables during the reporting period disaggregated by portfolio segment

7. **Major Categories** If major categories of loans or trade receivables are not presented separately in the statement of financial position, they would need to be presented separately in the notes to the financial statements. Additionally, the allowance for credit losses (also referred to allowance for doubtful accounts) and, where applicable, any unearned income and unamortized premiums and discounts, as well as net unamortized deferred fees and costs, need to be disclosed in the notes.

8. **Off-Balance-Sheet Exposure** Reporting entities need to disclose a description of the accounting policies and methodologies used in estimating liabilities for off-balance-sheet credit exposures and related charges associated with those disclosures. That description needs to identify factors that influenced management judgment (e.g., historical losses, existing economic conditions, etc.), and include a discussion of risk elements relevant to particular categories of financial instruments.

V. Investments in Marketable Securities

A. Uses

Funds not needed for the daily operations of the business are usually invested in short-term marketable securities to generate additional income. Some funds may be committed for longer periods by investing in securities to be held long term. Equity investments are assets that may be acquired for future income potential, appreciation, or control over the investee. As such, they generally occupy an auxiliary position in relation to a firm's primary activities. Investments may be classified as either temporary or long term.

1. **Temporary** Temporary investments are those that meet two tests: (a) marketability, and (b) intention by management to dispose of the investment for cash or other current assets if the need arises.

2. **Long-Term** Long-term investments are all other investments not meeting these two criteria. Investments in the form of common or preferred stock represent an equity interest in the investee, and are discussed in this chapter.

B. Applicability

The following applies to investments in equity securities that have a readily determinable fair value and to all investments in debt securities. It does **not** apply to investments in equity securities that, absent the election of the fair value option, would be required to be accounted for under the equity method nor to investments in consolidated subsidiaries. The focus of guidance is on portfolios (groups of stocks) rather than individual stocks.

C. Classification

Marketable securities are classified in one of three categories: held-to-maturity (HTM) securities, trading securities, or available-for-sale (AFS) securities.

1. **Held-to-Maturity (HTM) Securities** Debt securities that the enterprise has the positive intent and the ability to hold to maturity.

   a. Reported at amortized cost, though fair value must be disclosed.

   b. Not adjusted for unrealized holding gains and losses.

   c. If the fair value option is elected, cumulative unrealized gains and losses at the effective date shall be included in the cumulative effect adjustment. The amount of unrealized gains and losses previously unrecognized shall be separately disclosed.

2. **Trading Securities** Debt and equity securities that are bought and held principally for the purpose of selling them in the near term to generate profits on short-term differences in price.

   a. Reported at fair value, if readily determinable.

   b. Unrealized holding gains and losses are included in current earnings.

3. **Available-for-Sale (AFS) Securities** Debt and equity securities not classified as either held-to-maturity or trading securities.

   a. Reported at fair value, if readily determinable.

   b. Unrealized holding gains and losses are excluded from current earnings and are instead reported in other comprehensive income (OCI).

   c. If the fair value option is elected, cumulative unrealized gains and losses at the effective date shall be included in the cumulative effect adjustment. The amount of unrealized gains and losses reclassified from accumulated OCI shall be separately disclosed.

D. Acquisition Cost

Marketable debt and equity securities are recorded at cost, which includes the purchase price and other direct costs of acquisition, such as broker's fees and taxes. For debt securities purchased between interest dates, accrued interest is **not** part of the cost of the securities. Generally, the discount or premium on temporary investments in debt securities is not recorded separately in the accounts and not amortized because the investment is ordinarily held for only a short time and hence any amortized amount would be immaterial.

E. Year-End Valuation

HTM securities are reported at amortized cost. Trading securities and AFS securities are accounted for at fair value, determined at the balance sheet date. For trading securities, the excess of cost over fair value or fair value over cost is recorded directly against the investment account. The offsetting unrealized holding gain or loss shall be included in earnings on the income statement. The excess of cost over fair value or fair value over cost for AFS securities is recorded as a credit or debit in a Market Adjustment account. The offsetting unrealized gain or loss shall be excluded from earnings and be reported in an Other Comprehensive Income (OCI) account until realized.

Example 10 ▸ Available-for-Sale Portfolio, Unrealized Gain

The aggregate cost and fair value (FV) of Zeta Corp.'s investments (all classified as available-for-sale and first purchased in year 1) in marketable securities at 12/31 for years 1 and 2 are given below.

	December 31, Year 1		December 31, Year 2	
	Cost	FV	Cost	FV
Security W	$ 800	$1,300	$ 800	$1,100
Security X	800	1,000	800	700
Security Y	900	600	1,000*	900
Security Z	900	600	1,000*	1,400
	$3,400	$3,500	$3,600	$4,100

* Increases reflect net acquisitions during the period.

Required: Determine the following:

a. Amount to report for these investments on the 12/31, year 1 balance sheet.

b. Amount of unrealized gain or loss to be recognized in year 2.

c. Amount to report for these investments on the 12/31, year 2 balance sheet.

Solution:

a. The fair value of the securities at 12/31, year 1 ($3,500) is greater than its aggregate cost ($3,400). Therefore, the Market Adjustment—AFS account would have a $100 debit balance at 12/31, year 1 and the Unrealized Holding Gain or Loss (OCI) account would have a $100 credit balance at 12/31, year 1. The securities portfolio is presented in the asset section of the 12/31, year 1 balance sheet.

Investment in securities at fair value	$3,500

b. At the end of year 2, the fair value of the portfolio ($4,100) is $500 greater than its aggregate cost ($3,600). An additional $400 debit is required to bring the year-end balance in the valuation account to $500, resulting in the following journal entry:

Market Adjustment—AFS	400	
Unrealized Holding Gain or Loss (OCI)		400

This brings the Market Adjustment—AFS account balance up to the $500 ($4,100 – $3,600) difference between cost and fair value at year end. Since it pertains to the AFS portfolio, the net unrealized holding gain of $500 is reported in Accumulated Other Comprehensive Income.

c. The securities portfolio is presented in the asset section of the 12/31, year 2 balance sheet.

Investment in securities at fair value	$4,100

NOTE: If the securities are classified as current, they would appear in the current asset section of the balance sheet. If they are classified as noncurrent, they would appear in the long-term investment section.

Example 11 ▶ Available-for-Sale Portfolio, Unrealized Loss

Assume the fair value of the portfolio at 12/31, year 1 in Example 10 was $3,100 rather than $3,500 ($300 less than its aggregate cost). Therefore, the Market Adjustment—AFS account would have a $300 credit balance at 12/31, year 1 and the Unrealized Holding Gain or Loss (OCI) account would have a $300 debit balance at 12/31, year 1.

At 12/31, year 2, assume the fair value of the portfolio was $3,500 (only $100 less than its $3,600 aggregate cost). Therefore, the Market Adjustment—AFS account must be reduced by $200 with a corresponding reduction of the balance in the Unrealized Holding Gain or Loss (OCI) account. The journal entry is as follows:

Market Adjustment—AFS	200	
Unrealized Holding Gain or Loss (OCI)		200

This brings the Market Adjustment—AFS account balance down to the $100 ($3,600 – $3,500) difference between cost and fair value at year end. Because it applies to the AFS category, the net unrealized loss of $100 is reported in OCI. The security portfolio is presented in the asset section of the 12/31, year 2 balance sheet.

Investment in securities at fair value	$3,500

Example 12 ▶ Trading Securities Portfolio, Unrealized Gain or Loss

With the same facts as Example 10, except now the investments are all classified as trading securities. Now the unrealized holding gains and losses flow through the current income statement, rather than through other comprehensive income.

Required: Determine the following:

a. Amount of unrealized gain or loss to be recognized in year 1.

b. Amount of unrealized gain or loss to be recognized in year 2.

c. Amount to report for these investments on the 12/31, year 1 and year 2 balance sheet.

In Example 10, the unrealized holding gain of $100 would appear in the year 2 income statement.

Solution:

a. At the end of year 1, the unrealized holding gain of $100 would appear in the year 1 income statement. The $3,500 fair value of the portfolio in year 1 is $100 greater than its $3,400 aggregate cost. The journal entry is as follows:

Investment in Security W	500	
Investment in Security X	200	
Investment in Security Y		300
Investment in Security Z		300
Unrealized Holding Gain or Loss (Income)		100

b. At the end of year 2, the unrealized holding gain of $400 would appear in the year 2 income statement. The $4,100 fair value of the portfolio in year 2 is $400 greater than the total of the $3,500 year 1 fair value plus $200 new acquisitions in year 2. The journal entry is as follows:

Investment in Security Y	200	
Investment in Security Z	700	
Investment in Security W		200
Investment in Security X		300
Unrealized Holding Gain or Loss (Income)		400

c. The investments would be reported at their fair value in both year 1 and year 2.

NOTE: In this example, both year 1 and year 2 had unrealized holding gains. The method would be the same in a situation that may result in an unrealized holding loss. Compare the current fair value to the book value and the result is either an unrealized holding gain or loss.

F. **Other Than Temporary Decline in Fair Value**
If the decline in fair value for AFS or HTM securities is determined to be other than temporary, the cost basis of the individual security is written down to fair value that becomes the new cost basis and a realized loss is recognized in current earnings.

1. **Subsequent Increases** The new cost basis is not changed for subsequent recoveries in fair value. Subsequent increases in fair value of AFS securities are accounted for as unrealized gains by debiting the Market Adjustment account and crediting the Unrealized Holding Gain or Loss (OCI) account.

2. **Subsequent Decreases** Subsequent decreases in fair value of AFS securities, if not other-than-temporary, are accounted for as unrealized losses by debiting the Unrealized Holding Gain or Loss (OCI) account and crediting the Market Adjustment account.

G. **Transfers Between Categories**
Securities may be transferred among the three classifications: HTM, trading, and AFS. Reclassification should be rare.

1. **Transfers From Trading** If a security is transferred from the trading category, any previously recognized unrealized holding gain or loss should not be reversed. Additionally, the security should be transferred at fair value with a gain or loss recognized upon transfer.

2. **Transfers to Trading** If a security is transferred into the trading category, any unrealized holding gain or loss related to this security should be recognized in earnings immediately.

3. **Transfers From HTM to AFS** If a debt security is transferred from HTM to AFS category, any unrealized holding gain or loss related to this security should be recognized in an Other Comprehensive Income account consistent with the treatment for AFS securities.

4. **Transfers From AFS to HTM** If a debt security is transferred from AFS to HTM category, any unrealized holding gain or loss related to this security should still be reported in an Other Comprehensive Income account and amortized over the security's remaining life.

H. **Sale**
The realized gain or loss from the sale of a debt or equity security is the difference between the net proceeds received from the sale (i.e., the gross selling price of the security less brokerage commissions and taxes) and the cost or unamortized cost of the security, or in the case of trading securities its fair value at the most recent balance sheet date.

1. **Previously Recognized Losses or Recoveries** In determining the realized gain or loss on the sale of available-for sale securities, no regard is given to previously recognized unrealized losses or recoveries or to the amount accumulated in the Market Adjustment account.

2. **Reclassification Adjustments** Reclassification adjustments are made to avoid double counting in comprehensive income gains or losses realized and included in net income of the current period that were previously included in other comprehensive income as unrealized gains or losses. Reclassification adjustments for unrealized gains and losses on certain investments in debt and equity securities may be summarized on the face of the financial statement in which comprehensive income is reported or disclosed in the notes to the financial statements.

Exhibit 2 ▸ Marketable Securities Summary

	Held-to-Maturity	Available-for-Sale	Trading
Type of security	Debt	Debt or Equity	Debt or Equity
Accounting at acquisition	Cost (purchase price plus other direct costs of acquisition)	Cost (purchase price plus other direct costs of acquisition)	Cost (purchase price plus other direct costs of acquisition)
End-of-year valuation	Amortized cost	Fair value	Fair value
Valuation adjustments	Not adjusted for fair value	Market adjustment account	Adjust investment account
Change in fair value	Not applicable	Reported in OCI	Reported in income
Other than temporary declines in fair value below cost	Reported in income	Reported in income	Reported in income
Balance sheet classification	Noncurrent asset (Unless maturing within one year)	Either current or noncurrent asset	Current asset
Dividends and interest earned	Reported in income using interest method to amortize associated premium or discount	Reported in income using interest method to amortize associated premium or discount	Reported in income using interest method to amortize associated premium or discount*

* Generally, the amount of amortization for short-term investments is immaterial and therefore not recorded.

VI. Derivatives & Hedges

A. Definitions

1. **Financial Instrument** A financial instrument is cash, evidence of an ownership interest in an entity, or a contract that does both of the following: (a) imposes on one entity a contractual obligation to deliver cash or another financial instrument to a second entity or to exchange other financial instruments on potentially unfavorable terms with the second entity; or (b) conveys to that second entity a contractual right to receive cash or another financial instrument from the first entity or to exchange other financial instruments on potentially favorable terms with the first entity.

2. **Firm Commitment** A firm commitment is an agreement with an unrelated party, binding on both parties and usually legally enforceable, with the following characteristics: the agreement specifies all significant terms, including the quantity to be exchanged, the fixed price, and the timing of the transaction (the fixed price may be expressed as a specified amount of an entity's functional currency or of a foreign currency, or as a specified interest rate or specified effective yield); and the agreement includes a disincentive for nonperformance that is sufficient to make performance probable.

3. **Forecasted Transaction** A forecasted transaction is a transaction that is expected to occur for which there is no firm commitment, and does not give an entity any present rights to future benefits or a present obligation for future sacrifices.

4. **Derivative** A derivative is a financial instrument or other contract that derives its value from the movement of prices, interest rates, or foreign exchange rates associated with an underlying asset or financial instrument. For example, an option to purchase a piece of land is a derivative. As the value of the land increases or decreases, so too does the value of the option. Historically, a derivative was said to have "off-balance-sheet risk" because it could fluctuate in value after the initial agreement date, but these fluctuations would not be reflected in the balance sheet. Accounting standards have been changed to now bring these fluctuations "onto" the balance sheet.

B. Derivative Accounting

FASB ASC 815 defines what constitutes a derivative instrument, identifies which entities and derivative instruments are within the scope of the topic, and establishes the basic accounting for and financial reporting of non-hedging derivative instruments. In addition, FASB ASC 815 establishes conditions precedent to hedge accounting and common recognition, disclosure, and other accounting and financial reporting requirements for all types of hedges. FASB ASC 815 also sets out incremental guidance specific to accounting for and financial reporting of fair value, cash flow, and net investment hedges, respectively.

1. **Rights and Obligations** Derivatives are assets and liabilities because they are rights and obligations. The ability to settle a derivative in a gain position by receiving cash is evidence of the right to a future economic benefit and indicates the instrument is an asset. Similarly, the fact that a cash payment is required to settle a derivative in a loss position is evidence of the duty to sacrifice assets in the future and indicates the instrument is a liability.

2. **Characteristics** A derivate instrument is recorded in the balance sheet as either an asset or liability, measured at its fair value. Recognizing derivative assets and liabilities makes financial statements more complete and informative. Fair value is the amount at which an asset (liability) could be bought (incurred) or sold (settled) in a current transaction between willing parties other than in a forced or liquidation sale. Generally, quoted market prices, if available, are the best evidence of fair value. If quoted market prices are unavailable, the estimate of fair value should be based on the best information available in the circumstances. Changes in the fair value must be recognized currently in earnings unless specific hedge accounting criteria are met. An entity that does not report earnings, such as a nonprofit, generally is required to report such changes in value as part of the change in its net assets.

   A derivative has all of the following characteristics:

   a. An underlying is a specified interest rate, security price, commodity price, foreign exchange rate, index of prices or rates, or other variable (including the occurrence or nonoccurrence of a specified event such as a scheduled payment under a contract). An underlying may be a price or rate of an asset or liability, but it is not the asset or the liability.

   b. A notional amount is a number of currency units, shares, bushels, pounds, or other units specified in a derivative instrument. The notional amount is called a face amount in some contracts.

   c. A derivative instrument either requires little or no initial net investment, or one that is smaller than would be required for other types of contracts expected to have a similar response to market factor changes. For instance, in an interest-rate swap normally no initial net investment is required by either party to the swap.

   d. A derivative instrument requires or permits net settlement, can be readily settled net by a means outside the contract, or provides for delivery of an asset that puts the recipient in a position not substantially different from net settlement. In a plain-vanilla interest-rate swap, for example, the party that is out-of-the-money pays only the net difference between the variable and the fixed-rate payment.

3. **Types of Derivatives** Following are the four most common types of derivatives:

   a. Swap agreement: An interest rate swap agreement is an arrangement used to limit interest rate risk. Two companies swap interest payments, but not the principal. A company with a substantial amount of variable rate debt may wish to swap into fixed-rate debt to limit its exposure to rising interest rates. A company with a high fixed rate may wish to swap to a floating rate in anticipation of falling interest rates. Companies with lower credit ratings often cannot borrow in the fixed-rate market but can swap into it. Such transactions were previously considered off-balance sheet financing because only the original borrowings were reported on the balance sheet and the rights and obligations related to the interest payments per the swap agreement were not reported on the balance sheet, but only in the disclosures. This is an example of a derivative required to be reported on the balance sheet.

   b. Forward contract: A forward exchange contract is a private, non-standardized agreement to exchange different currencies at a specified future date and at a specified rate (the forward rate). A forward contract is a foreign currency transaction. The buying party assumes a *long* position, and the selling party assumes a *short* position. The buyer hopes or expects that the asset price is going to increase, while the seller hopes or expects that it will decrease. Forwards are not exchanged-traded; they are traded over-the-counter.

      The accounting for a gain or loss on a foreign currency transaction that is intended to hedge an identifiable foreign currency commitment is considered a foreign currency hedge and works like a fair value hedge. Gains and losses on this qualifying fair value hedge shall be recognized currently in earnings. The gain or loss realized on this forward exchange contract is computed by multiplying the foreign currency amount of the contact by the difference between the *spot* rate at the balance sheet date and the *spot* rate at the inception of the contract (or the spot rate last used to measure a gain or loss on that contract for an earlier period). The spot rate is the exchange rate for immediate delivery of currencies exchanged.

   c. Futures contract: Similar to a forward contract except that the terms of future contracts are standardized and these contracts are exchange-traded. The contract is between two parties to exchange a commodity or financial asset at a specified price (i.e., the futures price or strike price) with delivery occurring at a specified future date, the delivery date.

      A gain or loss on a speculative futures contract (that is, a contract that does **not** hedge an exposure) should be computed by multiplying the foreign currency amount of the futures contract by the difference between the *future* rate available for the remaining maturity of the contract and the contract future rate (or the forward rate last used to measure a gain or loss on that contract for an earlier period). No separate accounting recognition is given to the discount or premium on a speculative forward contract.

   d. Option: A contract between two parties for a future transaction on an asset at a specified (i.e., reference) price any time during a specified period in the future. The buyer of the option has the right, but not the obligation, to engage in that transaction, while the seller assumes the corresponding obligation to fulfill the transaction. The price of an option results from the difference between the reference price and the value of the underlying asset (usually stocks, bonds, a currency or a futures contract) plus a premium based on the time remaining until the expiration of the option.

      An option which conveys the right to buy at a specific price is a call; an option which conveys the right to sell at a specific price is a put. In return for assuming the obligation, called writing the option, the originator of the option collects a payment, the premium, from the buyer. The writer of an option must make good on delivering (or receiving) the underlying asset or its cash equivalent, if the option is exercised. If the option is not exercised by the expiration date, it becomes worthless.

4. **Exclusions** Although FASB defines "derivative" broadly, many transactions are excluded. The FASB expressly excluded various types of transactions even though they possess the three basic characteristics. For example, contracts for the purchase or sale of something to be used in the normal course of the contracting party's business (e.g., natural gas, corn, or electricity) are excluded, if it is probable that the contract will not settle net and will result in physical delivery.

   Exceptions are made for the following items:

   - Regular-way securities trades
   - Certain insurance contracts
   - Certain financial guarantees
   - Certain non-exchange-traded contracts (including weather derivatives)
   - Contracts between an acquirer and a seller to enter into a business combination at a future date
   - Most contracts in an entity's own stock
   - Contracts for stock-based compensation purposes

5. **Embedded Derivatives** Some contracts may not meet the definition of a derivative instrument in their entirety, but may contain embedded derivative instruments. An embedded derivative is a group of contract terms included in a host contract that, taken together, function as a derivative. Specifically, if the economic characteristics of an embedded derivative and its host contract are not closely related, the embedded derivative must be broken out (bifurcated) and accounted for like a stand-alone derivative instrument.

   An embedded derivative clearly and closely related to the host contract is not subject to FASB ASC 815 (i.e., does not have to be bifurcated). For example, terms of an interest-bearing note that tie the interest rate to an interest rate index may, collectively, be a derivative embedded in the note. Because the amount of interest due under the note is "clearly and closely related" to the note itself, the terms tying the interest rate to an index are not a derivative. Some interest-only and principal-only strips and foreign currency embedded derivatives are also not subject to GAAP.

6. **Unrealized Gains and Losses** Unrealized gains and losses resulting from changes in the fair value of a derivative will be accounted for in either current earnings or in other comprehensive income, depending on the intended use of the derivative.

   a. Nonhedging derivative: The gain or loss is recognized in earnings in the period of change for derivatives not held for hedging purposes.

   b. Fair value hedge: The gain or loss is recognized in earnings in the period of change, together with the offsetting loss or gain in the hedged item. Net losses or gains in the hedging activity indicates the effectiveness of the hedge; i.e., if the net loss or gain is zero, then the hedge was highly effective. The effect of that accounting is to reflect in earnings the extent to which the hedge is not effective in achieving offsetting changes in fair value. Thus both overhedged and underhedged positions will be included in income.

c. Cash flow hedge: The effective portion of the gain or loss is initially reported as a component of other comprehensive income (OCI) and subsequently reclassified into earnings when the forecasted transaction affects earnings. The overhedged ineffective portion of the gain or loss is reported in earnings immediately. For example, if the derivative is a hedge of anticipated cash flows associated with the acquisition of inventory, the gain or loss on the derivative would be included in income when the cost of sales is recognized. If, however, the forecasted cash flow were the acquisition of property and equipment, the gain or loss on the derivative would be recognized based on the depreciation of the property and equipment.

d. Foreign currency fair value hedge: The gain or loss on an unrecognized firm commitment or an available-for-sale security designated as a fair value foreign currency hedge is recognized currently in earnings. The gain or loss on the hedged item adjusts the carrying amount of the hedged item and is also recognized currently in earnings. (Note that this is the same treatment as for a fair value hedge.) If the hedged item is an available-for-sale security, the recognition of gain or loss in earnings rather than in other comprehensive income is an exception to the normal accounting treatment of gains and losses on available-for-sale securities, in order to offset the gain or loss on the hedging instrument that is reported in current earnings.

e. Foreign currency cash flow hedge: The effective portion of the gain or loss on a forecasted foreign-currency-denominated transaction or a forecasted intercompany foreign-currency-denominated transaction designated as a cash flow hedge is reported in other comprehensive income, and the ineffective portion is reported in earnings. Effectiveness is defined as the degree that the gain (loss) for the hedging instrument offsets the loss (gain) on the hedged item.

f. Hedge of net investment in foreign operation: The gain or loss on a hedging derivative instrument, or the foreign currency transaction gain or loss on a nonderivative hedging instrument, that is designated as an economic hedge, and is effective as an economic hedge, of the net investment in a foreign operation is reported in other comprehensive income, as part of the cumulative translation adjustment, to the extent it is effective as a hedge.

C. Hedge Accounting

1. **Overview** Hedging is a risk management strategy to protect against the possibility of loss, such as price fluctuations. FASB ASC 815's universe of conceivable hedges fall into two broad categories: those that address changes in the fair value of a hedged item and those that address the variability in a hedged item's future cash flows. The only qualifying hedge that falls outside these two categories is a hedge of a net investment in a foreign operation.

2. **Considerations** Hedge accounting is elective; therefore, management may choose whether or not to designate a transaction as a hedge. The most important factors to consider are:

   a. Not all activities that management considers hedging—in an economic sense—qualify for hedge accounting.

   b. The failure of certain market-risk exposures and derivative instruments to qualify for hedge accounting won't necessarily preclude earnings offset.

   For example, hedge accounting is not available for economic hedges of fair-value changes that already go to earnings. A hedge of changes in the fair value of an equity security due to changes in equity price cannot receive hedge accounting if that equity security is accounted for as a trading security under FASB ASC 320, *Investments—Debt and Equity Securities*, at fair value with all changes in fair value reported in earnings. The rationale is that the required mark-to-fair-value of a derivative instrument so employed already will affect earnings in the same period as the mark-to-fair-value on the hedged trading security.

3. **Exceptions** Hedge accounting, effectively, is a privilege, not a right. Specified qualifying conditions must be met and an item must meet specific criteria to be designated as being hedged. Further, hedge accounting is prohibited for a variety of transactions and positions, even if other hedge criteria can be met.

   None of the following transactions (or related forecasted transactions) qualify:

   - Assets, liabilities, or acquisitions thereof that will be remeasured with fair value changes reported currently in earnings
   - Noncontrolling interests (including preferred stock) in consolidated subsidiaries
   - Equity investments in consolidated subsidiaries
   - Anticipated business combinations, including anticipated acquisitions or disposals of subsidiaries, noncontrolling interests, or equity-method investees
   - Unrecorded intangibles, such as core deposit intangibles, not involving a firm commitment
   - Interest-rate risk of held-to-maturity debt securities
   - Price risk of major ingredients of nonfinancial assets or liabilities, such as effects of crude oil prices on the fair value of the oil content of gasoline or effects of copper prices on cash flows to purchase the copper content of bronze
   - Groups of assets or liabilities that are dissimilar or do not share the same risk (macro-hedges)
   - Future net income of a subsidiary
   - Transactions with stockholders as stockholders, such as projected purchases of treasury stock or payments of dividends
   - Intra-entity transactions (except for foreign-currency-denominated forecasted intra-entity transactions) between entities included in consolidated financial statements, including forecasted dividends from a subsidiary
   - The price of stock expected to be issued pursuant to a stock option plan for which recognized compensation expense is not based on changes in stock prices after the date of grant

4. **Hedge Designation and Effectiveness** At the inception of every hedging transaction, the entity must document the following information:

   a. Which instrument is the hedging instrument and which specific item it is hedging

   b. The nature of the risk being hedged (e.g., overall changes in fair value, interest rate risk, or foreign currency risk)

   c. The entity's risk management objective or strategy (e.g., to convert a floating-rate instrument to a fixed rate, or to hedge corn inventory from declines in the price of corn)

   d. The method the entity will use to assess and measure effectiveness (prospectively and retrospectively)

   e. The method the entity will use to measure hedge ineffectiveness

5. **Qualification** To qualify for hedge accounting, a derivative instrument has to be highly effective in achieving offsetting changes in fair value or offsetting cash flows for the risk being hedged. An entity must anticipate, measure, and account for hedge ineffectiveness. Even if a hedge is highly effective, all ineffectiveness is recognized currently in earnings.

6. **Benchmark Interest Rate** In interest rate hedges, an entity is permitted to designate, as the hedged risk, the risk of changes in a benchmark interest rate (e.g., in the United States, only the London InterBank Offered Rate (LIBOR) or U.S. Treasury rates). In a cash flow hedge, changes in cash flows due to changes in the benchmark interest rate cannot be designated as the hedged risk if the cash flows of the hedged item are explicitly based on a different index, such as prime rates, Fed fund rates, or commercial paper rates. Credit risk is defined as the issuer-specific spread over the benchmark interest rate and may be hedged separately from or in combination with the benchmark interest rate.

   For certain interest-rate-swap transactions, GAAP explicitly allows entities to apply a shortcut method to account for hedging relationships. Under this method, if certain key terms of the swap and hedged item match in a hedge of benchmark interest-rate risk, the entity may assume perfect effectiveness and follow hedge accounting, without having to reassess effectiveness prospectively.

7. **Fair Value Hedge** Derivatives that are fair value hedges are acquired to hedge against fluctuations in the fair value of recognized assets, recognized liabilities, or firm commitments. One of the primary criteria for determining a fair value hedge is that the hedged item is a single asset or liability, or is a portfolio of similar assets or a portfolio of similar liabilities. A fair value hedge derivative must be reported at fair value on the statement of financial position. Special rules for matching the gain or loss resulting from changes in the fair value of a derivative with changes in the value of the hedged asset, liability, or firm commitment are provided by GAAP. The investing party adjusts the carrying value of the hedged item for changes in the hedged item's value attributable to the hedged risk. The gain or loss from that adjustment flows to earnings and is then matched with the offsetting gain or loss resulting from the change in the derivative's fair value.

   Fair value hedge criteria include the following: (a) the hedged item is specifically identified as either all or a specific portion of a recognized asset or liability or of a firm commitment; (b) the hedged item is a single asset or liability, or is a portfolio of similar assets or a portfolio of similar liabilities. If similar assets or similar liabilities are aggregated and hedged as a portfolio, the individual assets or individual liabilities must share the risk exposure for which they are designated as being hedged; and (c) the hedged item presents an exposure to changes in fair value for the hedged risk that could affect reported earnings.

8. **Cash Flow Hedge** GAAP defines cash flow hedges as derivatives acquired to protect against variations in cash flow from forecasted transactions. A cash flow hedge must be reported on the statement of financial position at its fair value. GAAP provides for matching gain and loss from the change in the fair value of a cash flow hedge derivative with gain and loss from the hedged cash flow. To the extent the derivative is a highly effective hedge against expected variability in future cash flows, gains and losses from adjustments to its fair value are included on the statement of financial position equity section as "Other Comprehensive Income." As the hedged item affects earnings, the deferred gain or loss moves from other comprehensive income on the statement of financial position to earnings reflected on the income statement.

The overhedged ineffective portion of the gain or loss is reported in earnings immediately. For example, if the derivative is a hedge of anticipated cash flows associated with the acquisition of inventory, the gain or loss on the derivative would be included in income when the cost of sales is recognized. If, however, the forecasted cash flow were the acquisition of property and equipment, the gain or loss on the derivative would be recognized based on the depreciation of the property and equipment.

9. **Foreign Currency Hedges**

a. **Types** An entity may designate the following types of hedges of foreign currency exposure:

(1) A fair value hedge of an unrecognized firm commitment or an available-for-sale security.

(2) A cash flow hedge of a forecasted foreign-currency-denominated transaction or a forecasted intercompany foreign-currency-denominated transaction.

(3) A derivative instrument or a nonderivative financial instrument that may give rise to a foreign currency transaction gain or loss can be designated as hedging the foreign currency exposure of a net investment in a foreign operation.

b. **Reporting Gains & Losses**

(1) The gain or loss on a fair value foreign currency hedge is recognized currently in earnings. The gain or loss is computed by multiplying the foreign currency amount of the contract by the difference between the spot rate at the date of inception of the contract and the spot rate on the balance sheet (or settlement) date. The gain or loss on the hedged item adjusts the carrying amount of the hedged item and is recognized currently in earnings. If the hedged item is an available-for-sale security, the recognition of gain or loss in earnings rather than in other comprehensive income is an exception to the normal accounting treatment of gains and losses on available-for-sale securities, in order to offset the gain or loss on the hedging instrument that is reported in current earnings.

(2) The effective portion of the gain or loss on a derivative designated as a cash flow hedge is reported in other comprehensive income, and the ineffective portion is reported in earnings. Effectiveness is defined as the degree that the gain (loss) for the hedging instrument offsets the loss (gain) on the hedged item.

(3) The gain or loss on a hedging derivative instrument, or the foreign currency transaction gain or loss on a nonderivative hedging instrument, that is designated as and is effective as an economic hedge, of the net investment in a foreign operation is reported in other comprehensive income, as part of the cumulative translation adjustment, to the extent it is effective as a hedge.

Example 13 ▸ Hedge of Foreign Currency Exchange Rate Risk

On March 1, an entity anticipates acquiring equipment from a foreign manufacturer. The equipment is expected to be delivered in three months and will cost 1,200,000 FCU (Foreign Currency Units). The equipment will have a 5-year useful life and straight-line depreciation will be used. To hedge the foreign currency exchange rate exposure, the entity acquires forward contracts on the currency for delivery in three months. The current forward rate is $1 = 0.5 FCU. The spot (forward) rate for June 1 (at settlement) is $1 = 0.3 FCU. All of the hedging criteria are met. The entity takes a full year's depreciation in the year of requisition.

Required: Provide the journal entries to record the acquisition of the foreign currency derivative, unrealized gain, realization of gain, and depreciation expense.

Solution:

		Debit	Credit
3/1	Due from Broker (1,200,000/0.5)	2,400,000	
	Foreign Currency Derivative		2,400,000

Prior to settlement of contract:

		Debit	Credit
6/1	Due from Broker		
	[(1,200,000 FCU × $1/0.3 FCU) – $2,400,000]	1,600,000	
	Unrealized Gain on Derivative—OCI		1,600,000

Settlement of contract and acquisition of equipment: The entity would settle the contract and purchase the equipment, resulting in equipment recorded at $4,000,000.

Recorded each year for five years:

	Debit	Credit
Unrealized Gain on Derivative—OCI ($1,600,000/5)	320,000	
Gain on Derivatives		320,000
Depreciation Expense ($4,000,000/5)	800,000	
Accumulated Depreciation		800,000

Exhibit 3 ▸ Characterization of Hedging Strategies

Strategy	Hedge Type	Bottom-Line Effect on Income if Perfectly Effective
1. Swap interest rate from fixed to floating (same currency)	Fair Value	Creates floating interest rate in interest income or expense
2. Swap interest rate from floating to fixed (same currency)	Cash flow	Creates fixed interest rate in interest income or expense
3. Lock in fixed interest rate on anticipated debt offering with a futures contract	Cash flow	When debt is issued, creates desired fixed rate
4. Lock in price of raw materials with a forward purchase contract (no purchase order exists) Assume same currency	Cash flow	Cost of goods sold will reflect the locked in price of materials (ignoring any complications of inventory accounting)
5. Lock in minimum selling price of finished goods with an option (no sale contract with a customer exists) Assume same currency	Cash flow	Sales revenue will reflect a minimum price of inventory, plus cost of option
6. Lock in U.S. dollar equivalent of a purchase of machinery from a foreign supplier (currency amount per contract)	Cash flow or fair value hedge	No effect until machine is depreciated, using the locked-in U.S. dollar equivalent cost as its basis
7. Swap interest rate from floating to fixed and swap currency from foreign currency to functional currency (e.g., U.S. dollar)	Cash flow	Creates fixed U.S. dollar interest rate in interest income or expense
8. Lock in U.S. dollar equivalent of a forecasted sale of goods by a foreign subsidiary	Cash flow	Sales revenue will reflect the U.S. dollar equivalent of today's selling price of inventory

10. **Disclosures** The following disclosures are required for financial instruments:

    a. An entity that holds or issues hedging instruments must disclose its objectives for holding or issuing those instruments, the context needed to understand those objectives, and its strategies for achieving those objectives.

    b. The description must distinguish between instruments designated for fair value hedges, cash flow hedges, foreign currency hedges, and all other derivatives.

    c. The description must indicate the entity's risk management policy for each type of hedge, including a description of the items or transactions for which risks are hedged.

    d. For non-hedge derivatives, the description must indicate the purpose of the derivative activity.

    e. The entity is encouraged, but not required, to provide additional qualitative disclosures, including the entity's objectives and strategies within the context of an entity's overall risk management profile.

    f. For fair value hedges, the net gain or loss recognized in earnings during the reporting period representing the amount of the hedges' ineffectiveness and the component of the derivative instruments' gain or loss, if any, excluded from the assessment of hedge effectiveness and a description of where the net gain or loss is reported in the financial statements must be disclosed. When a hedged firm commitment no longer qualifies as a fair value hedge, the amount of net gain or loss recognized in earnings must be disclosed.

    g. For cash flow hedges, disclosure must include:

        (1) The net gain or loss recognized in earnings during the reporting period representing the amount of the hedges' ineffectiveness and the component of the derivative instruments' gain or loss, if any, excluded from the assessment of hedge effectiveness and a description of where the net gain or loss is reported in the financial statements.

        (2) A description of the transactions or other events that will result in the reclassification into earnings of gains and losses reported in accumulated other comprehensive income, and the estimated net amount of the existing gains or losses at the reporting date expected to be reclassified into earnings within the next 12 months.

        (3) The maximum length of time over which the entity is hedging its exposure to the variability in future cash flows for forecasted transactions excluding those forecasted transactions related to the payment of variable interest on existing financial instruments.

        (4) The amount of gains and losses reclassified into earnings as a result of the discontinuance of cash flow hedges because it is probable that the original forecasted transactions will not occur.

    h. For foreign currency hedge instruments, the net amount of gains or losses included in the cumulative translation adjustment during the reporting period must be disclosed.

    i. An entity must display as a separate classification within other comprehensive income the net gain or loss on derivative instruments designated and qualifying as cash flow hedging instruments that are reported in comprehensive income.

j. An entity must separately disclose, as part of the accumulated OCI disclosures, the beginning and ending accumulated derivative gain or loss, the related net change associated with current period hedging transactions, and the net amount of any reclassification into earnings.

D. General Disclosures

1. **Fair Value** An entity must disclose, either in the body of the financial statements or in the accompanying notes, the fair value of financial instruments for which it is practicable to estimate that value and the method(s) and significant assumptions used to estimate the fair value of financial instruments.

2. **Practicality** In the context of FASB ASC 825, practicable means that an estimate of fair value can be made without incurring excessive costs. If it is not practicable to estimate the fair value of a financial instrument or a class of financial instruments, the following should be disclosed: information pertinent to estimating the fair value of that financial instrument or class of financial instruments, such as the carrying amount, effective interest rate, and maturity; and the reasons why it is not practicable to estimate fair value.

3. **Concentration of Credit Risk** An entity must disclose all significant concentrations of credit risk arising from all financial instruments, whether from an individual counterparty or groups of counterparties. Credit risk is the possibility that a loss may occur from the failure of another party to perform according to the terms of a contract.

   a. Group concentrations of credit risk exist if a number of counterparties are engaged in similar activities and have similar economic characteristics that would cause their ability to meet contractual obligations to be similarly affected by changes in economic or other conditions.

   b. For each significant concentration, disclosure must be made as follows:

      - Information about the (shared) activity, region, or economic characteristic that identifies the concentration.
      - The maximum amount of loss exposure due to credit risk if all parties to the financial instruments failed completely to perform and the amounts due proved to be of no value to the entity.
      - The entity's policy of requiring collateral or other security to support financial instruments subject to credit risk, information about the entity's access to that collateral or security, and the nature and a brief description of the collateral or other security.
      - The entity's policy of entering into master netting arrangements to mitigate the credit risk and information about such arrangements and the extent the arrangements reduce the credit risk.

4. **Market Risk** An entity is encouraged, but not required to disclose quantitative information about the market risks of financial instruments that is consistent with the way it manages or adjusts those risks. Market risk is the possibility that future changes in market prices may make a financial instrument less valuable or more onerous.

Example 14 ▸ Hedge of Commodity Price Risk on Purchase of Inventories

Cereal Co. manufactures breakfast cereals and is concerned about the volatility of grain prices, since such volatility will significantly impact its profit margins on sales. Cereal Co. anticipates acquiring 10 million bushels of grain in six months at the then current spot rate. To protect against future price changes in the commodity on May 1, Cereal Co. acquires grain futures for 10 million bushels at the current spot rate for delivery in six months. The current price is $0.40 per bushel. Cereal Co. acquires the 10 million bushels of grain on October 1 at $0.45 per bushel. It then sells the finished products over the following three months. All hedging criteria are met.

Required: Provide the journal entries to record the commodity futures on the current date, prior to the settlement of the contract and a summary entry for the realization of the gain over the following three months as the inventory is sold. The entries to record the actual settlement of the contract and acquisition of inventory are not required.

Solution:

Date	Account	Debit	Credit
5/1	Investment in Grain Futures	4,000,000	
	Due to Broker		4,000,000
10/1	Investment in Grain Futures	500,000	
	Unrealized Gain on Derivative—OCI		500,000

Settlement of contract and acquisition of inventory: Cereal Co. would settle the contract and purchase inventory at the current market price. This results in inventory of $4,500,000.

3 months following, in proportion to sales of inventory:

Account	Debit	Credit
Unrealized Gain on Derivative—Accumulated OCI	500,000	
Gain on Derivatives		500,000

E. Transfers & Servicing of Financial Assets

Transfers of financial assets can take make different forms. A financial asset is defined to be cash, evidence of ownership interest in another entity, or a contract that conveys to one entity a right to receive cash or another financial instrument from a second entity, or the right to exchange other financial instruments on potentially favorable terms with the second entity.

If the transferor has no continuing involvement with the transferred asset or the transferee, the accounting is fairly simple. On the other hand, if the transferor retains some continuing interest, the accounting becomes more complicated. The issue is in determining whether the transaction was a sale of all or part of the assets or whether it was a secured borrowing.

1. **Transfers** Standards for transfers and servicing of financial assets and extinguishments of liabilities focus on control; an entity must recognize the financial and servicing assets it controls and the liabilities it has incurred, derecognize financial assets when control has been surrendered, and derecognize liabilities when extinguished. There are established guidelines to determine transfers of financial assets that are sales and transfers that are secured borrowing. All of this is based on a financial-components approach, which is the recognition that financial assets and liabilities can be divided into a variety of components. A transaction may be treated partially as a sale and partially as collateralized borrowing.

2. **Objectives** There are two broad objectives to consider. Each party to the transaction should:

   a. *Recognize* only assets it controls and liabilities it has incurred

   b. *Derecognize* assets only when control has been surrendered, and to derecognize liabilities only when they have been extinguished.

3. **Control Criteria** A transfer in which control is surrendered by the transferor shall be accounted for as a sale to the extent that consideration other than beneficial interests in the transferred assets is received in exchange. For control to be surrendered, *all of the following conditions* must be met.

   a. The transferred assets must be isolated from the transferor and must be beyond the reach of the transferor and its creditors, even in bankruptcy.

   b. Either the transferee obtains the rights to pledge or exchange the transferred assets, or the transferee is a qualified special purpose entity and the holders of the beneficial interest of that special purpose entity can pledge or exchange the interest. The transferor cannot place restrictions or conditions on what the transferee does with the transferred assets.

   c. The transferor does not maintain effective control over the transferred assets through repurchase or redemption agreements.

4. **Sale vs. Collateralized Borrowing** If the above conditions are met, the transfer is accounted for as a sale and the assets received and liabilities incurred in the exchange are measured at fair value. If not all of the above conditions are met, the exchange would be accounted for as collateralized borrowing.

   a. In April 2011, the FASB released Accounting Standards Update [ASU] 2011-03, *Reconsideration of Effective Control for Repurchase Agreements*. During the recent and, in some cases, continuing economic crisis, an issue bubbled-up that led to the FASB thinking that currently-utilized guidance needed to be amended. In particular, questions arose related to the necessity and usefulness of the collateral maintenance guidance for the transferor ability criterion when determining whether repurchase agreements (repos) should be accounted for as sales or as secured borrowings.

   b. It is not uncommon for government securities dealers, banks, other financial institutions, and corporate investors to use repo agreements to obtain or use short-term funds. Some agreements are similar to securities lending transactions in that the transferee has the right to sell or repledge the securities to a third party during the term of the agreement. In other situations, transferee entities do not have the right to sell or repledge the securities during the term of the agreement.

   c. Most repo agreements have ongoing collateral maintenance requirements so, as an example, when transferred assets increase in value, typically transferor entities receive additional cash from transferee entities; conversely, in circumstances where there is a decline in value of the transferred assets, cash is returned to the transferee entities. The goal behind these type arrangements is to minimize the credit exposure in repo agreements for both transferor and transferee entities.

   d. The transferor entity assurance that its ability to perform in accordance with its contractual rights or satisfy its contractual obligations should **not** be a determining factor as to whether an entity has, or does not have, effective control transferor entities in repo agreements are deemed to have effective control [i.e., the agreements would be accounted for as secured borrowings] if the following three conditions are satisfied:

      - The financial assets to be repurchased or redeemed are the same, or substantially the same, as those transferred.

      - The agreements are to repurchase or redeem the financial assets before maturity, at fixed or determinable prices.

      - The agreements are entered into contemporaneously with, or in contemplation of, the transfers.

5. **Servicing** An entity shall recognize and initially measure a servicing asset or servicing liability at fair value when entering a service contract in any of the following situations.

   a. A transfer of the financial assets that meets the requirements for sale accounting.

   b. A transfer of financial assets to a qualifying SPE in a guaranteed mortgage securitization in which the transferor retains all of the resulting securities and classifies them as either available-for-sale or trading securities.

   c. An acquisition or assumption of a servicing obligation that does not relate to financial assets of the servicer or its consolidated affiliates.

   d. An entity shall subsequently measure each class of servicing assets and servicing liabilities using one of the following methods.

      (1) Amortization method: Amortize in proportion to and over the period of estimated net servicing income or loss and assess for impairment or increased obligation based on fair value at each reporting date

      (2) Fair value measurement method: Measure at fair value each reporting date and report changes in fair value in earnings in the period in which the change occurs.

   e. An entity shall report recognized servicing assets and servicing liabilities measured using the fair value measurement method in a manner that separates their carrying amounts from the carrying amounts of those measured using the amortization method.

Example 15 ▶ Transfer & Servicing of Financial Assets

ABC Company originates $50,000 of loans that can be prepaid, yielding 10% interest income. ABC transfers 80% of the principal plus interest of 8.5% to another entity. ABC will continue to service the loans and will receive the interest income not sold. ABC has an option to purchase the loans, and there is a recourse obligation requiring ABC to repurchase delinquent loans.

ABC receives the following in the transfer (each amount represents fair value):

Cash	$40,000
Call option (to repurchase loans)	3,500
Recourse obligation	2,500
Servicing asset	3,000
20% interest retained	10,000

The fair value of the net proceeds received in the transfer is:

Cash	$40,000
Call option	3,500
Recourse obligation	(2,500)
Net proceeds	$41,000

Required:

a. Allocate the carrying amount ($50,000) between the portions sold and retained based upon the relative fair values.
b. Calculate the gain or loss on the sale.
c. Show the journal entries to record the transfer and to recognize the servicing asset.
d. Show how the amounts would appear on ABC's balance sheet after the transfer.

Solution:

a. Allocation of loan is as follows:

Interest	Fair Value	% Allocation of Total Fair Value	Carrying Amount
Interest sold	$41,000	75.9%	$37,950
Servicing asset	3,000	5.6%	2,800
20% interest retained	10,000	18.5%	9,250
Total	$54,000	100.0%	$50,000

b. The gain/loss on the sale is calculated as follows:

Net proceeds	$41,000
Carrying amount of loans sold	37,950
Gain on sale	$ 3,050

c. ABC would record the transfer and the servicing asset as follows:

	Debit	Credit
Cash	40,000	
Call option	3,500	
Loans		37,950
Recourse obligation		2,500
Gain on sale		3,050
Servicing asset	2,800	
Loans		2,800

d. The following amounts appear on ABC's balance sheet after the transfer:

Assets:		Liabilities:	
Cash	$40,000	Recourse obligation	$2,500
Loans	9,250		
Call option	3,500		
Servicing asset (carrying value)	2,800		

VII. Balance Sheet Offsetting

A. Overview

Offsetting allows the reporting of a recognized asset and a recognized liability as one net item on the financial statement. If the amounts are identical, then no amount would appear. If the amounts are different, then the net amount would be classified on the financial statement for the larger item.

1. **Applicability** Offsetting of assets and liabilities is not permitted except where a right of set-off exists. Generally, this is thought of in the context of unconditional receivables from and payables to another party. This principle also applies to conditional amounts recognized for contracts under which the amounts to be received or paid or items to be exchanged in the future depend on future interest rates, future exchange rates, future commodity prices, or other factors.

2. **Criteria** GAAP specifies four criteria that must be met for the right of offset to exist:

   a. Each of two parties owes the other determinable amounts.

   b. The reporting party has the right to set off the amount owed with the amount owed by the other party.

   c. The reporting party intends to set off.

   d. The right of setoff is enforceable a law.

3. Other Considerations

a. A debtor having a valid right of setoff may offset the related asset and liability and report the net amount.

b. If the parties meet all the criteria specified above, but maturities differ, only the party with the nearer maturity could offset because the party with the longer term maturity must settle in the manner that the other party selects at the earlier maturity date.

c. If a party does not intend to set off even though the ability to set off exists, an offsetting presentation in the statement of financial position is not representationally faithful.

d. The offset of cash or other assets against the tax liability or other amounts owing to governmental bodies is not acceptable unless it is clear that a purchase of securities is in substance an advance payment of taxes that will be payable in the relatively near future.

B. Repurchase and Reverse Repurchase Agreements

An entity may, but is not required to, offset amounts recognized as payables under repurchase agreements and amounts recognized as receivables under reverse repurchase agreements if certain conditions are met.

C. Disclosures

Offsetting (i.e., netting) of assets and liabilities is an important aspect of presentation in financial statements. Due to inconsistent offsetting requirements between U.S. GAAP and IFRS, amounts presented in the statements of financial position were significantly different, reducing the comparability of those statements.

A joint requirement issued by the FASB and IASB in December 2011 requires entities to disclose certain information for both financial and derivative instruments subject to offsetting requirements. Also included are derivative and other financial instruments and transactions that are subject to an enforceable master netting arrangement or similar agreement. The term "similar agreement" includes: derivative clearing agreements; global master repurchase agreements; and global master securities lending agreements. This includes the effect or potential effect of rights of setoff.

An entity shall disclose at the end of the reporting period the following quantitative information separately for qualified assets and liabilities:

1. The gross amounts of those recognized assets and those recognized liabilities

2. The amounts offset to determine the net amounts presented in the statement of financial position

3. The net amounts presented in the statement of financial position

4. The amounts subject to an enforceable master netting arrangement or similar agreement not otherwise included in (2. above), including:

a. The amounts related to recognized financial instruments and other derivative instruments that either management makes an accounting policy election not to offset; or that do not meet some or all of the disclosure guidance.

b. The amounts related to financial collateral (including cash collateral).

5. The net amount after deducting the amounts in (4) from the amounts in (3).

The required information shall be presented in a tabular format, separately for assets and liabilities, unless another format is more appropriate. The amounts included in the tables are limited to the amount that is actually subject to setoff. For example, if the gross amount of the derivative asset is larger than the gross amount of the derivative liability, the asset disclosure table will include the entire amount of the derivative asset and the entire amount of the derivative liability. However, the liability disclosure table will include the entire amount of the derivative liability, but only the amount of the derivative asset equal to the amount of the derivative liability.

An entity shall provide a description of the rights of setoff associated with an entity's recognized assets and recognized liabilities subject to an enforceable master netting arrangement or similar agreement, including the nature of those rights. For example, if an entity has a conditional right of setoff, the entity should describe the related conditions. For any financial collateral received or pledged, the entity should describe the terms of the collateral agreement.

CPA Exam Week Checklist

What to pack for exam week:

1. CPA exam registration material (Notice to Schedule and **two** proper forms of ID).
2. Hotel confirmation.
3. Cash and/or a major credit card.
4. Alarm clock—Don't rely on a hotel wake-up call.
5. Comfortable clothing that can be layered to suit varying temperatures.
6. An inexpensive watch (to leave in a testing site locker).
7. Appropriate review materials (don't take to exam site).
8. Healthy snack foods.

Evenings before exam sections:

1. Read through your Bisk Education chapter outlines for the next day's section(s).
2. Eat lightly and monitor your intake of alcohol and caffeine. Get a good night's rest.
3. Do not try to cram. A brief review of your notes will help to focus your attention on important points and remind you that you are well prepared, but too much cramming can shatter your self-confidence. If you have reviewed conscientiously, you already are well-prepared for the CPA exam.

The morning of each exam section:

1. Eat a satisfying breakfast. It will be several hours before your next meal. Eat enough to ward off hunger, but not so much that you feel uncomfortable.
2. Dress appropriately. Wear layers you can take off to suit varying temperatures in the room.
3. Arrive at the exam center at least 30 minutes early. Check in as soon as you are allowed to do so.

Dewitt Animal Hospital, P.C.
5620 Thompson Road
Dewitt, NY 13214
(315) 446-1200

SYRACUSE NY 130
29 JAN 2015 PM 3 L

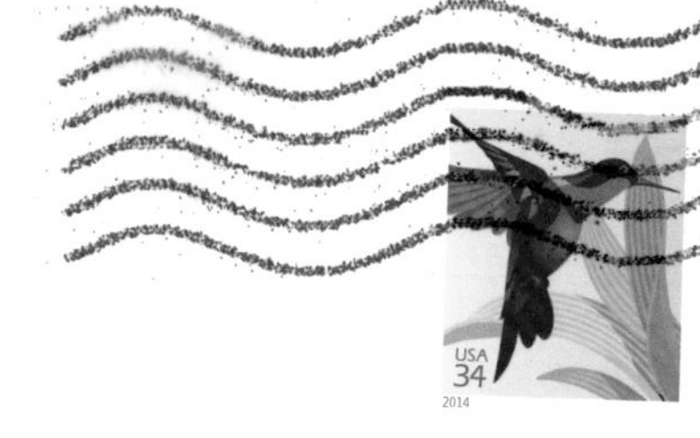

A reminder that Kritter is due for:
Dental Examination

Dan Coyle
158 Mountainview Ave
Syracuse, NY 13224

Please bring your pet in for a FREE oral health exam during the month of February!
Doctor's Hours: Mon-Fri 10:30 AM-12 PM; 2:30-5 PM.
Sat 10:30 AM-1:00 PM Evenings by appointment!

CHAPTER 2—CASH, RECEIVABLES & INVESTMENTS

Problem 2-1 MULTIPLE-CHOICE QUESTIONS

1. _______________ is (are) an economic benefit(s) owned by a firm that is (are) reasonably expected to be converted into cash or consumed during the entity's operating cycle or one year, whichever is longer.

   a. Restricted
   b. Current assets
   c. Notes receivable
   d. Accounts receivable (Editor, 6882)

2. The following trial balance of Trey Co. at December 31 of the current year has been adjusted except for income tax expense.

	Dr.	Cr.
Cash	$ 550,000	
Accounts receivable, net	1,650,000	
Prepaid taxes	300,000	
Accounts payable		$ 120,000
Common stock		500,000
Additional paid-in capital		680,000
Retained earnings		630,000
Foreign currency translation adjustment	430,000	
Revenues		3,600,000
Expenses	2,600,000	
	$5,530,000	$5,530,000

   - During the year, estimated tax payments of $300,000 were charged to prepaid taxes. Trey has not yet recorded income tax expense. There were no differences between financial statement and income tax income, and Trey's tax rate is 30%.
   - Included in accounts receivable is $500,000 due from a customer. Special terms granted to this customer require payment in equal semi-annual installments of $125,000 every April 1 and October 1.

   In Trey's December 31 year-end balance sheet, what amount should be reported as total current assets?

   a. $1,950,000
   b. $2,200,000
   c. $2,250,000
   d. $2,500,000 (11/94, FAR, #8, amended, 5273)

3. Trans Co. had the following balances at December 31, year 4:

Cash in checking account	$ 35,000
Cash in money market account	75,000
U.S. Treasury bill, purchased 11/1 year 4, maturing 1/31, year 5	350,000
U.S. Treasury bill, purchased 12/1 year 4, maturing 3/31, year 5	400,000

   Trans's policy is to treat as cash equivalents all highly-liquid investments with a maturity of three months or less when purchased. What amount should Trans report as cash and cash equivalents in its December 31, year 4, balance sheet?

   a. $110,000
   b. $385,000
   c. $460,000
   d. $860,000 (R/99, FAR #5, 6774)

4. At October 31 of the current year, Dingo, Inc. had cash accounts at three different banks. One account balance is segregated solely for a November 15 payment into a bond sinking fund. A second account, used for branch operations, is overdrawn. The third account, used for regular corporate operations, has a positive balance. How should these accounts be reported in Dingo's October 31 classified balance sheet?
   a. The segregated account should be reported as a noncurrent asset, the regular account should be reported as a current asset, and the overdraft should be reported as a current liability.
   b. The segregated and regular accounts should be reported as current assets, and the overdraft should be reported as a current liability.
   c. The segregated account should be reported as a noncurrent asset, and the regular account should be reported as a current asset net of the overdraft.
   d. The segregated and regular accounts should be reported as current assets net of the overdraft.

   (R/92, FAR #13, 3446)

5. The following are held by Smite Co.:

Cash in checking account	$20,000
Cash in bond sinking fund account	30,000
Post-dated check from customer dated one month from balance sheet date	250
Petty cash	200
Commercial paper (matures in two months)	7,000
Certificate of deposit (matures in six months)	5,000

   What amount should be reported as cash and cash equivalents on Smite's balance sheet?
   a. $57,200
   b. $32,200
   c. $27,450
   d. $27,200

   (R/05, FAR, #42, 7786)

6. Smith Co. has a checking account at Small Bank and an interest-bearing savings account at Big Bank. On December 31, year 1, the bank reconciliations for Smith are as follows:

Big Bank	
Bank balance	$150,000
Deposit in transit	5,000
Book balance	$155,000

Small Bank	
Bank balance	$ 1,500
Outstanding checks	(8,500)
Book balance	$ (7,000)

   What amount should be classified as cash on Smith's balance sheet at December 31, year 1?
   a. $148,000
   b. $151,000
   c. $155,000
   d. $156,000

   (R/08, FAR, #31, 8586)

7. Hilltop Co.'s monthly bank statement shows a balance of $54,200. Reconciliation of the statement with company books reveals the following information:

Bank service charge	$ 10
Insufficient funds check	650
Checks outstanding	1,500
Deposits in transit	350
Check deposited by Hilltop and cleared by the bank for $125, but improperly recorded by Hilltop as $152	

What is the net cash balance after the reconciliation?

a. $52,363
b. $53,023
c. $53,050
d. $53,077 (R/11, FAR, #36, 9886)

8. The following information relates to Jay Co.'s accounts receivable for the current year:

Accounts receivable, 1/1	$ 650,000
Credit sales for the year	2,700,000
Sales returns for the year	75,000
Accounts written off during year	40,000
Collections from customers during year	2,150,000
Estimated future sales returns at 12/31	50,000
Estimated uncollectible accounts at 12/31	110,000

What amount should Jay report for accounts receivable, before allowances for sales returns and uncollectible accounts, at December 31?

a. $1,200,000
b. $1,125,000
c. $1,085,000
d. $ 925,000 (5/93, PI, #12, amended, 4054)

9. Marr Co. had the following sales and accounts receivable balances, prior to any adjustments at year end:

Credit sales	$10,000,000
Accounts receivable	3,000,000
Allowance for uncollectible accounts (debit balance)	50,000

Marr uses 3% of accounts receivable to determine its allowance for uncollectible accounts at year end. By what amount should Marr adjust its allowance for uncollectible accounts at year end?

a. $0
b. $ 40,000
c. $ 90,000
d. $140,000 (R/11, FAR, #10, 9860)

10. Delta Inc. sells to wholesalers on terms of 2/15, net 30. Delta has no cash sales but 50% of Delta's customers take advantage of the discount. Delta uses the gross method of recording sales and trade receivables. Delta's trade receivables balances at December 31 revealed the following:

Age	Amount	Collectible
0-15 days	$100,000	100%
16-30 days	60,000	95%
31-60 days	5,000	90%
Over 60 days	2,500	$500
	$167,500	

In its December 31 balance sheet, what amount should Delta report for allowance for discounts?

a. $1,000
b. $1,620
c. $1,675
d. $2,000 (5/94, FAR, #15, amended, 4830)

11. Lew Co. sold 200,000 corrugated boxes for $2 each. Lew's cost was $1 per unit. The sales agreement gave the customer the right to return up to 60% of the boxes within the first six months, provided an appropriate reason was given. It was immediately determined, with appropriate reason, that 5% of the boxes would be returned. Lew absorbed an additional $10,000 to process the returns and expects to resell the boxes. What amount should Lew report as operating profit from this transaction?

a. $170,000
b. $179,500
c. $180,000
d. $200,000 (R/02, FAR, #8, 7063)

12. Foster Co. adjusted its allowance for uncollectible accounts at year end. The general ledger balances for the accounts receivable and the related allowance account were $1,000,000 and $40,000, respectively. Foster uses the percentage-of-receivables method to estimate its allowance for uncollectible accounts. Accounts receivable were estimated to be 5% uncollectible. What amount should Foster record as an adjustment to its allowance for uncollectible accounts at year end?

a. $10,000 decrease
b. $10,000 increase
c. $50,000 decrease
d. $50,000 increase (R/05, FAR, #25, 7769)

13. When the allowance method of recognizing uncollectible accounts is used, how would the collection of an account previously written off affect accounts receivable and the allowance for uncollectible accounts?

	Accounts receivable	Allowance for uncollectible accounts
a.	Increase	Decrease
b.	Increase	No effect
c.	No effect	Decrease
d.	No effect	Increase

(R/09, FAR, #29, 8779)

14. At January 1, Jam Co. had a credit balance of $260,000 in its allowance for uncollectible accounts. Based on past experience, 2% of Jam's credit sales have been uncollectible. During the year, Jam wrote off $325,000 of uncollectible accounts. Credit sales for the year were $9,000,000. In its December 31 year-end balance sheet, what amount should Jam report as allowance for uncollectible accounts?

a. $115,000
b. $180,000
c. $245,000
d. $440,000 (5/95, FAR, #9, amended, 5545)

15. Inge Co. determined that the net value of its accounts receivable at December 31 of the current year, based on an aging of the receivables, was $325,000. Additional information is as follows:

Allowance for uncollectible accounts—1/1	$ 30,000
Uncollectible accounts written-off during the year	18,000
Uncollectible accounts recovered during the year	2,000
Accounts receivable at 12/31	350,000

For the current year ending December 31, what would be Inge's uncollectible accounts expense?

a. $ 5,000
b. $11,000
c. $15,000
d. $21,000 (11/94, FAR, #45, 9048)

16. In its previous year-end balance sheet, Fleet Co. reported accounts receivable of $100,000 before allowance for uncollectible accounts of $10,000. Credit sales during the year were $611,000, and collections from customers, excluding recoveries, totaled $591,000. In the year, accounts receivable of $45,000 were written off and $17,000 were recovered. Fleet estimated that $15,000 of the accounts receivable at December 31 were uncollectible. In its December 31 current year balance sheet, what amount should Fleet report as accounts receivable before allowance for uncollectible accounts?

a. $58,000
b. $67,000
c. $75,000
d. $82,000 (R/00, FAR, #2, amended, 6897)

17. Which method of recording uncollectible accounts expense is consistent with accrual accounting?

	Allowance	Direct write-off
a.	Yes	Yes
b.	Yes	No
c.	No	Yes
d.	No	No

(5/95, FAR, #35, 5571)

18. Bee Co. uses the direct write-off method to account for uncollectible accounts receivable. During an accounting period, Bee's cash collections from customers equal sales adjusted for the addition or deduction of the following amounts:

	Accounts written-off	Increase in accounts receivable balance
a.	Deduction	Deduction
b.	Addition	Deduction
c.	Deduction	Addition
d.	Addition	Addition

(5/91, Theory, #9, 1784)

19. Which of the following statements is (are) true regarding account receivable discounts?

a. Forfeited discounts by the purchaser should be regarded as additional consideration received for the goods or services provided.
b. Forfeited discounts by the purchaser are included in the balances of sales and receivables.
c. Forfeited discounts by the purchaser are considered interest revenue.
d. Both A. and B. (Editor, 6096)

20. Which of the following is true regarding an entity that records a note receivable?

a. When a note is exchanged for cash and a promise to provide merchandise at a discount from market price, the note is presumed to have a present value at issuance equal to the cash proceeds exchanged.
b. Noninterest-bearing notes receivable and those with an unrealistic stated rate of interest are not reported on the balance sheet but disclosed in the notes to the financial statements.
c. Loan origination fees are expensed in full in the period incurred.
d. For interest-bearing notes calling for the prevailing rate of interest at the time of issuance, the present value of the note is the same as the face amount of the note. (Editor, 4426)

21. On August 15 of the current year, Benet Co. sold goods for which it received a note bearing the market rate of interest on that date. The four-month note was dated this July 15. Note principal, together with all interest, is due November 15. When the note was recorded on August 15, which of the following accounts increased?

    a. Unearned discount
    b. Interest receivable
    c. Prepaid interest
    d. Interest revenue (5/92, Theory, #21, amended, 2714)

22. Frame Co. has an 8% note receivable dated June 30, year 1, in the original amount of $150,000. Payments of $50,000 in principal plus accrued interest are due annually on July 1, year 2, year 3, and year 4. In its June 30, year 3, balance sheet, what amount should Frame report as a current asset for interest on the note receivable?

    a. $0
    b. $ 4,000
    c. $ 8,000
    d. $12,000 (11/93, PI, #17, amended, 4386)

23. Leaf Co. purchased from Oak Co. a $20,000, 8%, 5-year note that required five equal annual year-end payments of $5,009. The note was discounted to yield a 9% rate to Leaf. At the date of purchase, Leaf recorded the note at its present value of $19,485. What should be the total interest revenue earned by Leaf over the life of this note?

    a. $5,045
    b. $5,560
    c. $8,000
    d. $9,000 (11/94, FAR, #38, 5300)

24. January 1, Year 5, Elia Company sold a building which had a carrying amount of $350,000, receiving a $125,000 down payment and, as additional consideration, a $400,000 noninterest-bearing note due on January 1, Year 8. There was no established exchange price for the building and the note had no ready market. The prevailing rate of interest for a note of this type at January 1, Year 5, was 10%. The present value of 1 at 10% for three periods is 0.75.

    What amount of interest income should be included in Elia's Year 5 income statement?

    a. $0
    b. $30,000
    c. $35,000
    d. $40,000 (Editor, 9070)

25. On December 30 of the current year, Chang Co. sold a machine to Door Co. in exchange for a noninterest-bearing note requiring ten annual payments of $10,000. Door made the first payment on that same date. The market interest rate for similar notes at date of issuance was 8%. Information on present value factors is as follows:

Period	Present value of $1 at 8%	Present value of ordinary annuity of $1 at 8%
9	0.50	6.25
10	0.46	6.71

    In its December 31 year-end balance sheet, what amount should Chang report as note receivable?

    a. $45,000
    b. $46,000
    c. $62,500
    d. $67,100 (5/95, FAR, #8, amended, 5544)

26. Jole Co. lent $10,000 to a major supplier in exchange for a noninterest-bearing note due in three years and a contract to purchase a fixed amount of merchandise from the supplier at a 10% discount from prevailing market prices over the next three years. The market rate for a note of this type is 10%. On issuing the note, Jole should record

	Discount on note receivable	Deferred Charge
a.	Yes	Yes
b.	Yes	No
c.	No	Yes
d.	No	No

(R/01, FAR, #4, 6979)

27. On December 31, Key Co. received two $10,000 non-interest-bearing notes from customers in exchange for services rendered. The note from Alpha Co., which is due in nine months, was made under customary trade terms, but the note from Omega Co., which is due in two years, was not. The market interest rate for both notes at the date of issuance is 8%. The present value of $1 due in nine months at 8% is .944. The present value of $1 due in two years at 8% is .857. At what amounts should these two notes receivable be reported in Key's December 31 balance sheet?

	Alpha	Omega
a.	$ 9,440	$ 8,570
b.	$10,000	$ 8,570
c.	$ 9,440	$10,000
d.	$10,000	$10,000

(R/07, FAR, #34, 8355)

28. When a loan receivable is impaired but foreclosure is **not** probable, which of the following may the creditor use to measure the impairment?

    I. The loan's observable market price
    II. The fair value of the collateral if the loan is collateral dependent

    a. I only
    b. II only
    c. Either I or II
    d. Neither I nor II (11/96, FAR, #7, 6453)

29. Red Co. had $3 million in accounts receivable recorded on its books. Red wanted to convert the $3 million in receivables to cash in a more timely manner than waiting the 45 days for payment as indicated on its invoices. Which of the following would alter the timing of Red's cash flows for the $3 million in receivables already recorded on its books?

    a. Change the due date of the invoice
    b. Factor the receivables outstanding
    c. Discount the receivables outstanding
    d. Demand payment from customers before the due date (R/07, FAR, #22, 8343)

30. Ace Co. sold to King Co. a $20,000, 8%, 5-year note that required five equal annual year-end payments. This note was discounted to yield a 9% rate to King. The present value factors of an ordinary annuity of $1 for five periods are as follows:

8%	3.992
9%	3.890

    What should be the total interest revenue earned by King on this note?

    a. $9,000
    b. $8,000
    c. $5,560
    d. $5,050 (5/92, PI, #41, 2612)

31. Milton Co. pledged some of its accounts receivable to Good Neighbor Financing Corporation in return for a loan. Which of the following statements is correct?

    a. Good Neighbor Financing cannot take title to the receivables if Milton does not repay the loan. Title can only be taken if the receivables are factored.
    b. Good Neighbor Financing will assume the responsibility of collecting the receivables.
    c. Milton will retain control of the receivables.
    d. Good Neighbor Financing will take title to the receivables, and will return title to Milton after the loan is paid. (R/10, FAR, #30, 9330)

32. Which of the following describes portfolio segment disclosure in regards to credit losses?

    a. The level used by the entity in developing and documenting a systematic method for determining the allowance for credit losses
    b. The level based on initial measurement attributes, risk characteristics of the financing receivables, and methods used by reporting entities related to monitoring and assessing credit risk
    c. A fully aggregated basis of disclosure
    d. None of the above (Editor, 3434)

33. On July 1, year 1, Kay Corp. sold equipment to Mando Co. for $100,000. Kay accepted a 10% note receivable for the entire sales price. This note is payable in two equal installments of $50,000 plus accrued interest on December 31, year 1 and year 2. On July 1, year 2, Kay discounted the note at a bank at an interest rate of 12%. Kay's proceeds from the discounted note were

    a. $48,400
    b. $49,350
    c. $50,350
    d. $51,700 (11/90, PII, #1, amended, 0890)

34. A note receivable bearing a reasonable interest rate is sold to a bank with recourse. At the date of the discounting transaction, the notes receivable discounted account should be

    a. Decreased by the proceeds from the discounting transaction
    b. Increased by the proceeds from the discounting transaction
    c. Increased by the face amount of the note
    d. Decreased by the face amount of the note (5/89, Theory, #3, 1823)

35. On April 1, Aloe, Inc. factored $80,000 of its accounts receivable without recourse. The factor retained 10% of the accounts receivable as an allowance for sales returns and charged a 5% commission on the gross amount of the factored receivables. What amount of cash did Aloe receive from the factored receivables?

    a. $68,000
    b. $68,400
    c. $72,000
    d. $76,000 (R/10, FAR, #31, 9331)

36. In year 1, a company reported in other comprehensive income an unrealized holding loss on an investment in available-for-sale securities. During year 2, these securities were sold at a loss equal to the unrealized loss previously recognized. The reclassification adjustment should include which of the following?

    a. The unrealized loss should be credited to the investment account.
    b. The unrealized loss should be credited to the other comprehensive income account.
    c. The unrealized loss should be debited to the other comprehensive income account.
    d. The unrealized loss should be credited to beginning retained earnings. (R/11, FAR, #44, 9894)

37. At year end, Rim Co. held several investments with the intent of selling them in the near term. The investments consisted of $100,000, 8%, five-year bonds, purchased for $92,000, and equity securities purchased for $35,000. At year end, the bonds were selling on the open market for $105,000 and the equity securities had a market value of $50,000. What amount should Rim report as trading securities in its year-end balance sheet?

a. $ 50,000
b. $127,000
c. $142,000
d. $155,000 (R/05, FAR, #7, 7751)

38. At the end of year 1, Lane Co. held trading securities that cost $86,000 and which had a year-end market value of $92,000. During year 2, all of these securities were sold for $104,500. At the end of year 2, Lane had acquired additional trading securities that cost $73,000 and which had a year-end market value of $71,000. What is the impact of these stock activities on Lane's year 2 income statement?

a. Loss of $2,000
b. Gain of $10,500
c. Gain of $16,500
d. Gain of $18,500 (R/07, FAR, #4, 8325)

39. Nola has a portfolio of marketable equity securities which it does not intend to sell in the near term. How should Nola classify these securities, and how should it report unrealized gains and losses from these securities?

	Classify as	Report as a
a.	Trading securities	Component of income from continuing operations
b.	Available-for-sale securities	Component of other comprehensive income
c.	Trading securities	Component of other comprehensive income
d.	Available-for-sale securities	Component of income from continuing operations

(5/94, FAR, #14, amended, 4829)

40. Lee Corp. reported the following marketable equity security on its December 31 previous year balance sheet, classified as an available-for-sale security:

Neu Corp. common stock, at cost	$100,000
Market adjustment to reflect decline in fair value	(20,000)
Balance	$ 80,000

At December 31 of the current year, the fair value of Lee's investment in the Neu Corp. stock was $85,000. As a result of the current year increase in this stock's fair value, Lee's current year income statement should report

a. An unrealized gain of $5,000
b. A realized gain of $5,000
c. An unrealized loss of $15,000
d. No gain or loss (11/89, PII, #3, amended, 9049)

41. The following information was extracted from Gil Co.'s December 31, year-end balance sheet:

Noncurrent assets:	
Investments in available-for-sale marketable equity securities (carried at market)	$ 96,450
Accumulated other comprehensive income:	
Net unrealized loss on investments in marketable equity securities	(19,800)

Historical cost of the long-term investments in marketable equity securities was

a. $ 63,595
b. $ 76,650
c. $ 96,450
d. $116,250 (5/91, PII, #18, amended, 4566)

42. The following information pertains to Smoke Inc.'s investments in marketable equity securities, classified as available-for-sale:

    - On December 31 of the current year, Smoke has a security with a $70,000 cost and a $50,000 fair value. (No Market Adjustment account exists.)
    - A marketable equity security costing $50,000, has a $60,000 fair value on December 31 of the current year. Smoke believes the recovery from an earlier lower fair value is permanent.

    What is the net effect of the above two items on the balances of Smoke's Market Adjustment account for available-for-sale marketable equity securities as of December 31 of the current year?

    a. No effect
    b. Creates a $10,000 debit balance
    c. Creates a $20,000 credit balance
    d. Creates a $10,000 credit balance (5/92, PI, #14, amended, 4578)

43. When the fair value of an investment in debt securities exceeds its amortized cost, how should each of the following debt securities be reported at the end of the year?

	Debt securities classified as	
	Held-to-maturity	Available-for-sale
a.	Amortized cost	Amortized cost
b.	Amortized cost	Fair value
c.	Fair value	Fair value
d.	Fair value	Amortized cost

(11/96, FAR, #6, 6452)

44. Beach Co. determined that the decline in the fair market value (FMV) of an investment was below the amortized cost and permanent in nature. The investment was classified as available-for-sale on Beach's books. The controller would properly record the decrease in FMV by including it in which of the following?

    a. Other comprehensive income section of the income statement only
    b. Earnings section of the income statement and writing down the cost basis to FMV
    c. Extraordinary items section of the income statement, net of tax, and writing down the cost basis to FMV
    d. Other comprehensive income section of the income statement, and writing down the cost basis to FMV (R/07, FAR, #49, 8370)

Items 45 and 46 are based on the following information:

Sun Corp. had investments in equity securities classified as trading costing $650,000. On June 30 of the current year, Sun decided to hold the investments indefinitely and accordingly reclassified them from trading to available-for-sale on that date. The investment's fair value was $575,000 at December 31 of the previous year; $530,000 at this June 30; and $490,000 at December 31 of the current year.

45. What amount of loss from investments should Sun report in its current year income statement?

    a. $ 45,000
    b. $ 85,000
    c. $120,000
    d. $160,000 (5/93, PI, #3, amended, 4045)

46. What amount should Sun report as net unrealized loss on investments in equity securities in other comprehensive income at the end of the current year?

    a. $ 40,000
    b. $ 45,000
    c. $ 85,000
    d. $160,000 (5/93, PI, #4, amended, 4046)

47. Neron Co. has two derivatives related to two different financial instruments, instrument A and instrument B, both of which are debt instruments. The derivative related to instrument A is a fair value hedge, and the derivative related to instrument B is a cash flow hedge. Neron experienced gains in the value of instruments A and B due to a change in interest rates. Which of the gains should be reported by Neron in its income statement?

	Gain in value of debt instrument A	Gain in value of debt instrument B	
a.	Yes	Yes	
b.	Yes	No	
c.	No	Yes	
d.	No	No	(R/11, FAR, #33, 9883)

48. Which of the following statements is false with respect to derivative instruments?
    a. A derivative instrument has at least one underlying financial security.
    b. A derivative instrument has at least one notional amount or payment provision or both.
    c. A derivative instrument requires an initial net investment.
    d. A derivative instrument requires or permits net settlement, can be readily settled net by a means outside the contract, or provides for delivery of an asset that puts the recipient in a position not substantially different from net settlement. (Editor, 89532)

49. The primary criteria for determining a fair value hedge includes the fact that the hedged item does which of the following?
    a. Is specifically identified as a specific portion of a recognized asset or liability, or of a firm commitment
    b. Is a single asset or liability, or is a portfolio of similar assets or a portfolio of similar liabilities
    c. Presents an exposure to changes in fair value for the hedged risk that would not affect reported earnings
    d. Is/does all of the above (Editor, 89535)

50. A derivative financial instrument is best described as
    a. Evidence of an ownership interest in an entity such as shares of common stock
    b. A contract that has its settlement value tied to an underlying notional amount
    c. A contract that conveys to a second entity a right to receive cash from a first entity
    d. A contract that conveys to a second entity a right to future collections on accounts receivable from a first entity (R/10, FAR#39, 9339)

51. Which of the following is the characteristic of a perfect hedge?
    a. No possibility of future gain or loss
    b. No possibility of future gain only
    c. No possibility of future loss only
    d. The possibility of future gain and no future loss (R/08, FAR, #42, 8597)

52. Neely Co. disclosed in the notes to its financial statements that a significant number of its unsecured trade account receivables are with companies that operate in the same industry. This disclosure is required to inform financial statement users of the existence of
    a. Concentration of credit risk
    b. Concentration of market risk
    c. Risk of measurement uncertainty
    d. Off-balance sheet risk of accounting loss (R/10, FAR, #16, 9316)

53. On December 1 of the current year, Bann Co. entered into an option contract to purchase 2,000 shares of Norta Co. stock for $40 per share (the same as the current market price) by the end of the next two months. The time value of the option contract is $600. At the end of December, Norta's stock was selling for $43, and the time value of the option is now $400. If Bann does not exercise its option until January of the subsequent year, which of the following changes would reflect the proper accounting treatment for this transaction on Bann's December 31, year-end financial statements?

a. The option value will be disclosed in the footnotes only.
b. Other comprehensive income will increase by $6,000.
c. Net income will increase by $5,800.
d. Current assets will decrease by $200. (R/09, FAR, #36, 8786)

54. Which of the following risks are inherent in an interest rate swap agreement?

I. The risk of exchanging a lower interest rate for a higher interest rate
II. The risk of nonperformance by the counterparty to the agreement

a. I only
b. II only
c. Both I and II
d. Neither I nor II (11/96, FAR, #8, 6454)

55. On November 2, year 1, Platt Co. entered into a 90-day futures contract to purchase 50,000 Swiss francs when the contract quote was $0.70. The purchase was for speculation in price movement. The following exchange rates existed during the contract period:

	30-day futures	Spot rate
November 2, year 1	$0.62	$0.63
December 31, year 1	0.65	0.64
January 30, year 2	0.65	0.68

What amount should Platt report as foreign currency exchange loss in its income statement for the year ended December 31, year 1?

a. $2,500
b. $3,000
c. $3,500
d. $4,000 (R/02, FAR #4, 7059)

56. An entity may designate, as a type of hedge of foreign currency exposure, a derivative instrument or a nonderivative financial instrument that may give rise to a foreign currency transaction gain or loss as which of the following?

a. A fair value hedge
b. A cash flow hedge
c. A hedge of a net investment in a foreign operation
d. None of the above (Editor, 89584)

57. On December 12, year 1, Imp Co. entered into a forward exchange contract to purchase 100,000 euros in 90 days. The relevant exchange rates are as follows:

	Spot rate	Forward rate (for 3/12, yr 2)
December 12, year 1	$1.86	$1.80
December 31, year 1	1.96	1.83

Imp entered into the forward contract to hedge a commitment to purchase equipment being manufactured to Imp's specifications. At December 31, year 1, what amount of foreign currency transaction gain should Imp include in income from this forward contract?

a. $0
b. $ 3,000
c. $ 5,000
d. $ 10,000 (11/92, PI, #49, amended, 3282)

58. The functional currency of Nash Inc.'s subsidiary is the euro. Nash borrowed euros as a partial hedge of its investment in the subsidiary. In preparing consolidated financial statements, Nash's translation loss on its investment in the subsidiary exceeded its exchange gain on the borrowing. How should the effects of the loss and gain be reported in Nash's consolidated financial statements?

    a. The translation loss less the exchange gain is reported in other comprehensive income.
    b. The translation loss less the exchange gain is reported in net income.
    c. The translation loss is reported in other comprehensive income and the exchange gain is reported in net income.
    d. The translation loss is reported in net income and the exchange gain is reported in other comprehensive income. (5/92, Theory, #38, amended, 2731)

Problem 2-2 SIMULATION: Uncollectible Accounts

Sigma Co. began operations on January 1 of the previous year. On December 31 of the previous year, Sigma provided for uncollectible accounts based on 1% of annual credit sales. On January 1 of the current year, Sigma changed its method of determining its allowance for uncollectible accounts by applying certain percentages to the accounts receivable aging as follows:

Days past invoice date	Deemed to be uncollectible
0-30	1%
31-90	5%
91-180	20%
Over 180	80%

In addition, Sigma wrote off all accounts receivable that were over one year old. The following additional information relates to the previous and current years ended December 31:

	Current year	Previous year
Credit sales	$3,000,000	$2,800,000
Collections	2,915,000	2,400,000
Accounts written-off	27,000	None
Recovery of accounts previously written-off	7,000	None
Days past invoice date		
0-30	$300,000	$250,000
31-90	80,000	90,000
91-180	60,000	45,000
Over 180	25,000	15,000

1. Prepare a schedule showing the calculation of the allowance for uncollectible accounts at December 31 of the current year.

	A/R Amount	Percentage	Allowance
0 to 30 days			$
31 to 90 days			
91 to 180 days			
Over 180 days			
Accounts receivable			
Allowance for uncollectible accounts			$

2. Prepare a schedule showing the computation of the provision for uncollectible accounts for the year ended December 31 of the current year.

Balance December 31, previous year	$
Write-offs during the current year	
Recoveries during the current year	
Balance before the current year provisions	
Required allowance at December 31 of current year	
Current year provisions	$

(5/92, PI, #4, amended, 9018)

Problem 2-3 SIMULATION: Receivables

Fern Inc. had the following long-term receivable account balances at December 31, year 3:

Note receivable from the sale of an idle building	$900,000
Note receivable from an officer	400,000

Transactions during year 4 and other information relating to Fern's long-term receivables follows:

- The $900,000 note receivable is dated May 1, year 3, bears interest at 9%, and represents the balance of the consideration Fern received from the sale of its idle building to Bale Co. Principal payments of $300,000 plus interest are due annually beginning May 1, year 4. Bale made its first principal and interest payment on May 1, year 4. Collection of the remaining note installments is reasonably assured.

- The $400,000 note receivable is dated December 31, year 1, bears interest at 8%, and is due on December 31, year 6. The note is due from Jake White, president of Fern Inc., and is collateralized by 10,000 shares of Fern's common stock. Interest is payable annually on December 31, and all interest payments were made through December 31, year 4. The quoted market price of Fern's common stock was $45 per share on December 31, year 4.

- On April 1, year 4, Fern sold a patent to Fry Corp. in exchange for a $200,000 noninterest-bearing note due on April 1, year 6. There was no established exchange price for the patent, and the note had no ready market. The prevailing interest rate for this type of note was 10% at April 1, year 4. The present value of $1 for two periods at 10% is 0.826. The patent had a carrying amount of $80,000 at January 1, year 4, and the amortization for the year ended December 31, year 4 would have been $16,000. Fern is reasonably assured of collecting the note receivable from Fry.

- On July 1, year 4, Fern sold a parcel of land to Carr Co. for $600,000 under an installment sale contract. Carr made a $180,000 cash down payment on July 1, year 4, and signed a four-year 10% note for the $420,000 balance. The equal annual payments of principal and interest on the note will be $127,827, payable on July 1 of each year from year 5 through year 8. The fair value of the land at the date of sale was $600,000. The cost of the land to Fern was $450,000. Collection of the remaining note installments is reasonably assured.

1. Complete the long-term receivables section of Fern's December 31, year 4 balance sheet.

9% note receivable from sale of idle building, due in annual installments of $300,000 to May 1, year 6, less current installment	
8% note receivable from officer, due December 31, year 6, collateralized by 10,000 shares of Fern Inc. common stock with a fair value of $225,000	
Noninterest-bearing note from sale of patent, net of 10% imputed interest, due April 1, year 6	
Installment contract receivable, due in annual installments of $88,332 to July 1, year 7, less current installment	
Total long-term receivables	

2. Prepare a schedule showing current portion of long-term receivables and accrued interest receivable to be reported in Fern's December 31, year 4 balance sheet.

Current portion of long-term receivables:	
Note receivable from sale of idle building	$
Installment contract receivable	
Total	$
Accrued interest receivable:	
Note receivable from sale of idle building	$
Installment contract receivable	
Total	$

(5/91, PI, #4, amended, 9019t)

Problem 2-4 SIMULATION: Marketable Securities

Items 1 through 4 are based on the following:

Parcel Co. purchased various securities to be classified as held-to-maturity securities, trading securities, or available-for-sale securities. Determine the appropriate category for each security and enter in the cell. A category may be used once, more than once, or not at all.

Category Choices
Held-to-maturity Trading Available-for-sale

Security Purchases	Category
1. U.S. Treasury bonds that Parcel has both the positive intent and the ability to hold to maturity.	
2. Convertible preferred stock that Parcel does not intend to sell in the near term.	
3. Debt securities bought and held for the purpose of selling in the near term.	
4. $4 million debt security bought and held for the purpose of selling in three years to finance payment of Parcel's $3 million long-term note payable when it matures.	

Items 5 through 10 are based on the following chart:

The following information pertains to Parcel Co.'s portfolio of marketable investments for the current year ended December 31. Security CBA was purchased at par. All declines in fair value are considered to be temporary.

	Cost	Fair value, 12/31, Year 1	Year 2 Activity		Fair value, 12/31, Year 2
			Purchases	Sales	
Held-to-maturity securities Security CBA			$125,000		$120,000
Trading securities Security FED	$130,000	$140,000			$135,000
Available-for-sale securities Security IHG Security LKJ	 $170,000 $160,000	 $145,000 $165,000		 $155,000	 $150,000

Items 5 through 7 describe amounts to be reported in Parcel's current year financial statements. For each item, enter the correct amount to be reported, rounded to the nearest whole number. Ignore income tax considerations.

Item	Amount
5. Carrying amount of security CBA at 12/31 of the current year.	
6. Carrying amount of security FED at 12/31 of the current year.	
7. Carrying amount of security LKJ at 12/31 of the current year.	

Items 8 through 10 require two responses. For each item, indicate whether a gain (G) or a loss (L) is to be reported and enter the amount of that gain or loss from the choices provided.

Item	G or L	Amount
8. Recognized gain or loss on sale of security IHG.		
9. Unrealized gain or loss to be reported in current year income statement.		
10. Unrealized gain or loss to be reported at December 31 of the current year in accumulated other comprehensive income.		

(11/95, FAR, #61 - 70, amended, 6143t)

Problem 2-5 SIMULATION: Research

Question: How should derivative instruments be measured initially?

FASB ASC: ______ - ______ - ______ - ______

(9163)

Solution 2-1 MULTIPLE-CHOICE ANSWERS

Current Assets

1. (b) Current assets are economic benefits owned by a firm that are reasonably expected to be converted into cash or consumed during the entity's operating cycle or one year, whichever is longer. Restricted cash is cash held for a particular purpose and classified based upon the date of availability or disbursement. It is segregated from unrestricted cash. Notes receivable are claims usually not arising from sales in the ordinary course of business. Accounts receivable are used for claims arising from the sale of goods or the performance of services. (6882)

2. (a) The operating cycle of an enterprise is the *average* period of time between expenditures for goods and services and the date those expenditures are converted into cash. Since there is no indication that Trey's operating cycle is greater than one year, a twelve month time period should be used as the basis for determining the amount to be reported as total current assets. Included in Trey's accounts receivable is $500,000 due from a customer. *Special terms* granted to this customer require payment in equal semiannual installments of $125,000 every April 1 and October 1. Therefore, $250,000 (i.e., $125,000 semiannual payments to be received on 4/1 and 10/1 in two years) of this receivable should be excluded from current assets at 12/31 of the current year because this amount would be received after 12/31 of the following year. During the current year, estimated tax payments of $300,000 were charged to prepaid taxes. Since Trey's income tax expense for the current year is also $300,000 [i.e., ($3,600,000 – $2,600,000) × 30%], there are, in fact, no net prepaid taxes at 12/31 of the current year.

Cash	$ 550,000	
Accounts receivable, net ($1,650,000 – $250,000)	1,400,000	
Current assets, 12/31 current year	$1,950,000	(5273)

3. (c) The $400,000 U.S. Treasury bill purchased 12/1, year 4 and maturing 3/31, year 5 is not included as a cash equivalent because the maturity was more than three months at the time of purchase. Cash and cash equivalents reported at December 31, year 4, are as follows:

Cash in checking account	$ 35,000	
Cash in money market account	75,000	
U.S. Treasury Bills, purchased 11/1, year 4, maturing 1/31, year 5	350,000	
Total Cash & cash equivalents	$460,000	(6774)

4. (a) Cash that is segregated for the liquidation of long-term debts should be excluded from current assets. Hence, the account balance at the first bank which is segregated solely for payment into the bond sinking fund should be reported as a noncurrent asset. The bank overdraft at the second bank should be reported as a current liability because there is no available cash in another account at that bank to offset the overdrawn account (i.e., the bank overdraft should not be netted against the account used for regular operations held at the third bank). The cash in the regular account at the third bank is to be used for current operations, hence it should be reported as a current asset. (3446)

5. (d) Items in this question that are not considered cash equivalents are the cash in the bond sinking fund account ($30,000), the post dated check from a customer ($250), and the certificate of deposit that matures in six months ($5,000).

Cash in checking account	$20,000	
Petty cash	200	
Commercial paper (matures in two months)	7,000	
Total cash and cash equivalents	$27,200	(7786)

6. (c) Smith would classify the $150,000 bank balance and $5,000 deposit in transit for Big Bank as cash on the balance sheet. The bank balance of $1,500 in Small Bank is negated by the $8,500 in outstanding checks. Overdrafts in accounts with no available cash in another account at the same bank to offset are classified as current liabilities. They are not deducted from the total amount of cash at another bank. (8586)

7. (c) A common format of the bank reconciliation statement is to reconcile both book and bank balances to a common amount known as the "true balance" or net cash balance. This approach has the advantage of providing the cash figure to be reported in the balance sheet. Furthermore, journal entries necessary to adjust the books can be taken directly from the "book balance" section of the reconciliation. Net cash is the bank balance adjusted for outstanding checks and deposits in transit ($54,000 + 350 – 1,500 = $53,050). Net cash is also the book balance adjusted for unrecorded or misrecorded items, such as service charges, insufficient funds and errors. A normal book to bank reconciliation will compute the unadjusted book balance of $53,737. Net cash from the book side is $53,050 ($53,737 – $10 service charge – $650 insufficient funds – $27 net effect from the error). (9886)

Accounts Receivable

8. (c) Credit sales increase accounts receivable (A/R). Collections from customers, accounts written-off, and sales returns decrease A/R. Since the estimated future sales returns and the estimated uncollectible accounts are recorded in allowance accounts to A/R, they do not directly decrease the balance of the *Accounts Receivable* account.

Accounts Receivable		
Balance, 1/1	650,000	
Credit sales	2,700,000	2,150,000 Collections from customers
		40,000 Accounts written-off
		75,000 Sales returns
Balance, 12/31	1,085,000	

(4054)

9. (d) The amount of the adjustment to the uncollectible account is the difference between the existing balance and the desired ending balance. The uncollectible account currently has a debit balance of $50,000. To get the allowance account to the desired $90,000 credit balance (3% × 3,000,000) there would need to be a credit to allowance for uncollectible accounts and debit to uncollectible accounts expense for $140,000. (9860)

10. (a) Only the receivables which have aged 0-15 days are eligible for the discount. The discount is computed using 50% of the dollar amount eligible, not 50% of the discount. Only 50% of the customers take advantage of the discount.

Amount eligible for discount	$100,000
% of customers that take discount	× 50%
Amount of eligible amount taken	50,000
Discount allowed	× 2%
Allowance for discount	$ 1,000

(4830)

11. (c) An estimated loss from a loss contingency shall be accrued by a charge to income if both of the following conditions are met: (1) it is probable that an asset has been impaired or a liability has been incurred, and (2) the amount of the loss can be reasonably estimated.

Future returns and allowances should be anticipated. Accounting treatment depends on the likelihood that future events will confirm the contingent loss **and** whether the amount can be reasonably estimated. Where the likelihood of confirmation of a loss is considered probable and the loss can be reasonably estimated, the estimated loss should be accrued. If, however, only a range of possible loss can be estimated—and no amount in the range is a better estimate than the others—the minimum amount in the range should be accrued.

Sales revenue (200,000 × $2)	$ 400,000
Less: Cost (200,000 × $1)	(200,000)
Less: Processing costs	(10,000)
Less: Estimated returns ($200,000 × 5% = $10,000) × $1	(10,000)
Operating profit	$ 180,000

(7063)

12. (b) The allowance account balance would increase by the difference between the required amount and the balance at the end of the year.

Accounts receivable balance	$ 1,000,000
Times: % uncollectible	× 5%
Balance required	50,000
Less: End of year balance in allowance account	(40,000)
Adjustment to increase balance	$ 10,000

(7769)

13. (d) Journal entries to record the collection of an account previously written off as uncollectible are:

Accounts Receivable—Joe Doe	XX	
Allowance for Uncollectible Accounts		XX
To reopen account to balance when written off.		
Cash	XX	
Accounts Receivable—Joe Doe		XX
To record receipt of cash payment of receivable.		

These entries would increase cash and allowance for uncollectible accounts. They would have no net effect on net accounts receivable, net income, current assets, or working capital. (8779)

14. (a) Based on the information given, Jamin uses the percentage of sales method, under which bad debt expense is calculated as a percentage of credit sales (credit sales of $9,000,000 × 2% = $180,000), charged to *Bad Debt Expense,* and credited to the *Allowance for Uncollectible Accounts.* The allowance account balance is not considered in determining the amount of bad debt expense.

Allowance for Uncollectible Accounts

		260,000 Beg. bal. 1/1
Write-offs	325,000	
		180,000 Bad debt expense
		115,000 12/31 balance

(5545)

15. (b) After the allowance for uncollectible accounts at 12/31 is determined, uncollectible accounts expense can be analyzed.

Accounts receivable, 12/31	$ 350,000
Net realizable value of the receivables	(325,000)
Allowance for uncollectible accounts, 12/31	$ 25,000

Allowance for Uncollectible Accounts

		30,000 Balance, 1/1
Current year write-offs	18,000	2,000 Uncollectible accounts recovered
		14,000 Subtotal
		11,000 Uncollectible accounts expense (forced)
		25,000 Balance, 12/31

(9048)

16. (c) The A/R balance was increased by credit sales and decreased by collections from customers and by accounts written off. Accounts recovered resulted in an increase and a decrease of equal amount to the A/R balance.

Accounts Receivable

Balance, 1/1	100,000	
Credit sales	611,000	591,000 Customer collections
Accounts reinstated	17,000	45,000 Accounts written-off
		17,000 Accounts recovered
Balance, 12/31	**75,000**	

(6897)

17. (b) The allowance method of recording uncollectible account expense matches uncollectible account expense with the revenues generated by credit sales in the same period and therefore is consistent with accrual accounting. Since the write-off of an account receivable often occurs in a period after the revenues were generated, the direct write-off method of recording uncollectible account expense does not necessarily match uncollectible account expense with the revenues generated by credit sales in the same period. The direct write-off method is not consistent with accrual accounting. (5571)

18. (a) An increase in A/R indicates that there was an excess of sales over cash collections. A write-off of receivables will offset the gross increase in A/R without affecting cash. Regardless of the accrual method used to account for uncollectible accounts, the cash collections from customers equal sales adjusted for a deduction for an increase in A/R balance and a deduction for accounts written-off during the period. (1784)

19. (c) Conceptually, sales and receivables should be recorded net of any discounts for prompt payment. Failure by the purchaser to take advantage of the discount offered should not be regarded as additional consideration received for the goods or services provided. These additional amounts should be considered as interest revenue. If receivables are recorded at gross, such discounts should be anticipated at year-end and deducted from the accounts receivable. (6096)

Notes Receivable

20. (d) For interest-bearing notes calling for the prevailing rate of interest at the time of issuance, the present value of the note is the same as the face amount of the note. When a note is exchanged for cash and a promise to provide merchandise at a discount from market price, the issuer records the note at present value. The difference between fair value and cash payments is recognized as interest revenue over the contract life and is recorded as part of the cost of the related merchandise. For noninterest-bearing notes and those with an unrealistic stated rate of interest, the receivable must be reported at its present value or the fair value of the property, good, or service exchanged, whichever is more clearly determinable. Loan origination fees are deferred and amortized over the life of the loan as an adjustment to interest income. Such amounts, if material, are amortized using the interest method. (4426)

21. (b) When an interest-bearing instrument is sold between interest payment dates, the seller collects accrued interest from the buyer. The buyer will later collect interest for a full interest period at the next interest payment date. In the case at hand, inventory is being exchanged for the note. Because the market rate of interest is equal to the note's stated rate, the note's present value is equal to the face amount of the note plus the one month's accrued interest. The journal entry to record the exchange involves a debit to *Note Receivable* for its face amount, a debit to *Interest Receivable* for the one month of accrued interest, and a credit to Sales Revenue for the sum of the note's face amount and the one month of accrued interest. (2714)

22. (c) The note can be recorded at its face amount of $150,000 because there is no indication that the rate of interest (8%) stipulated by the parties to the transaction does not represent fair and adequate compensation for the use of the funds. Payments of $50,000 in principal plus accrued interest are due annually on July 1, year 2, year 3, and year 4. Frame should report the interest receivable as a current asset in its 6/30, year 3 balance sheet, because the amount is to be received within one year of the balance sheet date (i.e., it is to be received 7/1, year 3).

Carrying amount of note, 6/30, year 1	$150,000	
Less: Principal payment, 7/1, year 2	(50,000)	
Carrying amount of note, 7/1, year 2	100,000	
Times: Stated interest rate	× 8%	
Interest receivable, 6/30, year 3	$ 8,000	(4386)

23. (b) Total interest revenue earned over the life of the note is determined as the excess of the summation of the required annual year-end payments over the present value of the note.

Summation of required annual year-end payments ($5,009 × 5)	$ 25,045	
Less: Present value of note	(19,485)	
Interest revenue earned over life of note	$ 5,560	(5300)

24. (b) The recorded value of the Note Receivable is $300,000 (400,000 × .75). Interest income is $30,000 (300,000 × .10) (9070)

25. (c) The recording of notes receivable is at their present value. At December 31, Chang is owed 9 more annual payments of $10,000. The appropriate factor to apply is the present value of ordinary annuity of $1 at 8% for 9 periods, which is given as 6.25. $10,000 × 6.25 = $62,500. (5544)

26. (a) Notes receivable are reported net of any discount. If a non-interest-bearing (or low) note is exchanged for cash and a promise to provide future goods at lower-than-usual market prices, the issuer values the note at present value. The difference between present value and the cash payments is to be recognized as a part of the future goods' cost, i.e., a deferred charge. (6979)

27. (b) Notes receivable are claims usually not arising from sales in the ordinary course of business. Legally, the claim is evidenced by a note representing an unconditional promise to pay. Notes can be classified as interest-bearing, in which case the note pays an interest amount in addition to the face amount of the note, or non-interest bearing, in which case the interest is included in the face amount. The recording of notes receivable is at their present value. This is not intended to apply to receivables and payables arising from transactions with customers or suppliers in the normal course of business which are due in customary trade terms not exceeding approximately one year. Thus, the note from Alpha Co. would be reported at the $10,000 face value. The note from Omega would be discounted at $8,570 ($10,000 × .857). (8355)

28. (c) A creditor should consider a loan to be impaired when, "based on current information and events, it is probable that the creditor will be unable to collect all amounts due according to the contractual terms of the loan agreement." If foreclosure is not probable, the creditor measures the impaired loan at one of the following: (1) the loan's observable market price, (2) the fair value of collateral pledged, or (3) the present value of future principal and interest cash inflows, net of discounted disposal costs all discounted at the loan's effective interest rate. If foreclosure is probable, the second method is to be used to value a collateral dependent impaired loan. (6453)

29. (b) Only factoring the receivables would ensure altering the timing of cash flows for the $3 million in receivables already recorded on its books. Factoring the receivables outstanding is a transfer of the receivables to a factor (transferee) without recourse and is accounted for as any other sale of an asset: debit cash, credit the receivables, and record a gain or loss for the difference. Changing the due date of the invoice, discounting the receivables outstanding, and demanding payment from customers before the due date will not necessarily get the cash for receivables any quicker and alter the timing of cash flows. (8343)

Receivables as Sources of Cash

30. (c) The total amount of interest revenue to be earned by King over the life of the note is determined as the excess of the summation of the required annual year-end payments over the present value of the note discounted to yield 9% to King.

Summation of required annual year-end payments [5 × $5,010 (as determined below)]		$ 25,050
Face amount of note	$20,000	
Divide by: PV factor of an ordinary annuity of $1 for 5 periods at 8%	/ 3.992	
Required equal annual year-end payments under note	5,010	
Times: PV factor of an ordinary annuity of $1 for 5 periods at the yield rate of 9%	× 3.890	
Less: Present value of note		(19,490)
Interest revenue to be earned over note's life		$ 5,560

(2612)

31. (c) Receivables may be pledged as security for loans. Control of the receivables is retained and collections on the receivables are usually required to be applied to a reduction of the loan. Good Neighbor Financing could take title to the receivables if Milton doesn't pay the loan, does not assume the responsibility of collecting the receivables, and does not take title to the receivables until the loan is repaid. (9330)

32. (a) In order to achieve the disclosure objective, reporting entities need to provide disclosures on two levels of disaggregation: portfolio segment and class of financing receivable. A portfolio segment is defined as the level used by the entity in developing and documenting a systematic method for determining the allowance for credit losses. Class of financing receivables generally represents a disaggregation of a portfolio segment, based on initial measurement attributes, risk characteristics of the financing receivables, and methods used by reporting entities related to monitoring and assessing credit risk. (3434)

33. (d)

Face amount of note on 7/1, year 1	$100,000	
Less: Payment of first installment on 12/31, year 1	(50,000)	
Face amount of note on 12/31, year 1 (due 12/31, year 2)	50,000	
Add: Interest to maturity ($50,000 × 10% × 12/12)	5,000	
Maturity value of remaining portion of note	55,000	
Less: Bank discount ($55,000 × 12% × 6/12)	(3,300)	
Proceeds from discounted note	$ 51,700	(0890)

34. (c) A company that discounts a note receivable with recourse is contingently liable to the lender. It must pay the lender the amount due at maturity, if the maker of the note fails to pay the obligation. The contingent liability is usually shown in the accounts by recording the note discounted in a *Notes Receivable Discounted* account at the note's face amount. The *Notes Receivable Discounted* account is reported as a contra asset and deducted from *Notes Receivable* in the balance sheet.

Notes receivable	$ XXX		
Less: Notes receivable discounted	(XXX)	$XXX	(1823)

35. (a) Factoring is similar to a sale of receivables because it is generally without recourse and the factor generally handles the billing and collection function. Aloe would receive $68,000 from the factored receivables. The $80,000 factored amount less $8,000 (10% as an allowance for sales returns) and less $4,000 (for the 5% commission charged) equals $68,000. (9331)

Investments in Marketable Securities

36. (b) Available-for-Sale (AFS) securities are debt and equity securities not classified as either held-to-maturity or trading securities. Unrealized holding gains and losses are excluded from current earnings and are instead reported in other comprehensive income (OCI) until realized. In determining the realized gain or loss on the sale of available-for-sale securities, no regard is given to previously recognized unrealized losses or recoveries or to the amount accumulated in the Market Adjustment account. The realized loss reported from the sale of the marketable securities is determined as the difference between the proceeds received (i.e., the gross selling price of the shares less any brokerage commissions and taxes incurred in the sale) and the cost of the securities. Reclassification adjustments are made to avoid double counting in comprehensive income gains or losses realized and included in net income of the current period that were previously included in other comprehensive income as unrealized gains or losses. (9894)

37. (d) Trading securities can be debt and/or equity securities that are bought and held principally for the purpose of selling in the near term. Trading securities are reported at fair value ($105,000 + $50,000 = $155,000). (7751)

38. (b) Trading securities are debt and equity securities that are bought and held principally for the purpose of selling them in the near term. They are reported at fair value (market value) and any unrealized holding gains and losses are included in current earnings. At the end of year 1, the trading securities would have been valued at $92,000 and a gain of $6,000 ($92,000 year-end market value – $86,000 cost) would have been reported on the income statement. In year 2, there would be a gain of $12,500 ($104,500 selling price – $92,000 beginning value) from the initial set of securities and a $2,000 loss ($71,000 year-end market value – $73,000 cost) from the newly acquired trading securities. The net impact of these stock activities would be a $10,500 gain on the income statement in year 2. (8325)

39. (b) Marketable securities which an entity does not intend to sell in the near future are classified as available-for-sale (AFS) securities. Unrealized gains and losses for AFS securities are reported in other comprehensive income. If the entity did intend to sell the securities in the near future, then they would be classified as trading securities and any unrealized gains or losses would be reported as a component of income from continuing operations. (4829)

40. (d) At 12/31 of the previous year, the required balance of the *Market Adjustment—AFS* account was a $20,000 credit ($100,000 – $80,000). At 12/31 of the current year, the required balance of the *Market Adjustment—AFS* account is a $15,000 credit ($100,000 – $85,000). Thus, in the current year, the required balance of the *Market Adjustment—AFS* account decreased by $5,000. Changes in the *Market Adjustment* account related to the available-for-sale category are included in other comprehensive income. Thus, Lee does not recognize any gain or loss from a change in the *Market Adjustment—AFS* account on its income statement. (9049)

41. (d) The carrying amount of an available-for-sale marketable equity securities portfolio should be its market value. The amount by which aggregate cost of the portfolio exceeds market value should be accounted for as a valuation allowance. An amount equal to the valuation allowance is reported in accumulated other comprehensive income within owners' equity. Since the portfolio in question has a valuation allowance, its market value is less than cost. Thus, the historical cost of the portfolio is the sum of the amount of the valuation allowance of the portfolio and the market value of the portfolio. [($19,800 + $96,450 = $116,250)] (4566)

42. (d) The securities are measured at their fair value, with a *Market Adjustment* account established for the difference from cost. A $20,000 loss difference is offset by a $10,000 gain difference; the net is a $10,000 credit balance needed in the *Market Adjustment* account. (4578)

43. (b) At year-end, held-to-maturity securities are reported at amortized cost. Trading securities and available-for-sale (AFS) securities are accounted for at fair value. Unrealized holding gains and losses are included in current earnings for trading securities, and in other comprehensive income for AFS securities. (6452)

44. (b) If a decline in fair value for available-for-sale (AFS) or held-to-maturity is determined to be other than temporary, the cost basis of the individual security is written down to fair value which becomes the new cost basis and a realized loss is recognized in the earnings section of the income statement. Permanent declines in the fair market value of investments are not unusual in nature or infrequent in occurrence and so are not reported as extraordinary items. The investment would have been included in the other comprehensive income section of the income statement and written down to fair market value only if it was a temporary decline in fair value. (8370)

45. (a) The transfer of a security from the trading category of investments shall be accounted for at fair value. The unrealized holding loss resulting from the decrease in market value while classified as trading securities shall be included in earnings. As of the date of transfer, June 30 of the current year, the securities had experienced a decline in fair value of $45,000 ($575,000 – $530,000) from the end of the prior year. Upon transfer to a different category of investment, this unrealized loss is required to be included in earnings. (The decline from $650,000 to $575,000 would have been included as an unrealized loss on the previous year income statement.) (4045)

46. (a) Unrealized holding losses for available-for-sale (AFS) securities shall be excluded from earnings and reported in other comprehensive income until realized. The decrease in fair value over the time period in which the securities were classified as trading securities would have been reported in earnings. However, the decrease occurring after the transfer to the AFS category, $40,000 ($530,000 – $490,000), would be reflected in OCI. (4046)

Derivatives & Hedges

47. (b) The gain or loss of a fair value hedge (instrument A) is recognized in earnings in the period of change, together with the offsetting loss or gain in the hedged item. The effective portion of the gain or loss of a cash flow hedge (instrument B) is initially reported as a component of other comprehensive income (OCI) on the balance sheet, and subsequently reclassified into earnings when the forecasted transaction affects earnings. (9883)

48. (c) A derivative instrument either requires no initial net investment, or one that is smaller than would be required for other types of contracts expected to have a similar response to market factor changes. The other statements are true. (89532)

49. (b) One of the primary criteria for determining a fair value hedge is that the hedged item is specifically identified as either all or a specific portion of a recognized asset or liability, or of a firm commitment. The hedged item must be a single asset or liability, or a portfolio of similar assets or a portfolio of similar liabilities. The hedged item presents an exposure to changes in fair value for the hedged risk that could affect reported earnings. (89535)

50. (b) A derivative instrument is an instrument or other contract that has the following three characteristics: (1) at least one underlying and at least one notational amount or payment provision or both, (2) requires no initial net investment, or one that is smaller than would be required for other types of contracts expected to have a similar response to market factor changes, and (3) requires or permits net settlement, can be readily settled net by a means outside the contract, or provides for delivery of an asset that puts the recipient in a position not substantially different from net settlement. (9339)

51. (a) Hedging is a risk management strategy to protect against the possibility of loss, such as from price fluctuations. Generally, the strategy involves counterbalancing transactions in which a loss on one financial instrument or cash flow stream would be offset by a gain on the related derivative. A perfect hedge would result in no possibility of future gain or loss. (8597)

52. (a) Credit risk is the possibility that a loss may occur from the failure of another party to perform according to the terms of a contract. An entity must disclose all concentrations of credit risk arising from all financial instruments. Group concentrations of credit risk exist if a number of counterparties are engaged in similar activities and have similar economic characteristics that would affect their ability to meet contractual obligations affected by changes in economic or other conditions. Market risk is the possibility that future changes in market prices may make a financial instrument less valuable or more onerous. An entity is encouraged, but not required, to disclose quantitative information about the market risks of financial instruments. There is no note disclosure for risk of measurement uncertainty here. Accounts receivable uses an allowance for doubtful accounts to account for uncertainty of collection. There is no off-balance sheet risk of accounting loss here. Off-balance sheet risk is the risk of accounting loss from a financial instrument that exceeds the amount recognized for the instrument in the balance sheet. (9316)

53. (c) An option contract is a derivative. Derivatives are recognized as assets or liabilities on the financial statements and measures using fair value. Changes in fair value of non-hedge securities are reported as gains or losses in earnings. On December 1, Bann would initially record the option contract at $80,600 (2,000 shares × $40 market price on December 1 + $600 time value). At the end of December, the fair value of the option contract was $86,400 (2,000 shares × $43 market price on December 31 + $400 time value). Bann would report this change in fair value which would result in net income increasing by $5,800. (8786)

54. (c) An interest rate swap agreement is an arrangement used to limit interest rate risk. Two companies swap interest payments, but not the principal, in an agreement, such as an exchange of a variable interest rate for a fixed rate. The risk of accounting loss from an interest rate swap includes both (1) the risk of exchanging a lower interest rate for a higher rate and (2) the risk of nonperformance by the other party. (6454)

Foreign Currency Hedges

55. (a) A gain or loss on a speculative futures contract should be computed by multiplying the foreign currency amount of the futures contract by the difference between the future rate available for the remaining maturity of the contract and the contract future rate (or the forward rate last used to measure a gain or loss on that contract for an earlier period). No separate accounting recognition is given to the discount or premium. The spot rate is the exchange rate used for immediate delivery of currencies exchanged.

Foreign currency units to be purchased	50,000
Times: Excess of futures rate available for the remaining maturity of the contract and the contracted futures rate ($0.70 – $0.65)	× $0.05
Loss on futures contract	$ 2,500

(7059)

56. (c) An entity may designate a derivative instrument or a nonderivative financial instrument that may give rise to a foreign currency transaction gain or loss as a hedge of the foreign currency exposure of a net investment in a foreign operation. (89584)

57. (d) A forward exchange contract is an agreement to exchange different currencies at a specified future date and at a specified rate (the forward rate). A forward contract is a foreign currency transaction. The accounting for a gain or loss on a foreign currency transaction that is intended to hedge an identifiable foreign currency commitment (for example, an agreement to purchase or sell equipment) is considered a foreign currency hedge and works like a fair value hedge. Gains and losses on this qualifying fair value hedge shall be recognized currently in earnings.

The gain or loss realized on this forward exchange contract is computed by multiplying the foreign currency amount of the contract by the difference between the *spot* rate at the balance sheet date and the *spot* rate at the inception of the contract (or the spot rate last used to measure a gain or loss on that contract for an earlier period). The spot rate is the exchange rate for immediate delivery of currencies exchanged.

Foreign currency units to be purchased	100,000
Times: Excess of spot rate at the balance sheet date over the spot rate at the inception of the contract ($1.96 – $1.86)	× $0.10
Foreign currency transaction gain, year 1	$10,000

(3282)

58. (a) Translation adjustments are not included in determining net income, but in OCI. Gains and losses on foreign currency transactions that are designated as, and are effective as, economic hedges of a net investment in a foreign entity are not included in determining net income, but are reported in the same manner as translation adjustments. Therefore, the net translation loss is reported in OCI in Nash's consolidated financial statements. (2731)

PERFORMANCE BY SUBTOPICS

Each category below parallels a subtopic covered in Chapter 2. Record the number and percentage of questions you correctly answered in each subtopic area.

Current Assets

Question #	Correct √
1	
2	
3	
4	
5	
6	
7	
# Questions	7
# Correct	
% Correct	

Accounts Receivable

Question #	Correct √
8	
9	
10	
11	
12	
13	
14	
15	
16	
17	
18	
19	
# Questions	12
# Correct	
% Correct	

Notes Receivable

Question #	Correct √
20	
21	
22	
23	
24	
25	
26	
27	
28	
29	
# Questions	10
# Correct	
% Correct	

Receivables as Source of Cash

Question #	Correct √
30	
31	
32	
33	
34	
35	
# Questions	6
# Correct	
% Correct	

Investments in Marketable Securities

Question #	Correct √
36	
37	
38	
39	
40	
41	
42	
43	
44	
45	
46	
# Questions	11
# Correct	
% Correct	

Derivatives & Hedges

Question #	Correct √
47	
48	
49	
50	
51	
52	
53	
54	
# Questions	8
# Correct	
% Correct	

Foreign Currency Hedges

Question #	Correct √
55	
56	
57	
58	
# Questions	4
# Correct	
% Correct	

Solution 2-2 SIMULATION ANSWER: Uncollectible Accounts

1.

	A/R Amount	Percentage	Allowance	
0 to 30 days	$300,000	× 1%	$ 3,000	[1]
31 to 90 days	80,000	× 5%	4,000	[2]
91 to 180 days	60,000	× 20%	12,000	[3]
Over 180 days	25,000	× 80%	20,000	[4]
Accounts receivable	$465,000			[5]
Allowance for uncollectible accounts			$39,000	[6]

Explanations

[1] Accounts receivable 0 - 30 days past invoice date × percent deemed to be uncollectible (1%) = Amount to include in allowance for uncollectible accounts.

[2] Accounts receivable 31 - 90 days past invoice date × percent deemed to be uncollectible (5%) = Amount to include in allowance for uncollectible accounts.

[3] Accounts receivable 91 - 180 days past invoice date × percent deemed to be uncollectible (20%) = Amount to include in allowance for uncollectible accounts.

[4] Accounts receivable over 180 days past invoice date × percent deemed to be uncollectible (80%) = Amount to include in allowance for uncollectible accounts.

[5] Total Accounts receivable.

[6] Total allowance for uncollectible accounts.

2.

Balance December 31, previous year	$ 28,000	[1]
Write-offs during the current year	(27,000)	[2]
Recoveries during the current year	7,000	[3]
Balance before the current year provisions	8,000	[4]
Required allowance at December 31 of current year	39,000	[5]
Current year provisions	$ 31,000	[6]

Explanations

[1] Balance of allowance for uncollectible accounts 12/31 of previous year ($2,800,000 × .01)

[2] Accounts written off during the current year given in scenario information.

[3] Recoveries during the current year given in scenario information.

[4] Balance of allowance for uncollectible accounts before provision.

[5] Required allowance at 12/31 of the current year from part A

[6] Current year provision: Required provision less balance before provision ($39,000 – $8,000) (9018)

Solution 2-3 SIMULATION ANSWER: Receivables

1.

Long-Term Receivables Section of Balance Sheet

9% note receivable from sale of idle building, due in annual installments of $300,000 to May 1, year 6, less current installment	$ 300,000	[1]
8% note receivable from officer, due December 31, year 6, collateralized by 10,000 shares of Fern Inc. common stock with a fair value of $225,000	400,000	[2]
Noninterest-bearing note from sale of patent, net of 10% imputed interest, due April 1, year 6	177,590	[3]
Installment contract receivable, due in annual installments of $88,332 to July 1, year 7, less current installment	334,173	[4]
Total long-term receivables	$1,211,763	[5]

2.

Selected Balance Sheet Accounts

Current portion of long-term receivables:		
Note receivable from sale of idle building	$300,000	[6]
Installment contract receivable	85,827	[7]
Total	$385,827	[8]
Accrued interest receivable:		
Note receivable from sale of idle building	$ 36,000	[9]
Installment contract receivable	21,000	[10]
Total	$ 57,000	[11]

Explanations

[1,6]	Long-term portion of 9% note receivable at 12/31, year 4	
	Face amount, 5/1, year 3	$ 900,000
	Less: Installment received 5/1, year 4	(300,000)
	Balance, 12/31, year 4	600,000
	Less: Installment due 5/1, year 5	(300,000)
	Long-term portion, 12/31, year 4	$ 300,000
[2]	Note receivable is reported at book value	
[3]	Noninterest-bearing note, net of imputed interest at 12/31, year 4	
	Face amount, 4/1, year 4	$ 200,000
	Less: Imputed interest [$200,000 – $165,200 ($200,000 × 0.826)]	(34,800)
	Balance, 4/1, year 4	165,200
	Add: Interest earned to 12/31, year 4 [$165,200 × 10% × 9/12]	12,390
	Balance, 12/31, year 4	$ 177,590
[4, 7]	Long-term portion of installment contract receivable at 12/31, year 4	
	Contract selling price, 7/1, year 4	$ 600,000
	Less: Cash down payment	(180,000)
	Balance, 12/31, year 4	420,000
	Less: Installment due 7/1, year 5 [$127,827 – $42,000 ($420,000 × 10%)]	(85,827)
	Long-term portion, 12/31, year 4	$ 334,173

[5]	Sum of amounts entered in #1 through #4	
[8]	Sum of amounts entered in #6 through #7	
[9]	Accrued interest—note receivable, sale of idle building at 12/31, year 4 Interest accrued from 5/1 to 12/31, year 4 [$600,000 × 9% × 8/12]	$ 36,000
[10]	Accrued interest—installment contract at 12/31, year 4 Interest accrued from 7/1 to 12/31, year 4 [$420,000 × 10% × 1/2]	$ 21,000
[11]	Sum of amounts entered in #9 through #10	

(9019)

Solution 2-4 SIMULATION ANSWER: Marketable Securities

1. Held-to-maturity (HTM) securities are debt securities that the enterprise has the positive intent and the ability to hold to maturity.

2. Available-for-sale (AFS) securities are debt and equity securities not classified as either HTM or trading securities.

3. Trading securities are debt and equity securities that are bought and held principally for the purpose of selling them in the near term.

4. Available-for-sale (AFS) securities are debt and equity securities not classified as either HTM or trading securities.

5. $125,000. HTM securities are reported at amortized cost and are not adjusted for unrealized holding gains and losses, although fair value must be disclosed.

6. $135,000. Trading securities are reported at fair market value.

7. $150,000. AFS securities are reported at fair market value.

8. $15,000 loss. The recognized gain or loss from the sale of a debt or equity security is the difference between the net proceeds received from the sale and the cost or amortized cost of the security. $155,000 – $170,000 = $15,000 loss.

9. $5,000 loss. The $5,000 unrealized loss pertains to the trading securities, as these are the only securities for which unrealized holding gains and losses are included in current earnings. $135,000 fair value at 12/31, year 2 – $140,000 fair value at 12/31, year 1 = $5,000 unrealized loss.

10. $10,000 loss. The $10,000 loss pertains to security LKJ as AFS securities are the only securities for which net unrealized holding gains or losses are reported in accumulated other comprehensive income. $150,000 fair value at 12/31, year 2 – $160,000 cost = $10,000 net unrealized loss. (6143)

Solution 2-5 SIMULATION ANSWER: Research

FASB Accounting Standards Codification

FASB ASC: 815 - 10 - 30 - 1

30-1. All derivative instruments shall be measured initially at fair value. (9163)

Select Hot•Spot™ Video Description

CPA 3255 Cash, Receivables & Marketable Securities
In this video program, Robert Monette provides comprehensive coverage of cash and cash equivalents, accounts and notes receivable, investments in marketable debt and equity securities, fair value disclosure of financial instruments, derivative financial instruments and hedging activities...and more! Bob discusses 28 multiple-choice questions while explaining these concepts. Approximate video duration is 2 hours and 15 minutes. This does not include the time a candidate spends answering questions and taking notes.

Call our customer representatives toll-free at 1 (800) 874-7877 for more details about videos.

Subject to Change Without Notice

CHAPTER 3

INVENTORY

CHAPTER 3

INVENTORY

I. Overview

A. Definition

Inventory is defined as items of tangible personal property that are held for sale in the ordinary course of business, in the process of production for such sale, or which are to be currently consumed in the production of goods or services to be available for sale. The measuring of inventories involves two distinct problems: (1) determining **physical quantities** and (2) determining an appropriate **dollar valuation.**

The basic objective of inventory accounting is to identify, on a consistent basis, costs applicable to goods on hand at the end of the period and costs that should be included in the cost of goods sold for the period.

B. Ownership Criteria

Although ownership generally determines when items should be included in inventory, items purchased for which title (and, in some cases, even possession) remains with the vendor until paid for should be included in the buyer's inventories when the significant risks of ownership rest with the buyer. When the significant risks of ownership have not been transferred to the buyer and, therefore, revenue is not recognized by the seller, the goods should be included in the seller's inventories and excluded from the buyer's inventories.

1. **Goods in Transit From Vendor** If shipped "F.O.B. destination," the goods are **not** inventoriable until *received.* However, if shipped "F.O.B. shipping point," the goods should be inventoried when *shipped* by the vendor.

2. **Goods in Transit to Customer** The cost of inventory items sold "F.O.B. destination" should remain in inventory until the goods are *received* by the purchaser, while the cost of inventory items sold "F.O.B. shipping point" should be removed from inventory when the goods are *shipped.*

3. **Goods on Consignment** Goods *out* on consignment should be included in inventory at cost because title to the goods has not changed. Conversely, goods *held* on consignment should **not** be included in inventory. Costs incurred by a consignor on a transfer of goods to a consignee (e.g., shipping costs, warehousing costs, and in-transit insurance premiums) should be considered as inventory cost to the consignor.

4. **Transportation Charges** F.O.B. means "free on board" and requires the seller, at her/his expense, to deliver the goods to the destination indicated as F.O.B. Therefore, if goods are shipped F.O.B. *shipping point,* transportation charges are buyer's responsibility; if F.O.B. *destination,* they are seller's responsibility.

II. Measuring Inventories

A. Physical Quantities

Determination of physical inventory quantities is accomplished by the use of one or both of the following systems:

1. **Periodic Inventory System** This system is characterized by no entries being made to the inventory account during the period. Acquisitions of inventory goods are debited to "Purchases" while issuances are not recorded, so that at any point in time the balance in the inventory account reflects the amount at the *beginning* of the period. The inventory on hand is *periodically* determined by physical count. Cost of goods sold (CGS) is a residual amount obtained by subtracting the ending inventory from the sum of beginning inventory and net purchases.

2. **Perpetual Inventory System** A continuous record is maintained of items entering into and issued from inventory. The balance in the inventory account at any time reveals the inventory that should be on hand.

B. Acquisition & Production Cost

1. **Cost Method** The primary basis of accounting for inventories is cost. The cost of an inventory item is the cash price or fair value of other consideration given in exchange for it.

   a. With respect to merchandise inventory, this cost figure is net of trade and/or cash discounts, if any, but should include freight-in, taxes, insurance while in transit, warehousing costs, and similar charges paid by the purchaser to bring the article to its existing condition and location.

   b. The finished goods inventory of a manufacturer must include the cost of direct materials, direct labor and *both* variable and fixed manufacturing overhead, also called conversion expenditures. For goods manufactured, assembled, processed, or otherwise changed in form, content, or utility, wages of employees directly engaged in the production process and an allocated portion of indirect production expenses (overhead) should be included in inventory costs. Overhead should be allocated to inventory items on a rational and systematic basis, and should include both variable and fixed expenses.

      Interest cost should **not** be capitalized for inventories that are routinely manufactured or otherwise produced in large quantities on a repetitive basis.

   c. Freight-out is a selling expense and, thus, should **not** be included in the cost of inventory.

   d. Abnormal amounts of idle facility expense, freight, handling costs, and wasted materials (scrap and/or spoilage) should be recognized as current-period charges, not inventory cost. Inventory costs of primary products should be reduced by the net realizable value of scrap generated in the manufacturing process.

   e. Allocation of fixed production overheads to the costs of conversion should be based on the normal capacity of production facilities.

   f. A rebate or refund to be received under a binding arrangement should be recognized as a reduction of purchase costs. If earning the rebate or refund is probable and the amount is reasonably estimable, the rebate or refund to be received should be allocated on a systematic and rational basis to each of the underlying transactions that results in progress by the customer or reseller toward earning the rebate or refund. If earning the rebate or refund is not probable or the amount is not reasonably estimable, the rebate or refund to be received should only be recognized upon achievement of the milestones.

g. A *trade discount* is a deduction from the list or catalog price of merchandise to arrive at the gross selling price. Trade discounts are not recorded in the seller's or purchaser's accounting records. A *chain discount* occurs when a list price is subject to several trade discounts. In this situation, the amount of each trade discount is determined by multiplying (1) the list price of the merchandise **less** the amount of prior trade discounts by (2) the trade discount percentage.

Example 1 ▸ Chain Discount

Cairns Corp. purchased merchandise with a list price of $20,000, subject to trade discounts of 10% and 5%. Cairns should record the cost of this merchandise as $17,100, computed as follows:

List price	$20,000
Less: Trade discount—10%	(2,000)
Balance	18,000
Less: Trade discount—5%	(900)
Cost of the merchandise	$17,100

2. **Relative Sales Value Method** When a group of varying units are purchased at a single lump-sum price (sometimes called a "basket purchase"), the total cost of the units should be allocated to the various units on the basis of their relative sales value.

Example 2 ▸ Relative Sales Value Method

On May 1, Brevard Development Company purchased a tract of land for $600,000. Additional costs of $100,000 were incurred in subdividing the land during May through December. Of the tract acreage, 80% was subdivided into residential lots as shown below and 20% was conveyed to the city for roads and a park.

Lot class	Number of lots	Sales price per lot
A	100	$2,000
B	200	4,000
C	200	5,000

Under the relative sales value method, the cost allocated to each lot is determined as follows:

(A)	(B)	(C)	(D) (B × C)	(E)	(F)	(G) (E × F)	(H) (G / B)
Lot class	Number of lots	Sales price per lot	Total sales price	Relative sales price	Total cost	Cost allocated to lots	Cost per lot
A	100	$2,000	$ 200,000	10.0%	$700,000	$ 70,000	$ 700
B	200	4,000	800,000	40.0%	700,000	280,000	1,400
C	200	5,000	1,000,000	50.0%	700,000	350,000	1,750
			$2,000,000			$700,000	

3. **Cost Rule Exceptions**

a. When the utility of an inventory item is impaired, the pricing of the item is at cost or market, whichever is lower.

b. Replacement cost is justified for used, damaged, or repossessed inventory items. The valuation of these goods is based upon the hypothetical replacement cost of similar items in similar conditions of use.

c. Valuation at sales price is justifiable only by inability to determine appropriate approximate costs, immediate marketability at quoted market price, and the characteristic of units' interchangeability. Examples commonly given include precious metals and agricultural products with assured sales prices. When inventories are stated above cost, this fact is disclosed in the financial statements.

d. When there is a firm commitment to purchase goods in a future period at a set price (i.e., an enforceable contract exists), any loss resulting from a drop in the market value of such goods, or cancellation of the contract by the purchaser, should be recognized in the current period. There should be a note in the financial statements describing the nature of the contract. The journal entry would be a debit to Loss on Purchase Commitment and a credit to Allowance for Loss on Purchase Commitment.

Exhibit 1 ▶ Journal Entries for a Loss on Purchase Commitment

	Debit	Credit
Loss on Purchase Commitment	(Contract price – FV)	
Allowance for Loss on PC		(Contract price – FV)
To record estimated loss at the end of the period.		
Inventory (or purchases)	(Current FV)	
Allowance for Loss on PC	(Allowance account balance)	
Cash		(Contract price)
To record purchase in subsequent period.		

Had there been a further change in FV, it would be recorded by crediting or debiting an unrealized income (or loss) account, as appropriate.

C. Cost Flow Assumptions

The per-unit cost of inventory items purchased at different times will often vary. In order to allocate the total cost of goods available for sale (i.e., beginning inventory plus net purchases) between cost of goods sold and ending inventory, either the cost of specific items must be tracked or a *cost flow* method must be adopted. Generally, one method should be used for like groupings of inventories. However, a mixture of methods may be used for different groups or classifications of inventories of a particular enterprise, particularly when there are valid business reasons for doing so. When an entity changes to LIFO or to another method from LIFO, the entity should do so for all inventories unless a valid business reason exists for not doing so (e.g., an entity adopts LIFO only for U.S. inventories because other countries where the entity has inventories do not permit the LIFO cost method).

1. **Specific Identification** This costing method requires the ability to identify each unit sold or in inventory. The cost of goods sold is the cost of the specific items sold, and the ending inventory is the cost of the specific items still on hand. It is used when inventory goods are few in number, have individually high costs, and can be clearly identified.

2. **First-In, First-Out (FIFO)** This method assumes that the goods first acquired are the first sold. Hence, the earliest costs are charged to CGS and the ending inventories are stated in terms of the most recent costs. Use of FIFO necessitates maintaining records of separate lot prices (layers).

   a. FIFO is balance sheet-oriented, since it tends to report ending inventories at their approximate replacement cost. Income, however, may be misstated because old costs are matched to current revenues.

b. The easiest way to determine the cost of ending inventory under FIFO involves 4 simple steps: (a) determine the number of units in ending inventory; (b) segregate ending inventory into price layers, beginning with the most recent purchase prices; (c) determine the cost of each layer (i.e., unit cost multiplied by number of units); and (d) add up the cost of all the layers.

Example 3 ▸ FIFO

During the year, ABC Inc. determined ending inventory and cost of goods sold under the FIFO cost flow assumption as follows:

	Units	Unit cost	Total
Beginning inventory	100	$5	$ 500
Purchase, 1/12	200	6	1,200
Purchase, 8/25	150	7	1,050
Goods available for sale	450		2,750
Ending inventory	200*		1,350**
Cost of goods sold	250		$1,400

* Determined by physical count of inventory

** Determined by applying the most recent prices to the ending inventory quantity, as below:

8/25 layer	150	@ $7	$1,050
1/12 layer	50	@ 6	300
EI,	200		$1,350

3. **Last-In, First-Out (LIFO)** This method charges CGS with the latest acquisition costs, while ending inventories are reported at the older costs of the earliest units. The objective of LIFO is to charge against current revenues the cost of the goods acquired to replace those sold, rather than the original cost of the goods actually sold. Therefore, LIFO provides a better measure of earnings. However, balance sheet presentation may suffer because the inventory is presented at the oldest unit costs that may substantially differ from current replacement cost.

a. During periods of rising prices, the LIFO inventory cost-flow method reports a *higher* cost of sales and a lower amount for ending inventory than FIFO. During periods of falling prices, the reverse is true; the LIFO inventory cost flow method would report a lower cost of sales and a higher amount for ending inventory.

b. Under the FIFO cost-flow method, a perpetual system would result in the same dollar amount of ending inventory as a periodic inventory system. Under the LIFO cost-flow method, however, a perpetual system would generally **not** result in the same dollar amount of ending inventory as a periodic inventory system.

c. Quantity LIFO is generally limited to use in small businesses or where there is a small number of different inventory items. Application of quantity LIFO requires that records of separate lot prices be kept for each inventory item. At the end of the period, inventory items are valued at the oldest costs. Note that the same 4 steps used to value ending inventory under FIFO can be used for LIFO, except that step (b) now involves the oldest inventory layers.

d. Dollar value LIFO is widely used in practice. This procedure is designed to reduce clerical costs usually associated with LIFO and to minimize the probability of liquidating the LIFO inventory layers. The application of dollar-value LIFO is based on the use of the dollar value of inventory pools of similar items, rather than physical units, as a basis for allocating inventory costs. A base year dollar cost is determined in the year of adoption by dividing total inventory cost by number of units. The ending inventory in each subsequent period is costed at both the base year dollar amount and current year dollar costs. The ratio obtained by dividing these two amounts (Ending Inventory [EI] valued at current year costs over EI at base year cost), is the price index for the current period. A layer of inventory is added every time the ending inventory stated at base year dollars exceeds the beginning inventory (also stated at base year dollars). This new layer is costed by multiplying it by the specific price index for the current period. If an inventory liquidation has occurred, the reductions are taken from the most recent layers acquired. Several acceptable computational techniques are used with the dollar-value approach, including double extension, internal index, link chain, and external index.

A LIFO inventory liquidation occurs when the year-end inventory in a LIFO pool (as measured in specific goods or base-year costs) is less than the inventory at the beginning of the year, causing prior-year LIFO costs, instead of current-year costs, to be charged to cost of goods sold. The effects on income of a LIFO inventory liquidation resulting from sales of inventory to unrelated third parties should not be deferred at year-end under any circumstances.

Example 4 ▸ Quantity LIFO

Consider this data at the end of year 3:

	Quantity		Amount	
Beginning inventory (@ unit price):				
Year 1, base layer (@ $2.00)	120		$240	
Year 2 layer (@ $2.10)	40	160	84	$ 324
Year 3 Purchases:				
Jan. (@ $2.15)	100		215	
Apr. (@ $2.20)	200		440	
Aug. (@ $2.30)	250		575	
Nov. (@ $2.30)	300	850	690	1,920
Goods available for sale		1,010		2,244
Ending inventory, year 3		(290)		(605)*
Cost of goods sold		720		$1,639

* Computed as follows:

Base layer	120	@	$2.00	=	$240
Year 2 layer	40	@	2.10	=	84
Jan. purchase	100	@	2.15	=	215
Apr. purchase	30	@	2.20	=	66
EI Year 3	290				$605

Example 5 ▸ Dollar-Value LIFO

On the basis of the quantity and price information in Table 1, columns 1 and 2, a price index is computed (columns 3, 4, and 5). This price index is used to value each inventory layer in Table 2. The price indices in Table 1 are figured by comparing current year prices to the base year prices.

Table 1—Price Indices

Ending Inventory		1	2	3	4	5
				Base Year Amount (1A × $2.50) (1B × $4.00)	Current Year Amount (1 × 2)	Price Index (4 / 3)
Year	Item	Quantity	@*			
Year 1 (base)	A	10,000	$2.50	$25,000	$25,000	--
	B	6,000	4.00	24,000	24,000	--
Year 1 Total				$49,000	$49,000	1.00
Year 2	A	11,600	2.60	$29,000	$30,160	--
	B	6,100	4.25	24,400	25,925	--
Year 2 Total				$53,400	$56,085	1.05
Year 3	A	12,200	2.95	$30,500	$35,990	--
	B	6,200	4.45	24,800	27,590	--
Year 3 Total				$55,300	$63,580	1.15
Year 4	A	10,600	**	$26,500	**	--
	B	5,800	**	23,200	**	--
Year 4 Total				$49,700		**

* These unit prices may represent the weighted average of all purchase prices paid during the year or the latest price paid.

** No price indices are computed nor new layers added due to inventory liquidation.

Table 2—Valuation of the Ending Inventory, year 2 to year 4:

	12/31/yr 2	Layers	Index	Valuation
Total	$ 53,400			
Year 1 layer	(49,000)	$49,000	1.00	$49,000
Year 2 layer	$ 4,400	4,400	1.05	4,620
Total 12/31 year 2		$53,400		$53,620

	12/31/yr 3	Layers	Index	Valuation
Total	$ 55,300			
Year 1 layer	(49,000)	$49,000	1.00	$49,000
Year 2 layer	(4,400)	4,400	1.05	4,620
Year 3 layer	$ 1,900	1,900	1.15	2,185
Total 12/31 year 3		$55,300		$55,805

	12/31/yr 3	Reduction	12/31/yr 4	Index	Valuation
Year 1 layer	$49,000		$49,000	1.00	$49,000
Year 2 layer	4,400	$ 3,700	700	1.05	735
Year 3 layer	1,900	1,900	0	1.15	0
Total 12/31 year 4	$55,300	$ 5,600	$49,700		$49,735

Chain-link (or link-chain) method The chain-link method may also be used. In the chain-link method, a price change index is figured from year-beginning to year-end each year. To arrive at the price index for a current layer of inventory, the indices for all the intervening years from the current to the base year are multiplied together.

4. **Average Inventory Methods** These assume that cost of goods sold and ending inventory should be based on the average cost of the inventories available for sale during the period. A *weighted average* is generally used with a *periodic* inventory system while a *moving average* requires the use of a *perpetual* system. The weighted-average method costs inventory items on the basis of average prices paid, weighted according to the quantity purchased at each price. The moving average requires computation of a new average after each purchase. Issues are priced at the latest average unit cost.

Example 6 ▸ Average Inventory Methods

During the year, ABC Inc. purchased and sold several lots of inventory item X, as follows:

Purchases:	Units	Unit Cost	Extended Cost
2/15	10,000	$3.00	$30,000
6/1	5,000	3.30	16,500
8/10	6,000	3.38	20,280
Goods available	21,000		$66,780
Sales:			
7/1	7,000		
9/10	9,000		
Goods sold	16,000		
Ending inventory	5,000		

The cost of the ending inventory of item X using the *weighted-average* method is $15,900 determined as follows:

Ending inventory in units	5,000
Weighted average cost per unit ($66,780 / 21000)	× $3.18
Ending inventory	$15,900

The cost of the ending inventory of item X using the *moving-average* method is $16,100, determined as follows:

	1	2	3	4
Date	Units	@	Extended	Moving Avg. (3 / 1)
2/15	10,000	$3.00	$ 30,000	$3.00
6/1	5,000	3.30	16,500	--
	15,000		46,500	3.10
7/1	(7,000)	3.10	(21,700)	--
	8,000		24,800	3.10
8/10	6,000	3.38	20,280	--
	14,000		45,080	3.22
9/10	(9,000)	3.22	(28,980)	--
End inventory	5,000		$ 16,100	3.22

D. **Lower of Cost or Market (LCM)**

The cost basis (specific identification or cost flow assumption) ordinarily achieves the objective of properly matching inventory costs and revenue. This is only satisfactory, however, as long as the utility of the inventory equals or exceeds its cost. When the utility of inventory is impaired or otherwise reduced by damage, deterioration or any other cause, the decline in value should be charged against revenue in the period in which the decline occurred. The measurement of this decline is accomplished by pricing the inventory at cost or market, whichever is lower.

1. **Market** As used in the phrase *lower of cost or market,* market means current replacement cost (by purchase or reproduction) except for the following:

   a. Market should not exceed the net realizable value (estimated selling price in the ordinary course of business less reasonably predictable costs of completion and disposal). This would be the *maximum,* or *ceiling,* amount at which market could be valued.

   b. Market should not be less than the net realizable value minus normal profit. This would be the *minimum,* or *floor,* amount at which market could be valued.

Exhibit 2 ▸ Lower of Cost or Market Rule

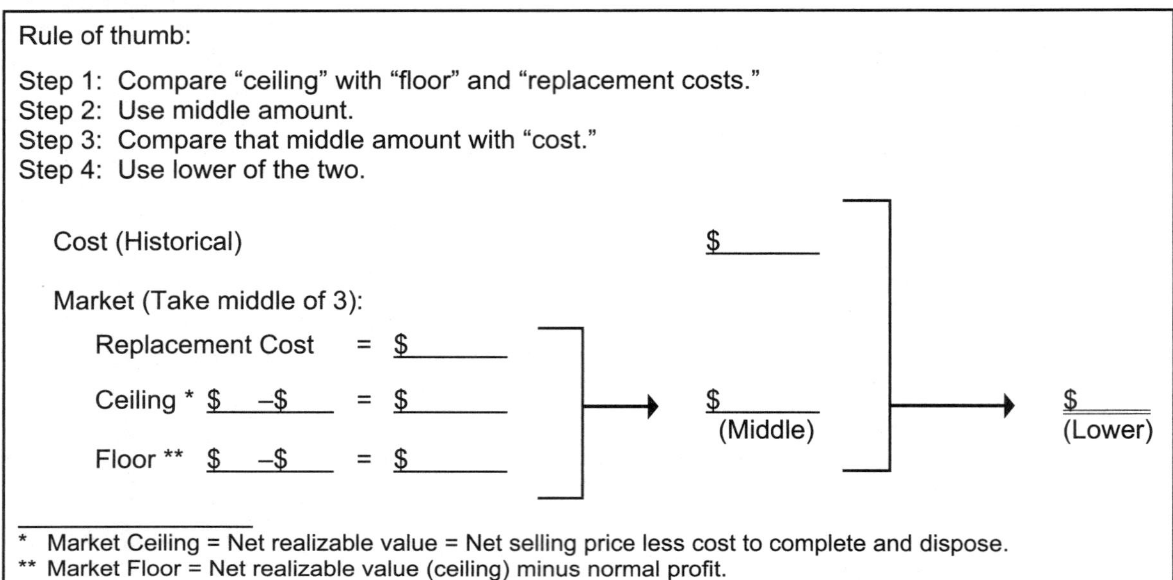

Example 7 ▸ Cost or Market, Whichever Is Lower Computation

Information related to Ellis Company's inventory at December 31 is given in columns 1 through 6. Lower of cost or market inventory calculations are illustrated in columns 7 through 10. The format shown in Exhibit 2 is also shown for inventory Item 1.

(1)	(2)	(3)	(4)	(5)	(6)	(7)	(8)	(9)	(10)
Item	Cost	Replacement Cost (Market)	Selling Price	Cost of Completion	Normal Profit	Ceiling Maximum (4) - (5)	Floor Minimum (7) - (6)	Market: Limited by Floor and Ceiling	Lower of Cost or Market
1	$20.50	$ 19.00	$ 25.00	$ 1.00	$ 6.00	$ 24.00	$ 18.00	$ 19.00	$19.00
2	25.00	17.00	30.00	2.00	10.00	28.00	18.00	18.00	18.00
3	10.00	12.00	15.00	1.00	3.00	14.00	11.00	12.00	10.00
4	40.00	55.00	60.00	6.00	4.00	54.00	50.00	54.00	40.00
	$95.50	$ 103.00	$130.00	$ 10.00	$23.00	$ 120.00	$ 97.00	$ 103.00	$87.00

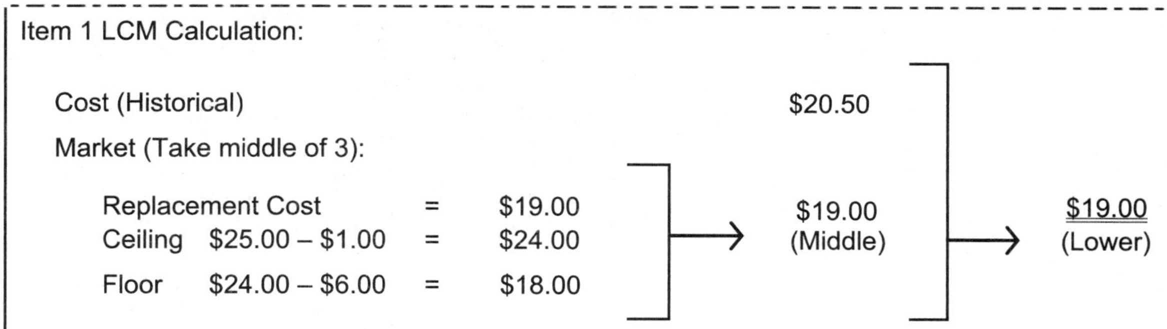

If the lower of cost or market is applied on an item-by-item basis, Item 1 would be written down $1.50 and Item 2 would be written down $7.00. However, Items 3 and 4 would not be written down as their costs are already lower than market.

2. **Applied Per Item or Groups** The rule of "cost or market, whichever is lower" may properly be applied either directly to each item or to one or more groups of the inventory. If LCM is applied item by item to each component in inventory, the lowest possible inventory balance is computed. If the inventory items are grouped into one or more groups and the LCM applied to each, decreases below cost of some items can be partially offset by increases above cost of others, resulting in a higher inventory balance.

Example 8 ▸ LCM Applied to Entire Inventory

Based on the information in Example 7, if lower of cost or market is applied to the entire inventory of Ellis Company, there is no write-down because the total cost of $95.50 is lower than the market of $103.00.

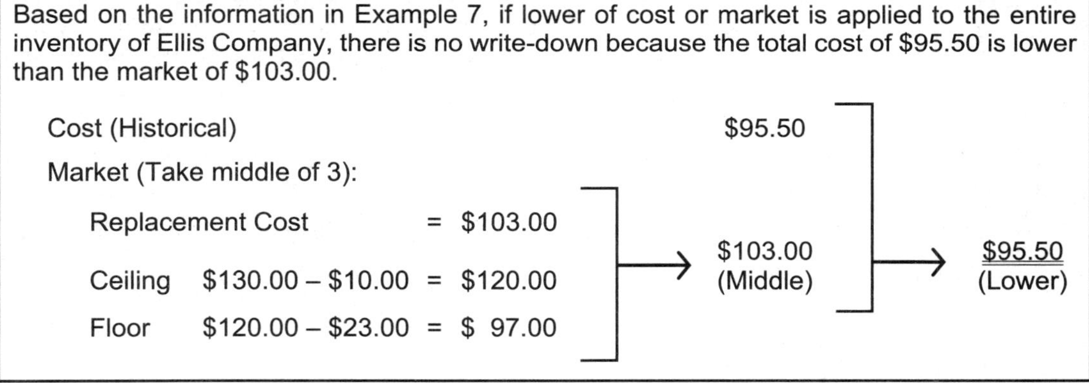

3. **Write-downs and Recoveries** Write-downs should be charged to expense in the period in which the conditions giving rise to the write-downs are first recognized. In addition, a write-down of inventory creates a new cost basis. Accordingly, a previously recorded write-down should not be reversed when the circumstances that gave rise to the write-down no longer exist. When a market write-down is necessary for finished goods, raw materials and work-in-process inventories also may have to be written down, unless they are readily marketable and may be sold for at least cost instead of being used in production.

4. **Conservatism and Matching Concepts** The LCM produces a realistic estimate of future cash flows to be realized from the sale of inventories. This is consistent with the principle of conservatism, and recognizes (matches) the anticipated loss in the income statement in the period in which the price decline occurs.

5. **Obsolete, Damaged and Excess Inventories** An essential part of the application of the lower of cost or market value concept is the reduction of the cost of obsolete, damaged, and excess inventories to market. Excess inventories are quantities of items that exceed anticipated sales or usage for a reasonable period. What constitutes a reasonable period will vary depending on the entity's business and the nature of the inventories. Obsolete, damaged, and excess inventories should be carried at net realizable value (which may be scrap value), with consideration being given to obsolescence risks for excess stock.

III. Inventory Estimation Methods

A. Gross Margin Method

This method rests on the assumption that the gross margin (GM) percentage is relatively stable. Cost of goods sold (CGS) is determined by applying the gross margin ratio to sales and subtracting this amount from the sales figure. Ending inventory is computed by subtracting the estimated CGS from the actual goods available for sale (GAFS), obtained from the beginning inventory and purchases accounts.

1. **Not GAAP** The gross margin method is **not** generally accepted for annual financial reporting purposes.

2. **Gross Margin Method Use** This method is used to (a) verify the accuracy of the year-end physical count, (b) estimate ending inventory and cost of goods sold for interim financial reporting, and (c) estimate inventory losses from theft and casualties (fires, floods).

Example 9 ▸ Gross Margin (Profit) Method

Maggie Company has a recent gross profit history of 40% of net sales. The following data are available from Maggie's accounting records for the three months ended March 31:

Inventory at 1/1	$ 650,000
Purchases	3,200,000
Net sales	4,500,000
Purchase returns	25,000

Required: Using the gross profit method, estimate the cost of the inventory at March 31.

Solution:

Beginning inventory		$ 650,000
Purchases		3,200,000
Purchase returns		(25,000)
Goods available for sale		3,825,000
Less: Estimated cost of goods sold:		
Net sales	$ 4,500,000	
Less: Gross margin (40% × $4,500,000)	(1,800,000)	(2,700,000)
Estimated ending inventory		$ 1,125,000

B. Retail Method

This method of inventory estimation is often used by retailers whose inventory goods are usually labeled upon receipt at their retail sales prices. This method requires that records be kept of beginning inventory and purchases for the period, both at cost and retail, additional markups and markdowns, and sales for the period. The ending inventory at cost is estimated by converting the ending inventory expressed in retail dollars to cost dollars, through the use of a cost/retail ratio. The retail method is generally applied under one of three following methods:

1. **Weighted Average, LCM** The weighted average is accomplished by combining beginning inventory and net purchases to determine a single cost/retail ratio. The LCM effect is achieved by including net markups, but **not** net markdowns, in the denominator of the ratio. This results in a larger denominator for the ratio and, thus, a lower ratio is obtained. Applying this lower ratio to ending inventory at retail, the inventory is reported at an amount below cost. This amount is intended to approximate lower of average cost or market.

2. **LIFO Retail** As a LIFO cost flow is assumed, (a) separate cost/retail ratios must be computed for beginning inventory and net purchases, and (b) LCM need not be used. Therefore, both net markups and net markdowns are included in the denominator of the purchases' cost/retail ratio. This results in a smaller denominator for the ratio and, thus, a higher ratio is obtained.

3. **Dollar-Value LIFO Retail** Combines retail and dollar-value LIFO methods. Under this method

   a. Ending inventory at retail is determined in the same manner as LIFO retail. Ending inventory at retail is then divided by the current price index to determine ending inventory at retail at base year dollars.

   b. Ending inventory at retail at base year dollars is then compared to beginning inventory at base year dollars. If the ending inventory at retail at base year dollars is larger, a new layer has been added; this layer is converted to current dollars by applying the current price index. If ending inventory at retail at base year dollars is smaller, liquidation takes place by layers, in LIFO order.

   c. Any incremental layer for the year, as determined in c. above, is then converted to cost by multiplying it by the cost/retail for purchases for the period. This layer is then added to the previous LIFO ending inventory at cost.

Example 10 ▸ Retail Methods

The LFGW Company commenced operations on January 1. An external price index is used for dollar-value LIFO computations. This index was 125 at January 1, and 150 at December 31. The following data was available from the records of the Company for the year ended December 31:

	Cost	Retail
Merchandise inventory January 1	$120,000	$200,000
Purchases, net	720,000	990,000
Markups, net		10,000
Markdowns, net		40,000
Sales, net		860,000

Required: Using the retail method, estimate merchandise inventory at December 31 under the following methods:

a. Weighted average, LCM
b. LIFO retail
c. Dollar-value LIFO retail

Solution:

a. Weighted Average, LCM:

	Cost		Retail		
Beginning inventory	$120,000		$ 200,000		
Purchases, net	720,000		990,000		
Markups, net	--		10,000		
WA/LCM cost/retail ratio	$840,000	/	$1,200,000	=	70%
Less: Sales, net			(860,000)		
Markdowns, net			(40,000)		
Ending inventory at retail			$ 300,000		
Ending inventory at cost ($300,000 × 70%)	$210,000				

b. LIFO Retail:

	Cost		Retail		
Beginning inventory	$120,000	/	$ 200,000	=	60%
Purchases, net	720,000		990,000		
Markups, net			10,000		
Markdowns, net			(40,000)		
Purchases cost/retail ratio	$720,000	/	$ 960,000	=	75%
Goods available for sale			$1,160,000		
Less: Sales, net			(860,000)		
Ending inventory at retail			$ 300,000		

Inventory layer	EI at retail		Cost/Retail ratio		EI at retail cost
Beginning	$200,000	×	60%	=	$120,000
Purchases	100,000	×	75%	=	75,000
	$300,000				$195,000

NOTE: Under a LIFO cost-flow assumption, the sum of ending inventory in retail dollars is composed of beginning inventory retail dollars (to the extent available) and a layer of purchase retail dollars for any increase in retail dollars for the period. The beginning inventory retail dollars and the purchase layer retail dollars are then converted to cost dollars by their separate cost/retail ratios.

c. Dollar-Value LIFO Retail:

	Cost	Retail
Ending inventory at retail at base year dollars ($300,000 / 1.20*)		$ 250,000
Base layer, January 1 year 1	$120,000	(200,000)
Incremental year 1 layer at base year dollars		$ 50,000
Incremental year 1 layer at current year dollars ($50,000 × 1.20)		$ 60,000
Incremental year 1 layer at cost ($60,000 × 75%)	45,000	
Ending inventory, dollar-value LIFO	$165,000	

*Current year external price index (150 / 125 = 1.20)

IV. Disclosures

A. Common Disclosures

The following disclosures related to inventory should be made in the financial statements or accompanying notes:

1. The basis of determining inventory amounts (e.g., the lower of cost or market) and the method of cost determination (e.g., first-in, first-out (FIFO), last-in, first-out (LIFO), average cost), including dollar amounts or percentage of inventories priced using each method should be disclosed. When the LIFO method is used, dollar amounts should be disclosed. The basis for stating any inventories at amounts that are above cost (e.g., precious metals, and so forth) should also be disclosed.

2. Amounts of major classes of inventories should be disclosed. For manufacturing companies, the categories, typically, would be raw materials, work-in-process, and finished goods. It is desirable to be more descriptive when possible. For example, "flour, sugar, and other ingredients" rather than "raw materials" could be used for a baking company. If it is not practical under a LIFO method to determine amounts assigned to major classes of inventories, the amounts of those classes may be stated under cost flow assumptions other than LIFO, with

the excess of such total amount over the aggregate LIFO amount presented as a deduction to arrive at the amount of the LIFO inventory.

3. Reserves resulting from inventory write-downs should be netted against the inventory amounts and desirably not disclosed.

4. When the LIFO method is used (note that the IRS has developed rules and regulations governing the financial statement treatment of LIFO inventories, and certain restrictions on disclosures regarding them):

   a. The dollar amount of inventories at current (e.g., FIFO) or replacement cost, or the excess of that amount over the stated LIFO value, and the basis of determining the current or replacement cost amount. In SEC filings, the excess of replacement or current cost over the stated LIFO value must be disclosed

   b. The effects on income of the liquidation of LIFO inventories and, for interim periods, the amount of any provision for temporary liquidation.

5. The amount of any substantial and unusual write-downs resulting from the application of the lower of cost or market rule (identified separately from cost of goods sold in the income statement, if material), including provisions for accrued net losses on firm, uncancelable, and unhedged purchase commitments for inventories (identified separately in the income statement, if material) should be disclosed.

6. Significant market declines after the balance sheet date not recognized in pricing the inventories should be disclosed.

7. Unusual or unusually significant purchase commitments should be disclosed.

8. Changes in pricing methods and the effects thereof should be disclosed.

9. Liens against and pledges of inventories should be disclosed.

B. Additional LIFO Disclosures

The following additional disclosures may be desirable, particularly in circumstances when alternative methods can result in significant differences in reported net income:

1. The method used in applying LIFO (e.g., dollar value, link chain method)

2. The approach used to price LIFO inventory increments (e.g., most recent acquisition price)

3. Pooling arrangements (e.g., a natural business unit pool)

4. The method used to price new items added to existing pools (e.g., reconstructed cost)

5. Other significant LIFO methods or approaches, when alternatives exist

6. Differences between the book and tax basis of LIFO inventories

7. Differences between the application of LIFO for financial reporting and for income tax purposes

8. Supplemental non-LIFO disclosures (e.g., disclosures pertaining to earnings information that would have been presented using a method other than LIFO in the financial statements)

Adaptive Testing

Each testlet is designed to cover all of the topics for an exam section. After the first testlet is finished, the software selects a second testlet based on the candidate's performance on the first testlet. If a candidate did well on the first testlet, the second testlet will be a little more difficult than average. The examiners plan on adaptive testing eventually allowing for less questions, resulting in more time for testing skills.

Initially, testlets with different levels of difficulty will have the same number of questions; however, the point value of a question from a "moderately difficult" testlet will be less than a question from a "difficult" testlet. Thus, some candidates may think that they are not doing well because they are finding the questions difficult; when in reality, they are getting difficult questions because of exceptional performance on previous testlets. Other candidates may think that they are doing well because they are finding the questions easy; when in reality, they are getting relatively easy questions because of poor performance on previous testlets.

The simulation testlet is not adaptive.

More helpful exam information is included in the **Exam Preparation Tips** appendix in this volume.

CHAPTER 3—INVENTORY

Problem 3-1 MULTIPLE-CHOICE QUESTIONS

1. Herc Co.'s inventory at December 31 of the previous year was $1,500,000, based on a physical count priced at cost, and before any necessary adjustment for the following:
   - Merchandise costing $90,000, shipped F.O.B. shipping point from a vendor on December 30 of the previous year, was received and recorded on January 5 of the current year.
   - Goods in the shipping area were excluded from inventory although shipment was not made until January 4. The goods, billed to the customer F.O.B. shipping point on December 30 had a cost of $120,000.

   What amount should Herc report as inventory in its December 31, previous year balance sheet?

   a. $1,500,000
   b. $1,590,000
   c. $1,620,000
   d. $1,710,000 (11/94, FAR, #13, amended, 5278)

2. Garson Co. recorded goods in transit purchased F.O.B. shipping point at year end as purchases. The goods were excluded from ending inventory. What effect does the omission have on Garson's assets and retained earnings at year end?

	Assets	Retained earnings
a.	No effect	Overstated
b.	No effect	Understated
c.	Understated	No effect
d.	Understated	Understated

(R/10, FAR, #5, 9305)

3. The following items were included in Opal Co.'s inventory account at December 31:

Merchandise out on consignment, at sales price, including 40% markup on selling price	$40,000
Goods purchased, in transit, shipped F.O.B. shipping point	36,000
Goods held on consignment by Opal	27,000

   By what amount should Opal's inventory account at December 31 be reduced?

   a. $103,000
   b. $ 67,000
   c. $ 51,000
   d. $ 43,000 (5/93, PI, #20, amended, 4062)

4. Nomar Co. shipped inventory on consignment to Seabright Co. that cost $20,000. Seabright paid $500 for advertising that was reimbursable from Nomar. At the end of the year, 70% of the inventory was sold for $30,000. The agreement states that a commission of 20% will be provided to Seabright for all sales. What amount of net inventory on consignment remains on the balance sheet for the first year for Nomar?

   a. $0
   b. $ 6,000
   c. $ 6,500
   d. $20,000 (R/06, FAR, #21, 8088)

5. During the current year, Kam Co. began offering its goods to selected retailers on a consignment basis. The following information was derived from Kam's current year accounting records:

Beginning inventory	$122,000
Purchases	540,000
Freight in	10,000
Transportation to consignees	5,000
Freight out	35,000
Ending inventory—held by Kam	145,000
—held by consignees	20,000

In its current year income statement, what amount should Kam report as cost of goods sold?

a. $507,000
b. $512,000
c. $527,000
d. $547,000 (5/95, FAR, #33, amended, 5569)

6. Which of the following statements regarding inventory accounting systems is true?

a. A disadvantage of the perpetual inventory system is that the inventory dollar amounts used for interim reporting purposes are estimated amounts.
b. A disadvantage of the periodic inventory system is that the cost of goods sold amount used for financial reporting purposes includes both the cost of inventory sold and inventory shortages.
c. An advantage of the perpetual inventory system is that the record keeping required to maintain the system is relatively simple.
d. An advantage of the periodic inventory system is that it provides a continuous record of the inventory balance. (R/05, FAR, #15, 7759)

7. Bren Co.'s beginning inventory at January 1 was understated by $26,000, and its ending inventory was overstated by $52,000. As a result, Bren's cost of goods sold for the year was

a. Understated by $26,000
b. Overstated by $26,000
c. Understated by $78,000
d. Overstated by $78,000 (11/94, FAR, #43, amended, 5305)

8. Seafood Trading Co. commenced operations during the year as a large importer and exporter of seafood. The imports were all from one country overseas. The export sales were conducted as drop shipments and were merely transshipped at Seattle. Seafood Trading reported the following data:

Purchases during the year	$12.0 million
Shipping costs from overseas	1.5 million
Shipping costs to export customers	1.0 million
Inventory at year end	3.0 million

What amount of shipping costs should be included in Seafood Trading's year-end inventory valuation?

a. $0
b. $250,000
c. $375,000
d. $625,000 (R/08, FAR, #32, 8587)

9. The following costs pertain to Den Co.'s purchase of inventory:

700 units of product A	$3,750
Freight-in	175
Cost of materials and labor incurred to bring product A to saleable condition	900
Insurance cost during transit of purchased goods	100
Total	$4,925

What amount should Den record as the cost of inventory as a result of this purchase?

a. $3,925
b. $4,650
c. $4,825
d. $4,925 (R/08, FAR, #8, 8563)

10. On July 1, Casa Development Co. purchased a tract of land for $1,200,000. Casa incurred additional costs of $300,000 during the remainder of the year in preparing the land for sale. The tract was subdivided into residential lots as follows:

Lot class	Number of lots	Sales price per lot
A	100	$24,000
B	100	16,000
C	200	10,000

Using the relative sales value method, what amount of costs should be allocated to the Class A lots?

a. $300,000
b. $375,000
c. $600,000
d. $720,000 (5/95, FAR, #10, amended, 5546)

11. On January 2 of the current year, LTTI Co. entered into a three-year, noncancelable contract to buy up to 1 million units of a product each year at $.10 per unit with a minimum annual guarantee purchase of 200,000 units. At year end, LTTI had only purchased 80,000 units and decided to cancel sales of the product. What amount should LTTI report as a loss related to the purchase commitment as of December 31 of the current year?

a. $0
b. $ 8,000
c. $12,000
d. $52,000 (R/10, FAR, #19, 9319)

12. A corporation entered into a purchase commitment to buy inventory. At the end of the accounting period, the current market value of the inventory was less than the fixed purchase price, by a material amount. Which of the following accounting treatments is most appropriate?

a. Describe the nature of the contract in a note to the financial statements, recognize a loss in the income statement, and recognize a liability for the accrued loss
b. Describe the nature of the contract and the estimated amount of the loss in a note to the financial statements, but do not recognize a loss in the income statement
c. Describe the nature of the contract in a note to the financial statements, recognize a loss in the income statement, and recognize a reduction in inventory equal to the amount of the loss by use of a valuation account
d. Neither describe the purchase obligation, nor recognize a loss on the income statement or balance sheet (R/08, FAR, #40, 8595)

13. Generally, which inventory costing method approximates most closely the current cost for each of the following?

	Cost of goods sold	Ending inventory
a.	LIFO	FIFO
b.	LIFO	LIFO
c.	FIFO	FIFO
d.	FIFO	LIFO

(11/91, Theory, #7, 2515)

14. A company decided to change its inventory valuation method from FIFO to LIFO in a period of rising prices. What was the result of the change on ending inventory and net income in the year of the change?

	Ending inventory	Net income	
a.	Increase	Increase	
b.	Increase	Decrease	
c.	Decrease	Decrease	
d.	Decrease	Increase	(11/95, FAR, #9, 6091)

15. The UNO Company was formed on January 2, year 1, to sell a single product. Over a two-year period, UNO's acquisition costs have increased steadily. Physical quantities held in inventory were equal to three months' sales at December 31, year 1, and zero at December 31, year 2. Assuming the periodic inventory system, the inventory cost method which reports the highest amount for each of the following is:

	Inventory December 31, Year 1	Cost of Sales Year 2	
a.	LIFO	FIFO	
b.	LIFO	LIFO	
c.	FIFO	FIFO	
d.	FIFO	LIFO	(Editor, 9050)

16. In January, Stitch, Inc. adopted the dollar-value LIFO method of inventory valuation. At adoption, inventory was valued at $50,000. During the year, inventory increased $30,000 using base-year prices, and prices increased 10%. The designated market value of Stitch's inventory exceeded its cost at year end. What amount of inventory should Stitch report in its year-end balance sheet?
    a. $80,000
    b. $83,000
    c. $85,000
    d. $88,000 (R/11, FAR, #27, 9877)

17. Assuming constant inventory quantities, which of the following inventory-costing methods will produce a lower inventory turnover ratio in an inflationary economy?
    a. FIFO (first in, first out)
    b. LIFO (last in, first out)
    c. Moving average
    d. Weighted average (R/11, FAR # 35,9885)

18. Jones Wholesalers stocks a changing variety of products. Which inventory costing method will be most likely to give Jones the lowest ending inventory when its product lines are subject to specific price increases?
    a. Specific identification
    b. Weighted average
    c. Dollar-value LIFO
    d. FIFO periodic (11/92, Theory, #15, 3448)

19. Nest Co. recorded the following inventory information during the month of January:

	Units	Unit cost	Total cost	Units on hand
Balance on 1/1	2,000	$1	$2,000	2,000
Purchased on 1/8	1,200	3	3,600	3,200
Sold on 1/23	1,800			1,400
Purchased on 1/28	800	5	4,000	2,200

Nest uses the LIFO method to cost inventory. What amount should Nest report as inventory on January 31 under each of the following methods of recording inventory?

	Perpetual	Periodic	
a.	$2,600	$5,400	
b.	$5,400	$2,600	
c.	$2,600	$2,600	
d.	$5,400	$5,400	(R/01, FAR, #2, 6977)

20. Estimates of price-level changes for specific inventories are required for which of the following inventory methods?

    a. Conventional retail
    b. Dollar-value LIFO
    c. Weighted average cost
    d. Average cost retail (11/93, Theory, #3, 4508)

21. Brock Co. adopted the dollar-value LIFO inventory method as of January 1, year 1. A single inventory pool and an internally computed price index are used to compute Brock's LIFO inventory layers. Information about Brock's dollar value inventory follows:

Date	At base year cost	At current year cost	At dollar-value LIFO
1/1, year 1	$40,000	$40,000	$40,000
Year 1, layer	5,000	14,000	6,000
12/31 year 1	45,000	54,000	46,000
Year 2, layer	15,000	26,000	?
12/31, year 2	$60,000	$80,000	$?

What was Brock's dollar-value LIFO inventory at December 31, year 2?

    a. $80,000
    b. $74,000
    c. $66,000
    d. $60,000 (11/93, PI, #20, amended, 4389)

22. Drew Co. uses the average cost inventory method for internal reporting purposes and LIFO for financial statement and income tax reporting. At December 31, the inventory was $375,000 using average cost and $320,000 using LIFO. The unadjusted credit balance in the LIFO Reserve account on December 31 was $35,000. What adjusting entry should Drew record to adjust from average cost to LIFO at December 31?

	Debit	Credit
a. Cost of Goods Sold	$55,000	
Inventory		$55,000
b. Cost of Goods Sold	$55,000	
LIFO Reserve		$55,000
c. Cost of Goods Sold	$20,000	
Inventory		$20,000
d. Cost of Goods Sold	$20,000	
LIFO Reserve		$20,000

(11/93, PI, #19, amended, 4388)

23. Trans Co. uses a periodic inventory system. The following are inventory transactions for the month of January:

1/1	Beginning inventory	10,000 units at $3
1/5	Purchase	5,000 units at $4
1/15	Purchase	5,000 units at $5
1/20	Sales at $10 per unit	10,000 units

Trans uses the average pricing method to determine the value of its inventory. What amount should Trans report as cost of goods sold on its income statement for the month of January?

    a. $ 30,000
    b. $ 37,500
    c. $ 40,000
    d. $100,000 (R/06, FAR, #40, 8107)

24. Ashe Co. recorded the following data pertaining to raw material X during January:

Date	Units Received	Cost	Issued	On Hand
1/01 Inventory		$8.00		3,200
1/11 Issue			1,600	1,600
1/22 Purchase	4,800	9.60		6,400

The moving-average unit cost of X inventory at January 31 is

a. $8.80
b. $8.96
c. $9.20
d. $9.60 (11/90, PI, #8, amended, 9051)

25. The replacement cost of an inventory item is below the net realizable value and above the net realizable value less a normal profit margin. The inventory item's original cost is above the net realizable value. Under the lower of cost or market method, the inventory item should be valued at

a. Original cost
b. Replacement cost
c. Net realizable value
d. Net realizable value less normal profit margin (R/11, FAR, #1, 9851)

26. The original cost of an inventory item is below both replacement cost and net realizable value. The net realizable value less normal profit margin is below the original cost. Under the lower of cost or market method, the inventory item should be valued at

a. Replacement cost
b. Net realizable value
c. Net realizable value less normal profit margin
d. Original cost (11/92, Theory, #14, 3447)

27. The original cost of an inventory item is below the net realizable value and above the net realizable value less a normal profit margin. The inventory item's replacement cost is below the net realizable value less a normal profit margin. Under the lower of cost or market method, the inventory item should be valued at

a. Original cost
b. Replacement cost
c. Net realizable value
d. Net realizable value less normal profit margin (5/97, FAR, #1, 6473)

28. Based on a physical inventory taken on December 31, Chewy Co. determined its chocolate inventory on a FIFO basis at $26,000 with a replacement cost of $20,000. Chewy estimated that, after further processing costs of $12,000, the chocolate could be sold as finished candy bars for $40,000. Chewy's normal profit margin is 10% of sales. Under the lower of cost or market rule, what amount should Chewy report as chocolate inventory in its December 31 balance sheet?

a. $28,000
b. $26,000
c. $24,000
d. $20,000 (11/93, PI, #21, amended, 4390)

29. Loft Co. reviewed its inventory values for proper pricing at year end. The following summarizes two inventory items examined for the lower of cost or market:

	Inventory item #1	Inventory item #2
Original cost	$210,000	$400,000
Replacement cost	150,000	370,000
Net realizable value	240,000	410,000
Net realizable value less profit margin	208,000	405,000

What amount should Loft include in inventory at year end, if it uses the total of the inventory to apply the lower of cost or market?

a. $520,000
b. $610,000
c. $613,000
d. $650,000 (R/07, FAR, #26, 8347)

30. At the end of the year, Ian Co. determined its inventory to be $258,000 on a FIFO (first in, first out) basis. The current replacement cost of this inventory was $230,000. Ian estimates that it could sell the inventory for $275,000 at a disposal cost of $14,000. If Ian's normal profit margin for its inventory was $10,000, what would be its net carrying value?

a. $244,000
b. $251,000
c. $258,000
d. $261,000 (R/08, FAR, #7, 8562)

31. The following information was obtained from Smith Co.:

Sales	$275,000
Beginning inventory	30,000
Ending inventory	18,000

Smith's gross margin is 20%. What amount represents Smith purchases?

a. $202,000
b. $208,000
c. $220,000
d. $232,000 (R/05, FAR, #41, 7785)

32. Fireworks, Inc. had an explosion in its plant that destroyed most of its inventory. Its records show that beginning inventory was $40,000. Fireworks made purchases of $480,000 and sales of $620,000 during the year. Its normal gross profit percentage is 25%. It can sell some of its damaged inventory for $5,000. The insurance company will reimburse Fireworks for 70% of its loss. What amount should Fireworks report as loss from the explosion?

a. $50,000
b. $35,000
c. $18,000
d. $15,000 (R/08, FAR, #33, 8588)

33. A flash flood swept through Hat, Inc.'s warehouse on May 1. After the flood, Hat's accounting records showed the following:

Inventory, January 1	$ 35,000
Purchases, January 1 through May 1	200,000
Sales, January 1 through May 1	250,000
Inventory not damaged by flood	30,000
Gross profit percentage on sales	40%

What amount of inventory was lost in the flood?

a. $ 55,000
b. $ 85,000
c. $120,000
d. $150,000 (R/06, FAR, #4, 8071)

34. The retail inventory method includes which of the following in the calculation of both cost and retail amounts of goods available for sale?

a. Purchase returns
b. Sales returns
c. Net markups
d. Freight in (11/90, Theory, #16, 1796)

35. Dean Company uses the retail inventory method to estimate its inventory for interim statement purposes. Data relating to the computation of the inventory at July 31 are as follows:

	Cost	Retail
Inventory, 2/1	$ 180,000	$ 250,000
Purchases	1,020,000	1,575,000
Markups, net		175,000
Sales		1,705,000
Estimated normal shoplifting losses		20,000
Markdowns, net		125,000

Under the approximate lower of average cost or market retail method, Dean's estimated inventory at July 31 is

a. $ 90,000
b. $ 96,000
c. $102,000
d. $150,000 (11/87, PI, #53, amended, 0919)

36. Hutch Inc. uses the conventional retail inventory method to account for inventory. The following information relates to current year operations:

	Average	
	Cost	Retail
Beginning inventory and purchases	$ 600,000	$920,000
Net markups		40,000
Net markdowns		60,000
Sales		780,000

What amount should be reported as cost of sales for the current year?

a. $480,000
b. $487,500
c. $520,000
d. $525,000 (5/92, PI, #49, amended, 2620)

37. On December 31 of the previous year, Jason Company adopted the dollar-value LIFO retail inventory method. Inventory data are as follows:

	LIFO Cost	Retail
Inventory, 12/31 previous year	$360,000	$500,000
Inventory, 12/31 current year	—	660,000
Increase in price level for current year		10%
Cost to retail ratio for current year		70%

Under the LIFO retail method, Jason's inventory at December 31 of the current year should be

a. $437,000
b. $462,000
c. $472,000
d. $483,200 (5/86, PI, #12, amended, 0927)

Problem 3-2 SIMULATION: Research

Question: What is the major objective in selecting a cost flow method for inventory?

FASB ASC: [ ] - [ ] - [ ] - [ ]

(9105)

Problem 3-3 SIMULATION: Cost of Goods Sold

Cork Co. sells one product, which it purchases from various suppliers.

Cork's trial balance at December 31 included the following accounts:

Sales (39,000 units @ $17)	$663,000
Sales discounts	9,500
Purchases	437,100
Purchase discounts	22,000
Freight-in	6,000
Freight-out	12,000

Cork Co.'s inventory purchases during the year were as follows:

	Units	Cost per unit	Total cost
Beg. inventory, Jan. 1	10,000	$8.30	$ 83,000
Purchases, quarters ended:			
March 31	14,000	8.35	116,900
June 30	17,000	8.00	136,000
September 30	15,000	7.60	114,000
December 31	9,000	7.80	70,200
	65,000		$520,100

Additional information:

Cork's accounting policy is to report inventory in its financial statements at the lower of cost or market, applied to total inventory. Cost is determined under the last-in, first-out (LIFO) method. Cork has determined that, at December 31, the replacement cost of its inventory was $8.20 per unit and the net realizable value was $9.00 per unit. Cork's normal profit margin is $1.10 per unit.

Prepare Cork's schedule of cost of goods sold, with a supporting schedule of ending inventory. Cork uses the direct method of reporting losses from market decline of inventory.

Schedule of Cost of Goods Sold

Beginning inventory	$
Add: Purchases	
Less: Purchase discounts	
Add: Freight-in	
Goods available for sale	$
Less: Ending inventory	
Cost of Goods Sold	$

Supporting Schedule of Ending Inventory

Inventory at cost (LIFO):

	Units	Cost per unit	Total cost
Beg. inventory, Jan. 1			
Purchases, quarters ended:			
Total			

(5/94, FAR, #4, amended, 4974t)

Problem 3-4 SIMULATION: Dollar-Value LIFO

On January 1, year 2, Gold Industries Inc. adopted the dollar-value LIFO method of determining inventory costs for financial and income tax reporting. The following information relates to this change:

- Gold has continued to use the FIFO method, which approximates current costs, for internal reporting purposes. Gold's FIFO inventories at December 31, year 2, year 3, and year 4 were $120,000, $157,500, and $215,000, respectively.

- The FIFO inventory amounts are converted to dollar-value LIFO amounts using a single inventory pool and cost indices developed using the link-chain method. Gold estimated that the current year cost change indices, which measure year-to-year cost changes, were 1.150 for year 3 and 1.100 for year 4.

Prepare a schedule showing the computation of Gold's dollar-value LIFO inventory at December 31, year 2 and year 3. Round to nearest dollar.

Computation of Dollar-Value LIFO Inventory

Year	**FIFO inventory**	**Current year cost change index**	**Link-chain cost index**	**Inventory at base year costs**
2	$120,000	1.000	1.000	$120,000
3	157,500	1.150	(a)	(c)
4	215,000	1.100	(b)	(d)
Year	**LIFO inventory layers at base year costs**	**Link-chain cost index**	**Year 2 dollar-value LIFO inventory**	**Year 3 dollar-value LIFO inventory**
2	$120,000	1.000	$120,000	$120,000
3	(e)	(a)	(h)	(j)
4	(f)	(b)		(k)
Totals	(g)		(i)	(l)

(11/92, PI, #4(b), amended, 6188t)

Solution 3-1 MULTIPLE-CHOICE ANSWERS

Ownership Criteria

1. (d) Goods should be included in the purchaser's inventory when legal title passes to the purchaser. Therefore, Herc should include the $90,000 cost of goods shipped to it F.O.B. shipping point in inventory at 12/31 because title of these goods passed to Herc when the goods were picked up by the common carrier on 12/30. Herc should also include the $120,000 cost of goods in its shipping area in inventory at 12/31. These goods should be included in inventory because shipment of these goods to the customer was not made until the current year. (5278)

2. (d) Goods purchased f.o.b. shipping point should be included in inventory when the goods are shipped. It states the goods are in transit, so they have been shipped. The goods were erroneously excluded from ending inventory, when they should have been included, meaning that inventory is understated. Inventory is an asset, so assets are understated. An understated inventory also would lead to an overstated cost of goods sold (goods available for sale – ending inventory = cost of goods sold). An overstated cost of goods sold would lead to an understated gross profit (revenue – cost of goods sold = gross profit) which in turn results in an understated retained earnings. (9305)

3. (d) Opal's inventory account should be reduced by $43,000 (i.e., $16,000 + $27,000) at 12/31. The merchandise out on consignment should be included in Opal's inventory at cost. Therefore, Opal's inventory must be reduced by the amount of the markup. Note that the question states that the merchandise out on consignment includes 40% *markup on selling price,* not a 40% markup on cost. The markup is easily calculated because the selling price is given. Selling price of $40,000 times 40% equals a markup of $16,000. Since Opal does not have title to the $27,000 of goods held on consignment, the cost of these goods should also be excluded from Opal's inventory. The cost of the $36,000 of goods in transit at 12/31, purchased F.O.B. shipping point, are properly included in Opal's inventory because title of the goods passed to Opal when the goods were shipped. (4062)

4. (b) Goods out on consignment should be included in inventory at cost because title to the goods has not changed. Of the $20,000 inventory Nomar shipped, only 70% ($14,000) was sold by Seabright. This leaves $6,000 to be included on the balance sheet for the first year for Nomar. The $500 Seabright paid for advertising is advertising expense and not included in inventory. (8088)

5. (b) Goods out on consignment remain the property of the consignor and must be included in the consignor's inventory at purchase price or production cost, including freight and other costs incurred to process the goods up to the time of sale.

Beginning inventory		$ 122,000
Purchases	$540,000	
Freight in	10,000	
Transportation to consignees	5,000	
Add: Inventoriable costs		555,000
Goods available for sale		677,000
Less: EI ($145,000 + $20,000)		(165,000)
Cost of goods sold		$ 512,000

(5569)

Measuring Inventories

6. (b) In the periodic system cost of goods sold (CGS) is a residual amount obtained by subtracting the ending inventory from the sum of beginning inventory and net purchases. The periodic system is characterized by no entries being made to the inventory account during the period. This amount would also include shortages as well as items actually sold, thus inaccurately reporting the true cost of goods sold. In a perpetual inventory system, record keeping is not simple; inventory dollar amounts are not estimated. The balance in the inventory account at any time reveals the inventory that should be on hand. (7759)

7. (c) An understatement of beginning inventory understates the cost of goods available for sale, thereby understating cost of goods sold. An overstatement of ending inventory also understates cost of goods sold. Therefore, cost of goods sold for the year is understated by the sum of the understatement of beginning inventory and the overstatement of ending inventory. (5305)

8. (c) Merchandise inventory should include freight-in, taxes, insurance while in transit, warehousing costs, and similar charges paid by the purchaser to bring the merchandise to its existing condition and location. Thus, the $1.5 million in shipping costs from overseas should be included in the inventory valuation. The shipping costs to export customers are a selling expense and should not be included in the cost of inventory. Seafood purchased $12 million in inventory during the year and has $3 million remaining in inventory at year end. The $12 million divided by $3 million means one-quarter of the inventory is still remaining. Thus, one-quarter of the $1.5 million, or $375,000, in shipping costs from overseas should be included in the year-end inventory valuation. (8587)

9. (d) The cost of merchandise inventory is net of any discounts but includes freight-in, taxes, insurance while in transit, warehousing costs, and similar charges paid to bring the article to its existing condition and location. The cost of the inventory would be the $3,750 purchase price, plus the $175 freight-in charge, plus the $900 costs of materials and labor to bring it to saleable condition, plus the $100 insurance cost during transit for a total of $4,925. (8563)

10. (c) Under the relative sales value method, the total cost of the individual units purchased at a single lump-sum price should be allocated to the various units on the basis of their relative sales value. The total cost includes the purchase price of $1,200,000 plus the additional costs of $300,000 to prepare the land for sale.

Lot class	Number of lots	Sales price per lot	Total sales for class
A	100	$24,000	$2,400,000
B	100	16,000	1,600,000
C	200	10,000	2,000,000
Total			$6,000,000

Class A lots ($2,400,000) / Total sales value ($6,000,000) = 40%.

Purchase price of entire tract	$1,200,000
Additional costs of preparing land for sale	300,000
Total cost	1,500,000
Class A lots relative value percentage	× 40%
Costs allocated to Class A lots	$ 600,000

(5546)

11. (d) When there is a firm commitment to purchase goods in a future period at a set price (i.e., an enforceable contract exists), any loss from a drop in the market value of such goods, or cancellation of the contract by the purchaser, should be recognized in the current period. The contract guaranteed LTTI purchase 200,000 units per year, so LTTI would recognize a loss for the 520,000 units that it had guaranteed to purchase throughout the life of the contract but had not yet purchased (120,000 current year units + 200,000 year 2 units + 200,000 year 3 units = 520,000 units). 520,000 × $0.10 = $52,000. (9319)

12. (a) When there is a firm commitment to purchase goods in a future period at a set price, an enforceable contract exists. Any loss resulting from a drop in the market value of such goods should be recognized in the current period. There should be a note in the financial statements describing the nature of the contract. The journal entry would be a debit to Loss on Purchase Commitment and a credit to Allowance for Loss on Purchase Commitment. (8595)

Cost Flow Assumptions

13. (a) In using LIFO, the cost of the last goods in are used in pricing the cost of goods sold. In using FIFO, the cost of the last goods in are used in pricing the ending inventory. Therefore, the LIFO method will result in having cost of goods sold most closely approximate current cost and the FIFO method will result in having ending inventory most closely approximate current cost. (2515)

14. (c) During periods of rising prices, the LIFO inventory cost flow method reports a higher cost of sales and a lower amount for ending inventory than FIFO. Therefore, a change from FIFO to LIFO during this period would result in a decrease in net income and a decrease in ending inventory. (6091)

15. (c) Under the last-in, first-out (LIFO) method of inventory valuation, the units remaining in ending inventory are costed at the oldest unit costs available. Under the first-in, first-out (FIFO) method of inventory valuation, the units remaining in ending inventory are costed at the most recent unit costs available. Therefore, because inventory acquisition costs increased steadily during year 1, the FIFO method of inventory valuation would report a higher amount for ending inventory than the LIFO method. The question indicates that there were no goods in inventory at 12/31, year 2. So, cost of goods sold for year 2 is comprised of the cost of inventory purchases made in year 2 and the cost of ending inventory at 12/31, year 1. Because the cost of the ending inventory at 12/31, year 1, is higher under FIFO, cost of goods sold for year 2 would also be higher under FIFO. (9050)

16. (b) Inventory is reported at the lower of cost or market. As indicated in the problem, market exceeded cost, so inventory should be stated at cost, using dollar value LIFO. The inventory layer added in the current year is computed in terms of base year cost. It then must be converted to current year cost because the layer was added during the current year. The index (1.1) is computed by dividing the ending inventory at current year cost ($88,000) by the ending inventory at base year cost ($80,000). The cost of ending inventory ($83,000) is the $50,000 cost of the beginning amount and the converted Year 1 layer. ($30.000 × 1.1 = $33,000). (9877)

17. (a) The inventory turnover ratio indicates the number of times inventory was acquired and sold (or used in production) during the period. It is computed by dividing Cost of Goods Sold by Average Inventory. Average inventory is generally determined by adding the beginning and ending inventories and dividing by two. The lower the numerator (i.e., Cost of Goods Sold), the lower the ratio. In times of rising prices, FIFO will give you the oldest/lowest Cost of Goods Sold, so FIFO will also compute the lowest inventory turnover ratio. (9885)

18. (c) The last-in, first-out (LIFO) methods of inventory valuation assign the oldest costs available to ending inventory. Therefore, when inventory is subject to specific price increases, the dollar-value LIFO method would report the lowest ending inventory of the inventory methods listed. (3448)

19. (b) Under the perpetual method, only 1,400 beginning inventory units remain, as 600 units were sold on 1/23, along with all units purchased on 1/8: (1,400 × $1) + (800 × $5). Under the periodic method, the beginning inventory and inventory first-in for the period is assumed to remain in inventory: (2,000 × $1) + (200 × $3). (6977)

20. (b) As a general rule, dollar-value LIFO uses a "double-extension method" to compute: (1) the value of the ending inventory in terms of base year prices, and (2) the value of ending inventory at current prices. The ratio of (2) over (1), above, provides the specific price index for valuing any layers of inventory added in the period. None of the other inventory methods require estimates of price-level changes for specific inventories. (4508)

21. (c) The price index is computed by dividing the ending inventory at current year cost by its base year cost.

Date	Layers at base year cost	Price index	Ending inventory at LIFO cost
01/01 Yr 1	$40,000	1.0000 [1]	$40,000
12/31 Yr 1	5,000	1.2000 [2]	6,000
12/31 Yr 2	15,000	1.3333 [3]	20,000
	$60,000		$66,000

[1] $40,000 / $40,000. [2] $54,000 / $45,000. [3] $80,000 / $60,000. (4389)

22. (d) Some companies use LIFO for tax and external reporting purposes, but they maintain a FIFO, average cost, or standard cost system for internal reporting purposes. The difference between the inventory method used for internal reporting purposes and LIFO is often referred to as the LIFO reserve. The LIFO reserve is a contra-inventory account that must be adjusted to its required balance at the financial statement date. At 12/31 Drew's inventory was $375,000 using average cost and $320,000 using LIFO. The required balance in the LIFO reserve at 12/31 is $55,000 (i.e., $375,000 – $320,000). Since the unadjusted LIFO reserve balance was $35,000, the reserve must be increased by $20,000 (i.e., $55,000 – $35,000). (4388)

23. (b) Average inventory methods assume that the cost of goods sold and ending inventory should be based on the average cost of the inventories available for sale (AFS) during the period. A weighted average method generally is used with a periodic inventory system. The weighted-average method costs inventory items on the basis of average prices paid, weighted according to the quantity purchased at each price.

Beg. Inventory, (10,000 × $3)	$ 30,000
Jan 5 purchase, (5,000 × $4)	20,000
Jan 15 purchase, (5,000 × $5)	25,000
Total cost of goods AFS	75,000
Divided by: Total units available	20,000
Weighted average cost per unit	$ 3.75
Times: Units sold during January	× 10,000
Cost of goods sold for January	$ 37,500

(8107)

24. (c) At 1/31, there were 6,400 units on hand at a total cost of $58,880 (1,600 @ $8.00 and 4,800 @ 9.60). The moving-average unit cost was therefore $9.20. (9051)

Lower of Cost or Market

25. (b) Valuation of inventory items is required at the lower of cost or replacement cost (commonly referred to as market). Market cannot exceed the net realizable value (ceiling) of the good (i.e., selling price less expected costs to sell), and market should not be less than this net realizable value reduced by an allowance for a normal profit margin (floor). In this problem, the replacement cost is between the ceiling and floor amounts, so it is used as the market value. Since the original cost is greater than replacement (i.e., market) cost, the item will be carried at the lower market/replacement cost. (9851)

26. (d) According to the lower of cost or market rule, market is defined as replacement cost. Market cannot exceed net realizable value and cannot be less than net realizable value less normal profit margin. In this instance, original cost is between net realizable value and net realizable value less normal profit margin. Since original cost is within the parameters for replacement cost and is less than replacement cost, the inventory should be reported at original cost. (3447)

27. (d) Under the lower of cost or market rule, market means current replacement cost with the exception that market value should not exceed the net realizable value (ceiling) and should not be less than the net realizable value minus normal profit (floor). Because in this question replacement cost is below the floor, this would be the minimum amount at which market could be valued. This market value is then compared to the original cost and the lower amount is used for the value of the inventory item. The question states that the original cost is above the net realizable value less a normal profit margin, thus, the market value is the lower amount. (6473)

28. (c) Under the lower of cost or market rule, replacement cost cannot exceed a "ceiling" of net realizable value (estimated selling price less estimated cost of completion and disposal) and cannot be below a "floor" of net realizable value reduced by a normal profit margin. The replacement cost is below the prescribed range [i.e., $20,000 < ($24,000 to $28,000)]. Therefore, the "floor" of $24,000 is the assigned market value. Because the assigned market value of $24,000 is below the historical cost of $26,000, the inventory should be valued at $24,000.

	Replacement Cost Parameters			
Cost	Replacement Cost	Ceiling (NRV)	Floor (NRV - NP)	
$2,600	$20,000	$28,000 [1]	$24,000 [2]	[1] $40,000 – $12,000 [2] $28,000 – ($40,000 × 10%)

(4390)

29. (b) In applying the lower of cost or market, one must first determine the market value. The market refers to the current replacement cost, yet it should not exceed a ceiling (the net realizable value) nor be less than a floor, the net realizable value minus normal profit. The market value is determined by comparing the ceiling, floor and replacement costs. The total inventory ceiling is $650,000 ($240,000 + $410,000), the total inventory floor is $613,000 ($208,000 + $405,000), and the total inventory replacement cost is $520,000 ($150,000 + $370,000). The middle number is selected as the market; here it is the $613,000 floor amount. The total inventory cost of $610,000 is the value of inventory at year end because it is lower than the $613,000 market value. (8347)

30. (b) Ian would report its inventory at the lower of cost or market. The market means current replacement cost except the market cannot exceed the net realizable value, known as the ceiling, or be less than the net realizable value minus normal profit, known as the floor. Net realizable value is the estimated selling price less reasonable costs of completion and disposal. The ceiling would be $261,000 ($275,000 selling price – $14,000 disposal costs) and the floor would be $251,000 ($275,000 selling price – $14,000 disposal costs – $10,000 normal profit margin). The replacement cost is only $230,000, so the market would be the minimum amount of $251,000. Comparing the lower of cost ($258,000) or market ($251,000) shows the market is lower. So Ian's inventory would be carried at $251,000. (8562)

Inventory Estimation Methods

31. (b)

Net Sales	$ 275,000
Less: Gross margin (20% × 275,000)	(55,000)
Estimated COGS	$ 220,000

Solve for Goods Available for Sale: (GAFS – COGS = EI)
GAFS – $220,000 = $18,000
GAFS = $238,000

Solve for Purchases: (BI – Purch = GAFS)
$30,000 – Purch = $238,000
Purchases = $208,000 (7785)

32. (d) The gross margin method of inventory estimation is used to estimate inventory losses from theft and casualties. First, calculate the goods available for sale, which is the beginning inventory of $40,000 plus purchases of $480,000 for a total of $520,000. Next, figure the estimated cost of goods sold, which is the net sale of $620,000 less the gross margin of $155,000 ($620,000 × 25%) for a total of $465,000. Subtracting the $465,000 estimated cost of goods sold from the $520,000 goods available for sale leaves $55,000 in estimated ending inventory. Now, subtract the $5,000 worth of damaged inventory Fireworks can sell and that leaves a $50,000 loss from the explosion. The insurance company reimburses Fireworks for 70% ($50,000 × 70% = $35,000) of that loss. Fireworks would report only $15,000 ($50,000 – $35,000) as loss from the explosion. (8588)

33. (a) The amount of inventory lost in the flood is calculated by determining the difference between the estimated ending inventory using the gross margin method and the actual physical inventory not damaged by the flood.

Beginning inventory, January 1		$ 35,000
Purchases, January 1 through May 1		200,000
Goods available for sale		235,000
Sales, January 1 through May 1	$ 250,000	
Less: Gross margin (40% × $250,000)	(100,000)	
Less: Estimated CGS		(150,000)
Estimated ending inventory		85,000
Less: Physical ending inventory		(30,000)
Estimated flood loss		$ 55,000

(8071)

34. (a) When the retail method is employed, purchase returns is included in the calculation of both cost and retail amounts of goods available for sale (AFS). Sales returns does not appear in the computation of the cost amount of goods AFS. Net markups appears in the retail amount of goods AFS (assuming the retail method is used to approximate a lower of average cost or market figure) but not in the cost amount of goods AFS. Freight in appears in the cost amount of goods available for sale but not in the retail amount of goods AFS. (1796)

35. (a)

	Cost	Retail
Inventory, 2/1	$ 180,000	$ 250,000
Purchases	1,020,000	1,575,000
Markups, net		175,000
Cost ratio	$1,200,000	2,000,000
Less: Sales		(1,705,000)
Markdowns, net		(125,000)
Est. normal shoplifting losses		(20,000)
Estimated ending inventory at retail		150,000
Cost-to-retail ratio ($1,200,000 / $2,000,000)		× 60%
Estimated ending inventory at cost		$ 90,000

(0919)

36. (d) Cost of sales is determined by subtracting the estimated ending inventory at cost from the cost of the beginning inventory and purchases (i.e., $600,000 – $75,000 = $525,000).

	Cost	Retail
Beg. inventory and purchases	$600,000	$ 920,000
Net markups		40,000
Close-to-retail amounts	$600,000	960,000
Less: Sales		(780,000)
Net Markdowns		60,000
Estimated EI at retail		120,000
Cost-to-retail ratio ($600,000 / $960,000)		× 62.5%
Estimated ending inventory at cost		$ 75,000

(2620)

37. (a)

Inventory at retail, 12/31 current year adjusted ($660,000 / 1.1)	$ 600,000
Beginning inventory at retail, base year price	(500,000)
New layer added in current year	100,000
Times: Price level adjustment	× 1.1
Current year layer, at LIFO retail	110,000
Times: Cost to retail ratio	× 0.70
Current year layer, at LIFO cost	77,000
Add: Beg. inventory, at LIFO cost	360,000
Ending inventory, 12/31 current year	$ 437,000

(0927)

PERFORMANCE BY SUBTOPICS

Each category below parallels a subtopic covered in Chapter 3. Record the number and percentage of questions you correctly answered in each subtopic area.

Ownership Criteria

Question #	Correct √
1	
2	
3	
4	
5	
# Questions	5
# Correct	
% Correct	

Measuring Inventories

Question #	Correct √
6	
7	
8	
9	
10	
11	
12	
# Questions	7
# Correct	
% Correct	

Cost Flow Assumptions

Question #	Correct √
13	
14	
15	
16	
17	
18	
19	
20	
21	
22	
23	
24	
# Questions	12
# Correct	
% Correct	

Lower of Cost or Market

Question #	Correct √
25	
26	
27	
28	
29	
30	
# Questions	6
# Correct	
% Correct	

Inventory Estimation Methods

Question #	Correct √
31	
32	
33	
34	
35	
36	
37	
# Questions	7
# Correct	
% Correct	

Solution 3-2 SIMULATION ANSWER: Research

FASB Accounting Standards Codification

FASB ASC: 330 - 10 - 30 - 9

30-9 Cost for inventory purposes may be determined under any one of several assumptions as to the flow of cost factors, such as first-in first-out (FIFO), average, and last-in first-out (LIFO). The major objective in selecting a method should be to choose the one which, under the circumstances, most clearly reflects periodic income.

Solution 3-3 SIMULATION ANSWER: Cost of Goods Sold

Schedule of Cost of Goods Sold

Beginning inventory	$ 83,000	1
Add: Purchases	437,100	2
Less: Purchase discounts	(22,000)	3
Add: Freight-in	6,000	4
Goods available for sale	504,100	5
Less: Ending inventory	(213,200)	6
Cost of Goods Sold	$ 290,900	7

Supporting Schedule of Ending Inventory
Inventory at cost (LIFO):

	A Units	B Cost per unit	C Total cost	
Beg. inventory, Jan. 1	10,000	$8.30	$ 83,000	8
Purchases, quarters ended:				
March 31	14,000	8.35	116,900	9
June 30	2,000	8.00	16,000	10
	26,000		$215,900	11

1. Beginning inventory given in scenario.
2. Purchases given in scenario.
3. Purchase discounts given in scenario.
4. Freight in given in scenario.
5. Sum of inventory adjustments.
6. Inventory at market: 26,000 units @ $8.20 = $213,200
7. Total cost of goods sold.

8 A. Units in beginning inventory given in scenario.
8 B. Cost per unit given in scenario.
8 C. Total cost: Beginning inventory × cost per unit = Total given in scenario.
9 A. Purchases for quarter ended March 31 given in scenario.
9 B. Cost per unit given in scenario.
9 C. Total cost of purchases for quarter ended March 31: Units × cost = Total given in scenario.
10 A.

Total units purchased for year	65,000
Less total units sold	39,000
Total units left in inventory	26,000
Units left in inventory (Beg. + March 31)	(24,000)
Units left in inventory purchased in quarter ended 6/30	2,000

10 B. Cost per unit given in scenario
10 C. Units left in inventory purchased in quarter ended 6/30 × cost per unit (2,000 × $8.00)
11 A. Number of units remaining in LIFO inventory.
11 C. Total cost of units left in LIFO inventory.

Solution 3-4 SIMULATION ANSWER: Dollar-Value LIFO

Computation of Dollar-Value LIFO Inventory

Year	FIFO inventory	Current year cost change index	Link-chain cost index	Inventory at base year costs
2	$120,000	1.000	1.000	$120,000
3	157,500	1.150	1.150 (a)	136,957 (c)
4	215,000	1.100	1.265 (b)	169,960 (d)

Year	LIFO inventory layers at base year costs	Link-chain cost index	Year 2 dollar-value LIFO inventory	Year 3 dollar-value LIFO inventory
2	$120,000	1.000	$ 120,000	$120,000
3	16,957 (e)	1.150 (a)	19,501 (h)	19,501 (j)
4	33,003 (f)	1.265 (b)		41,749 (k)
Totals	$169,960 (g)		$ 139,501 (i)	$181,250 (l)

Explanations

a. 1.000 × 1.150 = 1.150

In the link chain method, the current year indices are multiplied to arrive at the link chain indices.

b. 1.150 × 1.100 = 1.265

In the link chain method, the current year indices are multiplied to arrive at the link chain indices.

c. $157,500 / (1.000 × 1.150) = $136,957

FIFO inventory amounts converted to dollar-value LIFO using the year 3 link-chain index applied to year 3 FIFO inventory

d. $215,000 / (1.000 × 1.150 × 1.100) = $169,960

FIFO inventory amounts converted to dollar-value LIFO using the year 4 link-chain index applied to year 4 FIFO inventory

e. $136,957 – $120,000 = $16,957

Year 3 LIFO layer

f. $169,960 – $136,957 = $33,003

Year 4 LIFO layer

g. $120,000 + $16,957 + $33,003 = $169,960

Sum of LIFO layers for year 2, year 3, and year 4

h. $16,957 × 1.150 = $19,501

Year 3 dollar value LIFO layer

i. $120,000 + $19,501 = $139,501

Dollar-value LIFO inventory at December 31, year 3

j. See explanation for h.

k. $33,003 × 1.265 = $41,749

Year 4 dollar value LIFO layer

l. $120,000 + $19,501 + $41,749 = $181,250

Dollar-value LIFO inventory at December 31, year 4

CHAPTER 4

PROPERTY, PLANT & EQUIPMENT

CHAPTER 4

PROPERTY, PLANT & EQUIPMENT

I. Classification

A. Definition

Property, plant, and equipment typically consist of long-lived tangible assets used to create and distribute an entity's products and services and include: land and land improvements; buildings; machinery and equipment; and furniture and fixtures. Fixed assets are not for resale, and are subject to cost recovery through depreciation.

B. Characteristics

Productive assets are classified according to their characteristics, as follows:

1. **Limited Lives** Plant and equipment have limited service lives; thus, their costs must be allocated to the periods benefited by the application of depreciation charges.

2. **Indefinite Life** Land is deemed to have an indefinite life and, therefore, is not depreciated.

3. **Wasting Assets** Natural resources such as mineral, gas and oil deposits, and standing timber are considered wasting (nonregenerative) assets. Their costs must be allocated to inventory by the application of depletion charges because these resources are subject to exhaustion through extraction.

II. Initial Measurement

A. Valuation

Historical cost is the basis for valuation of PP&E. In general, the total cost of the asset should include the cash price paid and all costs incurred to bring that asset into a condition and location for its intended use.

B. Land and Land Improvements

Land purchased for the purpose of constructing new plant includes all costs incurred to prepare the land for its intended use. Costs include: purchase price and related commissions, title and recording fees; legal fees; site preparation (e.g., draining water bodies; clearing brush; demolition of an old building, less any scrap proceeds received); and any obligations assumed from the seller, such as mortgages, liens and back taxes. Land improvements are depreciable assets and include: lighting; fences, watering/sprinkler systems; sidewalks, paving; and landscaping.

C. Fixed Assets

Fixed assets such as buildings, machinery, equipment, furniture and fixtures, are to be recorded at their acquisition cost. Acquisition cost is defined as the cash price, or its equivalent, plus all other costs reasonably necessary to bring it to the location and to make it ready for its intended use. Machinery and equipment charges typically include: transportation, insurance while in-transit, special foundations, installation and test runs. Building costs generally include: cash price to purchase; building permits; architect fees; engineering fees; and interest.

Property, plant, and equipment may be acquired in various ways:

1. **Purchase for Cash** Record the asset net of any trade or quantity discounts available.

2. **Purchase on Deferred Payment Plan** The fixed asset should be recorded at its cash equivalent price. If the cash equivalent price is unavailable, an imputed interest rate should be used to record the asset at the present value of the payments to be made.

3. **Purchase by Issuance of Securities** The asset should be recorded at its fair value or the fair value of the securities issued, whichever is more clearly determinable. If there is an active market for the security and the additional securities issued can be reasonably expected to be absorbed without a decline in their value, the fair value of the securities should be used. If the securities exchanged are bonds and no established market exists, the asset should be recorded at the present value of the interest and principal payments to be made, discounted by use of an implicit or "imputed" rate. If equity securities are issued and no fair value is determinable, the appraisal value of the asset acquired should be used for the recording of the transaction.

4. **Group Purchases** If several dissimilar assets are purchased for a lump sum, the total amount paid should be allocated to each individual asset on the basis of its relative fair value.

Exhibit 1 ▸ Allocation Formula

Asset Y = Total cost of assets × FV of Y / Total FV

D. Nonmonetary Transactions

Both exchanges and nonreciprocal transfers that involve little or no monetary assets or liabilities are referred to as nonmonetary transactions.

1. **Definitions**

   a. **Monetary Assets and Liabilities** Assets and liabilities whose amounts are fixed in terms of units of currency by contract or otherwise. Examples are cash, accounts and notes receivable in cash, accounts and notes payable in cash.

   b. **Nonmonetary Assets and Liabilities** Assets and liabilities other than monetary ones. Examples are inventories; investments in common stocks; property, plant and equipment; and liabilities for rent collected in advance.

   c. **Exchanges** An exchange is a reciprocal transfer between an enterprise and another entity that results in the enterprise's acquiring assets (or services) or satisfying liabilities by surrendering other assets (or services) or through incurring liabilities. A reciprocal transfer of a nonmonetary asset shall be deemed an exchange only if the transferor has no substantial continuing involvement in the transferred asset such that the usual risks and rewards of ownership of the asset are transferred. If the cash received is 25 percent or more of the fair value in the exchange, then the transaction is treated as a monetary exchange.

   d. **Nonreciprocal Transfers** Transfer of assets or services in one direction, either from an enterprise to its owners (whether or not in exchange for their ownership interests) or another entity or from owners or another entity to the enterprise. An entity's reacquisition of its outstanding stock is an example of a nonreciprocal transfer. A nonmonetary asset received in a nonreciprocal transfer should be recorded at the fair value of the asset received with a credit to *APIC-Donated Services*. Donated services should not be recorded as income/gain or added to retained earnings when received from governmental entities. Assets donated by entities other than governmental units should be included in revenue in the period of receipt.

2. **Gains and Losses** In general, accounting for nonmonetary transactions should be based on the fair values of the assets involved. The acquisition cost of a nonmonetary asset is recorded at the fair value of the asset(s) surrendered, or the FV of the asset received if more clearly evident, and gains or losses should be recognized.

3. **Valuation** Nonmonetary exchanges should be based on recorded amounts (rather than fair values) of the exchanged assets if any of the following conditions apply:

   a. Neither the fair value of the assets received nor the fair value of the assets surrendered is determinable within reasonable limits. For purposes of applying this literature, fair values should be determined by referring to estimated realizable values in cash transactions of the same (or similar) assets, quoted market prices, independent appraisals, estimated fair values of assets (or services) received in exchange for the transferred assets, and/or any other available evidence. If either party involved in the nonmonetary exchange could have elected to receive cash (rather than the nonmonetary asset) in the transaction, the amount of cash that could have been received may be evidence of the fair value of the nonmonetary assets exchanged.

   b. The transaction is an exchange of a product or property held for sale in the ordinary course of business for a product or property to be sold in the same line of business to facilitate sales to customers (other than the parties to the exchange).

   c. The transaction lacks commercial substance.

4. **Commercial Substance** A nonmonetary exchange has commercial substance if the entity's future cash flows are expected to change significantly as a result of the exchange. The acquisition is recorded at the fair value of the asset surrendered or the fair value of the asset received, whichever is more clearly determinable. Gains or losses should be recognized as the earnings process has culminated for the asset exchanged. The entity's future cash flows are expected to significantly change if any of the following criteria are met:

   a. The configuration (risk, timing, and amount) of the future cash flows of the asset(s) received differs significantly from the configuration of the future cash flows of the asset(s) transferred.

   b. The entity-specific value of the asset(s) received differs from the entity-specific value of the asset(s) transferred, and the difference is significant in relation to the fair values of the assets exchanged. (A conclusive determination related to whether a transaction or exchange involves commercial substance, in some cases, can be based on a qualitative assessment rather than detailed calculations associated with the transaction or exchange.)

   c. If monetary consideration (boot) is paid and an asset is surrendered, the asset acquired is recorded at the FV of the asset given up plus the boot paid.

Example 1 ▸ Nonmonetary Exchange With Commercial Substance

Axel Company exchanged an asset with a book value of $15,000 for an asset from Berry Company with a fair value of $18,000, in an exchange that has commercial substance.

Solution:

	Debit	Credit
Asset received	18,000	
Asset given up		15,000
Gain on Exchange		3,000
To record the exchange.		

5. **No Commercial Substance** In a nonmonetary exchange that has no commercial substance, the assets exchanged are accounted for at book value (after reduction, if appropriate, for an indicated impairment of value) of the nonmonetary asset(s) given up; therefore, no gains or losses are normally recognized on the exchange itself. However, if the asset's carrying amount exceeds its fair value when exchanged, an impairment loss should be recognized. Also, the recipient of any boot would realize some amount of gain.

Example 2 ▸ Nonmonetary Exchange of Assets—No Commercial Substance

Axel Company exchanged an asset with a fair value of $15,000 and a carrying value of $12,000 for an asset from Berry Company with a fair value of $17,000 and a carrying value of $18,000.

Required: Prepare journal entries for (a) Axel and (b) Berry.

Solutions:

(a)	Asset received	12,000	
	Asset given up		12,000
	To record the exchange.		
(b)	Loss on impairment	1, 000	
	Asset given up		1,000
	To record the reduction for impairment.		
	Asset received	17,000	
	Asset given up		17,000
	To record the exchange.		

6. **Boot** A small monetary consideration that is sometimes included in exchanges of non monetary assets, even though the exchange is essentially nonmonetary. Exchanges of nonmonetary assets that would otherwise be based on recorded amounts may include an amount of boot.

   a. The recipient of the boot realizes a gain on the exchange to the extent the monetary receipt exceeds a proportionate share of the recorded amount of the asset surrendered (i.e., the sale portion). The portion of the cost applicable to the realized amount should be based on the ratio of the monetary consideration to the total consideration received or, if more clearly evident, the fair value of the nonmonetary asset transferred.

   b. The entity paying the monetary consideration should not recognize any gain but should record the asset received at the amount of the monetary consideration paid plus the recorded amount of the nonmonetary asset surrendered.

   c. If the terms of the transaction indicate a loss, the entire loss on the exchange should be recognized.

Example 3 ▶ Nonmonetary Exchange With Boot—No Commercial Substance

Beta Company exchanges asset A to Delta Company for asset C. Asset C has a book value of $12,000.

Required: Prepare journal entries to record this exchange under the following different conditions.

(a) Asset A has a book value of $11,000 and $3,000 cash is received.

(b) Asset A has a book value of $16,000 and $3,000 cash is received.

Solutions:

(a) *Beta's journal entry:*

	Debit	Credit
Asset C (see note 2)	8,800	
Cash	3,000	
Asset A		11,000
Gain on Exchange (see note 3)		800

Delta's journal entry:

	Debit	Credit
Asset A	11,000	
Loss on exchange (see note 4)	4,000	
Asset C		12,000
Cash		3,000

(b) *Beta's journal entry:*

	Debit	Credit
Asset C (see note 5)	12,000	
Cash	3,000	
Loss on Exchange (see note 6)	1,000	
Asset A		16,000

Delta's journal entry:

	Debit	Credit
Asset A (see note 7)	15,000	
Asset C		12,000
Cash		3,000

Note 1: BV of old asset × [boot / (boot + BV of new asset)] = portion of BV sold; $11,000 × [$3,000 / ($3,000 + $12,000)] = $2,200.

Note 2: BV of old asset – portion of BV sold = carrying amount of new asset; $11,000 – $2,200 = $8,800.

Note 3: Cash received – portion of BV sold = gain on sale of old asset; $3,000 – $2,200 = $800.

Note 4: BV of new asset – [BV of old asset + cash given] = gain (loss) on exchange; $11,000 – [$12,000 + $3,000] = ($4,000).

Note 5: BV of old asset × [boot / (boot + BV of new asset)] = portion of BV sold; $16,000 × [$3,000 / ($3,000 + $12,000)] = $3,200.

Note 6: The portion of BV sold being greater than cash received indicates a loss. [BV of new asset + cash received] – BV of old asset = gain (loss) on exchange; [$12,000 + $3,000] – $16,000 = $1,000.
If a loss is indicated, the entire amount of loss is recognized ($1,000).

Note 7: BV of new asset – [BV of old asset + cash given] = gain (loss) on exchange; $16,000 – [$12,000 + $3,000] = $1,000.
The entity paying the boot does not recognize gain, but instead records the asset received at the amount of cash given plus recorded amount of asset given.

Exhibit 2 ▸ Accounting for Nonmonetary Exchanges

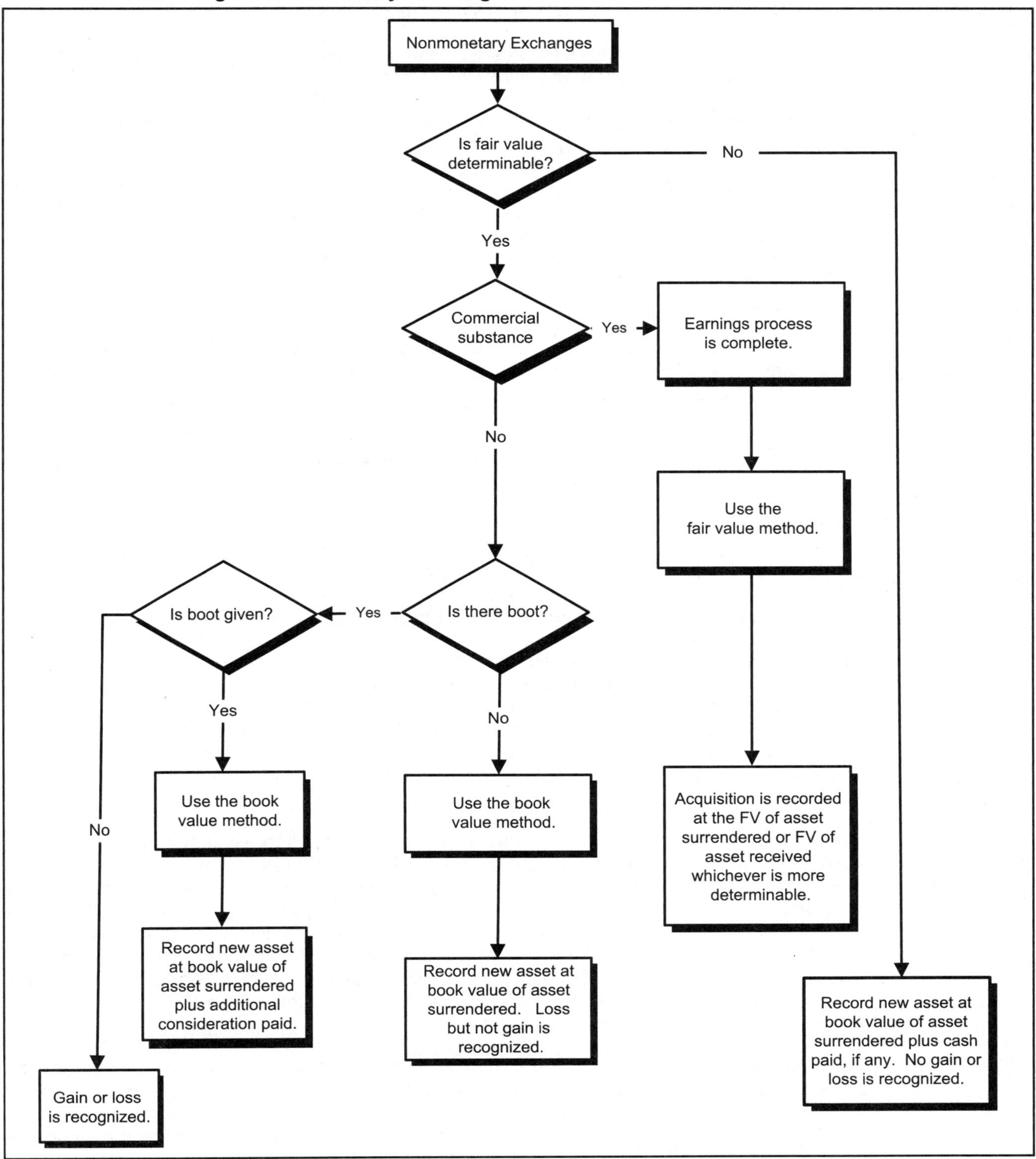

7. **Exceptions** The accounting guidance for nonmonetary transactions does not apply to the following transactions (in the following circumstances):

   a. An exchange of a business for a business or exchange of a part of an operating interest owned for a part of an operating interest owned by another party, a joint venture, in the oil and gas industry. This also includes a pooling of assets in a joint undertaking intended to find, develop, or produce oil or gas from a particular property or group of properties.

   b. Transfers of nonmonetary asset solely between companies (or persons) under common control. Examples include transfers between a parent company and subsidiaries of the parent; transfers between subsidiaries of the same parent; and transfers between a corporate joint venture and its owners. This also includes transfers of assets to an entity for an equity (ownership) interest in that entity. A transfer of a financial asset is also excluded.

   c. Acquired nonmonetary assets (or services) on issuance of the capital stock of an enterprise. This also includes stock that was issued or received in stock dividends and stock splits.

   d. Involuntary conversions of nonmonetary assets (for example, as a result of total or partial destruction, theft, seizure, or condemnation) to monetary assets that are then reinvested in other nonmonetary assets.

E. Self-Constructed

The cost of assets constructed for the use of the business should include all directly related costs, such as direct materials, direct labor, and additional overhead incurred. Interest costs incurred during the construction period must be capitalized. The interest cost capitalized is also a part of the cost of acquiring the asset and is written off over the estimated useful life of the asset.

1. **Eligible Assets** Assets qualifying for interest capitalization include assets constructed or produced for self-use on a repetitive basis, assets acquired for self-use through arrangements requiring down payments or progress payments, and assets constructed or produced as discrete projects for sale or lease (e.g., ships or real estate developments). Assets not qualifying for interest capitalization include inventories that are routinely manufactured on a repetitive basis, assets in use or ready for use, and assets not in use and not being prepared for use.

2. **Interest** The amount of interest cost to be capitalized is the interest cost incurred during the acquisition period that could have been avoided if expenditures for the asset had not been made. Interest "earned" by the entity is not offset to interest costs incurred in determining the amount of interest to be capitalized. If a specific interest rate is associated with the asset, that rate should be used to the extent that the average accumulated expenditures on the asset do not exceed the amount borrowed at the specific rate. If the average accumulated expenditures on an asset exceed the amount of specific new borrowings associated with the asset, the excess should be capitalized at the weighted average of the rates applicable to other borrowings of the enterprise.

3. **Capitalization Limits** The interest rate determined above is applied to the *average* amount of accumulated expenditures for the asset during the period. For example, if construction of a qualifying asset begins in January and the accumulated expenditures at year-end amount to $400,000, the interest rate is applied to the $200,000 average accumulated expenditure [($0 + $400,000) / 2]. The total interest cost capitalized in a period may **not** exceed the total interest cost incurred during that period. Interest *earned* by the enterprise during the period is **not** offset to interest costs incurred in determining the amount of interest to be capitalized.

Example 4 ▸ Capitalizing Interest on Assets Constructed for Self-Use

On January 1, year 2, Expansions Inc., borrowed $1,000,000 to finance the construction of a warehouse for its own use. The loan was to be repaid in 10 equal payments of $199,250, including interest of 15%, beginning on January 1, year 3. No other loans are presently outstanding. The total cost of labor, materials, and overhead assigned to the warehouse was $1,000,000. Construction was completed on December 30, year 2. The warehouse is depreciated using the straight-line method over an estimated useful life of 20 years, with no salvage value. The proceeds borrowed were invested in short-term liquid assets until needed to pay construction expenditures, yielding $24,000 interest income.

Required: Determine the capitalized cost of the asset, as of December 30, year 2, the interest expense for year 2 (assume no other debt outstanding), and the depreciation expense for year 3.

Solution:

Materials, labor, overhead, etc.	$1,000,000
Capitalized interest cost, [($0 + $1,000,000) / 2] × 0.15	75,000
Capitalized cost of asset	$1,075,000
Total interest cost incurred, year 1 ($1,000,000 × 0.15)	$ 150,000
Less capitalized interest cost	(75,000)
Interest expense, year 2	$ 75,000
Capitalized cost of asset	$1,075,000
Estimated useful life	/ 20
Depreciation expense, year 3	$ 53,750

Example 5 ▸ Partial Amount Borrowed

The same as in Example 1, except that Expansions Inc., needed to borrow only $300,000 (at 15%) to finance construction of the $1,000,000 warehouse. The remaining cash was provided from operations and from the sale of miscellaneous investments. During all of year 2, Expansions' only other long-term liabilities consisted of $2,000,000, 10%, 20-year bonds (sold at par in year 1) and a $500,000, 14%, interest-bearing note payable due in three years.

Required: Determine the amount of interest that should be capitalized in year 2.

Solution: Total interest cost incurred during the year is ($300,000 × 15%) + ($2,000,000 × 10%) + ($500,000 × 14%) = $315,000.

Accumulated average expenditures ($0 + $1,000,000) / 2	$500,000
Interest on new borrowings specifically associated with asset ($300,000 × 0.15)	$ 45,000
Weighted average rate on other borrowings, applied to accumulated average expenditures in excess of $300,000 ($200,000 × 0.108*)	21,600
Total interest cost capitalized during year 2	$ 66,600

*Computation of weighted average rate:

$$\frac{\text{Total interest}}{\text{Total principal}} = \frac{(\$2{,}000{,}000 \times 10\%) + (\$500{,}000 \times 14\%)}{\$2{,}000{,}000 + \$500{,}000} = 0.108$$

F. Donated

Donated assets should be recorded at their fair value along with any incidental costs incurred. When the asset is received from a governmental entity, no income is recognized, and the offsetting credit is to an owners' equity account, *Additional Paid-In Capital—Donated Assets.* Assets donated by entities other than governmental units are included in revenue in the period of receipt.

III. Subsequent Measurement

A. Betterments

The continued use of fixed assets will require further outlays to maintain their given level of services. Costs that extend the useful service life of the asset, increase or improve its output rate, or lower production costs are known as betterments or improvements and are capitalized (i.e., added to the assets' book value). Additionally, if an outlay will provide a service benefit beyond the current period, it is also a capital expenditure and is recorded as an asset.

B. Repairs and Maintenance

Expenditures that benefit only the current period (such as maintenance and repairs) are charged to expense as incurred and are referred to as revenue expenditures. The concept of materiality influences the decision whether to capitalize expenditures. Most companies expense all items costing less than a certain amount, regardless of their estimated useful lives. This is permissible as long as the total effect is immaterial **and** this policy is consistently applied.

Exhibit 3 ▸ Summary of Costs Subsequent to Acquisition of PP&E

Type of Expenditure	Expense	Capitalize	Comments
Additions		X	
Betterment and replacement (book value known)		X	• Remove cost and accumulated depreciation of old asset • Recognize any gain or loss • Capitalize replacement
Betterment and replacement (book value unknown)		X	• If the useful life is extended, debit accumulated depreciation for the cost of the replacement • If productivity is increased, capitalize the cost of the replacement
Ordinary repairs	X		
Extraordinary repairs		X	

IV. Cost Recovery

A. Depreciation

Depreciation is the process of allocating the depreciable cost of fixed assets over their estimated useful lives in a systematic and rational manner. This process matches the depreciable cost of the asset with revenues generated from its use. Depreciable cost is the capitalized cost less its estimated residual (salvage) value. Depreciation accounting recognizes both physical and functional causes of declining service potential. Physical causes include wear and tear, deterioration, and decay. Examples of functional factors are obsolescence and inadequacy. Depreciation is recorded by charging expense (or manufacturing overhead) and crediting accumulated depreciation. Property, plant, and equipment is not written up to reflect appraisal, market, or current values above cost. Various depreciation methods are used.

1. **Straight-Line Depreciation (SL)** The straight-line depreciation method is a fixed charge method where an equal amount of depreciable cost is allocated to each period. This method should be used when approximately the same amount of an asset's service potential is used up each period. If the reasons for the decline in service potential are unclear, then the selection of the straight-line method could be influenced by the ease of recordkeeping, its use for similar assets, and its use by others in the industry.

Exhibit 4 ▸ SL Depreciation Formula

$$\text{SL Depreciation} = \frac{\text{Historical Cost (HC)} - \text{Salvage Value (SV)}}{\text{Estimated Useful Life (EUL)}}$$

2. **Accelerated Depreciation** The rationale for using accelerated depreciation methods is based on two assumptions. First, an asset is more productive in the earlier years of its estimated useful life. Therefore, larger depreciation charges in the earlier years would be matched against the larger revenues generated in the earlier years. Second, an asset may become technologically obsolete prior to the end of its originally estimated useful life. The risk associated with estimated long-term cash flows is greater than the risk associated with near-term cash flows. Accelerated depreciation recognizes this condition.

   a. **Double-Declining-Balance (DDB)** A rate of depreciation twice the SL rate is applied to the *book value* (i.e., declining balance) of the asset to obtain the depreciation expense for the period. (Note that the SV is not used in the calculation of depreciation expense under DDB except as a lower bound for the asset's BV.)

   Exhibit 5 ▸ DDB Formula

   $$\textit{Depreciation for current period} = \frac{2}{\text{EUL}} \times (\text{HC} - \text{AD})$$

   Where: AD = Accumulated depreciation

   b. **Fixed-Percentage-of-Declining-Balance** A fixed percentage (usually 125 percent to 175 percent of the SL rate) is applied to the decreasing book value of the asset. It is similar to the DDB method in b., above, except that instead of double (i.e., 200 percent) the SL rate, a lower percentage is used.

   Example 6 ▸ Double-Declining-Balance Depreciation

Historical Cost (HC)	$1,200
Salvage Value (SV)	$ 100
Estimated Useful Life (EUL)	3 years

   Required: Calculate the depreciation using the DDB method.

   Solution: Original depreciable base = $1,200

	Fraction	×	Depreciable base	=	Depreciation Charge
Year 1	2/3		$1,200		$800
Year 2	2/3		$1,200 – $800 = $400		$267
Year 3	2/3		$1,200 – $1,067 = $133		$ 33*

   * May not depreciate below the salvage value ($133 × 2/3 = $89)

   c. **Sum-of-the-Years'-Digits (SYD)** A decreasing fraction is applied each year to the depreciable base (i.e., HC – SV). The denominator of the fraction is obtained by adding the number of years of EUL at the *beginning* of the asset's life (n). For instance, the denominator for an asset with n years would be computed as [n + (n – 1) + (n – 2) + ... + 1]. The use of the equation [n(n+1)/2] provides the same result and is more practical when n is a large number. Once determined, the denominator remains unchanged for all future computations. The numerator of the fraction is given by the remaining years of EUL, including the current year, and thus it decreases with time.

Example 7 ▸ Sum-of-the-Years'-Digits Depreciation

Historical Cost (HC)	$1,000
Salvage Value (SV)	$ 100
Estimated Useful Life (EUL)	3 years

Required: Calculate the depreciation using the SYD method.

Solution: Depreciable base (HC – SV): $1,000 – 100 = $900

Fraction denominator (remains unchanged): 3 + 2 + 1 = 6, or 3(3 + 1) / 2 = 6

Fraction numerator: Remaining years of life at the beginning of each period: 3, 2, 1

	Fraction	×	Depreciable base	=	Depreciation charge
Year 1	3/6		$900		$450
Year 2	2/6		900		300
Year 3	1/6		900		150

3. **Multiple-Asset Depreciation** In order to reduce the number of computations needed, assets are sometimes depreciated in groups, rather than individually. Two types are used.

   a. **Group Depreciation** Homogeneous assets having similar service lives are lumped together and one depreciation rate is applied to the entire group. Retirements are recorded by a credit to the asset for the amount of cost and a debit to accumulated depreciation for the same amount less any proceeds received in disposition. Note that **no** gains or losses are recognized.

   b. **Composite Depreciation** Similar to the group system but applied to groups of assets having a wider range of service lives. The composite rate is determined by calculating the annual depreciation expense for each asset, adding up these amounts, and expressing this as a percentage of the total cost of all the assets.

Example 8 ▸ Composite Depreciation

Asset class	Asset cost	–	Salvage value	=	Depr'n. base	/	EUL (yrs.)	=	SL Depr'n.
A	$120,000		$20,000		$100,000		10		$10,000
B	60,000		10,000		50,000		5		10,000
C	30,000		5,000		25,000		5		5,000
	$210,000		$35,000		$175,000				$25,000

Composite depreciation rate: ($25,000 / $210,000) = 11.905%
Composite life: ($175,000 / $25,000) = 7 years

The annual composite depreciation charge for the group of assets above would be $25,000 ($210,000 × 11.905%) and, assuming no additions or retirements, the group would be depreciated to the salvage value of its assets at the end of their seven-year average life. Additions are debited to the group at cost. Retirements are recorded by a credit to the asset account, a debit to cash or receivable for the consideration received, and the balance is debited to accumulated depreciation. No gains or losses are recognized.

4. **Variable Charge Methods** Depreciation is based upon the actual **usage** of the asset. Both of the two commonly used methods are represented by the same formula.

Exhibit 6 ▸ Variable Charge Depreciation Formula

$$\text{Depreciation expense} = \frac{HC - SV}{\text{Total expected output or usage}} \times \text{Current output or use}$$

   a. **Service Hours** The expected useful life (EUL) of the asset is determined on the basis of service hours, rather than years. Depreciation expense for the current period is a proportion of current hours of service to EUL (in service hours).

   b. **Units-of-Output** The EUL is stated in units of output, rather than years.

5. **Fractional-Year Depreciation** Assets are seldom acquired or disposed of at the exact date of the beginning or the end of the entity's accounting period. Fractional-year depreciation is generally accounted for under one of three different approaches.

   a. Depreciation for one entire year in the year of acquisition; none in the year of disposal.

   b. Half-year's depreciation in the year of acquisition and the year of disposal.

   c. Proportional depreciation based on the number of months the asset was used, both for the year of acquisition and disposal. When assets are acquired or retired during the year, the amount of depreciation is determined by allocating the annual depreciation based on the number of months that the asset was held during the period.

B. Depletion

Depletion refers to periodic allocation of acquisition costs of natural resources. A per-unit depletion rate is computed by dividing the depletable base of the natural resource (i.e., purchase price, exploring, drilling, and other development costs), less any estimated residual value, by the estimated number of units of the resource available for extraction. This unit rate is applied to the number of units extracted during the period to obtain the total amount of depletion for the period (i.e., inventoried and expensed). The unit rate is applied to the number of units sold during the period to determine the amount of depletion to be recognized as an expense.

V. Impairment

A. Categories

Assets are divided into three categories of impaired assets: held for use, held for disposal by sale, and held for disposal other than by sale. An asset group is a group of assets and liabilities that represents the unit of accounting for a long-lived asset to be held for use.

1. **Held for Sale** Criteria to determine when long-lived assets are held for sale, include requirements that (a) the asset is available for prompt sale as is, subject only to customary and usual sales terms for such assets; and (b) the asset sale is probable, and generally, to be completed within 12 months. The same accounting model is used for all long-lived assets to be sold, whether previously held and used or newly acquired. A long-lived asset to be sold is measured at the lower of its book or fair value less cost to sell and its depreciation (or amortization) discontinues. Therefore, discontinued operations are no longer valued at net realizable value (NRV) and future operating losses are no longer recognized before they occur.

2. **Assets Held for Use** Impairment is the condition that exists when the carrying amount of a long-lived asset, or asset group, exceeds its fair value. An impairment loss shall be recognized only if the carrying amount of a long-lived asset is not recoverable and exceeds its fair value. The carrying amount (book value) is not recoverable if it exceeds the sum of the undiscounted cash flows expected to result from the use and eventual disposition of the asset. That assessment shall be based on the carrying amount of the asset at the date it is tested for recoverability. A long-lived asset shall be tested for recoverability whenever events or changes in circumstances indicate that its carrying amount may not be recoverable. The amount of an impairment loss is the difference between an asset's book and fair value. The new book value is used as a basis for depreciation. Subsequent reversal of a previously recognized impairment loss is prohibited. Goodwill need not be allocated to long-lived assets to be tested for impairment.

Example 9 ▸ Impairment of Long-Lived Asset

In Z Co.'s review of long-lived assets to be held and used, an asset with a cost of $10,000 and accumulated depreciation of $5,500 was determined to have a fair value of $3,500.

Required: Determine the amount of impairment loss to be recognized if the expected future (undiscounted) cash flows is:

(a) $5,000

(b) $3,000

Solution a: The carrying value of $4,500 is less than the future cash flows of $5,000, so no loss is recognized even though the carrying value is greater than the fair value.

Solution b: The amount of impairment loss to be recognized is determined by calculating the difference between the carrying amount and the fair value. The carrying value of $4,500 is greater than future cash flows of $3,000 so an impairment loss of $1,000 is recognized.

3. **Disposals Other Than by Sale** Long-lived assets that will be abandoned, exchanged for a similar productive asset (exchanged), or distributed to owners in a spin-off (distributed) are required to be considered held and used until disposal. Also required is a revision in the depreciable life of a long-lived asset to be abandoned or recognition of an impairment loss when a long-lived asset is exchanged or distributed if book value exceeds fair value.

B. Classification

1. **Retroactive Classification** Retroactive classification of the asset is prohibited when the criteria for classification as held for sale are met before financial statement issuance, but after the balance sheet date.

2. **Reclassification** If a long-lived asset classified as held for sale is reclassified as held and used, the reclassified asset is valued at the lower of (a) fair value at the date that the asset is reclassified as held and used; or (b) book value before being classified as held for sale, adjusted for any depreciation (or amortization) that would have been recognized had the asset classification continuously been held and used.

VI. Disposal

A. Voluntary

Accounting for the voluntary disposal of an operational asset usually involves crediting the asset account for the cost of the asset, removing the accumulated depreciation by a debit to that account, debiting the appropriate account for any proceeds received, and recognizing a gain or loss on disposal (balancing figure). (Exceptions to this treatment are when multiple-asset depreciation methods are used. If the disposal qualifies as an exchange of nonmonetary assets, accounting should follow the guidelines of an acquisition by exchange.)

B. Involuntary

Property, plant, and equipment may be totally or partially destroyed by storm, fire, flood, or other similar causes. Damaged assets should be written down to their remaining value in use, if any, and a loss recognized in the current period.

1. **Casualty Losses** Property, plant, and equipment are usually insured against casualty losses. A gain or loss should be recognized depending on whether the amount due from the insurer exceeds the carrying amount of the loss.

2. **Recognition of Gain or Loss Regardless of Replacement** A gain or loss on the involuntary conversion (e.g., due to casualty, condemnation, theft, etc.) of a nonmonetary asset should be recognized even if the proceeds received as a result of the involuntary conversion (e.g., insurance settlement, condemnation award, etc.) are reinvested in a replacement nonmonetary asset. Removal and clean-up costs are used to determine the gain or loss recognized on the involuntary conversion. Incidental costs incurred in the acquisition of replacement property are capitalized as costs of acquiring the replacement property (i.e., they do not affect the gain or loss recognized on involuntary conversion).

Post Exam—Your Score

In each testing window, the AICPA transmits scores to NASBA in two waves—the first before the end of testing and the second after testing ends. First wave scores belong to candidates who tested in the first month of the window and were presented with content that does not require additional psychometric analysis. Second wave scores belong to candidates who tested in the second month of the window as well as to those who tested earlier but whose content required further analysis.

Please note that scores are NOT released by jurisdiction in a specific order, and also that the scores of candidates who test on the same day may well be reported at different times during the scoring cycle. For additional information about score release or score report content, contact your board of accountancy or its designated agent. (The AICPA does not provide score information to candidates.)

You can also contact your board of accountancy, or its designated agent, for instructions on requesting a score review. A score review is the verification of a candidate's Uniform CPA Examination score. It involves making certain that the approved answer key was used and that it was applied correctly. It is not an opportunity to "find additional points" or to have new responses considered.

Because all scores undergo several quality control checks before they are reported, a score review seldom results in a score change. However, the score review option is available to candidates who would like to have their scores checked one more time. Note that the option to apply for a score review is available only for a short period of time after your score has been reported to you and requires a fee be paid to request it within that deadline.

In the jurisdictions that allow appeals, the appeal process provides Uniform CPA Examination candidates with the opportunity to appeal failing scores. You should consider requesting an appeal only if you want to review your incorrect responses because you believe that there is a multiple-choice question or objective simulation problem that you would like to challenge.

Contact your board of accountancy, or its designated agent, to determine whether the appeal option is available in your jurisdiction and, if it is, to obtain detailed instructions. In order to qualify for an appeal, you will be required to submit a formal request, obtain your board's approval, and pay the required fee. Note that the option to apply for an appeal is available only for a short period of time after your score has been reported to you.

CHAPTER 4—PROPERTY, PLANT & EQUIPMENT

Problem 4-1 MULTIPLE-CHOICE QUESTIONS

1. Cart Co. purchased an office building and the land on which it is located for $750,000 cash and an existing $250,000 mortgage. For realty tax purposes, the property is assessed at $960,000, 60% of which is allocated to the building. At what amount should Cart record the building?

   a. $500,000
   b. $576,000
   c. $600,000
   d. $960,000 (R/06, FAR, #3, 8070)

2. Oak Co., a newly formed corporation, incurred the following expenditures related to land and building:

County assessment for sewer lines	$ 2,500
Title search fees	625
Cash paid for land with building to be demolished	135,000
Excavation for construction of basement	21,000
Removal of old building $21,000 less salvage of $5,000	16,000

   At what amount should Oak record the land?

   a. $138,125
   b. $153,500
   c. $154,125
   d. $175,625 (R/07, FAR, #7, 8328)

3. Talton Co. installed new assembly line production equipment at a cost of $185,000. Talton had to rearrange the assembly line and remove a wall to install the equipment. The rearrangement cost $12,000 and the wall removal cost $3,000. The rearrangement did not increase the life of the assembly line but it did make it more efficient. What amount of these costs should be capitalized by Talton?

   a. $185,000
   b. $188,000
   c. $197,000
   d. $200,000 (R/10, FAR, #33, 9333)

4. Young Corp. purchased equipment by making a down payment of $4,000 and issuing a note payable for $18,000. A payment of $6,000 is to be made at the end of each year for three years. The applicable rate of interest is 8%. The present value of an ordinary annuity factor for three years at 8% is 2.58, and the present value for the future amount of a single sum of one dollar for three years at 8% is .735. Shipping charges for the equipment were $2,000, and installation charges were $3,500. What is the capitalized cost of the equipment?

   a. $19,480
   b. $21,480
   c. $24,980
   d. $27,500 (R/09, FAR, #4, 8754)

5. Pine City owned a vacant plot of land zoned for industrial use. Pine gave this land to Medi Corp. solely as an incentive for Medi to build a factory on the site. The land had a fair value of $300,000 at the date of the gift. This nonmonetary transaction should be reported by Medi as

   a. Extraordinary income
   b. Additional paid-in capital
   c. A credit to retained earnings
   d. A memorandum entry (11/91, PII, #9, 2457)

6. Bensol Co. and Sable Co. exchanged similar trucks with fair values in excess of carrying amounts. In addition, Bensol paid Sable to compensate for the difference in truck values. As a consequence of the exchange, which lacked commercial substance, Sable recognizes:

   a. A gain equal to the difference between the fair value and carrying amount of the truck given up.
   b. A gain determined by the proportion of cash received to the total consideration.
   c. A loss determined by the proportion of cash received to the total consideration.
   d. Neither a gain nor a loss. (R/93, FAR #37, 4542)

7. Which of the following statements describes the proper accounting for losses when nonmonetary assets are exchanged for other nonmonetary assets?

   a. A loss is recognized immediately, because assets received should not be valued at more than their cash equivalent price.
   b. A loss is deferred so that the asset received in the exchange is properly valued.
   c. A loss, if any, which is unrelated to the determination of the amount of the asset received should be recorded.
   d. A loss can occur only when assets are sold or disposed of in a monetary transaction.
   (R/09, FAR, #46, 8796)

8. Which of the following statements correctly describes the proper accounting for nonmonetary exchanges that are deemed to have commercial substance?

   a. It defers any gains and losses
   b. It defers losses to the extent of any gains
   c. It recognizes gains and losses immediately
   d. It defers gains and recognizes losses immediately (R/11, FAR, #49, 9899)

9. Dahl Co. traded a delivery van and $5,000 cash for a newer van owned by West Corp. The transaction had commercial substance. The following information relates to the values of the vans on the exchange date:

	Carrying value	Fair value
Old van	$30,000	$45,000
New van	40,000	50,000

   Dahl's income tax rate is 30%. What amounts should Dahl report as gain on exchange of the vans?

   a. $15,000
   b. $ 1,000
   c. $ 700
   d. $0 (11/92, PI, #21, amended, 3279)

10. On January 1, Feld traded a delivery truck and paid $10,000 cash for a tow truck owned by Baker. The delivery truck had an original cost of $140,000, accumulated depreciation of $80,000, and an estimated fair value of $90,000. Feld estimated the fair value of Baker's tow truck to be $100,000. The transaction had commercial substance. What amount of gain should be recognized by Feld?

    a. $0
    b. $ 3,000
    c. $10,000
    d. $30,000 (R/09, FAR, #21, 8771)

11. Campbell Corp. exchanged delivery trucks with Highway, Inc. Campbell's truck originally cost $23,000, its accumulated depreciation was $20,000, and its fair value was $5,000. Highway's truck originally cost $23,500, its accumulated depreciation was $19,900, and its fair value was $5,700. Campbell also paid Highway $700 in cash as part of the transaction. The transaction lacks commercial substance. What amount is the new book value for the truck Campbell received?

    a. $5,700
    b. $5,000
    c. $3,700
    d. $3,000 (R/11, FAR, #50, 9900)

12. Yola Co. and Zaro Co. are fuel oil distributors. To facilitate the delivery of oil to their customers, Yola and Zaro exchanged ownership of 1,200 barrels of oil without physically moving the oil. Yola paid Zaro $30,000 to compensate for a difference in the grade of oil. On the date of the exchange, cost and market values of the oil were as follows:

	Yola Co.	Zaro Co.
Cost	$100,000	$126,000
Market values	120,000	150,000

In Zaro's income statement, what amount of gain should be reported from the exchange of the oil?

a. $0
b. $ 4,800
c. $24,000
d. $30,000 (5/92, PII, #11, 2643)

13. During the year, Bay Co. constructed machinery for its own use and for sale to customers. Bank loans financed these assets both during construction and after construction was complete. How much of the interest incurred should be reported as interest expense in the year-end income statement?

	Interest incurred for machinery for own use	Interest incurred for machinery held for sale
a.	All interest incurred	All interest incurred
b.	All interest incurred	Interest incurred after completion
c.	Interest incurred after completion	Interest incurred after completion
d.	Interest incurred after completion	All interest incurred

(5/91, Theory, #23, amended, 1788)

14. Sun Co. was constructing fixed assets that qualified for interest capitalization. Sun had the following outstanding debt issuances during the entire year of construction:

$6,000,000 face value, 8% interest
$8,000,000 face value, 9% interest

None of the borrowings were specified for the construction of the qualified fixed asset. Average expenditures for the year were $1,000,000. What interest rate should Sun use to calculate capitalized interest on the construction?

a. 8.00%
b. 8.50%
c. 8.57%
d. 9.00% (R/10, FAR, #17, 9317)

15. Cole Co. began constructing a building for its own use in January of the current year. During the year, Cole incurred interest of $50,000 on specific construction debt, and $20,000 on other borrowings. Interest computed on the weighted-average amount of accumulated expenditures for the building during the year was $40,000. What amount of interest cost should Cole capitalize?

a. $20,000
b. $40,000
c. $50,000
d. $70,000 (5/94, FAR, #17, amended, 4832)

16. On January 2 of the current year, Cruises, Inc. borrowed $3 million at a rate of 10% for three years and began construction of a cruise ship. The note states that annual payments of principal and interest in the amount of $1.3 million are due every December 31. Cruises used all proceeds as a down payment for construction of a new cruise ship that is to be delivered two years after start of construction. What should Cruise report as interest expense related to the note in its income statement for the second year?

a. $0
b. $300,000
c. $600,000
d. $900,000 (R/05, FAR, #44, 7788)

17. Which of the following is an example of an asset that qualifies for interest cost capitalization?
    a. Asset constructed or produced as a discrete project for sale or lease, such as a ship
    b. Item of inventory routinely manufactured on a repetitive basis
    c. Asset in use or ready for use
    d. Asset not in use and not being prepared for use (Editor, 89547)

18. During the previous year, Yvo Corp. installed a production assembly line to manufacture furniture. In the current year, Yvo purchased a new machine and rearranged the assembly line to install this machine. The rearrangement did not increase the estimated useful life of the assembly line, but it did result in significantly more efficient production. The following expenditures were incurred in connection with this project:

Machine	$75,000
Labor to install machine	14,000
Parts added in rearranging the assembly line to provide future benefits	40,000
Labor and overhead to rearrange the assembly line	18,000

What amount of the above expenditures should be capitalized in the current year?
    a. $147,000
    b. $107,000
    c. $ 89,000
    d. $ 75,000 (11/90, PII, #4, amended, 0934)

19. Dell Printing Co. incurred the following costs for one of its printing presses:

Purchase of collating and stapling attachment	$84,000
Installation of attachment	36,000
Replacement parts for overhaul of press	26,000
Labor and overhead in connection with overhaul	14,000

The overhaul resulted in a significant increase in production. Neither the attachment nor the overhaul increased the estimated useful life of the press. What amount of the above costs should be capitalized?
    a. $0
    b. $ 84,000
    c. $120,000
    d. $160,000 (5/90, PI, #16, amended, 0940)

20. A building suffered uninsured water and related damage. The damaged portion of the building was refurbished with upgraded materials. The cost and related accumulated depreciation of the damaged portion are identifiable. To account for these events, the owner should
    a. Capitalize the cost of refurbishing and record a loss in the current period equal to the carrying amount of the damaged portion of the building
    b. Capitalize the cost of refurbishing by adding the cost to the carrying amount of the building
    c. Record a loss in the current period equal to the cost of refurbishing and continue to depreciate the original cost of the building
    d. Record a loss in the current period equal to the sum of the cost of refurbishing and the carrying amount of the damaged portion of the building (11/90, Theory, #13, 1794)

21. A manufacturing firm purchased used equipment for $135,000. The original owners estimated that the residual value of the equipment was $10,000. The carrying amount of the equipment was $120,000 when ownership transferred. The new owners estimate that the expected remaining useful life of the equipment was 10 years, with a salvage value of $15,000. What amount represents the depreciable base used by the new owners?
    a. $105,000
    b. $110,000
    c. $120,000
    d. $125,000 (R/08, FAR, #9, 8564)

22. On January 1, year 1, Crater Inc. purchased equipment having an estimated salvage value equal to 20% of its original cost at the end of a 10-year life. The equipment was sold December 31, year 5, for 50% of its original cost. If the equipment's disposition resulted in a reported loss, which of the following depreciation methods did Crater use?

    a. Double-declining-balance
    b. Sum-of-the-years'-digits
    c. Straight-line
    d. Composite (5/93, Theory, #27, amended, 4215)

23. A depreciable asset has an estimated 15% salvage value. Under which of the following methods, properly applied, would the accumulated depreciation equal the original cost at the end of the asset's estimated useful life?

	Straight-line	Double-declining balance
a.	Yes	Yes
b.	Yes	No
c.	No	Yes
d.	No	No

(R/08, FAR, #34, 8589)

24. Carr, Inc. purchased equipment for $100,000 on January 1, year 2. The equipment had an estimated 10-year useful life and a $15,000 salvage value. Carr uses the 200% declining balance depreciation method. In its year 3 income statement, what amount should Carr report as depreciation expense for the equipment?

    a. $13,600
    b. $16,000
    c. $17,000
    d. $20,000 (R/09, FAR, #11, 8761)

25. A fixed asset with a five-year estimated useful life and no residual value is sold at the end of the second year of its useful life. How would using the sum-of-the-years'-digits method of depreciation instead of the double-declining-balance method of depreciation affect a gain or loss on the sale of the fixed asset?

	Gain	Loss
a.	Decrease	Decrease
b.	Decrease	Increase
c.	Increase	Decrease
d.	Increase	Increase

(5/90, Theory, #20, 1808)

26. Spiro Corp. uses the sum-of-the-years'-digits method to depreciate equipment purchased in January of the current year for $20,000. The estimated salvage value of the equipment is $2,000 and the estimated useful life is four years. What should Spiro report as the asset's carrying amount as of December 31 in the third year?

    a. $1,800
    b. $2,000
    c. $3,800
    d. $4,500 (R/99, FAR, #7, amended, 6776)

27. Which of the following uses the straight-line depreciation method?

	Group depreciation	Composite depreciation
a.	No	No
b.	Yes	No
c.	Yes	Yes
d.	No	Yes

(5/93, Theory, #28, 4216)

28. A company using the composite depreciation method for its fleet of trucks, cars, and campers retired one of its trucks and received cash from a salvage company. The net carrying amount of these composite asset accounts would be decreased by the

    a. Cash proceeds received and original cost of the truck
    b. Cash proceeds received
    c. Original cost of the truck less the cash proceeds
    d. Original cost of the truck (5/88, Theory, #9, 1833)

29. On January 3, Quarry Co. purchased a manufacturing machine for $864,000. The machine had an estimated eight-year useful life and a $72,000 estimated salvage value. Quarry expects to manufacture 1,800,000 units over the life of the machine. During the year, Quarry manufactured 300,000 units. Quarry uses the units-of-production depreciation method. In its December 31 balance sheet, what amount of accumulated depreciation should Quarry report for the machine?

    a. $ 99,000
    b. $108,000
    c. $132,000
    d. $144,000 (R/03, FAR, #15, amended 7617)

30. Turtle Co. purchased equipment on January 2, year 1, for $50,000. The equipment had an estimated five-year service life. Turtle's policy for five-year assets is to use the 200% double-declining depreciation method for the first two years of the asset's life, and then switch to the straight-line depreciation method. In its December 31, year 3, balance sheet, what amount should Turtle report as accumulated depreciation for equipment?

    a. $30,000
    b. $38,000
    c. $39,200
    d. $42,000 (R/94, FAR # 18, 4833)

31. In January, Vorst Co. purchased a mineral mine for $2,640,000 with removable ore estimated at 1,200,000 tons. After it has extracted all the ore, Vorst will be required by law to restore the land to its original condition at an estimated cost of $180,000. Vorst believes it will be able to sell the property afterwards for $300,000. During the year, Vorst incurred $360,000 of development costs preparing the mine for production and removed and sold 60,000 tons of ore. In its year-end income statement, what amount should Vorst report as depletion?

    a. $135,000
    b. $144,000
    c. $150,000
    d. $159,000 (5/95, FAR, #36, amended, 5572)

32. Cantor Co. purchased a coal mine for $2,000,000. It cost $500,000 to prepare the coal mine for extraction of the coal. It was estimated that 750,000 tons of coal would be extracted from the mine during its useful life. Cantor planned to sell the property for $100,000 at the end of its useful life. During the current year, 15,000 tons of coal were extracted and sold. What would be Cantor's depletion amount per ton for the current year?

    a. $2.50
    b. $2.60
    c. $3.20
    d. $3.30 (R/06, FAR, #25, 8092)

33. Which of the following conditions must exist in order for an impairment loss to be recognized?

    I. The carrying amount of the long-lived asset is less than its fair value.
    II. The carrying amount of the long-lived asset is not recoverable.

    a. I only
    b. II only
    c. Both I and II
    d. Neither I nor II (R/06, FAR, #19, 8086)

34. Four years ago on January 2, Randall Co. purchased a long-lived asset. The purchase price of the asset was $250,000, with no salvage value. The estimated useful life of the asset was 10 years. Randall used the straight-line method to calculate depreciation expense. An impairment loss on the asset of $30,000 was recognized on December 31 of the current year. The estimated useful life of the asset at December 31 of the current year did not change. What amount should Randall report as depreciation expense in its income statement for the next year?

    a. $20,000
    b. $22,000
    c. $25,000
    d. $30,000 (R/11, FAR, #18, 9868)

35. Last year, Katt Co. reduced the carrying amount of its long-lived assets used in operations from $120,000 to $100,000, in connection with its annual impairment review. During the current year, Katt determined that the fair value of the same assets had increased to $130,000. What amount should Katt record as restoration of previously recognized impairment loss in the current year's financial statements?

    a. $0
    b. $10,000
    c. $20,000
    d. $30,000 (R/10, FAR, #6, 9306)

36. When should a long-lived asset be tested for recoverability?

    a. When external financial statements are being prepared
    b. When events or changes in circumstances indicate that its carrying amount may **not** be recoverable
    c. When the asset's carrying amount is **less** than its fair value
    d. When the asset's fair value has decreased, and the decrease is judged to be permanent (R/10, FAR, #35, 9335)

37. When equipment is retired, accumulated depreciation is debited for the original cost less any residual recovery under which of the following depreciation methods?

	Composite depreciation	Group depreciation
a.	No	No
b.	No	Yes
c.	Yes	No
d.	Yes	Yes

(R/84, 1888)

38. Newt Co. sold a warehouse and used the proceeds to acquire a new warehouse. The excess of the proceeds over the carrying amount of the warehouse sold should be reported as a(an):

    a. Reduction of the cost of the new warehouse.
    b. Gain from discontinued operations, net of income taxes.
    c. Part of continuing operations.
    d. Extraordinary gain, net of taxes. (R/10, FAR #34, 9334)

39. Weir Co. uses straight-line depreciation for its property, plant, and equipment, which, stated at cost, consisted of the following:

	12/31/Yr2	12/31/Yr1
Land	$ 25,000	$ 25,000
Buildings	195,000	195,000
Machinery and equipment	695,000	650,000
	915,000	870,000
Less: Accumulated depreciation	(400,000)	(370,000)
	$ 515,000	$ 500,000

Weir's depreciation expense for year 2 and year 1 was $55,000 and $50,000, respectively. What amount was debited to accumulated depreciation during year 2 because of property, plant, and equipment retirements?

a. $40,000
b. $25,000
c. $20,000
d. $10,000 (11/93, PI, #23, amended, 4392)

40. On December 31 of the current year a building owned by Carr Inc. was destroyed by fire. Carr paid $12,000 for removal and clean-up costs. The building had a book value of $250,000 and a fair value of $280,000 on December 31. What amount should Carr use to determine the gain or loss on this involuntary conversion?

a. $250,000
b. $262,000
c. $280,000
d. $292,000 (5/91, PI, #27, amended, 0933)

41. Lano Corp.'s forest land was condemned for use as a national park. Compensation for the condemnation exceeded the forest land's carrying amount. Lano purchased similar, but larger, replacement forest land for an amount greater than the condemnation award. As a result of the condemnation and replacement, what is the net effect on the carrying amount of forest land reported in Lano's balance sheet?

a. The amount is increased by the excess of the replacement forest land's cost over the condemned forest land's carrying amount.
b. The amount is increased by the excess of the replacement forest land's cost over the condemnation award.
c. The amount is increased by the excess of the condemnation award over the condemned forest land's carrying amount.
d. No effect, because the condemned forest land's carrying amount is used as the replacement forest land's carrying amount. (5/92, Theory, #13, 2706)

42. On July 1, one of Rudd Co.'s delivery vans was destroyed in an accident. On that date, the van's carrying amount was $2,500. On July 15, Rudd received and recorded a $700 invoice for a new engine installed in the van in May, and another $500 invoice for various repairs. In August, Rudd received $3,500 under its insurance policy on the van, which it plans to use to replace the van. What amount should Rudd report as gain (loss) on disposal of the van in its year-end income statement?

a. $1,000
b. $ 300
c. $0
d. $ (200) (5/92, PI, #45, amended, 2616)

43. A state government condemned Cory Co.'s parcel of real estate. Cory will receive $750,000 for this property, which has a carrying amount of $575,000. Cory incurred the following costs as a result of the condemnation:

Appraisal fees to support a $750,000 value	$2,500
Attorney fees for the closing with the state	3,500
Attorney fees to review contract to acquire replacement property	3,000
Title insurance on replacement property	4,000

What amount of cost should Cory use to determine the gain on the condemnation?

a. $581,000
b. $582,000
c. $584,000
d. $588,000 (11/91, PI, #19, 2407)

Problem 4-2 SIMULATION: Depreciation/Recording

Items 1 through 8 are based on the following transactions:

- On January 2, year 2, Mink Co. purchased a manufacturing machine for $648,000. The machine has a five year estimated life and a $90,000 estimated salvage value. Mink expects to manufacture 1,395,000 units over the life of the machine. During year 3, Mink manufactured 280,000 units.
- During year 3, Mink purchased an office building and the land on which it is located by paying $720,000 cash and assuming an existing mortgage of $180,000. The property is assessed at $870,000 for realty tax purposes, of which 60% is allocated to the building.
- During year 3, Mink leased construction equipment under a 7-year capital lease requiring annual year-end payments of $90,000. Mink's incremental borrowing rate is 9%, while the lessor's implicit rate, which is not known to Mink, is 8%. Present value factors for an ordinary annuity for seven periods are 5.21 at 8% and 5.03 at 9%. Fair value of the equipment is $460,000.
- During year 3, Mink paid $60,000 and gave a plot of undeveloped land with a carrying amount of $340,000 and a fair value of $480,000 to Klub Co. in exchange for a plot of undeveloped land with a fair value of $520,000. The land was carried on Klub's books at $360,000. This transaction has commercial substance.

Items 1 through 4 represent various depreciation methods. For each item, calculate depreciation expense for year 3 (the second year of ownership) for the manufacturing machine described above using the method listed. Round all amounts to the nearest whole number.

Depreciation method	Amount
1. Units of production	
2. Sum-of-the-years'-digits	
3. Double-declining-balance	
4. Straight-line	

For items 5 through 8, calculate the amount to be recorded for each item. Round all amounts to the nearest whole number.

Asset	Amount
5. Building	
6. Leased equipment	
7. Land received from Klub on Mink's books	
8. Land received from Mink on Klub's books	

(11/94, FAR, #2, amended, 5321)

Problem 4-3 SIMULATION: Classification/Treatment

During year 4, Fur began a project to construct new corporate headquarters. Fur purchased land with an existing building for $840,000. The land was valued at $800,000 and the building at $40,000. Fur planned to demolish the building and construct a new office building on the site.

For each expenditure in items **1 through 9,** select from the list below the appropriate accounting treatment.

Treatment Choices
L. Classify as land and do not depreciate. B. Classify as building and depreciate. E. Expense.

Expenditure	Treatment
1. Moving costs of $142,000.	
2. $55,000 cost of razing existing building.	
3. $13,200 liability insurance premium during the construction period.	
4. $19,000 payment of delinquent real estate taxes assumed by Fur on purchase.	
5. Purchase of building for $40,000.	
6. Interest of $194,000 on construction financing paid during construction.	
7. Interest of $151,000 on construction financing incurred after completion of construction.	
8. Purchase of land for $800,000.	
9. Costs of $25,000 for current year security contract on the property.	

(11/92, P1, #4(a), amended, 3292)

Problem 4-4 SIMULATION: Capitalization

Peabody Inc. uses the calendar year as its reporting period. During year 1, the company completed numerous property, plant and equipment transactions. In particular, Peabody Inc. incurred long-term debt to build a new warehouse storage facility at its current location. An unrelated building contractor managed the new warehouse construction project. Peabody Inc. has a policy of capitalizing expenditures with a unit cost of at least $1,000 and a useful life greater than one year. The company prorates depreciation expense in the year of acquisition based on the date of purchase. Peabody Inc. had the following property, plant and equipment transactions during the year. For each transaction, choose the correct accounting treatment from the selection list. Each accounting treatment may be used once, more than once, or not at all.

Accounting Treatment	
A. Capitalize and depreciate	D. Expense at time incurred
B. Capitalize, do not depreciate	E. Expense monthly
C. Capitalize and amortize	F. Partially capitalize and partially expense

1. Peabody Inc. had the following property, plant and equipment transactions during the year. For each transaction, choose the correct accounting treatment from the selection list. Each accounting treatment may be used once, more than once, or not at all.

Asset	**Cost**	**Accounting treatment**
20 new desk-top computers for support personnel	$24,000	
Cost of parking lot for new warehouse	$10,000	
New process costing software—this software will need to be replaced in 6 years	$18,000	
Painting all of the ceiling tiles in the hallways and common areas of the property	$ 9,000	
Replacing office windows cracked as a result of an explosion at a neighboring manufacturing plant	$13,000	
Replace the cooling system in the company's current facility with a more modern and fuel efficient model	$35,000	

2. Peabody Inc. purchased or constructed the following assets during year 2. Calculate the amount that the company should capitalize for each of the following property, plant and equipment assets. Enter your answer in the appropriate shaded space provided.

Item	Amount
Land for the new warehouse:	
Purchase price	$350,000
Demolition of existing structures on property	115,000
Proceeds from the sale of scrap from the old buildings on the site	45,000
Costs incurred to grade and pave driveways and parking lots	35,000
Lawn and garden sprinkler systems for the property	21,000
Legal fees incurred to purchase the property and paid at settlement	22,500
Capitalized cost of the land	$
Construction of new warehouse:	
Construction began March 15 and ended August 31	
Borrowings to finance construction	$275,000
Interest incurred from 3/15 through 8/31	12,100
Interest incurred from 9/1 through 12/31	8,800
Total cost of labor, materials, and overhead to construct the warehouse	315,000
Costs incurred to grade and pave driveways and parking lots	36,000
Costs to repair water line ruptured during excavation	5,800
Capitalized cost of the warehouse	$
New machine:	
Cost of machine	$ 38,000
Sales tax paid on machine	2,280
Finance charges on purchase loan	2,950
Installation costs	4,100
Capitalized cost of the new machine	$

(R/05, FAR, P2a, amended, 8524)

Problem 4-5 SIMULATION: Depreciation/Disposition

Meathead Inc. purchased a new piece of equipment with a cost of $44,700 and a $7,000 residual value and placed it into service on May 1, year 3. The equipment was installed at an additional cost of $4,300. The estimated life of the equipment is six years.

1. Calculate the depreciation expense for this asset for year 3 and year 4. Enter your answers in the appropriate shaded space provided. Round to the nearest dollar.

Depreciation Method	Year 3	Year 4
Straight-line method:		
Depreciation expense	$	$
Double-declining-balance method:		
Depreciation expense	$	$

(R/05, FAR, P2b, amended, 9106)

2. Calculate the gain or loss on each of the following dispositions of property, plant and equipment assets. Place your answer in the shaded space provided. A loss should be indicated by a negative number. Enter a negative number with a leading minus (–) sign.

Furniture sold	
Original cost of the furniture	$14,000
Accumulated depreciation on the furniture	10,200
Fair market value of replacement furniture	17,500
Sales price of the furniture sold	3,600
Gain or loss recognized	$
Pickup truck exchanged for a new pickup truck	
Original cost of truck	$25,500
Accumulated depreciation of truck	23,000
Sticker price of new truck	29,000
Fair market value of the new truck	26,000
Cash paid to dealer	23,500
Gain or loss recognized	$
Equipment destroyed by fire	
Original cost of equipment	$17,500
Accumulated depreciation	3,500
Insurance proceeds	15,000
Cost to replace equipment	23,000
Gain or loss recognized	$

Problem 4-6 SIMULATION: Research

Question: In concept, interest cost is capitalizable for what assets?

FASB ASC: [ ] - [ ] - [ ] - [ ]

(9107)

Solution 4-1 MULTIPLE-CHOICE ANSWERS

Initial Measurement

1. (c) Assets are to be recorded at their acquisition cost, which is defined as the cash price or its equivalent. The acquisition cost of the office building and the land together is $1,000,000; the total of the $750,000 cash and $250,000 mortgage. The property is assessed with 60% allocated to the building. Cart would record the building at $600,000 ($1,000,000 × 60%) and the land at the remaining $400,000. (8070)

2. (c) Assets are to be recorded at their acquisition cost; defined as the cash price, or equivalent, plus all other costs reasonably necessary to make it ready for its intended use. The land is recorded at the $135,000 cash paid for the land plus the additional costs: the $2,500 for county assessment for sewer lines, the $625 for title search fees, and the $16,000 for removal of old building less salvage value ($21,00 – $5,000) = $154,125. The $21,000 excavation cost for construction of a basement is part of the cost of the new building, not the land. (8328)

3. (d) Assets are to be recorded at their acquisition cost. Acquisition cost is defined as the cash price, or equivalent, plus all costs reasonably necessary to bring it to the location and to make it ready for its intended use. Both the $12,000 rearrangement cost and $3,000 removal cost were necessary to bring the asset to its location and make it ready for its intended use. Talton would capitalized $200,000 ($185,000 + $12,000 + $4,000 = $200,000). (9333)

4. (c) Assets are to be recorded at their acquisition cost. Acquisition cost is defined as the cash price, or its equivalent, plus all the costs reasonably necessary to bring it to the location and to make it ready for its intended use. The cash price, or its equivalent, would be the $4,000 down payment plus the $15,480 present value of the $6,000 payments, an ordinary annuity, (2.58 × $6,000). Add to that price of $19,480 the $2,000 in shipping charges to get the equipment to its location and the $3,500 of installation charges to get it ready for its intended use, for a capitalized total cost of $24,980. (8754)

5. (b) The contribution of land by a governmental unit to an enterprise for industrial use is an example of a nonreciprocal transfer. A nonmonetary asset received in a nonreciprocal transfer should be recorded at the fair value of the asset received. The corresponding credit for a corporation is *Additional Paid-In Capital—Donated Assets.* Donated assets should *not* be recorded as income or gain or added to retained earnings when received from governmental entities. Assets donated by entities other than governmental units should be included in revenue in the period of receipt. (2457)

Nonmonetary Transactions

6. (b) Sable exchanged a truck with a fair value in excess of its carrying amount for a similar truck and received monetary consideration. Hence, Sable experiences a gain on the exchange. The recipient of monetary consideration in an exchange measured based on the recorded amount recognizes a portion of the gain experienced. The amount of the gain recognized is based on the ratio of the monetary consideration to the total consideration received. (4542)

7. (a) In general, accounting for nonmonetary transactions (those involving nonmonetary assets or liabilities) should be based on the fair values of the assets involved. The acquisition is recorded at the fair value of the asset surrendered or the fair value of the asset received, whichever is more clearly determinable, and gains or losses should be recognized. The rationale associated with immediate gain/loss, recording the transactions at fair value, is that the exchange represents the culmination of the earnings process associated with the assets surrendered. The best statement describing the proper accounting for losses when nonmonetary assets are exchanged is that a loss is recognized immediately, because assets received should not be valued at more than their cash equivalent price. (8796)

8. (c) In an exchange with commercial substance, the transaction is accounted for at the fair value of the asset received or the asset given up, whichever is more clearly evident, and a gain or loss is recognized on the exchange. (9899)

9. (a) Dahl is giving boot in an exchange with commercial substance. Dahl has a realized gain on its old van of $15,000:

Cash paid	$ 5,000
Book value of truck given up	30,000
Total consideration given up	35,000
Fair value of truck received	(50,000)
Gain on exchange	$ 15,000

The journal entry to be recorded in Dahl's books is:

Truck received	50,000	
Cash paid		5,000
Truck given up		30,000
Gain		15,000

(3279)

10. (d) In general, accounting for nonmonetary transactions (those involving nonmonetary assets or liabilities) should be based on the fair values (FV) of the assets involved. The acquisition is recorded at the FV of the asset surrendered or the FV of the asset received, whichever is more clearly determinable, and gains or losses should be recognized. Nonmonetary exchanges should be based on recorded amounts, rather than FV, of the exchanged assets if any of the following apply: 1) neither the FV of the assets received nor FV of the assets surrendered is reasonably determinable, or 2) the transaction is an exchange of a product or property held for sale in the ordinary course of business for a product or property to be sold in the same line of business to facilitate sales to customers, or 3) the exchange lacks commercial substance. This situation does not fall into any category warranting the exchange to be based on recorded amounts so it would be based on FV. Feld would realize a gain of $30,000 on this transaction. The entry would be:

Equipment (tow truck FV)	100,000	
Accumulated Depreciation	80,000	
Cash		10,000
Equipment (delivery truck)		140,000
Gain		30,000

(8771)

11. (c) In general, accounting for nonmonetary transactions should be based on the fair values (FV) of the assets involved. Nonmonetary exchanges should be based on recorded amounts, rather than FV, of the exchanged assets if any of the following apply: 1) neither the FV of the assets received nor FV of the assets surrendered is reasonably determinable, or 2) the transaction is an exchange of a product or property held for sale in the ordinary course of business for a product or property to be sold in the same line of business to facilitate sales to customers, or 3) the exchange lacks commercial substance. Since the above transaction lacks commercial substance, the new book value for the truck Campbell received ($3,700) is determined as follows:

New Truck (plug)	3,700	
Accm. Depr. Old Truck	20,000	
Old Truck (cost)		23,000
Cash		700

(9900)

12. (b) The transaction is an exchange of a product held for sale in the ordinary course of business for a product to be sold in the same line of business to facilitate sales to customers other than parties to the exchange and does not result in the culmination of an earnings process. The nonmonetary exchange shall be measured based on the recorded amount of the nonmonetary assets relinquished. Only to the extent cash (boot) has been received has a portion of the asset exchanged been sold and a gain can be recognized. The fair value of the asset acquired is reduced by the portion of the gain realized which is not recognized. The gain recognized on the exchange is determined by the ratio of the cash to the total consideration received (asset received and cash).

Cash received		$ 30,000
Fair value of inventory received		120,000
Total fair value received		150,000
Carrying amount of inventory exchanged		(126,000)
Gain realized on exchange		$ 24,000
Cash	$ 30,000	
Total fair value received	/ 150,000	
Extent earnings process culminated		× 20%
Gain recognized on exchange		$ 4,800

(2643)

Self Constructed

13. (d) Interest cost during construction is to be capitalized on assets that are constructed for an enterprise's own use or assets intended for sale or lease that are constructed as discrete projects. However, interest cost shall not be capitalized for inventories that are routinely manufactured or otherwise produced in large quantities on a repetitive basis. Once the constructed assets are completed, all interest should be expensed as incurred. In the question at hand, it is not clear, but it is assumed that the machinery constructed for sale is routinely manufactured in large quantities on a repetitive basis. Therefore, the interest during construction should be capitalized only for the equipment constructed for Bay's own use. The interest incurred during construction of the inventory items should be expensed. The interest incurred after completion should be expensed on both groups of equipment. (1788)

14. (c) The cost of assets constructed for the use of the business should include all directly related costs; cost of direct materials, cost of direct labor, additional overhead incurred, and interest costs incurred during the construction period. If the average accumulated expenditures of an asset exceed the amount of any specific borrowings associated with the asset, the excess should be capitalized at the weighted average of interest rates applicable to other borrowings of the business. There was no specific borrowing mentioned, so the interest rate would simply be the weighted average. (($6,000,000 × 0.08) + ($8,000,000 × 0.09)) / $14,000,000 = 8.57%. (9317)

15. (b) The amount of interest that may be capitalized is based on the weighted-average amount of accumulated expenditures. The weighted-average amount of accumulated expenditures applies the avoidable interest concept. This concept limits the amount of interest to be capitalized to the lower of the actual interest cost incurred during the period or avoidable interest. Avoidable interest is the amount of interest cost incurred during the period that theoretically could have been avoided if expenditures for the asset had not been made. (4832)

16. (a) None of the interest is expensed; it is all capitalized. Assets qualifying for interest capitalization include assets constructed or produced for self-use on a repetitive basis, assets acquired for self-use through arrangements requiring down payments or progress payments, and assets constructed or produced as discrete projects for sale or lease (e.g., ships or real estate developments). (7788)

17. (a) Assets qualifying for interest capitalization include assets constructed or produced as discrete projects for sale or lease; for example, ships or real estate developments. Assets qualifying for interest capitalization do not include inventories that are routinely manufactured on a repetitive basis, assets in use or ready for use, or assets not in use and not being prepared for use. (89547)

Subsequent Measurement

18. (a) All of the expenditures related to the purchase of the new machine ($75,000 + $14,000) and the rearrangement of the assembly line to install this machine ($40,000 + $18,000) should be capitalized. The costs associated with the rearrangement of the assembly line are capitalized because the rearrangement has resulted in significantly more efficient production, the benefits of which extend beyond the current period. (0934)

19. (d) The collating and stapling attachment is an addition to the printing press and so its cost (including installation cost) should be capitalized. The overhaul resulted in a significant increase in the productivity of the printing press; therefore, its cost (replacement parts, labor and overhead) should also be capitalized. The total cost capitalized is $160,000 (i.e., $84,000 + $36,000 + $26,000 + $14,000). (0940)

20. (a) The damaged portion of the building was refurbished with upgraded materials which indicates that a "betterment" is involved. There are future benefits due to the refurbishing expenditures; thus, they should be capitalized. The cost and related accumulated depreciation of the damaged portion of the building are identifiable so they should be removed from the books (with a resulting debit to "loss" for the difference) because this portion of the building has been replaced and upgraded. (1794)

Cost Recovery

21. (c) The asset would be recorded at $135,000, its acquisition cost to the new owners. The salvage value would be the $15,000 estimated by the new owners. The carrying amount and residual value of the previous owners does not matter to the new owners. The depreciable base would be $120,000; the $135,000 acquisition cost less the $15,000 estimated salvage value. (8564)

22. (c) The carrying amount of the equipment at the date of sale is computed by subtracting the accumulated depreciation on the equipment from the cost of the equipment. Under the straight-line method, the accumulated depreciation on the equipment at the date of sale is equal to 40% of the original cost of the equipment [i.e., (100% – 20%) × 1/10 × 5]. Thus, under the straight-line method, the carrying amount of the equipment at the date of sale is 60% (i.e., 100% – 40%) of the original cost of the equipment. Since the equipment was sold for only 50% of its original cost, use of the straight-line depreciation method would have resulted in a loss being recognized on the sale equal to 10% (i.e., 60% – 50%) of the original cost of the equipment. (4215)

23. (d) Under neither the straight-line method nor the double-declining balance method of depreciation would the accumulated depreciation equal the original cost at the end of the asset's estimated useful life. The straight-line method depreciates the cost less salvage value evenly over the estimated useful life of the asset. The double-declining balance method uses a rate of depreciation twice that of the straight-line rate, but the asset cannot be depreciated below the salvage value. (8589)

24. (b) The straight-line (SL) depreciation method is a fixed charge method where an equal amount of depreciable cost is allocated to each period. The SL formula is (historical cost – salvage value) / estimated useful life. The 200% declining balance depreciation method, also known as double-declining balance (DDB), uses a rate of depreciation twice the SL rate applied to the book value (i.e., declining balance) of the asset to obtain the depreciation expense for the period. The salvage value is not used in the calculation except as a lower bound for the asset's book value. The DDB formula is (2 / estimated useful life) × (historical cost – accumulated depreciation).

Year 2: (2/10) × ($100,000 – 0) = $20,000
Year 3: (2/10) × ($100,000 – $20,000) = $16,000 (8761)

25. (b) A gain or loss on the sale of a fixed asset is computed by comparing the proceeds received from its sale to its carrying amount at the date of sale. To determine the carrying amount of the fixed asset at the sale date, two years of depreciation must be subtracted from its cost. Because the cost of the fixed asset is not given, there are two options: (1) determine depreciation as a percent or fraction of the unknown cost of the fixed asset, "x," or (2) plug in any value for the cost of the machine and simply compute depreciation under both methods based on this amount. We chose the latter approach, assigning to the machine a cost of $300. Now we can compare the carrying amount of the fixed asset at the sale date under both methods. The fixed asset has a greater carrying amount at the date of sale under the SYD method. Therefore, using the SYD method of depreciation, instead of the DDB method of depreciation, decreases any gain and increases any loss recognized on the sale of the fixed asset.

Cost of fixed asset	$ 300	
Depreciation to date of sale:		
Yr. 1: 5/15 × ($300 – $0)	(100)	
Yr. 2: 4/15 × ($300 – $0)	(80)	
Carrying amount, date of sale, SYD	$ 120	
Cost of fixed asset	$ 300	
Depreciation to date of sale:		
Yr. 1: 2/5 × ($300 – $0)	(120)	
Yr. 2: 2/5 × ($300 – $120)	(72)	
Carrying amount, date of sale, DDB	$ 108	(1808)

26. (c)

Asset cost		$ 20,000	
Year 1 [(4/10)($20,000 – 2,000)]	$7,200		
Year 2 [(3/10)($20,000 – 2,000)]	5,400		
Year 3 [(2/10)($20,000 – 2,000)]	3,600		
Depreciation		(16,200)	
Carrying amount, 12/31, year 3		$ 3,800	(6776)

27. (c) The composite depreciation method refers to the depreciation of a collection of assets that are dissimilar. The group depreciation method refers to the depreciation of a collection of assets that are similar in nature. From an accounting standpoint, there is no distinction between the two methods. The same procedures are followed for both, and both utilize the straight-line depreciation method. (4216)

28. (b) Under the composite or group method of depreciation, no gain or loss is recognized upon the retirement of a plant asset. This practice is justified because some assets will be retired before the average service life and others after the average service life. Accumulated depreciation is debited for the difference between original cost and the cash received; no gain or loss is recorded on the disposition. The net carrying amount of these composite asset accounts is decreased by the cash proceeds received of $3,000 (cost removed of $18,000 minus accumulated depreciation removed of $15,000).

Cash	3,000		
Accumulated Depreciation	15,000		
Truck		18,000	(1833)

29. (c) Units-of-output depreciation takes into account salvage value and the number of units produced by the asset. Cost – salvage/expected output × current output:

$$\frac{\$864{,}000 - \$72{,}000}{1{,}800{,}000} = \frac{\$792{,}000}{\$1{,}800{,}000} = \$0.44 \times 300{,}000 = \$132{,}000 \quad (7617)$$

30. (b) On December 31, year 3 Turtle reports $32,000 + $6,000 = $38,000 as accumulated depreciation. Double-declining-balance is computed using twice the straight-line rate, which in this case is 40% (1/5 = 0.20; 0.20 × 2 = .40). In year 3, depreciation is computed by dividing the remaining life of 3 years = $6,000.

	Book value beginning of year	Rate	Depreciation Expense	Accumulated Depreciation	Book Value End of Year
Year 1	$50,000	40%	$20,000	$20,000	$30,000
Year 2	30,000	40%	12,000	32,000	18,000

(4833)

31. (b)

Purchase price of mine	$2,640,000
Development costs to prepare for production	360,000
Estimated restoration costs	180,000
Estimated residual value	(300,000)
Depletion base of mine	2,880,000
Estimated tons of removable ore	/ 1,200,000
Depletion charge per ton	2.40
Tons sold in the year	× 60,000
Depletion expense for the year	$ 144,000

(5572)

32. (c) Assets are to be recorded at their acquisition cost. Acquisition cost is the cash price, or its equivalent, plus all costs reasonably necessary to bring it to the location and to make it ready for its intended use. Depletion refers to periodic allocation of acquisition costs of natural resources. A per-unit depletion rate is computed by dividing the acquisition cost of the natural resource (i.e., purchase price, and other development costs), less any estimated residual value, by the estimated number of units of the resource available for extraction.

Purchase price of coal mine	$2,000,000
Plus: Mine preparation costs	500,000
Mine total acquisition cost	2,500,000
Less: Value at end of useful life	(100,000)
Net depletable amount	2,400,000
Divided by: Estimated number of units available for extraction	/ 750,000
Depletion amount per ton	$ 3.20

(8092)

Impairment

33. (b) Recognition of an impairment loss is only required if a long-term asset's, or asset group's, carrying amount is not recoverable and exceeds its fair value. (8086)

34. (a) Impairment is the condition that exists when the carrying amount of a long-lived asset exceeds its fair value. The amount of an impairment loss is the difference between an asset's book and fair value. The new book value is depreciated over the remaining useful life. Subsequent reversal of a previously recognized impairment loss is prohibited. This is classified as a change in accounting estimate and is reported in the period of change. There are no pro forma reports for prior periods, and amounts reported in financial statements of prior periods are not restated. Randall should report $20,000 ($250,000 cost – $100,000 accumulated depreciation – $30,000 impairment loss = $120,000 remaining basis depreciated over 6 years of remaining life) as depreciation expense in its income statement for the next year. (9868)

35. (a) Subsequent reversal or restoration of a previously recognized impairment loss is prohibited. (9306)

36. (b) Recoverability is associated with an impairment loss. An impairment loss is recognized only if the carrying amount of a long-lived asset is not recoverable and exceeds its fair value. The carrying amount (book value) is not recoverable if it exceeds the sum of the undiscounted cash flows expected to result from the use and eventual disposition of the asset. That assessment shall be based on the carrying amount of the asset at the date it is tested for recoverability. A long-lived asset (asset group) shall be tested for recoverability whenever events or changes in circumstances indicate that its carrying amount may not be recoverable. (9335)

Disposal

37. (d) Under both the group depreciation and the composite depreciation methods, assets are depreciated on the basis of their average lives. New assets are recorded at cost, and retirements are accounted for by crediting Assets for the original cost of the equipment and debiting Accumulated Depreciation for the original cost less proceeds received; thus, no gain or loss is recognized on disposal. The theoretical justification for this is that some assets will be retired early, while some will be used longer than originally estimated. The same approach is used under both group and composite depreciation—the only difference is that "group depreciation" refers to pools of assets that are similar in nature, whereas "composite" refers to essentially dissimilar assets. (1888)

38. (c) Accounting for the voluntary disposal of an operational asset usually involves crediting the asset account for the cost of the asset, removing the accumulated depreciation by a debit to that account, debiting the appropriate account for any proceeds received, and recognizing a gain or loss on disposal. The gain or loss would normally simply be part of continuing operations, as is the case in this scenario. (9334)

39. (b) Weir's *Accumulated Depreciation* account increased by $30,000 ($400,000 – $370,000) during year 2, despite the fact that $55,000 of depreciation expense was recorded during year 2. Therefore, the debit to accumulated depreciation during year 2 because of plant and equipment retirements was $25,000 (i.e., $55,000 – $30,000). (4392)

40. (b)

Building carrying amount, 12/31	$ 250,000	
Removal and clean-up costs	12,000	
Amount to determine gain or loss on involuntary conversion	$ 262,000	(0933)

41. (a) The condemnation of the forest land represents an example of an involuntary conversion of a nonmonetary asset to a monetary asset. Any gain or loss realized on the property converted is recognized in income even though the enterprise reinvests or is obligated to reinvest the monetary assets in replacement nonmonetary assets. Since any gain or loss realized on the property converted is recognized in income, the replacement nonmonetary asset is recorded at cost. Because the cost of the replacement forest land exceeds the condemnation award which exceeds the condemned forest land's carrying amount, the debit to *Forest Land* to record the cost of the replacement property exceeds the credit to *Forest Land* to remove the carrying amount of the condemned property, and, thus, the carrying amount of *Forest Land* in the balance sheet increases by the amount of this excess. (2706)

42. (b) A gain or loss on the involuntary conversion (e.g., casualty, condemnation, theft) of a nonmonetary asset should be recognized in income even if the proceeds received as a result of the involuntary conversion are reinvested in a replacement nonmonetary asset. The normal maintenance performed on the van (i.e., the various repairs) should not be capitalized. Normal maintenance does not enhance the service potential of the van, it serves only to maintain a given level of services from the van. On the other hand, the cost of the new engine should be capitalized because the expenditure for the new engine is nonrecurring in nature, enhances the service potential of the van, and is expected to yield benefits over a number of accounting periods.

Insurance proceeds		$ 3,500	
Carrying amount, 7/1	$ 2,500		
Cost of new engine installed prior to conversion	700		
Carrying amount of van		(3,200)	
Gain recognized on involuntary conversion		$ 300	(2616)

43. (a) The amount of cost that should be used to determine the gain on condemnation is $581,000 (i.e., the property's carrying amount of $575,000 plus the $2,500 appraisal fee plus the $3,500 attorney fees for the closing with the state). The attorney fees to review the contract and the title insurance are costs of acquiring the replacement property. (2407)

PERFORMANCE BY SUBTOPICS

Each category below parallels a subtopic covered in Chapter 4. Record the number and percentage of questions you correctly answered in each subtopic area.

Initial Measurement

Question #	Correct √
1	
2	
3	
4	
5	
# Questions	5
# Correct	________
% Correct	________

Nonmonetary Transactions

Question #	Correct √
6	
7	
8	
9	
10	
11	
12	
# Questions	7
# Correct	________
% Correct	________

Self Constructed

Question #	Correct √
13	
14	
15	
16	
17	
# Questions	5
# Correct	________
% Correct	________

Subsequent Measurement

Question #	Correct √
18	
19	
20	
# Questions	3
# Correct	________
% Correct	________

Cost Recovery

Question #	Correct √
21	
22	
23	
24	
25	
26	
27	
28	
29	
30	
31	
32	
# Questions	12
# Correct	________
% Correct	________

Impairment

Question #	Correct √
33	
34	
35	
36	
# Questions	4
# Correct	________
% Correct	________

Disposal

Question #	Correct √
37	
38	
39	
40	
41	
42	
43	
# Questions	7
# Correct	________
% Correct	________

Solution 4-2 SIMULATION: Depreciation/Recording

1. **Units of production = $112,000**

Cost of machine	$ 648,000
Less: Estimated salvage value	(90,000)
Depreciable base of machine	558,000
Divide by: Estimated useful life in units	/1,395,000
Depreciation charge per unit of output	0.40
Times: Units produced in year 3	× 280,000
Depreciation charge recorded for year 3	$ 112,000

2. **Sum-of-the-years'-digits = $148,800**

Cost of machine, 1/2, year 2	$ 648,000
Less: Estimated salvage value	(90,000)
Depreciable base of machine	558,000
Times: Fraction for second year of 5 year life*	× 4/15
Depreciation charge for year 3	$ 148,800

* The numerator of the fraction is the number of years of useful life remaining at 1/1, year 3 (i.e., 5 – 1). The denominator is the sum of the years of the estimated useful life of the machine.

3. **Double-declining-balance = $155,520**

The depreciation charge for the first year must be computed before the second year can be computed.

Cost of machine, 1/2, year 2	$ 648,000
Less: Accumulated depreciation, 1/2, year 2	(0)
Carrying amount of machine, 1/2, year 2	648,000
Times: Twice the SL rate [(100% / 5) × 2]	× 40%
Depreciation charge for year 2	$ 259,200
Cost of machine, 1/2, year 2	$ 648,000
Less: Accumulated depreciation, 1/1, year 3	(259,200)
Carrying amount of machine, 1/1, year 3	388,800
Times: Twice the SL rate	× 40%
Depreciation charge for year 3	$ 155,520

4. **Straight-line = $111,600**

Cost of machine	$ 648,000
Less: Estimated salvage value	(90,000)
Depreciable base of machine	558,000
Divide by: Estimated useful life in years	/ 5
Annual depreciation charge	$ 111,600

5. $540,000

The cost of the office building and land is $900,000, the sum of the $720,000 cash payment made and the $180,000 existing mortgage assumed by Mink. Since 60% of the property tax assessment on the building and land is allocated to the building, it can be inferred that the fair value of the building is 60% of the sum of the fair values of the building and the land. Thus, Mink should record the building at $540,000, 60% of the $900,000 cost of the building and land.

6. $452,700

At the inception of a capital lease, the lessee records an asset and the corresponding lease liability at the lesser of the present value of the minimum lease payments or the fair value of the leased property. The lessor's implicit rate in the lease of 8% is not known to the lessee. Therefore, the present value of the minimum lease payments should be computed using the lessee's incremental borrowing rate of 9%. The leased equipment is recorded at the present value of the minimum lease payments of $452,700 (i.e., $90,000 × 5.03) because this amount is less than the $460,000 fair value of the equipment.

7. $520,000

In an exchange with commercial substance, the transaction is recorded at the fair value of the asset received or the asset given up, whichever is greater (more clearly evident), and a gain or loss is recognized on the exchange.

Book value of land given up	$ 340,000
Cash paid	60,000
Total consideration given up	400,000
Fair value of land received	520,000
Gain on exchange of land	$ 120,000

8. $480,000

In an exchange with commercial substance, the transaction is recorded at the fair value of the asset received or the asset given up, whichever is greater (more clearly evident), and a gain or loss is recognized on the exchange.

FV of land received	$ 480,000
Cash received	60,000
Total consideration received	540,000
Book value of land given up	360,000
Gain on exchange of land	$ 180,000

Solution 4-3 SIMULATION: Classification/Treatment

1. E The moving costs should be expensed as incurred; they should not be included in the cost of the land or building.

2. L Since the existing building was torn down to prepare the site for the new building, the cost of demolition of the existing building, less any salvage proceeds, is a cost of getting the land ready for its intended use and should be included in the cost of the land.

3. B The liability insurance premium incurred during the construction period should be capitalized in the Building account because it was a reasonable and necessary cost of constructing the building.

4. L The payment of accrued or delinquent property taxes on the land at the time of purchase should be capitalized in the Land account.

5. L Where a building is to be constructed on a newly acquired site with an existing building on it, the amount paid for the existing building should be capitalized in the Land account.

6. B The new office building requires a period of time to get it ready for its intended use. Therefore, the interest cost on the construction financing incurred during the construction period should be capitalized as part of the historical cost of constructing the building.

7. E The interest cost on the construction financing incurred after completion of the construction should be expensed. Interest capitalization ceases when the asset is substantially complete and ready for its intended use.

8. L The purchase price of the land should be capitalized in the *Land* account.

9. E The cost of the current year security contract on the property should be expensed as a period cost. These costs do not extend the useful life of the property, nor do they improve the quality or quantity of output.

Solution 4-4 SIMULATION: Capitalization

1.

Asset	Cost	Accounting treatment
20 new desk-top computers for support personnel	$24,000	Capitalize and depreciate
Cost of parking lot for new warehouse	$10,000	Capitalize and depreciate
New process costing software—this software will need to be replaced in 6 years	$18,000	Capitalize and amortize
Painting all of the ceiling tiles in the hallways and common areas of the property	$ 9,000	Expense at time incurred
Replacing office windows cracked as a result of an explosion at a neighboring manufacturing plant.	$13,000	Expense at time incurred
Replace the cooling system in the company's current facility with a more modern and fuel efficient model.	$35,000	Capitalize and depreciate

2.

	Item	Amount
Land for the new warehouse:		
X	Purchase price	$350,000
X	Demolition of existing structures on property	115,000
X	Proceeds from the sale of scrap from the old buildings on the site	45,000
	Costs incurred to grade and pave driveways and parking lots	35,000
	Lawn and garden sprinkler systems for the property	21,000
X	Legal fees incurred to purchase the property and paid at settlement	22,500
	Capitalized cost of the land	**$442,500**
Construction of new warehouse (Construction began March 15 and ended August 31):		
	Borrowings to finance construction	$275,000
X	Interest incurred from 3/15 through 8/31	12,100
	Interest incurred from 9/1 through 12/31	8,800
X	Total cost of labor, materials, and overhead to construct the warehouse	315,000
	Costs incurred to grade and pave driveways and parking lots	36,000
	Costs to repair water line ruptured during excavation	5,800
	Capitalized cost of the warehouse	**$327,100**
New machine:		
X	Cost of machine	$ 38,000
X	Sales tax paid on machine	2,280
	Finance charges on purchase loan	2,950
X	Installation costs	4,100
	Capitalized cost of the new machine	**$ 44,380**

Editor's Note: Items marked "X" are included in the related calculations.

Solution 4-5 SIMULATION: Depreciation/Disposition

1.

	Year 3	Year 4
Straight-line method:		
Cost (purchase price + installation cost)	49,000	49,000
Less: Residual value	7,000	7,000
Divided by estimated life (in years)	6	6
Times amount of year in service	8/12	12/12
Depreciation expense	**$ 4,667**	**$ 7,000**
Double-declining-balance method:		
Cost (purchase price + installation cost)	49,000	49,000
Less: Accumulated depreciation	0	10,889
Divided by ½ the estimated life (in years)	3	3
Times amount of year in service	8/12	12/12
Depreciation expense	**$10,889**	**$12,704**

2.

Furniture sold		
X	Original cost of the furniture	$14,000
X	Accumulated depreciation on the furniture	10,200
	Fair market value of replacement furniture	17,500
X	Sales price of the furniture sold	3,600
	Gain or loss recognized	**$ (200)**
Pickup truck exchanged for a new pickup truck		
X	Original cost of truck	$25,500
X	Accumulated depreciation of truck	23,000
	Sticker price of new truck	29,000
X	Fair market value of the new truck	26,000
X	Cash paid to dealer	23,500
	Gain or loss recognized	**$ 0**
Equipment destroyed by fire		
X	Original cost of equipment	$17,500
X	Accumulated depreciation	3,500
X	Insurance proceeds	15,000
	Cost to replace equipment	23,000
	Gain or loss recognized	**$ 1,000**

Editor's Note: Items marked "X" are considered in the related calculations.

Solution 4-6 SIMULATION: Research

FASB Accounting Standards Codification

FASB ASC:	835	-	20	-	15	-	2

15-2 In concept, interest cost is capitalizable for all assets that require a period of time to get them ready for their intended use (acquisition period). However, in many cases, the benefit in terms of information about the entity's resources and earnings may not justify the additional accounting and administrative cost involved in providing the information. The significance of the effect of interest capitalization in relation to the entity's resources and earnings is the most important consideration in assessing its benefit. The ease with which qualifying assets and related expenditures can be separately identified and the number of assets subject to interest capitalization are important factors in assessing the cost of implementation.

Select Hot•Spot™ Video Description

CPA 3248 Inventory, Fixed Assets & Intangible Assets
This program highlights several important accounting topics. It provides extensive coverage of accounting for inventory in costing, measurement, and valuation. This includes the lower of cost or market, periodic and perpetual inventory systems, specific identification, the gross profit method, FIFO, LIFO, weighted and moving averages, the retail method, and dollar-value LIFO. This program also covers the most important aspects of fixed assets. This includes valuation, improvements, impairments, exchanges, and depreciation of fixed assets. Other topics discussed are research and development costs, intangibles, and software costs. During this video, Bob Monette goes through numerous examples and 30 multiple-choice questions covering these topics. Approximate video duration is 2 hours and 45 minutes. This does not include the time a candidate spends answering questions and taking notes.

CHAPTER 5

INTANGIBLES, R&D, SOFTWARE & OTHER ASSETS

CHAPTER 5

INTANGIBLES, R&D, SOFTWARE & OTHER ASSETS

I. Intangible Assets

A. Overview

Intangible assets are assets without physical substance that provide economic benefits through the rights and privileges associated with their possession. While goodwill is an intangible asset, the term intangible asset is used to refer to an intangible asset other than goodwill. An intangible asset may be classified as identifiable or unidentifiable. Examples of identifiable intangible assets include patents, franchises, licenses, leaseholds, leasehold improvements, copyrights, and trademarks.

1. **Patent** A patent represents a special right to a particular product or process that has value to the holder of the right. Only the external acquisition costs, which includes items such as legal costs associated with obtaining a patent on a new product, of a patent are capitalized. Research and development costs incurred to internally develop a patent are expensed as incurred. In addition, the cost of a competing patent acquired to protect an existing patent and the cost of a successful legal defense of an existing patent should also be capitalized. The cost of an unsuccessful defense, along with any amounts previously capitalized for the patent, is expensed in the period in which an unfavorable court decision is rendered.

2. **Franchise** A franchise represents a special right to operate under the name and guidance of another enterprise over a limited geographic area. A franchise is always externally purchased; it cannot be internally developed. Capitalize all significant costs incurred to acquire the franchise (e.g., purchase price, legal fees, etc.). If the acquisition cost of the franchise requires future cash payments, these payments should be capitalized at their present value using an appropriate interest rate. On the other hand, periodic service fees charged as a percentage of revenues are not capitalized; these costs represent a current operating expense of the franchisee.

3. **License** A license is a permit issued by a governmental agency allowing an entity to conduct business in a certain specified geographical area. Capitalize significant costs incurred to acquire the license and amortize the cost over the lesser of its useful or legal life.

4. **Leasehold** A leasehold is a right to use rented properties, usually for a number of years. In some situations, for example, a ten-year lease may require the immediate cash payment of the annual rent for the first and tenth years. The prepayment of the rent for the tenth year would be recorded as a leasehold and would be classified as an intangible asset until the tenth year, when it would be charged to rent expense.

5. **Leasehold Improvement** A leasehold improvement is an improvement made by the lessee to leased property for which benefits are expected beyond the current accounting period. Leasehold improvements are not separable from the leased property and revert to the lessor at the end of the lease term. The cost of leasehold improvements should be capitalized and amortized over the lesser of their estimated useful life or the remaining term of the lease. If a lease has a renewal option, which the lessee intends to exercise, the leasehold improvement should be amortized over the *lesser* of its estimated useful life or the sum of the remaining term of the lease **and** the period covered by the renewal option.

6. **Copyright** A copyright is an exclusive right granted by the federal government giving the owner protection against the illegal reproduction by others of the owner's written works, designs, and literary productions. Although the copyright period is for the life of the creator plus 70 years, the cost of a copyright should be amortized over its useful life.

7. **Trademark** A trademark is a symbol, design, or logo that is used in conjunction with a particular product, service, or enterprise. Generally, only the external acquisition costs of trademarks are capitalized; internal acquisition costs usually are expensed when incurred. Amortize any capitalized costs over the useful life of the trademark.

B. **Initial Recognition & Measurement**
An intangible asset may be externally acquired or internally developed. It may be acquired individually or with a group of other assets.

1. **Externally Acquired** Acquired intangible assets initially are recognized and measured based on fair value. If acquired as a group of assets in a transaction other than a business combination, the cost is allocated to individual assets based on their relative fair values and shall not give rise to goodwill. Intangible assets acquired in a business combination are discussed in the chapter on consolidated financial statements as deemed necessary.

2. **Internally Developed** The costs of internally developing, maintaining, or restoring intangible assets (including goodwill) that are not specifically identifiable and that have indeterminate lives, are expensed when incurred.

C. **After Acquisition**
Accounting for a recognized intangible asset is based on its useful life. An intangible asset with a finite useful life is amortized; an intangible with an indefinite useful life is not amortized. The useful life of an intangible asset to an entity is the period over which the asset is expected to contribute directly or indirectly to the future cash flows of that entity.

1. **Useful Life Estimate** The estimate of the useful life should be based upon the analysis of all pertinent factors, in particular:

   a. The expected use of the asset by the entity.

   b. The expected useful life of another asset or group of assets to which the useful life of the intangible asset may relate.

   c. Any legal, regulatory, or contractual provisions that may limit the useful life.

   d. The entity's own historical experience in renewing or extending similar arrangements. In the absence of that experience, the assumptions that market participants would use about extension or renewal.

   e. The effects of obsolescence, demand, competition and other economic factors.

   f. The level of maintenance expenditures required to obtain the expected future cash flows from the asset.

2. **Finite Useful Life** Intangible assets with finite useful lives are amortized over their useful lives, without the constraint of an arbitrary ceiling. The useful life is the period over which the asset is expected to contribute directly or indirectly to future cash flows. The estimate of the useful life should take into consideration all pertinent factors, including the expected use of the asset by the entity; any legal, regulatory, or contractual provisions that may limit the useful life and such provisions that might result in renewal or extension of the useful life without substantial cost; the effects of obsolescence, demand, competition, and other economic factors; and the expected maintenance expenditures required.

   a. The method of amortization should reflect the pattern in which the economic benefits of the intangible asset are consumed or used up. If that pattern cannot be reliably determined, a straight-line amortization method shall be used. The amount to be amortized shall be the amount initially assigned to the asset less any residual value.

   b. The residual value of an intangible asset shall be assumed to be zero unless at the end of its useful life to the entity the asset is expected to continue to have a useful life to another entity and (1) the reporting entity has a commitment from a third party to purchase the asset at the end of its useful life or (2) the residual value can be determined by reference to an exchange transaction in an existing market for that asset and that market is expected to exist at the end of the asset's useful life.

   c. Each reporting period, the remaining useful life of an intangible asset being amortized should be evaluated to determine whether events and circumstances warrant a revision to the remaining period of amortization.

3. **Indefinite Useful Life** An intangible asset with an indefinite useful life is not amortized. If no legal, regulatory, contractual, competitive, economic, or other factors limit the useful life, it is considered to be indefinite. The term indefinite does not mean infinite. Goodwill and intangible assets with indefinite useful lives are not amortized, but rather are tested at least annually for impairment.

   Each reporting period, an entity shall evaluate the remaining useful life of the intangible asset to determine whether events and circumstances continue to support an indefinite life. If it's determined the asset has a finite useful life, the asset shall be tested for impairment and then be amortized prospectively over its estimated remaining useful life. It is then accounted for in the same manner as other intangible assets with finite useful lives.

4. **Impairment** Prior to the issuance of ASU No. 2012-02, *Intangibles-Goodwill and Other (Topic 350): Testing Indefinite-Lived Intangible Assets for Impairment,* in July 2012, all intangible assets that are not amortized (e.g., indefinite-lived trademarks, licenses, and distribution rights) were to be tested for impairment at lease annually. If the carrying amount of an intangible asset exceeds its fair value, an impairment loss in an amount equal to that excess is recognized. After an impairment loss is recognized, the adjusted carrying amount of the asset is its new basis. Subsequent reversal of a previously recognized impairment loss is prohibited.

   With the release of ASU No. 2012-12, (testable beginning April 2013), an entity is now permitted to make a qualitative evaluation about the likelihood of impairment of an indefinite-lived intangible asset to determine whether it should apply the quantitative test and calculate the fair value (similar to the revised impairment testing for goodwill; see the next section for more information). If an organization concludes that it is more likely than not (i.e., a likelihood of more than 50 percent) that the indefinite-lived intangible asset is impaired, then the entity is required to determine the fair value and compare that amount to the carrying amount, recognizing the impairment loss, if any. Conversely, if the entity concludes otherwise, then it is not required to take any further action. An organization can bypass the qualitative assessment and proceed directly to calculating fair value, if it so chooses.

5. **Goodwill Impairment Testing** Before being amended by ASU 2011-08, the guidance in GAAP included the requirement for reporting entities to test goodwill for impairment, at least annually, using a two-step process. The ASU 2011-08 amendments were intended to have the end-result of reducing the complexity and costs incurred by reporting entities by *allowing* the use of a qualitative evaluation about the likelihood of goodwill being impaired in advance of making decisions about whether the fair value of reporting units needs to be calculated.

   a. Reporting entities now have the *option* of first assessing qualitative factors [events and circumstances] to determine whether it is more-likely-than-not (i.e., a likelihood of greater than 50%) that the fair value of a reporting unit is less than the carrying amount of that reporting unit. This is an optional step, so the qualitative assessment could be bypassed for any reporting unit in any period by proceeding directly to performing the first step of the two-step process.

   b. If, after considering all relevant events and circumstances, using the qualitative assessment, a conclusion is reached that it is *not* more-likely-than-not that the fair value of a reporting unit is less than its carrying amount, then performing the two-step process would not be necessary. However, if the converse is true, then the requirement still is retained related to performing the first step in the two-step impairment testing process, as that work is done today.

   c. In evaluating whether it is more-likely-than-not that the fair value of a reporting unit is less than its carrying amount, some examples of events and circumstances that need to be considered, among others, include:

   - Macroeconomic conditions
   - Industry and market considerations
   - Cost factors
   - Overall financial performance
   - Other relevant entity-specific events
   - Events affecting a reporting unit
   - Where applicable, a sustained decrease, both absolute and relative to peer entities, in share price.

   These events and circumstances are not intended to be all-inclusive. Other relevant events and circumstances might be identified that need to be considered in this overall qualitative assessment. It is important to consider positive and mitigating events and circumstances that may affect the determination of whether it is more-likely-than-not that the fair value of a reporting unit is less than its carrying amount. In circumstances where reporting entities have a recent fair value calculation for a reporting unit, this information may be useful in considering whether fair value exceeds the carrying amount by a substantial margin, and that assessment also would be helpful in determining whether the first step within the goodwill impairment test needs to be performed.

Exhibit 1 ▸ Goodwill Assessment

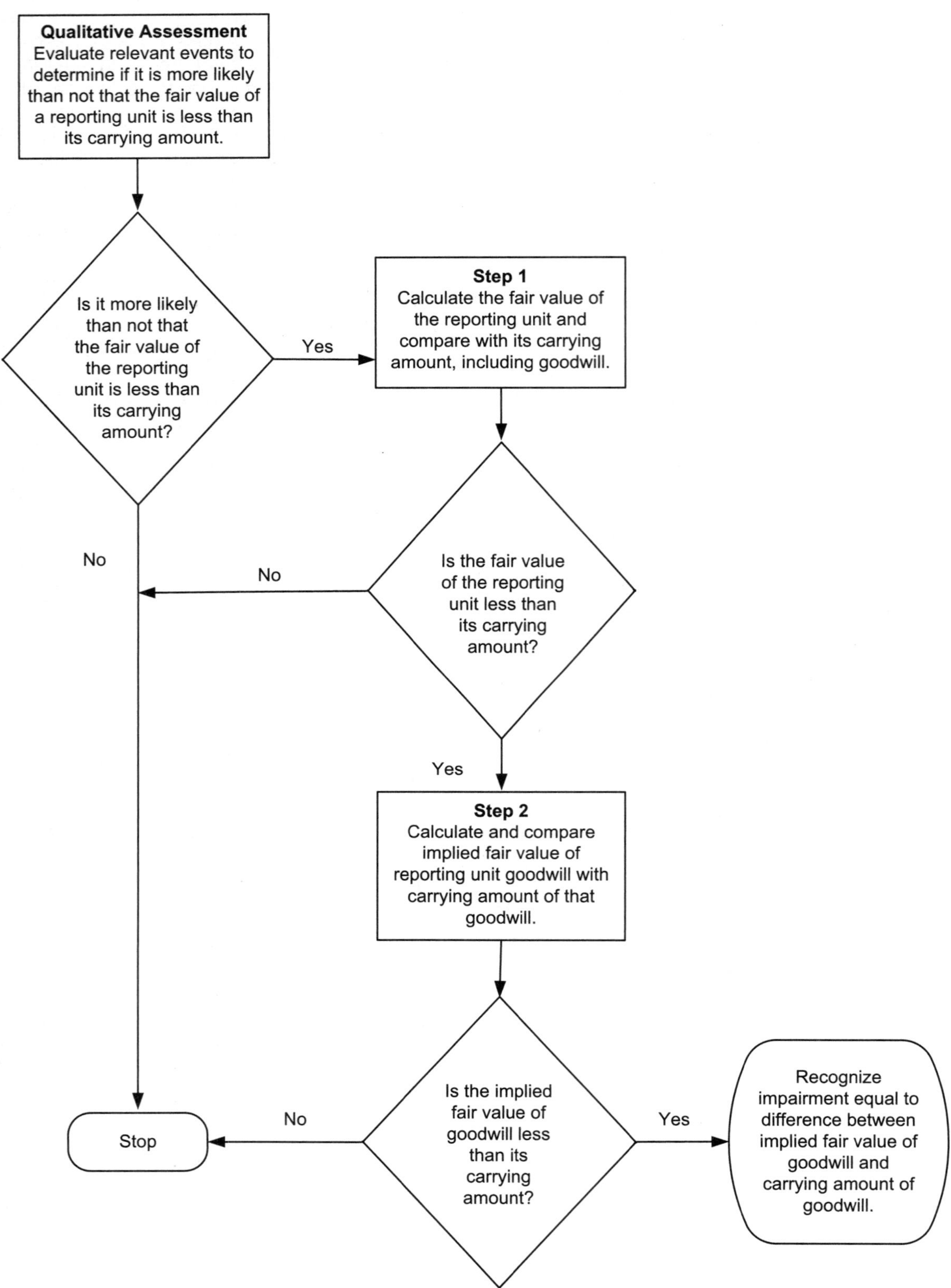

d. Accounting for goodwill is based on reporting units, (the units of the combined entity into which an acquired entity is integrated) as an aggregate view of goodwill. Goodwill is tested for impairment at a reporting unit level. A reporting unit is an operating segment or one level below an operating segment, referred to as a component. A component of an operating segment is a reporting unit if the component constitutes a business for which discrete financial information is available and segment management regularly reviews the operating results of that component.

e. The first step is a screen for potential impairment, and the second step measures the amount of impairment, if any.

(1) **Step One** The first step used to identify potential impairment compares reporting unit's fair value with its carrying amount, including goodwill. If the fair value exceeds its carrying amount, the reporting unit's goodwill is considered not impaired and the second step is unnecessary. If the carrying amount exceeds its fair value, the second step is performed.

For reporting units with zero or negative carrying amounts, they are *required* to perform Step 2 if it is *more likely than not* that a goodwill impairment exits. An entity should consider whether there are any adverse qualitative factors indicating that an impairment may exist.

(2) **Step Two** The second step compares the implied fair value of reporting unit's goodwill with its carrying amount. If the carrying amount exceeds the implied fair value of that goodwill, an impairment loss is recognized in an amount equal to that excess. The loss recognized cannot exceed the goodwill's carrying amount. After an impairment loss is recognized, the adjusted carrying amount of goodwill is its new accounting basis. Subsequent reversal of a previously recognized goodwill impairment loss is prohibited.

f. The guidance in International Accounting Standard (IAS) 36, *Impairment of Assets,* requires reporting entities to test goodwill for impairment using a single-step *quantitative* test performed at the level of a cash-generating unit or group of cash-generating units. That test needs to be performed at least annually, and then the test needs to be performed between annual tests whenever there is an indication of impairment. An impairment loss is recognized in circumstances where there is an excess of the carrying amount over the recoverable amount. Additionally, the amount of the impairment loss is not limited to the carrying amount of goodwill recorded in the cash-generating unit.

D. **Presentation**
Goodwill is presented as a separate line item. At a minimum, all other intangible assets are aggregated and presented as a separate line item in the statement of financial position. This does not preclude presentation of more detailed information.

1. **Expense & Losses** The amortization expense and impairment losses for intangible assets are presented in income statement line items within continuing operations. Goodwill impairment losses are presented as a separate line item in the income statement before the subtotal of income from continuing operations unless the impairment is associated with a discontinued operation. An impairment loss resulting from impairment testing is **not** recognized as a change in accounting principle.

2. **Disclosures**

a. **Acquisition Period**

(1) **Intangible Assets Subject to Amortization** In total and by major intangible asset class; the total amount, the amount of any significant residual value, and the weighted-average amortization period.

(2) **Intangible Assets Not Subject to Amortization** The total amount assigned and the amount assigned to any major intangible asset class.

(3) **Intangible Assets With Renewal or Extension Terms** The weighted-average period prior to the next renewal or extension by major intangible asset class.

(4) **Other Information** The amount of research and development assets acquired, other than a business combination, and written off in the period and the line item in the income statement in which the amounts written off are aggregated.

b. **Subsequent Periods**

(1) **Intangible Assets Subject to Amortization** The gross carrying amount and accumulated amortization, in total and by major intangible asset class, the aggregate amortization expense for the period, and the estimated aggregate amortization expense for each of the five succeeding fiscal years.

(2) **Intangible Assets Not Subject to Amortization** The total carrying amount and the carrying amount for each major intangible asset class.

(3) **Renewal or Extension Policy** The entity's accounting policy on the treatment of costs incurred to renew or extend the term of a recognizable intangible asset.

(4) **Intangible Assets Renewed or Extended in the Period** The weighted-average period prior to the next renewal or extension by major intangible class and for entities that capitalize renewal or extension costs, the total amount of costs incurred in the period to renew or extend the term of a recognized intangible asset, by major intangible asset class.

(5) **Goodwill** In total and for each reportable segment, the changes in the carrying amount of goodwill during the period showing separately:

(a) The gross amount and accumulated impairment losses at the beginning of the period

(b) Additional goodwill recognized during the period

(c) Adjustments resulting from the subsequent recognition of deferred tax assets during the period

(d) Goodwill included in a disposal group classified as held for sale and goodwill derecognized during the period without having previously been reported in a disposal group classified as held for sale

(e) Impairment losses recognized during the period

(f) Net exchange differences arising during the period due to any foreign currency translation

(g) Any other changes in the carrying amounts during the period

(h) The gross amount and accumulated impairment losses at the end of the period

c. **Periods When Impairment Loss is Recognized** The disclosures for periods that impairment loss is recognized include descriptions of the impaired asset, the facts and circumstances leading to the impairment, the amount of the impairment loss and the method for determining fair value, the caption in the income statement that includes the impairment loss, and any other potentially significant information.

II. Research & Development

A. Overview

Research activities are those aimed at the discovery of knowledge that will be useful in developing or significantly improving products or processes. *Development* activities are those concerned with translating research findings and other knowledge into plans or designs for new or significantly improved products or processes.

1. **R&D Examples** Examples of activities that are typically included in R&D

a. Laboratory research aimed at discovery of new knowledge

b. Searching for applications of new research findings or other knowledge

c. Conceptual formulation and design of product or process alternatives

d. Testing in search for or evaluation of product or process alternatives

e. Modification of the formulation or design of a product or process

f. Design, construction, and testing of pre-production prototypes and models

g. Design of tools, jigs, molds, and dies involving new technology

h. Pilot plant costs if **not** of a scale economically feasible for commercial production

i. Engineering activities until product meets specific functional and economic requirements and is ready for manufacture

2. **Non-R&D Examples** Examples of activities that are excluded from R&D

   a. Engineering follow-through in early stages of commercial production

   b. Quality control during commercial production including routine testing of products

   c. Troubleshooting in connection with breakdowns during commercial production

   d. Routine, ongoing efforts to improve existing products

   e. Adaptation of existing capability to meet particular requirements or customer's needs as part of continuing commercial activity

   f. Seasonal or other periodic design changes to existing products

   g. Routine design of tools, jigs, molds, and dies

   h. Construction, relocation, rearrangement, or start-up activities (including design and construction engineering) of facilities or equipment other than (1) pilot plants; and (2) facilities or equipment whose only use is for a particular R&D project

   i. Legal work to secure, sell, or license patents

B. Accounting

1. **Revenue Recognition** Research and/or development arrangements often include payment provisions for which a portion of the consideration to be received is contingent upon "milestone events." Examples of these types of events would include successful completion of phases in certain studies within the medical profession, or achieving specified results from other research or development work. Frequently, reporting entities recognize payments received as a result of reaching these types of milestones in their entirety upon achieving specific milestones. This revenue recognition approach is often referred to as the milestone method (see Chapter 11 for additional information on the milestone method).

   The milestone method of revenue recognition, which is, at its core, an application of the proportional performance method, is not the only revenue recognition method that is available for research and development arrangements. With the issuance of ASU 2010-17, there will still very likely be many reporting entities that continue to utilize other revenue recognition methods, including methods that represent variations of the proportional performance method. With that said, reporting entities will need to utilize revenue recognition methods that are selected on a consistent basis when considering how revenue should be recognized for similar arrangements.

2. **Expense R&D Costs** Future economic benefits deriving from R&D activities, if any, are uncertain in their amount and timing. Due to these uncertainties, most R&D costs are required to be charged to expense the year in which incurred. Capitalization of R&D costs, except as indicated below, is not acceptable.

3. **Alternative Future Uses** Materials, equipment, facilities, or intangibles purchased from others that are acquired for a particular R&D project and have *no alternative use* in other R&D projects or in normal operations should be *expensed* in the period in which acquired. However, these items should be recorded as *assets* if *alternative future uses* are expected, whether in other R&D activities or in normal operations. Assets recorded for R&D costs with alternative future uses should be amortized over their useful lives by periodic charges to R&D expense. If, at any point, these assets are no longer deemed to have alternative future uses, the remaining unamortized cost is charged to R&D expense for the period.

4. **Other Issues** R&D costs conducted for others under contract may be carried as assets. Contractually reimbursable R&D costs are not expensed as R&D.

5. **Acquired In-Proces Research and Development** In-process research and development (IPR&D) acquired as part of a business combination is initially valued at fair value. The IPR&D is then carried as an "indefinite-lived" intangible asset (which means it is not amortized). Once the resulting process is in use, the intangible asset is then amortized over its useful life. If the project fails, the intangible asset is expensed in its entirety.

Example 1 ▸ Research & Development

In the current year, Futura Inc. began an extensive research and development program. The following R&D related costs were incurred during the year:

Jan. 2:	Purchase of general purpose lab building (10-year life)	$150,000
Jan. 5:	Purchase of general purpose lab equipment (5-year life)	25,000
Jan. 7:	Purchase of a machine to be used exclusively on Project X (4-year life)	8,000
Jan. 30:	Acquired materials and supplies, as follows:	
	Materials to be used in Project X	10,000
	Miscellaneous lab supplies for several projects	12,000

In addition, $40,000 of direct labor costs was incurred on various R&D projects and $3,000 of overhead costs was appropriately allocated to R&D activities during the year. All but $4,000 of the materials purchased for Project X and $5,000 of the general purpose supplies were consumed during the year.

Required: Determine Futura's R&D expense for the year.

Solution: The cost of equipment and materials to be used on a single R&D project (i.e., having no alternative future uses) should be expensed as R&D when incurred.

Depreciation on lab building ($150,000 / 10)	$15,000
Depreciation on general purpose lab equipment ($25,000 / 5)	5,000
Machine to be used exclusively on Project X	8,000
Materials for Project X	10,000
Miscellaneous lab supplies ($12,000 – $5,000)	7,000
Direct labor	40,000
Appropriately allocated overhead	3,000
Total R&D expense for the year	$88,000

C. **Disclosures**
Total R&D costs expensed in each period for which an income statement is presented must be clearly disclosed.

III. Computer Software

A. To Be Sold, Leased, or Otherwise Marketed

The following applies only to computer software to be sold, leased, or otherwise marketed as a separate product or as a part of a product or process. If part of a product or process, it only applies if the software and software-related elements are more than incidental to the products or services as a whole.

1. **R&D Costs** Costs incurred internally in creating a computer software product are charged to expense when incurred as research and development until technological feasibility has been established for the product. Technological feasibility is established only upon completion of a detailed program design or, in its absence, completion of a working model. All costs of planning, designing, coding, and testing activities that are necessary to establish technological feasibility are expensed as research and development when incurred.

2. **Production Costs** The costs of producing product masters incurred subsequent to establishing technological feasibility are capitalized. Capitalized software costs are amortized on a product-by-product basis. These costs include coding and testing performed subsequent to establishing technological feasibility. Capitalization of computer software costs shall cease when the product is available for general release to customers. Costs of maintenance and customer support shall be charged to expense when related revenue is recognized or when those costs are incurred, whichever occurs first.

    a. Those costs for software that is to be used as an integral part of a product or process shall not be capitalized until both the technological feasibility has been established for the software and all research and development activities for the other components of the product or process have been completed.

    b. An entity may capitalize an allocated amount of indirect costs, such as overhead related to programmers and the facilities they occupy. However, an allocation of general and administrative expenses is not appropriate because those costs relate to the period in which they are incurred.

3. **Purchased Software** Some entities purchase software as an alternative to developing it internally. Purchased computer software may be modified or integrated with another product or process.

    a. The cost of purchased computer software to be sold, leased, or otherwise marketed that has no alternative future use shall be accounted for the same as the costs incurred to develop such software internally.

    b. An entity shall capitalize the total cost of purchased software if the technological feasibility of the software has been established. Otherwise, the cost will be charged to research and development.

    c. If purchased software has an alternative future use, the cost shall be capitalized when the software is acquired and accounted for in accordance with its use. The alternative future use test also applies to purchased software that will be integrated with a product or process in which the research and development activities for the other components are not complete.

4. **Inventory Costs** Costs incurred for (a) duplicating the computer software, documentation and training materials from product masters and (b) physically packaging the product for distribution are capitalized as inventory on a unit-specific basis. Capitalized inventory costs shall be charged to cost of sales when revenue from the sale of those units is recognized.

5. **Amortization** Amortization starts when the product is available for release to customers.

    a. The annual amortization is the **greater** of the amount computed using (1) the ratio that current gross revenues for a software product bear to the total of current and anticipated future gross revenue for that product, or (2) the straight-line method over the remaining estimated economic life of the product, including the current period being reported on.

    b. Amortization shall be based on estimated future revenues. Because of the uncertainties involved in estimating revenue, amortization shall not be less than straight-line amortization over the product's remaining estimated economic life.

    c. Because amortization expense of capitalized software costs relates to a software product that is marketed to others, the expense shall be charged to cost of sales or a similar expense category.

Example 2 ▸ Amortization Expense

On December 31 of year 1, the Clone Company had $200,000 of capitalized costs for a new computer software product with an economic useful life of five years. Sales for year 2 were thirty percent of expected total sales of the software.

Required: Determine the amortization expense for year 2.

Solution: Under the percent of revenue approach, the amortization expense for year 2 would be $60,000 ($200,000 × 30%). Under the straight-line approach, the amortization would be $40,000 ($200,000 / 5 years). The amortization for year 2 is $60,000, determined under the percent of revenue approach, because it results in a greater amortization charge.

6. **Net Realizable Value Test** At each balance sheet date, the unamortized capitalized costs of a computer software product shall be compared to the net realizable value of that product. The amount by which the unamortized capitalized costs of a computer software product exceed the net realizable value of that asset shall be written off.

   a. The net realizable value is the estimated future gross revenues from that product reduced by the estimated future costs of completing and disposing of that product, including the costs of performing maintenance and customer support required to satisfy the entity's responsibility set forth at the time of sale.

   b. The reduced amount of capitalized computer software costs that have been written down to net realizable value at the close of an annual fiscal period shall be considered to be the cost for subsequent accounting purposes, and the amount of the write-down shall not be subsequently restored.

7. **Other Presentation** In an entity's balance sheet, capitalized software costs having a life of more than one year or one operating cycle shall be presented as an other asset because the costs are an amortizable intangible asset. Guidance applicable to intangible assets applies.

8. **Disclosures** An entity must disclose the unamortized computer software costs included in each balance sheet presented and the total amount charged to expense for both the amortization of capitalized software costs and amounts written down to net realizable value.

B. **Developed or Obtained for Internal Use**

1. **Preliminary Project Stage** Computer software costs that are incurred in the preliminary project stage should be expensed as incurred. Activities in this stage include conceptual formulation and evaluation of alternatives, determination of existence of needed technology, and final selection of alternatives.

2. **Application Development Stage**

   a. Most costs in this stage are capitalized, including external direct costs, payroll and payroll-related costs for those who are directly involved with the project, and interest costs. Activities in this stage include design of the chosen path, design of the software configuration, coding, installation to hardware, and testing. Capitalization of the costs should cease when the software project is substantially complete and ready for its intended use, which generally is after all substantial testing is completed.

   b. Training costs and data conversion costs are generally expensed.

3. **Post-Implementation/Operation Stage**

   a. Internal and external training and maintenance costs should be expensed as incurred. The costs of upgrades are capitalized.

   b. Capitalized costs are amortized over the estimated useful life, and adjusted periodically with changes in the estimates of the useful life or when the value of the asset is impaired.

   c. If, after the development of internal-use software is completed, the entity decides to market the software, net proceeds received from the license should be applied against the carrying amount of the software.

IV. Other Assets

A. Prepaid Expenses

Under accrual accounting, revenues and expenses are recognized when earned or incurred, respectively. Thus when a firm pays in advance for a good or service such as insurance, rent, interest, etc., the cost of the item is first recorded as an asset—*Prepaid Expense.*

1. **Current vs. Noncurrent** In a classified balance sheet, a prepaid expense should be separated into a current and a noncurrent portion. In general, the current portion of the prepaid expense is the amount that expires within the next 12 months.

2. **Realized Expense** As the benefits from the prepayment are realized (i.e., the costs expire), the prepaid expenses are reduced and charged to an appropriate expense account, such as insurance expense, rent expense, interest expense, etc.

Example 3 ▸ Prepaid Insurance

On April 1, Denso Co. purchased for $120,000 a 4-year blanket casualty insurance policy covering all its buildings, equipment, and inventory. Denso is a calendar year corporation that issues a classified balance sheet.

Required: Provide the journal entries if Denso Co. initially records this policy as an asset and as an expense. Show the proper balance sheet presentation at December 31.

Solution: Premium, $120,000 / Number of months, 48 = Monthly expense, $2,500

1. Journal entries if initially recorded as an asset

Date	Account	Debit	Credit
4/1	Prepaid Insurance	120,000	
	Cash		120,000
12/31	Insurance Expense ($2,500/month × 9 months)	22,500	
	Prepaid Insurance		22,500

2. Journal entries if initially recorded as an expense

Date	Account	Debit	Credit
4/1	Insurance Expense	120,000	
	Cash		120,000
12/31	Prepaid Insurance [$120,000 – ($2,500 × 9)]	97,500	
	Insurance Expense		97,500

3. Balance sheet presentation, December 31

Current Assets	
Prepaid insurance (12 mos. × $2,500)	$30,000
Noncurrent Assets	
Prepaid insurance (27 mos. × $2,500)	$67,500

B. Cash Surrender Value of Life Insurance

Companies frequently insure the lives of key executives. Insurance premiums paid on many such life insurance policies consist of an amount for life insurance and a balance that constitutes a form of savings. The savings portion is manifested in the growing cash surrender value (amount realizable by the owner of the policy should the policy be canceled). Investments in life insurance contracts need to be reflected in financial statements as assets, measured at the amounts that could be realized under the contracts as of the financial statement date. The amount to be reported as life insurance expense for a year is the annual premium paid, less (1) the increase in cash surrender value and (2) any dividends received.

Contractual terms of insurance policies need to be considered in determining amounts that could be realized under a variety of insurance contracts. When it is probable that contractual terms would limit the amount that could be realized under the contracts, the limitations need to be considered in determining realizable amounts. The key here is that amounts that would be recoverable at the discretion of insurance entities issuing the policies need to be excluded from amounts that could be realized under life insurance contracts. Reporting entities need to determine amounts that will be realized under life insurance contracts assuming surrender of an individual-life by individual-life policy, or certificate by certificate in a group policy. Amounts that ultimately would be realized upon surrender of a final policy, or final certificate in a group policy, need to be included in the amount that could be realized under the insurance contract.

Using the guidance in GAAP for defined benefit plans, insurance contracts with insurance entities, other than those that are in substance annuities, need to be accounted for as investments and measured at fair value. That guidance also contains the clear stipulation that, for some contracts, the best available evidence of the fair value might well be contract value. If a contract has a determinable cash surrender value or conversion value that amount generally is presumed to be the fair value of the contract.

C. Special Purpose Funds

These funds result from the setting aside of specific assets, usually under the custody of a trustee, for a particular purpose. Some funds may be voluntarily created, such as preferred stock acquisition funds and plant expansion funds. Other funds result from contractual obligations, such as debt retirement funds. The fund is established by crediting cash or other assets and debiting the fund account. The fund is affected by (1) additions or withdrawals to the fund, (2) earnings on the fund, (3) gains or losses on the disposal of assets in the fund, and (4) expenses of operating the fund. The exchange of one asset for another within the fund (such as the exchange of cash for an investment) will not have any net effect on the balance of the fund. The fund balance at the end of the period is presented as a net amount, a separate line item, generally under *Investments and Funds.* The fund accounts for its own investments and generally records its own revenues and expenses.

Don't forget the helpful hints in the material at the front and back of this text!

Now that you have had a chance to become familiar with the text format, you may want to skim the **Getting Started, Exam Preparation Tips,** and **Research Skills** sections of the book again. These sections provide information on how to:

- Integrate materials so that they work best for you
- Develop effective techniques and strategies for passing the exam
- Organize a personalized training plan which uses your time wisely
- Structure an efficient search of an electronic database in order to select appropriate guidance
- Answer all question types

Remember, with the techniques and information in your material,

A passing score is well within reach!

CHAPTER 5—INTANGIBLES, R&D, SOFTWARE & OTHER ASSETS

Problem 5-1 MULTIPLE-CHOICE QUESTIONS

1. To be considered intangible, an asset must be which of the following?

   a. Classified as identifiable.
   b. Without physical substance.
   c. Internally developed.
   d. All of the above. (Editor, 4213)

2. Grayson Co. incurred significant costs in defending its patent rights. Which of the following is the appropriate treatment of the related litigation costs?

   a. Litigation costs would be capitalized regardless of the outcome of the litigation.
   b. Litigation costs would be expensed regardless of the outcome of the litigation.
   c. Litigation costs would be capitalized if the patent right is successfully defended.
   d. Litigation costs would be capitalized only if the patent was purchased rather than internally developed. (R/11, FAR, #15, 9865)

3. During the year, Jase Co. incurred research and development costs of $136,000 in its laboratories relating to a patent that was granted on July 1. Costs of registering the patent equaled $34,000. The patent's legal life is 20 years, and its estimated economic life is 10 years. In its December 31 balance sheet, what amount should Jase report as patent, net of accumulated amortization?

   a. $ 32,300
   b. $ 33,000
   c. $161,500
   d. $165,000 (5/95, FAR, #13, amended, 5549)

4. On January 2, Rafa Co. purchased a franchise with a useful life of ten years for $50,000. An additional franchise fee of 3% of franchise operation revenues must be paid each year to the franchisor. Revenues from franchise operations amounted to $400,000 during the year. In its December 31 balance sheet, what amount should Rafa report as an intangible asset-franchise?

   a. $33,000
   b. $43,800
   c. $45,000
   d. $50,000 (5/94, FAR, #20, amended, 4835)

5. On December 1, of the current year, Clark Co. leased office space for five years at a monthly rental of $60,000. On the same date, Clark paid the lessor the following amounts:

First months' rent	$ 60,000
Last months' rent	60,000
Security deposit (refundable at lease expiration)	80,000
Installation of new walls and offices	$360,000

   What should be Clark's current year expense relating to utilization of the office space?

   a. $ 60,000
   b. $ 66,000
   c. $120,000
   d. $140,000 (11/92, PI, #56, amended, 3288)

6. Green Co. incurred leasehold improvement costs for its leased property. The estimated useful life of the improvements was 15 years. The remaining term of the nonrenewable lease was 20 years. These costs should be

   a. Expensed as incurred
   b. Capitalized and depreciated over 15 years
   c. Capitalized and depreciated over 20 years
   d. Capitalized and expensed in the year in which the lease expires (R/06, FAR, #35, 8102)

7. A company recently acquired a copyright that now has a remaining legal life of 30 years. The copyright initially had a 38-year useful life assigned to it. An analysis of market trends and consumer habits indicated that the copyrighted material will generate positive cash flows for approximately 25 years. What is the remaining useful life, if any, over which the company can amortize the copyright for accounting purposes?

   a. 0 years
   b. 25 years
   c. 30 years
   d. 38 years (R/10, FAR, #36, 9336)

8. During January, Yana Co. incurred landscaping costs of $120,000 to improve leased property. The estimated useful life of the landscaping is fifteen years. The remaining term of the lease is eight years, with an option to renew for an additional four years. However, Yana has not reached a decision with regard to the renewal option. In Yana's December 31 balance sheet, what should be the net carrying amount of landscaping costs?

   a. $0
   b. $105,000
   c. $110,000
   d. $112,000 (11/97, FAR, #8, amended, 6488)

9. On January 2, Judd Co. bought a trademark from Krug Co. for $500,000. Judd retained an independent consultant, who estimated the trademark's remaining life to be 50 years. Its unamortized cost on Krug's accounting records was $380,000. In Judd's December 31 balance sheet, what amount should be reported as accumulated amortization?

   a. $ 7,600
   b. $ 9,500
   c. $10,000
   d. $12,500 (11/93, PI, #25, amended, 4394)

10. On June 30, Union Inc. purchased goodwill of $125,000 when it acquired the net assets of Apex Corp. During the year, Union incurred additional costs of developing goodwill, by training Apex employees ($50,000) and hiring additional Apex employees ($25,000). Union's December 31 balance sheet should report goodwill of

    a. $200,000
    b. $175,000
    c. $150,000
    d. $125,000 (5/91, PI, #28, amended, 0998)

11. Which of the following is an adverse qualitative factor related to goodwill?

    a. Unanticipated competition
    b. Loss of key personnel
    c. Adverse action or assessment by a regulator
    d. All of the above (Editors, 89441)

12. On January 2, year 1, Lava Inc. purchased a patent for a new consumer product for $90,000. At the time of purchase, the patent was valid for 15 years; however, the patent's useful life was estimated to be only 10 years due to the competitive nature of the product. On December 31, year 4, the product was permanently withdrawn from sale under governmental order because of a potential health hazard in the product. What amount should Lava charge against income during year 4, assuming amortization is recorded at the end of each year?

    a. $ 9,000
    b. $54,000
    c. $63,000
    d. $72,000 (11/93, PI, #54, amended, 4423)

13. A company reported $6 million of goodwill in last year's statement of financial position. How should the company account for the reported goodwill in the current year?

    a. Determine the current year's amortizable amount and report the current-year's amortization expense
    b. Determine whether the fair value of the reporting unit is greater than the carrying amount and report a gain on goodwill in the income statement
    c. Determine whether the fair value of the reporting unit is **less** than the carrying amount and report an impairment loss on goodwill in the income statement
    d. Determine whether the fair value of the reporting unit is greater than the carrying amount and report the recovery of any previous impairment in the income statement (R/10, FAR, #37, 9337)

14. Northstar Co. acquired a registered trademark for $600,000. The trademark has a remaining legal life of five years, but can be renewed every 10 years for a nominal fee. Northstar expects to renew the trademark indefinitely. What amount of amortization expense should Northstar record for the trademark in the current year?

    a. $0
    b. $ 15,000
    c. $ 40,000
    d. $120,000 (R/10, FAR, #7, 9307)

15. Johan Co. has an intangible asset, which it estimates will have a useful life of 10 years, while Abco Co. has goodwill, which has an indefinite life. Which company should report amortization in its financial statements?

	Johan	Abco
a.	Yes	Yes
b.	Yes	No
c.	No	Yes
d.	No	No

(R/07, FAR, #11, 8332)

16. After an impairment loss is recognized, the adjusted carrying amount of the intangible asset shall be its new accounting basis. Which of the following statements about subsequent reversal of a previously recognized impairment loss is correct?

    a. It is prohibited.
    b. It is required when the reversal is considered permanent.
    c. It must be disclosed in the notes to the financial statements.
    d. It is encouraged, but not required. (R/09, FAR, #18, 8768)

17. Goodwill should be tested for value impairment at which of the following levels?

    a. Entire business as a whole
    b. Each identifiable long-term asset
    c. Each acquisition unit
    d. Each reporting unit (R/07, FAR, #43, 8364)

18. Which of the following is a research and development cost?

    a. Development or improvement of techniques and processes
    b. Offshore oil exploration that is the primary activity of a company
    c. Research and development performed under contract for others
    d. Market research related to a major product for the company (R/06, FAR, #31, 8098)

19. Which of the following is an example of activities that would typically be excluded in research and development costs?

    a. Design, construction, and testing of preproduction prototypes and modes
    b. Laboratory research aimed at discovery of new knowledge
    c. Quality control during commercial production, including routine testing of products
    d. Testing in search for, or evaluation of, product or process alternatives (R/05, FAR, #45, 7789)

20. Which of the following expenditures qualifies for asset capitalization?
    a. Cost of materials used in prototype testing
    b. Costs of testing a prototype and modifying its design
    c. Salaries of engineering staff developing a new product
    d. Legal costs associated with obtaining a patent on a new product (R/08, FAR, #20, 8575)

21. Cody Corp. incurred the following costs during the year:

Design of tools, jigs, molds, and dies involving new technology	$125,000
Modification of the formulation of a process	160,000
Troubleshooting in connection with break-downs during commercial production	100,000
Adaptation of an existing capability to a particular customer's need as part of a continuing commercial activity	110,000

    In its year-end income statement, Cody should report research and development expense of
    a. $125,000
    b. $160,000
    c. $235,000
    d. $285,000 (11/90, PI, #42, amended, 1000)

22. During the current year, Beta Motor Co. incurred the following costs related to a new solar-powered car:

Salaries of laboratory employees researching how to build the new car	$250,000
Legal fees for the patent application for the new car	20,000
Engineering follow-up during the early stages of commercial production (the follow-up occurred during the current year)	50,000
Marketing research to promote the new car	30,000
Design, testing, and construction of a prototype	400,000

    What amount should Beta Motor report as research and development expense in its income statement for the current year?
    a. $250,000
    b. $650,000
    c. $720,000
    d. $750,000 (R/10, FAR, #44, 9344)

23. Stam Co. incurred the following research and development project costs during the current year:

Equipment purchased for current and future projects	$100,000
Equipment purchased for current projects only	200,000
Research and development salaries for current projects	400,000
Legal fees to obtain patent	50,000
Material and labor costs for prototype product	600,000

    The equipment has a five-year useful life and is depreciated using the straight-line method. What amount should Stam recognize as research and development expense at year end?
    a. $ 450,000
    b. $1,000,000
    c. $1,220,000
    d. $1,350,000 (R/08, FAR, #45, 8600)

24. Miller Co. incurred the following computer software costs for the development and sale of software programs during the current year:

Planning costs	$ 50,000
Design of the software	150,000
Substantial testing of the project's initial stages	75,000
Production and packaging costs for the first month's sales	500,000
Costs of producing product masters after technology feasibility was established	200,000

The project was not under any contractual arrangement when these expenditures were incurred. What amount should Miller report as research and development expense for the current year?

a. $200,000
b. $275,000
c. $500,000
d. $975,000 (R/02, FAR #9, 7064)

25. Which of the following computer software costs should be expensed?

a. Conceptual formulation of alternatives in the preliminary project stage
b. Design of the software configuration during the application development stage
c. The costs of upgrades during the post-implementation/operation stage
d. Installation to hardware during the application development stage (Editor, 89614)

26. During the year, Pitt Corp. incurred costs to develop and produce a routine, low-risk computer software product, as follows:

Design of tools, jigs, molds, and dies involving new technology	$125,000
Completion of detail program design	13,000
Costs incurred for coding and testing to establish technological feasibility	10,000
Other coding costs after establishment of technological feasibility	24,000
Other testing costs after establishment of technological feasibility	20,000
Costs of producing product masters for training materials	15,000
Duplication of computer software and training materials from product masters (1,000 units)	25,000
Packaging product (500 units)	9,000

In Pitt's December 31 balance sheet, what amount should be capitalized as software cost, subject to amortization?

a. $54,000
b. $57,000
c. $59,000
d. $69,000 (5/91, PI, #22, amended 0996)

27. On December 31, year 1, Bit Co. had capitalized costs for a new computer software product with an economic life of five years. Sales for year 2 were 30 percent of expected total sales of the software. At December 31, year 2, the software had a net realizable value equal to 90 percent of the capitalized cost. What percentage of the original capitalized cost should be reported as the net amount on Bit's December 31, year 2 balance sheet?

a. 70%
b. 72%
c. 80%
d. 90% (5/92, Theory, #14, amended, 2707)

28. Yellow Co. spent $12,000,000 during the current year developing its new software package. Of this amount, $4,000,000 was spent before it was at the application development stage and the package was only to be used internally. The package was completed during the year and is expected to have a four-year useful life. Yellow has a policy of taking a full-year's amortization in the first year. After the development stage, $50,000 was spent on training employees to use the program. What amount should Yellow report as an expense for the current year?

    a. $1,600,000
    b. $2,000,000
    c. $6,012,500
    d. $6,050,000 (R/06, FAR, #37, 8104)

29. Under East Co.'s accounting system, all insurance premiums paid are debited to prepaid insurance. For interim financial reports, East makes monthly estimated charges to insurance expense with credits to prepaid insurance. Additional information for the year ended December 31, year 2, is as follows:

Prepaid insurance at December 31, year 1	$105,000
Charges to insurance expense during year 2 (including a year-end adjustment of $17,500)	437,500
Prepaid insurance at December 31, year 2	122,500

    What was the total amount of insurance premiums paid by East during year 2?

    a. $332,500
    b. $420,000
    c. $437,500
    d. $455,000 (5/91, PI, #30, amended, 9058)

30. An analysis of Thrift Corp.'s unadjusted prepaid expense account at December 31, year 2, revealed the following:

    - An opening balance of $1,500 for Thrift's comprehensive insurance policy. Thrift had paid an annual premium of $3,000 on July 1, year 1.
    - A $3,200 annual insurance premium payment made July 1, year 2.
    - A $2,000 advance rental payment for a warehouse Thrift leased for one year beginning January 1, year 3.

    In its December 31, year 2 balance sheet, what amount should Thrift report as prepaid expenses?

    a. $5,200
    b. $3,600
    c. $2,000
    d. $1,600 (5/93, PI, #27, amended, 4069)

31. The premium on a three-year insurance policy expiring on December 31, year 3, was paid in total on January 2, year 1. If the company has a 6-month operating cycle, then on December 31, year 1, the prepaid insurance reported as a current asset would be for

    a. 6 months
    b. 12 months
    c. 18 months
    d. 24 months (5/90, Theory, #6, amended, 1758)

32. On May 1 of the current year, Marno County issued property tax assessments for the fiscal year ending the following June 30. The first of two equal installments was due on November 1 of this year. On September 1, Dyur Co. purchased a 4-year old factory in Marno subject to an allowance for accrued taxes. Dyur did not record the entire year's property tax obligation, but instead records tax expenses at the end of each month by adjusting prepaid property taxes or property taxes payable, as appropriate. The recording of the November 1, payment by Dyur should have been allocated between an increase in prepaid property taxes and a decrease in property taxes payable in which of the following percentages?

	Increase in prepaid property taxes	Decrease in property taxes payable	
a.	66-2/3%	33-1/3%	
b.	0%	100%	
c.	50%	50%	
d.	33-1/3%	66-2/3%	(5/91, Theory, #13, amended, 2045)

33. On January 1, year 1, Sip Co. signed a 5-year contract enabling it to use a patented manufacturing process beginning in year 1. A royalty is payable for each product produced, subject to a minimum annual fee. Any royalties in excess of the minimum will be paid annually. On the contract date, Sip prepaid a sum equal to two years' minimum annual fees. In year 1, only minimum fees were incurred. The royalty prepayment should be reported in Sip's December 31, year 1 financial statements as

   a. An expense only
   b. A current asset and an expense
   c. A current asset and noncurrent asset
   d. A noncurrent asset (11/92, Theory, #28, amended, 3461)

34. Ott Company acquired rights to a patent from Grey under a licensing agreement that required an advance royalty payment when the agreement was signed. Ott remits royalties earned and due, under the agreement, on October 31 each year. Additionally, on the same date, Ott pays, in advance, estimated royalties for the next year. Ott adjusts prepaid royalties at year-end. Information for the current year ended December 31 is as follows:

Date		Amount
01/01	Prepaid royalties	$ 65,000
10/31	Royalty payment (charged to royalty expense)	110,000
12/31	Year-end credit adjustment to royalty expense	25,000

In its December 31 balance sheet, Ott should report prepaid royalties of

   a. $25,000
   b. $40,000
   c. $85,000
   d. $90,000 (11/86, PI, #1, amended, 0986)

35. Upon the death of an officer, Jung Co. received the proceeds of a life insurance policy held by Jung on the officer. The proceeds were not taxable. The policy's cash surrender value had been recorded on Jung's books at the time of payment. What amount of revenue should Jung report in its statements?

   a. Proceeds received
   b. Proceeds received less cash surrender value
   c. Proceeds received plus cash surrender value
   d. None (11/95, FAR, #35, 6117)

36. On January 2, year 1, Jann Co. purchased a $150,000 whole-life insurance policy on its president. The annual premium is $4,000. The company is both the owner and the beneficiary. Jann charged officers' life insurance expense as follows:

Year 1	$ 4,000
Year 2	3,600
Year 3	3,000
Year 4	2,200
Total	$12,800

In its December 31, year 4, balance sheet, what amount should Jann report as investment in cash surrender value of officers' life insurance?

a. $0
b. $ 3,200
c. $12,800
d. $16,000 (5/97, FAR, #2, amended, 6474)

37. In year 1, Chain Inc. purchased a $1,000,000 life insurance policy on its president, of which Chain is the beneficiary. Information regarding the policy for the year ended December 31, year 6, follows:

Cash surrender value, 1/1, year 6	$ 87,000
Cash surrender value, 12/31, year 6	108,000
Annual advance premium paid 1/1, year 6	40,000

During year 6, dividends of $6,000 were applied to increase the cash surrender value of the policy. What amount should Chain report as life insurance expense for year 6?

a. $40,000
b. $25,000
c. $19,000
d. $13,000 (11/92, PI, #51, amended, 3284)

38. An issuer of bonds uses a sinking fund for the retirement of the bonds. Cash was transferred to the sinking fund and subsequently used to purchase investments. The sinking fund

I. Increases by revenue earned on the investments
II. Is **not** affected by revenue earned on the investments
III. Decreases when the investments are purchased

a. I only
b. I and III
c. II and III
d. III only (11/91, Theory, #36, 2544)

39. On March 1, year 1, a company established a sinking fund in connection with an issue of bonds due in year 8. At December 31, year 5, the independent trustee held cash in the sinking fund account representing the annual deposits to the fund and the interest earned on those deposits. How should the sinking fund be reported in the company's balance sheet at December 31, year 5?

a. The entire balance in the sinking fund account should appear as a current asset.
b. The entire balance in the sinking fund account should appear as a noncurrent asset.
c. Only the accumulated deposits should appear as a noncurrent asset.
d. The cash in the sinking fund should appear as a current asset. (11/93, Theory, #43, amended, 4548)

40. The following information relates to noncurrent investments that Fall Corp. placed in trust as required by the underwriter of its bonds:

Bond sinking fund balance, 12/31, year 1	$ 450,000
Year 2 additional investment	90,000
Dividends on investments	15,000
Interest revenue	30,000
Administration costs	5,000
Carrying amount of bonds payable	1,025,000

What amount should Fall report in its December 31, year 2 balance sheet related to its noncurrent investment for bond sinking fund requirements?

a. $585,000
b. $580,000
c. $575,000
d. $540,000 (5/93, PI, #16, amended, 4058)

Problem 5-2 SIMULATION: Accounting Treatment

Advance Corporation is involved in a number of projects related to its future success. Some of these projects are considered operational activities while others are considered research and development (R&D) activities. Advance must determine the proper accounting treatment in assessing certain expenditures for the year.

Select the proper accounting treatment for each of the expenditures listed below. Each choice may be used once, more than once, or not at all.

Answer Choices	
A. Record as receivable	E. Expense as consumed as R&D expense
B. Capitalize and amortize	F. Expense immediately as R&D
C. Capitalize and depreciate (as normally)	G. Expense as manufacturing cost
D. Capitalize and depreciate as R&D expense	H. Expense as operating expense

Expenditure	**Choice**
1. Executive salaries	
2. Costs incurred to upgrade current production facility	
3. Legal fees to obtain a patent on a new rocket engine	
4. Salaries of research staff designing new rocket engine	
5. Marketing research costs to promote new rocket engine	
6. Costs incurred to improve engine currently in production	
7. Commissions to sales staff marketing new rocket engine	
8. Material, labor, and overhead costs of new rocket engine	
9. Purchase of materials to be used on current and future R&D projects	
10. Costs incurred to successfully defend patent on the new rocket engine	
11. Acquisition of machinery to be used on current and future R&D projects	
12. Engineering costs to advance new rocket engine to full production stage	
13. Acquisition of R&D equipment for use on new rocket engine project only	
14. Research costs by ElectroMags Corp under contract for new rocket engine	
15. Research costs incurred under contract for Propel, Inc., and billed monthly	
16. Costs incurred in testing new rocket engine prototype and design modifications	
17. Construction of long-range research facility for use in current and future projects	
18. Costs of quality control in early stages of new rocket engine commercial production	
19. Costs of adapting existing capability to meet a customer's need as commercial activity	

(11/90, Theory, #4, 6190t)

Problem 5-3 SIMULATION: Research

... is the cost of purchased or leased software for use in research and development activities

(9109)

Solution 5-1 MULTIPLE-CHOICE ANSWERS

Intangibles

1. (b) Intangible assets are assets without physical substance that provide economic benefits through the rights and privileges associated with their possession. Intangibles may be classified as identifiable or unidentifiable and externally acquired or internally developed. (4213)

2. (c) Legal fees in a successful defense are capitalized because they offer probable future benefits. They are amortized over the remaining useful life of the patent. (9865)

3. (a) Research and development costs are expensed as incurred. Only the costs of acquiring a patent should be capitalized. Thus, only the cost of registering the patent, $34,000, is capitalized. The capitalized cost of an intangible asset is amortized over the asset's economic life. One-half year of amortization is $1,700 ($34,000 / 10 years × 1/2 year). [($34,000 – $1,700) = $32,300] (5549)

4. (c) The 3% of revenues fee is expensed in the period incurred, not capitalized and amortized. The franchise is amortized over its determinable useful life of 10 years.

Franchise	$50,000	
Amortization ($50,000 × 10%)	(5,000)	
Intangible asset, 12/31	$45,000	(4835)

5. (b) The new walls and offices are leasehold improvements since they are not separable from the leased property and revert to the lessor at the end of the lease term. They are amortized over the lease term. The prepayment of the last month's rent was made to secure the lease and should be reported as a leasehold within intangible assets.

Rent for December	$60,000	
Amortization of leasehold improvements for December ($360,000 / 60)	6,000	
Total expense relating to use of office space	$66,000	(3288)

6. (b) A leasehold improvement is an improvement made by the lessee to a leased property for which benefits are expected beyond the current accounting period. The cost of leasehold improvements should be capitalized and amortized over the lesser of the estimated useful life or the remaining term of the lease. If a lease has a renewal option, which the lessee intends to exercise, the leasehold improvement should be amortized over the lesser of its estimated useful life or the sum of the remaining term of the lease and the period covered by the renewal option. The leasehold improvement costs incurred by Green Co. would be capitalized and depreciated over 15 years, the estimated useful life. (8102)

7. (b) A copyright is an exclusive right granted by the federal government giving the owner protection against the illegal production by others. Although the copyright period is for the life of the creator plus 70 years, the cost of a copyright should be amortized over its useful life. Generating positive cash flows for approximately 25 years would indicate a useful life of 25 years for the copyright. (9336)

8. (b) The landscaping costs are leasehold improvements and should be capitalized and amortized over the lesser of the estimated useful life or the remaining term of the lease, including renewal options. The remaining term of the lease, with or without the renewal option, is less than the estimated useful life of 15 years. Because Yana Co. has not reached a decision to exercise the option to renew for the additional four years, the landscaping costs should be amortized over the 8-year remaining term of the lease. At December 31, one year of amortization, $15,000 ($120,000 / 8 years) should be expensed. Cost of $120,000 less amortization of $15,000 equals a net carrying amount of $105,000. (6488)

9. (c) The $500,000 acquisition cost of the trademark is amortized over the useful life, resulting in accumulated amortization of $10,000 at 12/31. The unamortized cost on Krug's books is irrelevant in determining Judd's acquisition cost. (4394)

10. (d) Costs of goodwill from a business combination accounted for as a purchase should be capitalized. However, costs of developing, maintaining, or restoring goodwill should be expensed when incurred. Thus, the goodwill of $125,000 from the acquisition of the net assets of Apex should be capitalized, while the additional costs of developing goodwill should be expensed as incurred. (0988)

Intangibles After Acquisition

11. (d) All of the factors listed are considered adverse qualitative factors related to testing goodwill impairment. (89441)

12. (c) The patented product was withdrawn from sale under governmental order. Therefore, the unamortized cost of the patent at 12/31, year 4 should be charged to income.

Purchase price of patent	$ 90,000
Less: Amortization prior to year 4 ($90,000 × 3/10)	(27,000)
Unamortized cost of patent, year 4	$ 63,000

(4423)

13. (c) Goodwill is not amortized; it is tested for impairment at least annually using a two-step process. The first step is a screen for potential impairment and the second step measures the amount of impairment, if any. The first step is to compare the reporting unit's fair value with its carrying amount, including goodwill. If the fair value exceeds its carrying amount, the reporting unit's goodwill is considered not impaired and no further action is necessary. There is no gain ever associated with goodwill. If the fair value is less than the carrying amount the second step compares the implied fair value of the reporting unit's goodwill with its carrying amount. If the carrying amount exceeds the implied fair value of that goodwill, an impairment loss is recognized in an amount equal to the excess. The loss recognized cannot exceed the goodwill's carrying amount. After an impairment loss is recognized, the adjusted carrying amount of goodwill is its new accounting basis. Subsequent reversal of previously recognized goodwill impairment is prohibited. (9337)

14. (a) A trademark is an identifiable tangible asset. With an externally acquired trademark, normally the acquisition costs are capitalized and amortized over the useful life of the trademark. If an intangible asset has an indefinite life, as is the case with the trademark in this question, it is not amortized but rather tested at least annually for impairment until its useful life is determined to be no longer indefinite. If the trademark had been internally developed the costs would have been expensed as incurred. (9307)

15. (b) Intangible assets with finite useful lives are amortized over their useful lives, without constraint of an arbitrary ceiling. Goodwill and intangible assets with indefinite useful lives are not amortized, but rather are tested at least annually for impairment. (8332)

16. (a) An impairment loss is recognized if the carrying amount of an intangible asset is not recoverable and its carrying amount exceeds its fair value. After an impairment loss is recognized, the adjusted carrying amount of the asset is its new accounting basis. Subsequent reversal of a previously recognized impairment loss is prohibited under U.S. GAAP. (8768)

17. (d) Accounting for goodwill is based on reporting units as an aggregate view of goodwill. Goodwill is tested for impairment at a reporting unit level. A reporting unit is an operating segment or one level below an operating segment, referred to as a component. A component of an operating segment is a reporting unit if the component constitutes a business for which discrete financial information is available and segment management regularly reviews the operating results of that component. (8364)

R&D Costs

18. (a) Research activities are those aimed at the discovery of knowledge that will be useful in developing or significantly improving products or processes and development activities are those concerned with translating research findings and other knowledge into plans or designs for new or significantly improved products, techniques, or processes. Offshore oil exploration as a primary activity is the main job function and not a R&D cost. Research and development under contract for others is a service and not a R&D cost. Market research for a product is a company expense and not a R&D cost. (8098)

19. (c) Quality control during commercial production including routine testing of products is an example of an activity typically excluded in research and development costs. Laboratory research aimed at discovery of new knowledge, testing in search for or evaluation of product or process alternatives design, construction, and testing of pre-production prototypes and models are examples of activities typically included in research and development costs. (7789)

20. (d) The external acquisition costs of a patent, which includes the legal costs associated with obtaining a patent on a new product, qualifies for asset capitalization. Cost of materials used in prototype testing, costs of testing a prototype and modifying its design, and salaries of engineering staff developing a new product are all examples of research and development costs. These research and development costs are not capitalized, but instead expensed in the year in which incurred. (8575)

21. (d) The design of tools, jigs, molds, and dies involving new technology ($125,000) and the modification of the formulation of a process ($160,000) typically would be included in R&D. Troubleshooting in connection with breakdowns during commercial production and the adaptation of an existing capability to a particular customer's need as part of a continuing commercial activity typically are excluded from R&D. (1000)

22. (b) Research activities are those aimed at the discovery of knowledge that will be useful in developing or significantly improving products or processes. Development activities are those concerned with translating research findings and other knowledge into plans or designs for new or significantly improved products or processes. Future economic benefits deriving from research and development (R&D) activities, if any, are uncertain in their amount and timing. Due to these uncertainties, most R&D costs are required to be charged to expense the year in which incurred. The major exception is that assets recorded for R&D costs with alternative future uses should be amortized over their useful lives by periodic charges to R&D expense. Another exception is that R&D costs conducted for others under contract are not expensed as R&D costs. The only items that qualify as R&D are the salaries of laboratory employees researching how to build the new car and the design, testing, and construction of a prototype. ($250,000 + $400,000 = $650,000) (9344)

23. (c) Future economic benefits deriving from research and development (R&D) activities, if any, are uncertain in their amount and timing. Due to these uncertainties, most R&D costs are required to be charged to expense the year in which incurred. However, any materials, equipment, facilities, or intangibles purchased that have alternative future uses should be recorded as assets. Assets recorded for R&D costs with alternative future uses should be amortized over their useful lives by periodic charges to R&D expense. Stam should recognize only the amortization amount of $20,000 as R&D expense for the $100,000 worth of equipment purchased for current and future projects. Stam should also recognize the $200,000 of equipment purchased for current projects only, the $400,000 of R&D salaries for current projects, and the $600,000 of material and labor costs for a prototype product as R&D expense at year end for a total of $1,220,000. The legal fees to obtain a patent would not be included in R&D expense. Only R&D costs incurred to internally develop a patent would be expensed as incurred. (8600)

Computer Software

24. (b) R&D costs incurred internally in creating a computer software product are charged to expense when incurred as research and development until technological feasibility has been established for the product. Technological feasibility is established only upon completion of a detailed program design or, in its absence, completion of a working model. All costs of planning, designing, coding, and testing activities that are necessary to establish technological feasibility are expensed as research and development when incurred.

The costs of producing product masters incurred subsequent to establishing technological feasibility ($200,000) are capitalized. Capitalization of computer software costs ceases when the product is available for general release to customers. Capitalized software production costs are reported at the lower of unamortized cost or net realizable value. Costs incurred for (1) duplicating the computer software and training materials from product masters and (2) physically packaging the product for distribution ($75,000) are capitalized as inventory. Capitalized inventory costs are expensed when the inventory is sold. (7064)

25. (a) Computer software costs that are incurred in the preliminary project stage should be expensed as incurred. Activities in this stage include: conceptual formulation and evaluation of alternatives; determination of existence of needed technology; and final selection of alternatives. (89614)

26. (c) Costs of producing product masters, including coding and testing, incurred subsequent to establishing technological feasibility should be capitalized. Thus, the costs of producing product masters for training materials, the coding costs, and testing costs incurred after establishment of technological feasibility should be capitalized ($15,000 + $24,000 + $20,000 = $59,000). (0996)

27. (a) The annual amortization of the capitalized software cost is the greater of: (1) the ratio of current revenues to current and future revenues (e.g., 30%) or (2) the straight-line method over the remaining useful life of the software including the period to be reported upon (e.g., 1 / 5 = 20%). Because the software has a net realizable value of 90% of the capitalized cost, it can be reported on the balance sheet at 70% (i.e., 1 - 30%) of its capitalized cost. (2707)

28. (d) Internal use computer software costs that are incurred in the preliminary project stage should be expensed as incurred. Most costs incurred in the application development stage are capitalized and should not cease until the software project is substantially complete and ready for its intended use. Training costs and data conversion costs are generally expensed in the application development stage. In the post-implementation/ operation stage, training and maintenance costs should be expensed as incurred while the costs of upgrades or enhancements are capitalized. The annual amortization cost is calculated by taking the remaining $8,000,000 (12,000,000 less the $4,000,000 spent) and dividing by the four-year useful life.

Preliminary project costs	$4,000,000
Post development training costs	50,000
Year 1 amortization expense	2,000,000
Current year expense	$6,050,000

(8104)

Prepaid Expenses

29. (d) The insurance premiums paid can be determined by the analysis of the *Prepaid Insurance* account (work backwards through the account).

Prepaid Insurance			
Balance, 12/31, year 1 (given)	105,000		
Premiums paid (forced)	**455,000**		
Balance before charges to expense (subtotal)	560,000	437,500	Charge to expense in year 2 (given)
Balance, 12/31, year 2 (given)	122,500		

(9058)

30. (b) The amount to be reported as prepaid expenses is comprised of (1) the $1,600 (i.e., $3,200 × 6/12) portion of the annual insurance premium payment made 7/1, year 2 that pertains to year 3 and (2) the $2,000 advance one-year rental payment for the lease which begins in year 3. The $1,500 opening balance of the prepaid expense account pertains to insurance coverage that expired during year 2. (4069)

31. (b) The operating cycle of an enterprise is the average period of time between the expenditure of cash for goods and services and the date those goods and services are converted into cash. Thus, it is the average length of time from cash expenditure, to inventory, to sale, to accounts receivable, and back to cash. A 1-year time period is to be used as a basis for the segregation of current assets in cases where there are several operating cycles occurring within a year. Since the company in question has a six-month operating cycle, it has two operating cycles within a year. Thus, the 1-year (i.e., twelve month) time period should be used as the basis for determining the amount of prepaid insurance to be reported as a current asset. (1758)

32. (d) On September 1, year 1, Dyur Co. would have credited two months of taxes from the seller to *Property Taxes Payable.* At the end of September and October, Dyur would have recorded one month of property taxes each month by a credit to *Property Taxes Payable.* When the payment was made for six months of taxes on November 1, year 1, the payment would be for the four months prior to that date that have already been accrued and for the two months that follow the payment date which should be recorded as Prepaid Property Taxes. Therefore, 2/3 of the payment should be allocated to a decrease in property taxes payable and 1/3 of the payment should be recorded as an increase in prepaid property taxes. (2045)

33. (b) Royalties were prepaid equal to the sum of two year's minimum annual fees on the contract date. Only the minimum annual fees were incurred in the first year of the contract. Since the second year's minimum annual fees will be consumed in the upcoming year, half of the royalty prepayment should be reported as an expense and half should be reported as a current asset at the end of the first contract year. (3461)

34. (d)

Prepaid royalties, 1/1	$ 65,000	
Royalty payment, 10/31	110,000	
Less: Royalty exp. ($110,000 – $25,000)	(85,000)	
Prepaid royalties, 12/31	$ 90,000	(0986)

Life Insurance: CSV

35. (b) The cash surrender value has been accounted for as an asset and has reduced insurance expense over the years the premium payments have been made. The receipt of life insurance proceeds is first applied to the cash surrender value to remove the asset and the balance is recorded as revenue. (6117)

36. (b) The annual premium on a whole-life insurance policy includes a portion to cash surrender value. The balance is reported as life insurance expense. Jann Co. paid a total of $16,000 in premiums from ($4,000 × 4 years). Of this amount, $12,800 was charged to life insurance expense, and the balance of $3,200 ($16,000 – $12,800) is reported as an investment in cash surrender value. (6474)

37. (c) Premiums paid on this policy consist of an amount for life insurance and a balance which constitutes a form of savings. In this question, the cash surrender value of the policy increased by $21,000 (i.e., $108,000 – $87,000) in year 6. This amount, which includes the dividends of $6,000 applied to increase the cash surrender value of the policy, is subtracted from the premium paid to determine the life insurance expense for the year (i.e., $40,000 – $21,000 = $19,000). (3284)

Special Purpose Funds

38. (a) The sinking fund is affected by (1) additions or withdrawals to the fund, (2) fund earnings, (3) gains or losses on the disposal of fund assets, and (4) fund operating expenses. The exchange of one asset for another within the fund (such as the exchange of cash for an investment) will not have any net effect on the fund balance. (2544)

39. (b) Because the bond sinking fund is earmarked for the retirement of long-term debt, its entire balance (i.e., all contributions to the fund plus all interest accumulations added to the fund balance to date) should be reported as a noncurrent asset in the investments section of the balance sheet. (4548)

40. (b) The bond sinking fund balance increases as a result of the additional investment and the income on the investments in the fund (i.e., the dividend and interest revenue). It decreases due to the expenses of the fund (i.e., the administrative costs incurred). The carrying amount of the bonds payable does not affect the bond sinking fund balance.

Bond sinking fund, 12/31, year 1	$450,000	
Add: Additional investment, year 2	90,000	
Dividends on investments	15,000	
Interest revenue	30,000	
Less: Administrative costs	(5,000)	
Bond sinking fund, 12/31, year 2	$580,000	(4058)

PERFORMANCE BY SUBTOPIC

Each category below parallels a subtopic covered in Chapter 5. Record the number and percentage of questions you correctly answered in each subtopic area.

Intangibles

Question #	Correct√
1	
2	
3	
4	
5	
6	
7	
8	
9	
10	
# Questions	10
# Correct	______
% Correct	______

Intangibles After Acquisition

Question #	Correct √
11	
12	
13	
14	
15	
16	
17	
# Questions	7
# Correct	______
% Correct	______

R&D Costs

Question #	Correct √
18	
19	
20	
21	
22	
23	
# Questions	6
# Correct	______
% Correct	______

Computer Software

Question #	Correct √
24	
25	
26	
27	
28	
# Questions	5
# Correct	______
% Correct	______

Prepaid Expenses

Question #	Correct √
29	
30	
31	
32	
33	
34	
# Questions	6
# Correct	______
% Correct	______

Life Insurance: CSV

Question #	Correct √
35	
36	
37	
# Questions	3
# Correct	______
% Correct	______

Special Purpose Funds

Question #	Correct √
38	
39	
40	
# Questions	3
# Correct	______
% Correct	______

Solution 5-2 SIMULATION ANSWER: Accounting Treatment

1. H Expense as operating expense (general and admin)
2. C Capitalize and depreciate (as normally)
3. B Capitalize and amortize
4. F Expense immediately as R&D
5. H Expense as operating expense (selling)
6. G Expense as manufacturing cost
7. H Expense as operating expense (selling)
8. F Expense immediately as R&D
9. E Expense as consumed as R&D expense
10. B Capitalize and amortize
11. D Capitalize and depreciate as R&D expense
12. F Expense immediately as R&D
13. F Expense immediately as R&D
14. F Expense immediately as R&D
15. A Record as receivable (reimbursable expense)
16. F Expense immediately as R&D
17. D Capitalize and depreciate as R&D expense
18. G Expense as manufacturing cost
19. G Expense as manufacturing cost

Solution 5-3 SIMULATION ANSWER: Research

FASB Accounting Standards Codification

FASB ASC:	730	-	10	-	25	-	3

25-3 When software for use in research and development activities is purchased or leased, its cost shall be accounted for as specified by (c) in the preceding paragraph 730-10-25-1. That is, the cost shall be charged to expense as incurred unless the software has alternative future uses (in research and development or otherwise).

Wondering how to find 20 hours a week for study time?

Robert Monette used this method to find 20 hours a week to study while working 40 hours a week. (Ask a customer service representative about a copy of Bob's demo video, *How to Pass the CPA Exam.*) Notice how this plan leaves most of the weekend free, ensuring time for you to take care of yourself, spend time with your family, meet with friends and, in general, take care of your other commitments.

Lunch hours, Monday through Friday	5 hours
Three hours, after work, Monday through Thursday	12 hours
Three hours, Saturday morning	3 hours
Sunday, total break from studying	0 hours
Weekly total	20 hours

This plan may work for you, or it may not. Consider Bob's plan and adapt it to your situation. For example, perhaps you prefer to study an hour before work Tuesday through Thursday, and relax on Saturday as well as Sunday.

Also consider how you use time. When you watch a video lecture, read text, or answer questions, do so in an environment without distractions.

A passing score is well within reach!

CHAPTER 6

BONDS

CHAPTER 6

BONDS

I. Investment in Bonds

A. Overview

Bonds are contractual agreements wherein the issuer (borrower) promises to pay the purchaser (lender) a principal amount at a designated future date. In addition, the issuer makes periodic interest payments based on the face amount of the bond and the stated rate of interest.

1. **Held-to-Maturity Securities** Held-to-maturity (HTM) securities are defined as debt securities that the enterprise has the intent and the ability to hold to maturity. HTM securities are accounted for under the **amortized cost** method discussed here. Trading and available-for-sale securities are not accounted for under the amortized cost method. Temporary fluctuations in the market value of bonds classified as HTM are not recognized in the accounts.

2. **Debenture Bonds** Unsecured bonds; they are not supported by a lien or mortgage on specific assets.

3. **Term Bonds** Bonds maturing at a specified date.

4. **Callable Bonds** Bonds that may be retired at the issuer's option.

5. **Serial Bonds** Bonds providing for repayment of principal in a series of installments.

6. **Convertible Bonds** Bonds that may be converted to stock at the bondholder's option.

B. Acquisition

Initial recording will be at an amount equal to the purchase price of the bond plus other direct costs of acquisition (e.g., broker's fees). The market price of a bond is determined based on the "market interest rate" that takes into consideration the stated (face) interest rate of the bonds, the credit worthiness of the debtor, the maturity date of the bonds, and other factors. The market price of the bond is equal to the present value of the bond's interest and principal payments, discounted using the market interest rate for that type of bond. If bonds are bought between interest dates, the purchaser will have to pay an additional amount for the interest accrued on the bond since the last interest date (or the bond date, if before the first interest date). This additional amount is **not** part of the cost of the bond investment, but must be recorded separately as purchased interest (i.e., interest receivable).

Example 1 ▸ Acquisition of Bond & Interest Payment

X buys at par on September 1 a 10%, $1,000 bond issued on June 1 of the same year. Interest dates are June 1 and December 1.

Investment in Bonds	1,000	
Interest Receivable (10% × $1,000 × 3 months/12 months)	25	
Cash		1,025
To record the purchase of bonds on September 1.		
Cash (10% × $1,000 × 6/12)	50	
Interest Receivable		25
Interest Income		25
To record receipt of the interest proceeds on December 1.		

C. Premium or Discount

A premium or discount on bonds arises when the stated interest rate of the bonds is higher or lower, respectively, than the current market interest rate for similar securities. Bond premium or discount generally is **not** separately recorded by the investor (i.e., the bond investment is recorded at a net amount). Premiums or discounts on bonds held as a long-term investment must be amortized from date of acquisition to maturity date and the interest method should be used to amortize these differences. Other methods of amortization (straight-line), may be used if the effects are not material. The premium amortization decreases both the bond investment and investment income, while the discount amortization increases these accounts.

Example 2 ▸ Bonds Acquired at a Discount

On June 30, year 1, ABC Corp. purchased 100 new bonds issued by XYZ Inc., with a total face amount of $100,000 and a 10% stated interest rate. The bonds mature in ten years and pay interest semiannually, on June 30 and December 31 (20 semiannual payments). The effective yield for similar securities is 12% annually and is reflected in the $88,530 purchase price paid by ABC Corp.

Required: Show how the appropriate purchase price of $88,530 for the $100,000 face amount of bonds is determined using the appropriate present value (PV) tables in Appendix D. In addition, prepare the journal entry to record the acquisition of the bonds.

Solution:

Maturity (face) amount to be received	$ 100,000	
PV factor for a single amount (6%, 20 periods)—Table 2	× 0.311805	
Present value of the maturity amount		$31,180.50
Semiannual interest payment to be received ($100,000 × 10% × 6/12)	5,000	
PV factor for an ordinary annuity (6%, 20 periods)—Table 4	× 11.469921	
Present value of future interest payments		57,349.60
Present value of the bonds		$88,530.10
Bond Investment	88,530	
Cash		88,530

Example 3 ▸ Interest Income & Discount Amortization

Required: Refer to Example 2. Provide ABC Corporation's entries to record interest income and discount amortization for the year ending December 31, year 1, assuming (1) straight-line and (2) effective interest methods of discount amortization.

Solution:

(1) *Straight-Line Method:*

Cash ($100,000 × 0.05)	5,000	
Bond Investment [($100,000 – $88,530) / 20]	574*	
Interest Income		5,574

(2) *Effective Interest Method:*

Cash ($100,000 × 0.05)	5,000	
Bond Investment (balancing amount)	312*	
Interest Income ($88,530 × .06)		5,312

* **NOTE:** The total amortization of the bond investment discount will be the same over the 10-year life of the bonds under either the straight-line or the interest method. As noted earlier, the amortization of the bond investment discount increases the bond *Investment* and *Interest Income* accounts. The amortization of a bond investment premium would decrease these accounts.

Exhibit 1 ▶ Bond Premiums and Discounts

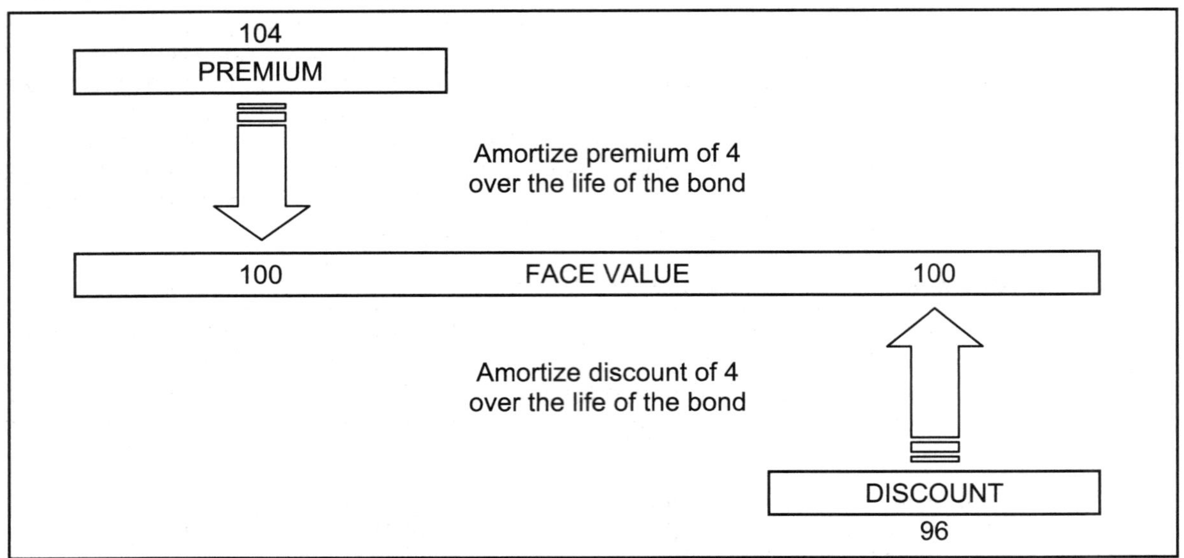

Exhibit 2 ▶ Effective Interest Method

Bond issued at:	Effective interest rate	×	Carrying value	=	Amount of interest income/expense
Discount	Constant		Increasing		Increasing
Premium	Constant		Decreasing		Decreasing

D. Interest Accrual

The bond interest payment date and the investor's year-end may not coincide. In this case, the investor must accrue the interest income earned through year-end, including the required amortization of premium or discount.

Example 4 ▶ Different Year-End and Payment Dates

Refer to Example 2, except that ABC's year-end is March 31.

Required: Provide ABC's journal entries on March 31, year 2, to record interest and discount amortization under both the straight-line and the interest methods.

Solution:

(1) *Straight-Line Method:*

	Debit	Credit
Accrued Interest Receivable ($100,000 × 0.05 × 3/6)	2,500	
Bond Investment ($574 × 3/6)*	287	
Interest Income		2,787

(2) *Interest Method:*

	Debit	Credit
Accrued Interest Receivable	2,500	
Bond Investment (balancing amount)	165	
Interest Income [($88,530 + $312) × 0.06 × 3/6]		2,665

* On March 31, year 2, ABC records interest income for 3 months of the six month payment. The 10% rate is an annual rate.

E. Sale of Bond Investments

The sale of bonds held for investment results in a gain or loss equal to the difference between the carrying amount of the bonds and the proceeds received on their disposal. This gain or loss is **not** an extraordinary item.

1. **Carrying Amount** In determining the carrying amount of the bonds, adjustment must be made for premium or discount amortization to date of sale.

2. **Bonds Sold Between Interest Dates** If the bonds are sold between interest dates, part of the proceeds must be assigned to the interest accrued since the last interest date.

Example 5 ▸ Sale of Bond Investment

Refer to the facts of Example 2. On August 31, year 5, ABC sold the 100 bonds to LMN Inc. for $92,000, which included interest accrued on the bonds. ABC amortized the original discount on the bonds under the straight-line method.

Required: Determine the gain (or loss) to be recognized by ABC on the sale of the bonds.

Solution:

Proceeds received	$92,000
Less: Amount attributable to accrued interest, $100,000 × 0.05 × 2/6	(1,667)
Sale price of bonds	90,333
Carrying amount*	93,313
Gain (loss) on sale of bonds	$ (2,980)

Computations:

* Original purchase price, June 30, year 1	$88,530
Plus discount amortization:	
Through June 30, year 5 ($574 × 8)	4,592
July 1 to August 31, year 5 ($574 × 2/6)	191
Carrying amount of the bonds	$93,313

II. Bonds Payable

A. Overview

Bonds payable represent a contractual obligation to make periodic interest payments on the amount borrowed and to repay the principal upon maturity. Therefore, when a company sells a bond issue it is in effect selling two cash flows.

1. **Principal** The receipt of the bond principal at its maturity

2. **Interest** The receipt of the periodic interest payments. The bonds' stated interest rate and face amount determine the amount of periodic interest payments.

B. Disclosures

The combined aggregate amount of maturities and sinking fund requirements for all long-term borrowings must be disclosed for each of the five years following the date of the latest balance sheet presented.

C. Bond Issuance

When bonds are issued, only the face amount of the bonds is recorded in the *Bonds Payable* account. The bond discount or premium, if any, is recorded in a separate account and reported in the balance sheet as a direct deduction from or addition to the face amount of the bond.

Example 6 ▶ Bond Issuance

On January 1, year 1, Maple Company issued five-year bonds with a face amount of $200,000 and a stated interest rate of 8%, payable semiannually on June 30 and December 31. The bonds were priced to yield 6%. The present value factor for the present value of $1 for 10 periods at 3% is 0.74409; the factor for the present value of an ordinary annuity of $1 for 10 periods at 3% is 8.53020.

Required: Determine the total issue price of the bonds. Record their issuance.

Solution:

Present value of principal payment [$200,000 × 0.74409 (PV of $1 for 10 periods at 3%)]	$148,818
Present value of periodic interest payments [($200,000 × 8% / 2) × 8.53020]	68,242
Amount received from the issuance of the bonds	$217,060

The stated rate of interest (8%) is above the market rate (6%). Therefore, these bonds were sold at a premium. The following entry is made to record the bond issuance.

Cash	217,060	
Bonds Payable		200,000
Bond Premium (difference)		17,060

D. **Bond Selling Price**
To estimate the proceeds to be received from the issuance of bonds payable (ignoring bond issue costs), the present values of the bond principal and interest payments must be determined. The prevailing market (yield) rate is used to discount the cash flows to arrive at their present value.

1. **Premium** A bond will sell at a **premium** (more than par) when the stated interest rate is *greater* than the market rate for similar debt.

2. **Discount** A bond will sell at a **discount** (less than par) when the stated interest rate is *less* than the market rate.

3. **Par** A bond will sell at **par** when the stated interest rate *equals* the market rate.

E. **Bond Issue Costs**
Bond issue costs include legal fees, accounting fees, underwriting commissions, registration, printing and engraving, and other such costs incurred in preparing and selling a bond issue.

1. **Classification** Bond issue costs should be classified as a deferred charge (i.e., asset) and amortized over the life of the bonds as an increase to interest expense. (Alternately, under the Statements of Financial Accounting Concepts, issuance costs could be accounted for either as an expense in the period incurred or as a reduction of the noncurrent debt liability, and accounted for the same as debt discount.)

2. **Amortization** The amortization of bond issue costs is affected when a bond issue is sold between interest dates because the issue costs should be amortized over the period from the date of sale (not the date of the bond) to the maturity date.

F. **Bond Retirement**

1. **Debt Extinguishment** A debtor considers debt to be extinguished for financial reporting purposes in the following situations:

   a. The debtor pays the creditor and is relieved of all its obligations with respect to the debt, including the debtor's reacquisition of its outstanding debt securities through cancellation or holding as treasury bonds.

b. The debtor legally is released from being the primary obligor under the debt, either judicially or by the creditor.

2. **Extinguishment vs. Refunding** Extinguishment includes the reacquisition of debt securities regardless of whether the securities are canceled or held as so-called treasury bonds. Refunding refers to achieving the reacquisition by the use of proceeds from issuing other securities.

3. **Principal and Related Amounts** When all or part of a bond issue is retired before maturity, it is necessary to write off both the principal and the pro rata portion of the unamortized premium or discount on the retired bonds. If bond issue costs were incurred and recorded as an asset (i.e., as a deferred charge), it is also necessary to write off a pro rata portion of the bond issue costs (when a bond issue is retired before maturity). The amount of such write-off increases any loss or reduces any gain recognized on the retirement.

4. **Extraordinary Item** Entities must evaluate whether early debt extinguishment is extraordinary using the same criteria as other events.

Example 7 ▸ Bond Retirement

On January 1, year 1, Ben Corporation issued $600,000 of 5% ten-year bonds at 103. Ben records amortization using the straight-line method (i.e., the amount is considered immaterial). On December 31, year 5, when the fair value of the bonds was 97, Ben repurchased $300,000 of the bonds in the open market at 97. Ben has an effective income tax rate of 30%. Ben has recorded interest and amortization for year 5. Ben should record this retirement as follows:

Bonds Payable ($600,000 × 0.50)	300,000	
Bond Premium ($9,000 × 0.50)	4,500	
Taxes Payable ($13,500 × 0.30)		4,050*
Cash ($300,000 × 0.97)		291,000
Gain on Bond Retirement		9,450*

***Computations:**

Original carrying amount ($600,000 × 103%)		$ 618,000
Premium to be amortized ($618,000 – $600,000)	$18,000	
Amortization [($18,000 / 10) × 5 yrs.]	9,000	9,000
Carrying amount of bonds, 12/31, year 5		609,000
Portion of bonds retired		× 50%
Carrying amount of bonds retired		304,500
Purchase price ($300,000 × 97%)		291,000
Gain on bond retirement, before income taxes		$ 13,500

NOTE: The gain, net of the related income tax effects, is $9,450 [$13,500 × (1 – 30%)]. This gain would be considered extraordinary only when it meets the criteria of being both unusual and infrequent considering the environment in which the company operates.

Example 8 ▸ Write-Off of Bond Issue Costs

If bond issue costs of $10,000 were recorded as an asset in the issuance of the bonds in Example 7, the gain on retirement before income taxes would be $11,000 [$13,500 – ($10,000 × 5/10 × 50%)].

III. Premium & Discount Amortization

A. Straight-Line Method

Straight-line amortization calls for the amortization of an equal amount of premium or discount each period over the life of the bonds. The straight-line method is acceptable only when the premium or discount is immaterial, because it fails to determine the periodic interest expense in terms of the effective rate of interest.

Example 9 ▸ Straight-Line Amortization

To amortize the premium in Example 6 using the straight-line method, divide the premium by the number of interest periods: $17,060 / 10 = $1,706.

B. Effective Interest Method

The effective interest method of amortization calls for recognizing interest expense at the effective interest rate at which the bonds were sold. Thus, this interest method overcomes the criticism of the straight-line method because it offers a more accurate measurement of interest expense. Use of the effective interest method results in a constant rate of interest when applied to the carrying amount of the bonds at the beginning of the period. As with long-term notes payable, other amortization methods may be used when the results do not differ materially from those obtained with the effective interest method.

Example 10 ▸ Effective Interest Method Amortization

To amortize the premium in Example 6 using the effective interest method, multiply the carrying amount of the bond issue ($217,060) by the effective yield (3%). This equals interest expense for the period ($6,512). The difference between the cash interest payment and the interest expense equals the amount of premium amortization for the period ($8,000 – $6,512 = $1,488). This procedure is followed each period until the maturity date when the premium (or discount) will be fully amortized.

Example 11 ▸ Interest Payments

Required: Record the first four interest payments for the bonds illustrated in Example 6, rounding amounts to the nearest dollar.

Solution:

6/30, year 1:	Interest Expense [($200,000 + 17,060) × 0.03]	6,512	
	Bond Premium (to balance)	1,488	
	Cash ($200,000 × 0.04)		8,000
12/31, year 1:	Interest Expense [($200,000 + 15,572*) × 0.03]	6,467	
	Bond Premium (to balance)	1,533	
	Cash ($200,000 × 0.04)		8,000
6/30, year 2:	Interest Expense [($200,000 + 14,039*) × 0.03]	6,421	
	Bond Premium (to balance)	1,579	
	Cash ($200,000 × 0.04)		8,000
12/31, year 2:	Interest Expense [($200,000 + 12,460*) × 0.03]	6,374	
	Bond Premium (to balance)	1,626	
	Cash ($200,000 × 0.04)		8,000

* 12/31, year 1: $17,060 – $1,488 = $15,572; 6/30/X2, $15,572 – $1,533; 12/31/X2, $14,039 – $1,579

Exhibit 3 ▸ Bond Premium Amortization Table

(1) Period	(2) Cash interest payments	(3) 3% × Prior (6) interest expense	(4) (2) – (3) Premium amortization	(5) Prior (5) – (4) unamortized premium	(6) $200,000 + (5) Carrying amount
0	—	—	—	$17,060.00	$217,060.00
1	$8,000	$6,511.80	$1,488.20	15,571.80	215,571.80
2	8,000	6,467.15	1,532.85	14,038.95	214,038.95
3	8,000	6,421.17	1,578.83	12,460.12	212,460.12
4	8,000	6,373.80	1,626.20	10,833.92	210,833.92
5	8,000	6,325.02	1,674.98	9,158.94	209,158.94
6	8,000	6,274.77	1,725.23	7,433.71	207,433.71
7	8,000	6,223.01	1,776.99	5,656.72	205,656.72
8	8,000	6,169.70	1,830.30	3,826.42	203,826.42
9	8,000	6,114.79	1,885.21	1,941.21	201,941.21
10	8,000	6,058.79*	1,941.21	0	200,000.00

* $0.55 difference due to rounding

C. **Amortization Effects**
Amortization of a bond premium decreases interest expense and the carrying amount of the bond for the issuer, while the amortization of a bond discount increases the issuer's interest expense and the carrying amount of the bond.

D. **Interest & Year-End Dates Differ**
An adjusting entry is required when interest dates do not coincide with the end of the accounting period, to record accrued interest expense and bond premium or discount amortization.

Example 12 ▸ Interest and Year-End Dates Differ

In Example 6, assume the end of the accounting period comes 3 months after the bonds are issued. The required entry at 3/31, year 1 would be the following.

	Dr	Cr
Interest Expense ($6,512 × 3/6)	3,256	
Bond Premium ($1,488 × 3/6)	744	
Accrued Interest Payable ($8,000 × 3/6)		4,000

E. **Issuance Between Interest Dates**
Bonds payable are often sold between interest dates. If bond issue costs or a bond premium or discount is involved, it must be amortized over the period the bonds are outstanding.

Example 13 ▸ Issuance Between Interest Dates

On March 1 of the current year, Trisha Company issued 12% ten-year bonds with a face amount of $1,000. The bonds are dated January 1 of this year, and interest is payable semiannually on January 1 and July 1. The bonds were sold at par and accrued interest.

Required: Provide journal entries to record the bond issuance and the first interest payment.

Solution:

The issuance of the bonds would be recorded as follows.

	Dr	Cr
Cash	1,020	
Bonds Payable (face amount)		1,000
Accrued Interest Payable ($1,000 × 0.12 × 2/12)		20

The payment of interest on July 1 would be recorded as follows.

	Dr	Cr
Interest Expense (to balance)	40	
Accrued Interest Payable (from above)	20	
Cash ($1,0000 × 0.12 × 6/12)		60

IV. Bonds With Additional Features

A. Serial Bonds

A set of bonds issued at the same time but having different maturity dates. These are also called installment bonds because they provide a series of installments for repayment of principal.

1. **Present Values** To determine the selling price of serial bonds, compute the present value of the principal and interest payments for each series separately, then total the present value of each series.

2. **Declining Principal** The amortization of bond premium or discount on serial bonds requires the recognition of a declining debt principal. Successive bond years cannot be charged with equal amounts of premium or discount because of a shrinking debt and successively smaller interest payments.

3. **Amortization of Premium/Discount** Bond premium or discount, if material, should be amortized using the effective interest method.

B. Bonds With Detachable Stock Warrants

When bonds are issued with detachable stock warrants, allocation of the proceeds between the warrants and the debt security based on relative fair values is required. If the FV of one security is not determinable, the proceeds are assigned based on the FV of the other security. The rationale behind this allocation is that, even if the warrants are exercised, the debt will still remain. There are two separate elements, the debt and the warrants. The warrants are accounted for as paid-in capital.

Example 14 ▶ Detachable Stock Warrants

On November 1, year 1, two hundred $1,000, 8% bonds due October 31, year 5, were sold at 103 with one detachable stock purchase warrant attached to each bond. The fair value of the bonds without the stock warrants is 98. The fair value of the warrants has not been determined. Each warrant entitles the holder to purchase ten shares of common stock (par $10) at $30 per share.

Borrower			Investor (net)		
Cash	206,000		Bond Investment	196,000	
Bond Discount	4,000		Stock Warrants	10,000	
Bond Payable		200,000	Cash		206,000
APIC-Stock Warrants		10,000			

Computations:

Cash proceeds [(200 × $1,000) × 103%]	$206,000
Proceeds allocated to bonds (200 × $1,000 × 98%)	196,000
Proceeds allocated to warrants (remainder)	$ 10,000
Bond discount ($200,000 – $196,000)	$ 4,000

If 100 of the 200 stock purchase warrants are exercised:

Borrower			Investor (net)		
Cash (100 × 10 × $30)	30,000		Inv. in Common Stock		
APIC-Stock Warrants			(1,000 × $35)	35,000	
($10,000 × 100/200)	5,000		Stock Warrants		
Common Stock			($10,000 × 100/200)		5,000
(1,000 × $10 PV)		10,000	Cash (100 × 10 × $30)		30,000
APIC-Common St. (to bal.)		25,000			

C. Convertible Bonds

Convertible bonds provide the bond holder the option of converting the bond to capital stock, typically common stock. Convertible debt securities are those debt securities which are convertible into common stock of the issuer or an affiliated company at a specified price at the option of the holder and which are sold at a price or have a value at issuance not significantly in excess of the face amount. The terms of such securities generally include (1) an interest rate which is lower than the issuer could establish for nonconvertible debt, (2) an initial conversion price which is greater than the market value of the common stock at time of issuance, and (3) a conversion price which does not decrease except pursuant to antidilution provisions. In most cases such securities also are callable at the option of the issuer and are subordinated to nonconvertible debt. No proceeds from the debt issue are to be assigned to the conversion feature (even though the convertible bonds may sell for substantially more than similar nonconvertible bonds). The reason for no allocation to equity is that the debt cannot be separated from the conversion feature, as would be the case with detachable stock warrants.

1. **Book Value Method** The conversion of the bonds into common stock is generally recorded by crediting the paid-in capital accounts for the carrying amount of the debt at the date of the conversion; thus, no gain or loss is recognized upon conversion. Costs associated with the conversion are **not** recognized as an expense. The paid-in capital accounts are credited for the carrying amount of the debt converted, **less** any costs associated with the conversion.

2. **Market Value Method** Alternately, the market value method recognizes a gain or loss on retirement equal to the difference between the carrying amount of the debt at the date of the conversion and the fair value of the shares issued upon conversion.

Example 15 ▸ Bond Conversion

Bonds with a face amount of $10,000 and a carrying amount of $10,400 are converted into 100 shares of $50 par common stock with $90 fair value.

Required: Record the conversion of the bonds in the books of the issuer under (a) the book value method, and (b) the market value method.

Solution:

		Debit	Credit
(a)	*Book Value Method:*		
	Bonds Payable	10,000	
	Bond Premium	400	
	Common Stock (100 × $50 PV)		5,000
	Add'l. Paid-In Capital (to balance)		5,400
(b)	*Market Value Method:*		
	Bonds Payable	10,000	
	Bond Premium	400	
	Common Stock (100 × $50 PV)		5,000
	Add'l. Paid-In Capital [100 × ($90 FV – $50 PV)]		4,000
	Gain on Conversion ($10,400 – $9,000)		1,400

3. **Induced Conversions** Generally a gain or loss is required to be recognized on the *retirement* of debt, including certain convertible debt. However, this does not apply to debt that is *converted* to equity securities of the debtor pursuant to conversion privileges provided in the terms of the debt at issuance. As illustrated in Example 15, the conversion of convertible debt securities to stock may or may not result in gain recognition, depending on whether the book value or the market value method is used. (However, the same method must be consistently applied.)

a. This applies to a specific situation in which a debtor attempts to induce prompt conversion of convertible debt to equity securities. To achieve this, the debtor may offer debt holders a higher conversion ratio, payment of additional consideration, or other favorable changes to the original terms of conversion. The conversion must occur pursuant to changed conversion privileges that are exercisable only for a limited period of time. The changed terms are applicable to the issuance of all of the equity securities issuable pursuant to the original conversion privileges for each debt instrument that is converted.

The changed terms may involve reduction of the original conversion price, thereby resulting in the issuance of additional shares of stock, issuance of warrants or other securities not provided for in the original conversion terms, or payment of cash or other consideration to those debt holders who convert during the specified time period.

b. When convertible debt is converted to equity securities of the debtor pursuant to an inducement offer described in a., above, the debtor enterprise should recognize an expense equal to the fair value of all securities and other consideration transferred in excess of the fair value of securities issuable pursuant to the original conversion terms.

(1) This expense should **not** be reported as an extraordinary item.

(2) The fair value of the securities or other consideration should be measured as of the date the inducement offer is accepted by the convertible debt holder. Normally this will be the date the debt holder converts the convertible debt into equity securities or enters into a binding agreement to do so.

c. This does not apply to conversions pursuant to other changes in conversion privileges or to changes in terms of convertible debt instruments that are different from those described above.

V. Bond Journal Entries

A. Premiums & Discounts

Example 16 ▸ Straight-Line Premium Amortization

On January 1, year 1, a $1,000 face value, two-year bond, with a 10% coupon rate of interest is sold for 104. The effective yield is 7.8%. Interest is paid semi-annually on June 30 and December 31. Use the straight-line method to amortize the premium.

Borrower			Investor		
January 1, year 1					
Cash	1,040		Invest. in Bond	1,040	
Bond Payable		1,000	Cash		1,040
Premium		40			
June 30, year 1					
Interest Expense	40		Cash	50	
Premium	10		Invest. in Bond		10
Cash		50	Interest Income		40
Same journal entries for next 3 periods.			Same journal entries for next 3 periods.		
December 31, year 2					
Bond Payable	1,000		Cash	1,000	
Cash		1,000	Invest. in Bond		1,000

Example 17 ▸ Straight-Line Discount Amortization

Same as Example 16, except that the bond is sold for 96 and the effective interest rate is 12.3%.

Borrower			Investor		
January 1, year 1					
Cash	960		Invest. in Bond	960	
Discount	40		Cash		960
Bond Payable		1,000			
June 30, year 1					
Interest Expense	60		Cash	50	
Cash		50	Invest. in Bond	10	
Discount		10	Interest Income		60
Same journal entries for next 3 periods.			Same journal entries for next 3 periods.		
December 31, year 2					
Bond Payable	1,000		Cash	1,000	
Cash		1,000	Invest. in Bond		1,000

Example 18 ▸ Effective Interest Method of Premium Amortization

Same as Example 16, except use the effective interest method to amortize the premium.

Borrower			Investor		
January 1, year 1					
Cash	1,040.00				
Bond Payable		1,000.00	Invest. in Bond	1,040.00	
Premium		40.00	Cash		1,040.00
June 30, year 1					
Interest Expense			Cash	50.00	
[($1,000 + $40) × 3.9%]	40.56		Invest. in Bond		9.44
Premium	9.44		Interest Income		40.56
Cash		50.00			
December 31, year 1					
Interest Expense			Cash	50.00	
[($1,000 + 30.56) × 3.9%]	40.19		Invest. in Bond		9.81
Premium	9.81		Interest Income		40.19
Cash		50.00			
June 30, year 2					
Interest Expense			Cash	50.00	
[(1,000 + 20.75) × 3.9%]	39.81		Invest. in Bond		10.19
Premium	10.19		Interest Income		39.81
Cash		50.00			
December 31, year 2					
Interest Expense			Cash	50.00	
[(1,000 + 10.56) × 3.9%]	39.41		Invest. in Bond		10.59
Premium	10.59		Interest Income		39.41
Cash		50.00			
Bond Payable	1,000.00		Cash	1,000.00	
Cash		1,000.00	Invest. in Bond		1,000.00

(Amortization of Premium: 9.44 + 9.81 + 10.19 + 10.59 = 40.03 **NOTE:** Difference due to rounding.)

Example 19 ▸ Effective Interest Method of Discount Amortization

Same as Example 17, except use the effective interest method to amortize the discount.

Borrower			Investor		
January 1, year 1					
Cash	960.00		Invest. in Bond	960.00	
Discount	40.00		Cash		960.00
Bond Payable		1,000.00			
June 30, year 1					
Interest Expense			Cash	50.00	
[(1,000 – 40) × 6.15%]	59.04		Invest. in Bond	9.04	
Cash		50.00	Interest Income		59.04
Discount		9.04			
December 31, year 1					
Interest Expense			Cash	50.00	
[($1,000 – 30.96) × 6.15%]	59.60		Invest. in Bond	9.60	
Cash		50.00	Interest Income		59.60
Discount		9.60			
June 30, year 2					
Interest Expense			Cash	50.00	
[(1,000 – 21.36) × 6.15%]	60.19		Invest. in Bond	10.19	
Cash		50.00	Interest Income		60.19
Discount		10.19			
December 31, year 2					
Interest Expense			Cash	50.00	
[(1,000 – 11.18) × 6.15%]	60.81		Invest. in Bond	10.81	
Cash		50.00	Interest Income		60.81
Discount		10.81			

(Amortization of discount: 9.04 + 9.60 + 10.19 + 10.81 = 39.63 **NOTE:** Difference due to rounding.)

B. Midperiod Issue

Example 20 ▸ Issuance Between Interest Dates

$1,000 face value, 2-year bond with a 10% coupon rate of interest is sold on April 1 of the current year at par. Interest is paid semi-annually on June 30 and December 31.

Borrower			Investor		
April 1					
Cash	1,025		Invest. in Bond	1,000	
Bond Payable		1,000	Interest Receivable	25	
Interest Payable		25	Cash		1,025
June 30					
Interest Expense	25		Cash	50	
Interest Payable	25		Interest Income		25
Cash		50	Interest Receivable		25

C. Warrants

Example 21 ▸ Detachable Warrants

On January 1 of the current year, 100 bonds with $1,000 face values and each with 20 detachable stock warrants (100 × 20 = 2,000) are sold at 105. Twenty warrants and $800 may be converted into one share of $200 par value common stock. The warrants have a fair value of $12,000 and expire on July 1. One half of the warrants are exercised on June 30 and the other half expire on July 1.

Borrower			Investor		
January 1					
Cash	105,000		Invest. in Bond	93,000	
Discount	7,000		Warrants	12,000	
Bond Payable		100,000	Cash		105,000
APIC—Warrants		12,000			
June 30					
Cash	40,000		Invest. in Stock	46,000	
APIC—Warrant	6,000		Cash		40,000
Common Stock		10,000	Warrants		6,000
APIC		36,000			
July 1					
APIC—Warrant	6,000		Loss on Investment	6,000	
APIC		6,000	Warrants		6,000

Computations:

Warrant	$12,000 × 50% =	$ 6,000
Cash	$ 800 × 50 =	40,000
		46,000
Common stock	$200 par × 50 =	(10,000)
APIC		$ 36,000

D. Convertible Bonds

Example 22 ▸ Convertible Bonds, Book Value Method

On January 1 of the current year, 100 bonds with $1,000 face values and each with 20 nondetachable stock warrants (100 × 20 = 2,000) are sold at 105. Twenty warrants, one bond, and $800 may be converted into one share of $200 par value common stock. 50% of the bonds are converted on June 30, and the book value method is used to record the conversion.

Borrower			Investor		
January 1					
Cash	105,000		Invest. in Bond	105,000	
Bond Payable		100,000	Cash		105,000
Premium		5,000			
June 30					
Cash	40,000		Invest. in Stock	92,500	
Bond Payable	50,000		Cash		40,000
Premium	2,500		Invest. in Bond		52,500
Common Stock		10,000			
APIC		82,500			

Computations:

Bond	$1,000 × 50 =	$ 50,000
Premium	$5,000 × 50% =	2,500
Cash	$ 800 × 50 =	40,000
		92,500
Common stock	$200 par × 50 =	(10,000)
APIC		$ 82,500

Example 23 ▸ Convertible Bonds, Market Value Method

On January 1 of the current year, 100 bonds with $1,000 face values and each with 20 nondetachable stock warrants (100 × 20 = 2,000) are sold at 105. Twenty warrants, one bond, and $800 may be converted into one share of $200 par value common stock. All of the bonds are converted on June 30. The market value method is used to record the conversion and the fair value of the stock on the date of conversion is $2,000.

Borrower			Investor		
January 1					
Cash	105,000		Invest. in Bond	105,000	
Bond Payable		100,000	Cash		105,000
Premium		5,000			
June 30					
Cash	80,000		Invest. in Stock	200,000	
Bond Payable	100,000		Cash		80,000
Premium	5,000		Invest. in Bond		105,000
Loss on Conversion	15,000		Gain on Conversion		15,000
Common Stock		20,000			
APIC		180,000			

Computations:

Bond	$1,000 × 100 =	$100,000	Common stock	$ 20,000	
Cash	$ 800 × 100 =	80,000	APIC	180,000	
Common stock	$200 par × 100 =	20,000			$200,000
APIC	($2,000 – 200) × 100 =	180,000	Bond	100,000	
			Premium	5,000	
			Cash	80,000	
					(185,000)
			Gain		$ 15,000

CHAPTER 6—BONDS

Problem 6-1 MULTIPLE-CHOICE QUESTIONS

1. An investor purchased a bond classified as a long-term investment between interest dates at a discount. At the purchase date, the carrying amount of the bond is more than the

	Cash paid to seller	Face amount of bond
a.	No	Yes
b.	No	No
c.	Yes	No
d.	Yes	Yes

(5/91, Theory, #4, 1781)

2. On July 1, year 6, Fox Company purchased 400 of the $1,000 face amount, 8% bonds of Dey Corporation for $369,200 to yield 10% per annum. The bonds, which mature on July 1, year 11, pay interest semiannually on January 1 and July 1. Fox uses the effective interest method of amortization and the bonds are appropriately recorded as a long-term investment.

   The bonds should be reported on Fox's December 31, year 6, balance sheet at?

   a. $397,540
   b. $374,120
   c. $371,660
   d. $366,740 (Editor, 89431)

3. When an investor entity purchases bonds, it must do which of the following?

   a. Record the bond investment initially at the purchase price of the bond plus other direct costs of acquisition, such as broker's fees
   b. Pay an additional amount for the interest accrued on the bonds since the last interest date (or the bond date, if no interest payment dates have yet occurred), if the bonds are bought between interest dates
   c. Record the additional amount paid, for interest accrued on bonds bought between interest dates, as purchased interest in a separate account, such as interest receivable
   d. All of the above (Editor, 89603)

4. In the previous year, Lee Co. acquired, at a premium, Enfield Inc. 10-year bonds as a long-term investment. At December 31 of the current year, Enfield's bonds were quoted at a small discount. Which of the following situations is the most likely cause of the decline in the bonds' market value?

   a. Enfield issued a stock dividend.
   b. Enfield is expected to call the bonds at a premium, which is less than Lee's carrying amount.
   c. Interest rates have declined since Lee purchased the bonds.
   d. Interest rates have increased since Lee purchased the bonds. (5/93, Theory, #11, amended, 4199)

5. On October 1, year 2, Park Co. purchased 200 of the $1,000 face amount, 10% bonds of Ott, Inc., for $220,000, including accrued interest of $5,000. The bonds, which mature on January 1, year 9, pay interest semiannually on January 1 and July 1. Park used the straight-line method of amortization and appropriately recorded the bonds as a long-term investment. On Park's December 31, year 3 balance sheet, the bonds should be reported at

   a. $215,000
   b. $214,400
   c. $214,200
   d. $212,000 (11/90, PI, #4, amended, 0971)

6. On July 1, year 1, Pell Co. purchased Green Corp. ten-year, 8% bonds with a face amount of $500,000 for $420,000. The bonds mature on June 30, year 9 and pay interest semiannually on June 30 and December 31. Using the interest method, Pell recorded bond discount amortization of $1,800 for the six months ended December 31, year 1. From this long-term investment, Pell should report year 1 revenue of

   a. $16,800
   b. $18,200
   c. $20,000
   d. $21,800 (5/90, PI, #46, amended, 0976)

7. Jent Corp. purchased bonds at a discount of $10,000. Subsequently, Jent sold these bonds at a premium of $14,000. During the period that Jent held this investment, amortization of the discount amounted to $2,000. What amount should Jent report as gain on the sale of bonds?

   a. $12,000
   b. $22,000
   c. $24,000
   d. $26,000 (5/94, FAR, #43, 4858)

8. Album Co. issued 10-year $200,000 debenture bonds on January 2. The bonds pay interest semiannually. Album uses the effective interest method to amortize bond premiums and discounts. The carrying value of the bonds on January 2 was $185,953. A journal entry was recorded for the first interest payment on June 30, debiting interest expense for $13,016 and crediting cash for $12,000. What is the annual stated interest rate for the debenture bonds?

   a. 6%
   b. 7%
   c. 12%
   d. 14% (R/05, FAR, #27, 7771)

9. A company issued a bond with a stated rate of interest that is less than the effective interest rate on the date of issuance. The bond was issued on one of the interest payment dates. What should the company report on the first interest payment date?

   a. An interest expense that is less than the cash payment made to bondholders
   b. An interest expense that is greater than the cash payment made to bondholders
   c. A debit to the unamortized bond discount
   d. A debit to the unamortized bond premium (R/09, FAR, #44, 8794)

10. A company issues bonds at 98, with a maturity value of $50,000. The entry the company uses to record the original issue should include which of the following?

   a. A debit to bond discount of $1,000
   b. A credit to bonds payable of $49,000
   c. A credit to bond premium of $1,000
   d. A debit to bonds payable of $50,000 (R/09, FAR, #50, 8800)

11. When purchasing a bond, the present value of the bond's expected net future cash inflows discounted at the market rate of interest provides what information about the bond?

   a. Price
   b. Par
   c. Yield
   d. Interest (R/11, FAR, #38, 9888)

12. The following information pertains to Camp Corp.'s bond issuance on July 1, year 1:

Face amount	$800,000
Term	10 years
Stated interest rate	6%
Interest payment dates	Annually on July 1
Yield	9%

	At 6%	At 9%
Present value of 1 for 10 periods	0.558	0.422
Future value of 1 for 10 periods	1.791	2.367
Present value of ordinary annuity of 1 for 10 periods	7.360	6.418

What should be the issue price for each $1,000 bond?

a. $1,000
b. $ 864
c. $ 807
d. $ 700 (Editor, 89434)

13. During the year, Lake Co. issued 3,000 of its 9%, $1,000 face value bonds at 101½. In connection with the sale of these bonds, Lake paid the following expenses:

Promotion costs	$ 20,000
Engraving and printing	25,000
Underwriters' commissions	200,000

What amount should Lake record as bond issue costs to be amortized over the term of the bonds?

a. $0
b. $220,000
c. $225,000
d. $245,000 (11/92, PI, amended, #37, 3270)

14. How should bond issue costs be recorded?

a. Expensed in the period incurred
b. Classified as an asset
c. Amortized from the date of the bond, rather than the date of sale, to the maturity date
d. All of the above (Editor, 89606)

15. On June 30, Huff Corp. issued at 99, one thousand of its 8%, $1,000 bonds. The bonds were issued through an underwriter to whom Huff paid bond issue costs of $35,000. On June 30, Huff should report the bond liability at

a. $ 955,000
b. $ 990,000
c. $1,000,000
d. $1,025,000 (11/90, PI, #24, amended, 1031)

16. A 15-year bond was issued in year 1 at a discount. During year 11, a 10-year bond was issued at face amount with the proceeds used to retire the 15-year bond at its face amount. The net effect of the year 11 bond transactions was to increase long-term liabilities by the excess of the 10-year bond's face amount over the 15-year bond's

a. Face amount
b. Carrying amount
c. Face amount less the deferred loss on bond retirement
d. Carrying amount less the deferred loss on bond retirement (5/91, Theory, #5, amended, 1782)

17. On July 31 of the current year, Dome Co. issued $1,000,000 of 10%, 15-year bonds at par and used a portion of the proceeds to call its 600 outstanding 11%, $1,000 face value bonds, due in ten years on July 31, at 102. On that date, unamortized bond premium relating to the 11% bonds was $65,000. In its year-end income statement, what amount should Dome report as gain or loss, before income taxes, from retirement of bonds?

    a. $ 53,000 gain
    b. $0
    c. $ (65,000) loss
    d. $ (77,000) loss

    (11/94, FAR, #42, amended, 5304)

18. On January 1, year 1, Fox Corp. issued 1,000 of its 10%, $1,000 bonds for $1,040,000. These bonds were to mature on January 1, year 11, but were callable at 101 any time after December 31, year 4. Interest was payable semiannually on July 1 and January 1. On July 1, year 6, Fox called all of the bonds and retired them. Bond premium was amortized on a straight-line basis. Before income taxes, Fox's gain or loss in year 6 on this early extinguishment of debt was

    a. $30,000 gain
    b. $12,000 gain
    c. $10,000 loss
    d. $ 8,000 gain

    (5/90, PI, #40, amended, 9064)

19. On January 2 of the current year, West Co. issued 9% bonds in the amount of $500,000, which mature in ten years. The bonds were issued for $469,500 to yield 10%. Interest is payable annually on December 31. West uses the interest method of amortizing bond discount. In its June 30 current year balance sheet, what amount should West report as bonds payable?

    a. $469,500
    b. $470,475
    c. $471,025
    d. $500,000

    (11/94, FAR, #24, amended, 5288)

20. When the effective interest method of amortization is used for bonds issued at a premium, the amount of interest payable for an interest period is calculated by multiplying the

    a. Face value of the bonds at the beginning of the period by the contractual interest rate
    b. Face value of the bonds at the beginning of the period by the effective interest rates
    c. Carrying value of the bonds at the beginning of the period by the contractual interest rate
    d. Carrying value of the bonds at the beginning of the period by the effective interest rates

    (R/11, FAR, #43, 9893)

21. Webb Co. has outstanding a 7%, 10-year $100,000 face-value bond. The bond was originally sold to yield 6% annual interest. Webb uses the effective interest rate method to amortize bond premium. On June 30, year 2, the carrying amount of the outstanding bond was $105,000. What amount of unamortized premium on bond should Webb report in its June 30, year 3 balance sheet?

    a. $1,050
    b. $3,950
    c. $4,300
    d. $4,500

    (11/93, PI, #36, amended, 4405)

22. Foley Co. is preparing the electronic spreadsheet below, to amortize the discount on its 10-year, 6%, $100,000 bonds payable. Bonds were issued on December 31 to yield 8%. Interest is paid annually. Foley uses the effective interest method to amortize bond discounts.

	A	B	C	D	E
1	Year	Cash paid	Interest expense	Discount amortization	Carrying amount
2	1				$86,580
3	2	$6,000			

Which formula should Foley use in cell E3 to calculate the bonds' carrying amount at the end of year 2?

a. E2 + D3
b. E2 – D3
c. E2 + C3
d. E2 – C3 (R/07, FAR, #20, 8341)

23. On January 1, a company issued a $50,000 face value, 8% five-year bond for $46,139 that will yield 10%. Interest is payable on June 30 and December 31. What is the bond carrying amount on December 31 of the current year?

a. $46,139
b. $46,446
c. $46,768
d. $47,106 (R/08, FAR, #12, 8567)

24. On June 1 of the current year, Cross Corp. issued $300,000 of 8% bonds payable at par with interest payment dates of April 1 and October 1. In its income statement for the current year ended December 31, what amount of interest expense should Cross report?

a. $ 6,000
b. $ 8,000
c. $12,000
d. $14,000 (R/05, FAR, #4, amended, 7748)

25. On November 1 of the current year, Mason Corp. issued $800,000 of its 10-year, 8% term bonds dated October 1 of the current year. The bonds were sold to yield 10%, with total proceeds of $700,000 plus accrued interest. Interest is paid every April 1 and October 1. What amount should Mason report for interest payable in its December 31 current year balance sheet?

a. $17,500
b. $16,000
c. $11,667
d. $10,667 (11/92, PI, #23, amended, 3256)

26. On July 1 of the current year, Eagle Corp. issued 600 of its 10%, $1,000 bonds at 99 plus accrued interest. The bonds are dated April 1 of the current year, and mature in 10 years. Interest is payable semiannually on April 1 and October 1. What amount did Eagle receive from the bond issuance?

a. $579,000
b. $594,000
c. $600,000
d. $609,000 (5/95, FAR, #19, amended, 5555)

27. Hancock Co.'s December 31, year 1 balance sheet contained the following items in the long-term liabilities section:

Unsecured	
9.375% registered bonds ($25,000 maturing annually beginning in year 5)	$275,000
11.5% convertible bonds, callable beginning in year 10, due year 21	125,000
Secured	
9.875% guaranty security bonds, due 2020	$250,000
10.0% commodity backed bonds ($50,000 maturing annually beginning in year 6)	200,000

What are the total amounts of serial bonds and debenture bonds?

	Serial bonds	Debenture bonds
a.	$475,000	$400,000
b	$475,000	$125,000
c.	$450,000	$400,000
d.	$200,000	$650,000

(5/91, PI, #47, amended, 9062)

28. What type of bonds in a particular bond issuance will **not** all mature on the same date?

a. Debenture bonds
b. Serial bonds
c. Term bonds
d. Sinking fund bonds

(R/08, FAR, #13, 8568)

29. Bonds with detachable stock warrants were issued by Flack Co. Immediately after issue, the aggregate market value of the bonds and the warrants exceeds the proceeds. Is the portion of the proceeds allocated to the warrants less than their market value, and is that amount recorded as contributed capital?

	Less than warrants' market value	Contributed capital
a.	No	Yes
b.	Yes	No
c.	Yes	Yes
d.	No	No

(11/91, Theory, #37, 2545)

30. On December 31 of the current year, Moss Co. issued $1,000,000 of 11% bonds at 109. Each $1,000 bond was issued with 50 detachable stock warrants, each of which entitled the bondholder to purchase one share of $5 par common stock for $25. Immediately after issuance, the market value of each warrant was $4. On December 31, what amount should Moss record as discount or premium on issuance of bonds?

a. $ 40,000 premium
b. $ 90,000 premium
c. $110,000 discount
d. $200,000 discount

(5/94, FAR, #34, amended, 4849)

31. On July 28, Vent Corp. sold $500,000 of 4%, eight-year subordinated debentures for $450,000. The purchasers were issued 2,000 detachable warrants, each of which was for one share of $5 par common stock at $12 per share. Shortly after issuance, the warrants sold at a market price of $10 each. What amount of discount on the debentures should Vent record at issuance?

a. $50,000
b. $60,000
c. $70,000
d. $74,000

(R/08, FAR, #36, 8591)

32. Which of the following statements characterizes convertible debt?
    a. The holder of the debt must be repaid with shares of the issuer's stock.
    b. No value is assigned to the conversion feature when convertible debt is issued.
    c. The transaction should be recorded as the issuance of stock.
    d. The issuer's stock price is **less** than market value when the debt is converted. (R/08, FAR, #37, 8592)

33. Which of the following is generally associated with the terms of convertible debt securities?
    a. An interest rate that is lower than nonconvertible debt
    b. An initial conversion price that is less than the market value of the common stock at time of issuance
    c. A noncallable feature
    d. A feature to subordinate the security to nonconvertible debt (R/07, FAR, #47, 8368)

34. On January 2, year 1, Burnt Co. issued 10-year convertible bonds at 105. During year 4, these bonds were converted into common stock having an aggregate par value equal to the total face amount of the bonds. At conversion, the market price of Burnt's common stock was 50 percent above its par value. Depending on whether the book value method or the market value method was used, Burnt would recognize gains or losses on conversion when using the

	Book value method	Market value method
a.	Either gain or loss	Gain
b.	Either gain or loss	Loss
c.	Neither gain nor loss	Loss
d.	Neither gain nor loss	Gain

(11/90, Theory, #30, amended, 9063)

35. On January 1, Stunt Corp. had outstanding convertible bonds with a face value of $1,000,000 and an unamortized discount of $100,000. On that date, the bonds were converted into 100,000 shares of $1 par stock. The market value on the date of conversion was $12 per share. The transaction will be accounted for with the book value method. By what amount will Stunt's stockholders' equity increase as a result of the bond conversion?
    a. $ 100,000
    b. $ 900,000
    c. $1,000,000
    d. $1,200,000 (R/09, FAR, #34, 8784)

Problem 6-2 SIMULATION: Bond Interest Expense

On January 1, year 1, the Pinehurst Company, Inc. a privately-held company, issued $3,000,000, three-year, 12.00% bonds, dated January 1, year 1. The bonds provided for semi-annual interest payments to be made on June 30 and December 31 of each year. The bonds were issued when the market interest rate was 10.00% and the bond issue price was $3,152, 270. Pinehurst Company, Inc uses the effective interest method for amortizing bond discounts and premiums. The bonds are term bonds that mature on December 31, year 3. Pinehurst Company, Inc.'s fiscal year for financial reporting purposes is December 31.

Complete the bond amortization table for the Pinehurst Company, Inc. bonds (issued 1/1/2001) **through the term** of the bonds. Round all amounts to the nearest dollar.

	A	B	C	D	E	F
1	**Date**	**Interest Payment**	**Interest Expense**	**Increase (Decrease) in Carrying Amount of Bonds**	**Unamortized (Discount) or Premium**	**Carrying Amount of Bonds**
2	01/01/01					$3,152,270
3						
4						
5						
6						
7						
8						

(R/08, FAR, P3, amended, 8606b/9111)

Problem 6-3 SIMULATION: Bond Investment Transactions

The following bonds related transactions took place by Ray Company over the course of several years:

- On September 30, year 2, Ray purchased 300 new bonds issued by Bob Corp., with a face amount of $300,000 and a 5% stated interest rate. The bonds mature in eight years and pay interest quarterly, at the end of March, June, September, and December. The effective yield for similar securities is 8% annually.
- On October 31, year 6, Ray sold the 300 Bob bonds to Hope Inc. for $280,000, which included interest accrued on the bonds. Ray amortized the original discount on the bonds using the straight-line method.
- On January 1, year 7, Ray issued five-year bonds with a face amount of $150,000 and a stated interest rate of 9%, payable semiannually on June 30 and December 31. The bonds were priced to yield 6%.
- On June 1, year 8, Ray issued 7% ten-year bonds with a face amount of $180,000. The bonds are dated January 1, year 8, and interest is payable on January 1 and July 1. The bonds were sold at par and accrued interest.
- On August 15, year 9, Ray converted bonds with a face amount of $175,000 and a carrying amount of $182,000 into 1000 shares of $110 par common stock with $169 fair value.

Note: Round all computation amounts to the nearest dollar.

1. Prepare the journal entry to record the acquisition of the Bob bonds on September 30, year 2.

Bond Investment		
Cash		

2. Prepare the journal entry to record the interest income and discount amortization of the Bob bonds for the year ending December 31, year 2, assuming the straight.

Cash		
Bond Investment		
Interest Income		

3. Prepare the journal entry to record the interest income and discount amortization of the Bob bonds for the year ending December 31, year 2, if the effective interest method of discount amortization was used.

Cash		
Bond Investment		
Interest Income		

4. Prepare the journal entry to record the sale of the Bob bonds on October 31, year 6.

Cash		
Bond Investment		
Interest Income		

5. Prepare the journal entry to record the issuance of bonds on January 1, year 7.

Cash		
Bonds Payable		

6. Prepare the journal entry to record the issuance of bonds on June 1, year 8.

Cash		
Bonds Payable		
Accrued Interest Payable		

7. Prepare the journal entry to record the bond conversion on August 15, year 9 using the book value method.

Bonds Payable		
Common Stock		
Additional Paid-In Capital		

8. Prepare the journal entry to record the bond conversion on August 15, year 9 using the market value method.

Bonds Payable		
Common Stock		
Additional Paid-In Capital		

(5/98, FAR, #1, 6611)

Problem 6-4 SIMULATION: Balance Sheet Presentation

The following amortization table is for $1,000,000, five-year, 10% bonds, dated and issued on January 2, 2013 by Lakehurst Company. The bonds provided for semi-annual interest payments to be made on June 30 and December 31 of each year. The bonds were issued when the market interest rate was 8.00%.

- Lakehurst Company, Inc. uses the effective interest method for amortizing bond discounts and premiums
- The bonds are term bonds that mature on December 31, 2013.
- Lakehurst Company, Inc.'s fiscal year for financial reporting purposes is December 31.

Date	Interest Payment	Interest Expense	**Increase** (Decrease) **in Carrying Amount of Bonds**	Unamortized (Discount) or Premium	Carrying Amount of Bonds
01/02/13				$81,109	$1,081,109
06/30/13	$50,000	$43,244	($6,756)	$74,353	$1,074,353
12/31/13	$50,000	$42,974	($7,026)	$67,327	$1,067,327
06/30/14	$50,000	$42,693	($7,307)	$60,020	$1,060,020
12/31/14	$50,000	$42,401	($7,599)	$52,421	$1,052,421
06/30/15	$50,000	$42,097	($7.903)	$44,518	$1,044,518
12/31/15	$50,000	$41,781	($8,219)	$36,299	$1,036,299
06/30/16	$50,000	$41,452	($8,548)	$27,751	$1,027,751
12/31/16	$50,000	$41,110	($8,890)	$18,861	$1,018,861
06/30/17	$50,000	$40,754	($9,246)	$9,615	$1,009,615
12/31/17	$50,000	$40,385	($9,615)	$0	$1,000,000

Use values in the amortization table to complete the liabilities section of Lakehurst Company, Inc.'s December 31, 2013, balance sheet and excerpts from the income statement for the year ending December 31, 2013. Insert the appropriate values in the cells below. Round all amounts to nearest whole dollar.

Balance Sheet—Liabilities:	
Accounts payable and other liabilities	$ 150,000
Bonds Payable	
Unamortized premium/discount	
Total liabilities	$
Income Statement:	
Sales	$1,000,000
Expenses before interest and taxes	500,000
Interest Expense	
Net income before taxes	$

(R/08, FAR, P3, amended, 8606c/9112)

Problem 6-5 SIMULATION: Bond Terms

The following are terms and concepts involving bonds. From the list provided, select the best response choice for each term or concept. Each response **can be used once, and only once.**

	Response Choices
A.	Mature at a specified date
B.	May be retired at the issuer's option
C.	May be converted to stock at bondholder's option
D.	Provide for repayment of principal in a series of installments
E.	Unsecured; not supported by a lien or mortgage on specific assets
F.	When selling a bond and the stated interest rate equals the market rate
G.	When selling a bond and the stated interest rate is less than the market rate
H.	Reacquisition of debt securities by the use of proceeds from issuing other securities
I.	When selling a bond and the stated interest rate is greater than the market rate for similar debt
J.	Includes legal fees, accounting fees, underwriting commissions, registration, printing and engraving
K.	Reacquisition of debt securities regardless of whether the securities are canceled or held as so-called treasury bonds
L.	Represents a contractual obligation to make periodic interest payments on the amount borrowed and to repay the principal upon maturity

	Terms & Concepts	Choice
1.	Premium	
2.	Issue Costs	
3.	Term Bonds	
4.	Callable Bonds	
5.	Extinguishment	
6.	Convertible Bonds	

	Terms & Concepts	Choice
7.	Debenture Bonds	
8.	Bonds Payable	
9.	Serial Bonds	
10.	Refunding	
11.	Discount	
12.	Par	

(11/98, FAR, #17, amended, 9113)

Problem 6-6 SIMULATION: Research

Question: In determining an appropriate interest rate, what are the considerations that may affect selection of a rate?

FASB ASC: _____ - _____ - _____ - _____

(9156)

Solution 6-1 MULTIPLE-CHOICE ANSWERS

Investment in Bonds

1. (b) A bond issued between interest payment dates requires the investor to pay the seller for accrued interest in addition to the price of the bond. A bond issued at a discount is a bond issued at a price below the bond's face amount. Hence, at the date of purchase, the carrying amount of a bond purchased at a discount between interest payment dates is less than the cash paid to the seller and is also less than the face amount of the bond. (1781)

2. (c) Fox purchased bonds with a full 6 months interest accrued. Discounts are typically not shown in a separate account for bond investments, but netted against the carrying amount. The most efficient method to determine the carrying amount for the bond investment is to plug the following journal entry:

Investment in Bonds	plug		$371,660	
Interest Receivable	16,000		$400,000 * 8% * 6/12	
Interest Income		18,460	$369,200 * 10% * 6/12	
Cash		369,200	given in problem	(89431)

3. (d) Although an investor entity initially records bonds held for investment at an amount equal to the purchase price of the bond plus other direct costs of acquisition, such as broker's fees, it is also true that: (1) if it buys bonds between interest dates, it will have to pay an additional amount for the interest accrued on the bond since the last interest date (or the bond date, if before the first interest date); and (2) it must record the additional amount paid due to purchasing the bonds between interest dates as purchased interest, such as interest receivable, rather than adding it to the cost of the bond investment. Since the answers for a., b., and c. are all correct, the best answer for this question is d., *all of the above*. (89603)

4. (d) The purchaser of a bond acquires the right to receive two cash flows: a lump sum paid at maturity for the face amount of the bond, and an annuity consisting of periodic interest payments over the life of the bond. The price the market is willing to pay for the bond is equal to the present value of these two cash flows, discounted at the prevailing market interest rate for bonds having the same maturity and perceived degree of risk. When interest rates increase, the present value of the two cash flows decreases, causing the market value of the bonds to decline. The issuance of a stock dividend should not cause a decline in the market value of the bonds. If the bonds currently are quoted at a small discount and the bonds are expected to be called at a premium (i.e., above face amount), this situation would most likely have the effect of causing a rise in the market value of the bonds. A decline in interest rates would cause a rise in the bond's market value. (4199)

5. (d) The carrying amount of the bonds is determined by subtracting the amortization of the bond premium from the date of purchase from the cost of the bond investment.

Bond cost, 10/1, year 2 ($220,000 – $5,000)		$ 215,000	
Bond investment cost, 10/1, year 2	$ 215,000		
Less: Face amount of bonds (200 × $1,000)	(200,000)		
Bond premium	15,000		
Divided by: Months to maturity (10/1, year 2 to 1/1, year 9)	÷ 75		
Monthly premium amortization	200		
Times: Months from issue	× 15		
Less amortization of premium to 12/31		(3,000)	
Bond carrying amount, 12/31, year 3		$ 212,000	(0971)

6. (d) Bonds purchased at a discount are purchased at less than their face amount. The subsequent amortization of the discount increases the carrying amount of the bond investment and the amount of interest income recognized.

Simple interest, 7/1, year 1 - 12/31, year 1 [$500,000 × (8% / 2)]	$ 20,000	
Amortization of discount on bond investment (given)	1,800	
Interest revenue recognized in year 1	$ 21,800	(0976)

7. (b) Since the bond was purchased at a discount, the initial carrying value of the bond investment is $10,000 less than the face amount. The amortization of the discount increases the bond investment and so, on the date of sale the bond investment is carried on Jent Corp.'s books at $8,000 less (i.e., $10,000 – 2,000) than the face amount. Therefore, the sale of the bond at a premium (i.e., at $14,000 more than the face amount of the bond) results in recognition of a $22,000 gain (i.e., $8,000 + $14,000). (4858)

Bonds Payable

8. (c) The bonds' stated interest rate and face amount determine the amount of periodic interest payments. The interest payment recorded on June 2 was for 6 months. To arrive at the annual rate multiply the semi-annual interest payment by 2 and divide by the face amount of the bond.

$12,000 × 2 = 24,000 / 200,000 = 12% (7771)

9. (b) A bond that is issued with a stated rate of interest that is less than the effective rate on the issuance date is a bond issued with a discount. A bond issued at a discount will have an increasing carrying value and an increasing amount of interest expense. On the first interest payment date the company should report an interest expense that is greater than the cash payment made to bondholders. (8794)

10. (a) A bond issued at 98 indicates the bond was issued at a 2% discount. The entry the company would use to record the original issue would be a debit to cash for $49,000, a debit to bond discount for $1,000 and a credit to bonds payable for $50,000. (8800)

11. (a) To estimate the proceeds to be received from the purchase and associated issuance of bonds payable (ignoring bond issue costs), the present values of the bond principal and interest payments must be determined. The prevailing market (yield) rate is used to discount the cash flows to arrive at their present value, which is the selling price of the bond. (9888)

12. (c) The total amount consists of 2 calculations: the present value of the interest annuity and the present value of the principle. Interest is paid annually, so there are 10 compounding periods. The discount rate is always the market/yield rate, which is 9% annually. The annual interest payment is computed using the face interest rate $48,000 [$800,000 * 6%]. The total amount for the bonds is $645,664: the pv of the interest annuity $308,064 [$48,000 * 6.418] + the pv of the principle $337,600 [$800,000 * .422]. The issue price per bond would be: $645,664 / 800 bonds = $807, rounded. (89434)

13. (d) Engraving and printing costs, accounting and legal fees, commissions paid to underwriters, promotion costs, and other similar charges are incurred when bonds are issued. Bond issue costs should be recorded as a deferred charge and amortized over the life of the debt, in a manner similar to that used for discount on bonds. Therefore, $245,000 (i.e., $20,000 + $25,000 + $200,000) should be recorded as bond issue costs to be amortized over the term of the bonds. (3270)

14. (b) Bond issue costs should be classified as a deferred charge (i.e., asset). (89606)

15. (b) The $35,000 of bond issue costs should be reported as a deferred charge (i.e., an asset) and amortized over the term of the bonds. The bond liability should be reported at the sum of the face amount of the bonds less the related discount.

Face amount of bonds ($1,000 × 1,000)	$1,000,000
Discount on bonds [$1,000,000 – ($1,000,000 × 99%)]	(10,000)
Amount to be reported as bond liability, 6/30	$ 990,000

(1031)

16. (b) The new 10-year bond was issued at its face amount which, from the facts, either equals or exceeds the face amount of the 15-year bond which exceeds the carrying amount of the 15-year bond because the 15-year bond was issued at a discount (a price less than the face amount). The excess of the retirement price (face amount) of the 15-year bond over its carrying amount will be recorded as a loss at retirement. Therefore, the issuance of the new bond and the retirement of the old bond will have the net effect of increasing the total of long-term liabilities by the excess of the new bond's face amount over the old bond's carrying amount. (1782)

17. (a) A gain is recognized because the cost to redeem the bonds is less than the carrying amount of the bonds.

Face amount of bonds retired (600 × $1,000)	$ 600,000	
Add: Unamortized bond premium	65,000	
Bond carrying amount at retirement date	665,000	
Less: Cost to retire ($600,000 × 102%)	(612,000)	
Pretax gain on retirement of bonds	$ 53,000	(5304)

Premium & Discount Amortization

18. (d)

Face amount of bonds (1,000 × $1,000)		$1,000,000
Premium at issuance ($1,040,000 – $1,000,000)	$ 40,000	
Amortized to extinguishment date ($40,000 × 11/20*)	(22,000)	
Add unamortized premium at extinguishment		18,000
Bond carrying amount at extinguishment		1,018,000
Cost to reacquire ($1,000,000 × 101%)		(1,010,000)
Pretax gain on early extinguishment of debt		$ 8,000

* The interest on the 10-year bonds was payable semiannually. Therefore, there were 20 (i.e., 10 × 2) interest dates over the life of the bonds. The premium must be amortized up to the date of retirement (i.e., 7/1, year 6—the eleventh interest date). (9064)

19. (b) $469,500 + $975 = $470,475

Bonds payable carrying amount, 1/2	$ 469,500	
Effective interest rate (10% × 6/12)	× 5%	
Interest expense, 1/2 - 6/30	23,475	
Interest payment [$500,000 × (9% × 6/12)]	(22,500)	
Amortization of discount, 1/2 - 6/30	$ 975	(5288)

20. (a) The effective interest method of amortization calls for recognizing interest expense at the effective interest rate at which the bonds were sold. Thus, this interest method overcomes the criticism of the straight-line method because it offers a more accurate measurement of interest expense. To amortize a premium using the effective interest method, multiply the carrying amount of the bond issue by the effective yield. This equals interest expense for the period. The difference between the cash interest payment and the interest expense equals the amount of premium amortization for the period. The cash payment is always computed by multiplying the face amount of the bond by the face or stated interest rate. (9893)

21. (c)

Unamortized bond premium, 6/30, year 2 ($105,000 – $100,000)		$ 5,000	
Bonds payable carrying amount, 6/30, year 2	$ 105,000		
Times: Annual effective interest rate	× 6%		
Interest expense, 6/30, year 2 - 6/30, year 3	6,300		
Annual interest payment ($100,000 × 7%)	(7,000)		
Bond premium amortization, 6/30, year 2 - 6/30, year 3		(700)	
Unamortized bond premium, 6/30, year 3		$ 4,300	(4405)

22. (a) Amortization of a bond discount increases the carrying amount of the bond. Adding the bonds' year 1 carrying amount (cell E2) the discount amortization (cell D3) would net the bond's carrying amount at the end of year 2 (cell E3). Amortization of a bond premium decreases the carrying amount of the bond. Interest expense is not subtracted or added to the carrying amount directly. (8341)

23. (c) In determining the carrying amount of bonds, an adjustment is made for premium or discount amortization to the date of sale. Amortization of a bond premium decreases interest expense and the carrying amount of the bond, while the amortization of a bond discount increases the issuer's interest expense and carrying amount of the bond.

Date	Interest Paid (4%)	Interest Expense (5%)	Amortization	Carrying Value
1/1				$46,139
6/30	$2,000	$2,307	$307	46,446
12/31	2,000	2,322	322	46,768

(8567)

24. (d) Interest expense from June 1 to December 31 is for 7 months.

$300,000
× 8%
24,000
× 7/12
$ 14,000

(7748)

25. (b) Interest payable is the cash interest accumulated that is not yet paid at the balance sheet date. The bonds have a semiannual interest payment of $32,000 [i.e., $800,000 × (8% / 2)]. Since the bonds are dated 10/1, Mason should report three months of interest payable, or $16,000 (i.e., $32,000 × 3/6), at 12/31. (3256)

26. (d)

Bond Price ($1,000 × 99% × 600 bonds)	$594,000
Plus: Accrued interest at stated interest rate (10% × $1,000 × 600 bonds × 3/12)	15,000
Proceeds from bond issuance	$609,000

(5555)

Bonds With Additional Features

27. (a) Bond issues maturing on a single date are called term bonds, whereas bond issues maturing in installments are called serial bonds. Since the registered bonds and the commodity-backed bonds both mature in installments, the total amount of serial bonds is $475,000 (i.e., $275,000 + $200,000). Debenture bonds are unsecured bonds; they are not supported by a lien or mortgage on specific assets. Since the registered bonds and the convertible bonds are unsecured, the total amount of debenture bonds is $400,000 (i.e., $275,000 + $125,000). (9062)

28. (b) Serial bonds are a set of bonds issued at the same time but having a different maturity date; thus providing a series of installments for repayment of principal. A debenture bond is just an unsecured bond. A term bond is an issue of bonds that all have the same maturity date. Most corporate bonds are term bonds. Sinking fund bonds require the debtor to periodically set aside sums to give assurance to investors and would mature normally on a set date. (8568)

29. (c) The proceeds from the issuance of bonds with detachable stock purchase warrants should be allocated to the two securities based on the relative market values of the securities involved. The amount allocated to the warrants is reported as paid-in capital (i.e., contributed capital). Since the aggregate market value of the bonds and the warrants exceeds the proceeds, the amount of proceeds allocated to the bonds and the amount of proceeds allocated to the warrants will be less than the market values of the respective securities. (2545)

30. (c) Since the fair market value of the bonds is not determinable, the incremental method is used to determine the value of the bonds and warrants. That is, the market value is used for the warrants and the remainder of the purchase price is allocated to the bonds.

Purchase price (1,000 bonds × $1,000 × 109%)	$1,090,000
Fair value of the warrants (1,000 × 50 × $4)	(200,000)
Portion allocated to bonds	$ 890,000
Face value of bonds	$1,000,000
Portion allocated to bonds	(890,000)
Discount on bonds	$ 110,000

(4849)

31. (c) When bonds are issued with detachable stock warrants there must be an allocation of the proceeds between the warrants and the debt security based on relative fair values. Vent would debit Cash $450,000, credit Bond Payable $500,000, and credit APIC-Stock Warrants for their fair value of $20,000 (2,000 detachable warrants at the market price of $10). The entry needs a $70,000 debit to balance and that is the discount on the debentures. (8591)

32. (b) Convertible debt securities are those debt securities which are convertible into common stock of the issuer or an affiliated company at a specified price at the option of the holder and which are sold at a price or have a value at issuance not significantly in excess of the face amount. The terms of such securities generally include (1) an interest rate which is lower than the issuer could establish for nonconvertible debt, (2) an initial conversion price which is greater than the market value of the common stock at time of issuance, and (3) a conversion price which does not decrease except pursuant to antidilution provisions. No proceeds from the debt issue are to be assigned to the conversion feature (even though the convertible bonds may sell for substantially more than similar nonconvertible bonds). The reason for no allocation to equity is that the debt cannot be separated from the conversion feature, as would be the case with detachable stock warrants. The holder of the debt need not be repaid with shares of the issuer's stock and the transaction should not be recorded as the issuance of stock. (8592)

33. (a) Convertible debt securities are debt securities that are convertible into common stock of the issuer or an affiliated company at a specified price at the option of the holder. The terms of such securities generally include (1) an interest rate that is lower than the issuer could establish for nonconvertible debt, (2) an initial conversion price that is greater than the market value of the common stock at time of issuance, and (3) a conversion price that does not decrease except pursuant to antidilution provisions. (8368)

34. (c) A major characteristic of the book value method is that neither a gain nor a loss is recognized on the conversion of bonds to stock; the carrying amount of debt is taken out of the debt accounts and recorded in stockholders' equity accounts. The market value method may result in a gain or loss because the stock is to be recorded at the market value of the stock (or bonds) and the carrying amount of the debt is to be removed from liability accounts. A difference between the market value of the stock and the carrying amount of the debt is to be recorded as a gain or loss, whichever is appropriate. Because of the relationships of amounts involved, it is evident that the market value of the stock exceeds the carrying amount of the debt; therefore, a loss will be recorded on the conversion. Those relationships are as follows: (1) the aggregate par value of the stock was equal to the total face amount (par value) of the bonds, (2) the market value of the stock is 50% above its par, and (3) the carrying amount of the debt is less than 5% above its par (the bonds were issued in a prior year at a 5% premium and at least 30% of that premium had been amortized prior to year 4). (9063)

35. (b) Convertible bonds provide the bondholder the option of converting the bond to capital stock, typically common stock. Using the book value method, the conversion of the bonds into common stock is generally recorded by crediting the paid-in capital accounts for the carrying amount of the debt at the date of the conversion, less any cost associated with the conversion. The carrying amount of the bonds on the date of conversion is the $1,000,000 face value less the $100,000 unamortized discount. The market value is not considered when using the book value method. The journal entry:

Bonds Payable	1,000,000	
Bond Discount		100,000
Common Stock (100,000 × $1 par)		100,000
APIC (to balance)		800,000

The $100,000 credit to common stock and $800,000 credit to APIC would increase stockholders' equity $900,000. (8784)

PERFORMANCE BY SUBTOPICS

Each category below parallels a subtopic covered in Chapter 6. Record the number and percentage of questions you correctly answered in each subtopic area.

Investment in Bonds

Question #	Correct √
1	
2	
3	
4	
5	
6	
7	
# Questions	7
# Correct	________
% Correct	________

Bonds Payable

Question #	Correct √
8	
9	
10	
11	
12	
13	
14	
15	
16	
17	
# Questions	10
# Correct	________
% Correct	________

Premium & Discount Amortization

Question #	Correct √
18	
19	
20	
21	
22	
23	
24	
25	
26	
# Questions	9
# Correct	________
% Correct	________

Bonds With Additional Features

Question #	Correct √
27	
28	
29	
30	
31	
32	
33	
34	
35	
# Questions	9
# Correct	________
% Correct	________

Solution 6-2 SIMULATION ANSWER: Bond Interest Expense

	A	B	C	D	E	F
1	**Date**	**Interest Payment**	**Interest Expense**	**Increase (Decrease) in Carrying Amount of Bonds**	**Unamortized (Discount) or Premium**	**Carrying Amount of Bonds**
2	01/01/01				152,270	3,152,270
3	06/30/01	180,000	157,613	(22,387)	129,883	3,129,883
4	12/31/01	180,000	156,494	(23,506)	106,377	3,106,377
5	06/30/02	180,000	155,319	(24,681)	81,696	3,081,696
6	12/31/02	180,000	154,085	(25,915)	55,781	3,055,781
7	06/30/03	180,000	152,789	(27,211)	28,570	3,028,570
8	12/31/03	180,000	151,429	(28,570)	0	3,000,000

Explanations:

Column A, rows 3 - 8: The dates will be June 30 and December 31 of each of the three years.

Column B, rows 3 - 8: The $180,000 interest payment will be the same for each period.

Column C, rows 3 - 8: To calculate interest expense, multiply the carrying amount of the bonds from the previous period by the 0.05 interest rate. For example, row 3 would be $3,152,270 × 0.05 = $157,613

Column D, rows 3 - 8: The change in carrying amount of bonds is the difference between the interest payment and interest expense. If the interest payment is greater than interest expense there is a decrease in the carrying amount of bonds. If the interest payment is less than interest expense there is an increase in the carrying amount of the bonds. For example, row 3 would be $180,000 – $157,613 = a $22,387 decrease.

Column E, row 2: The unamortized (discount) or premium is the difference between the carrying amount of the bonds and the face amount of the bonds. If the carrying amount of the bonds is greater than the face amount there is an unamortized premium. If the carrying amount of the bonds is less than the face amount there is an unamortized discount. In this case, $3,152,270 – $3,000,000 = an $152,270 premium.

Column E, rows 3 - 8: There are two ways to calculate the unamortized premium. One is to take that amount from the previous period and increase or decrease it by the increase (decrease) in carrying amount of bonds. For example, row 3 would be $152,270 – $22,387 = $129,883. The other is to simply take the carrying amount of the bonds and subtract the face amount. For example, row 3 would be $3,129,883 – $3,000,000 = $129,883.

Column F, rows 3 - 8: The carrying amount of the bonds is calculated by applying the increase or decrease in carrying amount of the bonds to the carrying amount of bonds from the previous period. For example, row 3 would be $3,152,270 – $22,387 = $3,129,883.

Solution 6-3 SIMULATION ANSWER: Bond Investment Transactions

1. Bond Investment	247,196	
Cash		247,196

2. Cash	3,750	
Bond Investment	1,650	
Interest Income		5,400

3. Cash	3,750	
Bond Investment	1,194	
Interest Income		4,944

4. Cash	280,000	
Bond Investment		274,146
Interest Income		1,250
Gain on Sale of Bonds		4,604

5. Cash	169,193	
Bonds Payable		150,000
Bond Premium		19,193
6. Cash	185,250	
Bonds Payable		180,000
Accrued Interest Payable		5,250

7. Bond Payable	175,000	
Bond Premium	7,000	
Common Stock		110,000
Additional Paid-In Capital		72,000

8. Bond Payable	175,000	
Bond Premium	7,000	
Common Stock		110,000
Additional Paid-In Capital		59,000
Gain on Conversion		13,000

Explanations:

1.

Maturity (face) amount to be received	$ 300,000	
Present value factor for a single amount (2%, 32 periods)	× 0.530633	
Present value of the maturity amount		$159,190
Quarterly interest payment to be received ($300,000 × 5% × 3/12)	3,750	
Present value factor for an ordinary annuity (2%, 32 periods)	× 23.46833	
Present value of future interest payments		88,006
Present value of the bonds		$247,196

2.

Cash:

Maturity (face) amount	$ 300,000
Times: Quarterly stated interest rate (5% × 3/12)	× 0.0125
	$ 3,750

Bond Investment:

Maturity (face) amount	$ 300,000
Less: Bond investment amount	247,196
Discount	52,804
Divided by: Number of periods	/ 32
Discount amortization	$ 1,650

Interest Income: Plug figure, balancing amount. $3,750 + $1,650 = $5,400

3.

Cash:

Maturity (face) amount	$ 300,000
Times: Quarterly stated interest rate (5% × 3/12)	× 0.0125
	$ 3,750

Interest Income:

Bond investment amount	$ 247,196
Times: Quarterly effective interest rate (8% × 3/12)	× 0.02
	$ 4,944

Bond Investment:
Plug figure, balancing amount. $4,944 – $3,750 = $1,194

4.

Cash:
Proceeds received, given in situation.

Bond Investment:

Original purchase price, September 30, year 2	$ 247,196
Plus discount amortization: Through September 30, year 6 ($1,650 × 16)	26,400
October 1 to October 31, year 6 ($1,650 × 1/3)	550
Carrying amount of the bonds	$ 274,146

Interest Income:

Maturity (face) amount	$ 300,000
Times: Quarterly stated interest rate (6% × 3/12)	× 0.0125
	3,750
Times: Portion accrued (October)	1/3
Interest earned	$ 1,250

Gain (loss) on sale of Bonds:

Cash proceeds received	$ 280,000
Less: Amount attributable to accrued interest ($300,000 × 0.0125 × 1/3)	1,250
Sale price of bonds	278,750
Carrying amounts of bonds	274,146
Gain on sale of bonds	$ 4,604

The sale price is greater than the carrying amount of bonds indicating a gain.

5.

Cash:

Maturity (face) amount	$ 150,000	
Present value factor of $1 for 10 periods at 3%	×0.744094	
Present value of principal payment		$111,614
Semiannual interest payment ($150,000 × 9% /2)	6,750	
Present value factor for an ordinary annuity (3%, 10 periods)	×8.530203	
Present value of periodic interest payments		57,579
Amount received from the issuance of bonds		$169,193

Bonds Payable:
Maturity (face) amount, provided in situation.

Bond Premium:

Plug figure, difference between the cash received and bonds payable amount. The stated rate of interest (9%) is above the market rate (6%). Therefore, these bonds were sold at a premium.

6.

Cash:
Plug figure, total of bonds payable and accrued interest payable

Bonds Payable:
Maturity (face) amount, provided in situation.

Accrued Interest Payable:

Maturity (face) amount	$ 180,000
Times: Stated interest rate	× 0.07
	12,600
Times: Portion accrued (January through May)	5/12
Interest payable	$ 5,250

7.

Bonds Payable:
Maturity (face) amount, provided in situation.

Bond Premium:
The bond premium is the difference between the face amount and carrying amount of the bonds. The carrying amount is higher than the face amount. Therefore, these bonds were converted at a premium.

Common Stock:
1000 shares × $110 par value = $110,000

Additional Paid-In Capital:
Plug figure to balance

8.

Bonds Payable:
Maturity (face) amount, provided in situation.

Bond Premium:
The bond premium is the difference between the face amount and carrying amount of the bonds. The carrying amount is higher than the face amount. Therefore, these bonds were converted at a premium.

Common Stock: 1000 shares × $110 par value = $110,000

Additional Paid-In Capital: 1000 shares × ($169 fair value – $110 par value) = $59,000

Gain on Conversion:
Plug figure, $182,000 – $169,000 = $13,000
The fair value of the shares issued on conversion were more than the carrying amount of the debt. Therefore, there is a gain on the conversion.

Solution 6-4 SIMULATION ANSWER: Balance Sheet Presentation

Bonds payable = $1,000,000; the face amount of the bonds.
Unamortized premium/discount = $67,327; the amount at December 31, 2013.
Total liabilities = $1,217,327; the sum of $150,000 + $1,000,000 + $67,327.

Interest expense = $86,218; the $43,244 from June 30, 2013 plus the $42,974 from December 31, 2013.
Net income before taxes = $413,782; the $1,000,000 in sales – $500,000 expenses – $86,218 interest expense.

Solution 6-5 SIMULATION ANSWER: Bond Terms

1. I When selling a bond and the stated interest rate is greater than the market rate for similar debt
2. J Includes legal fees, accounting fees, underwriting commissions, registration, printing and engraving
3. A Mature at a specified date
4. B May be retired at the issuer's option
5. K Reacquisition of debt securities regardless of whether the securities are canceled or held as so-called treasury bonds
6. C May be converted to stock at bondholder's option
7. E Unsecured; not supported by a lien or mortgage on specific assets
8. L Represents a contractual obligation to make periodic interest payments on the amount borrowed and to repay the principal upon maturity
9. D Provide for repayment of principal in a series of installments
10. H Reacquisition of debt securities by the use of proceeds from issuing other securities
11. G When selling a bond and the stated interest rate is less than the market rate
12. F When selling a bond and the stated interest rate equals the market rate

---

Solution 6-6 SIMULATION ANSWER: Research

<u>FASB Accounting Standards Codification</u>

FASB ASC: 835 - 30 - 25 - 13

25-13 The selection of a rate may be affected by many considerations. For instance, where applicable, the choice of a rate may be influenced by the following:

a. An approximation of the prevailing market rates for the source of credit that would provide a market for sale or assignment of the note
b. The prime or higher rate for notes which are discounted with banks, giving due weight to the credit standing of the maker
c. Published market rates for similar quality bonds
d. Current rates for debentures with substantially identical terms and risks that are traded in open markets
e. The current rate charged by investors for first or second mortgage loans on similar property.

CHAPTER 7

LIABILITIES

CHAPTER 7

LIABILITIES

I. Current Liabilities

A. Definition

Liabilities are obligations, based on past transactions, to convey assets or perform services in the future. The definition of *current* liabilities is logically correlated with the definition of current assets. Current assets are economic benefits owned by a firm that are reasonably expected to be converted into cash or consumed during the entity's operating cycle or one year, whichever is longer. The term current liabilities is used principally to designate obligations whose liquidation is reasonably expected to require the use of existing resources properly classifiable as current assets, or the creation of other current liabilities. Accounting for, and classification of, current liabilities is affected by the degree of certainty attached to the future payments.

B. Valuation

Ideally, liabilities should be recorded based on the present value of the future outlays involved. In the case of current liabilities, the difference between the present value and the amount to be paid is not likely to be material; therefore, the reporting of current liabilities is at their face amount.

C. Definitely Determinable Liabilities

The amounts and due dates of definitely determinable liabilities are established with considerable certainty. This certainty may be established by statutory law, contractual provision, or trade custom.

1. **Accounts Payable** Liabilities incurred in obtaining goods and services from vendors in the entity's ordinary course of business.

   a. Generally, accounts payable are not secured by collateral and do not require the periodic payment of interest.

   b. Accounts payable should reflect the cost of those goods and services that have been appropriately included in inventory (or other asset account) or expensed.

      (1) Materials purchased, F.O.B. shipping point, are inventoriable when shipped; thus, a liability should be recorded at that time.

      (2) Under an F.O.B. destination point contract, the goods and the related liability should not be recorded until the goods are received.

2. **Notes Payable** Loans obtained from banks and other lending institutions represent current liabilities if they are due in the succeeding operating period. These notes may be either *interest-bearing* or *noninterest-bearing.* Notes payable are handled much like bonds payable. They have a principal component and interest component that must be calculated each period.

Example 1 ▸ Interest-Bearing Note Payable

ABC Inc. borrowed $5,000 from a local bank at the market rate of interest of 8% on June 30, year 1. The principal plus the interest is due June 30, year 2.

Required: Provide ABC's journal entries.

Solution:

Date	Account	Debit	Credit
6/30, year 1	Cash	5,000	
	Notes Payable, Short-Term		5,000
12/31, year 1	Interest Expense ($5,000 × 0.08 × 6/12)	200	
	Accrued Interest Payable		200
6/30, year 2	Notes Payable, Short-Term	5,000	
	Accrued Interest Payable	200	
	Interest Expense	200	
	Cash		5,400

Example 2 ▸ Noninterest-Bearing Note Payable

ABC borrowed $5,000 on June 30, year 1 and signed an 8% noninterest-bearing note due in one year.

Required: Provide ABC's journal entries.

Solution:

Date	Account	Debit	Credit
6/30, year 1	Cash (face amount less discount)	4,600	
	Discount on Notes Payable ($5,000 × 0.08)	400	
	Notes Payable, Short-Term		5,000
12/31, year 1	Interest Expense ($400 × 6/12)	200	
	Discount on Notes Payable		200
6/30, year 2	Notes Payable, Short-Term	5,000	
	Interest Expense ($400 × 6/12)	200	
	Discount on Notes Payable		200
	Cash		5,000

NOTE: The effective interest rate on the discounted note is approximately 8.7% ($400 / $4,600) since less cash is received than the amount on which the interest rate is computed.

3. **Dividends Payable** When declared, cash and property dividends represent legal obligations due within one year and are reported as current liabilities. Stock dividends and undeclared dividends on cumulative preferred stock are not reported as liabilities; however, cumulative preferred stock dividends in arrears must be disclosed in the notes to the statements.

4. **Advances & Returnable Deposits** Advanced payments received from customers and others are liabilities until the transaction is completed; returnable deposits are liabilities until the relationship with the third party is terminated.

5. **Accrued Liabilities (Expenses)** An accrued expense is an expense incurred, but not yet paid in cash.

   a. An example of an accrued expense is salaries incurred for the last week of the accounting period that are not payable until the subsequent accounting period. Accrued payroll liabilities include social security taxes and federal unemployment taxes borne by the employer.

   b. Federal income taxes withheld from employees and the employees' share of social security taxes are **not** classified as accrued payroll expenses by the employer.

Exhibit 1 ▸ Accrued Expenses Journal Entry

Expense	XX	
Payable or Accrued Liability		XX

6. **Deferred Revenues** Deferred revenue is revenue collected in cash, but not yet earned. An example of deferred revenue is rent collected in advance by a lessor in the last month of the accounting period, which represents the rent for the first month of the subsequent accounting period. Other examples include subscriptions collected in advance and gift certificates issued but not yet redeemed. When gift certificates are issued, a deferred revenue account should be increased by the face amount of the gift certificates. This deferred revenue account is decreased when the gift certificates are redeemed or lapse.

Exhibit 2 ▸ Deferred Revenues Journal Entry

Cash	XX	
Unearned Revenues (a liability account)		XX

Exhibit 3 ▸ Formerly Deferred Revenues Now Earned Journal Entry

Unearned Revenues	XX	
Revenue		XX

7. **Current Maturities of Long-Term Debt** The portion of long-term debt due within the next fiscal period is classified as a current liability if payment is expected to require the use of current assets or the creation of other current liabilities. The liability is not classified as current if the maturing portion will be paid from the proceeds of a new bond issue or noncurrent assets (e.g., a bond sinking fund).

D. **Liabilities Dependent on Operating Results**

1. **Income Tax Liability** In accordance with federal and state tax laws, a corporation computes income taxes payable based on operating results for the period.

   a. Income taxes payable within the next period or operating cycle, whichever is longer, are classified as current liabilities.

   b. Taxable income and pretax accounting income may differ and, therefore, income tax payable (based on taxable income) and income tax expense (based on pretax accounting income) may differ substantially. This gives rise to deferred taxes. Deferred taxes should be netted out in their current and noncurrent portions for balance sheet presentation.

2. **Employee Bonuses** Bonus agreements based on profits usually fall into one of two classes: (1) the bonus is based on net income after income taxes, but before deducting the bonus, **or** (2) the bonus is based on net income after deducting both income taxes and the bonus. The amount of the bonus is determined by solving simultaneous equations that describe the terms of the bonus agreement.

Exhibit 4 ▸ Bonuses Based on Profits

B = Bonus
Br = Bonus rate
I = Income before income taxes and bonus
T = Tax
Tr = Tax rate

1. Bonus computed on net income after income taxes but before deducting the bonus; solve these simultaneous equations:
   a. B = Br(I – T)
   b. T = Tr(I – B)

2. Bonus computed on net income after deducting both income taxes and the bonus; solve these simultaneous equations:
   a. B = Br(I – T – B)
   b. T = Tr(I – B)

Example 3 ▸ Employee Bonus

Generous Corp. provides a bonus to its employees equal to 10% of net income (i.e., after deducting taxes and bonus). Income from operations for the year was $90,000. Assume a 40% tax rate.

Required: Compute the employee bonus liability for Generous Corp.

Solution:

Step 1: Substitute the value of T, as given in Exhibit 4, equation 2.b., into equation 2.a.

B = Br(I – T – B) B = Br[I – Tr (I – B) – B]

Step 2: Substitute the known values and solve for B.

B = 0.10 [$90,000 – 0.4 ($90,000 – B) – B]
B = 0.10 [$90,000 – $36,000 + 0.4B – B]
B = $9,000 – $3,600 + 0.04B – 0.1B = $5,400 – 0.06B
1.06B = $5,400
B = $5,094

E. **Contingent Liabilities**

Contingent liabilities arise from events or circumstances occurring before the balance sheet date, the resolution of which is contingent upon a future event or circumstance. The distinction between contingencies and other liabilities hinges on the uncertainty as to the existence of the liability and **not** on the uncertainty as to the amount of the liability.

1. **Examples** Examples of contingent liabilities include (a) obligations related to product warranties, (b) obligations related to product coupons and premiums, (c) obligations related to product defects, (d) pending or threatened litigation, and (e) actual or possible claims and assessments.

2. **Classification** Accounting treatment depends on the likelihood that future events will confirm the contingent loss **and** whether the amount can be reasonably estimated.

   a. Probable means the event is likely to occur. Where the likelihood of confirmation of a loss is considered probable and the loss can be reasonably estimated, the estimated loss should be accrued by a charge to income and the nature of the contingency should be disclosed. If, however, only a range of possible loss can be estimated—and no amount in the range is a better estimate than the others—the minimum amount in the range should be accrued. In addition, the nature of the contingency and the additional exposure to loss should be disclosed.

   b. Reasonably possible means the likelihood of the future event is more than remote, but less than probable. Where the loss is considered reasonably possible, no charge should be made to income **but** the nature of the contingency should be disclosed. This treatment also applies to probable losses that cannot be reasonably estimated.

   c. Remote means there is a slight chance of the event occurring. Where likelihood of loss is considered remote, disclosure normally is **not** required. Exceptions include guarantees of indebtedness of others, banks' standby letters of credit, and guarantees to repurchase receivables.

3. **No Disclosure**

   a. No disclosure is required for a loss contingency concerning an unasserted claim or assessment when no claimant has shown an awareness of such unless it is considered probable that the claim will be asserted, **and** there is a reasonable possibility of an unfavorable result.

   b. General, unspecified business risks are not loss contingencies; no accrual or disclosure is required.

4. **Gain Contingencies** Gain contingencies should be disclosed but not recognized as income. Care should be taken to avoid misleading implications as to the likelihood of realization.

5. **Postemployment Benefits** Postemployment benefits that do not meet the conditions for accrual as a compensated absence should be accounted for as a probable or reasonably possible contingency.

6. **Environmental Remediation Liabilities** The accrual of an environmental liability is required if information available prior to issuance of the financial statements indicates that it is *probable* that a liability has been incurred at the date of the financial statements and the amount of the loss can be *reasonably estimated.*

   a. If a claim has been asserted and an entity can be held responsible for it, then condition probable is met. If an entity has been notified by the EPA or a relevant state agency, for example, that the entity is a potentially responsible party (PRP) and the entity had some involvement, then it is probable that the entity will incur some costs.

   b. A variety of factors should be considered in making the estimate, including pre-cleanup activities, such as testing, engineering studies, and feasibility studies, conducted to define the extent of the damage; remedial activities to clean up the environmental damage; government oversight and enforcement costs, which includes fines and penalties; and operation and maintenance activities, including post-remediation monitoring.

   c. An entity's balance sheet may include several assets that relate to an environmental remediation obligation, including receivables from other PRPs that are not providing initial funding, anticipated recoveries from insurers, and anticipated recoveries from prior owners.

Exhibit 5 ▸ Contingencies

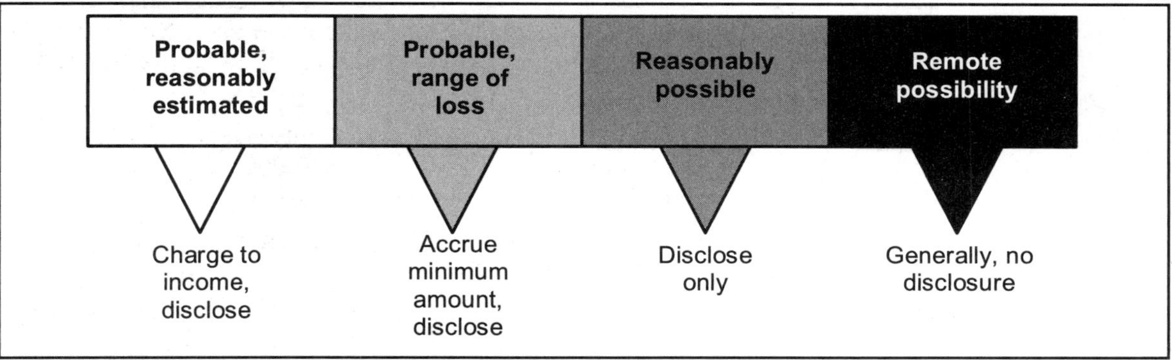

F. Estimated Liabilities

Estimated liabilities are known liabilities whose amount is uncertain at the end of the accounting period. Derivative instruments that represent obligations that meet the definition of liabilities are measured at fair value and reported as liabilities in the financial statements.

1. **Product Warranties & Guarantees** A warranty or guarantee is a promise made by the seller to the buyer to make good certain deficiencies in the product during a specified period of time after the sale. Product guarantees and warranties create a liability for the seller from the date of the sale to the end of the warranty period. Recording of the liability may take place either at the point of sale or at the end of the accounting period.

   a. When the liability is recorded at the point of sale, an entry is made to record the warranty expense and estimated warranty liability on that date. Any direct costs for servicing customer claims are debited to estimated warranty liability and credited to cash or other assets.

Exhibit 6 ▸ Recording at Point of Sale

Warranty Expense	XX	
Estimated Warranty Liability		XX
To record estimated warranty expense at point of sale		
Estimated Warranty Liability	XX	
Cash or Other Assets		XX
To record actual warranty expenditures as incurred		

   b. When the liability is recorded at the end of the accounting period, any direct costs for servicing customer claims are debited to warranty expense and credited to cash or other assets. An estimate of the year's warranty liability is made based on past experience and current estimates. If the estimated liability exceeds the amounts actually charged, the difference is debited to warranty expense and credited to estimated warranty liability. No additional entry is necessary if the estimated liability does not exceed the amounts actually charged.

Exhibit 7 ▸ Recording at End of Accounting Period

Warranty Expense	XX	
Cash or Other Assets		XX
To record actual warranty expenditures as incurred		
Warranty Expense	XX	
Estimated Warranty Liability		XX
To record remaining estimated warranty expense at end of accounting period		

Example 4 ▶ Product Warranty

A new product introduced by Shoddy Corporation carries a two-year warranty against defects. The estimated warranty costs related to dollar sales are 3% in the year of sale and 5% in the year after sale.

Year	Sales	Actual Warranty Expenditures
1	$400,000	$10,000
2	500,000	35,000

Required: Determine Shoddy's estimated warranty liability as of December 31, year 2, and its warranty expense for year 2.

Solution:

Sales (year 1 and year 2)	$900,000
Estimated warranty cost percentage (3% and 5%)	× 8%
Estimated warranty costs for year 1 and year 2 sales	72,000
Warranty expenditures to date ($10,000 + $35,000)	(45,000)
Estimated warranty liability, 12/31, year 2	$ 27,000

The warranty expense recognized in year 2 is $40,000 [$500,000 × (3% + 5%)].

2. **Premiums** In order to increase sales and promote certain products, companies may offer premiums to those customers who return boxtops, coupons, labels, wrappers, etc., as proof of purchase. The cost of these premiums represents an expense that should be matched against revenue from the sales benefited. At the end of the accounting period, an expense account should be debited and a liability account credited for the cost of outstanding premiums *expected* to be redeemed in subsequent periods.

Example 5 ▶ Premiums

The Whole Grain Cereal Company offers a T-shirt to those customers who present 10 cereal boxtops. Whole Grain purchases 2,000 T-shirts at a unit cost of $2.50. Between the time the premiums were offered and the end of the accounting period, 25,000 boxes of cereal were sold. Whole Grain expects that 80% of the boxtops will be returned. A total of 2,000 boxtops had been received as of the end of the accounting period.

Required: Provide journal entries for Whole Grain to account for the premiums.

Solution:

	Debit	Credit
Premium Merchandise Inventory	5,000	
Cash (2,000 × $2.50)		5,000
To record the purchase of 2,000 T-shirts		
Premium Expense [(2,000* / 10) × $2.50]	500	
Premium Merchandise Inventory		500
To record the redemption of 2,000 boxtops for 200 shirts		
Premium Expense	4,500	
Estimated Premium Liability [(2,000* – 200) × $2.50]		4,500
To record the estimated premium liability at year-end		
Estimated Premium Liability [(4,000 / 10) × $2.50]	1,000	
Premium Merchandise Inventory		1,000
To record the redemption of 4,000 boxtops in the subsequent period		

* (25,000 × 0.80) / 10

3. **Compensated Absences and Postemployment Benefits** The following does not apply to postemployment benefits provided through a pension or postretirement benefit plan, individual deferred compensation arrangements, or special or contractual termination benefits.

   a. A liability is accrued at year-end for the estimated cost of material compensated absences and postemployment benefits.

      (1) Compensated absences include vacation, occasional sick days, and holidays. The substance of the employer's sick leave policy takes precedence over its form. An employer generally is not required to accrue a liability for nonvesting accumulating rights to receive sick pay benefits. However, future compensation for sick leave is accrued if employees customarily are paid or allowed compensated absences for accumulated, nonvesting sick leave days, even though employees are not actually absent as a result of illness.

      (2) Postemployment benefits to be provided to former or inactive employees prior to retirement include salary continuation, severance benefits, continuation of other fringe benefits such as insurance, job training, and disability related benefits such as workers' compensation.

   b. A liability for employees' compensation for future absences and postemployment benefits should be accrued if **all** the following conditions are met. If the first three conditions are met, but no amount is accrued due to inability to estimate future payments for compensated absences or postemployment benefits, this fact must be disclosed. Postemployment benefits that do not meet these conditions are accounted for as contingencies.

      (1) Payment of the compensation is **probable.**

      (2) The obligation relates to employee rights that **vest or accumulate.** Vested rights are those for which the employer is obligated to pay to the employee, regardless of termination of employment. Accumulated rights are those that may be carried forward to one or more future periods, even though there might be a limitation on the amounts carried forward.

      (3) The obligation is for employee services **already** rendered.

      (4) The amount can be reasonably **estimated.**

   c. If the first three conditions are met, but no amount is accrued due to inability to estimate future payments for compensated absences or postemployment benefits, this fact must be disclosed.

   d. Postemployment benefits that do not meet the conditions of FASB ASC 712, *Compensation—Nonretirement Postemployment Benefits*, are accounted for in accordance with FASB ASC 450, *Contingencies.*

Exhibit 8 ▸ Compensated Absences

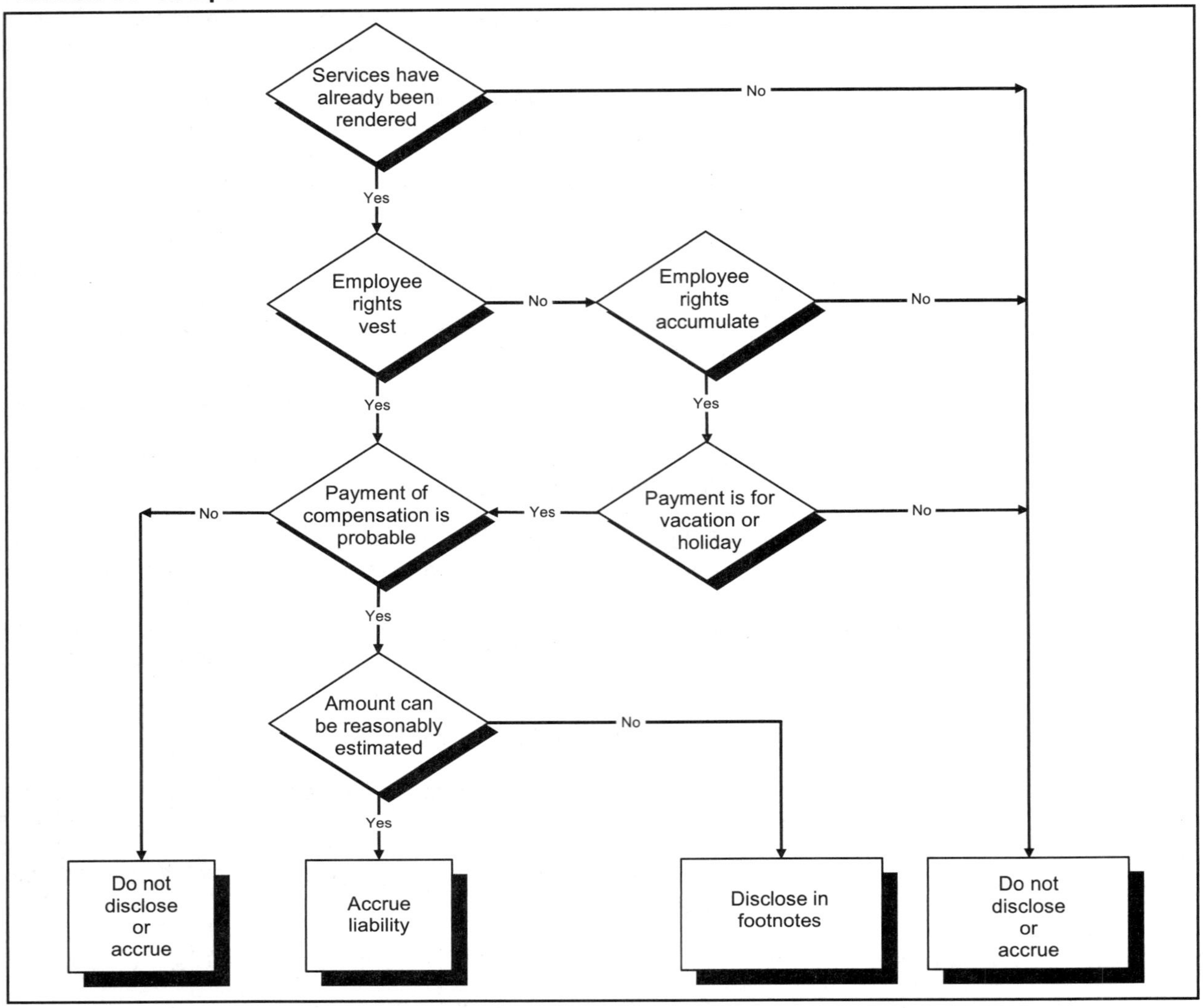

Services have already been rendered
No
Yes
Employee rights vest
No
Employee rights accumulate
No
Yes
Yes
Payment of compensation is probable
No
Yes
Payment is for vacation or holiday
No
Yes
Amount can be reasonably estimated
No
Yes
Do not disclose or accrue
Accrue liability
Disclose in footnotes
Do not disclose or accrue

II. Long-Term Liabilities

A. Definition

Long-term liabilities are all obligations not expected to be liquidated by the use of existing current assets or by the creation of current liabilities. Examples include: (1) long-term notes payable, (2) refinancing of short-term obligations, and (3) bonds payable. As bonds payable are discussed in a separate chapter, they are not discussed here.

B. Disclosures

The combined aggregate amount of maturities and sinking fund requirements for all long-term borrowings must be disclosed for each of the five years following the date of the latest balance sheet period.

C. Notes Payable

1. **Note Issued for Cash** When a note is issued solely for cash, it is generally presumed to have a present value at issuance equal to the cash proceeds exchanged. If special rights or privileges are included in the transaction, they must be measured separately.

2. **Note Exchanged for Property, Goods, or Services** When a note is exchanged for property, goods, or services, it is assumed that the rate of interest stipulated by the note is fair and adequate compensation. Therefore, unless the interest rate is not stated or is unreasonable, the note should be recorded at its face amount because this amount would approximate the note's present value.

3. **Interest Rate Not Stated or Unreasonable**

   a. Record the note at the fair value of the property, goods, or services exchanged or at the amount that approximates the market value of the note, whichever is more clearly determinable.

   b. In the absence of established exchange prices for the related property, goods, or services or evidence of the market value of the note, the note is recorded at its present value by discounting all future payments on the note using an imputed interest rate. The imputed interest rate is determined by considering the debtor's credit standing, prevailing rates for similar debt, and rates at which the debtor can obtain funds. The difference between the present value and the face amount of the note is recorded as a discount or premium.

   c. The discount or premium is amortized as interest expense over the life of the note in such a way as to result in a constant rate of interest when applied to the carrying amount of the note at the beginning of any given period. The use of amortization methods other than the effective interest method is allowed (e.g., straight-line) if the results do not differ materially from those obtained with the effective interest method.

Example 6 ▸ Unstated Interest Rate

XYZ Company acquires a patent on January 1, year 1, in exchange for a three-year noninterest-bearing note of $100,000. There was no established exchange price for the patent and the note has no ready market. The prevailing rate of interest for a note of this type is 8% at the date of the exchange. (The imputed interest rate is the prevailing interest rate of 8%.) The PV interest factor for an amount in three years discounted at 8% is 0.79383 (see Appendix D, Table 2).

Required: Provide the journal entries to record the patent and the note, the interest expense at year-ends, and the payment of the note.

Solution:

Date	Account	Debit	Credit
1/1, year 1	Patent ($100,000 × .79383)	79,383	
	Discount on Note Payable ($100,000 – $79,383)	20,617	
	Note Payable		100,000
12/31, year 1	Interest Expense [($100,000 – $20,617) × 0.08]	6,351	
	Discount on Note Payable		6,351
12/31, year 2	Interest Expense [($100,000 – $14,266*) × 0.08]	6,859	
	Discount on Note Payable		6,859
12/31, year 3	Interest Expense [($100,000 – $7,407**) × 0.08]	7,407	
	Discount on Note Payable		7,407
12/31, year 3	Note Payable	100,000	
	Cash		100,000

* $20,617 – $6,351
** $14,266 – $6,859

Example 7 ▸ Unreasonable Interest Rate

The same as Example 6, except that the note specifies annual interest payments of 5% on December 31. This rate is considered unreasonably low based on the current market rate of 8%. The interest factor for a three-year annuity at 8% is 2.57710 (see Appendix D, Table 4).

Required: Provide the journal entries to record the patent and the note, the interest expense at year-ends, and the payment of the note.

Solution:

Date	Account	Debit	Credit
1/1, year 1	Patent	92,268	
	Discount on Note Payable ($100,000 – 92,268)	7,732	
	Note Payable		100,000

Present value of principal ($100,000 × 0.79383)	$ 79,383
Present value of interest payments ($5,000 × 2.57710)	12,885
Present value of note	$ 92,268

Date	Account	Debit	Credit
12/31, year 1	Interest Expense [($100,000 – $7,732) × 0.08]	7,381	
	Cash ($100,000 × 0.05)		5,000
	Discount on Note Payable (to balance)		2,381
12/31, year 2	Interest Expense [($100,000 – $5,351*) × 0.08]	7,572	
	Cash ($100,000 × 0.05)		5,000
	Discount on Note Payable (to balance)		2,572
12/31, year 3	Interest Expense [($100,000 – $2,779**) × 0.08]	7,778	
	Cash ($100,000 × 0.05)		5,000
	Discount on Note Payable (to balance)		2,778
12/31, year 3	Note Payable	100,000	
	Cash		100,000

* $7,732 – $2,381
** $5,351 – $2,572

D. Refinancing of Short-Term Obligations

The following are guidelines for the classification of short-term obligations that are expected to be refinanced on a long-term basis.

1. **Reclassification to Noncurrent Liabilities** Short-term obligations are those scheduled to mature within one year or operating cycle, whichever is longer. Generally, short-term obligations are classified as current liabilities, since they will require the use of working capital during the ensuing period. However, if they are to be refinanced on a long-term basis they will be appropriately classified as noncurrent liabilities.

2. **Refinancing Defined** Refinancing a short-term obligation on a long-term basis means either of the following.

   a. Replacing it with long-term obligations or equity securities.

   b. Renewing, extending, or replacing it with short-term obligations for an uninterrupted period greater than one year (or operating cycle) from the balance sheet date.

3. **Reclassification Requirements** Exclusion from current liabilities requires that two conditions be met:

   a. The enterprise must intend to refinance the obligation on a long-term basis.

   b. The enterprise must have the ability to consummate the refinancing. Evidence of the ability to consummate the refinancing is provided by either of the following.

      (1) A refinancing that occurs after the balance sheet date but before the balance sheet is issued.

      (2) A financing agreement before the balance sheet is issued that permits the refinancing and extends beyond one year or operating cycle. If any violation of the agreement has occurred, a waiver from the lender must be obtained. Further, the lender must be expected to be financially capable of honoring the agreement.

4. **Portions of Past Obligations Not Refinanced** If post-balance sheet refinancing of a short-term obligation has taken place, any portion **not** refinanced must be shown as a current liability.

5. **Limitations on Exclusions From Current Liabilities** If a financing agreement provides evidence of the ability to refinance, the amount excluded from current liabilities is limited to the amount available for refinancing under the agreement. Limitations on the amount excluded arise from the following.

   a. Obligations in excess of the amount available for refinancing under the agreement.

   b. Restrictions imposed by other agreements on the use of funds obtained under the refinancing arrangement.

   c. Agreements that do not specify that a fixed amount of funds will be available. In this case, only an amount equal to the minimum sum expected to be available at any date during the period can be excluded. If the minimum sum cannot be reasonably estimated, the obligation must be shown as a current liability.

Example 8 ▸ Exclusions From Current Liabilities

> The First National Bank agrees to lend ABC Corporation, on a revolving credit basis, an amount equal to 75% of the Company's receivables. ABC plans to continue the revolving credit. During the year the receivables are expected to range between a low of $500,000 in the first quarter to a high of $2,000,000 in the fourth quarter. The minimum amount available for refinancing of short-term liabilities is $375,000 based on the expected low for trade receivables of $500,000. For balance sheet presentation, the maximum amount that can be excluded from current liabilities is $375,000.

6. **Repaid From Current Assets** Short-term obligations repaid after the balance sheet date and subsequently refinanced before the issuance of the balance sheet must be classified as current liabilities as of the balance sheet date because current assets were used for the repayment.

E. Asset Retirement Obligations

Asset retirement obligations (AROs) are used to determine the liability on assets that occur during the life of the assets. An ARO handles the costs associated with the retirement of long-term assets. Obligations for dismantlement, restoration, and abandonment costs are accounted for as AROs.

1. **Initial Recognition & Measurement** An ARO is recorded at fair value in the accounting period in which it occurs and in which its amount can be reasonably measured. If an active market for the ARO doesn't exist to provide fair value, the expected present value technique using discounted cash flows is the best way to determine the fair value of the asset.

2. **Asset Retirement Cost** Upon initial recognition of a liability for an ARO, an entity shall capitalize an asset retirement cost by increasing the carrying amount of the related long-lived asset by the same amount as the liability and, depending on prior accounting treatment, further adjusting for previously recorded depreciation.

3. **Subsequent Measurement** AROs incur depreciation and accretion expenses each year.

   a. The capitalized asset retirement cost is allocated as depreciation expense over the estimated useful life of the asset using a systematic and rational method. The depreciation charge is calculated as the increased asset base divided by the asset's useful life on the date of initial recording.

   b. Accretion expense is calculated by multiplying the balance of the recorded liability by the company's credit-adjusted discount rate each year, and is simply the amortization of the present value discount associated with the ARO's initial recording. Accretion expense is offset with an increase to the liability account, and, at the end of the asset's life, the liability account will have a balance equal to the amount needed to settle the retirement obligation.

III. Debt Extinguishment

A. Derecognition

FASB ASC 860, *Transfers and Servicing,* provides accounting and reporting standards for transfers and servicing of financial assets and extinguishments of liabilities. Those standards are based on consistent application of a "financial-components approach" that focuses on control. Under the financial-components approach, an entity must:

1. **Recognize After Transfer** Recognize the financial and servicing assets it controls and the liabilities it has incurred, after a transfer of financial assets has occurred

2. **Surrender** Derecognize the financial assets once control has been surrendered

3. **Extinguishment** Derecognize liabilities once extinguished

B. Conditions

A liability should not be removed from the financial statements until it has been extinguished, which occurs if either of the following conditions are met.

1. **Payment** The debtor pays the creditor and is relieved of its obligation for the liability. This may include delivering cash, other financial assets, goods, or services, or reacquiring outstanding debt securities; or

2. **Release** The debtor is legally released from being the primary obligor on the liability, either by the creditor or the courts, such as in the case of bankruptcy.

C. In-Substance Defeasance

In-substance defeasance is no longer accounted for as an extinguishment of debt. In-substance defeasance is a situation where a debt remains outstanding, but the debtor places risk-free monetary assets, such as U.S. government securities, in a trust that restricts the use of the assets to meeting all of the cash flow requirements on the debt. Previously, this was allowed to be accounted for as an extinguishment of debt; the liability was removed from the balance sheet and the trust was not recognized as an asset on the balance sheet. This type of transaction is to be accounted for as a separate asset and liability.

D. Extinguishment vs. Refunding

Extinguishment includes the reacquisition of debt securities regardless of whether the securities are canceled or held as so-called treasury bonds. Refunding refers to achieving the reacquisition by the use of proceeds from issuing other securities.

E. Gain or Loss

All extinguishments are fundamentally alike. Therefore, the extinguishment of debt, irrespective of the method used (except certain conversions of convertible bonds into stock or extinguishment through a troubled debt restructuring) should involve recognition of a gain or loss in the period in which the extinguishment took place. The gain or loss is the difference between the reacquisition price and the net carrying amount of the extinguished debt. Entities must evaluate whether early debt extinguishment is extraordinary considering their environments.

IV. Troubled Debt Restructurings-Creditors

A. Definition

A troubled debt restructuring (TDR) of receivables occurs when a creditor, for economic or legal reasons related to the debtor's financial difficulties, grants a concession to the debtor that the creditor would not otherwise consider. In evaluating whether a restructuring constitutes a troubled debt restructuring, a creditor must separately conclude that both of the following exist: the restructuring constitutes a concession; and the debtor is experiencing financial difficulties.

Generally, a debtor who can obtain funds from other than the existing creditor at an interest rate near the current rate for nontroubled debt is not involved with a troubled debt restructuring, even though the debtor may be experiencing difficulty. In a troubled debt restructuring, the creditor is granting the concession in order to protect as much of the investment as possible.

When receivables are restructured as TDRs, there is a presumption that the receivables are impaired and, thereby, are subject to a specific impairment measurement methodology.

B. TDR Examples

Troubled debt restructurings may include, but they are not necessarily limited to one or a combination of the following:

- Transfer from debtors to creditors of receivables from third parties, real estate, or other assets to satisfy fully or partially debt obligations under debt arrangements.
- Issuance or other tendering of equity interests to creditors to satisfy fully or partially debt obligations, unless the equity interests are granted pursuant to existing terms for converting debt into equity interests in debtors.
- Modification of terms of debt arrangements.

The modifications could be one of several items, including: reducing [absolutely of contingently] the stated interest rates for the remaining original lives of debt arrangements; extending maturity dates at stated interest rates lower than current market rates for new debt with similar risks; reducing [absolutely or contingently] face amounts or maturity amounts of debt as stated in debt arrangements; and/ or reducing [absolutely or contingently] accrued interest associated with debt arrangements.

C. Granting a Concession

A concession either stems from an agreement between the creditor and the debtor or is imposed by law or a court. A restructuring that results in only a delay in payment that is insignificant is not a concession. This concession may take either of two forms: (1) transfer of assets or an equity interest in the debtor in satisfaction of the debt, or (2) a modification of the terms of the obligation, including a reduction of the interest rate, extension of the maturity date, or reduction of the face amount of the debt and accrued interest. In considering whether concessions have been granted to debtors, creditors need to undertake an evaluation by considering the following:

1. When debtors do not otherwise have access to funds at market rates for debt with similar risk characteristics as the debt being restructured, the restructuring would be considered to be at a below-market rate, which may indicate that creditors have granted a concession.

2. Temporary or permanent increases in contractual interest rates as a result of restructurings would not preclude the restructuring from being considered to include concessions in that the new contractual interest rate on restructured debt still could be below market interest rates for new debt with similar risk characteristics. In these circumstances, creditors would need to consider all aspects of the restructuring in determining whether concessions have been granted. When assessments are made the concessions have been granted, creditors would need to make a separate assessment about whether debtors are experiencing financial difficulties to determine whether the restructurings constitute troubled debt restructurings.

3. Restructurings that result in delays in payments that are insignificant would not constitute concessions. However, it is important to consider various factors in considering whether restructurings resulting in delayed payments in fact should be considered insignificant, as discussed below.

4. Insignificant delays in contractual cash flows would be considered concessions under the amended guidance. ASU 2011-02 includes factors that may indicate that modifications resulting in contractual cash flow delays would be insignificant as follows:

    - The amount of the restructured payments subject to delay is insignificant related to unpaid principal or collateral value of the debt and will result in an insignificant shortfall in contractual amounts that are due.

    - The delay in timing of the restructured payment period is insignificant in relation to the frequency of payments due under the debt, the original contractual maturity of the debt, and/or the original expected duration of the debt.

D. Determining Financial Difficulty

If it has been determined that the creditor has made a concession, then a separate assessment must be made to determine whether a debtor is experiencing financial difficulties in order to meet the criteria of a TDR. A creditor should consider the following:

- A debtor is currently in payment default on any of its debt, or a creditor determines that it is probable that the debtor will be in payment default in the foreseeable future.

- The debtor has declared, or is in the process of declaring, bankruptcy.

- There is substantial doubt as to whether the debtor will continue to be a going concern

- The debtor has securities that have been delisted, are in the process of being delisted, or are under threat of being delisted, from an exchange.

- The creditor forecasts that the debtor's entity-specific cash flows will be insufficient to service any of its debt.

- Without the current modification, the debtor cannot obtain funds from sources other than the existing creditors at an effective interest rate.

E. Effective Interest Rate Test

One of the areas where creditors might have inappropriately been using guidance developed for debtors relates to the effective interest rate test. That test involves comparing the effective interest rate of debt immediately before and after restructurings take place. From the perspective of debtors, if that effective interest rate is lower immediately following the restructuring, they would conclude that interest rate concessions have been granted. This particular guidance is intended only for use when debtors are attempting to determine whether troubled debt restructurings have occurred.

F. Settlement

When the creditor receives assets or an equity interest as full settlement of a receivable, they are recorded at fair value of the assets/equity or the receivables, whichever is more clearly determinable, at the time of the restructuring. The excess of the carrying amount of the receivable over the fair value of the assets received is recognized as a loss.

Example 9 ▸ Troubled Debt Restructuring

On January 1, year 2, Risky Developers Inc. borrowed $100,000 from Easymoney Corp. The promissory note calls for 10% interest, payable annually on Dec. 31, and matures on Dec. 31, year 4. Risky made the first interest payment on time, but defaulted on the payment due Dec. 31, year 3. On July 1, year 4, Risky and Easymoney reached an agreement whereby the entire obligation would be discharged by the transfer of a parcel of land valued at $40,000 and Risky preferred stock with a par and fair value of $35,000. The land had been purchased by Risky in year 1 for $50,000.

Required: Provide the journal entries for both the debtor and creditor.

Solution:

Debtor:

	Debit	Credit
Note Payable, Including Accrued Interest [$100,000 + 10% ($100,000) + 10% ($110,000) (6/12)]	115,500	
Loss on Disposal of Land, Ordinary	10,000	
Land		50,000
Preferred Stock		35,000
Gain on Debt Restructuring [$115,500 – ($40,000 + $35,000)]		40,500

Creditor:

	Debit	Credit
Land	40,000	
Investment in Risky Preferred Stock	35,000	
Loss on Settlement of Receivable (ordinary)	40,500	
Notes Receivable, Including Accrued Interest		115,500

G. Disclosures

Creditors are required to disclose the following:

- On the statement of financial position, the total recorded investment in impaired loans at the end of the period; the amount of the recorded investment for which there is an allowance for credit losses; the amount of the allowance; and the amount of the recorded investment for which there is no related allowance.
- The creditor's policy for recognizing interest income on impaired loans, including how cash receipts were recorded.
- The average recorded investment in the impaired loans during each period and the related amount of interest income.
- Amounts of any commitment(s) to lend additional funds to any debtor who is a party to a restructuring.

H. Modification of Terms—Debtor Accounting

A troubled debt restructuring may involve a reduction of interest rate, a partial forgiveness of principal and interest payments, and/or extension of maturity date. Accounting for debtors is determined by whether the sum of the cash payments under the new terms (not discounted to present value) equal or exceed the amount of the obligation.

1. **Payments Less Than Obligation** When the aggregate payments under new terms are **less** than the amount of the obligation, the debtor reduces the carrying amount of the payable to the aggregate future cash payments.

   a. The debtor records gain equal to the difference between the carrying amount of the payable (including accrued interest) and the aggregate future payments required under the new terms.

   b. Future payments are recorded as a reduction of principal, and no interest expenses are recognized.

2. **Payments Equal To or More Than Obligation** When the aggregate payments under new terms are equal to or more than the amount of the obligation, the debtor

   a. Does not change the amount of the obligation, nor is any gain or loss recorded.

   b. Allocates subsequent payments between interest and principal on the basis of a constant rate of interest (i.e., the interest method).

3. **Debtor & Creditor Accounting Differ** Note that the debtor and creditor account for the modification differently. The debtor uses the aggregate of future cash payments and the creditor uses the present value of future cash payments.

V. Debt Covenant Compliance

Debt covenants can impose a heavy burden on an entity. Companies may have to sell assets in order to maintain compliance with leverage requirements, or sell additional shares to raise funds. Violations can result in stiff penalties, including declaration by the bank that the debtor is in default. An entity can be required to become compliant (i.e., "cure the default") within a grace period. If they cannot become compliant with the debt covenant, the lender can reset the covenant or impose a penalty ranging from prearranged fees to calling default on the loan.

A. Covenants

Debt covenants are agreements between an entity and its creditors that dictate the manner in which a company manages its finances while indebted to the bank. Covenants may change if debt is restructured.

There are two types of covenants: "affirmative covenants" (actions you can and should perform) and "negative covenants" (actions you cannot perform). Debt covenants are usually located in "negative covenants." Covenant documentation will include information on the types of covenants to be complied with, when updated financials are to be provided for compliance testing, and what the penalties are for covenant violation. Non-ratio covenants can include prohibitions on certain activities, such as the transfer ownership, issuing additional debt, or the distribution of dividends. Covenants can also include restrictions on how the borrowed funds may be used.

B. Compliance Ratios

One of the more common ratios is the debt service coverage ratio. It is the ratio of cash available for debt servicing of interest, principal and lease payments. It is a popular benchmark used in the measurement of an entity's ability to produce enough cash to cover its debt (including lease) payments. Typically, banks will require a greater than one-to-one ratio. This covenant can be calculated pre- or post-distributions. Other types of debt covenants include: maintenance of a minimum current ratio, minimum debt-to-equity ratio, or minimum level of shareholders' equity.

C. Compliance Audits

Debt covenant compliance can be maintained through mandatory audits. Auditors may periodically review the financial files and records to ensure no new debt was acquired and all debt payments were made on time. Auditors may also verify all necessary authorizations were given before major financial transactions. Lawyers may review legal records to ensure there are no unreported lawsuits against the debtor.

D. Classification

If one of the following situations exists, the debt would be classified as current unless the debt is expected to be refinanced on a long-term basis, in which case the debt would be classified as noncurrent:

1. **Modification of Agreement** The borrower has met the covenant requirement in the prior quarter but before the balance sheet date negotiates a modification of the loan agreement that eliminates the covenant requirement at the balance sheet date or modifies the requirement so that the borrower will comply. Absent the modification, the borrower would have been in violation of the covenant at the balance sheet date. The same or a more restrictive covenant must be met at the compliance date in three months, and it is probable that the borrower will fail to meet that requirement at that subsequent date.

2. **Waiver** The borrower is in violation of the current covenant requirement at the balance sheet date and, after the balance sheet date but before the financial statements are issued or are available to be issued, obtains a waiver. The same or a more restrictive covenant must be met at the compliance date in three months, and it is probable that the borrower will fail to meet that requirement at that subsequent date.

In the following situations the debt would be classified as noncurrent, in which case the borrower would be required to disclose the adverse consequences of its probable failure to satisfy future covenants:

- The debt covenants are applicable only after the balance sheet date, and it is probable that the borrower will fail to meet the covenant requirement at the compliance date three months after the balance sheet date.

- The borrower meets the current covenant requirement at the balance sheet date, and it is probable that the borrower will fail to meet the same covenant requirement at the compliance date in three months.

- The borrower meets the current covenant requirement, and it is probable that the borrower will fail to meet a more restrictive covenant requirement applicable at the compliance date in three months.

VI. Highlights of Federal Bankruptcy Law

A. Chapter 7 Bankruptcy

FAR exams have often included a multiple choice question on this topic, generally concerning the rules of priority and distribution. Bankruptcies are also tested in Regulation. Chapter 7 of the *Federal Bankruptcy Code* covers straight bankruptcies or liquidations. It involves the collection of the debtor's nonexempt property, the liquidation or sale of such property, and the distribution of the proceeds to the creditors by the trustee as provided by the Code. After distribution of the proceeds, the debtor is relieved from having to satisfy any personal liability concerning any of the discharged debts.

B. Priority of Claims

Claims filed by the creditors against the bankrupt debtor are classified according to their *priority,* that is, the order in which they will receive any of the liquidation proceeds that are ultimately distributed. Secured claims (i.e., secured by a lien on property) are entitled to first priority, but only on the distribution of the proceeds from the liquidation of their collateral, and only to the extent the loan is secured. If the value of the collateral is **less** than the amount of the claim, the excess amount of the claim is unsecured. Unsecured claims do not have a lien on any property of the debtor. There are many different classes of unsecured claims and their priority depends upon the nature of the claim.

C. Distribution Rules

Under a Chapter 7 case, claims of a higher priority are satisfied before those of a next priority class. If the assets are insufficient to satisfy all the claims within a particular class, they will be satisfied pro rata for that class. Any liquidation proceeds and/or other assets remaining after satisfying **all** claims are returned to the debtor.

Example 10 ▶ Bankruptcy Distribution

ABC Company filed a petition for a bankruptcy under Chapter 7. Creditors have secured claims of $300,000 and unsecured claims of $625,000. The following list of assets has been obtained.

	Amount secured	Amount received upon liquidation
Asset #1	$100,000	$100,000
Asset #2	75,000	50,000
Asset #3	125,000	150,000
Assets without security interests	--	300,000
	$300,000	$600,000

Required: Determine the distribution of the proceeds received from liquidation.

Solution: Claims secured by Asset #1 and Asset #3 are fully secured and will be satisfied in full ($100,000 and $125,000, respectively). The excess $25,000 of proceeds received over the amount of the secured claim for Asset #3 will go towards satisfying unsecured claims. As for Asset #2, its secured creditor is only partially secured, since the amount received for the asset is less than the amount of the claim; therefore, this creditor is now an unsecured creditor in the amount of $25,000. There is, ultimately, $325,000 [$600,000 – ($100,000 + $50,000 + $125,000)] left to be distributed to the unsecured claims. Since the unsecured claims total $650,000 ($625,000 of original unsecured claims plus $25,000 unsecured claim from creditor of Asset #2), the unsecured creditors will each receive one-half of their claims. Therefore, Asset #2's secured creditor will receive $62,500 [$50,000 + ($25,000 × 50%)].

CHAPTER 7—LIABILITIES

Problem 7-1 MULTIPLE-CHOICE QUESTIONS

1. __________ are expenses incurred, but not yet paid in cash.
   a. Dividends payable
   b. Advances
   c. Accrued expenses
   d. Returnable deposits (Editor, 89620)

2. Wilk Co. reported the following liabilities at December 31 of the current year:

Accounts payable-trade	$ 750,000
Short-term borrowings	400,000
Bank loan, current portion $100,000	3,500,000
Other bank loan, matures June 30 next year	1,000,000

   The bank loan of $3,500,000 was in violation of the loan agreement. The creditor had not waived the rights for the loan. What amount should Wilk report as current liabilities at December 31 this year?
   a. $1,250,000
   b. $2,150,000
   c. $2,250,000
   d. $5,650,000 (R/02, FAR, #6, amended, 7061)

3. Black Co. requires advance payments with special orders for machinery constructed to customer specifications. These advances are nonrefundable. Information for the current year is as follows:

Customer advances—prior year balance 12/31	$118,000
Advances received with orders in the current year	184,000
Advances applied to orders shipped in the current year	164,000
Advances applicable to orders canceled in the current year	50,000

   In Black's current year December 31 balance sheet, what amount should be reported as a current liability for advances from customer?
   a. $0
   b. $ 88,000
   c. $138,000
   d. $148,000 (11/94, FAR, #25, amended, 9065)

4. Brite Corp. had the following liabilities at December 31 of the current year:

Accounts payable	$ 55,000
Unsecured notes, 8%, due 7/1 next year	400,000
Accrued expenses	35,000
Contingent liability	450,000
Deferred income tax liability	25,000
Senior bonds, 7%, due 3/31 next year	1,000,000

   The contingent liability is an accrual for possible losses on a $1,000,000 lawsuit filed against Brite. Brite's legal counsel expects the suit to be settled in 2 years, and has estimated that Brite will be liable for damages in the range of $450,000 to $750,000. The deferred income tax liability is not related to an asset for financial reporting and is expected to reverse in 2 years.

   What amount should Brite report in its current year December 31 balance sheet for current liabilities?
   a. $ 515,000
   b. $ 940,000
   c. $1,490,000
   d. $1,515,000 (5/94, FAR, #11, amended, 4826)

5. On December 31, Roth Co. issued a $10,000 face value note payable to Wake Co. in exchange for services rendered to Roth. The note, made at usual trade terms, is due in nine months and bears interest, payable at maturity, at the annual rate of 3%. The market interest rate is 8%. The compound interest factor of $1 due in nine months at 8% is .944. At what amount should the note payable be reported in Roth's December 31 balance sheet?

   a. $10,300
   b. $10,000
   c. $ 9,652
   d. $ 9,440 (11/93, PI, #27, amended, 4396)

6. On October 1 of the prior year, Fleur Retailers signed a 4-month, 16% note payable to finance the purchase of holiday merchandise. At that date, there was no direct method of pricing the merchandise, and the note's market rate of interest was 11%. Fleur recorded the purchase at the note's face amount. All of the merchandise was sold by December 1 of the prior year Fleur's prior year financial statements reported interest payable and interest expense on the note for three months at 16%. All amounts due on the note were paid February 1 of the current year. Fleur's prior year cost of goods sold for the holiday merchandise was

   a. Overstated by the difference between the note's face amount and the note's October 1 present value
   b. Overstated by the difference between the note's face amount and the note's October 1 present value plus 11% interest for two months
   c. Understated by the difference between the note's face amount and the note's October 1 present value
   d. Understated by the difference between the note's face amount and the note's October 1 present value plus 16% interest for two months (5/92, Theory, #18, amended, 2711)

7. Fay Corp. pays its outside salespersons fixed monthly salaries and commissions on net sales. Sales commissions are computed and paid on a monthly basis (in the month following the month of sale), and the fixed salaries are treated as advances against commissions. However, if the fixed salaries for salespersons exceed their sales commissions earned for a month, such excess is not charged back to them. Pertinent data for the month of March for the three salespersons are as follows:

Salesperson	Fixed salary	Net sales	Commission rate
A	$10,000	$ 200,000	4%
B	14,000	400,000	6%
C	18,000	600,000	6%
	$42,000	$1,200,000	

   What amount should Fay accrue for sales commissions payable at March 31?

   a. $70,000
   b. $68,000
   c. $28,000
   d. $26,000 (R/89, FAR #16, amended, 1054)

8. Acme Co.'s accounts payable balance at December 31 was $850,000 before necessary year-end adjustments, if any, related to the following information:

   - At December 31, Acme has a $50,000 debit balance in its accounts payable resulting from a payment to a supplier for goods to be manufactured to Acme's specifications.
   - Goods shipped F.O.B. destination on December 20 were received and recorded by Acme on January 2, the invoice cost was $45,000.

   In its December 31 balance sheet, what amount should Acme report as accounts payable?

   a. $850,000
   b. $895,000
   c. $900,000
   d. $945,000 (R/10, FAR, #8, 9308)

9. Rabb Co. records its purchases at gross amounts but wishes to change to recording purchases net of purchase discounts. Discounts available on purchases recorded from last October 1 to this September 30 totaled $2,000. Of this amount, $200 is still available in the accounts payable balance. The balances in Rabb's accounts as of and for the current year ended September 30 before conversion are:

Purchases	$100,000
Purchase discounts taken	800
Accounts payable	30,000

What is Rabb's current year accounts payable balance as of September 30 after the conversion?

a. $29,800
b. $29,200
c. $28,800
d. $28,200 (11/92, PI, #21, amended, 3254)

10. Kew Co.'s accounts payable balance at December 31 of the prior year was $2,200,000 before considering the following data:

- Goods shipped to Kew F.O.B. shipping point on December 22 of the prior year were lost in transit. The invoice cost of $40,000 was not recorded by Kew. On January 7 of the current year, Kew filed a $40,000 claim against the common carrier.
- On December 27 of the prior year, a vendor authorized Kew to return, for full credit, goods shipped and billed at $70,000 on December 3 of the prior year. The returned goods were shipped by Kew on December 28 of the prior year. A $70,000 credit memo was received and recorded by Kew on January 5 of the current year.
- Goods shipped to Kew F.O.B. destination on December 20 of the prior year, were received on January 6 of the current year. The invoice cost was $50,000.

What amount should Kew report as accounts payable in its prior year December 31 balance sheet?

a. $2,170,000
b. $2,180,000
c. $2,230,000
d. $2,280,000 (5/91, PI, #34, amended, 1015)

11. On March 1 of the prior year, Fine Co. borrowed $10,000 and signed a two-year note bearing interest at 12% per annum compounded annually. Interest is payable in full at maturity on February 28 of next year. What amount should Fine report as a liability for accrued interest at December 31 of the current year?

a. $0
b. $1,000
c. $1,200
d. $2,320 (11/95, FAR, #16, amended, 6098)

12. On September 30, World Co. borrowed $1,000,000 on a 9% note payable. World paid the first of four quarterly payments of $264,200 when due on December 30. In its December 31, balance sheet, what amount should World report as note payable?

a. $735,800
b. $750,000
c. $758,300
d. $825,800 (R/10, FAR, #9, 9309)

13. Barnel Corp. owns and manages 19 apartment complexes. On signing a lease, each tenant must pay the first and last months' rent and a $500 refundable security deposit. The security deposits are rarely refunded in total, because cleaning costs of $150 per apartment are almost always deducted. About 30% of the time, the tenants are also charged for damages to the apartment, which typically cost $100 to repair. If a one-year lease is signed on a $900 per month apartment, what amount would Barnel report as refundable security deposit?

    a. $1,400
    b. $ 500
    c. $ 350
    d. $ 320 (11/92, PI, #26, 3259)

14. Lime Co.'s payroll for the month ended January 31 is summarized as follows:

Total wages	$10,000
Federal income tax withheld	1,200

    All wages paid were subject to FICA. FICA tax rates were 7% each for employee and employer. Lime remits payroll taxes on the 15th of the following month. In its financial statements for the month ended January 31, what amounts should Lime report as total payroll tax liability and as payroll tax expense?

	Liability	Expense
a.	$1,200	$1,400
b.	$1,900	$1,400
c.	$1,900	$ 700
d.	$2,600	$ 700

(11/95, FAR, #13, amended, 6095)

15. In its current year financial statements, Cris Co. reported interest expense of $85,000 in its income statement and cash paid for interest of $68,000 in its cash flow statement. There was no prepaid interest or interest capitalization either at the beginning or end of the current year. Accrued interest at December 31 of the prior year was $15,000. What amount should Cris report as accrued interest payable in its current year December 31 balance sheet?

    a. $ 2,000
    b. $ 15,000
    c. $ 17,000
    d. $ 32,000 (11/94, FAR, #18, 5282)

16. Ross Co. pays all salaried employees on a Monday for the five-day workweek ended the previous Friday. The last payroll recorded for the year ended December 31, year 2, was for the week ended December 25, year 2. The payroll for the week ended January 1, year 3, included regular weekly salaries of $80,000 and vacation pay of $25,000 for vacation time earned in year 2 not taken by December 31, year 2. Ross had accrued a liability of $20,000 for vacation pay at December 31, year 1. In its December 31, year 2 balance sheet, what amount should Ross report as accrued salary and vacation pay?

    a. $64,000
    b. $68,000
    c. $69,000
    d. $89,000 (11/93, PI, #28, amended, 4397)

17. Under state law, Acme may pay 3% of eligible gross wages or it may reimburse the state directly for actual unemployment claims. Acme believes that actual unemployment claims will be 2% of eligible gross wages and has chosen to reimburse the state. Eligible gross wages are defined as the first $10,000 of gross wages paid to each employee. Acme had five employees, each of whom earned $20,000 during the year. In its December 31 balance sheet, what amount should Acme report as accrued liability for unemployment claims?

    a. $1,000
    b. $1,500
    c. $2,000
    d. $3,000 (5/94, FAR, #22, 4837)

18. Kent Co., a division of National Realty Inc., maintains escrow accounts and pays real estate taxes for National's mortgage customers. Escrow funds are kept in interest-bearing accounts. Interest, less a 10% service fee, is credited to the mortgagee's account and used to reduce future escrow payments. Additional information follows:

Escrow accounts liability, 1/1	$ 700,000
Escrow payments received during the year	1,580,000
Real estate taxes paid during the year	1,720,000
Interest on escrow funds during the year	50,000

What amount should Kent report as escrow accounts liability in its December 31 balance sheet?

a. $510,000
b. $515,000
c. $605,000
d. $610,000 (11/93, PI, #32, amended, 4401)

19. Todd Care Co. offers three payment plans on its 12-month contracts. Information on the three plans and the number of children enrolled in each plan for the September 1, year 1, through August 31, year 2, contract year follows:

Plan	Initial payment per child	Monthly fees per child	Number of children
#1	$500	$—	15
#2	200	30	12
#3	—	50	9
			36

Todd received $9,900 of initial payments on September 1, year 1, and $3,240 of monthly fees during the period September 1 through December 31, year 1. In its December 31, year 1 balance sheet, what amount should Todd report as deferred revenues?

a. $3,300
b. $4,380
c. $6,600
d. $9,900 (11/92, PI, #29, amended, 3262)

20. Cado Co.'s payroll for the month ended January 31 is summarized as follows:

Total wages	$100,000
Amount of wages subject to payroll taxes:	
FICA	80,000
Unemployment	20,000
Payroll tax rates:	
FICA for employer and employee	7% each
Unemployment	3%

In its January 31 balance sheet, what amount should Cado accrue as its share of payroll taxes?

a. $ 6,200
b. $ 10,000
c. $ 11,800
d. $ 17,000 (R/03, FAR, #10, 7606)

21. As of December 15 of the current year, Aviator had dividends in arrears of $200,000 on its cumulative preferred stock. Dividends for this year of $100,000 have not yet been declared. The board of directors plan to declare cash dividends on its preferred and common stock on January 16 of next year. Aviator paid an annual bonus to its CEO based on the company's annual profits. The bonus for this year was $50,000, and it will be paid on February 10 of next year. What amount should Aviator report as current liabilities on its current year balance sheet at December 31?

    a. $ 50,000
    b. $150,000
    c. $200,000
    d. $350,000 (R/05, FAR, #35, amended, 7779)

22. Ivy Co. operates a retail store. All items are sold subject to a 6% state sales tax, which Ivy collects and records as sales revenue. Ivy files quarterly sales tax returns when due, by the 20th day following the end of the sales quarter. However, in accordance with state requirements, Ivy remits sales tax collected by the 20th day of the month following any month such collections exceed $500. Ivy takes these payments as credits on the quarterly sales tax return. The sales taxes paid by Ivy are charged against sales revenue. Following is a monthly summary appearing in Ivy's first quarter sales revenue account:

	Debit	Credit
January	$ —	$10,600
February	600	7,420
March	—	8,480
	$600	$26,500

    In its March 31 balance sheet, what amount should Ivy report as sales taxes payable?

    a. $ 600
    b. $ 900
    c. $1,500
    d. $1,590 (5/95, FAR, #15, amended, 5551)

23. Pine Corp. is required to contribute, to an employee stock ownership plan (ESOP), 10% of its income after deduction for this contribution but before income tax. Pine's income before charges for the contribution and income tax was $75,000. The income tax rate is 30%. What amount should be accrued as a contribution to the ESOP?

    a. $7,500
    b. $6,818
    c. $5,250
    d. $4,773 (5/91, PI, #36, 1016)

24. After three profitable years, Dodd Co. decided to offer a bonus to its branch manager, Cone, of 25% of income over $100,000 earned by his branch. Year 2, income for Cone's branch was $160,000 before income taxes and Cone's bonus. Cone's bonus is computed on income in excess of $100,000 after deducting the bonus, but before deducting taxes. What is Cone's bonus for the year 2?

    a. $12,000
    b. $15,000
    c. $25,000
    d. $32,000 (R/09, FAR, #42, 8792)

25. Ace Co. settled litigation on February 1 of the current year for an event that occurred during the prior year. An estimated liability was determined as of December 31 of the prior year. This estimate was significantly less than the final settlement. The transaction is considered to be material. The financial statements for prior year-end have not been issued. How should the settlement be reported in Ace's prior year-end financial statements?

    a. Disclosure only of the settlement
    b. Only an accrual of the settlement
    c. Neither a disclosure nor an accrual
    d. Both a disclosure and an accrual (R/02, FAR, #10, amended, 7065)

26. During Year 4, a former employee of Dane Co. began a suit against Dane for wrongful termination in November Year 3. After considering all of the facts, Dane's legal counsel believes that the former employee will prevail and will probably receive damages of between $1,000,000 and $1,500,000, with $1,300,000 being the most likely amount. Dane's financial statements for the year ended December 31, Year 3, will not be issued until February Year 4. In its December 31, Year 3, balance sheet, what amount should Dane report as a liability with respect to the suit?

    a. $0
    b. $1,000,000
    c. $1,300,000
    d. $1,500,000 (R/09, FAR, #30, 8780)

27. Management can estimate the amount of loss that will occur if a foreign government expropriates some company assets. If expropriation is reasonably possible, a loss contingency should be

    a. Disclosed but not accrued as a liability
    b. Disclosed and accrued as a liability
    c. Accrued as a liability but not disclosed
    d. Neither accrued as a liability nor disclosed (11/94, FAR, #26, 5289)

28. Eagle Co. has cosigned the mortgage note on the home of its president, guaranteeing the indebtedness in the event that the president should default. Eagle considers the likelihood of default to be remote. How should the guarantee be treated in Eagle's financial statements?

    a. Disclosed only
    b. Accrued only
    c. Accrued and disclosed
    d. Neither accrued nor disclosed (11/95, FAR, #17, 6099)

29. What is the underlying concept governing the generally accepted accounting principles pertaining to recording gain contingencies?

    a. Conservatism
    b. Relevance
    c. Consistency
    d. Reliability (11/95, FAR, #3, 6085)

30. During January of the current year, Haze Corp. won a litigation award for $15,000 which was tripled to $45,000 to include punitive damages. The defendant, who is financially stable, has appealed only the $30,000 punitive damages. Haze was awarded $50,000 in an unrelated suit it filed, which is being appealed by the defendant. Counsel is unable to estimate the outcome of these appeals. In its current year financial statements, Haze should report what amount of pretax gain?

    a. $15,000
    b. $45,000
    c. $50,000
    d. $95,000 (11/92, PII, #53, amended, 3387)

31. Wall Co. sells a product under a two-year warranty. The estimated cost of warranty repairs is 2% of net sales. During Wall's first two years in business, it made the following sales and incurred the following warranty repair costs:

Year 1	
Total sales	$250,000
Total repair costs incurred	4,500
Year 2	
Total sales	$300,000
Total repair costs incurred	5,000

What amount should Wall report as warranty expense for year 2?

a. $1,000
b. $5,000
c. $5,900
d. $6,000 (R/09, FAR, #43, 8793)

32. Oak Co. offers a three-year warranty on its products. Oak previously estimated warranty costs to be 2% of sales. Due to production advances at the start of the year, Oak now believes 1% of sales to be a better estimate of warranty costs. Warranty costs of $80,000 and $96,000 were reported in the two prior years. Sales for the year were $5,000,000. What amount should be disclosed in Oak's current year financial statements as warranty expense?

a. $ 50,000
b. $ 88,000
c. $ 100,000
d. $ 138,000 (11/95, FAR, #44, amended, 6126)

33. In December, Mill Co. began including one coupon in each package of candy that it sells and offering a toy in exchange for 50 cents and five coupons. The toys cost Mill 80 cents each. Eventually 60% of the coupons will be redeemed. During December, Mill sold 110,000 packages of candy and no coupons were redeemed. In its December 31 balance sheet, what amount should Mill report as estimated liability for coupons?

a. $ 3,960
b. $ 10,560
c. $ 19,800
d. $ 52,800 (5/95, FAR, #21, amended, 5557)

34. Baker Co. sells consumer products that are packaged in boxes. Baker offered an unbreakable glass in exchange for two box tops and $1 as a promotion during the current year. The cost of the glass was $2.00. Baker estimated at the end of the year that it would be probable that 50% of the box tops will be redeemed. Baker sold 100,000 boxes of the product during the current year and 40,000 box tops were redeemed during the year for the glasses. What amount should Baker accrue as an estimated liability at the end of the current year, related to the redemption of box tops?

a. $0
b. $ 5,000
c. $ 20,000
d. $ 25,000 (R/07, FAR, #40, 8361)

35. At December 31 of the current year, Taos Co. estimates that its employees have earned vacation pay of $100,000. Employees will receive their vacation pay next year. Should Taos accrue a liability at December 31 if the rights to this compensation accumulated over time or if the rights are vested?

	Accumulated	Vested
a.	Yes	No
b.	No	No
c.	Yes	Yes
d.	No	Yes

(11/92, Theory, #25, 3458)

36. In June, Northan Retailers sold refundable merchandise coupons. Northan received $10 for each coupon redeemable from July 1 to December 31 for merchandise with a retail price of $11. At June 30, how should Northan report these coupon transactions?

    a. Unearned revenues at the merchandise's retail price
    b. Unearned revenues at the cash received amount
    c. Revenues at the merchandise's retail price
    d. Revenues at the cash received amount (11/92, Theory, #7, amended, 3440)

37. Regal Department Store sells gift certificates, redeemable for store merchandise, that expire one year after their issuance. Regal has the following information pertaining to its gift certificates sales and redemptions:

Unredeemed at 12/31 of prior year	$ 75,000
Current year sales	250,000
Redemptions of prior year sales	25,000
Redemptions of current year sales	175,000

    Regal's experience indicates that 10% of gift certificates sold will not be redeemed. In its current year December 31 balance sheet, what amount should Regal report as unearned revenue?

    a. $125,000
    b. $112,500
    c. $100,000
    d. $ 50,000 (11/92, PI, #30, amended, 3263)

38. ABC borrowed $5,000 on June 30th and signed an 8-percent noninterest-bearing note due in one year. The 8 percent represents the ____________ of the note.

    a. Interest rate
    b. Effective rate
    c. Discount rate
    d. None of the above (Editor, 89619)

39. Long-term liabilities include which of the following?

    a. Dividends payable
    b. Accounts payable
    c. Refinancing of short-term obligations
    d. Loss contingencies concerning unasserted claims (Editor, 89625)

40. House Publishers offered a contest in which the winner would receive $1,000,000, payable over 20 years. On December 31 of the prior year, House announced the winner of the contest and signed a note payable to the winner for $1,000,000, payable in $50,000 installments every January 2. Also on that December 31, House purchased an annuity for $418,250 to provide the $950,000 prize monies remaining after the first $50,000 installment, which was paid on January 2 of this year. In its prior year December 31 balance sheet, what amount should House report as note payable-contest winner, net of current portion?

    a. $368,250
    b. $418,250
    c. $900,000
    d. $950,000 (11/94, FAR, #22, amended, 5286)

41. Godart Co. issued $4,500,000 notes payable as a scrip dividend that matured in five years. At maturity, each shareholder of Godart's three million shares will receive payment of the note principal plus interest. The annual interest rate was 10%. What amount should be paid to the stockholders at the end of the fifth year?

    a. $ 450,000
    b. $2,250,000
    c. $4,500,000
    d. $6,750,000 (R/06, FAR, #17, 8084)

42. On December 30 of the current year, Bart Inc. purchased a machine from Fell Corp. in exchange for a noninterest-bearing note requiring eight payments of $20,000. The first payment was made on December 30, and the others are due annually on December 30. At date of issuance, the prevailing rate of interest for this type of note was 11%. Present value factors are as follows:

Period	PVA of ordinary annuity of 1 at 11%	PV of annuity in advance of 1 at 11%
7	4.712	5.231
8	5.146	5.712

On Bart's current year December 31 balance sheet, the note payable to Fell was

a. $ 94,240
b. $102,920
c. $104,620
d. $114,240 (5/90, PI, #29, amended, 1045)

43. On October 1 of the prior year, Fleur Retailers signed a 4-month, 16% note payable to finance the purchase of holiday merchandise. At that date, there was no direct method of pricing the merchandise, and the note's market rate of interest was 11%. Fleur recorded the purchase at the note's face amount. All of the merchandise was sold by December 1 of the prior year Fleur's prior year financial statements reported interest payable and interest expense on the note for three months at 16%. All amounts due on the note were paid February 1 of the current year. As a result of Fleur's accounting treatment of the note, interest, and merchandise, which of the following items was reported correctly?

	Prior year 12/31 retained earnings	Prior year 12/31 interest payable
a.	Yes	Yes
b.	No	No
c.	Yes	No
d.	No	Yes

(5/92, Theory, #19, amended, 2712)

44. An entity would ***not*** be in compliance with authoritative guidance on long-term liabilities if it did which of the following?

a. Recognized an asset retirement obligation as a liability at fair value in the period in which it was incurred, if subject to reasonable estimation
b. Classified as a long-term liability the repayment of short-term obligations after the balance sheet date, and subsequently refinanced them as long-term obligations before the balance sheet was issued
c. Discounted its asset retirement obligation liability, and recognized accretion expense using the credit-adjusted risk-free interest rate in effect at initial recognition
d. None of the above (Editor, 89626)

45. Cali Inc. had a $4,000,000 note payable due on March 15 of the current year. On January 28 of the current year, before the issuance of its prior year financial statements, Cali issued long-term bonds in the amount of $4,500,000. Proceeds from the bonds were used to repay the note when it came due. How should Cali classify the note in its prior year December 31 financial statements?

a. As a current liability, with separate disclosure of the note refinancing
b. As a current liability, with no separate disclosure required
c. As a noncurrent liability, with separate disclosure of the note refinancing
d. As a noncurrent liability, with no separate disclosure required (5/95, FAR, #5, 5541)

46. A company has the following liabilities at year end:

Mortgage note payable; $16,000 due within 12 months	$355,000
Short-term debt that the company is refinancing with long-term debt	175,000
Deferred tax liability arising from depreciation	25,000

What amount should the company include in the current liability section of the balance sheet?

a. $0
b. $ 16,000
c. $ 41,000
d. $191,000 (R/09, FAR, #40, 8790)

47. Included in Lee Corp.'s liability account balances at December 31, year 3, were the following:

14% note payable issued October 1, year 3, maturing September 30, year 4	$125,000
16% note payable issued April 1, year 1, payable in six equal annual installments of $50,000 beginning April 1, year 2	200,000

Lee's December 31, year 3 financial statements were issued on March 31, year 4. On January 15, year 4, the entire $200,000 balance of the 16% note was refinanced by issuance of a long-term obligation payable in a lump sum. In addition, on March 10, year 4, Lee consummated a noncancelable agreement with the lender to refinance the 14%, $125,000 note on a long-term basis, on readily determinable terms that have not yet been implemented. Both parties are financially capable of honoring the agreement, and there have been no violations of the agreement's provisions. On the December 31, year 3 balance sheet, the amount of the notes payable that Lee should classify as short-term obligations is

a. $175,000
b. $125,000
c. $ 50,000
d. $0 (11/90, PI, #11, amended, 1026)

48. On December 31, year 1, Taylor, Inc. signed a binding agreement with a bank for the refinancing of an existing note payable scheduled to mature in February, year 2. The terms of the refinancing included extending the maturity date of the note by three years. On January 15, year 2, the note was refinanced. How should Taylor report the note payable in its December 31, year 1, balance sheet?

a. A current liability
b. A long-term liability
c. A long-term note receivable
d. A current note receivable (R/07, FAR, #3, 8324)

49. Finch Co. reported a total asset retirement obligation of $257,000 in last year's financial statements. This year, Finch acquired assets subject to unconditional retirement obligations measured at undiscounted cash flow estimates of $110,000 and discounted cash flow estimates of $68,000. Finch paid $87,000 toward the settlement of previously recorded asset retirement obligations and recorded an accretion expense of $26,000. What amount should Finch report for the asset retirement obligation in this year's balance sheet?

a. $238,000
b. $264,000
c. $280,000
d. $306,000 (R/10, FAR, #10, 9310)

50. On October 15, Year 1, Kam Corp. informed Finn Co. that Kam would be unable to repay its $100,000 note due on October 31 to Finn. Finn agreed to accept title to Kam's computer equipment in full settlement of the note. The equipment's carrying value was $80,000 and its fair value was $75,000. A similar event occurred last year with another creditor. What amounts should Kam report as ordinary gain (loss) and extraordinary gain for the year ended September 30, Year 2?

	Ordinary gain (loss)	Extraordinary gain (loss)
a.	$ (5,000)	$17,500
b.	$0	$20,000
c.	$0	$14,000
d.	$20,000	$0

(R/92, #59, amended, 3290)

51. In a troubled debt restructuring, the total fair value of the consideration given to discharge the obligation will __________ the recorded amount of the debt.

a. Always be less than
b. Always be more than
c. Always equal
d. Equal or exceed (Editor, 89627)

52. In year 2, May Corp. acquired land by paying $75,000 down and signing a note with a maturity value of $1,000,000. On the note's due date, December 31, year 7, May owed $40,000 of accrued interest and $1,000,000 principal on the note. May was in financial difficulty and was unable to make any payments. May and the bank agreed to amend the note as follows:

    - The $40,000 of interest due on December 31, year 7, was forgiven.
    - The principal of the note was reduced from $1,000,000 to $950,000 and the maturity date extended 1 year to December 31, year 8.
    - May would be required to make one interest payment totaling $30,000 on December 31, year 8.

    As a result of the troubled debt restructuring, May should report a gain, before taxes, in its year 7 income statement of

    a. $40,000
    b. $50,000
    c. $60,000
    d. $90,000 (Editor, 9030)

53. Allen Small obtains a 30 year mortgage loan that requires monthly principal and interest payments. In year 4, Allen Small lost his job, and experiences financial difficulties resulting in two missed payments. On the basis of Mr. Small's financial hardship, Mr. Allen and his mortgage loan company agree on a forbearance arrangement and repayment plan. The mortgage company agrees not to take any foreclosure action if the debtor increases its next four monthly payments such that each payment includes one fourth of the delinquent amount plus interest. The agreement does not result in the mortgage company charging Mr. Allen interest on the past due interest.

    At the end of the forbearance arrangement, Mr. Allen will be considered current in relation to the debt's original terms; have repaid all past due amounts; and will have resumed making monthly payments set out under the debt's original terms.

    Does the restructuring of Mr. Allen's debt qualify as a concession?

    a. Yes, because the delay in payment is considered significant.
    b. No, because the delay in payment in considered insignificant.
    c. No, because Mr. Allen's financial difficulties have been for less than one year.
    d. Yes, because the amount of the missed payments is considered significant relative to the unpaid principal and interest. (Editor, 89429)

Items 54 and 55 are based on the following:

The following information pertains to the transfer of real estate pursuant to a troubled debt restructuring by Knob Co. to Mene Corp. in full liquidation of Knob's liability to Mene.

Carrying amount of liability liquidated	$150,000
Carrying amount of real estate transferred	100,000
Fair value of real estate transferred	90,000

54. What amount should Knob report as the total amount of pretax gain (loss) as a result of this troubled debt restructuring?

    a. $(10,000)
    b. $0
    c. $ 50,000
    d. $ 60,000 (11/93, PI, #57, amended, 4427)

55. At what amount should Mene record the real estate transferred?

    a. $ 60,000
    b. $ 90,000
    c. $100,000
    d. $150,000 (11/93, PI, #58, amended, 4428)

56. For a troubled debt restructuring involving only a modification of terms, which of the following items specified by the new terms would be compared to the carrying amount of the debt to determine if the debtor should report a gain on restructuring?

a. The total future cash payments
b. The present value of the debt at the original interest rate
c. The present value of the debt at the modified interest rate
d. The amount of future cash payments designated as principal repayments (R/01, FAR, #9, 6984)

57. Kent Co. filed a voluntary bankruptcy petition, and the statement of affairs reflected the following:

	Book value	Estimated current value
Assets:		
Assets pledged with fully secured creditors	$ 300,000	$370,000
Assets pledged with partially secured creditors	180,000	120,000
Free assets	420,000	320,000
	$ 900,000	$810,000
Liabilities (book value):		
Liabilities with priority	$ 70,000	
Fully secured creditors	260,000	
Partially secured creditors	200,000	
Unsecured creditors	540,000	
	$1,070,000	

Assume that the assets are converted to cash at the estimated current values and the business is liquidated. What amount of cash will be available to pay unsecured nonpriority claims?

a. $240,000
b. $280,000
c. $320,000
d. $360,000 (11/90, PI, #31, amended, 1037)

58. Kamy Corp. is in liquidation under Chapter 7 of the Federal Bankruptcy Code. The bankruptcy trustee has established a new set of books for the bankruptcy estate. After assuming custody of the estate, the trustee discovered an unrecorded invoice of $1,000 for machinery repairs performed before the bankruptcy filing. In addition, a truck with a carrying amount of $20,000 was sold for $12,000 cash. This truck was bought and paid for in the year before the bankruptcy. What amount should be debited to estate equity as a result of these transactions?

a. $0
b. $1,000
c. $8,000
d. $9,000 (5/92, PII, #10, 2642)

Problem 7-2 SIMULATION: Adjustments/Disclosures

Buzz Co., a toy manufacturer, is in the process of preparing its financial statements for the year ended December 31, year 2. Buzz expects to issue its year 2 financial statements on March 1, year 3.

Items 1 through 12 represent various information that has not been reflected in the financial statements. For each item, determine if an adjustment is required and enter the appropriate amount if appropriate. Also, determine (Yes/No) if additional disclosure is required, either on the face of the financial statements or in the notes to the financial statements.

	Information Amounts	Adjustment Amount	Disclosure Yes/No
1.	Buzz offers an unconditional warranty on its toys. Based on past experience, Buzz estimates its warranty expense to be 2% of sales. Sales during year 2 were $12,500,000.		
2.	Buzz owns a small warehouse located on the banks of a river in which it stores inventory worth approximately $600,000. Buzz is not insured against flood losses. The river last overflowed its banks thirty years ago.		
3.	During year 2, Buzz began offering certain health care benefits to its eligible retired employees. Buzz's actuaries have determined that the discounted expected cost of these benefits for current employees is $200,000.		
4.	On August 22, year 2, Buzz initiated a lawsuit seeking $350,000 in damages from patent infringement.		
5.	On September 30, year 2, a safety hazard related to one of Buzz's toy products was discovered. It is considered probable that Buzz will be liable for an amount in the range of $50,000 to $250,000.		
6.	On October 15, year 2, Buzz guaranteed a bank loan of $200,000 for its president's personal use.		
7.	On November 17, year 2, a former employee filed a lawsuit seeking $150,000 for unlawful dismissal. Buzz's attorneys believe the suit is without merit. No court date has been set.		
8.	On December 31, year 2, Buzz's board of directors voted to discontinue the operations of its computer games division and sell all the assets of the division. The division was sold on February 15, year 3. On December 31, year 2, Buzz estimated that losses from operations, net of tax, for the period January 1, year 3, through February 15, year 3, would be $300,000 and that the gain from the sale of the division's assets, net of tax, would be $150,000. These estimates were materially correct. The year 2 division loss was $400,000.		
9.	On January 2, year 3, inventory purchased F.O.B. shipping point from a foreign country was detained at that country's border because of political unrest. The shipment is valued at $150,000. Buzz's attorneys have stated that it is probable that Buzz will be able to obtain the shipment.		
10.	On January 30, year 3, Buzz issued $12,000,000 bonds at a premium of $600,000.		
11.	On February 3, year 3, a warehouse containing a substantial portion of Buzz's inventory was destroyed by fire. Buzz expects to recover the entire loss, except for a $300,000 deductible, from insurance.		
12.	On February 4, year 3, the IRS assessed Buzz an additional $450,000 for the year 1 tax year. Buzz's tax attorneys and tax accountants have stated that it is likely that the IRS will agree to a $150,000 settlement.		

(5/96, FAR, #16, amended, 4948t)

Problem 7-3 SIMULATION: Interest Expense & Long-Term Liabilities

The following is the long-term liabilities section of Rocko Co.'s December 31, year 2 balance sheet:

Long-term liabilities:		
Note payable—bank; 18 principal payments of $6,000, plus 11% interest due annually on September 30	$108,000	
Less: Current portion	(6,000)	$102,000
Capital lease obligation—20 payments of $8,000 due annually on January 1	61,250	
Less: Current portion	(650)	60,600
Deferred income tax liability		27,000
Total long-term liabilities		$189,600

- Rocko's incremental borrowing rate on the date of the lease was 13% and the lessor's implicit rate, which was known by Rocko, was 12%.

- The only difference between Rocko's taxable income and pretax accounting income is depreciation on a machine acquired on January 1, year 2, for $350,000. The machine's estimated useful life is five years, with no salvage value. Depreciation is computed using the straight-line method for financial reporting purposes and the MACRS method for tax purposes. Depreciation expense for tax and financial reporting purposes for year 3 through year 6 is as follows:

Year	Tax depreciation	Financial depreciation	Tax depreciation over (under) financial depreciation
3	$90,000	$70,000	$ 20,000
4	45,000	70,000	(25,000)
5	40,000	70,000	(30,000)
6	35,000	70,000	(35,000)

The enacted federal income tax rates are 25% for years 2 and 3, and 30% for years 4 through 6.

- Included in Rocko's December year 2 balance sheet was a deferred tax asset of $12,000.

- For the year ended December 31, year 3, Rocko's income before income taxes was $540,000.

- On July 1, year 3, Rocko received proceeds of $545,523 from a $600,000 bond issuance. The bonds mature in 20 years and interest of 9% is payable each January 1 through July 1. The bonds were issued at a price to yield the investors 10%. Rocko uses the effective interest method to amortize the bond discount.

1. Prepare a schedule showing the calculation of Rocko's interest expense for the year ended December 31, year 3. Enter amount rounded to nearest whole dollar in the appropriate cell.

Note payable—bank:	
1/1 to 9/30	
10/1 to 12/31	
Capital lease obligation 1/1 to 12/31	
Bonds payable 7/1 to 12/31	
Total interest expense	

2. Prepare the long-term liabilities section of Rocko's December 31, year 3 balance sheet. Enter amount rounded to nearest whole dollar in the appropriate cell.

Long-term liabilities:		
Note payable–bank	$	
Less current portion		$
Capital lease obligation	$	
Less current portion		
9% bonds payable due June 30, year 23, less unamortized discount		
Deferred income tax liability		
Total long-term liabilities		$

(5/92, FAR, #5, amended, 6192)

Problem 7-4 SIMULATION: Reporting Commitments/Contingencies

Items 1 through 6 represent various commitments and contingencies of Rocko, Co. at December 31, year 5, and events subsequent to December 31, year 5, but prior to the issuance of the year 5 financial statements. Rocko, Co. is preparing its financial statements for the year ended December 31, year 5. For each item, select the reporting requirement from the choices below. A choice may be selected once, more than once, or not at all.

Reporting Requirement Choices			
A.	Accrual only	D.	Disclosure only
B.	Both accrual and disclosure	N.	Neither accrual nor disclosure

Commitments and Contingencies	**Choice**
1. A former employee of Rocko has brought a wrongful-dismissal suit against Rocko. Rocko's lawyers believe the suit to be without merit.	
2. A government contract completed during year 5 is subject to renegotiation. Although Rocko estimates that it is reasonably possible that a refund of approximately $100,000-$200,000 may be required by the government, it does not wish to publicize this possibility.	
3. On December 1, year 5, Rocko was awarded damages of $90,000 in a patent infringement suit it brought against a competitor. The defendant did not appeal the verdict, and payment was received in January, year 6.	
4. At December 31, year 5, Rocko had outstanding purchase orders in the ordinary course of business for purchase of a raw material to be used in its manufacturing process. The market price is currently higher than the purchase price and is not anticipated to change within the next year.	
5. On January 6, year 6, Rocko redeemed its outstanding bonds and issued new bonds with a lower rate of interest. The reacquisition price was in excess of the carrying amount of the bonds.	
6. Rocko has been notified by a governmental agency that it will be held responsible for the cleanup of toxic materials at a site where Rocko formerly conducted operations. Rocko estimates that it is probable that its share of remedial action will be approximately $400,000.	

(11/95, FAR, #78-83, amended 6152)

Problem 7-5 SIMULATION: Research

Question: What does refinancing a short-term obligation on a long-term basis mean?

FASB ASC: ______ - ______ - ______ - ______

(9116)

Solution 7-1 MULTIPLE-CHOICE ANSWERS

Current Liabilities

1. (c) Accrued expenses are expenses incurred, but not yet paid in cash. When declared, cash and property dividends represent legal obligations due within one year and are reported as current liabilities. Advanced payments received from customers and others are liabilities until the transaction is completed. Returnable deposits are liabilities until the relationship with the third party is terminated. (89620)

2. (d) Current liabilities are obligations whose liquidation is expected to require the use of existing current assets or the creation of other current liabilities. Current assets are assets that are reasonably expected to be converted into cash or used during the normal operating cycle of the business or one year, whichever is longer. Even though the bank loan appears to be long term, it is in violation of the loan agreement. The creditor has not waived their rights to demand payment of the loan, therefore, Wilk should report the entire balance of the loan as a current liability, not just the amount that would be due within one year if it was not in violation of the loan agreement. The "other bank loan" will mature in less than one year and is classified as a current liability. Of course, accounts payable and short-term borrowings are also current. [$750,000 + $400,000 + $3,500,000 + $1,000,000 = $5,650,000] (7061)

3. (b) Advanced payments received from customers are liabilities until the transaction is completed or canceled.

Customer Deposits			
		118,000	Balance, 01/01
Advances applied to orders shipped	164,000	184,000	Advances received with orders
Advances applicable to orders canceled	50,000		
		88,000	Balance, 12/31

(9065)

4. (c) The accounts payable and accrued expenses are current. Since the senior bonds are due within one year, they should be reported in the balance sheet as a current liability. Since the contingent liability is possible, not probable, it should not be accrued as a liability but should be disclosed in a footnote. The deferred income tax liability is not related to an asset for financial reporting and is expected to reverse more than one year after the balance sheet date, so it should be reported as a noncurrent liability.

Accounts payable	$ 55,000
Unsecured notes, due July 1	400,000
Accrued expenses	35,000
Senior bonds, due March 31	1,000,000
Current liabilities	$1,490,000

(4826)

5. (b) The note payable arose from a transaction with a vendor in the normal course of business and is due in customary trade terms not exceeding one year; therefore, the note can be reported at its face amount of $10,000, despite the fact that the 3% stated interest rate of the note does not approximate the prevailing market interest rate of 8% for similar notes at the date of the transaction. (4396)

6. (c) The note should not be recorded at its face amount because its stated interest rate of 16% does not approximate the market rate of interest of 11% for similar notes. When a note which does not bear the market rate of interest is exchanged for property, goods, or services, the note is to be recorded at the fair value of the property, goods, or services or the fair value of the note, whichever is more clearly determinable. Since neither of these amounts are determinable for the note in question, the note should be recorded at its present value. The interest rate to be used in the discounting process is the borrower's incremental borrowing rate (market rate) at the date the note is issued (11% in this case). Because the market rate of 11% is less than the stated rate of the note of 16%, the present value of the note is greater than the face amount of the note. Therefore, the correct journal entry at the date the note was issued would involve a debit to *Purchases* for the present value of the note, a credit to *Note Payable* for the face amount of the note, and a credit to *Premium on Note Payable* for the excess of the note's present value over its face amount. Fleur recorded the purchase at the note's face amount which understated the cost of the merchandise which was subsequently sold in the prior year. Therefore, prior year cost of goods sold is understated by the amount of the unrecorded premium on the note (i.e., the excess of the note's present value over its face amount). (2711)

Determinable Liabilities

7. (c) Salespersons receive sales commissions only to the extent that their sales commissions earned exceed their fixed salaries for that month.

Salesperson	Sales commissions	Fixed salary	Accrued commissions
A	$ 8,000 ($200,000 × 4%)	$10,000	$0
B	24,000 ($400,000 × 6%)	14,000	10,000
C	36,000 ($600,000 × 6%)	18,000	18,000
			$28,000

(1054)

8. (c) Accounts payable is a liability account incurred in obtaining goods and services from vendors in the entity's ordinary course of business. Accounts payable should reflect the cost of those goods or services that have been appropriately included in inventory (or other asset account) or have been expensed. The $50,000 debit for goods to be manufactured should not have been posted to the accounts payable account. The $50,000 payment would be classified as a prepaid asset and not as a reduction of any liability because the goods haven't been received yet. Adding the $50,000 to the $850,000 brings the accounts payable account to $900,000 on December 31. The $45,000 does not go into accounts payable until January 2 of the next year because the goods were shipped F.O.B. destination. Under an F.O.B. destination contract, the goods and related liability are not recorded until the goods are received. (9308)

9. (a) After the conversion, the accounts payable balance will be reported net of purchase discounts. The gross balance of the accounts payable of $30,000 is reduced by the $200 of discounts still available in the accounts payable balance to arrive at the net amount of $29,800. (3254)

10. (a) The cost of goods should be included in accounts payable when legal title passes from the seller to the purchaser. Kew should include the $40,000 cost of the goods lost in transit in accounts payable at 12/31 of the prior year. The goods were shipped F.O.B. shipping point, and the title of these goods passed to Kew when the vendor delivered the goods to the common carrier on 12/22. Since the vendor authorized Kew to return goods for full credit before year-end, and Kew shipped the goods before year-end, the 12/31 accounts payable balance should be reduced by $70,000, the cost of the goods returned. The $50,000 cost of the goods that were shipped from a vendor F.O.B. destination on 12/20 should not be included in accounts payable at 12/31. Title of these goods did not pass to Kew until Kew received the goods on 1/6 of the current year. Thus, accounts payable should be reported at $2,170,000 ($2,200,000 + $40,000 – $70,000). (1015)

11. (d)

March 1, prior year to Feb. 28, current year ($10,000 @ 12% × 12/12)	$ 1,200
March 1 to Dec. 31, current year [12% ($10,000 + $1,200) × 10/12]	1,120
Total accrued interest, December 31 of the current year	$ 2,320

(6098)

12. (c) The $264,200 payment includes both principal and interest. The amount of interest is $1,000,000 (amount of note) × 0.09 (the 9% interest) ÷ 4 (payments are quarterly) = $22,500. Subtracting $22,500 from $264,200 leaves $231,700 as principal. Subtracting the $231,700 of principle from the $1,000,000 note balance results in $758,300 should be reported as note payable on the December 31 balance sheet. (9309)

13. (b) The lessor should report the full amount of the $500 refundable security deposit as a liability until the lessor has earned a portion of it by cleaning or repairing vacated apartments. Revenue is not recognized until it has been earned. Deferred revenue is reported as a liability. (3259)

14. (d)

	Liability	Expense
FIT withheld	$1,200	
FICA employee portion ($10,000 @ 7%)	700	
FICA employer portion ($10,000 @ 7%)	700	$700
Totals	$2,600	$700

(6095)

15. (d)

Interest expense	$85,000
Cash paid for interest	(68,000)
Increase in accrued interest payable	17,000
Accrued interest payable, 12/31 prior year	15,000
Accrued interest payable, 12/31 current year	$32,000

(5282)

16. (d)

Accrued salary, 12/31, year 2 ($80,000 × 4/5*)	$64,000
Accrued vacation time earned in year 2	25,000
Accrued salary and vacation time, 12/31, year 2	$89,000

* Four days of the 5-day workweek ended 1/1 pertain to year 2. (4397)

17. (a) 2% of $10,000 × 5 employees = $1,000. Acme has chosen to reimburse the state for actual claims instead of using the 3% of eligible gross wages rate. The liability is computed using eligible gross wages, not total wages, for each employee. The actual unemployment claim is accrued, not the state rate times actual wages. (4837)

18. (c)

Escrow liability, 1/1	$ 700,000
Add: Escrow payments received during year	1,580,000
Add: Interest on escrow funds during year	50,000
Less: 10% service fee ($50,000 × 10%)	(5,000)
Less: Real estate taxes paid	(1,720,000)
Escrow liability, 12/31	$ 605,000

(4401)

19. (c) Todd received $9,900 [i.e., ($500 × 15) + ($200 × 12)] of initial payments on its 12-month contracts for the 9/1, year 1 through 8/31, year 2 contract year. Since four months of the initial payments on the contracts have been earned as of 12/31, year 1, eight months of the initial payments on the contracts should be reported as deferred revenue at that date (i.e., $9,900 × 8/12 = $6,600). (3262)

20. (a) ($80,000 × .07) + ($20,000 × .03) = ($5,600 + $600) = $6,200 (7606)

21. (a) When declared, cash and property dividends represent legal obligations due within one year and are reported as current liabilities. Stock dividends and undeclared dividends on cumulative preferred stock are not reported as liabilities. The dividends for the current year have not yet been declared, and are not reported as liabilities. Cumulative preferred stock dividends in arrears must be disclosed in the notes to the statements, and are not reported as liabilities. The only amount that should be reported as a current liability is the $50,000 bonus. (7779)

Dependent Liabilities

22. (b) Ivy Co. should report sales taxes based on February and March sales as sales taxes payable in its March 31 balance sheet. The taxes based on January sales were paid in February because they exceeded $500 ($10,600 sales / 1.06 = sales of $10,000; $10,600 – $10,000 = $600 in sales taxes). This is the $600 debit in February.

	(a) Total credits to sales revenue account	(b) Sales without taxes (a / 1.06)	(a – b) Sales taxes
March	$7,420	$7,000	$420
February	8,480	8,000	480
Total sales taxes payable, March 31			$900

(5551)

23. (b) Where C = contribution:

$$C = 0.10\ (\$75{,}000 - C);\ C = \$7{,}500 - 0.10C$$
$$1.10\ C = \$7{,}500$$
$$C = \$6{,}818$$

(1016)

24. (a) The amount of the bonus is determined by solving the proper equation that describes the terms of the bonus agreement. Using B to represent the bonus, B equals 25% of the total of income before taxes less $100,000 less B. The answer is computed as follows:

$$B = 0.25 \times (\$160{,}000 - \$100{,}000 - B)$$
$$B = 0.25 \times (\$60{,}000 - B)$$
$$B = \$15{,}000 - .25B$$
$$1.25B = \$15{,}000$$
$$B = \$12{,}000$$

(8792)

Contingent Liabilities

25. (d) An estimated loss from a loss contingency shall be accrued by a charge to income if both of the following conditions are met: (1) it is probable that an asset has been impaired or a liability has been incurred, and (2) the amount of the loss can be reasonably estimated. When the amount of loss is known, as with a settlement after the balance sheet date but before issuance of the financial statements, that amount should be accrued and disclosed in the financial statements. (7065)

26. (c) Contingent liabilities arise from events or circumstances occurring before the balance sheet date, the resolution of which is contingent on a future event or circumstance. Pending or threatened litigation is one example of a contingent liability. The accounting treatment depends on the likelihood that future events will confirm the contingent loss and whether the amount can be reasonably estimated. Where the likelihood of confirmation of a loss is considered probable and the loss can be reasonable estimated, the estimated loss should be accrued by a charge to income and the nature of the contingency should be disclosed. If, however, only a range of possible loss can be estimated, with no amount in the range better than any other, the minimum amount in the range should be accrued. The wrongful termination event took place in Year 3 and because a loss from it is considered probable it should be reported in the December 31, Year 3, balance sheet. The most likely amount (reasonably estimated) would be reported. (8780)

27. (a) Since the contingent loss from the expropriation of assets is judged to be reasonably possible, it should be disclosed in the footnotes, but not accrued. A contingent loss is accrued only in situations where the loss is probable and estimable. (5289)

28. (a) Contingent liabilities that are considered to have a remote possibility of loss normally do not require disclosure. Exceptions include the guarantees of indebtedness of others, in which case disclosure, but not accrual, is required. (6099)

29. (a) Gain contingencies should be disclosed in the financial statements in a footnote rather than being reflected in income because doing so could result in recognizing income prior to its realization. This treatment reflects the principle of conservatism which means that accountants who are selecting between two possible alternatives should choose the accounting alternative which is least likely to overstate assets and income. (6085)

30. (a) Haze should report a pretax gain of $15,000 (i.e., $45,000 – $30,000) for the amount of litigation award from the financially stable defendant that is not being appealed. The portion of the litigation awards that are being appealed (i.e., $30,000 and $50,000) represent gain contingencies and, thus, should not be accrued before realization; however, should be disclosed in the financial statement notes. (3387)

Estimated Liabilities

31. (d) A warranty or guarantee is a promise made by the seller to the buyer to make good certain deficiencies in the product during a specified period of time after the sale. Obligations related to product warranties and product defects are an example of loss contingencies. An estimated loss from a loss contingency shall be accrued by a charge to income if both of the following conditions are met; 1) information available prior to the issuance of the financial statements indicates that it is probable that an asset had been impaired or a liability had been incurred at the date of the financial statements, and 2) the amount of the loss can be reasonably estimated. It is probable that repairs are required and the 2% of net sales is a reasonable estimate so there is a charge to income through warranty expense. Proper accrual of the warranty expense for year 2 would be 2% of the net sales from year 2 (0.02 × $300,000 = $6,000). (8793)

32. (a) As Oak believes 1% of sales to be the best estimate of warranty costs, warranty expense should be accrued accordingly. ($5,000,000 × 1% = $50,000). The technological advance applied only to current year sales; thus, in this case, the estimates of warranty costs reported in the two prior years are not changed. (6126)

33. (a)

Cost of toys to Mill Co., each	$ 0.80
Less: Cash to be received with redemption	(0.50)
Net cost to Mill Co. for each toy	$ 0.30
Total packages of candy sold in December	$ 110,000
Times: Anticipated redemption rate	× 60%
Total coupons anticipated to be redeemed	66,000
Divided by: Number of coupons required for each toy	/ 5
Anticipated number of toys needed	13,200
Times: Net cost to Mill Co. for each toy (above)	× $0.30
Total estimated coupon liability, 12/31	$ 3,960

(5557)

34. (b) In order to increase sales and promote certain products, companies may offer premiums to those customers who return box tops, coupons, labels, wrappers, etc., as proof of purchase. The cost of these premiums represents an expense that should be matched against revenue from the sales benefited. At the end of the accounting period, an expense account should be debited and a liability account credited for the cost of outstanding premiums expected to be redeemed in subsequent periods. There were 50,000 box tops expected to be redeemed (100,000 sold × 50% probable redemption). As 40,000 box tops were redeemed during the year, an estimated 10,000 box tops will be redeemed in the future. The premium required two box tops and $1 per redemption. An estimated 10,000 box tops equates to an estimated 5,000 unbreakable glasses (10,000 / 2). The glasses cost $2 each, or $10,000 total ($2 × 5,000). The company also estimated receiving $5,000 ($1 × 5,000) in the redemption. The estimated liability at the end of the current year related to the premium is $5,000 ($10,000 glasses cost – $5,000 received with box tops). (8361)

35. (c) An employer must accrue a liability for employees' rights to receive vacation pay benefits if four conditions are met. Three of these conditions are met in the question data. These are: (1) the obligation is attributable to employees' services already rendered, (2) payment of the compensation is probable, and (3) the amount can be reasonably estimated (i.e., the employees have earned vacation pay of $100,000 that they will receive next year). The fourth condition necessary for accrual is that the employees' rights to receive the vacation pay benefits vest or accumulate. (3458)

36. (b) When the refundable merchandise coupons are sold, the sales price collected represents unearned revenue. Earned revenue will be recognized later when the coupons are redeemed. (3440)

37. (d) Of the $250,000 of gift certificates sold in the current year, only $225,000 [i.e., $250,000 × (100% – 10%)] are expected to be redeemed. Since $175,000 of the gift certificates sold in the current year were redeemed in the current year, $50,000 should be reported as unearned revenue at 12/31 of the current year. (At 12/31 there is no liability for unredeemed gift certificates sold in the prior year because the certificates expire one year after their issuance.) (3263)

Long-Term Liabilities

38. (c) Loans obtained from banks and other lending institutions represent current liabilities if they are due in the succeeding operating period. These notes may be either interest-bearing or noninterest-bearing. A noninterest-bearing note is a note without period interest payments, but is selling at a discount and matures at face value. The 8 percent represents the discount rate of this note. (89619)

39. (c) Long-term liabilities are all obligations not expected to be liquidated by the use of existing current assets or by the creation of current liabilities. Examples include: long-term notes payable; refinancing of short-term obligations; and bonds payable. When declared, cash and property dividends represent legal obligations due within one year and are reported as current liabilities, within a dividend payable account. Accounts payable are liabilities incurred in obtaining goods and services from vendors in the entity's ordinary course of business. Contingent liabilities arise from events or circumstances occurring before the balance sheet date, the resolution of which is contingent upon a future event or circumstance. No disclosure is required for a loss contingency concerning an unasserted claim unless it is considered probable that the claim will be asserted, and there is a reasonable possibility of an unfavorable result. (89625)

40. (b) The amount that should be reported as the noncurrent portion of *Note Payable to Contest Winner* at 12/31 of the prior year is $418,250, the cost of the annuity purchased to provide for the $950,000 of prize monies to be paid after 12/31 of the current year. This is the most objective available evidence of the present value of the prize money due. (5286)

41. (d) The amount paid to the stockholders at the end of the fifth year should be the accumulated annual interest, $4,500,000 × 10% × 5 yrs = $2,250,000 over the five years, plus the notes payable issue amount of $4,500,000. (8084)

42. (a) The factor for the present value of an annuity in advance is used because the first payment of the note was made immediately (i.e., 12/30).

Periodic annual payments	$ 20,000	
Times: Present value of an annuity in advance of $1 at 11% for 8 periods	× 5.712	
Present value of all cash flows	114,240	
Less: Payment, 12/30	(20,000)	
Carrying amount of note, 12/31	$ 94,240	(1045)

43. (d) The four-month note was issued on October 1 of the prior year. Fleur reported three months of interest payable at December 31 of the prior year, computed using the stated rate of the note. Therefore, interest payable is correctly reported at December 31 of the prior year. On the other hand, retained earnings is overstated at December 31 of the prior year, because (1) the prior year cost of goods sold was understated by the full amount of the unrecorded note premium, and (2) interest expense reported for the note for the prior year was overstated by 3/4 of the amount of the note premium (i.e., the amount of the note premium that should have been amortized for the three months the note was outstanding during the prior year). (2712)

44. (b) Short-term obligations repaid after the balance sheet date and subsequently refinanced before the issuance of the balance sheet must be classified as current liabilities as of the balance sheet date, because current assets were used for the repayment. An asset retirement obligation must be recognized as a liability at fair value in the period in which it is incurred, if it is subject to reasonable estimation. (89626)

45. (c) The portion of long-term debt due within the next fiscal period is classified as a current liability if payment is expected to require the use of current assets or the creation of other current liabilities. Short-term debt expected to be refinanced on a long-term basis is to be excluded from current liabilities when the enterprise has the intent and ability to refinance the obligation on a long-term basis. One way intent and ability are demonstrated is by post-balance-sheet-date issuance of a long-term obligation or equity securities. Separate disclosure of such refinancing is required. (5541)

46. (b) The term current liabilities is used primarily to designate obligations whose liquidation is reasonably expected to require the use of existing resources classified as current assets, or the creation of other current liabilities. Long-term liabilities are all obligations not expected to be liquidated by the use of existing current assets or by the creation of current liabilities. Short-term obligations are those scheduled to mature within one year or operating cycle, whichever is longer, and generally are classified as current liabilities. However, if they are to be refinanced on a long-term basis they will be appropriately classified as long-term liabilities. Income taxes payable within the next period, or operating cycle, are classified as current liabilities. A deferred tax liability is over a longer period of time and not considered a current liability. The only amount that would be reported is the $16,000 due within 12 months from the mortgage note payable. (8790)

47. (d) The entire $200,000 balance of the 16% note is properly excluded from short-term obligations because before the balance sheet was issued, Lee refinanced the note by issuance of a long-term obligation. The $125,000, 14% note is also properly excluded from short-term obligations because before the balance sheet was issued, Lee entered into a financing agreement that clearly permits Lee to refinance the short-term obligation on a long-term basis on terms that are readily determinable, and all of the following conditions are met: (1) the agreement is noncancelable as to all parties and extends beyond one year; (2) at the balance sheet date, and at the date of its issuance, Witt is not in violation of the agreement; and (3) the lender is financially capable of honoring the agreement. (1026)

48. (b) Long-term liabilities are all obligations not expected to be liquidated by the use of existing current assets or by the creation of current liabilities. Examples include: (1) long-term notes payable, (2) refinancing of short-term obligations, and (3) bonds payable. The binding agreement to refinance the existing note payable, extending the maturity date three years, changed the note payable classification from a current liability to a long-term liability. A note payable would not be reported as a receivable. (8324)

49. (b) An asset retirement obligations (ARO) must be recorded at fair value in the accounting period in which it occurs and in which its amount can be reasonably measured. If an active market for the ARO doesn't exist to provide fair value, the expected present value technique using discounted cash flows is the best way to determine the fair value of the asset. AROs incur depreciation and accretion expenses each year. Accretion expense is offset with an increase to the liability account, and, at the end of the asset's life, the liability account will have a balance equal to the amount needed to settle the retirement obligation. So the amount reported for the asset retirement obligation in this year's balance sheet would be the starting amount of $257,000 from last year's financial statements less $87,000 paid towards settlement of previously recorded AROs plus the $68,000 cash flow estimate for newly acquired AROs plus the $26,000 accretion expense. $257,000 – $87,000 + $68,000 + $26,000 = $264,000 (9310)

50. (d) The debtor recognizes an ordinary loss equal to the excess of the carrying amount over the fair value of the computer equipment transferred [$75,000 – $80,000 = ($5,000)] and an ordinary gain equal to the difference between the carrying amount of the obligation and the fair value of the equipment transferred at the restructure date [$100,000 – $75,000 = $25,000]. A similar event occurred last year so there is no evidence that the early debt extinguishment meets the criteria to be classified as extraordinary. The net ordinary gain equals $20,000 [($5,000) + $25,000]. (3290)

Troubled Debt & Bankruptcy

51. (a) In a troubled debt restructuring, the total fair value of the consideration given to discharge the obligation will always be less than the recorded amount of the debt. If the fair value of the consideration equals or exceeds the amount of the debt, the transaction will not be classified as a troubled debt restructuring. (89627)

52. (c) The debtor adds up total cash to be paid to the bank $980,000 ($950,000 principal and $30,000 interest) and compares this amount to the $1,040,000 due from the original transaction. The difference is a recognized gain of $60,000 in the year of restructuring. (9030)

53. (b) Since the creditor expects to collect all the amounts due for the periods of delay, and the length of delay resulting from the forbearance arrangement is considered insignificant in relation to the frequency of payments due, the delay is considered insignificant and the restructuring is not a concession. (89429)

54. (c) In a troubled debt restructuring, the debtor recognizes a gain on the retirement of debt, equal to the difference between the carrying amount of the obligation settled and the fair value of the assets and/or equity interest transferred to the creditor. Also, to the extent assets are transferred pursuant to the restructuring, the debtor will recognize an ordinary gain or loss equal to the difference between the fair value and the carrying amount of the assets transferred. The net gain reported in income from continuing operations. [$60,000 + ($10,000) = $50,000]

Carrying amount of liability liquidated	$ 150,000
Fair value of real estate transferred	(90,000)
Ordinary gain on retirement of debt	$ 60,000
Carrying amount of real estate transferred	$ 100,000
Fair value of real estate transferred	(90,000)
Ordinary loss on transfer of asset	$ (10,000)

(4427)

55. (b) In a troubled debt restructuring, the creditor, Mene, records the assets and/or equity securities (real estate transferred), at fair value, $90,000. (4428)

56. (a) Accounting for debtors when the restructuring is a modification of terms is determined by whether the sum of the cash payments under the new terms (not discounted to present value) equal or exceed the amount of the obligation. (6984)

57. (d) Secured creditors are paid first with the proceeds from the sale of specific assets upon which they have liens. Any excess proceeds from such sales are first applied against the liabilities with priority, and then to the unsecured creditors. If the claims of partially secured creditors exceed the proceeds from the sale of the assets pledged with such creditors, such excess constitutes an unsecured claim.

Total cash available		$ 810,000
Payments to fully secured creditors	$260,000	
Payments to partially secured creditors	120,000	
Payments to creditors with priority	70,000	(450,000)
Cash for unsecured nonpriority claims		$ 360,000

(1037)

58. (d) A trustee in a bankruptcy case takes over the assets of the debtor corporation and is accountable for those assets until released by the bankruptcy court. In liquidation (Chapter 7) cases, the trustee often establishes a new set of books for the bankruptcy estate. The assets are recorded at carrying amounts rather than at expected realizable values because of subjectivity in estimating realizable amounts at the time of filing. The trustee records gains and losses and liquidation expenses directly in the *Estate Equity* account. Any unrecorded assets or liabilities that are discovered by the trustee are also entered in the *Estate Equity* account. Therefore, $9,000 [i.e., $1,000 + ($20,000 – $12,000)] should be debited to *Estate Equity* as a result of the discovery of the unrecorded invoice and the sale of the truck. (2642)

PERFORMANCE BY SUBTOPICS

Each category below parallels a subtopic covered in Chapter 7. Record the number and percentage of questions you correctly answered in each subtopic area.

Current Liabilities

Question #	Correct √
1	
2	
3	
4	
5	
6	
# Questions	6
# Correct	______
% Correct	______

Determinable Liabilities

Question #	Correct √
7	
8	
9	
10	
11	
12	
13	
14	
15	
16	
17	
18	
19	
20	
21	
# Questions	15
# Correct	______
% Correct	______

Dependent Liabilities

Question #	Correct √
22	
23	
24	
# Questions	3
# Correct	______
% Correct	______

Contingent Liabilities

Question #	Correct √
25	
26	
27	
28	
29	
30	
# Questions	6
# Correct	______
% Correct	______

Estimated Liabilities

Question #	Correct √
31	
32	
33	
34	
35	
36	
37	
# Questions	7
# Correct	______
% Correct	______

Long-Term Liabilities

Question #	Correct √
38	
39	
40	
41	
42	
43	
44	
45	
46	
47	
48	
49	
50	
# Questions	13
# Correct	______
% Correct	______

Troubled Debt & Bankruptcy

Question #	Correct √
51	
52	
53	
54	
55	
56	
57	
58	
# Questions	8
# Correct	______
% Correct	______

Solution 7-2 SIMULATION ANSWER: Adjustments/Disclosures

Explanations	Amount	Yes/No
1. Based on past experience, it is probable that customers will make claims under unconditional warranty and a reasonable estimate of the costs can be made. Therefore, an accrual must be made for $250,000 (i.e., $12,500,000 × 2%).	$250,000	No
2. General, unspecified business risks, including the practice of self-insurance of catastrophes, are not considered loss contingencies. Therefore, no accrual is required.	None	No
3. Accrual of the liability for postemployment benefits to be provided to former or inactive employees prior to retirement is required. Therefore, the $200,000 of expected costs for benefits for current employees must be accrued in the financial statements. Additional information relating to the postemployment benefit plan, including a description of the plan, must be disclosed in the notes.	$200,000	Yes
4. The lawsuit initiated by Buzz represents a gain contingency. Gain contingencies should be disclosed but not recognized as income. In addition, care should be taken to avoid misleading implications as to the likelihood of realization. Gain contingencies should be disclosed, but not recognized as income. NOTE: In the AICPA Unofficial Answers to Exam Questions, the answer is listed as N. The Editors believe this is erroneous, as it contradicts Standards.	None	Yes
5. Where the likelihood of confirmation of a loss is considered probable and the loss can be reasonably estimated, the estimated loss should be accrued by a charge to income. If only a range of possible loss can be estimated, the minimum amount in the range should be accrued. Therefore, accrue the $50,000 minimum loss. The nature of the contingency and exposure to an additional potential $400,000 loss should be disclosed.	$ 50,000	Yes
6. Certain types of loss contingencies must be disclosed regardless of the probability of loss. These exceptions include guarantees of indebtedness of others, banks' standby letters of credit, and guarantees to repurchase receivables. Therefore, the guarantee of the president's loan must be disclosed in the financial statements.	None	Yes
7. Where the likelihood of loss is considered remote (i.e., the suit is believed to be without merit by attorneys), no accrual is required.	None	No
8. An estimated loss on the sale of the component is indication of an impairment, and this devaluation is included in discontinued operations in the fiscal period incurred. A gain is not recognized until the sale period. Buzz will report a $400,000 loss from discontinued operations in its December 31, year 2 financial statements. In addition, the financial statement notes must disclose the following information: (1) the circumstances leading to the disposal; (2) any impairment loss; (3) if applicable, revenue amounts and pretax profit or loss; (4) if applicable, the segment in which the long-lived asset (or disposal group) is reported.	$400,000	Yes
9. Subsequent events that arose after the balance sheet date do not result in adjustments to the account balances of the previous period and do not normally require disclosure in the financial statements.	None	No
10. Subsequent events that arose after the balance sheet date do not result in adjustments to the account balances of the previous period. Some events, including the purchase of a business, the loss of inventories or plant assets due to a casualty, and the sale of a bond or capital stock issue, must be disclosed in order to prevent the financial statements from being misleading. Thus, the bond issue must be disclosed in the financial statements.	None	Yes

11. Subsequent events that arose after the balance sheet date do not result in adjustments to the account balances of the previous period. Some events, including the purchase of a business, the loss of inventories or plant assets due to a casualty, and the sale of a bond or capital stock issue, must be disclosed in order to prevent the financial statements from being misleading. Thus, the loss must be disclosed in the financial statements.	None	Yes
12. Where the likelihood of confirmation of a loss is considered probable and the loss can be reasonably estimated, the estimated loss should be accrued by a charge to income. Since the lawyers believe it is likely (i.e., probable) that the IRS will agree to a $150,000 settlement, an estimated loss of $150,000 should be accrued in the December 31, year 2 financial statements. The nature of the contingency should be disclosed.	$150,000	Yes

---

Solution 7-3 SIMULATION ANSWER: Interest Expense & Long-Term Liabilities

1.

Calculation of Interest Expense

Note payable—bank	
1/1 to 9/30 ($108,000 × 11% × 9/12)	$ 8,910
10/1 to 12/31 ($102,000 × 11% × 3/12)	2,805
	$ 11,715
Capital lease obligation 1/1 to 12/31 ($60,600 × 12%)	7,272
Bonds payable 7/1 to 12/31 ($545,523 × 10% × 6/12)	27,276
Total interest expense	$ 46,263

2.

Long-Term Liabilities Section of Balance Sheet

Long-term liabilities:		
Note payable–bank (17 payments × $6,000)	$ 102,000	
Less current portion (Given in the scenario)	(6,000)	
		$ 96,000
Capital lease obligation (Given in the scenario)	$ 60,600	
Less current portion [$8,000 – ($60,600 × .12)]	(728)	
		59,872
9% bonds payable due June 30, year 23, less unamortized discount (see explanation next page)		545,799*
Deferred income tax liability [($25,000 + $30,000 + $35,000) × .30]		27,000**
Total long-term liabilities		$728,671

* Face amount of bonds less proceeds received equals beginning unamortized discount ($600,000 – $545,523 = $54,477). The bonds payable amount less actual interest amount equals amount of discount amortized ($27,276 – $27,000 = $276). Then $54,477 – $276 = $54,201 of unamortized discount.

** The entire deferred tax liability is classified as noncurrent as the underlying asset generating the temporary difference is also noncurrent. [($25,000 + $30,000 + $35,0000) × .30] Note that for year 2, there would have been a noncurrent deferred tax asset of $5,000 ($20,000 × 25%) in addition to the noncurrent deferred tax liability of $27,000.

Solution 7-4 SIMULATION ANSWER: Reporting Commitments/Contingencies

Explanations	Choice
1. Two conditions must be met for a loss contingency to be accrued as a charge to income as of the date of the financial statements. It must be probable that as of the date of the financial statements an asset has been impaired or a liability incurred, and the amount of the loss must be reasonably estimated. In this case the loss would not be accrued as the possibility of loss has been judged remote by Rocko's lawyers. If one or both of the conditions for loss accrual are not met and the loss contingency is classified as probable or reasonably possible, financial statement disclosure is required. In this case, the loss contingency is remote.	N
2. Two conditions must be met for a loss contingency to be accrued as a charge to income as of the date of the financial statements. It must be probable that as of the date of the financial statements an asset has been impaired or a liability incurred, and the amount of the loss must be reasonably estimated. In this case, an asset has not been impaired, nor a liability incurred, so no accrual is required. If one or both of the conditions for loss accrual are not met and the loss contingency is classified as probable or reasonably possible, financial statement disclosure is required, therefore disclosure is required in this case.	D
3. Because the damages were awarded prior to the balance sheet date and were received prior to issuance of the financial statements, the award should be both accrued and disclosed in the financial statements.	B
4. Because the outstanding purchase orders occurred in the ordinary course of business and the raw materials have not yet been received, the purchase is not required to be accrued. Because the price difference is only a market price difference occurring in the ordinary course of business, disclosure it not required.	N
5. Events that did not exist at the balance sheet date but arose subsequent to that date should not result in adjustment to the financial statements. Some of these events, however, may require disclosure in order to prevent the financial statements from being misleading. Examples of events that require disclosure include sale of bonds or capital stock and the redemption of outstanding bonds.	D
6. Two conditions must be met for a loss contingency to be accrued as a charge to income as of the date of the financial statements. It must be probable that as of the date of the financial statements an asset has been impaired or a liability incurred, and the amount of the loss must be reasonably estimated. In this case, a liability has been incurred and the amount is reasonably estimated, so accrual is required. If the loss contingency is classified as probable or reasonably possible, financial statement disclosure is required.	B

Solution 7-5 SIMULATION ANSWER: Research

FASB Accounting Standards Codification

FASB ASC: 470 - 10 - 45 - 12B

45-12B Refinancing a short-term obligation on a long-term basis means either replacing it with a long-term obligation with equity securities or renewing, extending, or replacing it with short-term obligations for an uninterrupted period extending beyond one year (or the operating cycle, if applicable) from the date of an entity's balance sheet.

Select Hot•Spot™ Video Description

CPA 2090 Bonds & Other Liabilities

This lecture examines bonds from both the issuer's and investor's perspectives. Learn both the straight-line and effective interest methods of amortizing bond discounts and premiums. Term, serial, convertible, secured, and debenture bonds are discussed. Coverage also includes troubled debt restructuring, contingencies, subsequent events, warranty and coupon liabilities, and compensated absences. Robert Monette reinforces these concepts with 29 multiple-choice questions and a simulation. Approximate duration of the video is 3 hours. This does not include the time a candidate spends answering questions and taking notes.

CHAPTER 8

LEASES

CHAPTER 8

LEASES

I. Leases Overview

A. Introduction

A lease is an agreement conveying the right to use property, plant, or equipment (land and/or depreciable assets) usually for a stated period of time. A lease that transfers substantially all of the benefits and risks incidental to the ownership of property should be accounted for as an acquisition of an asset and the incurrence of a liability by the lessee, and as a sale or financing agreement by the lessor. All other leases should be accounted for as operating leases.

1. **Lessor/Lessee** The lessor leases the asset to the lessee. Lease payments are made by the lessee to the lessor.

2. **Lease Term** The fixed noncancelable term of the lease plus the following.

   a. All periods, if any, covered by bargain renewal options.

   b. All periods for which failure to renew the lease imposes a penalty on the lessee in an amount such as to make renewal reasonably assured.

   c. All periods preceding the date that a bargain purchase option becomes exercisable.

   d. All periods representing renewals or extensions of the lease term at the lessor's option.

   In no case, however, should the lease term extend beyond the date at which a bargain purchase option becomes exercisable.

B. Definitions

1. **Minimum Lease Payments** The definition of minimum lease payments (MLP) parallels that of the lease term, above. If the lease contains a bargain purchase option, only the minimum rental payments over the lease term up to the date at which the bargain purchase option becomes exercisable and the payment called for by the bargain purchase option are included in the MLP. Otherwise, MLP includes the following.

   a. Minimum rental payments called for by the lease over the lease term.

   b. Any guarantee by the lessee, or a third party related to the lessee, of a residual value of the leased asset at the end of the lease.

   c. Any penalty that the lessee may be required to pay upon failure to renew the lease. However, if the penalty is such that renewal has been assumed and the lease term accordingly extended, the amount of the penalty should not be included in the MLP.

   d. For lessors, in addition to the above amounts, minimum lease payments also include any guarantee of the residual value by a third party unrelated to either the lessor or lessee if the third party is financially capable of discharging its obligations.

   e. Minimum lease payments do not include executory costs paid by either the lessor or the lessee, nor do they include any contingent rentals.

2. **Executory Costs** Executory costs are expenditures such as insurance, maintenance and taxes required to be paid on the asset during the asset's economic life. They are considered period costs which should be expensed when paid or accrued by either the lessor or lessee.

   a. If the lessor retains the responsibility to pay, the portion of the minimum lease payments representing these executory costs should be removed from the lessee's minimum lease payments (if the portion is unknown, it should be estimated).

   b. If the lessee retains the responsibility to pay, executory costs are not included in minimum lease payments. Rather they are charged to an appropriate expense account (e.g., insurance expense, property taxes, repairs and maintenance, etc.).

3. **Incremental Borrowing Rate** The incremental borrowing rate is the discount rate the lessee would pay in the lending market to purchase the asset leased. The lessee uses the incremental borrowing rate in computing the present value of the minimum lease payments, unless both of the following requirements are satisfied.

   a. The lessee knows or can practicably discover the lessor's implicit interest rate used in the lease.

   b. That implicit interest rate is lower than the lessee's incremental borrowing rate.

4. **Lessor's Implicit Interest Rate** If both requirements above are satisfied, the lessor's interest rate implicit in the lease is used in computing the present value of the minimum lease payments for asset and liability recording, instead of the lessee's incremental borrowing rate. The lessor's interest rate implicit in the lease is the interest rate that will discount the minimum lease payments plus unguaranteed residual value to the fair value of the leased property at the lease inception date.

5. **Residual Value** The residual value is the estimated fair value of the leased property at the end of the lease term.

   a. The guaranteed residual value is a specifically determinable amount payable at termination of the lease. The payment may constitute a purchase payment for the leased property, or it may be made to satisfy a deficiency below a "stated amount" which the lessee guarantees the lessor on realization of the property. The "stated amount" would be the guaranteed residual value. The guaranteed residual value is included in the minimum lease payments for both lessors and lessees.

   b. The unguaranteed residual value is not guaranteed by the lessee or by a third party related to the lessee. The unguaranteed residual value is not included in MLP by either lessor or lessee. The lessor's gross investment in the lease is equal to the sum of MLP plus the unguaranteed residual value of the leased property.

6. **Termination** Previous guidance called for recognizing lease termination costs in the period of commitment to an exit or disposal plan. Lease termination costs related with exit or disposal activities is recognized in periods when obligations to others exist, not necessarily in the period of commitment to a plan.

II. Classification Criteria

A. Lessee

1. **Capital Lease** Classify and account for the lease as a capital lease if at the date of the lease agreement (date of lease inception), the lease satisfies at least one of the following four criteria. However, if the beginning of the lease term falls within the last 25% of the total estimated economic life of the leased asset, then criteria c. and d. listed below are inapplicable. The lease then should be classified as a capital lease only if it meets a. or b.

Exhibit 1 ▸ Lessee Criteria

Lessee must meet just **ONE** condition to capitalize.

TO	Transfers Ownership at end of lease (upon final payment or required buyout)
BOP	Bargain Purchase Option
75	75% of asset economic life is committed in lease term
90	90% of leased property FMV $\leq$ PV of future lease payments

   a. The lease transfers ownership of the property to the lessee by the end of the lease.

   b. The lease contains a bargain purchase option.

   c. The lease term is equal to 75% or more of the estimated economic life of the leased property (as determined at the inception of the lease).

   d. The present value of the minimum lease payments (excluding executory costs) equals or exceeds 90% of the fair value of the leased property at lease inception.

2. **Operating Lease** If a lease does not satisfy at least one of the four criteria for a capital lease, then the lessee must classify and account for the lease as an operating lease.

B. Lessor

1. **Types of Leases** Lessor classifies leases meeting all the following criteria as either sales-type or direct financing type leases.

   a. The lease is a capital lease for the lessee. It is important to note that the lessor always uses the interest rate implicit in the lease in calculating the present value of the minimum lease payments.

   b. Collectibility of the minimum lease payments is reasonably predictable.

   c. No important uncertainties exist regarding the unreimbursable costs yet to be incurred by the lessor under the lease.

2. **Sales-Type Leases** Sales-type leases are, in substance, sales of assets on an installment basis.

   a. Sales-type leases contain a manufacturer's or dealer's profit (or loss). This profit (or loss) is the difference between the cost or carrying amount of the asset and its fair value. A second type of profit, interest income, is also recognized in a sales-type lease.

   b. Manufacturer's or dealer's profit should be recognized in full at the lease's inception while interest income should be recognized over the period of the lease using the interest method.

3. **Direct Financing** Direct financing leases differ from sales-type leases in that only interest income arises. Thus, no manufacturer's or dealer's profit results from a direct financing lease.

    a. Unearned interest income represents the difference between the lessor's gross investment in the lease (lessor's minimum lease payments plus unguaranteed residual value) and the cost or carrying amount of the leased asset (plus initial direct costs). The unearned interest income should also be recognized over the period of the lease by the interest method.

    b. The lessor's net investment in the capital lease is equal to the present value of the gross investment in the lease (i.e., the gross investment less the unearned interest income).

4. **Operating Leases** Leases that do not meet all the criteria for sales-type or direct financing leases are operating leases.

Exhibit 2 ▸ Capital Lease Criteria

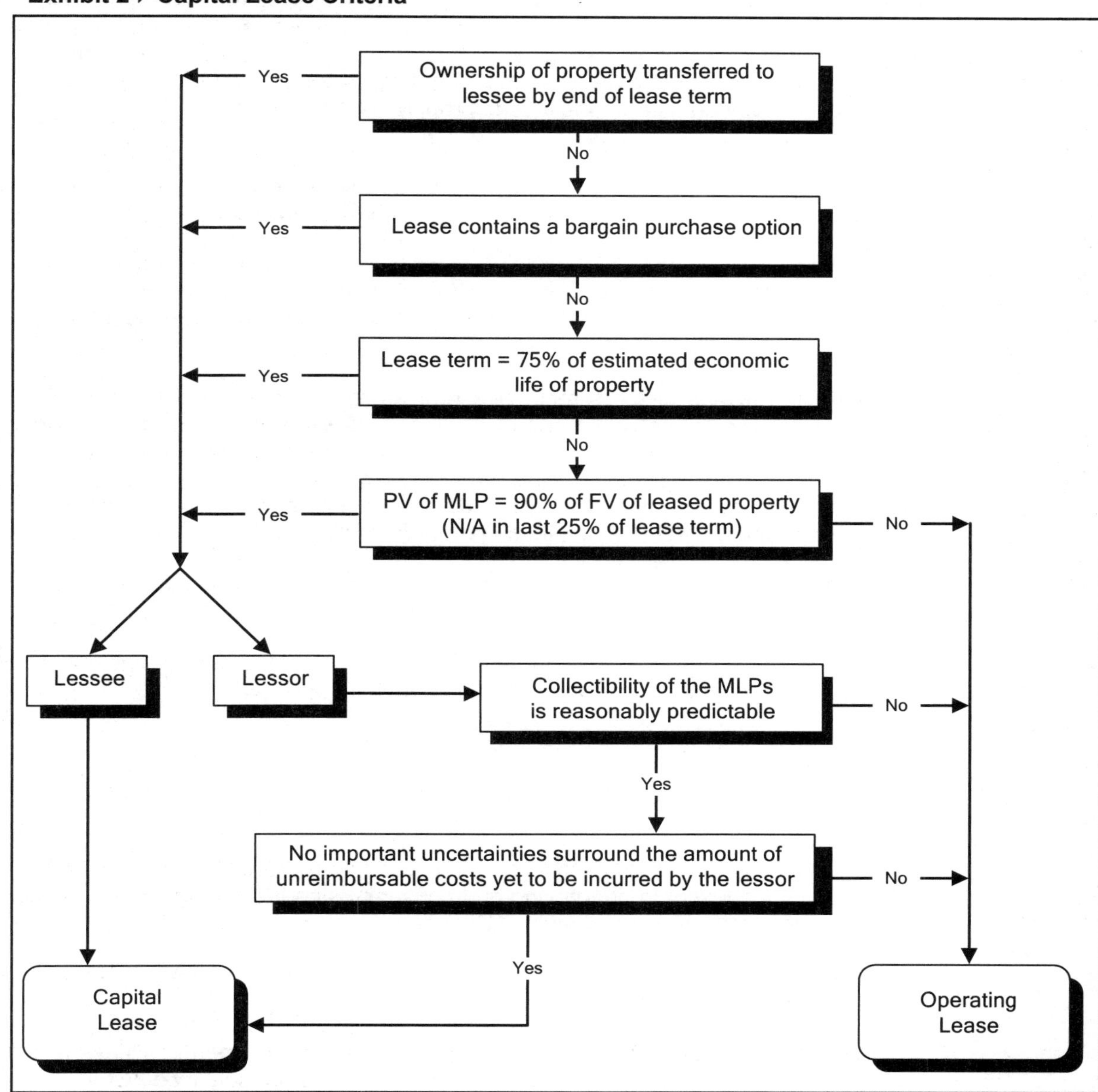

III. Operating Leases

A. Definition

All leases that do not meet the four criteria for capital leases are operating leases. Operating leases do not involve a transfer of the risks and benefits of ownership (as do capital leases). The leased property is not transferred from the books of the lessor to the lessee; it is included with or near the property, plant, and equipment in the balance sheet of the lessor.

Termination costs should be recognized for an operating lease when an entity terminates the lease in accordance with the lease terms. A liability for costs that will continue to be incurred under the operating lease for its remaining term without economic benefit to the entity shall be measured at its fair value at the date the entity ceases using the right conveyed by the lease contract.

B. Lessee

Under operating leases, lessees recognize rent as expense over the lease term as it becomes payable according to the provisions of the lease. If the rentals vary from a straight-line basis (e.g., the lessee pays a "lease bonus" at the inception of the lease or the lease agreement specifies scheduled rent increases over the lease term), the expense should continue to be recognized on a straight-line basis unless another systematic and rational basis is more representative of the time pattern in which the benefit from the leased property is diminished.

1. **Rental Expense** The rental expense recognized by the lessee for an operating lease is comprised of (a) the periodic rental payments as they become payable if equal in amount (or on a straight-line basis if not equal in amount) and (b) the amortization of any lease bonus.

2. **Disclosures** For operating leases with an initial or remaining noncancelable term in excess of 1 year the lessee must disclose the future minimum rental payments required, in aggregate, for each of the next 5 years and a general description of leasing arrangements.

C. Lessor

Under operating leases, lessors recognize rent as revenue over the lease term as it becomes receivable according to the provisions of the lease. If the rentals vary from a straight-line basis (e.g., the lessee pays a "lease bonus" at the inception of the lease or the lease agreement specifies scheduled rent increases over the lease term), the revenue should continue to be recognized on a straight-line basis unless another systematic and rational basis is more representative of the time pattern in which the benefit from the leased property is diminished.

1. **Rental Income** The net rental income recognized by the lessor for an operating lease is comprised of the following:

   a. The periodic rental payments as they become receivable if equal in amount (or on a straight-line basis if not equal in amount).

   b. The amortization of any lease bonus.

   c. Depreciation—The lessor depreciates the leased property using its normal depreciation policy.

   d. The amortization of any initial direct costs (e.g., commissions, legal fees, etc.) incurred by the lessor in negotiating and consummating the operating lease–Initial direct costs are amortized in a straight-line manner.

   e. Executory costs incurred—The lessor recognizes executory costs as expenses when they are incurred.

2. **Advances** Rent received in advance by the lessor for an operating lease is a deferred revenue which should be recognized as revenue in the period specified by the lease.

3. **Impairment** The lessor includes a leased asset subject to an operating lease in testing for impairment of long-lived assets.

4. **Disclosures** The lessor must disclose the cost and carrying amount, if different, of property leased or held for leasing, by major class and total accumulated depreciation; the minimum future rentals on noncancelable leases, in aggregate, for each of the next 5 years; and a general description of leasing arrangement.

Example 1 ▸ Operating Lease

On January 1, year 1, Montalba Company, a lessor of office machines, purchased for $700,000 a new machine, which is expected to have a ten-year life, and will be depreciated at a rate of $70,000 per year. The same day the machine was leased to Norton Company for a four-year period expiring January 1, year 5, at an annual rental of $120,000. Norton also paid $72,000 to Montalba on January 1, year 1, as a lease bonus. Montalba paid $16,000 of commissions associated with negotiating the lease in January of year 1. During year 1, Montalba incurred insurance and other related costs of $18,000 under the lease. There is no provision for the renewal of the lease or purchase of the machine by Norton at the expiration of the lease term.

Required:

a. Compute Norton Company's rental expense for the year ended December 31, year 1.

b. Compute Montalba Company's operating profit for this leased asset for the year ended December 31, year 1.

Solution: Both Norton and Montalba account for the lease as an operating lease because it fails to meet capital lease criteria.

a.	Equal annual rental payment		$120,000
	Amortization of lease bonus ($72,000 / 4 years)		18,000
	Rental expense, year 1		$138,000
b.	Equal annual rental payment		$120,000
	Amortization of lease bonus ($72,000 / 4 years)		18,000
	Rental revenue		138,000
	Less: Depreciation	$70,000	
	Amortization of initial direct costs ($16,000 / 4 years)	4,000	
	Executory costs	18,000	(92,000)
	Operating profit on leased asset, year 1		$ 46,000

IV. Lessee's Capital Leases

A. Initial Recording

Lessee must record a capital lease in an amount equal to (a) the fair value of the leased property at the inception date or, (b) the present value of the minimum lease payments (using the present value discount rate), whichever is lower. The same amount is recorded on the lessee's books both as an asset, "Leased Asset Under Capital Leases" and as a liability, "Obligations Under Capital Leases."

1. **Interest Factors** Where the annual rental is payable at the beginning of each lease year, the factor for the present value of annuity in advance (also referred to as an annuity due) is to be used to determine the present value of the minimum lease payments. If, however, the annual rental is payable at the end of each lease year, the factor for the present value of ordinary annuity (also referred to as an annuity in arrears) should be used.

2. **Bargain Purchase Options** The payment called for by a bargain purchase option should be capitalized at its present value. A purchase option is considered to be a bargain purchase option when the lessee can purchase the leased property for significantly less than the expected fair value of the property at the date the option becomes exercisable.

3. **Guarantee of Residual Value** Any guarantee of the residual value of the leased property by the lessee or a third party related to the lessee should be capitalized at its present value. A guarantee of the residual value of the leased property by a third party unrelated to the lessee should not be capitalized.

4. **Balance Sheet Classification** The obligation under capital lease is classified as both current and noncurrent, with the current portion being that amount that will be paid on the principal during the next year.

B. Amortization

1. **Leased Asset** Amortization should be consistent with the lessee's normal depreciation policy for similar owned assets.

   a. If the lease qualifies as a capital lease because it satisfies either the first two lease classification criteria (i.e., the lease agreement transfers ownership of the asset by the end of the lease term or contains a bargain purchase option), the lessee must amortize the leased asset over the remaining estimated economic life of the asset.

   b. If the lease is classified as a capital lease because it satisfies criteria other than the first two lease classification criteria, the lessee will amortize the leased asset over the lease term (rather than the life of the asset).

   c. For capital leases where there is a transfer of ownership (i.e., there is a title transfer or the lease contains a bargain purchase option), the leased asset is amortized to its expected residual value, if any, to the lessee at the end of the lease term.

2. **Lease Liability**

   a. The effective interest method is used to amortize the lease liability.

   b. Each lease payment made by the lessee is allocated between interest expense and the reduction of the lease obligation; it is not recorded as rent expense. Under this method, each successive uniform payment is comprised of a decreasing amount of interest expense and an increasing amount of reduction of the lease obligation.

   c. Although the asset and liability balances at the inception of the lease are the same present value amount (or fair value if lower at lease inception), each balance will be amortized at different rates during the asset life or lease term.

Example 2 ▸ Lessee's Accounting for Capital Leases

Lessor and Lessee enter into a lease for a computer on January 1, year 1. The lease duration is 3 years, noncancelable, with 2 renewal options of 1 year each. The lease provides for a termination penalty assuring renewal of the lease for 2 years after the 3-year regular term ends. The leased equipment consists of a computer which has a cost and fair value to lessor at lease inception of $100,000. The estimated economic life of the asset is 6 years. The asset has no residual value. The lessee uses the straight-line depreciation method for fixed assets. The lease rental is $27,991/year, which includes executory costs, payable at the beginning of each year. Lessor pays executory costs of $4,800/year, at beginning of each year. The lessee's incremental rate is 10%. The lessor's implicit rate is 8% and is known to the lessee.

Required: Record in lessee's books all entries related to the lease during the first year. Show supporting computations.

Solution: The lease is a capital lease because its term (5 years) exceeds 75% of the computer's estimated economic life (6 years). Additionally, the present value of the minimum lease payments ($100,000) exceeds 90% of the fair value of the computer ($100,000). See Schedule 3, below, for computation of PV of MLP.

Date	Account	Debit	Credit
01/01, year 1	Leased Equipment Under Capital Leases	100,000	
	Obligation Under Capital Leases		100,000
	To record capitalized lease. See Schedule 3.		
	Executory Expenses (detailed)	4,800	
	Obligation Under Capital Leases	23,191	
	Cash		27,991
	To record first year's minimum lease payment and executory costs. See Schedule 2.		
12/31, year 1	Amortization Expense on Leased Equipment	20,000	
	Accumulated Amortization of Leased Equipment Under Capital Leases		20,000
	To record the amortization of the asset based on the straight-line depreciation method over the lease term (no transfer of ownership; no bargain purchase option). Computation: $100,000 / 5 = $20,000. See Schedule 1 for lease term determination.		
12/31, year 1	Interest Expense	6,145	
	Accrued Interest Payable		6,145
	*To record interest expense on lease obligation ($76,809*8%)*		
01/01, year 2	Executory Expenses (detailed)	4,800	
	Accrued Interest Payable	6,145	
	Obligation Under Capital Leases	17,046	
	Cash		27,991
	To record second-year's minimum lease payment and executory costs. See Schedule 4.		

12/31, year 2 The entries to record depreciation and interest expense would be similar to the prior year's. The depreciation amount remains constant; the interest amount is from Schedule 4.

Schedule 1: Lease Term

Noncancelable term	3 years
Additional period for which termination penalty assures renewal	2 years
Total lease term	5 years

Schedule 2: Minimum Lease Payments

Yearly lease payments including yearly executory costs	$ 27,991
Yearly executory costs	(4,800)
Net yearly lease payments	23,191
Lease term (years)	× 5
Total lessee MLP	$115,955

Schedule 3: Present Value of Minimum Lease Payments

Since the lease payments are payable in advance, the present value factor is derived as follows: Choose from Appendix D the appropriate factor for the present value of an ordinary annuity of $1 per period for 4 periods at 8% (3.3121). To this 4-period factor add 1.000 (3.3121 + 1.000 = 4.3121) in order to find the present value of an annuity in advance payable in 5 years at 8%.

Minimum lease payments net of executory costs	$ 23,191
Factor for annuity in advance at 8%	× 4.3121
PV of MLP ($1.91 difference due to rounding)	$100,000

Since the lessor's implicit interest rate was known and was lower than the lessee's incremental borrowing rate of 10%, the lessor's implicit rate of 8% was used to calculate the present value of the asset and the liability on the lessee's books.

Schedule 4: Lease Payments and Interest Accruals (Lessee)

Date	Description	8% Interest expense	Lease payment amount	Interest	Amortization of principal	Balance of lease obligation
01/01, year 1	Initial bal.					$100,000
01/01, year 1	Payment		$23,191		$23,191	76,809
01/01, year 2	Payment		23,191	$6,145	17,046	59,763
01/01, year 3	Payment		23,191	4,781	18,410	41,353
01/01, year 4	Payment		23,191	3,308	19,883	21,470
01/01, year 5	Payment		23,191	1,718	21,470	0*

* All calculations and balances rounded to balance.

Schedule 5: Partial Balance Sheet, December 31, Year 1 (Lessee)

Assets		**Liabilities**	
Land, buildings, and equipment:		Current liabilities:	
Leased equipment	$100,000	Accrued interest payable	$ 6,145
Less: accumulated amortization	20,000	Obligations under capital lease, current portion	17,046
Net Value	$ 80,000	Noncurrent liabilities:	
		Obligations under capital leases, exclusive of current portion	$59,763

C. Impairment/Termination Loss Recognition

Assets subject to capital leases should be reviewed by the lessee whenever circumstances indicate that the carrying amount of the asset may not be recoverable. The review consists of estimating the future net cash flows; and, without discounting or considering interest charges, if the future cash flows is less than the carrying amount of the asset, impairment loss is recognized. Impairment loss recognized is the amount by which the carrying amount of the asset exceeds the fair value of the asset.

A termination of a capital lease before the expiration of the lease term shall be accounted for by the lessee by removing the asset and obligation, with gain or loss recognized for the difference.

D. **Disclosures**
For capital leases, the lessee is required to disclose:

1. **Gross Assets** The gross amount of assets recorded under capital leases as of the date of each balance sheet presented by major classes according to nature or function.

2. **P.V.M.L.P** The present value of future minimum lease payments as of the date of the latest balance sheet presented, in the aggregate and for each of the five succeeding fiscal years.

V. Lessor's Capital Leases

A. **Sales-Type Leases**
The lessor accounts for a sales-type lease by recording the following.

1. **Gross Investment in Lease** The lessor's gross investment in the lease is equal to the sum of the following:

   a. Guaranteed residual value is included in the minimum lease payments of both parties. Residual value or rental payments beyond the lease, guaranteed by a financially capable third party unrelated to either lessee or lessor, are also included in the lessor's minimum lease payments.

   b. Unguaranteed residual value accruing to lessor is the estimated fair value of the leased property at the end of the lease term, exclusive of any portion guaranteed by the lessee or a third party unrelated to the lessor.

2. **Net Investment in Lease** Present value of lessor's gross investment in the lease. In equation form: *Net investment in lease = PV of (MLP + Unguaranteed residual value).*

3. **Unearned Interest Income** Difference between the gross investment in the lease and the present value of its two components (i.e., the MLP and the unguaranteed residual value). Unearned interest income is reported as a contra-asset to gross investment in the lease. It is amortized as interest income by the "interest method" over the lease term.

4. **Sales Price in Lease** Equal to the present value of the lessor's minimum lease payments.

   a. Present value computed using the lessor's implicit interest rate.

   b. Unguaranteed residual value is not included in the lessor's minimum lease payments.

   c. Since the lessor's implicit interest rate is used, the present value of the lessor's minimum lease payments will equal the fair value of the leased asset less the present value of any unguaranteed residual value accruing to the lessor.

5. **Cost of Sales** Book value or carrying amount of asset leased out reduced by the present value of the unguaranteed residual value accruing to the lessor. In equation form: *Cost of sales = Book value – PV of unguaranteed residual value*

6. **Initial Direct Costs** Costs incurred by the lessor that are directly associated with negotiating and consummating completed leasing transactions. Examples include commissions, legal fees, cost of preparing documents and the applicable portion of the compensation of employees directly involved with completed leasing transactions. It does not include executory costs, administrative expenses or expenses of negotiating leases that are not consummated.

7. **Manufacturer's or Dealer's Profit** Equal to the present value of the minimum lease payments reduced by the cost of sales and by the initial direct costs. In equation form: *Manufacturer's or dealer's profit = PV of MLP – (Cost of sales + Initial direct costs)*

8. **Disclosures** The lessor must disclose the net investment components, including future MLP, unguaranteed residual value, unearned income, and the future MLP to be received in each of the succeeding 5 years.

Example 3 ▶ Sales-Type Lease

Lessor and lessee sign a lease on January 1, year 1 containing the following terms:

- Lease duration: 5 years beginning January 1, year 1.
- Leased asset's estimated economic life: 6 years
- Estimated residual value: $14,000, unguaranteed.
- Lease payments: $50,000/year, payable at year-end.
- Leased asset's manufacturing cost: $150,000
- Lease closing costs: $2,000 (initial direct costs)
- Lease provisions: Lease does not contain a bargain renewal or a bargain purchase option.
- Implicit lease interest rate: 10%

Lessor has determined that the collectibility of lease payments is reasonably predictable and there are no important uncertainties regarding costs yet to be incurred by the lessor.

Required:

a. Is this an operating, sales-type, or direct financing lease? Support your answer.

b. Provide lessor's journal entries during the first year of the lease.

c. Provide lessor's journal entry at the end of the lease.

Solution:

a. Lease Classification—The lease satisfies the tests for classification as a sales-type lease.

Test 1: The lease term exceeds 75% of the estimated economic life of the leased property. Furthermore, the lease does not begin during the last 25% of the asset's total economic life. (5-year lease / 6-year economic life = 83%)

Test 2: Collectibility of lease rentals is reasonably assured, and there are no important uncertainties regarding lessor costs yet to be incurred.

Test 3: Sales-Type Test—The present value of the minimum lease payments (as determined in Schedule 1, below) exceeds the cost of the asset to the lessor, less the present value of the unguaranteed residual value accruing to the lessor, resulting in a manufacturer's or dealer's profit.

b. Journal entries to record lease during first year

01/01, year 1	Gross Investment in Lease (Schedule 1)	264,000	
	Cost of Goods Leased (Schedule 2)	141,307	
	Selling Expenses (Schedule 2)	2,000	
	Sales Revenue (Schedule 2)		189,540
	Equipment		150,000
	Unearned Interest Income (Schedule 1)		65,767
	Cash		2,000
	To record sale of property under lease to lessee.		
12/31, year 1	Cash	50,000	
	Gross Investment in Lease		50,000
	Unearned Interest Income	19,823	
	Interest Income (Schedule 3)		19,823
	To record first year's lease payment and interest income earned.		

c. Journal entry at end of the lease

12/31, year 5	Equipment	14,000	
	Gross Investment in Lease		14,000
	To record receipt of the leased asset by lessor at the end of lease term and removal of lease receivable from books.		

Schedule 1: Lessor's Gross Investment in the Lease, PV, and Unearned Interest Income

Annual lease payment		$ 50,000
Lease term (years)		× 5
Summation of MLP		250,000
Add: Unguaranteed residual value		14,000
Gross investment in lease		$ 264,000
PV of MLP, $50,000 × PVA (n=5, i=10%); $50,000 × 3.7908	$189,540	
PV of unguaranteed residual value, $14,000 × PV (n=5, i=10%); $14,000 × 0.6209	8,693	
PV of investment in lease		(198,233)
Unearned interest income		$ 65,767

Schedule 2: Lessor's Cost of Sales and Manufacturer's or Dealer's Profit

Sales price (i.e., PV of MLP)		$ 189,540
Manufacturing cost of asset	$150,000	
Less: PV of unguaranteed residual accruing to lessor	(8,693)	
Cost of goods leased		(141,307)
Gross margin		48,233*
Less: Initial direct costs		(2,000)
Manufacturer's or dealer's profit		$ 46,233*

* Not required for this problem, shown for illustrative purposes.

Schedule 3: Lease Payments and Interest Accruals

Date	Lease payment	Interest income on net investment in lease (10%)	Reduction of investment in lease	Net investment in lease
01/01, year 1				$198,233
12/31, year 1	$50,000	$19,823	$30,177	168,056
12/31, year 2	50,000	16,806	33,194	134,862
12/31, year 3	50,000	13,486	36,514	98,348
12/31, year 4	50,000	9,835	40,165	58,183
12/31, year 5	50,000	5,818	44,182	14,000*

* This balance remaining in the net investment account represents the estimated residual value of the leased asset at the end of the term ($1 difference due to rounding).

B. Direct Financing Leases

A direct financing lease is a lease that meets the same criteria as a sales-type lease except it does not give rise to a manufacturer's or dealer's profit (i.e., the cost or carrying amount of the asset is equal to its fair value). The only income that arises from this type of lease is interest income.

1. **Gross Investment in Lease** The sum of MLP (net of lessor-paid executory costs) and unguaranteed residual value should be recorded as gross investment in the lease.

2. **Unearned Income** The difference between gross investment in the lease and cost or carrying amount of the leased property should be recorded as unearned income.

3. **Initial Direct Costs** Initial direct costs should be added to the net investment in a direct financing lease and amortized over the life of the lease. It is not acceptable to recognize a portion of the unearned income at inception of the lease to offset initial direct costs.

4. **Net Investment in Lease** The net investment in the lease is the gross investment in the lease plus any unamortized initial direct costs less the unearned income.

5. **Amortization** The unearned income and any initial direct costs should be amortized over the lease term using the "interest" method.

6. **Disclosures** The lessor must disclose the net investment components, including future MLP, unguaranteed residual value, unearned income, and the future MLP to be received in each of the succeeding 5 years.

Example 4 ▸ Direct Financing Lease

Lessor and lessee sign a lease on January 1, year 1. The lease contains the following terms:

Lease duration: 3 years beginning January 1, year 1
Estimated economic life: 4 years
Unguaranteed residual value: $5,200 at the end of year 3
Annual lease payments: (payable at year-end) $19,277
Leased asset cost (same as FV): $50,000
Lessor implicit rate: 12%
Lessee incremental borrowing rate: 12.5%
Present value of minimum lease payments: $50,000 [($19,277 × 2.4018) + ($5,200 × 0.7117)]

Required:

a. Classify the lease from the viewpoint of the lessor. Support your answer.

b. Provide lessor's entries to account for the lease during the lease term. Show supporting computations.

Solution:

a. One or more of the various criteria for classification as a capital lease are met because the lease term equals 75% of the equipment's estimated economic life and the present value of the minimum lease payments exceeds 90% of the fair value of the leased property at lease inception date. The cost and fair value of the property are identical; therefore, no manufacturer's or dealer's profit exists. The second test for direct financing lease classification is also satisfied because the lease in this example is assumed to be one in which (a) the collectibility of the minimum lease payments is reasonably assured and (b) there are no further unreimbursable costs yet to be incurred by the lessor.

b. Journal entries to record the lease during each of the three years of the lease term.

01/01, year 1	Gross Investment in Lease (Schedule 1)	63,031	
	Equipment		50,000
	Unearned Interest Income		13,031
	To record the lease at inception.		
12/31, year 1	Cash (Schedule 2)	19,277	
	Gross Investment in Lease		19,277
	Unearned Interest Income (Schedule 2)	6,000	
	Interest Income		6,000
	To record receipt of MLP and recognition of interest income.		
12/31, year 2	Cash (Schedule 2)	19,277	
	Gross Investment in Lease		19,277
	Unearned Interest Income (Schedule 2)	4,407	
	Interest Income		4,407
	To record the second year's receipt of MLP and recognition of interest income.		

12/31, year 3	Cash (Schedule 2)	19,277	
	Gross Investment in Lease		19,277
	Unearned Interest Income (Schedule 2)	2,622	
	Interest Income		2,622
	To record the third year's receipt of MLP and recognition of interest income.		
12/31, year 4	Equipment (Schedule 2)	5,200	
	Gross Investment in Lease		5,200
	To record the return of the equipment.		

Schedule 1: Gross Investment in Lease, Book Value, and Unearned Interest Income

Annual lease payment	$ 19,277
Lease term (years)	× 3
Summation of MLP	57,831
Add: Unguaranteed residual value	5,200
Gross investment in lease	63,031
Book value of the equipment (equal to its FV)	(50,000)
Unearned interest income	$ 13,031

Schedule 2: Lease Payments and Interest Income Recognized

Date	Lease Payment	Interest on Net Investment (12%)	Reduction of Net Investment in Lease	Balance of Net Investment
01/01, year 1				$50,000
12/31, year 1	$19,277	$6,000	$13,277	36,723
12/31, year 2	19,277	4,407	14,870	21,853
12/31, year 3	19,277	2,622	16,655	5,200*

* Balance remaining represents the estimated residual value of the leased asset (rounded).

VI. Sale-Leaseback Transactions

A. Definition

Sale-leaseback transactions involve the sale of property to a purchaser-lessor and a lease of the same property back to the seller-lessee. The economic purpose of this type of transaction is that the seller-lessee obtains financing for the use of the property and the purchaser-lessor (usually a financial institution or investor) obtains interest income. Tax considerations may also play an important role in sale-leaseback transactions. Sale-leaseback accounting is required for specified lease amendments with economic effects similar to sale-leaseback transactions.

B. Seller-Lessee

If the lease meets any of the four criteria for classification as a capital lease, the lessee accounts for it as a capital lease. Otherwise, the lease is treated as an operating lease.

1. **Gains and Losses** A gain or loss on the sale of the asset generally will be deferred and amortized.

   a. If a capital lease, the gain or loss will be deferred and amortized in proportion to the amortization of the leased asset. For instance, in a capital lease where there is no ownership transfer and the asset is amortized in a straight-line manner, the deferred gain or loss will be amortized in a straight-line manner over the term of the lease. If ownership transfers, the gain or loss will be amortized over the estimated life of the asset. If the leased asset is amortized under another method, such as DDB or SYD, the same method should be used to amortize the deferred gain or loss. At the time of sale, the deferred gain or loss should be reported as an asset valuation allowance.

   b. If an operating lease, the gain or loss will be deferred and amortized in proportion to the related gross rentals charged to expense during the period. This usually will result in straight-line amortization. At the time of sale, a deferred gain should be reported as a deferred credit.

Example 5 ▸ Sale-Leaseback Capital Lease

On January 1 of the current year, ABC Co. sold equipment to XYZ Inc., having a $100,000 BV and $130,000 FV. Simultaneously, ABC agreed to lease back the equipment for five years, at an annual rental of $34,295, due at year-end (implicit interest rate of 10%). The estimated useful life of the equipment was 5 years, with no residual value. ABC Co. depreciates similar assets on a straight-line basis. ABC Co. would record the first year's entries as follows.

Date	Account	Debit	Credit
01/01	Cash	130,000	
	Equipment (net)		100,000
	Deferred Gain		30,000
	To record the sale of equipment		
	Leased Equipment Under Capital Lease	130,000	
	Obligation Under Capital Lease		130,000
	To record the lease back of equipment		
12/31	Interest Expense (10% × 130,000)	13,000	
	Obligation Under Capital Lease ($34,295 – $13,000)	21,295	
	Cash		34,295
	To record interest expense		
	Amortization Expense on Leased Equipment	26,000	
	Accumulated Amortization ($130,000 / 5)		26,000
	To record amortization expense		
	Deferred Gain ($30,000 / 5)	6,000	
	Amortization Expense on Leased Equipment		6,000
	To record the deferred gain		

2. Deferment Requirement Exceptions

a. If the seller-lessee retains only a minor portion of the remaining use of the property sold, the sale and leaseback are recorded as two separate transactions (i.e., the entire gain or loss is recognized at the point of sale). Professional judgment is required for determining whether the portion of remaining use retained by the seller-lessee is "minor." In general, if the PV of the rental payments under the leaseback agreement is less than 10% of the FV of the property sold, the seller-lessee will be deemed to retain a "minor" portion.

b. If the seller-lessee retains more than a minor portion of the leased asset but less than substantially all of its remaining use and realizes a gain on the sale, the excess gain (if any) is recognized at the date of sale, as follows.

(1) Gain in excess of the PV of MLP should be recognized at the date of sale. The remaining portion of the gain should be deferred and amortized. PV of MLP is determined using the smaller of lessee's incremental borrowing rate or interest rate implicit in the lease.

(2) The excess gain over the recorded amount of the leased asset should be recognized at the date of sale. The remaining portion of the gain should be deferred and amortized.

c. If the fair value of the property at the time of the transaction is less than its undepreciated cost, a loss should be recognized immediately up to the amount of the difference between undepreciated cost and fair value.

C. Purchaser-Lessor

A lessor will account for a sale-leaseback transaction in the same manner as for other leases, that is, as if the property had been purchased from and leased to two separate parties.

Example 6 ▸ Loss on Sale-Leaseback

Equipment with a book value of $15,000 is sold for $10,000 and simultaneously leased back by the seller. The fair market value and the present value of the lease payments is $13,000.

Required: Determine the amount of loss to be recognized at the date of sale and the amount to be deferred.

Solution: Of the loss of $5,000, the $2,000 difference between book value and fair value is a real (economic) loss and should be recognized immediately. The remaining amount of $3,000 is deferred and amortized.

Equipment book value	$ 15,000	
Sales price	(10,000)	
Total loss		$5,000
Equipment book value	15,000	
Fair value	(13,000)	
Loss recognized at date of sale		2,000
Loss deferred		$3,000

Select Hot•Spot™ Video Description

CPA 2080 Leases and Pensions
This program highlights several important lease and pension topics, including: operating leases, capital leases, sales-type leases, direct financing-type leases, sale-leaseback transactions, defined contribution plans, defined benefit plans, projected benefit obligation (PBO), and postretirement benefits. During this video, Bob Monette goes through various examples, problems, and 30 multiple-choice questions covering these topics. Approximate video duration is 3 hours. This does not include the time a candidate spends answering questions and taking notes.

Call our customer representatives toll-free at 1 (800) 874-7877 for more details about videos.

Subject to Change Without Notice

CHAPTER 8—LEASES

Problem 8-1 MULTIPLE-CHOICE QUESTIONS

1. Which of the following is not included in a "lease term"?

   a. All periods, if any, covered by bargain renewal options
   b. All periods preceding the date that a bargain purchase option becomes exercisable
   c. All periods representing renewals or extensions of the lease term at the lessor's option
   d. All periods beyond the date at which a bargain purchase option becomes exercisable

   (Editor, 89628)

2. Executory costs, which are incurred as part of a lease, are which of the following?

   a. Expenditures, such as insurance, maintenance, and taxes, required to be paid on an asset during its economic life
   b. Capitalized by either the lessor or the lessee, depending on which party has the responsibility to pay these costs
   c. Included in the lessee's minimum lease payments
   d. None of the above (Editor, 89630)

3. Lease M does not contain a bargain-purchase option, but the lease term is equal to 90% of the estimated economic life of the leased property. Lease P does not transfer ownership of the property to the lessee at the end of the lease term, but the lease term is equal to 75% of the estimated economic life of the leased property. How should the lessee classify these leases?

	Lease M	Lease P
a.	Capital lease	Operating lease
b.	Capital lease	Capital lease
c.	Operating lease	Capital lease
d.	Operating lease	Operating lease

   (11/92, Theory, #27, 3460)

4. Douglas Co. leased machinery with an economic useful life of six years. For tax purposes, the depreciable life is seven years. The lease is for five years, and Douglas can purchase the machinery at fair market value at the end of the lease. What is the depreciable life of the leased machinery for financial reporting?

   a. Zero
   b. Five years
   c. Six years
   d. Seven years (R/02, far #2, 7057)

5. Bain Co. entered into a 10-year lease agreement for a new piece of equipment worth $500,000. At the end of the lease, Bain will have the option to purchase the equipment. Which of the following would require the lease to be accounted for as a capital lease?

   a. The lease includes an option to purchase stock in the company.
   b. The estimated useful life of the leased asset is 12 years.
   c. The present value of the minimum lease payments is $400,000.
   d. The purchase option at the end of the lease is at fair market value. (R/07, FAR, #25, 8346)

6. Which of the following is not a criterion for the lessor to classify a lease as either a sales-type or direct-financing-type lease?

   a. The lease is a capital lease for the lessee.
   b. Collectibility of the minimum lease payments is reasonably predictable.
   c. The incremental borrowing rate is used to calculate the present value of the minimum lease payments.
   d. No important uncertainties exist regarding the unreimbursable costs yet to be incurred by the lessor under the lease. (Editors, 9144)

7. Able Co. leased equipment to Baker under a noncancellable lease with a transfer of title. Will Able record depreciation expense on the leased asset and interest revenue related to the lease?

	Depreciation expense	Interest revenue
a.	Yes	Yes
b.	Yes	No
c.	No	No
d.	No	Yes

(R/10, FAR, #43, 9343)

8. Which of the following describes the lessee's incremental borrowing rate?
   a. The discount rate the lessee would pay in the lending market to purchase the asset leased
   b. The rate of change for the fair value of the leased property from the start of the lease to the end of the lease term
   c. The interest rate that will discount the minimum lease payments plus unguaranteed residual value to the fair value of the leased property at the lease inception date
   d. None of the above

(Editor, 89631)

9. On January 1, Mollat Co. signed a 7-year lease for equipment having a 10-year economic life. The present value of the monthly lease payments equaled 80% of the equipment's fair value. The lease agreement provides for neither a transfer of title to Mollat, nor a bargain-purchase option. In its current year income statement, Mollat should report
   a. Rent expense equal to the current year lease payments
   b. Rent expense equal to the current year lease payments less interest expense
   c. Lease amortization equal to one-tenth of the equipment's fair value
   d. Lease amortization equal to one-seventh of 80% of the equipment's fair value

(5/92, Theory, #34, amended, 2727)

10. On April 1, year 1, Hall Fitness Center leased its gym to Dunn Fitness Center under a four-year operating lease. Hall normally charges $6,000 per month to lease its gym, but as an incentive, Hall gave Dunn half off the first year's rent, and one quarter off the second year's rent. Dunn's rental payments were as follows:

Year 1	12 × $3,000 = $36,000
Year 2	12 × $4,500 = $54,000
Year 3	12 × $6,000 = $72,000
Year 4	12 × $6,000 = $72,000

Dunn's rent payments were due on the first day of the month, beginning on April 1, year 1. What amount should Dunn report as rent expense in its monthly income statement for April, year 3?
   a. $3,000
   b. $4,500
   c. $4,875
   d. $6,000

(R/11, FAR, #11, 9861)

11. A company enters into a three-year operating lease agreement effective January 1, year 1. The amounts due on the first day of each year are $25,000 in year 1, $30,000 in year 2, and $35,000 in year 3. What amount, if any, is the related liability on the first day of year 2?
   a. $0
   b. $ 5,000
   c. $ 60,000
   d. $ 65,000

(R/11, FAR, #46, 9896)

12. Main, a pharmaceutical company, leased office space from Ash. Main took possession and began to use the building on July 1, 2010. Rent was due the first day of each month. Monthly lease payments escalated over the 5-year period of the lease as follows:

Period	Lease payment
July 1, 2010 - September 30, 2010— rent abatement during move-in, construction	$ 0
October 1, 2010 - June 30, 2011	17,500
July 1, 2011 - June 30, 2012	19,000
July 1, 2012 - June 30, 2013	20,500
July 1, 2013 - June 30, 2014	23,000
July 1, 2014 - June 30, 2015	24,500

What amount would Main show as deferred rent expense at December 31, 2013?

a. $50,658
b. $52,580
c. $68,575
d. $71,550 (R/07, FAR, #42, 8363)

13. As an inducement to enter a lease, Graf Co., a lessor, granted Zep Inc., a lessee, twelve months of free rent under a 5-year operating lease. The lease was effective on January 1, year 1, and provides for monthly rental payments to begin January 1, year 2. Zep made the first rental payment on December 30, year 1. In its year 1 income statement, Graf should report rental revenue in an amount equal to

a. Zero
b. Cash received during year 1
c. One-fourth of the total cash to be received over the life of the lease
d. One-fifth of the total cash to be received over the life of the lease (11/94, FAR, #41, amended, 5303)

14. When should a lessor recognize in income a nonrefundable lease bonus paid by a lessee on signing an operating lease?

a. When received
b. At the inception of the lease
c. At the expiration of the lease
d. Over the life of the lease (11/95, FAR, #34, 6116)

15. On January 1 of the current year, Wren Co. leased a building to Brill under an operating lease for ten years at $50,000 per year, payable the first day of each lease year. Wren paid $15,000 to a real estate broker as a finder's fee. The building is depreciated $12,000 per year. For the year, Wren incurred insurance and property tax expense totaling $9,000. Wren's net rental income for the year should be

a. $27,500
b. $29,000
c. $35,000
d. $36,500 (11/90, PI, #37, amended, 1194)

16. At the inception of a capital lease, the guaranteed residual value should be

a. Included as part of minimum lease payments at present value
b. Included as part of minimum lease payments at future value
c. Included as part of minimum lease payments only to the extent that guaranteed residual value is expected to exceed estimated residual value
d. Excluded from minimum lease payments (11/94, FAR, #20, 5284)

17. On December 30 of the current year, Haber Co. leased a new machine from Gregg Corp. The following data relate to the lease transaction at the inception of the lease:

Lease term	10 years
Annual rental payable at the end of each lease year	$100,000
Estimated life of machine	12 years
Implicit interest rate	10%
Present value of an annuity of $1 in advance for 10 periods at 10%	6.76
Present value of an annuity of $1 in arrears for 10 periods at 10%	6.15
Fair value of the machine	$700,000

The lease has no renewal option, and the possession of the machine reverts to Gregg when the lease terminates. At the inception of the lease, Haber should record a lease liability of

a. $0
b. $615,000
c. $630,000
d. $676,000

(11/89, PI, #27, amended, 1203)

18. Robbins Inc. leased a machine from Ready Leasing Co. The lease qualifies as a capital lease and requires 10 annual payments of $10,000 beginning immediately. The lease specifies an interest rate of 12% and a purchase option of $10,000 at the end of the tenth year, even though the machine's estimated value on that date is $20,000. Robbins' incremental borrowing rate is 14%.

The present value of an annuity due of $1 at:	The present value of $1 at:
12% for 10 years is 6.328	12% for 10 years is .322
14% for 10 years is 5.946	14% for 10 years is .270

What amount should Robbins record as lease liability at the beginning of the lease term?

a. $62,160
b. $64,860
c. $66,500
d. $69,720

(5/92, PI, #34, amended, 2605)

19. On December 29, year 1, Action Corp. signed a 7-year capital lease for an airplane to transport its sports team around the country. The airplane's fair value was $841,500. Action made the first annual lease payment of $153,000 on December 31, year 1. Action's incremental borrowing rate was 12%, and the interest rate implicit in the lease, which was known by Action, was 9%. The following are the rounded present value factors for an annuity due:

9% for 7 years	5.5
12% for 7 years	5.1

What amount should Action report as capital lease liability in its December 31, year 1 balance sheet?

a. $841,500
b. $780,300
c. $688,500
d. $627,300

(11/92, PI, #33, amended, 3266)

20. Koby Co. entered into a capital lease with a vendor for equipment on January 2 for seven years. The equipment has no guaranteed residual value. The lease required Koby to pay $500,000 annually on January 2, beginning with the current year. The present value of an annuity due for seven years was 5.35 at the inception of the lease. What amount should Koby capitalize as leased equipment?

a. $ 500,000
b. $ 825,000
c. $ 2,675,000
d. $ 3,500,000

(R/06, FAR, #16, 8083)

21. Neal Corp. entered into a 9-year capital lease on a warehouse on December 31, year 1. Lease payments of $52,000, which include real estate taxes of $2,000, are due annually, beginning on December 31, year 2, and every December 31 thereafter. Neal does not know the interest rate implicit in the lease; Neal's incremental borrowing rate is 9%. The rounded present value of an ordinary annuity for nine years at 9% is 5.6. What amount should Neal report as capitalized lease liability at December 31, year 1?

    a. $280,000
    b. $291,200
    c. $450,000
    d. $468,000 (11/93, PI, #39, amended, 4408)

22. Steam Co. acquired equipment under a capital lease for six years. Minimum lease payments were $60,000 payable annually at year end. The interest rate was 5% with an annuity factor for six years of 5.0757. The present value of the payments was equal to the fair market value of the equipment. What amount should Steam report as interest expense at the end of the first year of the lease?

    a. $0
    b. $ 3,000
    c. $15,227
    d. $18,000 (R/08, FAR, #19, 8574)

23. Oak Co. leased equipment for its entire 9-year estimated life, agreeing to pay $50,000 at the start of the lease term on December 31, year 1, and $50,000 annually on each December 31 for the next eight years. The present value on December 31, year 1, of the nine lease payments over the lease term, using the rate implicit in the lease which Oak knows to be 10%, was $316,500. The December 31, year 1, present value of the lease payments using Oak's incremental borrowing rate of 12% was $298,500. Oak made a timely second lease payment. What amount should Oak report as capital lease liability in its December 31, year 2 balance sheet?

    a. $350,000
    b. $243,150
    c. $228,320
    d. $0 (11/93, PI, #35, amended, 4404)

24. Cott, Inc. prepared an interest amortization table for a five-year lease payable with a bargain-purchase option of $2,000, exercisable at the end of the lease. At the end of the five years, the balance in the leases payable column of the spreadsheet was zero. Cott asked Grant, CPA, to review the spreadsheet to determine the error. Only one error was made on the spreadsheet. Which of the following statements represents the best explanation for this error?

    a. The beginning present value of the lease did **not** include the present value of the bargain-purchase option.
    b. Cott subtracted the annual interest amount from the lease payable balance instead of adding it.
    c. The present value of the bargain-purchase option was subtracted from the present value of the annual payments.
    d. Cott discounted the annual payments as an ordinary annuity, when the payments actually occurred at the beginning of each period. (R/99, FAR, #19, 6788)

25. On January 1 of the current year, Nori Mining Co. (lessee) entered into a 5-year lease for drilling equipment. Nori accounted for the acquisition as a capital lease for $240,000, which includes a $10,000 bargain-purchase option. At the end of the lease, Nori expects to exercise the bargain-purchase option. Nori estimates that the equipment's fair value will be $20,000 at the end of its 8-year life. Nori regularly uses straight-line depreciation on similar equipment. For the current year ended December 31, what amount should Nori recognize as depreciation expense on the leased asset?

    a. $48,000
    b. $46,000
    c. $30,000
    d. $27,500 (11/93, PI, #55, amended, 4424)

26. On January 1 of the current year, Tell Co. leased equipment from Swill Co. under a nine-year sales-type lease. The equipment had a cost of $400,000, and an estimated useful life of 15 years. Semiannual lease payments of $44,000 are due every January 1 and July 1. The present value of lease payments at 12% was $505,000, which equals the sales price of the equipment. Using the straight-line method, what amount should Tell recognize as depreciation expense on the equipment in the current year?

    a. $26,667
    b. $33,667
    c. $44,444
    d. $56,111 (R/05, FAR, #24, 7768)

27. On January 1, year 1, West Co. entered into a 10-year lease for a manufacturing plant. The annual minimum lease payments are $100,000. In the notes to the December 31, year 2 financial statements, what amounts of subsequent years' lease payments should be disclosed?

	Amount for required period	Aggregate amount for period thereafter
a.	$100,000	$0
b.	$300,000	$500,000
c.	$500,000	$300,000
d.	$500,000	$0

(11/89, PI, #53, amended, 9069)

28. On July 1, year 1, South Co. entered into a 10-year operating lease for a warehouse facility. The annual minimum lease payments are $100,000. In addition to the base rent, South pays a monthly allocation of the building's operating expenses, which amounted to $20,000 for the year ended June 30, year 2. In the notes to South's June 30, year 2 financial statements, what amounts of subsequent years' lease payments should be disclosed?

    a. $100,000 per annum for each of the next five years and $500,000 in the aggregate
    b. $120,000 per annum for each of the next five years and $600,000 in the aggregate
    c. $100,000 per annum for each of the next five years and $900,000 in the aggregate
    d. $120,000 per annum for each of the next five years and $1,080,000 in the aggregate (11/93, PI, #42, amended, 4411)

29. Peg Co. leased equipment from Howe Corp. on July 1 of the current year for an 8-year period. Equal payments under the lease are $600,000 and are due on July 1 of each year. The first payment was made on July 1 of the current year. The rate of interest contemplated by Peg and Howe is 10%. The cash selling price of the equipment is $3,520,000, and the cost of the equipment on Howe's accounting records is $2,800,000. The lease is appropriately recorded as a sales-type lease. What is the amount of profit on the sale and interest revenue that Howe should record for the current year ended December 31?

	Profit on sale	Interest revenue
a.	$720,000	$176,000
b.	$720,000	$146,000
c.	$ 45,000	$176,000
d.	$ 45,000	$146,000

(11/89, PI, #34, amended, 1204)

30. Winn Co. manufactures equipment that is sold or leased. On December 31, year 1, Winn leased equipment to Bart for a 5-year period ending December 31, year 6, at which date ownership of the leased asset will be transferred to Bart. Equal payments under the lease are $22,000 (including $2,000 executory costs) and are due on December 31 of each year. The first payment was made on December 31, year 1. Collectibility of the remaining lease payments is reasonably assured, and Winn has no material cost uncertainties. The normal sales price of the equipment is $77,000, and cost is $60,000. On December 31, year 1, what amount of income should Winn realize from the lease transaction?

    a. $17,000
    b. $22,000
    c. $23,000
    d. $33,000 (11/90, PI, #33, amended, 1193)

31. A lease is recorded as a sales-type lease by the lessor. The difference between the gross investment in the lease and the sum of the present values of the two components of the gross investment (the net receivable) should be
    a. Amortized over the period of the lease as interest revenue using the interest method
    b. Amortized over the period of the lease as interest revenue using the straight-line method
    c. Recognized in full as interest revenue at the lease's inception
    d. Recognized in full as manufacturer's or dealer's profit at the lease's inception (5/87, Theory, #27, 9066)

32. In sales-type leases, the lessor must disclose which of the following?
    a. The cost and carrying amount, if different, of property leased or held for leasing, by major class and total accumulated depreciation
    b. A general description of leasing arrangements
    c. Net investment components
    d. All of the above (Editor, 89636)

33. On August 1 of the current year, Kern Company leased a machine to Day Company for a 6-year period requiring payments of $10,000 at the beginning of each year. The machine cost $48,000, which is the fair value at the lease date, and has an estimated life of eight years with no residual value. Kern's implicit interest rate is 10% and present value factors are as follows:

Present value of an annuity due of $1 at 10% for 6 periods	4.791
Present value of an annuity due of $1 at 10% for 8 periods	5.868

    Kern appropriately recorded the lease as a direct-financing lease. At the inception of the lease, the gross lease receivables account balance should be
    a. $60,000
    b. $58,680
    c. $48,000
    d. $47,910 (5/85, PI, #6, amended, 9067)

34. Glade Co. leases computer equipment to customers under direct-financing leases. The equipment has no residual value at the end of the lease, and the leases do not contain bargain-purchase options. Glade wishes to earn 8% interest on a 5-year lease of equipment with a fair value of $323,400. The present value of an annuity due of $1 at 8% for five years is 4.312. What is the total amount of interest revenue that Glade will earn over the life of the lease?
    a. $ 51,600
    b. $ 75,000
    c. $129,360
    d. $139,450 (11/95, FAR, #29, 6111)

35. What are the components of the lease receivable for a lessor involved in a direct-financing lease?
    a. The minimum lease payments plus any executory costs
    b. The minimum lease payments plus residual value
    c. The minimum lease payments **less** residual value
    d. The minimum lease payments **less** initial direct costs (R/11, FAR, #42, 9892)

36. In a sale-leaseback agreement, what is considered a "minor" portion for retaining use of the property?
    a. Less than 10%
    b. Less than 20%
    c. Less than 30%
    d. Less than 50% (Editors, 9145)

37. Rig Co. sold its factory at a gain, and simultaneously leased it back for 10 years. The factory's remaining economic life is 20 years. The lease was reported as an operating lease. At the time of sale, Rig should report the gain as

a. An extraordinary item, net of income tax
b. An asset valuation allowance
c. An item of other comprehensive income
d. A deferred credit (5/92, Theory, #32, amended, 2725)

38. In a sale-leaseback transaction, a gain resulting from the sale should be deferred at the time of the sale-leaseback and subsequently amortized when

I. The seller-lessee has transferred substantially all the risks of ownership.
II. The seller-lessee retains the right to substantially all of the remaining use of the property.

a. I only
b. II only
c. Both I and II
d. Neither I nor II (11/95, FAR, #11, 6093)

39. The following information pertains to a sale and leaseback of equipment by Mega Co. on December 31 of the current year:

Sales price	$400,000
Carrying amount	$300,000
Monthly lease payment	$ 3,250
Present value of lease payments	$ 36,900
Estimated remaining life	25 years
Lease term	1 year
Implicit rate	12%

What amount of deferred gain on the sale should Mega report at December 31 of the current year?

a. $0
b. $ 36,900
c. $ 63,100
d. $100,000 (5/92, PI, #31, amended, 2600)

40. On June 30 of the current year, Lang Co. sold equipment with an estimated useful life of eleven years and immediately leased it back for ten years. The equipment's carrying amount was $450,000; the sales price was $430,000; and the present value of the lease payments, which is equal to the fair value of the equipment, was $465,000. In its June 30 current year balance sheet, what amount should Lang report as deferred loss?

a. $35,000
b. $20,000
c. $15,000
d. $0 (11/92, PI, #35, amended, 3268)

Problem 8-2 SIMULATION: Operating Lease

On April 21 of the current year, Smiley Inc. purchased a machine for $1,600,000 for the purpose of leasing it. The machine is expected to have an 8-year life, no residual value, and will be depreciated on the straight-line basis. The machine was leased to Gutter Company on May 1 this year for a 5-year period at a monthly rental of $22,000. There is no provision for the renewal of the lease or purchase of the machine by the lessee at the expiration of the lease term. Smiley paid $80,000 of commissions associated with negotiating the lease in April. Enter amount in the appropriate cell. Round all amounts to the nearest dollar.

1. What expense should Gutter Company record as a result of the facts given for the current year ended December 31?

Rental Expense	$

2. What income or loss before income taxes should Smiley record as a result of the facts given for the current year ended December 31?

Rental Income		$
Deduct:		
Depreciation	$	
Amortization	$	
Income From Operating Lease		$

(7/10, amended, 9118)

Problem 8-3 SIMULATION: Capital Lease

Theo Corporation, a lessor of office machines, purchased a new machine for $650,000 on December 31, year 2, which was delivered the same day (by prior arrangement) to Ortiz Company, the lessee. The following information relating to the lease transaction is available:

- The leased asset has an estimated useful life of nine years which coincides with the lease term.
- At the end of the lease term, the machine will revert to Theo, at which time it is expected to have a residual value of $70,000 (none of which is guaranteed by Ortiz).
- Theo's implicit interest rate is 8%, which is known by Ortiz.
- Ortiz's incremental borrowing rate is 10% at December 31, year 2.
- Lease rentals consist of nine equal annual payments, the first of which was paid on December 31, year 2.
- The lease is appropriately accounted for as a direct-financing lease by Theo and as a capital lease by Ortiz. Both lessor and lessee are calendar year corporations and depreciate all fixed assets on the straight-line basis.

Information of present value factors is as follows:

Present value of $1 for nine periods at 8%	0.500249
Present value of $1 for nine periods at 10%	0.424098
Present value of an annuity of $1 in advance for nine periods at 8%	6.746639
Present value of an annuity of $1 in advance for nine periods at 10%	6.334926

1. Compute the annual rental under the lease. Enter amounts, rounded to the nearest dollar, in the shaded areas.

Cost of leased machine	$
Deduct PV of estimated residual value	
Net investment to be recovered	
PV of an annuity of $1 in advance for 9 periods at 8%	
Annual Rental	

2. Compute the amounts of the gross lease rentals receivable and the unearned interest revenue that Theo should disclose at the inception of the lease on December 31, year 2. Show computations in good form, rounded to the nearest dollar.

Gross lease rentals receivable		$
Deduct recovery of net investment in machine on capital lease:		
Cost of machine	$	
Residual value of machine		
Unearned interest revenue		$

3. What expense should Ortiz record for the year ended December 31, year 3? Show supporting computations in good form, rounded to the nearest dollar.

Liability under capital lease	$
Deduct lease payment on December 31, year 2	
Balance December 31, year 2	
Interest rate	
Interest expense year ended December 31, year 3	$
Plus: amortization (i.e. depreciation) expense	
Total expense on lease	$

(8/03, amended, 9022)

Problem 8-4 SIMULATION: Research

Question: How shall assets recorded under capital leases by the lessee be identified?

FASB ASC: ____ - ____ - ____ - ____

(9119)

Solution 8-1 MULTIPLE-CHOICE ANSWERS

Definitions & Classification

1. (d) The lease term includes all periods, if any, covered by bargain renewal options; all periods preceding the date that a bargain purchase option becomes exercisable; and all periods representing renewals or extensions of the lease term at the lessor's option. In no case should the lease term extend beyond the date at which a bargain purchase option becomes exercisable. (89628)

2. (a) As part of a lease agreement, executory costs are expenditures, such as insurance, maintenance, and taxes, required to be paid on an asset during the asset's economic life. Executory costs are considered period costs that should be expensed when paid or accrued by either the lessor or lessee. If the lessor pays executory costs, the portion of the minimum lease payments representing these executory costs should be removed from the lessee's minimum lease payments. (89630)

3. (b) A lease shall be classified as a capital lease by the lessee if at inception the lease meets one of four criteria: (1) the lease transfers ownership of the property to the lessee by the end of the lease term; (2) the lease contains a bargain-purchase option; (3) the lease term is equal to 75% or more of the property's estimated economic life; (4) the present value of the minimum lease payment (excluding executory costs) equals or exceeds 90% of the fair value of the leased property. Since both leases meet the third criterion, both leases are capital leases. (3460)

4. (b) If the lease qualifies as a capital lease because it satisfies either of the first two lease classification criteria (i.e., the lease agreement transfers ownership of the asset by the end of the lease term or contains a bargain purchase option), the lessee must amortize the leased asset over the remaining estimated economic life of the asset. If the lease is classified as a capital lease because it satisfies criteria other than the first two lease classification criteria, the lessee will amortize the leased asset over the lease term (rather than the life of the asset). In this question, the only evidence given that this is a capital lease is that it is being leased for 5 of the 6 years (83.3%) of estimated economic useful life. Therefore, by not meeting either of the first two criteria, it must be depreciated over the term of the lease. (7057)

5. (b) A lessee must classify and account for a lease as a capital lease if at the date of the lease agreement the lease satisfies any one of the following four criteria: (1) the lease transfers ownership of the property to the lessee at the end of the lease; (2) the lease contains a bargain-purchase option; (3) the lease term is

equal to 75% or more of the estimated economic life of the leased property (as determined at inception of the lease); or (4) the present value of the minimum lease payments equals or exceeds 90% of the fair value of the leased property at lease inception. The only criteria met is that the 10-year lease term is more than 75% of the 12-year estimated economic life of the new equipment (12 × 0.75 = 9). (8346)

6. (c) The incremental borrowing rate being used is not a criteria for the lessor to classify a lease as either a sales-type or direct-financing-type lease. The lessor always uses the interest rate implicit in the lease in calculating the present value of the minimum lease payments. (9144)

7. (d) A noncancellable lease with a transfer of title is considered a capital lease. The lessor, Able, does not record depreciation expense. Instead the lessee, Baker, would amortize the equipment using the lessee's normal depreciation policy for similar owned assets. Able would record interest revenue related to the lease whether it was treated as a sales-type lease or direct financing-type lease. (9343)

Operating Leases

8. (a) The lessee incremental borrowing rate is the discount rate the lessee would pay in the lending market to purchase the asset leased. (89631)

9. (a) The lessee has entered into an operating lease because none of the capital lease criteria are met. The lease does not transfer ownership of the equipment to the lessee by the end of the lease term nor does it contain a bargain-purchase option. The lease term is less than 75% (i.e., 7 / 10 = 70%) of the estimated economic life of the equipment and the present value of the minimum lease payments at the beginning of the lease term is *less than* 90% (i.e., 80% < 90%) of the fair value of the equipment. The lessee records neither an asset nor an obligation for an operating lease; instead, the lessee records its lease payments as rent expense. (2727)

10. (c) Accrual accounting recognizes expense in the period incurred, rather than only when the related cash is paid. The lease incentive is allocated ratably over the lease term as a reduction to rent expense.

Monthly rental payment	$ 6,000
Amortization of lease incentive ($36,000 + 18,000) / 48	(1,125)
Rental expense	$ 4,875

(9861)

11. (b) The lease liability on the first day of year 2 would be $5,000. Under operating leases, lessees recognize rent as expense over the lease term as it becomes payable according to the provisions of the lease. If the rentals vary from a straight-line basis (e.g., the lessee pays a "lease bonus" at the inception of the lease or the lease agreement specifies scheduled rent increases over the lease term), the expense should continue to be recognized on a straight-line basis unless another systematic and rational basis is more representative of the time pattern in which the benefit from the leased property is diminished. Annual lease expense of $30,000 (3-year average) would be recognized on this lease.

The year 1 journal entry would be:

Rent expense	30,000	
Cash		25,000
Rent payable		5,000

(9896)

12. (d) All leases that do not meet the four criteria for capital leases are operating leases. For operating leases, even if the rent payments vary from a straight-line basis, the expense is recognized on a straight-line basis (unless another systematic and rational basis is more representative of the time in which the benefit from the leased property lessens). The $1,201,500 total of the lease payments [($17,500 × 9) + ($19,000 × 12) + ($20,500 × 12) + ($23,000 × 12) + ($24,500 × 12)] is recognized on a straight-line basis. Thus, the monthly rent expense is $20,025 ($1,201,500 total divided by 60 months). A total of $841,050 has been incurred ($20,025 × 42 months for July 1, 2010 to December 31, 2013), whereas only $769,500 [($17,500 × 9) + ($19,000 × 12) + ($20,500 × 12) + ($23,000 × 6)] has been paid as of December 31, 2013. The difference of $71,550 is the deferred rent expense. (8363)

13. (d) Revenue from an operating lease is recognized on a straight-line basis, even if the payments vary. Therefore, the total amount of rental revenue from the operating lease is allocated ratably over the 5-year lease term. (5303)

14. (d) If rental payments vary from a straight-line basis (e.g., the lessee pays a "lease bonus" at the lease inception or the lease agreement schedules rent increases over the lease term), the expense for the lessee and the revenue for the lessor are recognized on a straight-line basis unless another systematic and rational basis is more representative of the time pattern in which the benefit derives from the leased property. (6116)

15. (a)

Annual rental payment		$ 50,000
Less: Depreciation	$12,000	
Executory costs (insurance and property taxes)	9,000	
Amortization of initial direct costs ($15,000 / 10 years)	1,500	(22,500)
Net rental income		$ 27,500

(1194)

Lessee's Capital Lease

16. (a) A capital lease refers to a capitalized lease from a lessee's viewpoint. Any guarantee by the lessee of the residual value at the lease term expiration is included in minimum lease payments (MLP). When the lessee agrees to make up any deficiency below a stated amount in the lessor's realization of the residual value, the guarantee to be included in the MLP shall be the stated amount, rather than an estimate of the deficiency. The lessee records the MLP at present value. (5284)

17. (b) The lease is a capital lease because the lease term is equal to 75% or more (10 / 12 = 83.3%) of the estimated useful life of the leased property. Therefore, the lessee, at the lease inception, records the asset and the corresponding lease liability at the lesser of the present value (PV) of the minimum lease payments (MLP) or the fair value of the lease property. Because the annual rental is payable at the *end* of each lease year, the PV factor for an annuity in *arrears* is to be used (i.e., the PV factor for an annuity in advance can only be used when the first annual rental payment is made immediately). The capital lease obligation is recorded at the PV of the MLP ($100,000 × 6.15 = $615,000) because it is less than the fair value of the machine ($700,000). (1203)

18. (c) The lessee records a capital lease as an asset and an obligation at an amount equal to the lesser of the fair value of the leased property (not provided) or the present value (PV) of the minimum lease payments (MLP). The MLP include the minimum rental payments called for by the lease over the lease term and payment called for by the bargain-purchase option (BPO). The purchase option qualifies as a BPO because the lessee is permitted to purchase the leased property for a price which is significantly lower than the expected fair value of the property at the option's exercise date (i.e., $10,000 < $20,000). Since the annual rental payment is payable at the *beginning* of each lease year, the PV factor for an *annuity due* is used. The PV of the MLP is computed using the lessor's implicit interest rate of 12%, since it is both known to the lessee (i.e., it was specified in the lease) and lower than the lessee's incremental borrowing rate.

PV of annual payments ($10,000 × 6.328)	$63,280
PV of bargain-purchase option ($10,000 × 0.322)	3,220
Capital lease liability at beginning of lease term	$66,500

(2605)

19. (c) The lessee records a capital lease as an asset and an obligation at an amount equal to the lesser of the present value (PV) of the minimum lease payments (MLP) or the fair value of the leased property. The PV of MLP is computed using the lessor's implicit rate in the lease of 9%, since it is known to the lessee and lower than the lessee's incremental borrowing rate. Since the annual rental payment is payable at the *beginning* of each lease year, the PV factor for an *annuity due* is used. The capital lease obligation is recorded at the PV of the MLP ($153,000 × 5.5 = $841,500) on 12/29 because this amount does not exceed the fair value of the leased property (i.e., $841,500). The capital lease liability in the 12/31, year 1 balance sheet reflects the first annual rental payment made 12/29 ($841,500 – $153,000 = $688,500). (3266)

20. (c) A lessee must record a capital lease in an amount equal to either the fair value of the leased property at the inception date or the present value of the minimum lease payments using the present value discount rate, whichever is lower. As no fair value of the leased property was provided, the present value discount rate must be used. Koby should capitalize $500,000 × 5.35 = $2,675,000. (8083)

21. (a) At a capital lease inception, the lessee records an asset and corresponding lease liability at the lesser of the fair value of the leased property (not provided in this problem) or the present value of the minimum lease payments (MLP). The lessee's incremental borrowing rate of 9% is used because the lessee does not

know the rate implicit in the lease. The lessee's obligation to pay executory costs (such as insurance, maintenance, and taxes) are excluded from the amount of the annual MLP, thus, the amount of Neal's MLP is $50,000 (i.e., $52,000 – $2,000). Neal's first MLP is not due until 12/31, year 2. Thus, in its 12/31, year 1 balance sheet, Neal should report a capitalized lease liability of $280,000 (i.e., $50,000 × 5.6). (4408)

22. (c) You must first calculate the present value of the minimum lease payments. The present value of the minimum lease payments is the minimum lease payment amount of $60,000 times the annuity factor of 5.0757 equaling $304,542. Because no payment is made until the end of the year, you would take that amount of $304,542 times the interest rate of 5% and get interest expense of $15,227 at the end of the first year of the lease. (8574)

23. (b)

Balance before payment, 12/31, year 1		$316,500	
Less: Minimum lease payment, 12/31, year 1		(50,000)	
Balance after MLP, 12/31, year 1		266,500	
MLP, 12/31, year 2	$ 50,000		
Less: Portion allocable to interest ($266,500 × 10%)	(26,650)		
Less principal reduction from 12/31, year 2 MLP		(23,350)	
Balance after MLP, 12/31, year 2		$243,150	(4404)

24. (a) If the bargain-purchase option (BPO) had been included in the capitalized lease amount, the final balance would have equaled the amount of the BPO. Since the balance was zero, the BPO must have been excluded. Subtracting the annual interest amount from the lease payable balance would have resulted in a negative balance, rather than zero. Subtracting the present value of the BPO from the present value of the annual payments would have caused the beginning lease payable balance to be understated and a negative balance before the lease end. Discounting the annual payments as an ordinary (paid in arrears, rather than in advance) annuity, would have resulted in an understated beginning lease payable balance and a negative balance before the lease end. (6788)

25. (d) If a lease qualifies as a capital lease because it contains a bargain-purchase option (BPO), then the lessee depreciates the leased asset over its estimated economic life. The leased asset is recorded on the books at $240,000 and is depreciated over its estimated economic life of 8 years, since the lessee expects to exercise the BPO. The lessee amortizes the leased asset in the same manner as owned assets. The equipment's salvage value is its estimated fair value at the end of its estimated life. The annual depreciation expense Nori recognizes on the equipment is $27,500 [i.e., ($240,000 – $20,000) / 8]. (4424)

26. (d) If the lease is classified as a capital lease because it satisfies criteria other than the first two lease classification criteria (transfer of ownership or bargain-purchase option), the lessee will amortize the leased asset over the lease term (rather than the life of the asset). Depreciation is calculated on the present value of the minimum lease payments because that amount equaled the fair value of the leased property at inception. ($505,000 / 9 years = $56,111) (7768)

27. (c) West discloses the minimum lease payments (MLP) of $500,000 ($100,000 × 5) pertaining to the next five succeeding fiscal years *and* the $300,000 [$100,000 × (10 – 2 – 5)] of MLP pertaining to the fiscal years after this 5-year period. (9069)

28. (c) For operating leases having initial or remaining noncancelable lease terms in excess of one year, the lessee should disclose future minimum lease payments (MLP) required as of the latest balance sheet date for *each of the five succeeding fiscal years and in the aggregate*. Since South is required to make annual MLP of $100,000 over the remaining noncancelable 9-year (i.e., 10 – 1) lease term, South should disclose $100,000 per annum for each of the next five years and $900,000 (i.e., $100,000 × 9) in the aggregate for the subsequent years' lease payments in the financial statement notes. (4411)

Lessor's Capital Lease

29. (b) The interest revenue is determined by applying the interest rate implicit in the lease to the lessor's net receivable. The excess of the fair value of leased property at the lease inception over its cost or carrying amount is dealer's profit from a sales-type lease and recognized fully at lease inception.

Cash selling price of equipment	$ 3,520,000
Equipment cost	(2,800,000)
Profit on sale	$ 720,000
Gross investment before receipt, 7/1 ($600,000 × 8)	$ 4,800,000
Less: Receipt, 7/1	(600,000)
Gross investment after receipt, 7/1	4,200,000
Less: Unearned interest revenue ($4,800,000 – $3,520,000)	(1,280,000)
Net receivable, 7/1	2,920,000
Times: Implicit interest rate (10% / 2)	× 5%
Interest revenue	$ 146,000

(1204)

30. (a) The lease qualifies as a sales-type lease because (1) the lease transfers ownership of the property to the lessee by the end of the lease term, (2) collectibility of the minimum lease payments is reasonably assured, and (3) no important uncertainties surround the amount of unreimbursable costs yet to be incurred by the lessor under the lease. In year 1, the lessor should recognize a manufacturer's profit of the excess of the normal sales price of the equipment over its cost ($77,000 – $60,000 = $17,000). The lessor does not recognize any interest income from this lease in year 1 because the lease term began on December 31. (1193)

31. (a) In a sales-type lease, the lessor recognizes two types of income: (1) manufacturer's or dealer's profit, and (2) interest income. The profit is the excess of the fair value of the leased property over the cost at the lease inception, and it is recognized fully at lease inception. The difference between the gross investment in the lease and the sum of the present values of the two components of the gross investment is unearned income. The unearned income is amortized over the lease term as interest revenue using the interest method. (9066)

32. (c) In sales-type and direct financing leases, the lessor must disclose the net investment components, including: future MLP; unguaranteed residual value; unearned income; and the future MLP to be received in each of the succeeding 5 years. For operating leases, the lessor must disclose: the cost and carrying amount, if different, of property leased or held for leasing, by major class and total accumulated depreciation; the minimum future rentals on noncancelable leases, in aggregate, for each of the next 5 years; and a general description of leasing arrangements. (89636)

33. (a) The gross lease receivable under a direct-financing lease is the sum of the minimum lease payments (net of executory costs) plus the unguaranteed residual value accruing to the lessor. In this question, there is no unguaranteed residual involved; therefore, the receivable is calculated as 6 annual payments of $10,000, or $60,000. (9067)

34. (a) The unearned interest income is the difference between the lessor's gross investment in the lease and the fair value of the leased asset. The fair value of the equipment is divided by the present value of an annuity due at 8% to get the annual payment. The annual payment times the number of payments is the gross investment. [$323,400 / 4.312 = $75,000; $75,000 × 5 = $375,000; $375,000 – $323,400 = $51,600] (6111)

35. (b) A direct financing lease is a lease that meets the same criteria as a sales-type lease except it does not give rise to a manufacturer's or dealer's profit (i.e., the cost or carrying amount of the asset is equal to its fair value). The only income that arises from this type of lease is interest income. The sum of minimum lease payment (net of lessor-paid executory costs) and unguaranteed residual value should be recorded as gross investment in the lease. (9892)

Sale-Leaseback Transaction

36. (a) Professional judgment is required for determining whether the portion of remaining use of the property retained by the seller-lessee is "minor." In general, if the PV of the rental payments under the leaseback agreement is less than 10% of the FV of the property sold, the seller-lessee will be deemed to retain a "minor" portion. (9145)

37. (d) This situation is a sale-leaseback transaction. Any profit or loss on the sale should be deferred and amortized in proportion to the related gross rental charged to expense over the lease term, if an operating lease (or in proportion to the amortization of the leased asset, if a capital lease). Thus, at the time of sale, the gain on the factory sale is reported as a deferred credit. Gains or losses on sale-leaseback transactions are not reported

as extraordinary items or as items of other comprehensive income. Since the seller-lessee does not report an asset for the leased property under an operating lease, the gain on the sale-leaseback cannot be reported as an asset valuation allowance. The gain on the sale-leaseback is reported as a deferred credit in the liabilities section of the balance sheet. (2725)

38. (b) A sale-leaseback transaction in which the seller-lessee has transferred substantially all the risks of ownership is in substance a sale and should be accounted for on the separate terms of the sale and of the leaseback, unless the rentals called for by the leaseback are unreasonable in relation to current market conditions. A gain on the sale is recognized at the point of sale and is not deferred. A sale-leaseback transaction in which the seller-lessee retains the right to substantially all of the remaining use of the property is in substance a financing transaction and the gain should be deferred and amortized. (6093)

39. (a) Gains and losses on sale-leaseback transactions generally are deferred and amortized over the term of the lease. There are two exceptions to this general rule: (1) where the seller-lessee retains only a *minor* portion of the use of the property, or (2) where the seller-lessee retains more than a minor portion but less than substantially all of the use of the property. The seller-lessee is deemed to have retained a *minor* portion of the use of the property if the present value of the minimum lease payments is less than 10% of the fair value of the property. In this case, the sale and leaseback are accounted for as two separate transactions and the full amount of the gain or loss realized on the sale of the property is recognized at the date of sale. In this question, the present value of the minimum lease payments is less than 10% of the fair value of the property [i.e., $36,900 < ($400,000 × 10%)]. Therefore, the seller-lessee recognizes the full $100,000 (i.e., $400,000 sales price – $300,000 carrying amount) profit from the equipment sale at the sale date. No portion of the profit from the sale would be reported as deferred revenue. (2600)

40. (b) Since the fair value of the asset sold is more than its carrying amount (i.e., $465,000 > $450,000), the $20,000 (i.e., $450,000 – $430,000) indicated loss on the sale is in substance a prepayment of rent. Thus, the $20,000 indicated loss should be deferred and amortized as prepaid rent. (3268)

PERFORMANCE BY SUBTOPICS

Each category below parallels a subtopic covered in Chapter 8. Record the number and percentage of questions you correctly answered in each subtopic area.

Definitions & Classifications

Question #	Correct √
1	
2	
3	
4	
5	
6	
7	
# Questions	7
# Correct	______
% Correct	______

Operating Leases

Question #	Correct √
8	
9	
10	
11	
12	
13	
14	
15	
# Questions	8
# Correct	______
% Correct	______

Lessee's Capital Lease

Question #	Correct √
16	
17	
18	
19	
20	
21	
22	
23	
24	
25	
26	
27	
28	
# Questions	13
# Correct	______
% Correct	______

Lessor's Capital Lease

Question #	Correct √
29	
30	
31	
32	
33	
34	
35	
# Questions	7
# Correct	______
% Correct	______

Sale-Leaseback Transaction

Question #	Correct √
36	
37	
38	
39	
40	
# Questions	5
# Correct	______
% Correct	______

Solution 8-2 SIMULATION ANSWER: Operating Lease

1.

Rental Expense ($22,000 × 8 months)	$176,000

2.

Rental Income ($22,000 × 8 months)		$ 176,000
Deduct:		
Depreciation [($1,600,000 / 8) × 8/12]	$133,333	
Amortization ($80,000 × 8/60)	$ 10,667	(144,000)
Income From Operating Lease		$ 32,000

Solution 8-3 SIMULATION ANSWER: Capital Lease

1.

Cost of leased machine	$ 650,000
Deduct PV of estimated residual value [$70,000 × 0.500249] (present value of $1 at 8% for 9 periods)	(35,017)
Net investment to be recovered	614,983
PV of an annuity of $1 in advance for 9 periods at 8%	/ 6.746639
Annual Rental	$ 91,154

2.

Gross lease rentals receivable ($91,154 × 9)		$ 820,386
Deduct recovery of net investment in machine on capital lease:		
Cost of machine	$650,000	
Residual value of machine	(70,000)	(580,000)
Unearned interest revenue		$ 240,386

3.

Liability under capital lease (initial value) [$91,154 × 6.746639] (present value of an annuity of $1 in advance for 9 periods at 8%*)	$ 614,983
Deduct lease payment on December 31, year 2	(91,154)
Balance December 31, year 2 (after initial payment)	523,829
Interest rate	× 8%*
Interest expense year ended December 31, year 3	$ 41,906
Depreciation expense [$614,983 / 9]	68,331
Total expense on lease	$ 110,237

* Ortiz must use Theo's implicit rate of 8% since it is known and lower than Ortiz's incremental borrowing rate of 10%.

Solution 8-4 SIMULATION ANSWER: Research

FASB Accounting Standards Codification

FASB ASC: 840 - 30 - 45 - 1

45-1 Assets recorded under capital leases and the accumulated amortization thereon shall be separately identified in the lessee's balance sheet or in footnotes thereto.

CHAPTER 9

POSTEMPLOYMENT BENEFITS

CHAPTER 9

POSTEMPLOYMENT BENEFITS

I. Postemployment Benefits Overview

A. Fundamentals

There are many similarities in accounting for pensions and accounting for other postretirement benefits. This chapter illustrates accounting for pensions in detail and then highlights the differences in accounting for postretirement benefits. There are three fundamental aspects that shape financial reporting in the application of accrual accounting to pensions.

1. **Delaying Recognition of Certain Events** Changes in the pension obligation and changes in the value of assets set aside to meet those obligations are not recognized as they occur. They are systematically and gradually recognized over subsequent periods.

2. **Reporting Net Cost** A single net cost amount is reported in the employer's financial statements. This net cost aggregates at least three items that might be reported separately for any other part of an entity's operations, including the compensation cost of the benefits promised, the interest cost resulting from deferring the payment of those benefits, and the return from investing the assets related to those benefits.

3. **Offsetting Liabilities and Assets** The employer's balance sheet reflects as a net amount the recognized values of assets contributed to a plan and the liabilities for pensions recognized as net pension cost of past periods. These assets and liabilities are netted, even though the liabilities have not been satisfied, the assets may still be controlled, and the employer is still subject to both the risks and rewards involved.

B. Disclosures

Uniform disclosures about pension and nonpension benefit plans are required to provide information to financial statement users about benefit plans sponsored by employers. Additional disclosures about the assets, obligations, cash flows, and net periodic benefit cost of defined benefit pension plans and other defined benefit postretirement plans are also required. The required information should be provided separately for pension plans and for other postretirement benefit plans. In addition, disclosure of significant events occurring during the period that are not otherwise apparent in the disclosures is required.

1. A reconciliation of beginning and ending balances of the projected benefit obligation showing separately the effects during the period of the following components: service cost, interest cost, contributions by plan participants, actuarial gains and losses, foreign currency exchange rate changes, benefits paid, plan amendments, business combinations, divestitures, curtailments, settlements, and special termination benefits.

2. A reconciliation of beginning and ending balances of the fair value of plan assets showing separately the effects during the period attributable to the following: actual return on plan assets, foreign currency exchange rate changes, contributions by the employer, contributions by employees or retirees, benefits paid, business combinations, divestitures, curtailments, and settlements.

3. The funded status of the plans and the amounts recognized in the balance sheet showing separately the assets and current and noncurrent liabilities recognized.

4. The amount of net periodic benefit cost recognized, showing separately the following components: service cost, interest cost, expected return on plan assets, gain or loss, prior service cost or credit, transition asset or obligation, and gain or loss recognized due to settlements or curtailments.

5. Separately, the net gain or loss and net periodic service cost or credit recognized in other comprehensive income for the period, and reclassification adjustments of other comprehensive income for the period, as those amounts, including amortization of the net transition asset or obligation are recognized as components of net periodic benefit cost.

6. Separately, the net gain or loss, net prior service cost or credit, and net transition asset or obligation amounts in accumulated other comprehensive income that have not yet been recognized as components of net periodic benefit cost.

7. Separately, the portion of the net gain or loss, net prior service cost or credit, and net transition asset or obligation remaining in accumulated other comprehensive income that is expected to be recognized as a component of net periodic benefit cost over the fiscal year that follows the employer's most recent balance sheet presented.

8. The amount and timing of any plan assets expected to be returned to the business during the 12-month period, or operating cycle, that follows the most recent annual balance sheet presented.

9. Key assumptions, on a weighted average basis, used in the accounting for the plans. These include assumed discount rates, rates of compensation increase, expected long-term rates of return on plan assets, and any assumptions used to determine the benefit obligation and net benefit cost.

10. Assumed health care cost trend rate(s) for the next year and a general description of the direction and pattern of change as well as the ultimate trend rate(s) and when the rate is expected to occur.

11. The effect of a one-percentage-point increase and decrease in the assumed health care costs trend rates on: the aggregate of the service and interest cost; and the accumulated post-retirement benefit obligations for health care benefits.

12. The amounts and types of securities of the employer and related parties included in plan assets, the approximate amount of future annual benefits of plan participants covered by insurance contracts issued by the employer or related parties and the plan during the period.

13. Any alternative amortization method used to amortize prior service amounts or net gains and losses.

14. Any substantive commitment, such as a past practice or history of regular benefit increases, used as the basis for accounting for the benefit obligation.

15. The cost of providing special or contractual termination benefits recognized during the period and a description of the nature of the event.

16. An explanation of any significant change in the benefit obligation or plan assets not readily apparent from the other disclosures.

C. Defined Contribution Plans

Defined contribution plans are plans in which the terms specify how contributions to the individual participants' accounts are to be determined (not the benefits to be received). These plans provide an individual account for each participant. Employers are required to recognize the funded status of pensions and other postretirement benefit plans on their balance sheets.

1. **Objective** The objective behind preparing financial statements of defined contribution plans is to provide information that is useful in assessing present and future ability of the plans to pay benefits. Financial statements need to provide information about plan resources and how stewardship responsibilities for those resources has been discharged, results of transactions and events that affect the information about resources, and other factors necessary for users to understand information provided in the statements. In particular, for defined contribution plans, the net assets available to pay benefits equal the sum of individual account balances of plan participants.

2. **Types of Plans** Generally, defined contribution plans fall into the following categories:

   - Profit-Sharing Plans: These defined contribution plans are not pension plans or stock bonus plans. Employer contributions may be discretionary or may be based on a fixed formula or other factors.

   - Money-Purchase Pension Plans: These defined contribution plans involve employer contributions based on fixed formulas that are not related to profits and are designated to be pension plans.

   - Stock-Bonus Plans: These are defined contribution plans where distributions normally are made in stock of employer entities, unless participants elect otherwise.

3. **Benefits** Participant benefits are determined by: the amounts contributed to the participants' account(s); returns earned on investments of contributions; and allocations of forfeitures of other participants' benefits.

4. **Net Pension Cost** The net pension cost is the contribution called for by the plan for the period in which the individual renders services. If the plan calls for contributions for periods after the individual has rendered services (e.g., after retirement), the cost should be accrued during the employee's service period.

5. **Participant Loans** Typically, these loans arise when participants take out a loan from their plan assets. These loans represent an extension of credit to plan participants by defined contribution plans. Participant loans should be classified as notes receivable, and valued at their outstanding principal amount, plus accrued but unpaid interest. Additionally, no valuation reserves should be determined.

6. **Contributions & Contributions Receivable** Contributions to and receivables associated with defined contribution plans take a variety of forms. These contributions and receivables most often relate to employer, employee, and/or rollover contributions. Additionally, the contributions may be of a discretionary or mandatory manner, and they may be in the form of cash or noncash items. Where applicable, contributions receivable need to be reflected in the financial statements to include an allowance for uncollectible amounts.

   Generally, employer contributions receivable for defined contribution plans are recorded when the eligibility to receive the contributions is based on service, or other criteria, that existed as of the year-end of the plan. This guidance is different from guidance used in defined benefit retirement plan statements where contributions in excess of the minimum funding are made to fund future benefit payments under the plan.

7. **Uncertain Tax Positions** One of the required disclosures in financial statements of defined contribution plans relates to the federal income tax status of the plan, if a favorable determination letter has not been obtained or maintained. It is important to consider currently-applicable disclosure requirements associated with uncertain tax positions in FASB ASC 740, entitled *Income Taxes.* The disclosure requirements apply not only to for-profit entities, but they also are applicable in financial statements of not-for-profit entities and benefit plans. Although qualified benefit plans generally are not subject to taxation, certain activities of those plans may be taxable.

The tax-exempt status of a defined contribution plan is a position that may be subject to uncertainty. Even when there are no uncertain tax positions that are subject to the general disclosure requirements, the description of open tax years that remain subject to examination would be a required disclosure even in financial statements of benefit plans.

8. **Forfeitures** When participants terminate employment with plan sponsors, they may not be fully-vested in employer contributions that have been allocated to their accounts. The forfeited nonvested portion of those accounts remains as a plan asset that is held and maintained by the plan. The forfeitures account (i.e., a suspense account) may only be used or allocated in accordance with provisions of the plan document.

   In some cases the amount of forfeitures could be material to the financial statements so that there could be the potential for improper use of a significant amount of funds. Plan documents typically specify how forfeitures are to be utilized. When plan documents allow for forfeitures to be offset against future employer contributions and plan administrators do so with the next employer contributions, the forfeiture balance at the end of the year typically is offset against the year-end employer contributions receivable balance. Forfeitures should not be shown separately on the face of the financial statements; rather forfeited amounts should be combined in the appropriate investment classification.

9. **Risks & Uncertainties** Defined contribution plans, like other reporting entities outside the plan financial reporting arena, need to include in their financial statement note disclosures information concerning:

   - The nature of their operations.
   - Use of estimates in preparation of their financial statements.
   - Certain significant estimates included in the financial statements.
   - Current vulnerability due to certain concentrations.

   On the certain significant estimates issue, financial statement disclosure is needed when information that is known and available prior to the financial statements being issued or available to be issued, depending on whether the plans are considered to be issuers or non-issuers, indicates that it is both at least reasonably possible that estimates will change in the near term due to one or more confirming events and the effect of the change would be material to the statements.

   Not uncommonly, plan participants may be concentrated in specific industries that carry certain risks. Additionally, plans also may hold investments and other assets, other than financial instruments, that are concentrated in particular industries or in particular geographic areas. In these circumstances, financial statements need to disclose the concentrations.

10. **Disclosures** In developing note disclosures, defined contribution plans need to disclose identification of any investments, including self-directed and participant-directed investments that represent 5% or more of net assets available for benefits. When any of those investments are nonparticipant-directed, they should be identified as such.

D. Multiemployer Plans

Multiemployer pension plans are frequently used by employers to provide benefits to union employees who may work for multiple employers during their working lives and, thereby, accrue benefits in one plan for their retirement. These plans generally receive contributions from two or more unrelated employers based on one or more collective-bargaining arrangements. Assets in these plans that are contributed by one employer may be used to fund benefits provided to employees of other employers participating in the plans in that plan assets, once they have been contributed, are not restricted to individual employers. Several employers participate in the individual plans, and a single employer actually may participate in more than one multiemployer plan.

1. **Individually Significant** Multiemployer pension plans must be assessed to determine which plans are considered to be individually significant in that some of the disclosure requirements only relate to those plans. Factors other than the amounts of employer contributions to the plans (e.g., the severity of the unfunded status of the plans) may need to be considered. All of the relevant facts and circumstances associated with individual plans (e.g., expected future contribution requirements, number of employees participating in the plans, potential withdrawal liabilities, etc.) should be considered in determining whether the individually significant threshold is met.

2. **Disclosures** For each individually significant multiemployer plan that provides pension benefits, employers have extensive reporting requirements. The essential elements related to the disclosures also address contributions made to each individually-significant plan and the total contributions made to all other plans in the aggregate. Additionally, disclosures need to include a description of the nature and effect of any changes affecting comparability from period to period for each period where a statement of income or statement of activities is included in the financial statements. These type significant changes might include, among other things, issues related to business combinations or divestitures, changes in contractual employer contribution rates, and changes in the number of employees covered by the plans during each year.

   Where plan-level information is not available in the public domain, employers are also required to disclose the following information about each significant plan:

   - A description of the nature of plan benefits.
   - A qualitative description of the extent to which employers could be responsible for obligations of the plans, including benefits earned by employees during employment with other employers.
   - Other qualitative information, to the extent available, as of the most recent date available, to help users of the financial statements understand financial information about the plans (e.g., total plan assets, actuarial present value of accumulated plan benefits, total contributions received by the plans).

3. **Other Postretirement Benefit Plans** For other postretirement benefit plans, employers are required to disclose a description of the nature and effect of any changes that affect comparability of total employer contributions from period to period, as well as:

   - Amounts of contributions made to the plans for each annual period where an income statement or statement of activities is presented.
   - The nature of the benefits.
   - Which employees are covered by the plans (i.e., active versus retired employees).

II. Single-Employer Defined Benefit Pension Plans

A. Overview

A defined benefit pension plan is a plan that defines an amount of pension benefit to be provided, usually as a function of one or more factors such as age, years of service, or compensation. The fundamental objective in defined benefit plan reporting is to provide a measure of pension cost that reflects the terms of the underlying plan and recognizes the compensation cost of an employee's pension benefits over the employee's approximate service period. The following definitions apply specifically to accounting for pensions. Most of these terms apply also to accounting for postretirement benefits, with minor modification.

1. **Accumulated Benefit Obligation** The actuarial present value of benefits (whether vested or nonvested) attributed by the pension benefit formula to employee services rendered before a specified date and based on employee services and compensation (if applicable) before that date. The accumulated benefit obligation differs from the projected benefit obligation in that it includes no assumption about future compensation levels. For plans with flat-benefit or non-pay-related pension benefit formulas, the accumulated benefit obligation and the projected benefit obligation are the same.

2. **Actuarial Present Value** The value, as of a specified date, of an amount or series of amounts payable or receivable thereafter, with each amount adjusted to reflect (a) the time value of money (through discounts for interest), and (b) the probability of payment (by means of decrements for events such as death, disability, withdrawal, or retirement) between the specified date and the expected date of payment.

3. **Amortization** In pension accounting, amortization is also used to refer to the systematic recognition in net pension cost over several periods of amounts previously recognized in other comprehensive income, that is, prior service costs or credits, gains or losses, and any transition asset or obligation existing at the date of initial application of these standards.

4. **Annuity Contract** A contract in which an insurance company unconditionally undertakes a legal obligation to provide specified pension benefits to specific individuals in return for a fixed consideration or premium.

5. **Assumptions** Estimates of the occurrence of future events affecting pension costs, such as mortality, withdrawal, disablement and retirement, changes in compensation and national pension benefits, and discount rates to reflect the time value of money.

6. **Attribution** The process of assigning benefits or costs to periods of employee service.

7. **Contributory Plan** A pension plan under which employees contribute part of the cost. In some contributory plans, employees wishing to be covered must contribute; in other contributory plans, participants' contributions result in increased benefits.

8. **Expected Return on Plan Assets** An amount calculated as a basis for determining the extent of delayed recognition of the effects of changes in the fair value of assets. The expected return on plan assets is determined based on the expected long-term rate of return on plan assets and the market-related value of plan assets.

9. **Funding Policy** The program regarding the amounts and timing of contributions by the employer(s), participants, and any other sources, to provide the benefits a pension plan specifies.

10. **Gain or Loss** A change in the value of either the projected benefit obligation or the plan assets resulting from experience different from that assumed or from a change in an actuarial assumption. Gains and losses that are not recognized in net periodic pension cost when they arise are recognized in other comprehensive income. Those gains or losses are subsequently recognized as a component of net periodic benefit cost based on amortization.

11. **Market-Related Value of Plan Assets** A balance used to calculate the expected return on plan assets. Market-related value can be either fair value or a calculated value that recognizes changes in fair value in a systematic and rational manner over not more than five years.

12. **Pension Benefit Formula** The basis for determining payments to which participants may be entitled under a pension plan. Pension benefit formulas usually refer to the employee's service or compensation or both.

13. **Plan Assets** Assets (usually stocks, bonds, and other investments) that have been segregated and restricted (usually in a trust) to provide benefits. Plan assets include amounts contributed by the employer (and by employees for a contributory plan) and amounts earned from investing the contributions, less benefits paid.

14. **Prior Service Cost** The cost of retroactive benefits granted in a plan amendment.

15. **Projected Benefit Obligation** The actuarial present value as of a date of all benefits attributed by the pension benefit formula to employee service rendered prior to that date. The projected benefit obligation is measured using assumptions as to future compensation levels if the pension benefit formula is based on those future compensation levels (pay-related, final-pay, final-average-pay, or career-average-pay plans). Plans not based on future compensation levels are called non-pay-related or flat-benefit plans. The projected benefit obligation is a measure of benefits attributed to service to date assuming that the plan continues in effect and that estimated future events (such as compensation increases, turnover, and mortality) occur.

16. **Retroactive Benefits** Benefits granted in a plan amendment (or initiation) that are attributed by the pension benefit formula to employee services rendered in periods prior to the amendment. The cost of the retroactive benefits is referred to as prior service cost.

17. **Unfunded Accumulated Postretirement Benefit Obligation** The accumulated postretirement benefit obligation in excess of the fair value of plan assets.

18. **Unfunded Projected Benefit Obligation** The excess of the projected benefit obligation over the fair value of plan assets.

19. **Unrecognized Net Gain or Loss** The cumulative net gain or loss that has not been recognized as a part of net periodic pension cost.

20. **Vested Benefit Obligation** The actuarial present value of vested benefits (benefits for which the employee's right to receive a present or future pension benefit is no longer contingent on remaining in the service of the employer).

B. Net Periodic Pension Cost

This is the amount recognized in an employer's financial statements as the cost of a pension plan for a period. Components of net periodic pension cost are service cost, interest cost, actual return on plan assets, gain or loss, amortization of prior service cost or credit, and amortization of the transition asset or obligation existing at the date of initial application. Note that net periodic pension cost may be an expense for the period (e.g., pension cost related to administrative or marketing personnel) or it may be inventoriable as manufacturing overhead (e.g., pension cost related to factory personnel). Pension cost consists of six components.

Exhibit 1 ▸ Net Periodic Pension Cost Components

S	**S**ERVICE COST (+)
I	**I**NTEREST COST (+)
R	**R**ETURN ON PLAN ASSETS (–)
P	**P**RIOR SERVICE COST (+) OR CREDIT (–) AMORTIZATION
A	**A**CTUARIAL GAINS (–) OR LOSSES (+)
T	**T**RANSITION ASSET (–) OR OBLIGATION (+) AMORTIZATION
=	**NET PENSION EXPENSE**

Exhibit 2 ▸ Elements of Pension Cost

Decreases Pension Cost	Increases Pension Cost
Actual Return on Plan Assets	Service Cost
Actuarial Gain Amortized	Interest Cost
Actuarial Loss Deferred	Actuarial Loss Amortized
Prior Service Credit Amortization	Actuarial Gain Deferred
Amortization of Net Transition Asset	Prior Service Cost Amortization
	Amortization of Net Obligation Recognized

1. **Service Cost** The service cost component is the actuarial present value of benefits attributed by the pension benefit formula to the employee's service during the period (i.e., the benefits earned during the period). Service costs are based on actuarial assumptions (reflecting time value of money, mortality, turnover, early retirement, etc.). Service costs reflect future compensation levels to the extent that the pension benefit formula defines pension benefits as a function of future compensation levels.

2. **Interest on PBO** This component is the increase in the projected benefit obligation (PBO) due to the passage of time. The interest rate to be used in the calculation is the rate at which the pension benefit could be effectively settled (i.e., the assumed discount rate). This same assumed discount rate is used in the measurement of the projected, accumulated, and vested benefit obligations, and the service cost component of net periodic pension cost.

3. **Return on Plan Assets** This component of net periodic pension cost reduces the pension cost for the period. It is based on the fair value of plan assets at the beginning and end of the period, adjusted for contributions and benefit payments.

   a. Algebraically, ARPA = End FV – Beg. FV – C + B

      Where:
      ARPA = Actual return on plan assets
      End FV = FV of plan assets at end of period
      Beg. FV = FV of plan assets at beginning of period
      C = Contributions to the plan during the period
      B = Benefits paid during the period

   b. For purposes of presenting the net periodic pension cost, the disclosure of the actual return on plan assets is required, as indicated here. However, net periodic pension cost is subsequently adjusted for the difference between actual return and expected return. The net effect of this is that net pension cost for any given period reflects the expected return for that period. The difference between the expected and actual return is included in accumulated other comprehensive income (OCI) and subject to amortization in future periods.

Example 1 ▸ Return on Plan Assets

The following facts pertain to the ABC Co. pension plan for year 7.

Expected return on plan assets	15%
FV of plan assets, on 1/1, year 7	$100,000
on 12/31, year 7	$130,000
Contributions to pension plan	$ 14,000
Benefits paid to retired employees	$ 8,000

Required: Determine the actual return on plan assets (ARPA) component of net pension cost for year 7. Assume contribution and benefit payments were made at year-end.

Solution: ARPA = $130,000 – $100,000 – $14,000 + $8,000 = $24,000

4. **Prior Service Cost Amortization** This is the spreading of the cost of retroactive benefits generated by a plan amendment that granted increased benefits based on service rendered in prior periods.

   a. Retroactively increasing benefits increases the projected benefit obligation at the date of the amendment and the cost shall be recognized as a charge to other comprehensive income. These costs are to be amortized as a component of net periodic pension cost by assigning an equal amount to each year of future service of each employee active at the date of the amendment who is expected to receive benefits under the plan. Prior service cost is incurred with the expectation that the employer will realize economic benefits in future periods. Plan amendments can reduce projected benefit obligations. These reductions reduce any other prior service costs and any excess is amortized. Other comprehensive income is adjusted each period as prior service cost is amortized.

   b. Since the amortization of prior service costs, as described in a., above, can be quite complex, the use of alternative approaches that would amortize the cost over a shorter period of time is permitted. For example, a straight-line method that amortizes the cost over the average remaining service life of the active participants is acceptable. The alternative method used shall be disclosed.

   c. Retroactively reducing benefits decreases the projected benefit obligation and shall be recognized as a prior service credit to other comprehensive income. This credit will be used to first reduce any remaining prior service cost included in accumulated other comprehensive income. Any remaining prior service credit shall be amortized as a component of net periodic pension cost on the same basis as the cost of a benefit increase.

Exhibit 3 ▸ Prior Service Cost

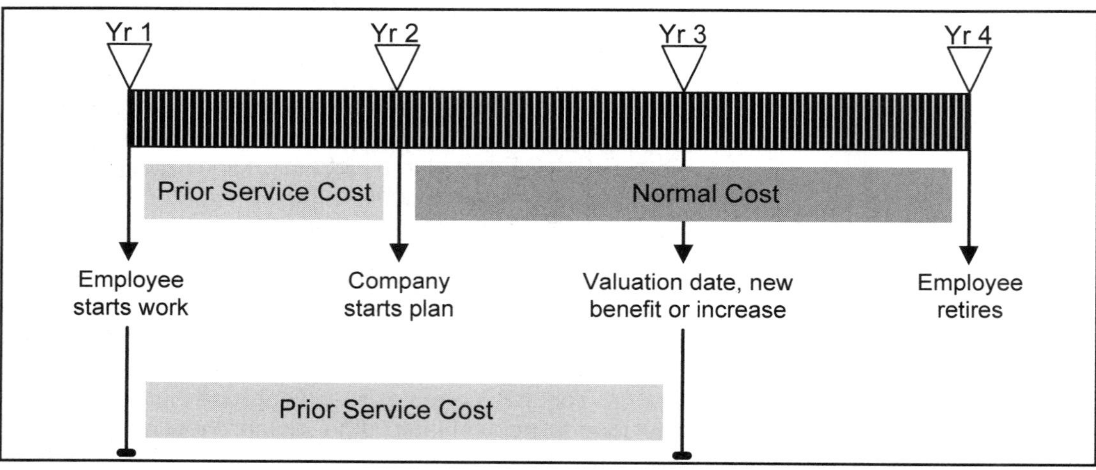

5. **Actuarial Gains and Losses** This refers to changes in the amount of either the projected benefit obligation or plan assets resulting from experience different from that assumed, and also changes in assumptions. It includes both realized and unrealized gains and losses.

   The gain or loss component of net periodic pension cost consists of the sum of: (1) the difference between the actual return on plan assets and the expected return on plan assets and (2) the amortization of the net gain or loss recognized in accumulated other comprehensive income. It is the net effect of delayed recognition of gains and losses in determining net periodic pension cost (the net change in the gain or loss) in accumulated other comprehensive income except that it does not include changes in the projected benefit obligation occurring during the period and deferred for later recognition in net periodic pension cost.

a. Because gains and losses may reflect refinements in estimates and those in one period may be offset in another period, recognition of gains and losses as components of net pension cost of the period in which they arise is not required. However, immediate recognition of gains and losses as a component of net periodic pension cost is permitted if that method is applied consistently, and is applied to all gains and losses on both plan assets and obligations. Gains and losses that are not recognized immediately as a component of net periodic pension cost shall be recognized as increases or decreases in other comprehensive income as they arise.

b. Asset gains and losses are differences between the actual return on plan assets during a period and the expected return on plan assets for that period. These include both changes reflected in the market-related value of plan assets and changes not yet reflected in the market-related value (that is, the difference between the fair value of assets and the market-related value). Gains or losses on transferable securities issued by the employer and included in plan assets are also included in asset gains and losses. Asset gains and losses not yet reflected in market-related value are not required to be amortized.

c. As noted above, recognition of the difference between the actual return on plan assets during a period and the expected return on plan assets for that period, a net gain or loss, is recognized in other comprehensive income in the period it arises. The amount recognized in other comprehensive income is also a component of net periodic pension cost for the current period. Thus, the amount recognized in other comprehensive income and the actual return on plan assets, when aggregated, equal the expected return on plan assets. The amount recognized in accumulated other comprehensive income affects future net periodic pension cost through subsequent amortization, if any, of the net gain or loss.

d. As a minimum, amortization of a net gain or loss included in accumulated other comprehensive income (excluding asset gains and losses not yet reflected in market-related value) shall be included as a component of net periodic pension cost for the year if, as of the beginning of the year, the unrecognized net gain or loss exceeds 10 percent of the greater of the projected benefit obligation or the market-related value of plan assets.

The excess must be amortized, at a minimum, over the average remaining service period of the active employees expected to receive benefits under the plan. Other methods of amortization may be used, but the amortization amount computed under such methods cannot be less than the minimum amortization described above. In addition, the method used should be applied consistently, applied similarly to both gains and losses, and disclosed.

Example 2 ▸ Actuarial Gains and Losses

Refer to Example 1, plus the following information as of the beginning of year 7.

Projected benefit obligation	$135,000
Accumulated gain (loss) in other comprehensive income (OCI)	$ 20,000
Average remaining service period of active employees	20 years

Required: Determine

a. The difference between the actual and expected return on plan assets for year 7.
b. The amortization of the net gain or loss accumulated in OCI.
c. The gain or loss pension cost component recognized in year 7.
d. The accumulated gain or loss carried forward in OCI to year 8.

Solution:

a. Difference between actual and expected returns on plan assets, year 7:

Actual return on plan assets (determined in Example 1)	$ 24,000
Expected return on plan assets ($100,000 FV on 1/1, year 7 × 15%)	(15,000)
Difference between the actual and expected returns on assets	$ 9,000

b. Amortization of the net gain(loss) in other comprehensive income:

Accumulated gain (loss) in other comprehensive income	$ 20,000
10% of the greater of projected benefit obligation ($135,000) or market related value of assets on January 1 ($100,000)	(13,500)
Net gain(loss) subject to amortization	6,500
Divided by average remaining service period of employees	/ 20
Amortization of gain in other comprehensive income	$ 325

c. Gains and losses for year 7:

Excess actual return on plan assets over expected return, deferred (a)	$ 9,000
Less: Amortization of accumulated gain (loss) in OCI (b)	(325)
Gain recognized	$ 8,675

d. Accumulated gain (loss) in OCI carried forward to year 8:

Accumulated gain (loss) in OCI, 1/1, year 7	$ 20,000
Less amortization to date	(325)
Plus difference between actual and expected returns on plan assets during year 7 (a)	9,000
Accumulated gain in OCI	$ 28,675

NOTE: The actual return ($24,000) is a reduction in net pension expense and the gain ($8,675) increases net pension expense. The net amount ($15,325) represents the expected return ($15,000) and the amortization of gains ($325) accumulated in other comprehensive income.

6. **Transition Asset or Obligation** The plan sponsor must determine, as of the measurement date for the beginning of the fiscal year, the amount of (a) the projected benefit obligation, and (b) the fair value of plan assets plus previously recognized unfunded accrued pension cost, or less previously recognized prepaid pension cost.

   The difference between these two amounts, whether it represents a net transition asset (and gain) or a net obligation (and loss or cost), should be amortized on a straight-line basis over the average remaining service period of employees expected to receive benefits under the plan. However, if the average remaining service period is less than 15 years, the employer may elect to use a 15-year period.

C. Recognition of Liabilities & Assets

The recognition of a liability, or asset, is required if the projected benefit obligation differs from the fair value of the plan assets. A liability is required if the projected benefit obligation exceeds the fair value of the plan assets. This liability amount equals the unfunded projected benefit obligation. An asset is recognized if the fair value of the plan assets exceeds the projected benefit obligation. The asset amount equals the overfunded projected benefit obligation.

1. **Presentation on the Balance Sheet** The aggregate amount of all overfunded plans shall be listed as an asset and separately the aggregate amount of all underfunded plans shall be listed as a liability. In a classified balance sheet the liability for underfunded plans will be classified as a current liability, a noncurrent liability, or a combination of both. The asset for an overfunded plan shall be classified as a noncurrent asset.

2. **Tax Effects** The asset or liability may result in a temporary difference for tax consequences. The deferred tax effects of any temporary differences shall be recognized in income tax expense for the year and allocated to various financial components, including other comprehensive income.

3. **New Determination** When there is a new determination of the funded status of a plan as an asset or liability, or when net gains or losses, prior service costs or credits, or the net transition asset or obligation are amortized as components of net periodic pension cost, the related balances for those net gains or losses, prior service costs or credits, and transition asset or obligation in accumulated other comprehensive income shall be adjusted as necessary and reported in other comprehensive income.

4. **Multiple Plans** Employers with more than one postretirement benefit plan are required to aggregate all overfunded plans and report one net asset amount and to aggregate all underfunded plans and report one net liability amount. The current and noncurrent portions of the liability are reported separately in a classified balance sheet.

   A current liability is reported for the amount by which the fair value of plan assets is exceeded by the expected benefits to be paid over the next 12 months or over the operating cycle if it is longer. This is determined on a plan-by-plan basis. The entire amount of expected benefits to be paid over the next 12 months or operating cycle will be classified as current for plans with no plan assets, such as many supplemental executive-retirement and postretirement medical plans. Net postretirement benefit assets will always be classified as noncurrent.

D. Measurement of Plan Assets

The funded-status amount is measured as the difference between the fair value of plan assets and the benefit obligation, with the benefit obligation including all actuarial gains and losses, prior service cost, and any remaining transition amounts. If the benefit obligation is larger than the fair value of plan assets, the plan is underfunded, and a net liability is reported. Conversely, if the fair value of the plan assets is larger, the plan is overfunded, and a net asset is reported on the balance sheet.

1. **Year-End** The measurement of plan assets and benefit obligations shall be as of the date of the employer's fiscal year-end balance sheet unless:

   a. The plan is sponsored by a subsidiary that is consolidated using a fiscal period that differs from its parent's.

   b. The plan is sponsored by an investee that is accounted for using the equity method of accounting.

2. **Interim-Period** Unless there is a remeasurement of both plan assets and benefit obligations during the fiscal year, the funded status reported shall be the same asset or liability recognized in the previous year-end balance sheet, adjusted for

   a. Subsequent accruals of net periodic pension cost that exclude the amortization of amounts previously recognized in comprehensive income.

   b. Contributions to a funded plan, or benefit payments.

Example 3 ▸ Recognition of Liabilities & Assets

Scenario 1: Taylor Co. implemented a defined benefit plan for its employees several years ago and adopted FASB rules on 12/31 of year 7. On 12/31, year 7, Taylor Co.'s projected benefit obligation was $225,000, the fair value of its plan assets was $190,000, and the accrued pension cost already on the books was $15,000.

Required: Determine as of 12/31, year 7, Taylor Co.'s year 7 (a) liability or asset required, if any, (b) the additional liability or asset adjustment to be reported in other comprehensive income (ignore income taxes) required, if any, and (c) any appropriate journal entry.

Solution:

	Projected benefit obligation	$ 225,000
	Less: FV of plan assets	(190,000)
(a)	Unfunded projected benefit obligation (liability required)	$ 35,000
	Minimum liability required (a)	$ 35,000
	Less: Accrued pension cost (account used to recognize liability prior to FASB adoption)	(15,000)
(b)	Additional liability required to be reported in OCI	$ 20,000

(c)	12/31	Other Comprehensive Income (b)	20,000	
		Accrued Pension Cost	15,000	
		Underfunded Pension Liability		35,000

Scenario 2: Same as scenario 1, except instead of a $15,000 accrued pension cost there is a $15,000 prepaid pension cost on the books.

Required: Determine as of 12/31, year 7, Taylor Co.'s year 7 (a) liability or asset required, if any, (b) the additional liability or asset adjustment to be reported in other comprehensive income (ignore income taxes), required, if any, and (c) any appropriate journal entry.

Solution:

	Projected benefit obligation	$ 225,000
	Less: FV of plan assets	(190,000)
(a)	Unfunded projected benefit obligation (liability required)	$ 35,000
	Minimum liability required (a)	$ 35,000
	Plus: Prepaid pension cost (account used to recognize asset prior to FASB adoption)	15,000
(b)	Additional liability required to be reported in OCI	$ 50,000

(c)	12/31	Other Comprehensive Income (b)	50,000	
		Prepaid Pension Cost		15,000
		Underfunded Pension Liability		35,000

Scenario 3: Same as scenario 1, except instead of a $225,000 projected benefit obligation it is only $190,000, equaling the fair value of plan assets.

Required: Determine as of 12/31, year 7, Taylor Co.'s year 7 (a) liability or asset required, if any, (b) the additional liability or asset adjustment to be reported in other comprehensive income (ignore income taxes) required, if any, and (c) any appropriate journal entry.

Solution:

	Projected benefit obligation	$ 190,000
	Less: FV of plan assets	(190,000)
(a)	Fully funded projected benefit obligation (no liability or asset required)	$ 0
	Minimum liability required (a)	$ 0
	Less: Accrued pension cost (account used to recognize liability prior to FASB adoption)	(15,000)
(b)	Liability required to be removed from OCI	$ (15,000)

(c)	12/31	Accrued Pension Cost (b)	15,000	
		Other Comprehensive Income		15,000

Scenario 4: Same as scenario 1, except instead of a $225,000 projected benefit obligation it is only $205,000.

Required: Determine as of 12/31, year 7, Taylor Co.'s year 7 (a) liability or asset required, if any, (b) the additional liability or asset adjustment to be reported in other comprehensive income (ignore income taxes) required, if any, and (c) any appropriate journal entry.

Solution:

	Projected benefit obligation	$ 205,000
	Less: FV of plan assets	(190,000)
(a)	Unfunded projected benefit obligation (liability required)	$ 15,000
	Minimum liability required (a)	$ 15,000
	Less: Accrued pension cost (account used to recognize liability prior to FASB adoption)	(15,000)
(b)	Additional liability or asset required to be reported in OCI	$ 0

(c)	12/31	Accrued Pension Cost	15,000	
		Underfunded Pension Liability		15,000

Scenario 5: Same as scenario 1, except instead of a $225,000 projected benefit obligation it is only $200,000.

Required: Determine as of 12/31, year 7, Taylor Co.'s year 7 (a) liability or asset required, if any, (b) the additional liability or asset adjustment to be reported in other comprehensive income (ignore income taxes) required, if any, and (c) any appropriate journal entry.

Solution:

	Projected benefit obligation	$ 200,000
	Less: FV of plan assets	(190,000)
(a)	Unfunded projected benefit obligation (liability required)	$ 10,000
	Minimum liability required (a)	$ 10,000
	Less: Accrued pension cost (account used to recognize liability prior to FASB adoption)	(15,000)
(b)	Additional asset required to be reported in OCI	$ (5,000)

(c)	12/31	Accrued Pension Cost	15,000	
		Underfunded Pension Liability		10,000
		Other Comprehensive Income (b)		5,000

Scenario 6: Same as scenario 1, except instead of a $225,000 projected benefit obligation it is only $175,000.

Required: Determine as of 12/31, year 7, Taylor Co.'s year 7 (a) liability or asset required, if any, (b) the additional liability or asset adjustment to be reported in other comprehensive income (ignore income taxes) required, if any, and (c) any appropriate journal entry.

Solution:

	FV of plan assets	$ 190,000
	Less: Projected benefit obligation	(175,000)
(a)	Overfunded projected benefit obligation (asset required)	$ 15,000
	Minimum asset required (a)	$ 15,000
	Plus: Accrued pension cost (account used to recognize liability prior to FASB adoption)	15,000
(b)	Additional asset required to be reported in OCI	$ 30,000

(c)	12/31	Accrued Pension Cost	15,000	
		Overfunded Pension Liability	15,000	
		Other Comprehensive Income (b)		30,000

Example 4 ▸ Comprehensive Defined Benefit Pension Plan

XYZ Corp. has an employee who is estimated to be retiring in 5 years (on 12/31, year 5). This employee is entered into a defined benefit pension plan at 1/1, year 1. The plan pays a lump sum upon retirement of $1,000 for each year of service after the date of entry into the plan. On 1/1, year 3, XYZ Corp. amended the plan to pay $1,500 for each year of service upon retirement, retroactive for one year of prior service.

Assume an appropriate discount rate (from an actuary) of 10%, and an expected and actual return on plan assets of 10%. Additionally, assume funding by XYZ Corp. of $700 at 12/31 of years 1 and 2, $1,500 at 12/31 of years 3 and 4, and $1,578 at 12/31 of year 5.

Required: Show the calculation of the projected benefit obligation and the net periodic pension cost and the necessary journal entries at 12/31 of years 1, 2, 3, 4 and 5.

Solution:

12/31, yr 1	Projected benefit obligation (P.V. at 10% of $1,000 in 4 years = 0.6830 × $1,000)		$ 683	
	Service cost (0.6830 × $1,000)		$ 683	
	Interest on projected benefit obligation		0	
	Expected return on plan assets		0	
	Prior service cost		0	
	Gains and losses		0	
	Net periodic pension cost		$ 683	
12/31, yr 1	Pension Expense	683		
	Overfunded Pension Asset	17		
	Cash			700
12/31, yr 2	Projected benefit obligation (P.V. at 10% of $2,000 in 3 years = 0.751315 × $2,000)		$1,503	
	Service cost (0.7513 × $1,000)		$ 751	
	Interest on (beginning) projected benefit obligation (10% × 683)		69	
	Actual return on plan assets (10% × $700)		(70)	
	Prior service costs		0	
	Gains and losses		0	
	Net periodic pension cost		$ 749	
12/31, yr 2	Pension Expense	750		
	Overfunded Pension Asset			17
	Underfunded Pension Liability			33
	Cash			700
12/31, yr 3	Projected benefit obligation [P.V. at 10% in 2 years = 0.8264 × ($1,000 + $1,500 + $1,500)]		$3,306	
	Service cost (0.8264 × $1,500)		$1,240	
	Interest on projected benefit obligation (10% × 1,878*)		188	
	Actual return on plan assets [10% × ($700 + $700 + $70)]		(147)	
	Amortization of prior service costs ($376** / 3)		125	
	Gains and losses		0	
	Net periodic pension cost		$1,406	

* Prior year's adjusted projected benefit obligation (0.7513 × $2,500 = $1,878)
** Prior service costs = P.V. of $500 = 0.7513 × $500 = $376

12/31, yr 3	Pension Expense	1,406	
	Other Comprehensive Income (PSC)	250	
	Underfunded Pension Liability		156
	Cash		1,500

Note: The $250 is the portion of prior service cost not yet expensed.

12/31, yr 4	Projected benefit obligation [P.V. at 10% in 1 year = 0.9091 × ($1,000 + $1,500 + $1,500 + 1,500)]		$5,000
	Service cost (0.9091 × $1,500)		$1,364
	Interest on projected benefit obligation (10% × 3,306)		331
	Actual return on plan assets [10% × ($700 + $700 + $70 +$1,500 + $147)]		(312)
	Amortization of prior service costs ($376 / 3)		125
	Gains and losses		0
	Net periodic pension cost		$1,508
12/31, yr 4	Pension Expense	1,508	
	Underfunded Pension Liability	117	
	Other Comprehensive Income (PSC)		125
	Cash		1,500
12/31, yr 5	Projected benefit obligation (P.V. at 10% of $7,000 in 0 years)		$7,000
	Service cost		$1,500
	Interest on projected benefit obligation (10% × $5,000)		500
	ARPA [10% ($700 + $700 + $70 + $1,500 + $147 + $1,500 + 312)]		(493)
	Amortization of prior service costs ($375.66 / 3)		125
	Gains and losses		0
	Net periodic pension cost		$1,632
12/31, yr 5	Pension Expense	1,632	
	Underfunded Pension Liability	71	
	Other Comprehensive Income (PSC)		125
	Cash		1,578
Summary:	Total pension expense ($683 + $749 + $1,406 + $1,508 + $1,632)		$5,978
	Total return on plan assets ($0 + $70 + $147 + $312 + 493)		$1,022
	Total funding (cash) payments ($700 + $700 + $1,500 + $1,500 + $1,578)		5,978
	Amount due to retiring employee		$7,000

NOTE: This example accounted for one employee enrolled in a pension plan. The example could easily be extended to combined groups of similar employees to account for all participants of a plan. Additionally, although pensions would usually pay participants on a periodic basis after retirement, these payments could be transformed into an equivalent lump-sum distribution at the date of retirement.

III. Benefit Settlement & Curtailment

A. Settlements

Settlement is an irrevocable action that relieves the employer or plan of primary responsibility for a benefit obligation and eliminates significant risks related to the obligation and the assets used to effect the settlement. A gain or loss must be recognized in earnings when a pension obligation is settled. The amount of the gain or loss is limited to the unrecognized net gain or loss from realized or unrealized changes in the amount of either projected benefit obligation or plan assets resulting from experience different from that assumed or from changes in assumptions. In simple language, either all or a pro rata share of the unrecognized gain or loss is recognized when a plan is settled. If full settlement takes place, all unrecognized net gains or losses are recognized. If only a portion of the plan is settled, a pro rata share of the unrecognized net gains or losses is recognized.

B. Curtailments

Curtailment is an event that significantly reduces the expected years of future service of present employees or eliminates, for a significant number of employees, the accrual of defined benefits for some or all of their future services. The unrecognized prior service cost associated with years of service no longer expected to be rendered as the result of the curtailment is a loss. Unrecognized prior service cost includes any remaining unrecognized net obligation existing at the date of initial application of the authoritative guidance. Note, in the case of a curtailment, the projected benefit obligation may also be decreased or increased.

C. **Settlements vs. Curtailments**

1. **Purchase Annuity Contracts** If an employer purchases nonparticipating annuity contracts for vested benefits and continues to provide defined benefits for future service, either in the same plan or in a successor plan, a settlement has occurred, but not a curtailment.

2. **Benefits Reduced** If benefits to be accumulated in future periods are reduced (for example, because half of a work force is dismissed or a plant is closed), but the plan remains in existence and continues to pay benefits, to invest assets, and to receive contributions, a curtailment has occurred, but not a settlement.

3. **Plan Terminated** If a plan is terminated (that is, the obligation is settled and the plan ceases to exist) and not replaced by a successor defined benefit plan, both a settlement and a curtailment have occurred (whether or not the employees continue to work for the employer).

D. **Termination Benefits**
Employers may provide benefits to employees related to the employees being terminated from employment. The benefits provided may represent contractual termination benefits, special termination benefits, one-time termination benefits, or other postemployment benefits. In certain circumstances, termination benefits fall within the scope of more than one of these types of benefits.

1. **Contractual Employee Termination Benefits** Contractual employee termination benefits are those provided in accordance with an existing plan or agreement that specifies termination benefits are due only upon the occurrence of a specified event. This type circumstance is encountered in situations to include, among other things, where reporting entities close a plant. In these circumstances, the expense and related liability associated with the benefits to be received need to be recorded when it is probable that the employees will be entitled to receive the benefits and the amount of the benefits can be reasonably estimated.

   The liability for contractual termination benefits is essentially recorded pretty using the guidance associated with accounting for loss contingencies. Losses associated with contingencies are recognized when it is both probable that they will be incurred and the amount of any loss is reasonably estimable.

2. **Special Employee Termination Benefits** Special employee termination benefits are those provided in circumstances where employer entities offer termination benefits for a short period of time in exchange for voluntary termination of employees. For example, when reporting entities deem it necessary to downsize a work force. The expense and related liability associated with the benefits to be received is recorded when employees accept the termination benefit offer and the amount of the benefits can be reasonably estimated.

3. **One-Time Employee Termination Benefits** One-time employee termination benefits are those provided in circumstances where employees are involuntarily terminated and benefits received by employees are not provided by employers and received by employees under terms of ongoing benefit arrangements, enhancements to ongoing benefit arrangements that would be applicable to future events, or voluntary termination benefits. These type situations are encountered when reporting entities plan to reduce their operating costs due to phasing-out of certain product lines, etc.

   Unlike the guidance associated with contractual employee termination benefits and special employee termination benefits, with one-time employee termination benefits the expense and related liability associated with the benefits are recorded only when all of the following conditions have been satisfied:

   - Management, having the authority to do so, commits to a plan of termination.

- The plan identifies the number of employees to be terminated, their job classifications or functions and their locations, and the expected completion date.
- The plan establishes the term of the benefit arrangement in sufficient detail to enable employees to determine the types and amounts of benefits they will receive if they are involuntarily terminated.
- The benefit arrangement has been communicated to employees (where that date often is referred to as the "communication date").
- Actions required to complete the plan indicate that it is unlikely that significant changes to the plan will be made or that the plan will be withdrawn.

Once all of the above-noted conditions are satisfied, the recognition pattern is determined by whether future services are required by employees to receive the termination benefits. Reporting entities need to immediately recognize costs in circumstances where future services are not required; if future services are required, the costs should be recognized ratably over the required future service period.

4. **Other Postemployment Employee Benefits** Other postemployment employee benefits are those provided in accordance with mutually-understood benefit arrangements between employers and employees or former employees. Mutually-understood benefit arrangements might be achieved through either written plans or through consistent practice that results in the conclusion that these type plans are substantive plans.

   Other postemployment benefits need to be recorded when existing situations or sets of circumstances indicate that an obligation has been incurred related to the mutual understanding of benefits to which employees will be entitled, it is probable that the benefits will be paid, and the amount of the benefits can be reasonably estimated.

E. Segment Disposal

If the gain or loss from a settlement or curtailment is directly related to a disposal of a segment of a business, it should be included in determining the gain or loss associated with that event and recognized. Recognizing lease termination costs and specified employee severance plan costs related with exit or disposal activities in periods when obligations to others exists, not necessarily in the period of commitment to a plan is required.

IV. Other Postretirement Benefits

A. Attribution Method

This essentially represents an extension of the measurement principles related to defined benefit pension plans (modified for different fact circumstances) to postretirement benefits other than pensions. It focuses primarily on postretirement health care benefits. Both accounting for pensions and accounting for postretirement benefits other than pensions assign benefit costs on a years-of-service approach.

1. **Required** An employer's obligation for postretirement benefits expected to be provided to or for an employee is to be fully accrued by the date that employee attains full eligibility for all of the benefits expected to be received by that employee (the full eligibility date), even if the employee is expected to render additional service beyond that date.
2. **Attribution Period** The beginning of the attribution (accrual) period is the employee's date of hire, unless the plan only grants credit for service from a later date. An equal amount of the postretirement benefit obligation is attributed to each year of service in the attribution period unless the plan attributes a disproportionate share of the expected benefits to employees' early years of service.

B. Net Postretirement Benefit Cost

The components of the calculation of net benefit cost for postretirement benefits are essentially the same as the components for the calculation of net period pension cost, with some differences.

There are some modifications in terminology due to the different benefit agreements being measured and differences in the treatment of transition amounts.

1. **Amortization Over 20 Years** In accounting for postretirement benefits other than pensions, amortization of the transition obligation (and loss or cost) or transition asset (and gain), included in accumulated other comprehensive income existing at the date of the initial application is amortized on a straight-line basis over the employees' average remaining service period. However, if the average remaining service period is less than 20 years, the employer may elect to use a 20-year period. (With pensions, if the average remaining service period is less than 15 years, the employer may elect to use a 15-year period.)

2. **Option of Immediate Recognition** The transition amounts for postretirement benefits other than pensions may be recognized immediately in net income as a change in accounting principle, as an alternative to amortization. This option is not available in accounting for pension costs.

C. Recognition of Liabilities & Assets
A liability or an asset is recognized for a postretirement benefit plan in the same manner as for a pension plan, with the exception that there is no minimum liability requirement for a postretirement benefit plan and thus no intangible asset requirement.

Exhibit 4 ▸ Components of Benefit Cost, Postretirement vs. Pension

	Other Postretirement	Pension
1. Service Cost	Actuarial present value of postretirement benefit obligation attributed to current period.	Actuarial present value of pension benefit obligation attributed to current period.
2. Interest Cost	Increase in the accumulated postretirement benefit obligation to recognize the effects of the passage of time (uses assumed discount rates).	Increase in the projected benefit obligation to recognize the effects of the passage of time (uses assumed discount rates).
3. Actual Return on Plan Assets	Change in fair value of plan assets during the period after adjusting for contributions and benefit payments.	Change in fair value of plan assets during the period after adjusting for contributions and benefit payments.
4. Prior Service Cost	Change in accumulated retirement benefit obligation for new or amended benefits granted to plan participants.	Change in projected benefit obligation for new or amended benefits granted to plan participants.
5. Gains and Losses	Change in accumulated retirement benefit obligation and plan assets from experience different from that assumed or from changes in assumptions. May be recognized immediately or delayed with minimum amortization required.	Change in projected benefit obligation and plan assets from experience different from that assumed or from changes in assumptions. May be recognized immediately or delayed with minimum amortization required.
6. Transition Amounts	Overfunded or underfunded accumulated retirement benefit obligation at transition. May delay or immediately recognize amounts. If delay, amortize over service lives with option for 20-year amortization period when service lives are less than 20 years. If immediate, recognize in net income as a change in accounting principle.	Overfunded or underfunded projected benefit obligation at transition. Must delay recognition and amortize over service lives with option for 15-year amortization period when service lives are less than 15 years.
= Net Cost	Net Postretirement Benefit Cost	Net Period Pension Cost

Exhibit 5 ▶ Liability/Asset Recognition for Other Postretirement Benefits Versus Pensions

	Other Postretirement Benefits	Pensions
Accrued/Prepaid Cost	Accrued postretirement benefit cost (liability) recognized when net cost exceeds the amount contributed. Prepaid postretirement benefit cost (asset) recognized when amount contributed exceeds net cost.	Unfunded accrued pension cost (liability) recognized when net periodic pension cost exceeds amount contributed. Prepaid pension cost (asset) recognized when amount contributed exceeds net periodic pension cost.
Minimum Liability	No minimum liability required.	Minimum liability is excess of Accumulated Benefit Obligation* over fair value of plan assets at financial statement date.
Intangible Asset	No intangible asset required.	Intangible asset is the amount of additional liability needed to equal the minimum liability. Intangible asset may not exceed the amount of unrecognized prior service cost; if excess exists, it is reported net of income tax effect in other comprehensive income.

* *Do not be confused about the use of the Accumulated Benefit Obligation in this comparison table. When pension plans are pay related, the Projected Benefit Obligation would be used for interest calculations, transition amounts, etc.*

Boards of Accountancy

Certified Public Accountants are licensed to practice by Boards of Accountancy in 54 jurisdictions. Application forms and requirements to sit for the CPA exam should be requested from your particular board. IT IS EXTREMELY IMPORTANT THAT YOU COMPLETE THE APPLICATION FORM CORRECTLY AND RETURN IT TO YOUR STATE BOARD BEFORE THE SPECIFIED DEADLINE. Errors or delays may result in the rejection of your application. Be extremely careful in filling out the application and be sure to enclose all required materials. In many jurisdictions, complete applications must be received by the board at least **ninety** days before the examination date. Requirements as to education, experience, internship, and other matters vary. If you have not done so already, take a moment to contact the appropriate board for specific current requirements. Complete the application in a timely manner.

It may be possible to sit for the exam in another state as an out-of-state candidate. Candidates wishing to do so should contact the Board of Accountancy in their home jurisdiction as well as the other jurisdiction.

Approximately one month before the exam, check to see that your application to sit for the exam has been processed. DON'T ASSUME THAT YOU ARE PROPERLY REGISTERED UNLESS YOU HAVE RECEIVED YOUR NOTICE TO SCHEDULE.

The AICPA publishes a booklet entitled *The Uniform CPA Examination Candidate Bulletin: Information for Applicants*. You may download a copy from the AICPA's exam website.

Addresses of State Boards are on the site of the National Association of the State Boards of Accountancy (http://www.nasba.org).

CHAPTER 9—POSTEMPLOYMENT BENEFITS

Problem 9-1 MULTIPLE-CHOICE QUESTIONS

1. Which of the following is a (are) fundamental aspect(s) that shape financial reporting in the application of accrual accounting to pensions?

   a. Immediate recognition of certain events
   b. Reporting gross cost
   c. Offsetting liabilities and assets
   d. All of the above (Editors, 6159)

2. Note section disclosures in the financial statements for pensions do **not** require inclusion of which of the following?

   a. The components of period pension costs
   b. The amount of unrecognized prior service cost
   c. The differences in executive and non-executive plans
   d. A detailed description of the plan including employee groups covered (R/05, FAR, #50, 7794)

3. Which of the following information should be included in disclosures by a company providing health care benefits to its retirees?

   I. The assumed health care cost trend rate used to measure the expected cost of benefits covered by the plan
   II. The accumulated post-retirement benefit obligation

   a. I and II
   b. I only
   c. II only
   d. Neither I nor II (5/93, Theory, #30, amended, 4218)

4. _______________ is the contribution called for by the plan for the period in which the individual renders services.

   a. Defined contribution
   b. Defined benefit pension
   c. Net pension cost
   d. Attribution (Editors, 3566)

5. In the terminology of single-employer defined benefit pension plans, _____________ means the actuarial present value, as of a date, of all benefits attributed by the pension benefit formula to employee service rendered prior to that date, and may be measured using assumptions as to future compensation levels.

   a. Accumulated benefit obligation
   b. Projected benefit obligation
   c. Unfunded accumulated benefit obligation
   d. Vested benefit obligation (Editors, 5740)

6. What is the present value of all future retirement payments attributed by the pension benefit formula to employee services rendered prior to that date only?

   a. Service cost
   b. Interest cost
   c. Projected benefit obligation
   d. Accumulated benefit obligation (R/06, FAR, #49, 8116)

7. Visor Co. maintains a defined benefit pension plan for its employees. The service cost component of Visor's net periodic pension cost is measured using the

   a. Unfunded accumulated benefit obligation
   b. Unfunded vested benefit obligation
   c. Projected benefit obligation
   d. Expected return on plan assets (11/93, Theory, #30, 4535)

8. Interest cost included in the net pension cost recognized by an employer sponsoring a defined benefit pension plan represents the

   a. Shortage between the expected and actual returns on plan assets
   b. Increase in the fair value of plan assets due to the passage of time
   c. Increase in the projected benefit obligation due to the passage of time
   d. Amortization of the discount on prior service cost (5/92, Theory, #20, amended, 2713)

9. Effective January 1 of the previous year, Flood Co. established a defined benefit pension plan with no retroactive benefits. The first of the required equal annual contributions was paid on December 31 of that previous year. A 10% discount rate was used to calculate service cost and a 10% rate of return was assumed for plan assets. All information on covered employees for the previous and current year is the same. How should the service cost for the current year compare with the previous year, and should the previous year balance sheet report an underfunded or an overfunded funding status?

	Service cost for current year compared to the previous year	Funding status reported on the previous year balance sheet
a.	Equal to	Underfunded
b.	Equal to	Overfunded
c.	Greater than	Underfunded
d.	Greater than	Overfunded

(11/90, Theory, #21, amended, 2059)

10. For a defined benefit pension plan, the discount rate used to calculate the projected benefit obligation is determined by the

	Expected return on plan assets	Actual return on plan assets
a.	Yes	Yes
b.	No	No
c.	Yes	No
d.	No	Yes

(5/91, Theory, #37, 2057)

11. Parker Co. amended its pension plan on January 2 of the current year. It also granted $600,000 of unrecognized prior service costs to its employees. The employees are all active and expect to provide 2,000 service years in the future, with 350 service years this year. What is Parker's unrecognized prior service cost amortization for the year?

   a. $0
   b. $ 2,000
   c. $105,000
   d. $600,000 (R/07, FAR, #9, 8330)

12. On July 31 of the current year, Tern Co. amended its single employee defined benefit pension plan by granting increased benefits for services provided prior to the current year. This prior service cost will be reflected in the financial statement(s) for

   a. Years before the current year only
   b. The current year only
   c. The current year, and years before and following the current year
   d. The current year and following years only (11/92, Theory, #26, amended, 3459)

13. The following information pertains to Lee Corp.'s defined benefit pension plan for the current year:

Service cost	$160,000
Actual and expected gain on plan assets	35,000
Unexpected loss on plan assets related to a disposal of a subsidiary	40,000
Amortization of prior service cost	5,000
Annual interest on pension obligation	50,000

What amount should Lee report as pension expense in its current year-end income statement?

a. $250,000
b. $220,000
c. $210,000
d. $180,000 (5/92, PII, #14, amended, 2646)

14. The following information pertains to Seda Co.'s pension plan for the current year:

Actuarial estimate of projected benefit obligation at 1/1	$72,000
Assumed discount rate	10%
Service costs for the year	18,000
Pension benefits paid during the year	15,000

If no change in actuarial estimates occurred during the year, Seda's projected benefit obligation at December 31 of the current year was

a. $64,200
b. $75,000
c. $79,200
d. $82,200 (11/90, FAR, #16, amended, 1223)

15. The following information pertains to Gali Co.'s defined benefit pension plan for the current year:

Fair value of plan assets at 1/1	$350,000
Fair value of plan assets at 12/31	525,000
Employer contributions	110,000
Benefits paid	85,000

In computing pension expense, what amount should Gali use as actual return on plan assets?

a. $ 65,000
b. $150,000
c. $175,000
d. $260,000 (5/95, FAR, #39, amended, 5575)

16. When a single employer has a defined benefit pension plan and records actuarial gains and losses to the extent recognized, it is not in compliance with authoritative guidance if it does which of the following?

a. Excludes unrealized gains and losses from its computations and analyses
b. Computes part of the gain or loss on plan assets as the difference between the actual return on assets and the expected return on assets, for a given accounting period
c. Determines the expected return on assets by considering the expected long-term rate of return and the market-related value of plan assets
d. Determines the expected long-term rate of return as the average rate of earnings expected on the funds invested, including the return expected to be available for reinvestment (Editor, 3539)

17. Which of the following components should be included in net pension cost by an employer sponsoring a defined benefit pension plan?

	Amortization of unrecognized prior service cost	Fair value of plan assets
a.	Yes	No
b.	Yes	Yes
c.	No	Yes
d.	No	No

(R/89, FAR #20, 2069)

18. A pension liability, or asset, is required if the projected benefit obligation differs from
    a. The vested benefit obligation
    b. The accumulated benefit obligation
    c. Contributions to the plan
    d. The fair value of plan assets (Editors, 9147)

19. A company has a defined benefit pension plan for its employees. On December 31, year 1, the accumulated benefit obligation is $45,900, the projected benefit obligation is $68,100, and the fair value of the plan assets is $62,000. What amount, if any, related to the defined benefit plan should be recognized in the balance sheet at December 31, year 1?
    a. An asset of $16,100
    b. A liability of $6,100
    c. Nothing, as the fair value of the plan assets exceeds the accumulated benefit obligation
    d. An unrealized loss of $6,100 (R/11, FAR, #20, 9870)

20. Dell Co. established a defined benefit pension plan on January 1, year 1. Dell amortizes the prior service cost over 16 years and funds prior service cost by making equal payments to the fund trustee at the end of each of the first ten years. The service (normal) cost is fully funded at the end of each year. The following data are available for year 1:

Service (normal) cost for the year	$220,000
Prior service cost:	
Amortized	83,400
Funded	114,400

Dell's pension asset at December 31, prior to comparing the fair value of plan assets to the projected benefit obligation, is
    a. $114,400
    b. $ 83,400
    c. $ 31,000
    d. $0 (5/91, PI, #32, amended, 1220)

21. On January 2, year 2, Loch Co. established a noncontributory defined benefit plan covering all employees and contributed $1,000,000 to the plan. At December 31, year 2, Loch determined that the service and interest costs on the plan were $620,000 for the year. The expected and the actual rate of return on plan assets for the year was 10%. There are no other components of Loch's pension expense. Prior to comparing the fair value of plan assets to the projected benefit obligation, what amount should Loch report in its December 31, year 2 balance sheet as a pension asset?
    a. $280,000
    b. $380,000
    c. $480,000
    d. $620,000 (11/93, PI, #26, amended, 4395)

22. On January 2, East Corp. established a defined benefit pension plan. The plan's service cost of $150,000 was fully funded at the end of the year. In the year, prior service cost was funded by a contribution of $60,000 and amortization of prior service cost was $24,000. At December 31, what amount should East report as a pension asset prior to comparing the fair value of plan assets to the projected benefit obligation?

    a. $90,000
    b. $84,000
    c. $60,000
    d. $36,000 (5/93, PI, #28, amended, 4070)

23. The difference between the fair value of plan assets and the benefit obligation is the ______________.

    a. funded-status amount.
    b. Minimum pension liability.
    c. Accumulated benefit obligation.
    d. None of the above. (Editor, 3418)

24. Webb Co. implemented a defined benefit pension plan for its employees on January 1, year 5. During years 5 and 6, Webb's contributions fully funded the plan. The following data are provided:

	Year 8 Estimated	Year 7 Actual
Projected benefit obligation, December 31	$750,000	$700,000
Accumulated benefit obligation, December 31	20,000	500,000
Plan assets at fair value, December 31	675,000	600,000
Projected benefit obligation in excess of plan assets	75,000	100,000
Pension expense	90,000	75,000
Employer's contribution	?	50,000

    What amount should Webb contribute in order to report an underfunded pension liability of $15,000 in its December 31, year 8 balance sheet?

    a. $ 50,000
    b. $ 60,000
    c. $ 75,000
    d. $ 100,000 (5/92, PI, #25, amended, 2593)

25. Payne Inc., implemented a defined benefit pension plan for its employees on January 2, year 3. The following data are provided for the year, as of December 31, year 3:

Projected benefit obligation	$103,000
Plan assets at fair value	78,000
Net periodic pension cost	90,000
Employer's contribution	70,000

    What amount should Payne record as additional pension liability at December 31, year 3?

    a. $0
    b. $ 5,000
    c. $20,000
    d. $45,000 (5/94, FAR, #28, amended, 4843)

26. Nome Co. sponsors a defined benefit plan covering all employees. Benefits are based on years of service and compensation levels at the time of retirement. Nome determined that, as of September 30, year 2, its projected benefit obligation was $380,000, and its plan assets had a $290,000 fair value. Nome's September 30, year 2 trial balance showed a pension asset of $20,000. To report the proper pension liability in its September 30, year 2 balance sheet, what amount should Nome report as an adjustment?

    a. $110,000
    b. $360,000
    c. $380,000
    d. $400,000 (11/92, PI, #25, amended, 3258)

27. How should plan investments be reported in a defined benefit plan's financial statements?

    a. At actuarial present value
    b. At cost
    c. At net realizable value
    d. At fair value (R/11, FAR, #22, 9872)

28. An entity sponsors a defined benefit pension plan that is underfunded by $800,000. A $500,000 increase in the fair value of plan assets would have which of the following effects on the financial statements of the entity?

    a. An increase in the assets of the entity
    b. An increase in accumulated other comprehensive income of the entity for the full amount of the increase in the value of the assets
    c. A decrease in accumulated other comprehensive income of the entity for the full amount of the increase in the value of the assets
    d. A decrease in the liabilities of the entity (R/10, FAR, #15, 9315)

29. Which of the following is a pension plan settlement?

    a. An employer purchases nonparticipating annuity contracts for vested benefits and continues to provide defined benefits for future service in the same plan.
    b. Benefits to be accumulated in future periods are reduced, but the plan remains in existence and continues to pay benefits, to invest assets, and to receive contributions.
    c. A plan is terminated and not replaced by a successor defined benefit plan.
    d. Both A. and C. (Editors, 6503)

30. On September 1, year 1, Howe Corp., offered special termination benefits to employees who had reached the early retirement age specified in the company's pension plan. The termination benefits consisted of lump-sum and periodic future payments. Additionally, the employees accepting the company offer receive the usual early retirement pension benefits. The offer expired on November 30, year 1. Actual or reasonably estimated amounts at December 31, year 1, relating to the employees accepting the offer are as follows:

    - Lump-sum payments totaling $475,000 were made on January 1, year 2.
    - Periodic payments of $60,000 annually for three years will begin January 1, year 3. The present value at December 31, year 1, of these payments was $155,000.
    - Reduction of accrued pension costs at December 31, year 1, for the terminating employees was $45,000.

    In its December 31, year 1, balance sheet, Howe should report a total liability of special termination benefits of:

    a. $475,000
    b. $585,000
    c. $630,000
    d. $655,000 (R/88, #29, amended, 1227)

31. Bounty Co. provides postretirement health care benefits to employees who have completed at least 10 years service and are aged 55 years or older when retiring. Employees retiring from Bounty have a median age of 62, and no one has worked beyond age 65. Fletcher is hired at 48 years old. The attribution period for accruing Bounty's expected postretirement health care benefit obligation to Fletcher is during the period when Fletcher is age

    a. 48 to 65
    b. 48 to 58
    c. 55 to 65
    d. 55 to 62 (11/93, Theory, #27, 4532)

32. An employer's obligation for postretirement health benefits that are expected to be fully provided to or for an employee must be fully accrued by the date the

    a. Benefits are paid.
    b. Benefits are utilized.
    c. Employee retires.
    d. Employee is fully eligible for benefits. (R/06, FAR, #28, 8095)

33. As of December 31 of the current year, the accumulated postretirement benefit obligation and plan assets of a defined benefit postretirement plan sponsored by Crouse, Inc., were:

Accumulated postretirement benefit obligation	$500,000
Plan assets at fair value	425,000
Transition obligation	$ 75,000

    Crouse elected to apply GAAP provisions for employers' accounting for postretirement benefits other than pensions, in its financial statements for the current year ended December 31 and recognize the transition amount on a delayed basis as a component of net periodic postretirement benefit cost. The average remaining service period of active plan participants expected to receive benefits was estimated to be 10 years at the date of transition. Some participants' estimated service periods are 25 years. To minimize an accrual for postretirement benefit cost, what amount of transition obligation should Crouse amortize?

    a. $3,000
    b. $3,750
    c. $5,000
    d. $7,500 (R/89, FAR, #172, 3329)

34. For a defined benefit postretirement plan, an employer recognizes a transition obligation or transition asset, determined as the measurement date for the beginning of the fiscal year in which GAAP employers' accounting for postretirement benefits other than pensions is applied. The transition obligation or transition asset may be recognized

	Immediately in net income of the period of change as the effect of a change in accounting principle	On a delayed basis as a component of net periodic postretirement benefit cost
a.	Yes	Yes
b.	Yes	No
c.	No	Yes
d.	No	No

    (R/90, #291,3644)

35. How does the accounting for postretirement benefits other than pensions differ from the accounting for pensions?

    a. Accounting for postretirement benefits differs by assigning benefit costs on a years-of-service approach.
    b. Accounting for postretirement benefits differs by allocating benefit costs over the approximate service years of employees.
    c. Accounting for postretirement benefits differs by allowing the option of recognizing immediately in net income, as a change in accounting, the transition amounts for postretirement benefits other than pensions.
    d. None of the above. (Editors, 5739)

Problem 9-2 SIMULATION: Pension Costs

The following information pertains to Athena Co.'s defined benefit pension plan.

Discount rate	7%
Expected rate of return	9%
Average service life	10 years

	At January 1, year 3	At December 31, year 3
Projected benefit obligation	$800,000	$1,220,000
Fair value of pension plan assets	960,000	1,080,000
Unrecognized prior service cost	280,000	
Unamortized prior pension gain	108,000	

Service cost for the current year was $90,000. There were no contributions made or benefits paid during the year. Athena's unfunded accrued pension liability was $8,000 at January 1, year 3. Athena uses the straight-line method of amortization over the maximum period permitted.

1. Calculate the amounts to be recognized as components of Athena's net periodic pension cost at December 31, year 3. Round all amounts to the nearest dollar.

Interest cost	
Expected return on plan assets	
Actual return on plan assets	
Amortization of prior service costs	
Minimum amortization of pension gain included in accumulated other comprehensive income	

2. Determine whether the following components increase (I) or decrease (D) Athena's pension liability.

Service cost	
Deferral of gain on pension plan assets	
Actual return on plan assets	
Amortization of prior service costs	
Amortization of pension gain included in accumulated other comprehensive income	

(5/93, P1, #4(61-70), amended, 4100)

Problem 9-3 SIMULATION: Research

Question: If the projected benefit obligation exceeds the fair value of plan assets, how shall the employer account for the difference in the statement of financial position?

FASB ASC: [ ] [ ] [ ] [ ]

(89449)

Solution 9-1 MULTIPLE-CHOICE ANSWERS

Postemployment Benefit Overview

1. (c) There are three fundamental aspects shape financial reporting in the application of accrual accounting to pensions. They are: delaying recognition of certain events; reporting net cost; and offsetting liabilities and assets. (6159)

2. (c) The differences in executive and non-executive plans is not a required disclosure. The components of period pension costs is a required disclosure. The amount of unrecognized prior service cost and a detailed description of the plan including employee groups covered are required disclosures. (7794)

3. (a) An employer sponsoring a benefit plan should disclose, among other things, the assumed health care cost trend rate(s) for the next year and a general description of the direction and pattern of change as well as the ultimate trend rate(s) and when the rate is expected to occur. The employer must also disclose the accumulated post-retirement benefit obligation. (4218)

4. (c) The net pension cost is the contribution called for by the defined contribution plan for the period in which the individual renders services. (3566)

Net Periodic Pension Cost

5. (b) A projected benefit obligation is the actuarial present value, as of a date, of all benefits attributed by the pension formula to employee service rendered prior to that date. The projected benefit obligation is measured using assumptions as to future compensation levels if the pension benefit formula is based on those future compensation levels (pay-related, final-pay, final-average-pay, or career-average-pay plans). (5740)

6. (d) An accumulated benefit obligation is the actuarial present value of benefits attributed by the pension benefit formula to employee services rendered before a specified date and based on employee services and compensation prior to that date. Service and interest costs are components of the net periodic pension cost. The projected benefit obligation is the actuarial present value as of a date of all benefits attributed by the pension benefit formula to employee service rendered prior to that date. (8116)

7. (c) The service cost component of net periodic pension cost is a portion of the projected benefit obligation. Therefore, it is measured using the projected benefit obligation. (4535)

8. (c) Interest cost included in net pension cost is the increase in the projected benefit obligation due to the passage of time. (2713)

9. (d) Service cost for a period is the increase in the projected benefit obligation due to services rendered by employees during that period. All information on covered employees for the previous and current year is the same, and the current year is one year closer to the payment of retirement benefits. Service cost will be greater in the current year as compared to the previous year because the present value computation will be greater due to one less year of discounting. The plan requires equal annual contributions, but service costs are less in the beginning and more later. The contribution in the previous year will exceed the previous year service costs, resulting in an overfunded pension status to be reported on the previous year balance sheet. (2059)

10. (b) The projected benefit obligation is determined using the settlement rate and not the expected or actual return on plan assets. These two rates, however, do have an impact on the determination of net periodic pension cost. (2057)

11. (c) Prior service cost amortization is the spreading of the cost of retroactive benefits generated by a plan amendment that granted increased benefits based on service rendered in prior periods. These costs are to be amortized as a component of net periodic pension cost by assigning an equal amount to each year of future service of each employee active at the date of the amendment who is expected to receive benefits under the plan. The $600,000 unrecognized prior service costs divided by the 2,000 future service years equals $300 to be amortized per service year. In the current year there were 350 service years provided. Multiplying the 350 service years by the $300 to be amortized per service year results in $105,000 unrecognized prior service cost amortization for the year. (8330)

12. (d) The plan amendment granted increased benefits for services provided prior to the current year. Because the plan amendment was granted with the expectation that Tern will realize economic benefits in future periods, the cost of providing the retroactive benefits should not be included in pension cost entirely in the year of amendment. Instead, the prior service cost should be recognized during the future service periods of those employees active at the date of the amendment who are expected to receive benefits under the plan (i.e., in current and following years). (3459)

13. (d) A loss on plan assets related to a subsidiary disposal is not included in the determination of net pension cost. A gain or loss directly related to a disposal is recognized as a part of the gain or loss associated with that event.

Service cost	$ 160,000
Annual interest on pension obligation	50,000
Actual and expected gain on plan assets	(35,000)
Amortization of prior service cost	5,000
Net pension cost	$ 180,000

(2646)

14. (d) Interest cost represents the increase in the projected benefit obligation due to the passage of time, and is computed by multiplying the projected benefit obligation at 1/1 by the assumed discount (settlement) rate. The projected benefit obligation is increased by the interest costs and service costs for the year and decreased by any pension benefits paid during the year.

Projected benefit obligation at 1/1	$ 72,000
Interest cost for the year ($72,000 × 10%)	7,200
Service costs for the year	18,000
Pension benefits paid during the year	(15,000)
Projected benefit obligation, 12/31	$ 82,200

(1223)

15. (b)

Increase in fair value of plan assets ($525,000 – $350,000)	$ 175,000
Less: Increase due to employer contributions	(110,000)
Add: Decrease due to benefit payments	85,000
Actual return on plan assets	$ 150,000

(5575)

16. (a) Actuarial gains and losses to the extent recognized refers to changes in the amount of either the projected benefit obligation or plan assets resulting from experience different from that assumed, and also changes in assumptions. It includes both realized and unrealized gains and losses. (3539)

17. (a) The following components are included in net pension cost: (1) service cost, (2) interest cost, (3) actual return on plan assets, if any, (4) amortization of unrecognized prior service cost, if any, (5) gain or loss (including the effects of changes in assumptions) to the extent recognized, and (6) amortization of the unrecognized net obligation (and loss or cost) or unrecognized net asset (and gain) existing at the date of initial application of GAAP. The fair value of plan assets should *not* be included in net pension cost. (2069)

Recognition of Pension Liabilities & Assets

18. (d) The recognition of a liability, or asset, is required if the projected benefit obligation differs from the fair value of the plan assets. A liability is required if the projected benefit obligation exceeds the fair value of the plan assets. This liability amount equals the unfunded projected benefit obligation. An asset is recognized if the fair value of the plan assets exceeds the projected benefit obligation. The asset amount equals the overfunded projected benefit obligation. (9147)

19. (b) The amount of the total liability to be recognized equals the unfunded projected benefit obligation.

Projected benefit obligation	$ 68,100
Less: Plan assets at fair value	(62,000)
Amount of total liability to be recognized	$ 6,100

(9870)

20. (c) During the year, Dell accrued pension cost of $303,400 ($220,000 + $83,400) and made funding payments of $334,400 ($220,000 + $114,400). At 12/31, Dell's pension asset is $31,000 ($334,400 – $303,400), prior to comparing the fair value of plan assets to the projected benefit obligation. (1220)

21. (c) Loch contributed $1,000,000 to the plan. Therefore, in its 12/31, year 2 balance sheet, Loch should report a pension asset of $480,000 (i.e., $1,000,000 – $520,000) prior to comparing the fair value of plan assets to the projected benefit obligation.

Service and interest cost	$ 620,000
Less: Actual return on plan assets ($1,000,000 × 10%)	(100,000)
Pension cost	$ 520,000

(4395)

22. (d) In the current year, East accrued pension cost of $174,000 (i.e., $150,000 service cost + $24,000 prior service cost amortization) and made funding payments of $210,000 (i.e., $150,000 for service cost + $60,000 for prior service cost). The amount of East's pension asset at 12/31 is $36,000 (i.e., $210,000 funding payments – $174,000 pension cost), prior to comparing the fair value of plan assets to the projected benefit obligation. (4070)

23. (a) The funded-status amount is measured as the difference between the fair value of plan assets and the benefit obligation, with the benefit obligation including all actuarial gains and losses, prior service cost, and any remaining transition amounts. The minimum pension liability was the previous requirement and measured as the excess of the accumulated benefit obligation over the fair value of plan assets. The accumulated benefit obligation is the actuarial present value of benefits attributed by the pension benefit formula to employee services rendered before a specified date and based on employee services and compensation (if applicable) prior to that date. (3418)

24. (b) The pension liability in year 8 would be the amount the projected benefit obligation exceeded the fair value of plan assets. (i.e., $750,000 – $675,000 = $75,000). In order to report a pension liability of $15,000 in its 12/31, year 8 balance sheet, Webb must make a funding payment of $60,000 (i.e., $75,000 – $60,000) in year 8. (2593)

25. (b) The amount of the total liability to be recognized equals the unfunded projected benefit obligation.

Projected benefit obligation	$103,000
Less: Plan assets at fair value	(78,000)
Amount of total pension liability	$ 25,000

Payne would have already recorded a pension liability in the difference between the net periodic pension cost and the employer's contribution.

Net periodic pension cost	$ 90,000
Less: Employer's contribution	(70,000)
Pension liability recognized	$ 20,000

So, the additional pension liability is $25,000 – $20,000 = $5,000. (4843)

26. (a) The excess of the projected benefit obligation over the fair value of plan assets (i.e., $90,000) is the amount of the pension liability to be reported in the 9/30 balance sheet. The pension asset of $20,000 and the adjustment of $110,000 are netted into one amount and reported as pension liability in the amount of $90,000.

Projected benefit obligation	$ 380,000
Less: Fair value of plan assets	(290,000)
Unfunded projected benefit obligation	90,000
Add: Pension asset on books	20,000
Liability adjustment	$ 110,000

(3258)

27. (d) For purposes of reporting overfunded and underfunded plans, along with required disclosures, plan investments shall be measured at their fair value as of the measurement date. (9872)

Settlement & Curtailment

28. (d) The recognition of a liability, or asset, is required if the projected benefit obligation differs from the fair value of plan assets for a defined benefit pension plan. A defined pension plan that is underfunded indicates the projected benefit obligation exceeds the fair value of plan assets and a liability is required. A $500,000 increase in the fair value of plan assets would lower the amount underfunded to only $300,000 and would in effect decrease the liabilities of the entity. (9315)

29. (d) If benefits to be accumulated in future periods are reduced, but the plan remains in existence and continues to pay benefits, to invest assets, and to receive contributions, a curtailment has occurred, but not a settlement. If a plan is terminated and not replaced by a successor, both a settlement and a curtailment have occurred. A settlement has also occurred if an employer purchases nonparticipating annuity contracts for vested benefits and continues to provide defined benefits for future service in the same plan. Since answers A. and C. are correct, answer D., both A. and C., is the best choice. (6503)

30. (c) An employer may provide benefits to employees in connection with their termination of employment. Special termination benefits are termination benefits that are offered for only a short period of time. An employer that offers special termination benefits to employees recognizes a liability and a loss when the employees accept the offer and the amount can be reasonably estimated. The cost of termination benefits recognized as a liability and loss is the amount of any lump-sum payments and the present value of any expected future payments. The amount to be reported as the total liability for special termination benefits at December 31, year 1, for the company in question is determined as follows:

Lump-sum payments made 1/1, year 2	$475,000
Present value of periodic payments beginning 1/1, year 3	155,000
Liability for special termination benefits, 12/31, year 1	$630,000

The reduction of accrued pension cost for the terminating employees does not affect the liability reported for special termination benefits. (1227)

Other Postretirement Benefits

31. (b) The attribution period for accruing the expected postretirement health care benefit obligation begins with the date of hire and ends at the full eligibility date. Bounty provides postretirement health care benefits to employees who have completed at least 10 years of service and are aged 55 years or older when retiring. Fletcher is hired at 48 years old. Therefore, the attribution period for accruing Bounty's expected postretirement health care benefit obligation to Fletcher is during the period when Fletcher is aged 48 to 58, because at age 58, Fletcher will have completed 10 years of service and be 55 years or older. (4532)

32. (d) An employer's obligations for postretirement benefits expected to be provided to or for an employee be fully accrued by the date that employee attains full eligibility for all of the benefits expected to be received by that employee, any beneficiaries, and covered dependents (the full eligibility date), even if the employee is expected to render additional service beyond that date. (8095)

33. (b) The $75,000 of transition obligation at the beginning of the current year, the first fiscal year in which Crouse applied GAAP, is computed as the excess at that date of the accumulated postretirement benefit obligation over the fair value of plan assets (i.e., $500,000 – $425,000). Typically, if the transition amount is recognized on a delayed basis as a component of net periodic postretirement benefit cost, it should be amortized on a straight-line basis over the average remaining service period of employees expected to receive benefits under the plan. However, because the average remaining service period is less than 20 years (i.e., 10 < 20), Crouse may elect to use a 20-year period. Therefore, the amount of transition obligation that Crouse should amortize to minimize its accrual for postretirement benefit cost is $3,750 (i.e., $75,000 / 20). (3329)

34. (a) A transition obligation or transition asset may be recognized immediately in net income of the period of change as the effect of a change in accounting principle, or on a delayed basis as a component of net periodic postretirement benefit cost. (3644)

35. (c) The transition amounts for postretirement benefits other than pensions may be recognized immediately in net income as a change in accounting principle, as an alternative to amortization. This option is not available in accounting for pension costs. (5739)

PERFORMANCE BY SUBTOPICS

Each category below parallels a subtopic covered in Chapter 9. Record the number and percentage of questions you correctly answered in each subtopic area.

Postemployment Benefit Overview

Question #	Correct √
1	
2	
3	
4	
# Questions	4
# Correct	______
% Correct	______

Net Periodic Pension Cost

Question #	Correct √
5	
6	
7	
8	
9	
10	
11	
12	
13	
14	
15	
16	
17	
# Questions	13
# Correct	______
% Correct	______

Recognition of Pension Liabilities & Assets

Question #	Correct √
18	
19	
20	
21	
22	
23	
24	
25	
26	
27	
# Questions	10
# Correct	______
% Correct	______

Settlement & Curtailment

Question #	Correct √
28	
29	
30	
# Questions	3
# Correct	______
% Correct	______

Other Postretirement Benefits

Question #	Correct √
31	
32	
33	
34	
35	
# Questions	5
# Correct	______
% Correct	______

Solution 9-2 SIMULATION ANSWER: Pension Costs

1.

Interest cost.	$ 56,000	[1]
Expected return on plan assets.	$ 86,400	[2]
Actual return on plan assets.	$120,000	[3]
Amortization of prior service costs.	$ 28,000	[4]
Minimum amortization of pension gain included in accumulated other comprehensive income.	$ 1,200	[5]

Explanations

[1] Interest cost included in net periodic pension cost is determined as the increase in the projected benefit obligation due to the passage of time.

Projected benefit obligation, 1/1	$800,000
Times: Discount rate at which pension benefits could be effectively settled	× 7%
Interest cost for the year	$ 56,000

[2] The expected return on plan assets is determined based on the expected long-term rate of return on plan assets and the market-related value of plan assets. The market-related value of plan assets is either fair value or a calculated value that recognizes changes in fair value in a systematic and rational manner over not more than five years.

Fair value of plan assets, 1/1	$960,000
Times: Expected rate of return	× 9%
Expected return on plan assets	$ 86,400

[3] For a funded plan, the actual return on plan assets is determined based on the fair value of plan assets at the beginning and the end of the period, adjusted for contributions and benefit payments. Therefore, since there were no contributions made or benefits paid during the year, the actual return on Athena's plan assets is $120,000 (i.e., $1,080,000 – $960,000), the increase in the fair value of plan assets in the year.

[4] Prior service cost is the increase in the projected benefit obligation at the date of a plan amendment (or initiation of a plan). Prior service cost is amortized during the future service periods of those employees active at the date of the amendment (or initiation) who are expected to receive benefits under the plan. Since the amortization of prior service cost can be quite complex, a straight-line method that amortizes the cost over the average remaining service life of the active participants is acceptable. Therefore, the amount of prior service cost that Athena should include in the calculation of year 3 net periodic pension cost is $28,000 (i.e., $280,000 ÷ 10).

[5] The minimum amortization of pension gain included in accumulated OCI that Athena should include in the calculation of net pension cost is determined, as of the beginning of the year, as the amount by which the unrecognized pension gain exceeds 10% of the greater of the projected benefit obligation or the market-related value of plan assets, divided by the average remaining service period of active employees expected to receive benefits under the plan.

Accumulated pension gain in OCI, 1/1	$108,000
Less: 10% of fair value of plan assets (i.e., the market-related value of plan assets), 1/1 ($960,000* × 10%)	(96,000)
Excess of pension gain	$ 12,000
Divide by: Average service life	÷ 10
Minimum amortization of pension gain	$ 1,200

* At 1/1, the fair value of plan assets exceeds the projected benefit obligation (i.e., $960,000 > $800,000).

2.

Service cost.	I	[6]
Deferral of gain on pension plan assets.	I	[7]
Actual return on plan assets.	D	[8]
Amortization of prior service costs.	I	[9]
Amortization of pension gain included in accumulated other comprehensive income.	D	[10]

Explanations

[6] Service cost is the actuarial present value of benefits attributed by the pension benefit formula to employee service during that period. Since service cost increases net pension cost, it also increases the pension liability.

[7] Since the deferral of the gain on pension plan assets increases net pension cost, it also increases the pension liability.

[8] Since the actual return on plan assets decreases net pension cost, it also decreases the pension liability.

[9] Since the amortization of prior service costs increases net pension cost, it also increases the pension liability.

[10] Since the amortization of unrecognized pension gain decreases net pension cost, it also decreases the pension liability.

Solution 9-3 SIMULATION ANSWER: Research

FASB Accounting Standards Codification

FASB ASC: 715 - 30 - 25 - 1

25-1 If the projected benefit obligation exceeds the fair value of plan assets, the employer shall recognize in its statement of financial position a liability that equals the unfunded projected benefit obligation. If the fair value of plan assets exceeds the projected benefit obligation, the employer shall recognize in its statement of financial position an asset that equals the overfunded projected benefit obligation.

CHAPTER 10

EQUITY

CHAPTER 10

EQUITY

I. Overview

A. Equity

Equity (also called shareholders' equity, stockholders' equity, or owners' equity) is the residual interest in the assets of an entity after deducting its liabilities (also known as net assets). In a business enterprise, the equity is the ownership interest. In other words, it is the combined total of contributed capital and all other increments in capital from profitable operations or other sources. It is usually shown on the statement of financial position (i.e., balance sheet) as the last section, following liabilities.

Equity may take several forms, depending on the type of ownership involved.

1. **Proprietorship** A sole proprietorship's equity consists of a single proprietor's equity account, *Owner's Equity* or *Net Worth.* This is the sum of the beginning capital balance, plus additional investments during the period, plus net income (or minus net loss) minus withdrawals. Because of the simplicity of this concept, we will not review it any further.

2. **Partnership** A partnership's equity consists of one capital account for each partner. A partner's investments and allocations of income and withdrawals are recorded in her/his individual capital account.

3. **Corporation** A corporation's equity consists of three main components: contributed capital, which includes capital stock and additional paid-in capital; retained earnings; and the accumulated balance of other comprehensive income (OCI).

B. Equity Reclassification

Certain instruments previously classified as equity are required to be classified as liabilities, even though this classification is inconsistent with the current definition of a liability.

1. **Applicability** This applies to issuer's classification and measurement of freestanding financial instruments, including those that comprise more than one option or forward contract. The following instruments are required to be reclassified as liabilities:

   a. A financial instrument that is mandatorily redeemable, issued in the form of shares—that embodies an unconditional redemption obligation requiring a transfer of assets at a specified or determinable date(s) or upon an event that is certain to occur.

   b. A financial instrument other than outstanding shares, that, at inception, embodies an obligation to repurchase the issuer's equity shares, or is indexed to an obligation to repurchase the issuer's equity shares, and requires or may require settlement of the obligation by the transfer of assets.

   c. A financial instrument that embodies an unconditional obligation that the issuer must or may settle by issuing a variable number of its equity shares, whether or not it is an outstanding share, if, at inception, the monetary value of the obligation is based solely or predominantly on any of the following: a fixed monetary amount known at inception; variations in something other than the fair value of the issuer's equity shares; or variations inversely related to changes in the fair value of the issuer's equity shares.

2. **Exempt**

   a. Features embedded in a financial instrument that is not a derivative in its entirety, such as conversion or conditional redemption features.

   b. Classification or measurement of convertible bonds, puttable stock or other outstanding shares that are conditionally redeemable

   c. Certain financial instruments indexed partly to the issuer's equity shares and partly, but not predominantly, to something else.

   d. Nonsubstantive or minimal features are to be disregarded.

   e. Forward contracts to repurchase an issuer's equity shares that require physical settlement in exchange for cash are initially measured at the fair value of the shares at inception, adjusted for any consideration or unstated rights or privileges, which is the same as the amount that would be paid under the conditions specified in the contract if settlement occurred immediately. Disclosures are required about the terms of the instruments and settlement alternatives.

3. **Impact on Private Companies**

   a. Many privately-held businesses (including partnerships) require shares be sold back to the company upon termination of the agreement or death of the owner.

   b. Events certain to occur (termination of the agreement or death of a shareholder) require classification of mandatorily redeemable shares of stock as liabilities, thus eliminating the equity of many privately-held businesses.

   c. Publicly traded companies generally do not have these types of agreements.

Example 1 ▸ Equity Reclassification

Balance Sheet

Total Assets	$2,000,000
Liabilities other than shares	$1,400,000
Shares subject to mandatory redemption	600,000
Total Liabilities	$2,000,000

Note: The balance of the equity section is zero. "Shares subject to mandatory redemption" includes the value of common stock plus retained earnings as described in the notes to the financial statements.

Notes to the Financial Statements

Shares, all subject to mandatory redemption upon death of the holders, consist of:

Common stock, $100 par value, 10,000 shares authorized, 4,000 shares issued	$ 400,000
Retained earnings attributable to those shares	200,000
Total subject to mandatory redemption	$ 600,000

II. Capital

A. Terms

1. **Contributed Capital** Contributed capital represents injections of capital by stockholders, and consists of:

   a. Capital stock is the par or stated value of the stock purchased by owners.

   b. Additional paid-in capital (APIC) is paid-in capital in excess of par or stated value.

2. **Legal Capital** The portion of contributed capital required by statute to be retained in the business for the protection of creditors is called legal capital. Legal or stated capital is usually valued as the total par or stated value of all shares issued. If stock is issued without a par or stated value, the total amount received for the stock is used. The following limitations are placed upon the corporation by law to safeguard its legal capital.

   a. Legal capital may not be used as a basis for dividends.

   b. Acquisition of treasury stock is limited to the amount of retained earnings.

   c. The amount of legal capital cannot be reduced arbitrarily by the corporation.

3. **Par Value** Stock with a specified par value per share printed on the certificate. Generally, the stockholder's maximum liability to creditors in the case of insolvency is par value. The par value of all shares issued and subscribed will normally represent the legal or stated capital.

4. **No-Par Value** Stock with no specific par value assigned to it. No-par stock avoids the contingent liability involved with the issuance of par value stock at a price below par (discount). Additionally, the stated or assigned consideration received for all no-par value shares generally represents the legal or stated capital of the corporation.

5. **No-Par With Stated Value** Essentially treated in the same manner as par value stock.

6. **Securities** Securities are the evidence of debt or ownership or a related right. The term securities generally includes options and warrants as well as debt and stock.

7. **Participation Rights** Participation rights are contractual rights of security holders to receive dividends or returns from the security issuer's profits, cash flows, or returns on investments.

8. **Stock Rights** Represents privileges extended by corporations to acquire additional shares of capital stock under prescribed conditions within a stated time period. Corporations often issue stock rights to existing common stockholders if additional common shares are to be issued to give them the opportunity to purchase a proportionate number of shares of the new offering.

   a. No entry is required when stock rights are issued to existing stockholders (other than a memorandum entry); therefore, common stock, additional paid-in capital, and retained earnings are **not** affected when stock rights are issued. With respect to stock rights, only common stock and additional paid-in capital increase when stock rights are exercised. Retained earnings is not affected when stock rights are exercised.

   b. An entry is required only when stock rights are exercised. Cash is debited for the number of common shares acquired times the exercise price of the shares. Common stock is credited for the par or stated value of the shares issued. Additional paid-in capital is credited for the excess of the cash received over the par or stated value of the shares.

Exhibit 1 ▸ Stock Rights

	Dr.	Cr.
Cash (shares × exercise price)	XXX	
Common Stock (shares × par/stated value)		XXX
Additional Paid-In Capital (to balance)		XXX

   c. No entry is required when stock rights are issued to existing stockholders (other than a memorandum entry); therefore, no entry is required when stock rights expire. Common stock, additional paid-in capital, and retained earnings are **not** affected when stock rights lapse.

9. **Stock Warrants** Physical evidence of stock rights. The warrants specify the number of rights conveyed, the number of shares to which the rightholders are entitled, the price at which the rightholders may purchase the additional shares, and the life of the rights (i.e., the time period over which the rights may be exercised).

B. Preferred Stock

Preferred stock is a security that has certain preferences or priorities not found in common stock: preference as to assets in the event of a liquidating distribution; generally, absence of voting rights (must be prohibited specifically in the charter); and preference as to dividends at a stated percentage of par or, if no-par, at a stated dollar amount and paid before dividends on common stock.

1. Features

a. **Redeemable** Shareholders may redeem shares, at their option, at a specified price per share.

b. **Convertible** Shareholders may exchange shares, at their option, for common stock.

Exhibit 2 ▸ Conversion

Account	Debit	Credit
Preferred Stock	(shs. × par)	
Add'l. PIC—Preferred	(if any)	
Common Stock		(shs. × par)
Add'l. PIC—Common		(to balance)

c. **Callable** The corporation may, at its option, purchase preferred stock for the purpose of canceling it.

Exhibit 3 ▸ Cancellation

Account	Debit	Credit
Preferred Stock	(par)	
Add'l. PIC—Preferred	(if any)	
Retained Earnings	("loss")	
Cash		(call price)
Add'l. PIC—Retirement of PS		("gain")

2. Preferred Stock Dividends

a. **Cumulative** If all or part of the stated dividend on cumulative preferred stock is not paid in a given year, the unpaid portion accumulates (i.e., dividends in arrears). No dividends can be paid on common stock until the accumulated dividends are paid on the preferred stock. Dividends in arrears are not a liability; however, they should be disclosed parenthetically or in the footnotes to the financial statements.

b. **Noncumulative** If a dividend on noncumulative preferred stock is not paid in a given year, the dividend is lost forever.

c. **Fully Participating** Entitled to share excess dividends on a pro rata basis (based on par or stated value) with common stock. For instance, 4% fully participating preferred stock will earn not only a 4% return, but also, if amounts paid on common stock exceed 4%, then dividends will be shared ratably with the common stockholders.

d. **Partially Participating** Limited in its participation with common stock to some additional percentage of par or stated value or a specified dollar amount per share as stated on the stock certificate. For instance, the stock certificate may specify that 6% preferred will participate up to a maximum of 9% of par value, or 6% preferred will participate only in distributions in excess of a 10% rate on common stock.

e. **Nonparticipating** Limited to receiving dividends at the preferential rate.

C. **Common Stock**

Common stock represents the residual ownership interest in the corporation. Distributions on common stock are generally subordinate to the rights of other securities. Thus, holders of common stock usually bear the greatest financial risks, but may also enjoy the greatest potential rewards. The four basic rights of a common stockholder are:

- Voting rights.
- Dividend rights.
- Preemptive rights to purchase stock issued by the corporation.
- Rights to share in the distribution of assets if the corporation is liquidated.

D. **Issuance**

The issuance of stock is generally recorded by debiting cash or the appropriate asset accounts for the fair value of the consideration received. *Capital Stock* is credited for the par or stated value of the shares issued, and the balancing figure is credited to *Additional Paid-In Capital.* A shareholder who acquires stock from the corporation at less than par value incurs a contingent liability to the corporation's creditors for the difference between the par value and the issue price. The issuance of stock at a discount is illegal in most states today.

Example 2 ▸ Stock Issue

500 shares of $10 par value common stock are sold for $30 per share.

Cash (500 shares × $30)	15,000	
Common Stock (500 shares × $10 par value)		5,000
APIC—Common (to balance)		10,000

E. **Additional Paid in Capital**

Additional paid in capital (APIC) is contributed capital in excess of the par or stated value. APIC can be created through other transactions, such as the sale of treasury stock at a gain, quasi-reorganizations, conversion of bonds, and the declaration of a small stock dividend.

F. **Property Other Than Cash**

Where stock is issued for noncash consideration, the property received and the amount of contributed capital should be recorded at the fair value of the property received or the market value of the stock, whichever is more objectively determinable. If fair values are not determinable, then appraised values or values set by the board of directors may be used.

Exhibit 4 ▸ Stock Exchanged for Property

Assets	(FV)	
Common Stock		(par or stated value)
APIC—Common Stock		(to balance)

G. **Subscription**

A subscription is a contract to purchase one or more shares of stock in the future. Usually, shares of stock are not issued until the full subscription price is paid. If a subscriber defaults on a subscription contract, amounts paid to the corporation may be: returned in full; retained by the corporation, and an equivalent number of shares issued; or retained to cover any losses on resale and the balance, if any, returned.

Example 3 ▶ Subscription Issue

ABC Corp. received subscriptions for 20,000 shares of $50 par value common stock at $75 per share. ABC required an initial payment of 25% of the subscription price.

Date of subscription contract		
Cash (20,000 × $75 × 25%)	375,000	
Subscriptions Receivable (20,000 × $75 × 75%)	1,125,000	
Common Stock Subscribed (20,000 × $50)		1,000,000
APIC—Common Stock (20,000 × $25)		500,000
Cash receipt and issuance of stock		
Cash	1,125,000	
Subscriptions Receivable		1,125,000
Common Stock Subscribed	1,000,000	
Common Stock		1,000,000

H. **Lump-Sum Purchase Price**
When a corporation sells two or more classes of stock for a lump sum, the proceeds are allocated among several classes of stock by one of two methods.

1. **Proportional Method** Allocation of the lump sum between the classes of stock in accordance with their relative fair values.

2. **Incremental Method** Allocation of the lump sum based on the known fair value of one security with the remainder of the lump sum being allocated to the other security.

I. **Going Concern Incorporation**
An unincorporated firm (i.e., a sole proprietorship or a partnership) may decide to adopt the corporate form. To achieve this, the new corporation issues stock (and possibly debt securities) in exchange for the assets of the going concern. The newly created corporation does not recognize gain or loss on the issuance of securities in exchange for the business' assets.

1. **Fair Value** The acquired assets are recorded at their fair values. Current liabilities assumed generally are recorded at face amount and long-term liabilities at their present value.

2. **Par or Stated Value** The issued stock is recorded at par or stated value. Any excess of net assets acquired over par or stated value of the capital stock is credited to *Additional Paid-in Capital.*

Example 4 ▶ Going Concern Incorporation

On January 1, year 2, Kyle Fleming decided to incorporate his automobile repair and restoration business, Fleming Automotive. To this effect, he transferred the assets and liabilities of his business to a new corporation, Auto Concepts, Inc., receiving in exchange all 1,000 shares of its $10 par value stock.

Fleming Automotive
Balance Sheet, as of December 31, Year 3

Current assets (fair value, $25,000)	$ 20,000
Equipment (appraised value, $130,000)	150,000
Less, accumulated depreciation	(60,000)
Total assets	$110,000
Liabilities	$ 30,000
Kyle Fleming, Capital	80,000
Total liabilities and equity	$110,000

Required: Provide the journal entry to record the incorporation of the business.

Solution:

Current Assets	25,000	
Equipment	130,000	
Liabilities		30,000
Common Stock, $10 Par		10,000
Add'l. Paid-in Capital (balancing figure)		115,000

J. Disclosures

1. **Rights and Privileges of Securities Outstanding** An entity is required to disclose in the financial statements, in summary form, the pertinent rights and privileges of the various securities outstanding. Examples include dividend and liquidation preferences, participation rights, call prices and dates, conversion or exercise prices or rates and pertinent dates, sinking-fund requirements, unusual voting rights, and significant terms of contracts to issue additional shares.

2. **Number of Shares Issued** An entity is required to disclose the number of shares issued upon conversion, exercise, or satisfaction of required conditions during at least the most recent annual fiscal period and any subsequent interim period presented.

3. **Liquidation Preference of Preferred Stock**

   a. If an entity issues preferred stock or other senior stock that has a preference in involuntary liquidation considerably in excess of the par or stated value of the shares, the entity is required to disclose this information in the equity section of the statement of financial position. The disclosure may be made parenthetically or "in short," but not on a per-share basis or in the notes.

   b. In addition, the entity is required to disclose, either on the statement of financial position or in the notes, the aggregate or per-share amounts at which preferred stock may be called or is subject to redemption through sinking-fund operations, and the aggregate or per share amounts of arrearages in cumulative preferred dividends.

4. **Redeemable Stock** The amount of redemption requirements related to redeemable stock must be disclosed for all issues of capital stock that are redeemable at fixed or determinable prices on fixed or determinable dates in each of the five years following the date of the latest statement of financial position presented.

III. Retained Earnings

A. Classification

The *Retained Earnings* account is the final terminus for all profit and loss accounts. The balance represents the accumulated income of the corporation, less dividends declared and amounts transferred to paid-in capital accounts. Retained earnings should not include the following: gains from treasury stock transactions; gifts of property; additions to owners' equity attributable to reappraisals of property; or accumulated balance of other comprehensive income.

1. **Appropriated Retained Earnings** The portion unavailable for dividends. Some reasons for appropriation are to create a reserve for plant expansion, to satisfy legal requirements of a bond indenture, or to provide a cushion for expected future losses. Owing to the application of most state corporate laws, retained earnings is often appropriated in the amount of the cost of treasury stock acquired under either the cost or par value methods.

Exhibit 5 ▸ Appropriation of Retained Earnings

Retained Earnings	XXX	
Appropriated RE—Plant Construction		XXX

Costs associated with the construction of the plant are not charged to the appropriation. When the appropriation is no longer needed, the entry is reversed.

2. **Unappropriated Retained Earnings** That portion of retained earnings available for dividend distribution.

B. **Statement of Changes in Retained Earnings**
Disclosure of changes in the separate accounts comprising stockholders' equity (in addition to retained earnings) is required to make the financial statements sufficiently informative. Disclosure may take the form of separate statements or may be made in the basic financial statements or notes thereto.

Exhibit 6 ▸ Statement of Changes in Retained Earnings

Retained earnings, Jan. 1, year 1, as reported	XXX
+/– Cumulative effect of retroactive changes in accounting principles	XXX
+/– Prior period adjustments	XXX
Retained earnings, Jan. 1, year 1, as adjusted	XXX
+ Net income (– Net loss)	XXX
– Dividends declared	(XXX)
Retained earnings, Dec. 31, year 1	XXX

C. **Quasi-Reorganization**
A reorganization or revision of the capital structure, which is permitted in some states. This procedure eliminates an accumulated deficit as if the company had been legally reorganized without much of the cost and difficulty of a legal reorganization. Thus, the corporation will be able to pay dividends again. It involves the following steps.

1. **Assets Revalued** Assets are revalued at net realizable value, but there is no net asset increase. (Any loss on revaluation increases the deficit.)

2. **Deficit** A minimum of the amount of the adjusted deficit must be available in paid-in capital (PIC). This might be created by donation of stock from shareholders or reduction of the par value.

3. **Elimination** The deficit is charged against PIC and thus is eliminated.

D. **Effect of Various Transactions**
Frequently, CPA exam questions ask about the effect of common transactions.

1. **Increases** In general, retained earnings (RE) is increased only as a result of net income generated by the firm. In addition, retained earnings may increase as a result of a prior period adjustment (e.g., the correction of an error) or certain special changes in accounting principle (e.g., change from the completed contract to the percentage of completion method of accounting for long-term construction contracts).

2. **Decreases** Retained earnings decreases as a result of dividends (cash, property, or stock) and net losses suffered by the firm. In addition, treasury stock transactions, certain stock splits, prior period adjustments, and certain special changes in accounting principle may also reduce retained earnings.

Exhibit 7 ▸ Transactions Affecting Retained Earnings

Transactions	Effect on RE	Amount
Operations—gains and losses	Increase **or** decrease	Net income or net loss
Dividends—cash or property	Decrease	Amount of cash or FV of property distributed (Note that gain or loss is also recognized on declaration of property dividends.)
Stock dividends:		
1. Small (≤ 20 to 25%)	Decrease	FV of stock distributed
2. Large (> 25%)	Decrease	Par value of stock distributed
Stock splits:		
1. Par reduced proportionally	No change	-0-
2. Par not reduced	Decrease	Par value of new shares
Acquisition of treasury stock:		
1. Cost method	No change	-0-
2. Par value method	No change **or** decrease	-0- [if cost ≤ (par + APIC)] Purchase price in excess of par and pro rata APIC
Sale of treasury stock:		
1. Cost method	No change **or** decrease	-0- (if sale price > cost) Excess of cost over sale price, but offset first to APIC on TS transactions
2. Par value method	No change	-0-
Prior period adjustments	Increase **or** decrease	Amount of adjustment, net of income tax
Certain changes in accounting principle	Increase **or** decrease	Amount of adjustment, net of income tax

E. Accumulated Other Comprehensive Income

Accumulated other comprehensive income (AOCI) is used to accumulated unrealized gains and unrealized losses on those items in the income statement that are classified within Other Comprehensive Income (OCI). An entity is required to display the accumulated balance of OCI separately from retained earnings, capital stock, and additional paid-in capital in the equity section of a statement of financial position. An entity must disclose accumulated balances for each classification as a separate component of equity on the face of the statement of financial position, in the statement of changes in equity, or in the notes to the financial statements. The classifications must correspond to classifications used elsewhere in the same set of statements for components of OCI, and may include: unrealized holding gains and losses on available-for-sale securities; foreign currency translation gains or losses; pension plan gains or losses; pension prior service costs or credits; and deferred gains or losses on the effective portion of cash flow hedges.

Once a gain or loss is realized, it is moved out of AOCI and into net income to determine comprehensive income, and eventually to retained earnings.

IV. Treasury Stock

A. Overview

Treasury stock is the corporation's common or preferred stock that has been reacquired by purchase, by settlement of an obligation to the corporation, or through donation. Acquisition of treasury stock reduces assets and total stockholders' equity (unless donated) while the reissuance of treasury stock increases assets and total stockholders' equity. There are two basic methods to account for treasury stock: the cost method and the par value method. The cost method is used more commonly. Treasury stock is not an asset. No gains or losses are recognized on treasury stock transactions. Retained earnings may be decreased, but never increased, by treasury stock transactions.

Total stockholders' equity is the same under both the cost and par value methods. Total stockholders' equity decreases by the cost of treasury shares acquired and increases by the proceeds received from the reissuance of treasury stock, regardless of whether the treasury stock is accounted for by the cost or the par value method. In many states, retained earnings must be appropriated in the amount of the cost of treasury stock.

B. Cost Method

The cost method views the purchase and subsequent disposition of stock as one transaction. The treasury stock is recorded (debited), carried, and reissued at the acquisition cost.

1. **Reissued in Excess of Acquisition Cost** If the stock is reissued at a price in *excess* of the acquisition cost, the excess is credited to an appropriately titled paid-in capital account (e.g., *Additional Paid-In Capital From Treasury Stock Transactions*).

2. **Reissued at Less Than Acquisition Cost** If the stock is reissued at less than the acquisition cost, the deficit is first charged against any existing balance in the *Additional Paid-In Capital From Treasury Stock Transactions* account. The excess, if any, is then charged against *Retained Earnings.*

3. **Balance Sheet Presentation** Under the cost method, treasury stock is presented on the balance sheet as an unallocated reduction of total stockholders' equity (i.e., contributed capital and retained earnings).

C. Par Value Method

The par value method views the purchase and subsequent disposition of stock as two distinct transactions. Under this method, the acquisition of the treasury shares is viewed as a constructive retirement of the stock. Since capital stock is carried on the balance sheet at par (or stated value), the acquisition of treasury stock is also recorded at par (or stated value), by debiting *Treasury Stock.* Likewise, *Additional Paid-In Capital—Common Stock* is charged with a pro rata amount of any excess over par or stated value recorded on the original issuance of the stock. Note that the effect of these two entries is to remove the treasury stock from the accounts, i.e., as if it had been retired.

1. **Cost Less Than Price** If the acquisition cost of the treasury stock is less than the price at which the stock was originally issued, the difference is credited to *APIC From Treasury Stock.*

2. **Cost Exceeds Price** On the other hand, if the acquisition cost exceeds the stock's original issue price, then the excess is debited to *APIC From Treasury Stock,* but only to the extent of any existing balance (i.e., from prior treasury stock transactions). The excess, if any, is debited to *Retained Earnings.*

3. **Reissuance** The reissuance of treasury stock under the par value method is accounted for in the same manner as an original stock issuance. However, any reissuances of treasury stock at less than par value will reduce (debit) *Additional Paid-In Capital From Treasury Stock* until that balance is exhausted, then debit *Retained Earnings* for any excess.

Example 5 ▸ Treasury Stock Transactions Comparison

Cost Method			Par Value Method		
Original Issue of 1,000 shares of $10 par value common stock at $15 per share:					
Cash (1,000 shares @ $15)	15,000		Cash (1,000 shares @ $15)	15,000	
Common Stock (1,000 sh. @ $10)		10,000	Common Stock (1,000 sh. @ $10)		10,000
APIC—CS (1,000 sh. @ $5)		5,000	APIC—CS (1,000 sh. @ $5)		5,000
Acquisition of 100 shares at $18 per share:					
Treasury Stock	1,800		Treasury Stock (100 sh. @ $10)	1,000	
Cash (100 sh. @ $18)		1,800	APIC—CS (100 sh. @ $5)	500	
			Retained Earnings (to balance)	300	
			Cash		1,800
Acquisition of 50 shares at $9 per share:					
Treasury Stock	450		Treasury Stock (50 sh. @ $10)	500	
Cash (50 sh. @ $9)		450	APIC—CS (50 sh. @ $5)	250	
			Cash (50 sh. @ $9)		450
			APIC—TS (to balance)		300
Reissuance of 50 shares at $20 per share (FIFO):					
Cash (50 sh. @ $20)	1,000		Cash (50 sh. @ $20)	1,000	
Treasury Stock (50 sh. @ $18)		900	Treasury Stock (50 sh. @ $10)		500
APIC—TS (to balance)		100	APIC—TS (to balance)		500
Reissuance of 50 shares at $9 per share (FIFO):					
Cash (50 sh. @ $9)	450		Cash (50 sh. @ $9)	450	
APIC—TS (up to existing bal.)	100		APIC—TS (to balance)	50	
Retained Earnings (to balance)	350		Treasury Stock (50 sh. @ $10)		500
Treasury Stock (50 sh. @ $18)		900			

D. Retirement

A corporation may decide to retire some or all of its treasury stock. Retired stock is classified as authorized and unissued (i.e., as if it had never been issued). Accounting for the retirement of treasury stock depends on the method used initially to record it, i.e., cost or par value method.

Example 6 ▸ Retirement of Treasury Stock

Cost Method			Par Value Method		
Original Issue of 20 shares of $100 par value common stock at $105 per share:					
Cash (20 shares @ $105)	2,100		Cash (20 shares @ $105)	2,100	
Common Stock (20 sh. @ $100)		2,000	Common Stock (20 sh. @ $100)		2,000
APIC—CS (20 sh. @ $5)		100	APIC—CS (20 sh. @ $5)		100
a.					
Acquisition of 20 shares at $110 per share:					
Treasury Stock	2,200		Treasury Stock (20 sh. @ $100)	2,000	
Cash (20 sh. @ $110)		2,200	APIC—CS (20 sh. @ $5)	100	
			Retained Earnings (to balance)	100	
			Cash (20 sh. @ $110)		2,200
Retirement of the 20 shares acquired at $110 per share:					
Common Stock (20 sh. @ $100)	2,000		Common Stock (20 sh. @ $100)	2,000	
APIC—CS (20 sh. @ $5)	100		Treasury Stock		2,000
Retained Earnings (to balance)	100				
Treasury Stock (20 sh. @ $110)		2,200			

b.
Acquisition of 20 shares at $98 per share:

Treasury Stock	1,960		Treasury Stock (20 sh. @ $100)	2,000	
Cash (20 sh. @ $98)		1,960	APIC—CS (20 sh. @ $5)	100	
			Cash (20 sh. @ $98)		1,960
			APIC—TS (to balance)		140

Retirement of the 20 shares acquired at $98 per share:

Common Stock (20 sh. @ $100)	2,000		Common Stock (20 sh. @ $100)	2,000	
APIC—CS (20 sh. @ $5)	100		Treasury Stock		2,000
Treasury Stock (20 sh. @ $98)		1,960			
APIC—TS (to balance)		140			

V. Distributions

A. Definition

Dividends represent the distribution to stockholders of a proportionate share of retained earnings or, as in the case of liquidating dividends, a return of capital. Dividends (except stock dividends) reduce stockholders' equity through the distribution of assets or the incurrence of a liability.

B. Significant Dates

1. **Declaration** The date of declaration is the date on which dividends are formally declared by the board of directors and the declared dividends (except stock dividends) become a liability.

Exhibit 8 ▶ Recording Dividend Liability

Retained Earnings	XXX	
Dividends Payable		XXX

2. **Record** The date of record is the date used to establish those stockholders who will receive the declared dividends. No journal entry is required unless the number of shares outstanding have changed from the date of declaration.

3. **Payment** The distribution of assets is made on the date of payment.

Exhibit 9 ▶ Dividend Payment

Dividends Payable	XXX	
Cash or Other Property		XXX

Exhibit 10 ▶ Cash Dividend

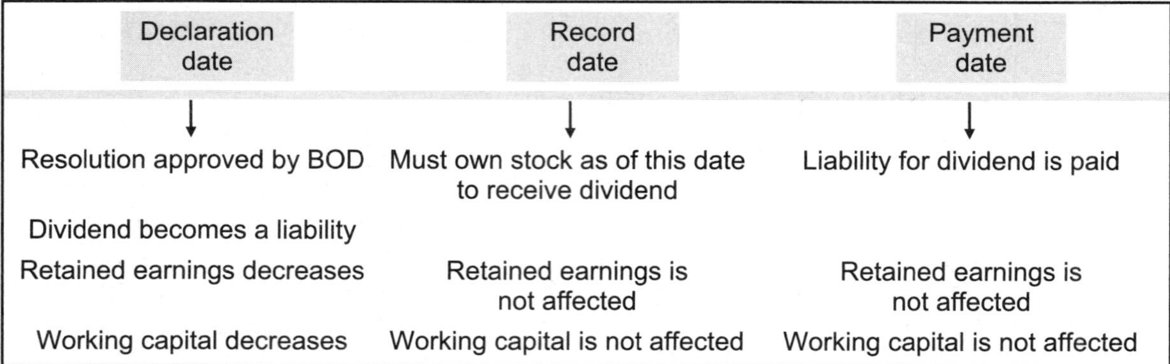

C. Property Dividends

At the date of declaration, property dividends are recorded at the fair value of assets given up, and any difference between fair value and carrying amount of the asset is recorded as a gain or loss as a component of income from continuing operations.

Example 7 ▸ Property Dividend

ABC Company transfers marketable debt securities that cost $1,500 to shareholders by declaring a property dividend. The fair value of the securities was $2,000 at the date of declaration.

Date of declaration		
Retained Earnings	2,000	
Property Dividends Payable		2,000
Investment in Marketable Securities	500	
Gain on Investment in Marketable Securities		500
Date of payment		
Property Dividends Payable	2,000	
Investment in Marketable Securities		2,000

NOTE: Any change in the fair value of the asset to be distributed between the date of declaration and date of payment is ignored.

D. Liquidating Dividends

Liquidating dividends are distributions in excess of retained earnings and, therefore, represent a return of investment rather than a share in profits.

Exhibit 11 ▸ Liquidating Dividend

Date of declaration		
Retained Earnings (nonliquidating portion)	XXX	
Paid-In Capital in Excess of Par (liquidating portion)	XXX	
Dividends Payable		XXX
Date of payment		
Dividends Payable	XXX	
Cash		XXX

E. Stock Dividends

Issuance by a corporation of its own common shares to its common shareholders without consideration and under conditions indicating such action is prompted mainly by a desire to give the recipient shareholders some ostensibly separate evidence of a part of their respective interests in accumulated corporate earnings without distribution of cash or other property. The following guidance does **not** apply when each shareholder is given an election to receive cash or shares.

1. **General Effect** A stock dividend takes nothing from the property of the corporation and adds nothing to the interests of the stockholders; that is, the corporation's property is not diminished and the interests of the stockholders are not increased. The proportional interest of each shareholder remains the same.

2. **Shareholder Income** The shareholder has no income as a result of the stock dividend because the stock dividend (or stock split) is not a distribution, division, or severance of the corporate assets. There is nothing resulting that the shareholder can realize without parting with some proportionate interest in the corporation. The cost of the shares held *before* the stock dividend is allocated to all of the shares held after the receipt of the dividend.

3. **Recording** In recording the stock dividend, a charge is made to retained earnings (thereby making a portion of retained earnings no longer available for distribution) and credits are made to paid-in capital accounts; total stockholders' equity is not affected. The amount of retained earnings capitalized depends on the size of the stock dividend and the apparent effect which the dividend has on the market value of the shares.

Exhibit 12 ▸ Stock Dividend

<u>Small Stock Dividend Declaration & Issuance</u>		
Retained Earnings	(FV)	
Common Stock		(Par)
Add'l. PIC—CS		(Balance)
<u>Large Stock Dividend Declaration & Issuance</u>		
Retained Earnings	(Par)	
Common Stock		(Par)

a. When the stock dividend is relatively small (not in excess of 20 to 25 percent of outstanding stock) the fair value (at the date of declaration) of the additional shares should be transferred from retained earnings to paid-in capital.

b. When the stock dividend is large (greater than 25% of the outstanding shares) only the par or stated value of the additional shares is to be capitalized.

F. **Stock Splits**
Increase the number of shares outstanding and proportionately decrease the par or stated value of the stock. There is no change in the dollar amount of capital stock, additional paid-in capital, retained earnings, or total stockholders' equity. Stock splits are issued mainly to reduce the unit market price per share of the stock, in order to obtain a wider distribution. Reverse stock splits simply decrease shares outstanding and proportionately increase the par or stated value of the stock.

Example 8 ▸ Stock Split

ABC Corp. declares a 3-for-1 stock split on common stock in order to increase trading of the stock on the open market. Prior to the split, the corporation had 300,000 shares of $12 par value common stock issued and outstanding. The journal entry to record the stock split would be:

Common Stock (par $12; 300,000 shares outstanding)	3,600,000	
Common Stock (par $4; 900,000 shares outstanding)		3,600,000

NOTE: The corporation may elect to record the stock split in a memorandum entry.

Exhibit 13 ▸ Total Stockholders' Equity

	RETAINED EARNINGS	PAR VALUE PER SHARE	TOTAL PAR VALUE	ADD'L. PAID-IN CAPITAL	# OF SHARES OUTST.	TOTAL S.H. EQUITY
Small stock dividend	⇓ by FV of shares issued	**x**	⇑	⇑	⇑	**x**
Large stock dividend	⇓ by par value of shares issued	**x**	⇑	**x**	⇑	**x**
Stock split	**x**	⇓	**x**	**x**	⇑	**x**

⇑ = increase; ⇓ = decrease; **x** = no change

VI. Employees & Stock

A. Share-Based Payment Plans

An employee stock option is issued as a form of noncash compensation. The employee can exercise the option at a particular price (set on the grant day) to purchase a specific number of shares of the company's stock. There is usually a holding period before the options can be exercised. Options are not only used as compensation, but also to retain and attract key employees. Employees try to profit be exercising their options at a higher price than when they were granted.

Since most employee stock options are non-transferable, and are not immediately exercisable, the IRS considers that their fair value cannot be readily determinable, and therefore no taxable event occurs when an employee receives a grant. Generally, the employee pays ordinary income tax on the difference between the exercise price and the current stock price when the options are exercised. Companies can deduct this amount as compensation expense.

Basically, the appropriate accounting treatment for share-based payment plans is determined by whether the plan is noncompensatory or compensatory.

B. Noncompensatory Plans

Noncompensatory plans (employee-share purchase plans) pose no unique accounting problems. These plans are adopted primarily to raise capital and induce widespread stock ownership among a company's employees. When the stock is issued, it is accounted for as an ordinary issue of stock. An employee share purchase plan that satisfies all of the following criteria does not give rise to recognizable compensation cost (that is, the plan is noncompensatory):

1. **Conditions** The plan satisfies at least one of the following conditions:

   a. The terms of the plan are no more favorable than those available to all holders of the same class of shares.

   b. Any purchase discount from the market price does not exceed the per-share amount of share issuance costs that would have been incurred to raise a significant amount of capital by a public offering. A purchase discount of 5 percent or less from the market price shall be considered to comply with this condition without further justification. A purchase discount greater than 5 percent that cannot be justified under this condition results in compensation cost for the entire amount of the discount.

2. **Participation** Substantially all employees that meet limited employment qualifications may participate on an equitable basis.

3. **Option Features** The plan incorporates no option features, other than the following:

   a. Employees are permitted a short period of time—not exceeding 31 days—after the purchase price has been fixed to enroll in the plan.

   b. The purchase price is based solely on the market price of the shares at the date of purchase, and employees are permitted to cancel participation before the purchase date and obtain a refund of amounts previously paid (such as those paid by payroll withholdings).

C. Compensatory Plans

Compensatory plans are those that do not meet the criteria for noncompensatory plans. If the employee pays less than the quoted market price of the stock at the measurement date, compensation expense must be measured and allocated to the appropriate periods of the employee's services. If the plan is deemed to be compensatory, then compensation cost will need to be recognized using the fair value method of option pricing.

1. **Employee** The definition of an employee includes elected outside members of the company's board of directors. An individual is considered an employee if the company granting the options has sufficient control over the individual as to establish an employer-employee relationship.

2. **Measurement Date** The measurement date is the date of the grant. When the measurement date occurs subsequent to the grant date, compensation expense is recorded and accrued at the end of each period based on the quoted market price at the end of the period, the estimated number of shares earned, and the option price.

3. **Measurement Method** Entities are required to adopt a fair value based method of accounting for stock-based compensation plans.

   a. Fair value is defined as the amount at which willing parties in a current transaction would buy or sell an asset, other than in a forced or liquidation sale. The fair value based method calls for recognizing compensation cost of stock-based compensation based on the grant-date fair value of the award (with limited exceptions).

   b. The use of a valuation model is required to estimate the value of the stock-based compensation granted. Entities can use the Black-Scholes, binomial, or similar pricing model which takes into account the following information as of the grant date: (1) the exercise price, (2) the expected life of the option, (3) the current price of the stock, (4) the expected volatility of the stock, (5) the expected dividends on the stock, and (6) the risk-free interest rate for the expected term of the option.

   Exhibit 14 ▸ Black-Scholes Pricing Model

D	—	Dividends expected on the stock
E	—	Exercise price
V	—	Volatility of the stock
I	—	Interest rate (risk free rate) for the expected term of the option
L	—	Life of the option
S	—	Stock current price

   c. When options or other equity instruments are exchanged for goods or services with a nonemployee, the transaction will need to be reflected at fair value. In such a case, the value received may be more readily determinable than the value of the options given.

4. **Future Services** If the stock or options are granted as compensation for future services, *Deferred Compensation Cost* is debited and the amount is recognized as compensation expense in the appropriate period. *Deferred Compensation Expense* is a contra-equity account.

Example 9 ▸ Compensatory Plan

An option is granted on January 1, year 1, to a key executive to purchase 5,000 shares of $20 par common stock at $40 per share when the market price is $46 per share. The key executive is awarded the option based on services to be rendered equally over four years. The options are worth $160,000.

Required: Make journal entries to record: (1) compensation cost on the measurement date, (2) annual compensation expense, and (3) issuance of the stock if the option is exercised at the end of year 4.

Solution: On the balance sheet, deferred compensation cost is recorded as a deduction from stock options outstanding; it is not an asset. The "net" of these two accounts represents the compensation that the employee has earned to date.

(1)	*January 1, year 1*		
	Deferred Comp. Cost (value of options at date of grant)	160,000	
	Stock Options Outstanding		160,000
(2)	*December 31, year 1, year 2, year 3, and year 4*		
	Compensation Expense ($160,000 / 4)	40,000	
	Deferred Compensation Cost		40,000
(3)	*December 31, year 4*		
	Cash (5,000 shares × $40)	200,000	
	Stock Options Outstanding	160,000	
	Common Stock (5,000 × $20)		100,000
	Add'l. Paid-In Cap., Common (to balance)		260,000

5. **Previously Rendered Service** Where the employee works for several periods before the stock is issued, the employer accrues a portion of the compensation expense from the stock issuance.

6. **Unearned Stock Compensation** Where the stock is issued before some or all of the services are performed, the compensation that is unearned is shown as a separate reduction to shareholder equity, and is recognized as an expense over the years in which services are performed.

7. **Unexercised Stock Options for Nonvested Employees** If a stock option is not exercised because an employee fails to fulfill an obligation under the option agreement, the estimate of compensation expense recorded in previous periods should be adjusted by decreasing compensation expense in the year of forfeiture.

8. **Expired Stock Options of Vested Employees** Previously recognized compensation cost is not reversed if a vested employee's stock option expires unexercised.

9. **Adjustments to Compensation Expense** Adjustments to compensation expense in subsequent periods may be necessary as new estimates are determined.

10. **Repriced Options** When a company directly or indirectly reprices options, it has changed the terms of the plan, which would convert the award from a fixed to a variable award as of the date of the reprising. Accounting for variable awards includes an element of compensation expense.

11. **Employee Stock Ownership Plans (ESOP)** An ESOP is a tax-qualified, defined-contribution retirement plan which makes a company's employees partial owners. Contributions are made by the employer, and can grow tax-deferred, just as with an IRA. Contributions must be invested in the company's stock.

    a. The compensation expense that an entity recognizes for an ESOP is the amount contributed (or committed to be contributed) for the period. When a noncash asset or the entity's stock is contributed to the plan, the fair value of the asset or stock is used to measure compensation expense.

    b. When an obligation of an ESOP is covered by an employer's guarantee or a commitment by the employer to make future contributions to the plan sufficient to meet debt service requirements, the obligation is presented as a liability in the employer's balance sheet. When the employer's liability is recorded, an offsetting debit is recorded that is reported as a reduction of stockholders' equity. Therefore, an employer reports a reduction of stockholders' equity equal to the obligation reported for the plan.

Example 10 ▸ ESOP

On May 1 of the current year, Harrell Corporation established an employee stock ownership plan and contributed $20,000 cash and 1,000 shares of its $10 par value common stock to the ESOP. On this date the market price of the stock was $23 a share.

Required: Determine the amount of compensation expense that Harrell should report in its current year income statement.

Solution:

Cash contributed	$20,000
Fair value of common stock contributed (1,000 shares × $23)	23,000
Compensation expense recognized in the year	$43,000

D. Disclosure

Prominent disclosures about the method of accounting for stock-based employee compensation and the effect of the method used on the reported results are required in both annual and interim financial statements. The following information must be disclosed regardless of the method used.

- The number and weighted-average exercise prices of options: (a) for those outstanding at the beginning of the year, (b) for those outstanding at the end of the year, (c) for those exercisable at the end of the year, (d) for those granted during the year, (e) for those exercised during the year, (f) for those forfeited during the year, and (g) for those expired during the year.
- The weighted-average grant-date fair value of options granted during the year.
- The number and weighted-average grant-date fair value of equity instruments other than options.
- A description of the method and significant assumptions used during the year to estimate the fair values of options.
- Total compensation cost recognized in income for stock-based employee compensation awards.
- The terms of significant modifications of outstanding awards.
- The method of reporting the change in accounting principles when a change to the fair value based method is adopted.

VII. Partnership Formation

A. Revised Uniform Partnership Act

The **Revised Uniform Partnership Act** (RUPA) defines a partnership as an association of two or more persons to carry on, as co-owners, a business for profit. In addition to setting forth the legal rights and liabilities of the partners, the RUPA has some impact on accounting for partnership transactions. Accounting for partnerships must comply with the legal requirements as set forth by the RUPA (e.g., liquidation payments to partnership creditors before any distribution to partners) or other applicable state laws, as well as complying with the partnership agreement itself.

B. Identifiable Assets Contributed

All identifiable assets (e.g., cash, inventory, land, patents, etc.) contributed to the partnership are recorded by the partnership at their fair values (i.e., book values are ignored). All liabilities that the partnership assumes are recorded at their present values. If a partner contributes a noncash asset to the partnership (e.g., land or equipment) subject to a mortgage, the contributing partner's capital account is credited for the fair value of the noncash asset less the mortgage assumed by the partnership.

Example 11 ▸ Identifiable Assets Contributed

Alice and Brenda form a partnership: Alice contributes cash of $60,000; Brenda contributes a building with a fair value of $90,000 subject to a mortgage loan of $30,000.

Required: Provide the journal entry to record the partnership formation.

Solution:

Cash	60,000	
Building	90,000	
Mortgage Loan on Building		30,000
Alice, Capital		60,000
Brenda, Capital ($90,000 – $30,000)		60,000

C. Unidentifiable Assets Contributed

When one or more partners contribute unidentifiable assets (e.g., managerial expertise or personal business reputation), the formation of the partnership may be recorded under the bonus method or the goodwill method.

1. **Bonus Method** The bonus method assumes that unidentifiable assets contributed to the partnership do **not** constitute a partnership asset with a measurable cost. Only identifiable assets contributed to the partnership, such as cash, inventory, patents, and equipment are recognized by the partnership. The bonus method allocates invested capital, equal to the fair value of the identifiable net assets contributed to the partnership, to the partners according to a specified ratio.

Example 12 ▸ Bonus Method

Alice and Brenda form a partnership. Alice contributes cash of $40,000 and her considerable managerial expertise; Brenda contributes a building with a fair value of $90,000 subject to a mortgage loan of $30,000. Alice and Brenda are to be given equal capital balances using the bonus method.

Required: Provide the journal entry to record the partnership formation.

Solution:

Cash	40,000	
Building	90,000	
Mortgage Loan on Building		30,000
Alice, Capital		50,000
Brenda, Capital		50,000

The bonus method allocates the $100,000 [i.e., ($40,000 + $90,000) – $30,000] of invested capital to Brenda and Alice equally. Alice is receiving a capital bonus of $10,000 from Brenda because she is given a capital balance of $50,000, although she has only contributed identifiable assets of $40,000 to the partnership.

2. **Goodwill Method** All assets contributed to the partnership, such as cash, inventory, patents, equipment, and managerial expertise are recognized by the partnership. The goodwill method credits the contributing partner's capital account for the fair value of the identifiable and unidentifiable assets contributed less the amount of any assumed liabilities.

Example 13 ▸ Goodwill Method

Same situation as in Example 12, except that the goodwill method is to be used.

Required: Provide the journal entry to record the partnership formation.

Solution:

	Debit	Credit
Cash	40,000	
Building	90,000	
Goodwill	20,000	
Mortgage Loan on Building		30,000
Alice, Capital		60,000
Brenda, Capital		60,000

The goodwill method considers Alice's managerial expertise to be a partnership asset with a measurable cost. Since Alice is to be given a $60,000 capital balance while only contributing identifiable assets with a fair value of $40,000, an implied value of $20,000 can be assigned to her managerial expertise. The goodwill method capitalizes the apparent value of Alice's contribution. Brenda is given a $60,000 capital balance, equal to the fair value of the building she contributed to the partnership less the mortgage assumed by the partnership (i.e., $90,000 – $30,000).

D. Owners' Equity Accounts

The capital account is an equity account used to account for permanent withdrawals, additional contributions and net income or loss. Other important accounts include the drawing account and loans to or from partners. The drawing account is used to account for normal withdrawals. It is closed at the end of the period into the capital account. Loan accounts are established for amounts intended as loans, rather than as additional capital investments. In liquidation proceedings, a loan to or from a partner is treated as a decrease or increase to the partner's capital account, respectively.

E. Profit & Loss Division

The method of division used is generally the method specified in the partnership agreement. The profit and loss sharing ratio may be entirely independent of the partners' ownership interests.

1. **No Arrangement Specified** If no profit and loss sharing arrangement is specified in the partnership agreement, RUPA requires that profits and losses be shared equally.

2. **No Arrangement for Losses** If the agreement specifies how profits are to be shared, but is silent as to losses, losses are to be shared in the same manner as profits. Conversely, if the agreement specifies the sharing of losses, but is silent as to profits, profits are shared in the same manner as losses.

3. **Equally or Specified Ratio** Equally or in accordance with a specified ratio set forth in the partnership agreement

4. **Capital Balance** According to the ratio of partners' capital balances as of a particular date or according to their weighted-average capital balances for the period

Example 14 ▸ Division of Profits

Adams, Burks, and Crew are partners in a going concern with capital accounts at the beginning of the period of $40,000, $24,000, and $28,000, respectively. Partnership income was $25,000. Adams, Burks, and Crew had drawings of $2,000, $1,000, and $2,000 respectively.

The partnership agreement provides that:

a. All partners are to receive interest of 6% on beginning capital balances.
b. Burks is to receive a $4,000 annual salary and Crew a $5,000 annual salary.
c. The remaining income is to be divided 30% to Adams; 25% to Burks; and 45% to Crew.

Required: Compute the ending capital balances of each partner.

Solution:

	Adams	Burks	Crew	Total
Beginning capital balances	$40,000	$24,000	$28,000	$ 92,000
6% interest on beginning capital balances	2,400	1,440	1,680	5,520
Guaranteed payments		4,000	5,000	9,000
Division of remaining income ($25,000 – $5,520 – $9,000)	3,144	2,620	4,716	10,480
Capital balances before drawings	45,544	32,060	39,396	117,000
Drawings	(2,000)	(1,000)	(2,000)	(5,000)
Ending capital balances	$43,544	$31,060	$37,396	$112,000

VIII. New Partner Admission

A. Overview

A new partner may be admitted to the partnership by purchasing the interest of one or more of the existing partners or by contributing cash or other assets (i.e., investment of additional capital).

B. Purchase

When a new partner enters the partnership by purchasing some or all of the interest of an existing partner, the price paid for that interest is irrelevant to the partnership accounting records because it is a private transaction between the buyer and seller. The assets and liabilities of the partnership are not affected. The capital account of the new partner is recorded by merely relabeling the capital account of the old partner.

Example 15 ▸ Partnership Interest Purchase

Henry and Gerald are partners with capital accounts of $40,000 and $60,000, respectively. Rocky purchases Henry's interest for $50,000.

Required: Provide the journal entry to record this transaction.

Solution: After Rocky's purchase, total partnership capital continues to equal $100,000 (i.e., $40,000 + $60,000).

	Debit	Credit
Henry, Capital	40,000	
Rocky, Capital		40,000

C. Additional Asset Investment

A new partner may be granted an interest in the partnership in exchange for contributed identifiable assets and/or goodwill (e.g., business expertise, an established clientele, etc.). The admission of the new partner and contribution of assets may be recorded on the basis of the bonus method or the goodwill method.

1. **Bonus Method** Admittance of a new partner involves debiting cash or other identifiable assets for the fair value of the assets contributed and crediting the new partner's capital for the agreed (i.e., purchased) percentage of total capital. Total capital equals the carrying amount of the net assets prior to admittance of the new partner, plus the fair value of the identifiable assets contributed by the new partner. A difference between the fair value of the identifiable assets contributed and the interest granted to the new partner results in the recognition of a bonus.

Example 16 ▸ Bonus Method

Henry and Gerald are partners with capital accounts of $40,000 and $60,000, respectively; income and losses are shared equally (50%). The partnership records new partners using the bonus method. Rocky invests additional assets for a 1/3 ownership interest.

Required: Provide the journal entries to record Rocky's admission, if (a) Rocky invests $50,000; (b) Rocky invests $56,000; and (c) Rocky invests $44,000.

Solution:

(a) **No Bonus Recognized** Following the admittance of Rocky, the identifiable net assets of the partnership will have a carrying amount of $150,000 ($40,000 + $60,000 + $50,000). One-third of this amount, or $50,000, is assigned to Rocky's capital account. Since this is equal to the fair value of the identifiable assets contributed by Rocky ($50,000), no bonus results.

Cash (or other identifiable assets, as appropriate)	50,000	
Rocky, Capital (1/3 × $150,000)		50,000

After Rocky's admission, total partnership capital equals the carrying amount of the identifiable net assets of the partnership (i.e., $40,000 + $60,000 + $50,000 = $150,000).

(b) **Bonus to Old Partners** The total capital of the new partnership equals $156,000. Rocky's 1/3 interest of this new total is $52,000. The $4,000 excess of identifiable assets contributed by Rocky over his initial capital balance is divided among the old partners as a bonus on the basis of their profit and loss sharing ratio.

Cash	56,000	
Henry, Capital ($4,000 × 50%)		2,000
Gerald, Capital ($4,000 × 50%)		2,000
Rocky, Capital		52,000

After Rocky's admission, Henry's and Gerald's capital balances are $42,000 (i.e., $40,000 + $2,000) and $62,000 (i.e., $60,000 + $2,000), respectively, and total partnership capital equals the recorded amount of the identifiable net assets of the partnership (i.e., $42,000 + $62,000 + $52,000 = $156,000).

(c) **Bonus to New Partner** Since Rocky contributes $44,000, the total net assets of the new partnership will be $144,000. Rocky's 1/3 share of this is $48,000. The $4,000 difference between the fair value of the identifiable assets contributed by Rocky ($44,000) and the amount to be credited to him ($48,000) is allocated among the old partners in accordance with their profit and loss sharing ratio.

Cash	44,000	
Henry, Capital ($4,000 × 50%)	2,000	
Gerald, Capital ($4,000 × 50%)	2,000	
Rocky, Capital		48,000

After Rocky's admission, Henry's and Gerald's capital balances are $38,000 (i.e., $40,000 – $2,000) and $58,000 (i.e., $60,000 – $2,000), respectively, and total partnership capital equals the recorded amount of the identifiable net assets of the partnership (i.e., $38,000 + $58,000 + $48,000 = $144,000).

a. When the fair value of the identifiable assets contributed by an incoming partner exceeds the amount of ownership interest to be credited to the capital account, the old partners recognize a bonus equal to this excess. This bonus is allocated on the basis of the same ratio used for income allocation (unless otherwise specified in the partnership agreement). Recording involves crediting the old partners' capital accounts for the allocated amounts of the bonus.

b. An incoming partner may contribute identifiable assets having a fair value less than the partnership interest granted to that new partner. Similarly, the new partner may not contribute any identifiable assets at all. The incoming partner is therefore presumed to contribute an unidentifiable asset, such as managerial expertise or personal business reputation. In this case, a bonus is granted to the new partner, and the capital accounts of the old partners are reduced on the basis of their profit and loss ratio.

2. **Goodwill Method** This method attempts to revalue the net worth of the partnership on the basis of the fair value of assets received in exchange for a percentage ownership interest. Following the admission of the new partner, the total capital (i.e., net worth) of the partnership is revalued to approximate its fair value. Existing identifiable assets must be revalued at their fair value; any excess valuation implied in the purchase price is recorded as goodwill.

Example 17 ▸ Goodwill Method

Same as Example 16, except the partnership records admissions of new partners under the goodwill method.

Required: Provide the journal entries to record Rocky's admission, as if (a) Rocky invests $56,000 and if (b) Rocky invests $44,000.

Solution:

(a) **Goodwill to Old Partners** As Rocky is to be credited with a 1/3 interest for $56,000, the implied capital (total fair value) of the partnership is $168,000 (i.e., $56,000 × 3). The $12,000 difference between the actual capital ($156,000) and the implied capital ($168,000) is recorded as goodwill attributable to the old partners in accordance with their profit and loss sharing ratio (50% each as stated above).

Goodwill	12,000	
Henry, Capital		6,000
Gerald, Capital		6,000
Cash	56,000	
Rocky, Capital		56,000

After Rocky's admission, Henry's and Gerald's capital balances are $46,000 (i.e., $40,000 + $6,000) and $66,000 (i.e., $60,000 + $6,000), respectively, and total partnership capital equals the fair value of the net assets of the partnership (i.e., $46,000 + $66,000 + $56,000 = $168,000).

(b) **Goodwill to New Partner** As Rocky is to receive a 1/3 interest for $44,000, the old partners are to have a 2/3 interest. If 2/3X = $100,000 (old partners' capital), the implied value for 100% is $150,000 (100,000 / 2/3). Thus, Rocky's capital will be $50,000 consisting of $44,000 contributed and $6,000 goodwill.

Cash	44,000	
Goodwill	6,000	
Rocky, Capital		50,000

After Rocky's admission, Henry's and Gerald's capital balances are $40,000 and $60,000, respectively, and total partnership capital equals the fair value of the net assets of the partnership (i.e., $40,000 + $60,000 + $50,000 = $150,000).

a. When a new partner's asset contribution is greater than the ownership interest s/he is to receive, the excess assets are accounted for as goodwill attributable to the old partners.

b. When a new partner's identifiable asset contribution is less than the ownership interest s/he is to receive, the excess capital allowed to the new partner is considered as goodwill attributable to her/him. This assumes that the recorded amounts of the old partners' capital accounts adequately reflect the fair value of the partnership's assets; otherwise, write off the excess carrying amount.

IX. Partner Withdrawal

A. Overview

Admission of a new partner is not the only manner by which a partnership can undergo a change in composition. Over the life of any partnership, partners may leave the organization. Some method of equitably settling the withdrawing partner's interest in the business property is necessary. The withdrawal of a partner generally is recorded using either the bonus or the goodwill method.

B. Bonus Method

The difference between the balance of the withdrawing partner's capital account and the amount s/he is paid is the amount of the "bonus." The "bonus" is allocated among the remaining partners' capital accounts in accordance with their profit and loss ratios. Although the partnership's identifiable assets may be revalued to their fair value at the date of withdrawal, any goodwill implied by an excess payment to the retiring partner is **not** recorded.

Example 18 ▸ Bonus Method Withdrawal

On May 1, Able decided to retire from the partnership. By mutual agreement, the assets are to be adjusted to their fair value of $260,000 at May 1, and the partnership will pay Able $60,000 for Able's partnership interest. No goodwill is to be recorded. The balance sheet for the partnership of Able, Baker, and Cain, together with their respective profit and loss ratios, was as follows:

Assets, at cost	$200,000	Accounts Payable	$ 20,000
		Able, Capital (20%)	40,000
		Baker, Capital (20%)	50,000
		Cain, Capital (60%)	90,000
			$200,000

Required: Provide the journal entries to record this transaction and determine the balances of Baker's and Cain's capital accounts after Able's retirement.

Solution: The entry to adjust the partnership assets to their fair value is as follows.

Identifiable Assets ($260,000 – $200,000)	60,000	
Able, Capital ($60,000 × 20%)		12,000
Baker, Capital ($60,000 × 20%)		12,000
Cain, Capital ($60,000 × 60%)		36,000

After this entry, Able has a capital balance of $52,000 ($40,000 + $12,000). Under the bonus method, the additional payment of $8,000 ($60,000 payment – $52,000 capital balance) made to Able is recorded as a decrease in the remaining partners' capital accounts. As Baker and Cain have been receiving 20% and 60% of all profits and losses, respectively, 25% [0.2 / (0.2 + 0.6)] of this reduction is allocated to Baker and 75% [0.6 / (0.2 + 0.6)] to Cain:

Able, Capital	52,000	
Baker, Capital (25% × $8,000)	2,000	
Cain, Capital (75% × $8,000)	6,000	
Cash		60,000

After this entry, Baker's capital balance is $60,000 ($50,000 + $12,000 – $2,000) and Cain's capital balance is $120,000 ($90,000 + $36,000 – $6,000).

C. Goodwill Method

The partners may elect to record the implied goodwill in the partnership based on the payment to the withdrawing partner. The amount of the implied goodwill is allocated to all of the partners in accordance with their profit and loss ratios. After the allocation of the implied goodwill of the partnership, the balance in the withdrawing partner's capital account should equal the amount s/he is to receive in final settlement of her/his interest.

Example 19 ▸ Goodwill Method Withdrawal

Same as Example 18, except that goodwill is to be recorded in the transaction, as implied by the excess payment to Able.

Required: Provide the journal entries to record this transaction and determine the balances of Baker's and Cain's capital accounts after Able's retirement.

Solution: The entry to adjust the partnership assets to their fair value is the same.

Identifiable Assets ($260,000 – $200,000)	60,000	
Able, Capital ($60,000 × 20%)		12,000
Baker, Capital ($60,000 × 20%)		12,000
Cain, Capital ($60,000 × 60%)		36,000

After this entry, Able has a capital balance of $52,000 ($40,000 + $12,000). Able's capital account must be increased by $8,000 to equal her $60,000 cash distribution. To accomplish this, goodwill is recognized for some amount, of which, $8,000 represents 20%, Able's profit and loss percentage. Therefore, the amount of goodwill to be recorded is $40,000 ($8,000 / 20%). The entries to record the implied goodwill of the partnership and the payment to Able in final settlement of her interest are as follows.

Goodwill	40,000	
Able, Capital ($40,000 × 20%)		8,000
Baker, Capital ($40,000 × 20%)		8,000
Cain, Capital ($40,000 × 60%)		24,000
Able, Capital ($52,000 + $8,000)	60,000	
Cash		60,000

After this entry, Baker's capital balance is $70,000 ($50,000 + $12,000 + $8,000) and Cain's capital balance is $150,000 ($90,000 + $36,000 + $24,000).

X. Partnership Liquidation

A. Overview

Liquidation is the process of converting partnership assets into cash and distributing the cash to creditors and partners. If the sale of partnership assets does not provide sufficient cash to pay both creditors and partners, then the creditors have priority on any distribution. No distribution is made to any partner until all possible losses and liquidation expenses have been paid or provided for.

1. **Premature Distribution** An individual prematurely distributing cash to a partner whose capital account later shows a deficit may be held personally liable if the insolvent partner is unable to repay such a distribution. The liquidation of a partnership may take place over a period of several months. The proceeds of a liquidation may be distributed in a lump sum after all assets have been sold and all creditors satisfied, or the proceeds may be distributed to partners in installments as excess cash becomes available.

2. **Loans** In liquidation proceedings, a loan to a partner from the partnership is treated as a decrease to the partner's capital account. A loan from a partner to the partnership is treated as an increase to the partner's capital account.

B. Lump-Sum Distribution

The first step in the liquidation process is to sell all noncash assets and allocate the resulting gain or loss to the capital accounts of the partners in accordance with their profit and loss sharing ratio. The second step is to satisfy the liabilities owing to creditors other than partners. The third step is to satisfy liabilities owing to partners other than for capital and profits. The final step is to distribute any cash remaining to the partners for capital and finally for profits. Any deficiency (i.e., debit balance) in a solvent partner's capital will require that partner to contribute cash equal to the debit balance. If the deficient partner is insolvent, the debit balance must be absorbed by the remaining partners (usually in accordance with their profit and loss sharing ratio).

Example 20 ▸ Lump-Sum Distribution

XYZ Partnership is to be liquidated and excess cash, if any, is to be distributed to the partners in a lump sum. The balance sheet of the XYZ Partnership is shown with the profit-loss ratio indicated in parentheses next to each partner's capital account. A loss of $108,000 was realized on the sale of noncash assets.

Cash	$ 22,000	Liabilities	$ 18,000
Other assets	128,000	X, Capital (50%)	44,000
Total assets	$150,000	Y, Capital (30%)	44,000
		Z, Capital (20%)	44,000
		Total liabilities and capital	$150,000

Required: Provide a schedule showing the liquidation of assets and distribution of proceeds to creditors and partners.

Solution: XYZ Partnership—Liquidation Statement Schedule

		Other		Capital		
	Cash	Assets	Liabs.	X(50%)	Y(30%)	Z(20%)
Balances before realization	$ 22,000	$ 128,000	$ 18,000	$ 44,000	$ 44,000	$ 44,000
Sale of assets at loss of $108,000	20,000	(128,000)		(54,000)	(32,400)	(21,600)
Balances after realization	42,000	$ 0	18,000	(10,000)	11,600	22,400
Payment of liabilities	(18,000)		(18,000)			
Balances	24,000		$ 0	(10,000)	11,600	22,400
Distribution of X's deficit	0			10,000	(6,000)	(4,000)
Balances	24,000			$ 0	5,600	18,400
Final distribution of cash	(24,000)				(5,600)	(18,400)
Balances	$ 0				$ 0	$ 0

C. Installment Distributions

Installment distributions may be made to partners on the basis of a Schedule of Safe Payments, in conjunction with a Liquidation Schedule similar to the one used for lump-sum liquidations. The Schedule of Safe Payments takes a conservative approach to the distribution by assuming that non-cash assets are worthless; thus no distribution may be made to partners on the basis of the value of partnership assets, until the assets are sold.

Example 21 ▸ Installment Distributions

Refer to Example 20. Liquidation of XYZ's partnership assets took place as per the schedule below. Disposal expenses to be incurred during the liquidation period were estimated at $5,000; this amount is to be held in escrow until the final liquidation.

Date	Carrying Amount	Sale Price	(Loss)
June 24	$ 40,000	$ 5,000	$ (35,000)
July 7	60,000	13,000	(47,000)
August 3	28,000	2,000	(26,000)
	$128,000	$20,000	$(108,000)

Required: What is the safe amount of cash that may be distributed to each partner following each sale of partnership noncash assets? Show supporting schedule(s).

Solution: XYZ Partnership—Liquidation Statement Schedule

	Cash	Other Assets	Liabs.	Capital X(50%)	Capital Y(30%)	Capital Z(20%)
Balances before realization	$ 22,000	$128,000	$ 18,000	$ 44,000	$ 44,000	$ 44,000
June 24 sale	5,000	(40,000)		(17,500)	(10,500)	(7,000)
Balance	27,000	88,000	18,000	26,500	33,500	37,000
Liabilities paid	(18,000)		(18,000)			
Balance	9,000	88,000	$ 0	26,500	33,500	37,000
Cash distribution*	(4,000)					(4,000)
Balance	5,000	88,000		26,500	33,500	33,000
July 7 sale	13,000	(60,000)		(23,500)	(14,100)	(9,400)
Balance	18,000	28,000		3,000	19,400	23,600
Cash distribution*	(13,000)				(1,400)	(11,600)
Balance	5,000	28,000		3,000	18,000	12,000
August 3 sale	2,000	(28,000)		(13,000)	(7,800)	(5,200)
Payment of liquidation costs	(5,000)			(2,500)	(1,500)	(1,000)
Balance	2,000	$ 0		(12,500)	8,700	5,800
Allocation of debit balance	0			12,500	(7,500)	(5,000)
Balance	2,000			$ 0	1,200	800
Cash distribution**	(2,000)				(1,200)	(800)
	$ 0				$ 0	$ 0

* See accompanying Schedule of Safe Cash Distribution.
** Note that final cash distribution may be made on the basis of balances shown in the partners' capital accounts, since all assets have been sold and liabilities paid.

XYZ Partnership—Schedule of Safe Cash Distribution

Date	Description	Capital Balances X(50%)	Capital Balances Y(30%)	Capital Balances Z(20%)	Total(100%)
June 25	Acct. bal. following sale of assets & pmt. of liabilities**	$ 26,500	$ 33,500	$ 37,000	$ 97,000
	Estimated cost of disposal	(2,500)	(1,500)	(1,000)	(5,000)
	Balance	24,000	32,000	36,000	92,000
	Maximum loss possible	(44,000)	(26,400)	(17,600)	(88,000)
	Balance	(20,000)	5,600	18,400	4,000
	Allocation of debit balance	20,000	(12,000)	(8,000)	
	Balance	$ 0	(6,400)	10,400	4,000
	Allocation of debit balance		6,400	(6,400)	
	Safe cash distribution*		$ 0	$ 4,000	$ 4,000
July 7	Acct. bal. following sale of fixed assets**	$ 3,000	$ 19,400	$ 23,600	$ 46,000
	Max. loss possible including $5,000 est. expense)	(16,500)	(9,900)	(6,600)	(33,000)
		(13,500)	9,500	17,000	13,000
	Allocation of debit balance	13,500	(8,100)	(5,400)	
	Safe cash distribution*	$ 0	$ 1,400	$ 11,600	$ 13,000

* To Liquidation Statement.
** From Liquidation Statement.

Select Hot•Spot™ Video Descriptions

CPA 3440 Owners' Equity & Miscellaneous Topics
This program highlights several important accounting topics. It provides extensive coverage of accounting for stockholders' equity. This includes the components of stockholders' equity, dividends, stock splits, stock options, and treasury stock. Also covered in this program are the most important aspects of partnership accounting, foreign operations and financial analysis with emphasis on earnings per share. During this video, Bob Monette goes through numerous examples and 37 multiple-choice questions covering these topics. Approximate video duration is 3 hours. This does not include the time a candidate spends answering questions and taking notes.

CPA 3220 Revenue Recognition & Income Statement Presentation
This program includes extensive coverage of the income statement components, what is included in each component, and how components are presented in the financial statements. Learn what comprehensive income includes and how it is presented. In-depth coverage includes accounting for long-term contracts, installment sales, discontinued operations, extraordinary items, prior period adjustments, changes in accounting principles, changes in estimates, changes in entity...and more! Robert Monette discusses 50 multiple-choice questions, a simulation, and several examples. Approximate video duration is 3 hours and 55 minutes. This does not include the time a candidate spends answering questions and taking notes.

Call our customer representatives toll-free at 1 (800) 874-7877 for more details about videos.

Subject to Change Without Notice

CHAPTER 10—EQUITY

Problem 10-1 MULTIPLE-CHOICE QUESTIONS

1. On January 2 of the current year, Smith purchased the net assets of Jones' Cleaning, a sole proprietorship, for $350,000, and commenced operations of Spiffy Cleaning, a sole proprietorship. The assets had a carrying amount of $375,000 and a market value of $360,000. In Spiffy's cash-basis financial statements for the current year ended December 31, Spiffy reported revenues in excess of expenses of $60,000. Smith's drawings during the year were $20,000. In Spiffy's financial statements, what amount should be reported as Capital—Smith?

   a. $390,000
   b. $400,000
   c. $410,000
   d. $415,000 (11/94, FAR, #36, amended, 5298)

2. Zinc Co.'s adjusted trial balance at December 31 includes the following account balances:

Common stock, $3 par	$600,000
Additional paid-in capital	800,000
Treasury stock, at cost	50,000
Net unrealized loss on AFS marketable equity securities	20,000
Retained earnings: Appropriated for uninsured earthquake losses	150,000
Retained earnings: Unappropriated	200,000

   What amount should Zinc report as total stockholders' equity in its December 31 balance sheet?

   a. $1,680,000
   b. $1,720,000
   c. $1,780,000
   d. $1,820,000 (5/92, PI, #5, amended, 2572)

3. On April 1 of the current year, Hyde Corp., a newly formed company, had the following stock issued and outstanding:

   - Common stock, no par, $1 stated value, 20,000 shares originally issued for $30 per share.
   - Preferred stock, $10 par value, 6,000 shares originally issued for $50 per share.

   Hyde's April 1 statement of stockholders' equity should report

	Common stock	Preferred stock	Additional paid-in capital	
a.	$ 20,000	$ 60,000	$820,000	
b.	$ 20,000	$300,000	$580,000	
c.	$600,000	$300,000	$0	
d.	$600,000	$ 60,000	$240,000	(5/93, PI, #6, amended, 4048)

4. An accumulated balance of other comprehensive income (OCI) is a component of which of the following?

   a. Corporation's equity
   b. Partnership's equity
   c. Sole proprietorship's equity
   d. All of the above (Editor, 89637)

5. A company issued rights to its existing shareholders without consideration. The rights allowed the recipients to purchase unissued common stock for an amount in excess of par value. When the rights are issued, which of the following accounts will be increased?

	Common stock	Additional paid-in capital	
a.	Yes	Yes	
b.	Yes	No	
c.	No	No	
d.	No	Yes	(11/95, FAR, #21, 6103)

6. In September of year 2, West Corp. made a dividend distribution of one right for each of its 120,000 shares of outstanding common stock. Each right was exercisable for the purchase of 1/100 of a share of West's $50 variable rate preferred stock at an exercise price of $80 per share. On March 20 of year 6, none of the rights had been exercised, and West redeemed them by paying each stockholder $0.10 per right. As a result of this redemption, West's stockholders' equity was reduced by

   a. $ 120
   b. $ 2,400
   c. $12,000
   d. $36,000 (11/95, FAR, #22, amended, 6104)

7. Quoit Inc. issued preferred stock with detachable common stock warrants. The issue price exceeded the sum of the warrants' fair value and the preferred stocks' par value. The preferred stocks' fair value was not determinable. What amount should be assigned to the warrants outstanding?

   a. Total proceeds
   b. Excess of proceeds over the par value of the preferred stock
   c. The proportion of the proceeds that the warrants' fair value bears to the preferred stocks' par value
   d. The fair value of the warrants (5/93, Theory, #13, 4201)

8. On November 2 of year 2, Fins Inc. issued warrants to its stockholders giving them the right to purchase additional $20 par value common shares at a price of $30. The stockholders exercised all warrants on March 1 of year 3. The shares had market prices of $33, $35, and $40 on November 2, year 2, December 31, year 2, and March 1, year 3, respectively. What were the effects of the warrants on Fins' additional paid-in capital and net income?

	Additional paid-in capital	Net income
a.	Increased in year 3	No effect
b.	Increased in year 2	No effect
c.	Increased in year 3	Decreased in years 2 and 3
d.	Increased in year 2	Decreased in years 2 and 3

(11/93, Theory, #15, 4520)

9. During the previous year, Brad Co. issued 5,000 shares of $100 par convertible preferred stock for $110 per share. One share of preferred stock can be converted into three shares of Brad's $25 par common stock at the option of the preferred shareholder. On December 31 of the current year, when the market value of the common stock was $40 per share, all of the preferred stock was converted. What amount should Brad credit to Common Stock and to Additional Paid-In Capital—Common Stock as a result of the conversion?

	Common stock	Additional paid-in capital
a.	$375,000	$175,000
b.	$375,000	$225,000
c.	$500,000	$ 50,000
d.	$600,000	$0

(11/94, FAR, #29, amended, 5292)

10. At December 31 of year 1 and year 2, Carr Corp. had outstanding 4,000 shares of $100 par value 6% cumulative preferred stock and 20,000 shares of $10 par value common stock. At December 31, year 1, dividends in arrears on the preferred stock were $12,000. Cash dividends declared in year 2 totaled $44,000. Of the $44,000, what amounts were payable on each class of stock?

	Preferred stock	Common stock
a.	$44,000	$0
b.	$36,000	$ 8,000
c.	$32,000	$ 12,000
d.	$24,000	$ 20,000

(5/93, PII, #4, amended, 4113)

11. ___________ stock avoids the contingent liability involved with the issuance of other types of stocks at a discounted price.

    a. Par value
    b. No-par value
    c. No-par with stated value
    d. None of the above (Editor, 89638)

12. If 500 shares of $10 par value common stock are sold for $40 per share, the entry would be debit cash $20,000 and credit, which of the following accounts for how much?

    a. Common Stock $20,000
    b. Common Stock $5,000; Additional Paid-in Capital—Common $15,000
    c. Common Stock $15,000; Retain Earnings $5,000
    d. Retained Earnings $5,000; Common Stock $15,000 (Editor, 89644)

13. East Co. issued 1,000 shares of its $5 par common stock to Howe as compensation for 1,000 hours of legal services performed. Howe usually bills $160 per hour for legal services. On the date of issuance, the stock was trading on a public exchange at $140 per share. By what amount should the additional paid-in capital account increase as a result of this transaction?

    a. $135,000
    b. $140,000
    c. $155,000
    d. $160,000 (11/94, FAR, #28, 5291)

14. On December 1 of the current year, shares of authorized common stock were issued on a subscription basis at a price in excess of par value. A total of 20% of the subscription price of each share was collected as a down payment on December 1 with the remaining 80% of the subscription price of each share due in the next year. Collectibility was reasonably assured. At December 31 the stockholders' equity section of the balance sheet would report additional paid-in capital for the excess of the subscription price over the par value of the shares of common stock subscribed and

    a. Common stock issued for 20% of the par value of the shares of common stock subscribed
    b. Common stock issued for the par value of the shares of common stock subscribed
    c. Common stock subscribed for 80% of the par value of the shares of common stock subscribed
    d. Common stock subscribed for the par value of the shares of common stock subscribed (11/88, Theory, #17, amended, 1996)

15. On July 1 of the current year, Cove Corp., a closely held corporation, issued 6% bonds with a maturity value of $60,000, together with 1,000 shares of its $5 par value common stock, for a combined cash amount of $110,000. The market value of Cove's stock cannot be ascertained. If the bonds were issued separately, they would have sold for $40,000 on an 8% yield to maturity basis. What amount should Cove report for additional paid-in capital on the issuance of the stock?

    a. $75,000
    b. $65,000
    c. $55,000
    d. $45,000 (11/92, PII, #44, amended, 3378)

16. The condensed balance sheet of Adams & Gray, a partnership, at December 31, year 1, follows:

Current assets	$250,000	Liabilities	$ 20,000
Equipment (net)	30,000	Adams, capital	160,000
Total assets	$280,000	Gray, capital	100,000
		Total liabilities and capital	$280,000

On December 31, year 1, the fair values of the assets and liabilities were appraised at $240,000 and $20,000, respectively, by an independent appraiser. On January 2 of year 2, the partnership was incorporated and 1,000 shares of $5 par value common stock were issued. Immediately after the incorporation, what amount should the new corporation report as additional paid-in capital?

a. $275,000
b. $260,000
c. $215,000
d. $0 (5/93, PII, #6, amended, 4115)

17. A retained earnings appropriation can be used to

a. Absorb a fire loss when a company is self-insured
b. Provide for a contingent loss that is probable and reasonable
c. Smooth periodic income
d. Restrict earnings available for dividends (5/92, Theory, #37, 2730)

18. At December 31, year 1, Eagle Corp. reported $1,750,000 of appropriated retained earnings for the construction of a new office building, which was completed in year 2 at a total cost of $1,500,000. In year 2, Eagle appropriated $1,200,000 of retained earnings for the construction of a new plant. Also, $2,000,000 of cash was restricted for the retirement of bonds due in year 3. In its year 2 balance sheet, Eagle should report what amount of appropriated retained earnings?

a. $1,200,000
b. $1,450,000
c. $2,950,000
d. $3,200,000 (5/93, PII, #5, amended, 4114)

19. The primary purpose of a quasi-reorganization is to give a corporation the opportunity to

a. Obtain relief from its creditors
b. Revalue understated assets to their fair values
c. Eliminate a deficit in retained earnings
d. Distribute the stock of a newly-created subsidiary to its stockholders in exchange for part of their stock in the corporation (11/94, FAR, #37, 5299)

20. The stockholders' equity section of Brown Co.'s December 31, year 1, balance sheet consisted of the following:

Common stock, $30 par, 10,000 shares authorized and outstanding	$ 300,000
Additional paid-in capital	150,000
Retained earnings (deficit)	(210,000)

On January 2, year 2, Brown put into effect a stockholder-approved quasi-reorganization by reducing the par value of the stock to $5 and eliminating the deficit against additional paid-in capital. Immediately after the quasi-reorganization, what amount should Brown report as additional paid-in capital?

a. $ (60,000)
b. $ 150,000
c. $ 190,000
d. $ 400,000 (11/95, FAR, #25, amended, 6107)

21. The following changes in Vel Corp.'s account balances occurred during the current year:

	Increase
Assets	$89,000
Liabilities	27,000
Capital stock	60,000
Additional paid-in capital	6,000

Except for a $13,000 dividend payment and the year's earnings, there were no changes in retained earnings for the year. What was Vel's net income for the year?

a. $ 4,000
b. $ 9,000
c. $13,000
d. $17,000 (5/93, PII, #3, amended, 4112)

22. In general, retained earnings may increase as a result of which of the following?

a. Prior adjustments
b. Net losses suffered by the firm
c. Stock dividends
d. All of the above (Editor, 89647)

23. Nest Co. issued 100,000 shares of common stock. Of these, 5,000 were held as treasury stock at December 31 of year 3. During year 4, transactions involving Nest's common stock were as follows:

May 3 — 1,000 shares of treasury stock were sold.
August 6 — 10,000 shares of previously unissued stock were sold.
November 18 — A 2-for-1 stock split took effect.

Laws in Nest's state of incorporation protect treasury stock from dilution. At December 31 of year 4, how many shares of Nest's common stock were issued and outstanding?

	Shares Issued	Shares Outstanding
a.	220,000	212,000
b.	220,000	216,000
c.	222,000	214,000
d.	222,000	218,000

(11/95, FAR, #18, amended, 6100)

24. On December 1 of the current year, Line Corp. received a donation of 2,000 shares of its $5 par value common stock from a stockholder. On that date, the stock's market value was $35 per share. The stock was originally issued for $25 per share. By what amount would this donation cause total stockholders' equity to decrease?

a. $70,000
b. $50,000
c. $20,000
d. $0 (5/93, PI, #11, amended, 4053)

25. Selected information from the accounts of Row Co. at December 31 follows:

Total income since incorporation	$420,000
Total cash dividends paid	130,000
Total value of property dividends distributed	30,000
Excess of proceeds over cost of treasury stock sold, accounted for using the cost method	110,000

In its December 31 financial statements, what amount should Row report as retained earnings?

a. $260,000
b. $290,000
c. $370,000
d. $400,000 (5/96, FAR, #1, 6274)

26. Murphy Co. had 200,000 shares outstanding of $10 par common stock on March 30 of the current year. Murphy reacquired 30,000 of those shares at a cost of $15 per share, and recorded the transaction using the cost method on April 15. Murphy reissued the 30,000 shares at $20 per share, and recognized a $50,000 gain on its income statement on May 20. Which of the following statements is correct?

    a. Murphy's comprehensive income for the current year is correctly stated.
    b. Murphy's net income for the current year is overstated.
    c. Murphy's net income for the current year is understated.
    d. Murphy should have recognized a $50,000 loss on its income statement for the current year.

    (R/05, FAR, #31, 7775)

27. Grid Corp. acquired some of its own common shares at a price greater than both their par value and original issue price but less than their book value. Grid uses the cost method of accounting for treasury stock. What is the impact of this acquisition on total stockholders' equity and the book value per common share?

	Total stockholders' equity	Book value per share
a.	Increase	Increase
b.	Increase	Decrease
c.	Decrease	Increase
d.	Decrease	Decrease

(11/91, Theory, #40, 2548)

28. During the current year, Onal Co. purchased 10,000 shares of its own stock at $7 per share. The stock was originally issued at $6. The firm sold 5,000 of the treasury shares for $10 per share. The firm uses the cost method to account for treasury stock. What amount should Onal report in its income statement for these transactions?

    a. $0
    b. $ 5,000 gain
    c. $10,000 loss
    d. $15,000 gain

    (R/09, FAR, #16, 8766)

29. Porter Co. began its business last year and issued 10,000 shares of common stock at $3 per share. The par value of the stock is $1 per share. During January of the current year, Porter bought back 500 shares at $6 per share, which were reported by Porter as treasury stock. The treasury stock shares were reissued later in the current year at $10 per share. Porter used the cost method to account for its equity transactions. What amount should Porter report as paid-in capital related to its treasury stock transactions on its balance sheet for the current year?

    a. $ 1,500
    b. $ 2,000
    c. $ 4,500
    d. $20,000

    (R/06, FAR, #41, 8108)

30. Baker Co. issued 100,000 shares of common stock in the current year. On October 1, Baker repurchased 20,000 shares of its common stock on the open market for $50.00 per share. At that date, the stock's par value was $1.00 and the average issue price was $40.00 per share. Baker uses the cost method for treasury stock transactions. On December 1, Baker reissued the stock for $60.00 per share. What amount should Baker report as treasury stock gain at December 31?

    a. $0
    b. $200,000
    c. $400,000
    d. $980,000

    (R/07, FAR, #27, 8348)

31. At December 31, year 7, Rama Corp. had 20,000 shares of $1 par value treasury stock it had acquired in year 7 at $12 per share. In May, year 8, Rama issued 15,000 of these treasury shares at $10 per share. The cost method is used to record treasury stock transactions. Rama is located in a state where laws relating to acquisition of treasury stock restrict the availability of retained earnings for declaration of dividends. At December 31, year 8, what amount should Rama show in notes to financial statements as a restriction of retained earnings as a result of its treasury stock transactions?

    a. $ 5,000
    b. $10,000
    c. $60,000
    d. $90,000 (5/89, PII, #6, amended, 1103)

32. The par-value method of accounting for treasury stock differs from the cost method in that

    a. Any gain is recognized upon repurchase of stock but a loss is treated as an adjustment to retained earnings.
    b. No gains or losses are recognized on the issuance of treasury stock using the par-value method.
    c. It reverses the original entry to issue the common stock with any difference between carrying amount and purchase price adjusted through paid-in capital and/or retained earnings and treats a subsequent reissuance like a new issuance of common stock.
    d. It reverses the original entry to issue the common stock with any difference between carrying amount and purchase price being shown as an ordinary gain or loss and does **not** recognize any gain or loss on a subsequent resale of the stock. (5/89, Theory, #10, 1993)

33. Lem Co., which accounts for treasury stock under the par value method, acquired 100 shares of its $6 par value common stock for $10 per share. The shares had originally been issued by Lem for $7 per share. By what amount would Lem's additional paid-in capital from common stock decrease as a result of the acquisition?

    a. $0
    b. $100
    c. $300
    d. $400 (R/11, FAR, #30, 9880)

34. On incorporation, Dee Inc., issued common stock at a price in excess of its par value. No other stock transactions occurred except treasury stock was acquired for an amount exceeding this issue price. If Dee uses the par value method of accounting for treasury stock appropriate for retired stock, what is the effect of the acquisition on the following?

	Net common stock	Additional paid-in capital	Retained earnings
a.	No effect	Decrease	No effect
b.	Decrease	Decrease	Decrease
c.	Decrease	No effect	Decrease
d.	No effect	Decrease	Decrease

(5/91, Theory, #18, 1972)

35. Two years ago, Fogg Inc. issued $10 par value common stock for $25 per share. No other common stock transactions occurred until March 31 of the current year, when Fogg acquired some of the issued shares for $20 per share and retired them. Which of the following statements correctly states an effect of this acquisition and retirement?

    a. Current year net income is decreased
    b. Current year net income is increased
    c. Additional paid-in capital is decreased
    d. Retained earnings is increased (5/93, Theory, #10, amended, 4198)

36. On December 31 of the current year, Pack Corp.'s board of directors canceled 50,000 shares of $2.50 par value common stock held in treasury at an average cost of $13 per share. Before recording the cancellation of the treasury stock, Pack had the following balances in its stockholder's equity accounts:

Common Stock	$540,000
Additional paid-in capital	750,000
Retained earnings	900,000
Treasury stock, at cost	650,000

In its balance sheet at December 31, Pack should report common stock outstanding of

a. $0
b. $250,000
c. $415,000
d. $540,000 (11/92, PII, #50, amended, 3384)

37. Park Corp.'s stockholders' equity accounts at December 31 of the previous year were as follows:

Common stock, $20 par	$8,000,000
Additional paid-in capital	2,550,000
Retained earnings	1,275,000

All shares of common stock outstanding at December 31 of the previous year were issued originally for $26 a share. On January 4 of the current year, Park reacquired 20,000 shares of its common stock at $24 a share and retired them. Immediately after the shares were retired, the balance in additional paid-in capital would be

a. $2,430,000
b. $2,470,000
c. $2,510,000
d. $2,590,000 (5/88, PI, #42, amended, 1106)

38. A company declared a cash dividend on its common stock on December 15 of the previous year, payable on January 12 of the current year. How would this dividend affect stockholders' equity on the following dates?

	December 15, previous year	December 31, previous year	January 12, current year
a.	Decrease	No effect	Decrease
b.	Decrease	No effect	No effect
c.	No effect	Decrease	No effect
d.	No effect	No effect	Decrease

(5/91, Theory, #17, amended, 1971)

39. East Corp., a calendar-year company, had sufficient retained earnings in year 1 as a basis for dividends, but was temporarily short of cash. East declared a dividend of $100,000 on April 1, year 1, and issued promissory notes to its stockholders in lieu of cash. The notes, which were dated April 1, year 1, had a maturity date of March 31, year 2, and a 10% interest rate. How should East account for the scrip dividend and related interest?

a. Debit retained earnings for $110,000 on April 1, year 1.
b. Debit retained earnings for $110,000 on March 31, year 2.
c. Debit retained earnings for $100,000 on April 1, year 1, and debit interest expense for $10,000 on March 31, year 2.
d. Debit retained earnings for $100,000 on April 1, year 1, and debit interest expense for $7,500 on December 31, year 1. (5/94, FAR, #31, amended, 4846)

40. On June 27 of the current year, Brite Co. distributed to its common stockholders 100,000 outstanding common shares of its investment in Quik Inc., an unrelated party. The carrying amount on Brite's books of Quik's $1 par common stock was $2 per share. Immediately after the distribution, the market price of Quik's stock was $2.50 per share. In its income statement for the current year ended June 30, what amount should Brite report as gain before income taxes on disposal of the stock?

    a. $250,000
    b. $200,000
    c. $ 50,000
    d. $0 (5/93, PI, #45, amended, 4086)

41. Instead of the usual cash dividend, Evie Corp. declared and distributed a property dividend from its overstocked merchandise. The excess of the merchandise's carrying amount over its market value should be

    a. Ignored
    b. Reported as a separately disclosed reduction of retained earnings
    c. Reported as an extraordinary loss, net of income taxes
    d. Reported as a reduction in income before extraordinary items (5/92, Theory, #36, 2729)

42. On January 2 of the current year, Lake Mining Co.'s board of directors declared a cash dividend of $400,000 to stockholders of record on January 18 and payable on February 10 of the current year. The dividend is permissible under law in Lake's state of incorporation. Selected data from Lake's previous year December 31 balance sheet are as follows:

Accumulated depletion	$100,000
Capital stock	500,000
Additional paid-in capital	150,000
Retained earnings	300,000

    The $400,000 dividend includes a liquidating dividend of

    a. $0
    b. $100,000
    c. $150,000
    d. $300,000 (5/94, FAR, #32, amended, 4847)

43. Ole Corp. declared and paid a liquidating dividend of $100,000. This distribution decreases Ole's

	Paid-in capital	Retained earnings
a.	No	No
b.	Yes	Yes
c.	No	Yes
d.	Yes	No

(11/91, PII, #6, amended, 2454)

44. Stock dividends on common stock should be recorded at their fair market value by the investor when the related investment is accounted for under which of the following methods?

	Cost	Equity
a.	Yes	Yes
b.	Yes	No
c.	No	Yes
d.	No	No

(11/94, FAR, #39, 5301)

45. Plack Co. purchased 10,000 shares (2% ownership) of Ty Corp. on February 14 of the current year. Plack received a stock dividend of 2,000 shares on April 30 when the market value per share was $35. Ty paid a cash dividend of $2 per share on December 15. In its current year income statement, what amount should Plack report as dividend income?

    a. $20,000
    b. $24,000
    c. $90,000
    d. $94,000 (R/01, FAR, #5, 6980)

46. Universe Co. issued 500,000 shares of common stock in the current year. Universe declared a 30% stock dividend. The market value was $50 per share, the par value was $10, and the average issue price was $30 per share. By what amount will Universe decrease stockholders' equity for the dividend?

    a. $0
    b. $1,500,000
    c. $4,500,000
    d. $7,500,000 (R/05, FAR, #30, 7774)

47. The following stock dividends were declared and distributed by Sol Corp.:

Common shares outstanding	Fair value	Par value
10%	$15,000	$10,000
28%	40,000	30,800

    What aggregate amounts should be debited to retained earnings for these stock dividends?

    a. $40,800
    b. $45,800
    c. $50,000
    d. $55,000 (5/91, PII, #12, 1093)

48. How would a stock split affect each of the following?

	Assets	Total stockholders' equity	Additional paid-in capital
a.	Increase	Increase	No effect
b.	No effect	No effect	No effect
c.	No effect	No effect	Increase
d.	Decrease	Decrease	Decrease

    (5/85, Theory, #17, 2012)

49. Long Co. had 100,000 shares of common stock issued and outstanding at January 1 of the current year. During the year, Long took the following actions:

    Mar. 15—Declared a 2-for-1 stock split, when the fair value of the stock was $80 per share.
    Dec. 15—Declared a $.50 per share cash dividend.

    In Long's statement of stockholders' equity for the current year, what amount should Long report as dividends?

    a. $ 50,000
    b. $100,000
    c. $850,000
    d. $950,000 (11/94, FAR, #31, amended, 5294)

50. On which of the following dates is a public entity required to measure the cost of employee services in exchange for an award of equity interests, based on the fair market value of the award?

    a. Date of grant
    b. Date of restriction lapse
    c. Date of vesting
    d. Date of exercise (R/10, FAR, #14, 9314)

51. On June 1 of the previous year, Oak Corp. granted stock options valued at $8,000 to certain key employees as additional compensation for the year. The options were for 1,000 shares of Oak's $2 par value common stock at an option price of $15 per share. Market price of this stock on June 1 of the previous year was $20 per share. The options were exercisable beginning January 2 of the current year and expire on December 31 of next year. On April 1 of the current year, when Oak's stock was trading at $21 per share, all the options were exercised. What amount of pretax compensation should Oak report in the previous year in connection with the options?

a. $8,000
b. $5,000
c. $2,500
d. $2,000 (11/92, PII, #56, amended, 3390)

52. On January 2 of the current year, Kine Co. granted Morgan, its president, compensatory stock options to buy 1,000 shares of Kine's $10 par common stock. The options call for a price of $20 per share and are exercisable for 3 years following the grant date. The options are valued at $35,000 on the date of the grant. Morgan exercised the options on December 31 of the current year. The market price of the stock was $50 on January 2 and $70 on December 31. By what net amount should stockholders' equity increase as a result of the grant and exercise of the options?

a. $20,000
b. $30,000
c. $50,000
d. $70,000 (5/94, FAR, #33, amended, 4848)

53. On January 2, year 3, Farm Co. granted an employee an option valued at $32,000 to purchase 1,000 shares of Farm's $10 common stock at $40 per share. The option became exercisable on December 31, year 3, after the employee had completed one year of service, and was exercised on that date. The market prices of Farm's stock were as follows:

January 2, year 3	$50
December 31, year 3	65

What amount should Farm recognize as compensation expense for year 3?

a. $0
b. $30,000
c. $32,000
d. $60,000 (11/94, FAR, #33, amended, 9027)

54. Avers and Smith formed a partnership. Avers contributed cash of $50,000. Smith contributed property with a $36,000 carrying amount, a $40,000 original cost, and a fair value of $80,000. The partnership assumed the $35,000 mortgage attached to the property. What should Smith's capital account be on the partnership formation date?

a. $36,000
b. $40,000
c. $45,000
d. $80,000 (11/98, FAR, #9, amended, 6736)

55. On May 1, Cobb and Mott formed a partnership and agreed to share profits and losses in the ratio of 3:7, respectively. Cobb contributed a parcel of land that cost him $10,000. Mott contributed $40,000 cash. The land was sold for $18,000 on that same date, immediately after formation of the partnership. What amount should be recorded in Cobb's capital account on formation of the partnership?

a. $18,000
b. $17,400
c. $15,000
d. $10,000 (5/89, PII, #9, amended, 1308)

56. Which of the following statements concerning identifiable assets is ***false***?

    a. Accounting for partnerships must comply with the legal requirements as set forth by the Revised Uniform Partnership Act or other applicable state laws, as well as complying with the partnership agreement itself.
    b. All identifiable assets contributed to the partnership are recorded by the partnership at their fair values.
    c. All liabilities that the partnership assumes are recorded at their book values.
    d. If a partner contributes a noncash asset to the partnership subject to a mortgage, the contributing partner's capital account is credited for the fair value of the noncash asset less the mortgage assumed by the partnership. (Editor, 89594)

57. Abel and Carr formed a partnership and agreed to divide initial capital equally, even though Abel contributed $100,000 and Carr contributed $84,000 in identifiable assets. Under the bonus approach to adjust the capital accounts, Carr's unidentifiable asset should be debited for

    a. $46,000
    b. $16,000
    c. $ 8,000
    d. $0 (5/91, PII, #1, 1300)

58. Which of the following is ***true*** regarding unidentifiable assets in a partnership?

    a. In the formation of a partnership, no unidentifiable assets are contributed.
    b. Since unidentifiable assets cannot be accurately recorded, they are unrecognized until the partnership is liquidated.
    c. Managerial expertise cannot be recorded in the formation of a partnership.
    d. None of the above is true. (Editor, 89595)

59. The Flat and Iron partnership agreement provides for Flat to receive a 20% bonus on profits before the bonus. Remaining profits and losses are divided between Flat and Iron in the ratio of 2 to 3, respectively. Which partner has a greater advantage when the partnership has a profit or when it has a loss?

	Profit	Loss
a.	Flat	Iron
b.	Flat	Flat
c.	Iron	Flat
d.	Iron	Iron

(11/91, Theory, #15, 2523)

60. The Low and Rhu partnership agreement provides special compensation to Low for managing the business. Low receives a bonus of 15 percent of partnership net income before salary and bonus, and also receives a salary of $45,000. Any remaining profit or loss is to be allocated equally. During the current year, the partnership had net income of $50,000 before the bonus and salary allowance. As a result of these distributions, Rhu's equity in the partnership would

    a. Increase
    b. Not change
    c. Decrease the same as Low's
    d. Decrease (5/89, Theory, #12, amended, 1994)

61. During the current year, Young and Zinc maintained average capital balances in their partnership of $160,000 and $100,000, respectively. The partners receive 10% interest on average capital balances, and residual profit or loss is divided equally. Partnership profit before interest was $4,000. By what amount should Zinc's capital account change for the year?

    a. $ 1,000 decrease
    b. $ 2,000 increase
    c. $11,000 decrease
    d. $12,000 increase (11/95, FAR, #23, 6105)

62. The partnership agreement of Axel, Berg & Cobb provides for the year-end allocation of net income in the following order:

    - First, Axel is to receive 10% of net income up to $100,000 and 20% over $100,000.
    - Second, Berg and Cobb each are to receive 5% of the remaining income over $150,000.
    - The balance of income is to be allocated equally among the three partners.

    The partnership's net income was $250,000 before any allocations to partners. What amount should be allocated to Axel?

    a. $101,000
    b. $103,000
    c. $108,000
    d. $110,000 (11/91, PII, #11, amended, 2459)

63. Blau and Rubi are partners who share profits and losses in the ratio of 6:4, respectively. On May 1 of the current year, their respective capital accounts were as follows:

Blau	$60,000
Rubi	50,000

    On that date, Lind was admitted as a partner with a one-third interest in capital and profits for an investment of $40,000. The new partnership began with total capital of $150,000. Immediately after Lind's admission, Blau's capital should be

    a. $50,000
    b. $54,000
    c. $56,667
    d. $60,000 (11/89, PII, #19, amended, 1307)

64. Kern and Pate are partners with capital balances of $60,000 and $20,000, respectively. Profits and losses are divided in the ratio of 60:40. Kern and Pate decided to form a new partnership with Grant, who invested land valued at $15,000 for a 20% capital interest in the new partnership. Grant's cost of the land was $12,000. The partnership elected to use the bonus method to record the admission of Grant into the partnership. Grant's capital account should be credited for

    a. $12,000
    b. $15,000
    c. $16,000
    d. $19,000 (5/93, PII, #19, 4127)

65. When Mill retired from the partnership of Mill, Yale, and Lear, the final settlement of Mill's interest exceeded Mill's capital balance. Under the bonus method, the excess

    a. Was recorded as goodwill
    b. Was recorded as an expense
    c. Reduced the capital balances of Yale and Lear
    d. Had **no** effect on the capital balances of Yale and Lear (11/94, FAR, #35, 5297)

66. On June 30 of the current year the condensed balance sheet for the partnership of Eddy, Fox, and Grimm, together with their respective profit and loss sharing percentages, was as follows:

Assets, net of liabilities	$320,000
Eddy, capital (50%)	160,000
Fox, capital (30%)	96,000
Grimm, capital (20%)	64,000
Total Equity	$320,000

Eddy decided to retire from the partnership and by mutual agreement is to be paid $180,000 out of partnership funds for his interest. Total goodwill implicit in the agreement is to be recorded. After Eddy's retirement, what are the capital balances of the other partners?

	Fox	Grimm
a.	$ 84,000	$56,000
b.	$102,000	$68,000
c.	$108,000	$72,000
d.	$120,000	$80,000

(11/88, PI, #26, 9072)

67. In a partnership liquidation proceeding, where a partnership converts its assets into cash and distributes the cash to creditors and partners, the partnership does which of the following?

a. Gives priority to creditors on any distribution
b. May hold each partner personally liable if a partner or other individual prematurely distributes cash to another partner whose capital account later shows a deficit, and the latter partner is unable to repay the premature distribution
c. Is required to distribute the liquidation's proceeds to partners in a lump sum, after all assets have been sold and all creditors have been satisfied
d. None of the above

(Editor, 89600)

68. The following condensed balance sheet is presented for the partnership of Alfa and Beda, who share profits and losses in the ratio of 60:40, respectively:

Cash	$ 45,000	Accounts payable	$120,000
Other assets	625,000	Alfa, capital	348,000
Beda, loan	30,000	Beda, capital	232,000
	$700,000		$700,000

Alfa and Beda decide to liquidate the partnership. If the other assets are sold for $500,000, what amount of the available cash should be distributed to Alfa?

a. $255,000
b. $273,000
c. $327,000
d. $348,000

(5/95, FAR, #24, 5560)

69. On January 1 of the current year, the partners of Cobb, Davis, and Eddy, who share profits and losses in the ratio of 5:3:2, respectively, decided to liquidate their partnership. On this date the partnership condensed balance sheet was as follows:

Cash	$ 50,000	Liabilities	$ 60,000
Other assets	250,000	Cobb, capital	80,000
	$300,000	Davis, capital	90,000
		Eddy, capital	70,000
			$300,000

On January 15 of the current year, the first cash sale of other assets with a carrying amount of $150,000 realized $120,000. Safe installment payments to the partners were made the same date. How much cash should be distributed to each partner?

	Cobb	Davis	Eddy
a.	$15,000	$51,000	$44,000
b.	$40,000	$45,000	$35,000
c.	$55,000	$33,000	$22,000
d.	$60,000	$36,000	$24,000

(5/87, PI, #33, amended, 1310)

Problem 10-2 SIMULATION: Stockholders' Equity

Stream Co.'s stockholders' equity account balances at December 31, year 4, were as follows:

Common stock	$ 900,000
Additional paid-in capital	1,500,000
Retained earnings	1,965,000

The following year 5 transactions and other information relate to the stockholders' equity accounts:

- Stream had 500,000 authorized shares of $5 par common stock, of which 180,000 shares were issued and outstanding.
- On March 5, year 5, Stream acquired 6,000 shares of its common stock for $9 per share to hold as treasury stock. The shares were originally issued at $12 per share. Stream uses the cost method to account for treasury stock. Treasury stock is permitted in Stream's state of incorporation.
- On July 15, year 5, Stream declared and distributed a property dividend of inventory. The inventory had a $100,000 carrying value and a $80,000 fair market value.
- On January 2, year 3, Stream granted stock options to employees to purchase 30,000 shares of Stream's common stock at $15 per share, which was the market price on the grant date. The options are valued at $45,000 and may be exercised within a three-year period beginning January 2, year 5. On October 1, year 5, employees exercised all 30,000 options when the market value of the stock was $23 per share. Stream issued new shares to settle the transaction.
- Stream's net income for year 5 was $260,000.
- Stream intends to issue new stock options to key employees in year 6. Stream's management is aware that the "fair value" method of accounting for stock options is required (hint: this is a compensatory plan).

Prepare the stockholders' equity section of Stream's December 31, year 5, balance sheet. Round to nearest whole dollar.

Common stock, $5 par value, 500,000 shares authorized, 210,000 shares issued, 204,000 shares outstanding		$
Additional paid-in capital		
Retained earnings:		
Beginning balance	$1,965,000	
Add: Net income		
Less: Property dividend distributed		
Ending balance		
Subtotal		
Less: Common stock in treasury		
Total stockholders' equity		$

(5/95, FAR, #2, amended, 6502)

Problem 10-3 SIMULATION: Equity Worksheet

Quonset, Inc. is a public company whose shares are actively traded in the over-the-counter market. The company's stockholders' equity account balances at December 31, year 5, were as follows:

Common stock: $1 par value; 1,450,000 shares authorized; 750,000 shares issued and outstanding	$ 750,000
Additional paid-in capital	3,000,000
Retained earnings	3,500,000
Total stockholders' equity	$7,250,000

During the year ended December 31, year 6, transactions and other information relating to Quonset's stockholders' equity were as follows:

- On February 1, year 6, Quonset issued 15,000 shares of common stock to Carson Co. in exchange for land. On the date issued, the stock had a market price of $14 per share. The land had a carrying value on Carson's books of $150,000 and an assessed value for property taxes of $100,000.
- On March 5, year 6, Quonset purchased 25,000 of its shares to hold as treasury stock at $10 per share. The shares were originally issued at $11 per share. Quonset uses the cost method to account for treasury stock. Treasury stock is permitted in Quonset's state of incorporation.
- On March 15, year 6, Quonset purchased a portfolio of marketable securities to be held as available-for-sale securities.
- On June 5, year 6, Quonset declared a property dividend of inventory. The inventory had a $85,000 carrying value and a $75,000 fair market value.
- On July 1, year 6, Quonset declared and issued a 16% stock dividend. The stock had a market value of $12 per share.
- On December 5, year 6, Quonset declared a cash dividend of $1 per share to all common stockholders of record on December 15, year 6. The dividend was paid on January 5, year 7.
- Net income for year 6 was $1,332,000.
- At December 31, year 6, unrealized gain on the portfolio of marketable securities purchased during the year was $75,000, net of tax.

Using the stockholders' equity balances as of December 31, year 5, and the transactions and other information relating to Quonset's stockholders' equity during year 6, complete the following worksheet analysis of stockholders' equity for year 6. Ignore the effect of income taxes. Enter increases to stockholders' equity as positive numbers and decreases to stockholders' equity as negative numbers. If there is no amount to enter in a particular shaded cell, enter a value of zero (0).

Accounts	Number of shares issued and outstanding	Common stock	Additional paid-in capital	Retained earnings	Accumulated other comprehensive income (loss)	Treasury stock	Total stockholders' equity
Beginning balances							
Issuance of shares for property							
Purchase of treasury stock							
Property dividends distributed							
Stock dividend issued							
Cash dividend							
Net income for the year							
Unrealized gain (loss) on marketable securities available for sale							
Ending balances							

(4/07, amended, 8372)

Problem 10-4 SIMULATION: Retained Earnings

Trask Corp., a public company whose shares are traded in the over-the-counter market, had the following stockholders' equity account balances at December 31, year 5:

Common stock	$ 7,875,000
Additional paid-in capital	15,750,000
Retained earnings	16,445,000
Treasury common stock	750,000

Transactions during year 6, and other information relating to the stockholders' equity accounts, were as follows:

- Trask had 4,000,000 authorized shares of $5 par value common stock; 1,575,000 shares were issued, of which 75,000 were held in treasury.
- On January 21, year 6, Trask issued 50,000 shares of $100 par value, 6% cumulative preferred stock in exchange for all of Rover Co.'s assets and liabilities. On that date, the net carrying amount of Rover's assets and liabilities was $5,000,000. The carrying amounts of Rover's assets and liabilities equaled their fair values. On January 22, year 6, Rover distributed the Trask shares to its stockholders in complete liquidation and dissolution of Rover. Trask had 150,000 authorized shares of preferred stock.
- On February 17, year 6, Trask formally retired 25,000 of its 75,000 treasury common stock shares. The shares were originally issued at $15 per share and had been acquired on September 25, year 5, for $10 per share. Trask uses the cost method to account for treasury stock.
- Trask owned 15,000 shares of Harbor Inc. common stock purchased in year 3 for $600,000. The Harbor stock was included in Trask's short-term marketable securities portfolio. On March 5, year 6, Trask declared a property dividend of one share of Harbor common stock for every 100 shares of Trask common stock held by a stockholder of record on April 16, year 6. The market price of Harbor stock on March 5, year 6, was $60 per share. The property dividend was distributed on April 29, year 6.
- On January 2, year 4, Trask granted stock options valued at $600,000 to executive employees to purchase 200,000 shares of the company's common stock at $9 per share, when the market price on that date was $12 per share. The options are exercisable within a three-year period beginning January 2, year 6. On June 1, year 6, the executives exercised 150,000 of the options when the market value of the stock was $25 per share. Trask issued new shares to settle the transaction.
- On October 27, year 6, Trask declared a 2-for-1 stock split on its common stock and reduced the per share par value accordingly. Trask stockholders of record on August 2, year 6, received one additional share of Trask common stock for each share of Trask common stock held. The laws in Trask's state of incorporation protect treasury stock from dilution.
- On December 12, year 6, Trask declared the yearly cash dividend on preferred stock, payable on January 11, year 7, to stockholders of record on December 31, year 6.
- On January 16, year 7, before the accounting records were closed for year 6, Trask became aware that depreciation expense was understated by $350,000 for the year ended December 31, year 5. The after-tax effect on year 5 net income was $245,000. The appropriate correcting entry was recorded on the same day.
- Net income for year 6 was $2,400,000.

1. Prepare Trask's statement of retained earnings for the year ended December 31, year 6. Assume that Trask prepares only single-period financial statements.

Balance, December 31, year 5	
Less: Prior period adjustment	
Add: Income tax effect	
As restated	
Net income	
Subtotal	
Deduct dividends:	
Cash dividend on preferred stock	
Dividend in kind on common stock	
Balance, December 31, year 6	

2. Prepare the stockholders' equity section of Trask's balance sheet at December 31, year 6.

Preferred stock, $100 par value, 6% cumulative; 150,000 shares authorized; 50,000 shares issued and outstanding	
Common stock, $2.50 par value; 4,000,000 shares authorized; 3,400,000 shares issued	
Additional paid-in capital	
Retained earnings	
Subtotal	
Less: Common stock in treasury	
Total stockholders' equity (Preferred stock plus common stock)	

(11/93, P1, #4, amended, 9024)

Problem 10-5 SIMULATION: Research

The Hopeful company made open-market purchases of its own common stock with the intent to reissue the shares in the future. It is anticipated that the market price of the stock will be in excess of the purchase price when the stock is reissued. List the proper citation from the authoritative literature that provides guidance as to how the company should account for the excess of the market price at the time of re-issuance over the purchase price of the common stock.

FASB ASC: [ ] - [ ] - [ ] - [ ]

(9122)

Solution 10-1 MULTIPLE-CHOICE ANSWERS

Overview

1. (a)

Capital—Smith, 1/2 (i.e., cost of net assets contributed by owner at 1/2)	$350,000	
Income of sole proprietorship	60,000	
Less: Smith's drawings	(20,000)	
Capital—Smith, 12/31	$390,000	(5298)

2. (a)

Common stock, $3 par	$600,000		
Additional paid-in capital	800,000		
Total paid-in capital		$1,400,000	
Retained earnings, appropriated	150,000		
Retained earnings, unappropriated	200,000		
Total retained earnings		350,000	
Less: Treasury stock, at cost		(50,000)	
Less: Net unrealized loss on AFS securities		(20,000)	
Total stockholders' equity		$1,680,000	(2572)

3. (a) APIC = $580,000 + $240,000 = $820,000. If Hyde has only one APIC account, the issuance of the common and preferred stock would be recorded as follows.

Cash (20,000 × $30)	600,000		
Common Stock (20,000 × $1)		20,000	
Additional Paid-In Capital (to balance)		580,000	
Cash (6,000 × $50)	300,000		
Preferred Stock (6,000 × $10)		60,000	
Additional Paid-In Capital (to balance)		240,000	(4048)

4. (a) A corporation's equity consists of three main components: contributed capital, which includes capital stock and additional paid-in capital; retained earnings; and the accumulated balance of OCI. A partnership's equity consists of one capital account for each partner. A partner's investments and allocations of income and withdrawals are recorded in her/his individual capital account. A sole proprietorship's equity consists of a single proprietor's equity account, "Owner's Equity or Net Worth." This is the sum of the beginning capital balance, plus additional investments during the period, plus net income (or minus net loss) minus withdrawals. (89637)

Capital

5. (c) No entry (other than a memorandum entry) is made when stock rights are issued to existing stockholders without consideration. (6103)

6. (c) No entry (other than a memorandum entry) is made when stock rights are issued to existing stockholders. However, the redemption of the rights resulted in an outflow of cash. As this did not increase a noncash asset or reduce liabilities, it must affect an equity account. 120,000 × $0.10 = $12,000. (6104)

7. (d) The proceeds should be allocated between the preferred stock and the detachable stock purchase warrants based on their relative fair market values at date of issue. If the relative fair values are not known, then the fair value of either security is used. In this question, the fair value of the warrants is known, but the fair value of the preferred stock without the warrants is not. Therefore, the amount assigned to the warrants is the fair value of the warrants. The remaining amount of the proceeds is assigned to the preferred stock. (4201)

8. (a) Stock rights have no impact on net income. No entry is required when stock rights are issued to existing stockholders (other than a memorandum entry); therefore, APIC was not affected when the stock rights were issued. Stock issued upon the exercise of stock rights is recorded the same as any other issuance; therefore, when the stock rights were exercised, APIC increased by the excess of the $30 exercise price over the $20 par value of the common stock. (4520)

9. (a) *Common Stock* should be credited for $375,000 [i.e., (5,000 × 3) × $25], the par value of the common shares issued to effect the conversion. *Additional Paid-in Capital—Common Stock* should be credited for $175,000, the excess of the carrying amount of the preferred stock converted over the par value of common shares issued to effect the conversion [i.e., (5,000 × $110) – $375,000]. (5292)

10. (b)

Cash dividends declared in year 2		$ 44,000
Dividends in arrears at 12/31, year 1	$12,000	
Dividend for year 2 (4,000 × $100 × 6%)	24,000	
Cash dividends payable to preferred stock		(36,000)
Cash dividends payable to common stock		$ 8,000

(4113)

11. (b) No-par value stock avoids the contingent liability involved with the issuance of par value stock at a price below par (discount). Par value stock is stock with a specified par value per share printed on the certificate. The par value of all shares issued and subscribed will normally represent the legal or stated capital. (89638)

12. (b) The issuance of stock is generally recorded by debiting cash or the appropriate asset accounts for the fair value of the consideration received. Common Stock is credited for the par or stated value of the shares issued (not the entire amount), and the balancing figure is credited to Additional Paid-In Capital. Common Stock is credited $5,000 (500 shares × $10 per share), with the remaining $15,000 credited to Additional Paid-in Capital. (86644)

13. (a) The acquisition of services by issuance of common stock is a nonmonetary exchange that should be recorded at the fair value of the stock issued or the services performed, whichever is more clearly evident. The fair value of the stock issued should be used to record this transaction because (1) on the date of issuance, the stock was trading on a public exchange and, thus, had the more clearly evident fair value, and (2) the fair value of the stock issued is less than the amount usually billed for the services received. Thus, the increase in *Additional Paid-in Capital* as a result of the transaction is the excess of the fair value over the par value of the common stock multiplied by the number of shares issued. ($140 – $5 = $135 × 1,000 = $135,000) (5291)

14. (d) The common stock's par value is recorded as *Common Stock Subscribed* and the excess of the subscription price over the common stock's par value is recorded as APIC.

Cash (20% down payment)	XX	
Subscriptions Receivable (balance due)	XX	
Common Stock Subscribed(shares × par value)		XX
Additional Paid-In Capital (to balance)		XX

(1996)

15. (b) Since the market value of both securities is not determinable, the incremental method should be used to allocate the cash proceeds between the two securities. Since the market value of the bonds is known, the cash proceeds in excess of this amount are allocated to the common stock. The excess of the proceeds allocated to the common stock over the par value is recorded as APIC.

Lump sum cash proceeds	$110,000
Less: Market value of bonds	(40,000)
Cash proceeds allocated to common stock	70,000
Less: Par value of common stock (1,000 × $5)	(5,000)
APIC on issuance of common stock	$ 65,000

(3378)

16. (c) *Additional Paid-In Capital* is credited for the difference between the fair value of the net assets contributed and the stock's par value.

Assets (at fair value)	240,000	
Liabilities (at fair value)		20,000
Common Stock (1,000 × $5)		5,000
Additional Paid-In Capital (to balance)		215,000

(4115)

Retained Earnings

17. (d) The purpose of a retained earnings appropriation is to restrict a portion of retained earnings as to availability for dividends. A retained earnings appropriation is not used to absorb a fire loss when a company is self-insured, provide for a contingent loss that is probable and reasonably estimable, or to smooth periodic income. (2730)

18. (a) Since the new office building was completed in year 2, the retained earnings reported appropriated for that purpose at 12/31, year 1 should have been returned to unappropriated retained earnings in year 2. Restricted cash does not affect the amount of appropriated retained earnings. (4114)

19. (c) The primary purpose of a quasi-reorganization is to eliminate an accumulated deficit (negative retained earnings balance) so that the corporation has a "fresh start" with a zero balance in retained earnings. Although the accounting procedures for a quasi-reorganization involve restating assets to their fair values, this is not the primary purpose. There should be no net asset write-up. (5299)

20. (c) The balance in the APIC account after the quasi-reorganization is the beginning balance, plus the difference in the old and new par values, times the number of issued shares [($30 – $5) × 10,000 = $250,000], less the retained earnings deficit. $150,000 + $250,000 – $210,000 = $190,000. (6107)

21. (b) During the current year, stockholders' equity increased by $62,000 (i.e., $89,000 – $27,000). Since paid-in capital increased by $66,000 (i.e., $60,000 + $6,000), retained earnings must have decreased by $4,000 (i.e., $66,000 – $62,000). Since the only charge to retained earnings was for a $13,000 dividend payment, net income for the year must have been $9,000. (4112)

22. (a) In general, retained earnings is increased only as a result of net income generated by the firm, as well as a result of a prior period adjustment or certain special changes in accounting principle. Retained earnings decreases as a result of net losses suffered by the firm, and as a result of dividends (cash, property, or stock) and net losses suffered by the firm. In addition, treasury stock transactions, certain stock splits, prior period adjustments, and certain special changes in accounting principle may also reduce retained earnings. (89647)

Treasury Stock

23. (a)

	Shares Issued	Shares Outstanding
Beginning balance, shares	100,000	95,000
May 3, sale of treasury stock		1,000
Aug. 6, additional stock sold	10,000	10,000
Subtotal prior to stock split	110,000	106,000
Nov. 18, 2-for-1 stock split	× 2	× 2
Ending balance, shares	220,000	212,000

(6100)

24. (d) The question does not indicate whether the donated shares are accounted for as treasury stock under the cost or par value methods, or whether the donated shares were canceled and retired. Therefore, this question cannot be answered by constructing a journal entry to record the donation of the shares. Instead, the question can be answered by knowing that the donation of the common stock would be accounted for entirely within stockholders' equity accounts. Therefore, the amount reported for total stockholders' equity would be unchanged as a result of the donation of the stock. (4053)

25. (a) The excess of proceeds over cost of treasury stock sold, accounted for using the cost method, is credited to an appropriately titled paid-in capital account, such as *Additional Paid-In Capital From Treasury Stock Transactions.*

Income since incorporation	$ 420,000
Less: Cash dividends	(130,000)
Less: Property dividends	(30,000)
Retained earnings, 12/31	$ 260,000

(6274)

26. (b) The net income for the current year is overstated, because no gains or losses are recognized on treasury stock transactions. (7775)

27. (c) When treasury stock is acquired, total stockholders' equity decreases by the cost of the treasury shares, regardless of the method used to account for the treasury stock. The book value per common share is computed by dividing total stockholders' equity applicable to common stock by the number of common stock shares outstanding. The acquisition of treasury shares at a price less than their book value will reduce both the numerator and denominator of the book value ratio; however, the reduction of the numerator is less than the amount that was in there for these shares. The excess book value for those shares would now be spread over the remaining shares outstanding, resulting in an increase in the book value per common share. (2548)

28. (a) Treasury stock is the corporation's common or preferred stock that has been reacquired by purchase, by settlement of an obligation to the corporation, or through donation. The cost method views the purchase and subsequent disposition of stock as one transaction. The treasury stock is recorded (debited), carried, and reissued at the acquisition cost. If the stock is reissued at a price in excess of the acquisition cost, such as in this situation, the excess is credited to an appropriately titled paid-in capital account. There are no gains or losses reported in the income statement for these transactions. (8766)

29. (b) Treasury stock is the corporation's common or preferred stock that has been reacquired by purchase, by settlement of an obligation to the corporation, or through donation. The cost method views the purchase and subsequent disposition of stock as one transaction. The treasury stock is recorded (debited), carried, and then reissued at acquisition cost. If the stock is reissued at a price in excess of the acquisition cost, the excess is credited to an appropriately titled paid-in capital (PIC) account. If the stock is reissued at less than the acquisition cost, the deficit is first charged against any existing balance in the treasury stock paid-in capital account and then excess, if any, is then charged against retained earnings. Porter reissued the 500 shares of treasury stock at a price ($10 per share) in excess of the acquisition cost ($6 per share). The excess ($10 – $6 = $4 per share × 500 shares = $2,000) is credited to the PIC account related to treasury stock on Porter's balance sheet for the current year. (8108)

30. (a) No gains or losses are recognized on treasury stock transactions. If the stock is reissued at a price in excess of the acquisition cost, the excess is credited to an appropriately titled paid-in capital account. If the stock is reissued at less than the acquisition cost, the deficit is first charged against any existing balance in the appropriately named paid-in capital account. Any excess then is charged against *Retained Earnings*. (8348)

31. (c) The amount that Rama discloses as a restriction of retained earnings as a result of treasury stock held is $60,000 [(20,000 – 15,000) × $12 per share]. (1103)

32. (c) The theoretical justification for the par value method is that the purchase of treasury stock is in fact a constructive retirement of those shares; therefore, reacquired stock is recorded essentially by reversing the amounts at which the stock was originally issued and adjusting any difference to *APIC* or *Retained Earnings*. Reissuance of the stock is treated as if it were a new issue, i.e., the excess purchase price received over par is credited to *APIC*. (1993)

33. (b) Under the par value method, the acquisition of the treasury shares is viewed as a constructive retirement of the stock. Since capital stock is carried on the balance sheet at par (or stated value), the acquisition of treasury stock is also recorded at par (or stated value), by debiting *Treasury Stock*. Any *Additional Paid-In Capital—Common Stock* associated with the original issuance of the stock is also removed. If the acquisition cost exceeds the stock's original issue price, then the excess is debited to *Additional Paid-In Capital—Treasury Stock,* but **only** to the extent of any existing balance from prior treasury stock transactions. The remaining excess, if any, is then debited to *Retained Earnings.*

Treasury stock (100 sh @ $6)	600	
APIC-common stock (100 sh @ $7 - $6)	100	
Retained earnings (plug)	300	
Cash		1,000

(9880)

34. (b) The entry to record the acquisition of the treasury stock in excess of its original issue price using the par value method will involve a debit to *Treasury Stock* for the par value of the stock, a debit to *APIC* for the amount of the premium on the original issuance, a debit to *Retained Earnings* for the excess of the cost of the treasury stock over the original issuance price, and a credit to *Cash* for the cost of the treasury shares. When the par value method is used, the balance of the *Treasury Stock* account is contra to the *Common Stock* account. Therefore, the use of the par value method will result in a decrease in net common stock, a decrease in *APIC* and a decrease in *Retained Earnings*. (1972)

35. (c) The effect of the acquisition and retirement of each common share is to decrease APIC by $10 (i.e., $15 – $5). A corporation cannot record a gain or loss on the acquisition and retirement of its own common stock. Retained earnings can be decreased, but never increased, as a result of the acquisition and retirement of its own common stock.

Common Stock	10		
APIC—Common Stock	15		
Cash		20	
APIC—Retirement of Stock		5	(4198)

36. (c) Under the cost method, the cost of the treasury stock is reported as an unallocated reduction of the stockholders' equity. Under this method, the treasury stock did not reduce the *Common Stock* account prior to their cancellation.

Par value of common stock before recording cancellation of treasury stock	$ 540,000	
Less: Par value of treasury stock canceled (50,000 shares × $2.50 par value)	(125,000)	
Par value of common stock outstanding after cancellation of treasury stock	$ 415,000	(3384)

37. (b) In a treasury stock retirement, the Common Stock account decreases for the par value and the Additional Paid-In Capital account decreases up to the original increase to the APIC account when the retired shares were first issued. Immediately after the shares were retired, the APIC balance would be $2,470,000 (2,550,000 – $120,000 + $40,000).

Common Stock (20,000 × $20 PV)	400,000		
APIC – CS [$20,000 × (26 – $20 PV)]	120,000		
Cash (20,000 × $24)		480,000	
APIC - Retirement of CS (to balance)		40,000	(1106)

Distributions

38. (b) A cash dividend is recorded when declared by a debit to *Retained Earnings* and a credit to *Cash Dividends Payable.* There is no adjusting entry at the end of the period. The entry at the payment date includes a debit to *Cash Dividends Payable* and a credit to *Cash.* Generally, the cash dividend reduces stockholders' equity only at the declaration date. (1971)

39. (d) At the end of the year, interest is accrued. At the date of declaration, April 1, year 1, the journal entry is as follows:

Retained Earnings	100,000	
Notes Payable to Stockholders		100,000

And then on December 31, year 1, the entry is:

Interest Expense ($100,000 × 10% × 9/12)	7,500	
Interest Payable		7,500

The interest portion of the payment is not treated as part of the dividend. When the dividend is declared, it becomes a liability and is reported on the balance sheet. If the entry to accrue the interest expense is made on December 31, year 1, and is reversed on January 1, year 2, then interest expense would be debited for $10,000 on March 31, year 2. However, since answer (c) does not state this, assume that the reversing entry was not made. (4846)

40. (c) Property dividends are recorded at the property's fair value at the declaration date. The excess of the fair value over the carrying amount of the property distributed is recognized as a gain by the distributing corporation at the declaration date.

Fair value of distributed shares (100,000 × $2.50)	$ 250,000	
Less: Distributed share's carrying amount (100,000 × $2.00)	(200,000)	
Pretax gain on distributed shares	$ 50,000	(4086)

41. (d) Evie records the property dividend at the merchandise's fair value at the declaration date. Since the merchandise's carrying amount exceeds its fair value at the declaration date, Evie recognizes the excess as a loss in income from continuing operations. (2729)

42. (b) Any dividend that does not come out of retained earnings is a reduction of corporate paid-in capital and, to that extent, is a liquidating dividend.

Dividend	$ 400,000	
Retained earnings	(300,000)	
Liquidating dividend	$ 100,000	(4847)

43. (d) Any dividend not based on earnings must be a reduction of corporate paid-in capital and, to that extent, a liquidating dividend. Since no portion of the dividend is based on accumulated past earnings, paid-in capital decreases by the full dividend amount, while retained earnings is unaffected. The following journal entry illustrates the effects of the declaration of a $100,000 liquidating cash dividend.

Additional Paid-In Capital	100,000		
Cash Dividends Payable		100,000	(2454)

44. (d) Stock dividends received on common stock may be recorded only by memorandum entry, regardless of the method of accounting for the investment. Under the cost method, a new cost basis per share would be computed. Under the equity method, a new carrying amount per share would be computed. (5301)

45. (b) A stock dividend is not income under the cost or equity methods of accounting for equity investments, but it does impact the number of shares owned at the dividend declaration date. (10,000 + 2,000) × $2 = $24,000. (6980)

46. (a) Stock dividends operate to transfer a part of the retained earnings to contributed capital (capitalization of retained earnings). In recording the stock dividend, a charge is made to retained earnings (thereby making a portion of retained earnings no longer available for distribution) and credits are made to paid-in capital accounts. Because the declaration and issuance of a stock dividend decreases retained earnings and increases paid-in capital by equal amounts, total stockholders' equity is not affected. (7774)

47. (b) The issuance of a "small" stock dividend (i.e., less than 20 to 25% of the number of shares outstanding) should be recorded by capitalizing a portion of retained earnings equal to the fair value of the shares issued. On the other hand, the issuance of a "large" stock dividend (i.e., more than 20 to 25% of the number of shares outstanding) should be recorded by capitalizing a portion of retained earnings equal to the par value of the shares issued. Thus, *Retained Earnings* should be debited for (1) the fair value of the 10% stock dividend ($15,000) and (2) the par value of the 28% stock dividend ($30,800), for a total of $45,800. (1093)

48. (b) A stock split consists of a reduction in the par value per share, together with a proportional increase in the number of shares outstanding. For instance, in a 2-for-1 split, the par value per share is halved, while the number of shares outstanding is doubled. *Total* par value, additional paid-in capital, stockholders' equity, and total assets remain unchanged. (2012)

49. (b) The amount to be reported as dividends is determined as follows:

Common shares outstanding, 1/1	100,000	
Adjustment for 2-for-1 stock split, 3/15	× 2	
Common shares outstanding, declaration date	200,000	
Times: Cash dividend per common share	× $0.50	
Cash dividends declared during year	$ 100,000	(5294)

Employees and Stock

50. (a) An award of equity interests in exchange for employee services is considered a compensatory share-based payment plan. With a compensatory share-based payment plan the compensation cost is recognized using the fair value method of option pricing and the measurement date is the date of the grant. (9314)

51. (a) The cost of services received from employees in exchange for awards of share-based compensation generally shall be measured based on the grant-date fair value of the options. The account *Stock Options Outstanding* is increased on the grant date. The subsequent exercising, forfeiture, or lapsing of the stock options reduces this account.

Deferred Compensation Cost (value of options at date of grant)	8,000		
Stock Options Outstanding		8,000	(3390)

52. (a) Deferred compensation expense is a contra stockholders' equity account. Therefore, the net effect on stockholders' equity when the options are granted is zero. Stockholders' equity is increased $45,000 + $10,000 – $35,000 = $20,000.

Deferred Compensation Cost (value of options at date of grant)	35,000		
Stock Options Outstanding		35,000	
Cash (1,000 shares × $20)	20,000		
Stock Options Outstanding	35,000		
Common Stock (1,000 × $10)		10,000	
Add'l Paid-in Cap., Common Stock (to balance)		45,000	(4848)

53. (c) The cost of services received from employees in exchange for awards of share-based compensation generally shall be measured based on the grant-date fair value of the options. The account *Stock Options Outstanding* is increased on the grant date. The subsequent exercising, forfeiture, or lapsing of the stock options reduces this account.

<u>January 2, Year 3</u>			
Deferred Compensation Cost (value of options at date of grant)	32,000		
Stock Options Outstanding		32,000	
<u>December 31, Year 3</u>			
Wages and Compensation Expense	32,000		
Deferred Compensation Cost		32,000	
Cash (1,000 shares × $40)	40,000		
Stock Options Outstanding	32,000		
Common Stock (1,000 × $10)		10,000	
Add'l Paid-in Cap., Common Stock (to balance)		62,000	(9027)

Partnership Formation

54. (c) All identifiable assets contributed to a partnership are recorded by the partnership at their fair values. All liabilities that the partnership assumes are recorded at their present values. The contributing partner's capital account is credited for the fair value of the property less the assumed mortgage. Smith's capital account would be the fair value of the property of $80,000 less the mortgage assumed by the partnership of $35,000, for a balance of $45,000. (6736)

55. (a) Using historical cost for assets such as inventory, land, or equipment would be inequitable to any partner investing appreciated property. Therefore, the contribution of noncash assets to a partnership should be recorded based on fair values. The land was sold on the same date for $18,000, so that would be used for its fair value. (1308)

56. (c) Accounting for partnerships must comply with the legal requirements as set forth by the Revised Uniform Partnership Act or other applicable state laws, as well as complying with the partnership agreement itself. All liabilities that the partnership assumes are recorded at their present values. (89594)

57. (d) Carr must have made an intangible contribution to the partnership because Abel and Carr have agreed to divide initial capital equally, even though Carr contributed less in identifiable assets ($84,000 < $100,000). Because the bonus method is used to record the formation of the partnership, and the bonus method assumes that an intangible contribution does not constitute a partnership asset with a measurable cost, no unidentifiable asset (i.e., goodwill) is recognized by the partnership. The partnership formation adjusts the capital accounts of the two partners without recognizing goodwill.

Identifiable Assets ($100 + $84)	184,000		
Abel, Capital ($184,000 × 50%)		92,000	
Carr, Capital ($184,000 × 50%)		92,000	(1300)

58. (d) In the formation of a partnership, one or more of the partners may contribute an unidentifiable asset (e.g., managerial expertise or personal business reputation). Unidentifiable assets can be as valuable to the partnership as identifiable assets, such as cash, inventory, patents, and equipment. When one or more partners contribute unidentifiable assets, the formation of the partnership may be recorded under the bonus method or the goodwill method. Since answers a., b., and c. are incorrect, answer d. is the best choice. (89595)

59. (b) When there is a profit, Flat receives 20% of the profits before the bonus and 40% of the remaining 80% (i.e., 32%), for a total of 52% of the profits. In loss situations, Flat receives only 40% of the loss. Thus, Flat has a greater advantage whether the partnership has a profit or loss. (2523)

60. (d) Low's equity account would still have a net increase due to the salary and bonus. Only Rhu's account has a decrease.

Partnership profit prior to distributions	$ 50,000	
Less: Bonus to Low (15% × $50,000)	(7,500)	
Salary to Low	(45,000)	
Residual partnership loss	(2,500)	
Times: Rhu's loss percentage	× 50%	
Decrease in Rhu's equity in partnership	$ (1,250)	(1994)

61. (a) Young received $16,000 ($160,000 × 10%) and Zinc received $10,000 ($100,000 × 10%) for the interest on average capital balances. This makes the residual loss $22,000 ($4,000 – $16,000 – $10,000). As the residual loss is evenly divided between the two partners, Zinc gets $11,000 of loss. Zinc's interest allowance less Zinc's portion of the residual loss is the change in Zinc's capital balance. $10,000 – $11,000 = $1,000 decrease. (6105)

62. (c) The portion allocated to Alex is bonus ($40,000) and one-third of residual partnership profit ($204,000 × 1/3 = $68,000) for a total of $108,000.

	Partnership profit	
Profit prior to distribution	$250,000	
Deduct bonus to Axel [($100 × 10%) + ($250 – 100) × 20%]	(40,000)	
Less: Bonuses to Berg & Cobb [$250 – ($150 + $40)] × 5% × 2]	(6,000)	
Residual profit	$204,000	(2459)

Partnership Changes

63. (b) Because the total capital of the partners following the admission of Lind will be equal to the sum of the original partners' capital balances plus the cash contributed by Lind (i.e., $60,000 + $50,000 + $40,000 = $150,000), no goodwill is recognized.

Blau's capital balance, pre-admission		$60,000	
Credit to Lind for 1/3 of new partnership capital ($150,000 × 1/3)	$50,000		
Less: Cash contributed by Lind	40,000		
Bonus to Lind from Blau and Rubi	10,000		
Times: Blau's share of bonus [60% / (60% + 40%)]	× 60%		
Decrease in Blau's capital account		(6,000)	
Blau's capital balance, post-admission		$54,000	(1307)

64. (d) Under the bonus method, the total capital of the new partnership will equal the sum of the original partners' capital balances plus the fair value of the identifiable asset (i.e., land) contributed by the new partner. Immediately after admission, the balance of the new partner's capital account equals the total capital of the new partnership multiplied by the new partner's capital interest. After Grant's admission into the partnership, Kern's capital account balance would be $57,600 (i.e., $60,000 – $2,400), and Pate's capital account balance would be $38,400 (i.e., $40,000 – $1,600).

Original partnership capital ($60,000 + $20,000)	$80,000
Fair value of identifiable asset contributed by Grant	15,000
Total recorded capital of new partnership	95,000
Grant's capital interest	× 20%
Credit to Grant's capital account	$19,000

Land (fair value)	15,000		
Kern, Capital ($4,000 × 60%)	2,400		
Pate, Capital ($4,000 × 40%)	1,600		
Grant, Capital		19,000	(4127)

65. (c) The final settlement of Mill's interest exceeded his capital balance. The excess payment represents Mill's share of the unrecorded goodwill of the partnership. Under the bonus method, this excess payment would be recorded as a decrease in the remaining partners' capital accounts. (5297)

66. (c) The goodwill method looks upon this transaction as an indication that the partnership possesses an actual value of $360,000 ($180,000 / 50%) prior to Eddy's retirement. The partnership is reporting $320,000 in net assets, so a $40,000 valuation adjustment of is required. This adjustment is recorded as goodwill and is allocated to Eddy, Fox, and Grimm by their respective profit and loss sharing percentages. Immediately after Eddy's retirement, Fox's capital account balance is $108,000 ($96,000 + $12,000) and Grimm's capital account balance is $72,000 ($64,000 + $8,000).

Goodwill	40,000		
Eddy, Capital ($40,000 × 50%)		20,000	
Fox, Capital ($40,000 × 30%)		12,000	
Grimm, Capital ($40,000 × 20%)		8,000	
Eddy, Capital ($160,000 + $20,000)	180,000		
Cash		180,000	(9072)

67. (a) In a partnership liquidation, creditors have priority on any distribution. An individual prematurely distributing cash to a partner whose capital account later shows a deficit may be held personally liable if the insolvent partner is unable to repay such a distribution. The proceeds of a partnership liquidation may be distributed in a lump sum after all assets have been sold and all creditors satisfied, or the proceeds may be distributed to partners in installments as excess cash becomes available. (89600)

68. (b)

Total Cash to Distribute:	
Cash	$ 45,000
Plus: Sale of other assets	500,000
Less: Accounts payable to settle	(120,000)
Total available cash	$ 425,000

Distribution of Available Cash:	Alfa (60%)	Beda (40%)	
Beginning capital	$348,000	$232,000	
Reduce Beda capital for loan		(30,000)	
Allocate loss on sale of assets per profit and loss sharing ratio ($625,000 – $500,000)	(75,000)	(50,000)	
Distribution of cash	$273,000	$152,000	(5560)

69. (a) The maximum possible loss assumes that nothing will be received from the disposition of the remaining $100,000 of other assets. (in 000's)

	Cash	Other assets	Liabs.	Capital Cobb 50%	Capital Davis 30%	Capital Eddy 20%
Balances before realization	$ 50	$ 250	$60	$ 80	$ 90	$ 70
1/15 sale	120	(150)		(15)	(9)	(6)
Balance	170	100	60	65	81	64
Liabs. paid	(60)		(60)			
Balance	110	100	0	65	81	64
Maximum loss		(100)		(50)	(30)	(20)
Safe cash distribution	$110	$ 0	$ 0	$ 15	$ 51	$ 44

(1310)

PERFORMANCE BY SUBTOPICS

Each category below parallels a subtopic covered in Chapter 10. Record the number and percentage of questions you correctly answered in each subtopic area.

Overview

Question #	Correct √
1	
2	
3	
4	
# Questions	4
# Correct	______
% Correct	______

Capital

Question #	Correct √
5	
6	
7	
8	
9	
10	
11	
12	
13	
14	
15	
16	
# Questions	12
# Correct	______
% Correct	______

Retained Earnings

Question #	Correct √
17	
18	
19	
20	
21	
22	
# Questions	6
# Correct	______
% Correct	______

Treasury Stock

Question #	Correct √
23	
24	
25	
26	
27	
28	
29	
30	
31	
32	
33	
34	
35	
36	
37	
# Questions	15
# Correct	______
% Correct	______

Distributions

Question #	Correct √
38	
39	
40	
41	
42	
43	
44	
45	
46	
47	
48	
49	
# Questions	12
# Correct	______
% Correct	______

Employees and Stock

Question #	Correct √
50	
51	
52	
53	
# Questions	4
# Correct	______
% Correct	______

Partnership Formation

Question #	Correct √
54	
55	
56	
57	
58	
59	
60	
61	
62	
# Questions	9
# Correct	______
% Correct	______

Partnership Changes

Question #	Correct √
63	
64	
65	
66	
67	
68	
69	
# Questions	7
# Correct	______
% Correct	______

Solution 10-2 SIMULATION ANSWER: Stockholders' Equity

1	Common stock, $5 par value, 500,000 shares authorized, 210,000 shares issued, 204,000 shares outstanding		$1,050,000
2	Additional paid-in capital		1,800,000
3	Retained earnings:		
4	Beginning balance	$1,965,000	
5	Add: Net income	260,000	
6	Less: Property dividend distributed	(80,000)	
7	Ending balance		2,145,000
8			4,995,000
9	Less common stock in treasury, 6,000 shares at cost		(54,000)
10	Total stockholders' equity		$4,941,000

Explanations

1 Shares issued: 180,000 + 30,000 = 210,000 × $5 = $1,050,000

2 Additional paid-in capital: $1,500,000 + $345,000 - $45,000 = $1,800,000

	Debit	Credit
Cash (30,000 shares × $15)	450,000	
Stock Options Outstanding	45,000	
Common Stock (30,000 × $5)		150,000
Add'l Paid-in Cap., Common (to balance)		345,000

To record the exercise of options.

7 Ending balance of retained earnings: $1,965,000 + $260,000 – $80,000 = $2,145,000

8 Common stock + Additional Paid in Capital + ending balance of retained earnings = Subtotal:

Common stock	$1,050,000
Additional Paid in Capital	1,800,000
Ending balance of retained earnings	2,145,000
Subtotal	$4,995,000

9 6,000 shares of treasury stock @ $9.00 = $54,000 reduced stockholders equity when acquired.

10 Total stockholders' equity $4,995,000 – 54,000 = $4,941,000

Solution 10-3 SIMULATION ANSWER: Equity Worksheet

Accounts	Number of shares issued and outstanding	Common stock	Additional paid-in capital	Retained earnings	Accumulated other comprehensive income (loss)	Treasury stock	Total stockholders' equity
Beginning balances	750,000	750,000	3,000,000	3,500,000			7,250,000
Issuance of shares for property	15,000	15,000	195,000				210,000
Purchase of treasury stock	(25,000)					(250,000)	(250,000)
Property dividends distributed				(75,000)			(75,000)
Stock dividend issued	118,400	118,400	1,302,400	(1,420,800)			0
Cash dividend				(858,400)			(858,400)
Net income for the year				1,332,000			1,332,000
Unrealized gain (loss) on marketable securities available for sale					75,000		75,000
Ending balances	858,400	883,400	4,497,400	2,477,800	75,000	(250,000)	7,683,600

Solution 10-4 SIMULATION ANSWER: Retained Earnings

1. Trask's statement of retained earnings

Balance, December 31, year 5	$16,445,000
Less: Prior period adjustment from error understating depreciation	(350,000)
Add: Income tax effect	105,000
As restated (Beginning balance less adjustments)	16,200,000
Net income	2,400,000
Subtotal (Restated amount plus Net Income)	18,600,000
Deduct dividends	
Cash dividend on preferred stock [$5,000,000 × $.06]	(300,000)
Dividend in kind on common stock [15,000 @ $60]	(900,000)
Balance, December 31, year 6 (Net Income less dividends)	$17,400,000

2. Trask's stockholders' equity section, at December 31, year 6.

1	Preferred stock, $100 par value, 6% cumulative; 150,000 shares authorized; 50,000 shares issued and outstanding (Given)	$ 5,000,000
2	Common stock, $2.50 par value; 4,000,000 shares authorized; 3,400,000 shares issued	8,500,000
3	Additional paid-in capital	16,675,000
4	Retained earnings (See schedule #1 above)	17,400,000
5	Subtotal	47,575,000
6	Less: Common stock in treasury, 100,000 shares at cost [(100,000 × $5 cost), adjusted for 2-for-1 split]	(500,000)
7	Total stockholders' equity (Preferred stock plus common stock)	$47,075,000

[2] Number of common shares issued and outstanding:

Number of common shares issued, 12/31, year 5	1,575,000
Less: Common shares retired	(25,000)
Number of common shares issued, 6/1, year 6	150,000
	1,700,000
Two-for-one stock split, 10/27, year 6	× 2
Number of common shares issued after stock split	3,400,000
Less: Common shares held in treasury	(100,000)
Total number of common shares outstanding	3,300,000

Amount of common shares issued:

Amount of common shares issued, 12/31, year 5	$ 7,875,000
Less: Common shares retired at par value	(125,000)
Number of common shares issued, 6/1, year 6	750,000
Total amount of common shares issued	$ 8,500,000

[3] Amount of additional paid-in capital:

Amount at 12/31, year 5 (1,575,000 @ $10)	$15,750,000
Less: Treasury stock retired [25,000 shares @ $5 ($10 cost – $5 par value)]	(125,000)
APIC from exercise of stock options 6/1, year 6 (see below)	1,050,000
APIC calculation (stock option recording):	$16,675,000

	Debit	Credit
Cash [150,000 shares × $9]	1,350,000	
Stock Options Outstanding [$600,000 × (150,000/200,000)]	450,000	
Common Stock [150,000 shares × $5 par]		750,000
APIC [plug the difference]		1,050,000

Solution 10-5 SIMULATION ANSWER: Research

FASB Accounting Standards Codification

FASB ASC: 505 - 30 - 25 - 9

25-9 The difference between the repurchase and resale prices of a corporation's own stock shall be reflected as part of the capital of a corporation and allocated to the different components within stockholder equity as required by paragraph 505-30-30-7.

Simulation Preparation

Some candidates who are otherwise confident about the exam are overwhelmed by simulations. The following tips are designed to help you increase your confidence when presented with these lengthy questions.

As you progress through your study plan, work simulations from each major topic; waiting until the last month leaves you little time to prepare for this question type. The more uncomfortable that you are with simulations, the more important this becomes. You might not realize that you are uncomfortable with simulations if you don't try working some of them.

After working a simulation and checking your answers, reflect on the questions. If you had trouble with some aspect, evaluate whether you need to review the material, refine your answering technique, or merely gain confidence with this format.

Did you feel pressured for time? As you become more familiar with the material, your speed will increase. If you feel you are taking too long, it may indicate a need to consider alternative techniques to work the simulations. Specific information about techniques to solve simulations is in the **Exam Preparation Tips** appendix.

Once you know the content, you will be able to prepare a response regardless of the question format. Exam time is limited and you don't want the pressure of time considerations to distract you from providing your best answer to questions. Practice more simulations that may seem difficult; be prepared to answer simulations in any topic area.

Remember, with the techniques and information in your material,

A passing score is well within reach!

CHAPTER 11

REVENUE & EXPENSE RECOGNITION

CHAPTER 11

REVENUE & EXPENSE RECOGNITION

I. Conceptual Basis for Recognition

A. Overview

Revenue is usually the largest single item in the financial statements, and issues involving revenue recognition are among the most important and difficult that standard setters and accountants face. There is a significant gap between the broad conceptual guidance in the FASB's Concepts Statements and the detailed guidance in the authoritative literature, which tends to be industry or transaction-specific.

B. Accrual Accounting

Accrual accounting recognizes and reports the effects of transactions and other events on the assets and liabilities of a business enterprise in the time periods to which they relate rather than only when cash is received or paid. Accrual accounting attempts to match revenues and the expenses associated with those revenues in order to determine net income for an accounting period.

1. **Revenue and Gains Recognition** The recognition of revenue and gains of an entity during a period involves consideration of the following two factors, with sometimes one and sometimes the other being the more important consideration:

   a. Revenue and gains generally are not recognized until realized or realizable. Revenue and gains are realized when products (goods or services), merchandise, or other assets are exchanged for cash or claims to cash. Revenue and gains are realizable when related assets received or held are readily convertible to known amounts of cash or claims to cash.

   b. An entity's revenue-earning activities involve delivering or producing goods, rendering services, or other activities that constitute its ongoing major or central operations. Revenues are considered to have been earned when the entity has substantially accomplished what it must do to be entitled to the benefits represented by the revenues. Gains commonly result from transactions and other events that involve no earning process, and for recognizing gains, being earned is generally less significant than being realized or realizable.

2. **Expense Recognition** Expenses are recognized and recorded as follows:

   a. Some expenses are recognized and recorded on a presumed direct association with specific revenue.

   b. In the absence of a direct association with specific revenue, some expenses are recognized and recorded by attempting to allocate expenses in a systematic and rational manner among the periods in which benefits are provided.

   c. Some costs are associated with the current accounting period as expenses. Reasons for this could be any of the following:

      (1) Costs incurred during the period provide no discernible future benefits,

      (2) Costs recorded as assets in prior periods no longer provide discernible benefits

      (3) Allocating costs either on the basis of association with revenues or among several accounting periods is considered to serve no useful purpose.

3. **Accruals** An accrual represents a transaction that affects the determination of income for the period but has not yet been reflected in the cash accounts of that period.

   a. Accrued revenue is revenue earned but not yet collected in cash. An example of accrued revenue is accrued interest revenue earned on bonds from the last interest payment date to the end of the accounting period.

   b. An accrued expense is an expense incurred but not yet paid in cash. An example of an accrued expense is salaries incurred for the last week of the accounting period that are not payable until the subsequent accounting period.

4. **Deferrals** A deferral represents a transaction that has been reflected in the cash accounts of the period but has not yet affected the determination of income for that period.

   a. Deferred revenue is revenue collected or collectible in cash but not yet earned. An example of deferred revenue is rent collected in advance by a lessor in the last month of the accounting period, which represents the rent for the first month of the subsequent accounting period.

   b. A deferred (prepaid) expense is an expense paid or payable in cash but not yet incurred. An example of a deferred (prepaid) expense is an insurance premium paid in advance in the current accounting period, which represents insurance coverage for the subsequent accounting period.

C. Consignments

A consignment is a transfer of goods from the owner (consignor) to another person (consignee) who acts as a sales agent for the owner in a principal-agent relationship. The transfer is not a sale and the consignee never has title to the goods. When the consignee sells the goods, title passes directly from the consignor to the third party buyer.

1. **Consignor** Consignment sales revenue is recognized at the time of the sale at the sales price. The commission paid to the consignee is reported as a selling expense; it is not netted against sales revenue.

2. **Consigneee** Records revenue based on the amount retained (that is, the amount billed to the customer less the amount paid to the consignor).

Example 1 ▸ Consignment Sale

On October 10 of the current year, Dunn Co. consigned 50 freezers to Taylor Co. for sale at $1,000 each and paid $800 in transportation costs. On December 30, Taylor reported the sale of 20 freezers and remitted $18,000. The remittance was net of the agreed 10% commission.

Required: Determine the amount of consignment sales revenue for the year.

Solution: Consignment sales revenue is recognized at the time of the sale at the sales price. Thus, consignment sales revenue of $20,000 (20 freezers × $1,000 sales price) should be reported in the current year. The 10% commission should be reported as a selling expense; it should **not** be netted against sales revenue. The following journal entry would be used to record the consignment sale.

Account	Debit	Credit
Cash	18,000	
Consignment Sales Commissions	2,000	
Consignment Sales Revenues		20,000

D. Franchises

1. **Initial Franchise Fees** Initial franchise fees from an individual franchise sale ordinarily must be recognized (with an appropriate provision for estimated uncollectible amounts) when all material services or conditions relating to the sale have been substantially performed or satisfied by the franchisor.

2. **Substantial Performance** Services are considered to be substantially performed when all of the following conditions have been met:

   a. The franchisor has no remaining obligation or intent to refund any cash received or forgive any unpaid notes or receivables.

   b. Substantially all *initial* services of the franchisor required by the franchise agreement have been performed.

   c. No other material conditions or obligations related to the determination of substantial performance exist.

3. **Deferred Income** Sometimes, large initial franchise fees are required but continuing franchise fees are small in relation to future services. If it is probable that the continuing fee will not cover the cost of the continuing services to be provided by the franchisor and a reasonable profit on those continuing services, then a portion of the initial franchise fee should be deferred and amortized over the life of the franchise. The deferred amount should be enough to cover the estimated cost in excess of continuing franchise fees and provide a reasonable profit on the continuing services.

4. **Continuing Franchise Fees** Fees derived from ongoing services provided by the franchisor to the franchisee. Oftentimes, the fees are computed based on a percentage of franchise income. Continuing franchise fees are reported as revenue when the fees are earned and become receivable from the franchisee.

5. **Area Franchise Sales** If the franchisor's substantial obligations depend on the number of individual franchises established within the area, area franchise fees shall be recognized in proportion to the initial mandatory services provided. Revenue that may have to be refunded because future services are not performed shall not be recognized by the franchisor until the franchisee has no right to receive a refund.

6. **Collectibility of Franchise Fees** Installment or cost recovery accounting methods may be used to account for franchise fee revenue only in those exceptional cases when revenue is collectible over an extended period and no reasonable basis exists for estimating collectibility.

7. **Repossession of Franchise Rights** A franchisor may recover franchise rights through repossession if a franchisee decides not to open an outlet. If, for any reason, the franchisor refunds the consideration received, the original sale is cancelled, and revenue previously recognized shall be accounted for as a reduction in revenue in the period the franchise is repossessed. If franchise rights are repossessed but no refund is made, the franchisor shall apply the following guidance:

   a. The transaction shall not be regarded as a sale cancellation.

   b. No adjustment shall be made to any previously recognized revenue.

   c. Any estimated uncollectible amounts resulting from unpaid receivables shall be provided for.

8. **Costs** Costs related to continuing franchise fees should be expensed as incurred, and include:

   a. Direct incremental costs relating to franchise sales ordinarily are deferred until the related revenue is recognized; however, deferred costs must not exceed anticipated revenue less estimated additional related costs.

   b. Indirect costs of a regular and recurring nature irrespective of the level of sales should be expensed as incurred.

   c. Costs yet to be incurred should be accrued and charged against income no later than the period in which the related revenue is recognized.

Example 2 ▸ Franchise Fee Revenue

Bigger Burger, Inc., sold a fast food restaurant franchise to Donald. The sale agreement, signed on January 2, year 1, called for a $30,000 down payment plus two $10,000 annual payments, due January 2, year 2 and January 2, year 3, representing the value of initial franchise services rendered by Bigger Burger. The agreement required the franchisee to pay 5% of its gross revenues to the franchisor; deemed sufficient to cover the cost and a reasonable profit margin on continuing franchise services to be performed by Bigger Burger. The restaurant opened early in year 1, and its sales for the year amounted to $500,000.

Required: Assuming a 10% interest rate, determine Bigger Burger's year 1 total revenue from the Donald franchise.

Solution:

Initial franchise fee:		
Down payment	$30,000	
P.V. of installments ($10,000 × 1.7355)	17,355	$47,355
5% of gross sales (.05 × $500,000)		25,000
Interest income ($17,355 × .10)		1,735
Year 1 Total Revenue		$74,090

E. **Royalties**

Royalty revenue and royalty expense are recognized under the rules of accrual accounting.

1. **Revenue** Royalty revenue is recognized in the period(s) the royalties are earned. Royalties received in advance are not recognized as revenue at the date of the royalty agreement.

2. **Expense** Royalty expense is recognized in the period the royalties are incurred. Royalties paid in advance are not recognized as an expense at the date of the royalty agreement.

3. **Computation** In general, the amount of royalty revenue or expense to recognize during a period is computed by multiplying the period's sales applicable to the royalty agreement by the royalty percentage.

Example 3 ▸ Royalties

On January 2, year 1, Shaw Company sold the copyright to a book to Poe Publishers, Inc. for royalties of 20% of future sales. On the same date, Poe paid Shaw a royalty advance of $100,000 to be applied against royalties for year 2 sales. On September 30, year 1, Poe made a $42,000 royalty remittance to Shaw for sales in the six-month period ended June 30, year 1. In January year 2, before issuance of its year 1 financial statements, Shaw learned that Poe's sales of the book totaled $250,000 for the last half of year 1.

Required: Determine how much royalty revenue Shaw should report in year 1.

Solution: The $100,000 advance to be applied against royalties for year 2 sales is **not** used to compute royalty revenue. Neither royalty revenue nor royalty expense is recognized on the cash basis.

Royalties for Jan. 1 - June 30, year 1 (paid Sept. 30, year 1)	$42,000
Royalties for July 1 - Dec. 31, year 1 ($250,000 × 20%)	50,000
Royalty revenue for year 1	$92,000

F. Disclosures

A description of all significant accounting policies of the reporting entity should be included as an integral part of the financial statements. Disclosure of accounting policies should identify and describe the accounting principles followed by the reporting entity and the methods of applying those principles that materially affect the financial statements.

The standards state that the disclosure should include judgments as to the appropriateness of the principles relating to recognition of revenue and the allocation of asset costs to current and future periods. Importantly, it should encompass those accounting principles and methods that involve any of the following:

1. **Acceptable Alternatives** A selection from existing acceptable alternatives

2. **Industry Preferences** Principles and methods peculiar to the industry in which the reporting entity operates, even if such principles and methods are predominantly followed in that industry

3. **Application** Unusual or innovative applications of generally accepted accounting principles (and, as applicable, of principles and methods peculiar to the industry in which the reporting entity operates)

4. **Risks and Uncertainties** Entities should include in their financial statements disclosures about the nature of their operations and about the use of estimates in the preparation of financial statements. If certain criteria are met, additional disclosures may be required in regards to significant estimates and the entity's vulnerability due to certain concentrations (e.g., concentrations in the volume of business transacted with a particular customer or concentrations in revenue from particular products or services).

II. Other Comprehensive Basis of Accounting

A. Overview

The term "other comprehensive basis of accounting" (OCBOA) refers to basis of accounting other than GAAP. Unlike GAAP, there is no standard-setting organization for OCBOA. Other comprehensive basis of accounting include: historical cost, income tax, modified cash and cash.

The primary guidance for OCBOA financial statements is provided by SAS No. 62, *Special Reports,* (AU §623). AU §623.04 recognizes the following OCBOAs. A basis of accounting used to comply with regulatory or financial reporting provisions of a governmental agency whose jurisdiction the entity is subject to. The basis of accounting the reporting entity uses, or expects to use, to file its income tax return for the period covered by the financial statements. The cash receipts and disbursements basis of accounting, and modifications of the cash basis having substantial support, such as recording depreciation on fixed assets or accruing income taxes. A definite set of criteria having substantial support that is applied to all material items appearing in financial statements, such as the price-level basis of accounting.

B. Cash Basis

Under the pure cash basis, the effects of transactions and other events on the assets and liabilities of a business enterprise are recognized and reported only when cash is received or paid; while in accrual accounting, these effects are recognized and reported in the time periods to which they relate. Cash basis accounting does not attempt to match revenues and the expenses associated with those revenues. Under the pure cash basis, long-term assets are not capitalized, and, hence, no depreciation or amortization is recorded. Also, no accruals are made for taxes and no prepaid expenses are recorded.

The modified cash basis is a hybrid method that combines features of both the cash basis and the accrual basis of accounting. Modifications to the cash basis include such items as the capitalization of assets and the accrual of taxes. Modified cash basis financial statements are intended to provide more information to users than cash financial statements, while still avoiding the complexities of current value GAAP financial statements.

C. Income-Tax Basis

In income-tax basis accounting, the effects of events on a business enterprise are recognized when taxable income or deductible expense is recognized on the tax return. Nontaxable income and nondeductible expenses are still included in the determination of income.

D. Basic Financial Statements

Under GAAP, a complete set of financial statements consists of a statement of financial condition, a statement of changes in net worth, and the related notes. Each financial statement should include references to the notes and should state that the notes are an integral part of the financial statements.

The GAAP statement of financial condition, or balance sheet, is divided into four main sections: assets, liabilities, income tax effects, and net worth. In the asset section, the economic resources of the client (individual or group of individuals) are presented. Generally, assets should be presented in order of liquidity. The liability section of the statement of financial condition displays the client's debt. Liabilities should be presented in order of maturity. In the net worth section, a single amount is presented, and no attempt is made to differentiate among the types of net worth (such as donated capital, earned capital, and appreciated capital).

When an OCBOA is used, the design of the statement of financial condition should be similar, except for the following: the statement would not present an "income tax effect" section. It should not use terms normally associated with current value basis presentations, such as financial condition or net worth.

Exhibit 1 ▸ Revenue and Expense Item Effects

Revenue or Expense Item	Plus or Minus Adjustments to Derive Accrual Basis	Illustrative Amounts
Collections from sales		$190
Adjustments:		
1. Increase in accounts receivable	+	7
2. Decrease in accounts receivable	–	
3. Uncollectible accounts written off	+	5
Sales revenue		$202
Collections from other revenues		$184
Adjustments:		
1. Increase in revenue receivable	+	
2. Decrease in revenue receivable	–	(4)
3. Increase in unearned revenue	–	(10)
4. Decrease in unearned revenue	+	
Revenue recognized		$170
Payments for purchases		$ 91
Adjustments:		
1. Increase in inventory	–	(7)
2. Decrease in inventory	+	
3. Increase in accounts payable	+	9
4. Decrease in accounts payable	–	
Cost of goods sold		$ 93
Payment for Expenses		$ 92
Adjustments:		
1. Increase in prepaid expenses	–	(9)
2. Decrease in prepaid expenses	+	
3. Increase in accrued expenses payable	+	8
4. Decrease in accrued expenses payable	–	
Expenses recognized		$ 91

NOTE: This exhibit is for revenue or expense item effects, **not** the effects to income.

III. Personal Financial Statements

A. Overview

Personal financial statements are prepared for individuals either to formally organize and plan their financial affairs in general or for specific purposes, such as obtaining credit, income tax planning, retirement planning, gift and estate planning, or public disclosure of their financial affairs. Users of personal financial statements rely on them in determining whether to grant credit, in assessing the financial activities of individuals, in assessing the financial affairs of public officials and candidates for public office, and for similar purposes.

B. Basic Financial Statements

The basic financial statements typically present financial condition and changes in net worth, descriptions of accounting policies, and notes to the financial statements. Each financial statement should include references to the notes and should state that the notes are an integral part of the financial statements.

Assets and liabilities and changes in them should be recognized on the accrual basis, not on the cash basis. The most useful and readily understood presentation of assets and liabilities in personal financial statements is by order of liquidity and maturity, without classification as current and noncurrent, since the concept of working capital applied to business enterprises is inappropriate for personal financial statements.

1. **Financial Condition** The statement of financial condition is the basic personal financial statement. It presents the estimated current values of assets, the estimated current amounts of liabilities, estimated income taxes on the differences between the estimated current values of assets and the estimated current amounts of liabilities and their tax bases, and net worth at a specified date. The term net worth should be used in the statement to designate the difference between total assets and total liabilities, after deducting estimated income taxes on the differences between the estimated current values of assets and the estimated current amounts of liabilities and their tax bases.

   Significant assets and liabilities may represent limited business activities. That is, the activity does not constitute a separate trade or business. An investment in commercial real estate financed with a mortgage is an example of a limited business activity. Assets and liabilities related to a limited business activity should be reported as separate amounts and not netted against one another.

2. **Financial Net Worth** The statement of changes in net worth should present the major sources of increases in net worth: income, increases in the estimated current values of assets, decreases in the estimated current amounts of liabilities, and decreases in estimated income taxes on the differences between the estimated current values of assets and the estimated current amounts of liabilities and their tax bases. It should present the major sources of decreases in net worth: expenses, decreases in the estimated current values of assets, increases in the estimated current amounts of liabilities, and increases in estimated income taxes on the differences between the estimated current values of assets and the estimated current amounts of liabilities and their tax bases. One statement combining income and other changes is desirable because of the mix of business and personal items in personal financial statements. The presentation of a statement of changes in net worth is optional.

3. **Valuation** The estimated current value of an asset in personal financial statements is the amount at which the item could be exchanged between a buyer and seller, each of whom is well-informed and willing, and neither of whom is compelled to buy or sell. Costs of disposal, such as commissions, if material, should be considered in determining estimated current values. The estimated current values of some assets may be difficult to determine and the cost of obtaining estimated current values of some assets directly may exceed the benefits of doing so; therefore, judgment be exercised in determining estimated current values.

   Recent transactions involving similar assets and liabilities in similar circumstances ordinarily provide a satisfactory basis for determining the estimated current value of an asset and the estimated current amount of a liability. If recent sales information is unavailable, other methods that may be used include the capitalization of past or prospective earnings, the use of liquidation values, the adjustment of historical cost based on changes in a specific price index, the use of appraisals, or the use of the discounted amounts of projected cash receipts and payments. Specifically:

   a. Receivables should be presented at the discounted amounts of cash estimated to be collected, using appropriate interest rates at the date of the financial statements.

   b. Marketable securities include both debt and equity securities for which market quotations are available. The estimated current values of such securities are their quoted market prices.

c. The estimated current value of an investment in life insurance is the cash value of the policy less the amount of any loans against it. The face amount of life insurance the individuals own should be disclosed.

d. Investments in real estate (including leaseholds) should be presented in personal financial statements at their estimated current values.

e. Intangible assets should be presented at the discounted amounts of projected cash receipts and payments arising from the planned use or sale of the assets if both the amounts and timing can be reasonably estimated.

f. A provision should be made for estimated income taxes on the differences between the estimated current values of assets and the estimated current amounts of liabilities and their tax bases, including consideration of negative tax bases of tax shelters, if any. The provision should be computed as if the estimated current values of all assets had been realized and the estimated current amounts of all liabilities had been liquidated on the statement date, using applicable income tax laws and regulations, considering recapture provisions and available carryovers. The estimated income taxes should be presented between liabilities and net worth in the statement of financial condition. The methods and assumptions used to compute the estimated income taxes should be fully disclosed.

C. Disclosures

Determining the adequacy of disclosure is probably the most challenging aspect of preparing personal financial statements. Although there is no comprehensive list of what notes should be included in personal financial statements, the statements should include sufficient disclosures to make the financial statements adequately informative. Specifically, informative disclosures can be classified in the following categories: summary of significant accounting policies; financial statement items; presentation requirements; and other information.

Generally, notes are accumulated and presented on separate pages following the primary financial statements. The notes should be arranged in the same order as the amounts in the financial statements to which they relate.

D. Supplemental Information

Personal financial statement presentations may include a variety of information that supplements the basic financial statements, such as detailed schedules, summaries, consolidating information, comparisons, or statistical information. There is no authoritative guidance on what may or may not be presented as supplementary information.

IV. Long-Term Construction Contracts

A. Overview

Due to the length of time implicit in long-term construction contracts, significant problems often arise concerning the measurement and timing of income recognition. The two methods most commonly used in these types of contracts are the percentage of completion method and the completed contract method.

Use of the percentage of completion method or the completed contract method should not be acceptable alternatives for the same circumstances. Determination of which of the two methods is preferable should be based on a careful evaluation of the circumstances. The percentage of completion method is recommended when contract revenues, costs to complete and extent of progress toward completion can be reasonably estimated. If no dependable estimates can be made or inherent hazards are present, the completed contract method is preferable.

B. Percentage of Completion Method

The advantages of the percentage of completion method are the periodic recognition of income as it is earned, and the reflection of the status of uncompleted contracts that is provided through the current estimates of costs to complete or of progress toward completion. The disadvantage is that it is necessarily dependent upon estimates and, therefore, subject to uncertainty.

Income is recognized as work on the contract progresses. The amount of income recognized in the period is added to Construction in Progress. Estimates of contract revenue, costs to complete, and the extent of progress toward completion must be continually reevaluated throughout the life of a contract.

1. **Income Recognition** The meaningful measurement of the extent of progress toward completion is essential because this factor is used in determining the amounts of estimated contract revenue and the estimated gross profit that will be recognized in any given period.

   Income should be recognized on the basis of either of the following:

   a. The percentage derived from incurred costs to date over total expected costs; or

   $$\left(\frac{\textit{Actual cost to date}}{\textit{Estimated total cost}} \times \textit{Total estimated contract income}\right) - \textit{Income previously recognized} = \textit{Income to be recognized}$$

   b. Some other measure of progress toward completion as may be appropriate under the circumstances. Use of any given method depends on whether input measures (terms of efforts devoted to a contract) or output measures (terms of results achieved) are used. Output measures are generally the best method of progress toward completion but often they cannot be established and input measures must be used. The methods selected should be applied consistently to all contracts having similar characteristics. The percentage of completion may be based on estimates of completion to date developed by architects or engineers.

2. **Progress Billings** Progress billings and collections on progress billings are not generally accepted as a method of recognizing income because they often do not bear a meaningful relationship to the work performed on the contract. Typically, billings may be accelerated in the early stages of the contract to provide the contractor with the working capital needed to begin performance. If income were recognized on progress billings, it would be possible for a contractor to materially distort income merely by rendering progress billings without regard to any degree of progress on the contract. *Progress Billings* is a contra account to *Construction in Progress.*

3. **Loss Recognition** When current estimates of total contract costs indicate a loss, the loss should be recognized immediately and in full in the current period.

4. **Current Assets/Liabilities** Each contract may give rise to a current asset or liability.

   a. An excess of costs incurred and income recognized over progress billings should be reported as a current asset.

   b. An excess of progress billings over related costs and income recognized constitutes a current liability.

   c. Current assets and current liabilities pertaining to two or more contracts should not be netted out for financial statement presentation.

5. **Advantages** The principal advantages of the percentage of completion method are: periodic recognition of income as work is performed thus enhancing the interperiod comparability of the financial statements; and reflection of the status of uncompleted contracts provided through current estimates of completion costs.

6. **Disadvantage** The principal disadvantage is the necessity of relying on estimates of ultimate contract costs and of consequently accruing income based upon those estimates.

C. Completed Contract Method

This method may be used in circumstances in which financial position and results of operations would not vary materially from those resulting from the use of the percentage of completion method, e.g., when an entity has primarily short-term contracts. The completed contract method is preferable in circumstances in which estimates cannot meet the criteria for reasonable dependability or in which there are inherent hazards. Examples of inherent hazards are: contracts whose validity is seriously in question (i.e., which are less than fully enforceable); contracts whose completion may be subject to the outcome of pending legislation or pending litigation; or contracts exposed to the possibility of the condemnation or expropriation of the resulting properties.

No income is recognized on the contract until it is completed or substantially completed and the work accepted. However, if at any point expected contract costs exceed the contract price, losses are recognized immediately and in full in the current period.

1. **Balance Sheet Presentation** Excess of accumulated costs over related progress billings should be shown as a current asset on the balance sheet, while an excess of accumulated progress billings over related costs should be shown as a current liability. Contracts should be separated to accurately segregate asset and liability contracts.

2. **Advantage** The principal advantage of the completed contract method is that it is based on results as finally determined rather than on estimates for unperformed work which may involve unforeseen costs and possible losses.

3. **Disadvantage** The principal disadvantage is it does not reflect current performance when the life of the contract extends over several periods and thus diminishes the interperiod comparability of the financial statements.

Example 4 ▸ Percentage of Completion vs. Completed Contract

On January 1, year 1, Estimator, Inc. entered into two $1,800,000 fixed-price contracts to construct office buildings. The estimated time for both projects was three years.

Contract A	Year 1	Year 2	Year 3
Incurred costs to date	$ 250,000	$ 320,000	$1,530,000
Est. costs to complete	1,250,000	1,280,000	0
Total estimated costs	1,500,000	1,600,000	1,530,000
Billed during year	220,000	1,130,000	450,000
Collected during year	180,000	1,040,000	580,000

Contract B	Year 1	Year 2	Year 3
Incurred costs to date	$ 250,000	$ 320,000	$1,810,000
Est. costs to complete	1,250,000	1,490,000	0
Total estimated costs	1,500,000	1,810,000	1,810,000
Billed during year	220,000	1,130,000	450,000
Collected during year	180,000	1,040,000	580,000

Required: Prepare the journal entries and determine income (loss) recognized in all three years for both contracts under the percentage of completion method and the completed contract method (in 1,000s).

Solution:

<u>Percentage of Completion Entries:</u>
1. To record the costs of construction.
2. To record progress billings.
3. To record collections.
4. To recognize revenue and gross profit.
5. To record the completion of the contract.

Contract A		Year 1		Year 2		Year 3	
1.	Construction in Progress	250		70		1,210	
	Cash (or Accounts Payable)		250		70		1,210
2.	Accounts Receivable	220		1,130		450	
	Progress Billings		220		1,130		450
3.	Cash	180		1,040		580	
	Accounts Receivable		180		1,040		580
4.	Construction Expenses	250					
	Construction in Progress	50 [1]					
	Revenue from LT Contracts		300				
4.	Construction Expenses			70			
	Construction in Progress				10 [2]		
	Revenue from LT Contracts				60		
4.	Construction Expenses					1,210	
	Construction in Progress					230 [3]	
	Revenue from LT Contracts						1,440
5.	Progress Billings					1,800	
	Construction in Progress						1,800 [4]

[1] (250 / 1,500) × [1,800 – (250 + 1,250)] – 0 = 50
[2] (320 / 1,600) × [1,800 – (320 + 1,280)] – 50 = –10
[3] (1,530 / 1,530) × [1,800 – 1,530] – (50 – 10) = 230
[4] 250 + 50 + 70 – 10 + 230 + 1,210 = 1,800

Contract B		Year 1		Year 2		Year 3	
1.	Construction in Progress	250		70		1,490	
	Cash (or Accounts Payable)		250		70		1,490
2.	Accounts Receivable	220		1,130		450	
	Progress Billings		220		1,130		450
3.	Cash	180		1,040		580	
	Accounts Receivable		180		1,040		580
4.	Construction Expenses	250					
	Construction in Progress	50 [1]					
	Revenue from LT Contracts		300				
4.	Construction Expenses			70			
	Construction in Progress				60 [2]		
	Revenue from LT Contracts				10		
4.	Construction Expenses					1,490	
	Revenue from LT Contracts						1,490
5.	Progress Billings					1,800	
	Construction in Progress						1,800 [3]

[1] (250 / 1,500) × [1,800 – (250 + 1,250)] – 0 = 50
[2] Reverse recognized profit and recognize estimated loss in full. –50 + (1,800 – 1,810) = –60
[3] 250 + 50 + 70 – 60 + 1,490 = 1,800

Completed Contract Entries:
1, 2, and 3. The entries to record the costs of construction, progress billings, and collections are the same as entries 1, 2, and 3 for the percentage of completion method for both contracts.
4. To record the contract loss first evident in year 2 on Contract B.
5. To recognize revenue and gross profit and record the completion of the contract.

Contract A	Year 1		Year 2		Year 3	
5. Construction Expenses					1,530	
Construction in Progress						1,530
Progress Billings					1,800	
Revenue from LT Contracts						1,800

Contract B	Year 1		Year 2		Year 3	
4. Loss From LT Contracts			10			
Construction in Progress				10		
5. Construction Expenses					1,800	
Construction in Progress						1,800
Progress Billings					1,800	
Revenue from LT Contracts						1,800

Income (Loss) Recognized:

Contract A	Year 1	Year 2	Year 3	Total
% of Completion	$50	($10)	$230	$270
Completed Contract	0	0	270	270
Contract B				
% of Completion	50	(60)	0	(10)
Completed Contract	0	(10)	0	(10)

NOTE: Contract A has a loss in year 2, but overall the contract is profitable. Contract B has an overall loss, which is recognized in year 2, the year the loss is evident.

D. Determining the Profit Center

The basic presumption should be that each contract is the profit center for revenue recognition, cost accumulation, and income measurement. That presumption may be overcome only if a contract or a series of contracts meets the conditions described for combining or segmenting contracts.

1. **Combining Contracts** Combining contracts for profit recognition purposes may occur when a group of contracts are so closely related that they are, in effect, parts of a single project with an overall profit margin, such as when a group of contracts have been negotiated as a package with the objective of achieving an overall profit. The standards detail specific criteria that must be met for contracts to be combined for accounting purposes.

2. **Segmenting Contracts** A single contract or a group of contracts that otherwise meet the test for combining may include several elements or phases, each of which the contractor negotiated separately with the same customer and agreed to perform without regard to the performance of the others. A project consisting of a single contract or a group of contracts with segments that have different rates of profitability may be segmented if it meets specific criteria described in the accounting standards.

E. Disclosures

The following items require disclosure in the financial statements: the basic method of accounting used for contracts; departures from the basic accounting policy; methods of measuring extent of progress toward completion for contracts accounted for using the percentage of completion method; and specific criteria used to determine when a contract is substantially completed for contracts accounted for using the completed contract method. The effect of significant revisions of estimates should be disclosed if the effect is material.

V. Contract Accounting

A. Insurance

1. **Acquisition Costs** Acquisition costs are costs that vary with and are primarily related to the acquisition of insurance contracts. Costs that meet that definition are typically recognized as assets and are commonly referred to a *deferred acquisition costs*. Deferred acquisition costs are amortized over time using amortization methods dependent upon the nature of the underlying insurance product (e.g., proportional to revenues, based on a contract's estimated gross profit, or based on a contract's estimated gross margin). Other costs are charged to expense as incurred.

2. **Capitalized Costs** The following costs incurred in the acquisition of new and renewal contracts should be capitalized:

   a. Incremental direct costs are those costs that result directly from and are essential to the contract transaction(s) and would not have been incurred by the insurance entity had the contract transaction(s) not occurred.

   b. Certain other costs related directly to the following acquisition activities performed by the insurer for the contract, such as: underwriting; policy issuance and processing; medical and inspection costs; and sales force contract selling costs.

3. **Advertising Costs** Should be included in deferred acquisition costs only if the capitalization criteria are met.

4. **Other Costs** All other acquisition-related costs—including costs incurred by the insurer for soliciting potential customers, market research, training, administration, unsuccessful acquisition or renewal efforts, and product development—should be charged to expense as incurred.

B. Sales of Real Estate

1. **Full Accrual Method** For sales of real estate other than retail land sales, use of the full accrual method (i.e., recognition of all of the profit at the date of sale) depends on the existence of the following two conditions (part or all of the profit should be deferred until both conditions exist):

   a. The profit is determinable (i.e., the collectibility of the sales price is reasonably assured or an uncollectible amount can be estimated).

   b. The earnings process is virtually complete (i.e., the seller is not obligated to perform significant tasks after the sale to earn the profit).

2. **Collectibility** Collectibility is demonstrated by the buyer's commitment to pay as supported by substantial initial and continuing investments in the property such that the buyer's risk of loss through default motivates the buyer to honor the obligation to the seller.

3. **Profit** Profit on real estate transactions should not be recognized by the full accrual method unless all of the following criteria are met:

   a. A sale is consummated, meaning that: the parties are bound by the terms of a contract; all consideration has been exchanged; any permanent financing for which the seller is responsible has been arranged; and all conditions precedent to closing have been performed. These four conditions usually are met at the time of closing, not when an agreement to sell has been signed or at a preclosing.

   b. The buyer's initial and continuing investments are adequate to demonstrate a commitment to pay for the property.

c. The seller's receivable is not subject to future subordination.

d. The seller has transferred to the buyer the usual risks and rewards of ownership in a transaction that is in substance a sale and does not have a substantial continuing involvement with the property.

VI. Software Revenue Recognition

A. Revenue Criteria

If an arrangement to deliver software or a software system does not require significant production, modification, or customization of software, revenue should be recognized when all of the following criteria are met:

1. **Persuasive Evidence** If the vendor has a customary business practice of utilizing written contracts, evidence of the arrangement is provided only by a contract signed by both parties. Vendors that do not rely on signed contracts should have other forms of evidence to document the transaction, such as a purchase order or on-line authorization. Even if all other requirements in the guidance for recognition of revenue are met (including delivery), revenue should not be recognized on any element of the arrangement unless persuasive evidence of an arrangement exists.

2. **Delivery Has Occurred** The principle of not recognizing revenue before delivery applies whether the customer is a user or a reseller. For software that is delivered electronically, delivery has been met when the customer takes possession of the software via a download or has been provided with access codes that allow the customer to take immediate possession of the software on its hardware pursuant to an agreement or purchase order for the software.

   If uncertainty exists about customer acceptance after delivery, license revenue should not be recognized until acceptance occurs. Delivery should not be considered complete unless the destination is the customer's place of business or another site specified by the customer. If the customer specifies an intermediate site, but a substantial portion of the fee is not payable until the delivery by the vendor to another site specified by the customer, revenue should not be recognized until delivery is made to that other site. Revenue from transactions involving delivery agents of the vendor should be recognized when the software is delivered to the customer, not to the delivery agent.

3. **Vendor's Fee is Fixed or Determinable** A software licensing fee is not fixed or determinable if it is based on the number of units distributed or copied, or the expected number of users of the product. If an arrangement includes rights of return or rights to refunds without return, conditions that must be met for the vendor to recognize revenue include that the amount of future returns or refunds can be reasonably estimated in accordance with FASB ASC 605-15. *Any* extended payment terms may indicate that the fee is not fixed or determinable.

   a. If payment of a significant portion of the fee is not due until after expiration of the license or more than twelve months after delivery, the licensing fee should be presumed not to be fixed or determinable unless the vendor can demonstrate a standard business practice of using long-term or installment contracts and a history of successfully collecting under the original payment terms without making concessions. If it cannot be concluded that a fee is fixed or determinable at the outset of an arrangement, revenue should be recognized as payments become due.

b. For reseller arrangements, factors such as the following may indicate that the fixed or determinable fees and collectibility criteria have not been met.

(1) Payment is substantially contingent on the reseller's success in distributing the product.

(2) Resellers may not be able to honor a commitment to make fixed and determinable payments until they collect cash from their customers.

(3) Uncertainties indicate the amount of future returns cannot be reasonably estimated.

(4) Distribution arrangements with resellers require the vendor to rebate or credit a portion of the fee if the vendor subsequently reduces its price for a product and the reseller still has rights with respect to that product (price protection).

(5) Fees from licenses cancelable by the customer are neither fixed nor determinable until the cancellation privileges lapse. Fees from licenses with cancellation privileges that expire ratably over the license period are considered to become determinable ratably as the cancellation privileges lapse.

B. Multiple-Element Arrangements

1. **Software Arrangements** Software arrangements may consist of multiple elements, that is, additional software products, upgrades and enhancements, postcontract customer support (PCS), or services, including elements deliverable only on a when-and-if-available basis. If contract accounting does not apply, the vendor's fee must be allocated to the various elements based on vendor-specific objective evidence of fair values, regardless of any separate prices stated within the contract for each element.

2. **Vendor-Specific Objective Evidence of Fair Value** If sufficient vendor-specific objective evidence of fair values does not exist for the allocation of revenue to the various elements of an arrangement, all revenue from the arrangement should be deferred until such sufficient evidence exists, or until all elements have been delivered. Vendor-specific objective evidence of fair value is limited to the following:

   a. The price charged when the same element is sold separately

   b. For an element not yet being sold separately, the price established by management having the relevant authority

3. **Exceptions** Exceptions to this guidance are provided for PCS, services that do not involve significant customization, subscriptions, and arrangements in which the fee is based on the number of copies. In addition, SOP 98-9 amends this guidance for multiple-element arrangements in which there is vendor-specific objective evidence of the fair values of *all* undelivered elements, and vendor-specific objective evidence of fair value does not exist for one or more of the delivered elements. In such circumstances, it requires recognition of revenue in accordance with the residual method. Under the residual method, the total fair value of the undelivered elements is deferred, and the difference between the total arrangement fee and the amount deferred for the undelivered elements is recognized as revenue related to the delivered elements.

4. **Criterion of Collectibility** The portion of the fee allocated to an element should be recognized as revenue when all of the revenue recognition criteria have been met. In applying those criteria, the delivery of an element is considered not to have occurred if there are undelivered elements that are essential to the functionality of any delivered elements. In addition, no portion of the fee (including amounts otherwise allocated to delivered elements) meets the criterion of collectibility if the portion of the fee allocable to delivered elements is subject to forfeiture, refund, or other concession if the undelivered elements are not delivered.

   In order for the revenue related to an arrangement to be considered not subject to forfeiture, refund, or other concession, management must intend not to provide refunds or concessions that are not required under the provisions of the arrangement. The vendor's historical pattern of making refunds or other concessions that were not required under the original provisions (contractual or other) of other arrangements should be considered more persuasive than terms included in the arrangement that indicate that no concessions are required.

C. Service Elements

1. Separate accounting for a service element of an arrangement is required if both of the following criteria are met:

   a. The services are not essential to the functionality of any other element of the transaction.

   b. The services are described in the contract such that the total price of the arrangement would be expected to vary as the result of the inclusion or exclusion of the services.

2. FASB ASC 985 provides comprehensive guidance on different kinds of multiple-element arrangements, PCS, services, and contract accounting. In addition, it includes appendixes with examples of the application of certain provisions of this guidance and a flowchart illustrating a decision process for recognizing revenue on software arrangements.

VII. Alternative Revenue Recognition Methods

A. Installment

Under GAAP, revenue should ordinarily be accounted for at the time a transaction is completed, with appropriate provision for uncollectible accounts. Thus, revenues generally are recognized at the point of sale. There are several exceptions to this rule. The installment method is an exception to this because it allows revenue to be deferred and recognized each year in proportion to the receivables collected during that year.

1. **Applicability** The installment method of accounting for sales is not generally acceptable. There are exceptional cases where receivables are collectible over an extended period of time and, because of the terms of the transactions or other conditions, there is no reasonable basis for estimating the degree of collectibility. When such circumstances exist, and as long as they exist, the installment method of accounting may be used.

2. **Computation** Income recognized using the installment method of accounting generally equals cash collected multiplied by the gross profit percentage applicable to those sales. Selling and administrative expenses are not used to compute the gross profit rate. Receivable accounts and deferred profit accounts must be kept separately for each year because the gross profit rate will often vary from year to year. Where an installment receivable extends beyond one year, it should be recorded at the present value of the payments discounted at the market interest rate. At any time after the sale, the installment receivables' balance will be the present value of the remaining monthly payments discounted at the market interest rate at the time of the exchange.

Example 5 ▸ Installment Method

The Thomas Equipment Company reports income using the installment method of accounting and uses a perpetual inventory system. Installment sales during year 3 amounted to $400,000.

Year of sale	Gross profit percentage	Installment receivables on Jan. 1, year 3	Collected during Year 3	Installment receivables on Dec. 31, year 3
1	46%	$ 60,000	$ 60,000	--
2	42%	100,000	68,000	$ 32,000
3	40%	--	120,000	280,000

Required: Determine

1. The realized gross profit on installment sales during year 3 from all sales.
2. The balance in the deferred gross profit account at December 31, year 3.

Solution:

1. The realized gross profit on installment sales is $104,160.

Year of sale	Gross profit percentage		Year 3 collections		Realized gross profit
1	46%	×	$ 60,000	=	$ 27,600
2	42%	×	68,000	=	28,560
3	40%	×	120,000	=	48,000
					$104,160

2. The balance in the deferred gross profit account is $125,440.

Year of sale	Gross profit percentage		Installment receivables on Dec. 31, year 3		Deferred gross profit
2	42%	×	$ 32,000	=	$ 13,440
3	40%	×	280,000	=	112,000
					$125,440

B. **Cost Recovery**

The cost recovery method of revenue recognition is also not generally accepted; however, it may be used where (1) receivables are collectible over an extended period of time and there is no reasonable basis for estimating the degree of collectibility, (2) an investment is very speculative in nature, and/or (3) the final sale price is to be determined by future events.

1. **Applicability** The cost recovery method is the most conservative revenue recognition method. This method is used when the uncertainty of collection is so great that use of the installment method is precluded.

2. **Computation** All amounts collected are treated as a recoupment of the cost of the item sold, until the entire cost associated with the transaction has been recovered. Only at this point is profit recognized.

Example 6 ▸ Cost Recovery Method

On January 2, year 2, Old Mine Co. sold a gold mine that had become unprofitable to Golddiggers, Inc., a newly incorporated venture that hoped to wring additional profits from the mine by use of a revolutionary—but yet unproven—method of extraction. At the time of the sale, the gold mine had a carrying amount of $450,000 in Old Mine's books. The sales agreement called for a $100,000 down payment and two notes of $200,000 bearing interest of 10% with one note payable, including accrued interest, due on January 2, year 3 and one note payable, including accrued interest, due on January 2, year 4. Because of the extreme uncertainty concerning the eventual collection of the notes' proceeds, Old Mine appropriately accounted for this transaction under the cost recovery method. The notes were paid when due, including interest and principal.

Required: Determine Old Mine's income from this transaction for the years ending December 31, year 2, year 3, and year 4. Provide appropriate journal entries.

Solution:

Year	Amount collected	Unrecovered cost (Year 1: $450,000)	Deferred profit Dr. (Cr.)	Recognized profit (Cr.)
2	$100,000	$350,000	($50,000)	$ 0
3	220,000	130,000	(20,000)	0
4	242,000	0	70,000	(112,000)

	Account	Dr.	Cr.
Year 2:	Cash	100,000	
	Notes Receivable	400,000	
	Gold Mine (net)		450,000
	Deferred Profit		50,000
Year 3:	Cash [$200,000 + ($200,000 × 10%)]	220,000	
	Notes Receivable		200,000
	Deferred Profit		20,000
Year 4:	Cash [$220,000 + ($220,000 × 10%)]	242,000	
	Deferred Profit	70,000	
	Recognized Profit		112,000
	Notes Receivable		200,000

C. **Milestone Method**

Research and/or development arrangements often include payment provisions for which a portion of the consideration to be received is contingent upon "milestone events." Examples of these types of events would include successful completion of phases in certain studies within the medical profession, or achieving specified results from other research or development work. Frequently, reporting entities recognize payments received as a result of reaching these types of milestones in their entirety upon achieving specific milestones. This revenue recognition approach is often referred to as the milestone method. The milestone method is essentially an application of the proportional performance method, and is typically used in conjunction with revenue recognition for research and development arrangements.

1. **Characteristics** A milestone is an event having all of the following characteristics:

   a. There is substantive uncertainty at the date the arrangement is entered into that the event will be achieved. A vendor's assessment that it expects to achieve a milestone does not necessarily mean that there is not substantive uncertainty associated with achieving the milestone.

   b. The event can only be achieved based in whole or in part on either the vendor's performance or a specific outcome resulting from the vendor's performance.

   c. If achieved, the event would result in additional payments being due to the vendor.

2. **Excluded** A milestone does not include events for which the occurrence is either contingent solely upon the passage of time or the result of a counterparty's performance.

3. **Substantive** Determining whether a milestone is substantive is a matter of judgment; that assessment shall be performed only at the inception of the arrangement. The consideration earned from the achievement of a milestone shall meet all of the following for the milestone to be considered substantive:

   a. It is commensurate with either the vendor's performance to achieve the milestone or the enhancement of the value of the delivered item or items as a result of a specific outcome resulting from the vendor's performance to achieve the milestone.

   b. It relates solely to past performance.

   c. It is reasonable relative to all of the deliverables and payment terms (including other potential milestone consideration) within the arrangement.

4. **Not Substantive** A milestone shall not be considered substantive if any portion of the associated milestone consideration relates to the remaining deliverables in the unit of accounting (that is, it does not relate solely to past performance). To recognize the milestone consideration in its entirety as revenue in the period in which the milestone is achieved, the milestone shall be substantive in its entirety. Milestone consideration shall not be bifurcated into substantive and nonsubstantive components. Also, if a portion of the consideration earned from achieving a milestone may be refunded or adjusted based on future performance the related milestone cannot be considered substantive. If the consideration from an individual milestone is not considered to relate solely to past performance, the vendor is not precluded from using the milestone method for other milestones in the arrangement.

5. **Disclosures** The decision by vendors to use the milestone method of revenue recognition for research or development arrangements constitutes a policy decision. As such, there would be a need for policy note disclosure in use of this revenue recognition approach. An entity shall disclose its accounting policy for the recognition of milestone payments as revenue. For each arrangement that includes milestone consideration an entity shall disclose all of the following in the notes to financial statements:

   a. A description of the overall arrangement

   b. A description of each milestone and related contingent consideration

   c. A determination of whether each milestone is considered substantive

   d. The factors considered in determining whether the milestone(s) are substantive.

   e. The amount of consideration recognized during the period for the milestone(s).

D. Completion of Production

Revenue sometimes is recognized at completion of the production activity. The three necessary conditions rarely are present except in the case of certain precious metals and agricultural products. The recognition of revenue at completion of production is justified only if certain conditions are present.

1. **Market** There must be a relatively stable market for the product.

2. **Costs** Marketing costs must be nominal.

3. **Units** The units must be homogeneous.

E. **Right of Return**
Revenue from sales when the buyer has the right to return the product.

1. **Time of Sale** Revenue should be recognized at the time of sale only if all the following conditions are met.

   a. The seller's price to the buyer is substantially fixed or determinable at the date of sale.

   b. The buyer has paid the seller, or the buyer is obligated to pay the seller, and the obligation is not contingent on resale of the product.

   c. The buyer's obligation to the seller would not be changed in the event of theft, physical destruction, or damage of the product.

   d. The buyer acquiring the product for resale has economic substance apart from that provided by the seller.

   e. The seller does not have significant obligations for future performance to directly bring about resale of the product by the buyer.

   f. The amount of future returns can be reasonably estimated.

2. **Deferral** If these conditions are not met, revenue (and cost of sales) must be recognized when the return privilege has substantially expired or when these conditions are subsequently met, whichever occurs first.

3. **Costs or Losses** Any costs or losses that may be expected in connection with sales revenue recognized at the time of sale must be accrued.

4. **Applicability** These standards do not apply to:

   a. Accounting for revenue in service industries if part or all of the service revenue may be returned under cancellation privileges granted to the buyer.

   b. Transactions involving real estate or leases.

   c. Sales transactions in which a customer may return defective goods, such as under warranty provisions.

F. **Bill and Hold**

1. **Definition** In a "bill and hold" transaction, a customer agrees to purchase the goods but the seller retains physical possession until the customer requests shipment to a designated location. Normally, such an arrangement does not quality as a sale because delivery has not occurred. Under certain conditions, when a buyer has made an absolute purchase commitment and has assumed the risks and rewards of the purchased product but is unable to accept delivery because of a compelling business reason, bill and hold sales may qualify for revenue recognition.

2. **Conditions** SEC Accounting and Auditing Enforcement Release No. 108 specifies the following conditions that a bill and hold transaction of a public company should meet in order to quality for revenue recognition:

   a. The risks of ownership must have passed to the buyer.

   b. The customer must have made a fixed commitment to purchase the goods, preferably in writing.

c. The buyer, not the seller, must request that the transaction be on a bill and hold basis. The buyer must have a substantial business purpose for ordering the goods on a bill and hold basis.

d. There must be a fixed schedule for delivery of the goods. The date for delivery must be reasonable and must be consistent with the buyer's business purpose (e.g., storage periods are customary in the industry).

e. The seller must not have retained any specific performance obligations such that the earnings process in not complete.

f. The ordered goods must have been segregated from the seller's inventory and not be subject to being used to fill other orders.

g. The equipment must be complete and ready for shipment.

3. **Applicability** The individuals responsible for the preparation of financial statements should also consider the following factors:

   a. The date by which the seller expects payment, and whether it has modified its normal billing and credit terms for this buyer.

   b. The seller's past experience with and pattern of bill and hold transactions.

   c. Whether the buyer has the expected risk of loss in the event of a decline in the market value of the goods.

   d. Whether FASB ASC 835, *Interest,* pertaining to the need for discounting the related receivables, is applicable.

   e. Whether extended procedures are necessary in order to assure that there are no exceptions to the buyer's commitment to accept and pay for the goods sold (i.e., the business reasons for the bill and hold have not introduced a contingency to the buyer's commitment).

G. Issues Requiring Special Consideration

1. **Side Agreements** Side agreements are used to alter the terms and conditions of recorded sales transactions to entice customers to accept the delivery of goods and services. They may create obligations or contingencies relating to financing arrangements or to product installation or customization that may relieve the customer of some of the risks and rewards of ownership. Side agreements appear to be prevalent in high technology industries, particularly the computer hardware and software segments. The terms they provide may preclude revenue recognition.

2. **Channel Stuffing** Channel stuffing (also known as trade loading) is a marketing practice that suppliers sometimes use to boost sales by inducing distributors to buy substantially more inventory than they can promptly resell, particularly at or near the end of the reporting period. Inducements to overbuy may range from deep discounts on the inventory to threats of losing the distributorship if the inventory is not purchased. Channel stuffing without appropriate provision for sales returns is an example of booking tomorrow's revenue today in order to window-dress financial statements. Channel stuffing also may be accompanied by side agreements with distributors that essentially negate some of the sales by providing for the return of unsold merchandise beyond the normal sales return privileges. Even when there is no evidence of side agreements, channel stuffing may indicate the need to increase the level of anticipated sales returns above historical experience.

Out-of-State Candidates

Each state has separate requirements for candidates who wish to proctor within the state. Contact individual states or NASBA (www.nasba.org) for more information on individual states' requirements. Contact both the state where you plan to apply for a certificate and the state where you plan to sit for the examination.

Most states require candidates with degrees from schools outside of the United States to have their credentials evaluated by a member of the National Association of Credential Evaluation Services (NACES). View the NASBA web-site for a list of NACES members.

CHAPTER 11—REVENUE & EXPENSE RECOGNITION

Problem 11-1 MULTIPLE-CHOICE QUESTIONS

1. Which of the following indicates when revenues are usually recognized under GAAP?

   a. When the earnings process is complete or virtually complete
   b. When an exchange has taken place
   c. When cash has been collected
   d. When both a. and b. occur (Editor, 89537)

2. Under accrual accounting, expenses that are recognized and recorded on a presumed direct association with specific revenue are considered which of the following types of expenses?

   a. Immediate recognition
   b. Systematic and rational allocation
   c. Associating cause and effect
   d. None of the above (Editor, 89562)

3. A company provides the following information:

	Year 1	Year 2	Year 3
Cash receipts from customers			
From year 1 sales	$95,000	$120,000	
From year 2 sales		200,000	$ 75,000
From year 3 sales		50,000	225,000

   What is the accrual-based revenue for year 2?

   a. $200,000
   b. $275,000
   c. $320,000
   d. $370,000 (R/10, FAR, #29, 9329)

4. Ward, a consultant, keeps her accounting records on a cash basis. During the current year, Ward collected $200,000 in fees from clients. At December 31 of the previous year, Ward had accounts receivable of $40,000. At December 31 of the current year, Ward had accounts receivable of $60,000, and unearned fees of $5,000. On an accrual basis, what was Ward's service revenue for the current year?

   a. $175,000
   b. $180,000
   c. $215,000
   d. $225,000 (5/95, FAR, #25, amended, 5561)

5. UVW Broadcast Co. entered into a contract to exchange unsold advertising time for travel and lodging services with Hotel Co. As of June 30, advertising commercials of $10,000 were used. However, travel and lodging services were not provided. How should UVW account for advertising in its June 30 financial statements?

   a. Revenue and expense is recognized when the agreement is complete.
   b. An asset and revenue for $10,000 is recognized.
   c. Both the revenue and expense of $10,000 are recognized.
   d. Not reported (R/05, FAR, #29, 7773)

6. Tara Co. owns an office building and leases the offices under a variety of rental agreements involving rent paid in advance monthly or annually. Not all tenants make timely payments of their rent. Tara's balance sheets contained the following data:

	Year 1	Year 2
Rentals receivable	$ 9,600	$12,400
Unearned rentals	32,000	24,000

During year 2, Tara received $80,000 cash from tenants. What amount of rental revenue should Tara record for year 2?

a. $90,800
b. $85,200
c. $74,800
d. $69,200 (5/91, PI, #53, amended, 1117)

7. Zach Corp. pays commissions to its sales staff at the rate of 3% of net sales. Sales staff are not paid salaries but are given monthly advances of $15,000. Advances are charged to commission expense, and reconciliations against commissions are prepared quarterly. Net sales for the current year ended March 31 were $15,000,000. The unadjusted balance in the commissions expense account on March 31 was $400,000. March advances were paid on April 3. In its income statement for the current year ended March 31, what amount should Zach report as commission expense?

a. $465,000
b. $450,000
c. $415,000
d. $400,000 (5/93, PI, #49, amended, 4090)

8. Able Co. provides an incentive compensation plan under which its president receives a bonus equal to 10% of the corporation's income before income tax but after deduction of the bonus. If the tax rate is 40% and net income after bonus and income tax was $360,000, what was the amount of the bonus?

a. $36,000
b. $60,000
c. $66,000
d. $90,000 (11/94, Theory, #48, 5309)

9. Troop Co. frequently borrows from the bank to maintain sufficient operating cash. The following loans were at 12% interest rate, with interest payable at maturity. Troop repaid each loan on its scheduled maturity date.

Date of Loan	Amount	Maturity date	Term of loan
11/1, Yr 5	$10,000	10/31, Yr 6	1 year
2/1, Yr 6	30,000	7/31, Yr 6	6 months
5/1, Yr 6	16,000	1/31, Yr 7	9 months

Troop records interest expense when the loans are repaid, thus interest expense of $3,000 was recorded in year 6. If **no** correction is made, by what amount would year 6 interest expense be understated?

a. $1,080
b. $1,240
c. $1,280
d. $1,440 (5/97, FAR, #6, amended, 6478)

10. House Publishers offered a contest in which the winner would receive $1,000,000, payable over 20 years. On December 31, year 1, House announced the winner of the contest and signed a note payable to the winner for $1,000,000, payable in $50,000 installments every January 2. Also on December 31, year 1, House purchased an annuity for $418,250 to provide the $950,000 prize monies remaining after the first $50,000 installment, which was paid on January 2, year 2. In its year 1 income statement, what should House report as contest prize expense?

    a. $0
    b. $ 418,250
    c. $ 468,250
    d. $1,000,000 (11/94, FAR, #23, amended, 5287)

11. What is the appropriate treatment for goods held on consignment?

    a. The goods should be included in ending inventory of the consignor.
    b. The goods should be included in ending inventory of the consignee.
    c. The goods should be included in cost of goods sold of the consignee only when sold.
    d. The goods should be included in cost of goods sold of the consignor when transferred to the consignee. (R/10, FAR, #32, 9332)

12. Garnett Co. shipped inventory on consignment to Hart Co. that originally cost $50,000. Hart paid $1,200 for advertising that was reimbursable from Garnett. At the end of the year, 40% of the inventory was sold for $32,000. The agreement stated that a commission of 10% will be provided to Hart for all sales. What amount should Garnett report as net income for the year?

    a. $0
    b. $ 7,600
    c. $10,800
    d. $12,000 (R/05, FAR, #37, 7781)

13. Which of the following is (are) true under the consignment method of revenue recognition?

    a. A transfer of goods from the owner (consignor) to another person (consignee) is considered a sale.
    b. When a consignee sells the goods, title passes directly from the consignee to the third-party buyer.
    c. The commission paid by the consignor to the consignee is reported as a selling expense, rather than being netted against sales revenue.
    d. All of the above (89541)

14. Baker Co. has a franchise restaurant business. On January 15 of the current year, Baker charged an investor a franchise fee of $65,000 for the right to operate as a franchisee of one of Baker's restaurants. A cash payment of $25,000 towards the fee was required to be paid to Baker during the current year. Four subsequent annual payments of $10,000 with a present value of $34,000 at the current market interest rate represent the balance of the fee which is expected to be collected in full. The initial cash payment is nonrefundable and no future services are required by Baker. What amount should Baker report as franchise revenue during the current year?

    a. $0
    b. $25,000
    c. $59,000
    d. $65,000 (R/05, FAR, #34, 7778)

15. North Co. entered into a franchise agreement with South Co. for an initial fee of $50,000. North received $10,000 at the agreement's signing. The remaining balance was to be paid at a rate of $10,000 per year, beginning the following year. North's services per the agreement were not complete in the current year. Operating activities will commence next year. What amount should North report as franchise revenue in the current year?

    a. $0
    b. $10,000
    c. $20,000
    d. $50,000 (R/06, FAR, #33, 8100)

16. On December 31, year 3, Moon, Inc. authorized Luna Co. to operate as a franchisee for an initial franchise fee of $100,000. Luna paid $40,000 on signing the agreement and signed an interest-free note to pay the balance in three annual installments of $20,000 each, beginning December 31, year 4. On December 31, year 3, the present value of the note, appropriately discounted, is $48,000. Services for the initial fee will be performed in year 4. In its December 31, year 3, balance sheet, what amount should Moon report as unearned franchise fees?

    a. $0
    b. $ 48,000
    c. $ 88,000
    d. $100,000 (R/08, FAR, #35, 8590)

17. Wren Corp.'s trademark was licensed to Mont Co. for royalties of 15% of sales of the trademarked items. Royalties are payable semiannually on March 15 for sales in July through December of the prior year, and on September 15 for sales in January through June of the same year. Wren received the following royalties from Mont:

	March 15	September 15
Year 1	$10,000	$15,000
Year 2	12,000	17,000

    Mont estimated that sales of the trademarked items would total $60,000 for July through December, year 2. In Wren's year 2 income statement, the royalty revenue should be

    a. $26,000
    b. $29,000
    c. $38,000
    d. $41,000 (11/94, Theory, #40, amended, 5302)

18. Under a royalty agreement with another company, Wand Co. will pay royalties for the assignment of a patent for three years. The royalties paid should be reported as expense

    a. In the period paid.
    b. In the period incurred.
    c. At the date the royalty agreement began.
    d. At the date the royalty agreement expired. (5/95, FAR, #38, 5574)

19. Rill Co. owns a 20% royalty interest in an oil well. Rill receives royalty payments on January 31 for the oil sold between the previous June 1 and November 30, and on July 31 for oil sold between the previous December 1 and May 31. Production reports show the following oil sales:

June 1, year 1—November 30, year 1	$300,000
December 1, year 1—December 31, year 1	50,000
December 1, year 1—May 31, year 2	400,000
June 1, year 2—November 30, year 2	325,000
December 1, year 2—December 31, year 2	70,000

    What amount should Rill report as royalty revenue for year 2?

    a. $140,000
    b. $144,000
    c. $149,000
    d. $159,000 (11/95, FAR, #30, amended, 6112)

20. Compared to its current year cash basis net income, Potoma Co.'s current year accrual basis net income increased when it

    a. Declared a cash dividend in the previous year that it paid in the current year
    b. Wrote off more accounts receivable balances than it reported as uncollectible accounts expense in the current year
    c. Had lower accrued expenses on December 31 than on January 1 of the current year
    d. Sold used equipment for cash at a gain in the current year (11/93, Theory, #40, amended, 4545)

21. For an OCBOA presentation, which of the following statements is *false*?

    a. Under the pure cash basis, revenues are recognized when cash is received, rather than when earned.
    b. Under the pure cash basis, expenses are recognized when cash is disbursed rather than when incurred.
    c. Under the pure cash basis, long-term assets are not capitalized, and, hence, no depreciation or amortization is recorded.
    d. Under the pure cash basis, accruals should be made for taxes. (89505)

22. Which of the following is **not** a comprehensive basis of accounting other than generally accepted accounting principles?

    a. Cash receipts and disbursements basis of accounting
    b. Basis of accounting used by an entity to file its income tax return
    c. Basis of accounting used by an entity to comply with the financial reporting requirements of a government regulatory agency
    d. Basis of accounting used by an entity to comply with the financial reporting requirements of a lending institution. (11/98, FAR, #7, 6734)

23. A company records items on the cash basis throughout the year and converts to an accrual basis for year-end reporting. Its cash-basis net income for the year is $70,000. The company has gathered the following comparative balance sheet information:

	Beginning of year	End of year
Accounts payable	$3,000	$1,000
Unearned revenue	300	500
Wages payable	300	400
Prepaid rent	1,200	1,500
Accounts receivable	1,400	600

What amount should the company report as its accrual-based net income for the current year?

    a. $68,800
    b. $70,200
    c. $71,200
    d. $73,200 (R/11, FAR, #40, 9890)

24. The following information pertains to Eagle Co.'s sales for the year:

Cash sales	
Gross	$ 80,000
Returns and allowance	4,000
Credit sales	
Gross	$120,000
Discounts	6,000

On January 1, customers owed Eagle $40,000. On December 31, customers owed Eagle $30,000. Eagle uses the direct write-off method for bad debts. No bad debts were recorded in the year. Under the cash basis of accounting, what amount of net revenue should Eagle report for the year?

    a. $ 76,000
    b. $170,000
    c. $190,000
    d. $200,000 (11/94, Theory, #58, amended, 5318)

25. On April 1, Ivy began operating a service proprietorship with an initial cash investment of $1,000. The proprietorship provided $3,200 of services in April and received full payment in May. The proprietorship incurred expenses of $1,500 in April which were paid in June. During May, Ivy drew $500 against her capital account. What was the proprietorship's income for the two months ended May 31, under the following methods of accounting?

	Cash basis	Accrual basis
a.	$1,200	$1,200
b.	$1,700	$1,700
c.	$2,700	$1,200
d.	$3,200	$1,700

(11/93, PI, #43, amended, 4412)

26. Young & Jamison's modified cash-basis financial statements indicate cash paid for operating expenses of $150,000, end-of-year prepaid expenses of $15,000, and accrued liabilities of $25,000. At the beginning of the year, Young & Jamison had prepaid expenses of $10,000, while accrued liabilities were $5,000. If cash paid for operating expenses is converted to accrual-basis operating expenses, what would be the amount of operating expenses?

    a. $125,000
    b. $135,000
    c. $165,000
    d. $175,000 (R/10, FAR, #4, 9304)

27. Hahn Co. prepared financial statements on the cash basis of accounting. The cash basis was modified so that an accrual of income taxes was reported. Are these financial statements in accordance with the modified cash basis of accounting?

    a. Yes.
    b. No, because the modifications are illogical.
    c. No, because the modifications result in financial statements equivalent to those prepared under the accrual basis of accounting.
    d. No, because there is no substantial support for recording income taxes. (R/02, FAR, #5, 7060)

28. In financial statements prepared on the income-tax basis, how should the nondeductible portion of expenses, such as meals and entertainment, be reported?

    a. Included in the expense category in the determination of income
    b. Included in a separate category in the determination of income
    c. Excluded from the financial statements
    d. Excluded from the determination of income but included in the determination of retained earnings (11/95, FAR, #56, 6138)

29. Income tax-basis financial statements differ from those prepared under GAAP in that income tax-basis financial statements

    a. Do **not** include nontaxable revenues and non-deductible expenses in determining income.
    b. Include detailed information about current and deferred income tax liabilities.
    c. Contain **no** disclosures about capital and operating lease transactions.
    d. Recognize certain revenues and expenses in different reporting periods. (R/99, FAR, #2, 6771)

30. Which of the following bases of accounting is considered GAAP for personal financial statements?

    a. Historical cost basis
    b. Income tax basis
    c. Cash basis
    d. Estimated current value basis (Editor, 89514)

31. When personal financial statements are prepared, a presentation of financial data that is intended to disclose the estimated current values of assets, the estimated current amounts of liabilities, estimated income taxes on the differences between the estimated current values of assets and the estimated current amounts of liabilities and their tax bases, and net worth at a specified date is referred to as which of the following?

    a. The statement of financial condition
    b. The statement of changes in net worth
    c. The financial statement
    d. None of the above (Editor, 89516)

32. Which of the following is not a major source of increase in net worth in personal financial statements?

    a. Income
    b. Increases in the estimated current values of assets
    c. Decreases in the estimated current amounts of liabilities
    d. Increases in estimated income taxes on the differences between the estimated current values of assets and the estimated current amounts of liabilities and their tax bases (Editor, 89517)

33. Which of the following statements is true concerning the preparation of personal financial statements?

    a. Business interests that constitute a large part of a person's total assets should be combined with other investments.
    b. The estimated current value of an investment in a separate entity should be shown in one amount as an investment if the entity is marketable as a going concern.
    c. Assets and liabilities of the separate entity should be combined with similar personal items.
    d. The estimated current values of assets and the estimated current amounts of liabilities of limited business activities not conducted in a separate business entity should be combined. (Editor, 89518)

34. Personal financial statements should present ________________ at the discounted amounts of cash the person estimates will be collected, using appropriate interest rates at the date of the financial statements.

    a. Marketable securities
    b. Receivables
    c. Options
    d. Investments in life insurance (Editor, 89519)

35. In accounting for a long-term construction contract using the percentage of completion method, the progress billings on contracts account is a

    a. Contra current asset account
    b. Contra noncurrent asset account
    c. Noncurrent liability account
    d. Revenue account (11/85, Theory, #28, 1882)

36. Which of the following is a *disadvantage* of the percentage of completion method of accounting?

    a. It reflects the periodic recognition of income as it is earned.
    b. It reflects the status of uncompleted contracts that is provided through the current estimates of costs to complete or of progress toward completion.
    c. It is necessarily dependent upon estimates.
    d. All of the above are advantages of the percentage of completion method of accounting. (89508)

37. The calculation of the income recognized in the third year of a five-year construction contract accounted for using the percentage of completion method includes the ratio of

    a. Costs incurred in year 3 to total billings
    b. Costs incurred in year 3 to total estimated costs
    c. Total costs incurred to date to total billings
    d. Total costs incurred to date to total estimated costs (R/05, FAR, #8, 7752)

38. Lake Construction Company has consistently used the percentage of completion method of recognizing income. During year 1, Lake entered into a fixed-price contract to construct an office building for $10,000,000. Information relating to the contract is as follows:

	At December 31,	
	Year 1	Year 2
Percentage of completion	20%	60%
Estimated total cost at completion	$7,500,000	$8,000,000
Income recognized (cumulative)	500,000	1,200,000

Contract costs incurred during year 2 were

a. $3,200,000
b. $3,300,000
c. $3,500,000
d. $4,800,000 (11/87, PI, #21, amended, 1329)

39. The following data pertains to Pell Co.'s construction jobs, which commenced during the current year:

	Project 1	Project 2
Contract price	$420,000	$300,000
Costs incurred during the year	240,000	280,000
Estimated costs to complete	120,000	40,000
Billed to customers during the year	150,000	270,000
Received from customers during the year	90,000	250,000

If Pell used the percentage of completion method, what amount of gross profit (loss) would Pell report in its current year income statement?

a. $(20,000)
b. $ 20,000
c. $ 22,500
d. $ 40,000 (5/93, PI, #39, amended, 4080)

40. Frame construction company's contract requires the construction of a bridge in three years. The expected total cost of the bridge is $2,000,000, and Frame will receive $2,500,000 for the project. The actual costs incurred to complete the project were $500,000, $900,000, and $600,000, respectively, during each of the three years. Progress payments received by Frame were $600,000, $1,200,000, and $700,000, respectively. Assuming that the percentage-of-completion method is used, what amount of gross profit would Frame report during the last year of the project?

a. $120,000
b. $125,000
c. $140,000
d. $150,000 (R/11, FAR, #13, 9863)

41. Falton Co. had the following first-year amounts related to its $9,000,000 construction contract:

Actual costs incurred and paid	$2,000,000
Estimated costs to complete	6,000,000
Progress billings	1,800,000
Cash collected	1,500,000

What amount should Falton recognize as a current liability at year end, using the percentage-of-completion method?

a. $0
b. $200,000
c. $250,000
d. $300,000 (R/10, FAR, #11, 9311)

42. When should an anticipated loss on a long-term contract be recognized under the percentage of completion method and the completed contract method, respectively?

	Percentage of completion	Completed contract
a.	Over life of project	Contract complete
b.	Immediately	Contract complete
c.	Over life of project	Immediately
d.	Immediately	Immediately

(11/87, Theory, #16, 1850)

43. The following data pertains to Pell Co.'s construction jobs, which commenced during the current year:

	Project 1	Project 2
Contract price	$420,000	$300,000
Costs incurred during the year	240,000	280,000
Estimated costs to complete	120,000	40,000
Billed to customers during the year	150,000	270,000
Received from customers during the year	90,000	250,000

If Pell used the completed contract method, what amount of gross profit (loss) would Pell report in its current year income statement?

a. $ (20,000)
b. $0
c. $340,000
d. $420,000

(5/93, PI, #38, amended, 4079)

44. A company uses the completed contract method to account for a long-term construction contract. Revenue is recognized when recorded progress billings

	Are collected	Exceed recorded costs
a.	Yes	Yes
b.	No	No
c.	Yes	No
d.	No	Yes

(5/92, Theory, #44, 2737)

45. When would a company use the installment sales method of revenue recognition?

a. When collectibility of installment accounts receivable is reasonably predictable
b. When repossessions of merchandise sold on the installment plan may result in a future gain or loss
c. When installment sales are material, and there is no reasonable basis for estimating collectibility
d. When collection expenses and bad debts on installment accounts receivable are deemed to be immaterial

(R/09, FAR, #20, 8770)

46. The installment method of accounting for sales is acceptable under which of the following conditions?

a. Receivables are collected within a short period of time.
b. Circumstances exist such that collection of the sales price is not reasonably assured.
c. There is no reasonable basis for estimating the degree of collectability.
d. All of the above

(Editor, 89538)

47. Pie Co. uses the installment sales method to recognize revenue. Customers pay the installment notes in 24 equal monthly amounts, which include 12% interest. What is an installment note's receivable balance six months after the sale?

a. 75% of the original sales price
b. Less than 75% of the original sales price
c. The present value of the remaining monthly payments discounted at 12%
d. Less than the present value of the remaining monthly payments discounted at 12%

(11/92, Theory, #9, 3442)

48. Asp Co. appropriately uses the installment method of revenue recognition to account for its credit sales. The following information was abstracted from Asp's December 31, year 2, financial statements:

	Year 2	Year 1
Sales	$1,500,000	$1,000,000
Accounts receivable:		
Year 2 sales	900,000	
Year 1 sales	540,000	600,000
Deferred gross profit:		
Year 2 sales	252,000	
Year 1 sales	108,000	120,000

What was Asp's gross profit percentage for Year 2 sales?

a. 20%
b. 25%
c. 28%
d. 40% (R/09, FAR, #7, 8757)

49. Lang Co. uses the installment method of revenue recognition. The following data pertain to Lang's installment sales for the years ended December 31, year 1 and year 2:

	Year 1	Year 2
Installment receivables at year-end on year 1 sales	$60,000	$30,000
Installment receivables at year-end on year 2 sales	—	69,000
Installment sales	80,000	90,000
Cost of sales	40,000	60,000

What amount should Lang report as deferred gross profit in its December 31, year 2 balance sheet?

a. $23,000
b. $33,000
c. $38,000
d. $43,000 (11/95, FAR, #10, amended, 6092)

50. Cash collection is a critical event for income recognition in the

	Cost recovery method	Installment method
a.	No	No
b.	Yes	Yes
c.	No	Yes
d.	Yes	No

(11/93, Theory, #39, 4544)

51. Drew Co. produces expensive equipment for sale on installment contracts. When there is doubt about eventual collectibility, the income recognition method **least** likely to overstate income is

a. At the time the equipment is completed
b. The installment method
c. The cost recovery method
d. At the time of delivery (5/91, Theory, #8, 1896)

52. Wren Co. sells equipment on installment contracts. Which of the following statements best justifies Wren's use of the cost recovery method of revenue recognition to account for these installment sales?

a. The sales contract provides that title to the equipment only passes to the purchaser when all payments have been made.
b. No cash payments are due until one year from the date of sale.
c. Sales are subject to a high rate of return.
d. There is **no** reasonable basis for estimating collectibility. (5/94, FAR, #41, 4856)

53. Several of Fox Inc.'s customers are having cash flow problems. Information pertaining to these customers for the years ended March 31, year 1 and year 2, follows:

	3/31, year 1	3/31, year 2
Sales	$10,000	$15,000
Cost of sales	8,000	9,000
Cash collections		
on year 1 sales	7,000	3,000
on year 2 sales	—	12,000

If the cost recovery method is used, what amount would Fox report as gross profit from sales to these customers for the year ended March 31, year 2?

a. $ 2,000
b. $ 3,000
c. $ 5,000
d. $15,000 (11/92, PI, #43, amended, 3276)

54. Which of the following statements regarding the milestone method of revenue recognition is true?

a. It is an application of the proportional performance method.
b. It is the only revenue recognition method that is available for research and development arrangements.
c. With the issuance of ASU 2010-17, reporting entities will not be able to utilize other revenue recognition methods.
d. All of the above are true. (Editor, 3607)

55. Amar Farms produced 300,000 pounds of cotton during the year 1 season. Amar sells all of its cotton to Brye Co., which has agreed to purchase Amar's entire production at the prevailing market price. Recent legislation assures that the market price will not fall below $.70 per pound during the next two years. Amar's costs of selling and distributing the cotton are immaterial and can be reasonably estimated. Amar reports its inventory at expected exit value. During year 1, Amar sold and delivered to Brye 200,000 pounds at the market price of $.70. Amar sold the remaining 100,000 pounds during year 2 at the market price of $.72. What amount of revenue should Amar recognize in year 1?

a. $140,000
b. $144,000
c. $210,000
d. $216,000 (11/90, PII, #6, amended, 1321)

56. On January 1, Dell Inc. contracted with the city of Little to provide custom built desks for the city schools. The contract made Dell the city's sole supplier and required Dell to supply no less than 4,000 desks and no more than 5,500 desks per year for two years. In turn, Little agreed to pay a fixed price of $110 per desk. During the year, Dell produced 5,000 desks for Little. At December 31, 500 of these desks were segregated from the regular inventory and were accepted and awaiting pickup by Little. Little paid Dell $450,000 during the year. What amount should Dell recognize as contract revenue in this year?

a. $450,000
b. $495,000
c. $550,000
d. $605,000 (11/91, PI, #31, amended, 2419)

57. On December 30, Devlin Co. sold goods to Jensen Co. for $10,000, under an arrangement in which (1) Jensen has an unlimited right of return and (2) Jensen's obligation to pay Devlin is contingent upon Jensen's reselling the goods. Past experience has shown that Jensen ordinarily resells 60% of goods and returns the other 40%. What amount should Devlin include in sales revenue for this transaction on its December 31 income statement?

a. $10,000
b. $ 6,000
c. $ 4,000
d. $0 (R/06, FAR, #12, 8079)

58. Lin Co., a distributor of machinery, bought a machine from the manufacturer in November for $10,000. On December 30, Lin sold this machine to Zee Hardware for $15,000 under the following terms: 2% discount if paid within 30 days, 1% discount if paid after 30 days but within 60 days, or payable in full within 90 days if not paid within the discount periods. However, Zee had the right to return this machine to Lin if Zee was unable to resell the machine before expiration of the 90-day payment period, in which case Zee's obligation to Lin would be canceled. In Lin's net sales for the year ended December 31, how much should be included for the sale of this machine to Zee?

    a. $0
    b. $14,700
    c. $14,850
    d. $15,000 (5/87, PII, #20, amended, 9079)

59. In a ____________________, a customer agrees to purchase the goods, but the seller retains physical possession until the customer requests shipment to designated locations.

    a. Side agreement
    b. Bill and hold transaction
    c. Related-party transaction
    d. Trade loading transaction (Editor, 89507)

60. ____________________ is(are) used to alter the terms and conditions of recorded sales transactions to entice customers to accept the delivery of goods and services.

    a. Side agreements
    b. Channel stuffing
    c. Related-party transactions
    d. Trade loading (Editor, 89512)

Problem 11-2 SIMULATION: Cash Basis to Accrual Basis

The following information pertains to Count Candy, a calendar-year sole proprietorship, which maintained its books on the cash basis during the year.

Count has developed plans to expand into the wholesale candy market and is in the process of negotiating a bank loan to finance the expansion. The bank is requesting year 8 financial statements prepared on the accrual basis of accounting from Count. During the course of a review engagement, Drucilla, Count's accountant, obtained the following additional information.

1. Amounts due from customers totaled $40,000 at December 31, year 8.

2. An analysis of the receivables in item 1 revealed that an allowance for uncollectible accounts of $4,700 should be provided.

3. Unpaid invoices for candy purchases totaled $38,500 and $21,000, at December 31, year 8, and December 31, year 7, respectively.

4. The inventory totaled $91,000 based on a physical count of the goods at December 31, year 8. The inventory was priced at cost, which approximates market value.

5. On May 1, year 8, Count paid $10,800 to renew its comprehensive insurance coverage for one year. The premium on the previous policy, which expires on April 30, year 8, was $9,600.

6. On January 2, year 8, Count entered into a 30-year operating lease for the vacant lot adjacent to Count's retail store for use as a parking lot. As agreed in the lease, Count paved and fenced in the lot at a cost of $48,000. The improvements were completed on April 1, year 8, and have an estimated useful life of twenty years. No provision for depreciation or amortization has been recorded. Depreciation on furniture and fixtures was $15,000 for year 8.

7. Accrued expenses at December 31, year 7 and year 8, were as follows:

	Year 7	Year 8
Utilities	$1,200	$1,900
Payroll taxes	1,400	2,000
	$2,600	$3,900

8. Count is being sued for $500,000. Coverage under the comprehensive insurance policy is limited to $250,000. Count's attorney believes that an unfavorable outcome is probable and that a reasonable settlement estimate is $350,000.

9. The salaries account includes $5,000 per month paid to the proprietor. Count also receives $300 per week for living expenses.

Using this worksheet, prepare the adjustments necessary to convert the trial balance of Count Candy to the accrual basis of accounting for the year ended December 31, year 8. Formal journal entries are not required to support your adjustments. Use the numbers 1 through 9 in the Reference columns to cross-reference the postings placed in the adjustment columns to the additional information provided by the accountant. Select the additional account titles needed from the choices provided. Any choice may be used once, more than once, or not at all. Not all shaded areas must necessarily be filled.

Count Candy
Worksheet to Convert Trial Balance to Accrual Basis
December 31, Year 8

	Cash basis		Adjustments				Accrual Basis*	
Account title	**Dr.**	**Cr.**	**Ref.**	**Dr.**	**Ref.**	**Cr.**	**Dr.***	**Cr.***
Cash	32,800							
Accounts rec'ble, 12/31, Yr 7	20,400							
Inventory, 12/31, Yr 7	78,000							
Furniture & fixtures	147,400							
Land improvements	48,000							
Accumulated depreciation & amortization, 12/31, Yr 7		40,500						
Accounts payable, 12/31, Yr 7		21,000						
Count, Drawings								
Count, Capital, 12/31, Yr 7		155,800						
Sales		772,700						
Purchases	334,500							
Salaries	218,000							
Payroll taxes	16,500							
Insurance	10,800							
Rent	51,250							
Utilities	16,750							
Living expenses	15,600							
Totals	**990,000**	**990,000**						

* Completion of these columns is not required but may be useful in checking your work.

Title Choices for Additional Accounts		
Accrued expenses	Estimated liability from lawsuit	Lawsuit expenses
Allowance for uncollectible accounts	Estimated loss from lawsuit	Prepaid insurance
Bad debt expenses	Income summary—inventory	Unpaid expenses
Depreciation & amortization	Inventory adjustments	Uncollectible accounts

(11/95, FAR, #4, amended, 8522t)

Problem 11-3 SIMULATION: Long-Term Construction Projects

Paris Corp. began operation of its construction division on October 1, year 4, and entered into contracts for two separate projects. The Alpha project contract price was $750,000 and provided for penalties of $15,000 per week for late completion. Although during year 5 the Alpha project had been on schedule for timely completion, it was completed five weeks late in August year 6. The Sigma project's original contract price was $1,000,000. Change orders during year 6 added $50,000 to the original contract price.

The following data pertains to the separate long-term construction projects in progress:

	Alpha	Sigma
As of September 30, year 5:		
Costs incurred to date	$450,000	$515,000
Estimated costs to complete	50,000	515,000
Billings	395,000	550,000
Cash collections	345,000	455,000
	Alpha	**Sigma**
As of September 30, year 6:		
Costs incurred to date	$540,000	$900,000
Estimated costs to complete	—	225,000
Billings	675,000	885,000
Cash collections	675,000	780,000

- Paris accounts for its long-term construction contracts using the percentage of completion method for financial reporting purposes and the completed contract method for income tax purposes.
- Enacted tax rates are 20% for year 5 and 25% for future years.
- Paris's income before income taxes from all divisions, before considering revenues from long-term construction projects, was $375,000 for the year ended September 30, year 5. There were no other temporary or permanent differences.

1. Prepare a schedule showing Paris's balances in the following accounts at September 30, year 5, under the percentage of completion method:

   - Accounts receivable
   - Costs and estimated earnings in excess of billings
   - Billings in excess of costs and estimated earnings

	A	B	C
1	Accounts receivable		$
2	Costs and estimated earnings in excess of billings:		
3	Construction in progress	$	
4	Less: Billings		
5	Costs and estimated earnings in excess of billings		$
6	Billings in excess of costs and estimated earnings		$

2. Prepare a schedule showing Paris's gross profit (loss) recognized for the years ended September 30, year 5 and year 6, under the percentage of completion method.

	A	B	C
1	**For the Year Ended September 30, Year 5:**	**Alpha**	**Sigma**
2	Estimated gross profit (loss):		
3	Contract price	$	$
4	Less: Total costs		
5	Estimated gross profit (loss)	$	$
6	Percent complete:		
7	Costs incurred to date	$	$
8	Total costs	/	/
9	Percent complete		
10	Gross profit (loss) recognized	$	$
11	**For the Year Ended September 30, Year 6:**	**Alpha**	**Sigma**
12	Estimated gross profit (loss):		
13	Contract price	$	$
14	Less: Total costs		
15	Estimated gross profit (loss)	$	$
16	Percent complete:		
17	Costs incurred to date	$	$
18	Total costs	/	/
19	Percent complete		
20	Gross profit (loss)	$	$
21	Less: Gross (profit) loss recognized in prior year		
22	Gross profit (loss) recognized	$	$

(11/93, PI, #3, amended, 9008t)

Problem 11-4 SIMULATION: Research

Question: How and when are continuing franchise fees reported?

FASB ASC: ☐ - ☐ - ☐ - ☐

(9126)

Solution 11-1 MULTIPLE-CHOICE ANSWERS

Accrual Accounting

1. (d) Under GAAP, revenues are usually recognized when two conditions are met: the earnings process is complete or virtually complete; and an exchange has taken place. Revenues generally are recognized at the point of sale. (89537)

2. (c) Associating cause and effect involves expenses that are recognized and recorded on a presumed direct association with specific revenue. (89562)

3. (b) Accrual accounting recognizes and reports the effects of transactions and other events on the assets and liabilities of a business enterprise in the time periods to which they relate rather than only when cash is received or paid. The accrual-based revenue for year 2 would be all the $275,000 total cash receipts from customers for year 2 sales ($200,000 in year 2 + $75,000 in year 3 = $275,000). (9329)

4. (c)

Collection of fees in current year	$200,000	
Less: Accounts receivable, Jan. 1	(40,000)	
Plus: Accounts receivable, Dec. 31	60,000	
Less: Unearned revenue, Dec. 31	(5,000)	
Service revenue for current year	$215,000	(5561)

5. (b) Accrual accounting recognizes and reports the effects of transactions and other events on the assets and liabilities of a business enterprise in the time periods to which they relate rather than only when cash is received or paid. Revenues are recognized when earned. A deferred (prepaid) expense is an expense paid or payable in cash but not yet incurred. A prepaid expense is reported in the financial statements as an asset. (7773)

6. (a) The $2,800 increase in rentals receivable represents rental revenue earned but not yet received in cash. The $8,000 decrease in unearned rentals represents rental revenue earned that had been received in cash in a prior period.

Cash (given)	$80,000	
Rentals Receivable ($12,400 – $9,600)	2,800	
Unearned Rentals ($32,000 – $24,000)	8,000	
Rental Revenue (to balance)	$90,800	(1117)

7. (b) Accrual accounting recognizes expenses in the period they are incurred rather than when paid. Zach pays commissions to its sales staff at the rate of 3% of net sales. For the year ended 3/31, Zach should report commission expense of $450,000 ($15,000,000 × 3%). (4090)

8. (b) Net income after bonus and income taxes is $360,000. The income tax rate is 40%. Therefore, income after bonus but before income taxes is $600,000 [i.e., $360,000 / (100% – 40%)]. The bonus is equal to 10% of the corporation's income after bonus but before income taxes. Therefore, the amount of the bonus is $60,000 (i.e., $600,000 × 10%). (5309)

9. (a) Interest expense should be accrued in the period in which it is earned, rather than the period in which it is paid. In year 6, total interest expense of $4,080 should be reported, as shown below. If only $3,000 interest expense is recorded, the understatement is $1,080.

Loan Dates	Amount	Monthly Interest	Months in Year 6	Year 6 Interest
11/01, year 5 to 10/31, year 6	$10,000	$100	10	$ 1,000
02/01, year 6 to 07/31, year 6	30,000	300	6	1,800
05/01, year 6 to 01/31, year 7	16,000	160	8	1,280
Total interest				4,080
Less interest expense recorded				(3,000)
Understated interest				$ 1,080

(6478)

10. (c) On 12/31, year 1, House announced the contest winner and signed a note payable to the winner.

First installment of note payable, due 1/2, year 2	$ 50,000	
Cost of annuity purchased on 12/31, year 1 to provide prize monies remaining after first installment	418,250	
Contest prize expense for year 1	$468,250	(5287)

Consignments, Franchises, Royalties

11. (a) A consignment is a transfer of goods from the owner (consignor) to another person or entity (consignee) who acts as a sales agent for the owner in a principal-agent relationship. The transfer is not a sale and the consignee never has title to the goods. When the consignee sells the goods, title passes from the consignor to the buyer. Thus, goods held on consignment should be included in the ending inventory of the consignor, not the consignee. Also, the goods should be included in cost of goods sold of the consignor, never the consignee, when transferred to the buyer and not the consignee. (9332)

12. (b) Consignment sales revenue is recognized at the time of the sale at the sales price. The commission paid to the consignee is reported as a selling expense; it is not netted against sales revenue. Net income would be sales revenue less commissions and other expenses.

Inventory sale	$32,000	
Cost inventory sold ($50,000 × .4)	20,000	
Gross income	12,000	
Less: Commission	(3,200)	
Less: Advertising	(1,200)	
Net income	$ 7,600	(7781)

13. (c) The commission paid to the consignee is reported as a selling expense; it is not netted against sales revenue. In a consignment, the transfer of goods from the owner (consignor) to another person (consignee) is not a sale. The consignee acts as a sales agent for the owner in a principal-agent relationship. The consignee never has title to the goods. When the consignee sells the goods, title passes directly from the consignor to the third-party buyer. (89541)

14. (c) Initial franchise fees from franchise sales ordinarily must be recognized (with provision for estimated uncollectible amounts) when all material services or conditions relating to the sale have been substantially performed or satisfied by the franchisor. The balance is payable in 4 annual installments, and is expected to be collected in full, therefore the balance should be handled as a noninterest-bearing note. Accrual accounting treatment requires that the balance be reported at the present value of the future payments. ($25,000 + $34,000 = $59,000) (7778)

15. (a) Initial franchise fees from franchise sales ordinarily must be recognized (with provision for estimated uncollectible amounts) when all material services or conditions relating to the sale have been substantially performed or satisfied by the franchisor. North's services per the agreement were not complete in the current year so no franchise revenue would be reported by North in the current year. (8100)

16. (c) Initial franchise fees from franchise sales ordinarily must be recognized when all material services or conditions relating to the sale have been substantially performed or satisfied by the franchisor. Because services for the initial fee won't be performed until year 4, any amounts recognized on December 31, year 3 would be reported as unearned franchise fees. Moon would report the $40,000 cash and $48,000 present value of the note for a total of $88,000 as unearned franchise fees. Remember that notes receivable are recorded at their present value. Any discount or premium should be amortized over the life of the note. (8590)

17. (a) Accrual accounting recognizes revenue in the period(s) it is earned, rather than when the related cash is received.

Royalties for 1/1 to 6/30, year 2 (received 9/15)	$17,000	
Royalties for 7/1 to 12/31, year 2 ($60,000 × 15%)	9,000	
Royalty revenue, year 2	$26,000	(5302)

18. (b) Accrual accounting recognizes expenses in the period they are incurred, not paid. Royalties paid should not be recognized as an expense at the date the royalty agreement began or the date the royalty agreement expires. (5574)

19. (c) Royalty revenue and expense are recognized in the period in which the royalties are earned.

Dec. 1, year 1, to May 31, year 2	$400,000
Less: Month of December year 1	(50,000)
June 1, year 2, to Nov. 30, year 2	325,000
Month of December year 2	70,000
Total royalty revenue	745,000
Times: Percentage of Rill's ownership	20%
Rill's royalty revenue	$149,000

(6112)

OCBOA

20. (c) Potoma's accrued expenses decreased during the current year. Hence, Potoma's current year payments for expenses exceeded the amount of expense recognized on the accrual basis in the current year. The increased amount of expenses recognized in the current year under the cash basis increases Potoma's current year accrual basis net income as compared to its current year cash basis net income. The declaration or payment of a cash dividend does not affect net income computed under either the cash or accrual basis. Compared to its current year cash basis net income, Potoma's current year accrual basis net income decreased when it recognized uncollectible accounts expense in the current year. Potoma's current year cash basis net income is not affected by either the accounts receivable balances written off in the current year or the uncollectible account expense recognized in the current year. The sale of the used equipment at a gain increases net income under both the cash and accrual basis by equal amounts. (4545)

21. (d) Under the pure cash basis, revenues are recognized when cash is received, rather than when earned; expenses are recognized when cash is disbursed rather than when incurred; long-term assets are not capitalized, and, hence, no depreciation or amortization is recorded; and no accruals are made for taxes and no prepaid expenses are recorded. (89505)

22. (d) A comprehensive basis of accounting other than generally accepted accounting principles is one of the following: (1) a basis of accounting used to comply with regulatory requirements; (2) a basis used for tax purposes; (3) a cash basis; (4) a definite set of criteria having substantial support, such as the price-level basis of accounting. A basis of accounting used by an entity to comply with the financial reporting requirements of a lending institution does not fit any of the categories. (6734)

23. (c) In cash-basis accounting, the effects of transactions and other events on the assets and liabilities of a business enterprise are recognized and reported only when cash is received or paid; while in accrual accounting, these effects are recognized and reported in the time periods to which they relate. Cash-basis accounting does not attempt to match revenues and the expenses associated with those revenues. If liabilities have a net decrease, then cash is assumed to have been used, and cash net income would be lower than accrual. The same logic holds true for the asset side. If current assets increase, cash was consumed, so cash net income is less than accrual. A short-cut method is to journalize the net change of each account, and plug the difference to cash, as follows:

Accounts payable	2,000	
Prepaid Rent	300	
Unearned revenue		200
Wages payable		100
Accounts receivable		800
Cash		**1,200**

Overall, net cash decreased by $1,200, so Cash Net Income is $1,200 less than Accrual Net Income; Accrual Net Income was $71,200. (9890)

24. (d) The decrease in accounts receivable represents collections in the current period of credit sales of a prior period.

Gross cash sales	$ 80,000		
Less: Returns and allowances	(4,000)		
Receipts from cash sales		$ 76,000	
Gross credit sales	120,000		
Less: Discounts	(6,000)		
Net credit sales	114,000		
Add: Decrease in accounts receivable ($40,000 – 30,000)	10,000		
Receipts from credit sales		124,000	
Receipts from cash and credit sales		$200,000	(5318)

25. (d) The sole proprietor's drawing of $500 is recorded as a reduction of her capital account under both the cash basis and accrual basis methods of accounting.

	Cash	Accrual	
Revenue for services provided in April, payment received May	$ 3,200	$ 3,200	
April expenses, paid June	—	(1,500)	
Proprietorship's income for two months ended May 31	$ 3,200	$ 1,700	(4412)

26. (c) In converting cash paid for operating expenses from the modified cash-basis to accrual-basis adjustments must be made for the changes in prepaid expenses and accrued liabilities from the beginning of the year to the end of the year. An increase in prepaid expenses would require a minus $5,000 (the difference between $15,000 and $10,000) adjustment to derive the accrual basis. An increase in accrued liabilities would require a plus $20,000 (the difference between $25,000 and $5,000) adjustment to derive the accrual basis. [$150,000 – $5,000 + $20,000 = $165,000] (9304)

27. (a) A comprehensive basis of accounting other than generally accepted accounting principles is one of the following: (1) a basis of accounting used to comply with regulatory requirements; (2) a basis used for tax purposes; (3) a cash basis; (4) a definite set of criteria having substantial support, such as the price-level basis of accounting. Cash basis does not attempt to match revenues and the expenses associated with those revenues, therefore, conversion of income statement amounts from the cash basis to the accrual basis would be in accordance with the modified cash basis of accounting. (7060)

28. (a) In financial statements prepared on the income-tax basis, the nondeductible portion of expenses is included in the expense category in the determination of income. (6138)

29. (d) Tax-basis financial statements recognize certain revenues and expenses in different reporting periods than GAAP financial statements. Nontaxable income and nondeductible expenses are still included in the determination of income in tax-basis statements. Detailed information about current and deferred income tax liabilities is included in GAAP financial statements. Income tax-basis financial statements may include disclosures about capital and operating lease transactions. (6771)

Personal Financial Statements

30. (d) The estimated current value basis is considered GAAP for personal financial statements. The historical cost basis, the income tax basis, and the cash basis are considered OCBOA for personal financial statements. (89514)

31. (a) The statement of financial condition presents the estimated current values of assets, the estimated current amounts of liabilities, estimated income taxes on the differences between the estimated current values of assets and the estimated current amounts of liabilities and their tax bases, and net worth at a specified date. (89516)

32. (d) Increases in estimated income taxes on the differences between the estimated current values of assets and the estimated current amounts of liabilities and their tax bases represent a major source of decrease in net worth. (89517)

33. (b) The estimated current value of an investment in a separate entity, such as a closely held corporation, a partnership, or a sole proprietorship, should be shown in one amount as an investment if the entity is marketable as a going concern. (89518)

34. (b) Personal financial statements should present receivables at the discounted amounts of cash the person estimates will be collected, using appropriate interest rates at the date of the financial statements. (89519)

Long-Term Construction Contracts

35. (a) The percentage of completion method requires that revenues and gross profit be recognized each period based upon the progress of completion. Construction costs plus gross profit earned to date are accumulated in an inventory account, *Construction in Progress,* and progress billings are accumulated in a contra inventory account. (1882)

36. (c) Being dependent upon estimates (subject to uncertainty) is a disadvantage of the percentage of completion method of accounting. Reflecting the periodic recognition of income as it is earned and reflecting the status of uncompleted contracts that is provided through the current estimates of costs to complete or of progress toward completion are both advantages of the percentage of completion method of accounting. (89508)

37. (d) The ratio used for the percentage of completion method is incurred costs to date over total expected costs. Progress billings are not generally accepted as a method of recognizing income because billings do not necessarily relate to work actually performed on a contract. Costs incurred in year 3 to total estimated costs are not part of the cost of completion ratio. (7752)

38. (b) Amounts below are rounded (000s).

	Year 1		Year 2		
Contract price		$10,000		$10,000	
Estimated total cost at completion		(7,500)		(8,000)	
Estimated gross profit		$ 2,500		$ 2,000	
Estimated total cost at completion		$ 7,500		$ 8,000	
GP recognized to date	$ 500		$1,200		
Estimated total GP	/ 2,500		/ 2,000		
Percentage of completion		× 20%		× 60%	
Contract costs to date		1,500		4,800	
Contract costs, prior years		(0)		(1,500)	
Contract costs, current year		$ 1,500		$ 3,300	(1329)

39. (b) If the percentage of completion method is used, Pell recognizes a gross profit of $20,000 on the two projects combined because (1) $40,000 of the estimated gross profit on Project 1 is recognized in the current year, and (2) the full amount of the $20,000 anticipated loss on Project 2 is recognized in the current year because no portion of the anticipated loss can be deferred to future periods. Amounts below are rounded (000s).

	Project 1		Project 2		
Contract price		$420		$300	
Cost incurred to date	$240		$280		
Estimated costs to complete	120		40		
Less: Estimated total costs		(360)		(320)	
Estimated total gross profit (loss)		60		$ (20)	
Costs incurred to date	240				
Estimated total costs	/ 360				
Times: Percentage of completion		× 2/3			
Gross profit recognized		$ 40			(4080)

40. (d) In the final year of a contract accounted for by the percentage-of-completion method, the final income recognition would take place. The calculation would be the total revenue earned over the entire contract less the actual total costs incurred less the income previously recognized.

Contract price		$2,500,000
Costs incurred to date		2,000,000
Estimated total gross profit		$ 500,000
Costs incurred to date	$2,000,000	
Estimated total costs	/ 2,000,000	
Times estimated % of completion		× 100%
Gross profit recognizable to date		$ 500,000
Less: Gross profit recognized in year 1 & 2		350,000
Gross profit recognized in year 3		$ 150,000

(9863)

41. (a) Using the percentage-of-completion method of accounting for long-term construction contracts an excess of progress billings over related costs and income recognized constitutes a current liability. The amount of income to be recognized for the first year would be the amount of actual costs divided by the estimated total costs times the total estimated contract income ($2,000,000 ÷ $8,000,000 × $9,000,000 = $2,250,000). The $1,800,000 of progress billings does not exceed the amount of income to be recognized so there would be $0 current liability recognized at year-end from this contract. (9311)

42. (d) Under the conservatism principle, the full amount of an anticipated loss on a long-term construction contract must be recognized immediately under both the percentage of completion and completed contract methods. The recognition of an anticipated loss cannot be deferred to future periods under either method.(1850)

43. (a) If the completed contract method is used, Pell recognizes a gross loss of $20,000 on the two projects because (1) no portion of the $60,000 estimated gross profit on Project 1 can be recognized in the current year since the project is not completed at 12/31, and (2) the full amount of the $20,000 anticipated loss on Project 2 must be recognized in the current year because the anticipated loss cannot be deferred to future periods. Amounts below have been rounded (000s).

	Project 1		Project 2	
Contract price		$ 420		$ 300
Cost incurred to date	$ 240		$ 280	
Less: Estimated costs to complete	120		40	
Less: Estimated total costs		(360)		(320)
Estimated total gross profit		$ 60		$ (20)

(4079)

44. (b) Progress billings and collections on progress billings are not generally accepted as a method of recognizing income because they often do not bear a meaningful relationship to the work performed on the contract. If income were recognized on the basis of progress billings, it would be possible for a contractor to materially distort the contractor's income merely by rendering progress billings without regard to any degree of progress on the contract. (2737)

Alternative Recognition Models

45. (c) The installment method is an exception of normal GAAP revenue recognition and not allowed unless certain circumstances exist such that collection of sales is not reasonably assured. This method is permitted when receivables are collected over an extended period of time and, because of the terms of transactions or other conditions, there is no reasonable basis for estimating the degree of collectibility. The installment method allows revenue to be deferred and recognized each year in proportion to the receivables collected that year. (8770)

46. (b) The installment method of accounting for sales is not acceptable unless circumstances exist such that collection of the sales price is "not reasonably assured." (89538)

47. (c) Since the installment notes extend beyond one year, they are recorded at the present value of the payments discounted at the market interest rate (assumed here to be 12%). At any time after the sale, the installment note's receivable balance will be the present value of the remaining monthly payments discounted at 12%. (3442)

48. (c) The installment method is an exception of normal GAAP revenue recognition and not allowed unless certain circumstances exist such that collection of sales is not reasonably assured. The installment method allows revenue to be deferred and recognized each year in proportion to the receivables collected that year. Income recognized generally equals cash collected multiplied by the gross profit percentage applicable to those sales. Receivable accounts and gross profit accounts must be kept separately for each year because the gross profit rate will often vary from year to year. The gross profit percentage can be computed by either dividing the realized gross profit by collections or dividing the deferred gross profit by receivables for a particular year. The $252,000 deferred gross profit in Year 2 divided by the $900,000 accounts receivable in Year 2 equals a gross profit percentage of 28% for Year 2 sales. (8757)

49. (c)

Receivable on year 1 sales	$30,000		
@ GP% ($80,000 – $40,000)/$80,000	× 0.50	$15,000	
Receivable on year 2 sales	69,000		
@ GP% ($90,000 – $60,000)/$90,000	× 0.33	23,000	
Deferred gross profit, December 31, year 2		$38,000	(6092)

50. (b) Cash collection is a critical event for income recognition under both the cost recovery and installment methods of accounting. Under the cost recovery method, recognition of all gross profit is deferred until cash collections of revenue are equal to the cost of the item sold. All remaining cash collections are recorded as profit. Gross profit recognized using the installment method is generally computed by multiplying cash collected during the period by the gross profit percentage applicable to those sales. Since both the cost recovery and installment methods of accounting use the cash basis of accounting, neither is a generally accepted method. (4544)

51. (c) The cost recovery method defers the recognition of all gross profit until cash collections of revenue are equal to the cost of the item sold. All remaining cash collections are recorded as profit. The recognition of income at the time the equipment is completed or at the time of delivery would provide for the recognition of profits before any or much of the cash is received. These methods are, therefore, not appropriate for situations where there is doubt about the collectibility of the sales price. The use of the installment method would allow for the recognition of profits in proportion to the amount of the revenue collected in cash. The cost recovery method is less likely to overstate income than the installment method because it defers the recognition of profits longer than the installment method. (1896)

52. (d) The cost recovery method defers the recognition of all gross profit until cash collections of revenue are equal to the cost of the item sold. All remaining cash collections are recorded as profit. Though not generally accepted, the cost recovery method may be used where collectibility of proceeds is doubtful, where an investment is very speculative in nature, and/or where the final sale price is to be determined by future events. Therefore, Wren Co. would be justified in accounting for installment sales for which there is *no* reasonable basis for estimating collectibility under the cost recovery method. (4856)

53. (c) The cost recovery method defers the recognition of all gross profit until cash collections of revenue are equal to the cost of the item sold. All remaining cash collections are recorded as gross profit. No profit was recognized on the year 1 sales for the year ended 3/31, year 1 because the $7,000 collected in the period did not recover the $8,000 cost of sales. For the year ended 3/31, year 2 (1) collections to date on the year 1 sales were $10,000 (i.e., $7,000 + $3,000), permitting the recognition of $2,000 profit above the year 1 cost of sales of $8,000 and (2) collections on the year 2 sales were $12,000, permitting the recognition of $3,000 profit above the year 2 cost of sales of $9,000. The amount of gross profit that Fox should recognize for the year ended 3/31, year 2 is $5,000 (i.e., $2,000 + $3,000). (3276)

54. (a) The milestone method of revenue recognition, which is, at its core, an application of the proportional performance method, is not the only revenue recognition method that is available for research and development arrangements. There will still very likely be many reporting entities that continue to utilize other revenue recognition methods, including methods that represent variations of the proportional performance method.(3607)

55. (c) Amar recognizes revenue of $210,000 (i.e., 300,000 lbs. × $0.70/lb.) in year 1 for the cotton produced in year 1. It is appropriate for Amar to recognize revenue when the cotton is produced because (1) there is a relatively stable market for the cotton, (2) Amar's costs of selling and distributing the cotton are immaterial and can be reasonably estimated, and (3) the units of cotton are homogeneous. (1321)

56. (c) Dell should recognize contract revenue of $550,000 (5,000 × $110). Dell properly recognizes the full amount of the contract revenue pertaining to the 5,000 desks produced because (1) the number of desks produced is within the parameters of the contract for the year, and (2) the earnings process is virtually complete. (2419)

57. (d) Revenue from sales when the buyer has the right to return the product should be recognized at the time of sale **only** if all of several conditions are met. One condition is that the buyer has paid the seller, or is obligated to pay the seller, and the obligation is not contingent on resale of the product. While the amount of returns can be estimated based on past experience, the obligation for Jensen to pay Devlin is contingent upon Jensen reselling the goods. Thus, Devlin has no sales revenue for this transaction. (8079)

58. (a) Zee has the right to return the machine to Lin if Zee is not able to resell the machine before expiration of the 90-day payment period. If an enterprise sells its product but gives the buyer the right to return the product, revenue from the sales transaction is not recognized at the time of sale if the buyer is obligated to pay the seller and the obligation is contingent upon resale of the product. (9079)

59. (b) In a "bill and hold" transaction, a customer agrees to purchase the goods, but the seller retains physical possession until the customer requests shipment to designated locations. Side agreements are used to alter the terms and conditions of recorded sales transactions to entice customers to accept the delivery of goods and services. Trade loading (also known as channel stuffing) is a marketing practice that suppliers sometimes use to boost sales by inducing distributors to buy substantially more inventory than they can promptly resell. (89507)

60. (a) Side agreements are used to alter the terms and conditions of recorded sales transactions to entice customers to accept the delivery of goods and services. They may create obligations or contingencies relating to financing arrangements or to product installation or customization that may relieve the customer of some of the risks and rewards of ownership. Channel stuffing (also known as "trade loading") is a marketing practice that suppliers sometimes use to boost sales by inducing distributors to buy substantially more inventory than they can promptly resell. Trade loading (also known as "channel stuffing") is a marketing practice that suppliers sometimes use to boost sales by inducing distributors to buy substantially more inventory than they can promptly resell. (89512)

PERFORMANCE BY SUBTOPICS

Each category below parallels a subtopic covered in Chapter 11. Record the number and percentage of questions you correctly answered in each subtopic area.

Accrual Accounting

Question #	Correct √
1	
2	
3	
4	
5	
6	
7	
8	
9	
10	
# Questions	10
# Correct	______
% Correct	______

Consignments, Franchises, Royalties

Question #	Correct √
11	
12	
13	
14	
15	
16	
17	
18	
19	
# Questions	9
# Correct	______
% Correct	______

OCBOA

Question #	Correct √
20	
21	
22	
23	
24	
25	
26	
27	
28	
29	
# Questions	10
# Correct	______
% Correct	______

Personal Financial Statements

Question #	Correct √
30	
31	
32	
33	
34	
# Questions	5
# Correct	______
% Correct	______

Long-Term Construction Contracts

Question #	Correct √
35	
36	
37	
38	
39	
40	
41	
42	
43	
44	
# Questions	10
# Correct	______
% Correct	______

Alternative Recognition Methods

Question #	Correct √
45	
46	
47	
48	
49	
50	
51	
52	
53	
54	
55	
56	
57	
58	
59	
60	
# Questions	16
# Correct	______
% Correct	______

Solution 11-2 SIMULATION ANSWER: Cash Basis to Accrual Basis

	Cash basis		Adjustments				Accrual Basis*	
Account	**Dr.**	**Cr.**	**Rf**	**Dr.**	**Rf**	**Cr.**	**Dr.***	**Cr.***
Cash	32,800						32,800	
Accounts receivable, 12/31, year 7	20,400		[1]	**19,600**			40,000	
Inventory, 12/31, year 7	78,000		[4]	**13,000**			91,000	
Furniture & fixtures	147,400						147,400	
Land improvements	48,000						48,000	
Accumulated depreciation & amortization, 12/31, year 7		40,500			[6]	**16,800**		57,300
Accounts payable, 12/31, year 7		21,000			[3]	**17,500**		38,500
Count, Drawings			[9]	**75,600**			75,600	
Count, Capital, 12/31, year		155,800	[7]	**2,600**	[5]	**3,200**		156,400
Allowance for uncollectible accounts					[2]	**4,700**		4,700
Prepaid insurance			[5]	**3,600**			3,600	
Accrued expenses					[7]	**3,900**		3,900
Est. liability from lawsuit					[8]	**100,000**		100,000
Sales		772,700			[1]	**19,600**		792,300
Purchases	334,500		[3]	**17,500**			352,000	
Salaries	218,000				[9]	**60,000**	158,000	
Payroll taxes	16,500		[7]	**600**			17,100	
Insurance	10,800				[5]	**400**	10,400	
Rent	51,250						51,250	
Utilities	16,750		[7]	**700**			17,450	
Living expenses	15,600				[9]	**15,600**		
Income summary—inventory			[4]	**78,000**	[4]	**91,000**		13,000
Uncollectible accounts			[2]	**4,700**			4,700	
Depreciation & amortization			[6]	**16,800**			16,800	
Estimated loss from lawsuit			[8]	**100,000**			100,000	
Totals	**990,000**	**990,000**		**332,700**		**332,700**	**1,166,100**	**1,166,100**

These explanation reference numbers correspond with the entries on the lines with the same number.

[1] To convert year 8 sales to accrual basis.

Accounts receivable balances:	
December 31, year 8	$40,000
December 31, year 7	(20,400)
Increase in sales	$19,600

[2] To record provision for uncollectible accounts.

[3] To convert year 8 purchases to accrual basis.

Accounts payable balances:	
December 31, year 8	$ 38,500
December 31, year 7	(21,000)
Increase in purchases	$ 17,500

[4] To record increase in inventory from 12/31, year 7 to 12/31, year 8

Inventory balances:	
December 31, year 8	$ 91,000
December 31, year 7	(78,000)
Increase in inventory	$ 13,000

[5] To adjust prepaid insurance.

Prepaid balances:	
December 31, year 8 ($10,800 × 4/12)	$ 3,600
December 31, year 7 ($9,600 × 4/12)	(3,200)
Decrease in insurance expense	$ 400

[6] To record year 8 depreciation and amortization expense.

Cost of leasehold improvement	$48,000
Estimated life –	20 years
Amortization ($48,000 × 1/20 × 9/12)	1,800
Depreciation expense on fixtures and equipment	15,000
	$16,800

[7] To convert expenses to accrual basis.

	Balances, December 31		
	Year 8	Year 7	Increase in expenses
Utilities	$1,900	$ 1,200	$ 700
Payroll taxes	2,000	1,400	600
	$3,900	$ 2,600	$1,300

[8] To record lawsuit liability at 12/31, year 8.

Attorney's estimate of probable loss	$350,000
Amount covered by insurance	(250,000)
Count's estimated liability	$100,000

[9] To record Count's drawings for year 8.

Salary ($5,000 × 12)	$60,000
Living expenses ($300 × 52)	15,600
	$75,600

Solution 11-3 SIMULATION ANSWER: Long-Term Construction Projects

1.

	A	B	C
1	Accounts receivable		**$145,000**
2	Costs and estimated earnings in excess of billings:		
3	Construction in progress	$675,000	
4	Less: Billings	(395,000)	
5	Costs and estimated earnings in excess of billings		**$280,000**
6	Billings in excess of costs and estimated earnings		**$ 65,000**

C1 (Alpha $395,000 – $345,000) + (Sigma $550,000 – $455,000) = $145,000.

B3 [$450,000 / ($450,000 + $50,000)] × $750,000 = $675,000. An excess of costs incurred and income recognized over progress billings in the Alpha Project gave rise to a current asset.

B4 Given in scenario information

C5 Sum of 2 and 3

C6 $515,000 costs incurred to date (Sigma) – $30,000 estimated loss = $485,000.

Billings $550,000 – $485,000 = $65,000. An excess of progress billings over related costs and income in the Sigma Project gave rise to a current liability. The current asset and current liability should not be netted.

2.

	A	B	C
1	**For the Year Ended September 30, Year 5:**	**Alpha**	**Sigma**
2	Estimated gross profit (loss):		
3	Contract price	$ 750,000	$ 1,000,000
4	Less: Total costs	(500,000)	(1,030,000)
5	Estimated gross profit (loss)	**$ 250,000**	**$ (30,000)**
6	Percent complete:		
7	Costs incurred to date	$ 450,000	$ 515,000
8	Total costs	/ 500,000	/ 1,030,000
9	Percent complete	90%	50%
10	Gross profit (loss) recognized	**$ 225,000**	**$ (30,000)**

11	**For the Year Ended September 30, Year 6:**	**Alpha**	**Sigma**
12	Estimated gross profit (loss):		
13	Contract price	$ 675,000	$ 1,050,000
14	Less: Total costs	(540,000)	(1,125,000)
15	Estimated gross profit (loss)	**$ 135,000**	**$ (75,000)**
16	Percent complete:		
17	Costs incurred to date	$ 540,000	$ 900,000
18	Total costs	/ 540,000	/ 1,125,000
19	Percent complete	100%	80%
20	Gross profit (loss)	$ 135,000	$ (75,000)
21	Less: Gross (profit) loss recognized in prior year	(225,000)	30,000
22	Gross profit (loss) recognized	**$ (90,000)**	**$ (45,000)**

B3 Given in scenario information

B4 Year 5 costs incurred to date plus estimated costs to complete ($450,000 + $50,000)

B5 Contract price less total costs ($750,000 – $500,000)

C3 Given in scenario information

C4 Year 5 costs incurred to date plus estimated costs to complete ($515,000 + $515,000)

C5 Contract price less total costs ($1,000,000 – $1,030,000)

B7 Given in scenario information

B8 Year 5 costs incurred to date plus estimated costs to complete ($450,000 + $50,000)

B9 Costs incurred to date divided by total costs ($450,000 / $500,000)

B10 Percent completed × estimated gross profit (90% × $250,000)

C7 Given in scenario information

C8 Year 5 costs incurred to date plus estimated costs to complete ($515,000 + $515,000)

C9 Costs incurred to date divided by total costs ($515,000 / $1,030,000)

C10 Losses are recognized immediately and in full in the current period

B13 Original contract price less penalties [$750,000 – (5 × $15,000)]

B14 Year 6 costs incurred to date plus estimated costs to complete ($540,000 + 0)

B15 Contract price less total costs ($675,000 – $540,000)

C13 Original contract price plus change orders ($800,000 + $40,000)

C14 Year 6 costs incurred to date plus estimated costs to complete ($900,000 + $225,000)

C15 Original contract price plus change orders and less total costs ($1,000,000 + $50,000 – $1,125,000)

B17 Given in scenario information

B18 Given in scenario information

B19 Costs incurred to date divided by total costs ($540,000 / $540,000)

C17 Given in scenario information

C18 Year 6 costs incurred to date plus estimated costs to complete ($900,000 + $225,000)

C19 Costs incurred to date divided by total costs ($900,000 / $1,125,000)

B20 Contract price less total costs ($675,000 – $540,000)

B21 Gross (profit) loss recognized in prior year

B22 Current year gross profit (loss) less gross (profit) loss recognized in the prior year ($135,000 – $225,000)

C20 Current year gross profit (loss)

C21 Gross (profit) loss recognized in prior year

C22 Current year gross profit (loss) less gross (profit) loss recognized in the prior year [($75,000) – $30,000]

Solution 11-4 SIMULATION ANSWER: Research

FASB Accounting Standards Codification

FASB ASC:	952	-	605	-	25	-	12

25-12 Continuing franchise fees shall be reported as revenue as the fees are earned and become receivable from the franchisee. For guidance on related franchise costs, see Subtopic 952-720.

CHAPTER 12

REPORTING THE RESULTS OF OPERATIONS

CHAPTER 12

REPORTING THE RESULTS OF OPERATIONS

I. Reporting Considerations

A. Definitions

1. **Accounting Change** A change in (a) an accounting principle, (b) an accounting estimate, or (c) the reporting entity. The correction of an error in previously issued financial statements is not an accounting change.

2. **Error in Previously Issued Financial Statements** An error in recognition, measurement, presentation, or disclosure in financial statements resulting from mathematical mistakes, mistakes in the application of GAAP, or oversight or misuse of facts that existed at the time the financial statements were prepared. A change from an accounting principle that is not generally accepted to one that is generally accepted is a correction of an error.

3. **Prior Period Adjustment** A prior period adjustment consists of adjusting the financial statements of some prior period and restating those financial statements.

4. **Restatement** The process of revising previously issued financial statements to reflect the correction of an error in those financial statements.

5. **Retrospective Application** The application of a different accounting principle to one or more previously issued financial statements, or to the statement of financial position at the beginning of the current period, as if that principle had always been used, or a change to financial statements of prior accounting periods to present the financial statement of a new reporting entity as if it had existed in those prior years. (Synonymous with the term retroactive restatement)

6. **Impracticable** After making every reasonable effort, an entity is unable to comply because needed information is unable to be substantiated.

B. Change in Accounting Principle

A change in accounting principles represent a choice between and/or among generally accepted accounting principles when there are two or more generally accepted accounting principles that apply or when the accounting principle formerly used is no longer generally accepted. These changes could include changes in inventory pricing methods, changes in depreciation methods, changes in the method of accounting for long-term construction contracts, etc. A change in the method of applying an accounting principle is also considered a change in accounting principle.

In the preparation of financial statements, there is a presumption that an accounting principle, once adopted, should not be changed. Consistent application of accounting principles between reporting periods enhances the value of financial reporting by facilitating analysis and understanding of comparative accounting information.

1. **Identification** A change in accounting principle results from the adoption of a generally accepted accounting principle (GAAP) different from the GAAP previously used for reporting purposes. Adoption of a principle to record transactions for the first time or to record the effects of transactions that were previously immaterial is not a change in accounting principle. Neither is adoption or modification of an accounting principle brought about by transactions or events that are clearly different than those previously occurring:

2. **Justification** Once an accounting principle is adopted, it shall be used consistently in accounting for similar events and transactions. An entity may change an accounting principle only if:

   a. The change is required by a newly issued accounting pronouncement, or

   b. The entity can justify the use of an allowable alternative accounting principle on the basis it is preferable.

3. **Reporting** A change in accounting principle is reported through retrospective application of the new accounting principle to all prior periods, unless it is impracticable to do so. Retrospective application requires the following:

   a. The cumulative effect of the change to the new accounting principle on periods prior to those presented shall be reflected in the carrying amounts of assets and liabilities as of the beginning of the first period presented or earliest period to which the new accounting principle can be applied.

   b. An offsetting adjustment, if needed, shall be made to the opening balance of retained earnings for that period.

   c. Financial statements for each individual prior period presented shall be adjusted to reflect the period-specific effects of applying the new principle.

   d. Only the direct effects of a change in accounting principle are included in retrospective application, including any related income tax effects.

4. **Direct Effects of a Change in Accounting Principle** Those recognized changes in assets or liabilities necessary to effect a change in accounting principle. An example is an adjustment to an inventory balance to effect a change in inventory valuation method. Related changes, such as an effect on deferred income tax assets or liabilities or an impairment adjustment resulting from applying the lower-of-cost-or-market test to the adjusted inventory balance, also are examples of direct effects of a change in accounting principle.

5. **Indirect Effects of a Change in Accounting Principle** Any changes to current or future cash flows of an entity that result from making a change in accounting principle that is applied retrospectively. An example of an indirect effect is a change in nondiscretionary profit sharing or royalty payment that is based on a reported amount such as revenue or net income.

6. **Impracticability** If it is impracticable to determine the cumulative effect of applying a change in accounting principle to any prior period, the new accounting principle shall be applied as if the change was made prospectively as of the earliest date possible. It shall be deemed impracticable to apply the effects of a change in accounting principle only if any of the following conditions exist:

   a. After making every reasonable effort to do so, the entity is unable to apply the requirement.

   b. Retrospective application requires assumptions about management's intent in a prior period that cannot be independently substantiated.

   c. Retrospective application requires significant estimates of amounts, and it is impossible to distinguish objectively information about those estimates.

7. **Disclosures** The following disclosures are required in the fiscal period in which a change in accounting principle is made:

   a. The nature and reason for the change in accounting principle and the method of applying the change.

   b. A description of the prior-period information that has been retrospectively adjusted, if any.

   c. The effect of the change on income before extraordinary items, net income, and the related per share amounts for all periods presented, either on the face of the income statement or in the notes thereto.

   d. The cumulative effect of the change on retained earnings or other components of equity or net assets in the statement of financial position as of the beginning of the earliest period presented.

   e. If retrospective application to all prior periods is impracticable, disclosure of the reasons why and a description of the alternative method used to report the change.

   f. Presentation of the effect on financial statement subtotals and totals other than income from continuing operations and net income is not required.

C. **Change in Accounting Estimate**
A change that has the effect of adjusting the carrying amount of an existing asset or liability or altering the subsequent accounting for existing or future assets or liabilities. Essentially, accounting estimates change as new events occur, as more experience is acquired, and as additional information is obtained. Some items for which estimates are necessary are uncollectible receivables, inventory obsolescence, service lives and salvage values of depreciable assets, and warranty obligations.

1. **Justification** Changes in an estimate used in accounting are necessary consequences of periodic presentations of financial statements. Preparing financial statements requires estimating the effects of future events. Future events and their effects cannot be perceived with certainty. Therefore, estimating requires the exercise of judgment. Accounting estimates change as new events occur, as more experience is acquired, or as additional information is obtained.

2. **Change in Estimate Inseparable From Change in Principle** In some cases, a change in accounting estimate and a change in accounting principle are inseparable. One common example is a change in the method of depreciation affecting estimated future benefits. When the effects of the two changes cannot be separated, the change should be accounted for as a change in estimate.

3. **Examples of Changes in Estimate** Changes in the following items would usually require a change in accounting estimate.

   a. Useful lives and salvage values of depreciable assets

   b. Recovery periods benefited by a deferred cost

   c. Expected losses on receivables

   d. Warranty costs

4. **Period of Recognition** A change in accounting estimate should be accounted for in the period of change if the change only affects that period, or in the current and subsequent periods, if the change affects both, as a component of income from continuing operations. A change in estimate is applied prospectively; it does not require restatement or retrospective adjustment to prior period financial statements. The effects of the change in estimate on income *before* extraordinary items, *net income,* and related *per share* amounts should be disclosed in the period of the change or in future periods if the change affects those periods.

5. **Disclosure** No disclosure is required for estimates made in the ordinary course of accounting if the effects are not material or long-term. An example is the bad debt estimate.

Example 1 ▸ Change in Estimate

Machinery with a cost of $450,000 is being depreciated over a 15-year life. After 10 years, information becomes available that indicates a useful life of 20 years for the machinery. Accounting for the change in depreciation estimate in the eleventh year would be as follows:

Historical cost	$ 450,000
Depreciation to date ($30,000 × 10)	(300,000)
Remaining balance	$ 150,000
Balance to be depreciated over remaining useful life ($150,000 / 10)	$ 15,000

To record depreciation expense in the year of the change:

Depreciation Expense	15,000	
Accumulated Depreciation		15,000

The notes to the income statement would include the following disclosure:

Note A: During the eleventh year, the estimated useful life of certain machinery was changed from 15 years to 20 years. The effect of the change was to increase net income by $15,000 (ignoring taxes). Earnings per share amounts increased $1.50.

The financial statements of prior periods presented would **not** be restated, nor would the pro forma effects of retroactive application be reported.

D. Change in Reporting Entity

An accounting change that results in financial statements that are, in effect, the statements of a different reporting entity (i.e., a different group of companies comprise the reporting entity after the change).

1. **Reporting** Report the change by retrospectively applying the change to the financial statements of all prior periods presented to reflect the financial information for the new reporting entity for the periods. Do not report (a) the cumulative effect of the change on the amount of retained earnings at the beginning of the period in which the change is made or (b) pro forma effects on net income and earnings per share of retroactive application.

2. **Examples** A change in the reporting entity is limited mainly to (a) presenting consolidated or combined financial statements in place of financial statements of individual entities, (b) changing specific subsidiaries that make up the group of entities for which consolidated financial statements are presented, and (c) changing the entities included in combined financial statements.

3. **Disclosures** A description of both the nature of the change and the reason for it shall be disclosed in the period of the change. In addition, the effect of the change on income before extraordinary items, net income, other comprehensive income, and any related per-share amounts shall be disclosed for all periods presented.

E. **Prior Period Adjustment**
A prior period adjustment consists of adjusting the financial statements of some prior period and restating those financial statements.

1. **Examples** Several items qualify to be treated as a prior period adjustment. They include:

   a. Errors in financial statements result from mathematical mistakes, mistakes in the application of accounting principles, or the oversight or misuse of facts that existed at the time the financial statements were prepared. Errors commonly found in financial statements include the following:

      (1) Estimates based on unreasonable assumptions; for example, the use of an unrealistic depreciation rate.

      (2) Recording erroneous amounts for assets and equities. For example, incorrect footing of inventory totals would cause inventories to be misstated on the balance sheet.

      (3) Failure to record prepaid and accrued expenses.

      (4) The improper classification of assets as expenses and vice versa. The purchase price of a plant asset may be incorrectly charged to expense rather than an asset account.

      (5) In addition, the change from an accounting principle that is not generally accepted to one that is generally accepted is treated as the correction of an error; for example, a change from the direct write-off method to the allowance method of accounting for uncollectible accounts.

   b. Misapplied GAAP, including changes from a non-GAAP method of accounting to a GAAP method (i.e., cash basis to accrual basis)

   c. Retroactive restatements for newly issued GAAP pronouncements

2. **Classification of Errors** Accounting errors may be classified by time of discovery or according to their effect on the balance sheet, income statement, or both.

   a. Errors that occur in one accounting period and are discovered in a subsequent accounting period are more involved: the cumulative effect of each error on periods prior to the period of discovery is calculated and recorded as a direct adjustment to the beginning balance of retained earnings.

   b. Errors that occur and are discovered in the same accounting period may be corrected by reversing the incorrect entry and recording the correct one or by directly correcting the account balances with a single entry.

   c. Only balance sheet accounts are affected, for instance, if the *Inventory* account is debited instead of the *Equipment* account or if *Notes Payable* is credited, instead of *Accounts Payable.* When the error is discovered, an entry is recorded to correct the account balances.

d. Revenue or expense classification errors will affect only the income statement for the period. If *Sales Revenue* is credited instead of *Rent Revenue* or *Interest Expense* is debited instead of *Wage Expense,* the amounts presented on the income statement for these accounts will be misstated. Net income for the period, however, will not be affected. If the error is discovered prior to the year-end closings, an entry can be recorded to correct the account balances. If the error is discovered in a subsequent period, no correction is necessary. However, the restatement of comparative financial statements is required.

e. Some errors affect both the balance sheet and the income statement, and may be classified in the following two ways:

(1) **Counterbalancing Errors** Counterbalancing errors will "correct" themselves over two consecutive accounting periods. Generally, a counterbalancing error will cause a misstatement of net income and balance sheet accounts in one period that will be offset by an equal misstatement in the following period. Balance sheet accounts and combined net income for both periods will be stated correctly at the end of the second period (ignoring tax effects).

Example 2 ▸ Counterbalancing Errors

A company neglects to record accrued wage expense at the end of a fiscal period. In the first year, the error would have the following effects:

Income Statement	Balance Sheet
Wage expense understated	Liabilities understated
Net income overstated	Retained earnings overstated

In the second year, the payment of accrued wage expense will be charged to wage expense of the current year causing the following effects:

Income Statement	Balance Sheet
Wage expense overstated	Accounts are correctly stated due to the
Net income understated	counterbalancing effect on error.

(2) **Non-Counterbalancing Errors** Errors that are not counterbalancing cause successive balance sheet amounts and net income to be incorrectly stated until the errors are discovered and corrected. For example, suppose that instead of capitalizing the cost of an asset, the cost is charged to expense. In the year the error occurs, expenses will be overstated and net income understated. During the life of the asset, net income will be overstated by the amount of unrecorded depreciation. Additionally, assets on the balance sheet will be understated throughout the service life of the unrecorded asset.

3. **Reporting** The prior period adjustment must be highlighted on the statement of retained earnings. It is shown as an adjustment to the opening balance of retained earnings, reported net of tax. Intra-period tax allocations must be addressed as well.

4. **Disclosures** The entity shall disclose that its previously issued financial statements have been restated, along with a description of the error. They shall also disclose the following:

a. The effect of the error correction on each financial statement line item and any per-share amounts affected for each prior period presented.

b. The cumulative effect of the change on retained earnings or other appropriate components of equity or net assets in the statement of financial position, as of the beginning of the earliest period presented.

c. The resulting effects (both gross and net of applicable income tax) on the net income of prior periods should be disclosed in the annual report for the year in which the adjustments are made. When financial statements for a single period only are presented, this disclosure should indicate the effects of such restatement on the balance of retained earnings at the beginning of the period and on the net income of the immediately preceding period. When financial statements for more than one period are presented, which is ordinarily the preferable procedure; the disclosure should include the effects for each of the periods included in the statements. Such disclosures should include the amounts of income tax applicable to the prior period adjustments. Disclosure of restatements in annual reports issued subsequent to the first such post-revision disclosure would ordinarily not be required.

II. Income Statement

A. Concepts of Income

The determination and presentation of various items on the income statement are influenced by two alternative concepts, the current operating concept and the all-inclusive concept. Proponents of the all-inclusive approach insist that the income statement should include unusual and nonrecurring items in order to measure the long-range operating performance of the enterprise. Proponents of the current operating concept emphasize the importance of normal recurring operations in evaluating the performance of the entity. They contend that the inclusion of unusual and nonrecurring items in the income statement distorts net income. The method required reflects a compromise between the all-inclusive and current-operating concepts.

1. **Regular Item** All regular items of income and expense, including items that are unusual or infrequently occurring, are included in the determination of net income.

2. **Discontinued and Extraordinary Items** Income from discontinued operations and extraordinary items are reported separately from the results of continuing operations.

3. **Prior Period Items** Prior period adjustments are presented as adjustments to the beginning balance of retained earnings.

B. Continuing Operations

1. **Revenues and Expenses** Revenue and expense items (and gains and losses) that are considered to be of a usual and recurring nature are reported in income from continuing operations.

2. **Unusual or Infrequent Items** Items that are considered to be either unusual in nature or infrequent in occurrence are reported as a separate component of income from continuing operations. The nature and financial effects of this type of item should be disclosed on the face of the income statement, or alternatively, in the notes to the financial statements. These items should not be reported net of income taxes or in any other manner that would imply that they are extraordinary items.

3. **Tax Provision** The provision for income taxes associated with income from continuing operations should be presented as a single line item.

C. Discontinued Operations

The results of discontinued operations are reported separately from continuing operations. Discontinued operations refers to the operations of a component of an entity that has been disposed of or is still operating, but is the subject of a formal plan for disposal. A component of an entity is a segment, reporting unit, or asset group whose operations and cash flows are clearly distinguished from the rest of the entity, operationally as well as for financial reporting purposes.

Exhibit 1 ▸ Discontinued Operations: Component vs. Non-Component Disposals

Component Disposals	Non-Component Disposals
Two companies manufacture and sell consumer products with several product groups, with different product lines and brands. For both companies, a product group is the lowest level at which operations and cash flows can be distinguished.	
Caring Pharmaceuticals plans to sell the beauty product group and its operations.	Nesbit Household Products discontinues cosmetic brands associated with losses.
Two companies operate nationwide restaurant chains, each with numerous company-owned sites. For both companies, a single restaurant is the lowest level at which operations and cash flows can be distinguished.	
Cluck-to-Go decides to exit its northeast region. It removes its name from the northeast restaurants and sells the buildings.	New Wave Coffee sells all restaurants in its west coast region to franchisees. New Wave will receive franchise fees, provide advertising, and supply select ingredients.
Two companies operate retail home appliance chains, each with numerous company-owned sites. For both companies, a single store is the lowest level at which operations and cash flows can be distinguished.	
Cheap Freddie's closes stores in areas with declining populations, selling the buildings and moving remaining inventory to stores in other regions.	Never-a-care, Inc., closes pairs of Never-a-care Appliances stores and opens Never-a-cloud Superstores, central to former locations, with an expanded range of products.
Two sporting goods producers have golf club divisions that design, manufacture, market, and distribute golf clubs. For both companies, a division is the lowest level at which operations and cash flows can be distinguished.	
Committed Sports, Inc., agrees to a plan to sell the golf club division to an independent conglomerate.	Never Say Die Manufacturers sells its golf club manufacturing plants. Never Say Die plans to outsource its golf club manufacturing.

1. **Non-Component Assets** Income from continuing operations includes gains or losses from an asset (or asset group) that is classified as held for sale, but that is below the level of a component of the entity. If disposal will not occur for more than 12 months, costs to sell are discounted to present value.

2. **Income Statement** The results of operations of a component of an entity are reported as part of discontinued operations, for current and prior periods (in the periods in which they occur), provided that:

    a. Operations and cash flows have been (or will be) removed from the entity's ongoing operations due to the disposal transaction.

    b. The entity ceases any significant continuing involvement in the component's operations after the disposal transaction.

3. **Balance Sheet** The component is valued at current fair value less cost to sell. Asset(s) that are classified as held for sale, and their related liabilities, are presented separately in the asset and liability sections of the balance sheet (not offset and presented as a single item).

   a. No liability for future operating losses is recognized. Expected future operating losses that other buyers and sellers would not recognize as part of the fair value less cost to sell are not indirectly recognized as part of an expected loss on the sale by reducing the book value of the asset (or asset group) to an amount less than its current fair value less cost to sell. This provision is designed to limit *big bath accounting* (the inclusion of losses with a questionable relation to the disposal, in order that profits in future periods appear more favorable).

   b. While classified as held for sale, the asset is not depreciated or amortized, although accrual of other related expenses, such as interest or rent, continue.

   c. Lease termination costs and specified employee severance plan costs related with exit or disposal activities in periods when obligations to others exists, not necessarily in the period of commitment to a plan, are required to be recognized.

4. **Contingencies** Changes to the previously reported discontinued operations amounts are reported in current period statements as discontinued operations. Such adjustments may occur due to the resolution of contingencies regarding purchase price, purchaser indemnification, environmental warranty obligations, product warranty obligations, and directly-related employee benefit plan obligations.

Example 3 ▸ Discontinued Operations

On April 30 Empire Corporation, whose fiscal year-end is September 30, adopted a plan to discontinue the operations of Bello Division on November 30. Bello contributed a major portion of Empire's sales volume. Empire estimated that Bello would sustain a loss of $460,000 from May 1 through September 30 and would sustain an additional loss of $220,000 from October 1 to November 30. Empire also estimated that it would realize a gain of $600,000 on the sale of Bello's assets. At September 30, Empire determined that Bello had actually lost $1,120,000 for the fiscal year, of which $420,000 represented the loss from May 1 to September 30. Empire's tax rate is 30%.

Required: Determine the amounts that should be reported in the discontinued operations section of Empire's income statement for the year ended September 30, for income from operations of the discontinued segment, and the gain or loss on disposal of the discontinued segment.

Solution:

Discontinued operations	
Loss from operations of discontinued Bello Division	$1,120,000
Income taxes	(336,000)
Loss from discontinued operations	$ 784,000

D. Extraordinary Items

An extraordinary item should be classified separately in the income statement if it is material in relation to income before extraordinary items or to the trend of annual earnings before extraordinary items, or is material by other appropriate criteria. Items should be considered individually and not in the aggregate in determining whether an extraordinary event or transaction is material. If the item is determined to be extraordinary, it should be presented separately on the income statement net of related income tax after discontinued operations of a segment of a business (see Exhibit 1).

1. **Criteria** Most events and transactions affecting the operations of an enterprise are of a normal, recurring nature. For an occurrence to be classified as extraordinary it must meet both of the following criteria:

    a. The event or transaction that is unusual in nature should possess a high degree of abnormality and be of a type clearly unrelated to, or incidentally related to, the ordinary and typical activities of the entity, taking into account the environment in which the entity operates.

    b. The event or transaction that is infrequent in nature should be of a type that would not reasonably be expected to recur in the foreseeable future, taking into account the environment in which the entity operates.

2. **Non-Extraordinary Gains/Losses** The following gains and losses should not be reported as extraordinary items because they are usual in nature or may be expected to recur as a consequence of customary and continuing business activities. In certain circumstances, gains or losses such as a. and d., below, should be included in extraordinary items if they are the direct result of an event that meets the criteria for an extraordinary item.

    a. Write-down or write-off of receivables, inventories, equipment leased to others, and intangible assets

    b. Gains or losses from exchange or translation of foreign currencies, including those relating to major devaluations and revaluations

    c. Gains or losses on disposal of a segment of a business

    d. Other gains or losses from sale or abandonment of property, plant, or equipment used in the business

    e. Effects of a strike, including strikes against competitors and major suppliers

    f. Adjustments of accruals on long-term contracts

Exhibit 2 ▸ Summary of Item Placement on an Income Statement

Item	Criteria	Examples	Placement
Unusual or infrequent gains or losses	Unusual or infrequent but not both	Write-down or write-off of receivables, inventories, equipment leased to others, other gains or losses from the sale or abandonment or impairment of property, plant, or equipment used in the business	**C** D E
Changes in estimate	A revision of an accounting measurement	Changing the useful life of a depreciable asset from 5 to 7 years	**C** D E
Discontinued operations	The disposal of a component of the entity which represents separate operations and cash flows.	A component that has been sold, abandoned, or spun-off. The component's operations and cash flows must be clearly distinguished.	C **D** E
Extraordinary items	Both unusual and infrequent in nature	Casualty gains and losses	C D **E**

E. Format

1. **Comparative Statements** Comparative statements project more relevant and meaningful information than do noncomparative statements. Comparative statements prepared on a consistent basis from one period to the next are especially valuable because they measure the difference in operating results based on the same measurement criteria.

2. **Multiple-Step Format** The presentation of income from continuing operations in a multiple-step format emphasizes a functional or object classification of each statement item, and sets forth various intermediate levels of income.

Exhibit 3 ▸ Multiple-Step Format

Sales			$ 950,000
Less sales returns and allowances			(16,500)
Net sales			933,500
Beginning inventory		$ 230,000	
Purchases	$590,000		
Less purchase returns and allowances	(19,300)		
Net purchases		570,700	
Freight-in		2,000	
Goods available for sale		802,700	
Less ending inventory		(220,000)	
Cost of goods sold			(582,700)
Gross margin			350,800
Selling		150,000	
General & administrative		72,000	
Operating expenses			(222,000)
Income from operations			128,800
Rent	2,500		
Interest and dividends	6,700		
Gain on sale of machinery	8,000		
Other revenues		17,200	
Interest	5,200		
Loss on sale of investments	6,000		
Other expenses		(11,200)	
			6,000
Income from continuing operations before income taxes			134,800
Provision for income taxes			(60,660)
Income from continuing operations			74,140
Extraordinary item:			
Loss due to earthquake, less tax saving of $3,150			(3,850)
Net income			$ 70,290

3. **Single-Step Format** Income from continuing operations may be presented in a multiple-step format or a single-step format. Presentation of income from continuing operations in a single-step format is often used for publicly issued statements. Revenues are grouped under one classification while expenses are grouped under another classification.

Exhibit 4 ▶ Single-Step Format

Sales (less returns and allowances of $16,500)		$ 933,500
Rent		2,500
Interest and dividends		6,700
Gain on sale of machinery		8,000
Revenues		950,700
Cost of goods sold	$582,700	
Selling	150,000	
General & administrative	72,000	
Interest	5,200	
Loss on sale of investments	6,000	
Expenses		(815,900)
Income from continuing operations before income taxes		134,800
Provision for income taxes		(60,660)
Income from continuing operations		74,140
Extraordinary item:		
Loss due to earthquake, less tax saving of $3,150		(3,850)
Net income		$ 70,290

4. **Single-Year Presentation** The following format is for the presentation of the income statement for a single year.

Exhibit 5 ▶ Income Statement Presentation

Income from continuing operations before income taxes		$XXX
Provision for income taxes		XXX
Income (loss) from continuing operations (after income taxes)		XXX
Discontinued operations (Note X):		
Income (loss) from operations of discontinued Division A (including loss on disposal of $XXX)	$XXX	
Income taxes	XXX	
Income from discontinued operations		XXX
Income before extraordinary items		XXX
Extraordinary items (less applicable income taxes of $XXX)		XXX
Net income		$XXX

III. Earnings Per Share

A. Overview

Basic and diluted earnings per share data are required to be included in the financial statements of entities with publicly held common stock or potential common stock, if those securities trade in a public market. Potential common stock includes securities such as options, warrants, convertible securities, and contingent stock agreements.

1. **Earnings Per Share (EPS)** The amount of earnings attributable to each share of common stock. Note that EPS is computed for common stock only, not for preferred stock.

2. **Dilution (Dilutive)** Reduction in earnings per share due to the *assumed* conversion or exercise of certain securities into common stock.

3. **Antidilution (Antidilutive)** Increase in earnings per share or decrease in loss per share.

4. **Basic Earnings Per Share (Basic EPS)** The amount of earnings for the period available to each share of common stock outstanding during the reporting period.

5. **Diluted Earnings Per Share (Diluted EPS)** The amount of earnings for the period available to each share of common stock outstanding during the reporting period and to each share that would have been outstanding assuming the issuance of common shares for all dilutive potential common shares outstanding during the reporting period.

6. **Convertible Security** A security that is convertible into another security based on a conversion rate.

B. Basic EPS

1. **Formula** Basic EPS is computed by dividing income available to common stockholders (IAC) by the weighted-average number of shares outstanding during the period. Shares issued during the period and shares reacquired during the period are weighted for the portion of the period they were outstanding.

$$\text{Basic EPS} = \frac{\text{Income Available to Common Stockholders}}{\text{Weighted Average Number of Shares Outstanding}}$$

Example 4 ▸ Basic EPS

IAC is $100,000 and the weighted average number of shares of common stock outstanding is 250,000 shares.

Basic EPS is $100,000 / 250,000 shares = $0.40.

2. **Numerator** The numerator for basic EPS is fairly simple to determine. The income number used for basic EPS is income from continuing operations adjusted for the claims by senior securities. Senior security claims generally refer to preferred stock and are adjusted in the period earned.

   a. All preferred stock dividends declared reduce income to arrive at IAC.

   b. Cumulative preferred stock dividends of the current period, even though not declared, also reduce income to arrive at IAC.

   c. Dividends on common stock are not used in determining EPS.

Example 5 ▸ IAC—Noncumulative Preferred Stock

Corporation A has 10,000 shares of $100 par, noncumulative, 3% dividend, participating preferred stock. Net income has been $100,000 for each of the last four years. Dividends of $30,000 were paid in year 1, zero in year 2, $50,000 in year 3, and $60,000 in year 4. Income available to the common stockholders would be:

Year	Net Income	Preferred Dividends Earned	IAC
1	$100,000	$30,000	$ 70,000
2	$100,000	–	$100,000
3	$100,000	$50,000	$ 50,000
4	$100,000	$60,000	$ 40,000

Example 6 ▸ IAC—Cumulative Preferred Stock

Refer to Example 2, except that the preferred stock is cumulative. IAC would be:

Year	Net Income	Preferred Dividends Earned	IAC
1	$100,000	$30,000	$ 70,000
2	$100,000	$30,000*	$ 70,000
3	$100,000	$30,000**	$ 70,000
4	$100,000	$50,000***	$ 50,000

* The dividends in arrears are earned in year 2.

** The $50,000 declared in year 3 are $30,000 in arrears from year 2 and $20,000 of the $30,000 earned in year 3.

*** The $60,000 declared in year 4 are $10,000 in arrears from year 3, $30,000 earned in year 4, and $20,000 participation by the preferred stockholders in year 4.

3. **Denominator** The denominator is the weighted-average number of shares outstanding during the period. For basic EPS, this number will include shares outstanding the entire period, shares issued during the period, and shares where all of the conditions of issuance have been met.

   a. Issuance of stock and reacquisition of stock during the period changes the ownership structure and the shares only participate in earnings for the time that the stock is outstanding. For example, if a shareholder holds 10,000 shares the entire period and another shareholder purchases 10,000 in the middle of the year, you would not expect their EPS to be the same.

   b. Stock dividends, stock splits, and reverse stock splits change the total number of shares outstanding but not the proportionate shares outstanding. Stock dividends, stock splits, and reverse stock splits are reflected retroactively for all periods presented.

   c. When the purchase method is used, the weighted average is applied from the date of the business combination.

Example 7 ▸ Weighted Average Shares of Common Stock Outstanding

Date	Transaction	Change in Shares from Transaction	Total Shares Outstanding
1/1	Shares outstanding		10,000
4/1	Shares issued	8,000	18,000
6/1	Shares reacquired and held in treasury	(3,000)	15,000
7/1	Issued 10% stock dividend	1,500	16,500
8/1	Shares reacquired and held in treasury	(6,000)	10,500
9/1	Shares issued	12,000	22,500
12/1	Issued 2 for 1 stock split	22,500	45,000

Total Shares Outstanding		Months Outstanding		Stock Dividend		Stock Split		Weighted Average
10,000	×	3/12	×	1.10	×	2	=	5,500
18,000	×	2/12	×	1.10	×	2	=	6,600
15,000	×	1/12	×	1.10	×	2	=	2,750
16,500	×	1/12			×	2	=	2,750
10,500	×	1/12			×	2	=	1,750
22,500	×	3/12			×	2	=	11,250
45,000	×	1/12					=	3,750
Weighted average number of shares outstanding								34,350

Note: The stock dividend and stock split are applied retroactively to the beginning of the year from the date declared.

C. Diluted EPS

1. **Objective** The objective of reporting diluted EPS is to measure the performance of an entity over the reporting period while giving effect to all dilutive potential common shares that were outstanding during the period.

2. **Dilutive Security** With diluted EPS, the first step is to determine if a security is dilutive. A security is dilutive if the inclusion of the security in the computation of EPS results in a smaller EPS or increases the loss per share.

   a. **Potentially Dilutive** Securities that are potentially dilutive include convertible preferred stock, convertible debt, options, warrants, participating securities, different classes of common stock, and agreements to issue these securities or shares of common stock in the future, referred to as contingently issuable shares.

   b. **Anti-Dilutive Securities** Not all potential securities will be dilutive. When the per share effect of an individual security is greater than the total per share effect, the security is anti-dilutive. Anti-dilutive securities are excluded from diluted EPS. Thus it is necessary to calculate the per share effect of each potentially dilutive security and include only those which have a dilutive effect.

   c. **Categories of Potentially Dilutive Securities**

      (1) Convertible securities where the if-converted method is used

      (2) Options, warrants, and their equivalents where the treasury stock method is used

      (3) Contingently issuable shares

3. **If-Converted Method** Convertible securities may or may not be converted. If they are converted, they become common stock. The if-converted method assumes that they are converted; in other words, pretend that convertible securities are converted. The pretend conversion may impact the IAC and the weighted-average number of common shares outstanding.

   a. **Numerator**

      (1) **Convertible Debt** If the enterprise has convertible debt, the conversion would mean that the company does not have the interest expense for the debt and should be added back to income to arrive at IAC. The interest expense adjustment should be net of tax and increases income or decreases the loss for the period. If the tax amount impacts a nondiscretionary item such as bonuses, a further adjustment is necessary.

      (2) **Convertible Preferred Stock** If convertible preferred stock is assumed to be exercised, the entity would not have the corresponding preferred dividends, and income from continuing operations would not be reduced for preferred dividends. These adjustments do not have nondiscretionary or tax effects.

   b. **Denominator** Assuming convertible securities are converted to common stock increases the weighted average number of common shares outstanding.

Example 8 ▸ If-Converted Method

A company has IAC of $2,000,000 and weighted average common shares outstanding of 1,000,000. The company has a convertible bond that is convertible into 100,000 shares. This bond has been outstanding for the entire year, and the company reported $40,000 in related interest expense. The company has a profit-sharing plan of 10% of net income and a 40% tax rate. Additionally, the company has convertible preferred stock that is convertible into 50,000 common shares, and $125,000 of dividends were earned on this preferred stock during the period.

Basic EPS = $2,000,000 / 1,000,000	$ 2.00
Effect on IAC:	
Interest expense	$ 40,000
Increase in profit-sharing if converted	(4,000)
Effect before taxes	36,000
Tax effect ($36,000 × 40%)	(14,400)
Increase to IAC	$ 21,600
Effect on weighted average common shares:	
Additional shares issued if converted; increases the weighted average	100,000
Per share effect of the convertible debt = $21,600 / 100,000	$ 0.216

The convertible debt has a dilutive effect since the per share effect is less than basic EPS.

Effect on IAC:	
Dividends on preferred stock added back to IAC	$125,000
Effect on weighted average common shares:	
Additional shares issued if converted; increases the weighted average	50,000
Per share effect of the convertible preferred stock = $125,000 / 50,000	$ 2.50

The convertible preferred stock is anti-dilutive since $2.50 is greater than $2.00.

Diluted EPS is calculated as follows: $\frac{\$2,000,000 + \$21,600}{1,000,000 + 100,000} = \frac{\$2,021,600}{1,100,000}$ $ 1.838

Note: The adjustments for the convertible debt assumed converted are made because they are dilutive. No adjustments are made for the convertible preferred stock because they are anti-dilutive.

4. **Treasury Stock Method** Holders of options and warrants can exercise these securities for specified amounts of cash and receive common stock. The treasury stock method assumes that this cash is used to repurchase treasury stock at the average market price, and the net effect on the shares of common stock outstanding is the difference between the shares issued and the shares purchased.

   a. The treasury stock method is applied separately to each option and warrant to determine if the individual option or warrant is dilutive. Since the effect of options and warrants is only a denominator effect for the net additional shares that are issued, the per share effect of each option or warrant is $.00.

   b. If the average market price is higher than the exercise price, the item is "in the money," and the options or warrants are dilutive. If the average market price is less than the exercise price, the options or warrants are anti-dilutive.

Example 9 ▸ Treasury Stock Method

A company has IAC of $100,000 and 250,000 weighted-average common stock outstanding for the period. The average market price of the common stock is $22 per share. The following options and warrants are outstanding:

	Options	Warrants Series A	Warrants Series B
Shares of Common Stock Issuable	10,000	5,000	7,000
Exercise price per share	$20	$15	$24

Step 1: Determine if the options and warrants are dilutive

Options: Market ($22) > Exercise ($20); Determination: Dilutive

Warrants, Series A: Market ($22) > Exercise ($15); Determination: Dilutive

Warrants, Series B: Market ($22) < Exercise ($24); Determination: Anti-Dilutive

Step 2: Determine the incremental shares for dilutive securities

Additional Shares of Common Stock		10,000
Proceeds (10,000 shares × $20)	$200,000	
Divided by market price	/ 22	
Less: Treasury Stock Purchased		(9,091)
Incremental Shares		909
Per Share Effect of Options (0 / 909)		$ .00
Additional Shares of Common Stock		5,000
Proceeds (5,000 shares × $15)	$ 75,000	
Divided by market price	/ 22	
Less: Treasury Stock Purchased		(3,409)
Incremental Shares		1,591
Per Share Effect of Warrants, Series A (0 / 1,591)		$ .00

Step 3: Calculate Basic and Diluted EPS

Item	IAC	Shares	EPS
Basic EPS	$100,000	250,000	$0.400
Warrants, Series A	0	1,591	
Subtotal	$100,000	251,591	$0.397
Options	0	909	
Diluted EPS	$100,000	252,500	$0.396

5. **Contingently Issuable Shares** Contingent issuances involve the meeting of specific conditions for the issuance of additional shares.

   a. If the contingency involves only the passage of time, the securities are assumed issued and are used in computing diluted EPS.

   b. If the contingency has not been met, the number of shares that would be issued if the contingency had been met at the end of the contingency period is used in computing diluted EPS.

c. The number of shares contingently issuable may depend on the market price of the stock at a future date. In this case, computations of EPS should reflect the number of shares which would be issuable based on the market price at the close of the reporting period. For example, assume a company had a plan to issue 20,000 shares if the market price was $15 per share, 30,000 shares if the market price was $20 per share, and 50,000 shares if the market price was $30 per share. If the market price for the current period was $17 per share, EPS should show the 20,000 contingently issuable shares.

d. If the contingency is contingent on attainment or maintenance of earnings at a certain level, the number of shares would be considered outstanding and used in computing diluted EPS if the earnings amount is currently being achieved.

6. **Calculation of Diluted EPS** Diluted EPS should reflect the maximum dilution of all potentially dilutive securities that have a dilutive effect. To accomplish this, the security with the smallest individual per share effect is first introduced into total EPS and additional securities are introduced until either all dilutive securities are included or further introduction would be anti-dilutive.

Example 10 ▸ Calculation of Diluted EPS

A company has the following earnings and securities. The tax rate is 30% and there are no non-discretionary items.

Net income for the period			$100,000
Weighted average common shares outstanding			75,000
Dividends on preferred stock earned			$ 5,000
Convertible Bonds	Series A	Series B	
Face amount and carrying value	$40,000	$60,000	
Interest rate	10%	12%	
Number of shares issuable	10,000	4,400	
Options			
Number of shares issuable			7,500
Exercise price			$ 25
Market price			$ 35
Warrants			
Number of shares issuable			2,500
Exercise price			$ 32

Step 1: Determine Basic EPS

Net income	$100,000
Preferred dividends earned	(5,000)
IAC	$ 95,000
IAC / Weighted-average shares outstanding = $95,000 / 75,000	$ 1.2667

Step 2: Determine the per share effect of each dilutive security

Interest expense	$ 4,000
Taxes	(1,200)
Adjustment to IAC (increase)	$ 2,800
Adjustment to weighted-average shares (increase): Number of shares issuable	10,000
Per share effect of Series A Convertible Bonds ($2,800 / 10,000)	$ 0.28

Interest expense		$ 7,200
Taxes		(2,160)
Adjustment to IAC (increase)		$ 5,040
Adjustment to weighted-average shares (increase):		
Number of shares issuable		4,400
Per share effect of Series B Convertible Bonds ($5,040 / 4,400)		$ 1.1455
Additional Shares of Common Stock		7,500
Proceeds (7,500 shares × $25)	$187,500	
Divided by market price	/ 35	
Less: Treasury Stock Purchased		(5,357)
Incremental Shares		2,143
Per Share Effect of Options (0 / 2,143)		$ 0.00
Additional Shares of Common Stock		2,500
Proceeds (2,500 shares × $32)	$ 80,000	
Divided by market price	/ 35	
Less: Treasury Stock Purchased		(2,286)
Incremental Shares		214
Per Share Effect of Warrants (0 / 214)		$ 0.00

Step 3: Begin with the most dilutive security and include all with a dilutive effect

Item	IAC	Shares	EPS
Basic EPS	$95,000	75,000	$ 1.2667
Options	0	2,143	
Subtotal	95,000	77,143	$ 1.2315
Warrants	0	214	
Subtotal	95,000	77,357	$ 1.2281
Series A Bonds	2,800	10,000	
Diluted EPS	$97,800	87,357	$ 1.1195

NOTE: The EPS number is adjusted for the most dilutive effect. Since the per share effect ($0.28) of the Series A Bonds is less than the previously calculated EPS number ($1.2281) the Series A Bonds are dilutive. However, the per share effect of the Series B Bonds ($1.1455) is greater than the previously calculated EPS number ($1.1195), and the security is excluded because it is anti-dilutive. The options are included first because they are more dilutive than the warrants.

D. Financial Statement Presentation

EPS data is required to be presented for all periods for which an income statement or summary of earnings is presented. If the capital structure is complex for any of the periods presented, dual presentation must be provided for all the periods presented.

1. Location

a. EPS is reported on the face of the income statement for income from continuing operations and net income.

b. An entity that reports a discontinued operation or an extraordinary item is required to present EPS amounts for those line items either on the face of the income statement or in the notes to the financial statements.

2. **Simple Capital Structure** An entity has a simple capital structure if it has only common stock outstanding and has no dilutive securities. An entity with a simple capital structure is required to present only basic EPS.

3. **Complex Capital Structure** EPS reporting is more involved if the reporting enterprise has a complex capital structure. An entity's capital structure is complex if it has dilutive securities. Dilutive securities dilute earnings per common share.

   a. An entity with a complex capital structure is required to present both basic and diluted EPS for income from continuing operations and for net income on the face of the income statement with equal prominence.

   b. For each component of income, including discontinued operations and extraordinary items, an entity must present per share information either on the income statement face or in the notes to the financial statements.

Example 11 ▸ Income Statement Presentation of EPS

Asp Company presents the following income statement information. Asp has 40,000 common shares outstanding. Asp has only convertible cumulative 8% preferred stock with a par value of $100,000, that would require 5,000 shares of common stock, if converted. Asp displays all EPS information on the face of the income statement.

Income from continuing operations	$100,000
Discontinued operations	(40,000)
Income before extraordinary item	60,000
Extraordinary item—gain on debt extinguishment	25,000
Net income	$ 85,000

Required: Determine earnings per share.

Basic EPS from continuing operations

Income from continuing operations	$100,000
Preferred dividends earned	(8,000)
IAC	$ 92,000
IAC / Weighted average common shares = $92,000 / 40,000	$ 2.30
Effect on IAC ($100,000 × 8%)	$ 8,000
Effect on weighted-average shares	5,000
Per share effect of Preferred Stock ($8,000 / 5,000)	$ 1.60

Diluted EPS

Item	IAC	Shares	EPS
Basic EPS	$ 92,000	40,000	$ 2.30
Preferred Stock	8,000	5,000	
	$100,000	45,000	$ 2.22

Basic EPS for other income items

Item	IAC	Shares	EPS
Basic EPS	$ 92,000	40,000	$ 2.30
Discontinued operations	(40,000)	0	
EPS for income before EI	52,000	40,000	$ 1.30
Extraordinary item	25,000	0	
EPS for net income	$ 77,000	40,000	$ 1.93

Diluted EPS for other income items

Item	IAC	Shares	EPS
Basic EPS	$ 92,000	40,000	$ 2.30
Preferred stock	8,000	5,000	
EPS for income from cont. op	100,000	45,000	$ 2.22
Discontinued operations	(40,000)	0	
EPS for income before EI	60,000	45,000	$ 1.33
Extraordinary item	25,000	0	
EPS for net income	$ 85,000	45,000	$ 1.89

EPS information would be presented as:

	Income	Basic EPS	Diluted EPS
Income from continuing operations	$100,000	$ 2.30	$ 2.22
Discontinued operations	(40,000)	(1.00)	(.89)
Income before extraordinary item	60,000	1.30	1.33
Extraordinary item—gain on debt extin.	25,000	.63	.56
Net income	$ 85,000	$ 1.93	$ 1.89

NOTE: The diluted EPS amount for income for extraordinary items is greater than the basic EPS. The effect of the convertible preferred stock is included in all computations if it is dilutive in computing EPS for continuing operations.

4. **Disclosures** The following disclosures are required.

   a. A reconciliation of the numerators and the denominators of the basic and diluted per share computations for income from continuing operations. In this way, the financial statement reader can see the per share impact of each security.

   b. The effect that has been given to preferred dividends in determining the income available to common stockholders.

   c. Securities that could potentially dilute basic EPS in a future period, but that were anti-dilutive in the current period.

   d. A description of any transaction that occurs after the end of the period, but before the issuance of the financial statements that would have materially changed the number of common shares or potential common shares outstanding at the end of the period if the transaction had occurred before the end of the period. Examples would include issuance or acquisition of common shares, issuance or exercise/conversion of warrants, options, or convertible securities.

IV. Comprehensive Income

A. Recognition and Measurement

The recognition and measurement of comprehensive income is based upon current accounting standards (GAAP). Comprehensive income includes all changes in equity during a period except those resulting from investments by owners and distributions to owners. Comprehensive income is divided into net income and other comprehensive income.

1. **Components and Total Reported** All components of comprehensive income must be reported in the financial statements in the period in which they are recognized. A total amount for comprehensive income must be displayed in the financial statement where the components of OCI are reported.

2. **Interim-Period Reporting** An entity must report a total for comprehensive income in condensed financial statements of interim periods.

B. Other Comprehensive Income (OCI)

OCI includes revenues, expenses, gains, and losses that are excluded from net income. Instead, they are listed after net income on the income statement. These items have not yet been realized. In other words, the underlying transaction has not been completed or settled yet. For example, unrealized gains or losses resulting from changes in the *Investment in Bonds* account would be included in OCI. Once the bonds are sold, the gain or loss shifts out of OCI, higher up the income statement, so that it is part of net income. Other comprehensive income has no effect on direct adjustments to equity accounts, such as capital stock transactions and transactions related to retained earnings.

1. **Classification** An entity must classify items of other comprehensive income by their nature, in one of these classifications: foreign currency items, pension adjustments, unrealized gains and losses on certain investments in debt and equity securities, and gains and losses on cash flow hedging derivative instruments. Additional classifications or additional items within current classifications may result from future accounting standards.

   a. **Foreign Currency Items** Included in this classification are foreign currency translation adjustments and gains and losses on foreign currency transactions that are designated as, and are effective as, economic hedges of a net investment in a foreign entity. Also included is the effective portion of gains and losses on hedging derivative instruments in a hedge of a forecasted foreign-currency-denominated transaction, and the effective portion of the gain or loss in the hedging derivative or nonderivative instrument in a hedge of a net investment in a foreign operation.

   b. **Pension Adjustments** The amounts of net gain or loss, net prior service cost or credit, and net transition asset or obligation that are expected to be recognized as components of net periodic benefit cost.

   c. **Unrealized Gains and Losses on Certain Investments** Unrealized gains and losses on certain investments in debt and equity securities including

      (1) Unrealized holding gains and losses on available-for-sale (AFS) securities

      (2) Unrealized holding gains and losses that result from a debt security being transferred into the AFS category from the HTM category

      (3) Subsequent decreases or increases in the fair value of AFS securities previously written down as impaired

      (4) A change in the market value of a futures contract that qualifies as a hedge of an asset reported at fair value

   d. **Gains and Losses on Derivative Instruments** The effective portion of gains and losses on cash flow derivative instruments is reported as a component of OCI and reclassified into earnings when the hedged forecasted transaction affects earnings.

2. **Reclassification** Reclassification adjustments must be reported within other comprehensive income on the face of the statement that reports OCI.

   a. Adjustments must be made to avoid double counting in comprehensive income items that are displayed as part of net income for a period that also had been included as part of OCI in that period or earlier periods.

   b. Reclassification adjustments must be determined for each classification of OCI, except minimum pension liability adjustments. Minimum pension liability adjustments must be shown net.

C. Presentation

All non-owner changes in stockholders' equity must be presented either in a single continuous statement of comprehensive income or in two separate but consecutive condensed statements for both annual and interim reporting.

1. **One-Statement Approach** Since net income is a significant part of comprehensive income, the one-statement approach combines the statement of income and comprehensive income. In a single continuous statement, the entity is required to present the components of net income and total net income, the components of other comprehensive income and total other comprehensive income, along with the total of comprehensive income in that statement.

Exhibit 6 ▸ One-Statement Approach, With Tax Effect Shown Parenthetically

ABC Company
Statement of Income and Comprehensive Income
For the year ended December 31, Year 1

Revenues			$ 450,000
Expenses			(300,000)
Loss on sale of securities			(20,000)
Income from Continuing Operations, before taxes			130,000
Provision for taxes			(54,000)
Income from Continuing Operations			76,000
Discontinued Operations:			
Loss on operations of discontinued component		$(62,000)	
Income taxes		7,000	
Loss on Discontinued Operations			(55,000)
Income before Extraordinary Items			21,000
Extraordinary Gain, net of tax			18,000
Net Income			39,000
Other Comprehensive Income:			
Foreign currency adjustments, net of tax of $6,000		9,000	
Unrealized Loss on Marketable Securities:			
Unrealized holding loss arising during period, net of tax of $18,000	$ (42,000)		
Less: reclassification adjustment, net of tax of $6,000, for loss included in net income	14,000		
Pension adjustment, net of tax of $4,000		(6,000)	
Other Comprehensive Income			(25,000)
Comprehensive Income			$ 14,000

2. **Two-Statement Approach** In the two-statement approach, an entity is required to present components of net income and total net income in one statement and present the components of OCI, a total for OCI, and a total for comprehensive income in a second statement that immediately follows the first statements.

Exhibit 7 ▸ Two-Statement Approach, With Tax Effect Shown as a Single Amount*

ABC Company Statement of Income For the year ended December 31, Year 1			
Revenues			$ 450,000
Expenses			(300,000)
Loss on sale of securities			(20,000)
Income from Continuing Operations, before taxes			130,000
Provision for taxes			(54,000)
Income from Continuing Operations			76,000
Discontinued Operations			
Loss on operations of discontinued segment		$(62,000)	
Income Tax		7,000	
Loss on discontinued operations			(55,000)
Income before Extraordinary Items			21,000
Extraordinary Gain, net of tax			18,000
Net Income			$ 39,000

ABC Company Statement of Comprehensive Income For the year ended December 31, Year 1			
Net Income			$ 39,000
Other Comprehensive Income:			
Foreign currency adjustments		$ 15,000	
Unrealized Loss on Marketable Securities:			
Unrealized holding loss arising during period	$ (60,000)		
Less: reclassification adjustment for loss included in net income	20,000		
Pension adjustment		(10,000)	
Other Comprehensive Income, before tax		(35,000)	
Income tax expense		10,000	
Other Comprehensive Income			(25,000)
Comprehensive Income			$ 14,000

* Tax effect reflected in notes

3. **Reporting Related Income Tax**
An entity may display components of other comprehensive income in two alternative ways.

   a. Each of the components of comprehensive income may be reported on a net-of-tax basis.

   b. Each of the other comprehensive income items may be reported before tax, with one line reporting the tax provision of all of those elements. If this alternative is used, the tax provision for each individual item must be shown within the notes to the financial statements.

4. **FASB/IASB Amendments** The IASB and FASB issued joint amendments in 2011, effective in 2012. The amendments were intended to increase the prominence of other comprehensive income in financial statements and help financial statement users better understand the cause of a company's change in financial position and results of operations. Initially these amendments:

   a. Required an entity must present separately the items of OCI that would be reclassified to profit or loss in the future if certain conditions are met from those items that would never be reclassified to profit or loss. An entity that presents items of OCI before related tax effects would also have to allocate the aggregated tax amount between these sections.

   b. Do not change the existing option to present profit or loss and OCI in two statements.

c. Change the title of the statement of comprehensive income to the statement of profit or loss and other comprehensive income. However, an entity is still allowed to use other titles.

Subsequent to the issuance of ASU 2011-05, stakeholders raised concerns that the new presentation requirements about the reclassification of items out of accumulated other comprehensive income would be costly for preparers and add unnecessary complexity to financial statements. As a result of these concerns, the FASB issued ASU 2011-12, deferring the effective date for presentation of reclassification adjustments only. While the Board is considering the operational concerns about the presentation requirements for classification adjustments, entities will continue to report reclassifications out of accumulated comprehensive income consistent with the presentation requirements in effect before Update 2011-05.

V. Interim Financial Reporting

A. Concepts

Each interim period should be viewed as an integral part of an annual period and not as a separate, independent period. In order to maintain comparability between interim and annual financial statements, the principles and practices used to prepare the latest annual financial statements also should be used to prepare the interim statements. However, certain procedures applied to the annual statements may require modification at the interim reporting dates so that the results for the interim period may better relate to the results of operations for the annual period. At the end of each interim period, the company should make its best estimate of the effective tax rate expected to be applicable for the full fiscal year. This estimated effective tax rate should be used to provide for income taxes on a current year-to-date basis. The effective tax rate should reflect foreign tax rates, percentage depletion, and other available tax planning alternatives.

1. **Estimated Effective Tax Rate** In arriving at the estimated full year tax rate, no effect should be included for the income tax related to significant unusual or extraordinary items that will be separately reported or reported net of their related income tax effects for the interim period or for the fiscal year.

2. **Significant, Unusual, or Extraordinary Items** In arriving at the estimated full year tax rate, no effect should be included for the income tax related to significant unusual or extraordinary items that will be separately reported or reported net of their related income tax effects for the interim period or for the fiscal year.

3. **Nonordinary Items** Unusual or infrequently occurring items (nonordinary items) should be included in determining interim period income, but should be excluded in determining the full year effective income tax rate.

B. Continuing Operations

1. **Revenues** Revenues should be recognized as earned during an interim period on the same basis as followed for recognition of income for the full year. For example, revenues from long-term construction-type contracts accounted for under the percentage of completion method should be recognized in interim periods on the same basis as is followed for the full year. Losses from such contracts should be recognized in full during the interim period in which the existence of the losses becomes evident.

2. **Product Costs** Costs and expenses associated directly with products sold or services rendered for annual reporting purposes should be similarly treated for interim reporting purposes. Some exceptions are appropriate for valuing inventory at interim reporting dates.

   a. Some companies use estimated gross profit rates to estimate ending inventory and cost of goods sold during interim periods or use other methods different from those used at annual inventory dates. These companies should disclose the methods used at the interim date and any significant adjustments that result from reconciliation with the annual physical inventory.

b. Companies that use the LIFO method may encounter a liquidation of base period inventories at an interim date that is expected to be replaced by the end of the annual period. The inventory at the interim date should not give effect to the LIFO liquidation, and cost of sales for the interim reporting period should include the replacement cost of the liquidated LIFO base.

c. The use of lower of cost or market may result in inventory losses that should not be deferred beyond the interim period in which the decline occurs. Recoveries of these losses in subsequent periods should be recognized as gains, but only to the extent of losses recognized in previous interim periods of the same fiscal year. Temporary market declines need not be recognized at the interim date since no loss is expected to be incurred in the fiscal year.

d. Companies that use standard costs for valuing inventory at year-end should use the same procedures for valuing inventory at interim dates. Material and volume variances that are planned and expected to be absorbed by year-end should be deferred until the end of the year. Unplanned variances should be reported in the interim period in the same manner as year-end variances.

3. **Costs Other Than Product Costs** Costs and expenses other than product costs should be charged to income in interim periods as incurred, or be allocated among interim periods based on an estimate of time expired, benefit received, or activity associated with the periods. Procedures adopted for assigning specific cost and expense items to an interim period should be consistent with the bases followed by the company in reporting results of operations at annual reporting dates. However, when a specific cost or expense item charged to expense for annual reporting purposes benefits more than one interim period, the cost or expense item may be allocated to those interim periods.

   a. Some costs and expenses incurred in an interim period cannot be readily identified with the activities or benefits of other interim periods and should be charged to the interim period in which incurred.

   b. Arbitrary assignment of the amount of such costs to an interim period should not be made.

   c. Gains and losses that arise in any interim period similar to those that would not be deferred at year-end should not be deferred to later interim periods within the same fiscal year.

4. **Allocation of Indirect Cost Examples** The following examples may be helpful in applying the standards for allocation of costs and expenses not directly associated with revenues in interim financial statements.

   a. When a cost that is expensed for annual reporting purposes clearly benefits two or more interim periods (e.g., annual major repairs), each interim period should be charged for an appropriate portion of the annual cost by the use of accruals or deferrals.

   b. Property taxes (and similar costs such as insurance, interest, and rent) may be accrued or deferred at an annual reporting date to achieve a full year's charge of taxes to costs and expenses. Similar procedures should be adopted at each interim reporting date to provide an appropriate cost in each period.

   c. Advertising costs may be deferred within a fiscal year if the benefits of an expenditure clearly extend beyond the interim period in which the expenditure is made.

5. **Financial Statements** Interim period financial statements should bear a reasonable portion of such year-end adjustments as inventory shrinkage, allowance for uncollectible accounts, and discretionary year-end bonuses.

6. **Seasonal Variations** Companies whose revenues and expenses are subject to material *seasonal variations* should disclose the seasonal nature of their activities, and consider supplementing their interim reports with information for twelve-month periods ended at the interim date for the current and preceding years.

7. **Income Tax Provisions** At the end of each interim period the company should make its best estimate of the effective tax rate expected to be applicable for the full fiscal year. That rate should be used in providing for income taxes on a current year-to-date basis. The effective tax rate should reflect anticipated investment tax credits, foreign tax rates, percentage depletion, capital gains rates, and other available tax planning alternatives. However, in arriving at this effective tax rate no effect should be included for the tax related to significant unusual or extraordinary items that will be separately reported or reported net of their related tax effect in reports for the interim period or for the fiscal year.

   a. The tax effects of losses that arise in the early portion of a fiscal year should be recognized only when the tax benefits are expected to be realized during the year or recognizable as a deferred tax asset at the end of the year.

   b. The effect of a change in tax laws or rates on a deferred tax liability or asset shall not be apportioned among interim periods through an adjustment of the annual effective tax rate. The tax effect of a change in tax laws or rates on taxes payable or refundable for a prior year shall be recognized as of the enactment date of the change as tax expense (benefit) for the current year.

C. Discontinued Operations & Extraordinary Items

Extraordinary items and the gain or loss from disposal of a component of an entity and their related income tax effects should be included in the determination of net income for the interim period in which they occur. An item should be classified as extraordinary in the interim period if it is material in relation to annual net income. Extraordinary items and the gain or loss from discontinued operations should **not** be prorated among interim periods.

D. Contingencies & Uncertainties

Contingencies and other uncertainties that could be expected to affect the fairness of presentation of financial data at an interim date should be disclosed in interim reports in the same manner required for annual reports. Such disclosures should be repeated in interim and annual reports until the contingencies have been removed, resolved, or have become immaterial.

E. Accounting Changes

Each report of interim financial information should indicate any change in accounting principles or practices from those applied in (1) the comparable interim period of the prior annual period, (2) the preceding interim periods in the current annual period and (3) the prior annual report. Whenever possible, companies should adopt any accounting changes during the first interim period of a fiscal year. Changes in accounting principles and practices adopted after the first interim period in a fiscal year tend to obscure operating results and complicate disclosure of interim financial information.

1. **Change in Accounting Principle** Changes in an interim or annual accounting principle made in an interim period should be reported by retrospective application in the period in which the change is made. The required disclosures are also presented in this same period in which the change was made. Financial statements of subsequent periods need not repeat the required disclosures.

2. **Change in Accounting Estimate** The effect of a change in an accounting estimate, including a change in the estimated effective annual tax rate, should be accounted for in the period in which the change in estimate is made. No restatement of previously reported interim information should be made for changes in estimates, but the effect on earnings of a change in estimate made in a current interim period should be reported in the current and subsequent interim periods and continue to be reported in the interim financial information of the subsequent year for as many periods as necessary to avoid misleading comparisons. The disclosures related to changes in accounting estimate are also required.

3. **Correction of an Error** In determining materiality for the purpose of reporting the correction of an error, amounts should be related to the estimated income for the full fiscal year and also to the effect on the trend of earnings. Changes that are material with respect to an interim period but not material with respect to the estimated income for the full fiscal year or to the trend of earnings should be separately disclosed in the interim period.

F. Minimum Disclosures

Disclosure requirements apply to reporting summarized financial data to security holders of **publicly** traded companies. When summarized financial data are regularly reported on a quarterly basis, information with respect to the current quarter and the current year-to-date or the last-twelve-months-to-date should be furnished together with comparable data for the preceding year.

1. Sales or gross revenues, provision for income taxes, extraordinary items, cumulative effect of a change in accounting principles, net income, and comprehensive income

2. Primary and fully diluted earnings per share data for each period presented

3. Seasonal revenue, costs or expenses

4. Significant changes in estimates or provisions for income taxes

5. Disposal of a segment of a business and extraordinary, unusual, or infrequently occurring items

6. Contingent items

7. Changes in accounting principles or estimates

8. Significant changes in financial position

9. Information about reportable operating segments, including revenues from external customers, intersegment revenues, a measure of segment profit or loss, material changes in total assets, a description of differences in segments or measurement of segment profit or loss, and a reconciliation of the total of segment profit or loss to consolidated income.

What is eligible to be tested?

From the AICPA's *Uniform CPA Examination Candidate Bulletin*:

"Accounting and auditing pronouncements are eligible to be tested on the Uniform CPA Examination in the window beginning six months after a pronouncement's *effective* date, unless early application is permitted. When early application is permitted, the new pronouncement is eligible to be tested in the window beginning six months after the *issuance* date. In this case, both the old and new pronouncements may be tested until the old pronouncement is superseded.

See the **Exam Preparation Tips** section of this volume for additional information.

CHAPTER 12—REPORTING THE RESULTS OF OPERATIONS

Problem 12-1 MULTIPLE-CHOICE QUESTIONS

1. On August 31, Harvey Co. decided to change from the FIFO periodic inventory system to the weighted average periodic inventory system. Harvey is on a calendar year basis. The cumulative effect of the change is determined

   a. As of January 1
   b. As of August 31
   c. During the eight months ending August 31, by a weighted average of the purchases
   d. During the entire year by a weighted average of the purchases (5/93, Theory, #20, amended, 4208)

2. Which of the following would be accounted for as a change in accounting principle?

   a. A change in the method of inventory pricing, such as from LIFO to FIFO
   b. A change in depreciation method, such as from the double-declining-balance method to the straight-line method
   c. A change in the amortization method for an intangible asset
   d. All of the above (Editor, 89557)

3. Milt Co. began operations on January 1, year 1. On January 1, year 3, Milt changed its inventory method from LIFO to FIFO for both financial and income tax reporting. If FIFO had been used in prior years, Milt's inventories would have been higher by $60,000 and $40,000 at December 31, year 3 and year 2, respectively. Milt has a 30% income tax rate. What amount should Milt report as the cumulative effect of this accounting change in its income statement for the year ended December 31, year 3?

   a. $0
   b. $14,000
   c. $28,000
   d. $42,000 (11/92, PI, #60, amended, 3291)

4. At December 31, year 5, Off-Line Co. changed its method of accounting for demo costs from writing off the costs over two years to expensing the costs immediately. Off-Line made the change in recognition of an increasing number of demos placed with customers that did not result in sales. Off-Line had deferred demo costs of $500,000 at December 31, year 4, $300,000 of which were to be written off in year 5 and the remainder in year 6. Off-Line's income tax rate is 30%. In its December 31, year 5 income statement, what amount should Off-Line report as cumulative effect of change in accounting principle?

   a. $140,000
   b. $200,000
   c. $350,000
   d. $500,000 (R/99, FAR, #12, 6781)

5. Which of the following describes the appropriate reporting treatment for a change in accounting estimate?

   a. In the period of change with **no** future consideration
   b. By reporting *pro forma* amounts for prior periods
   c. By restating amounts reported in financial statements of prior periods
   d. In the period of change and future periods if the change affects both (R/08, FAR, #16, 8571)

6. In Year 7, Spirit, Inc. determined that the 12-year estimated useful life of a machine purchased for $48,000 in January Year 2 should be extended by three years. The machine is being depreciated using the straight-line method and has no salvage value. What amount of depreciation expense should Spirit report in its financial statements for the year ending December 31, Year 7?

   a. $2,800
   b. $3,200
   c. $4,200
   d. $4,800 (R/08, FAR, #14, 8569)

7. On January 2, year 1, Union Co. purchased a machine for $264,000 and depreciated it by the straight-line method using an estimated useful life of eight years with no salvage value. On January 2, year 4, Union determined that the machine had a useful life of six years from the date of acquisition and will have a salvage value of $24,000. An accounting change was made in year 4 to reflect the additional data. The accumulated depreciation for this machine should have a balance at December 31, year 4, of

   a. $176,000
   b. $160,000
   c. $154,000
   d. $146,000 (11/93, PI, #60, amended, 4429)

8. For the previous year, Pac Co. estimated its two-year equipment warranty costs based on $100 per unit sold in the previous year. Experience during the current year indicated that the estimate should have been based on $110 per unit. The effect of this $10 difference from the estimate is reported

   a. In current year income from continuing operations
   b. As an accounting change, net of tax, below current year income from continuing operations
   c. As an accounting change requiring the previous year financial statements to be restated
   d. As a correction of an error requiring the previous year financial statements to be restated

   (11/93, Theory, #23, amended, 4528)

9. Which of the following statements regarding changes in accounting estimates is false?

   a. Changes in accounting estimates differ from changes in accounting principles in that changes in estimates are simply necessary consequences of periodic financial reporting.
   b. Examples of changes in estimates reflected in the financial statements include changes in estimates related to uncollectible receivables.
   c. Examples of changes in estimates reflected in the financial statements do not include warranty costs.
   d. Accounting estimates change as new events occur, as more experience is acquired, and as additional information is obtained. (Editor, 8074)

10. Matt Co. included a foreign subsidiary in its current consolidated financial statements. The subsidiary was acquired six years ago and was excluded from previous consolidations. The change was caused by the elimination of foreign exchange controls. Including the subsidiary in the consolidated financial statements results in accounting change that should be reported

    a. By footnote disclosure only
    b. Currently and prospectively
    c. Currently with footnote disclosure of pro forma effects of retroactive application
    d. By retrospective application to the financial statements of all prior periods presented

    (5/92, Theory, #40, amended, 2733)

11. Which of the following statements is correct regarding accounting changes that result in financial statements that are, in effect, the statements of a different reporting entity?

    a. Cumulative-effect adjustments should be reported as separate items on the financial statements pertaining to the year of change.
    b. No restatements or adjustments are required if the changes involve consolidated methods of accounting for subsidiaries.
    c. No restatements or adjustments are required if the changes involve the cost or equity methods of accounting for investments.
    d. The financial statements of all prior periods presented should be reported by retrospective application.

    (5/94, FAR, #39, amended, 4854)

12. On January 2, Year 4, Raft Corp. discovered that it had incorrectly expensed a $210,000 machine purchased on January 2, Year 1. Raft estimated the machine's original useful life to be 10 years and its salvage value at $10,000. Raft uses the straight-line method of depreciation and is subject to a 30% tax rate. In its December 31, Year 4, financial statements, what amount should Raft report as a prior period adjustment?

    a. $102,900
    b. $105,000
    c. $165,900
    d. $168,000 (R/08, FAR, #15, 8570)

13. How should a company report its decision to change from a cash-basis of accounting to accrual-basis of accounting?

    a. As a change in accounting principle, requiring the cumulative effect of the change (net of tax) to be reported in the income statement
    b. Prospectively, with no amounts restated and no cumulative adjustment
    c. As an extraordinary item (net of tax)
    d. As a prior-period adjustment (net of tax), by adjusting the beginning balance of retained earnings (R/09, FAR, #47, 8797)

14. In which of the following situations should a company report a prior-period adjustment?

    a. A change in the estimated useful lives of fixed assets purchased in prior years
    b. The correction of a mathematical error in the calculation of prior years' depreciation
    c. A switch from the straight-line to double-declining balance method of depreciation
    d. The scrapping of an asset prior to the end of its expected useful life (R/05, FAR, #43, 7787)

15. Which of the following items requires a prior period adjustment to retained earnings?

    a. Purchases of inventory this year were overstated by $5 million.
    b. Available-for-sale securities were improperly valued last year by $20 million.
    c. Revenue of $5 million that should have been deferred was recorded in the previous year as earned.
    d. The prior year's foreign currency translation gain of $2 million was never recorded. (R/03, FAR, #1, 7603)

16. In single period statements, which of the following should be reflected as an adjustment to the opening balance of retained earnings?

    a. Effect of a failure to provide for uncollectible accounts in the previous period.
    b. Effect of a decrease in the estimated useful life of depreciable equipment.
    c. Cumulative effect of a change of income recognition from the installment sale method to recognition at point of sale.
    d. Cumulative effect of a change from an accelerated method to straight-line depreciation. (R/ 91, FAR #25, 2533)

17. During the current year, Orca Corp. decided to change from the FIFO method of inventory valuation to the weighted-average method. Inventory balances under each method were as follows:

	FIFO	Weighted-average
January 1	$71,000	$77,000
December 31	79,000	83,000

    Orca's income tax rate is 30%. Orca should report the cumulative effect of this accounting change as a(an):

    a. Prior period adjustment to the beginning balance of retained earnings
    b. Component of income from continuing operations.
    c. Extraordinary item.
    d. Component of income after extraordinary items. (R/95, FAR, #46, 5582)

18. The correction of an error in the financial statements of a prior period should be reported
    a. Net of applicable income taxes, in the current retained earnings statement after net income but before dividends
    b. As a prior period adjustment by restating the prior-period financial statements
    c. Net of applicable income taxes, in the current income statement after income from continuing operations and before extraordinary items
    d. Net of applicable income taxes, in the current income statement after income from continuing operations and after extraordinary items (11/93, Theory, #22, amended, 4527)

19. Which of the following errors results in an overstatement of both current assets and stockholders' equity?
    a. An understatement of accrued sales expenses.
    b. Noncurrent note receivable principal is misclassified as a current asset.
    c. Annual depreciation on manufacturing machinery is understated.
    d. Holiday pay expense for administrative employees is misclassified as manufacturing overhead.
    (5/93, Theory, #17, amended, 4205)

20. A material overstatement in ending inventory was discovered after the year-end financial statements of a company were issued to the public. What effect did this error have on the year-end financial statements?

	Current assets	Gross profit
a.	Understated	Overstated
b.	Overstated	Overstated
c.	Understated	Understated
d.	Overstated	Understated

(R/07, FAR, #1, 8322)

21. Conn Co. reported a retained earnings balance of $400,000 at December 31 of the previous year. In August of the current year, Conn determined that insurance premiums of $60,000 for the three-year period beginning January 1 of the previous year had been paid and fully expensed in that year. Conn has a 30% income tax rate. What amount should Conn report as adjusted beginning retained earnings in its current year statement of retained earnings?
    a. $420,000
    b. $428,000
    c. $440,000
    d. $442,000 (R/93, FAR #10, 4379)

22. Lore Co. changed from the cash basis of accounting to the accrual basis of accounting during the year. The cumulative effect of this change should be reported in Lore's financial statements as a
    a. Correction of an error
    b. Change in accounting principle
    c. Component of income before extraordinary item
    d. Component of income after extraordinary item (11/95, FAR, #43, amended, 6125)

23. Pear Co.'s income statement for the current year ended December 31, as prepared by Pear's controller, reported income before taxes of $125,000. The auditor questioned the following amounts that had been included in income before taxes:

Equity in earnings of Cinn Co.	$ 40,000
Dividends received from Cinn	8,000
Adjustments to profits of prior years for arithmetical errors in depreciation	(35,000)

Pear owns 40% of Cinn's common stock. Pear's December 31 income statement should report income before taxes of
    a. $ 85,000
    b. $117,000
    c. $120,000
    d. $152,000 (5/93, PI, #5, amended, 4047)

24. Which of the following statements concerning income determination is a true representation of the compromise between the all-inclusive and the current-operating concepts of income statement preparation?
    a. Inclusion of all regular items of income and expense, including unusual or infrequently occurring items, in the determination of net income
    b. Reporting of income from discontinued operations within the results of continuing operations
    c. Reporting of income from extraordinary items within the results of continuing operations
    d. All of the above (Editor, 89551)

25. In Baer Food Co.'s current year single-step income statement, the section titled "Revenues" consisted of the following:

Net sales revenue		$187,000
Results from discontinued operations:		
Loss from operations of segment (net of $1,200 tax effect)	$ (2,400)	
Gain on disposal of segment (net of $7,200 tax effect)	14,400	12,000
Interest revenue		10,200
Gain on sale of equipment		4,700
Total revenues		$213,900

In the revenues section of the income statement, Baer Food should have reported total revenues of

a. $216,300
b. $213,900
c. $203,700
d. $201,900 (5/91, PI, #3, amended, 1115)

26. On October 1, year 1, Acme Fuel Co. sold 100,000 gallons of heating oil to Karn Co. at $3 per gallon. Fifty-thousand gallons were delivered on December 15, year 1, and the remaining 50,000 gallons were delivered on January 15, year 2. Payment terms were: 50% due on October 1, year 1, 25% due on first delivery, and the remaining 25% due on second delivery. What amount of revenue should Acme recognize from this sale during year 1?
    a. $ 75,000
    b. $150,000
    c. $225,000
    d. $300,000 (5/92, PI, #37, amended, 2608)

27. The following costs were incurred by Griff Co., a manufacturer, during the year:

Accounting and legal fees	$ 25,000
Freight-in	175,000
Freight-out	160,000
Officers' salaries	150,000
Insurance	85,000
Sales representatives' salaries	215,000

What amount of these costs should be reported as general and administrative expenses for the year?

a. $260,000
b. $550,000
c. $635,000
d. $810,000 (11/93, PI, #52, amended, 4421)

28. During the current year, Fuqua Steel Co. had the following unusual financial events occur:
    - Bonds payable were retired five years before their scheduled maturity, resulting in a $260,000 gain. Fuqua has frequently retired bonds early when interest rates declined significantly.
    - A steel forming segment suffered $255,000 in losses due to hurricane damage. This was the fourth similar loss sustained in a 5-year period at that location.
    - A segment of Fuqua's operations, steel transportation, was sold at a net loss of $350,000. This was Fuqua's first divestiture of one of its operating segments.

    Before income taxes, what amount of gain (loss) should be reported separately as a component of income from continuing operations?

    a. $ 260,000
    b. $ 5,000
    c. $ (255,000)
    d. $ (350,000) (R/91, FAR #50, 2438)

29. The following information pertains to Deal Corp.'s current year cost of goods sold:

Inventory, 12/31 of the previous year	$ 90,000
Purchases	124,000
Write-off of obsolete inventory	34,000
Inventory, 12/31 of current year	30,000

    The inventory written off became obsolete due to an unexpected and unusual technological advance by a competitor. In its year-end income statement, what amount should Deal report as cost of goods sold?

    a. $218,000
    b. $184,000
    c. $150,000
    d. $124,000 (5/93, PI, #48, amended, 4089)

30. A material loss is presented separately as a component of income from continuing operations when it is
    a. An extraordinary item
    b. A cumulative-effect-type change in accounting principle
    c. Unusual in nature and infrequent in occurrence
    d. Not unusual in nature but infrequent in occurrence (5/95, FAR, #40, amended, 5576)

31. Hail damaged several of Toncan Co.'s vans. Hailstorms had frequently inflicted similar damage to Toncan's vans. Over the years, Toncan had saved money by not buying hail insurance and either paying for repairs, or selling damaged vans and then replacing them. The damaged vans were sold for less than their carrying amount. How should the hail damage cost be reported in Toncan's financial statements?
    a. The actual hail damage loss as an extraordinary loss, net of income taxes
    b. The actual hail damage loss in continuing operations, with **no** separate disclosure
    c. The expected average hail damage loss in continuing operations, with **no** separate disclosure
    d. The expected average hail damage loss in continuing operations, with separate disclosure (5/93, Theory, #35, amended, 4223)

32. Envoy Co. manufactures and sells household products. Envoy experienced losses associated with its small appliance group. Operations and cash flows for this group can be clearly distinguished from the rest of Envoy's operations. Envoy plans to sell the small appliance group with its operations. What is the earliest point at which Envoy should report the small appliance group as a discontinued operation?
    a. When Envoy classifies it as held for sale
    b. When Envoy receives an offer for the segment
    c. When Envoy first sells any of the assets of the segment
    d. When Envoy sells the majority of the assets of the segment (R/07, FAR, #12, 8333)

33. During January of the previous year, Doe Corp. agreed to sell the assets and product line of its Hart division. The sale on January 15 of the current year resulted in a gain on disposal of $900,000. Not considering any impairment losses, Hart's operating losses were $600,000 for the previous year and $50,000 for the current year period January 1 through January 15. Disregarding income taxes, what amount of net gain (loss) should be reported in Doe's comparative current and previous years income statements?

	Current Year	Previous Year
a.	$0	$ 250,000
b.	$250,000	$0
c.	$850,000	$ (600,000)
d.	$900,000	$ (650,000)

(11/95, FAR, #39, amended, 6121)

34. On April 30, Deer approved a plan to dispose of a segment of its business. For the period January 1 through April 30, the segment had revenues of $500,000 and expenses of $800,000. The assets of the segment were sold on October 15, at a loss for which no tax benefit is available. In its income statement for the calendar year how should Deer report the segment's operations from January 1 to April 30?

    a. $500,000 and $800,000 included with revenues and expenses, respectively, as part of continuing operations
    b. $300,000 reported as a net loss, as part of continuing operations
    c. $300,000 reported as an extraordinary loss
    d. $300,000 reported as a loss from discontinued operations (11/95, FAR, #40, amended, 6122)

35. Which of the following transactions qualify as a discontinued operation?

    a. Disposal of part of a line of business
    b. Planned and approved sale of a segment
    c. Phasing out of a production line
    d. Changes related to technological improvements (R/11, FAR, #7, 9857)

36. On October 1, year 4, Host Co. approved a plan to dispose of a segment of its business. Host expected that the sale would occur on April 1, year 5, at an estimated gain of $350,000. The segment had actual and estimated operating losses as follows:

1/1 to 9/30, year 4	$(300,000)
10/1 to 12/31, year 4	(200,000)
1/1 to 3/31, year 5	(400,000)

In its December 31, year 4, income statement, what should Host report as a loss from discontinued operations before income taxes?

    a. $200,000
    b. $250,000
    c. $500,000
    d. $600,000 (5/95, FAR, #44, amended, 5580)

37. A company decided to sell an unprofitable division of its business. The company can sell the entire operation for $800,000, and the buyer will assume all assets and liabilities of the operations. The tax rate is 30%. The assets and liabilities of the discontinued operation are as follows:

Buildings	$5,000,000
Accumulated depreciation	3,000,000
Mortgage on buildings	1,100,000
Inventory	500,000
Accounts payable	600,000
Accounts receivable	200,000

What is the after-tax net loss on the disposal of the division?

a. $ 140,000
b. $ 200,000
c. $1,540,000
d. $2,200,000 (R/11, FAR, #16, 9866)

38. An extraordinary gain should be reported as a direct increase to which of the following?

a. Net income
b. Comprehensive income
c. Income from continuing operations, net of tax
d. Income from discontinued operations, net of tax (R/07, FAR, #44, 8365)

39. In open-market transactions, Gold Corp. simultaneously sold its long-term investment in Iron Corp. bonds and purchased its own outstanding bonds. The broker remitted the net cash from the two transactions. Gold's gain on the purchase of its own bonds exceeded its loss on the sale of the Iron bonds. Gold should report the

a. Net effect of the two transactions as an extraordinary gain
b. Net effect of the two transactions in income before extraordinary items
c. Effect of its own bond transaction gain in income before extraordinary items, and report the Iron bond transaction as an extraordinary loss
d. Effect of its own bond transaction as an extraordinary gain, and report the Iron bond transaction loss in income before extraordinary items (11/95, FAR, #41, amended, 6123)

40. In September, Koff Co.'s operating plant was destroyed by an earthquake. Earthquakes are rare in the area in which the plant was located. The portion of the resultant loss not covered by insurance was $700,000. Koff's income tax rate is 40%. In its year-end income statement, what amount should Koff report as extraordinary loss?

a. $0
b. $280,000
c. $420,000
d. $700,000 (5/97, FAR, #5, amended, 6477)

41. Midway Co. had the following transactions during the current year:
    - $1,200,000 pretax loss on foreign currency exchange due to a major unexpected devaluation by the foreign government.
    - $500,000 pretax loss from discontinued operations of a division.
    - $800,000 pretax loss on equipment damaged by a hurricane. This was the first hurricane ever to strike in Midway's area. Midway also received $1,000,000 from its insurance company to replace a building, with a carrying value of $300,000, that had been destroyed by the hurricane.

    What amount should Midway report in its year-end income statement as extraordinary loss before income taxes?

    a. $ 100,000
    b. $1,300,000
    c. $1,800,000
    d. $2,500,000 (5/93, PI, #59, amended, 4098)

42. Jordan Co. had the following gains during the current period:

Gain on disposal of business segment	$500,000
Foreign currency translation gain	100,000

    What amount of extraordinary gain should be presented on Jordan's income statement for the current period?

    a. $0
    b. $100,000
    c. $500,000
    d. $600,000 (R/09, FAR, #5, 8755)

43. Ocean Corp.'s comprehensive insurance policy allows its assets to be replaced at current value. The policy has a $50,000 deductible clause. One of Ocean's waterfront warehouses was destroyed in a winter storm. Such storms occur approximately every four years. Ocean incurred $20,000 of costs in dismantling the warehouse and plans to replace it. The following data relate to the warehouse:

Current carrying amount	$ 300,000
Replacement cost	1,100,000

    What amount of gain should Ocean report as a separate component of income before extraordinary items?

    a. $1,030,000
    b. $ 780,000
    c. $ 730,000
    d. $0 (5/92, PI, #46, 2617)

44. A company's activities for year 2 included the following:

Gross sales	$3,600,000
Cost of goods sold	1,200,000
Selling and administrative expense	500,000
Adjustment for a prior-year understatement of amortization expense	59,000
Sales returns	34,000
Gain on sale of available-for-sale securities	8,000
Gain on disposal of a discontinued business segment	4,000
Unrealized gain on available-for-sale securities	2,000

    The company has a 30% effective income tax rate. What is the company's net income for year 2?

    a. $1,267,700
    b. $1,273,300
    c. $1,314,600
    d. $1,316,000 (R/11, FAR, #21, 9871)

45. On January 1, Brec Co. installed cabinets to display products in customers' stores. Brec expects to use these cabinets for five years. Brec's year-end multi-step income statement should include:

    a. One-fifth of the cabinet costs in cost of goods sold
    b. One-fifth of the cabinet costs in selling, general, and administrative expenses
    c. All of the cabinet costs in cost of goods sold
    d. All of the cabinet costs in selling, general, and administrative expenses (Editor, 9076)

46 Vane Co.'s trial balance of income statement accounts for the current year ended December 31 included the following:

	Debit	Credit
Sales		$575,000
Cost of sales	$ 240,000	
Administrative expenses	70,000	
Loss on sale of equipment	10,000	
Sales commissions	50,000	
Interest revenue		25,000
Freight out	15,000	
Loss on early retirement of LT debt	20,000	
Uncollectible accounts expense	15,000	
Totals	$ 420,000	$600,000

Vane's income tax rate is 30%. In Vane's year-end multiple-step income statement, What amount should Vane report as income after income taxes from continuing operations?

a. $126,000
b. $129,500
c. $140,000
d. $147,000 (5/94, FAR, #10, 4825)

47. In Dart Co.'s year 2 single-step income statement, as prepared by Dart's controller, the section titled "Revenues" consisted of the following:

Sales	$250,000
Purchase discounts	3,000
Recovery of accounts written off	10,000

In its year 2 single-step income statement, what amount should Dart report as total revenues?

a. $250,000
b. $253,000
c. $260,000
d. $263,000 (R/10, FAR, #2, 9302)

48. The senior accountant for Carlton Co., a public company with a complex capital structure, has just finished preparing Carlton's income statement for the current fiscal year. While reviewing the income statement, Carlton's finance director noticed that the earnings per share data has been omitted. What changes will have to be made to Carlton's income statement as a result of the omission of the earnings per share data?

    a. No changes will have to be made to Carlton's income statement. The income statement is complete without the earnings per share data.
    b. Carlton's income statement will have to be revised to include the earnings per share data.
    c. Carlton's income statement will only have to be revised to include the earnings per share data if Carlton's market capitalization is greater than $5,000,000.
    d. Carlton's income statement will only have to be revised to include the earnings per share data if Carlton's net income for the past two years was greater than $5,000,000. (R/10, FAR, #38, 9338)

49. Earnings per share data should be reported in the financial statements for

	Discontinued operations	An extraordinary item	
a.	Yes	No	
b.	Yes	Yes	
c.	No	Yes	
d.	No	No	(11/91, Theory, #16, amended, 2524)

50. Jen Co. had 200,000 shares of common stock and 20,000 shares of 10%, $100 par value cumulative preferred stock. No dividends on common stock were declared during the year. Net income was $2,000,000. What was Jen's basic earnings per share?

a. $ 9.00
b. $ 9.09
c. $10.00
d. $11.11 (R/07, FAR, #2, 8323)

51. During the current year, Comma Co. had outstanding: 25,000 shares of common stock, 8,000 shares of $20 par, 10% cumulative preferred stock, and 3,000 bonds that are $1,000 par and 9% convertible. The bonds were originally issued at par, and each bond was convertible into 30 shares of common stock. During the year, net income was $200,000, no dividends were declared, and the tax rate was 30%. What amount was Comma's basic earnings per share for the current year?

a. $3.38
b. $7.36
c. $7.55
d. $8.00 (R/05, FAR, #48, 7792)

52. In computing the weighted-average number of shares outstanding during the year, which of the following midyear events must be treated as if it had occurred at the beginning of the year?

a. Declaration and distribution of stock dividend
b. Purchase of treasury stock
c. Sale of additional common stock
d. Sale of preferred convertible stock (5/98, FAR, #5, 6608)

53. The following information pertains to Ceil Co., a company whose common stock trades in a public market:

Shares outstanding at 1/1	100,000
Stock dividend at 3/31	24,000
Stock issuance at 6/30	5,000

What is the weighted-average number of shares Ceil should use to calculate its basic earnings per share for the year ended December 31?

a. 120,500
b. 123,000
c. 126,500
d. 129,000 (R/07, FAR, #32, 8353)

54. Dilutive stock options would generally be used in the calculation of

	Basic earnings per share	Diluted earnings per share	
a.	No	No	
b.	No	Yes	
c.	Yes	Yes	
d.	Yes	No	(11/88, Theory, #33, amended, 9041)

55. A firm has basic earnings per share of $1.29. If the tax rate is 30%, which of the following securities would be dilutive?

    a. Cumulative 8%, $50 par preferred stock
    b. Ten percent convertible bonds, issued at par, with each $1,000 bond convertible into 20 shares of common stock
    c. Seven percent convertible bonds, issued at par, with each $1,000 bond convertible into 40 shares of common stock
    d. Six percent, $100 par cumulative convertible preferred stock, issued at par, with each preferred share convertible into four shares of common stock (R/10, FAR, #13, 9313)

56. The following information is relevant to the computation of Chan Co.'s earnings per share to be disclosed on Chan's income statement for the year ending December 31:

    - Net income for 2002 is $600,000.
    - $5,000,000 face value 10-year convertible bonds outstanding on January 1. The bonds were issued four years ago at a discount which is being amortized in the amount of $20,000 per year. The stated rate of interest on the bonds is 9%, and the bonds were issued to yield 10%. Each $1,000 bond is convertible into 20 shares of Chan's common stock.
    - Chan's corporate income tax rate is 25%.
    - Chan has no preferred stock outstanding, and no other convertible securities.

    What amount should be used as the numerator in the fraction used to compute Chan's diluted earnings per share assuming that the bonds are dilutive securities?

    a. $ 130,000
    b. $ 247,500
    c. $ 952,500
    d. $1,070,000 (R/08, FAR, #41, 8596)

57. Ian Co. is calculating earnings per share amounts for inclusion in the Ian's annual report to shareholders. Ian has obtained the following information from the controller's office as well as shareholder services:

Net income from January 1 to December 31	$125,000
Number of outstanding shares:	
January 1 to March 31	15,000
April 1 to May 31	12,500
June 1 to December 31	17,000

    In addition, Ian has issued 10,000 incentive stock options with an exercise price of $30 to its employees and a year-end market price of $25 per share. What amount is Ian's diluted earnings per share for the year ended December 31?

    a. $4.63
    b. $4.85
    c. $7.35
    d. $7.94 (R/09, FAR, #26, 8776)

58. When a full set of general-purpose financial statements are presented, comprehensive income and its components should

    a. Appear as a part of discontinued operations and extraordinary items
    b. Be reported net of related income tax effect, in total and individually
    c. Appear in a supplemental schedule in the notes to the financial statements
    d. Be displayed in a financial statement that has the same prominence as other financial statements (R/99, FAR, #1, 6770)

59. What is the purpose of reporting comprehensive income?

    a. To summarize all changes in equity from nonowner sources
    b. To reconcile the difference between net income and cash flows provided from operating activities
    c. To provide a consolidation of the income of the firm's segments
    d. To provide information for each segment of the business (R/11, FAR, #23, 9873)

60. A company reports the following information as of December 31:

Sales revenue	$800,000
Cost of goods sold	600,000
Operating expenses	90,000
Unrealized holding gain on available-for-sale securities, net of tax	30,000

    What amount should the company report as comprehensive income as of December 31?

    a. $ 30,000
    b. $110,000
    c. $140,000
    d. $200,000 (R/09, FAR, #9, 8759)

61. Which of the following is included in other comprehensive income?

    a. Unrealized holding gains and losses on trading securities
    b. Unrealized holding gains and losses that result from a debt security being transferred into the held-to-maturity category from the available-for-sale category
    c. Foreign currency translation adjustments
    d. The difference between the accumulated benefit obligation and the fair value of pension plan assets (R/10, FAR, #27, 9327)

62. In general, an enterprise preparing interim financial statements should

    a. Defer recognition of seasonal revenue
    b. Disregard permanent decreases in the market value of its inventory
    c. Allocate revenues and expenses evenly over the quarters, regardless of when they actually occurred
    d. Use the same accounting principles followed in preparing its latest annual financial statements (R/05, FAR, #10, 7754)

63. Bard Co., a calendar-year corporation, reported income before income tax expense of $10,000 and income tax expense of $1,500 in its interim income statement for the first quarter of the year. Bard had income before income tax expense of $20,000 for the second quarter and an estimated effective annual rate of 25%. What amount should Bard report as income tax expense in its interim income statement for the second quarter?

    a. $3,500
    b. $5,000
    c. $6,000
    d. $7,500 (R/10, FAR, #18, 9318)

64. How are discontinued operations and extraordinary items that occur at midyear initially reported?

    a. Disclosed only in the notes to the year-end financial statements
    b. Included in net income and disclosed in the notes to the year-end financial statements
    c. Included in net income and disclosed in the notes to interim financial statements
    d. Disclosed only in the notes to interim financial statements (R/10, FAR, #42, 9342)

65. Due to a decline in market price in the second quarter, Petal Co. incurred an inventory loss. The market price is expected to return to previous levels by the end of the year. At the end of the year the decline had not reversed. When should the loss be reported in Petal's interim income statements?

    a. Ratably over the second, third, and fourth quarters
    b. Ratably over the third and fourth quarters
    c. In the second quarter only
    d. In the fourth quarter only (5/93, Theory, #21, 9078)

66. On January 16, Tree Co. paid $60,000 in property taxes on its factory for the current calendar year. On April 2, Tree paid $240,000 for unanticipated major repairs to its factory equipment. The repairs will benefit operations for the remainder of the calendar year. What amount of these expenses should Tree include in its third quarter interim financial statements for the three months ended September 30?

    a. $0
    b. $15,000
    c. $75,000
    d. $95,000 (R/08, FAR, #44, 8599)

67. During the first quarter of the current year, Tech Co. had income before taxes of $200,000, and its effective income tax rate was 15%. Tech's previous year effective annual income tax rate was 30%, but Tech expects its current year effective annual income tax rate to be 25%. In its first quarter interim income statement, what amount of income tax expense should Tech report?

    a. $0
    b. $30,000
    c. $50,000
    d. $60,000 (5/93, PII, #17, amended, 4125)

Problem 12-2 SIMULATION: Accounting Classifications

On January 1 of year 5, Columbo Co. hired a new controller. During the year, the controller, working closely with Columbo's president and outside accountants, made changes in existing accounting policies, instituted new accounting policies, and corrected several errors from prior to year 5.

For each of the items listed below, select a classification from List A and the general accounting treatment required to report the change from List B. Place the letter answers in the shaded boxes next to each item.

Item	List A	List B
1. Columbo manufactures customized equipment to customer specifications on a contract basis. Columbo changed its method of accounting for these long-term contracts from the completed contract method to the percentage of completion method because Columbo is now able to make reasonable estimates of future construction costs.		
2. Based on improved collection procedures, Columbo changed the percentage of credit sales used to determine the allowance for uncollectible accounts from 3% to 2%.		

List A—Type of Change		List B—General Accounting Treatment	
A.	Change in accounting principle	Y.	Retrospective application
B.	Change in accounting estimate	Z.	Prospective application
C.	Correction of an error in previously presented financial statements		
D.	Neither an accounting change nor an error correction		

List A represents possible classifications of these transactions as a change in accounting principle, a change in accounting estimate, correction of an error in previously presented financial statements, or neither an accounting change nor an error correction.

List B represents the general accounting treatment required for these transactions. These treatments are:

- Retrospective application—Apply the cumulative effect resulting from the accounting change or error correction to the carrying amounts of assets and liabilities, with an adjustment to opening balance of retained earnings, in the current financial statements. Also apply adjustments to the financial statements for each individual prior period presented.
- Prospective approach—Report current year and future financial statements on the new basis, but do not adjust beginning retained earnings or include the cumulative effect of the change in the current year income statements.

For each of the items listed below, in addition to selecting a classification from List A and the general accounting treatment from List B, a **third** response is required. For these items, determine the amount of the change, if any, ignoring income tax effects. Place the letter and numerical answers in the shaded spaces provided next to the item.

Item	List A	List B	Amount
3. Effective January 1, year 5, Columbo changed from average cost to FIFO to account for its inventory. Cost of goods sold under each method was as follows: Time Frame / Average cost / FIFO Years prior to year 4: $63,000 / $68,000 Year 4: 66,000 / 72,000			
4. In January of year 4, Columbo purchased a machine with a four-year life and no salvage value for $50,000. The machine was depreciated using the straight-line method. On December 30 of year 5, Columbo discovered that depreciation on the machine had been calculated using a 30% rate.			

(11/97, FAR, #2, amended, 6492t)

Problem 12-3 SIMULATION: Financial Statement Categories

Hake Co. is in the process of preparing its financial statements for December 31, year 9.

The items listed below represent various transactions that occurred during year 9.

The following **two** responses are required for each item:

- Compute the amount of gain, loss, or adjustment to be reported in the year-end financial statements. Disregard income taxes and round all computations to the nearest dollar.
- Select from the list below the financial statement category in which the gain, loss, or adjustment should be presented. A category may be used once, more than once, or not at all.

	Financial Statement Categories
A.	Income from continuing operations
B.	Extraordinary item
C.	Prior period adjustment to beginning retained earnings
D.	Other comprehensive income

Item	Amount	Category
1. On June 30, after paying the semiannual interest due and recording amortization of bond discount, Hake redeemed its 10-year, 10%, $500,000 par bonds at 103. The bonds, which had a carrying amount of $460,000 on January 1, had originally been issued to yield 12%. Hake uses the effective interest method of amortization, and had paid interest and recorded amortization on June 30. Compute the amount of gain or loss on redemption of the bonds and select the proper category.		
2. As of January 1, Hake decided to change the method of computing depreciation on its sole piece of equipment from the sum-of-the-years'-digits method to the straight-line method. The equipment, acquired in January of year 6 for $740,000, had an estimated life of six years and a salvage value of $50,000. Compute the amount of depreciation expense that should be reported in year 9 and select the proper category.		

<table>
<tr><td>3. In October, Hake paid $275,000 to a former employee to settle a lawsuit out of court. The lawsuit had been filed in year 8, and at December 31, year 8, Hake had recorded a liability from lawsuit based on legal counsel's estimate that the loss from the lawsuit would be between $100,000 and $500,000. Compute the amount of gain or loss from settlement of the lawsuit and select the proper category.</td><td></td><td></td></tr>
<tr><td>4. In November, Hake purchased two marketable equity securities, I and II, which it bought and held principally to sell in the near term, and, in fact, sold on February 28, year 10. Relevant data is as follows:
<table><tr><td>Cost</td><td colspan="2">Fair Value</td></tr><tr><td></td><td>12/31, yr 9</td><td>2/28, yr 10</td></tr><tr><td>I. $150,000</td><td>$175,000</td><td>$190,000</td></tr><tr><td>II. 275,000</td><td>225,000</td><td>260,000</td></tr></table>Compute the amount of holding gain or loss at December 31, year 9, and select the proper category.</td><td></td><td></td></tr>
<tr><td>5. During the year, Hake received $1,500,000 from its insurance company to cover losses suffered during a hurricane. This was the first hurricane ever to strike in Hake's area. The hurricane destroyed a warehouse with a carrying amount of $640,000, containing equipment with a carrying amount of $370,000 and inventory with a carrying amount of $785,000 and a fair value of $900,000. Compute the amount of gain or loss from the hurricane and select the proper category.</td><td></td><td></td></tr>
<tr><td>6. At December 31, Hake prepared the following worksheet summarizing the translation of its wholly owned foreign subsidiary's financial statements into dollars. Hake had purchased the foreign subsidiary for $324,000 on January 2. On that date, the carrying amounts of the subsidiary's assets and liabilities equaled their fair values. Compute the amount of the foreign currency translation adjustment and select the proper category.
<table><tr><td>Net assets at</td><td>Foreign currency amounts</td><td>Applicable exchange rates</td><td>Dollars</td></tr><tr><td>January 2, year 9 (date of purchase)</td><td>758,000</td><td>$0.39</td><td>$226,200</td></tr><tr><td>Net income, year 9</td><td>190,000</td><td>0.37</td><td>70,300</td></tr><tr><td>Net assets at December 31, year 9</td><td>770,000</td><td></td><td>296,500</td></tr><tr><td>Net assets at December 31, year 9</td><td>770,000</td><td>0.34</td><td>261,800</td></tr></table></td><td></td><td></td></tr>
</table>

(5/95, FAR, #3, amended, 5607t)

Problem 12-4 SIMULATION: Income Statement

The following condensed trial balance of Probe Co., a publicly held company, has been adjusted except for income tax expense.

	12/31 Yr 3 Balances Dr. (Cr.)	12/31 Yr 2 Balances Dr. (Cr.)	Net change Dr. (Cr.)
Cash	$ 473,000	$ 817,000	$ (344,000)
Accounts receivable, net	670,000	610,000	60,000
Property, plant, and equipment	1,070,000	995,000	75,000
Accumulated depreciation	(345,000)	(280,000)	(65,000)
Dividends payable	(25,000)	(10,000)	(15,000)
Income taxes payable	35,000	(150,000)	185,000
Deferred income tax liability	(42,000)	(42,000)	—
Bonds Payable	(500,000)	(1,000,000)	500,000
Unamortized premium on bonds	(71,000)	(150,000)	79,000
Common stock	(350,000)	(150,000)	(200,000)
Additional paid-in capital	(430,000)	(375,000)	(55,000)
Retained earnings	(185,000)	(265,000)	80,000
Sales	(2,420,000)		
Cost of sales	1,863,000		
Selling and administrative expenses	220,000		
Interest income	(14,000)		
Interest expense	46,000		
Depreciation	88,000		
Loss on sale of equipment	7,000		
Gain on flood damage	(90,000)		
	$ 0	$ 0	$ 300,000

Additional information:

- During year 3, equipment with an original cost of $50,000 was sold for cash and equipment costing $125,000 was purchased.
- Insurance reimbursements exceeded the carrying amount of a warehouse and its contents destroyed in a year 3 flood. The flood was the first recorded flood at the warehouse's location.
- Probe's tax payments during year 3 were debited to *Income Taxes Payable.* For the year ended December 31, year 2, Probe recorded a deferred income tax liability of $42,000 based on temporary differences of $120,000 and an enacted tax rate of 35%. Probe's year 3 financial statement income before income taxes was greater than its year 3 taxable income, due entirely to temporary differences, by $60,000. Probe's cumulative net taxable temporary differences at December 31, year 3, were $180,000. Probe's enacted tax rate for the current and future years is 30%.
- 60,000 shares of common stock, $2.50 par, were outstanding on December 31, year 2. Probe issued an additional 80,000 shares on April 1, year 3.
- There were no changes to retained earnings other than dividends declared.

Prepare Probe Co.'s multiple-step income statement for the year ended December 31, year 3, with earnings per share information and supporting computations for current and deferred income tax expense.

	A	B	C
1	Sales		$
2	Cost of sales		
3	Gross profit		
4	Selling and administrative expenses	$	
5	Depreciation		
6	Operating income		
7	Other income (expenses):		
8	Interest income		
9	Interest expense		
10	Loss on sale of equipment		
11	Income before income tax and extraordinary item		
12	Income tax:		
13	Current		
14	Deferred		
15	Income before extraordinary item		
16	Extraordinary item:		
17	Gain on flood damage, net of income taxes of $27,000		
18	Net income		$
19	Earnings per share:		
20	Earnings before extraordinary item		$
21	Extraordinary item		
22	Net income		$

(R/03, FAR, 3, amended, 9006)

Problem 12-5 SIMULATION: Research

Question: When shall a reporting entity change an accounting principle?

FASB ASC: [ ] - [ ] - [ ] - [ ]

(9125)

Problem 12-6 SIMULATION: Earnings Per Share

Dixon Corporation's capital structure is as follows:

	December 31	
	Year 5	Year 4
Outstanding shares of:		
Common stock	432,000	360,000
Nonconvertible preferred stock	12,000	12,000
10% convertible bonds	$1,200,000	$1,200,000

- On October 1, year 5, Dixon sold 72,000 additional shares of common stock.
- Net income for the year ended December 31, year 5, was $900,000.
- During year 5, Dixon paid dividends of $3.50 per share on its nonconvertible preferred stock.
- The 10% convertible bonds are convertible into 50 shares of common stock for each $1,000 bond.
- Unexercised stock options to purchase 25,000 shares of common stock at $25.50 per share were outstanding at the beginning and end of year 5. The average market price of Dixon's common stock was $37.50 per share during year 5. The market price was $34 per share at December 31, year 5.
- Warrants to purchase 10,000 shares of common stock at $39 per share were attached to the preferred stock at the time of issuance. The warrants, which expire on December 31, year 9, were outstanding at December 31, year 5.
- Dixon's effective income tax rate was 35% for year 4 and year 5.

Compute the number of shares which should be used for the computation of basic earnings per share for the year ended December 31, year 5.

Dates	Shares	Months outstanding	Weighted shares
January 1 – September 30, year 5		×	
October 1, sold additional shares			
October 1 – December 30, year 5		×	
Total shares			
Total months			÷
Weighted-average number of shares outstanding			

Compute the basic earnings per share for the year ended December 31, year 5.

Income:	
Net income	$
Deduct dividends paid on preferred stock	
Net income, adjusted	
Weighted-average number of shares outstanding	
Basic earnings per share (* Round earnings per share to the nearest penny)	$

Compute the number of shares which should be used for the computation of diluted earnings per share for the year ended December 31, year 5.

Weighted-average number of shares outstanding			
Common stock equivalents:			
From stock options:			
Shares that would be issued upon exercise of options			
Cash proceeds that would be realized upon exercise	$		
Treasury shares that could be purchased			
Common stock equivalents			
Amount included in EPS computation			
From warrants:			
Shares that would be issued upon exercise of warrants			
Cash proceeds that would be realized upon exercise	$		
Treasury shares that could be purchased			
Common stock equivalents			
Amount included in EPS computation			
Shares assumed to be issued upon conversion of convertible bonds			
Total number of shares for diluted EPS computation			

Compute the diluted earnings per share for the year ended December 31, year 5.

Income:	
Net income	$
Deduct dividends paid on preferred stock	
Add interest expense (net of income tax effect) on convertible bonds	
Net income, adjusted	$
Number of shares for diluted EPS computation	
Diluted earnings per share (*Round earnings per share to the nearest penny)	$

(9134)

Solution 12-1 MULTIPLE-CHOICE ANSWERS

Accounting Changes

1. (a) A change from the FIFO periodic inventory system to the weighted average periodic inventory system is a change in accounting principle. The cumulative effect of the change is the difference between the amount of retained earnings at the beginning of the period of change and the amount of retained earnings that would have been reported at that date if the new accounting principle had been retrospectively applied for all affected periods. Since Harvey is on a calendar year basis, the cumulative effect of the change in accounting principle should be determined as of January 1. (4208)

2. (a) A change in the method of inventory pricing is accounted for as a change in accounting principle. A change in depreciation method for long-lived, nonfinancial assets and a change in amortization should both be accounted for as a change in accounting estimate affected by a change in accounting principle. (89557)

3. (a) A change from LIFO to another inventory method is a change in accounting principle that should be reported by retrospectively applying the new method to prior periods and adjusting the beginning balance of *retained earnings.* The cumulative effect of the accounting change is not reported in the income statement. (3291)

4. (d) A change in accounting estimate affected by a change in accounting principle is accounted for as a change in estimate. A change in accounting estimate shall be accounted for in (a) the period of change if the change affects that period only or (b) the period of change and future periods if the change affects both. A change in accounting estimate shall not be accounted for by restating or retrospectively adjusting amounts reported in financial statements of prior periods or by reporting pro forma amounts for prior periods. Because the change was made at December 31, the total of both the $300,000 and $200,000 would be recorded. (6781)

5. (d) A change in accounting estimate is reported in the period of change and future periods if the change affects both. There are no pro forma reports for prior periods, and amounts reported in financial statements of prior periods are not restated. (8571)

6. (a) Changing the estimated useful life of a machine is considered a change in accounting estimate and accounted for in the current and subsequent periods. The machine had been depreciated a total of $20,000 thus far, 5 years at $4,000 per year ($48,000 / 12 years straight-line = $4,000 per year). The original amount of $48,000 less the $20,000 depreciated so far equals $28,000 worth of useful life. Extending the useful life three years means it now has 10 years of useful life left (12 years originally less the 5 years gone by plus 3 more years). So the depreciation expense is $2,800 ($28,000 / 10) per year. (8569)

7. (d) The change in the estimated useful life of the machine is a change in accounting estimate. The effect of a change in accounting estimate is accounted for prospectively in the period of change and future periods, because both are affected.

Accumulated depreciation, 1/1, year 4 [($264,000 – $0) / 8] × 3 years		$ 99,000
Cost of machine	$264,000	
Accumulated depreciation, 1/1, year 4	(99,000)	
Carrying amount of machine, 1/1, year 4	165,000	
Less: Estimated salvage value	(24,000)	
Depreciable base of machine, 1/1, year 4	141,000	
Divide by: Estimated remaining useful life (6 – 3)	/ 3	
Depreciation for year 4		47,000
Accumulated depreciation, 12/31, year 4		$146,000

(4429)

8. (a) A change in estimated warranty costs is an example of a change in accounting estimate. The effect of a change in accounting estimate should be accounted for as a component of income from continuing operations entirely in the period of change if it affects that period only. Therefore, the effect of the additional $10 of estimated warranty costs for the previous and current years should be reported in current year income from continuing operations since the change in accounting estimate affected only the current year. (4528)

9. (c) Examples of changes in estimates reflected in the financial statements do include warranty costs. (8074)

10. (d) Since the subsidiary was excluded from previous consolidations, its inclusion in the current year's consolidated financial statements results in a change in accounting principle in which the financial statements, in effect, are those of a different reporting entity. The change in the reporting entity should be reported by retrospective application to the financial statements of all prior periods presented to reflect the new reporting entity. (2733)

11. (d) An accounting change that results in a change of entity should be reported by retrospective application to the financial statements of all prior periods presented to show the financial information for the new reporting entity for all periods. (4854)

Prior Period Adjustments

12. (b) Raft Corp. should have only expensed the depreciation expense of $60,000 over the previous 3 years [($210,000 cost less $10,000 salvage value) / 10 years useful life = $20,000 per year]. The difference of what was expensed ($210,000) and what should have been expensed ($60,000) is $150,000. The $150,000 times the 30% tax rate = $45,000. Therefore, $150,000 less $45,000 equals a prior period adjustment of $105,000. (8570)

13. (d) The change from cash-basis accounting to accrual-basis accounting is a change from an accounting principle that is not generally accepted to one that is generally accepted, which is considered a correction of an error. Correction of an error requires a prior-period adjustment, which is done net of tax, by adjusting the beginning retained earnings. (8797)

14. (b) Errors in financial statements result from mathematical mistakes, mistakes in the application of accounting principles, or the oversight or misuse of facts that existed at the time the financial statements were prepared. For an item to be classified as a prior-period adjustment, it must be an item of profit or loss related to the correction of an error in the financial statements of a prior period. Any error in the financial statements of a prior period discovered subsequent to their issuance shall be reported as a prior-period adjustment by restating the prior-period financial statements. Prior-period adjustments bypass the income statement. They are instead reported net of their income tax effect in the statement of retained earnings as an adjustment to the beginning balance of retained earnings. A change in accounting estimate should be accounted for in the period of change if the change only affects that period, or in the current and subsequent periods, if the change affects both, as a component of income from continuing operations. A change in estimate does not require the presentation of pro forma effects of retroactive application or restatement of prior-period financial statements. A change in accounting principle results from the adoption of a generally accepted accounting principle (GAAP) different from the GAAP previously used for reporting purposes. The term "accounting principle" includes not only accounting principles but also the methods of applying them. Most changes in accounting principle should be recognized by including the cumulative effect of the change in the net income of the period of the change. (7787)

15. (c) Errors in financial statements result from mathematical mistakes, mistakes in the application of accounting principles, or the oversight or misuse of facts that existed at the time the financial statements were prepared. Errors that occur in one accounting period and are discovered in a subsequent accounting period are more involved: the cumulative effect of each error on periods prior to the period of discovery is calculated and recorded as a direct adjustment to the beginning balance of retained earnings. Errors that occur and are discovered in the same accounting period may be corrected by reversing the incorrect entry and recording the correct one or by directly correcting the account balances with a single entry. Foreign currency gains and losses and available for sale securities are reported in other comprehensive income. (7603)

16. (c) A change from the installment sale method to the point of sale method of income recognition represents a change in accounting principle (this assumes that the installment sale method was appropriately being used because of not being able to reasonably estimate the collectibility of the related receivables). The cumulative effect of changing to the new accounting principle should be reported as an adjustment to the beginning balance of retained earnings in the period of change. The recognition of the effect of the failure to provide for uncollectible accounts in the previous period represents the correction of an error of a prior period and should be reported as a prior-period adjustment by restating prior-period financial statements. A decrease in the estimated life of depreciable assets represents a change in accounting estimate which is to be accounted for prospectively (in the period of change and future periods) as a component of income from continuing operations. A change in depreciation method is to be accounted for as a change in estimate effected by change in accounting principle; therefore, the effect would be reported in the period of change as a component of income from continuing operations. (2533)

17. (a) A change in inventory valuation method is a change in accounting principle, and the cumulative effect of the change in accounting principle should be reported as an adjustment to the beginning balance of retained earnings in the period of change. It is not reported in the income statement. (5582)

18 (b) The correction of an error in financial statements of a prior period is reported as a prior-period adjustment by restating the prior-period financial statements. (4527)

19. (d) Since holiday pay for administrative employees is a period cost, it should have been expensed when incurred. Instead, it was misclassified and inventoried as manufacturing overhead. This error overstates both inventory and net income, thus overstating both current assets and stockholders' equity. The understatement of an accrued expense overstates net income and stockholders' equity and understates current liabilities. Misclassifying noncurrent note receivable principal as a current asset overstates current assets and understates noncurrent assets but does not affect stockholders' equity. The understatement of depreciation expense overstates noncurrent assets, net income, and stockholders' equity. (4205)

20. (b) The current assets portion of the balance sheet would be overstated because the inventory account is part of current assets. Gross profit would be overstated because an overstatement in inventory results in an understatement of cost of goods sold. The ending inventory is subtracted from goods available for sale to get cost of goods sold. If costs of goods sold is understated, then gross profit is overstated. (8322)

21. (b) The recognition of the effect of fully expensing the premiums for the three-year insurance policy represents the correction of an error of a prior period. The correction of the error should be reported as prior-period adjustment by restating the prior-period financial statements. The correction results in $40,000 (i.e., $60,000 × 2/3) less insurance expense recognized in the previous year. This increases the balance of retained earnings as corrected by the retrospective application. However, the balance of retained earnings cannot be increased by the full $40,000, because the reduction in insurance expense would have increased the amount of income tax expense previously recognized by $12,000 (i.e., $40,000 × 30%). Thus, the balance of retained earnings corrected by the retrospective application is increased by $28,000 (i.e., $40,000 - $12,000). Therefore, the amount to be reported as corrected by the retrospective application is $428,000 (i.e., $400,000 + $28,000). (4379)

22. (a) The change from the cash basis of accounting (not GAAP) to the accrual basis of accounting (GAAP) is a correction of an error. The correction of an error in prior-period income is reported as a prior-period adjustment by restating prior-period financial statements. (6125)

23. (d) Since Pear owns 40% of Cinn's common stock, Pear has the ability to exercise significant influence over Cinn by virtue of its investment and should account for its investment in Cinn by the equity method. Therefore, Pear's $40,000 equity in Cinn's earnings is properly included in Pear's current year income before taxes. Under the equity method, the dividends received from Cinn reduce the carrying amount of the investment; they do not affect the amount of investment income that Pear recognizes. So, the $8,000 of dividends received from Cinn is erroneously included in current year income, before taxes are subtracted to correct that figure. The arithmetical errors in depreciation of prior years represents a correction of errors of prior periods. The correction of the errors should be reported as a prior-period adjustment by restating the prior-period financial statements. So, the $35,000 of arithmetical errors in depreciation of prior years that Pear had inadvertently subtracted from current year income before taxes are added back to correct that figure.

Income before taxes, before adjustment	$125,000	
Less: Dividends received from equity method investee	(8,000)	
Add: Arithmetical errors in depreciation of prior years	35,000	
Corrected income before taxes	$152,000	(4047)

Continuing Operations

24. (a) All regular items of income and expense, including items that are unusual or infrequently occurring, are included in the determination of net income. Income from discontinued operations and extraordinary items are reported separately from the results of continuing operations. (89551)

25. (d) The results from discontinued operations cannot be included in the revenues section of the single-step income statement. The results from discontinued operations is reported separately below income from continuing operations.

Net sales revenue	$187,000	
Interest revenue	10,200	
Gain on sale of equipment	4,700	
Total revenues reported in income from continuing operations	$201,900	(1115)

26. (b) Revenues are only considered earned when the entity has accomplished substantially what it must do to be entitled to the revenues. Although Acme has sold 100,000 gallons of heating oil to Karn during year 1, Acme has only delivered 50,000 of these gallons to Karn during year 1. Therefore, Acme should only recognize revenue of $150,000 (i.e., 50,000 gallons × $3) during year 1 from this sale. (2608)

27. (a) The freight-in cost is an inventoriable cost. The freight-out cost and the sales representatives' salaries should both be reported as selling expenses in the year.

Accounting and legal fees	$ 25,000	
Officers' salaries	150,000	
Insurance	85,000	
General and administrative expenses	$260,000	(4421)

28. (b) To be classified as an extraordinary item, an event must be both unusual in nature and infrequent in occurrence, taking into account the environment in which the entity operates. The loss due to hurricane damage is stated to be unusual in nature; however, since this was the fourth hurricane loss sustained in a 5-year period at that location, it is not infrequent in occurrence. Thus, the $255,000 loss due to hurricane damage should be reported separately as a component of income from continuing operations. Though stated as unusual, Fuqua frequently retired bonds early when interest rates declined significantly. Thus, the $260,000 gain on the early extinguishment of debt should be reported as an ordinary item. The $350,000 loss on the disposal of the steel transportation segment should be reported below income from continuing operations in the discontinued operations section of the income statement. $260,000 - $255,000 = $5,000. (2438)

29. (c) Because the amount of the write-off of obsolete inventory is material, it should be reported separately from cost of goods sold in income from continuing operations.

Inventory, 12/31 previous year		$ 90,000
Add: Purchases		124,000
Goods available for sale		214,000
Less: Inventory, 12/31 current year	$30,000	
Write-off of obsolete inventory	34,000	(64,000)
Cost of goods sold, current year		$150,000

(4089)

30. (d) A transaction that is unusual in nature or infrequent in occurrence, but not both, is reported as a component of income from continuing operations. A transaction must be both unusual in nature and infrequent in occurrence to be classified as an extraordinary item. (5576)

31. (b) To be classified as an extraordinary item, an event must be both unusual in nature and infrequent in occurrence, taking into account the environment in which the entity operates. The loss due to hailstorms is stated to occur frequently; therefore, it should be reported in income from continuing operations. The full amount of a realized loss must be recognized in income when it occurs. (4223)

Discontinued Operations

32. (a) The results of discontinued operations are reported separately from continuing operations. Discontinued operations refers to the operations of a component of an entity that has been disposed of or is still operating, but is subject of a formal plan for disposal. A component of an entity is defined as a segment, reporting unit, or asset group whose operations and cash flows are clearly distinguished from the rest of the entity, operationally as well as for financial reporting purposes. The small appliance group clearly qualifies as a component of an entity. When Envoy classifies the small appliance group as held for sale it is in effect implementing a formal plan for disposal. (8333)

33. (c) The income statement of a business enterprise for current and prior periods shall report the results of operations of the component in discontinued operations in the period(s) in which they occur. (6121)

34. (d) The operating results of a discontinued component are reported separately from results of continuing operations. Results of the discontinued operations are reported as discontinued operations in the period in which they occur. (6122)

35. (b) Discontinued operations refers to the operations of a component of an entity that has been disposed of or is still operating, but is the subject of a formal plan for disposal. A component of an entity is a segment, reporting unit, or asset group (not a part of a line of business) whose operations and cash flows are clearly distinguished from the rest of the entity, operationally as well as for financial reporting purposes. (9857)

36. (c) The income statement of a business enterprise for current and prior periods shall report the results of operations of the component in discontinued operations in the period(s) in which they occur. (5580)

37. (a) The results of discontinued operations are reported separately from continuing operations. Discontinued operations refers to the operations of a component of an entity that has been disposed of or is still operating, but is subject of a formal plan for disposal. A component of an entity is defined as a segment, reporting unit, or asset group whose operations and cash flows are clearly distinguished from the rest of the entity, operationally as well as for financial reporting purposes. The after-tax net loss on the disposal of the division is: (1 – .30) × 200,000 = $140,000.

The entry to record the sale is as follows:

Cash	800,000	
Accounts payable	600,000	
Mortgage payable	1,100,000	
Loss on disposal	200,000	
Building, net		2,000,000
Inventory		500,000
Accounts Receivable		200,000

(9866)

Extraordinary Items

38. (a) The format for the presentation of the income statement begins with a section for income from continuing operations, is followed by a section for discontinued operations, and then a section for extraordinary items. The sum of these three sections results in net income. Comprehensive income includes all changes to equity during a period except those resulting from investments by and distributions to owners. Comprehensive income is the sum of net income and other comprehensive income. (8365)

39. (b) An early extinguishment of debt must meet the same criteria as other events to be deemed extraordinary. There is no indication that this event is extraordinary for Gold. Gains or losses from the sale of long-term investments are reported as income from continuing operations. (6123)

40. (c) The loss due to the earthquake qualifies as an extraordinary item because it is **both** unusual in nature and infrequent in occurrence. An extraordinary item should be presented separately on the income statement, net of related income tax.

Loss not covered by insurance	$ 700,000	
Less: Tax benefit ($700,000 × 0.40)	(280,000)	
Extraordinary item, net of tax	$ 420,000	(6477)

41. (a) Gains or losses on disposal of a segment of a business and gains or losses from exchange or translation of foreign currencies, including those relating to major devaluations and revaluations, should not be reported as extraordinary items. To be classified as an extraordinary item, the item must be both unusual in nature and infrequent in occurrence, taking into account the environment in which the entity operates. The loss due to hurricane damage should be reported as an extraordinary item since the hurricane was the first ever to strike in Midway's area. Since the loss realized on the damage to the equipment and the gain realized on the destruction of the building are a direct result of the hurricane, they are considered to be extraordinary.

Pretax loss on damaged equipment		$ 800,000	
Proceeds from insurance company	$1,000,000		
Carrying amount of building	(300,000)		
Less: Pretax gain on destroyed building		(700,000)	
Extraordinary loss before income taxes		$ 100,000	(4098)

42. (a) Gains on disposal of a business segment and foreign currency translations are in most cases considered normal events and transactions affecting operations. For an occurrence of an underlying event or transaction to be classified as extraordinary it must meet both of the following criteria: 1) unusual in nature in that it possesses a high degree of abnormality and be of the type clearly unrelated to, or incidentally related to, the ordinary and typical activities of the entity, taking into account the environment in which the entity operates and 2) infrequent in occurrence in that it be of a type that would not reasonably be expected to recur in the foreseeable future, taking into account the environment in which the entity operates. The scenario does not indicate anything that would classify the gains as extraordinary. (8755)

Income Statement Format

43. (c) A gain or loss on the involuntary conversion (e.g., casualty, condemnation, theft) of a nonmonetary asset is recognized in income even if the proceeds received as a result of the involuntary conversion are reinvested in a replacement nonmonetary asset. The warehouse was destroyed in a severe winter storm, which occur approximately every four years. Since the occurrence of such storms is not infrequent, the gain on the involuntary conversion is reported as a separate component of income from continuing operations.

Insurance proceeds ($1,100,000 – $50,000)		$1,050,000	
Carrying amount at conversion date	$300,000		
Add: Dismantling cost	20,000		
Amount to determine gain		(320,000)	
Gain recognized on involuntary conversion		$ 730,000	(2617)

44. (c) The $2,000 unrealized holding gain for AFS is included in other comprehensive income, not the income statement. The prior period adjustment is reported as an adjustment to the beginning balance of retained earnings, net of their income tax effect, not in the income statement. All other items listed would in included in the computation of net income, as follows:

Sales		$ 3,600,000
Less Sales Returns		(34,000)
Cost of sale	$ 1,200,000	
Selling and administrative expenses	500,000	(1,700,000)
Gain on sale of available-for-sale securities		8,000
Gain on disposal of a discontinued business segment		4,000
Income before income taxes		$ 1,878,000
Income taxes		(563,400)
Income from continuing operations after taxes		$ 1,314,600

(9871)

45. (b) The cabinets are expected to provide benefits over five years; hence, they meet the definition of an asset (probable future economic benefits). The cabinets are used in the selling function; therefore, the expired portion of the cabinet costs should be classified as a selling expense and not as part of cost of goods sold. (9076)

46. (a) Gains and losses from the early retirement of debt are not assumed to be extraordinary.

Sales		$ 575,000
Interest revenue		25,000
Cost of sales	$ 240,000	
Administrative expenses	70,000	
Sales commissions	50,000	
Freight out	15,000	
Uncollectible accounts expense	15,000	
Loss on sale of equipment	10,000	
Loss on early retirement of debt	20,000	(420,000)
Income from continuing operations before taxes		180,000
Income taxes (30%)		(54,000)
Income from continuing op.		$ 126,000

(4825)

47. (a) A single-step income statement does not set forth various intermediate levels of income like a multiple-step format. In a single-step format revenues are grouped under one classification while expenses are grouped under another classification. Sales should be reported net of any returns and allowances and Dart should report total revenues of $250,000. Purchase discounts have nothing to do with sales revenue, and if it were a sales discount, sales are recorded net of any discounts. Recovery of accounts written off would merely adjust the allowance for uncollectible accounts and not affect total revenues. (9302)

48. (b) Earnings per share (EPS) data is required to be presented for all periods for which an income statement or summary of earnings is presented. An entity with a complex capital structure is required to present both basic and diluted EPS for income from continuing operations and for net income on the face of the income statement. There amount of market capitalization or net income makes no difference. (9338)

49. (b) Earnings per share amounts should be reported on the face of the income statement or in the notes to the financial statements for a discontinued operation or an extraordinary item. (2524)

Earnings Per Share

50. (a) Basic earnings per share (EPS) is computed by dividing income available to common stockholders by the weighted-average number of shares outstanding during the period. The income available for common stockholders is net income, less any adjustments for senior claims. Senior claims include preferred stock. The total adjustment for preferred dividends is $200,000 (20,000 shares × $100 par value × 10%). The net income of $2,000,000 less preferred dividends earned of $200,000 leaves $1,800,000 of income available to common stockholders. The $1,800,000 divided by 200,000 shares provides basic EPS of $9.00. (8323)

51. (b) To arrive at basic EPS, the income available to common stockholders is divided by the number of common shares outstanding. Income available to common stockholders is net income less dividends on preferred stock (not net of tax).

Net income	$200,000
Less: Dividends on preferred stock [(8,000 × $20) × 10%]	(16,000)
Income available to common s/h	184,000
Divide: Common shares outstanding	/25,000
Basic EPS	$ 7.36

$3.38 would be the diluted EPS if the bonds had been converted. $7.55 would be the EPS if dividends on preferred stock was added net of tax to net income for the year. EPS of $8 does not adjust for dividends paid on the cumulative preferred stock. (7792)

52. (a) In computing the weighted-average number of shares outstanding, stock dividends, stock splits, and reverse stock splits are reflected retroactively, because they change the total number of shares outstanding but not the proportionate shares outstanding. The purchase of treasury stock, the sale of additional common stock and preferred convertible stock affect the total number of shares and the proportionate shares outstanding. These shares participate in earnings for only the time the stock is outstanding. (6608)

53. (c) Basic earnings per share (EPS) is computed by dividing income available to common stockholders by the weighted-average number of shares outstanding during the period. Shares issued during the period and shares reacquired during the period are weighted for the portion of the period they were outstanding. Stock dividends, stock splits, and reverse stock splits change the total number of shares outstanding but not the proportionate shares outstanding. For this reason, stock dividends, stock splits, and reverse stock splits are reflected retroactively for all periods presented. The weighted-average number of shares used to calculate basic EPS is 126,500. It's comprised of 100% of the 100,000 shares that have been outstanding all year, 100% of the 24,000 stock dividend (reflected retroactively), and 50% of the 5,000 shares issued at 6/30 (outstanding 50% of the year). (8353)

54. (b) Stock options should be used in the calculation of diluted EPS if the effect is dilutive (their inclusion has the effect of decreasing the EPS amount or increasing the loss per share amount otherwise computed). (9041)

55. (c) A security is dilutive if the inclusion of the security in the computation of earnings per share (EPS) results in a smaller EPS or increases loss per share. Categories of potentially dilutive securities include (1) convertible securities where the if-converted method is used, (2) options, warrants, and their equivalents where the treasury stock method is used, and (3) contingently issuable shares. The cumulative 8%, $50 par preferred stock does not qualify as a potentially dilutive security so it must be one of the other three possible choices. To decide which security would be dilutive you need to look at the per share effect of each. The ten percent convertible bonds would increase the amount of income available to common stockholders by $70 [$1,000 bond × 10% = $100, then – ($100 × 30% tax effect)] and the weighted average number of shares outstanding by 20 shares for each bond converted. The $70 / 20 = a per share effect of $3.50. The seven percent convertible bonds would increase the amount of income available to common stockholders by $49 ($1,000 bond × 10% = $70, then – ($70 × 30% tax effect)]) and the weighted average number of shares outstanding by 40 shares for each bond converted. The $49 / 40 = a per share effect of $1.225. The six percent convertible preferred stock would increase the amount of income available to common stockholders by $6 ($100 bond × 6%) and the weighted average number of shares outstanding by 4 shares for each preferred share converted. The $6 / 4 = a per share effect of $1.50. Convertible preferred stock adjustments do not have tax effects. Only the seven percent convertible bonds have a dilutive effect because their per share effect o $1.225 is less than the basic EPS of $1.29. (9313)

56. (c) Diluted earnings per share is the amount of earnings for the period available to each share of common stock outstanding during the reporting period and to each share that would have been outstanding assuming the issuance of common shares for all dilutive potential common shares outstanding during the reporting period. Earnings per share calculations have the income available to common shareholders in the numerator and the weighted-average number of shares outstanding in the denominator. The income available to common stockholders starts with the net income of $600,000. There is no preferred stock outstanding, so there is no need to worry about any deduction for preferred dividends. The if-converted method is applied to the convertible bonds in assuming they are dilutive. The conversion means the company would not have the interest expense for the debt and it should be added back to income to arrive at income available to common stockholders. The interest for the year would be the face value of the bonds times the stated interest rate plus any amortization of the discount. [($5,000,000 × 9%) + $20,000 = $470,000] Taking in the effect of taxes would reduce the interest expense by 25%. [25% × $470,000 = $117,500; $470,000 – $117,500 = $352,500] Adding the $352,500 interest expense to the $600,000 net income results in $952,500 of income available to common stockholders in the numerator of the diluted earnings per share computation. (8596)

57. (d) Calculating diluted earnings per share (EPS) is a two-step process. The first step is to compute basic EPS and the second is to determine the per share effect of each dilutive security. Basic EPS is computed by dividing income available to shareholders (IAC) by the weighted-average number of shares outstanding during the period.

Shares Outstanding	Months Outstanding	Weighted Average
15,000	3/12	3,750
12,500	2/12	2,083.333
17,000	7/12	9,916.667
Totals	12/12	15,750

Basic EPS would be $125,000 / 15,750 = $7.94. The incentive stock options are potentially dilutive securities. A security is only dilutive if the inclusion of the security in the computation of EPS results in a smaller EPS or increases the loss per share. If the average market price is higher than the exercise price the options are dilutive. If the average market price is less than the exercise price the options are anti-dilutive. Since the market price of $25 is less than the exercise price of $30 these options are anti-dilutive and have no per share effect. The diluted EPS is the same as basic EPS. (8776)

Comprehensive Income

58. (d) Comprehensive income and all items that are required to be recognized as components of comprehensive income should be reported in a financial statement that is displayed with the same prominence as other financial statements. Discontinued operations and extraordinary items are components of the income statement, reported after income from continuing operations and before net income. If comprehensive income is reported in the same statement as net income, other comprehensive income (OCI) and comprehensive income are reported after net income. An entity may display components of OCI in either net-of-tax basis or summary net-of-tax basis. Comprehensive income must be shown on the face of one of the statements, not just in the notes to the financial statements. (6770)

59. (a) Comprehensive income is the change in equity (net assets) of a business entity as a result of transactions and other events from nonowner sources. It includes all changes in equity during a period except those resulting from investments by owners and distributions to owners. Comprehensive income is divided into net income and other comprehensive income. (9873)

60. (c) Comprehensive income includes all changes in equity during a period except those resulting from investments by owners and distributions to owners. Comprehensive income is divided into net income and other comprehensive income (OCI). It would include $110,000 from net income ($800,000 – $600,000 – $90,000) and $30,000 from OCI (the unrealized holding gain on available-for-sale securities). (8759)

61. (c) An entity must classify items of other comprehensive income (OCI) by their nature. One of the classifications is foreign currency which includes foreign currency translation adjustments and gains and losses on foreign currency transactions that are designated as and are effective as, economic hedges of a net investment in a foreign entity. Items included in OCI include unrealized holding gains and losses on available-for-sale (AFS) securities, not trading securities; unrealized holding gains and losses that result from a debt security being transferred into the AFS category from the held-to-maturity (HTM) category; not HTM category to AFS category; and, for pensions, the amounts of net gain or loss, net prior service cost or credit, and net transition asset or obligation that are expected to be recognized as components of net periodic benefit cost; not the difference between the accumulated benefit obligation and the fair value of pension plan assets. (9327)

Interim Reporting

62. (d) Each interim period should be viewed as an integral part of an annual period and not as a separate, independent period. In order to maintain comparability between interim and annual financial statements, the principles and practices used to prepare the latest annual financial statements should also be used to prepare the interim statements. Revenue should be recognized as earned during an interim period on the same basis as followed for recognition of income for the full year. Costs and expenses associated directly with products sold or services rendered for annual reporting purposes generally should be similarly treated for interim reporting purposes. (7754)

63. (c) Each interim period should be viewed as an integral part of an annual period and not as a separate, independent period. At the end of each interim period, an entity should make its best estimate of the effective tax rate expected to be applicable for the full fiscal year. This estimated tax rate should be used to provide for income taxes on a current year-to-date basis. Bard had an estimated effective tax rate of 25% and current year-to-date income of $30,000. $30,000 × .25 = $7,500 for current year-to-date income tax expense. Bard reported $1,500 income tax expense already in the first quarter. $7,500 – $1,500 = $6,000 income tax expense should be reported for the second quarter. (9318)

64. (c) Discontinued operations and extraordinary items should be included in the determination of net income for the interim period in which they occur. Discontinued operations and extraordinary items should not be prorated among interim periods. Disposal of a segment of a business (discontinued operations) and extra-ordinary, unusual, or infrequently occurring items are disclosed in the notes to interim financial statements. (9342)

65. (d) Inventory losses from market declines, which can reasonably be expected to be restored in the fiscal year, need not be recognized at the interim date since no loss is expected to be incurred in the fiscal year. Therefore, since Petal expected the market price to return to previous levels by the end of the year, Petal would not have recognized the inventory loss until the fourth quarter, when the decline had not reversed. (9078)

66. (d) For interim financial reporting, costs and expenses other than product costs should be charged to income in interim periods as incurred or be allocated among interim periods based on an estimate of time expired, benefit received, or activity associated with the periods. The $60,000 in property taxes is for the entire calendar year and would be allocated evenly as $15,000 of expenses for each quarter. The $240,000 for major repairs happened on April 2 and will benefit operations for just the remainder of the year. The $240,000 divided by the three remaining quarters equals $80,000 in expenses for each of those three quarters. The $15,000 plus $80,000 equals $95,000 in expenses to be reported in the third quarter of the interim financial statements for the three months ended September 30. (8599)

67. (c) At the end of each interim period, a company should make its best estimate of the effective tax rate expected to be applicable for the full fiscal year. The rate so determined should be used in providing for income taxes on a current year-to-date basis. The amount of income tax expense that Tech should report in its current year first quarter interim income statement is $50,000—Tech's current year first quarter's income before taxes of $200,000 multiplied by the 25% effective annual income tax rate Tech expects for the current year. (4125)

PERFORMANCE BY SUBTOPICS

Each category below parallels a subtopic covered in Chapter 12. Record the number and percentage of questions you correctly answered in each subtopic area.

Accounting Changes

Question #	Correct √
1	
2	
3	
4	
5	
6	
7	
8	
9	
10	
11	
# Questions	11
# Correct	______
% Correct	______

Prior-Period Adjustments

Question #	Correct √
12	
13	
14	
15	
16	
17	
18	
19	
20	
21	
22	
23	
# Questions	12
# Correct	______
% Correct	______

Continuing Operations

Question #	Correct √
24	
25	
26	
27	
28	
29	
30	
31	
# Questions	8
# Correct	______
% Correct	______

Discontinued Operations

Question #	Correct √
32	
33	
34	
35	
36	
37	
# Questions	6
# Correct	______
% Correct	______

Extraordinary Items

Question #	Correct √
38	
39	
40	
41	
42	
# Questions	5
# Correct	______
% Correct	______

Income Statement Format

Question #	Correct √
43	
44	
45	
46	
47	
48	
49	
# Questions	7
# Correct	______
% Correct	______

Earnings Per Share

Question #	Correct √
50	
51	
52	
53	
54	
55	
56	
57	
# Questions	8
# Correct	______
% Correct	______

Comprehensive Income

Question #	Correct √
58	
59	
60	
61	
# Questions	4
# Correct	______
% Correct	______

Interim Reporting

Question #	Correct √
62	
63	
64	
65	
66	
67	
# Questions	6
# Correct	______
% Correct	______

Solution 12-2 SIMULATION ANSWER: Accounting Classifications

1. A, Y Changing from the completed contract method to the percentage of completion method of accounting for long-term contracts is a change in accounting principle. An entity shall report a change in accounting principle through retrospective application of the new accounting principle to all prior periods, unless it is impracticable to do so.

2. B, Z Changing the percentage of credit sales used to determine the allowance for uncollectible accounts from 3% to 2% is a change in accounting estimate and applied prospectively. The allowance for uncollectible accounts and the related expense for current and future financial statements should be reported on the new basis, and beginning retained earnings should not be adjusted.

3. A, Y, $11,000

Changing from the average cost to FIFO methods of inventory is a change in accounting principle. An entity shall report a change in accounting principle through retrospective application of the new accounting principle to all prior periods, unless it is impracticable to do so. The offsetting adjustment required is the difference between the amount of retained earnings at the beginning of the period of a change and the amount of retained earnings that would have been reported at that date if the new accounting principle had been applied retroactively for all prior periods that would have been affected.

	FIFO	Average Cost	Difference
Prior to year 4	$68,000	$63,000	$ 5,000
Year 4	72,000	66,000	6,000
Cumulative effect			$11,000

4. C, Y, $2,500

The error in the calculation of depreciation resulted in the need for a correction of the error in previously presented financial statements. This requires a prior-period adjustment, which is retrospective application.

Incorrect depreciation calculation ($50,000 × 30%)	$ 15,000
Less: Correct depreciation calculation ($50,000 × 25%)	(12,500)
Adjustment to beginning retained earnings	$ 2,500

Solution 12-3 SIMULATION ANSWER: Financial Statement Categories

1. $52,400 loss, A

Gains or losses on the extinguishment of debt are reported as components of continuing operations. The bonds are redeemed for $515,000 ($500,000 × 1.03). The amortization of the bond discount at June 30, year 9, must be added to the carrying amount of the bonds on January 1, year 10, before the gain or loss on extinguishment may be computed.

$460,000 × 0.12 × 6/12	$ 27,600
$500,000 × 0.10 × 6/12	(25,000)
Amortization of discount	$ 2,600

The carrying value at the time of redemption was $462,600 ($460,000 + $2,600). The excess of the price paid to redeem the bonds ($515,000) over the carrying value ($462,600) is the loss on the bond redemption ($52,400).

2. $65,714, A

The SYD depreciation was computed as follows.

Year 6	($740,000 – $50,000) × 6/21	$197,143
Year 7	($740,000 – $50,000) × 5/21	$164,286
Year 8	($740,000 – $50,000) × 4/21	$131,429
		$492,858

The $740,000 cost less accumulated depreciation of $492,858 less salvage of $50,000 = $197,142 to be depreciated over the three remaining years. $197,142 ÷ 3 = $65,714.

3. $175,000 loss, A

In year 8, the loss was probable according to the attorney with an estimated loss between $100,000 and $500,000. Since no amount within the range is more probable than any other amount, the lowest amount of the loss in the estimated range should be recorded. Therefore, $100,000 would have been accrued in the year 8 financial statements. When the actual loss realized was $275,000 in year 9, the accrued liability of $100,000 would be debited, a current period loss (reported in income from continuing operations) for $175,000 would be debited, and a credit would be made to cash for $275,000.

4. $25,000 loss, A

The holding loss to be reported in income from continuing operations at December 31, year 9, is $25,000. The cost of securities I and II is $425,000 ($150,000 + $275,000), while the fair value at December 31, year 9, is $400,000 ($175,000 + $225,000). The difference between the two is the holding loss. The securities are classified as trading because they were bought and held to sell in the near term. Since the securities are trading securities, the holding loss is reported in income from continuing operations.

5. $295,000 loss, B

Book value of the warehouse	$ 640,000
Book value of the equipment	370,000
Book value of the inventory	785,000
Total loss	1,795,000
Less: Insurance proceeds	(1,500,000)
Extraordinary loss	$ 295,000

The loss is extraordinary because of the unusual and infrequent (this is the first hurricane ever to hit this area) nature of the event causing the loss. The book value of the inventory is used in the computation of the loss.

6. $34,700 loss, D

The adjustment due to translation is the difference between the net assets at December 31, year 9, after the remeasurement ($296,500) and the net assets at December 31, year 9, translated for the exchange rate at the balance sheet date ($261,800), or $34,700. The foreign currency translation adjustment should be reported in other comprehensive income. Any gain or loss on the *remeasurement* of the financial statements should be reflected in the income statement.

Solution 12-4 SIMULATION ANSWER: Income Statement

	A	B	C
1	Sales		$2,420,000
2	Cost of sales		1,863,000
3	Gross profit		557,000
4	Selling and administrative expenses	$220,000	
5	Depreciation	88,000	308,000
6	Operating income		249,000
7	Other income (expenses):		
8	Interest income	14,000	
9	Interest expense	(46,000)	
10	Loss on sale of equipment	(7,000)	(39,000)
11	Income before income tax and extraordinary item		210,000
12	Income tax:		
13	Current	45,000	
14	Deferred	12,000	57,000
15	Income before extraordinary item		153,000
16	Extraordinary item:		
17	Gain on flood damage, net of income taxes of $27,000		63,000
18	Net income		**$ 216,000**
19	Earnings per share:		
20	Earnings before extraordinary item		$ 1.275
21	Extraordinary item		.525
22	Net income		**$ 1.800**

Explanations

C1 Sales given in scenario information.

C2 Cost of sales given in scenario information.

C3 Sales less cost of sales ($2,420,000 – $1,863,000).

B4 Selling and administrative expenses given in scenario information.

B5 Depreciation given in scenario information.

C5 Total selling & administrative expenses plus depreciation ($220,000 + $88,000).

C6 Gross profit less expenses ($557,000 – $308,000).

B8 Interest income given in scenario information.

B9 Interest expense given in scenario information.

B10 Loss on sale of equipment given in scenario information.

C10 Total other income less expenses ($14,000 – $46,000 – $7,000).

C11 Sum of operating income and other income (expenses) ($249,000 – $39,000).

B13 Current income tax.

Income before income tax and extraordinary item	$210,000
Differences between financial statement and taxable income	(60,000)
Income subject to tax	150,000
Income tax rate	× 30%
Income tax excluding extraordinary item (current income tax expense)	$ 45,000

B14. Deferred income tax.

Cumulative temporary differences—12/31 year 3	$180,000
Income tax rate	× 30%
Deferred tax liability—12/31 year 3	54,000
Deferred tax liability—12/31 year 2	(42,000)
Deferred income tax expense for year 3	$ 12,000

C14 Total income taxes (current plus deferred) ($45,000 + $12,000).

C15 Income less taxes ($210,000 – $57,000).

C17 Gain on flood damage less taxes ($90,000 × .7).

C18 Income adjusted for extraordinary items ($153,000 + $63,000).

C20 Earnings per share before extraordinary item.

Earnings per share:	
January thru March 60,000 × 3 months	180,000
April thru December 140,000 × 9 months	1,260,000
Total	1,440,000
	/ 12
Weighted average number of shares outstanding for year 3	120,000
Income before extraordinary item	$ 153,000
Earnings per share ($153,000 / 120,000)	$ 1.275

C21 Extraordinary item per share: Extraordinary item divided by weighted average number of shares outstanding for year 3 ($63,000 / 120,000).

C22 Net income per share: Net income divided by weighted average number of shares outstanding for year 3 ($216,000 / 120,000)

Solution 12-5 SIMULATION ANSWER: Research

FASB Accounting Standards Codification

FASB ASC: 250 - 10 - 45 - 2

45-2 A reporting entity shall change an accounting principle only if either of the following apply:

a. The change is required by a newly issued Codification update.

b. The entity can justify the use of an allowable alternative accounting principle on the basis that is preferable.

Solution 12-6 SIMULATION ANSWER: Earnings Per Share

Number of Shares for Computation of Basic Earnings Per Share

	A	B	C	
Dates	**Shares**	**Months outstanding**	**Weighted shares**	
January 1 – September 30, year 5	360,000	× 9	3,240,000	[1]
October 1, sold additional shares	72,000			[2]
October 1 – December 30, year 5	432,000	× 3	1,296,000	[3]
Total shares			4,536,000	[4]
Total months			÷ 12	[5]
Weighted-average number of shares outstanding			**378,000**	[6]

1 A. Number of shares given in scenario; 360,000

1 B. 1/1 through 9/30 = 9 months

1 C. 360,000 × 9 = 3,240,000

2 A. Number of shares given in scenario; 72,000

3 A. Number of shares given in scenario; 432,000

3 B. 10/1 through 12/31 = 3 months

3 C. 432,000 × 3 = 1,296,000

4 C. 3,240,000 + 1,296,000 = 4,536,000

5 C. Total months in the period (year 5)

6 C. 4,536,000 / 12 = 378,000

Computation of Basic Earnings Per Share

Income:		
Net income	$900,000	[7]
Deduct dividends paid on preferred stock	(42,000)	[8]
Net income, adjusted	$858,000	[9]
Weighted-average number of shares outstanding	÷378,000	[10]
Basic earnings per share	**$ 2.27**	[11]

7. Net income given in scenario; $900,000
8. 12,000 shares × $3.50 = $42,000
9. $900,000 – $42,000 = $858,000
10. Number of shares from previous computation
11. $858,000 / 378,000 = $2.27

Number of Shares for Computation of Diluted Earnings Per Share

Weighted-average number of shares outstanding			378,000	[12]
Common stock equivalents:				
From stock options:				
Shares that would be issued upon exercise of options		25,000		[13]
Cash proceeds that would be realized upon exercise	$637,500			[14]
Treasury shares that could be purchased		17,000		[15]
Common stock equivalents—dilutive		8,000		[16]
Amount included in EPS computation			8,000	[17]
From warrants:				
Shares that would be issued upon exercise of warrants		10,000		[18]
Cash proceeds that would be realized upon exercise	$390,000			[19]
Treasury shares that could be purchased		10,400		[20]
Common stock equivalents—antidilutive		(400)		[21]
Amount included in EPS computation			0	[22]
Shares assumed to be issued upon conversion of convertible bonds			60,000	[23]
Total number of shares for diluted EPS computation			**446,000**	[24]

12. Number of shares from previous computation
13. Number of shares given in scenario; 72,000
14. 25,000 shares × $25.50 option price = $637,500
15. $637,500 / $37.50 avg. market price = 17,000 (The $34 market price at December 31, year 5 is not used because it's lower than the $37.50 average market price for year 5)
16. 25,000 – 17,000 = 8,000
17. The 8,000 shares are included because they are dilutive
18. Number of shares given in scenario; 10,000
19. 10,000 shares × $39 exercise price = $390,000
20. $390,000 / $37.50 avg. market price = 10,400 (The $34 market price at December 31, year 5, is not used because it's lower than the $37.50 average market price for year 5)
21. 10,000 – 10,400 = (400)
22. The shares are not included because they are antidilutive
23. $1,200,000 / $1,000 = 1,200 bonds; 1,200 bonds × 50 convertible shares = 60,000
24. 378,000 + 8,000 + 0 + 60,000 = 446,000

Computation of Diluted Earnings Per Share

Income:		
Net income	$ 900,000	[25]
Deduct dividends paid on preferred stock	(42,000)	[26]
Add interest expense (net of income tax effect) on convertible bonds	78,000	[27]
Net income, adjusted	$ 936,000	[28]
Number of shares for diluted EPS computation	÷ 446,000	[29]
Diluted earnings per share	**$ 2.10**	[30]

25. Net income given in scenario; $900,000

26. 12,000 shares × $3.50 = $42,000

27. $1,200,000 × 10% × (1.0 – .35 tax rate) = $78,000

28. $900,000 – $42,000 + $78,000 = $936,000

29. Total number of shares for diluted EPS computation from previous computation

30. $936,000 / 446,250 = $2.10

Boolean Search Skills

The three Boolean operators are OR, AND, and NOT. Boolean operators can be combined to refine searches. For example, the following parameters would find information on letters to a client's attorney inquiring about litigation, claims, and assessments: (attorney OR lawyer) AND (letter OR inquiry). If you get too many or too few results from a search, refine your search parameters until you find what you need. The exam doesn't limit candidates from repeating searches with refined parameters. A review of Boolean operators is provided here.

OR Operator

A search using "accounting OR auditing" will find all documents containing either the word "accounting" or the word "auditing." OR typically is used to search for terms that are used as synonyms, such as "management" and "client." As more terms are combined in an OR search, more documents are included in the results.

AND Operator

A search using "accounting AND auditing" will find all documents containing both the word "accounting" and the word "auditing." All other things being equal, a search using AND typically will find fewer documents than a search using OR, but more than a search using NOT. As more terms are combined in an AND search, fewer documents are included in the results.

NOT Operator

A search using "accounting NOT auditing" will find all documents containing the word "accounting" except those that also contain the word "auditing." All other things being equal, a search using NOT typically will find the fewest documents. As more terms are combined in a NOT search, fewer documents are included in the results.

CHAPTER 13

REPORTING: SPECIAL AREAS

CHAPTER 13

REPORTING: SPECIAL AREAS

I. Subsequent Events

A. Overview

Subsequent events are events or transactions that occur after the balance sheet date but before the financial statements are issued or are available to be issued.

1. **Evaluation Period** An entity that is either an SEC filer or a conduit bond obligor for conduit debt securities traded in public markets is required to evaluate subsequent events through the date financial statements are issued. For all other entities, including private companies and not-for-profit organizations, management will need to evaluate subsequent events through the date the financial statements are available to be issued.

2. **Financial Statement Issuance** Financial statements are considered issued when they are widely distributed to shareholders and other financial statement users for general use and reliance in a form or format that complies with GAAP. Financial statements are considered available to be issued when they are complete in form and format that complies with GAAP and all approvals necessary for issuance have been obtained.

3. **Other GAAP** If an event or transaction is within the scope of other applicable GAAP, then an entity shall follow the guidance in that applicable GAAP. Examples include: accounting for uncertainty in income taxes; earnings per share; and accounting for contingencies.

B. Recognized Events

An entity shall recognize in the financial statements the effects of all subsequent events that provide additional evidence about conditions that existed at the date of the balance sheet, including the estimates inherent in the process of preparing financial statements. The following are examples of recognized subsequent events:

1. **Litigation** If the events that gave rise to litigation had taken place before the balance sheet date and that litigation is settled, after the balance sheet date but before the financial statements are issued or are available to be issued, for an amount different from the liability recorded in the accounts, then the settlement amount should be considered in estimating the amount of liability recognized in the financial statements at the balance sheet date.

2. **Realization of Assets** Subsequent events affecting the realization of assets, such as receivables and inventories or the settlement of estimated liabilities, should be recognized in the financial statements when those events represent the culmination of conditions that existed over a relatively long period of time. For example, a loss on an uncollectible trade account receivable as a result of a customer's deteriorating financial condition leading to bankruptcy after the balance sheet date but before the financial statements are issued or are available to be issued ordinarily will be indicative of conditions existing at the balance sheet date. Thus, the effects of the customer's bankruptcy filing shall be considered in determining the amount of uncollectible trade accounts receivable recognized in the financial statements at the balance sheet date.

C. **Nonrecognized Events**
An entity shall **not** recognize subsequent events that provide evidence about conditions that did not exist at the date of the balance sheet but arose after the balance sheet date but before financial statements are issued or are available to be issued. The following are examples of nonrecognized subsequent events:

1. **Sale of Bonds or Capital Stock** Sale of a bond or capital stock issued after the balance sheet date but before financial statements are issued or are available to be issued.

2. **Business Combination** A business combination that occurs after the balance sheet date but before financial statements are issued or are available to be issued.

3. **Litigation** Settlement of litigation when the event giving rise to the claim took place after the balance sheet date but before financial statements are issued or are available to be issued.

4. **Loss of Plant or Inventories** Loss of plant or inventories as a result of fire or natural disaster that occurred after the balance sheet date but before financial statements are issued or are available to be issued.

5. **Losses on Receivables** Losses on receivables resulting from conditions (such as a customer's major casualty) arising after the balance sheet date but before financial statements are issued or are available to be issued.

6. **Changes in Fair Value** Changes in the fair value of assets or liabilities (financial or nonfinancial) or foreign exchange rates after the balance sheet date but before financial statements are issued or are available to be issued.

7. **Commitments or Contingent Liabilities** Entering into significant commitments or contingent liabilities, for example, by issuing significant guarantees after the balance sheet date but before financial statements are issued or are available to be issued.

D. **Disclosures**
An entity shall provide disclosures as follows.

1. **Evaluation Period** If an entity is not an SEC filer, then the entity shall disclose the date through which subsequent events have been evaluated, as well as whether that date is the date the financial statements were issued or the date the financial statements were available to be issued.

   Disclosure requirements associated with the date through which management has evaluated subsequent events, along with the basis for that date being the appropriate date, need to be implemented in full-disclosure financial statements without regard to whether the statements have been audited, reviewed, or compiled. Further, the disclosure needs to be made without regard to whether the statements are prepared using GAAP, or another comprehensive basis of accounting (OCBOA). Essentially, the disclosure is required regardless of the level of service performed on the financial statements, and regardless of the basis of accounting used in preparing the statements.

2. **Nonrecognized Subsequent Events** Some nonrecognized subsequent events may be of such a nature that they must be disclosed to keep the financial statements from being misleading. For such events an entity shall disclose the nature of the event and an estimate of its financial effect or a statement that such an estimate cannot be made. An entity also shall consider supplementing the historical financial statements with pro forma financial data.

3. **Revised/Reissued Financial Statements** Revised financial statements include restatements (i.e., correction of an error) and retroactive application of accounting principles. After the original issuance of the financial statements, events or transactions may have occurred that require disclosure in the revised financial statements to keep them from being misleading. An entity shall not recognize events occurring between the time the financial statements were issued or available to be issued and the time the financial statements were revised unless the adjustment is required by GAAP or regulatory requirements. Unless the entity is an SEC filer, the entity shall disclose the date through which subsequent events have been evaluated in the revised financial statements.

II. Related-Party Disclosures

A. Introduction

Related-party transactions require special consideration because related parties may be difficult to identify and related-party transactions may pose significant "substance over form" issues. Transactions between related parties include transactions among: (1) a parent company and its subsidiaries; (2) subsidiaries of a common parent; (3) an enterprise and its principal owners, management, or members of their immediate families; and (4) affiliates. Examples of related-party transactions include

1. Sales, purchases, and transfers of realty and personal property

2. Services received or furnished (e.g., accounting, management, engineering, and legal services)

3. Use of property and equipment by lease or otherwise

4. Borrowings, lendings, and guarantees

5. Intercompany billings based on allocations of common costs

6. Filings of consolidated tax returns

B. Considerations

Transactions involving related parties cannot be presumed to be carried out on an arm's-length basis, as the requisite conditions of competitive, free-market dealings may not exist.

1. **Representations** Representations about transactions with related parties, if made, should not imply that the related-party transactions were consummated on terms equivalent to those that prevail in arm's-length transactions unless such representations can be substantiated.

2. **Control Relationships** If the reporting enterprise and one or more other enterprises are under common ownership or management control and the existence of that control could result in operating results or financial position of the reporting enterprise significantly different from those that would have been obtained if the enterprises were autonomous, the nature of the control relationship should be disclosed even though there are no transactions between the enterprises.

3. **Significant Unusual Transactions** Some related party transactions may require special consideration. A series of sales may be executed with an undisclosed related party that individually are insignificant but in total are material.

   Significant, unusual, or highly complex transactions resulting in revenue recognition that are executed with customers who are not related parties similarly require special consideration because they also may pose "substance over form" questions and may involve the collusion of the entity and the customer in a fraudulent revenue recognition scheme.

C. Disclosures

Undisclosed related-party transactions may be used to fraudulently inflate earnings. Examples include the recording of sales of the same inventory back and forth among affiliated entities that exchange checks periodically to "freshen" the receivables, and sales with commitments to repurchase that, if known, would preclude recognition of revenue.

Financial statements should include disclosures of material related-party transactions, other than compensation arrangements, expense allowances, and other similar items in the ordinary course of business. However, disclosure of transactions that are eliminated in the preparation of consolidated or combined financial statements (e.g., intercompany sales) is not required. The disclosures should include the following:

1. **Nature** The nature of the relationship(s) involved.

2. **Description** A description of the transactions, including transactions to which no amounts or nominal amounts were ascribed, for each of the periods for which income statements are presented, and such other information necessary to an understanding of the effects of the transactions on the financial statements.

3. **Dollar Amounts of Transactions** The dollar amounts of transactions for each of the periods for which income statements are presented and the effects of any change in the method of establishing the terms from that used in the preceding period.

4. **Amounts Due From or Due To** Amounts due from or to related parties as of the date of each balance sheet presented and, if not otherwise apparent, the terms and manner of settlement.

III. Development Stage Enterprises

A. Introduction

An enterprise is in the development stage if "substantially all" of its efforts are devoted to establishing a new business and either principal operations have not begun or principal operations have begun, but revenue produced is insignificant. A development stage enterprise will typically be devoting most of its efforts to activities such as financial planning; raising capital; exploring for or developing natural resources; research and development; establishing sources of supply; acquiring property, plant, or equipment for other operating assets such as mineral rights; recruiting and training personnel, developing markets, and starting up production.

B. Presentation

Financial statements issued by a development stage enterprise should be presented in conformity with generally accepted accounting principles (GAAP) applicable to established operating enterprises.

1. **Special Accounting Practices** Special accounting practices that are based on a distinctive accounting for development stage enterprises are not acceptable.

2. **GAAP** Generally accepted accounting principles that apply to established operating enterprises govern the recognition of revenue by a development stage enterprise and determine whether a cost incurred by a development stage enterprise is to be charged to expense when incurred or is to be capitalized or deferred. Accordingly, capitalization or deferral of costs shall be subject to the same assessment of recoverability that would be applicable in an established operating enterprise. Costs of start-up activities, including organization costs, should be expensed as incurred.

3. **Differences** Financial reporting by a development stage enterprise differs from financial reporting for an established operating enterprise in regard only to the additional information.

C. **Required Statements**
The additional information to be included is as follows.

1. **Balance Sheet** Cumulative net losses are reported as part of stockholders' equity using terms such as "deficit accumulated during the development stage."

2. **Income Statement** Includes cumulative expenses and revenues from the inception of the development stage. Information on other comprehensive income, if any, may be combined with the income statement or presented separately.

3. **Statement of Cash Flows** Includes cumulative amounts from date of inception.

4. **Statement of Stockholders' Equity** Includes the following from the date of inception:

    a. Number of shares, warrants, etc., issued and date of issuance.

    b. Dollar amounts received for shares, etc., of each issuance. Noncash consideration received must be assigned a dollar value and must indicate the nature of the consideration and the valuation basis used.

D. **Disclosures**
Financial statements of a development stage enterprise should be identified as such and shall include the nature of the activities in which the enterprise is engaged. The financial statements for the first fiscal year in which an enterprise is no longer considered to be in the development stage shall disclose that in prior years it had been in the development stage. If financial statements for prior years are presented for comparative purposes, the cumulative amounts and additional disclosures need not be shown.

IV. Operating Segments

A. **Management Approach Method**
General-purpose financial statements are required to include selected information reported on a single basis of segmentation using the management approach method. The management approach is based on the way that management organizes the segments within the enterprise for making operating decisions and assessing performance. The components are called *operating segments.* Consequently, the segments are evident from the structure of the enterprise's internal organization, and financial statement preparers should be able to provide the required information in a cost-effective and timely manner.

1. **Objectives** The objective is to provide information about an enterprise to help financial statement users better understand the enterprise's performance, better assess its prospects for future net cash flows, and make more informed judgments about the enterprise as a whole.

2. **Requirements** An enterprise is required to report a measure of segment profit or loss, segment assets and certain related items, but not segment cash flow or segment liabilities.

3. **Applicability** This applies to public business enterprises; it does not apply to nonpublic enterprises or not-for-profit organizations.

4. **Operating Segments** Operating segments have three characteristics. Not every part of an entity is necessarily part of an operating segment.

    a. An operating segment is a component of an enterprise with revenue producing (even if no revenue is yet earned) and expense incurring activities.

    b. The operating results of an operating segment are regularly reviewed by the entity's chief operating decision maker.

    c. Discrete financial information is available for an operating segment.

5. **Chief Operating Decision Maker** The chief operating decision maker is identified by the function of allocating resources and assessing the performance of a segment, not necessarily by title. The chief operating decision maker may be, for example, the chief executive officer, the president, or the chief operating officer. It may be one person or it may be a group, such as the Chairman and the Board of Directors.

6. **Segment Manager** Generally, an operating segment has a segment manager directly accountable to the chief operating decision maker. The term segment manager is also identified by function, not necessarily by a specific title. The chief operating decision maker in some cases may also be the segment manager for an operating segment. The same person may be a segment manager for more than one operating segment.

7. **Reportable Segments** Reportable segments include operating segments that exceed the quantitative thresholds. Operating segments that do not meet any of the quantitative thresholds may be considered reportable, and separately disclosed, if management believes information about the segment would be useful to readers of financial statements. A reportable segment may also result from aggregating two or more segments in accordance with the aggregation criteria. Exhibit 1 summarizes identifying reportable operating segments. An enterprise shall report separately information about an operating segment that meets any of the following quantitative thresholds:

   a. Its reported revenue, including both sales to external customers and intersegment sales or transfers, is 10 percent or more of the combined revenue, internal and external, of all operating segments.

   b. The absolute amount of its reported profit or loss is 10 percent or more of the greater, in absolute amount, of (1) the combined reported profit of all operating segments that did not report a loss or (2) the combined reported loss of all operating segments that did report a loss.

   c. Its assets are 10 percent or more of the combined assets of all operating segments.

B. **Aggregation Criteria**

Operating segments often exhibit similar long-term financial performance if they have similar economic characteristics. Two or more operating segments may be aggregated into a single operating segment if aggregation is consistent with the basic principles of GAAP, if the segments have similar economic characteristics, and if the segments are similar in each of the following areas:

1. The nature of the products and services

2. The nature of the production processes

3. The type or class of customer for their products and services

4. The methods used to distribute their products or provide their services

5. The nature of the regulatory environment, if applicable; for example, banking, insurance, or public utilities

Exhibit 1 ▸ Diagram for Identifying Reportable Operating Segments

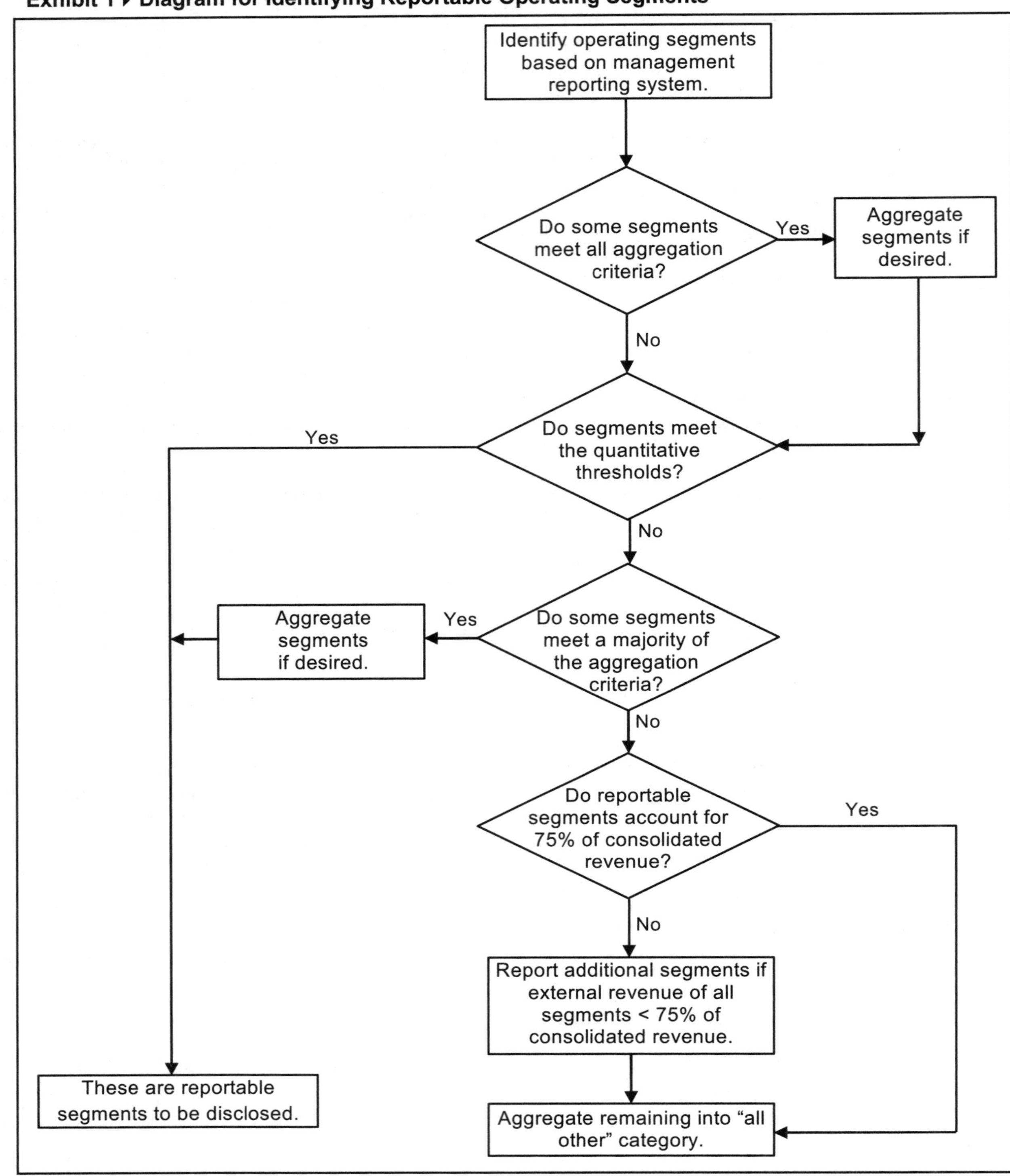

Example 1 ▸ Quantitative Thresholds

A, B, and C are operating segments of a public corporation. Pertinent information regarding sales, profit and loss, and assets of the three segments are given below.

	A	B	C	Combined	Elimination	Consolidated
Sales:						
Unaffiliated	$ 800	$ 20	$ 40	$ 860		$ 860
Intersegment	40	500		540	$(540)	
Total sales	$ 840	$ 520	$ 40	$1,400	$(540)	$ 860
Profit(loss)	$ 200	$(300)	$ 25	$ (75)		$ (75)
Assets	$1,200	$ 150	$400	$1,750		$1,750

Required: Determine which segments should be reported separately, based on the quantitative thresholds requirements.

Solution:

Revenue Test—10% of combined segment revenues equals $140 [10% × ($840 + $520 + $40)]; therefore, segments A and B meet the revenue requirement for segmental disclosure.

Profit(loss) Test—The absolute amount of combined reported losses of all segments having losses exceed the combined profits of the profitable segments (i.e., $300 exceeds $225). The reported profit of segment A ($200), and the absolute amount of loss of segment B ($300) is 10% or more of the absolute amount of combined reported loss of all operating segments ($300); therefore, segments A and B meet this test.

Assets Test—10% of combined assets equals $175 [10% × ($1,200 + $150 + $400]; therefore, segments A and C meet this test.

All three segments meet at least **one** of the quantitative thresholds criteria for reportable segments; consequently, segmental disclosure should be reported for three segments.

6. **Exceptions**

   a. **Combining Segments** An entity may combine information about operating segments not meeting the quantitative thresholds to produce a reportable segment only if the operating segments share a majority of the aggregation criteria.

   b. **Minimum Reportable Segments** If the total of external revenue reported by operating segments is less than 75 percent of total consolidated revenue, additional operating segments must be identified as reportable segments until at least 75 percent of total consolidated revenue is included in reportable segments.

   c. **"All Other" Category** Non-reportable business activities and operating segments are required to be combined and disclosed in an "all other" category separate from other reconciling items in the reconciliations. The revenue sources must be described.

   d. **Judgment** If management judges an operating segment to be of continuing significance even though it no longer meets the criteria for reportability, information about that segment should continue to be reported separately in the current period.

   e. **Restatement** Information from prior periods presented for comparative purposes must be restated to reflect the newly reportable segment as a separate segment, unless it is impracticable to do so, such as when the information is not available and the cost to develop the information would be excessive.

   f. **Practical Limit** There may be a practical limit to the number of reportable segments beyond which information may become overly detailed. No precise limit is set, but generally an enterprise should consider whether this limit has been reached as the number of reportable segments increases above 10.

C. **Disclosures**

1. **General** An enterprise must disclose the following general information.

   a. Factors used to identify reportable segments, such as differences in products and services, geographic areas, or regulatory environments.

   b. Types of products and services from which each reportable segment derives its revenues.

2. **Basis of Measurement**

   a. An enterprise shall report a measure of profit or loss and total assets for each reportable segment. These measures are generally based upon the measures as reported to, and used by, the chief operating decision maker, and may include revenues from external customers; revenues from transactions with other operating segments of the same enterprise; interest revenue; interest expense; depreciation, depletion, and amortization expense; unusual items; equity in the net income of investees accounted for by the equity method; income tax expense or benefit; extraordinary items; and significant other noncash items.

   b. An enterprise must report interest revenue separately from interest expense for each reportable segment unless a majority of the segment's revenues are from interest.

   c. If the specified amounts are included in the determination of segment assets reviewed by the chief operating decision maker, the enterprise is required to disclose the amount of investment in equity method investees, and total expenditures for additions to long-lived assets other than financial instruments, long-term customer relationships of a financial institution, mortgage and other servicing rights, deferred policy acquisition costs, and deferred tax assets.

   d. An enterprise must provide an explanation of the measurements used, at a minimum:

      (1) The basis of accounting for any transactions between reportable segments

      (2) The nature of any differences between the measurements applied to the reportable segments and the consolidated statements

      (3) The nature of any changes from prior periods in the measurement methods used

      (4) The nature and effect of any asymmetrical allocations to segments. For example, an enterprise might allocate depreciation expense to a segment without allocating the related depreciable assets to that segment.

3. **Reconciliations** An enterprise is required to report reconciliations of the totals of segment revenues, reported profit or loss, assets, and other significant items to corresponding enterprise amounts. All significant reconciling items must be separately identified and described.

4. **Interim Period Reporting** An enterprise is required to disclose information about each reportable segment in condensed financial statements of interim periods, including revenues from external customers, intersegment revenues, measures of segment profit or loss, material changes in total assets, descriptions of differences in measurement or segmentation, and a reconciliation of segments profit or loss to consolidated income.

5. **Enterprise-Wide Disclosures** If the following information is not provided as part of the segment information disclosed, it must also be disclosed.

   a. Revenues from external customers for each product and service or group of similar products and services unless it is impracticable to do.

   b. Revenues from external customers based on geographic area, including domestic revenues and foreign revenue.

c. Long-lived assets located in the enterprise's country of domicile, and located in foreign countries.

d. Information about major customers. Enterprises must disclose the total amount of revenues from each single customer that amounts to 10 percent or more of the enterprise's revenues and identify the segment(s) reporting the revenues. The identity of the customer need not be disclosed.

V. Foreign Operations

A. Introduction

The financial statements of separate entities within an enterprise, which may exist and operate in different economic and currency environments, are consolidated and presented as though they were the financial statements of a single enterprise. Because it is not possible to combine, add, or subtract measurements expressed in different currencies, it is necessary to translate into a single reporting currency those assets, liabilities, revenues, expenses, gains, and losses that are measured or denominated in a foreign currency. Accordingly, the translation of the financial statements of each component entity of an enterprise should accomplish the following objectives:

1. **Provide Information** Provide information that is generally compatible with the expected economic effects of a rate change on an enterprise's cash flows and equity.

2. **Reflect Financial Results** Reflect in consolidated statements the financial results and relationships of the individual consolidated entities as measured in their functional currencies in conformity with U.S. generally accepted accounting principles.

B. Functional Currency

The assets, liabilities, and operations of a foreign entity should be measured in its functional currency. An entity's functional currency is the currency of the primary economic environment in which the entity operates; normally, that is the currency of the environment in which an entity primarily generates and expends cash. An entity's functional currency is basically a matter of fact. In some cases, however, the nature of a foreign entity's operations is such that its functional currency is not clearly determinable.

Example 2 ▸ Functional Currency

Americana Inc., a U.S. company, owns 100 percent of the stock of Frenchie's, a self-contained subsidiary incorporated in the United Kingdom. Frenchie's records all its transactions in Pounds Sterling, even though the bulk of its operations are conducted in Germany (i.e., the Euro is the functional currency). In order to prepare its consolidated financial statements, Americana will first remeasure the Pound Sterling statements into Euros and then translate them into U.S. dollars.

1. **Determining Functional Currency** The functional currency of a foreign entity may be its local currency, the U.S. dollar, or another foreign currency.

   a. Where a foreign operation is relatively self-contained (i.e., most activities are performed independently of the parent company) and integrated within one country, the entity's functional currency will be the local currency. In this case, translation of financial statements from the functional currency into the parent's reporting currency (e.g., the U.S. dollar) will be required.

   b. Where the foreign operation is, in essence, an extension of the parent's U.S. operations (e.g., a sales branch that purchases all its inventory from the U.S. home office, in U.S. dollars), the functional currency will be the U.S. dollar.

      (1) If the foreign entity's books are kept in the local currency, then remeasurement into U.S. dollars will be required. A gain or loss from remeasurement will be included in the foreign entity's income from continuing operations.

(2) If the foreign entity keeps its books in U.S. dollars, then its trial balance can be directly incorporated into the reporting entity's financial statements. Transactions denominated in foreign currency will result in foreign currency gains and losses. The net gain (loss) will be the same as the remeasurement gain (loss). In other words, if the functional currency of the foreign entity is the U.S. dollar, the aggregate net gain or loss from exchange rate fluctuations will be the same whether the foreign entity keeps its books in the local currency or U.S. dollars.

c. A foreign entity may keep its books in the local currency (i.e., "recording currency"), yet have another foreign currency as functional currency. In this case, remeasuring of the recording currency statements into functional currency will be required.

d. Once the functional currency for a foreign entity is determined, that determination shall be used consistently unless significant changes in economic facts and circumstances indicate clearly that the functional currency has changed.

Exhibit 2 ▸ Functional Currency

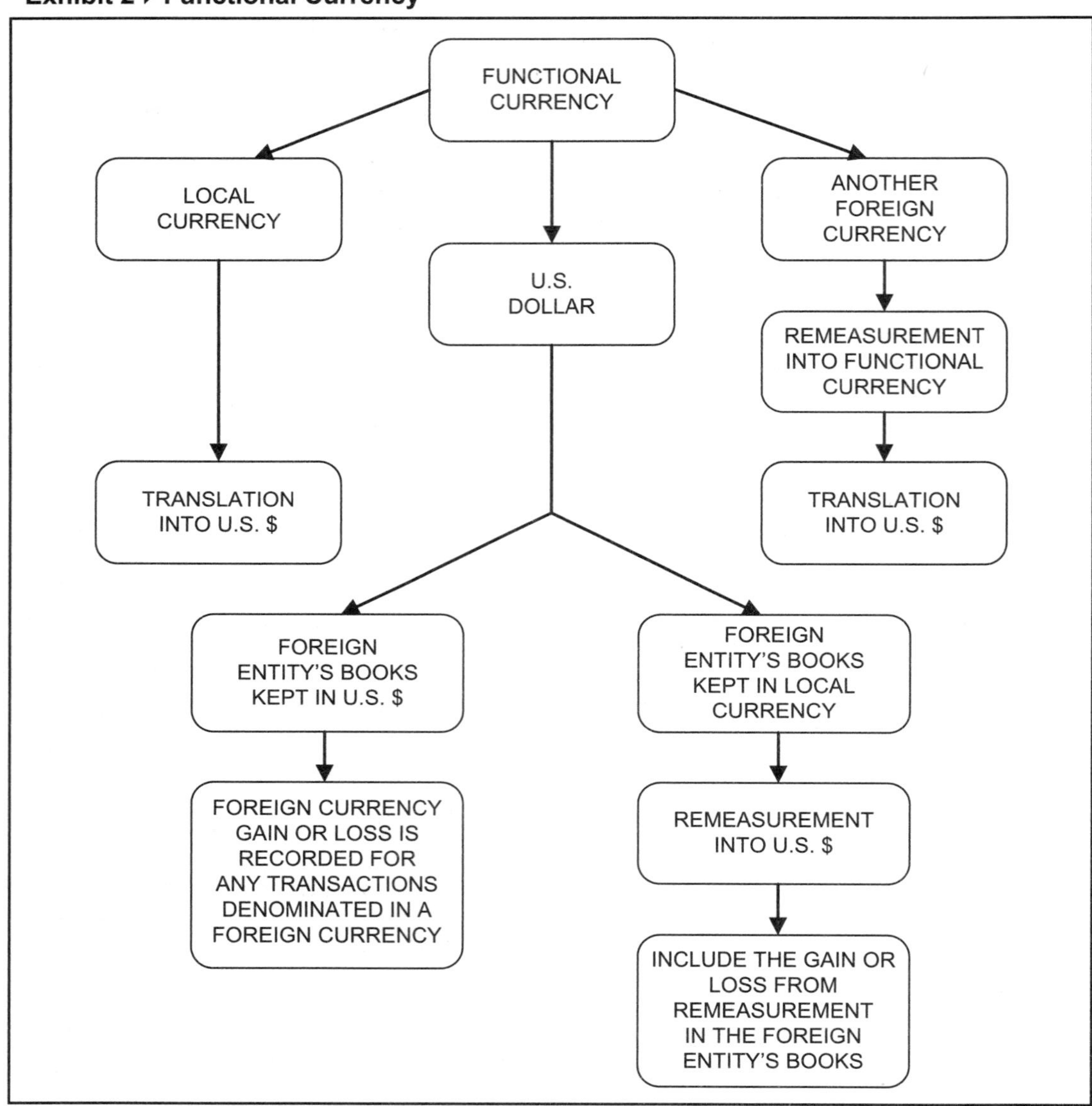

2. **Highly Inflationary Economies** Where a foreign country's cumulative inflation rate over the three-year period preceding the date of financial statements is approximately 100 percent or more, the local currency is not considered stable enough to be the functional currency. In this case, the reporting currency (e.g., the U.S. dollar) will be the functional currency, and **remeasurement** will be required.

3. **Economic Indicators** The following economic factors should be considered both individually and collectively when determining functional currency.

   a. **Cash Flow Indicators**

      (1) **Foreign** Cash flows related to the foreign entity's individual assets and liabilities are primarily in the foreign currency and do not directly impact the parent company's cash flows.

      (2) **Parent** Cash flows related to the foreign entity's individual assets and liabilities directly impact the parent's cash flows on a current basis and are readily available for remittance to the parent company.

   b. **Sales Price Indicators**

      (1) **Foreign** Sales prices for the foreign entity's products are not primarily responsive on a short-term basis to changes in exchange rates but are determined more by local competition or local government regulation.

      (2) **Parent** Sales prices for the foreign entity's products are primarily responsive on a short-term basis to changes in exchange rates; for example, sales prices are determined more by worldwide competition or by international prices.

   c. **Sales Market Indicators**

      (1) **Foreign** There is an active local sales market for the foreign entity's products, although there also might be significant amounts of exports.

      (2) **Parent** The sales market is mostly in the parent's country or sales contracts are denominated in the parent's currency.

   d. **Expense Indicators**

      (1) **Foreign** Labor, materials, and other costs for the foreign entity's products or services are primarily local costs, even though there also might be imports from other countries.

      (2) **Parent** Labor, materials, and other costs for the foreign entity's products or services, on a continuing basis, are primarily costs for components obtained from the country in which the parent company is located.

   e. **Financing Indicators**

      (1) **Foreign** Financing is primarily denominated in foreign currency, and funds generated by the foreign entity's operations are sufficient to service existing and normally expected debt obligations.

      (2) **Parent** Financing is primarily from parent or other dollar-denominated obligations, or funds generated by the foreign entity's operations are not sufficient to service existing and normally expected debt obligation without infusion of additional funds from the parent company. Infusion of additional funds from the parent company for expansion is not a factor, provided funds generated by the foreign entity's expanded operations are expected to be sufficient to service that additional financing.

f. **Intercompany Transactions & Arrangements Indicators**

(1) **Foreign** There is a low volume of intercompany transactions, and there is not an extensive interrelationship between the operations of the foreign entity and the parent company. However, the foreign entity's operations may rely on the parent's or affiliates' competitive advantages, such as patents and trademarks.

(2) **Parent** There is a high volume of intercompany transactions and there is an extensive interrelationship between the operations of the foreign entity and the parent company. Additionally, the parent's currency generally would be the functional currency if the foreign entity is a device or shell corporation for holding investments, obligations, intangible assets, etc., that could readily be carried on the parent's or an affiliate's books.

C. **Translation of Foreign Currency Statements**
Prior to translation, the foreign currency statements must be conformed to U.S. GAAP and be measured in the functional currency of the foreign entity (otherwise, remeasurement into the functional currency is required).

1. **Before Translation** If an entity does not maintain its books in its functional currency, remeasuring into the functional currency is required prior to translation into the reporting currency (i.e., the U.S. dollar). If the functional currency is the same as the reporting currency, remeasurement will eliminate the need for translation (i.e., the statements will be remeasured into U.S. dollars, and, thus, no translation will be required).

2. **Remeasurement Into Functional Currency** The remeasuring process should achieve the same result as if the books had been initially recorded in the functional currency.

a. This requires the remeasuring of certain accounts (nonmonetary items) at historical rates. All other accounts are remeasured at current rates.

b. The remeasuring process will result in exchange gains and losses. The net gain or loss from remeasurement should be recognized in income from continuing operations for the current period.

c. The following items should be remeasured at historical rates:

(1) Marketable securities carried at cost (equity securities and debt securities not intended to be held until maturity)

(2) Inventories carried at cost

(3) Prepaid expenses such as insurance, advertising, and rent

(4) Property, plant, and equipment (and its accumulated depreciation)

(5) Patents, trademarks, licenses, formulas, goodwill, and other intangible assets

(6) Common stock and preferred stock carried at issuance price

(7) Revenues and expenses related to nonmonetary items; for example: (a) Cost of goods sold; (b) Depreciation of property, plant, and equipment; and (c) Amortization of certain intangible items such as patents

Example 3 ▸ Remeasurement Into Functional Currency

Figueras S.A. is a Spanish sales subsidiary formed on January 1 of the current year, and is 100 percent owned by Americana Inc. Management has determined that Figueras S.A. is, in fact, a foreign extension of Americana's operations, and, thus, its functional currency is the U.S. dollar. The following additional information is available.

- No dividends were paid by Figueras S.A. during the year.
- Inventories are carried at weighted-average cost.
- Figueras' office is located in a building purchased on May 5.
- Figueras' trial balance (in Euros) is reproduced in column (1) of the trial balance.
- Exchange rate information for the year follows:

January 1	1 Euro	=	$1.00
May 5		=	.98
December 31		=	.90
Year's Average		=	.95

Based on the preceding information, Figueras' accounts have been remeasured as indicated in column (3) of the trial balance. The remeasured balance sheet and income statement are presented below.

Trial Balance [Dr. (Cr.)]

	(1) Euros	(2) Rate	(3) U.S. Dollars
Assets			
Cash	200,000 EUR	$ .90/EUR	$ 180,000
Inventory (w. avg. cost)	500,000	.95/EUR	475,000
Office building (net)	800,000	.98/EUR	784,000
Total assets	1,500,000		1,439,000
Liabilities			
Accounts payable	(300,000)	$ .90/EUR	(270,000)
Mortgage payable	(600,000)	.90/EUR	(540,000)
Total liabilities	(900,000)		(810,000)
Equity			
Common stock	(350,000)	$1.00/EUR	(350,000)
Retained earnings	0	*	0*
Total equity	(350,000)		(350,000)
Operations			
Sales	(700,000)	$ .95/EUR	(665,000)
Cost of goods sold	350,000	.95/EUR	332,500
General and administrative	100,000	.95/EUR	95,000
Exchange gain (to balance)	--		(41,500)
Total debits and credits	0 EUR		$ 0

* Because this was the first year of operations, the beginning RE balance is zero. Had the company been in operation for more than a year, the RE balance as remeasured at the end of the prior year would have been the amount entered in column (3).

Remeasured Balance Sheet

Assets		Liabilities	
Cash	$ 180,000	Accounts payable	$ 270,000
Inventory	475,000	Mortgage payable	540,000
Office building, net	784,000		810,000
		Equities	
		Common stock	350,000
		Retained earnings	279,000*
			629,000
Total assets	$1,439,000	Total liabilities & equity	$1,439,000

* Same as NI, since this was the first year of operations, and no dividends were paid.

Remeasured Income Statement

Sales	$ 665,000
Cost of goods sold	(332,500)
General and administrative	(95,000)
Exchange gain (from trial balance)	41,500
Net income	$ 279,000

3. **Translation Rates** Foreign currency financial statements should be translated by means of the following rates:

   a. All assets and liabilities = Current exchange rate at the balance sheet date.

   b. Revenues and expenses = Conceptually, the exchange rate at the time the revenue or expense was recognized. However, due to the impracticability of this where rates change frequently, a weighted-average exchange rate for the period may be used.

   c. Contributed capital = Historical exchange rate.

   d. Retained earnings = The translated amount of retained earnings for the prior period (i.e., beginning retained earnings), plus (less) net income (loss) at the weighted-average rate, less dividends declared during the period, at the exchange rate when declared.

4. **Translation Adjustments** Translation of foreign currency statements as indicated above will result in a translation adjustment. This translation adjustment is reported in other comprehensive income. It should not be included in the determination of net income.

5. **Sale or Disposal of Foreign Entity** The translation adjustments accumulated in other comprehensive income should be removed using a reclassification adjustment and reported as part of the gain or loss on the disposal of the investment.

Example 4 ▶ Translation Computation

Americana Inc., a U.S. corporation, owns 100% of the outstanding common stock of Kaiser Ltd., a German company. Kaiser's financial statements for the year ending December 31, year 1, are reproduced below. The statement amounts are in Euros (EUR).

Balance Sheet
December 31, Year 1

Assets	
Cash	150,000 EUR
Accounts receivable	200,000
Inventory	450,000
Plant and equipment (net)	1,200,000
Total assets	2,000,000 EUR
Liabilities and Equity	
Accounts payable	100,000 EUR
Notes payable	500,000
Common stock	400,000
Additional paid-in capital	300,000
Retained earnings	700,000
Total liabilities and equity	2,000,000 EUR

Income Statement
For the Year Ended December 31, Year 1

Sales	400,000 EUR
Cost of goods sold	(150,000)
Gross margin	250,000
Operating expenses	(100,000)
Net income	150,000 EUR

The following information is also available:

- On August 31, Kaiser paid a 50,000 EUR dividend.
- Kaiser's translated retained earnings as of January 1 was $600,000.
- The exchange rate when Americana acquired its investment in Kaiser was 1 EUR = U.S. $1.
- Exchange rate data for the year:

January 1	1 EUR = $0.95
August 31	1 EUR = 0.90
December 31	1 EUR = 0.80
Year's Average	1 EUR = 0.85

Required: Translate Kaiser's financial statements.

Solution:

	Balance Sheet		
Assets	Euros	Rate	U.S. Dollars
Cash	150,000 EUR	$0.80/EUR	$ 120,000
Accounts receivable	200,000	0.80/EUR	160,000
Inventory	450,000	0.80/EUR	360,000
Plant and equipment (net)	1,200,000	0.80/EUR	960,000
Total assets	2,000,000 EUR		$1,600,000
Liabilities and Equity			
Accounts payable	100,000 EUR	$0.80/EUR	$ 80,000
Notes payable	500,000	0.80/EUR	400,000
Common stock	400,000	1.00/EUR	400,000
Additional paid-in capital	300,000	1.00/EUR	300,000
Retained earnings*	700,000		682,500
Translation adjustment (bal. fig.)**	--		(262,500)
Total liabs. and equity	2,000,000 EUR		$1,600,000

* Translated retained earnings (RE) equals beginning RE as previously translated, plus net income at a weighted-average rate, less dividends, at the rate in effect when declared.
** The translation adjustment is reported in other comprehensive income.

Beginning RE (from information above)	$600,000
Net income (below)	127,500
Dividends (50,000 EUR × $.90/EUR)	(45,000)
Translated RE, Dec. 31	$682,500

	Income Statement		
	Euros	Rate	U.S. Dollars
Sales	400,000 EUR	$ .85/EUR	$ 340,000
Cost of goods sold	(150,000)	.85/EUR	(127,500)
Operating expenses	(100,000)	.85/EUR	(85,000)
Net income	150,000 EUR		$ 127,500

D. Foreign Currency Transactions

Foreign currency transactions are transactions denominated in a currency other than the entity's functional currency. Foreign currency transactions may produce receivables or payables that are fixed in terms of the amount of foreign currency that will be received or paid.

1. **Fluctuations** A change in exchange rates between the functional currency and the currency in which a transaction is denominated increases or decreases the expected amount of functional currency cash flows upon settlement of the transaction.

   a. That increase or decrease in expected functional currency cash flows is a foreign currency transaction gain or loss that generally should be included as a component of income from continuing operations for the period in which the exchange rate changes.

   b. Likewise, a transaction gain or loss (measured from the transaction date or the most recent intervening balance sheet date, whichever is later) realized upon settlement of a foreign currency transaction generally should be included as a component of income from continuing operations for the period in which the transaction is settled.

2. **Exceptions** Gains and losses on the following foreign currency transactions should not be included in determining net income but should be reported in the same manner as translation adjustments.

   a. Foreign currency transactions that are designated as, and effective as, economic hedges of a net investment in a foreign entity, commencing as of the designation date.

   b. Intercompany foreign currency transactions that are of a long-term investment nature (that is, settlement is not planned or anticipated in the foreseeable future), when the entities to the transaction are consolidated, combined, or accounted for by the equity method in the reporting enterprise's financial statements.

3. **General Rule** At the date a transaction is recognized, each asset, liability, revenue, expense, gain, or loss arising from the transaction should be measured and recorded in the functional currency of the recording entity by use of the exchange rate in effect at that date.

   a. At the date a transaction is recognized, each asset, liability, revenue, expense, gain, or loss arising from the transaction should be measured and recorded in the functional currency of the recording entity by use of the exchange rate in effect at that date.

   b. At each balance sheet date, recorded balances that are denominated in a currency other than the functional currency of the recording entity should be adjusted to reflect the current exchange rate. These adjustments should be currently recognized as transaction gains or losses and reported as a component of income from continuing operations.

Example 5 ▸ Exchange Rates

On November 1, year 2, Americana Inc. purchased equipment from an unrelated French company for 10,000 Euros, payable on January 30, year 7. The following exchange rate information is available:

November 1, year 2	1 Euro	=	$.90
December 31, year 2		=	.92
January 30, year 7		=	.93

Americana would account for this transaction as follows:

Nov. 1, year 2:		
Equipment	9,000	
Note Payable (10,000EUR × $.90/EUR)		9,000
Dec. 31, year 2:		
Exchange Loss [10,000EUR × ($.92/EUR – $.90/EUR)]	200	
Note Payable		200

The $200 transaction loss from November 1, year 2, to December 31, year 2, is included as a component of income from continuing operations for year 2.

Jan. 30, year 7:		
Note Payable ($9,000 + $200)	9,200	
Exchange Loss (to balance)	100	
Cash (10,000EUR × $.93/EUR)		9,300

The $100 transaction loss from December 31, year 2, to January 30, year 7, is included as a component of income from continuing operations for year 7.

NOTE: The recorded amount of the equipment is not affected by exchange rate fluctuations between the date of purchase and the date of payment.

E. Income Tax Consequences of Rate Changes

Exchange gains or losses from an entity's foreign currency transactions that are included in taxable income of an earlier or later year than the year in which they are recognized in financial income result in temporary differences. Foreign currency financial statement translation adjustments also should be accounted for as temporary differences.

VI. Changing Prices

A. Definitions

A business enterprise that prepares its financial statements in U.S. dollars and in conformity with U.S. generally accepted accounting principles is encouraged, though not required, to disclose supplementary information on the effects of changing prices. The following terms are defined:

1. **Current Cost/Constant Purchasing Power** A method of accounting based on measures of current cost or lower recoverable amount in units of currency, each of which has the same general purchasing power. For operations in which the dollar is the functional currency, the general purchasing power of the dollar is used, and the Consumer Price Index for All Urban Consumers (CPI-U) is the required measure of purchasing power.

2. **Historical Cost/Constant Purchasing Power** A method of accounting based on measures of historical prices in units of a currency, each of which has the same general purchasing power.

3. **Value in Use** The amount determined by discounting the future cash flows (including the ultimate proceeds of disposal) expected to be derived from the use of an asset at an appropriate rate that allows for the risk of the activities concerned.

4. **Purchasing Power Gain or Loss** The net gain or loss determined by restating in units of constant purchasing power the opening and closing balances of, and transactions in monetary assets and liabilities.

5. **Recoverable Amount** Current worth of the net amount of cash expected to be recoverable from the use or sale of an asset.

6. **Monetary Assets** Monetary assets are defined as money or a claim to receive a sum of money, the amount of which is fixed or determinable without reference to future prices of specific goods or services.

Exhibit 3 ▸ Monetary Assets

Time Deposits	Cash on hand and demand bank deposits
Bonds (other than convertible)	Foreign currency—on hand and claims to
Accounts and notes receivable	Preferred stock (nonconvertible and non-participating)
Loans to employees	Allowance for uncollectible accounts/notes receivable
Long-term receivables	Advances to unconsolidated subsidiaries
Refundable deposits	Cash surrender value of life insurance
Deferred tax assets	Advances to supplier—not on a fixed price contract

7. **Nonmonetary Assets**

   a. Goods held primarily for resale or assets held primarily for direct use in providing services for the business of the enterprise.

   b. Claims to cash in amounts dependent on future prices of specific goods or services.

   c. Residual rights such as goodwill or equity interests.

Exhibit 4 ▸ Nonmonetary Assets

Investment in common stocks (in most circumstances)
Inventories (other than inventories used on contracts)
Property, plant, and equipment (PP&E)
Accumulated depreciation of PP&E
Purchase commitments—portion paid on fixed-price contracts
Patents, trademarks, licenses, and formulas
Goodwill, other intangible assets and deferred charges

8. **Assets Requiring Individual Analysis**

   a. **Preferred Stock (Convertible or Participating) and Convertible Bonds** If the market values the security primarily as a bond, it is monetary; if it values the security primarily as stock, it is nonmonetary.

   b. **Inventories Used on Contracts** If the future cash receipts on the contracts will not vary due to future changes in specific prices, they are monetary. Goods used on contracts to be priced at market upon delivery are nonmonetary.

   c. **Pension, Sinking, and Other Funds Under an Enterprise's Control** The specific assets in the fund should be classified as monetary or nonmonetary.

9. **Monetary Liabilities** Monetary liabilities are obligations to pay a sum of money, the amount of which is fixed or determinable without reference to future prices of specific goods or services.

Exhibit 5 ▸ Monetary Liabilities

Accounts and notes payable	Obligations payable in foreign currency
Accrued expenses payable	Customer advances—not on fixed price contracts
Cash dividends payable	Accrued losses on firm purchase commitments
Refundable deposits	Bonds payable and other long-terms debt
Convertible bonds payable	Unamortized premium or discount and prepaid interest on bonds or notes payable
Deferred tax	

10. **Nonmonetary Liabilities**

    a. Obligations to furnish goods or services in quantities that are fixed or determinable without reference to changes in prices.

    b. Obligations to pay cash in amounts dependent on future prices of specific goods or services.

Exhibit 6 ▸ Nonmonetary Liabilities

Sales commitments—portion collected on fixed-price contracts
Obligations under warranties
Deferred investment tax credits
Minority interests in consolidated subsidiaries

11. **Liabilities Requiring Special Analysis** Liabilities requiring special analysis include deferred revenue. If an obligation to furnish goods or services is involved, deferred revenue is nonmonetary.

12. **Stockholders' Equity—Preferred Stock** Capital stock of the enterprise or of its consolidated subsidiaries subject to mandatory redemption at fixed amounts is considered a monetary item. Therefore, preferred stock, which is fixed in terms of dollars to be paid in liquidation, is classified as a monetary item.

B. Presentation

1. **Five-Year Summary** Enterprises are encouraged to provide information for each of the five most recent years for net sales and other operating revenues; income from continuing operations on a current cost basis; the purchasing power gain or loss on net monetary items; the increase or decrease in the current cost or lower recoverable amount of inventory and property, plant, and equipment, net of inflation; the aggregate foreign currency translation adjustment on a current cost basis, if applicable; net assets at year-end on a current cost basis; income per common share from continuing operations on a current cost basis; cash dividends declared per common share; and the market price per common share at year-end.

2. **Additional Current Year Disclosures** If income from continuing operations on a current cost/constant purchasing power basis would differ significantly from that reported in the primary financial statements, enterprises are encouraged to provide information about the current cost basis on the components, including the cost of goods sold, and the depreciation, depletion, and amortization expense. The information may be presented in a statement format or in a reconciliation format.

3. **Separate Disclosures** The enterprise is also encouraged to disclose separate amounts for the current cost of lower recoverable amount at the end of the current year of inventory and PPE; the increase or decrease in current cost or lower recoverable amount before and after adjusting for the effects of inflation of inventory and PPE for the current year; the principal types of information used to calculate the current cost of inventory, PPE, cost of goods sold, and depreciation depletion, and amortization expense; and any differences between the depreciation methods, estimates of useful lives, and salvage values of assets used for calculations of current cost/constant purchasing power depreciation and the methods and estimates used for calculations of depreciation in the primary financial statements.

C. Inventory and PP&E

Amounts of inventory and property, plant, and equipment (PP&E) are measured as follows.

1. **Inventory** The current cost of inventory owned by an enterprise is the current cost of purchasing the goods concerned or the current cost of the resources required to produce the goods concerned (including an allowance for overhead), whichever would be applicable in the circumstances of the enterprise.

Example 6 ▸ Current Cost of Inventory

Rice Wholesaling Corporation accounts for inventory on a FIFO basis. There were 8,000 units in inventory on January 1 of the current year. Costs were incurred and goods purchased as follows during the year.

Period	Historical costs	Units purchased	Units sold
1st quarter	$ 410,000	7,000	7,500
2nd quarter	550,000	8,500	7,300
3rd quarter	425,000	6,500	8,200
4th quarter	630,000	9,000	7,000
	$2,015,000	31,000	30,000

Rice estimates that the current cost per unit of inventory was $57 at January 1, and $71 at December 31.

Required: Determine the amount of December 31 inventory to be reported in Rice's voluntary supplementary information restated into current cost.

Solution: 9,000 units × $71 / unit = $639,000

Units in inventory, 1/1	8,000
Units purchased during the year	31,000
Units available for sale	39,000
Units sold during the year	(30,000)
Units in inventory, 12/31	9,000

NOTE: The FIFO inventory cost flow method used for the primary financial statements is irrelevant to the computation of the current cost of the year-end inventory.

2. **PP&E** The current cost of PP&E owned by an enterprise is the current cost of acquiring the same service potential as embodied by the asset owned; the information used to measure current cost reflects whatever method of acquisition would be currently appropriate in the circumstances of the enterprise. The current cost of a used asset may be calculated by measuring the current cost of:

   a. A new asset that has the same service potential as the used asset when it was new (the current cost of the asset as if it were new) and deducting an allowance for depreciation.

   b. A used asset of the same age and in the same condition as the asset owned.

c. A new asset with a different service potential and adjusting that cost for the value of the difference in service potential due to differences in life, output capacity, nature of service, and operating costs.

Example 7 ▸ Current Cost of PP&E

Poe Corporation calculates depreciation at 10 percent per annum, using the straight-line method. A full year's depreciation is charged in the year of acquisition. There were no year 3 plant asset disposals. Details of Poe's plant assets at December 31, year 3, are as follows:

Year acquired	Percent depreciated	Historical cost	Estimated current cost
1	30	$200,000	$280,000
2	20	60,000	76,000
3	10	80,000	88,000

Required: Determine the net current cost (after accumulated depreciation) of the plant assets at December 31, year 3, to be reported in Poe's voluntary supplementary information restated into current cost.

Solution:

Year	Estimated current cost	Percent not depreciated	Net current cost
1	$280,000	70%	$196,000
2	76,000	80%	60,800
3	88,000	90%	79,200
Net current cost of plant assets at 12/31, year 3			$336,000

3. **Recoverable Amount** The recoverable amount is the current worth of the net amount of cash expected to be recoverable from the use or sale of an asset. It may be measured by considering the value in use or current market value of the asset concerned. Value in use is used to determine the recoverable amount of an asset if immediate sale of the asset is not intended. Current market value is used to determine the recoverable amount only if the asset is about to be sold.

a. If the recoverable amount for a group of assets is judged to be materially and permanently lower than the current cost amount, the recoverable amount is used as a measure of the assets and of the expense associated with the use or sale of the assets.

b. Decisions on the measurement of assets at their recoverable amount need not be made by considering assets individually unless they are used independently of other assets.

Example 8 ▸ Current Cost or Lower Recoverable Amount of Inventory and PP&E

At December 31 of the current year, Jannis Corp. owned two assets as follows:

	Equipment	Inventory
Current cost	$100,000	$80,000
Recoverable amount	95,000	90,000

Required: Determine the amount of total assets that Jannis should report in voluntarily disclosed supplementary information about current cost at December 31.

Solution:

Equipment	$ 95,000	(Recoverable amount lower than current cost)
Inventory	80,000	(Current cost lower than recoverable amount)
Total assets at 12/31	$175,000	

4. **Change in Current Costs** The increase or decrease in the current cost amounts of inventory and PP&E represents the difference between the measures of the assets at their entry dates for the year and the measures of the assets at their exit dates for the year.

   a. Entry date is the beginning of the year or the acquisition date, whichever is applicable.

   b. Exit date is the end of the year or the date of use or sale, whichever is applicable.

   c. The inflation component of the increase in current cost amount is the difference between the nominal dollar and constant dollar measures.

5. **Restatement of Current Cost** Enterprises that do not have significant foreign operations are to use the CPI-U to restate current costs into units of constant purchasing power.

D. Income From Continuing Operations

An enterprise presenting the minimum information shall measure income from continuing operations on a current cost basis.

1. **Cost of Goods Sold** Cost of goods sold at current cost or lower recoverable amount at the date of sale. To compute cost of goods sold on a current cost basis, multiply the number of units sold by the average current cost of the units during the period. (Average current cost of the units during the period is the sum of the current cost of the units at the beginning and the end of the period, divided by two.)

Example 9 ▸ Current Cost of Cost of Goods Sold

Refer to Example 7 (Rice Wholesaling Corporation)

Required: Determine the cost of goods sold for the year restated into current cost.

Solution: The FIFO inventory cost flow method used for the primary financial statements is irrelevant to the current cost computation of the cost of goods sold for the year.

Average current cost per unit [($57 + $71) / 2]	$ 64
Units sold during the year	× 30,000
Cost of goods sold, average current cost	$1,920,000

2. **Cost Recovery Expense** Depreciation, depletion, and amortization expense on the basis of the average current cost of the assets, service potential or lower recoverable amount during the period of use. To compute depreciation on a current cost basis, divide the average current cost of the plant asset during the period by its estimated useful life. (Average current cost of the plant asset is the sum of the current cost of the plant asset at the beginning and the end of the period, divided by two.)

Example 10 ▸ Depreciation Expense Based on Average Current Cost

Kerr Company purchased a machine for $115,000 on January 1, the company's first day of operations. At the end of the year, the current cost of the machine was $125,000. The machine has no salvage value, a five-year life, and is depreciated by the straight-line method.

Required: Determine the amount of the current cost depreciation expense that would appear in voluntary supplementary current cost information for the first year ending December 31.

Solution:

Average current cost for the year ($115,000 + $125,000) / 2]	$120,000
Estimated useful life	/ 5
Current cost depreciation for the year	$ 24,000

3. **Other Revenues/Expenses and Gains/Losses** Other revenues, expenses, gains, and losses may be measured at the amounts included in the primary income statement.

E. **Purchasing Power Gain or Loss on Net Monetary Items**
The purchasing power gain or loss on net monetary items is the net gain or loss determined by restating in units of constant purchasing power the opening and closing balances of, and transactions in, monetary assets and monetary liabilities.

1. **Economic Significance** The economic significance of monetary assets and liabilities depends heavily on the general purchasing power of money, although other factors may affect their significance. The economic significance of nonmonetary items depends heavily on the value of specific goods and services.

2. **Gains** Purchasing power gains result from holding:

   a. Monetary liabilities during a period of inflation because the obligations will be settled with dollars that have less purchasing power.

   b. Monetary assets during a period of deflation because a fixed amount of money will purchase more goods and services following a period of deflation.

3. **Losses** Purchasing power losses result from holding:

   a. Monetary assets during a period of inflation because the fixed amount of money will purchase fewer goods and services following a period of inflation.

Example 11 ▸ Purchasing Power Loss on Net Monetary Items

Lang Company's monetary assets exceeded monetary liabilities by $3,000 at the beginning of the current year and $4,000 at the end of the current year. On January 1, the general price level was 125. On December 31, the general price level was 150.

Required: Determine Lang's purchasing power gain or loss on net monetary items.

Solution:

	Nominal Dollars	Conversion Factor	Restated into year's Dollars
Net monetary assets, 1/1	$3,000	150/125	$ 3,600
Change in net monetary assets during the year	1,000	*	1,000
Balance in net monetary assets, 12/31	$4,000	150/150	(4,000)
Purchasing power loss on net monetary assets			$ 600

*Assumed to be in average year's dollars.

b. Monetary liabilities during a period of deflation because the obligation will be settled with dollars that have more purchasing power.

Exhibit 7 ▸ Purchasing Power Gains and Losses

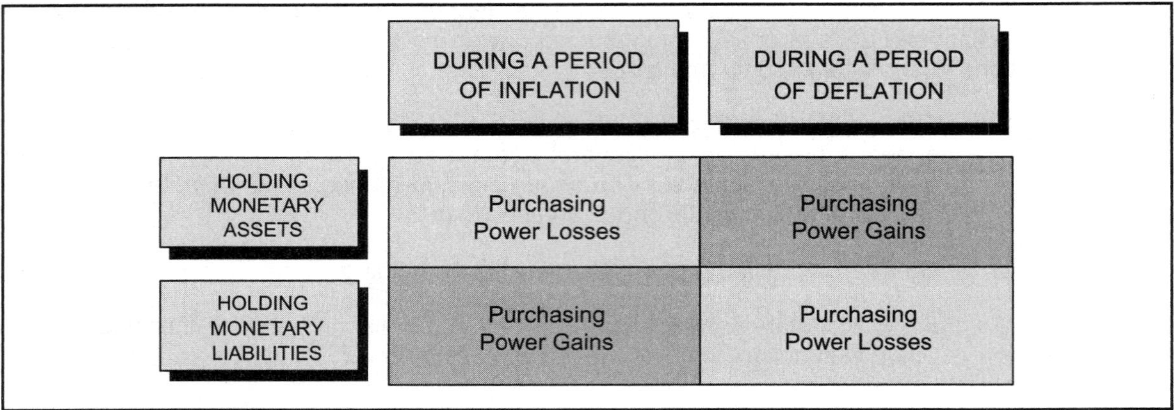

4. **Holding Nonmonetary Items** The holding of nonmonetary items during a period of changing prices does not give rise to purchasing power gains or losses.

F. **Holding Gains & Losses on Nonmonetary Assets**
Current cost financial statements measure and report both realized and unrealized holding gains and losses on nonmonetary assets. Realized holding gains and losses occur when the nonmonetary asset has been sold or consumed in the earnings process. An increase in the current cost of inventory items sold is an example of a realized holding gain. Unrealized holding gains and losses occur when the nonmonetary asset is held from period to period. A decrease in the current cost of inventory items on hand is an example of an unrealized holding loss.

CHAPTER 13—REPORTING: SPECIAL AREAS

Problem 13-1 MULTIPLE-CHOICE QUESTIONS

1. Which of the following items would most likely require a subsequent event adjustment to the financial statements for the year ended December 31, year 1?

   a. Uninsured loss of inventories purchased in year 1 as a result of a flood in year 2
   b. Settlement of litigation in year 2 over an event that occurred in year 2
   c. Loss on an uncollectible trade receivable recorded in year 1 from a customer that declared bankruptcy in year 2
   d. Proceeds from a capital stock issuance in year 2 which was being approved by the board of directors in year 1 (Editor, 89523)

2. Zero Corp. suffered a loss on an uncollectible trade account receivable due to a customer's bankruptcy that would have a material effect on its financial statements. This occurred suddenly due to a natural disaster ten days after Zero's balance sheet date, but one month before the issuance of the financial statements. Under these circumstances, the financial statements:

   a. Should be adjusted, but should not disclose the event
   b. Should be adjusted and should disclose the event
   c. Should not be adjusted should not disclose the event
   d. Should not be adjusted, but should disclose the event (Editor, 89522)

3. Which of the following statements is false concerning subsequent events?

   a. An entity shall not recognize events occurring between the time the financial statements were issued or were available to be issued and the time the financial statements were reissued unless the adjustment is required by GAAP or regulatory requirements.
   b. Some nonrecognized subsequent events may be of such a nature that they must be disclosed to keep the financial statements from being misleading.
   c. An entity shall not recognize subsequent events that provide evidence about conditions that did not exist at the date of the balance sheet but arose after the balance sheet date but before financial statements are issued or are available to be issued.
   d. An entity is not permitted to disclose any estimates inherent in the process of preparing financial statements when disclosing the effects of subsequent events that provide additional evidence about conditions existing at the date of the balance sheet. (Editor, 89525)

4. Dex Co. has entered into a joint venture with an affiliate to secure access to additional inventory. Under the joint venture agreement, Dex will purchase the output of the venture at prices negotiated on an arms'-length basis. Which of the following is(are) required to be disclosed about the related-party transaction?

   I. The amount due to the affiliate at the balance sheet date
   II. The dollar amount of the purchases during the year

   a. I only
   b. II only
   c. Both I and II
   d. Neither I nor II (R/06, FAR, #6, 8073)

5. Dean Co. acquired 100% of Morey Corp. prior to the current year. During the current year, the individual companies included in their financial statements the following:

	Dean	Morey
Officers' salaries	$ 75,000	$50,000
Officers' expenses	20,000	10,000
Loans to officers	125,000	50,000
Intercompany sales	150,000	—

What amount should be reported as related-party disclosures in the notes to Dean's year-end consolidated financial statements?

a. $150,000
b. $155,000
c. $175,000
d. $330,000 (11/90, PI, #53, amended, 1129)

6. Which type of material related-party transactions requires disclosure?

a. Only those not reported in the body of the financial statements
b. Only those that receive accounting recognition
c. Those that contain possible illegal acts
d. All those other than compensation arrangements, expense allowances, and other similar items in the ordinary course of business (11/95, FAR, #7, amended, 6089)

7. Lemu Co. and Young Co. are under the common management of Ego Co. Ego can significantly influence the operating results of both Lemu and Young. While Lemu had no transactions with Ego during the year, Young sold merchandise to Ego under the same terms given to unrelated parties. In the notes to their respective financial statements, should Lemu and Young disclose their relationship with Ego?

	Lemu	Young
a.	Yes	Yes
b.	Yes	No
c.	No	Yes
d.	No	No

(5/98, FAR, #6, 6609)

8. A development stage enterprise should use the same generally accepted accounting principles that apply to established operating enterprises for

	Revenue recognition	Deferral of expenses
a.	Yes	Yes
b.	Yes	No
c.	No	No
d.	No	Yes

(11/95, FAR, #4, 6086)

9. Which of the following statements is correct concerning start-up costs?

a. Costs of start-up activities, including organization costs, should be expensed as incurred.
b. Costs of start-up activities, including organization costs, should be capitalized and expensed only if an impairment exists.
c. Costs of start-up activities, including organization costs, should be capitalized and amortized on a straight-line basis over the lesser of the estimated economic life of the company, or 60 months.
d. Costs of start-up activities should be capitalized and amortized on a straight-line basis over the lesser of the estimated economic life of the company, or 60 months, while organization cost should be expensed as incurred. (R/07, FAR, #41, 8362)

10. Lind Corp. was a development stage enterprise from its inception on October 10, year 1 to December 31, year 2. The following were among Lind's expenditures for this period:

Leasehold improvements, equipment, and furniture	$1,200,000
Research and development	850,000
Laboratory operations	175,000
General and administrative	275,000

The year ended December 31, year 3 was the first year in which Lind was an established operating enterprise. For the period ended December 31, year 2, what total amount of expenditures should Lind have capitalized?

a. $2,500,000
b. $2,225,000
c. $2,050,000
d. $1,200,000 (5/90, PII, #52, amended, 1139)

11. Lex Corp. was a development stage enterprise from October 10, year 1 (inception), to December 31, year 2. The year ended December 31, year 3, is the first year in which Lex is an established operating enterprise. The following are among the costs incurred by Lex:

	For period 10/10 yr 1 to 12/31 yr 2	For year ended 12/31 yr 3
Leasehold improvements, equipment, and furniture	$1,000,000	$ 300,000
Security deposits	60,000	30,000
Research and development	750,000	900,000
Laboratory operations	175,000	550,000
General and administrative	225,000	685,000
Depreciation	25,000	115,000
	$2,235,000	$2,580,000

From its inception through the period ended December 31, year 3, what is the total amount of costs incurred by Lex that should be charged to operations?

a. $3,425,000
b. $2,250,000
c. $1,775,000
d. $1,350,000 (11/90, PI, #58, amended, 1131)

12. Deficits accumulated during the development stage of a company should be

a. Reported as organization costs
b. Reported as a part of stockholders' equity
c. Capitalized and written off in the first year of principal operations
d. Capitalized and amortized over a five-year period beginning when principal operations commence (11/90, Theory, #8, 1908)

13. Which of the following types of entities are required to report on business segments?

a. Nonpublic business enterprises
b. Publicly-traded enterprises
c. Not-for-profit enterprises
d. Joint ventures (R/07, FAR, #24, 8345)

14. Which of the following factors determines whether an identified segment of an enterprise should be reported in the enterprise's financial statements?

    I. The segment's assets constitute more than 10% of the combined assets of all operating segments.
    II. The segment's liabilities constitute more than 10% of the combined liabilities of all operating segments.

    a. I only
    b. II only
    c. Both I and II
    d. Neither I nor II (R/06, FAR, #30, amended, 8097)

15. Which of the following should be disclosed for each reportable operating segment of an enterprise?

	Profit or loss	Total assets
a.	Yes	Yes
b.	Yes	No
c.	No	Yes
d.	No	No

(R/06, FAR, #8, 8075)

16. Two or more operating segments may be aggregated into a single operating segment if aggregation is consistent with the objective and basic principles of FASB ASC 280, if the segments have similar economic characteristics, and if the segments are similar in which of the following areas?

    a. The nature of the products, services, production processes, and regulatory environment
    b. The methods used to distribute their products or provide their services
    c. The type or class of customer for their products and services
    d. All of the above (Editor, 89566)

17. Which of the following qualifies as an operating segment?

    a. Corporate headquarters, which oversees $1 billion in sales for the entire company
    b. North American segment, whose assets are 12% of the company's assets of all segments, and management reports to the chief operating officer
    c. South American segment, whose results of operations are reported directly to the chief operating officer, and has 5% of the company's assets, 9% of revenues, and 8% of the profits
    d. Eastern Europe segment, which reports its results directly to the manager of the European division, and has 20% of the company's assets, 12% of revenues, and 11% of profits (R/05, FAR, #40, 7784)

18. Correy Corp. and its divisions are engaged solely in manufacturing operations. The following data (consistent with prior years' data) pertain to Correy's operating segments for the current year ended December 31:

Operating Segment	Total revenue	Operating profit	Identifiable assets at 12/31
A	$10,000,000	$1,750,000	$20,000,000
B	8,000,000	1,400,000	17,500,000
C	6,000,000	1,200,000	12,500,000
D	3,000,000	550,000	7,500,000
E	4,250,000	675,000	7,000,000
F	1,500,000	225,000	3,000,000
	$32,750,000	$5,800,000	$67,500,000

In its segment information for the current year, how many reportable segments does Correy have?

    a. Three
    b. Four
    c. Five
    d. Six (5/90, PII, #56, amended, 1141)

19. Opto Co. is a publicly-traded, consolidated enterprise reporting segment information. Which of the following items is a required enterprise-wide disclosure regarding external customers?
    a. The fact that transactions with a particular external customer constitute more than 10% of the total enterprise revenues
    b. The identity of any external customer providing 10% or more of a particular operating segment's revenue
    c. The identity of any external customer considered to be "major" by management
    d. Information on major customers is **not** required in segment reporting (R/05, FAR, #14, 7758)

20. In preparing consolidated financial statements of a U.S. parent company with a foreign subsidiary, the foreign subsidiary's functional currency is the currency
    a. In which the subsidiary maintains its accounting records.
    b. Of the country in which the subsidiary is located.
    c. Of the country in which the parent is located.
    d. Of the environment in which the subsidiary primarily generates and expends cash.
    (R/99, FAR, #16, 6785)

21. When remeasuring foreign currency financial statements into the functional currency, which of the following items would be remeasured using historical exchange rates?
    a. Inventories carried at cost
    b. Marketable equity securities reported at market values
    c. Bonds payable
    d. Accrued liabilities (11/93, Theory, #36, 4541)

22. Park Co.'s wholly owned subsidiary, Schnell Corp., maintains its accounting records in euros. Because all of Schnell's branch offices are in Switzerland, its functional currency is the Swiss franc. Remeasurement of Schnell's current year financial statements resulted in a $7,600 gain, and translation of its financial statements resulted in an $8,100 gain. What amount should Park report as a foreign exchange gain in its income statement for the current year ended December 31?
    a. $0
    b. $ 7,600
    c. $ 8,100
    d. $15,700 (5/95, FAR, #31, amended, 5567)

23. A balance arising from the translation or remeasurement of a subsidiary's foreign currency financial statements is reported in the consolidated income statement when the subsidiary's functional currency is the

	Foreign currency	U.S. dollar
a.	No	No
b.	No	Yes
c.	Yes	No
d.	Yes	Yes

(5/90, Theory, #22, 2088)

24. A foreign subsidiary's functional currency is its local currency, which has not experienced significant inflation. The weighted average exchange rate for the current year would be the appropriate exchange rate for translating

	Salaries expense	Sales to external customers
a.	Yes	Yes
b.	Yes	No
c.	No	Yes
d.	No	No

(R/09, FAR, #6, 8756)

25. Certain balance sheet accounts of a foreign subsidiary of Rowan Inc., at December 31, have been translated into U.S. dollars as follows:

	Translated at	
	Current Rates	Historical Rates
Note receivable, long-term	$240,000	$200,000
Prepaid rent	85,000	80,000
Patent	150,000	170,000
	$475,000	$450,000

The subsidiary's functional currency is the currency of the country in which it is located. What total amount should be included in Rowan's December 31 consolidated balance sheet for the above accounts?

a. $450,000
b. $455,000
c. $475,000
d. $495,000 (5/90, PII, #44, amended, 9081)

26. Gordon Ltd., a 100% owned British subsidiary of a U.S. parent company, reports its financial statements in local currency, the British pound. A local newspaper published the following U.S. exchange rates to the British pound at year end:

Current rate	$1.50
Historical rate (acquisition)	1.70
Average rate	1.55
Inventory (FIFO)	1.60

Which currency rate should Gordon use to convert its income statement to U.S. dollars at year end?

a. 1.50
b. 1.55
c. 1.60
d. 1.70 (R/08, FAR, #43, 8598)

27. On October 1 of the current year, Mild Co., a U.S. company, purchased machinery from Grund, a German company, with payment due on April 1 of next year. If Mild's current year operating income included no foreign exchange transaction gain or loss, then the transaction could have

a. Resulted in an extraordinary gain
b. Been denominated in U.S. dollars
c. Caused a foreign currency gain to be reported as a contra account against machinery
d. Caused a foreign currency translation gain to be reported in other comprehensive income (11/93, Theory, #35, amended, 4540)

28. Which of the following statements regarding foreign exchange gains and losses is correct?

a. An exchange gain occurs when the exchange rate increases between the date a payable is recorded and the date of cash payment.
b. An exchange gain occurs when the exchange rate increases between the date a receivable is recorded and the date of cash receipt.
c. An exchange loss occurs when the exchange rate decreases between the date a payable is recorded and the date of the cash payment.
d. An exchange loss occurs when the exchange rate increases between the date a receivable is recorded and the date of the cash receipt. (R/03, FAR, #2, 7604)

29. Toigo Co. purchased merchandise from a vendor in England on November 20 for 500,000 British pounds. Payment was due in British pounds on January 20. The spot rates to purchase one pound were as follows:

November 20	$1.25
December 31	1.20
January 20	1.17

How should the foreign currency transaction gain be reported on Toigo's financial statements at December 31?

a. A gain of $40,000 as a separate component of stockholders' equity
b. A gain of $40,000 in the income statement
c. A gain of $25,000 as a separate component of stockholders' equity
d. A gain of $25,000 in the income statement (R/11, FAR, #45, 9895)

30. On October 1 of the current year, a U.S. company sold merchandise on account to a British company for 2,000 pounds (exchange rate, 1 pound = $1.43). At the company's December 31 fiscal year end, the exchange rate was 1 pound = $1.45. The exchange rate was 1 pound = $1.50 on collection in January of the subsequent year. What amount would the company recognize as a gain(loss) from foreign currency translation when the receivable is collected?

a. $0
b. $ 100
c. $ 140
d. $(140) (R/09, FAR, #41, 8791)

31. Which of the following gains/losses should not be included in determining net income, but should be reported in the same manner as translation adjustments?

a. Foreign currency transactions that are designated as, and are effective as, economic hedges of a net investment in a foreign entity, commencing as of the designation date
b. Intercompany foreign currency transactions that are of a long-term investment nature (that is, settlement is not planned or anticipated in the foreseeable future), when the entities to the transaction are consolidated, combined, or accounted for by the equity method in the reporting enterprise's financial statements
c. Both A. and B.
d. Neither A. nor B. (Editor, 89583)

32. Ball Corp. had the following foreign currency transactions during the current year:

- Goods purchased from a foreign supplier on January 20 for the U.S. dollar equivalent of $90,000. The invoice was paid on March 20, at the U.S. dollar equivalent of $96,000.
- On July 1, Ball borrowed the U.S. dollar equivalent of $500,000 evidenced by a note that was payable in the lender's local currency on July 1, in two years. On December 31, the U.S. dollar equivalents of the principal amount and accrued interest were $520,000 and $26,000, respectively. Interest on the note is 10% per annum.

In Ball's year-end income statement, what amount should be included as foreign exchange loss?

a. $0
b. $ 6,000
c. $ 21,000
d. $ 27,000 (11/90, PI, #43, amended, 1335)

33. The following information pertains to Flint Co.'s sale of 10,000 foreign currency units under a forward contract dated November 1 of the current year for delivery on January 31 of the following year:

	11/1	12/31
Spot rates	$0.80	$0.83
30-day future rates	0.79	0.82
90-day future rates	0.78	0.81

Flint entered into the forward contract in order to speculate in the foreign currency. In Flint's income statement for the current year ended December 31, what amount of loss should be reported from this forward contract?

a. $400
b. $300
c. $200
d. $0 (5/92, PI, #52, amended, 2623)

34. ________________________ is a method of accounting based on measures of historical prices in units of a currency, each of which has the same general purchasing power.

a. Current cost/constant purchasing power accounting
b. Current market value
c. Historical cost accounting
d. Historical cost/constant purchasing power accounting (Editor, 89575)

35. ________________________ is (are) defined as money or a claim to receive a sum of money, the amount of which is fixed or determinable without reference to future prices of specific goods or services.

a. Monetary assets
b. Monetary liabilities
c. The value in use
d. The recoverable amount (Editor, 89577)

36. Financial statements prepared under which of the following methods include adjustments for both specific price changes and general price-level changes?

a. Historical cost/nominal dollar
b. Current cost/nominal dollar
c. Current cost/constant dollar
d. Historical cost/constant dollar (11/95, FAR, #57, 6139)

37. The following assets were among those that appeared on Baird Co.'s books at the end of the year:

Demand bank deposits	$650,000
Net long-term receivables	400,000
Patents and trademarks	150,000

In preparing constant dollar financial statements, how much should Baird classify as monetary assets?

a. $1,200,000
b. $1,050,000
c. $ 800,000
d. $ 650,000 (5/90, PII, 50, 1245)

38. A company that wishes to disclose information about the effect of changing prices should report this information in

a. The body of the financial statements.
b. The notes to the financial statements.
c. Supplementary information to the financial statements.
d. Management's report to shareholders. (11/94, FAR, #4, amended, 5269)

39. In its financial statements, Hila Co. discloses supplemental information on the effects of changing prices. Hila computed the increase in current cost of inventory as follows:

Increase in current cost (nominal dollars)	$15,000
Increase in current cost (constant dollars)	$12,000

What amount should Hila disclose as the inflation component of the increase in current cost of inventories?

a. $ 3,000
b. $12,000
c. $15,000
d. $27,000 (5/94, FAR, #58, amended, 4873)

40. Manhof Co. prepares supplementary reports on income from continuing operations on a current cost basis. How should Manhof compute cost of goods sold on a current cost basis?

a. Number of units sold times average current cost of units during the year
b. Number of units sold times current cost of units at year end
c. Number of units sold times current cost of units at the beginning of the year
d. Beginning inventory at current cost plus cost of goods purchased less ending inventory at current cost (11/92, Theory, #40, amended, 3473)

41. When computing purchasing power gain or loss on net monetary items, which of the following accounts is classified as nonmonetary?

a. Advances to unconsolidated subsidiaries
b. Allowance for uncollectible accounts
c. Unamortized premium on bonds payable
d. Accumulated depreciation of equipment (11/93, Theory, #1, 4506)

42. In a period of rising general price levels, Pollard Corp. discloses income on a current cost basis. Which of the following contributes to Pollard's purchasing power loss on net monetary items?

a. Refundable deposits with suppliers
b. Equity investment in unconsolidated subsidiaries
c. Warranty obligations
d. Wages payable (5/92, Theory, #5, amended, 2697)

43. The following information pertains to each unit of merchandise purchased for resale by Vend Co.:

	March 1	December 31
Purchase price	$ 8	
Selling price	12	$ 15
Price level index	110	121
Replacement cost		10

Under current cost accounting, what is the amount of Vend's holding gain on each unit of this merchandise?

a. $0
b. $0.80
c. $1.20
d. $2.00 (5/92, PII, #13, amended, 2645)

Problem 13-2 SIMULATION: Functional Currency

Fiore, Inc. is an Italian subsidiary formed on July 1 of the current year, and is 100 percent owned by Florida Inc. Management has determined that Fiore is, in fact, a foreign extension of Florida's operations, and thus, its functional currency is the U.S. dollar.

The following additional information is available:

- No dividends were paid by Fiore during the year.
- Inventory was shipped from Florida on August 1.
- Fiore's office is located in a building purchased on October 1.
- Fiore's trial balance (in Euros) is provided.

Exchange rate information for the year follows:

July 1	1 Euro	=	$0.75
August 1		=	0.72
October 1		=	0.68
December 1		=	0.65
Year's Average		=	0.70

Compute the remeasured trial balance of Fiore in its functional currency.

Trial Balance

Account	Euros (debit/credit)	Exchange Rate	U.S. Dollars (debit/credit)
Cash	$ 150,000		
Account receivable (net)	100,000		
Inventory	320,000		
Office building (net)	840,000		
Accounts payable	(130,000)		
Mortgage payable	(700,000)		
Common stock	(440,000)		
Sales	(980,000)		
Costs of goods sold	550,000		
Selling expenses	110,000		
Operating expenses	180,000		
Exchange gain			
Totals	$ 0		

(07, FAR, Editors, 3597)

Problem 13-3 SIMULATION: Economic Indicators

Items 1 through 16 represent possible economic indicators that should be considered, both individually and collectively, when determining the functional currency pertaining to subsidiaries. The functional currency is the foreign currency or parent's currency that most closely correlates to these economic indicators.

Select **Yes** or **No** by each of the following items in determining whether they are, or are not, a type of economic indicator that should be considered.

	Economic Indicators	**(Yes or No)**
1.	Cash flow	
2.	Continent	
3.	Currency value	
4.	Engineering	
5.	Expense	
6.	Financing	
7.	Global environment	
8.	Global market	
9.	Intercompany arrangement	
10.	Intercompany transactions	
11.	Sales price	
12.	Sales market	
13.	Sales volume	
14.	Stock price	
15.	Stock market	
16.	Stock volume	

(07, FAR, Editors, 9110)

Problem 13-4 SIMULATION: Research

Question: What are the objectives of translating a foreign subsidiary's financial statements?

FASB ASC: [ ] - [ ] - [ ] - [ ]

(9137)

Solution 13-1 MULTIPLE-CHOICE ANSWERS

Subsequent Events

1. (c) There are two types of subsequent events: recognized and nonrecognized. The first type requires adjustment of the financial statements because it provides evidence about conditions that existed at the balance sheet date. The second type of subsequent event provides evidence about conditions that did not exist at the balance sheet date and does not require adjustment of the financial statements; however, if material in nature, the event(s) may require disclosure to keep the financial statements from being misleading. Loss on an uncollectible trade receivable recorded in year 1 from a customer that declared bankruptcy in year 2 is a classic example of providing evidence about conditions that existed at the balance sheet date and thus it requires a financial statement adjustment. (89523)

2. (d) There are two types of subsequent events. The first type requires adjustment of the financial statements because it provides evidence about conditions that existed at the balance sheet date. The second type of subsequent event provides evidence about conditions that did not exist at the balance sheet date and does not require adjustment of the financial statements; however, if material in nature, the event(s) may require disclosure to keep the financial statements from being misleading. This is an example of the second type, requiring disclosure only. (89522)

3. (d) Choices a, b, and c are all true. Choice d is false. An entity shall recognize in the financial statements the effects of all subsequent events that provide additional evidence about conditions that existed at the date of the balance sheet, including the estimates inherent in the process of preparing financial statements. (89525)

Related-Party Disclosures

4. (c) Transactions between affiliates are considered related-party transactions. Related-party disclosures should include, among other things, the dollar amount of purchases during the year and the amounts due from or to the affiliate at the balance sheet date. (8073)

5. (c) Financial statements should include disclosures of material related-party transactions other than (1) compensation arrangements, (2) expense allowances, (3) other similar items in the ordinary course of business, and (4) transactions that are eliminated in the preparation of consolidated or combined financial statements. Thus, Dean should report related-party disclosures totaling $175,000 ($125,000 + $50,000), the amount of the loans to officers. The amounts for officers' salaries, officers' expenses, and intercompany sales should not be disclosed as related-party transactions. (1129)

6. (d) All material related-party transactions that are not eliminated in consolidated or combined financial statements be disclosed. However, the following related-party transactions do not have to be disclosed: compensation arrangements, expense allowances, and similar items incurred in the ordinary course of business. (6089)

7. (a) If the reporting enterprise and one or more other enterprises are under common ownership or management control and the existence of that control could result in operating results or financial position of the reporting enterprise significantly different from those that would have been obtained if the enterprises were autonomous, the nature of the control relationship should be disclosed even though there are no transactions between the enterprises. Therefore, both Lemo and Young should disclose their relationship with Ego. (6609)

Developmental Stage Enterprises

8. (a) Financial statements issued by a development stage enterprise should be presented in conformity with GAAP applicable to established operating enterprises. Special accounting practices that are based on a distinctive accounting for development stage enterprises are not acceptable. Financial reporting by a development stage enterprise differs from financial reporting for an established operating enterprise in regard only to required additional information. (6086)

9. (a) Start-up activities, including organization costs, should be expensed as incurred. Organization costs are written off over 60 months for tax purposes, not for financial accounting purposes. (8362)

10. (d) Generally accepted accounting principles that apply to established operating enterprises determine whether a cost incurred by a development stage enterprise should be charged to expense when incurred or should be capitalized or deferred. Therefore, only the $1,200,000 cost of the leasehold improvements, equipment, and furniture should have been capitalized by Lind. The research and development costs, laboratory operations costs, and the general and administrative costs should have been expensed when incurred. (1139)

11. (a) Financial statements issued by a development stage enterprise should be presented in conformity with GAAP that apply to established operating enterprises. These accounting principles determine whether a cost incurred by a development stage enterprise should be charged to expense when incurred or should be capitalized or deferred. Lex should capitalize both the cost of the leasehold improvements, equipment, and furniture, and the cost of the security deposits.

Research and development ($750,000 + $900,000)	$1,650,000
Laboratory operations ($175,000 + $550,000)	725,000
General and administrative ($225,000 + $685,000)	910,000
Depreciation ($25,000 + $115,000)	140,000
Total amount of costs charged to operations	$3,425,000

(1131)

12. (b) The balance sheet of a development stage enterprise should include any cumulative net losses reported with a caption such as "deficit accumulated during the development stage" in the stockholders' equity section. It is never acceptable to capitalize a deficit. A deficit is a debit item that belongs in the equity section of the balance sheet, not in the asset section. (1908)

Operating Segments

13. (b) Public business enterprises are required to report on business segments. Public business enterprises are those business enterprises that have issued debt or equity securities that are traded in a public market. It does not apply to nonpublic business enterprises or not-for-profit enterprises. While joint ventures may be public enterprises, they are not necessarily so. Editor's Note: Remember, the AICPA examiners instruct candidates to select the best answer. (8345)

14. (a) Reportable segments include operating segments that exceed the quantitative thresholds. An enterprise shall report separately information about an operating segment that meets any of the following three quantitative thresholds: (1) its reported revenue, including both sales to external customers and intersegment sales or transfers, is 10% or more of the combined revenue, internal and external, of all operating segments, (2) the absolute amount of its reported profit or loss is 10% or more of the greater, in absolute amount, of (a) the combined reported profit of all operating segments that did not report a loss or (b) the combined reported loss of all operating segments that did report a loss, or (3) its assets are 10% or more of the combined assets of all operating segments. (8097)

15. (a) General-purpose financial statements are required to include selected information on an enterprise's operating segments. An enterprise is required to report a measure of segment profit or loss, segment assets and certain related items, but not segment cash flows or segment liabilities. (8075)

16. (d) Two or more operating segments may be aggregated into a single operating segment if aggregation is consistent with the objective and basic principles of FASB ASC 280, if the segments have similar economic characteristics, and if the segments are similar in each of the following areas: the nature of the products and services; the nature of the production processes; the type or class of customer for their products and services; the methods used to distribute their products or provide their services; and the nature of the regulatory environment, if applicable; for example, banking, insurance, or public utilities. Since answers a., b., and c. are needed, answer d., *all of the above*, is the best choice. (89566)

17. (b) Operating segments have three characteristics. The description in answer a contains no characteristics that would qualify it as an operating segment. The description in answer b meets all three characteristics of an operating segment as well as the quantitative thresholds criteria. The description in answer c meets the characteristics of an operating segment; it doesn't meet the quantitative thresholds criteria. The description in answer d meets the quantitative thresholds criteria but doesn't meet the characteristics of an operating segment. (7784)

18. (c) An operating segment is identified as a reportable segment if it meets one or more of the three tests: revenue, profit(loss), and assets. (1) Revenue test—Its revenue (including both sales to external customers and intersegment sales and transfers) is 10% or more of the combined revenue of all operating segments. (2) Profit(loss) test—Its profit or loss is 10% or more of the greater of the following two absolute amounts: Combined profits of all segments that did not report losses, or the sum of all losses for all segments reporting losses. (3) Assets test—Its assets are 10% or more of the combined assets of all operating segments. Segments A, B, C, and E have revenue greater than $3,275,000, which is 10% of the combined revenue. They also have profits greater than $580,000, which is 10% of the combined profits (no segments reported losses). Segments A, B, C, D, and E all have assets greater than $6,750,000, which is 10% of the combined assets. Only segment F does not meet at least one of the three tests. Therefore, Correy has five reportable segments. (1141)

19. (a) Information about major customers is required in an enterprise-wide disclosure. Enterprises must disclose the total amount of revenues from each single customer that amounts to 10% or more of the enterprise's revenues and identify the segment(s) reporting the revenues. Identity of the customer need not be disclosed. (7758)

Functional Currency/Translations

20. (d) An entity's functional currency is the currency of the primary economic environment in which the entity operates. Normally, that is the currency of the environment in which an entity primarily generates and expends cash. The functional currency of a foreign entity may be its local currency, the U.S. dollar, or another foreign currency. Where a foreign operation is relatively self-contained and integrated within one country, the entity's functional currency will be the local currency. Where the foreign operation is, in essence, an extension of the parent's U.S. operations, the functional currency will be the U.S. dollar. A foreign entity may keep its books in the local currency, yet have another foreign currency as functional currency; in which case remeasurement of the recording currency statements into functional currency will be required. (6785)

21. (a) If an entity does not maintain its books in its functional currency, remeasurement into the functional currency prior to translation into the reporting currency (i.e., the parent company's currency) is required. In this process, nonmonetary balance sheet items are remeasured using historical exchange rates. Hence, inventories carried at cost should be remeasured using historical exchange rates. Marketable equity securities, bonds payable, and accrued liabilities balance sheet items are remeasured using the current exchange rate. (4541)

22. (b) Park's foreign subsidiary does not maintain its accounting records in its functional currency (the Swiss franc). Therefore, the financial statements of the foreign subsidiary must be remeasured. The $7,600 remeasurement gain is reported in income from continuing operations. The $8,100 translation gain is reported in other comprehensive income. Translation gains and losses are not reported in income. (5567)

23. (b) The functional currency of a foreign entity may be its local currency (i.e., the foreign currency) or the reporting currency (e.g., the U.S. dollar). If the functional currency is the foreign currency, the foreign currency financial statements must be translated into U.S. dollars. The translation adjustments which result from this process are not reported in the consolidated income statement but are reported in other comprehensive income. If the functional currency is the U.S. dollar, the foreign currency financial statements must be remeasured into U.S. dollars. The foreign exchange gains/losses which result from this process are reported in the consolidated income statement. (2088)

24. (a) Foreign currency financial statements should be translated by means of the following rates: all assets and liabilities at the current exchange rate at the balance sheet date; revenues and expenses at the exchange rate at the time the revenue or expense was recognized, however due to the impracticability of this where rates change frequently, a weighted-average exchange rate for the period may be used; contributed capital at the historical exchange rate; and retained earnings at the translated amount of retained earnings for the prior period, plus (less net income(loss) at the weighted-average rate, less dividends declared during the period at the exchange rate when declared. The weighted average exchange rate would be an appropriate exchange rate for salaries expense and sales to external customers. (8756)

25. (c) Since the subsidiary's functional currency is the currency of the country in which it is located, all of its assets are translated at the current rate (i.e., the exchange rate in effect at the balance sheet date). (9081)

26. (b) The foreign currency income statement should conceptually use the exchange rate at the time the revenue or expense was recognized. However, due to the impracticability of this where rates change frequently, a weighted-average exchange rate for the period may be used. The current exchange rate would be used for all assets and liabilities at the balance sheet date. The historical exchange rate is used for contributed capital. There is no inventory (FIFO) exchange rate used in the financial statements. (8598)

Foreign Currency Transactions

27. (b) Foreign currency transactions are transactions denominated in a currency other than the entity's functional currency. Hence, no foreign currency transaction gain or loss would occur if the purchase of the machinery by the U.S. company is denominated in U.S. dollars. Foreign exchange transaction gains and losses are recognized as a component of income from continuing operations in the period they occur. (4540)

28. (b) Receivable: Rate increase results in a gain (receive more at settlement), rate decrease results in a loss (receive less at settlement). Payable: Rate increase results in a loss (pay more at settlement), rate decrease results in a gain (pay less at settlement). (7604)

29. (d) At the date the transaction is recognized, each asset, liability, revenue, expense, gain, or loss arising from the transaction should be measured and recorded in the functional currency of the recording entity by use of the exchange rate in effect at that date. Toigo would record a liability of $625,000 (500,000 × $1.25). At each balance sheet date, recorded balances that are denominated in a currency other than the functional currency of the recording entity should be adjusted to reflect the current exchange rate. These adjustments should be currently recognized as transaction gains or losses and reported as a component of income from continuing operations. Toigo would recognize a gain of $25,000 on the December 31 financial statements based on 500,000 pounds × $1.20 = $600,000 as of December 31. (9895)

30. (b) The exchange rate to be used for translation of foreign currency transactions is as follows. At the date the transaction is recognized, each asset, liability, revenue, expense, gain, or loss arising from the transaction should be measured and recorded in the functional currency of the recording entity by use of the exchange rate in effect at that date. At each balance sheet date, recorded balances that are denominated in a currency other than the functional currency of the recording entity should be adjusted to reflect the current exchange rate. These adjustments should be currently recognized as transaction gains or losses and reported as a component of income from continuing operations. Upon settlement, a transaction gain or loss, measured from the transaction date or the most recent intervening balance sheet date (whichever is later), should be included as a component of income from continuing operations for the period in which the transaction is settled. The U.S. company would recognize a gain of $100 when the receivable is collected (settlement date) based on 2,000 pounds × $0.05, the increase in the exchange rate of $1.45 on the balance sheet date to $1.50 on the settlement date. (8791)

31. (c) Gains and losses on the following foreign currency transactions should not be included in determining net income, but should be reported in the same manner as translation adjustments: foreign currency transactions that are designated as, and are effective as, economic hedges of a net investment in a foreign entity, commencing as of the designation date; or intercompany foreign currency transactions that are of a long-term investment nature (that is, settlement is not planned or anticipated in the foreseeable future), when the entities to the transaction are consolidated, combined, or accounted for by the equity method in the reporting enterprise's financial statements. Since answers a. and b. are correct, answer c., *both a. and b.*, is the best choice. (89583)

32. (d) The payables resulting from the merchandise purchased from the foreign supplier and the borrowing are transactions denominated in a foreign currency. The payable from the merchandise purchased was recorded at $90,000 on 1/20. It was paid on 3/20 at the U.S. dollar equivalent of $96,000, resulting in a $6,000 foreign exchange loss. The payable from the borrowing was recorded at $500,000 at 7/1. Accrued interest on the borrowing was $25,000 (i.e., $500,000 × 10% × 6/12) at 12/31. At 12/31, the U.S. dollar equivalents of principal and accrued interest were $520,000 and $26,000, respectively, resulting in an additional $21,000 [i.e., ($520,000 + $26,000) – ($500,000 + $25,000)] foreign exchange loss. Thus, the foreign exchange loss recognized in the year-end income statement is $27,000 (i.e., $6,000 + $21,000). (1335)

33. (a) A forward exchange contract (forward contract) is an agreement to exchange different currencies at a specified future date and at a specified rate (the forward rate). A forward contract is a foreign currency transaction. Therefore, a gain or loss on a forward contract is included in determining net income in accordance with the requirements for other foreign currency transactions. A gain or loss on a speculative forward contract (that is, a contract that does not hedge an exposure) is computed by multiplying the foreign currency amount of the contract by the difference between the forward rate available for the remaining maturity of the contract and the contracted forward rate (or the forward rate last used to measure a gain or loss on that contract for an earlier period).

Foreign currency units	10,000
Times: Excess of forward rate available for the remaining maturity of the contract and the contracted forward rate ($0.82 – $0.78)	× $0.04
Loss on forward contract	$ 400

(2623)

Changing Prices

34. (d) Historical cost/constant purchasing power accounting is a method of accounting based on measures of historical prices in units of a currency, each of which has the same general purchasing power. (89575)

35. (a) Monetary assets are defined as money or a claim to receive a sum of money, the amount of which is fixed or determinable without reference to future prices of specific goods or services. Monetary liabilities are obligations to pay a sum of money, the amount of which is fixed or determinable without reference to future prices of specific goods and services. The value in use is the amount determined by discounting the future cash flows (including the ultimate proceeds of disposal) expected to be derived from the use of an asset at an appropriate rate that allows for the risk of the activities concerned. (89577)

36. (c) Financial statements prepared under the current cost/constant dollar method of accounting include adjustments for both specific price changes and general price-level changes. Historical cost/nominal dollar is the generally accepted method of accounting based on measures of historical prices without restatement. Current cost/nominal dollar is a method of accounting in which adjustments for specific price changes are made but not for general price-level changes. Historical cost/constant dollar is a method of accounting in which adjustments are not made for specific price changes but are made for general price-level changes. (6139)

37. (b) Monetary assets represent a claim to receive a fixed sum of money or an amount determinable without reference to future prices of specific goods and services. The demand bank deposits and net long-term receivables are monetary assets as they represent claims to receive a fixed sum of money, the amounts of which can be determined without reference to future prices of specific goods and services. All assets that are not monetary are nonmonetary. The patents and trademarks do not represent a claim to receive cash, and hence are classified as nonmonetary assets. (1245)

38. (c) A company disclosing voluntary information about the effect of changing prices should report this information in the supplementary information to the financial statements. This information should not be reported in the body of the financial statements, the notes to the financial statements, or management's report to shareholders. (5269)

39. (a) The "inflation component" of the increase in the current cost amount is defined as the difference between the nominal dollars and constant dollars measures. (4873)

40. (a) To compute cost of goods sold on a current cost basis, multiply the number of units sold by the average current cost of the units during the year. (Average current cost of the units during the year is the sum of the current cost of the units at the beginning and the end of the year, divided by two.) (3473)

41. (d) In classifying balance sheet accounts as monetary or nonmonetary, a valuation account is classified the same as the account to which it relates. Accumulated depreciation on equipment is classified as nonmonetary because it is a valuation account to equipment, which is nonmonetary. Advances to unconsolidated subsidiaries is a receivable, and, thus, is monetary. Allowance for uncollectible accounts is a valuation allowance to accounts receivable, which is monetary. Premium on bonds payable is a valuation account to bonds payable, which is monetary. (4506)

42. (a) An entity suffers purchasing power losses in a period of rising general price levels from holding monetary assets. A monetary asset is money or a claim to receive a sum of money, the amount of which is fixed or determinable without reference to future prices of specific goods and services. A refundable deposit with a supplier is a monetary asset. An equity investment in unconsolidated subsidiaries is a nonmonetary asset. Warranty obligations are nonmonetary liabilities. Wages payable is a monetary liability. An entity would have purchasing power gains in a period of rising general price levels from holding monetary liabilities. (2697)

43. (d) Under current cost accounting, the amount of holding gain on a unit of inventory is the increase in current cost from holding the inventory from period to period. The inventory in question was purchased at $8 per unit and has a replacement cost of $10 on December 31. Therefore, under current cost accounting, Vend has a holding gain of $2 ($10 – $8) on each unit of the inventory (2645)

PERFORMANCE BY SUBTOPICS

Each category below parallels a subtopic covered in Chapter 13. Record the number and percentage of questions you correctly answered in each subtopic area.

Subsequent Events

Question #	Correct √
1	
2	
3	
# Questions	3
# Correct	______
% Correct	______

Related Party Disclosures

Question #	Correct √
4	
5	
6	
7	
# Questions	4
# Correct	______
% Correct	______

Developmental Stage Enterprises

Question #	Correct √
8	
9	
10	
11	
12	
# Questions	5
# Correct	______
% Correct	______

Operating Segments

Question #	Correct √
13	
14	
15	
16	
17	
18	
19	
# Questions	7
# Correct	______
% Correct	______

Functional Currency/ Translations

Question #	Correct √
20	
21	
22	
23	
24	
25	
26	
# Questions	7
# Correct	______
% Correct	______

Foreign Currency Transactions

Question #	Correct √
27	
28	
29	
30	
31	
32	
33	
# Questions	7
# Correct	______
% Correct	______

Changing Prices

Question #	Correct √
34	
35	
36	
37	
38	
39	
40	
41	
42	
43	
# Questions	10
# Correct	______

Solution 13-2 SIMULATION ANSWER: Functional Currency

Trial Balance

Account	Euros (debit/credit)	Exchange Rate	U.S. Dollars (debit/credit)
Cash	$ 150,000	$0.65	$ 97,500
Account receivable (net)	100,000	0.65	65,000
Inventory	320,000	0.72	230,400
Office building (net)	840,000	0.68	571,200
Accounts payable	(130,000)	0.65	(84,500)
Mortgage payable	(700,000)	0.65	(455,000)
Common stock	(440,000)	0.75	(330,000)
Sales	(980,000)	0.70	(686,000)
Costs of goods sold	550,000	0.72	396,000
Selling expenses	110,000	0.70	77,000
Operating expenses	180,000	0.70	126,000
Exchange gain			(7,600)
Totals	$ 0		$ 0

Explanations

Cash is remeasured at the current rate $0.65; $150,000 × 0.65 = $97,500

Accounts receivable is remeasured at the current rate of $0.65; $100,000 × 0.65 = $65,500

Inventory is remeasured at the historical rate of $0.72; $320,000 × 0.72 = $230,400

Office building is remeasured at the historical rate of $0.68; $840,000 × 0.68 = $571,200

Accounts payable is recorded at the current rate of $0.65; $(130,000) × 0.65 = $(84,500)

Mortgage payable is recorded at the current rate of $0.65; $(700,000) × 0.65 = $(455,000)

Common stock is recorded at the original issue rate of $0.75; $(440,000) × 0.75 = $(330,000)

Sales is recorded at the average exchange rate of 0.70; $(980,000) × 0.70 = $(686,000)

Cost of goods sold is remeasured at the historical rate of $0.72; $550,000 × 0.72 = $396,000

Selling expenses is recorded at the average exchange rate of 0.70; $110,000 × 0.70 = $77,000

Operating expenses is recorded at the average exchange rate of 0.70; $180,000 × 0.70 = $126,000

Solution 13-3 SIMULATION ANSWER: Economic Indicators

	Economic Indicators	**(Yes or No)**
1.	Cash flow	Yes
2.	Continent	No
3.	Currency value	No
4.	Engineering	No
5.	Expense	Yes
6.	Financing	Yes
7.	Global environment	No
8.	Global market	No
9.	Intercompany arrangement	Yes
10.	Intercompany transactions	Yes
11.	Sales price	Yes
12.	Sales market	Yes
13.	Sales volume	No
14.	Stock price	No
15.	Stock market	No
16.	Stock volume	No

Explanations

1. Cash flows related to the foreign entity's individual assets and liabilities are primarily in the foreign currency and do not directly impact the parent company's cash flows are indicative of using the foreign currency as the functional currency.

Cash flows related to the foreign entity's individual assets and liabilities directly impact the parent's cash flows on a current basis and are readily available for remittance to the parent company are indicative of using the parent's currency as the functional currency.

2. This is not a type of economic indicator identified in FASB authoritative literature.

3. This is not a type of economic indicator identified in FASB authoritative literature.

4. This is not a type of economic indicator identified in FASB authoritative literature.

5. Labor, materials, and other costs for the foreign entity's products or services are primarily local costs, even though there also might be imports from other countries are indicative of using the foreign currency as the functional currency.

Labor, materials, and other costs for the foreign entity's products or services, on a continuing basis, are primarily costs for components obtained from the country in which the parent company is located are indicative of using the parent's currency as the functional currency.

6. Financing is primarily denominated in foreign currency, and funds generated by the foreign entity's operations are sufficient to service existing and normally expected debt obligations are indicative of using the foreign currency as the functional currency.

Financing is primarily from the parent or other dollar-denominated obligations, or funds generated by the foreign entity's operations are not sufficient to service existing and normally expected debt obligations without the infusion of additional funds from the parent company are indicative of using the parent's currency as the functional currency. Infusion of additional funds from the parent company for expansion is not a factor, provided funds generated by the foreign entity's expanded operations are expected to be sufficient to service that additional financing.

7. This is not a type of economic indicator identified in FASB authoritative literature.

8. This is not a type of economic indicator identified in FASB authoritative literature.

9. There is not an extensive interrelationship between the operations of the foreign entity and the parent company, though the foreign entity's operations may rely on the parent's or affiliates' competitive advantages, such as patents and trademarks, is indicative of using the foreign currency as the functional currency.

There is an extensive interrelationship between the operations of the foreign entity and the parent company is indicative of using the parent's currency as the functional currency. Additionally, the parent's currency generally would be the functional currency if the foreign entity is a device or shell corporation for holding investments, obligations, intangible assets, etc., that could readily be carried on the parent's or an affiliate's books.

10. There is a low volume of intercompany transactions between the operations of the foreign entity and the parent company is indicative of using the foreign currency as the functional currency.

There is a high volume of intercompany transactions between the operations of the foreign entity and the parent company is indicative of using the parent's currency as the functional currency. Additionally, the parent's currency generally would be the functional currency if the foreign entity is a device or shell corporation for holding investments, obligations, intangible assets, etc., that could readily be carried on the parent's or an affiliate's books.

11. Sales prices for the foreign entity's products are primarily responsive on a short-term basis to changes in exchange rates; for example, sales prices are determined more by worldwide competition or by international prices is indicative of using the parent's currency as the functional currency.

12. There is an active local sales market for the foreign entity's products, although there also might be significant amounts of exports, is indicative of using the foreign currency as the functional currency.

The sales market is mostly in the parent's country or sales contracts are denominated in the parent's currency is indicative of using the parent's currency as the functional currency.

13. This is not a type of economic indicator identified in FASB authoritative literature.

14. This is not a type of economic indicator identified in FASB authoritative literature.

15. This is not a type of economic indicator identified in FASB authoritative literature.

16. This is not a type of economic indicator identified in FASB authoritative literature.

Solution 13-4 SIMULATION ANSWER: Research

FASB Accounting Standards Codification

FASB ASC:	830	-	10	-	10	-	2

10-2 The unity presented by such translation does not alter the underlying significance of the results and relationships of the constituent parts of the reporting entity. It is only through the effective operation of its constituent parts that the reporting entity as a whole is able to achieve its purpose. Accordingly, the translation of the financial statements of each component entity of a reporting entity should accomplish both of the following objectives:

a. Provide information that is generally compatible with the expected economic effects of a rate change on a reporting entity's cash flows and equity.

b. Reflect in consolidated statements the financial results and relationships of the individual consolidated entities as measured in their functional currencies in conformity with U.S. generally accepted accounting principles (GAAP).

FYI: Question Reference Numbers

This page is included due to questions editors have received from some candidates using previous editions of our review material; however, it is not essential for your review.

In the lower right-hand corner of a multiple-choice question, you may note a question reference. This reference is included primarily so that editors may trace a question to its source and readily track it from one edition to another and from one media to another.

The reference indicates the source of the question and, possibly, a similar question in the software. For instance, a question with reference 11/93, AUD., #4, 4241, was question number 4 from the November 1993 AICPA Auditing & Attestation examination. When the reference has an "R" instead of 5 or 11, the AICPA released the question from a "nondisclosed" exam without specifying the exam month.

Questions marked "Editors" are questions that are modeled after AICPA questions, but are not actually from the examiners. The examiners occasionally move topics from one exam section to another. You may see a question from a former AUD exam, for instance, in the REG or BEC volume. The following abbreviations indicate former exam section titles.

BLPR	Business Law & Professional Responsibilities	BL	Business Law
AR	Accounting & Reporting	PI	Accounting Practice, Part I
AUD	Auditing & Attestation	PII	Accounting Practice, Part II
FAR	Financial Accounting & Reporting	T	Accounting Theory

At first glance, candidates may assume that older questions are irrelevant for preparation for upcoming exams. Provided that they are updated appropriately, many early questions are excellent choices for review questions. When the exam was fully disclosed, editors noted that it was **more** likely that questions from early exams would reappear than questions from relatively recent exams. For instance, on a 1994 exam, it was more likely that an updated question from a 1988 exam would appear than an updated question from a 1993 exam. Second-guessing what questions the examiners will ask typically is more difficult and less reliable than merely learning the content eligible to be tested on the exam.

The four-digit number in these references often correspond to an ID number in our software, online courses, and/or Hot*Spot videos. Sometimes questions are removed from the software but not the book (and vice versa), so a question in the book is not necessarily in the software. Also, questions may vary slightly between the book, software, and videos. If you need help finding a question from the book in the software using this question ID number, please contact our technical support staff at support@cpaexam.com or 1-800-742-1309 and ask them to explain using the "jump" feature for questions.

CHAPTER 14

ACCOUNTING FOR INCOME TAXES

CHAPTER 14

ACCOUNTING FOR INCOME TAXES

I. Basic Concepts

A. Pretax Financial Income

Pretax financial income (often called pretax accounting income, and sometimes called book income, financial income, accounting income, or income for financial accounting purposes) is determined on the accrual basis. That is, expenses incurred for the period are deducted from revenues earned for the period to arrive at pretax financial income. Income tax expense (often called provision for income taxes) is then deducted from that subtotal to arrive at net income. An excess of expenses over revenues will cause a pretax financial loss. In situations where a loss situation results in a tax refund or tax savings, the provision is referred to as income tax benefit.

B. Taxable Income

Taxable income is determined by following the rules of the Internal Revenue Code. Deductions (called deductible amounts or tax deductible amounts or tax deductible expenses) allowed for the period and allowable exemptions are subtracted from income items (called taxable amounts or taxable revenues) for the period to arrive at taxable income (loss) for the period.

Exhibit 1 ▸ Financial vs Taxable Income

	Revenues earned		Taxable amounts
–	Expenses incurred	–	Deductible amounts
	Pretax financial income (loss)		Taxable income (loss)
–	Income tax expense (benefit)		
	Net income (loss)		

C. Objectives

The objectives of accounting for income taxes are to recognize (a) the amount of taxes payable or refundable for the current year and (b) deferred tax liabilities and assets for the future tax consequences of events that have been recognized in an enterprise's financial statements or tax returns. To implement the objectives, the following basic principles are applied in accounting for income taxes at the date of the financial statements:

- A current tax liability or asset is recognized for the estimated taxes payable or refundable on tax returns for the current year.
- A deferred tax liability or asset is recognized for the estimated future tax effects attributable to temporary differences and carryforwards.
- The measurement of current and deferred tax liabilities and assets is based on provisions of the enacted tax law; the effects of future changes in tax laws or rates are not anticipated.
- The measurement of deferred tax assets is reduced, if necessary, by the amount of any tax benefits that, based on available evidence, are not expected to be realized.

D. Income Taxes Currently Payable (Refundable)

Income taxes currently payable (refundable) is also called current tax expense (or benefit) and is determined by applying the provisions of the tax law to the taxable income or taxable loss figure for a period. The tax law provides that a net operating loss (NOL) may be carried back 2 years and forward 20 years.

Example 1 ▸ Income Taxes Currently Payable

Zanthe Corp. has taxable income for the year of $400,000 and a tax rate of 40%.

Required: Compute the amount of income taxes payable for the year.

Solution:

Taxable income	$400,000
Tax rate	× 40%
Income taxes currently payable	$160,000

Example 2 ▸ Income Taxes Currently Refundable

The Aspen Company has the following history of taxable income and taxes paid:

Year	Taxable income		Tax rate		Taxes paid
1	$ 60,000	×	50%	=	$30,000
2	50,000	×	45%	=	22,500
3	40,000	×	40%	=	16,000
4	80,000	×	35%	=	28,000

The tax rate for year 5 is 30%, and a 25% rate is enacted for year 6 and subsequent years. In year 5, Aspen reports a $200,000 excess of tax deductible expenses over taxable revenues on its tax return. This excess often is called a net operating loss (NOL).

Required: Compute the amount of taxes refundable due to a carryback of the year 5 NOL.

Solution: The $200,000 NOL in year 5 is first applied to year 3, which is the earliest of the two years prior to the loss year. The NOL exceeds the year 3 taxable income so the remaining NOL is then applied to the $80,000 taxable income of year 4 (in that order).

	Taxable income		Tax rate		Taxes paid
From year 3:	$ 40,000	×	40%	=	$ 16,000
From year 4:	80,000	×	35%	=	28,000
	$120,000				
Taxes refundable due to year 5 NOL					$ 44,000

NOTE: Because there was insufficient taxable income in the 2 years prior to year 5 to fully offset the NOL, there is an NOL carryforward for tax purposes of $80,000 (i.e., $200,000 – $120,000) at the end of year 5.

E. Income Tax Expense (Benefit)

Income tax expense (benefit) is the sum of current tax expense (benefit) and deferred tax expense (benefit). In the rare instances where taxable income is the same amount as pretax financial income, total income tax expense will equal income taxes currently payable. Income tax expense is often referred to as the provision for income taxes. There can be both a current portion and a deferred portion of the provision. A corporation often charges estimated tax payments to an account titled *Prepaid Income Taxes.* The balance of this account is used to offset the balance of the *Income Taxes Payable* account; the net amount is classified as a current asset if the prepaid account is larger or as a current liability if the payable account is larger.

Example 3 ▸ Current Income Tax Expense

Refer to Example 1. Pretax financial income for the year is also $400,000 (no differences in taxable income and pretax financial income).

Required: Prepare the journal entry to record income taxes for the year.

Solution:

Income Tax Expense—current	160,000	
Income Taxes Payable ($400,000 × 40%)		160,000

Discussion: Because there are no temporary differences, there are no deferred income taxes. There is only a current portion for the provision; hence, income tax expense (provision) is the same amount as income tax payable ($160,000). The expense account balance appears on the income statement and the payable account balance is reported as a current liability on the balance sheet.

Example 4 ▸ Deferred Income Tax Expense

Refer to Example 2. The pretax financial loss for year 5 was also $200,000 (no differences in taxable income and pretax financial income in any of the years affected). Aspen reports pretax financial income and taxable income of $92,000 for year 6 before consideration of the deduction for the NOL carryforward.

Required: Prepare the journal entry at the end of year 5 to record the benefits of the operating loss carryback and the expected future benefits of the $80,000 loss carryforward.

Solution:

Income Tax Refund Receivable	44,000	
Benefits of Loss Carryback (from Example 2)		44,000
Deferred Tax Asset ($80,000 × 25%)	20,000	
Benefits of Loss Carryforward		20,000

Discussion: The income tax refund receivable balance of $44,000 is classified as a current asset on the balance sheet. The deferred tax asset balance of $20,000 is classified as a current asset or a noncurrent asset, depending on whether the benefits of the NOL carryforward are expected to be realized in the year that immediately follows the balance sheet date (in which case, it would be classified as a current asset) or in a later year (noncurrent asset). The income statement for year 5 would report the following.

Operating loss before income taxes	$(200,000)
Benefits of loss carryback	44,000
Benefits of loss carryforward	20,000
Net loss, year 5	$(136,000)

The income taxes for year 6 are recorded as follows.

Income Tax Expense—current	3,000	
Income Tax Expense—deferred	20,000	
Income Taxes Payable [25% × ($92,000 – $80,000)]		3,000
Deferred Tax Asset (25% × $80,000)		20,000

The income statement for year 6 would report the following.

Income before income taxes		$ 92,000
Current tax expense	$ 3,000	
Deferred tax expense	20,000	
Total income tax expense		(23,000)
Net income		$ 69,000

F. **Reconciliation of Pretax Financial Income & Taxable Income**
Most revenues and most expenses are reported on the tax return in the same period that they are reported on the income statement. However, tax laws often differ from the recognition and measurement requirements of financial accounting standards, and it is common to find differences between the amount of pretax financial income (loss) and the amount of taxable income (loss) for a period.

Exhibit 2 ▸ Income Reconciliation

Pretax financial income for the current period can be reconciled with taxable income for the current period by using the following format.

Pretax financial income (loss)	$X,XXX
Excess of taxable revenues over revenues per books	+ XXX
Excess of deductible amounts over expenses per books	(XXX)
Excess of revenues per books over taxable revenues	(XXX)
Excess of expenses per books over deductible amounts	+ XXX
Taxable income (loss)	$X,XXX

II. Differences

A. **Temporary Differences**
A temporary difference is a difference between the tax basis of an asset or liability and its reported amount in the financial statements that will result in taxable or deductible amounts in future years when the reported amount of the asset is recovered or the liability is settled.

1. **Origin** The tax consequences of most events recognized in the current year's financial statements are included in determining income taxes currently payable. Because tax laws and financial accounting standards differ in their recognition and measurement of assets, liabilities, equity, revenues, expenses, gains, and losses, differences arise between the following.

   a. The amount of taxable income and pretax financial income for a year

   b. The tax basis of assets or liabilities and their reported amounts in financial statements

2. **Future Effects** Because it is assumed that the reported amounts of assets and liabilities will be recovered and settled, respectively, a difference between the tax basis of an asset or a liability and its reported amount in the balance sheet will result in a taxable or a deductible amount in some future year(s) when the reported amounts of assets are recovered and the reported amounts of liabilities are settled.

3. **Taxable & Deductible Temporary Differences** Temporary differences that will result in taxable amounts in future years when the related assets are recovered are often called taxable temporary differences. Likewise, temporary differences that will result in deductible amounts in future years when the related liabilities are settled are often called deductible temporary differences.

4. **Recognition & Measurement** The asset and liability method is required to be used in accounting and reporting for temporary differences. Under this method, a current or deferred tax liability or asset is recognized for the current or deferred tax consequences of all events that have been recognized in the financial statements, and the current or deferred tax consequences of an event are measured based on provisions of the enacted tax law to determine the amount of taxes payable or refundable currently or in future years.

Example 5 ▸ Temporary Differences

Pretax financial income for the current year for Zippy Corporation is $400,000, including revenue of $50,000, which will not be taxable until a future period. Deductible amounts of $30,000 on the current year tax return will be expensed on a future income statement. The tax rate is 40% for all years. There is no existing balance in any deferred tax account at the beginning of the year.

Required:

1. Compute taxable income for the year.
2. Prepare the journal entry to record income taxes for the year.

Solution:

1.

Pretax financial income	$400,000
Excess of revenues over taxable amounts	(50,000)
Excess of deductible amounts over expenses	(30,000)
Taxable income	$320,000

2.

Income Tax Expense—current	128,000	
Income Tax Expense—deferred	32,000	
Income Taxes Payable ($320,000 × 40%)		128,000
Deferred Tax Liability [($50,000 + $30,000) × 40%]		32,000

Discussion: Because differences between pretax financial income and taxable income in the year do cause differences between pretax financial income and taxable income in some other period, there are deferred taxes to compute and record. The amount due to the government (income taxes payable) is based on the amount of taxable income. The deferred tax amount is computed in accordance with the asset and liability method.

Under the liability method, the deferred tax consequences of the $80,000 ($50,000 + $30,000) future taxable amounts are calculated using enacted future tax rates (40%). The total income tax expense (provision) figure ($160,000) is the amount needed to balance the entry [current tax expense (provision) of $128,000 plus deferred tax expense (provision) of $32,000].

5. **Timing Sources** Differences between taxable income and pretax financial income that result from including revenues, expenses, gains, or losses in taxable income of an earlier or later year than the year in which they are recognized in financial income (referred to as "timing differences") create differences (sometimes accumulating over more than one year) between the tax basis of an asset or liability and its reported amount in the financial statements and, thus, are temporary differences.

Example 6 ▸ Taxable After Being Included in Financial Income

One example is the use of the accrual method for accounting for installment sales for computing financial income and the use of the installment (cash) method for tax purposes. This will cause an excess of the reported amount of an asset (receivable) over its tax basis that will result in a taxable amount in a future year(s) when the asset is recovered (when the cash is collected). This situation will result in future taxable amounts.

Example 7 ▸ Deductible After Being Included in Financial Income

Examples include accruals of items such as warranty expense and loss contingencies in computing financial income. Such items are deductible for tax purposes only when they are realized. This type of situation causes a reported amount of a liability to exceed its tax basis (zero) which will result in deductible amounts in a future year(s) when the liability is settled. This situation will result in future tax deductible amounts.

Example 8 ▸ Taxable Before Being Included in Financial Income

One example is accounting for revenue received in advance for rent or subscriptions. For tax purposes, the revenue is taxable in the period the related cash is received. The revenue is not included in the computation of financial income until the period in which it is earned. This situation causes a liability's reported amount on the balance sheet to exceed its tax basis (zero) which will result in future tax deductible amounts when the liability is settled. This case is said to result in future tax deductible amounts because of the future sacrifices required to provide goods or services or to provide refunds to those who cancel their orders. This situation will result in future tax deductible amounts.

Example 9 ▸ Deductible Before Being Included in Financial Income

These situations result in future taxable amounts. Typically, temporary differences of this type accumulate and then eliminate over several years. Future temporary differences for **existing** depreciable assets (in use at the balance sheet date) are considered in determining the future years in which existing temporary differences result in **net** taxable or deductible amounts.

a. One example is when a prepaid expense is deducted for tax purposes in the period it is paid, but deferred and deducted in the period the expense is incurred for purposes of computing financial (book) income.

b. The most commonly cited example is where a depreciable asset is depreciated faster for tax purposes than it is depreciated for book purposes. This will cause the asset's carrying amount to exceed its tax basis. Amounts received upon the future recovery of the asset's carrying amount (through use or sale) will exceed its tax basis and the excess will be a taxable amount when the asset is recovered.

Example 10 ▸ Multi-Year Temporary Differences

An enterprise acquired a depreciable asset at the beginning of year 1. The asset has a cost of $60,000, no residual value, is being depreciated over six years using the straight-line method for financial reporting purposes, and is being depreciated over three years using the straight-line method and the one-half year convention for tax purposes.

Year	Depreciation for financial reporting	Depreciation for tax purposes	Difference
1	$10,000	$10,000	$ --
2	10,000	20,000	(10,000)
3	10,000	20,000	(10,000)
4	10,000	10,000	--
5	10,000	--	10,000
6	10,000	--	10,000
	$60,000	$60,000	$ --

Required: Determine the cumulative temporary difference at the end of each year and describe its impact on future tax returns.

Solution:

1. At the end of year 1 there is no temporary difference. The carrying amount of the asset is $50,000 and its tax basis is $50,000 (i.e., $60,000 – $10,000).
2. At the end of year 2 the cumulative temporary difference is $10,000 and will result in a net future taxable amount of $10,000. This amount will reverse in year 5.
3. At the end of year 3 the cumulative temporary difference is $20,000 and will result in a net future taxable amount of $20,000. This amount will reverse equally in year 5 and year 6.
4. At the end of year 4 the cumulative temporary difference is $20,000 and will result in a net future taxable amount of $20,000. This amount will reverse equally in year 5 and year 6.
5. At the end of year 5 the cumulative temporary difference is $10,000 and will result in a future taxable amount of $10,000. This amount will reverse in year 6.
6. At the end of year 6 there is no more temporary difference because the asset is fully depreciated both for financial statements and tax purposes.

6. **Other Sources** Other situations that may cause temporary differences because of differences between the reported amount and the tax basis of an asset or liability, such as:

   a. A reduction in the tax basis of depreciable assets because of tax credits.

   b. Investment tax credits accounted for by the deferred method.

   c. An increase in the tax basis of assets because of indexing whenever the local currency is the functional currency.

   d. Assets acquired and liabilities assumed in a business combination or in an acquisition by a not-for-profit entity and assets and liabilities carried over to the records of a new entity formed by a merger of not-for-profits entities.

7. **Not Linked to Particular Item** Some temporary differences are deferred taxable income or tax deductions and have balances only on an income tax balance sheet and, therefore, cannot be identified with a particular asset or liability for financial reporting. There is no related, identifiable asset or liability for financial reporting, but there is a temporary difference that results from an event that has been recognized in the financial statements, and that difference will result in taxable or deductible amounts in future years. An example is a long-term contract that is accounted for by the percentage of completion method for financial reporting and by the completed contract method for tax purposes. The temporary difference (income on the contract) is deferred income for tax purposes that becomes taxable when the contract is completed.

Exhibit 3 ▸ Temporary Differences

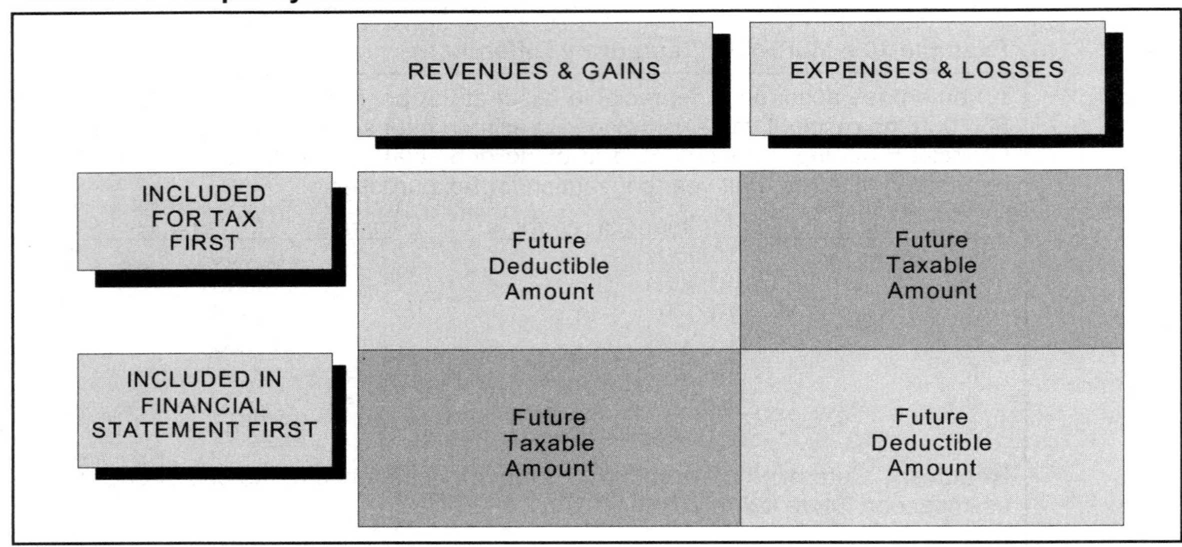

B. Permanent Differences

Some events recognized in financial statements do not have tax consequences under the regular U.S. tax system. Certain revenues are exempt from taxation and certain expenses are not deductible. Events that do not have tax consequences do not give rise to temporary differences and, therefore, do not give rise to deferred tax assets or liabilities. These differences that will not have future tax consequences are often referred to as permanent differences.

1. **Revenue Examples** Permanent differences resulting from revenues that are included in the computation of financial income, but are not included in computing taxable income, include: (a) interest earned on state and municipal obligations; (b) life insurance proceeds received by an enterprise on one of its officers; and (c) dividends received by one U.S. corporation from another U.S. corporation that are excluded from taxable income due to the dividends-received deduction (70%, 80%, or 100%).

2. **Expense Examples** Permanent differences resulting from expenses that are included in the computation of financial income, but are not included in computing taxable income, include: (a) expenses incurred in generating tax-exempt income; (b) premiums paid for life insurance on officers when the enterprise is the beneficiary; and (c) fines, penalties, and other costs incurred from activities that are a violation of the law.

3. **Deduction Example** An example of a permanent difference resulting from deductions that are allowed in computing taxable income but are not allowed in computing financial income is excess of percentage depletion (statutory allowance) over cost of natural resources.

Example 11 ▸ Permanent Differences

Pretax financial income for year 7 for Zippy Corporation is $300,000 including tax-exempt revenues of $40,000 and nondeductible expenses of $14,000. The tax rate for all years is 40%.

Required:

1. Compute the amount of taxable income for year 7.
2. Prepare the journal entry to record income taxes for year 7.
3. Show a condensed income statement for year 7.

Solution:

1.	Pretax financial income	$ 300,000		
	Tax-exempt revenues	(40,000)		
	Nondeductible expenses	14,000		
	Taxable income	$ 274,000		
2.	Income Tax Expense—current		109,600	
	Income Taxes Payable ($274,000 × 40%)			109,600
3.	Income before income taxes	$ 300,000		
	Current income tax expense	(109,600)		
	Net income	$ 190,400		

Discussion: Because differences between pretax financial income and taxable income in the year do not cause differences between pretax financial income and taxable income in any other period, there are no deferred taxes to compute and record. The amount due to the government is based on the amount of taxable income. Because there are no deferred taxes, the amount of income tax expense recorded is the same amount as income taxes payable. The effective tax rate ($109,600 / $300,000 = 36.53%) is less than the statutory rate due to an excess of tax-exempt revenues ($40,000) over nondeductible expenses ($14,000).

Exhibit 4 ▸ Summary of Temporary & Permanent Differences

	GAAP Financial Statements	IRC Tax Return	TEMP	PERM	NONE
GROSS INCOME:					
Gross Sales	Income Now	Income Now			✓
Installment Sales	Income Now	Income (Later) When Rec'd	✓		
Dividends Equity Method	Income-Sub Earnings	Income is Dividends	✓		
100/80/70% Exclusion	No Exclusion	Excluded Forever		✓	
Rents & Royalties in Advance	Income When Earned	Income When Received	✓		
State & Muni Bond Interest	Income	Never Income		✓	
Life Insurance Proceeds	Income	Never Income		✓	
Gain/Loss Treasury Stock	Not Reported	Not Reported			✓
ORDINARY EXPENSES:					
Officers Compensation (Top)	Expense	$1,000,000 Limit			✓
Bad Debt	Allowance	Direct Write Off	✓		
Interest Expense Business Loan	Expense	Expense			✓
Tax-Free Investment	Expense	Nondeductible		✓	
Taxable Investment	Expense	Up to Taxable Income			✓
Contributions	All Expensed	Limit to 10% of Income	✓		✓
Loss on Abandonment/Casualty	Expense	Expense			✓
Loss on Worthless Subsidiary	Expense	Expense			✓
Depreciation MACRS vs. S.L.	Slow Depreciation	Fast Depreciation	✓		
Section 179 Deduction	Not Allowed, Must Depreciate	For 2012, first $139,000 of $560,000, subtracting $1 for $1 any amount over $560,000	✓		
Bonus Depreciation	Not Allowed, Must Depreciate	For 2012, 50% on qualified asset after §179 deduction; new equipment only	✓		
Diff. Basis of Asset	Use GAAP Basis	Use IRC Basis		✓	
Purchased Goodwill	Gain/Loss; Tested each year for impairment	Amortize S/L 15 Yrs.	✓	✓	✓
Depletion % vs. S.L.	Cost Over Years	% of Sales	✓		
% in Excess of Cost	Not Allowed	% of Sales		✓	
Life Insurance Exp. (Corp. Gets)	Expense	No Deduction		✓	
Profit & Pension Expense	Expense Accrued	No Deduction Until Paid	✓		
Accrued Exp. (50% owner/family)	Expense Accrued	No Deduction Until Paid	✓		
Net Capital Gain	Income	Income			✓
Research & Development	Expense	Exp. / Amortize / Capital.	✓	✓	✓
SPECIAL ITEMS:					
Net Capital Loss	Report as Loss	Not Deductible	✓		
Carryover (3 Yrs. & 5 Yrs.)	Not Applicable	Unused Loss Allowed	✓		
Shareholder Dealing	Report as Loss	Not Deductible		✓	
Penalties	Expense	Not Deductible		✓	
Est. Liab. Contingency/Warranty	Expense-Accrued	No Deduction Until Paid	✓		
Federal Income Taxes	Expense	Not Deductible		✓	
Bond Sinking Trust Fund	Inc. / Exp. / Gain / Loss	Inc. / Exp. / Gain / Loss	✓	✓	✓
Lobbying / Political	Expense	No Deduction		✓	

Example 12 ▶ Temporary & Permanent Differences

Tigger Corporation has pretax financial income of $100,000 for year 1 (first year of operations). The following differences exist between pretax financial income and taxable income.

1. Interest on investments in tax-exempt securities amounts to $22,000.
2. Fines and violations of the law amount to $3,000.
3. An excess of accrued warranty expense over amounts paid to satisfy warranties during the year is $18,000.
4. An excess of installment sales revenue over the cash received is $31,000 (accrual basis used for financial reporting and cash basis used for tax return).
5. Premiums paid for life insurance on officers is $6,000. Tigger Corp. is the beneficiary.
6. Depreciation for books is $70,000, whereas depreciation using an accelerated method for tax purposes is $90,000.
7. Losses accrued for financial accounting purposes for litigation contingencies amounts to $16,000.

Required:

a. Identify each difference between pretax financial income and taxable income as being either a permanent or temporary difference and reconcile pretax financial income with taxable income.

b. Compute the net future taxable (deductible) amounts due to temporary differences existing at the end of the year.

c. Assuming a tax rate for the current and future years of 40%, compute the amount of income taxes currently payable and the amount of deferred income taxes. Prepare the journal entry to record income taxes for the year.

Solution a:

Pretax financial income	$100,000
Permanent differences:	
Tax-exempt revenue [1]	(22,000)
Nondeductible fines [2]	3,000
Life insurance premiums [5]	6,000
Temporary differences originating:	
Excess of warranty expense per books [3]	18,000
Excess of installment revenue per books [4]	(31,000)
Excess of depreciation per tax return [6]	(20,000)
Excess of accrued losses per books [7]	16,000
Taxable income	$ 70,000

Solution b:

Future warranty deductions [3]	$(18,000)
Future installment sale collections [4]	31,000
Excess of book depreciation over tax depreciation in future [6]	20,000
Future deductions for litigation [7]	(16,000)
Net future taxable amounts	$ 17,000

Solution c:

Taxable income	$70,000	Net future taxable amounts	$ 17,000
Current tax rate	× 40%	Enacted future tax rate	× 40%
Income taxes currently payable	$28,000	Deferred tax liability at 12/31	$ 6,800

NOTE: Because there is a flat tax rate for all future years, deferred taxes may be computed by one aggregate calculation; the future taxable and deductible amounts that will result from the elimination of existing temporary differences need not be scheduled for the individual future years affected.

NOTE: The temporary differences originating in the year that will cause future deductible amounts (accrual of warranty expense and loss contingency for book purposes) are added to pretax financial income to arrive at taxable income; temporary differences originating in the year that will cause future taxable amounts (installment sales method and accelerated depreciation for tax purposes) are deducted from pretax financial income to arrive at taxable income.

Income Tax Expense—current	28,000	
Income Tax Expense—deferred	6,800	
Income Taxes Payable ($70,000 × 40%)		28,000
Deferred Tax Liability ($6,800 – $0)		6,800

NOTE: The change required in the *Deferred Tax Liability* account is equal to its ending balance because there was a zero beginning balance.

III. Deferred Tax Liabilities & Assets

A. Recognition

Deferred tax liabilities or assets are recognized for the future tax consequences of the following:

a. Revenues, expenses, gains, or losses that are included in taxable income of an earlier or later year than the year in which they are recognized in financial income (i.e., temporary differences).

b. Other events that create differences between the tax bases of assets and liabilities and their amounts for financial reporting.

c. Operating loss or tax credit carrybacks for refunds of taxes paid in prior years and carryforwards to reduce taxes payable in future years.

B. Terms

1. **Deferred Tax Expense or Benefit** Deferred tax expense or benefit is the change during the year in an enterprise's deferred tax liabilities and assets.

2. **Total Income Tax Expense or Benefit** Total income tax expense (provision) or benefit for the year is the sum of deferred tax expense or benefit and current tax expense or benefit (income taxes currently payable or refundable).

3. **Basis** The recognition and measurement of a deferred tax liability or asset is based on the future effects on income taxes, as measured by the provisions of enacted tax laws, resulting from temporary differences and operating loss and tax credit carryforwards at the end of the current year.

4. **Jurisdictions** A deferred tax liability or asset is separately computed for each tax jurisdiction (i.e., for each federal, state, local, and foreign taxing authority) because the tax attributes related to one taxing authority cannot be used to directly offset tax attributes related to a different taxing authority.

C. Computation

The steps in the annual computation of deferred tax liabilities and assets are as follows.

1. **Identification** Identify (a) the types and amounts of existing temporary differences and (b) the nature and amount of each type of operating loss and tax credit carryforward and the remaining length of the carryforward period.

2. **Measuring Deferred Tax Liability** Measure the total deferred tax liability for taxable temporary differences using the applicable tax rate.

3. **Measuring Deferred Tax Asset** Measure the total deferred tax asset for deductible temporary differences and operating loss carryforwards using the applicable tax rate.

4. **Tax Credit Carryforwards** Measure deferred tax assets for each type of tax credit carryforward.

5. **Valuation Allowance** Reduce deferred tax assets by a valuation allowance if, based on the weight of available evidence, it is *more likely than not* (a likelihood of more than 50%) that some or all of the deferred tax assets will not be realized. The allowance must reduce the deferred tax asset to an amount that is more likely than not to be realized.

D. Enacted Tax Rate

The tax rate that is used to measure deferred tax liabilities and deferred tax assets is the enacted tax rate(s) expected to apply to taxable income in the years that the liability is expected to be settled or the asset recovered. Measurements are based on elections (for example, an election for loss carryforward instead of carryback) that are expected to be made for tax purposes in future years.

1. **Determining Applicable Tax Rate** Presently enacted changes in tax laws and rates that become effective for a particular future year or years must be considered when determining the tax rate to apply to temporary differences reversing in that year or years. Tax laws and rates for the current year are used if no changes have been enacted for future years.

2. **Measuring Asset or Liability** An asset for deductible temporary differences that are expected to be realized in future years through carryback of a future loss to the current or a prior year (or a liability for taxable temporary differences that are expected to reduce the refund claimed for the carryback of a future loss to the current or a prior year) is measured using tax laws and rates for the current or a prior year, that is, the year for which a refund is expected to be realized based on loss carryback provisions of the tax law.

3. **Future Years** Therefore, if there are no new tax rates enacted for future years, the current rate(s) is (are) used to compute deferred taxes, and aggregate calculations are acceptable. However, if there are new tax rates enacted for future years, a scheduling of the individual future years affected by existing temporary differences is required. The schedule shows in which future years existing temporary differences cause taxable or deductible amounts. The appropriate enacted tax rate is applied to each future taxable and deductible amount.

4. **Assumptions About Future Taxable Income** In determining the appropriate tax rate, an assumption must be made about whether the entity will report taxable income or loss in the various individual future years expected to be affected by the reversal of existing temporary differences.

    a. If taxable income is expected in the year that a future taxable (or deductible) amount is scheduled, use the enacted rate for that future year to calculate the related deferred tax liability (or asset).

b. If an NOL is expected in the year that a future taxable (or deductible) amount is scheduled, use the enacted rate of what will be the prior year the NOL will be carried back to or the enacted rate of the future year to which the carryforward will apply, whichever is appropriate, to calculate the related deferred tax liability (or asset).

E. Applicable Tax Rate

The objective is to measure a deferred tax liability or asset using the enacted tax rate(s) expected to apply to taxable income in the periods in which the deferred tax liability or asset is expected to be settled or realized.

1. **Flat Rate vs Graduated Rate** Under current U.S. federal tax law, if taxable income exceeds a specified amount, all taxable income is taxed, in substance, at a single flat tax rate. That tax rate is used for measurement of a deferred tax liability or asset by enterprises for which graduated tax rates are not a significant factor. Enterprises for which graduated tax rates are a significant factor measure a deferred tax liability or asset using the **average graduated tax rate** applicable to estimated annual taxable income in the periods in which the deferred tax liability or asset is estimated to be settled or realized.

2. **Other Tax Provisions** Other provisions of enacted tax laws are considered when determining the tax rate to apply to certain types of temporary differences and carryforwards (for example, the tax law may provide for different tax rates on ordinary income and capital gains). If there is a phased-in change in tax rates, determination of the applicable tax rate requires knowledge about when deferred tax liabilities and assets will be settled and realized.

Example 13 ▸ Annual Computation of Deferred Tax Liabilities & Assets

Bensen's first year of operations is year 1. For year 1, Bensen has pretax financial income of $150,000 and taxable income of $50,000. Taxable income is expected in all future years.

a. Tax rates enacted by the end of year 1 are as follows: year 1, 40%; year 2, 35%; years 3 through 6, 30%; and year 7, 25%.

b. Temporary differences and amounts existing at the end of year 1 are as follows.

Installment sale difference (taxable in year 2)	$ 30,000
Depreciation difference (see below)	90,000
Estimated expenses (deductible in year 7)	(20,000)
Net temporary difference	$100,000

c. The temporary difference related to depreciable assets will result in the following future taxable (deductible) amounts: for year 3, $50,000; for year 4, 40,000.

Solution:

Step 1: Identify the types and amounts of existing temporary differences and the nature and amount of each type of operating loss and tax credit carryforward and the remaining length of the carryforward period.

The installment sale causes a taxable temporary difference.

The estimated expenses accrued for accounting purposes and deferred for tax purposes cause a deductible temporary difference.

	Amount
Future taxable (deductible) types for temporary differences	
Installment sale	$ 30,000
Depreciation	90,000
Estimated expense	(20,000)

Step 2: Measure the total deferred tax liability for taxable temporary differences using the applicable tax rates.

	Amount	Rate	Deferred Tax Liab.
Future taxable types for temporary differences			
Installment sale	$30,000	35%	$ 10,500
Depreciation	90,000	30%	27,000
Total			$ 37,500

The enacted tax rate used to measure the deferred tax consequences of a future taxable amount is the rate at which the taxable amount will be taxed. The amount of temporary difference scheduled to reverse in year 2 and cause a taxable amount that year is tax effected at the 35% rate enacted for year 2. Similarly, the amount of temporary difference scheduled to reverse in year 3 ($50,000) and year 4 ($40,000) and result in a taxable amount those years is tax effected at the 30% tax rate already enacted for those years.

Step 3: Measure the total deferred tax asset for deductible temporary differences and operating loss carryforwards using the applicable tax rate.

	Amount	Rate	Deferred Tax Asset
Future deductible types for temporary differences			
Estimated expense	$(20,000)	25%	$ 5,000

The enacted tax rate used to measure the deferred tax consequences of a future deductible amount is the rate at which the deductible amount will provide tax benefits. Thus, the deductible amount scheduled for year 7 will provide tax benefits at a rate of 25%. (There are no operating loss carryforwards in this example.)

Step 4: Measure deferred tax assets for each type of tax credit carryforward. (There are no tax credit carryforwards in this example.)

Step 5: Reduce deferred tax assets by a valuation allowance if, based on the weight of available evidence, it is more likely than not (a likelihood of more than 50%) that some portion or all of the deferred tax assets will not be realized. The valuation allowance should be sufficient to reduce the deferred tax asset to the amount that is more likely than not to be realized. (There is no mention of any uncertainty regarding the future realization of the benefits associated with the deferred tax asset. Therefore, assume no valuation allowance is necessary.)

NOTE: Deferred tax liabilities and assets are not reported at discounted values.

Example 14 ▸ Income Tax Expense & Deferred Taxes

Refer to Example 13.

Required:

a. Prepare the journal entry to record income tax expense, deferred taxes, and income taxes payable for year 1.

b. Compute the total income tax expense for year 1. Indicate the portion that is current and the portion that is due to deferred tax expense or benefit. Draft the bottom portion of the income statement beginning with "Income before income taxes."

c. Indicate the proper classification(s) of deferred taxes for the December 31, year 1, balance sheet.

Solution a:

	Debit	Credit
Income Tax Expense—current	20,000	
Income Tax Expense—deferred	32,500	
Deferred Tax Asset	5,000	
Income Taxes Payable ($50,000 × 40%)		20,000
Deferred Tax Liability		37,500

To record income taxes for year 1, in one compound entry.

Balance of deferred tax liability, 12/31, year 1	$37,500*
Balance of deferred tax liability, 01/01, year 1	0
Increase in deferred tax liability	$37,500
Balance of deferred tax asset, 12/31, year 1	$ 5,000*
Balance of deferred tax asset, 01/01, year 1	0
Increase in deferred tax asset	$ 5,000

* These ending balances are the result of the annual computation of deferred tax liabilities and assets illustrated in Example 13. Beginning balances are the result of entries recorded in prior periods. There are no beginning balances because year 1 is Bensen's first year of operations.

Balance the entry by a debit or credit (whichever is appropriate) to *Income Tax Expense—Current* and *Income Tax Expense—Deferred.* Here, the net tax provision is $52,500. An alternative to the above entry is to record the current income tax expense and the deferred income taxes in separate entries.

Solution b: The effective tax rate is $52,500 / $150,000 = 35%.

Deferred tax liability, 12/31, year 1 (Example 13)	$37,500
Deferred tax liability, 01/01, year 1	--
Deferred tax expense, year 1 (increase required in deferred tax liability account)	$37,500
Deferred tax asset, 12/31, year 1 (Example 13)	$ 5,000
Deferred tax asset, 01/01, year 1	--
Deferred tax benefit, year 1 (increase required in deferred tax asset account)	$ 5,000
Deferred tax expense, year 1	$37,500
Deferred tax benefit, year 1	(5,000)
Net deferred tax expense, year 1	32,500
Current tax expense, year 1 ($50,000 × 40%)	20,000
Total income tax expense, year 1	$52,500

Income before income taxes		$150,000
Current tax expense	$20,000	
Deferred tax expense	32,500	
Provision for income taxes		(52,500)
Net income		$ 97,500

Solution c: Deferred income taxes should appear on the balance sheet at the end of year 1 in the following amounts and classifications.

Current liabilities:		Long-term liabilities:	
Deferred tax liability	$10,500	Deferred tax liability	$22,000

Explanation: The $10,500 deferred tax liability caused by the installment sale is classified as a current liability because the installment receivable is classified as a current asset (for the temporary difference to reverse in year 2, the receivable will be collected in year 2). The $27,000 net deferred tax liability related to the depreciation type temporary difference is classified as a noncurrent liability because the related assets (PP&E) are classified as noncurrent assets. The $5,000 deferred tax asset resulting from the expenses accrued for accounting purposes is classified as a noncurrent asset because the related accrued liability is a noncurrent liability (for the temporary difference to reverse in year 7, the accrued liability is expected to be settled in year 7, which makes the liability noncurrent).

Type of difference	Temporary difference	Tax rate	Deferred taxes	Current or noncurrent
Installment sale	$ 30,000	35%	$10,500	Current
Depreciation	90,000	30%	27,000	Noncurrent
Accrued expenses	(20,000)	25%	(5,000)	Noncurrent

The net current amount is a liability of $10,500. The net noncurrent amount is a liability of $22,000.

Example 15 ▸ Deferred Tax Liabilities & Assets

The first year of operations for the Pandora Corporation was year 1. Taxable income for year 1 was $120,000. Pandora was subject to enacted U.S. tax rates of 40% in year 1 and 30% in year 2 and later years. Taxable income is expected in all future years. At the end of year 1, there was only one future taxable temporary difference of $140,000, related to depreciation.

Deferred taxes at the end of year 1 (using the liability method):

	Amount	Rate	Deferred Tax Liab.
Future taxable amounts for temporary differences			
Depreciation	$140,000	30%	$42,000

Income taxes for year 1 were properly recorded as follows.

Income Tax Expense—current	48,000	
Income Tax Expense—deferred	42,000	
Income Taxes Payable ($120,000 × 40%)		48,000
Deferred Tax Liability		42,000

Pandora has taxable income for year 2 of $110,000. Enacted tax rates have not changed so the rate for year 2 and future years is 30%. At the end of year 2, cumulative taxable temporary differences related to depreciation are $180,000.

Required:

a. Compute the amount of deferred taxes to be reported on the balance sheet at the end of year 2.

b. Prepare the journal entry to record income taxes for year 2.

c. Draft the section of the income statement for year 2 that relates to reporting income taxes.

Solution a:

	Amount	Rate	Deferred Tax Liab.
Future taxable amounts for temporary differences			
Depreciation	$180,000	30%	$54,000

Solution b:

Income Tax Expense—current	33,000	
Income Tax Expense—deferred	12,000	
Income Taxes Payable ($110,000 × 30%)		33,000
Deferred Tax Liability ($54,000 – $42,000)		12,000

Deferred tax liability, end of year 2	$ 54,000
Deferred tax liability, end of year 1	(42,000)
Deferred tax expense, year 2 (increase in deferred tax liability account)	12,000
Current tax expense, year 2	33,000
Total tax expense (provision), year 2	$ 45,000

Solution c:

Income before income taxes		$150,000
Current tax expense	$33,000	
Deferred tax expense	12,000	
Income tax expense		(45,000)
Net income		$105,000

Income before taxes is verified as follows (no permanent differences):

Pretax financial income	$ X
Increase in cumulative taxable temporary differences ($180,000 – $140,000)	(40,000)
Taxable income	$110,000

Solve for X: X = $150,000

Example 16 ▸ Deferred Tax Liabilities & Assets

Jersey Corporation uses different depreciation methods for accounting and tax purposes which result in a $60,000 cumulative temporary difference at December 31, year 4. This temporary difference will reverse equally over the next 5 years. Taxable income for year 4 is $46,000. Jersey's balance sheet at December 31, year 3, reported a net deferred tax liability of $8,000 (noncurrent deferred tax liability of $28,000 and a noncurrent deferred tax asset of $20,000). Jersey expects taxable income in all future years.

1. At December 31, year 4, Jersey has a $17,000 liability reported because of the accrual of estimated litigation claims. Jersey expects to pay the claims and have tax deductible amounts in year 8 of $15,000 and in year 9 of $2,000.
2. The enacted tax rates as of the beginning of year 3 are as follows: 50% in years 3 to 5; 40% in years 6 to 7; and 30% in year 8 and later years.

Required:

a. Calculate the amount of net deferred taxes that should be reported on Jersey's balance sheet at December 31, year 4, and indicate whether that net amount is an asset or a liability.

b. Prepare the journal entry for Jersey to record income taxes for year 4.

Solution a: The $60,000 must be divided into three parts to account for the different tax rates.

	Amount	Rate	Deferred Tax Liab.
Future taxable amounts for temporary differences	$12,000	50%	$ 6,000
Depreciation—year 5	24,000	40%	9,600
Depreciation—years 6-7	24,000	30%	7,200
Depreciation—years 8-9	$60,000		$22,800

			Deferred Tax Asset
Future deductible amounts for temporary differences			
Litigation	$17,000	30%	$ 5,100

$22,800 + $(5,100) = $17,700 net deferred tax liability at December 31, year 4.

Solution b:

	Dr.	Cr.
Income Tax Expense—current	23,000	
Income Tax Expense—deferred ($14,900 – $5,200)	9,700	
Deferred Tax Liability ($28,000 – $22,800)	5,200	
Income Tax Payable ($46,000 × 50%)		23,000
Deferred Tax Asset ($20,000 – $5,100)		14,900

Deferred tax liability, 12/31, year 4—part (a)	$ 22,800
Deferred tax liability, 12/31, year 3	28,000
Deferred tax benefit, year 4 (decrease required in deferred tax liability account)	$ (5,200)
Deferred tax asset, 12/31, year 4—part (a)	$ 5,100
Deferred tax asset, 12/31, year 3	20,000
Deferred tax expense, year 4 (decrease required in deferred tax asset account)	$ 14,900
Deferred tax benefit, year 4	$ (5,200)
Deferred tax expense, year 4	14,900
Net deferred tax expense, year 4	9,700
Current tax expense, year 4	23,000
Total tax expense (provision) for year 4	$ 32,700

Example 17 ▸ Deferred Tax Liabilities & Assets

Jersey Corporation, from Example 16, expects taxable income in years 5 through 8 and an NOL in year 9, the benefits of which are expected to be realized by carryback.

Required:

a. Calculate the amount of net deferred taxes that should be reported on Jersey's balance sheet at December 31, year 4, and indicate whether that net amount is an asset or a liability.

b. Prepare the journal entry for Jersey to record income taxes for year 4.

Solution a: Because Jersey expects an NOL rather than taxable income in year 9, the tax rate to be used to tax effect the future taxable and deductible amounts scheduled for year 9 (due to temporary differences existing at the end of year 4) is the rate of the year to which the expected NOL of year 9 is to be carried back or forward. In this case, that would be year 7 (the data indicated an expected carry-back and the provisions of the tax code require carryback to the earliest of two years prior to the loss year). Thus, the taxable amount of $12,000 scheduled for year 9 will reduce a tax refund computed at the rate of 40% and the deductible amount of $2,000 scheduled for year 9 will increase a tax refund computed at the rate of 40%.

	Amount	Rate	Deferred Tax Liab.
Future taxable amounts for temporary differences			
Depreciation—year 5	$12,000	50%	$ 6,000
Depreciation—years 6-7, 9	36,000	40%	14,400
Depreciation—years 8-9	12,000	30%	3,600
	$60,000		$24,000

NOTE: The $60,000 must be divided into three parts to account for the different tax rates.

	Amount	Rate	Deferred Tax Asset
Future deductible amounts for temporary differences			
Litigation—year 8	$15,000	30%	$ 4,500
Litigation—year 9	2,000	40%	800
	$17,000		$ 5,300

$24,000 + $(5,300) = $18,700 deferred tax liability at December 31, year 4.

Solution b:

Income Tax Expense—current	23,000	
Income Tax Expense—deferred ($14,700 – $4,000)	10,700	
Deferred Tax Liability ($28,000 – $24,000)	4,000	
Income Tax Payable ($46,000 × 50%)		23,000
Deferred Tax Asset ($20,000 – $5,300)		14,700

F. Attributes of Asset & Liability Method

1. **Balance Sheet Approach** There is an emphasis on the amount to be reported as deferred taxes on the balance sheet (hence, it is said to be a balance sheet approach or balance sheet-oriented).

2. **Balance of Deferred Tax Asset or Liability** The balance in a deferred tax liability or asset account on a balance sheet is the amount of taxes expected to be paid or refunded (or saved) in the future as a result of the turn-around (reversal) of temporary differences existing at the balance sheet date.

3. **Calculation** The amount to be reported for deferred taxes on a balance sheet is calculated by using future tax rates (i.e., rates that have already been enacted for the future) and applying them to cumulative temporary differences based on when and how the temporary differences are expected to affect the tax return in the future.

4. **Effect on Income Statement** A temporary difference originating in the current period that causes an increase in a deferred tax liability will also cause a debit (charge) to the provision for deferred taxes on the income statement; an increase in deferred tax asset will result in a credit to the provision for deferred taxes.

5. **Deferred Tax Expense or Benefit** Deferred tax expense (benefit) on the income statement is a "residual" amount because it merely reflects the change in the balance sheet deferred tax account(s) from the prior year. The amount of deferred tax expense (benefit) for a year is a by-product of the year's deferred tax calculation because it is the net change during the year in the net deferred tax liability or asset amount.

6. **Increase/Decrease in Deferred Tax Asset/Liability** An increase in a deferred tax liability or a decrease in a deferred tax asset on the balance sheet results in a deferred tax expense on the income statement; an increase in a deferred tax asset or a decrease in a deferred tax liability on the balance sheet will cause a deferred tax benefit on the income statement.

7. **Subsequent Changes** The balance sheet deferred tax account(s) is(are) to be adjusted for any subsequent changes in the tax rates or laws.

8. **Single Tax Rate vs Different Tax Rates** If a single tax rate applies to all future years, an aggregate computation is appropriate. However, if different tax rates apply to individual future years, a scheduling of future taxable and deductible amounts (due to existing temporary differences) with a separate computation for each future year affected is required.

IV. Other Considerations

A. Valuation Allowance

1. **Deferred Tax Assets** Deferred tax assets are recorded for the future tax benefits of operating loss carryforwards, tax credit carryforwards, and deductible temporary differences existing at a balance sheet date. Deferred tax assets are to be reduced by a valuation allowance if it is more likely than not, a likelihood of more than 50%, that some or all of the deferred tax assets will not be realized. The valuation allowance should be sufficient to reduce the deferred tax asset to the amount that is more likely than not to be realized.

Example 18 ▸ Valuation Allowance

At December 31, year 1, at the end of XYZ's first year of operations, XYZ reports a net operating loss of $50,000 on its tax return. At December 31, year 1, XYZ has a temporary difference that will result in future deductible amounts of $80,000. The enacted tax rate for year 1 is 50%. The tax rate for year 2 and subsequent years is 40%. At the end of year 1, it is estimated that 30% of the company's deferred tax assets will not be realized in the future. In year 2, XYZ reports taxable income of $100,000 (before deduction of the NOL carryover and after deducting the $80,000 future deductible amount) and has no temporary differences at the end of year 2.

Required:

a. Prepare the journal entry(s) to record income taxes for year 1.

b. Draft the section of the year 1 income statement that reports income tax expense, beginning with the line "Income Before Income Taxes."

c. Prepare the appropriate journal entries to record income taxes and draft the section of the year 2 income statement that reports income tax expense.

Solution a:

Deferred Tax Asset	52,000	
Benefits of Loss Carryforward ($50,000 × 40%)		20,000
Income Tax Expense—deferred ($80,000 × 40%)		32,000
Benefits of Loss Carryforward ($20,000 × 30%)	6,000	
Income Tax Expense—deferred ($32,000 × 30%)	9,600	
Allowance to Reduce Deferred Tax Asset to Realizable Value		15,600

Solution b:

Operating loss before income taxes*		$(130,000)
Benefits of loss carryforward ($20,000 × 70%)	$14,000	
Deferred tax benefit ($32,000 × 70%)	22,400	
Income tax benefits		36,400
Net loss		$ (93,600)

* Pretax financial income $ X
Deductible temporary difference originating in Year 1 80,000
Taxable loss $(50,000) Solve for X: X = $(130,000)

Solution c:

Income Tax Expense—current ($100,000 × 40%)	40,000	
Income Tax Expense—deferred ($32,000 – $9,600)	22,400	
Allowance to Reduce Deferred Tax Asset to Realizable Value (balance of account)	15,600	
Income Taxes Payable [($100,000 – $50,000) × 40%]		20,000
Deferred Tax Asset (balance of account)		52,000
Benefits of Loss Carryforward (income tax expense) ($20,000 × 30%)		6,000

Income Statement:

Income before income taxes**		$ 180,000
Current tax expense	$40,000	
Deferred tax expense	22,400	
Benefits of loss carryforward	(6,000)	
Total income tax expense		(56,400)
Net income		$ 123,600

** Pretax financial income $ X
Reversing temporary difference (80,000)
Taxable loss $100,000 Solve for X: X = $180,000

The compound journal entry replaces the following three journal entries.

Income Tax Expense	40,000	
Income Tax Payable [($100,000 – $50,000) × 40%]		20,000
Benefit of Loss Carryforward		20,000

To record current income taxes.

Income Tax Expense—deferred	32,000	
Benefit of Loss Carryforward	20,000	
Deferred Tax Asset (balance of account)		52,000

To eliminate the deferred asset balance and to recognize deferred tax expense.

Allowance to Reduce Deferred Tax Asset to Realizable Value (balance of account)	15,600	
Benefits of Loss Carryforward ($20,000 × 30%)		6,000
Income Tax Expense—deferred (to balance)		9,600

To eliminate the allowance balance and to recognize the previously unrecognized benefits of the loss carryforward.

2. **Future Realization of Tax Benefit** Future realization of the tax benefit of an existing deductible temporary difference or carryforward ultimately depends on the existence of sufficient taxable income of the appropriate character (for example, ordinary income or capital gain) within the carryback, carryforward period available under the tax law. Whatever amount is allowed is multiplied by the effective tax rate to come up with the amount of tax benefit realized. The following four possible sources of taxable income may be available under the tax law to realize a tax benefit for deductible temporary differences and carryforwards:

   a. Future reversals of existing taxable temporary differences

   b. Future taxable income exclusive of reversing temporary differences and carryforwards

   c. Taxable income in prior carryback year(s) if carryback is permitted under the tax law

   d. Tax-planning strategies that would, if necessary, be implemented to the following, for example:

      (1) Accelerate taxable amounts to utilize expiring carryforwards

      (2) Change the character of taxable or deductible amounts from ordinary income or loss to capital gain or loss

      (3) Switch from tax-exempt to taxable investments

3. **Tax-Planning Strategies** In some circumstances, there are actions (including elections for tax purposes) that (1) are prudent and feasible, (2) an enterprise ordinarily might not take, but would take to prevent an operating loss or tax credit carryforward from expiring unused, and (3) would result in realization of deferred tax assets. These actions are referred to as *tax-planning strategies.* An enterprise shall consider tax-planning strategies in determining the amount of valuation allowance required. Significant expenses to implement a tax-planning strategy or any significant losses that would be recognized if that strategy were implemented (net of any recognizable tax benefits associated with those expenses or losses) shall be included in the valuation allowance.

4. **Evidence to Determine Need for Valuation Allowance** All available evidence, both positive and negative, should be considered to determine whether, based on the weight of that evidence, a valuation allowance is needed. Information about an enterprise's current financial position and its results of operations for the current and preceding years ordinarily is readily available. That historical information is supplemented by all currently available information about future years. Sometimes, however, historical information may not be available (for example, start-up operations), or it may not be as relevant (for example, if there has been a significant, recent change in circumstances) and special attention is required.

5. **Negative Evidence** Forming a conclusion that a valuation allowance is not needed is difficult when there is negative evidence such as cumulative losses in recent years. Other examples of negative evidence include (but are not limited to) the following:

   a. A history of operating loss or tax credit carryforwards expiring unused

   b. Losses expected in early future years (by a presently profitable entity)

   c. Unsettled circumstances that, if unfavorably resolved, would adversely affect future operations and profit levels on a continuing basis in future years

   d. A carryback, carryforward period that is so brief that it would limit realization of tax benefits if (1) a significant deductible temporary difference is expected to reverse in a single year or (2) the enterprise operates in a traditionally cyclical business

6. **Positive Evidence Examples** Examples (not prerequisites) of positive evidence that might support a conclusion that a valuation allowance is not needed when there is negative evidence include (but are not limited to) the following:

   a. Existing contracts or firm sales backlog that will produce more than enough taxable income to realize the deferred tax asset based on existing sales prices and cost structures.

   b. An excess of appreciated asset value over the tax basis of the entity's net assets in an amount sufficient to realize the deferred tax asset.

   c. A strong earnings history exclusive of the loss that created the future deductible amount (tax loss carryforward or deductible temporary difference) coupled with evidence indicating that the loss (for example, an unusual, infrequent, or extraordinary item) is an aberration rather than a continuing condition.

7. **Weighing Evidence** An enterprise must use judgment in considering the relative impact of negative and positive evidence. The weight given to the potential effect of negative and positive evidence should be commensurate with the extent to which it can be objectively verified. The more negative evidence that exists the more positive evidence is necessary and the more difficult it is to support a conclusion that a valuation allowance is not needed for some portion or all of the deferred tax asset.

8. **Change in Valuation Allowance** The effect of a change in the beginning-of-the-year balance of a valuation allowance that results from a change in circumstances that causes a change in judgment about the realizability of the related deferred tax asset in future years ordinarily shall be included in income from continuing operations.

B. Enacted Change in Tax Laws or Rates

1. **Adjustment of Deferred Tax Liability or Asset** A deferred tax liability or asset is adjusted for the effect of a change in tax laws or rates. The deferred tax previously provided on items that will become taxable or deductible in any future year affected by the rate change is to be adjusted downward or upward to reflect the new rate. This cumulative effect is included in income from continuing operations for the period that includes the enactment date. Adjustments of a deferred tax liability or asset for enacted changes in tax laws or rates are a component of income tax expense attributable to continuing operations.

2. **Interim Period** If the date of enactment occurs during an interim period, the effect of the change on the existing balance of a deferred tax liability or asset must be recognized in the interim period that includes the enactment date.

Example 19 ▸ Enacted Change in Tax Laws or Rates

Sean Corporation began operations in year 1. Taxable income for year 1 was $22,000. Pretax financial income for year 1 was $32,000. The tax rates enacted as of the beginning of year 1 were 50% for year 1 and 40% for year 2 and later years. At December 31, year 1, Sean Corporation had the following cumulative temporary differences.

1. The reported amount of installment receivables was in excess of the tax basis of those receivables which will result in future taxable amounts of $12,000 ($6,000 in each of years 3 and 4).
2. The reported amount of an estimated litigation liability was $2,000. There was no such liability for tax purposes (i.e., its tax basis was zero). The liability was expected to be paid (and then result in a tax deductible amount) in year 4.

The net deferred tax liability of $4,000 at the end of year 1 was calculated as follows.

	Amount	Rate	Deferred Tax Liability (Asset)
Future taxable amounts	$12,000	40%	$4,800
Future deductible amount	(2,000)	40%	(800)
Net deferred tax liability (asset)			$4,000

The journal entry to record income taxes for year 1 was as follows.

Income Tax Expense—current	11,000	
Income Tax Expense—deferred	4,000	
Deferred Tax Asset	800	
Income Taxes Payable ($22,000 × 50%)		11,000
Deferred Tax Liability		4,800

During year 2, a new tax rate of 30% was enacted for year 4. There were no new temporary differences originating in year 2, and none of the temporary differences existing at the beginning of year 2 reversed so the cumulative temporary differences existing at the end of year 2 were the same as those that existed at the end of year 1. Taxable income for year 2 amounted to $25,000. Pretax financial income was also $25,000.

Required: Record all journal entries related to income taxes for year 2.

Solution:

Income Tax Expense—current	10,000	
Deferred Tax Liability ($4,800 – $4,200)	600	
Income Tax Benefit—change in rates ($4,000 – $3,600)		400
Income Taxes Payable ($25,000 × 40%)		10,000
Deferred Tax Asset ($800 – $600)		200

Discussion: A change in an enacted tax rate causes an immediate cumulative effect on the income tax provision. The deferred tax previously provided on items that will become taxable or deductible in any future year affected by the rate change is to be adjusted to reflect the new rate. To determine the adjustment needed because of the change in the tax rate for year 4, prepare the scheduling process as it would have been prepared at the end of year 1, if the new rate for year 4 had been known at that point in time.

Future taxable amounts	Amount	Rate	Deferred Tax Liability (Asset)
Year 3	$ 6,000	40%	$2,400
Year 4	6,000	30%	1,800
Future deductible amount	(2,000)	30%	(600)
Net deferred tax liability (asset)			$3,600

Comparing this schedule with the schedule used in year 1, we find that the deferred tax liability account needs to decrease by $600 ($4,800 – $4,200) and the deferred tax asset account needs to decrease by $200 ($800 – $600). A comparative income statement would report the following.

	Year 1		Year 2	
Income before income taxes		$ 32,000		$25,000
Current	$11,000		$10,000	
Deferred	4,000			
Adjustment due to rate change			(400)	
Income tax expense		(15,000)		(9,600)
Net income		$ 17,000		$15,400

C. Change in Enterprise Tax Status
A deferred tax liability or asset is recognized for temporary differences at the date that a nontaxable enterprise becomes a taxable enterprise (e.g., partnership to corporation or S corporation to C corporation). A deferred tax liability or asset should be eliminated at the date that an enterprise ceases to be a taxable enterprise (e.g., corporation to partnership or C corporation to S corporation). The effect of recognizing or eliminating a deferred tax liability or asset is included in income from continuing operations.

V. Uncertain Tax Positions

A. Recognition

GAAP prescribes a recognition threshold and measurement attribute for the financial statement recognition and measurement of a tax position taken or expected to be taken in a tax return. A "tax position" for this purpose includes a current or future reduction in taxable income reported or expected to be reported on a tax return, the decision not to report a transaction in a tax return, and an assertion that a company is not subject to taxation. Because of the way a tax position is defined, the guidance applies to not-for-profit organizations, real estate investment trusts, regulated investment companies, and other entities that are potentially subject to income taxes if conditions specified by the tax law are not met. The recognition and measurement principles also apply to evaluating the potential treatment of tax planning strategies used to support the reliability of deferred tax assets.

B. Scope

1. **Applicability** The guidance applies to all tax positions, regardless of their level of uncertainty or the nature of the position; however, the recognition and measurement requirements are likely to have the most impact on positions for which current or future deductions may be disallowed or reduced in a tax examination.

2. **Examples** These situations include the uncertainty is about the timing, the amount, or the validity of the deduction. The following tax positions are among those subject to the guidance:

   a. A deduction taken on the tax return for a current expenditure that the taxing authority may assert should be capitalized and amortized over future periods

   b. A decision that certain income is nontaxable under the tax law

   c. The determination of the amount of taxable income to report on intercompany transfers between subsidiaries in different tax jurisdictions

   d. The calculation of the amount of a research and experimentation credit

   e. The determination as to whether a spin-off transaction is taxable or nontaxable

   f. The determination as to whether an entity qualifies as a real estate investment trust or regulated investment company

   g. The determination as to whether an entity is subject to tax in a particular jurisdiction

C. Two-Step Process
Applying the guidance to determine how to recognize tax benefits in the financial statements is a two-step process where recognition (Step 1) and measurement (Step 2) should be evaluated separately.

1. **Step 1: Recognition** GAAP provides a "more-likely-than-not" recognition threshold that must be met before a tax benefit can be recognized in the financial statements. For each tax position, an enterprise must make a hypothetical assessment: if a dispute with the taxing authority were taken to the court of last resort, is it more likely than not that the tax position would be sustained as filed? If it is, the recognition threshold is met.

   a. GAAP does not prescribe the type of evidence required to support meeting the more-likely-than-not threshold, stating that it depends on the individual facts and circumstances.

      (1) A position may be supported, in whole or in part, by unambiguous tax law, prior experience with the taxing authority, and analysis that considers all relevant facts, circumstances, and regulations, including widely understood administrative practices and precedents of the taxing authority.

      (2) Tax positions supported by "administrative practices and precedents" are those positions which are accepted by the taxing authorities even though the treatment may not be specified by the tax law or the positions may be considered technical violations of the tax law.

   b. If the tax position does not meet the more-likely-than-not recognition threshold, its tax benefit is not recognized in the financial statements. As a result, financial statement tax expense will be higher than what is reflected in the tax return by the full benefit of the tax position. An enterprise would increase financial statement tax expense by:

      (1) Recognizing a liability for unrecognized tax benefits

      (2) Reducing an income tax refund receivable

      (3) Reducing a deferred tax asset (e.g., if the as-filed tax position increases a net operating loss carryforward)

      (4) Increasing a deferred tax liability (e.g., if the as-filed tax position increases an asset's tax basis)

      (5) Doing a combination of any of the above

   c. For each tax position, an enterprise should reassess whether the more-likely-than-not recognition threshold is met at the end of each reporting period. A tax position should also be recognized when either of the following occur:

      (1) The tax matter is ultimately resolved through negotiation or litigation

      (2) The statute of limitations for the relevant taxing authority to examine the tax position has expired

2. **Step 2: Measurement of the Tax Benefit** For tax positions that meet the more-likely-than-not recognition threshold, the next step is to determine how much of a tax benefit to recognize in the financial statements. Enterprises should recognize the largest amount of tax benefit that is greater than 50 percent likely of being realized upon ultimate settlement with the taxing authority. In this step, the enterprise should also presume that the taxing authority has full knowledge of all relevant information.

   a. An enterprise should consider the amounts and probabilities of the outcomes that could be realized upon ultimate settlement. In many cases this will be a settlement with the relevant taxing authority. An enterprise starts with the largest possible outcome and evaluates whether there is a greater than 50 percent chance it would realize that amount in ultimate settlement. If not, it evaluates the next largest possible outcome. This evaluation continues until the probability of occurrence for an amount is greater than 50 percent. That amount gets recognized in the financial statements as a tax benefit.

   b. An enterprise has a high degree of confidence in the technical merits of a tax position if it believes that position is based on clear and unambiguous tax law. In this case, the tax position will meet the recognition threshold. In determining the amount to recognize in the financial statements, the enterprise will conclude that there is a greater than 50 percent chance that it will ultimately realize the full tax benefit. Accordingly, it should recognize the full benefit in the financial statements.

   c. The difference between the financial statement tax benefit and the full benefit is recognized as a higher tax expense in the same way that a tax position that has not met the recognition threshold is recognized. Again, the use of a valuation allowance to reflect the higher tax expense is not permitted.

D. Classification of the Liability

Whether to classify the uncertain income tax liability as a current or noncurrent liability depends on when the enterprise anticipates paying cash to settle it. If the enterprise anticipates payment of cash to the taxing authority within one year (or within its operating cycle, if longer) the liability should be classified as a current liability—otherwise, it should be classified as a noncurrent liability. In determining the classification of its uncertain income tax liability, an enterprise should consider all relevant factors, including the expected timing of an examination, related appeals, and settlement.

E. Changed Evaluations

With new information, management may change its judgment over how much of a tax benefit it should recognize in the financial statements (e.g., recognition, derecognition, measurement). Depending on when the related tax position was taken—prior fiscal year or interim period in the same fiscal year—changes in judgment are accounted for differently in interim financial statements. GAAP prescribes the following accounting:

1. **Prior Period** The effect of a change in judgment over a tax position taken in a prior annual period is recorded entirely in the interim period in which the judgment changes (similar to taxes on an unusual, infrequently occurring, or extraordinary item).

2. **Current Period** The effect of a change in judgment over a tax position taken in an interim period in the same fiscal year is partially recognized in the quarter the judgment changes, with the remainder being recognized over the remaining interim periods (incorporated into the annual estimated effective tax rate).

Example 20 ▸ Income Tax Liability

In its Year 7 tax return, an enterprise that has a 40% tax rate takes a $100 tax deduction that provides a tax benefit of $40. The enterprise concludes that there is a greater than 50% chance that, if the taxing authority were to examine the tax position, the position would be sustained as filed. Accordingly, the tax deduction meets the more-likely-than-not recognition threshold.

Although the tax position meets the more-likely-than-not recognition threshold, the enterprise believes it would negotiate a settlement if the tax position were challenged by the taxing authority. Accordingly, the enterprise develops the following possible outcomes and probabilities based on the assumptions that the tax position is examined and disputed, and that the enterprise negotiates a settlement with the taxing authority:

Possible Estimated Outcome	Individual Probability of Occurrence	Cumulative Probability of Occurrence
$40	31	31
$30	20	51
$20	20	71
$20	20	91
$ 0	9	100

Based on the possible outcomes and related probabilities, the enterprise should recognize a tax benefit of $30, because that is the largest benefit that is greater than 50% likely of being realized in ultimate settlement. Accordingly, the enterprise should record a $10 uncertain income tax liability (assuming the tax position does not affect a deferred tax asset or liability).

Sample Journal Entries:

Using the same information from the chart above, further assume that the enterprise has:

- Taxable income of $150 before taking the $100 tax deduction
- A 40% tax rate
- Concluded that the full tax benefit should be recognized for all other tax positions
- No temporary differences or carryforwards

The following journal entries should be recorded by the enterprise (the journal entries are grossed up for illustration purposes and do not include interest and penalties):

	Dr.	Cr.
Current tax expense	60	
Current tax liability		60

To record current tax expense on the $150 of income before taking the $100 deduction ($150 × 40%)

	Dr.	Cr.
Current tax liability	40	
Current tax expense		40

To adjust current tax expense for the $100 deduction taken on the tax return ($100 × 40%)

	Dr.	Cr.
Current tax expense	10	
Uncertain income tax liability		10

To recognize an uncertain income tax liability for the difference between the benefit reflected in the tax return ($40) and the largest benefit that is greater than 50% likely of being realized ($30).

F. Disclosures

GAAP requires significant annual disclosures in the notes to the financial statements, related to uncertain income tax positions. A significant additional requirement is a table disclosing the beginning and ending balances of unrecognized tax benefits.

1. **Required Items** The following items must be separately presented in the table, which is required at the end of each annual period:

   a. The gross amounts of the increases and decreases in unrecognized tax benefits as a result of tax positions taken during a prior period

   b. The gross amounts of the increases and decreases in unrecognized tax benefits as a result of tax positions taken during the current period

   c. The amount of decreases in unrecognized tax benefits relating to settlements with taxing authorities

   d. Reductions to unrecognized tax benefits as a result of lapse of the applicable statute of limitations

2. **Table** The table is required for unrecognized tax benefits on an aggregate, worldwide basis. No disaggregated information for individual tax positions or jurisdictions is required. Companies must also disclose the amount of unrecognized tax benefits that, if recognized, would change the effective rate.

3. **Qualitative and Quantitative Disclosures** Qualitative and quantitative disclosures related to estimates of unrecognized tax benefits are also required if it is "reasonably possible" the estimate will significantly change in the 12 months after the balance sheet date. This disclosure must include the nature of the uncertainty, the nature of the events that could cause the change, and an estimate of the range of reasonably possible changes or a statement that an estimate of the changes cannot be made. Companies must also disclose the classification of interest and penalties, the amount of interest and penalties included in the income statement each period, and the amount of interest and penalties accrued in the statement of financial position. A description of open tax years by major jurisdiction is also required.

VI. Presentation & Disclosure

A. Balance Sheet

In a classified balance sheet, deferred tax assets and liabilities are separated and reported in a net current and a net noncurrent amount.

1. **Classification Based on Related Asset** Deferred tax assets and liabilities are classified as current or noncurrent based on the classification of the related asset or liability for financial reporting. A deferred tax liability or asset that is not related to an asset or liability for financial reporting, including deferred tax assets related to carryforwards, is classified according to the expected reversal date of the temporary difference.

2. **Jurisdiction** The valuation allowance for a particular tax jurisdiction is to be allocated between current and noncurrent deferred tax assets for that jurisdiction on a pro rata basis. Deferred tax liabilities and assets attributable to different tax jurisdictions should not be offset.

Example 21 ▸ Balance Sheet Presentation of Deferred Taxes

Molly Corporation has a tax rate for all periods at 40% and the following temporary differences at December 31 of the current year:

1. Installment receivables appearing on their GAAP balance sheet have a zero tax basis. These receivables are to be collected equally over the next three years and will result in reporting $20,000 gross profit each year for tax purposes. Only one-third of the receivables are classified as a current asset.
2. An accrued payable of $45,000 appearing in the current liability section of the GAAP balance sheet has a zero tax basis.
3. Depreciable assets have an excess of carrying amount over tax basis of $50,000.

Required: Compute deferred taxes at December 31 and indicate how they should be classified on the balance sheet at that date.

Solution: $8,000 + $(18,000) = $(10,000) current; $16,000 + $20,000 = $36,000 noncurrent

Temporary difference	Future taxable (deductible) amount	Rate	Deferred tax liability (asset)	Current or noncurrent
Installment sales	$ 20,000	40%	$ 8,000	Current
Installment sales	40,000	40%	16,000	Noncurrent
Accrued expenses	(45,000)	40%	(18,000)	Current
Depreciation	50,000	40%	20,000	Noncurrent

Current assets:		Long-term liabilities:	
Deferred tax asset	$ 10,000	Deferred tax liability	$36,000

Discussion: The deferred tax liability related to the installment sales is one-third current and two-thirds noncurrent because of the classification of the related receivables. The deferred tax asset stemming from the accrual of expenses for books is a current asset because of the current classification of the related accrued payable. The deferred tax liability resulting from different depreciation policies for financial statements and tax returns is classified as noncurrent because the related plant assets have a noncurrent balance sheet classification. The current deferred tax items are netted (liability of $8,000 and asset of $18,000) to arrive at an asset of $10,000; the noncurrent items (liabilities of $16,000 and $20,000) are netted to arrive at a liability of $36,000.

3. **Disclosures** The following are to be disclosed.

   a. Total of all deferred tax liabilities and total of all deferred tax assets

   b. Total valuation allowance recognized for deferred tax assets and the net change during the year in the total valuation allowance

   c. Approximate tax effect of each type of temporary difference and carryforward that gives rise to a significant portion of deferred tax liabilities and deferred tax assets (before allocation of valuation allowances)

B. Income Statement

1. **Allocation** Income tax expense or benefit for the year is to be allocated among continuing operations, discontinued operations, extraordinary items, and items of other comprehensive income (e.g., foreign currency translation adjustments and market value adjustments attributable to available-for-sale marketable equity securities). The process of allocating income taxes to key components of the financial statements is called intraperiod tax allocation. Thus, items such as discontinued operations, extraordinary items, and prior period adjustments are reported net of the related income tax effects.

a. The amount allocated to continuing operations is the tax effect of the pretax income or loss from continuing operations that occurred during the year, plus or minus income tax effects of (1) changes in circumstances that cause a change in judgment about the realization of deferred tax assets in future years, (2) changes in tax laws or rates, and (3) changes in tax status. The remainder is allocated to items other than continuing operations.

b. If there is only one item other than continuing operations, the portion of income tax expense or benefit for the year that remains after the allocation to continuing operations is allocated to that item. If there are two or more items other than continuing operations, the amount that remains after the allocation to continuing operations shall be allocated among those other items in proportion to their individual effects on income tax expense or benefit for the year.

Example 22 ▸ Intraperiod Tax Allocation

Kelly Corporation's pretax financial income and taxable income are the same. Kelly's ordinary loss from continuing operations is $5,000. Kelly also has an extraordinary gain of $9,000 that is a capital gain for tax purposes. The tax rate is 40% on ordinary income and 30% on capital gains. Income taxes currently payable are $1,200 ($4,000 at 30%).

Required: Determine the amount of income tax expense (benefit) to allocate to continuing operations and the amount to allocate to the extraordinary item.

Solution:

Total income tax expense	$1,200
Tax benefit allocated to the loss from operations	1,500
Incremental tax expense allocated to the extraordinary gain	$2,700

The effect of the $5,000 loss from continuing operations was to offset an equal amount of capital gains that otherwise would be taxed at a 30% tax rate. Thus, $1,500 ($5,000 at 30%) of tax benefit is allocated to continuing operations. The $2,700 incremental effect of the extraordinary gain is the $1,200 of total tax expense and the $1,500 tax benefit from continuing operations.

c. The manner of reporting the tax benefit of an operating loss carryforward or carryback is determined by the source of income or loss of the current year that enabled its recognition. For example, if income from continuing operations in the current year permits recognition of an operating loss carryforward that arose from a discontinued operation of a prior year, the tax benefit attributable to that operating loss carryforward is allocated to income from continuing operations and not by (1) the source of the operating loss carryforward or taxes paid in a prior year or (2) the source of expected future income that will result in realization of a deferred tax asset for an operating loss carryforward from the current year. Thus, the benefit of an NOL carryback would be classified as a component of continuing operations if the income earned in the current year was due to continuing operations even though the NOL resulted from an extraordinary loss in a prior period. (There are a few exceptions to this guideline, including one that deals with business combinations and another involving quasi-reorganizations.)

d. Stockholders' equity is charged or credited for the income tax effects of the following.

(1) Adjustments of the opening balance of retained earnings for certain changes in accounting principles or a correction of an error

(2) Gains and losses recognized in comprehensive income, but excluded from net income (e.g., foreign currency translation adjustments, market value adjustments attributable to certain investments in debt and equity securities, and minimum pension liability adjustments)

(3) An increase or decrease in contributed capital (e.g., expenditures reported as a reduction of the proceeds from issuing capital stock)

(4) Expenses for employee stock options recognized differently for financial reporting and tax purposes

2. **Components of Income Tax Expense** The significant components of income tax expense attributable to continuing operations for each year presented are disclosed in the financial statements or notes thereto. Those components would include the following.

a. Current tax expense or benefit

b. Deferred tax expense or benefit (exclusive of the effects of other components listed below)

c. Investment tax credits

d. Government grants (to the extent recognized as a reduction of income tax expense)

e. The benefits of operating loss carryforwards

f. Tax expense that results from allocating certain tax benefits either directly to contributed capital or to reduce other noncurrent intangible assets of an acquired entity

g. Adjustments of a deferred tax liability or asset for enacted changes in tax laws or rates or a change in the tax status of the enterprise

h. Adjustments of the beginning-of-the-year balance of a valuation allowance because of a change in circumstances that causes a change in judgment about the reliability of the related deferred tax asset in future years

3. **Reconciliation** A public enterprise discloses a reconciliation using percentages or dollar amounts of a reported amount of income tax expense attributable to continuing operations for the year to an amount of income tax expense that would result from applying domestic federal statutory tax rates to pretax income from continuing operations.

4. **Losses & Carryforwards** The amounts and expiration dates of operating loss and tax credit carryforwards for tax purposes must be disclosed.

VII. Business Combinations & Investments in Common Stock

A. Business Combinations

1. **Valuation Allowance** Changes in a valuation allowance for an acquired entity's deferred tax asset within the measurement period that result from new information about facts and circumstances that existed at the acquisition date shall be recognized through a corresponding adjustment to goodwill. However, once goodwill is reduced to zero, an acquirer shall recognize any additional decrease in the valuation allowance as a bargain purchase. All other changes shall be reported as a reduction or increase to income tax expense (or a direct adjustment to contributed capital as required).

2. **Acquired Income Tax Positions** The acquirer shall recognize changes in any acquired tax positions. Tax positions will be evaluated for recognition, derecognition, and measurement using consistent criteria.

B. Cost Method Investments

1. **No Temporary Differences** The basis for income recognition on investments accounted for by the cost method (i.e., the investor does not have the ability to exercise significant influence over the investee, less than 20% ownership) is dividends received, both for financial accounting and tax purposes. Thus, no temporary differences result from cost method investments.

2. **Dividends Received Deduction** Tax law has generally allowed corporate shareholders owning less than 20% of the stock of a qualifying domestic corporation to deduct 70% of the dividends received. That portion of the dividends received is an event recognized in the financial statements that does not have a tax consequence because it is exempt from taxation. Therefore, the financial accounting tax expense and the tax liability from cost-method investment income will be the same because no tax deferrals result.

Example 23 ▸ Cost Method Investments

Investments, Inc., owns a 10% interest in Goodbuy Co. Goodbuy reported net income of $500,000 and declared and paid dividends of $300,000.

Required: Assuming a 30% effective tax rate, determine Investments' tax expense and liability in connection with its ownership interest in Goodbuy.

Solution:

Dividends paid by Goodbuy	$300,000
Investments, Inc.'s ownership interest	× 10%
Dividends received	30,000
70% dividends received deduction	(21,000)
Taxable dividend income	9,000
Effective tax rate	× 30%
Tax expense **and** liability (no deferrals)	$ 2,700

C. Equity Method Investments

1. **GAAP Basis & Tax Basis Differ** When a company has investments accounted for under the "equity method" (i.e., 20% to 50% ownership, "significant influence") investment income is recognized on a different basis for financial accounting and tax purposes.

2. **Dividends Received Deduction** Tax law has generally allowed corporate shareholders owning 20% or more, but less than 80% of the stock of a qualifying domestic corporation to deduct 80% of the dividends received. That portion of the dividends received that is excluded from taxable income is an event recognized in the financial statements that does not have a tax consequence because it is exempt from taxation.

3. **Income Taxes** Income taxes on income from equity method investments are accounted for under the assumption that the investor will eventually receive her/his share in the undistributed income of the equity-method investee.

   a. Therefore, an equity-method investee's undistributed income should be treated as a temporary difference.

b. The tax effect of this temporary difference depends on whether the investor ultimately expects to receive the undistributed income as dividends or as a realized gain upon disposal of the investment (or as a combination of both).

(1) If the undistributed income is expected to be received as dividends, the computation of temporary differences should allow for the dividends-received deduction.

(2) If the undistributed income is expected to be received as a realized gain upon disposal of the investment, the computation of temporary differences should **not** include the dividends-received deduction.

Example 24 ▸ Equity Method Investments

Ivy, Inc., owns 30% of Goodbuy's common stock and no preferred stock. During the current year, Goodbuy reported income of $500,000 and paid $300,000 dividends on common stock and $50,000 on preferred stock. Ivy's tax rate is 30%, including federal and state taxes.

Required: Record Ivy's tax expense, liability and related deferrals, assuming no transactions occurred in the year other than those dealing with investments and that undistributed income is expected to be received as dividends.

Solution:

	Debit	Credit
Tax Expense—current	5,400	
Tax Expense—deferred	2,700	
Taxes Payable ($18,000 [1] × 30%)		5,400
Deferred Tax Liability ($9,000 [2] × 30%)		2,700

[1]	Dividends paid to Ivy ($300,000 × 30%)	$ 90,000
	Less 80% deduction	(72,000)
	Dividends included in taxable income	$ 18,000
[2]	Ivy's equity in Goodbuy's income [($500,000 – $50,000) × 30%]	$135,000
	Dividends paid to Ivy ($300,000 × 30%)	(90,000)
	Undistributed income	45,000
	Less 80% deduction	(36,000)
	Temporary difference	$ 9,000

CHAPTER 14—ACCOUNTING FOR INCOME TAXES

Problem 14-1 MULTIPLE-CHOICE QUESTIONS

1. Busy Co. applied the provisions of the tax law to its taxable loss figure for the period. What period of time is Busy allowed to carryback and carryforward a net operating loss?

	Carryback	Carryforward
a.	2 years	15 years
b.	2 years	20 years
c.	3 years	15 years
d.	3 years	20 years

(Editors, 9146)

2. In year 2, Ajax, Inc. reported taxable income of $400,000 and pretax financial statement income of $300,000. The difference resulted from $60,000 of nondeductible premiums on Ajax's officers' life insurance and $40,000 of rental income received in advance. Rental income is taxable when received. Ajax's effective tax rate is 30%. In its year 2 income statement, what amount should Ajax report as income tax expense-current portion?

   a. $ 90,000
   b. $102,000
   c. $108,000
   d. $120,000

(R/10, FAR, #40, 9340)

3. Mobe Co. reported the following operating income (loss) for its first three years of operations:

Year 1	$ 300,000
Year 2	(700,000)
Year 3	1,200,000

   For each year, there were no deferred income taxes, and Mobe's effective income tax rate was 30%. In its year 2 income tax return, Mobe elected to carry back the maximum amount of loss possible. In its year 3 income statement, what amount should Mobe report as total income tax expense?

   a. $120,000
   b. $150,000
   c. $240,000
   d. $360,000

(5/95, FAR, #43, amended, 5579)

4. Ajax Corp. has an effective tax rate of 30%. On January 1, Year 2, Ajax purchased equipment for $100,000. The equipment has a useful life of 10 years. What amount of current tax benefit will Ajax realize during Year 2 by using the 150% declining balance method of depreciation for tax purposes instead of the straight-line method?

   a. $1,500
   b. $3,000
   c. $4,500
   d. $5,000

(R/09, FAR, #10, 8760)

5. On January 2, year 1, Ross Co. purchased a machine for $70,000. This machine has a 5-year useful life, a residual value of $10,000, and is depreciated using the straight-line method for financial statement purposes. For tax purposes, depreciation expense was $25,000 for year 1 and $20,000 for year 2. Ross' year 2 income, before income taxes and depreciation expense, was $100,000 and its tax rate was 30%. If Ross had made **no** estimated tax payments during year 2, what amount of current income tax liability would Ross report in its December 31, year 2 balance sheet?

   a. $26,400
   b. $25,800
   c. $24,000
   d. $22,500

(5/92, PI, #26, amended, 2595)

6. Pine Corp.'s books showed pretax income of $800,000 for the current year ended December 31. In the computation of federal income taxes, the following data were considered:

Gain on an involuntary conversion (Pine has elected to replace the property within the statutory period using total proceeds.)	$350,000
Depreciation deducted for tax purposes in excess of depreciation deducted for book purposes	50,000
Federal estimated tax payments	70,000
Enacted federal tax rates	30%

What amount should Pine report as its current federal income tax liability on its December 31 balance sheet?

a. $ 50,000
b. $ 65,000
c. $120,000
d. $135,000 (11/90, PI, #16, amended, 3311)

7. Zeff Co. prepared the following reconciliation of its pretax financial statement income to taxable income for the current year ended December 31, its first year of operations:

Pretax financial income	$160,000
Nontaxable interest received on municipal securities	(5,000)
Long-term loss accrual in excess of deductible amount	10,000
Depreciation in excess of financial statement amount	(25,000)
Taxable income	$140,000

Zeff's tax rate for the year is 40%.

In its December 31 balance sheet, what should Zeff report as deferred income tax liability?

a. $2,000
b. $4,000
c. $6,000
d. $8,000 (11/95, FAR, #38, amended, 6120)

8. Ram Corp. prepared the following reconciliation of income per books with income per tax return for the current year ended December 31:

Book income before income taxes	$ 750,000
Add temporary difference:	
Construction contract revenue which will reverse in four years	100,000
Deduct temporary difference:	
Depreciation expense which will reverse in equal amounts in each of the next four years	(400,000)
Taxable income	$ 450,000

Ram's effective income tax rate for the year is 34%. What amount should Ram report in its current year income statement as the current provision for income taxes?

a. $ 34,000
b. $153,000
c. $255,000
d. $289,000 (11/90, PII, #7, amended, 3432)

9. Because Jab Co. uses different methods to depreciate equipment for financial statement and income tax purposes, Jab has temporary differences that will reverse during the next year and add to taxable income. Deferred income taxes that are based on these temporary differences should be classified in Jab's balance sheet as a

a. Contra account to current assets
b. Contra account to noncurrent assets
c. Current liability
d. Noncurrent liability (5/94, FAR, #24, 4839)

10. When accounting for income taxes, a temporary difference occurs in which of the following scenarios?
    a. An item is included in the calculation of net income, but is neither taxable nor deductible.
    b. An item is included in the calculation of net income in one year and in taxable income in a different year.
    c. An item is **no** longer taxable due to a change in the tax law.
    d. The accrual method of accounting is used. (R/10, FAR, #41, 9341)

11. In its current year income statement, Cere Co. reported income before income taxes of $300,000. Cere estimated that, because of permanent differences, taxable income would be $280,000. During the year Cere made estimated tax payments of $50,000, which were debited to income tax expense. Cere is subject to a 30% tax rate. What amount should Cere report as income tax expense?
    a. $34,000
    b. $50,000
    c. $84,000
    d. $90,000 (11/94, Theory, #51, amended, 5312)

12. Fern Co. has net income, before taxes, of $200,000, including $20,000 interest revenue from municipal bonds and $10,000 paid for officers' life insurance premiums where the company is the beneficiary. The tax rate for the current year is 30%. What is Fern's effective tax rate?
    a. 27.0%
    b. 28.5%
    c. 30.0%
    d. 31.5% (R/11, FAR, #34, 9884)

13. Orleans Co., a cash basis taxpayer, prepares accrual basis financial statements. In its current year balance sheet, Orleans' deferred income tax liabilities increased compared to the previous year. Which of the following changes would cause this increase in deferred income tax liabilities?

    I. An increase in prepaid insurance
    II. An increase in rent receivable
    III. An increase in warranty obligations

    a. I only
    b. I and II
    c. II and III
    d. III only (5/92, Theory, #9, amended, 3625)

14. Which of the following should be disclosed in a company's financial statements related to deferred taxes?

    I. The types and amounts of existing temporary differences
    II. The types and amounts of existing permanent differences
    III. The nature and amount of each type of operating loss and tax credit carryforward

    a. I and II only
    b. I and III only
    c. II and III only
    d. I, II, and III (R/06, FAR, #20, 8087)

15. At the end of year 1, Cody Co. reported a profit on a partially completed construction contract by applying the percentage of completion method. By the end of year 2, the total estimated profit on the contract at completion in year 3 had been drastically reduced from the amount estimated at the end of year 1. Consequently, in year 2, a loss equal to one-half of the previous year profit was recognized. Cody used the completed contract method for income tax purposes and had no other contracts. The year 2 balance sheet should include a deferred tax

	Asset	Liability
a.	Yes	Yes
b.	No	Yes
c.	Yes	No
d.	No	No

(11/91, Theory, #4, amended, 9080)

16. Rein Inc. reported deferred tax assets and deferred tax liabilities at the end of the previous year and at the end of the current year. For the current year ended, Rein should report deferred income tax expense or benefit equal to the

    a. Decrease in the deferred tax assets
    b. Increase in the deferred tax liabilities
    c. Sum of the net changes in deferred tax assets and deferred tax liabilities
    d. Amount of the current tax liability plus the sum of the net changes in deferred tax assets and deferred tax liabilities (11/92, Theory, #41, amended, 3474)

17. In year 1, Lobo Corp. reported for financial statement purposes the following revenue and expenses which were not included in taxable income:

Premiums on officers' life insurance under which the corporation is the beneficiary	$ 5,000
Interest revenue on qualified state or municipal bonds	10,000
Depreciation deducted for income tax purposes in excess of depreciation reported for financial statement purposes	10,000
Estimated future warranty costs to be paid in year 2 and year 3	60,000

    Lobo's enacted tax rate for the current and future years is 30%. Lobo expects to operate profitably in the future. There were no temporary differences in prior years. The deferred tax benefit is

    a. $18,000
    b. $19,500
    c. $21,000
    d. $22,500 (5/90, PI, #41, amended, 3315)

18. In its year 1 income statement, Tow Inc. reported proceeds from an officer's life insurance policy of $90,000 and depreciation of $250,000. Tow was the owner and beneficiary of the life insurance on its officer. Tow deducted depreciation of $370,000 in its year 1 income tax return when the tax rate was 30%. Data related to the reversal of the excess tax deduction for depreciation follow:

Year	Reversal of excess tax deduction	Enacted tax rates
2	$50,000	35%
3	40,000	35%
4	20,000	25%
5	10,000	25%

    There are no other temporary differences. Tow expects to report profits (rather than losses) for tax purposes for all future years. In its December 31, year 1 balance sheet, what amount should Tow report as a deferred income tax liability?

    a. $36,000
    b. $39,000
    c. $63,000
    d. $66,000 (11/91, PI, #35, amended, 3307)

Use the following information for Questions 19 and 20.

Paxton Inc.'s reconciliation between financial statement and taxable income for year 6 follows. Pretax financial income	$750,000
Permanent difference	(25,000)
	725,000
Temp difference: depreciation	(60,000)
Temp difference: disallowed warranty expense	50,000
Taxable income	$715,000

19. The enacted tax rate was 30% for year 6 and 35% for years thereafter. Paxton estimates that 10% of any deferred tax asset will never be realized. In its December 31, year 6 balance sheet, what amount would Paxton report as deferred income tax asset?
    a. $17,500
    b. $21,000
    c. $15,750
    d. $18,900

    (Editor, 9158)

20. The enacted tax rate was 30% for year 6 and 35% for years thereafter. Paxton estimates that 10% of any deferred tax asset will never be realized. In its December 31, year 6 balance sheet, what amount would Paxton report as deferred income tax liability?
    a. $18,000
    b. $21,000
    c. $18,900
    d. $17,500

    (Editor, 9159)

21. Concerning the measurement of deferred tax accounts, which of the following statements is false?
    a. A current tax liability or asset is recognized for the estimated taxes payable or refundable on tax returns for the current year.
    b. A deferred tax liability or asset is recognized for the estimated future tax effects attributable to temporary differences and carryforwards.
    c. The measurement of current and deferred tax liabilities and assets is based on the provisions of future changes in tax laws and rates.
    d. The measurement of deferred tax assets is reduced, if necessary, by the amount of any tax benefits that, based on available evidence, are not expected to be realized. (Editor, 89654)

22. Mill, which began operations on January 1, year 1, recognizes income from long-term construction contracts under the percentage of completion method in its financial statements and under the completed contract method for income tax reporting. Income under each method follows:

Year	Completed contract	Percentage of completion
1	$ —	$300,000
2	400,000	600,000
3	700,000	850,000

    The income tax rate was 30% for years 1 through 3. For years after year 3, the enacted tax rate is 25%. There are no other temporary differences. Assuming Mill does not expect any tax losses in the near future, Mill should report in its December 31, year 3 balance sheet, a deferred income tax liability of
    a. $ 87,500
    b. $ 105,000
    c. $ 162,500
    d. $ 195,000

    (11/91, PI, #38, amended, 3303)

23. Black Co., organized on January 2, year 1, had pretax financial statement income of $500,000 and taxable income of $800,000 for the year ended December 31, year 1. The only temporary differences are accrued product warranty costs, which Black expects to pay as follows:

Year 2	$ 100,000
Year 3	50,000
Year 4	50,000
Year 5	100,000

The enacted income tax rates are 25% for year 1, 30% for years 2 through 4, and 35% for year 5. Black believes that future years' operations will produce profits. In its December 31, year 1, balance sheet, what amount should Black report as deferred tax asset?

a. $50,000
b. $75,000
c. $90,000
d. $95,000 (11/98, FAR, #10, amended, 6737)

24. Quinn Co. reported a net deferred tax asset of $9,000 in its December 31, year 1 balance sheet. For year 2, Quinn reported pretax financial statement income of $300,000. Temporary differences of $100,000 resulted in taxable income of $200,000 for year 2. At December 31, year 2, Quinn had cumulative taxable differences of $70,000. Quinn's effective income tax rate is 30%. In its December 31, year 2 income statement, what should Quinn report as deferred income tax expense?

a. $12,000
b. $21,000
c. $30,000
d. $60,000 (11/90, PI, #48, amended, 5578)

25. Which of the following is true regarding the enacted tax rate?

a. The enacted tax rate is the expected tax rate applied to taxable income in the years that the liability is expected to be settled or the asset recovered, and is used to measure deferred tax liabilities and deferred tax assets.
b. The presently enacted changes in tax rates and laws must be considered when determining the tax rate to apply to temporary differences reversing in that year(s).
c. The enacted tax rate is the tax rate for the current year if no changes have been enacted for future years.
d. All of the above are true. (Editor, 89660)

26. Under current generally accepted accounting principles, which approach is used to determine income tax expense?

a. Asset and liability approach
b. "With and without" approach
c. Net of tax approach
d. Periodic expense approach (Editor, 6786)

27. Senlo Co. uses a one-year operating cycle and recognizes profits for financial statement and tax purposes during its two years of operation. Depreciation for tax purposes exceeded depreciation for financial statement purposes each year. These temporary differences are expected to reverse in years 3, 4, and 5. At the end of year 2, the deferred tax liability shown as a noncurrent liability is based on the

a. Enacted tax rates for years 3, 4, and 5
b. Enacted tax rates for years 4 and 5
c. Enacted tax rate for year 3
d. Tax rates for years 1 and 2 (11/90, Theory, #27, amended, 3633)

28. During the first quarter of the calendar year, Worth Co. had income before taxes of $100,000, and its effective income tax rate was 15%. Worth's effective annual income tax rate for the previous year was 30%. Worth expects that its effective annual income tax rate for the current year will be 25%. The statutory tax rate for the current year is 35%. In its first quarter interim income statement, what amount of income tax expense should Worth report?

    a. $15,000
    b. $25,000
    c. $30,000
    d. $35,000

    (R/07, FAR, #50, 8371)

29. A deferred tax asset of $100,000 was recognized in the year 1 financial statements by the Chaise Company when a loss from discontinued segments was carried forward for tax purposes. A valuation allowance of $100,000 was also recognized in the year 1 statements because it was considered more likely than not that the deferred tax asset would not be realized. Chaise had no temporary differences. The tax benefit of the loss carried forward reduced current taxes payable on year 3 continuing operations. The year 3 income statement would include the tax benefit from the loss brought forward in

    a. Income from continuing operations
    b. Gain or loss from discontinued segments
    c. Extraordinary gains
    d. Cumulative effect of accounting changes

    (5/90, Theory, #25, amended, 3632)

30. Dodd Corp. is preparing its December 31 current year financial statements and must determine the proper accounting treatment for the following situations:

    - For the current year ended December 31, Dodd has a loss carryforward of $180,000 available to offset future taxable income. However, there are no temporary differences. Based on an analysis of both positive and negative evidence, Dodd has reason to believe it is more likely than not that the benefits of the entire loss carryforward will be realized within the carryforward period.
    - On 12/31 of this year, Dodd received a $200,000 offer for its patent. Dodd's management is considering whether to sell the patent. The offer expires on 2/28 of next year. The patent has a carrying amount of $100,000 at 12/31.

    Assume a current and future income tax rate of 30%. In its current year income statement, Dodd should recognize an increase in net income of

    a. $0
    b. $ 54,000
    c. $ 70,000
    d. $124,000

    (5/90, PII, #60, amended, 3433)

31. On its current year December 31 balance sheet, Shin Co. had income taxes payable of $13,000 and a current deferred tax asset of $20,000 before determining the need for a valuation account. Shin had reported a current deferred tax asset of $15,000 at December 31 of the previous year. No estimated tax payments were made during the current year. At December 31, current year, Shin determined that it was more likely than not that 10% of the deferred tax asset would not be realized. In its current year income statement, what amount should Shin report as total income tax expense?

    a. $ 8,000
    b. $ 8,500
    c. $10,000
    d. $13,000

    (11/95, FAR, #36, amended, 6118)

32. Brass Co. reported income before income tax expense of $60,000 for Year 3. Brass had no permanent or temporary timing differences for tax purposes. Brass has an effective tax rate of 30% and a $40,000 net operating loss carryforward from Year 2. What is the maximum income tax benefit that Brass can realize from the loss carryforward for Year 3?

    a. $12,000
    b. $18,000
    c. $20,000
    d. $40,000 (R/09, FAR, #8, 8758)

33. Concerning valuation allowances for income taxes, which of the following statements is false?

    a. For each tax position, an enterprise should reassess whether the more-likely-than-not recognition threshold is met at the end of each reporting period.
    b. A tax position should also be recognized when the tax matter is ultimately resolved through negotiation or litigation or when the statute of limitations for the relevant taxing authority to examine the tax position has expired.
    c. When a tax position no longer meets the more-likely-than-not threshold, any previously recognized tax benefit is derecognized in its entirety in the financial statements.
    d. An enterprise may use a valuation allowance to derecognize the benefit. (Editor, 89664)

34. Lion Co.'s income statement for its first year of operations shows pretax income of $6,000,000. In addition, the following differences existed between Lion's tax return and records:

	Tax return	Accounting records
Uncollectible accounts expense	$ 220,000	$250,000
Depreciation expense	860,000	570,000
Tax-exempt interest revenue	—	50,000

    Lion's current year tax rate is 30% and the enacted rate for future years is 40%. What amount should Lion report as deferred tax expense in its income statement for the year?

    a. $148,000
    b. $124,000
    c. $104,000
    d. $ 78,000 (R/09, FAR, #13, 8763)

35. Which of the following tax positions is unlikely to be affected by the accounting for uncertain tax positions?

    a. A deduction taken on the tax return for a current expenditure that the taxing authority may assert should be capitalized and amortized over future periods.
    b. The calculation of the amount of a research and experimentation credit.
    c. The determination as to whether an entity is subject to tax in a particular jurisdiction.
    d. Deductions for ordinary salaries paid to employees. (Editor, 89663)

36. Concerning income tax guidance provided by GAAP, which of the following statements is (are) true?

    a. GAAP does not provide guidance on accounting for uncertainty in income taxes recognized in an enterprise's financial statements.
    b. GAAP does not prescribe a recognition threshold and measurement attribute for the financial statement recognition and measurement of a tax position taken or expected to be taken in a tax return.
    c. GAAP provides guidance on derecognition, classification, interest and penalties, accounting in interim periods, disclosure, and transition related to uncertain tax positions.
    d. All of the above (Editor, 89662)

37. Hut Co. has temporary taxable differences that will reverse during the next year and add to taxable income. These differences relate to noncurrent assets. Deferred income taxes based on these temporary differences should be classified in Hut's balance sheet as a

 a. Current asset
 b. Noncurrent asset
 c. Current liability
 d. Noncurrent liability (11/97, FAR, #11, 6491)

38. At December 31, Bren Co. had the following deferred income tax items:

 - A deferred income tax liability of $15,000 related to a noncurrent asset
 - A deferred income tax asset of $3,000 related to a noncurrent liability
 - A deferred income tax asset of $8,000 related to a current liability

 Which of the following should Bren report in the noncurrent section of its December 31 balance sheet?

 a. A noncurrent tax asset of $3,000 and a noncurrent liability of $15,000
 b. A noncurrent tax liability of $12,000
 c. A noncurrent tax asset of $11,000 and a noncurrent liability of $15,000
 d. A noncurrent tax liability of $4,000 (5/95, FAR, #17, amended, 5553)

39. In year 1, Rand Inc. reported for financial statement purposes the following items, which were not included in taxable income:

Installment gain to be collected equally in years 2 through 4	$1,500,000
Estimated future warranty costs to be paid equally in years 2 through 4	2,100,000

 Rand had the installment gain arise from the sale of an investment. There were no temporary differences in prior years. Rand expects taxable income in all future years. Rand's enacted tax rates are 25% for year 1 and 30% for years 2 through 4. In Rand's December 31, year 1 balance sheet, what amounts of the net deferred tax asset should be classified as current and noncurrent?

	Current	Noncurrent
a.	$60,000	$100,000
b.	$60,000	$120,000
c.	$50,000	$100,000
d.	$50,000	$120,000

(5/91, PI, #31, amended, 3319)

40. Stockholders' equity is charged or credited for the income tax effects of which of the following?

 a. Foreign currency translation adjustments
 b. Expenditures reported as a reduction of the proceeds from issuing capital stock
 c. Both A. and B.
 d. None of the above (Editor, 89667)

41. Income tax expense or benefit for the year should be allocated among

	Discontinued operations	Prior period adjustments
a.	Yes	Yes
b.	Yes	No
c.	No	Yes
d.	No	No

(Editors, 3636)

42. Generally, the manner of reporting the tax benefit of an operating loss carryforward or carryback is determined by the source of the

	Income or Loss in the current year	Operating loss carryforward or taxes paid in a prior year
a.	Yes	Yes
b.	Yes	No
c.	No	Yes
d.	No	No

(Editors, 3631)

43. Purl Corporation's income statement for the year ended December 31 shows the following:

Income before income tax and extraordinary item	$900,000
Gain on life insurance coverage—included in the above $900,000 income amount	100,000
Extraordinary item—loss due to earthquake damage	300,000

Purl's tax rate for the year is 30%. How much should be reported as the provision for income tax in Purl's income statement?

a. $150,000
b. $180,000
c. $240,000
d. $270,000 (Editors, 3321)

44. Which of the following statements is false regarding business combinations?

a. The acquirer should not adjust the accounting for prior business combinations for previously recognized changes in acquired tax uncertainties or previously recognized changes in the valuation allowance for acquired deferred tax assets.
b. The acquirer should recognize, as an adjustment to income tax expense (or a direct adjustment to contributed capital in accordance with GAAP changes in the valuation allowance for acquired deferred tax assets.
c. The acquirer should recognize changes in the acquired income tax positions in accordance with GAAP.
d. Both B. and C. are true. (Editor, 89668)

45. On January 1 of the current year, Lundy Corp. purchased 40% of the voting common stock of Glen Inc., and appropriately accounts for its investment by the equity method. During the year, Glen reported earnings of $225,000 and paid dividends of $75,000. Lundy assumes that all of Glen's undistributed earnings will be distributed as dividends in future periods when the enacted tax rate will be 30%. Ignore the dividends-received deduction. Lundy's current enacted income tax rate is 25%. Lundy uses the liability method to account for temporary differences and expects to have taxable income in all future periods. The increase in Lundy's deferred income tax liability for this temporary difference is

a. $45,000
b. $37,500
c. $27,000
d. $18,000 (5/89, PI, #40, amended, 3323)

46. Leer Corp.'s pretax income in the current year was $100,000. The temporary differences between amounts reported in the financial statements and the tax return are as follows:

- Depreciation in the financial statements was $8,000 more than tax depreciation.
- The equity method of accounting resulted in financial statement income of $35,000. A $25,000 dividend was received during the year, which is eligible for the 80% dividends received deduction.

Leer's effective income tax rate was 30%. In its current year income statement, Leer should report a current provision for income taxes of

a. $26,400
b. $23,400
c. $21,900
d. $18,600 (11/91, PI, #48, amended, 3312)

47. Taft Corp. uses the equity method to account for its 25% investment in Flame Inc. During the current year, Taft received dividends of $30,000 from Flame and recorded $180,000 as its equity in the earnings of Flame. Additional information follows:

    - All the undistributed earnings of Flame will be distributed as dividends in future periods.
    - The dividends received from Flame are eligible for the 80% dividends received deduction.
    - There are no other temporary differences.
    - Enacted income tax rates are 30% for this year and thereafter.

    In its December 31 balance sheet, what amount should Taft report for deferred income tax liability?

    a. $ 9,000
    b. $ 10,800
    c. $ 45,000
    d. $ 54,000

    (5/93, PI, #35, amended, 4076)

Problem 14-2 SIMULATION: Tax Differences

Items 1 through 4 describe circumstances resulting in differences between financial statement income and taxable income. Select the **best** answer for each item. An answer may be selected once, more than once, or not at all. For each numbered item, determine whether the difference is:

List	
A.	A temporary difference resulting in a deferred tax asset
B.	A temporary difference resulting in a deferred tax liability
C.	A permanent difference

Circumstance	Difference
1. Costs of guarantees and warranties are estimated.	
2. Interest is received on an investment in tax-exempt municipal obligations.	
3. A landlord collects some rents in advance. Rents received are taxable in the period in which they are received.	
4. For plant assets, the depreciation expense deducted for tax purposes is in excess of the depreciation expense used for financial reporting purposes.	

Items 5 through 8 represent amounts omitted from the following worksheet. The partially completed worksheet contains a reconciliation between financial statement income and taxable income for the three years ended April 30, year 8, and additional information. The tax rate changes were enacted at the beginning of each tax year and were not known at the end of the prior year. For each item, determine the amount omitted from the worksheet and enter in the cell. Round to nearest whole dollar. An answer may be used once, more than once, or not at all.

	April 30, Year 6	April 30, Year 7	April 30, Year 8
Pretax financial income	$1,000,000	$1,250,000	$1,450,000
Permanent differences	200,000	200,000	200,000
Temporary differences	100,000	150,000	200,000
Taxable income	$ 700,000	$ 900,000	$1,050,000
Cumulative temporary differences (future taxable amounts)	$ 100,000	$ (6)	$ 450,000
Tax rate	25%	30%	35%
Deferred tax liability	$ 25,000	$ 75,000	$ (8)
Deferred tax expense	$ —	$ (7)	$ —
Current tax expense	$ (5)	$ —	$ —

Item	Amount
5. Current tax expense for the year ended April 30, year 6.	
6. Cumulative temporary differences at April 30, year 7.	
7. Deferred tax expense for the year ended April 30, year 7.	
8. Deferred tax liability at April 30, year 8.	

(5/97, FAR, #1, amended, 6479t)

Problem 14-3 SIMULATION: Tax Effects

The following condensed trial balance of Colin Corp., a publicly owned company, has been adjusted except for income tax expense:

	Debit	Credit
Total assets	$33,560,000	
Total liabilities		$12,700,000
6% cumulative preferred stock		2,500,000
Common stock		15,000,000
Retained earnings		3,100,000
Machine sales		950,000
Service revenues		350,000
Interest revenues		20,000
Gain on sale of factory		200,000
Cost of sales—machines	475,000	
Cost of services	150,000	
Administrative exp.	400,000	
R & D expenses	165,000	
Interest expense	10,000	
Loss from asset disposal	60,000	
	$34,820,000	**$34,820,000**

- The weighted average number of common shares outstanding during year 5 was 250,000. The potential dilution from the exercise of stock options held by Colin's officers and directors was not material.
- There were no dividends-in-arrears on Colin's preferred stock at July 1, year 4. On May 1, year 5, Colin's directors declared a 6% preferred stock dividend to be paid in August year 5.
- During year 5, one of Colin's foreign factories was expropriated by the foreign government, and Colin received a $800,000 payment from the foreign government in settlement. The carrying value of the plant was $600,000. Colin has never disposed of a factory.
- Administrative expenses includes a $10,000 premium payment for a $2,000,000 life insurance policy on Colin's president, of which the corporation is the beneficiary.
- Colin depreciates its assets using the straight-line method for financial reporting purposes and an accelerated method for tax purposes. There were no other temporary differences. The differences between book and tax depreciation are as follows:

June 30	Financial statements over (under) tax depreciation
Year 5	$(25,000)
Year 6	15,000
Year 7	10,000

- Colin's enacted tax rate for the current and future years is 25%.

1. Using the single-step format, prepare Colin's income statement for the year ended June 30, year 5.

Revenues:		
Machine sales		
Service revenues		
Interest revenue		
Total revenue		
Expenses:		
Cost of sales—machines		
Cost of services		
Administrative expense		
Research and development expense		
Interest expense		
Loss from asset disposal		
Current income tax expense		
Deferred income tax expense		
Total expenses and losses		
Income before extraordinary gain		
Extraordinary gain, net of income taxes of $50,000		
Net income		
Earnings (loss) per share:		
Income before extraordinary gain		
Net income		

2. Prepare a schedule reconciling Colin's financial statement net income to taxable income for the year ended June 30, year 5.

Net income	
Add: Taxes on extraordinary gain	
Provision for income tax	
Financial statement income before income taxes	
Permanent difference—officer's life insurance	
Temporary difference—excess of tax over financial statement depreciation	
Taxable income	

(R/03, FAR, amended, 9010)

Problem 14-4 SIMULATION: Deferred Taxes

Stanhope, Inc., a C corporation, is a distributor of personal electronics and has reported a net income for each year since inception. Its taxable income has consistently resulted in an effective tax rate of 33%. (Ignore state income taxes.) You have been assigned to compute the company's deferred portion of federal income taxes for inclusion in its financial statements for year 2 and to provide the company's controller with a schedule that supports your computation. Your schedule should identify deductible and taxable temporary differences and components of the deferred tax computations.

The controller has provided you with the following reconciliation of Stanhope's pretax accounting income to taxable income for year 2 and the additional information shown below. Use this information to answer the subsequent questions.

Stanhope, Inc.
Reconciliation of Pretax Accounting Income to Taxable Income
Year ended December 31, year 2

Pretax accounting income		$678,000
Expenses recorded on books this year not deductible for tax purposes:		
Meals and entertainment expenses	$12,000	
Bad debts expense provision	15,000	27,000
Subtotal		705,000
Income recorded on books this year not subject to tax:		
Tax-exempt interest income	15,000	
Unrealized gain (loss) on trading securities	8,000	
Deductions on tax return not charged against book income this year:		
Depreciation expense	63,000	
Bad debts written off and charged against allowance account	5,000	91,000
Taxable income		$614,000

1. The Allowance for doubtful accounts (bad debts) as of December 31, year 1, was $11,000. During year 2, uncollectible accounts totaling $5,000 were written off and charged against the allowance account. A provision for bad debts of $15,000 was charged to operations at the end of the year to result in an Allowance for doubtful accounts balance at December 31, year 2, of $21,000.
2. At the end of the year, there were net unrealized gains on trading securities of $8,000. There were no unrealized gains/losses on trading securities at the beginning of the year.
3. The company uses straight-line depreciation for financial reporting (GAAP) purposes and accelerated methods for income tax purposes. Balances and activity in the accumulated depreciation account for GAAP and income tax purposes are summarized below:

	GAAP	Tax	Difference
Accumulated depreciation, December 31, year 1	1,314,000	2,018,000	704,000
Year 2 depreciation expense	196,000	259,000	63,000
Accumulated depreciation, December 31, year 2	1,510,000	2,277,000	767,000

Use the information on the previous page to complete the worksheet, as follows:

- In column A, select a line item from the choices below that will result in a temporary difference.
- In column B, enter the total temporary difference that would result in a deferred tax asset or liability.
- Enter the total deferred tax asset or liability in the appropriate column, C or D, based on the temporary difference you recorded in column B.

Selection list for description of temporary differences	
Accumulated depreciation, excess of tax over GAAP	Unrealized gain (loss) on trading securities
Accumulated depreciation, excess of GAAP over tax	Meals and entertainment expenses
Allowance for doubtful accounts	Tax-exempt interest income
Bad debts expense provision	Bad debts written off

	A	**B**	**C**	**D**
	Description of temporary differences	**Temporary differences**	**Deferred tax assets**	**Deferred tax liabilities**
1				
2				
3				
4				
5				
6	Totals			

Use the information from your completed worksheet to prepare the applicable line items for Stanhope, Inc.'s balance sheet as of December 31, year 2. If there is no balance in an account, enter a value of zero (0).

Assets:	
Deferred taxes, current asset	
Deferred taxes, noncurrent asset	
Liabilities:	
Deferred taxes, current liability	
Deferred taxes, noncurrent liability	

(R/09, FAR, P3, amended, 8749)

Problem 14-5 SIMULATION: Research

Question: The management of Stanhope, Inc. inquired whether changes in tax laws and rates during the current year would affect the computation of Stanhope's deferred tax liabilities and deferred tax assets. Find authoritative guidance that responds to this inquiry.

FASB ASC: ______ - ______ - ______ - ______

(9129)

Solution 14-1 MULTIPLE-CHOICE ANSWERS

Basic Concepts

1. (b) The tax law provides that a net operating loss may be carried back 2 years and forward 20 years. (9146)

2. (d) Pretax financial statement income is determined on the accrual basis. Most revenues and expenses are reported on the tax return in the same period that they are reported on the income statement. However, tax laws often differ from the recognition and measurement requirements of financial accounting standards, and it is common to find differences between the amount of pretax financial income and the amount of taxable income for a period. The $60,000 difference for officer's life insurance premiums is a permanent difference that does not give rise to any deferred tax assets or liabilities. The $40,000 difference for rental income received in advance is a temporary difference that will result in a deductible amount when the liability is settled. The income tax expense for the year is the $400,000 taxable income × the 30% tax rate = $120,000. (9340)

3. (c) The maximum Mobe could carry back to year 1 was $300,000. The remaining $400,000 of the operating loss ($700,000 – $300,000) would be carried forward to year 3, thereby reducing taxable operating income to $800,000 ($1,200,000 – $400,000)

Operating income for year 3	$1,200,000	
Less: Operating loss carryforward	(400,000)	
Net taxable income	800,000	
Effective tax rate	× 30%	
Current tax expense, year 3	$ 240,000	(5579)

4. (a) Using the straight-line method of depreciation, Ajax would have a depreciation expense of $10,000 ($100,000 purchase price / 10 years). The current tax benefit would be $3,000 ($10,000 depreciation expense × 30% effective tax rate). Using the 150% declining balance method of depreciation, Ajax would have a depreciation expense of $15,000 ($100,000 purchase price / 10 years × 150%). The current tax benefit would be $4,500 ($15,000 depreciation expense × 30% effective tax rate). The amount of tax benefit realized by using the 150% declining method instead of the straight-line method would be the difference ($4,500 – $3,000). (8760)

5. (c)

Pretax income before depreciation	$ 100,000	
Depreciation for tax purposes	(20,000)	
Taxable income	80,000	
Tax rate expected	× 30%	
Current income tax expense	24,000	
Estimated tax payments	(0)	
Current income tax liability	$ 24,000	(2595)

6. (a)

Pretax financial income	$ 800,000	
Gain on involuntary conversion deferred for tax purposes	(350,000)	
Excess depreciation for tax purposes	(50,000)	
Taxable income	400,000	
Enacted tax rate	× 30%	
Estimated payments	$ 120,000	
Liability	(70,000)	
Taxes payable	$ 50,000	(3311)

7. (c) Since both temporary items are noncurrent, the amount of the deferred tax liability to be reported is computed by considering the future tax effects of the cumulative net taxable type temporary differences. ($25,000 – $10,000) × 40% = $6,000. Being the first year of operations, the temporary differences originating in the current year are the cumulative temporary differences existing at the balance sheet date. (6120)

8. (b) The current portion of the provision for income taxes (which is the same as the amount of taxes due to the government for the current period) is computed by multiplying the taxable income figure by the statutory tax rate for the current period. The statutory tax rate is not given. However, because there are no permanent differences and because there are no temporary differences which are expected to reverse at tax rates different from the current statutory rate, the effective rate for the current year must be the same as the statutory tax rate. Thus, $450,000 × 34% = $153,000. (3432)

Differences

9. (d) The deferred tax liability is classified as noncurrent because it is related to the equipment, a non-current asset. Deferred tax accounts are reported on the balance sheet as assets and liabilities, not as contra accounts. (4839)

10. (b) A temporary difference occurs when an item is included in the calculation of net income in one year and in taxable income in a different year. It is the difference between the tax basis of an asset or liability and its reported amount in the financial statements that will result in taxable or deductible amounts in future years when the reported amount of the asset is recovered or liability is settled. An item included in the calculation of net income, but is neither taxable nor deductible is a permanent difference. An item that is no longer taxable due to a change in the tax law is not a temporary difference. Although the accrual method of accounting is used for pretax for financial statement income, that in itself does not cause a temporary difference. The pretax financial income and taxable income could be the same amounts. (9341)

11. (c) No temporary differences exist at the beginning or end of the year. Therefore, the amount to be reported as income tax expense is computed by multiplying Cere's taxable income for the year by the enacted tax rate for the year. (5312)

12. (b) The effective tax rate (28.5%) is the amount due to the government ($57,000) divided by net income before taxes ($200,000). The amount due to the government $57,000 ($190,000 × 30%) is net income before taxes adjusted for tax-exempt revenues and nondeductible expenses $190,000 ($200,000 – 20,000 + 10,000) times the current year tax rate (30%). (9884)

Deferred Taxes

13. (b) An increase in prepaid insurance can cause an increase in deferred tax liabilities because an expense deducted this period for tax purposes but deferred for financial accounting purposes will cause future taxable amounts. An increase in rent receivable can cause an increase in deferred tax liabilities because a revenue accrued for book purposes but not recognized for tax purposes until it is collected will give rise to future taxable amounts. A deferred tax liability represents the deferred tax consequences attributable to taxable temporary differences. An increase in cumulative temporary differences giving rise to future taxable amounts results in an increase in deferred tax liabilities. An increase in warranty obligation can cause an increase in deferred tax assets rather than deferred tax liabilities. An expense accrued for book purposes, but deducted for tax purposes when paid, causes a temporary difference which gives rise to future deductible amounts. A deferred tax asset is the deferred tax consequences attributable to deductible temporary differences and carryforwards. (3625)

14. (b) The recognition and measurement of a deferred tax liability or asset is based on the future effects on income taxes, as measured by the provisions of enacted tax laws, resulting from temporary differences and operating loss and tax credit carryforwards at the end of the current year. An enterprise is to identify (disclose) the types and amounts of existing temporary differences and the nature and amount of each type of operating loss and tax credit carryforward (and remaining length of carryforward). (8087)

15. (b) At the end of year 1, a cumulative difference exists which is equal to the contract profit recognized on the income statement in the previous year. The cumulative difference will result in future taxable amounts, so a deferred tax liability is established for an amount equal to the cumulative temporary difference multiplied by the tax rate enacted for the year(s) in which the temporary difference is expected to reverse. In year 2, half of the cumulative temporary difference reverses because of the recognition of a loss to offset half of the profit reported in the previous year. With no change in enacted future tax rates, this reversal results in a decrease in the related deferred tax liability account. Therefore, at the end of year 2, Cody has a deferred tax liability balance equal to half of the balance that was in that account at the end of year 1. (9080)

16. (c) Deferred income tax expense or benefit is calculated using the asset and liability method. Under this approach, deferred income tax expense or benefit is equal to sum of the net changes in deferred taxes assets and deferred tax liabilities on the balance sheet. Deferred income tax expense or benefit is equal to sum of the net changes in both deferred taxes assets and deferred tax liabilities. Answer (d) describes the amount of total income tax expense, assuming no estimated payments have been made. (3474)

17. (a) The amount of deferred tax benefit to be applied against current income tax expense is computed by considering the tax effects of the difference for accrued product warranty costs. Product warranty costs are accrued in computing financial income and deductible for tax purposes only when paid. This causes the product warranty liability to exceed its tax basis (zero), which will result in deductible amounts in years when the warranty liability is settled. A deferred tax asset (DTA) is recognized for the tax benefit of the future deductible amounts ($60,000 × 30% = $18,000). There is no apparent need for a valuation allowance against that DTA; Lobo expects to operate profitably in the future. Lobo had no temporary differences in prior years. Recognition of the DTA requires a debit to *Deferred Tax Asset* and a credit to *Income Tax Expense* for $18,000. The credit to the expense account is called a deferred tax benefit of $18,000 to be applied against current income tax expense (current tax expense is computed by multiplying the taxable income figure by the current tax rate). The insurance premiums and interest revenue do not affect the recognition of the DTA because they are events recognized in financial statements that do not have tax consequences. The insurance premiums are not tax deductible, and the municipal bond interest is exempt from taxation. (3315)

18. (b) The proceeds from the officer's life insurance policy is a tax-exempt revenue; therefore, no current or future tax consequences will result and no deferred taxes are to be recorded for this difference. The $120,000 ($370,000 – $250,000) difference due to depreciation is the only temporary difference existing at the balance sheet date. The tax rate that is used to measure the deferred tax consequences is the enacted tax rate(s) expected to apply to taxable income in the years that this difference reverses.

	Amount	Rate	Def. Tax Liab.
Depreciation			
Years 2 - 3	$90,000	35%	$31,500
Years 4 - 5	$30,000	25%	7,500
Total Deferred tax liability			$39,000

(3307)

19. (c) A deferred tax asset is generated from a temporary difference that is classified as a future deductible amount, computed using future tax rates. The warranty expense is not deductible currently for tax purposes, but will be in the future once the expense is paid, although it is estimated that 10% will never be realized. The deferred tax asset is computed as follows: (50,000 – 5,000) × 35% = $15,750. (9158)

20. (b) A deferred tax liability is generated from a temporary difference that is classified as a future taxable amount, computed using future tax rates. The excess depreciation expense is deductible currently for tax purposes, but not for book purposes. The deferred tax liability is computed as follows: 60,000 × 35% = $21,000. (9159)

21. (c) The measurement of current and deferred tax liabilities and assets is based on provisions of the enacted tax law; the effects of future changes in tax laws or rates are not anticipated. (89654)

22. (c) The $650,000 [($300,000 + $600,000 + $850,000) – ($400,000 + $700,000)] of contract income recognized in the financial statements in excess of that included in taxable income results in taxable amounts in future years. The enacted tax rate for later years is used to determine the deferred income tax liability ($650,000 × 25% = $162,500). (3303)

23. (d) A deferred tax asset or liability is calculated by multiplying temporary differences by the enacted tax rate expected to apply to taxable income in the periods in which the deferred tax liability or asset is expected to be settled or realized.

	Amount		Rate		Def. Tax Asset
Years 2 - 4	$200,000	×	30%	=	$60,000
Years 5	$100,000	×	35%	=	35,000
Total Deferred tax asset					$95,000

(6737)

24. (c) Deferred income tax expense reported for a period is determined by the net change during the year in the deferred tax accounts on the balance sheet. For Quinn, the elimination of the beginning $9,000 net deferred tax asset and the creation of the ending $21,000 ($70,000 cumulative taxable differences × 30% effective income tax rate) net deferred tax liability results in $30,000 of deferred income expense for year 2. (5578)

25. (d) The tax rate that is used to measure deferred tax liabilities and deferred tax assets is the enacted tax rate(s) expected to apply to taxable income in the years that the liability is expected to be settled or the asset recovered. Presently enacted changes in tax laws and rates that become effective for a particular future year or years must be considered when determining the tax rate to apply to temporary differences reversing in that year(s). Tax laws and rates for the current year are used if no changes have been enacted for future years. Since answers a., b., and c. are correct, answer d., *all of the above*, is the best answer choice. (89660)

26. (a) The asset and liability method must be used in accounting and reporting for temporary differences between the amount of taxable income and pretax financial income and the tax bases of assets or liabilities and their reported amounts in financial statements. Under this method, a current or deferred tax liability or asset is recognized for the current or deferred tax consequences of all events that have been recognized in the financial statements. (6786)

Other Considerations

27. (a) A difference caused by the excess of depreciation taken for tax purposes over the depreciation reported for financial statement purposes will result in taxable amounts in the periods that the difference reverses. The deferred tax liability related to this difference at the end of year 2 is calculated by scheduling the taxable amounts that are to occur in each future year because of the temporary difference and by applying enacted tax rates for those years to the amount of taxable amounts scheduled for those years. Deferred tax accounts are classified based on the classification of a related asset or liability. Depreciation relates to plant assets, which are noncurrent assets. Hence, the entire related deferred tax liability is a noncurrent liability. (3633)

28. (b) The objectives of accounting for income taxes are to recognize the amount of taxes payable or refundable for the current year and deferred tax liabilities and assets for the future tax consequences of events that have been recognized in an enterprise's financial statements or tax returns. One of the following basic principles applied in accounting for income taxes at the date of the financial statements is that a current tax liability or asset is recognized for the estimated taxes payable or refundable on tax returns for the current year. The effective annual income tax rate for the entire year will be 25%, thus $25,000 (25% of the first quarter $100,000 income) should be reported as income tax expense in the first quarter interim income statement. The first quarter effective rate, previous year effective rate, and statutory tax rate are not considered. (8371)

29. (a) Except for certain areas such as business combinations and quasi-reorganizations, the manner of reporting the tax benefits of an operating loss carryforward or carryback is determined by the source of income or loss in the current year and not by the source of the operating loss carryforward or taxes paid in a prior year. Therefore, the tax benefit of the operating loss in question reduces income tax expense from income from continuing operations because the realization of the tax benefit results from income from continuing operations. If realization of the tax benefit resulted from an extraordinary gain, the tax benefit would have been reported as an extraordinary item. (3632)

30. (b) A deferred tax asset (DTA) is recognized for the future benefits of a loss carryforward. Therefore, Dodd will increase income by $54,000 ($180,000 × 30% future tax rate) when the benefits of the NOL carryforward are recorded by a debit to *Deferred Tax Asset* and a credit to *Benefits of Loss Carryforward* (a component of income tax expense on the income statement). No valuation allowance is required (which would reduce the DTA and the described impact on income) because the company expects the benefits of the loss carryforward to be realized in the future. The potential gain of $100,000 (i.e., $200,000 offer – $100,000 carrying amount) from the possible sale of the patent should *not* be recognized. Dodd Corp. has not sold the patent as of December 31; it is only considering whether to sell the patent. The excess of fair value over book value of the patent does serve as some positive evidence in evaluating the realizability of the DTA related to the tax loss carryforward. (3433)

31. (c)

Income taxes payable	$ 13,000	
Plus: Deferred tax expense due to valuation allowance (10% × $20,000)	2,000	
Less: Deferred tax benefit due to increase in deferred tax asset ($20,000 – $15,000)	(5,000)	
Total income tax expense	$ 10,000	(6118)

32. (a) Future realization of the tax benefit of an existing deductible temporary difference or carryforward ultimately depends on the existence of sufficient taxable income of the appropriate character within the carryback, carryforward period available under law. Whatever amount is allowed is multiplied by the effective tax rate to come up with the tax benefit realized. Brass had $60,000 reported income which was sufficient income to cover the entire $40,000 net operating loss carryforward. With an effective tax rate of 30%, Brass can realize an income tax benefit of $12,000 ($40,000 × 30%). (8758)

33. (d) Using a valuation allowance to derecognize the benefit is not permitted. (89664)

34. (c) Deferred tax liabilities or assets are recognized for the future tax consequences of, among other things, revenues, expenses, gains, or losses that are included in taxable income of an earlier or later year than the year in which they are recognized. The difference in uncollectible accounts expense between the tax return and the accounting records would result is a $30,000 deferred tax asset. The difference in depreciation expense between the tax return and the accounting records would result in a $290,000 deferred tax liability. The difference in tax-exempt interest revenue between the tax return and the accounting records results in no tax asset or liability because the revenue was tax exempt. This results in a net future tax liability of $260,000. The $260,000 times the future tax rate of 40% equals $104,000. (8763)

Uncertain Tax Positions

35. (d) Tax benefits associated with positions that are highly certain and not likely to be questioned by the taxing authorities, such as deductions for ordinary salaries paid to employees, are unlikely to be affected by the guidance related to uncertain tax positions. (89663)

36. (c) GAAP provides guidance for uncertainty in income taxes recognized in an enterprise's financial statements and prescribes a recognition threshold and measurement attribute for the financial statement recognition and measurement of a tax position taken or expected to be taken in a tax return. (89662)

Presentation and Disclosures

37. (d) Deferred taxable temporary differences create deferred tax liabilities. Deferred tax items are classified as current or noncurrent based on the related asset or liability. Since the related item is noncurrent, the deferred tax liability is noncurrent. (6491)

38. (b) In a classified balance sheet, deferred tax assets (DTA) and liabilities are reported in a net current and a net noncurrent amount. The classification of an individual deferred tax amount is based on the classification of the related asset or liability for financial reporting. The deferred tax liability of $15,000 related to a noncurrent asset is netted with the DTA of $3,000 related to a noncurrent liability for a noncurrent tax liability of $12,000. The DTA of $8,000 related to a current liability is a current tax asset. (5553)

39. (b) The classification of each deferred tax amount is based on the classification of the related asset or liability for financial reporting. The deferred tax liability arising from the installment sale is 1/3 current ($450,000 / 3 = $150,000) and 2/3 noncurrent because the related receivable is classified as 1/3 current and 2/3 noncurrent. The deferred tax asset arising from the accrual of warranty costs is 1/3 current ($630,000 / 3 = $210,000) and 2/3 noncurrent because the related warranty obligation is 1/3 current (one-third of the warranty liability comes due within one year of the balance sheet date). $150,000 + $(210,000) = $(60,000) current; $300,000 + $(420,000) = $(120,000) noncurrent.

Temporary difference	Future taxable (deductible) amount	Tax rate	Deferred tax liability (asset)	
Installment sale	$ 1,500,000	30%	$ 450,000	
Accrued costs	(2,100,000)	30%	(630,000)	(3319)

40. (c) Stockholders' equity is charged or credited for the income tax effects of foreign currency translation adjustments and expenditures reported as a reduction of the proceeds from issuing capital stock. Since answers a. and b. are correct, answer c., *both a. and b.*, is the best choice. (89667)

41. (a) Income tax expense or benefit for the year shall be allocated among continuing operations, discontinued operations, extraordinary items, and items charged or credited directly to shareholders' equity' such as prior period adjustments, certain changes in accounting principles, and changes in market values of investments in marketable equity securities classified as noncurrent assets. (3636)

42. (b) Except for certain areas such as business combinations and quasi-reorganizations, the manner of reporting the tax benefits of an operating loss carryforward or carryback is determined by the source of the income or loss in the current year and *not* by the source of the operating loss carryforward or taxes paid in a prior year. Thus, for example, the tax benefit of an operating loss carryforward reduces income tax expense from continuing operations if realization of the tax benefit results from income from continuing operations; likewise, that tax benefit is reported as an extraordinary item if realization of the tax benefit results from an extraordinary gain. (3631)

43. (c)

Income before income taxes and extraordinary item	$900,000
Less: Nontaxable gain on life insurance coverage	(100,000)
Income before taxes and taxable extraordinary item	$800,000
Times: Applicable tax rate	× 30%
Provision for income taxes	$240,000

(3321)

Business Combinations and Investments

44. (a) For business combinations, the acquirer should adjust the accounting for prior business combinations for previously recognized changes in acquired tax uncertainties or previously recognized changes in the valuation allowance for acquired deferred tax assets. (89668)

45. (d) The investor recognizes investment income for financial purposes based on its equity in the investee's earnings; for tax purposes, investment income is recognized on the cash basis when dividends are received. Deferred taxes are recorded on this temporary difference. In this question, we are told to ignore the 80% dividends-received deduction (DRD).

Equity in investee's earnings, book ($225,000 × 40%)	$ 90,000
Less: Dividends received ($75,000 × 40%)	(30,000)
Temporary difference (without DRD)	60,000
Times: Enacted tax rate for future	× 30%
Increase in deferred tax liability	$ 18,000

(3323)

46. (b)

Pretax financial income	$ 100,000
Less: Investment income (book) in excess of dividend income (tax) [$35,000 – ($25,000 × 20%)]	(30,000)
Add: Depreciation recorded in financial statements in excess of tax deduction	8,000
Taxable income	$ 78,000
Effective tax rate	× 30%
Current provision for income taxes	$ 23,400

(3312)

47. (a) The investor recognizes investment income for financial purposes based on its equity in the investee's earnings; for income tax purposes, investment income is recognized when cash dividends are received. Deferred income taxes are recorded on this temporary difference which will result in a future taxable amount.

Equity in investee's earnings, book	$ 180,000
Less: Dividends received	(30,000)
Temporary difference before DRD consideration	150,000
Less: Dividends-received deduction applicable to temporary difference ($150,000 × 80%)	(120,000)
Taxable portion of temporary difference	30,000
Times: Enacted tax rate for future periods	× 30%
Deferred tax liability	$ 9,000

(4076)

PERFORMANCE BY SUBTOPICS

Each category below parallels a subtopic covered in Chapter 14. Record the number and percentage of questions you correctly answered in each subtopic area.

Basic Concepts

Question #	Correct √
1	
2	
3	
4	
5	
6	
7	
8	
# Questions	8
# Correct	______
% Correct	______

Differences

Question #	Correct √
9	
10	
11	
12	
# Questions	4
# Correct	______
% Correct	______

Deferred Taxes

Question #	Correct √
13	
14	
15	
16	
17	
18	
19	
20	
21	
22	
23	
24	
25	
26	
# Questions	14
# Correct	______
% Correct	______

Other Considerations

Question #	Correct √
27	
28	
29	
30	
31	
32	
33	
34	
# Questions	8
# Correct	______
% Correct	______

Uncertain Tax Positions

Question #	Correct √
35	
36	
# Questions	2
# Correct	______
% Correct	______

Presentation and Disclosures

Question #	Correct √
37	
38	
39	
40	
41	
42	
43	
# Questions	7
# Correct	______
% Correct	______

Business Combinations and Investments

Question #	Correct √
44	
45	
46	
47	
# Questions	4
# Correct	______
% Correct	______

Solution 14-2 SIMULATION ANSWER: Tax Differences

Circumstance	Difference
1. Costs of guarantees and warranties are estimated.	A
2. Interest is received on an investment in tax-exempt municipal obligations.	C
3. A landlord collects some rents in advance. Rents received are taxable in the period in which they are received.	A
4. For plant assets, the depreciation expense deducted for tax purposes is in excess of the depreciation expense used for financial reporting purposes.	B

1. A Costs of guarantees and warranties that are estimated and accrued for financial reporting create a temporary difference that results in a deferred tax asset. Such items will result in deductible amounts in future years for tax purposes when the liability is settled. This is similar to a prepaid expense in that both situations result in assets.

2. C Interest received on an investment in tax-exempt securities is a permanent difference because tax-exempt income is recognized in the financial statements, but does not have tax consequences under the regular U.S. tax system. Therefore, this difference will not reverse in future tax periods.

3. A When revenue is received in advance, the temporary difference results in a deferred tax asset. For tax purposes, the revenue is taxable in the period the related cash is received. The revenue is not included in the computation of financial income until the period in which it is earned. In other words, a larger amount of taxes is due for the current period, and is similar to a prepaid expense.

4. B When an asset is depreciated faster for tax purposes than it is depreciated for financial accounting purposes, the temporary difference results in a deferred tax liability. In other words, the current amount due for taxes is less because of the larger depreciation deduction for tax purposes. Temporary differences of this type reverse themselves over time, and the entity has a deferred tax liability in the meantime.

5.

Taxable income	$700,000
Tax rate	× 25%
Current tax expense	$175,000

6.

Temporary differences, year 6	$100,000
Temporary differences, year 7	150,000
Cumulative temporary differences	$250,000

7.

Deferred tax liability, year 7	$ 75,000
Deferred tax liability, year 6	(25,000)
Deferred tax expense, year 7	$ 50,000

8.

Cumulative temporary differences	$450,000
Tax rate	× 35%
Deferred tax liability, April 30, year 8	$157,500

Solution 14-3 SIMULATION ANSWER: Tax Effects

Revenues:			
Machine sales	$ 950,000		[1]
Service revenues	350,000		[2]
Interest revenue	20,000		[3]
Total revenues		$ 1,320,000	[4]
Expenses:			
Cost of sales—machines	475,000		[5]
Cost of services	150,000		[6]
Administrative expenses	400,000		[7]
Research and development expenses	165,000		[8]
Interest expense	10,000		[9]
Loss from asset disposal	60,000		[10]
Current income tax expense	11,250		[11]
Deferred income tax expense	6,250		[12]
Total expenses and losses		(1,277,500)	[13]
Income before extraordinary gain		42,500	[14]
Extraordinary gain, net of income taxes of $50,000		150,000	[15]
Net income		**$ 192,500**	[16]
Earnings (loss) per share:			
Income before extraordinary gain		$ (0.43)	[17]
Net income		$ 0.17	[18]

Explanations:

[1] Machine sales given in scenario.

[2] Service revenues given in scenario.

[3] Interest revenue given in scenario.

[4] Total revenues: Sum of all sales and revenues ($950,000 + $350,000 + $20,000 = $1,320,000).

[5] Cost of sales given in scenario.

[6] Cost of services given in scenario.

[7] Administrative expense given in scenario.

[8] Research and development expense given in scenario.

[9] Interest expense given in scenario.

[10] Loss from asset disposal given in scenario.

[11] Current tax expense

($475,000 + $150,000 + $400,000 + $165,000 + $10,000 + 60,000 = $1,260,000 total non-tax expenses/ losses)

[($1,320,000 total revenues – $1,260,000 total non-tax expenses/losses + $10,000 life insurance premium permanent difference – $25,000 year 5 temporary difference) × .25 tax rate = $6,000]

[12] ($25,000 × .25 = $6,250)

[13] Total expenses and losses.

[14] Income before extraordinary gain.

[15] Extraordinary gain on sale of factory net of taxes

($800,000 – $600,000 = $200,000)

($200,000 × .25 = $50,000)

($200,000 – $50,000 = $150,000)

[16] Net income: Income before extraordinary gain plus extraordinary gain ($42,500 + $150,000).

[17] Income before extraordinary gain less stock dividend divided by number of shares outstanding ($42,500 – $150,000) / 250,000 = ($0.43).

[18] Net income less stock dividend divided by number of shares outstanding [($192,500 – $150,000) / 250,000 = $0.17].

Net income	$192,500	[19]
Add: Taxes on extraordinary gain	50,000	[20]
Provision for income taxes	17,500	[21]
Financial statement income before income taxes	260,000	[22]
Permanent difference—officer's life insurance	10,000	[23]
Temporary difference—excess of tax over financial statement depreciation	(25,000)	[24]
Taxable income	**$245,000**	[25]

[19] Net income calculated in part A

[20] ($200,000 × .25 = 50,000)

[21] Current income tax expense plus deferred income tax expense ($11,250 + $6,250)

[22] ($192,500 + $50,000 + $17,500 = $260,000)

[23] Permanent difference given in scenario (life insurance premium).

[24] Temporary difference given in scenario.

[25] Total taxable income.

Solution 14-4 SIMULATION ANSWER: Deferred Taxes

	A	B	C	D
	Description of temporary differences	**Temporary differences**	**Deferred tax assets**	**Deferred tax liabilities**
1	Allowance for doubtful accounts	21,000	6,930	
2	Accumulated depreciation, excess of tax over GAAP	767,000		253,110
3	Unrealized gain (loss) on trading securities	8,000		2,640
4				
5				
6	Totals		6,930	255,750

Explanations

Row 1: The Allowance for doubtful accounts (bad debts) is a temporary difference in that for financial reporting an allowance method is used to record bad debts expense for the year whereas for income tax purposes a direct write off method is used. The amount of the temporary difference is $21,000; the $11,000 starting balance less $5,000 actually written off plus the additional $15,000 charged. This results in a deferred tax asset of $6,930, $21,000 × 33% (the enacted tax rate), because this amount is expected to be written off for income tax purposes in future years.

Row 2: The Accumulated depreciation, excess of tax over GAAP is a temporary difference in that for financial reporting the straight-line depreciation rate is used and for income tax purposes accelerated methods are used. The amount of the temporary difference is $767,000 (the amount provided as the difference at December 31, year 2). This results in a deferred tax liability of $253,110, the $767,000 × 33% (the enacted tax rate), because more income will be taxable in future years.

Row 3: The Unrealized gain (loss) on trading securities is a temporary difference in that for financial reporting the unrealized gain (loss) is reported in current income and for income tax purposes it is not. The amount of the temporary difference is $8,000 (the amount provided at December 31, year 2). This results in a deferred tax liability of $2,640, $8,000 × 33% (the enacted tax rate), because more income will be taxable in future years.

Row 4, columns C and D: The total sum of deferred tax assets and deferred tax liabilities, respectively.

Assets:		
Deferred taxes, current asset	4,290	[1]
Deferred taxes, noncurrent asset	-	[2]
Liabilities:		
Deferred taxes, current liability	-	[3]
Deferred taxes, noncurrent liability	253,110	[4]

[1] The allowance for doubtful accounts and unrealized gain on trading securities are allowance-type accounts that will be reviewed annually and as such are considered current. They equal a net $4,290 asset.

[2] There are no noncurrent deferred tax assets.

[3] There are no current deferred taxes liabilities

[4] No information was given stating the depreciable asset's carrying amount will be recovered through use or sale within the next year so it is implied that it is noncurrent.

Solution 14-5 SIMULATION ANSWER: Research

FASB Accounting Standards Codification

FASB ASC:	740	-	10	-	35	-	4

35-4 Deferred tax liabilities and assets shall be adjusted for the effect of a change in tax laws or rates. A change in tax laws or rates may also require a reevaluation of a valuation allowance for deferred tax assets.

CHAPTER 15

STATEMENT OF CASH FLOWS

CHAPTER 15

STATEMENT OF CASH FLOWS

I. Overview

A. Purpose

A business enterprise that provides a set of financial statements that reports both financial position and results of operations should also provide a statement of cash flows for each period for which results of operations are provided. The primary purpose of a statement of cash flows is to provide relevant information about the cash receipts and cash payments of an enterprise during a period.

1. **Information Use** The information provided in a statement of cash flows helps investors, creditors, and others to assess the following:

   a. The enterprise's ability to generate positive future net cash flows

   b. The enterprise's ability to meet its obligations, its ability to pay dividends, and its needs for external financing

   c. The reasons for differences between net income and associated cash receipts and payments

   d. The effects on an enterprise's financial position of both its cash and noncash investing and financing transactions during the period

2. **Information to Report** To achieve its purpose of providing information to help investors, creditors, and others make these assessments, a statement of cash flows should report the cash effects during a period of an enterprise's operations, its investing transactions, and its financing transactions. Related disclosures should report the effects of investing and financing transactions that affect an enterprise's financial position, but do **not** directly affect cash flows during the period.

B. Focus

A statement of cash flows should explain the change during the period in cash and cash equivalents.

1. **Cash Equivalents** Cash equivalents are short-term, highly liquid investments that are both (a) readily convertible into known amounts of cash and (b) so near their maturity that they present insignificant risk of changes in value because of changes in interest rates. Generally, only investments with original maturities to the entity holding the investment of **three months or less** qualify under this definition. Examples include Treasury bills, commercial paper, and money market funds.

2. **Investments** Cash purchases and sales of investments considered to be cash equivalents generally are part of the enterprise's cash management activities rather than part of its operating, investing, and financing activities, and details of those transactions need **not** be reported in a statement of cash flows.

3. **Policy** An enterprise should establish a policy concerning which short-term, highly liquid investments that satisfy the cash equivalents definition are treated as cash equivalents. An enterprise's policy for determining which items are treated as cash equivalents should be disclosed.

C. Content & Form

1. **Classification of Cash Receipts & Payments** A statement of cash flows should classify cash receipts and cash payments as resulting from investing, financing, or operating activities. A statement of cash flows should report the following:

   a. Net cash provided or used by operating, investing, and financing activities

   b. The net effect of those flows on cash and cash equivalents during the period in a manner that reconciles beginning and ending cash and cash equivalents

2. **Cash Flows From Operating Activities**

   a. **Direct Method** Under this method, enterprises are encouraged to report major classes of gross cash receipts and gross cash payments and their arithmetic sum—the net cash flow from operating activities.

      (1) At a minimum, the following classes of operating cash receipts and payments should be separately reported.

         (a) Cash collected from customers

         (b) Interest and dividends received

         (c) Other operating cash receipts, if any

         (d) Cash paid to employees and other suppliers of goods or services, including suppliers of insurance, advertising, and the like

         (e) Interest paid

         (f) Income taxes paid

         (g) Other operating cash payments, if any

      (2) Enterprises are encouraged to provide further breakdowns of operating cash receipts and payments that they consider meaningful and feasible; for example, a retailer or manufacturer might decide to further divide cash paid to employees and suppliers into payments for costs of inventory and payments for selling, general, and administrative expenses. If the direct method of reporting net cash flow from operating activities is used, a reconciliation of net income to net cash flow from operating activities should be provided in a separate schedule.

   b. **Indirect Method** Net cash flow from operating activities may also be reported under the indirect method by adjusting net income to reconcile it to net cash flow from operating activities. That requires adjusting net income to remove the effects of the following.

      (1) All deferrals of past operating cash receipts and payments, such as changes during the period in inventory and deferred income

      (2) All accruals of expected operating cash receipts and payments, such as changes during the period in receivables and payables

      (3) Items whose cash effects are investing cash flows, such as depreciation and gains and losses on sales of property, plant, and equipment and discontinued operations

      (4) Items whose cash effects are financing cash flows, such as gains and losses on extinguishment of debt

c. **Reconcile Net Income** The reconciliation of net income to net cash flow from operating activities should separately report all major classes of reconciling items. The reconciliation may be either reported within the statement of cash flows or provided in a separate schedule, with the statement of cash flows reporting only the net cash flow from operating activities. In addition, if the indirect method is used, amounts of interest paid (net of amounts capitalized) and income taxes paid during the period should be provided in related disclosures.

3. **Cash Flows From Investing and Financing Activities** Both investing cash inflows and outflows and financing cash inflows and outflows should be reported **separately** in a statement of cash flows. For example, outlays for acquisitions of property, plant, and equipment should be reported separately from proceeds from sale of property, plant, and equipment; proceeds of borrowings should be reported separately from repayments of debt; and proceeds from issuing stock should be reported separately from outlays to reacquire the enterprise's stock.

4. **Noncash Investing & Financing Activities** Information about all investing and financing activities of an enterprise during a period that affects recognized assets or liabilities, but does not result in cash receipts or cash payments in the period, should be reported in related disclosures.

   a. Examples of noncash investing and financing transactions are: converting debt to equity; acquiring assets by assuming *directly related liabilities,* such as purchasing a building by incurring a mortgage to the seller; obtaining an asset by entering into a capital lease; and exchanging noncash assets or liabilities for other noncash assets or liabilities.

   b. If a transaction is part cash and part noncash, only the cash portion should be reported in a statement of cash flows.

5. **Per Share Information** Financial statements should not report an amount of cash flow per share.

D. **Preparation**
In simple situations, efficient preparation of the statement of cash flows may be accomplished by analysis of transactions and other events, the income statement, the statement of retained earnings, and comparative balance sheets. More complex problems may require a more systematic approach to the preparation of the statement, such as the T-account method or the worksheet method. However, these methods are merely aids in preparing the statement; no formal entries are made in the company's books. **NOTE:** Use of these methods is **not** required to solve CPA exam problems, but may be helpful.

1. **Cash and Cash Equivalents** Determine the change in cash and cash equivalents for the period.

2. **Operating Activities** Determine net cash flow from operating activities either by the direct method or the indirect method.

3. **Nonoperating Accounts** Analyze changes in the nonoperating accounts to determine the effect on cash. Investing and financing activities affecting cash are reported in the statement; significant noncash investing and financing activities are reported in related disclosures.

4. **Prior-Period Adjustments** Sometimes there is a need to consider how prior-period adjustments impact the current-period statement of cash flows. These types of adjustments need to be reflected in the financial statements as adjustments to the beginning balance of retained earnings. The offsetting debit or credit often has the result of changing specific asset or liability accounts. Information about all investing and financing activities during a period that affected recognized assets or liabilities, but did not result in cash receipts or cash payments during a particular period, must be reported in the disclosures to the financial statements. The difference between the current statement of financial position in an account and that same account in the restated beginning statement of financial position that resulted from a prior-period adjustment, even if not presented, should be disclosed in the notes to the financial statements and clearly referenced in the statement of cash flows.

5. **Presentation Guidelines**

   a. Information should be presented using the following format for the statement of cash flows:

      (1) Net cash flow from operating activities—direct method or indirect method

      (2) Net cash flow from investing activities

      (3) Net cash flow from financing activities

      (4) Net increase (decrease) in cash and cash equivalents

      (5) Cash and cash equivalents at beginning of year

      (6) Cash and cash equivalents at end of year

   b. Report significant noncash investing and financing activities in related disclosures. In addition, disclose the enterprise's policy for determining which items are treated as cash equivalents.

   c. If the direct method of reporting net cash flow from operating activities is used, provide a reconciliation of net income to net cash flow from operating activities in a separate schedule.

   d. If the indirect method is used, amounts of interest paid (net of amounts capitalized) and income taxes paid during the period should be provided in related disclosures.

II. Receipt & Payment Classification

A. Operating Activities

1. **Nature** Cash flows from operating activities are generally the cash effects of transactions and other events that enter into the determination of net income, including interest and taxes. Operating activities generally involve producing and delivering goods and providing services.

2. **Cash Inflows**

   a. Cash receipts from sales of goods or services, including receipts from collection or sale of accounts receivable and notes receivable from customers arising from those sales

   b. Cash receipts from returns on loans, other debt instruments of other entities, and equity securities, including: interest and distributions that constitute returns on equity investments (i.e., dividends).

c. Cash receipts from sales and maturities of trading securities, if applicable. Trading securities are classified based on the nature and purpose for which the securities were purchased.

d. All other cash receipts that do not stem from transactions defined as investing or financing activities; such as amounts received to settle lawsuits; proceeds of insurance settlements not related to investing or financing activities, and refunds from suppliers

3. **Cash Outflows**

a. Cash payments to acquire materials for manufacture or goods for resale, including principal payments on accounts and notes payable to suppliers for those materials or goods

b. Cash payments to other suppliers and employees for other goods or services

c. Cash payments to governments for taxes

d. Cash payments to lenders and other creditors for interest

e. Cash payments for purchases of trading securities, if applicable. Trading securities are classified based on the nature and purpose for which the securities were purchased.

f. All other cash payments that do not stem from transactions defined as investing or financing activities, such as payments to settle lawsuits, cash contributions to charities, and cash refunds to customers

B. **Investing Activities**

1. **Nature** Primarily includes sales and purchases on non-current assets

2. **Cash Inflows** Receipts from disposing of loans; debt or equity instruments; or property, plant, and equipment including directly related proceeds of insurance settlements, such as the proceeds of insurance on a building that is damaged or destroyed.

CASH FLOWS FROM INVESTING ACTIVITIES

H	HELD TO MATURITY
A	AVAILABLE FOR SALE
P	PROPERTY
P	PLANT
E	EQUIPMENT
E	EQUITY INVESTMENTS

a. Receipts from collections or sales of loans made by the enterprise and of other entities' debt instruments (other than cash equivalents and certain debt instruments that are acquired specifically for resale) that were purchased by the enterprise.

b. Receipts from sales of equity instruments of other enterprises (other than certain equity instruments that are acquired specifically for resale) and from returns of investments in those instruments. These include held as available-for-sale securities. Trading securities are classified based on the nature and purpose for which the securities were acquired (normally operating).

c. Receipts from sales of property, plant, and equipment, and other productive assets.

d. Collections from advances/loans to related parties.

3. **Cash Outflows**

a. Disbursements for loans made by the enterprise.

b. Payments to acquire debt instruments of other entities (other than cash equivalents and certain debt instruments that are acquired specifically for resale).

c. Payments to acquire equity instruments of other entities (other than certain equity instruments carried in a trading account). These would include available-for-sale or held-to-maturity securities. Trading securities are classified based on the nature and purpose for which the securities were acquired (normally operating).

d. Advances/loans made to related parties.

e. Payments at the time of purchase, or soon before or after purchase, to acquire property, plant, and equipment, and other productive assets.

(1) Generally, only advance payments, the down payment, or other amounts paid at the time of purchase or soon before or after purchase of property, plant, and equipment and other productive assets are *investing cash outflows.*

(2) Generally, principal payments on seller-financed debt directly related to a purchase of property, plant, and equipment or other productive assets are *financing cash outflows.*

C. Financing Activities

CASH FLOWS FROM FINANCING ACTIVITIES	
PRINC	DEBT PRINCIPAL
DIV	PAY DIVIDENDS
I	ISSUE STOCK
TS	TREASURY STOCK

1. **Nature** Includes transactions whereby cash is obtained from or returned to owners and creditors. The net change in overdrafts for the period is also a financing activity.

2. **Derivatives** Cash flows from derivatives that contain a financing component and are accounted for as fair-value or cash-flow hedges are required to be classified in the same cash flow category as the items being hedged. When a hedge of an identifiable transaction or event is discontinued, the subsequent cash flows are to be classified consistent with the nature of the instrument.

3. **Cash Inflows**

a. Proceeds from issuing equity instruments (e.g., common and preferred stock).

b. Proceeds from issuing bonds, mortgages, notes, and from other short- or long-term borrowing.

c. Advances/loans from related parties.

4. **Cash Outflows**

a. Payments of dividends or other distributions to owners, including outlays to reacquire the enterprise's equity instruments (e.g., treasury stock).

b. Repayments of amounts borrowed.

c. Other principal payments to creditors who have extended long-term credit.

d. Repayments of advances/loans to related parties.

III. Illustrative Problem

A. Given Information for the Current Year

1. On January 8, the company sold marketable equity securities for cash. These securities had a cost of $9,200.
2. On July 17, three acres of land were sold for cash of $32,000.
3. On September 3, the company purchased equipment for cash.
4. On November 10, bonds payable were issued by the company at par for cash.
5. On December 15, the company declared and paid an $8,000 dividend to common stockholders.
6. General and administrative expenses include $3,000 of bad debt expense.
7. No dividends were received during the year from the 30% owned investee.
8. The company's preferred stock is convertible into common stock at a rate of one share of preferred for two shares of common. The preferred stock and common stock have par values of $2 and $1, respectively.
9. For purposes of the statement of cash flows, the company considers all highly liquid debt instruments purchased with a maturity of three months or less to be cash equivalents.

Required: Prepare a statement of cash flows for the Wolverine Company.

Exhibit 1 ▸ Income Statement

Wolverine Company
Income Statement Data
For the Year Ended December 31, Current Year

Sales		$ 242,807
Gain on sale of available-for-sale securities		2,400
Equity in earnings of 30% owned company		5,880
Gain on sale of land		10,700
		261,787
Cost of sales	$138,407	
General and administrative expenses	25,010	
Depreciation	1,250	
Interest expense	1,150	
Income taxes	34,952	(200,769)
Net income		$ 61,018

Exhibit 2 ▸ Comparative Balance Sheet

Wolverine Company
Comparative Balance Sheet
December 31, Current Year

	Current Year	Previous Year	Change
Assets			
Cash	$ 46,400	$ 25,300	$ 21,100
Available-for-sale securities	7,300	16,500	(9,200)
Accounts receivable	50,320	25,320	25,000
Allowance for uncollectible accounts	(1,000)	(1,000)	—
Inventory	48,590	31,090	17,500
Investment in 30% owned company	67,100	61,220	5,880
Land	18,700	40,000	(21,300)
Building	79,100	79,100	—
Equipment	81,500	—	81,500
Less accumulated depreciation	(16,250)	(15,000)	(1,250)
Total Assets	$381,760	$262,530	$119,230
Liabilities			
Accounts payable	$ 17,330	$ 21,220	$ (3,890)
Income taxes payable	4,616	—	4,616
Bonds payable	115,000	50,000	65,000
Less unamortized discount	(2,150)	(2,300)	150
Deferred tax liability	846	510	336
Stockholders' Equity			
Preferred stock	—	30,000	(30,000)
Common stock	110,000	80,000	30,000
Retained earnings	136,118	83,100	53,018
Total Liabilities and Stockholders' Equity	$381,760	$262,530	$119,230

B. **Change in Cash & Cash Equivalents**
The increase in cash and cash equivalents is $21,100. The marketable equity securities are not considered to be cash equivalents. Cash equivalents are short-term, highly liquid investments, such as Treasury bills, commercial paper, and money market funds.

C. **Net Cash Flow From Operating Activities**
This amount is determined by using either the direct method or the indirect method.

1. **Direct Method** Under this method, enterprises report major classes of gross cash receipts and gross cash payments and their arithmetic sum—the net cash flow from operating activities. When the direct method is used, a reconciliation of net income to net cash flow from operating activities should be provided in a separate schedule. Presented below are the Wolverine Company's cash flows from operating activities for the current year ended December 31 using the direct method.

Example 1 ▸ Direct Method of Determining Net Cash From Operating Activities

Wolverine Company
Cash Flows From Operating Activities
For the Year Ended December 31, Current Year
Increase (Decrease) in Cash and Cash Equivalents

Cash flows from operating activities:	
Cash received from customers [1]	$ 214,807
Cash paid for inventory [2]	(159,797)
Cash paid for general and administrative expenses [3]	(22,010)
Interest paid [4]	(1,000)
Income taxes paid [5]	(30,000)
Net cash provided by operating activities	$ 2,000

[1] Cash received from customers is determined by subtracting the increase in accounts receivable (A/R) from sales; the increase in A/R represents sales that were not collected in cash. Under the direct method, the allowance for uncollectible accounts is used to determine cash collected from customers if write-offs occur during the period.

Sales	$ 242,807
Beginning balance of A/R	25,320
Write-offs	(3,000)
Ending balance of A/R	(50,320)
Cash from customers	$ 214,807

[2] The increase in inventory is added to cost of sales to determine inventory purchases. The decrease in accounts payable is added to inventory purchases to determine cash payments for inventory.

Cost of sales	$ 138,407
Add: Increase in inventory	17,500
Inventory purchases	155,907
Add: Decrease in accounts payable	3,890
Cash paid for inventory	$ 159,797

[3]

General & administrative expense	$ 25,010
Bad debt expense	(3,000)
Cash paid for G&A exp.	$ 22,010

[4] The bond discount amortization increased interest expense, but did not involve an outflow of cash; therefore, it is subtracted from interest expense to determine cash payments for interest.

Interest expense	$ 1,150
Less: Bond discount amortization	(150)
Interest paid	$ 1,000

[5] The increase in income taxes payable increased current income tax expense and the increase in the deferred tax liability caused the recognition of deferred income tax expense, but they did not involve an outflow of cash. Therefore, these increases are subtracted from income tax expense to determine cash used to pay income taxes.

Income tax expense	$ 34,952
Less: Increase in income taxes payable	(4,616)
Increase in deferred tax liability	(336)
Income taxes paid	$ 30,000

2. **Indirect Method** Net cash flow from operating activities is reported under this method by converting net income to net cash flow from operating activities. Presented below are the Wolverine Company's cash flows from operating activities for the current year ended December 31 using the indirect method.

Example 2 ▸ Indirect Method of Determining Net Cash From Operating Activities

Wolverine Company
Cash Flows From Operating Activities
For the Year Ended December 31, Current Year
Increase (Decrease) in Cash and Cash Equivalents

Net income		$ 61,018
Adjustments to reconcile net income to net cash provided by operating activities:		
Depreciation [1]	$ 1,250	
Bond discount amortization [1]	150	
Deferred income taxes [1]	336	
Gain on sale of available-for-sale securities [2]	(2,400)	
Gain on sale of land [2]	(10,700)	
Equity in earnings of equity method investee in excess of cash dividends [2]	(5,880)	
Increase in net accounts receivable [3]	(25,000)	
Increase in inventory [4]	(17,500)	
Decrease in accounts payable [5]	(3,890)	
Increase in income taxes payable [6]	4,616	
Total adjustments		(59,018)
Net cash provided by operating activities [7]		$ 2,000

[1] To convert net income to net cash flow from operating activities, noncash charges to income for depreciation, bond discount amortization, and deferred income taxes are added back to net income because those items did not involve a cash outflow.

[2] The noncash credits to income for the gain on sale of AFS securities, the gain on sale of land, and the equity in earnings of equity method investee in excess of cash dividends received must be deducted from net income for this conversion because those items did not produce an inflow of cash. The *Available-for-Sale Securities* account is not an operating asset; therefore, the net change in the account is not used to convert net income to net cash flow from operating activities.

[3] The $25,000 [i.e., ($50,320 – $1,000) – ($25,320 – $1,000)] increase in **net** accounts receivable represents sales that were not collected in cash. This amount must be deducted to convert net income to net cash flow from operating activities. Under the indirect method, the allowance for uncollectible accounts is used to determine the change in **net** accounts receivable during the period.

[4] The increase in inventories is an operating use of cash; the incremental investment in inventories reduced cash without increasing cost of sales. This amount must be deducted to convert net income to net cash flow from operating activities.

[5] The decrease in accounts payable is due to cash payments for inventory exceeding the amount of inventory purchases. This amount must be deducted to convert net income to net cash flow from operating activities.

[6] The increase in income taxes payable represents current income tax expense not paid out in cash. This amount must be added to convert net income to net cash flow from operating activities.

[7] When the indirect method is used, amounts of interest paid (net of amounts capitalized) and income taxes paid during the period are provided in related disclosures.

D. Analysis of Nonoperating Accounts

1. **Marketable Equity Securities** The proceeds from the sale resulted in an $11,600 cash inflow due to an investing activity. The $2,400 gain on the sale is a noncash credit to income; therefore, it does not involve an inflow of cash. The gain on the sale is not used to determine net cash flow from operating activities under the direct method. If the indirect method is used, the gain is deducted from net income to determine net cash flow from operating activities.

Exhibit 3 ▸ Sale of Securities

Cash (to balance)	11,600	
Available-for-Sale Securities (cost from additional information)		9,200
Gain on Sale (from income statement)		2,400

2. **Equity Method Investment** The increase in the account of $5,880 represents Wolverine's equity in the investee's earnings for the year since no cash dividends were received from the investee during the year. This noncash credit to income is not used to determine net cash flow from operating activities under the direct method. If the indirect method is used, this amount is deducted from net income to determine net cash flow from operating activities.

3. **Land** The decrease in the account is due to the sale of land. The proceeds from the sale resulted in a $32,000 cash inflow due to an investing activity. The $10,700 gain on the sale is a noncash credit to income; therefore, it does not represent an inflow of cash. The gain on the sale is not used to determine net cash flow from operating activities under the direct method. If the indirect method is used, the gain is deducted from net income to determine net cash flow from operating activities.

4. **Equipment** The $81,500 ($81,500 – $0) purchase of equipment for cash is a cash outflow due to an investing activity.

5. **Accumulated Depreciation** There were no disposals of plant assets during the year; the $1,250 increase in the account is due to additional depreciation expense. Depreciation does not involve a cash outflow. Depreciation is not used to determine net cash flow from operating activities if the direct method is used. If the indirect method is used, depreciation is added to net income to determine net cash flow from operating activities.

6. **Bonds Payable** The $65,000 ($115,000 – $50,000) proceeds from the issuance of bonds payable is a cash inflow due to a financing activity.

7. **Unamortized Bond Discount** The bond discount amortization does not involve an outflow of cash. The bond discount amortization is not used to determine net cash flow from operating activities if the direct method is used. If the indirect method is used, the bond discount amortization is added to net income to determine net cash flow from operating activities.

Exhibit 4 ▸ Interest Expense

Interest Expense (from income statement)	1,150	
Bond Discount ($2,300 – $2,150)		150
Cash (to balance)		1,000

8. **Deferred Tax Liability** The $336 increase in the deferred tax liability resulted in recognition of $336 of deferred income tax expense. The deferred income tax expense do not involve an outflow of cash. The deferred income taxes not used to determine net cash flow from operating activities if the direct method is used. If the indirect method is used, the deferred income taxes are added to net income to determine net cash flow from operating activities.

9. **Preferred and Common Stock** The conversion of $30,000 of preferred stock into common stock is a noncash financing transaction; therefore, it is reported in related disclosures to the statement.

10. **Retained Earnings** The $8,000 cash dividends paid during the year is a cash outflow due to a financing activity. If the dividends had been declared during the year, but not paid in the year, they would **not** have been reported in the statement of cash flows because their declaration would not have affected cash. Neither the declaration or issuance of a stock dividend nor the appropriation of retained earnings affects the enterprise's assets or liabilities; therefore, these transactions are not investing or financing transactions and need **not** be reported in related disclosures to the statement.

Exhibit 5 ▸ Explanation of Retained Earnings Increase

Retained earnings 1/1	$ 83,100
Add: Net income for the year	61,018
Less: Cash dividends declared in the year	(8,000)
Retained earnings, 12/31	$136,118

E. Direct Method

Presented below is the Wolverine Company's statement of cash flows for the current year ended December 31, using the direct method of reporting cash flows from operating activities. Note that the reconciliation of net income to net cash provided by operating activities on the direct-method statement is identical to the data reported in the statement under the heading "Cash Flow from Operating Activities" under the indirect method. (Compare the shaded areas.)

Exhibit 6 ▸ Direct Method Statement of Cash Flows

Wolverine Company
Statement of Cash Flows
For the Year Ended December 31, Current Year
Increase (Decrease) in Cash

Cash flows from operating activities:		
Cash received from customers	$ 214,807	
Cash paid for inventory	(159,797)	
Cash paid for general and administrative expenses	(22,010)	
Interest paid	(1,000)	
Income taxes paid	(30,000)	
Net cash provided by operating activities		$ 2,000
Cash flows from investing activities:		
Proceeds from sale of land	32,000	
Proceeds from sale of available-for-sale securities	11,600	
Purchase of equipment for cash	(81,500)	
Net cash used in investing activities		(37,900)
Cash flows from financing activities:		
Dividends paid	(8,000)	
Proceeds from issuance of bonds payable	65,000	
Net cash provided by financing activities		57,000
Net increase in cash		21,100
Cash at beginning of year		25,300
Cash at end of year		$ 46,400

Reconciliation of net income to net cash provided by operating activities:

Net income		$ 61,018
Adjustments to reconcile net income to net cash provided by operating activities:		
Depreciation	$ 1,250	
Bond discount amortization	150	
Deferred income taxes	336	
Gain on sale of available-for-sale securities	(2,400)	
Gain on sale of land	(10,700)	
Equity in earnings of equity method investee in excess of cash dividends	(5,880)	
Increase in net accounts receivable	(25,000)	
Increase in inventory	(17,500)	
Decrease in accounts payable	(3,890)	
Increase in income taxes payable	4,616	
Total adjustments		(59,018)
Net cash provided by operating activities		$ 2,000

Supplemental schedule of noncash investing and financing activities:

Additional common stock was issued upon the conversion of $30,000 of preferred stock.

Disclosure of Accounting Policy—For purposes of the statement of cash flows, the Company considers all highly liquid debt instruments purchased with a maturity of three months or less to be cash equivalents.

F. Indirect Method

Presented below is the Wolverine Company's statement of cash flows for the current year ended December 31, using the indirect method of reporting cash flows from operating activities.

Exhibit 7 ▸ Indirect Method Statement of Cash Flows

Wolverine Company
Statement of Cash Flows
For the Year Ended December 31, Current Year
Increase (Decrease) in Cash

Cash flows from operating activities:		
Net income		$ 61,018
Adjustments to reconcile net income to net cash provided by operating activities:		
Depreciation	$ 1,250	
Bond discount amortization	150	
Deferred income taxes	336	
Gain on sale of available-for-sale securities	(2,400)	
Gain on sale of land	(10,700)	
Equity in earnings of equity method investee in excess of cash dividends	(5,880)	
Increase in net accounts receivable	(25,000)	
Increase in inventory	(17,500)	
Decrease in accounts payable	(3,890)	
Increase in income taxes payable	4,616	
Total adjustments		(59,018)
Net cash provided by operating activities		$ 2,000

Cash flows from investing activities:		
Proceeds from sale of land	$ 32,000	
Proceeds from sale of available-for-sale securities	11,600	
Purchase of equipment for cash	(81,500)	
Net cash used in investing activities		(37,900)
Cash flows from financing activities:		
Dividend paid	(8,000)	
Proceeds from issuance of bonds payable	65,000	
Net cash provided by financing activities		57,000
Net increase in cash		21,100
Cash at beginning of year		25,300
Cash at end of year		$ 46,400

Supplemental disclosures of cash flow information:

Cash paid during the year for:	
Interest (net of amount capitalized)	$ 1,000
Income taxes	$ 30,000

Supplemental schedule of noncash investing and financing activities:

Additional common stock was issued upon the conversion of $30,000 of preferred stock.

Disclosure of Accounting Policy: For purposes of the statement of cash flows, the company considers all highly liquid debt instruments purchased with a maturity of three months or less to be cash equivalents.

Select Hot•Spot™ Video Descriptions

CPA 2035 Accounting for Income Taxes
Robert Monette demonstrates accounting for income taxes using examples and 17 multiple choice questions. He explains how temporary and permanent differences between financial and taxable income arise. Bob shows how current tax expense, deferred tax assets, deferred tax liabilities, deferred tax expense, deferred tax benefit, the valuation allowance account, and future tax rates are used to prepare journal entries. He also discusses income tax issues pertaining to financial statement presentation and equity method investments. Approximate time is 1 hour and 55 minutes.

CPA 2033 Statement of Cash Flows
Get in-depth coverage for both the direct and indirect methods of preparing the Statement of Cash Flows. Remove the mystery from the operating, investing, and financing sections of this statement and learn easy ways of remembering just what goes in each. In addition, learn when, where, and how to include noncash transactions. Robert Monette explains the answers to 15 multiple choice questions and 2 simulations while demonstrating how to approach questions on cash flows. Approximate time is 2 hours.

CHAPTER 15—STATEMENT OF CASH FLOWS

Problem 15-1 MULTIPLE-CHOICE QUESTIONS

1. The primary purpose of a statement of cash flows is to provide relevant information about
   a. Differences between net income and associated cash receipts and disbursements
   b. An enterprise's ability to generate future positive net cash flows
   c. The cash receipts and cash disbursements of an enterprise during a period
   d. An enterprise's ability to meet cash operating needs (5/94, FAR, #5, 4820)

2. Which is the most appropriate financial statement to use to determine if a company obtained financing during a year by issuing debt or equity securities?
   a. Balance sheet
   b. Statement of cash flows
   c. Statement of changes in stockholders' equity
   d. Income statement (R/03, FAR, #18, 7620)

3. Mend Co. purchased a three-month U.S. Treasury bill. Mend's policy is to treat as cash equivalents all highly liquid investments with an original maturity of three months or less when purchased. How should this purchase be reported in Mend's statement of cash flows?
   a. As an outflow from operating activities
   b. As an outflow from investing activities
   c. As an outflow from financing activities
   d. Not reported (11/95, FAR, #47, 6129)

4. Inch Co. had the following balances at December 31, year 2:

Cash in checking account	$ 35,000
Cash in money market account	75,000
U.S. Treasury bill, purchased 12/1, year 2 maturing 2/28, year 3	200,000
U.S. Treasury bill, purchased 12/1, year 1 maturing 5/31, year 3	150,000

   Inch's policy is to treat as cash equivalents all highly-liquid investments with a maturity of three months or less when purchased. What amount should Inch report as cash and cash equivalents in its December 31, year 2 balance sheet?
   a. $110,000
   b. $235,000
   c. $310,000
   d. $460,000 (R/00, FAR, #1, amended, 6896)

5. The following information was taken from the current year financial statements of Planet Corp.:

Accounts receivable, January 1	$ 21,600
Accounts receivable, December 31	30,400
Sales on account and cash sales	438,000
Uncollectible accounts	1,000

   No accounts receivable were written off or recovered during the year. If the direct method is used in the current year statement of cash flows, Planet should report cash collected from customers as
   a. $447,800
   b. $446,800
   c. $429,200
   d. $428,200 (5/91, PI, #8, amended, 1234)

6. A company's accounts receivable decreased from the beginning to the end of the year. In the company's statement of cash flows (direct method), the cash collected from customers would be

   a. Sales revenues plus accounts receivable at the beginning of the year
   b. Sales revenues plus the decrease in accounts receivable from the beginning to the end of the year
   c. Sales revenues less the decrease in accounts receivable from the beginning to the end of the year
   d. The same as sales revenues (11/88, Theory, #34, 9044)

7. In a statement of cash flows, which of the following would increase reported cash flows from operating activities using the direct method? (Ignore income tax considerations.)

   a. Dividends received from investments
   b. Gain on sale of equipment
   c. Gain on early retirement of bonds
   d. Change from straight-line to accelerated depreciation (5/92, Theory, #7, 2699)

8. Duke Co. reported cost of goods sold as $270,000 for the current year. Additional information is as follows:

	December 31	January 1
Inventory	$60,000	$45,000
Accounts payable	26,000	39,000

   If Duke uses the direct method, what amount should Duke report as cash paid to suppliers in its current year statement of cash flows?

   a. $242,000
   b. $268,000
   c. $272,000
   d. $298,000 (11/93, PI, #9, amended, 4378)

9. Rory's Co.'s prepaid insurance was $50,000 at December 31, year 2, and $25,000 at December 31, year 1. Insurance expense was $20,000 for year 2 and $15,000 for year 1. What amount of cash disbursements for insurance would be reported in Rory's year 2 net cash flows from operating activities presented on a direct basis?

   a. $55,000
   b. $45,000
   c. $30,000
   d. $20,000 (11/90, PII, #17, amended, 1238)

10. Which of the following is **not** disclosed on the statement of cash flows when prepared under the direct method, either on the face of the statement or in a separate schedule?

    a. The major classes of gross cash receipts and gross cash payments
    b. The amount of income taxes paid
    c. A reconciliation of net income to net cash flow from operations
    d. A reconciliation of ending retained earnings to net cash flow from operations (11/95, FAR, #48, 6130)

11. Would the following be added back to net income when reporting operating activities' cash flows by the indirect method?

	Excess of treasury stock acquisition cost over sales proceeds (cost method)	Bond discount amortization
a.	Yes	Yes
b.	No	No
c.	No	Yes
d.	Yes	No

    (11/91, Theory, #21, 2529)

12. Reed Co.'s current year statement of cash flows reported cash provided from operating activities of $400,000. For the year, depreciation of equipment was $190,000, impairment of goodwill was $5,000, and dividends paid on common stock were $100,000. In Reed's current year statement of cash flows, what amount was reported as net income?

    a. $105,000
    b. $205,000
    c. $305,000
    d. $595,000 (R/05, FAR, #1, amended, 7745)

13. New England Co. had net cash provided by operating activities of $351,000; net cash used by investing activities of $420,000; and cash provided by financing activities of $250,000. New England's cash balance was $27,000 on January 1. During the year, there was a sale of land that resulted in a gain of $25,000 and proceeds of $40,000 were received from the sale. What was New England's cash balance at the end of the year?

    a. $ 27,000
    b. $ 40,000
    c. $208,000
    d. $248,000 (R/06, FAR, #42, 8109)

14. When an entity prepares a statement of cash flows, it should do which of the following?

    a. Report significant noncash investing and financing activities in the body of the statement of cash flows
    b. Provide a reconciliation of net income to net cash flow from operating activities in a separate schedule, if the direct method of reporting net cash flow from operating activities is used
    c. Disclose amounts of interest paid (net of amounts capitalized) and income taxes paid during the period, if the direct method is used
    d. None of the above (Editor, 89589)

15. In the statement of cash flows, advances from related parties would be reflected in which of the following sections?

    a. Operating
    b. Investing
    c. Financing
    d. Either a. or b., depending upon the amount (Editor, 9017)

16. Which of the following information should be disclosed as supplemental information in the statement of cash flows?

	Cash flow per share	Conversion of debt to equity
a.	Yes	Yes
b.	Yes	No
c.	No	Yes
d.	No	No

(5/95, FAR, #49, 5585)

17. Deed Co. owns 2% of Beck Cosmetic Retailers. A property dividend by Beck consisted of merchandise with a fair value lower than the listed retail price. Deed in turn gave the merchandise to its employees as a holiday bonus. How should Deed report the receipt and distribution of the merchandise in its statement of cash flows?

    a. As both an inflow and outflow for operating activities
    b. As both an inflow and outflow for investing activities
    c. As an inflow for investing activities and outflow for operating activities
    d. As a noncash activity (11/92, Theory, #21, 3454)

18. During the current year, Ace Co. amortized a bond discount. Ace prepares its statement of cash flows using the indirect method. In which section of the statement should Ace report the amortization of the bond discount?

    a. Supplemental disclosures
    b. Operating activities
    c. Investing activities
    d. Financing activities (R/07, FAR, #48, 8369)

19. Lino Co.'s worksheet for the preparation of its statement of cash flows included the following:

	December 31	January 1
Accounts receivable	$29,000	$23,000
Allowance for uncollectible accounts	1,000	800
Prepaid rent expense	8,200	12,400
Accounts payable	22,400	19,400

    Lino's net income is $150,000. What amount should Lino include as net cash provided by operating activities in the statement of cash flows?

    a. $151,400
    b. $151,000
    c. $148,600
    d. $145,400 (11/93, PI, #5, amended, 4374)

20. Karr Inc. reported net income of $300,000 for the year. During the year, Karr sold equipment costing $25,000, with accumulated depreciation of $12,000, for a gain of $5,000. In December, Karr purchased equipment costing $50,000 with $20,000 cash and a 12% note payable of $30,000. Depreciation expense for the year was $52,000. Changes occurred in several balance sheet accounts as follows:

Equipment	$25,000 increase
Accumulated depreciation	40,000 increase
Note payable	30,000 increase

    In Karr's statement of cash flows, net cash provided by operating activities should be

    a. $340,000
    b. $347,000
    c. $352,000
    d. $357,000 (11/93, PI, #6, amended, 4375)

21. Paper Co. had net income of $70,000 during the year. Dividend payment was $10,000. The following information is available:

Mortgage repayment	$20,000
Available-for-sale securities purchased	10,000 increase
Bonds payable—issued	50,000 increase
Inventory	40,000 increase
Accounts payable	30,000 decrease

    What amount should Paper report as net cash provided by operating activities in its statement of cash flows for the year?

    a. $0
    b. $10,000
    c. $20,000
    d. $30,000 (R/07, FAR, #8, 8329)

22. Baker Co. began its operations during the current year. The following is Baker's balance sheet at December 31:

Assets	
Cash	$192,000
Accounts receivable	82,000
Total assets	$274,000
Liabilities and stockholders' equity	
Accounts payable	$ 24,000
Common stock	200,000
Retained earnings	50,000
Total liabilities and stockholders' equity	$274,000

Baker's net income for the current year was $78,000 and dividends of $28,000 were declared and paid. Common stock was issued for $200,000. What amount should Baker report as cash provided by operating activities in its statement of cash flows for the current year?

a. $ 20,000
b. $ 50,000
c. $192,000
d. $250,000 (R/09, FAR, #48, 8798)

23. A company acquired a building, paying a portion of the purchase price in cash and issuing a mortgage note payable to the seller for the balance. In a statement of cash flows, what amount is included in investing activities for the transaction?

a. Cash payment
b. Acquisition price
c. Zero
d. Mortgage amount (5/90, Theory, #27, 9042)

24. In preparing its cash flow statement for the current year ended December 31, Reve Co. collected the following data:

Gain on sale of equipment	$ (6,000)
Proceeds from sale of equipment	10,000
Purchase of A.S. Inc. bonds (par value $200,000)	(180,000)
Amortization of bond discount	2,000
Dividends declared	(45,000)
Dividends paid	(38,000)
Proceeds from sale of treasury stock (carrying amount $65,000)	75,000

In its current year December 31 statement of cash flows, what amount should Reve report as net cash used in investing activities?

a. $170,000
b. $176,000
c. $188,000
d. $194,000 (5/95, FAR, #47, amended, 5583)

25. Which of the following would be reported as an investing activity in a company's statement of cash flows?

a. Collection of proceeds from a note payable
b. Collection of a note receivable from a related party
c. Collection of an overdue account receivable from a customer
d. Collection of a tax refund from the government (R/10, FAR, #3, 9303)

26. For the year ended December 31, Ion Corp. had cash inflows of $25,000 from the purchases, sales, and maturities of held-to-maturity securities and $40,000 from the purchases, sales, and maturities of available-for-sale securities. What amount of net cash from investing activities should Ion report in its cash flow statement?

    a. $0
    b. $25,000
    c. $40,000
    d. $65,000 (R/09, FAR, #1, 8751)

27. Green Co. had the following equity transactions at December 31:

Cash proceeds from sale of investment in Blue Co. (carrying value – $60,000)	$75,000
Dividends received on Grey Co. stock	10,500
Common stock purchased from Brown Co.	38,000

    What amount should Green recognize as net cash from investing activities in its statement of cash flows at December 31?

    a. $37,000
    b. $47,500
    c. $75,000
    d. $85,500 (R/09, FAR, #27, 8777)

28. In a statement of cash flows, proceeds from issuing equity instruments should be classified as cash inflows from

    a. Lending activities
    b. Operating activities
    c. Investing activities
    d. Financing activities (11/89, Theory, #29, 1913)

29. A company acquired a building, paying a portion of the purchase price in cash and issuing a mortgage note payable to the seller for the balance. In a statement of cash flows, what amount is included in financing activities for the transaction?

    a. Cash payment
    b. Acquisition price
    c. Zero
    d. Mortgage amount (5/90, Theory, #28, 9043)

30. In a statement of cash flows, which of the following items is reported as a cash outflow from financing activities?

    I. Payments to retire mortgage notes
    II. Interest payments on mortgage notes
    III. Dividend payments

    a. I, II, and III
    b. II and III
    c. I only
    d. I and III (5/91, Theory, #31, 1902)

31. In preparing its cash flow statement for the current year ended December 31, Reve Co. collected the following data:

Gain on sale of equipment	$ (6,000)
Proceeds from sale of equipment	10,000
Purchase of A.S. Inc. bonds (par value $200,000)	(180,000)
Amortization of bond discount	2,000
Dividends declared	(45,000)
Dividends paid	(38,000)
Proceeds from sale of treasury stock (carrying amount $65,000)	75,000

In its current year December 31 statement of cash flows, what amount should Reve report as net cash provided by financing activities?

a. $20,000
b. $27,000
c. $30,000
d. $37,000 (5/95, FAR, #48, amended, 5584)

32. During the current year, Xan Inc. had the following activities related to its financial operations:

Payment for the early retirement of long- term bonds payable (carrying amount $370,000)	$375,000
Distribution of cash dividend declared in previous year to preferred shareholders	31,000
Carrying amount of convertible preferred stock in Xan, converted into common shares	60,000
Proceeds from sale of treasury stock (carrying amount at cost, $43,000)	50,000

In Xan's current year statement of cash flows, net cash used in financing operations should be

a. $265,000
b. $296,000
c. $356,000
d. $358,000 (11/93, PI, #8, amended, 4377)

Problem 15-2 SIMULATION: Cash Flows Statements—Direct

Presented below are the condensed statement of income for the year ended December 31, year 8, and the condensed statements of financial position of Garfield Consulting Associates as of December 31, year 8 and year 7.

Fee revenue	$ 2,701,000
Operating expenses	(1,950,000)
Operating income	751,000
Equity in earnings of Zap, Inc. (net of $5,000 amortization of excess of cost over book value)	229,000
Net income	$ 980,000

Assets	**Year 8**	**Year 7**	**Net change increase (decrease)**
Cash	$ 871,000	$ 398,000	$473,000
Accounts receivable, net	464,000	382,000	82,000
Investment in Zap Inc., at equity	555,000	465,000	90,000
Property and equipment	1,240,000	1,055,000	185,000
Accumulated depreciation	(195,000)	(125,000)	(70,000)
Excess of cost over book value of investment in Zap Inc. (net)	160,000	165,000	(5,000)
Total assets	$3,095,000	$2,340,000	$755,000
Liabilities and Partners' Equity			
Accounts payable and accrued expenses	$ 330,000	$ 275,000	$ 55,000
Mortgage payable	235,000	265,000	(30,000)
Partners' equity	2,530,000	1,800,000	730,000
Total liabilities and partners' equity	$3,095,000	$2,340,000	$755,000

Additional information:

- On December 31, year 7, partners' capital and profit sharing percentages were as follows:

	Capital	Profit sharing %
Melody	$ 990,000	55%
Stacey	810,000	45%
	$1,800,000	

- On January 1, year 8, Melody and Stacey admitted Mario to the partnership for a cash payment of $450,000 to Garfield Consulting Associates as the agreed amount of Mario's beginning capital account. In addition, Mario paid a $80,000 cash bonus directly to Melody and Stacey. This amount was divided $50,000 to Melody and $30,000 to Stacey. The new profit sharing arrangement is as follows:

Melody	40%
Stacey	35%
Mario	25%

- On July 1, year 8, Garfield purchased and paid for an office computer costing $85,000, including $8,500 for sales tax, delivery, and installation. There were no dispositions of property and equipment during year 8.

- Throughout year 8, Garfield owned 30% of Zap Inc.'s, common stock. As a result of this ownership interest, Garfield can exercise significant influence over Zap's operating and financial policies. During year 8, Zap paid dividends totaling $390,000 and reported net income of $780,000. Garfield's year 8 amortization of excess of cost over book value in Zap was $5,000.

- Partners' drawings for year 8 were as follows:

Melody	$341,000
Stacey	251,000
Mario	181,000
	$773,000

1. Using the direct method, prepare Garfield's statement of cash flows for the year ended December 31, year 8.

	A	B	C
1	Cash flows from operating activities:		
2	Cash received from customers		
3	Cash paid to suppliers and employees		
4	Dividends received from affiliate		
5	Net cash provided by operating activities		
6	Cash flows from investing activities:		
7	Purchased property and equipment		
8	Cash flows from financing activities:		
9	Principal payment of mortgage payable		
10	Proceeds for admission of new partner		
11	Drawings against partners' capital accounts		
12	Net cash used in financing activities		
13	Net increase in cash		
14	Cash at beginning of year		
15	Cash at end of year		

2. Prepare a reconciliation of net income to net cash provided by operating activities.

	A	B	C
1	Net income		
2	Adjustments to reconcile net income to net cash provided by operating activities:		
3	Depreciation and amortization		
4	Undistributed earnings of affiliate		
5	Change in assets and liabilities:		
6	Increase in accounts receivable		
7	Increase in accounts payable and accrued expenses		
8	Total adjustments		
9	Net cash provided by operating activities		

(11/90, PI, #5, amended, 9009t)

Problem 15-3 SIMULATION: Cash Flows Indirect Method

Comparative balance sheets for Bayshore Industries, Inc. as of December 31, year 2 and year 1 are presented below. See next page for additional information.

Bayshore Industries, Inc.
Balance Sheets
December 31, Year 2 and Year 1

	Year 2	Year 1	Change
Assets			
Current assets			
Cash and cash equivalents	$ 216,000	$ 144,000	$ 72,000
Trade receivables—net	3,434,000	1,971,000	1,463,000
Inventory	810,000	216,000	594,000
Prepaid expenses	18,000	--	18,000
Total current assets	4,478,000	2,331,000	2,147,000
Property and equipment	7,780,000	7,740,000	40,000
Less: accumulated depreciation	576,000	455,000	121,000
Property and equipment—net	7,204,000	7,285,000	(81,000)
Intangibles, less accumulated amortization of $14,400—year 2 and $7,200—year 1	21,600	28,800	(7,200)
Total assets	$11,703,600	$9,644,800	$2,058,800
Liabilities and Stockholders' Equity			
Current liabilities			
Accounts payable and accrued expenses	$ 872,600	$ 396,800	$ 475,800
Line of credit	108,000	90,000	18,000
Current portion of long-term debt	29,000	27,000	2,000
Total current liabilities	1,009,600	513,800	495,800
Long-term debt	3,069,000	3,098,000	(29,000)
Total liabilities	4,078,600	3,611,800	466,800
Stockholders' equity			
Common stock	9,000	9,000	0
Additional paid-in capital	5,400,000	5,400,000	0
Retained earnings	2,216,000	624,000	1,592,000
Total stockholders' equity	7,625,000	6,033,000	1,592,000
Total liabilities and stockholders' equity	$11,703,600	$9,644,800	$2,058,800

The Statement of Income and Retained Earnings for Bayshore Industries, Inc. for Year 2, as well as additional information regarding the company's operations for the year, is presented below.

Bayshore Industries, Inc. Statement of Income and Retained Earnings For the year ended December 31, Year 2	
Net sales	$19,800,000
Cost of sales	9,000,000
Gross profit on sales	10,800,000
Operating expenses	
Selling expenses	3,600,000
General and administrative expenses	4,050,000
Other operating expenses	393,300
Total operating expenses	8,043,300
Operating income	2,756,700
Other income and expenses	
Gain/loss on property and equipment disposals	18,000
Interest income	9,000
Interest expense	(252,000)
Other income and expenses—net	(225,000)
Income before income taxes	2,531,700
Provision for income taxes	759,700
Net income	1,772,000
Retained earnings – beginning	624,000
Dividends paid	180,000
Retained earnings – ending	$ 2,216,000

Additional information on transactions during the year ended December 31, year 2:

- All accounts receivable relate to customer sales.
- All accounts payable relate to suppliers.
- All fixed assets were acquired for cash.
- A building with original cost of $360,000 and accumulated depreciation of $319,500 was sold for $58,500.
- The company had no new debt in year 2.
- Interest paid in current year was $250,000.
- Cash paid for income taxes in current year were $700,000.
- There were no noncash financing or investing transactions during the year.

Using the indirect method, prepare the portions of the Statement of Cash Flows of Bayshore Industries, Inc. shown below for the year ended December 31, Year 2. For each of the shaded lines you feel may be necessary, choose an activity name from the selection list on the following page. Some of the shaded cells in the table may not be used in the completion of this task. Each item in the selection list may be used once, more than once, or not at all. Next to each activity, enter the appropriate value. Enter negative numbers with a leading minus (–) sign. (Editor's Note: The selection list is reproduced on the next page.)

1	Cash flows from operating activities:	
2		$
3		
4		
5		
6		
7		
8		
9		
10	Net cash provided by operating activities	$
11		
12	Cash flows from investing activities:	
13		$
14		
15		
16	Net cash used in investing activities	$
17		
18	Cash flows from financing activities:	
19		$
20		
21		
22		
23	Net cash used by financing activities	$
24		
25	Net increase (decrease) in cash and cash equivalents	$
26		
27	Supplemental disclosures:	
28		$
29		$

Selection List

A. Increase/decrease in prepaid expenses
B. Cash paid for income taxes
C. Net income/loss
D. Depreciation and amortization expense
E. Allowance for bad debts
F. Cash collected from licensees
G. Increase/decrease in intangibles
H. Proceeds from/repayment of line of credit
I. Deferred income taxes
J. Dividends received
K. Increase/decrease in trade receivables – net
L. Increase/decrease in accounts payable and accrued expenses
M. Interest received
N. Purchases of property and equipment
O. Increase/decrease in inventory
P. Dividends paid
Q. Cash paid to suppliers and employees
R. Gain/loss on property and equipment disposals
S. Repayment of long-term debt
T. Cash received from lessees
U. Collections from customers
V. Interest paid
W. Proceeds from plant and equipment disposals
X. Proceeds from issuance of common stock
Y. Proceeds from issuance of long-term debt

(R/06, FAR, P2, 8118)

Problem 15-4 SIMULATION: Cash Flows Direct Method

Comparative balance sheets for Flax Corp. as of December 31, year 2 and year 1 are presented below. Use this information to answer the subsequent questions.

	December 31	
	Year 2	Year 1
Debits:		
Cash	$ 35,000	$ 32,000
Accounts receivable	33,000	30,000
Inventory	31,000	47,000
Property, plant, and equipment	100,000	95,000
Unamortized bond discount	4,500	5,000
Cost of goods sold	250,000	380,000
Selling expenses	141,500	172,000
General and administrative expenses	137,000	151,300
Interest expense	4,300	2,600
Income tax expense	20,400	61,200
	$756,700	$976,100
Credits:		
Allowance for uncollectible accounts	$ 1,300	$ 1,100
Accumulated depreciation	16,500	15,000
Trade accounts payable	25,000	17,500
Income taxes payable	21,000	27,100
Deferred income taxes	5,300	4,600
8% callable bonds payable	45,000	20,000
Common stock	50,000	40,000
Additional paid-in capital	9,100	7,500
Retained earnings	44,700	64,600
Sales	538,800	778,700
	$756,700	$976,100

Additional Information

- Flax Corp. uses the direct method to prepare its statement of cash flows.
- Flax purchased $5,000 in equipment during year 2.
- Flax allocated one-third of its depreciation expense to selling expenses and the remainder to general and administrative expenses.

For the following items, what amounts should Flax report in its statement of cash flows for the year ended December 31, year 2?

Item	Amount
1. Cash collected from customers	
2. Cash paid for goods to be sold	
3. Cash paid for interest	
4. Cash paid for income taxes	
5. Cash paid for selling expenses	

(3/11, amended, 9130)

Problem 15-5 SIMULATION: Cash Flow Categories: Indirect Method

The following are descriptions of items that will be reported in the statement of cash flows prepared using the indirect method or disclosed in the related notes. For each item, select from the following list where the amount should be reported or disclosed. An answer may be selected once, more than once, or not at all. Select the **best** answer for each item.

Item	Location
1. Proceeds received from sale of bonds	
2. Interest paid	
3. Amortization of bond premium	
4. Gain on early extinguishment of debt	
5. Loss on sale of machinery	
6. Payment of cash dividends	
7. Exchange of land for equipment	
8. Purchase of patent	
9. Reissuance of Treasury stock	

Classification	
O.	Operating activities
I.	Investing activities
F.	Financing activities
S.	Supplemental schedule

(11/98, amended, 6746)

Problem 15-6 SIMULATION: Research

Question: What is the primary purpose of a statement of cash flows?

FASB ASC: ______ - ______ - ______ - ______

(9131)

Solution 15-1 MULTIPLE-CHOICE ANSWERS

Purpose & Focus

1. (c) The primary purpose of a statement of cash flows is to provide relevant information about the cash receipts and cash disbursements of an enterprise during a period. (4820)

2. (b) The primary purpose of a statement of cash flows is to provide relevant information about the cash receipts and cash payments of an enterprise during a period. The information provided in a statement of cash flows helps investors, creditors, and others to assess the effects on an enterprise's financial position of both its cash and non-cash investing and financing transactions during the period. Related disclosures should report the effects of investing and financing transactions that affect an enterprise's financial position, but do not directly affect cash flows during the period. Neither the balance sheet nor the income statement would show changes in the balances of debt or equity accounts. The statement of changes in stockholders' equity would not indicate changes in debt accounts. (7620)

3. (d) The exchange of cash for a cash equivalent is not reported on the Statement of Cash Flows. (6129)

4. (c) Cash is by definition the most liquid asset of an enterprise; thus, it is usually the first item presented in the current assets section of the balance sheet. The U.S. Treasury bill purchased on 12/1, year 1, is not a cash equivalent because the maturity of the instrument was more than three months from the purchase date. (6896)

Cash in checking account	$ 35,000
Cash in money market account	75,000
U.S. Treasury Bill purchased 12/1, year 2	200,000
Total cash and cash equivalents on 12/31, year 2	$310,000

Content & Form

5. (c) Accounts receivable have increased by $8,800 (i.e., $30,400 – $21,600) from the beginning to the end of the year, which means that cash collected from customers is less than the sales revenues reported on the accrual basis by this amount. Thus, the amount of cash collected from customers is $429,200 (i.e., $438,000 – $8,800). (It is important to note that since the direct method is used to determine cash flows from operating activities, the Allowance for Uncollectible Accounts is not used in determining cash collected from customers.) (1234)

6. (b) Accounts receivable have decreased from the beginning to the end of the year, which means that cash collected from customers is greater than sales revenues reported on an accrual basis. The cash collected from customers is determined by adding the decrease in accounts receivable from the beginning to the end of the year to sales revenues. (9044)

7. (a) Cash dividends received from investments produce a cash inflow due to operating activities so they increase the reported cash flow from operating activities using the direct method. The proceeds from the sale of equipment are to be classified as an inflow from investing activities; any associated gain on the sale will not impact the reported cash flows from operating activities using the direct method. The payment to retire bonds is a cash outflow due to financing activities; any associated gain will not impact the reported cash flows from operating activities using the direct method. A change from the straight-line method to an accelerated depreciation method does not affect cash nor does it impact the computation of net cash flows from operating activities using the direct method. (2699)

8. (d) Inventories have increased by $15,000 (i.e., $60,000 – $45,000) from the beginning to the end of the year, which means that inventory purchases were greater than cost of goods sold by this amount. Thus, the amount of inventory purchases is $285,000 (i.e., $270,000 + $15,000). Accounts payable have decreased by $13,000 (i.e., $39,000 – $26,000) from the beginning to the end of the year, which means that cash payments for inventories were greater than inventory purchases by this amount. The amount of cash paid to suppliers for inventories is $298,000 (i.e., $285,000 + $13,000). (4378)

9. (b) The cash disbursements for insurance in year 2 are composed of both the insurance expense for the year and the increase in the prepaid insurance account. Therefore the amount of insurance disbursements can be calculated as the ending balance of the prepaid insurance account minus the beginning balance of the account plus the insurance expense for the period. (1238)

Insurance expense for year 2	$20,000
Increase in prepaid insurance ($50,000 – $25,000)	25,000
Cash disbursements for insurance in year 2	$45,000

10. (d) A reconciliation of ending retained earnings to net cash flow from operations is not disclosed on the Statement of Cash Flows under either method. The major classes of gross cash receipts and payments, the amount of income taxes paid, and a reconciliation of net income to net cash flow from operations all appear on the face of the Statement of Cash Flows or in a separate schedule when the direct method is used. (6130)

11. (c) When using the cost method, an excess of treasury stock acquisition cost over sales proceeds is recorded by a charge to an additional paid-in capital account or to the *Retained Earnings* account, **not** an income statement account. Therefore, this "loss" is **not** an adjustment in converting net income on an accrual basis to net cash provided by operating activities. The amortization of bond discount decreases net income (because of the increase in interest expense) but has no effect on cash. Thus, it is added to net income when using the indirect method of computing net cash provided by operating activities. (2529)

12. (b) Net cash provided by operating activities is adjusted to remove the effects of depreciation expense and goodwill impairment (see editor's note) expense. ($400,000 – $190,000 – $5,000 = $205,000) Dividends paid on common stock are not reported in operating activities. (7745)

13. (c) A statement of cash flows should report the cash provided or used by operating, investing, and financing activities. It should also report the net effect of those flows on cash and cash equivalents during the period in such a manner that reconciles the beginning and ending cash and cash equivalents. The $40,000 sale of land proceeds already is incorporated in the cash flows from investing activities. (8109)

Beginning cash balance, Jan 1	$ 27,000
Plus: Cash from operating activities	351,000
Less: Cash for investing activities	(420,000)
Plus: Cash for financing activities	250,000
Cash balance, Dec 31	$ 208,000

Preparation

14. (b) If the direct method of reporting net cash flow from operating activities is used, an entity should provide a reconciliation of net income to net cash flow from operating activities in a separate schedule. An entity should report significant noncash investing and financing activities, and amounts of interest paid (net of amounts capitalized) and income taxes paid during the period in related disclosures. (89589)

15. (c) Advances from related parties, like other advances, should be reflected in the statements as financing activities, and repayments of the advances should also be reflected in the statements within the financing section. (9017)

16. (c) Financial statements shall not report an amount of cash flow per share. The conversion of debt to equity is a noncash financing activity because the transaction affects the enterprise's liabilities but it does not result in cash receipts or payments during the period. The conversion of debt to equity should be disclosed as supplemental information in the statement of cash flows. (5585)

17. (d) The receipt and distribution of the merchandise affected recognized assets but did not result in cash receipts or cash payments in the period. Hence, it should be reported in the statement of cash flows as a non-cash activity. (3454)

Operating Activities

18. (b) Operating activities include all transactions and other events that are not defined as investing or financing activities. Cash flows from operating activities are generally the cash effects of transactions and other events that enter into the determination of net income, including cash receipts from returns on loans, other debt instruments of other entities, and equity securities—interest and dividends. Bond discount amortization increases interest expense, but does not involve any outflow of cash. It is subtracted from interest expense to determine cash payments for interest, an operating activity. (8369)

19. (a) The increase in net A/R represents sales that were not collected in cash; therefore, this amount must be subtracted from net income to compute net cash from operating activities. The decrease in prepaid rent expense represents expenses recognized that were not paid in cash, and thus must be added for the adjustment. The increase in A/P represents purchases that were not paid out in cash, and thus must be added for the adjustment. (4374)

Net income		$150,000
Increase in net accounts receivable ($29,000 – $1,000) – ($23,000 – $800)]	$(5,800)	
Decrease in prepaid rent expense ($12,400 – $8,200)	4,200	
Increase in accounts payable ($22,400 – $19,400)	3,000	
Adjustments		1,400
Net cash provided by operating activities		$151,400

20. (b) Depreciation is a noncash expense; therefore, it is added back to net income to compute net cash provided by operating activities. The gain on the sale of equipment was added to determine net income, but it did not represent an inflow of cash. Therefore, the gain must be subtracted for the adjustment. (4375)

Net income		$300,000
Depreciation expense	$52,000	
Gain on sale of equipment	(5,000)	
Adjustments		47,000
Net cash provided by operating activities		$347,000

21. (a) The determination of net cash flow from operating activities is determined by using either the direct method or indirect method. Using the indirect method, net cash flow is reported by converting net income to net cash flow from operating activities. Only the inventory and accounts payable accounts effect operating activities. The available-for-sale securities purchase would affect investing activities while the mortgage repayment, issuance of bonds payable, and dividend payment would affect financing activities. To calculate the net cash provided by operating activities in the statement of cash flows, using the indirect method, start with the net income of $70,000. The $40,000 increase in inventory would be deducted from net income because the incremental increase in inventories reduces cash without increasing cost of sales. The $30,000 decrease in accounts payable also would be deducted from net income because this represents credit sales exceeding the amount of collections. The result ($70,000 – $40,000 – $30,000 = $0) is the amount of net cash provided by operating activities. (8329)

22. (a) Cash flows from operating activities are generally the cash effects of transactions and other events that enter into the determination of net income. Both the $28,000 from dividends that were declared and paid and the $200,000 from issuance of common stock are cash flows from financing activities, not operating. With the limited information provided it is best to use the indirect method to compute the cash provided by operating activities. Computation under this method is done by converting net income to net cash flow from operating activities. Start with net income and then make adjustments to reconcile net income to net cash provided by operating activities. Take the $78,000 net income less the $82,000 increase in accounts receivable plus the $24,000 increase in accounts payable and the result is $20,000 net cash provided by operating activities. (8798)

Investing Activities

23. (a) To answer this question, reconstruct separate journal entries for the portion of the building acquired by issuing the mortgage note payable to the seller and the portion of the building acquired by paying cash. (9042)

Building	XX	
Mortgage Note Payable		XX
Building	XX	
Cash		XX

The portion of the building acquired by issuing the mortgage note payable to the seller (i.e., a seller-financed debt) is a noncash investing and financing activity. This portion of the transaction affects the enterprise's recognized assets and liabilities, but it does not result in cash receipts or payments. Therefore, this portion of the transaction should be reported in related disclosures and not in the body of the statement of cash flows. The portion of the building acquired by paying cash should be reported as a cash outflow due to an investing activity. Cash outflows for investing activities include payments at the time of purchase to acquire PP&E.

24. (a) If an exam question does not specify that a debt or equity investment is a cash equivalent or classed as a trading security, then the cash flows from the purchase, sale, or maturity should be classed as cash flows from investing activities. (5583)

Purchase of bond investment	$180,000
Proceeds from sale of equipment	(10,000)
Net cash used in investing activities	$170,000

25. (b) Collection of a note receivable from a related party would be reported as an investing activity. Collection of proceeds from a note payable would be reported as a financing activity. Collection of an overdue account receivable from a customer and a tax refund from the government would be reported as operating activities. (9303)

26. (d) Cash flows from investing activities includes purchases, sales, and maturities of debt and equity securities; excluding those acquired specifically for resale. This would include available-for-sale and held-to-maturity securities. ($25,000 + $40,000 = $65,000) (8751)

27. (a) Cash flows from investing activities include 1) making and collecting loans (excluding those acquired specifically for resale), 2) acquiring and disposing of property, plant and equipment, and other productive assets, and 3) purchases, sales, and maturities of debt and equity securities (excluding those acquired specifically for resale). The sale of investment in Blue Co. would be an investing activity cash inflow of $75,000 and the common stock purchase from Brown Co. would be an investing activity cash outflow of $38,000. The $75,000 cash in less $38,000 cash out equals net $37,000 cash from investing activities. Dividends received on stock are classified as cash flows from operating activities. (8777)

Financing Activities

28. (d) Cash inflows from financing activities are (1) proceeds from issuing equity instruments and (2) proceeds from issuing bonds, mortgages, notes, and from other short- or long-term borrowing. (1913)

29. (c) The portion of the building acquired by paying cash should be reported as a cash outflow due to an investing activity. The portion of the building acquired by issuing the mortgage note payable to the seller (i.e., a seller-financed debt) is a noncash investing and financing activity. This portion of the transaction affects the enterprise's recognized assets and liabilities, but it does not result in cash receipts or payments. Therefore, this portion of the transaction should be reported in related disclosures and not in the statement body. (9043)

30. (d) Cash outflows from financing activities include payments of amounts borrowed and payments of dividends to owners. Interest payments, interest receipts, and dividends received are all operating activities. (1902)

31. (d) (5584)

Proceeds from sale of treasury stock	$ 75,000
Dividends paid	(38,000)
Net cash provided by financing activities	$ 37,000

32. (c) Cash inflows from financing activities include proceeds from issuing equity securities (e.g., treasury stock). Cash outflows for financing activities include payments of dividends and repayments of amounts borrowed. Conversion of preferred stock into common stock is a noncash financing activity. (4377)

Payment for early retirement of bonds payable	$(375,000)
Payment of preferred stock dividend	(31,000)
Proceeds from sale of treasury stock	50,000
Net cash used in financing operations	$(356,000)

PERFORMANCE BY SUBTOPICS

Each category below parallels a subtopic covered in Chapter 15. Record the number and percentage of questions you correctly answered in each subtopic area.

Purpose & Focus

Question #	Correct √
1	
2	
3	
4	
# Questions	4
# Correct	______
% Correct	______

Content & Form

Question #	Correct √
5	
6	
7	
8	
9	
10	
11	
12	
13	
# Questions	9
# Correct	______
% Correct	______

Preparation

Question #	Correct √
14	
15	
16	
17	
# Questions	4
# Correct	______
% Correct	______

Operating Activities

Question #	Correct √
18	
19	
20	
21	
22	
# Questions	5
# Correct	______
% Correct	______

Investing Activities

Question #	Correct √
23	
24	
25	
26	
27	
# Questions	5
# Correct	______
% Correct	______

Financing Activities

Question #	Correct √
28	
29	
30	
31	
32	
# Questions	5
# Correct	______
% Correct	______

Solution 15-2 SIMULATION ANSWER: Cash Flows Statements—Direct

1.

	A	B	C
1	Cash flows from operating activities:		
2	Cash received from customers	$ 2,619,000	
3	Cash paid to suppliers and employees	(1,825,000)	
4	Dividends received from affiliate	117,000	
5	Net cash provided by operating activities		$ 911,000
6	Cash flows from investing activities:		
7	Purchased property and equipment		(85,000)
8	Cash flows from financing activities:		
9	Principal payment of mortgage payable	(30,000)	
10	Proceeds for admission of new partner	450,000	
11	Drawings against partners' capital accounts	(773,000)	
12	Net cash used in financing activities		(353,000)
13	Net increase in cash		473,000
14	Cash at beginning of year		398,000
15	Cash at end of year		**$ 871,000**

Explanations

B2. Cash received from customers: Fee revenue less ending accounts receivable balance plus beginning accounts receivable balance ($2,701,000 – $464,000 + $383,000).

B3. Cash paid to suppliers and employees: Operating expenses less depreciation less ending accounts payable balance plus beginning accounts payable balance ($1,950,000 – $70,000 – $330,000 + $275,000).

B4. Dividends received from affiliate: Garfield's share of dividends declared by Zap (30% × $390,000).

C5. Sum of cash flows from operating activities ($2,619,000 – $1,825,000 + 117,000).

C7. Net change in property plant and equipment given in scenario.

B9. Change in mortgage payable given in scenario.

B10. Proceeds from admission of new partner given in additional information.

B11. Drawings against partners' capital accounts given in additional information.

C12. Sum of cash flows from financing activities (–$30,000 + $450,000 – $773,000).

C13. Net increase in cash: Sum of net cash flow provided by operating activities, investing activities and financing activities ($911,000 – $85,000 – $353,000).

C14. Cash at beginning of year given in scenario information.

C15. Cash at end of year: Sum of net increase in cash and cash at beginning of year ($473,000 + $398,000).

2.

	A	B	C
1	Net income		$980,000
2	Adjustments to reconcile net income to net cash provided by operating activities:		
3	Depreciation and amortization	$ 75,000	
4	Undistributed earnings of affiliate	(117,000)	
5	Change in assets and liabilities:		
6	Increase in accounts receivable	(82,000)	
7	Increase in accounts payable and accrued expenses	55,000	
8	Total adjustments		(69,000)
9	Net cash provided by operating activities		**$911,000**

Explanations

C1. Net income given in scenario information.

B3. Sum of amortization and depreciation ($70,000 + 5,000).

B4. Undistributed earnings of affiliate: Sum of Garfield's share (30%) of Zap, Inc's reported net income ($780,000) and cash dividends paid ($390,000) for year 8 ($234,000 – $117,000).

B6. Increase in accounts receivable given in scenario information.

B7. Increase in accounts payable and accrued expenses given in scenario information.

C8. Total adjustments: Sum of increase in depreciation and amortization and decrease in undistributed earnings of affiliate and increase in accounts receivable and accounts payable ($75,000–$117,000 – 82,000 + $55,000).

C9. Net cash provided by operating activities: Sum of net income and adjustments ($980,000 – $69,000). (9009)

Solution 15-3 SIMULATION ANSWER: Cash Flows Indirect Method

1	Cash flows from operating activities:	
2	Net income/loss (C)	$ 1,772,000
3	Depreciation and amortization expense (D)	447,700
4	Increase/decrease in trade receivables—net (K)	(1,463,000)
5	Increase/decrease in inventory (O)	(594,000)
6	Increase/decrease in prepaid expenses (A)	(18,000)
7	Gain/loss on property and equipment disposals (R)	(18,000)
8	Increase/decrease in accounts payable and accrued expenses (L)	475,800
9		
10	**Net cash provided by operating activities**	**$ 602,500**
11		
12	Cash flows from investing activities:	
13	Purchases of property and equipment (N)	(400,000)
14	Proceeds from plant and equipment disposals (W)	58,500
15		
16	**Net cash used in investing activities**	**$ (341,500)**
17		
18	Cash flows from financing activities:	
19	Proceeds from/repayment of line of credit (H)	18,000
20	Repayment of long-term debt (S)	(27,000)
21	Dividends paid (P)	(180,000)
22		
23	**Net cash used by financing activities**	**$ (189,000)**
24		
25	**Net increase (decrease) in cash and cash equivalents**	**$ 72,000**
26		
27	Supplemental disclosures:	
28	Interest paid (V)	$ 250,000
29	Cash paid for income taxes (B)	$ 700,000

Explanations

Cash Flows From Operating Activities (lines 2-8): Cash flows from operating activities are generally the cash effects of transactions and other events that enter into the determination of net income. These answers may be on any of lines 2-8, but the letter and amount must be together.

C2 Positive cash flow from net income, as shown on the statement of income and retained earnings

C3 Positive cash flow from the total of (1) increase in accumulated depreciation [576,000 – 455,000 = 121,000], plus (2) increase in accumulated amortization [14,400 – 7,200 = 7,200], plus (3) the accumulated depreciation on the building that was sold

C4 Negative cash flow from increase in trade receivables [3,434,000 – 1,971,000 = 1,463,000]

C5 Negative cash flow from increase in inventory [810,000 – 216,000 = 594,000]

C6 Negative cash flow from increase in prepaid expenses [18,000 – 0 = 18,000]

C7 Negative cash flow from gain on sale of building [58,500 sale price – 40,500 book value = 18,000] (The 360,000 cost – 319,500 accumulated depreciation = 40,500 book value)

C8 Positive cash flow from increase in accounts payable and accrued expenses [872,600 – 396,800 = 475,800]]

C10 Net Cash Provided by Operating Activities: 602,500

Cash Flows From Investing Activities (lines 13 and 14): Cash inflows from investing activities include: receipts from disposing of loans; debt or equity instruments; or property, plant, and equipment including directly related proceeds of insurance settlements, such as the proceeds of insurance on a building that is damaged or destroyed. Cash outflows include: disbursements for loans; payments to acquire debt instruments of other entities; and payments to acquire equity instruments of other entities (other than certain equity instruments carried in a trading account). These answers may be on lines 13 or 14, but the letter and amount must be together.

C13 Negative cash flow from total increase in property and equipment [7,780,000 – (7,740,000 – 360,000 from building sold) = 400,000]

C14 Positive cash flow from proceeds of building sold, as provided in additional information for year 2

C16: Net Cash Provided by Investing Activities: –341,500

Cash Flows From Financing Activities (lines 19-21): Cash inflows from financing activities are (1) proceeds from issuing equity instruments and (2) proceeds from issuing bonds, mortgages, notes, and from other short- or long-term borrowing. Cash outflows from financing activities include payments of dividends to owners, repayments of amounts borrowed, and other principal payments to creditors who have extended long-term credit. These answers may be on any of lines 19-21, but the letter and amount must be together.

C19 Positive cash flow from increase in line of credit [108,000 – 90,000 = 18,000]

C20 Negative cash flow from repayment of long-term debt, as shown on the year 1 balance sheet (Note this was "current portion" of long-term debt)

C21 Negative cash flow from dividends paid, as shown on the statement of income and retained earnings

C23: Net Cash Provided by Financing Activities: –189,000

Supplemental Disclosures (lines 28 and 29): These answers may be on either line 28 or 29, but the letter and amount must be together.

C28 As provided in additional information for year 2

C29 As provided in additional information for year 2 (8118)

Solution 15-4 SIMULATION ANSWER: Cash Flows Direct Method

Item	Amount
1. Cash collected from customers	$535,800
2. Cash paid for goods to be sold	$226,500
3. Cash paid for interest	$ 3,800
4. Cash paid for income taxes	$ 25,800
5. Cash paid for selling expenses	$141,000

Explanations

1. Accounts receivable have increased by $3,000 (i.e., $33,000 – $30,000) from the beginning to the end of the year, which means that cash collected from customers is less than the sales revenues reported on the accrual basis by this amount. Thus, the amount of cash collected from customers is $535,800 (i.e., $538,800 – $3,000). (It is important to note that since the direct method is used to determine cash flows from operating activities, the *Allowance for Uncollectible Accounts* is not netted against *Accounts Receivable* in determining cash collected from customers.)

2. (d) Inventories have decreased by $16,000 (i.e., $47,000 – $31,000) from the beginning to the end of the year, which means that inventory purchases were less than cost of goods sold by this amount. Thus, the amount of inventory purchases is $234,000 (i.e., $250,000 – $16,000). Accounts payable have increased by $7,500 (i.e., $25,000 – $17,500) from the beginning to the end of the year, which means that cash payments for inventories were less than inventory purchases by this amount. Thus, the amount of cash paid for inventories is $226,500 (i.e., $234,000 – $7,500).

2. (c) Unamortized bond discount decreased by $500 (i.e., $5,000 – $4,500) from the beginning to the end of the year. The bond discount amortization decreases net income (because of the increase in interest expense) but has no affect on cash. Therefore, the amount of cash paid for interest is $3,800 (i.e., $4,300 – $500).

4. (a) Since income taxes payable decreased from the beginning to the end of the year, the amount of cash paid for income taxes is greater than income tax expense reported on an accrual basis by this amount. The increase in deferred income taxes is a noncash expense (i.e., it increases income tax expense but has no affect on cash), therefore it is subtracted from income tax expense to determine the amount of cash paid for income taxes.

Income tax expense	$ 20,400
Add: Decrease in income taxes payable ($27,100 – $21,000)	6,100
Less: Increase in deferred income taxes ($5,300 – $4,600)	(700)
Cash paid for income taxes	$ 25,800

5. (c) (9130)

Selling expenses	$141,500
Less: Allocated portion of depreciation expense [($16,500 – $15,000) / 3]	(500)
Cash paid for selling expenses	$141,000

Solution 15-5 SIMULATION ANSWER: Cash Flow Categories: Indirect Method

Item	Location
1. Proceeds received from sale of bonds	F
2. Interest paid	S
3. Amortization of bond premium	O
4. Gain on early extinguishment of debt	O
5. Loss on sale of machinery	O
6. Payment of cash dividends	F
7. Exchange of land for equipment	S
8. Purchase of patent	O
9. Reissuance of Treasury stock	F

Editor's Note: all replies are for the indirect method only

1. The proceeds received from the sale of bonds are reported in the financing section of the statement of cash flows.

2. Interest paid is provided in related disclosures. The net income amount shown in the operating section is net of interest paid and income taxes paid; so separate disclosure is needed for the statement to reflect this information.

3. Amortization of bond premium is shown in the statement of cash flows as an adjustment to net income in the operating section.

4. Items whose cash effects are financing cash flows, such as gain on early debt extinguishment, are shown in the statement of cash flows as adjustments to net income in the operating section.

5. Loss on the sale of long-term assets is shown in the statement of cash flows as an adjustment to net income in the operating section.

6. Payment of cash dividends is reported in the financing section of the statement of cash flows.

7. Significant investing and financing activities, such as exchanges of land, do not affect cash and are reported in a supplemental schedule.

8. Purchase of a patent, which is a long-term asset, is recorded in the operating section of the statement of cash flows.

9. Reissuance of treasury stock is classified as a financing activity. (6746)

Solution 15-6 SIMULATION ANSWER: Research

<u>FASB Accounting Standards Codification</u>

FASB ASC: 230 - 10 - 10 - 1

10-1 The primary objective of a standard of cash flows is to provide relevant information about the cash receipts and cash payments of an entity during a period. (9131)

Wondering how to allocate your study time?

In your excitement to answer multiple-choice questions, don't forget that the examiners ask questions in simulation format as well!

The first pass through a chapter:

1. Strive to answer **all** the multiple-choice questions.

2. Choose one or more of the simulations to answer completely. Read the questions and possible responses, if given, for the simulations that you don't answer. Just reviewing simulation questions and any possible responses will assist you in being more comfortable about how simulations can be formatted.

3. At the very beginning of your review, don't worry about whether you finish questions within any specific time period. As you become more familiar with the content and the way the examiners ask questions, your speed will increase. Start noticing your time when you are on the first pass through your fourth or fifth chapter.

When you review the chapter later:

1. Answer **at least** those multiple-choice questions and any simulations that you did not understand the first time. (If you had a lucky guess, did you really understand?)

2. Select a new simulation, if available, to answer completely. Again, read the questions and responses for the simulations that you don't answer.

When you review the chapter for the final time (for some chapters, the second time **may be** the final time):

1. Answer the questions "cold turkey" (without reviewing the text materials just before answering questions). Before answering questions, only review the notes you would review just before the exam. For a whole exam section, this should take less than five minutes.

2. Answer **at least** those multiple-choice and simulation questions that you did not understand the first time.

3. Attempt to complete any simulations you haven't answered already.

Remember, with the techniques and information in your material,

A passing score is well within reach!

CHAPTER 16

BUSINESS COMBINATIONS AND CONSOLIDATIONS

CHAPTER 16

BUSINESS COMBINATIONS AND CONSOLIDATIONS

I. Investments in Equity Securities

A. Introduction

An investment in the equity securities of a corporation confers upon the investor the right to share in the earnings of the investee. If the investment is in the voting common stock of the investee, the investor is also entitled to participate, at least indirectly, in the investee's management. All equity securities initially are recorded at cost, which includes broker's fees, taxes, and any other direct costs of acquisition. The degree of influence that the investor is deemed to have over the investee by virtue of the investment determines the method of accounting for that investment. When a company owns stock in another corporation, its investment should be accounted for under one of three methods.

1. **Cost Method** The cost method is appropriate where the investor is **not** deemed to have a significant level of influence over the investee by virtue of the investment. In this case, the investor recognizes dividends as income when received.

2. **Equity Method** The equity method is required where the investor is deemed to have significant influence over the investee by virtue of the investment, but consolidated financial statements are not appropriate. Under the equity method, the investor recognizes as income its pro rata share of the investee's earnings or losses in the periods in which they are reported by the investee, while cash dividends received reduce the carrying amount of the investment. The equity method is more consistent with accrual accounting than the cost method, because the equity method recognizes income when earned rather than when dividends are received.

3. **Consolidated Financial Statements** Consolidated financial statements are required when a company owns more than 50% of the voting stock of another firm, with few exceptions. (Consolidated financial statements are covered in Chapter 17)

Exhibit 1 ▸ Accounting for Investments

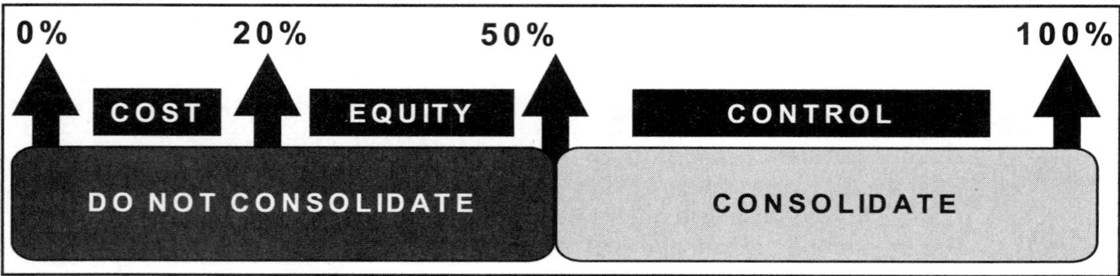

B. Cost Method

1. **Cost Method Criteria** The cost method is appropriate when the investor is **not** deemed to be able to exercise significant influence over the investee by virtue of the investment. Factors such as participation in policy-making or directorship indicate significant influence. In the absence of other evidence, ownership of 20% or more of the voting stock of an investee indicates significant influence. The cost method typically is used in the following situations.

   a. The investment is in nonvoting stock, such as preferred stock.

b. The number of shares of voting common stock owned represent less than 20% of the common stock outstanding.

c. The investment is of a temporary nature due to circumstances outside the investor's control.

2. **Upon Acquisition** Upon acquisition, the investment is recorded at cost. "Cost" also includes broker's fees and other direct costs of acquisition. In a lump-sum purchase, the purchase price is allocated to the various types of securities on the basis of their relative fair values.

3. **Trading and Available-for-Sale Securities** Investments in equity securities are classified as either (a) trading securities or (b) available-for-sale (AFS) securities. Dividends received are accounted for in current income. Changes in fair value (at year-end) of trading or AFS securities' portfolios are recorded through a valuation allowance account's addition or subtraction for both unrealized holding gains and losses. For trading securities, these changes are reported in current income. For AFS securities, these changes are reported in other comprehensive income.

4. **Investment Account** The investment account is not adjusted to reflect the investor's share of the investee's earnings or dividend distributions of earnings subsequent to acquisition. An adjustment must be made, however, for liquidating dividends (i.e., dividend distributions in excess of earnings subsequent to acquisition). Stock dividends and splits are recorded only by a memo entry, the carrying amount of the investment being allocated to the total number of shares owned.

5. **Stock Rights** If stock rights are received (rights to buy additional shares usually received to satisfy the investor's preemptive right to maintain its existing level of ownership in the investee), the carrying amount of the investment should be allocated between the investment and the rights. The allocation should be based on the ratio of the market value of the stock to the market value of the rights. This procedure is also used for the receipt of stock warrants. A stock warrant is physical evidence of stock rights.

6. **Upon Disposal** Upon disposal, a realized gain or loss should be recognized to the extent that the proceeds received differ from the carrying amount of the investment. The carrying amount of the shares sold may be determined by specific identification, FIFO, or the average method.

C. Equity Method

1. **Criteria** The equity method is based upon the premise that the investor owns a sufficiently large proportion of voting shares of the investee to allow the investor to exert significant influence over the policies of the investee, particularly the dividend policy.

a. **Significant Influence** The equity method of accounting for investments is required for investments where the investor is able to exercise significant influence over the operating and financial policies of the investee by virtue of the investment. If 20% or more of the outstanding voting stock of the investee is owned by the investor, a presumption of significant influence exists. Significant influence may be indicated by the following.

(1) Representation on the board of directors

(2) Participation in policy-making decisions

(3) Level of intercompany transactions or dependency

(4) Concentration of ownership in the hands of a small group of stockholders

b. **Consolidation** Consolidation is required of all majority-owned subsidiaries. The equity method is not a valid substitute for consolidation.

2. **Exceptions** The exception to the presumption that an investor owning 20% or more of the voting stock of an investee has significant influence over the investee is if the investment is operating in a foreign country where severe operating restrictions exist. Additionally, there are situations where the 20% ownership presumption may be overcome.

    a. **No Significant Influence** Opposition by the investee, such as litigation or complaints to governmental regulatory authorities, challenges the investor's ability to exercise significant influence.

    b. **By Agreement** The investor and investee sign an agreement under which the investor surrenders significant rights as a shareholder.

    c. **Other Owners** Majority ownership of the investee is concentrated among a small group of shareholders who operate the investee without regard to the views of the investor.

    d. **Lack of Information** The investor needs or wants more financial information to apply the equity method than is available to the investee's other shareholders (for example, the investor wants quarterly financial information from an investee that publicly reports only annually), tries to obtain that information, and fails.

    e. **No Representation** The investor tries and fails to obtain representation on the investee's board of directors.

3. **Upon Acquisition** Upon acquisition, the investment should be recorded at cost. If the investor owned less than 20% of the voting stock of the investee and subsequently increased the ownership percentage to 20% or more, the equity method should be retroactively applied in a manner consistent with the accounting for a step-by-step acquisition of a subsidiary. Retroactive adjustment to the investor's *Investment* and *Retained Earnings* accounts is required.

4. **Subsequent to Acquisition** Subsequent to acquisition, the *Investment* and the *Investment Income* accounts periodically must be adjusted in a manner analogous to a consolidated investment. (The equity method is sometimes referred to as a "one line consolidation.") Steps an investor would follow in applying the equity method include:

    a. **Investee's Earnings** Periodically, the investor recognizes its share of the investee's earnings. This is done by debiting the *Investment* account and crediting *Investment Income* for an amount proportionate to the ownership interest. The investor's share of investee earnings or losses is computed after deducting any cumulative preferred dividends of the investee. If the investor also owns shares of preferred stock, the investor should account for them under the cost method because they are nonvoting securities. Income on preferred stock would be recorded simply as dividend income as the preferred dividends are declared. Finally, when the investor's and the investee's fiscal years do not coincide, the investor may report its share of investee income from the most recent financial statements of the investee, so long as the time lag is consistent from period to period.

    b. **Dividends** Dividends declared by the investee represent a distribution of earnings previously recognized. The investor records the declaration of dividends by debiting a receivable and crediting the *Investment* account, since the distribution reduces the owners' equity of the investee. Dividends declared by the investee do not affect the *Investment Income* account.

    c. **Goodwill** The price paid for the common stock of the investee will seldom, if ever, equal the book value of the shares acquired. Any excess purchase price over the underlying equity is usually regarded as purchased goodwill.

d. **Excess Purchase Price** Specific investee assets may have fair values that differ from their book values. Any excess purchase price identified directly with individual assets (e.g., inventory, buildings, equipment, patents) having a limited useful life is amortized over the appropriate time period. The proper entry is to debit *Investment Income* and credit the *Investment* account for the amortization amount. The opposite entry is made if the fair value of the asset is less than its book value.

e. **Intercompany Profits & Losses** Intercompany profits and losses are eliminated until realized.

Example 1 ▸ Intercompany Profits & Losses

Investee Co., sells inventory to Investor, Inc., and recognizes a profit on the sale. At year-end Investor has not resold 25% of this inventory. Investor, Inc., must then reduce both its *Investment Income* and *Investment* accounts by an amount equal to 25% of the inter-company profits contained in the ending inventory.

f. **Intercompany Receivables and Payables** Intercompany receivables and payables between affiliates should not be eliminated unless the requirements for consolidation are met (i.e., > 50% ownership).

g. **Capital Transactions** Investee's capital transactions are accounted for as if the investee were a consolidated subsidiary. For instance, a sale by the investee of its common stock to third parties, at a price greater than book value, results in an increase in the carrying amount of the investment and a corresponding increase in the investor's additional paid-in capital. No income is recorded if the investee declares stock dividends or splits since the investor continues to own the same portion of the investee as before the stock split or dividend. The investor needs only to make a memo entry.

h. **Deferred Income Taxes** Deferred income taxes should be recognized for the temporary difference caused by the difference between the income recognized using the equity method and the dividends received from the investee. Corporate shareholders that own 20% or more (but less than 80%) of the stock of the distributing corporation are allowed an 80% dividend deduction. This portion of the dividends received is an event recognized in the financial statements that does not have a tax consequence because it is exempt from taxation. Events that do not have tax consequences do not give rise to temporary differences and are often referred to as "permanent differences."

i. **Changes in Common Stock Market Value** Changes in the market value of the investee's common stock do **not** affect the *Investment* account or the *Investment Income* account.

Example 2 ▸ Equity Method Application

On January 2 Company R purchased 20% of the outstanding common stock of Company E for $25,000. Any excess of the purchase price over the book value of the securities acquired is attributable to goodwill. Company E's net income for the year was $10,000. Cash dividends amounting to $4,000 were declared and paid. During the year, Company E sold inventory to R for $8,000, recording a $2,000 profit on the sale; 50% of this inventory ($4,000) had not been resold by Company R at year-end.

The owners' equity section of Company E at the time of acquisition is summarized below.

Common stock ($1 par)	$ 10,000
Additional paid-in capital	40,000
Retained earnings	50,000
Book value of Company E's net assets, Jan. 2	$100,000

Required: Provide the journal entries to record the acquisition and subsequent accounting for Company R's investment in Company E.

Solution: Entry to record acquisition of the 20% interest in E's common stock outstanding.

Investment in E	25,000		
Cash		25,000	

Entry to record R's share of E's net income for the year.

Investment in E (20% × $10,000)	2,000		
Investment Income		2,000	

Entry to reduce the investment in E for the amount of the dividend distribution received.

Cash ($4,000 × 20%)	800		
Investment in E		800	
E's profit on sale of inventory to R			$2,000
Sale price of inventory			/ 8,000
E's gross margin ratio			25%
E's inventory still in R's ending inventory (in dollars)			× 4,000
E's recorded profit on R's ending inventory			$1,000

Investment Income ($1,000 × 20%)	200		
Investment in E		200	

Entry to adjust for Co., R's share of intercompany unrealized profits.

Note: The $5,000 of goodwill attributable to the investment in E is not recorded separately. It is recognized as a portion of the investment price that should be tested periodically for impairment.

5. **Changes From Equity Method** Upon disposal of an equity method investment, the investor should recognize a gain or loss equal to the difference between the carrying amount of the investment and its sale price. Note that the carrying amount of the investment must be adjusted to the date of disposal. If, as a result of a partial disposal, the ownership percentage becomes less than 20%, the investor should stop accruing its share of investee income. A change in the method of accounting must be made to the cost method. The cost basis for accounting purposes is the carrying amount of the investment at the date of the change. Any dividends in future years that exceed the investor's share of the investee's income for such future years (i.e., liquidating dividends) should be applied to reduce the *Investment* account.

6. **Changes to Equity Method** Where the investor's level of ownership increases, so that use of the equity method is required, the investment account, results of operations, and retained earnings of the investor must be retroactively adjusted. This adjustment must be consistent with the accounting for a step-by-step subsidiary acquisition. The amount of the adjustment to prior periods is for the difference between the amounts that were recognized in prior periods under the cost method and the amounts that would have been recognized if the equity method had been used. The adjustments are made based on the ownership interest that existed at the time the income was earned.

Example 3 ▸ Changes to Equity Method

On January 2, year 1, Amsted Corporation purchased 10% of the outstanding shares of Cable Company common stock for $250,000 and recorded the investment using the cost method. On January 2, year 3, Amsted purchased an additional 20% of Cable's stock for $600,000. Now having a 30% interest and significant influence, Amsted uses the equity method. Cable Co.'s net income and dividends paid are as follows.

Year	Cable Co., net income	Cable Co., dividends paid to Amsted
1	$250,000	$10,000
2	500,000	15,000
3	600,000	60,000

Required: Provide the journal entry for the January 2, year 3, transaction retroactively reflecting the change from the cost to equity method.

Solution:

Investment in Cable Co., Stock	650,000	
Cash		600,000
Retained earnings		50,000*

* **Computations:**	Year 1	Year 2	Total
Amsted Corp., equity in earnings of Cable Co., 10%	$ 25,000	$ 50,000	$ 75,000
Dividends received	(10,000)	(15,000)	(25,000)
Prior period adjustment	$ 15,000	$ 35,000	$ 50,000

7. **Losses** A loss in the value of an equity method investment should be recognized if such loss is other than temporary. A loss in value may be evidenced by a poor earnings record, inability to recover the carrying amount of the investment, or similar causes. An investor should reduce its investment for its pro rata share of investee losses. However, if the investee continuously reports net losses, the investor should discontinue applying the equity method after the investment has been written down to zero. The investor should then record her/his share of further investee losses by memo entry only. If the investee becomes profitable in the future, the investor should resume applying the equity method only after its share of net income equals its share of net losses not previously recognized.

8. **Financial Statement Presentation** The investor's investment in common stock should be disclosed as a single line item on the balance sheet. The investor's share of investee's earnings is disclosed as a single line item on the income statement. An **exception** arises for investee's extraordinary items and prior period adjustments. If material, these items should be separately reported in the investor's financial statements.

Exhibit 2 ▸ T-Account Summary of the Equity Method

Equity Investment in X Co. (balance sheet)	
Original cost of investment Pro rata share of investee's income since acquisition Retroactive adjustment due to change from cost to equity method (dr. or cr.)	Pro rata share of investee's losses since acquisition Pro rata share of investee's dividends declared Disposal of investee stock

Investment Income, X Co. (income statement)	
Pro rata share of investee's losses since acquisition	Pro rata share of investee's income since acquisition

NOTE: The investment income account is **not** affected by dividends declared by the investee.

D. Joint Ventures

1. **Definition** A joint venture is a business arrangement in which investors agree to develop, for a finite time, a separate economic entity to take on a particular project. The investors own, operate and jointly control the venture, exercising shared control over the entity and share revenues, expenses and assets. A joint venture could be a partnership, corporation, or be unincorporated.

2. **Accounting Recommendations** The AICPA Accounting Standards Executive Committee (AcSEC) published several recommendations regarding the accounting for joint ventures, as follows:

   a. The equity method should be applied to investments in unincorporated joint ventures subject to joint control

   b. Majority interests in unincorporated joint ventures should be consolidated

   c. Investments in joint ventures not subject to joint control should be accounted for by proportionate consolidation

   d. Additional supplementary disclosures regarding the assets, liabilities, and result of operations are required for all material investments in unincorporated joint ventures

3. **Income Taxes** Use of the equity method results in the recognition of income based on the undistributed earnings of the investee. The investor has no tax liability for equity method income until those earnings are distributed, unless the entity is an S corporation. The equity method will create temporary timing differences that need to be considered when deferred tax assets and liabilities are computed.

4. **Intra-Entity Profits and Losses** Intra-entity profits and losses are eliminated until realized by the investor or investee as if the investee were consolidated. Intra-entity profits and losses on assets are eliminated, creating income tax consequences on the intra-entity transactions, except for:

   a. A transaction accounted for as a deconsolidation of a subsidiary or a derecognition of a group of assets.

   b. A transaction that is accounted for as a change in ownership.

II. Business Combinations

A. Overview

A business combination is a transaction or event in which two or more entities combine to form a single entity, with the acquirer obtaining control. Control is defined as ownership of a majority voting interest; as a general rule ownership by one company, directly or indirectly, of over fifty percent of the outstanding voting shares of another company. Transactions sometimes referred to as "true mergers" or "mergers of equals" are also business combinations. Business combinations are accounted for using the acquisition method of accounting.

1. **Identification** An entity shall determine whether a transaction (or event) is a business combination by applying the definition above, which requires that the assets acquired and liabilities assumed constitute a business.

    a. A business is defined as an integrated set of activities and assets that is capable of being conducted and managed for the purpose of providing a return in the form of dividends, lower costs, or other economic benefits directly to investors or other owners, members, or participants.

    b. If not a business, the entity shall account for the transaction as an asset acquisition.

2. **Chain of Interests** On occasion, intercorporate stock ownership arrangements may indicate a chain of interests (e.g., A owns 80 percent of B, B owns 60 percent of C) the product of which (e.g., 80% × 60% = 48%) does not represent control of the lower level subsidiary. In this instance, the preparation of consolidated statements is warranted, notwithstanding the 48 percent indirect interest of A Company in C Company. The product of the percentages of stock ownership in the chain is not a determinant in establishing a minimal condition for preparation of consolidated financial statements.

3. **Exceptions** GAAP provides that a majority-owned subsidiary should not be consolidated if control does not rest with the majority owner. For example, if the subsidiary is in legal reorganization, in bankruptcy, or operates under foreign exchange restrictions, controls or other governmentally imposed uncertainties so severe that they cast significant doubt on the parent's ability to control the subsidiary.

B. Acquisition Method

An entity is required to account for each business combination by applying the acquisition method. The acquisition method was previously called the purchase method but had some changes to improve reporting. It applies to all business entities, including mutual entities that previously used the pooling-of-interests method of accounting. Applying the acquisition method requires:

- Indentifying the acquirer
- Determining the acquisition date
- Recognizing and measuring identifiable assets acquired, liabilities assumed, and any noncontrolling interest in the acquiree
- Recognizing and measuring goodwill or a gain from a bargain purchase

1. **Indentifying the Acquirer and Acquisition Date** The acquirer is the entity that obtains control of the acquiree. The acquirer is usually the entity that transfers cash or other assets, or incurs liabilities, or issues its equity interests. Other factors that may identify the acquirer are the larger size of the entities involved and the entity initiating the combination.

   The acquisition date is the date on which the acquirer obtains control of the acquiree (typically the closing date). It is the only relevant date for recognition and measurement and is used to measure the fair value of the consideration paid. When the acquirer issues equity instruments as full or partial payment for the acquiree, for example, the fair value of the acquirer's equity instruments will be measured at the acquisition date.

2. **Business Combination Achieved in Stages** When an acquirer obtains control of an acquiree in which it previously held an equity interest immediately before the acquisition date it is call a business combination achieved in stages. This is sometimes also referred to as a step acquisition.

   a. The acquisition method requires the acquirer to recognize the identifiable assets and liabilities, as well as the noncontrolling interest in the acquiree, at the full amounts of their fair values.

   b. The acquirer shall remeasure its previously held equity interest in the acquiree at its acquisition-date fair value and recognize the resulting gain or loss, if any, in earnings.

   c. In prior reporting periods, the acquirer may have recognized changes in the value of its equity interest in the acquiree in other comprehensive income (OCI). If so, the amount recognized in OCI shall be reclassified and included in the calculation of gain or loss as of the acquisition date.

3. **Business Combination Achieved Without the Transfer of Consideration** An acquirer sometimes obtains control of an acquiree without transferring consideration. For example, the acquiree repurchases a sufficient number of its own shares for an existing investor, the acquirer, to obtain control; minority veto rights lapse that previously kept the acquirer from controlling an acquiree in which the acquirer held the majority voting interest; or the acquirer and acquiree agree to combine businesses by contract alone. The acquirer transfers no consideration in exchange for control of an acquiree and holds no equity interests in the acquiree, either on the acquisition date or previously.

4. **Measurement Period** If the initial accounting for a business combination is incomplete by the end of the reporting period in which the combination occurs, the acquirer shall report provisional amounts in its financial statements for the following items: the identifiable assets acquired, liabilities assumed, and any noncontrolling interest in the acquiree; the consideration transferred for the acquiree (or the other amount used in measuring goodwill); the equity interest in the acquiree previously held by the acquirer for business combinations achieved in stages; and the resulting goodwill recognized or the gain on a bargain purchase recognized.

   a. The acquirer shall retrospectively adjust the provisional amounts recognized at the acquisition date to reflect new information obtained about facts and circumstances that existed as of the acquisition date that, if known, would have affected the amounts recognized as of that date.

   b. The acquirer also shall recognize additional assets and liabilities if new information is obtained about facts and circumstances that existed as of the acquisition date that, if known, would have resulted in the recognition of those assets and liabilities as of that date.

c. The acquirer recognizes an increase (decrease) in the provisional amount recognized for an identifiable asset (liability) by means of a decrease (increase) in goodwill. The acquirer shall recognize any adjustments to the provisional amounts as if the accounting for the business combination had been completed at the acquisition date.

d. The measurement period ends when the acquirer receives the information it was seeking about facts and circumstances that existed as of the acquisition date or learns that more information is not obtainable, however, it shall not exceed one year from the acquisition date.

e. After the measurement period ends, the acquirer shall not revise the accounting for the business combination but to correct an error.

5. **Identifying the Business Combination Transaction** The acquirer and the acquiree may have a preexisting relationship or other arrangement before negotiations for the business combination began, or they may enter into an arrangement during the negotiations that is separate from the business combination.

   a. The acquirer shall identify any amounts that are not part of what the acquirer and the acquiree (or its former owners) exchanged in the business combination, that is, the amounts that are not part of the exchange for the acquiree.

   b. The acquirer shall recognize as part of applying the acquisition method only the consideration transferred for the acquiree and the assets acquired and liabilities assumed in the exchange for the acquiree.

   c. A transaction entered into by or on behalf of the acquirer primarily for the benefit of acquirer or the combined entity, rather than primarily for the benefit of the acquiree (or its former owners) before the combination, is likely to be a separate transaction. The following are examples of separate transactions that are not to be included in applying the acquisition method:

      (1) A transaction that in effect settles preexisting relationships between the acquirer and acquiree

      (2) A transaction that compensates employees or former employees of the acquiree for future services

      (3) A transaction that reimburses the acquiree or its former owners for paying the acquirer's acquisition related costs.

6. **Acquisition Costs** Acquisition related costs are those costs the acquirer incurs to effect a business combination. Those costs shall include finders fees; advisory, legal, accounting, valuation, and other professional or consulting fees; general administrative costs, including the costs of maintaining an internal acquisitions department; and costs of registering and issuing debt and equity securities. The acquirer shall account for acquisition-related costs as expenses in the periods in which the costs are incurred and the services are received, with one exception. The costs to issue debt or equity securities shall be recognized in accordance with other applicable GAAP.

7. **Income Tax Issues** The acquirer shall recognize, as an adjustment to income tax expense in income from continuing operations (or if appropriate a direct adjustment to contributed capital), changes in the valuation allowance for acquired deferred tax assets. The acquirer shall recognize changes in the acquired tax positions in accordance with GAAP authoritative guidance on accounting for income taxes.

8. **Disclosures**

   a. The notes to the financial statements of a combined entity in the period in which a material business combination is completed should include, at a minimum, the following information:

   - The name and description of the acquiree, the acquisition date, and the percentage of voting equity interests acquired
   - The primary reasons for the business combination and a description of how the acquirer obtained control of the acquiree
   - The acquisition-date fair value of the total consideration transferred and the acquisition-date fair value of each major class of consideration
   - The amounts recognized as of the acquisition date for each major class of assets acquired and liabilities assumed
   - The amounts recognized, the nature of recognized and unrecognized contingencies, and an estimate of the range of outcomes for assets and liabilities arising from contingencies
   - The amount recognized, a description and basis of determination, and an estimate of the range of outcomes for contingent consideration arrangements and indemnification assets
   - Transactions that are recognized separately from the acquisition of assets and assumptions of liabilities in the business combination
   - A qualitative description of the factors that make up the goodwill recognized and the total amount of goodwill that is expected to be deductible for tax purposes
   - In a bargain purchase: the amount of any gain recognized in a bargain purchase and the line item in the income statement in which the gain is recognized, and a description of the reasons why the transaction resulted in a gain
   - In a business combination achieved in stages: the acquisition-date fair value of the equity interest in the acquiree held by the acquirer immediately before the acquisition date, and the amount of any gain or loss recognized as a result of remeasuring to fair value the equity interest in the acquiree held by the acquirer before the business combination and the line item in the income statement in which that gain or loss is recognized.

   b. For transactions that are not part of the exchange for the acquiree, but rather are accounted for separately from the business combination, the following should be disclosed:

   - A description of each transaction and how it was accounted for
   - The amounts recognized and the line item in the financial statements where each amount is recognized
   - The method used to determine the settlement amount when the transaction is the effective settlement of a preexisting relationship

- The amount of acquisition related costs and the financial statement line item where the items are recognized

- The amount of issuance costs that are not recognized as an expense and a description of how they are recognized.

c. If the acquirer is a public entity, the following should be disclosed:

- The amounts of revenue and earnings of the acquiree since the acquisition date included in the consolidated income statement for the reporting period

- The revenue and earnings of the combined entity for the current reporting period as though the acquisition date had been as of the beginning of the annual reporting period

- If comparative financial statements are presented, the revenue and earnings of the combined entity for the comparable prior reporting period as though the acquisition date had been as of the beginning of the comparable prior annual reporting period

- The nature and amount of any material, nonrecurring pro forma adjustments due to the combination.

C. Identifiable Assets and Liabilities

1. Recognition Principle As of the acquisition date, the acquirer shall recognize, separately from goodwill, the identifiable assets acquired, the liabilities assumed, and any noncontrolling interest in the acquiree at their full fair value on the acquisition date.

GAAP provides exceptions from or modifications to fair value measurement for income taxes, employee benefit arrangements, reacquired rights, assets held for sale, indemnification assets, and share-based payment awards. All other elements, including contingent liabilities that meet the recognition threshold, are measured at full fair value whether the acquirer acquires 100 percent or a lesser amount (i.e., a partial acquisition).

a. An asset is identifiable if it either:

(1) Is capable of being separated or divided from the entity and sold, transferred, licensed, rented, or exchanged either individually or together with a related contract, identifiable asset, or liability, regardless of whether the entity intends to do so; or

(2) Arises from contractual or other legal rights, regardless of whether those rights are transferable or separable from the entity or from other rights and obligations.

b. To qualify as part of applying the acquisition method, the identifiable assets acquired and liabilities assumed must:

(1) Meet the definitions of assets and liabilities at the acquisition date. For example, costs the acquirer expects but is not obligated to incur in the future to effect its plan are not liabilities at the acquisition date; and

(2) Be part of what the acquirer and acquiree exchanged in the business combination transaction rather than the result of separate transactions.

2. **Measurement Principle** The acquirer shall measure the identifiable assets acquired, the liabilities assumed, and any noncontrolling interest in the acquiree at their acquisition-date fair values.

   a. The acquirer shall not recognize a separate valuation allowance because the effects of uncertainty about future cash flows are included in the fair value measure. For example, the acquirer is required to measure acquired receivables, including loans, at their acquisition-date fair value so the acquirer does not recognize a separate valuation allowance for the contractual cash flows that are deemed to be uncollectible at that date.

   b. For competitive or other reasons, the acquirer may intend not to use an acquired asset or may intend to use the asset in a way that is not its highest and best use. The acquirer must still measure the asset at fair value for its highest and best use, both initially and for purposes of subsequent impairment testing.

3. **Exceptions**

   a. The acquirer shall recognize all the assets acquired and liabilities assumed that arise from contingencies related to contracts. For all other contingencies, the acquirer will assess whether it is **more likely than not** as of the acquisition date that the contingency gives rise to an asset or liability. If the criterion is met, the acquirer will recognize the asset or liability at that date; if not met, the acquirer will not recognize an asset or liability.

   b. The acquirer's application of the recognition principle and conditions may result in some assets and liabilities that the acquiree had not previously recognized in their financial statements. For example, the acquirer recognizes the acquired intangible assets, such as brand name, patent, or customer relationships, that the acquiree did not recognize as assets because it developed them internally and charged the related costs to expense.

4. **Contingency Disclosures**

   a. For contingent consideration arrangements and indemnification assets, the following should be disclosed: amounts, descriptions of arrangements, and estimates of the range of outcomes.

   b. For assets and liabilities arising from contingencies, disclose the following:

      (1) The amounts recognized at the acquisition date or an explanation of why no amount was recognized

      (2) The nature of recognized and unrecognized contingencies

      (3) An estimate of the range of outcomes (undiscounted) for contingencies (recognized and unrecognized) or, if a range cannot be estimated, that fact and the reasons why.

D. Goodwill or a Gain From a Bargain Purchase

1. **Goodwill** An asset representing future economic benefits arising from other assets acquired in a business combination that are not individually identified and separately recognized. The requirement to measure the noncontrolling interest results in recognizing the goodwill attributable to the noncontrolling interest in addition to that attributable to the acquirer. The acquirer is allocated their portion first and then any remaining goodwill is attributed to the noncontrolling interest.

   a. Goodwill is recognized as of the acquisition date and measured as the excess of (1) over (2) below:

   (1) The aggregate of the consideration transferred plus the fair value of any noncontrolling interest plus, in a business combination achieved in stages, the acquisition-date fair value of the acquirer's previously held equity interest.

   (2) The net of the acquisition-date amounts of the identifiable assets acquired and the liabilities assumed.

   b. In a business combination in which the acquirer and acquiree exchange only equity interests, the acquisition-date fair value of the acquiree's equity interests may be more reliable than the acquisition-date fair value of the acquirer's equity interests. If so, the acquirer shall determine the amount of goodwill by using the acquisition-date fair value of the acquiree's equity interests instead of the acquisition-date fair value of the equity interests transferred.

   c. In a business combination in which no consideration is transferred, the acquirer shall determine the amount of goodwill using the acquisition-date fair value of the acquirer's interest in the acquiree determined using a valuation technique in place of the acquisition-date fair value of the consideration in (a.(1)) above.

Example 4 ▶ Goodwill, 100% Acquisition

On January 1, year 1, Parent Inc., (P) acquired all of Subsidiary Corp.'s (S) 100,000 shares of outstanding stock for $800,000 cash. This was the first acquisition of any of S's shares by P. The net book value of S is $700,000.

Required: Determine the total amount of goodwill recognized on the acquisition date for each of the following situations.

a. The fair value of S's assets and liabilities is equal to the book value.

b. The fair value of S's assets and liabilities is equal to the book value, except for land. Land is undervalued on the books by $50,000.

Solution:

a. The net book value of S is $700,000 and the fair value of the assets and liabilities is equal to the book value so the fair value of S is also worth $700,000. P acquired S for $800,000 cash; $800,000 cash – $700,000 fair value of S = $100,000 of total goodwill would be recognized on the acquisition date.

b. The net book value of S is $700,000 and the fair value of the assets and liabilities is equal to the book value except for land, which is undervalued on the books by $50,000. Because the land is undervalued, it must first be written up to fair value before determining the amount of goodwill. The fair value of S is worth the $700,000 book value + $50,000 land = $750,000. P acquired S for $800,000 cash; $800,000 cash – $750,000 fair value of S = $50,000 of total goodwill would be recognized on the acquisition date.

d. If an acquirer obtains less that 100 percent of the acquiree, goodwill is allocated to both the controlling and noncontrolling interests. The amount of goodwill allocated to the controlling interest is the difference between the fair value of the controlling interest and the controlling interest's share in the fair value of the identifiable net assets acquired. Any remaining goodwill is allocated to the noncontrolling interest.

Example 5 ▸ Goodwill With Noncontrolling Interest

On January 1, year 1, Parent Inc., (P) acquired 80% of Subsidiary Corp.'s (S) 100,000 shares of outstanding stock for $750,000 cash. This was the first acquisition of any of S's shares by P. The net book value of S is $700,000 and the fair value of S's assets and liabilities is equal to the book value. The fair value of the noncontrolling interest is determined to be $150,000.

Required: Determine the total amount of goodwill and the amount attributed to both P and the noncontrolling interest recognized on the acquisition date.

Solution:

The net book value of S is $700,000 and the fair value of the assets and liabilities is equal to the book value so the fair value of S is also worth $700,000. P acquired S for $750,000 cash and the fair value of the noncontrolling interest is $150,000. The $750,000 cash + $150,000 fair value of noncontrolling interest – $700,000 fair value of S = $200,000 of total goodwill recognized on the acquisition date. The goodwill is allocated to P and the noncontrolling interest as follows:

Fair value of P's 80% interest	$ 750,000
Less: Fair value of P's share of S's fair value ($700,000 × 80%)	(560,000)
P's share of goodwill	$ 190,000
Total goodwill	$ 200,000
Less: P's share of goodwill	(190,000)
Noncontrolling interest share of goodwill	$ 10,000

Note: The total goodwill is first applied to the controlling interest (P). If in this example there was only $150,000 of goodwill it all would be allocated to the controlling interest. The goodwill is not apportioned according to the ratio of ownership. For example, the controlling interest does **not** get 80% of $200,000, or just $160,000, and the noncontrolling interest is not allocated 20% of $200,000, or the other $40,000.

2. Gain From Bargain Purchase A bargain purchase is a business combination in which the fair value of the recognized identifiable net assets acquired exceeds the fair value of the acquirer's interest in the acquiree plus the recognized amount of any noncontrolling interest in the acquiree. In such cases, the acquirer should reassess whether it has correctly identified all of the assets acquired and all of the liabilities assumed and should recognize any additional assets or liabilities that are noted in that review. The objective of the review is to ensure that the measurements appropriately reflect consideration of all available information as of the acquisition date.

If the excess remains after reassessing all assets and liabilities and reviewing the procedures used to measure their amounts, the acquirer shall recognize the resulting gain in earnings on the acquisition date. The gain shall be attributed to the acquirer.

Example 6 ▸ Bargain Purchase With Noncontrolling Interest

On January 1, year 1, Parent Inc., (P) acquired 80% of Subsidiary Corp.'s (S) 100,000 shares of outstanding stock for $500,000 cash. This was the first acquisition of any of S's shares by P. The net book value of S is $700,000 and the fair value of S's assets and liabilities is equal to the book value. The fair value of the noncontrolling interest is determined to be $150,000.

Required: Determine the total amount of the bargain purchase and the amount attributed to both P and the noncontrolling interest recognized on the acquisition date.

Solution:

The net book value of S is $700,000 and the fair value of the assets and liabilities is equal to the book value so the fair value of S is also worth $700,000. P acquired S for $500,000 cash and the fair value of the noncontrolling interest is $150,000. The $500,000 cash + $150,000 fair value of noncontrolling interest – $700,000 fair value of S = $50,000 of bargain purchase recognized on the acquisition date. The entire gain in a bargain purchase is attributed to the acquirer. Thus P recognizes a $50,000 gain and the noncontrolling interest doesn't have any.

3. **Consideration Transferred** The consideration transferred in a business combination shall be measured at fair value, which shall be calculated as the sum of the acquisition-date fair values of the assets transferred by the acquirer, the liabilities acquired by the acquirer to former owners of the acquiree, and the equity interests issued by the acquirer.

   a. Potential forms of consideration include cash, other assets, a business or a subsidiary of the acquirer, contingent consideration, common or preferred equity instruments, options, warrants, and member interests of mutual entities.

   b. The consideration transferred may include assets or liabilities of the acquirer that have carrying amounts that differ from their fair values at the acquisition date. If so, the acquirer shall remeasure the transferred assets or liabilities to their fair values as of the acquisition date and recognize the resulting gains and losses, if any, in earnings. If the transferred assets or liabilities remain within the combined entity after the business combination the acquirer retains control of them. In that case, the acquirer shall measure those assets and liabilities at their carrying amounts immediately before the acquisition date and shall not recognize any gain or loss.

   c. The consideration the acquirer transfers in exchange for the acquiree includes any asset or liability resulting from a contingent consideration arrangement. The acquirer shall recognize the acquisition-date fair value of contingent consideration as part of the consideration transferred in exchange for the acquiree.

      (1) The acquirer shall classify an obligation to pay contingent consideration as a liability or as equity in accordance with applicable GAAP.

      (2) The acquirer shall classify as an asset a right to the return of previously transferred consideration if specified conditions are met.

4. **Disclosures** The notes to the financial statements of a combined entity should include, at a minimum, the following:

   - A qualitative description of the factors that make up the goodwill recognized
   - The amount of goodwill that is expected to be deductible for income tax purposes
   - The amount of goodwill by reportable segment.

III. Consolidations

A. Overview

Subsequent to a business combination, the newly affiliated companies continue to maintain their separate accounting records. Consolidated financial statements are required when a company owns more than 50% of the voting stock of another firm, with few exceptions.

1. **Policy** All subsidiaries—that is, all entities in which a parent has a controlling financial interest—shall be consolidated. A difference in fiscal periods of a periods of a parent and subsidiary does not justify the exclusion of the subsidiary from consolidation. Consolidation procedures must be performed every period in which financial statements are presented. Consolidated financial statements shall disclose the consolidation policy that is being followed. In most cases this is made apparent by the headings or other information in the financial statements, but in some cases a footnote is required.

2. **Exceptions** A majority-owned entity shall not be consolidated if control is temporary or does not rest with the majority owner. For example, if the entity is in legal reorganization or in bankruptcy or operates under foreign exchange restrictions, controls, or other governmentally imposed uncertainties so severe that they cast significant doubt on the parent's ability to control the entity.

3. **Consolidation Versus Equity Method** Under both the equity method and consolidations, the income and balance sheet effects of intercompany transactions are eliminated. For consolidations, the details for all of the entities are shown on the financial statements. Conversely, under the equity method, the investment is shown as a single amount on the investor balance sheet, and earnings or losses are usually represented by a single amount on the income statement; hence, the equity method is often referred to as a one-line consolidation.

B. Procedures

When a subsidiary is initially consolidated during the year, the consolidated financial statements shall include the subsidiary's revenues, expenses, gains and losses only from the date the subsidiary is initially consolidated. In the preparation of consolidated financial statements, intercompany balances and transactions shall be eliminated. The eliminations and adjustments made as part of the consolidation procedures are **not** entered into the books of any of the companies; these are simply worksheet entries that are never formally journalized. Consolidation procedures involve the following:

1. **Eliminate Capital and Investment Accounts** Entries to eliminate the subsidiary's capital accounts (except for noncontrolling interest, if any), and the parent's investment account. Any shares of the parent held by a subsidiary shall not be treated as outstanding shares and, therefore, shall be eliminated in the consolidated financial statements and reflected as treasury shares.

2. **Eliminate Intercompany Balances** This includes intercompany open account balances, security holdings, sales and purchases, interest, dividends, etc.

3. **Eliminate Intercompany Transactions** Consolidated financial statements should not include gain or loss on transactions among entities in the consolidated group. Accordingly, any intercompany income or loss on assets remaining within the group shall be eliminated. If income taxes have been paid on intercompany profits on assets remaining within the consolidated group, those taxes shall be deferred or the intercompany profits to be eliminated in consolidation shall be appropriately reduced.

Example 7 ▸ 100% Acquisition

The December 31, year 3, trial balances of Parent Inc., (P) and Subsidiary Corporation (S) are reproduced in the first two columns of the worksheet solution. P acquired its 100% interest in the common stock of S on January 1, year 3, for $120,000 cash. At the time of acquisition, S had assets with a book value of $110,000 and liabilities with a book value $15,000. The recorded amounts of all assets and liabilities of S were deemed to approximate their FV, except land, which was undervalued by $25,000 in S's books. S had $20,000 of net income for the year and as of December 31 P had not recorded any portion of S's net income.

Required: Provide elimination entries to consolidate the financial statements of P and S.

Solution: Three steps are recommended before attempting to complete the consolidation worksheet.

Step 1: Determine the fair value of S at the time of the 100% stock acquisition by P.

BV of assets assumed – BV of liabilities acquired +/– fair value adjustments = FV of S at acquisition

$110,000 – $15,000 = BV of S	$ 95,000
Fair value adjustments	25,000
FV of S, January 1, year 3	$ 120,000

Step 2: Determine amount of noncontrolling interests (NCI), if any.

P acquired 100% interest so there is no NCI.	$ 0

Step 3: Determine amount of goodwill or bargain purchase, if any.

Purchase price	$ 120,000
Plus: FV of NCI (Step 2)	0
Less: FV of S (Step 1)	(120,000)
Goodwill	$ 0

Consolidation Worksheet, 100% Ownership

	Trial Balance Dr. (Cr.)		Eliminations		Controlling R/E	Consolidated Balance Sheet	
	P	S	Dr.	Cr.	Dr. (Cr.)	Dr.	Cr.
Current assets	50,000	20,000				70,000	
Land	200,000	105,000	[1] 25,000			330,000	
Investment in S	120,000		[2] 20,000	[1] 25,000			
				[3] 115,000			
Liabilities	(70,000)	(10,000)					80,000
C/S, $1 par (P)	(100,000)						100,000
R/E, Dec. 31, yr 3 (P)	(200,000)			[2] 20,000	(220,000)		
C/S, $2 par (S)		(20,000)	[3] 20,000				
R/E, Dec 31, yr 3 (S)		(95,000)	[3] 95,000				
	0	0	160,000	160,000			
Consolidated R/E					(220,000)		220,000
						400,000	400,000

Worksheet entries:

[1] To write land up to FV at time of acquisition.
[2] To record net income of S accruing to P (100%).
[3] To eliminate 100% of S capital account balances.

Example 8 ▸ 100% Acquisition With Goodwill

Same scenario as Example 7, except P acquired 100% interest in the common stock of S for $150,000 cash.

Required: Provide elimination entries to consolidate the financial statements of P and S.

Solution: Three steps are recommended before attempting to complete the consolidation worksheet.

Step 1: Determine the fair value of S at the time of the 100% stock acquisition by P.

BV of assets assumed – BV of liabilities acquired +/– fair value adjustments = FV of S at acquisition

$110,000 – $15,000 = BV of S	$ 95,000
Fair value adjustments	25,000
FV of S, January 1, year 3	$ 120,000

Step 2: Determine amount of noncontrolling interests (NCI), if any.

P acquired 100% interest so there is no NCI.	$ 0

Step 3: Determine amount of goodwill or bargain purchase, if any.

Purchase price	$ 150,000
Plus: FV of NCI (Step 2)	0
Less: FV of S (Step 1)	(120,000)
Goodwill	$ 30,000

Consolidation Worksheet, 100% Ownership

	Trial Balance Dr. (Cr.)		Eliminations		Controlling R/E	Consolidated Balance Sheet	
	P	S	Dr.	Cr.	Dr. (Cr.)	Dr.	Cr.
Current assets	50,000	20,000				70,000	
Land	200,000	105,000	[1] 25,000			330,000	
Investment in S	150,000		[3] 20,000	[1] 25,000 [2] 30,000 [4] 115,000			
Goodwill			[2] 30,000			30,000	
Liabilities	(70,000)	(10,000)					80,000
C/S, $1 par (P)	(100,000)						100,000
R/E, Dec. 31, yr 3 (P)	(230,000)			[3] 20,000	(250,000)		
C/S, $2 par (S)		(20,000)	[4] 20,000				
R/E, Dec 31, yr 3 (S)		(95,000)	[4] 95,000				
	0	0	190,000	190,000			
Consolidated R/E					(250,000)		250,000
						430,000	430,000

Worksheet entries:

[1] To write land up to FV at time of acquisition.
[2] To record the goodwill at time of acquisition.
[3] To record net income of S accruing to P (100%).
[4] To eliminate 100% of S capital account balances.

Example 9 ▶ 80% Acquisition

Same scenario as Example 7, except P acquired only 80% interest in S for $96,000 cash.

Required: Provide elimination entries to consolidate the financial statements of P and S.

Solution: Three steps are recommended before attempting to complete the consolidation worksheet.

Step 1: Determine the fair value of S at the time of the 100% stock acquisition by P.

BV of assets assumed – BV of liabilities acquired +/– fair value adjustments = FV of S at acquisition

$110,000 – $15,000 = BV of S	$ 95,000
Fair value adjustments	25,000
FV of S, January 1, year 3	$ 120,000

Step 2: Determine amount of noncontrolling interests (NCI), if any, at acquisition.

Because no fair value of NCI was given, you must infer what the fair value would be based upon the price paid by P.

80% of X = $96,000; X = $96,000 / 0.80 = $120,000	$ 120,000
Times: NCI of 20%	0.20
Fair value of NCI	$ 24,000

Step 3: Determine amount of goodwill or bargain purchase, if any, at acquisition.

Purchase price	$ 96,000
Plus: FV of NCI (Step 2)	24,000
Less: FV of S (Step 1)	(120,000)
Goodwill	$ 0

Consolidation Worksheet, 80% Ownership

	Trial Balance Dr. (Cr.)		Eliminations		Noncontrolling Interest	Controlling R/E	Consolidated Balance Sheet	
	P	S	Dr.	Cr.	Dr. (Cr.)	Dr. (Cr.)	Dr.	Cr.
Current assets	50,000	20,000					70,000	
Land	200,000	105,000	[1] 25,000				330,000	
Investment in S	96,000		[2] 16,000	[1] 20,000				
				[3] 92,000				
Liabilities	(70,000)	(10,000)						80,000
C/S, $1 par (P)	(100,000)							100,000
R/E, Dec. 31, yr 3 (P)	(176,000)			[2] 16,000		(192,000)		
C/S, $2 par (S)		(20,000)	[3] 20,000					
R/E, Dec 31, yr 3 (S)		(95,000)	[3] 95,000					
NCI				[1] 5,000	(5,000)			
				[3] 4,000	(4,000)			
				[3] 19,000	(19,000)			
	0	0	156,000	156,000				
NCI					(28,000)			28,000
Consolidated R/E						(192,000)		192,000
							400,000	400,000

Worksheet entries:

[1] To write land up to FV at time of acquisition. (P allocated 80% of $25,000 = $20,000; rest to NCI)

[2] To record net income of S accruing to P (80% × $20,000 = $16,000).

[3] To eliminate 80% of S capital account balances attributed to P and record noncontrolling interest.

Note: Notice that NCI at the acquisition date had a fair value of $24,000 and in the consolidated worksheet has a balance of $28,000. The difference, 428,000 – $24,000 = $4,000 is the amount of S's income that was not attributable to P.

C. Intercompany Transactions

1. **Receivables and Payables** Originate from intercompany transactions such as the sale of inventory and fixed assets or the rendering of services. These receivables and payables appear in the affiliated company's trial balance at the end of the period; note, however, that no asset or liability exists outside the consolidated group. Elimination of the receivable/payable simply involves a "worksheet entry" reversing the original recording.

2. **Loans** These must also be eliminated from consolidated statements, in a manner similar to that used for receivables and payables. In addition, interest income and expense and interest accruals must be eliminated.

Example 10 ▸ Intercompany Loans

P lent $10,000 on June 1, year 1 to S, its 90% owned subsidiary. The note is to be repaid May 30, year 2, with 12% interest. Partial trial balances of P and S are reproduced below.

	P	S
Note receivable—S	10,000	
Accrued interest on note	600	
Note payable—P		(10,000)
Accrued interest on note		(600)
Sales revenue	(50,000)	(20,000)
Interest revenue	(600)	0
Expenses	36,000	17,000
Interest expense		600
	$ 0	$ 0

Required: Provide the elimination entries related to the intercompany note. Also, compute consolidated net income and allocate it to controlling and noncontrolling interest.

Solution: Note that whereas interest is not an expense for the consolidated entity, it is nevertheless a cost of doing business for S. It must be included in S's net income in order to determine the noncontrolling interest in S's net income.

	Dr	Cr
Notes Payable	10,000	
Accrued Interest Payable	600	
Notes Receivable		10,000
Accrued Interest Receivable		600
To eliminate intercompany receivable/payable and related accrued interest		
Interest Income	600	
Interest Expense		600
To eliminate interest income and expense on intercompany notes		

	P	S	Consolidated
Sales Revenue (CR)	$(50,000)	$(20,000)	$ (70,000)
Expenses	36,000	17,000	53,000
Noncontrolling interest in net income, 10% × ($20,000 – $17,000 – $600)			240
Controlling interest in net income			$ (16,760)

3. **Sales and Cost of Goods Sold** The sale and CGS are recorded twice: first, the seller records a sale and related CGS as the merchandise is "sold" to the affiliated buyer; secondly, the buyer resells the goods to outsiders, also recording a sale and CGS. For consolidated purposes, however, it is obvious that only one sale has occurred.

4. **Gross Profit** When one company sells merchandise to its affiliate at a price above cost, the ending inventory of the buyer contains an element of unrealized gross profit. The gross profit is not realized to the economic entity until it is sold to outsiders. The preparation of consolidated financial statements requires that unrealized gross profit be eliminated.

5. **Noncontrolling Interest** Noncontrolling interest in the subsidiary's income must be based on the sales and CGS originally reported by the subsidiary. As was the case in interaffiliate interest income and expense, the noncontrolling interest income should reflect the expense incurred (or revenues obtained) in intercompany transactions. The sale, however, may not be recognized until after the goods have been sold to an outside buyer.

Example 11 ▸ Intercompany Sales of Inventory

Parent sells merchandise to its 90% owned Sub at 25% above cost. The following chart summarizes the transactions in intercompany sales at year-end.

	Parent's sales price (= cost to Sub)	Cost	Parent's gross profit	
Beginning inventory 1/1	$ 50,000	$ 40,000	$ 10,000	(realized)
Sales	200,000	160,000	40,000	
Total	250,000	200,000	50,000	
Ending inventory 12/1	(75,000)	(60,000)	(15,000)	(unrealized)
Cost of goods sold	$175,000	$140,000	$ 35,000	

Required: Provide the consolidation elimination entries.

Solution:

		Dr.	Cr.
(1)	R/E	10,000	
	CGS		10,000
	To adjust beginning R/E and CGS for the overstated beginning inventory		
(2)	Sales	200,000	
	Purchases		200,000
	To eliminate intercompany sales and purchases		
(3)	CGS	15,000	
	Inventory		15,000
	To eliminate unrealized gross profit in ending inventory		

6. **Sales of Fixed Assets** Sales of fixed assets between members of an affiliated group may result in the recognition of gain or loss by the seller, if the selling price differs from the carrying amount of the asset. Again, no gain or loss has taken place for the consolidated entity; assets have merely been transferred from one set of books to another. Additional complications result from the fact that the buyer of the asset will record it in its books at the agreed upon purchase price; subsequent depreciation charges will be based upon this purchase price, thus requiring adjustment. In summary, an interaffiliate sale of fixed assets involves the following.

   a. In the year of sale, restore the carrying amount of the asset to its original BV and eliminate the gain (loss) recorded by the seller.

b. For each period, adjust depreciation expense and accumulated depreciation to reflect the original BV of the asset.

c. For periods subsequent to the year of sale, R/E must be adjusted to eliminate the gain (loss) contained therein. If the parent is the seller, controlling interest R/E absorbs the entire adjustment. If a less than 100 percent owned subsidiary is the seller, the adjustment to R/E should be allocated to the controlling and noncontrolling interests on the basis of their ownership ratio.

Example 12 ▸ Intercompany Sale of Depreciable Assets

Parent sells machinery for $1,500 to its wholly owned subsidiary. The machinery cost Parent $2,000 and accumulated depreciation at date of sale was $1,000. Parent had been depreciating the machinery on the SL method over a 10-year life. Sub continues this depreciation method.

Required: Provide the elimination entries at the end of years 1 and 2.

Solution: The debit to RE is $400 ($500 – $100). Thus, the yearly indirect increase in consolidated income (from decreasing depreciation expense) will cause the $500 gain to be fully recognized by the seller by the end of the fifth year, when the asset is fully depreciated.

Year 1	Gain on Intercompany Sale of Assets	500	
	Machinery	500	
	Accumulated Depreciation		1,000
	To eliminate gain and restore asset and accumulated depreciation accounts to their original balances		
	Accumulated Depreciation	100*	
	Depreciation Expense ($500 / 5)		100*
	To adjust consolidated depreciation charges		

* Gain / Life remaining to buyer = Depreciation elimination per year

Year 2	Retained Earnings	400	
	Machinery	500	
	Accumulated Depreciation		800
	Depreciation Expense		100

7. **Intercompany Bonds** A direct sale and purchase of bonds between affiliates poses problems similar to the interaffiliate lending and borrowing transactions already discussed. Intercompany receivables and payables (including accrued interest) must be eliminated, as well as interest income/expense. Note that in a direct acquisition of bonds, no gain or loss results to either party, even if a premium or discount is involved, since the net carrying amount of the bond liability on the issuer's books will always equal the bond investment amount on the purchaser's books.

Example 13 ▸ Direct Sale of Bonds

Parent purchases $100,000 bonds from Sub on December 31, year 1. The bonds' stated interest rate is 10%. Parent pays $110,000 for the bonds. The effective interest rate of the bonds is 8%.

Required: Prepare the consolidation elimination entry at the date of the transaction and at December 31, year 2.

Solution: On December 31, year 1, the following journal entries were made on the books of the acquirer and the issuer.

Acquirer (Parent)			Issuer (Sub)		
Investment in Bonds	110,000		Cash	110,000	
Cash		110,000	Bonds Payable		100,000
			Premium on Bonds		10,000

The consolidation elimination entry required is

Bond Premium	10,000	
Bonds Payable	100,000	
Investment in Bonds		110,000

During Year 2, the following journal entries would be made to record income and expenses.

Acquirer			Issuer		
Cash	10,000		Interest Expense	8,800*	
Interest Income		8,800*	Bond Premium	1,200	
Bond Investment		1,200	Cash		10,000

* Interest income or expense = Effective interest rate × Net carrying amount (8% × $110,000).

The consolidation elimination entries required at the end of Year 2 are as follows.

Interest Income	8,800	
Interest Expense		8,800
Bonds Payable	100,000	
Bond Premium	8,800	
Investment in Bonds		108,800

8. **Third Party** A member of an affiliated group may issue its bonds to outsiders. These bonds may then be purchased from the outside parties by a second affiliate.

   a. For consolidated purposes, the bonds have been retired, since they are no longer held by outsiders.

   b. A gain or loss will typically result from the acquisition by the second affiliate of bonds originally issued by the first affiliate to outsiders. This occurs because the FV of bonds at the time of reacquisition is likely different than the carrying amount of the bond obligation on the issuer's books. No gain or loss is recorded by individual affiliates, yet a gain or loss on retirement must be recognized at the consolidated level.

   c. This gain or loss will be periodically recognized by the issuer as the difference between interest expense to the issuer and interest income to the purchaser. Upon maturity of the bond issue, the entire consolidated gain (loss) realized at the time of reacquisition of the bond will have been amortized and no further adjustments will be necessary.

Example 14 ▶ Bonds Originally Issued to Third Parties (face amount)

P owns a 90% interest in S, acquired several years ago. P accounts for its investment in S under the equity method. No intercompany sales of fixed assets or inventories have taken place.

- On January 1, year 1, S issued to outsiders $100,000, 8%, 10-year bonds at face amount. Interest is paid annually, on December 30.
- On January 1, year 3, P bought the entire bond issue, when the prevailing interest rate for that type of bond was 12%.
- Operating income before interest charges and revenue was as follows:

Year	P	S
3	$55,000	$33,000
4	60,000	30,000

- Present value rates provided are:

  Present value of $1 in 8 years at 12% is 0.40388
  Present value of $1 annuity due in 8 years at 12% is 4.96764

Required: Provide elimination entries and allocate consolidated income to the noncontrolling and controlling interest for (a) year 3, and (b) year 4. Round all calculations to the nearest dollar and ignore income taxes.

Solution: A gain is calculated and recognized as follows.

$100,000 × 0.40388 =	$40,388
$ 8,000 × 4.96764 =	39,741
	$80,129

Carrying amount of bonds in S books	$100,000
Less: Price paid by P to acquire bonds	(80,129)
Gain on retirement	$ 19,871

a. The following entries would have been made by P and S during year 3

P			S		
Cash	8,000		Interest Expense	8,000	
Investment in S Bonds	1,615		Cash		8,000
Interest Income		9,615			

Elimination entries are illustrated by the following partial consolidation worksheet:

	P Dr. (Cr.)	S Dr. (Cr.)	Eliminations Dr.	Eliminations Cr.	Consolidated Income Statement Dr. (Cr.)
Invest. in S bonds ($80,129 + $1,615)	81,744			81,744	
Bonds payable		(100,000)	100,000		
Operating income (excluding interest)	(55,000)	(33,000)			(88,000)
Interest income	(9,615)		9,615		
Interest expense		8,000		8,000	
Gain on retirement of S bonds				19,871	(19,871)
			109,615	109,615	
Consolidated NI (Cr)					(107,856)

Noncontrolling interest, 10% ($33,000 – $8,000 – $1,615 + $19,871)*	$ 4,326
Controlling interest, $55,000 + $9,615 + (90% × $43,256)	103,545
	$107,871

* The entire gain on retirement is allocated to S, and interest expense is adjusted to reflect the current rate (12%). To understand the reasoning behind this, assume two transactions:

(1) S retires $100,000 BV bonds at a cost of $80,144, realizing a $19,856 gain.

(2) S reissues debt for $80,144 at face value. The interest rate on this debt is the prevailing rate, or 12%; therefore, interest expense for Year 3 is $8,000 + $1,617 = $9,617 (i.e., 12% × $80,144).

b. The following entries would have been made by P and S during year 4.

P			S		
Cash	8,000		Interest Expense	8,000	
Bond Investment	1,809		Cash		8,000
Interest Income					
($81,744 × 12%)		9,809			

	P Dr. (Cr.)	S Dr. (Cr.)	Eliminations Dr.	Eliminations Cr.	Consolidated Income Statement Dr.(Cr.)
Invest. in S bonds					
(81,744 + 1,809)	83,553			83,553	
Bonds payable		(100,000)	100,000		
Operating income					
(excluding interest)	(60,000)	(30,000)			(90,000)
Interest income	(9,811)		9,811		
Interest expense		8,000		8,000	
Retained earnings, P	(XXX)			16,430*	
Retained earnings, S		(XX)		1,826*	
			109,809	109,809	
Consolidated NI (Cr)					(90,000)

Noncontrolling interest, 10% × ($30,000 – $8,000 – $1,809)	$ 2,019
Controlling interest, $60,000 + $9,809 + (90% × $20,191)	87,981
	$ 90,000

* Consolidated R/E must include the gain on retirement of the bonds ($19,871) less the amount amortized prior to year 4 ($1,615 additional interest expense charged to S in year 3, see part a, above). The remaining adjustment to R/E of $18,256 is allocated to the controlling and minority interests in proportion to their ownership percentage.

Example 15 ▶ Bonds Originally Issued to Third Parties at Discount

P owns a 90% interest in S, acquired several years ago. P accounts for its investment in S under the equity method. No intercompany sales of fixed assets or inventories have taken place.

- On January 1, year 1, S issued to outside parties $100,000, 8% bonds to yield 9% and due to mature on December 31, year 4.
- On January 1, year 3, P bought the entire bond issue, when the prevailing interest rate for that type of bond was 12%.
- Operating income before interest charges and revenue was as follows:

Year	P	S
3	$80,000	$35,000
4	90,000	38,000

- Present value rates provided are:

  Present value of $1 in 4 years at 9% is 0.70843
  Present value of $1 annuity due in 4 years at 9% is 3.23972
  Present value of $1 in 2 years at 12% is 0.79719
  Present value of $1 annuity due in 2 years at 12% is 1.69005

Required: Provide the consolidation worksheet entries to eliminate the intercompany bonds and allocate consolidated net income to the minority and controlling interests for (a) year 3, and (b) year 4. Round all calculations to the nearest dollar and ignore income taxes..

Solution:

$100,000 × 0.70843	$ 70,843
$ 8,000 × 3.23972	25,918
Bond issue price, January 1, year 1	96,761
Face amount	100,000
Discount, January 1, year 1	$ 3,239

Table 1—S Discount Amortization Schedule

Date	Cash payment	Interest expense	Amortization	Carrying amount
Jan. 1, year 1				$ 96,761
Dec. 31, year 1	$8,000	$8,708	$708	97,469
Dec. 31, year 2	8,000	8,772	772	98,241
Dec. 31, year 3	8,000	8,842	842	99,083
Dec. 31, year 4	8,000	8,917	917	100,000

$100,000 × 0.79719	$79,719
$ 8,000 × 1.69005	13,520
Retirement price	93,239
Carrying amount in S books (Table 1)	98,241
Consolidated gain on retirement	$ 5,002

Table 2—P Discount Amortization Schedule

Date	Cash payment	Interest expense	Amortization	Carrying amount
Jan. 1, year 3				$ 93,239
Dec. 31, year 3	$8,000	$11,189	$3,189	96,428
Dec. 31, year 4	8,000	11,572*	3,572*	100,000

* Remaining amortization amount, $1 difference in calculation due to rounding

a. Year 3 Partial Consolidation Worksheet

	P Dr. (Cr.)	S Dr. (Cr.)	Eliminations Dr.	Eliminations Cr.	Consolidated Income Statement Dr.(Cr.)
Investment in S bonds (Table 2)	96,428			96,428	
Bonds payable		(100,000)	100,000		
Discount (Table 1)		917		917	
Operating income (Cr) (excluding interest)	(80,000)	(35,000)			(115,000)
Int. income (Table 2)	(11,189)		11,189		
Int. expense (Table 1)		8,842		8,842	
Gain on retirement				5,002	(5,002)
			111,189	111,189	
Consolidated NI (Cr)					(120,002)
Noncontrolling interest, 10% ($35,000 – $11,189 + $5,002)					$ 2,881
Controlling interest, $80,000 + $11,189 + 90% ($28,813)					117,121
					$ 120,002

b. Year 4 Partial Consolidation Worksheet

	P Dr. (Cr.)	S Dr. (Cr.)	Eliminations Dr.	Eliminations Cr.	Consolidated Income Statement Dr.(Cr.)
Investment in S bonds (Table 2)	100,000			100,000	
Bonds payable		(100,000)	100,000		
Operating income (Cr) (excluding interest)	(90,000)	(38,000)			(128,000)
Int. income (Table 2)	(11,572)		11,572		
Int. expense (Table 1)		8,917		8,917	
R/E, P	(XXXX)			2,390*	
R/E, S		(XX)		265*	
			111,572	111,572	
Consolidated NI (Cr)					(128,000)
Noncontrolling interest, 10% ($38,000 – $11,572)					$ 2,643
Controlling interest, $90,000 + $11,572 + 90% ($26,428)					125,357
					$ 128,000

---

* Gain on requirement of S bonds		$ 5,002
Interest income, P	$ 8,842	
Interest expense, S	(11,189)	
Less: Year 3 amortization:		(2,347)
Unamortized gain, adjust beginning R/E		$ 2,655
Noncontrolling interest, 10%		$ 265 (Rounded down to keep even)
Controlling interest, 90%		2,390
		$ 2,655

IV. Variable Interest Entities

A. Overview

Financial statements should include the consolidated financial results of all entities in which the reporting entity has a controlling financial interest. There are ways to have a controlling financial interest other than through ownership of a majority voting interest, and conversely, ownership of a majority voting interest may not provide a controlling financial interest. For example, a majority-owned subsidiary should not be consolidated if another party has a controlling financial interest.

B. Definitions

1. **Legal Entity** GAAP defines an entity as any legal structure used to conduct activities or to hold assets. Entities subject to GAAP guidance include: corporations, partnerships, limited liability companies, majority-owned subsidiaries, and grantor trusts.

2. **Variable Interest** Variable interests are investments or other interests that will absorb portions of a variable interest entity's expected losses or receive portions of the entity's expected residual returns. Generally, assets create variability and are not variable interests, while liabilities, equity, and guarantees absorb the variability and are variable interests. For example, the fair value of an equity interest in an entity increases and decreases with increases and decreases in the fair value of the entity's net assets, and the fair value of an obligation under a guarantee of the entity's debt increases and decreases with decreases and increases in the fair value of the entity's net assets.

3. **Variable Interest Entity** A variable interest entity, ordinarily referred to as a VIE, is a legal entity subject to consolidation according to GAAP. Generally, whether an entity is subject to consolidation under GAAP, and is therefore a VIE, depends on whether the entity's equity investors have a sufficient amount of equity investment at risk and the characteristics of a controlling financial interest. In those cases, focusing on voting interests is usually ineffective for determining if a controlling financial interest exists.

4. **Primary Beneficiary** The entity that consolidates a variable interest entity is called the primary beneficiary of that variable interest entity. An entity should determine whether it is the primary beneficiary of a variable interest entity at the time the entity becomes involved with the variable interest entity and should reconsider, on an ongoing basis, whether it is the primary beneficiary of the variable interest entity.

   Only one entity (if any) is expected to be identified as the primary beneficiary of a VIE. Although more than one entity could meet the losses/benefits criterion, only one entity (if any) will have the power to direct the activities of a VIE that most significantly impact the entity's economic performance.

C. Controlling Interest

In assessing whether an entity has a controlling financial interest in another entity, it should consider the entity's purpose and design, including the risks that the entity was designed to create and pass through to its variable interest holders. If equity is sufficient and the equity investors have the characteristics of a controlling financial interest, the entity is not subject to consolidation under the VIE model and, therefore, is not a VIE. However, it would be subject to consolidation under the voting interest entity model if a single equity investor holds a majority voting interest or has a controlling financial interest some other way. If equity is not sufficient or the equity investors do not have the characteristics of a controlling financial interest, the entity is subject to consolidation under the VIE model and, therefore, is a variable interest entity.

Further consideration is required when any of the following conditions exist:

- The reporting entity, its related parties, or both participated significantly in designing the entity.
- The entity is designed so that substantially all of its activities involve or are conducted on behalf of the reporting entity and its related parties.
- The reporting entity and its related parties provide more than half of the equity investment and similar forms of subordinated financial support for the entity.
- The entity's activities are primarily related to securitizations or other forms of asset-backed financings or single-lessee leasing arrangements.

D. Identification of a VIE

A legal entity is subject to consolidation under the variable interest entities guidance if, by design, any of the following conditions exist (the phrase by design refers to legal entities that meet these conditions because of the way they are structured):

1. **Risk** The total equity investment (equity investments in a legal entity are interests that are required to be reported as equity in that entity's financial statements) at risk is not sufficient to permit the legal entity to finance its activities without additional subordinated financial support provided by any parties, including equity holders

2. **Lack of Criteria** As a group, the holders of the equity investment at risk lack any one of the following three characteristics:

   a. The power, through voting rights or similar rights, to direct the activities of a legal entity that most significantly affect the entity's economic performance.

   b. The obligation to absorb the expected losses of the legal entity.

   c. The right to receive the expected residual returns of the legal entity.

3. **Measurement** GAAP provides guidance related to the initial and subsequent measurement of assets, liabilities, and noncontrolling interests of newly consolidated variable interest entities. The subsequent accounting for a consolidated variable interest entity is essentially the same as the accounting for any other consolidated subsidiary.

E. Characteristics

The reporting entity with a variable interest or interests that provide the reporting entity with a controlling financial interest in a variable interest entity will have both of the following characteristics:

1. The power to direct the activities of a variable interest entity that most significantly affect the variable interest entity's economic performance.

2. The obligation to absorb losses of the variable interest entity that could potentially be significant to the variable interest entity or the right to receive benefits from the variable interest entity that could potentially be significant to the variable interest entity.

Generally, the assessments of whether an entity is a VIE and, if so, whether consolidation is required should be made based on when the reporting entity first becomes involved with the entity, which ordinarily is near its inception, and should only be reconsidered if one or more prescribed reconsideration events occur.

F. Disclosures

Beginning with calendar-year 2010 financial statements, it became significant to note that VIE disclosures have been significantly-enhanced even in circumstances where reporting entities are not deemed to be primary beneficiaries of affiliated entities. Disclosures about variable interest entities may be reported in the aggregate for similar entities where it is determined that separating the disclosures would not provide more useful information for decision-making by end-users of the statements.

1. **Aggregated Entities** When disclosures of similar entities are aggregated, disclosures would need to include information about how those entities have been aggregated. Additionally, disclosures need to clearly-distinguish between information disclosed about consolidated VIEs and disclosures about VIEs where reporting entities have made the assessment that there is no need to consolidate the entities in that they are not primary beneficiaries of the VIEs.

2. **Primary Beneficiary** The following types of issues, while not an all-inclusive listing, need to be addressed in financial statements of reporting entities that are deemed to be primary beneficiaries of VIEs:

   - Methodologies used in determining that reporting entities constitute primary beneficiaries, including significant judgments and assumptions used in making those determinations.

   - When there is a change in primary beneficiary status in the current reporting period, the primary factors resulting in that change and any effects of the change in the financial statements.

   - Any explicit or implicit financial or other support that has been provided to the affiliated entities that were not previously required contractually, to include the type and amount of support, and including circumstances where reporting entities provided help to VIEs in obtaining support, along with the primary reasons that the support was provided.

   - Qualitative and quantitative information about involvement of reporting entities with VIEs, to include information about both explicit arrangements and implicit variable interests.

   - The nature, purpose, size, activities, and financing of the VIEs.

   - Any gain or loss recognized on initial consolidation of VIEs.

   - Classification and carrying amounts of liabilities, to include qualitative information about the relationship between those assets and liabilities.

   - Information related to creditors or beneficial interest holders of VIEs having or lacking recourse to the general credit of the primary reporting entities.

   - Terms and arrangements that could require primary beneficiaries to provide financial support to VIEs, to include events or circumstances that could expose reporting entities to potential losses.

3. **Non Primary Beneficiaries** Depending on facts and circumstances associated with each arrangement, reporting entities that are not primary beneficiaries will need to have fairly-robust disclosures addressing relationships with affiliated entities, including:

- Methodologies used in determining that reporting entities are not primary beneficiaries, including significant judgments and assumptions used in making those determinations.
- When there is a change in primary beneficiary status in the current reporting period, the primary factors resulting in that change and any effects of the change in the financial statements.
- Any explicit or implicit financial or other support that has been provided to the affiliated entities that were not previously required contractually, to include the type and amount of support, and including circumstances where reporting entities provided help to VIEs in obtaining support, along with the primary reasons that the support was provided.
- Qualitative and quantitative information about involvement of reporting entities with VIEs, to include information about both explicit arrangements and implicit variable interests.
- The nature, purpose, size, activities, and financing of the VIEs.
- Classification and carrying amounts of assets and liabilities in the financial statements that relate to variable interests in VIEs.
- The maximum exposure to loss due to involvement with VIEs, how that maximum exposure has been determined, and the significant sources of exposure to the VIEs, or a statement that the maximum exposure to loss cannot be quantified.
- When a conclusion has been reached that power is shared related to directing activities of VIEs that most significantly-impact economic performance of the VIEs, and the significant factors considered, along with judgments made, in making those assessments.

V. Noncontrolling Interests

A. Similar Economic Interests

The FASB's view is that the consolidated financial statements should be presented as if the parent company investors and the other minority investors in partially owned subsidiaries have similar economic interests in a single entity. Therefore, minority shareholders are viewed as having an interest in the consolidated reporting entity. As a result, the investments of these minority shareholders, previously recorded between liabilities and equity (i.e., the "mezzanine" section), are now reported as equity in the parent company's consolidated financial statements.

B. Reporting of Gains and Losses

Since the noncontrolling interests are considered equity of the entire reporting entity, transactions between the parent company and the noncontrolling interests are treated as transactions between shareholders, provided that the transactions do not create a change in control. This means that no gains or losses are recognized in earnings for transactions between the parent company and the noncontrolling interests, unless control is achieved or lost.

C. **Step Acquisitions**

Under GAAP, when a business combination is achieved in stages, the acquirer's interest in the acquiree includes the acquisition-date fair value of the equity interest the acquirer held in the acquiree before control is obtained. The carrying amounts of the previously acquired tranches are adjusted to fair value as of the date control is obtained (the acquisition date), and the acquirer recognizes the differences as a gain or loss in income at the acquisition date. Amounts the acquirer previously recognized in accumulated other comprehensive income (e.g., cumulative translation adjustments recognized during the period the equity method was used to account for the investment tranches) would be included in the gain or loss recognized in income at the date control is obtained.

D. **Transactions**

1. **Acquiring Noncontrolling Interests—No Change in Control** The purchase of additional interests in a partially owned subsidiary is treated as an equity transaction if there is no change in control. If the parent company purchases additional shares of stock in the partially owned subsidiary, and the fair value of the interest acquired exceeds its carrying value, the adjustment will reduce the parent company's equity. For example, assume that a parent company that owns 60 percent of the voting equity interests of a subsidiary acquires an additional 10 percent from the minority shareholders for $100 million. Further, assume that the carrying value of that interest is $65 million. Since there was no change in control, the parent company would record an adjustment (in this case a decrease) to its equity for the difference between the fair value of that interest of $100 million and the related carrying value of $65 million, or $35 million.

2. **Parent Company Sale to Third Parties—No Change in Control** Transactions such as the sale of subsidiary stock by the parent or the issuance of stock by the partially owned subsidiary, which under previous accounting generally resulted in gains or losses, is now recorded in stockholders' equity as long as there is no change in control of the subsidiary.

3. **Step Acquisitions—Change in Control** If the parent company obtains control by increasing its ownership from, for instance, 40 percent to 65 percent, the parent would adjust its initial investment (i.e., the 40 percent) to fair value by recording a gain or loss based on the difference between the fair value and the carrying value of the investment. The remeasurement guidance is likely to have more of an impact on the recognition of gains, since companies are required to periodically evaluate their investments for impairment.

4. **Parent Company Sale to Third Parties—Change in Control** Transactions between the parent company and third parties (noncontrolling interests) that result in a change of control will generate gains or losses to be recorded in earnings. If a company sells shares of its subsidiary such that it no longer controls the subsidiary, the company would recognize a gain or loss in earnings on the shares sold and adjust the retained equity investment to fair value, with any difference from its carrying value recognized as a gain or loss in earnings.

5. **Multiple Transactions** GAAP contains guidance designed to prevent manipulation of income through a series of planned transactions designed to take advantage of the fact that obtaining or surrendering control over an investee is a remeasurement event through income. GAAP identifies the following four conditions, one or more of which may indicate that multiple arrangements should be accounted for as a single transaction: the arrangements are entered into at the same time or in contemplation of one another; they form a single transaction designed to achieve an overall commercial effect; the occurrence of one arrangement depends on the occurrence of at least one other arrangement; or one arrangement considered on its own is not economically justified, but the arrangements are economically justified when considered together.

E. Measurement

An acquirer will sometimes be able to measure the acquisition-date fair value of a noncontrolling interest on the basis of active market prices for the equity shares not held by the acquirer. In other situations an active market price for equity shares will not be available and the acquirer would use other valuation techniques. The fair values of the acquirer's interest in the acquiree and the non-controlling interest on a per-share basis might differ. The main difference is likely to be the inclusion of a control premium in the per-share fair value of the acquirer's interest.

Example 16 ▸ Noncontrolling Interest

On January 1, year 1, Parent Inc., (P) acquired 80% of Subsidiary Corp.'s (S) 100,000 shares of outstanding stock for $800,000 cash. This was the first acquisition of any of S's shares by P.

Required: Determine the amount attributed to noncontrolling interest at the acquisition date for each of the following situations.

a. The active market price of S's shares on the acquisition date is $8.00 per share.
b. The fair value of the noncontrolling interest was determined [given] to be $150,000.
c. No active market price of S's shares or fair value of the noncontrolling interest is provided.

Solution:

a. P acquired 80% of S's 100,000 shares outstanding = 80,000 shares. With P owning 80,000 shares, that leaves 20,000 shares remaining for noncontrolling interests (100,000 – 80,000). The 20,000 shares × $8.00 active market price = $160,000 fair value attributed to the non-controlling interest on the acquisition date.

b. If the fair value of the noncontrolling interest is given, use it. There may have been some other viable valuation technique used to determine that fair value. In this case the $150,000 fair value provided would be attributed to the noncontrolling interest on the acquisition date.

c. If no market price for S's shares is provided and no fair value of the noncontrolling interest is given you must infer what the fair value of the noncontrolling interest is worth. P paid $800,000 for 80% of S's 100,000 outstanding shares. By dividing $800,000 by 80% we can infer that the total (100%) fair value of S must be worth $1,000,000. The noncontrolling interest owns 20%; $1,000,000 × 20% = $200,000 fair value attributed to the noncontrolling interest on the acquisition date.

F. Presentation and Disclosures

Net income includes both the parent's and the minority shareholders' share of earnings. This differs from previous presentation guidance in which net income represented only the parent's share. To provide consistency with past reporting, a new category called "net earnings attributable to the parent company," which is similar to net income under the prior standards, is used. Despite this change, earnings per share is still determined on the basis of net earnings attributable to the parent company's shareholders, consistent with previous calculations.

For each business combination in which the acquirer holds less than 100 percent of the equity interests in the acquiree, the following should be disclosed: the fair value of the noncontrolling interest in the acquiree at the acquisition date; and the valuation technique(s) and significant inputs used to measure the fair value of the noncontrolling interest.

A parent with one or more less-than-wholly-owned subsidiaries shall disclose the following for each reporting period.

1. Separately, on the face of the consolidated financial statements, the amounts of consolidated net income and consolidated comprehensive income and the related amounts of each attributable to the parent and the noncontrolling interest.

2. Either in the notes or on the face of the consolidated income statement, amounts attributable to the parent for the income from continuing operations, discontinued operations, and extraordinary items, if reported in the consolidated financial statements.

3. Either in the consolidated statement of changes in equity, if presented, or in the notes to consolidated financial statements, a reconciliation at the beginning and the end of the period of the carrying amount of total equity (net assets), equity (net assets) attributable to the parent, and equity (net assets) attributable to the noncontrolling interest. That reconciliation shall separately disclose net income, transactions with owners acting in their capacity as owners (showing separately contributions from and distributions to owners), and each component of other comprehensive income.

VI. Other Issues

A. Deconsolidation

A parent shall deconsolidate a subsidiary as of the date the parent ceases to have a controlling financial interest in the subsidiary. The following are examples of events that result in deconsolidation of a subsidiary: a parent sells all or part of its ownership interest in its subsidiary, and as a result, the parent no longer has a controlling financial interest in the subsidiary; the expiration of a contractual agreement that gave control of the subsidiary to the parent; the subsidiary issues shares, which reduces the parent's ownership interest in the subsidiary so that the parent no longer has a controlling financial interest in the subsidiary; or the subsidiary becomes subject to the control of a government, court, administrator, or regulator.

1. **Recognition** If a parent deconsolidates a subsidiary through a nonreciprocal transfer to owners, such as a spinoff, they shall use nonmonetary transaction accounting guidance in reporting the transaction. Otherwise, a parent shall account for the deconsolidation of a subsidiary by recognizing a gain or loss in net income attributable to the parent, measured as the difference between:

   a. The aggregate of:

      - The fair value of any consideration received
      - The fair value of any retained noncontrolling investment in the former subsidiary at the date the subsidiary is deconsolidated
      - The carrying amount of any noncontrolling interest in the former subsidiary (including any accumulated other comprehensive income attributable to the noncontrolling interest) at the date the subsidiary is deconsolidated.

   b. The carrying amount of the former subsidiary's assets and liabilities.

2. **Disclosures** If a subsidiary is deconsolidated, the parent shall disclose:

   - The amount of any gain or loss recognized in accordance with the deconsolidation
   - The portion of any gain or loss related to the remeasurement of any retained investment in the former subsidiary to its fair value
   - The caption in the income statement in which the gain or loss is recognized unless separately presented on the face of the income statement

- A description of the valuation technique(s) used to measure the fair value of any direct or indirect retained investment in the former subsidiary and information that enables users of the parent's financial statements to assess the inputs used to develop the fair value

- The nature of continuing involvement with the subsidiary after it has been deconsolidated

- Whether the transaction that resulted in the deconsolidation was with a related party and whether the former subsidiary will be a related party after deconsolidation.

B. Push-Down Accounting

Our review of business combinations has focused on (1) the recording by the parent company and (2) the required consolidation procedures. Historically, where separate incorporation is maintained, the subsidiary's financial records are not affected by either the acquisition or the consolidation.

Under push-down accounting, however, the subsidiary records purchase price allocations and subsequent amortization. The subsidiary records the allocations attributed to its identifiable net assets (e.g., inventory, land, building, equipment) and goodwill with a balancing entry to an *Additional Paid-In Capital* account. Every year thereafter, the subsidiary recognizes depreciation expense, as appropriate, on these various allocations.

Because the allocations and amortization are already entered into the records of the subsidiary, the use of push-down accounting simplifies the consolidation process. In addition, push-down accounting provides better internal reporting. Since the subsidiary's separate figures may include additional depreciation expense resulting from the purchase, the net income reported by the subsidiary is a good representation of the impact that the acquisition has on the earnings of the business combination.

C. Combined Financial Statements

Combined financial statements are often prepared for a group of related companies (e.g., a group of unconsolidated subsidiaries) or a group of commonly controlled companies (e.g., one individual owns a controlling financial interest in several entities that are related in their operations). Consolidated statements are not appropriate if there is no investment by one affiliate in another to eliminate. Combined financial statements are prepared by combining the individual companies' financial statement classifications into one set of financial statements. Intercompany transactions, balances, and profits or losses are eliminated in the same manner as in consolidated statements.

D. Parent-Company Financial Statements

In addition to consolidated financial statements, parent-company financial statements may be needed to indicate the position of bondholders and other creditors or preferred shareholders of the parent. Parent-company financial statements are not a valid substitute for consolidated financial statements. Consolidating financial statements, in which one column is used for the parent and other columns for subsidiaries is often used to effectively present the pertinent information.

Select Hot•Spot™ Video Description

CPA 4205 Nonprofit Accounting
Following previous exam emphasis, this program concentrates on accounting for nonprofits such as private, not-for-profit hospitals, private, nonprofit colleges & universities, and voluntary health & welfare organizations. Robert Monette discusses problem-solving techniques while covering 30 multiple-choice questions. Approximate duration of the video is 1 hour and 45 minutes. This does not include the time a candidate spends answering questions and taking notes.

Call our customer representatives toll-free at 1 (800) 874-7877 for more details about videos.

Subject to Change Without Notice

CHAPTER 16—BUSINESS COMBINATIONS AND CONSOLIDATIONS

Problem 16-1 MULTIPLE-CHOICE QUESTIONS

1. Peel Co. received a cash dividend from a common stock investment. Should Peel report an increase in the investment account if it uses the cost method or the equity method of accounting?

	Cost	Equity
a.	No	No
b.	Yes	Yes
c.	Yes	No
d.	No	Yes

(11/93, Theory, #9, 4514)

2. Pal Corp.'s current year dividend income included only part of the dividend received from its Ima Corp. investment. The balance of the dividend reduced Pal's carrying amount for its Ima investment. This reflects that Pal accounts for its Ima investment by the

   a. Cost method, and only a portion of Ima's current year dividends represent earnings after Pal's acquisition
   b. Cost method, and its carrying amount exceeded the proportionate share of Ima's market value
   c. Equity method, and Ima incurred a loss in the current year
   d. Equity method, and its carrying amount exceeded the proportionate share of Ima's market value

(11/92, Theory, #30, amended, 3463)

3. Wood Co. owns 2,000 shares of Arlo, Inc.'s 20,000 shares of $100 par, 6% cumulative, nonparticipating preferred stock, and 1,000 shares (2%) of Arlo's common stock. During the current year, Arlo declared and paid dividends of $240,000 on preferred stock. No dividends had been declared or paid the previous year. Also, Wood received a 5% common stock dividend from Arlo when the quoted market price of Arlo's common stock was $10 per share. What amount should Wood report as dividend income in its year-end income statement?

   a. $12,000
   b. $12,500
   c. $24,000
   d. $24,500

(5/95, FAR, #29, amended, 5565)

4. An investor uses the cost method to account for an investment in common stock classified as an available-for-sale security. Dividends received this year exceeded the investor's share of investee's undistributed earnings since the date of investment. The amount of dividend revenue that should be reported in the investor's income statement for this year would be

   a. The portion of the dividends received this year that were in excess of the investor's share of investee's undistributed earnings since the date of investment
   b. The portion of the dividends received this year that were **not** in excess of the investor's share of investee's undistributed earnings since the date of investment
   c. The total amount of dividends received this year
   d. Zero

(11/91, Theory, #10, amended, 2518)

5. Information pertaining to dividends from Wray Corp.'s common stock investments for the current year ended December 31 follows:

    - On September 8, Wray received a $50,000 cash dividend from Seco, Inc., in which Wray owns a 30% interest. A majority of Wray's directors are also directors of Seco.
    - On October 15, Wray received a $6,000 liquidating dividend from King Co. Wray owns a 5% interest in King Co.
    - Wray owns a 2% interest in Bow Corp., which declared a $200,000 cash dividend on November 27, to stockholders of record on December 15, payable on January 5 of next year.

    What amount should Wray report as dividend income in its income statement for the current year ended December 31?

    a. $60,000
    b. $56,000
    c. $10,000
    d. $ 4,000 (11/92, PI, #44, amended, 3277)

6. Larkin Co. has owned 25% of the common stock of Devon Co. for a number of years, and has the ability to exercise significant influence over Devon. The following information relates to Larkin's investment in Devon during the most recent year:

Carrying amount of Larkin's investment in Devon at the beginning of the year	$200,000
Net income of Devon for the year	600,000
Total dividends paid to Devon's stockholders during the year	400,000

    What is the carrying amount of Larkin's investment in Devon at year end?

    a. $100,000
    b. $200,000
    c. $250,000
    d. $350,000 (R/11, FAR, #6, 9856)

7. Anchor Co. owns 40% of Main Co.'s common stock outstanding and 75% of Main's noncumulative preferred stock outstanding. Anchor exercises significant influence over Main's operations. During the current period, Main declared dividends of $200,000 on its common stock and $100,000 on its noncumulative preferred stock. What amount of dividend income should Anchor report on its income statement for the current period related to its investment in Main?

    a. $ 75,000
    b. $ 80,000
    c. $120,000
    d. $225,000 (R/08, FAR, #10, 8565)

8. Puff Co. acquired 40% of Straw, Inc.'s voting common stock on January 2 of the current year for $400,000. The carrying amount of Straw's net assets at the purchase date totaled $900,000. Fair values equaled carrying amounts for all items except equipment, for which fair values exceeded carrying amounts by $100,000. The equipment has a five-year life. During the year, Straw reported net income of $150,000. What amount of income from this investment should Puff report in its year-end income statement?

    a. $40,000
    b. $52,000
    c. $56,000
    d. $60,000 (R/01, FAR, #6, 6981)

Items 9 through 11 are based on the following:

Grant, Inc. acquired 30% of South Co.'s voting stock for $200,000 on January 2, year 3. Grant's 30% interest in South gave Grant the ability to exercise significant influence over South's operating and financial policies. During year 3, South earned $80,000 and paid dividends of $50,000. South reported earnings of $100,000 for the six months ended June 30, year 4, and $200,000 for the year ended December 31, year 4. On July 1, year 4, Grant sold half of its stock in South for $150,000 cash. South paid dividends of $60,000 on October 1, year 4.

9. Before income taxes, what amount should Grant include in its year 3 income statement as a result of the investment?

   a. $15,000
   b. $24,000
   c. $50,000
   d. $80,000 (11/95, FAR, #26, amended, 6108)

10. In Grant's December 31, year 3 balance sheet, what should be the carrying amount of this investment?

    a. $200,000
    b. $209,000
    c. $224,000
    d. $230,000 (11/95, FAR, #27, amended, 6109)

11. In its year 4 income statement, what amount should Grant report as gain from the sale of half of its investment?

    a. $24,500
    b. $30,500
    c. $35,000
    d. $45,500 (11/95, FAR, #28, amended, 6110)

12. On January 1 of the current year, Point, Inc. purchased 10% of Iona Co.'s common stock. Point purchased additional shares bringing its ownership up to 40% of Iona's common stock outstanding on August 1. During October, Iona declared and paid a cash dividend on all of its outstanding common stock. How much income from the Iona investment should Point's year-end income statement report?

    a. 10% of Iona's income for January 1 to July 31, plus 40% of Iona's income for August 1 to December 31
    b. 40% of Iona's income for August 1 to December 31 only
    c. 40% of Iona's total year income
    d. Amount equal to dividends received from Iona (11/93, Theory, #8, amended, 4513)

13. When the equity method is used to account for investments in common stock, which of the following affect(s) the investor's reported investment income?

	A change in market value of investee's common stock	Cash dividends from investee
a.	Yes	Yes
b.	Yes	No
c.	No	Yes
d.	No	No (5/96, FAR, #2, 6275)

14. Bort Co. purchased 2,000 shares of Crel Co. common stock on March 5, year 1, for $72,000. Bort received a $1,000 cash dividend on the Crel stock on July 15, year 1. Crel declared a 10% stock dividend on December 15, year 1, to stockholders of record as of December 31, year 1. The dividend was distributed on January 15, year 2. The market price of the stock was $38 on December 15, year 1, $40 on December 31, year 1, and $42 on January 15, year 2. What amount should Bort record as dividend revenue for the year ended December 31, year 1?

    a. $1,000
    b. $8,600
    c. $9,000
    d. $9,400 (R\92, FAR #43, 2614)

15. Penn, Inc., a manufacturing company, owns 75% of the common stock of Sell, Inc., an investment company. Sell owns 60% of the common stock of Vane, Inc., an insurance company. In Penn's consolidated financial statements, should consolidation accounting or equity method accounting be used for Sell and Vane?

    a. Consolidation used for Sell and equity method used for Vane
    b. Consolidation used for both Sell and Vane
    c. Equity method used for Sell and consolidation used for Vane
    d. Equity method used for both Sell and Vane (11/92, Theory, #31, 3464)

16. The authoritative guidance on business combinations states which of the following?

    a. A business combination occurs when an acquirer obtains control over one or more businesses.
    b. If intercorporate stock ownership arrangements result in a parent company owning less than 50 percent of a third lower-level subsidiary, through the parent's second subsidiary (a chain of interests), consolidated financial statements should not be prepared.
    c. Consolidation of majority-owned subsidiaries is not required if a large minority interest exists in the subsidiaries.
    d. Consolidation of majority-owned subsidiaries is not required if a subsidiary is in a foreign location. (Editor, 89678)

17. A transaction is accounted for as a business combination. Which of the following expenses related to the business combination should be included, in total, in the determination of net income of the combined corporation for the period in which the expenses are incurred?

	Fees of finders and consultants	Registration fees for equity securities issued
a.	Yes	Yes
b.	Yes	No
c.	No	Yes
d.	No	No

(R/01, FAR, #7, amended, 6982)

18. Sayon Co. issues 200,000 shares of $5 par value common stock to acquire Trask Co. in an acquisition method business combination. The market value of Sayon's common stock is $12. Legal and consulting fees incurred in relationship to the purchase are $110,000. Registration and issuance costs for the common stock are $35,000. What should be recorded in Sayon's additional paid-in capital account for this business combination?

    a. $1,545,000
    b. $1,400,000
    c. $1,365,000
    d. $1,255,000 (R/08, FAR, #39, 8594)

19. In a transaction accounted for as a business combination, the appraised values of the identifiable net assets acquired exceeded the acquisition price. How should the excess appraised value be reported?

    a. As negative goodwill
    b. As extraordinary gain
    c. As a reduction of the values assigned to noncurrent assets and extraordinary gain for any unallocated portion
    d. As an ordinary gain (11/95, FAR, #53, amended, 6135)

20. A subsidiary, acquired for cash in a business combination, owned inventories with a market value different than the carrying amount as of the date of combination. A consolidated balance sheet prepared immediately after the acquisition would include this difference as part of

    a. Deferred credits
    b. Goodwill
    c. Inventories
    d. Retained earnings (11/86, Theory, #3, 2034)

21. An entity is required to account for each business combination by applying the acquisition method. In applying the acquisition method, which of the following is **not** required?

    a. Determining the acquisition date
    b. Recognizing and measuring identifiable assets acquired, liabilities assumed, and any noncontrolling interest in the acquiree
    c. Allocating the excess of fair value over purchase price as a pro rata reduction of acquired assets
    d. Recognizing and measuring goodwill or a gain from a bargain purchase (Editors, 8980)

22. Company J acquired all of the outstanding common stock of Company K in exchange for cash. The acquisition price exceeds the fair value of net assets acquired. How should Company J determine the amounts to be reported for the plant and equipment and long-term debt acquired from Company K?

	Plant and equipment	Long-term debt
a.	K's carrying amount	K's carrying amount
b.	K's carrying amount	Fair value
c.	Fair value	K's carrying amount
d.	Fair value	Fair value

(11/90, Theory, #4, 2019)

23. When an entity acquires a controlling interest in another entity, __________ are expensed as incurred.

    a. Finders' fees
    b. Consultants' fees
    c. Indirect expenses related to the acquisition
    d. All of the above (Editor, 89679)

24. On September 1, Pappy, Corp. acquired 80% of the outstanding common stock of Sibb Co. for $1,440,000 cash. At September 1, Sibb's balance sheet showed a carrying amount of net assets of $1,080,000 and the fair value of Sibb's property, plant, and equipment exceeded its carrying amount by $290,000. Also at that date, the fair value of the noncontrolling interest was determined to be $310,000. There was no goodwill impairment recorded during the year. In its December 31 year-end consolidated balance sheet, what amount of goodwill, related to the acquisition of Sibb, should Pappy report?

    a. $290,000
    b. $344,000
    c. $380,000
    d. $430,000 (Editors, 8983)

25. Under the acquisition method, which of the following would be considered a bargain purchase?

    a. The net of the book value of assets acquired and liabilities assumed exceeds the aggregate of the consideration transferred plus the fair value of any noncontrolling interest
    b. The net of the fair value of assets acquired and liabilities assumed exceeds the aggregate of the consideration transferred plus the fair value of any noncontrolling interest
    c. The aggregate of the consideration transferred plus the fair value of any noncontrolling interest exceeds the net of the book value of assets acquired and liabilities assumed
    d. The aggregate of the consideration transferred plus the fair value of any noncontrolling interest exceeds the net of the fair value of assets acquired and liabilities assumed (Editors, 8985)

26. Birk Co. purchased 30% of Sled Co.'s outstanding common stock on December 31 of the current year for $200,000. On that date, Sled's stockholders' equity was $500,000, and the fair value of its identifiable net assets was $600,000. On December 31, what amount of goodwill should Birk attribute to this acquisition?

    a. $0
    b. $20,000
    c. $30,000
    d. $50,000 (R/00, FAR, #4, 6899)

27. Damon Co. purchased 100% of the outstanding common stock of Smith Co. in an acquisition by issuing 20,000 shares of its $1 par common stock that had a fair value of $10 per share and providing contingent consideration that had a fair value of $10,000 on the acquisition date. Damon also incurred $15,000 in direct acquisition costs. On the acquisition date, Smith had assets with a book value of $200,000, a fair value of $350,000, and related liabilities with a book and fair value of $70,000. What amount of gain should Damon report related to this transaction?

    a. $ 55,000
    b. $ 70,000
    c. $ 80,000
    d. $250,000 (R/11, FAR, #47, 9897)

28. Which of the following statements is ***false*** concerning goodwill?

    a. Goodwill is recognized as the excess of the acquisition-date fair value of the purchase price over the recognized amounts of assets, liabilities, and noncontrolling interests.
    b. Goodwill is impaired if carrying value exceeds the fair value of the purchase price.
    c. If an acquirer obtains less than 100 percent of the acquiree at the acquisition date, goodwill is allocated to the controlling and noncontrolling interests.
    d. The amount of goodwill allocated to the noncontrolling interest is the difference between the fair value of the controlling interest and the controlling interest's share in the fair value of the identifiable net assets acquired. (Editor, 89680)

29. Jane Co. owns 90% of the common stock of Dun Corp. and 100% of the common stock of Beech Corp. On December 30, Dun and Beech each declared a cash dividend of $100,000 for the current year. What is the total amount of dividends that should be reported in the December 31 consolidated financial statements of Jane and its subsidiaries, Dun and Beech?

    a. $ 10,000
    b. $100,000
    c. $190,000
    d. $200,000 (R/11, FAR, #29, 9879)

30. Consolidated financial statements are typically prepared when one company has a controlling financial interest in another **unless**

    a. The subsidiary operates under foreign exchange restrictions.
    b. The fiscal year-ends of the two companies are more than three months apart.
    c. The two companies are in unrelated industries, such as manufacturing and real estate.
    d. Such control is likely to be temporary. (5/94, FAR, #7, amended, 4822)

31. Sun Co. is a wholly owned subsidiary of Star Co. Both companies have separate general ledgers, and prepare separate financial statements. Sun requires stand-alone financial statements. Which of the following statements is correct?

    a. Consolidated financial statements should be prepared for both Star and Sun.
    b. Consolidated financial statements should only be prepared by Star and **not** by Sun.
    c. After consolidation, the accounts of both Star and Sun should be changed to reflect the consolidated totals for future ease in reporting.
    d. After consolidation, the accounts of both Star and Sun should be combined together into one general-ledger accounting system for future ease in reporting. (R/05, FAR, #49, 7793)

32. A 70%-owned subsidiary company declares and pays a cash dividend. Under the acquisition method, what effect does the dividend have on the retained earnings and noncontrolling interest balances in the parent company's consolidated balance sheet?

    a. No effect on either retained earnings or noncontrolling interest
    b. No effect on retained earnings and a decrease in noncontrolling interest
    c. Decreases in both retained earnings and noncontrolling interest
    d. A decrease in retained earnings and no effect on noncontrolling interest

    (11/92, Theory, #34, amended, 3467)

33. On January 2, of the current year, Peace Co. paid $310,000 to purchase 75% of the voting shares of Surge Co. Peace reported retained earnings of $80,000, and Surge reported contributed capital of $300,000 and retained earnings of $100,000. The purchase differential was attributed to depreciable assets with a remaining useful life of 10 years. Peace used the equity method in accounting for its investment in Surge. Surge reported net income of $20,000 and paid dividends of $8,000 during the current year. Peace reported income, exclusive of its income from Surge, of $30,000 and paid dividends of $15,000 during the current year. What amount will Peace report as dividends declared and paid in its current year's consolidated statement of retained earnings?

    a. $ 8,000
    b. $15,000
    c. $21,000
    d. $23,000 (R/08, FAR, #17, 8572)

34. Sun, Inc. is a wholly owned subsidiary of Patton, Inc. On June 1 of the current year, Patton declared and paid a $1 per share cash dividend to stockholders of record on May 15. On May 1 of this year Sun bought 10,000 shares of Patton's common stock for $700,000 on the open market, when the book value per share was $30. What amount of gain should Patton report from this transaction in its consolidated income statement for the current year ended December 31?

    a. $0
    b. $390,000
    c. $400,000
    d $410,000 (11/94, FAR, #56, amended, 5317)

35. On January 1, Owen Co. purchased all of Sharp Corp.'s common stock for $1,200,000. On that date, the fair values of Sharp's assets and liabilities equaled their carrying amounts of $1,320,000 and $320,000, respectively. During the year, Sharp paid cash dividends of $20,000. Select information from the separate balance sheets and income statements of Owen and Sharp as of December 31, are as follows:

	Owen	Sharp
Balance sheet accounts		
Investment in subsidiary	$1,300,000	—
Retained earnings	1,240,000	560,000
Total stockholders' equity	2,620,000	1,120,000
Income statement accounts		
Operating income	420,000	200,000
Equity in earnings of Sharp	120,000	—
Net income	400,000	140,000

    In Owen's December 31 consolidated balance sheet, what amount should be reported as total retained earnings?

    a. $1,240,000
    b. $1,360,000
    c. $1,380,000
    d. $1,800,000 (5/94, FAR, #56, amended, 4871)

36. Rowe Inc. owns 80% of Cowan Co.'s outstanding capital stock. On November 1, Rowe advanced $100,000 in cash to Cowan. What amount should be reported related to the advance in Rowe's consolidated balance sheet as of December 31?

    a. $0
    b. $ 20,000
    c. $ 80,000
    d. $100,000 (R/11, FAR, #8, 9858)

37. Wright Corp. has several subsidiaries that are included in its consolidated financial statements. In its December 31 trial balance, Wright had the following intercompany balances before eliminations:

	Debit	Credit
Current receivable due from Main Co.	$ 32,000	
Noncurrent receivable from Main	114,000	
Cash advance to Corn Corp.	6,000	
Cash advance from King Co.		$ 15,000
Intercompany payable to King		101,000

In its December 31 consolidated balance sheet, what amount should Wright report as intercompany receivables?

a. $152,000
b. $146,000
c. $ 36,000
d. $0 (5/93, PI, #14, amended, 4056)

38. Clark Co. had the following transactions with affiliated parties during the current year:

- Sales of $60,000 to Dean, Inc., with $20,000 gross profit. Dean had $15,000 of this inventory on hand at year end. Clark owns a 15% interest in Dean and exerts no significant influence.
- Purchases of raw materials totaling $240,000 from Kent Corp., a wholly owned subsidiary. Kent's gross profit on the sale was $48,000. Clark had $60,000 of this inventory remaining on December 31.

Before eliminating entries, Clark had consolidated current assets of $320,000. What amount should Clark report in its December 31 consolidated balance sheet for current assets?

a. $320,000
b. $317,000
c. $308,000
d. $303,000 (5/93, PI, #9, amended, 4051)

Items 39 and 40 are based on the following:

Selected information from the separate and consolidated balance sheets and income statements of Pare, Inc. and its subsidiary, Shel Co., as of December 31, and for the current year ended is as follows:

Balance sheet accts	Pare	Shel	Consolidated
Accounts receivable	$ 52,000	$ 38,000	$ 78,000
Inventory	60,000	50,000	104,000
Income statement accts			
Revenues	$400,000	$ 280,000	$ 616,000
Cost of goods sold	(300,000)	(220,000)	(462,000)
Gross profit	$100,000	$ 60,000	$ 154,000

39. What was the amount of intercompany sales from Pare to Shel during the year?

a. $ 6,000
b. $12,000
c. $58,000
d. $64,000 (5/95, FAR, #50, amended, 5586)

40. In Pare's consolidating worksheet, what amount of unrealized intercompany profit was eliminated?

a. $ 6,000
b. $12,000
c. $58,000
d. $64,000 (5/95, FAR, #52, amended, 5588)

41. During the current year, Pard Corp. sold goods to its 80%-owned subsidiary, Seed Corp. At December 31, one-half of these goods were included in Seed's ending inventory. Reported selling expenses were $1,100,000 and $400,000 for Pard and Seed, respectively. Pard's selling expenses included $50,000 in freight-out costs for goods sold to Seed. What amount of selling expenses should be reported in Pard's year-end consolidated income statement?

    a. $1,500,000
    b. $1,480,000
    c. $1,475,000
    d. $1,450,000 (11/91, PI, #53, amended, 2441)

42. Water Co. owns 80% of the outstanding common stock of Fire Co. On December 31, Fire sold equipment to Water at a price in excess of Fire's carrying amount, but less than its original cost. On a consolidated balance sheet at December 31, the carrying amount of the equipment should be reported at

    a. Water's original cost
    b. Fire's original cost
    c. Water's original cost less Fire's recorded gain
    d. Water's original cost less 80% of Fire's recorded gain (11/90, Theory, #2, amended, 2017)

43. Zest Co. owns 100% of Cinn, Inc. On January 2, Zest sold equipment with an original cost of $80,000 and a carrying amount of $48,000 to Cinn for $72,000. Zest had been depreciating the equipment over a five-year period using straight-line depreciation with no residual value. Cinn is using straight-line depreciation over three years with no residual value. In Zest's December 31, consolidating worksheet, by what amount should depreciation expense be decreased?

    a. $0
    b. $ 8,000
    c. $16,000
    d. $24,000 (R/07, FAR, #37, amended, 8358)

44. Which of the following is true, if a member of an affiliated group issues its bonds to outsiders, followed thereafter by a second affiliate purchasing those same bonds from the outside party?

    a. The bonds are still considered outstanding, for consolidated purposes.
    b. A gain or loss typically results from the acquisition of the bonds by the second affiliate, because the fair value of the bonds at the time of reacquisition is likely to be different than the carrying amount of the bonds on the books of the issuer.
    c. The full amount of the gain or loss on acquisition is recorded by the individual affiliate purchasing the bonds, immediately at the time of acquisition.
    d. None of the above occurs. (Editor, 89685)

45. Wagner, a holder of a $1,000,000 Palmer, Inc. bond, collected the interest due on March 31 of the current year, and then sold the bond to Seal, Inc. for $975,000. On that date, Palmer, a 75% owner of Seal, had a $1,075,000 carrying amount for this bond. What was the effect of Seal's purchase of Palmer's bond on the retained earnings and noncontrolling interest amounts reported in Palmer's March 31 consolidated balance sheet?

	Retained earnings	Noncontrolling interest
a.	$100,000 increase	$0
b.	$ 75,000 increase	$ 25,000 increase
c.	$0	$ 25,000 increase
d.	$0	$100,000 increase

(5/92, PI, #4, amended, 2571)

46. GAAP defines ______________ as any legal structure used to conduct activities or to hold assets.

    a. An entity
    b. A variable interest entity
    c. A business
    d. A special purpose entity (Editor, 89683)

47. __________ in a variable interest entity is a (are) contractual, ownership, or other pecuniary interest(s) in an entity that change(s) with changes in the entity's net asset value.

a. The primary beneficiary
b. Variable interests
c. Subordinated financial support
d. Expected variability (Editor, 89684)

48. On January 2, year 3, Pare Co. purchased 75% of Kidd Co.'s outstanding common stock. Selected balance sheet data at December 31, year 3, is as follows:

	Pare	Kidd
Total assets	$420,000	$180,000
Liabilities	120,000	60,000
Common Stock	100,000	50,000
Retained earnings	200,000	70,000
	$420,000	$180,000

During year 3, Pare and Kidd paid cash dividends of $25,000 and $5,000, respectively, to their shareholders. There were no other intercompany transactions. In Pare's December 31, year 3, consolidated balance sheet, what amount should be reported as noncontrolling interest in net assets?

a. $0
b. $ 30,000
c. $ 45,000
d. $105,000 (11/95, FAR, #50, amended, 6132)

49. On June 30, Peppy, Corp. purchased for cash at $17.50 per share 80% of Spunky Company's 100,000 total shares of outstanding common stock. The active market price for shares on that date was $15 per share. At June 30, Spunky's balance sheet showed a carrying amount of net assets of $1,500,000 and the fair value of Spunky's assets and liabilities equaled their carrying amounts except for property, plant, and equipment which exceeded its carrying amount by $250,000. In its June 30 consolidated balance sheet, what amount should Peppy report as noncontrolling interest?

a. $250,000
b. $300,000
c. $350,000
d. $400,000 (Editors, 8982)

50. On February 1, Pizza, Inc. acquired 75% of the outstanding common stock of Sausage Co. for $750,000 cash. At February 1, Sausage's balance sheet showed a carrying amount of net assets of $1,100,000 and the fair value of Sausage's assets and liabilities equaled their carrying amounts except for property, plant, and equipment which exceeded its carrying amount by $200,000. On February 1, what amount would be attributed as fair value for the noncontrolling interest?

a. $325,000
b. $300,000
c. $275,000
d. $250,000 (Editors, 8981)

51. If an acquirer obtains less than 100 percent of the acquiree at the acquisition date, goodwill is allocated to which of the following?

a. The controlling interests
b. The noncontrolling interests
c. Both A. and B.
d. None of the above (Editor, 89681)

52. A parent decides to spin off a subsidiary and deconsolidates it through a nonreciprocal transfer to owners. How shall the parent account for and report the transaction?
    a. As a noncontrolling interest
    b. As a nonmonetary transaction
    c. As an extraordinary gain or loss in net income
    d. As an ordinary gain or loss in net income attributable to the parent (Editors, 8986)

53. Historically, where separate incorporation is maintained, the subsidiary's financial records are which of the following?
    a. Not affected by either the acquisition or the consolidation
    b. Affected by the acquisition, but not the consolidation
    c. Not affected by the acquisition, but affected by the consolidation
    d. Affected by the acquisition and the consolidation (Editor, 89686)

54. Combined statements may be used to present the results of operations of

	Companies under common management	Commonly controlled companies
a.	No	Yes
b.	Yes	No
c.	No	No
d.	Yes	Yes

(5/93, Theory, #8, 4196)

55. For which of the following reporting units is the preparation of combined financial statements most appropriate?
    a. A corporation and a majority-owned subsidiary with nonhomogeneous operations
    b. A corporation and a foreign subsidiary with nonintegrated homogeneous operations
    c. Several corporations with related operations with some common individual owners
    d. Several corporations with related operations owned by one individual (11/91, Theory, #8, 2516)

56. Which of the following items should be treated in the same manner in both combined financial statements and consolidated statements?

	Different fiscal periods	Foreign operations	Noncontrolling interest
a.	No	No	No
b.	No	Yes	Yes
c.	Yes	Yes	Yes
d.	Yes	No	No

(11/89, Theory, #40, amended, 2026)

57. The following information pertains to shipments of merchandise from Home Office to Branch during the current year:

Home Office's cost of merchandise	$160,000
Intracompany billing	200,000
Sales by Branch	250,000
Unsold merchandise at Branch on December 31	20,000

In the combined income statement of Home Office and Branch for the year ended December 31, what amount of the above transactions should be included in sales?
    a. $250,000
    b. $230,000
    c. $200,000
    d. $180,000 (11/92, PII, #60, amended, 3394)

58. Mr. Cord owns four corporations. Combined financial statements are being prepared for these corporations, which have intercompany loans of $200,000 and intercompany profits of $500,000. What amount of these intercompany loans and profits should be included in the combined financial statements?

	Intercompany Loans	Intercompany Profits
a.	$200,000	$0
b.	$200,000	$500,000
c.	$0	$0
d.	$0	$500,000

(11/90, PI, #60, 1273)

Problem 16-2 SIMULATION: Cost & Equity Methods

Brooks, an investor in Acre Co., asked Jones, CPA, for advice on the propriety of Acre's financial reporting for two of its investments. Jones obtained the following information related to the investments from Acre's December 31, current year financial statements:

- 20% ownership interest in Korn Co., represented by 300,000 shares of outstanding common stock purchased on January 2 of the current year for $900,000.
- 20% ownership interest in Ward Co., represented by 40,000 shares of outstanding common stock purchased on January 2 of the current year for $600,000.
- On January 2, the carrying values of the acquired shares of both investments equaled their purchase price.
- Korn reported earnings of $600,000 for the current year ended December 31, and declared and paid dividends of $150,000 during the year.
- Ward reported earnings of $490,000 for the current year ended December 31, and declared and paid dividends of $80,000 during the year.
- On December 31, Korn's and Ward's common stock were trading over-the-counter at $20 and $22 per share, respectively.
- The investment in Korn is accounted for using the equity method.
- The investment in Ward is accounted for as available-for-sale securities.

Jones recalculated the amounts reported in Acre's December 31, current year financial statements, and determined that they were correct. Stressing that the information available in the financial statements was limited, Jones advised Brooks that, assuming Acre properly applied generally accepted accounting principles, Acre may have appropriately used two different methods to account for its investments in Korn and Ward, even though the investments represent equal ownership interests.

Prepare a schedule indicating the amounts Acre should report for the two investments. Ignore income taxes.

	Amounts
Korn:	
Investment in Korn, January 2	
Dividend rec'd	
Carrying amount	
Ward:	
Investment in Ward, January 2	
Divided income	
Unrealized gain	
Korn:	
Balance Sheet, December 31	
Acre reported its investment in Korn at a carrying amount of	
Statement of Income and Comprehensive Income, December 31	
Acre's equity in Korn's earnings	
Ward:	
Balance Sheet, December 31	
Acre reported its investment in Ward at a fair value of	
Statement of Income and Comprehensive Income, December 31	
Dividend income	
Unrealized gain	

(11/98, FAR, #2, amended, 6750t)

Problem 16-3 SIMULATION: Consolidated Amounts

The separate condensed balance sheets and income statements of Purl Corp. and its wholly owned subsidiary, Scott Corp., are as follows:

BALANCE SHEETS
December 31, Year 2

Assets	Purl	Scott
Current assets	$ 310,000	$135,000
Property, plant, and equipment (net)	625,000	280,000
Investment in Scott (equity method)	400,000	—
Total assets	$1,335,000	$415,000
Liabilities and Stockholders' Equity		
Current liabilities	$ 270,000	$125,000
Stockholders' equity		
Common stock ($10 par)	300,000	50,000
Additional paid-in capital	—	10,000
Retained earnings	765,000	230,000
Total stockholders' equity	1,065,000	290,000
Total liabilities and stockholders' equity	$1,335,000	$415,000

INCOME STATEMENTS
For the Year Ended December 31, Year 2

	Purl	Scott
Sales	$2,000,000	$750,000
Cost of goods sold	1,540,000	500,000
Gross margin	460,000	250,000
Operating expenses	260,000	150,000
Operating income	200,000	100,000
Equity in earnings of Scott	70,000	—
Income before income taxes	270,000	100,000
Provision for income taxes	60,000	30,000
Net income	$ 210,000	$ 70,000

Additional information

- On January 1, year 2, Purl purchased for $360,000 all of Scott's $10 par, voting common stock. On January 1, year 2, the fair value of Scott's assets and liabilities equaled their carrying amount of $410,000 and $160,000, respectively, except that the fair values of certain items identifiable in Scott's inventory were $10,000 more than their carrying amounts. These items were still on hand at December 31, year 2.
- During year 2, Purl and Scott paid cash dividends of $100,000 and $30,000, respectively. For tax purposes, Purl receives the 100% exclusion for dividends received from Scott.
- There were no intercompany transactions, except for Purl's receipt of dividends from Scott and Purl's recording of its share of Scott's earnings.
- Both Purl and Scott paid income taxes at the rate of 30%.

Item	Amount
1. Total current assets	
2. Total assets	
3. Total retained earnings	
4. Net income	

(9138)

Problem 16-4 SIMULATION: Consolidated Trial Balance

On April 1 of the current year, Jared, Inc., purchased 80% of the common stock of Munson Manufacturing Company for $6,000,000. At the date of purchase the book and fair values of Munson's assets and liabilities were as follows:

	Book Value	Fair Value
Cash	$ 200,000	$ 200,000
Notes receivable	85,000	85,000
Accounts receivable, net	980,000	980,000
Inventories	828,000	700,00
Land	1,560,000	2,100,00
Machinery and equipment	7,850,000	10,600,000
Accumulated depreciation	(3,250,000)	(4,000,000)
Other assets	140,000	50,000
	$8,393,000	$10,715,000
Notes payable	$ 115,000	$ 115,000
Accounts payable	400,000	400,000
Subordinated 7% debentures	5,000,000	5,000,000
Common stock; par value $10 per share; authorized, issued, and outstanding 100,000 shares	1,000,000	--
Additional paid-in capital (common stock)	872,000	--
Retained earnings	1,006,000	
	$8,393,000	

By the year-end, December 31, the following transactions had occurred during the year:

- The balance of Munson's net accounts receivable at April 1 had been collected.
- The inventory on hand at April 1 had been charged to cost of sales. Munson used a perpetual inventory system in accounting for inventories.
- Prior to this year, Jared had purchased at face value $1,500,000 of Munson's 7% subordinated debentures. These debentures mature in seven years on October 31, with interest payable annually on October 31.
- As of April 1, the machinery and equipment had an estimated remaining life of six years. Munson uses the straight-line method of depreciation. Munson's depreciation expense calculation for the nine months ended December 31 was based upon the old depreciation rates.
- The other assets consist entirely of long-term investments made by Munson and do not include any investment in Jared.
- During the last nine months of the year, the following intercompany transactions occurred between Jared and Munson:

Intercompany sales:	Jared to Munson	Munson to Jared
Net sales	$158,000	$230,000
Included in purchaser's inventory at December 31	36,000	12,000
Balance unpaid at December 31	16,800	22,000

Jared sells merchandise to Munson at cost. Munson sells merchandise to Jared at regular selling price including a normal gross profit margin of 35 percent. There were no intercompany sales between the two companies prior to April 1. Accrued interest on intercompany debt is recorded by both companies in their respective accounts receivable and accounts payable accounts. This business combination is being accounted for under the acquisition method.

Complete the worksheet to prepare the consolidated trial balance for Jared, Inc., and its subsidiary, Munson Manufacturing Company, at December 31.

Jared's revenue and expense figures are for the twelve-month period while Munson's are for the last nine months of the year. You may assume that both companies made all the adjusting entries required for separate financial statements unless stated to the contrary. Round all computations to the nearest dollar. Ignore income taxes.

Jared, Inc., and Subsidiary
Worksheet to Prepare Consolidated Trial Balance
December 31, Current Year

	Jared, Inc.	Munson Mfg. Co.	Adjustment and Eliminations		Consolidated Balances
	Dr.(Cr.)	Dr.(Cr.)	Debit	Credit	Dr.(Cr.)
Cash	$ 822,000	$ 530,000			
Notes receivable	--	85,000			
Accounts receivable, net	2,758,000	1,368,400			
Inventories	3,204,000	1,182,000			
Land	4,000,000	1,560,000			
Machinery and equipment	15,875,000	7,850,000			
Acc. depr.—mach. and equip.	(6,301,000)	(3,838,750)			
Buildings	1,286,000	--			
Acc. depr.—buildings	(372,000)	--			
Investment in Munson Mfg. Co.	6,000,000	--			
Investment in Munson bonds	1,500,000	--			
Other assets	263,000	140,000			
Goodwill					
Notes payable	--	(115,000)			
Accounts payable	(1,364,000)	(204,000)			
Long-term debt	(10,000,000)	--			
Subordinated debentures—7%	--	(5,000,000)			
Common stock	(2,400,000)	(1,000,000)			
Additional paid-in capital	(240,000)	(872,000)			
Retained earnings	(12,683,500)	(1,006,000)			
Noncontrolling interest					
Sales	(18,200,000)	(5,760,000)			
Cost of sales	10,600,000	3,160,000			
Selling, G&A expenses	3,448,500	1,063,900			
Depr. exp.—mach. and equip.	976,000	588,750			
Depr. exp.—buildings	127,000	--			
Interest revenue	(105,000)	(1,700)			
Interest expense	806,000	269,400			
Totals	$ 0	$ 0			

(R/03, FAR, #51, amended, 9005)

Problem 16-5 SIMULATION: Research

Question: What is the purpose of consolidated financial statements?

FASB ASC: [ ] - [ ] - [ ] - [ ]

(9139)

Solution 16-1 MULTIPLE-CHOICE ANSWERS

Cost Method

1. (a) The receipt of a cash dividend from a common stock investment should not be reported as an increase in the *Investment* account under either the cost or equity methods. Under the cost method, (1) dividends received up to the investor's share of the investee's earnings subsequent to the date of the investment are recorded as dividend income and (2) dividends received in excess of the investor's share of the investee's earnings since the date of the investment represent a liquidating dividend and are recorded as a decrease to the *Investment* account. Under the equity method, the receipt of a cash dividend from the investee always is recorded as a decrease to the *Investment* account. (4514)

2. (a) Dividend income is not recognized under the equity method of accounting for investments in common stock. Under this method, the investor's share of dividends declared by the investee reduce the carrying amount of the investment. Pal recognized dividend income from the investment in the current year. Hence it must account for the investment by the cost method. Under this method, investment income reported for the year is usually the investor's share of dividends declared by the investee during the year. The exception is where the investor's share of dividends declared by the investee exceeds the investor's share of investee earnings subsequent to the date of the investment. In this case, the excess amount represents a liquidating dividend that is recorded as a reduction of the carrying amount of the investment and not as dividend income. Since only part of the dividends that Pal received in the current year was recorded as dividend income, only a portion of the current year dividends represent earnings subsequent to the date of Pal's investment (i.e., the balance of the current year dividends represent liquidating dividends). (3463)

3. (c) Wood owns 10% of Arlo's preferred stock and would have received $24,000 ($240,000 dividends × 10%) in dividends in the current year on this preferred stock. Although this amount represents the dividend preference for the previous year, due to the 6% cumulative feature of the stock, as well as for the current year, the revenue is not recognized until the dividends are actually declared in the current year. Stock dividends received are not recognized as income because they are not a distribution, division, or severance of the corporate assets. (5565)

4. (b) When the cost method is used to account for investments in common stock, dividends received up to the investor's share of the investee's earnings subsequent to the date of investment are recorded as dividend income. Dividends received in excess of the investor's share of the investee's earnings since the date of investment represent a liquidating dividend and should be recorded as a decrease to the investment account. (2518)

5. (d) Of the dividends listed, only the $4,000 (i.e., $200,000 × 2%) cash dividend receivable from Bow should be reported as dividend income. Wray owns only a 2% interest in Bow; thus, Wray does not have the ability to exercise significant influence over Bow by virtue of the investment. Therefore, the investment should be accounted for under the cost method. The cash dividend received from Seco should be recorded as a reduction of the carrying amount of the investment in Seco reported in Wray's balance sheet because the investment should be accounted for under the equity method (i.e., Wray owns a 30% interest in Seco and a majority of Wray's directors are also directors of Seco). The liquidating dividend received from King should be recorded as a reduction of the carrying amount of the investment in King reported in Wray's balance sheet. (3277)

Equity Method

6. (c) Because Larkin exercises significant influence over Devon, Larkin would use the equity method to account for its common stock investment in Devon. Larkin would debit the Investment account for 25% of $600,000 ($150,000) since net income would increase the owner's equity in Devon, and would credit the Investment account for 25% of $400,000 ($100,000) since the dividend distribution reduces the owner's equity in Devon. (9856)

7. (a) Anchor would report $75,000 in dividend income on its income statement for the current period related to its investment in Main. The $75,000 comes from the 75% of $100,000 dividend that Anchor would receive on the noncumulative preferred stock. Anchor would also recognize $80,000, 40% of the $200,000 common stock dividend, but not on the income statement. Because Anchor exercises significant influence over Main's operations, Anchor would use the equity method to account for its common stock investment in Main. Anchor would credit the Investment account since the distribution reduces the owner's equity of Main. (8565)

8. (b) If fair value exceeds the net assets' carrying value, the excess is allocated among most undervalued assets. Then consideration is given to the existence of goodwill. As the related undervalued asset is depreciated or sold, the investment account is adjusted. Straw's fair value is $900,000 + $100,000 = $1,000,000. Puff's investment in Straw is 40% × $1,000,000 = $400,000, the same as the purchase price. Puff offsets its share of Straw's income with the depreciation of its share of the difference in the carrying and fair value of equipment. {[$150,000 – ($100,000 / 5 years)] × 40% = $52,000} (6981)

9. (b) As Grant has 20% or more ownership in South, the amount of investment income in Grant's income statement is Grant's percentage of ownership times South's earnings. [$80,000 × 30% = $24,000] (6108)

10. (b) As Grant has 20% or more ownership in South, the carrying amount of the investment is the original purchase price plus Grant's share in South's earnings ($80,000 × 30% = $24,000), less the dividends paid to Grant ($50,000 × 30% = $15,000). [$200,000 + $24,000 – $15,000 = $209,000] (6109)

11. (b) The balance in Grant's Investment in South account at the beginning of year 4 is $209,000. Grant has equity in South's earnings of $30,000 ($100,000 × 30%), which increases the investment account. South did not pay any dividends during the first six months of year 4, so the balance in Investment in South is $239,000 at the date of sale. Half of the investment was sold, so half of the balance in the account is Grant's carrying value for the stock sold ($239,000 × 50% = $119,500). The gain is the sale price less the carrying value ($150,000 – $119,500 = $30,500). (6110)

12. (a) On 8/1, when Point increased its investment in Iona's common stock from 10% to 40%, Point gained the ability to exercise significant influence over the financial and operating policies of Iona and accordingly should report its investment using the equity method. The change from the cost method to the equity method should be made by retroactively restating all prior periods in which the investment was held as if the equity method were used from inception. Therefore, the amount Point should report as income from the Iona investment in its year-end income statement is 10% of Iona's income from 1/1 to 7/31, plus 40% of Iona's income for 8/1 to 12/31. (4513)

13. (d) Under the equity method of accounting for investments in common stock, the investment is recorded at cost. Changes in the market value of the investee's common stock do not affect the Investment account or the Investment Income account. The investor recognizes as income its share of the investee's earnings or losses in the periods in which they are reported by the investee. Dividends declared by the investee represent a distribution of earnings previously recognized and, thus, do not affect the Investment Income account. (6275)

14. (a) Only the $1,000 cash dividend received from Crel should be reported as dividend revenue. Apparently, Bort does not have the ability to exercise significant influence over the financial and operating policies of Crel by virtue of its 2,000 share investment. No income is recognized from the receipt of the stock dividend. Bort's proportionate interest in Crel did not change and Crel's underlying assets and liabilities did not change as a result of the stock dividend. (2614)

Business Combinations

15. (b) Penn should consolidate both Sell and Vane. Penn has a controlling financial interest in Sell through direct ownership of a majority voting interest (i.e., 75%). The intercorporate stock ownership arrangement with respect to Vane indicates a chain of interests, the product of which (i.e., 75% × 60% = 45%) does not represent control of the lower level subsidiary, where control is defined in terms of the 50% stock ownership minimum. Notwithstanding the 45% indirect interest of Penn in Vane, the preparation of consolidated statements is warranted in this instance. While the product of equities in a chain of interests does factor into the determination of consolidated net income and consolidated retained earnings that should be recorded, it is not a determinant in establishing a minimal condition for preparation of consolidated financial statements. Penn controls Sell and Sell controls Vane, so with no evidence presented that control of Sell or Vane doesn't rest with Penn, one must assume control is apparent and consolidation is appropriate. (3464)

16. (a) A business combination occurs when an acquirer obtains control over one or more businesses. When intercorporate stock ownership arrangements have a chain of interests' feature, where the parent company owns less than 50 percent of a third company through the parent's main subsidiary, the preparation of consolidated statements is still required. Consolidation of a majority-owned subsidiary is still required even if the subsidiary has a large minority interest or is physically located in a foreign location. (89678)

17. (b) Acquisition related costs are those costs the acquirer incurs to effect a business combination. Those costs shall include finders' fees; advisory, legal, accounting, valuation, and other professional or consulting fees; general administrative costs, including the costs of maintaining an internal acquisitions department; and costs of registering and issuing debt and equity securities. The acquirer shall account for acquisition-related costs as expenses in the periods in which the costs are incurred and the services are received, with one exception; the costs to issue debt or equity securities shall be recognized in accordance with other applicable GAAP. (6982)

18. (c) In an acquisition method business combination, if the purchaser issues its own equity securities as part of the consideration the securities must be credited to additional paid-in capital based on their fair value. Costs of registering and issuing equity securities are a reduction of the fair value of the securities in additional paid-in capital. Direct acquisition costs incurred (e.g., finders' fees, legal and consulting fees) must be capitalized as part of the total purchase price. Any indirect and general expenses related to the acquisition are expensed as incurred. The market value of Sayon's common stock is $7 more than the par value ($12 – $5 = $7). The $7 times 200,000 shares equals $1,400,000 Sayon would initially record, but then it must subtract the $35,000 registration and issuance costs for a total amount of $1,365,000 that should be recorded in Sayon's additional paid-in capital account. The $110,000 in legal and consulting fees would be capitalized as part of the total purchase price, but would not affect the additional paid-in capital account. (8594)

19. (d) Under the acquisition method, current assets and noncurrent marketable securities of the acquired company are always recorded at their fair values and all liabilities assumed are recorded at their fair value (present value). If the purchase price is less than the fair value of the identifiable net assets, any excess is considered a bargain purchase. The acquirer recognizes an ordinary gain in earnings on the acquisition date. (6135)

20. (c) Under the acquisition method, a consolidated balance sheet prepared immediately after the acquisition includes the assets of the subsidiary at their fair values. The difference would be part of inventories. (2034)

21. (c) Allocating the excess of fair value over purchase price as a pro rata reduction of acquired assets is not a part of applying the acquisition method. Applying the acquisition method requires (1) identifying the acquirer, (2) determining the acquisition date, (3) recognizing and measuring identifiable assets acquired, liabilities assumed, and (4) recognizing and measuring goodwill or a gain from a bargain purchase. (8980)

22. (d) In a transaction accounted for as a business combination, all identifiable assets acquired and liabilities assumed are assigned their fair values at the date of acquisition. (2019)

23. (d) Finders' fees and consultants' fees are all examples of transactions costs, and are excluded from the acquisition accounting. In addition, indirect and general expenses related to the acquisition are expensed as incurred. (89679)

24. (c) Goodwill is the excess of the consideration transferred plus the fair value of any noncontrolling interest over the fair value of the identifiable net assets (INA) acquired.

Investment cost (80%)		$ 1,440,000	
Noncontrolling interest (20%)		310,000	
Carrying amount of INA	$1,080,000		
Fair value of plant assets in excess of carrying amount	290,000		
Less: Fair value of INA acquired		(1,370,000)	(8983)
Goodwill		$ 380,000	

25. (b) Under the acquisition method, assets acquired and liabilities assumed by the acquirer are always recorded at their fair values. If the net of the fair value of assets acquired and liabilities assumed exceeds the aggregate of the consideration transferred plus the fair value of any noncontrolling interest, that excess is called a bargain purchase. The acquirer recognizes an ordinary gain in earnings on the acquisition date. (8985)

26. (b) Goodwill is recognized at an amount equal to the excess of the cost of the enterprise acquired over the fair value of the identifiable net assets (INA).

Purchase price of 30% of Sled Co's O/S common stock		$ 200,000	
Fair value of Sled's INA	$600,000		
Times: % acquired by Birk	× 30%		
Less: Sled's INA acquired by Birk		(180,000)	
Goodwill		$ 20,000	(6899)

27. (b) Under the acquisition method, current assets, and noncurrent marketable securities of the acquired company are always recorded at their fair values and all liabilities assumed are recorded at their fair value (present value). If the fair value of the consideration transferred (including contingent consideration) is less than the fair value of the identifiable net assets, any excess is considered a bargain purchase. The acquirer recognizes a gain in earnings on the acquisition date. (9897)

28. (d) The amount of goodwill allocated to the controlling interest is the difference between the fair value of the controlling interest and the controlling interest's share in the fair value of the identifiable net assets acquired. (89680)

Consolidations

29. (a) Jane will report just the $10,000 ($100,000 × 10%) in dividends that Dun paid to minority owners during the year. The $90,000 paid by Dun to Jane and the $100,000 paid by Beech to Jane are eliminated on a consolidated statement of retained earnings. (9879)

30. (a) A majority-owned subsidiary should **not** be consolidated if control does not rest with the majority owner, for example, if the subsidiary is in legal reorganization or in bankruptcy or operates under foreign exchange restrictions, controls, or other governmentally imposed uncertainties so severe that they cast significant doubt on the parent's ability to control the subsidiary. Consolidation of majority-owned subsidiaries is required even if they have "nonhomogeneous" operations, control is likely to be temporary, or there is a difference in fiscal periods. (4822)

31. (b) Consolidated statements are required when a company owns more than 50% of the voting stock in another company. Star owns more than 50% of Sun; Sun does not own more than 50% of Star, therefore, Star would prepare consolidated financial statements and Sun would not. Consolidating entries are prepared on a worksheet only and are not formally entered into the books of either company. Consolidating procedures must be preformed every period in which financial statements are presented. (7793)

32. (b) Under the acquisition method, the amount of consolidated retained earnings is equal to the parent company's retained earnings because the subsidiary's stockholders' equity accounts are eliminated in the consolidation process. Thus, the cash dividend declared by the subsidiary has no effect on consolidated retained earnings. The noncontrolling interest balance reported in the consolidated statements is based upon the balances of the subsidiary's stockholders' equity accounts. Since the cash dividend declared and paid by the subsidiary decreases the amount of the subsidiary's retained earnings, the noncontrolling interest balance reported in the consolidated balance sheet decreases. (3467)

33. (b) Peace will report just the $15,000 in dividends they paid during the year as dividends declared and paid in its current year's consolidated statement of retained earnings. The 75% portion of the $8,000 in dividends paid by Surge will be treated by Peace as a reduction in the carrying amount of the investment in Surge (8572)

34. (a) When parent shares are obtained by a subsidiary, no gain or loss is reported from the transaction in the consolidated income statement. Any dividends paid to the subsidiary on this stock are eliminated in the consolidation process because they are considered intercompany cash transfers. (5317)

35. (a) Under the acquisition method, consolidated retained earnings are comprised solely of the *parent's* retained earnings at the balance sheet date since the subsidiary's owners' equity accounts are eliminated in the process of consolidation. Total consolidated stockholders' equity will equal the total stockholders' equity reported by the parent company (assuming no intercompany transactions). (4871)

Intercompay Transactions

36. (a) Consolidated financial statements should not include intercompany payables, receivables, or advances pertaining to consolidated subsidiaries. Intercompany advances must be eliminated from consolidated statements, in a manner similar to that used for receivables and payables. In addition, interest income and expense and interest accruals must be eliminated. (9858)

37. (d) Consolidated financial statements should not include any intercompany payables, receivables, or advances pertaining to consolidated subsidiaries. (4056)

38. (c) When one company sells merchandise to an affiliate at a price above cost, the ending inventory of the buyer contains an element of unrealized gross profit. The gross profit is not realized to the economic entity until the inventory is sold to an unaffiliated company. The preparation of the consolidated financial statements requires that the unrealized gross profit be eliminated from inventory. Dean is not an affiliate of Clark because Clark cannot exercise significant influence over Dean by virtue of its investment (i.e., Clark owns only a 15% interest in Dean). Therefore, no elimination entry should be made for the transaction with Dean.

Consolidated current assets before elimination entries	$320,000	
Less: Unrealized gross profit on intercompany inventory transfer to wholly-owned subsidiary [($60,000 / $240,000) × $48,000]	(12,000)	
Consolidated current assets to be reported in consolidated balance sheet	$308,000	(4051)

39. (d) Intercompany sales are eliminated in the preparation of consolidated financial statements. The amount of intercompany sales can be computed by subtracting consolidated revenues from the sum of the revenues reported in the separate financial statements of Pare and Shel [i.e., ($400,000 + $280,000) – $616,000 = $64,000]. (5586)

40. (a) Unrealized profit on intercompany inventory transactions is eliminated in the preparation of consolidated financial statements. The amount of unrealized intercompany profit from inventory transactions is computed by subtracting the amount reported for consolidated inventory from the sum of inventory reported in the separate financial statements of Pare and Shel [i.e., ($60,000 + $50,000) – $104,000 = $6,000]. (5588)

41. (d) No portion of the $50,000 freight costs on the intercompany inventory transfer is reported as selling expense in the consolidated income statement. Although this expense is "freight-out" to Pard, for consolidated purposes, it is not freight-out to a buyer. It is part of the inventory cost and when the related goods are sold, the freight costs will increase the amount reported as cost of goods sold in the consolidated income statement. (2441)

42. (c) Consolidated statements should not include gain or loss on transactions among the companies in the group. Any intercompany profit or loss on assets remaining within the group should be eliminated and is not affected by the existence of a minority interest. Therefore, the carrying amount of the equipment should be reported at the cost of the equipment to the purchasing affiliate (Water) less the entire gain recorded by the selling affiliate (Fire). (2017)

43. (b) Sales of fixed assets between members of an affiliated group will result in the recognition of gain or loss by the seller, if the selling price differs from the carrying amount of the asset. However, no gain or loss has taken place for the consolidated entity; assets merely have been transferred from one set of books to another. The buyer of the asset will record it in its books at the purchase price; subsequent depreciation charges will be based upon this purchase price, thus requiring adjustment if the price is different from the book value. The equipment was being depreciated by the seller at a rate of $16,000 per year ($80,000 original cost / 5 years) and had been depreciated $32,000 ($80,000 original cost – $48,000 book value with no residual value) before being sold. The buyer will record depreciation expense of $24,000 ($72,000 cost / 3 years). With intercompany sales of fixed assets, in the year of the sale the carrying amount of the asset is restored to its original book value and the gain (loss) recorded by the seller is eliminated. For each period depreciation expense and accumulated depreciation are adjusted to reflect the original book value of the asset. The consolidating worksheet in this problem should decrease depreciation expense $8,000, the difference between the $24,000 recorded by the buyer based on the purchase price and the $16,000 determined based on the carrying amount. (8358)

44. (b) A gain or loss will typically result from the acquisition by the second affiliate, in the open market, of bonds originally issued by the first affiliate to outsiders. This occurs because the fair value of the bonds at the time of reacquisition is likely to be different than the carrying amount of the bond obligation on the books of the issuer. For consolidated purposes, the bonds have been retired, since outsiders no longer hold them. No gain or loss on acquisition is recorded by the individual affiliate, yet a gain or loss on retirement must be recognized at the consolidated level. (89685)

45. (a) An investment by one member of a consolidated group of companies in the bonds of another member of that group is, in substance, the same thing as the purchase by a member of its own bonds. Although the bonds cannot physically be retired, since two separate entities are involved in the transaction, from a consolidated viewpoint, the transaction is treated as a constructive retirement of the bonds to the extent of the investment in the bonds. Thus, the consolidated financial statements will reflect any gain or loss on the retirement of bonds in the year of purchase. This is true despite the fact that the books of the affiliates involved in the transaction continue to reflect the *Investment in Bonds* and *Bond Payable* accounts, respectively. Thus, the consolidated entity in question recognizes a gain of $100,000 (i.e., $1,075,000 carrying amount of bond – $975,000 cost to subsidiary) on the bond retirement. Gains and losses on the early retirement of bonds can only be reflected on the books of the issuer. Thus, Palmer, the parent company, is attributed the entire $100,000 gain on the retirement, thereby increasing consolidated *Retained Earnings* by the same amount. Since no portion of the gain on retirement is attributed to the subsidiary, the amount reported in the consolidated financial statements for the 25% noncontrolling interest in the subsidiary is unaffected by the intercompany bond transaction. (2571)

Variable Interest Entities

46. (a) An "entity" is any legal structure used to conduct activities or to hold assets. A "variable interest entity" is defined based on the characteristics of the entity. To be considered a business, the entity must meet the requirements set forth in GAAP. A special purpose entity (SPE) is not recognized in U.S. GAAP. (89683)

47. (b) Variable interests in a variable interest entity are contractual, ownership, or other pecuniary interests in an entity that change with changes in the entity's net asset value. A primary beneficiary refers to an enterprise that consolidates a variable interest entity under the provisions of GAAP. Subordinated financial support refers to variable interests that will absorb some or all of an entity's expected losses if they occur. Expected variability is the sum of the absolute values of the expected residual return and the expected loss. (89684)

Noncontrolling Interests

48. (b) Without any specific information provided about amounts on the acquisition date and reported net income you must infer the noncontrolling interest is worth 25% of Kidd's net assets. Kidd's net assets are $180,000 – $60,000 = $120,000. $120,000 × 25% = $30,000. (6132)

49. (b) An acquirer can measure the acquisition-date fair value of a noncontrolling interest on the basis of active market prices for the equity shares not held by the acquirer. The active market prices for the acquiree's equity shares on that date was $15 per share. Peppy purchased 80% of the 100,000 total common shares outstanding, or 80,000 shares of Spunky (.80 × 100,000 = 80,000). If Peppy owns 80,000 shares, that means 20,000 shares (100,0000 – 80,000 = 20,000) are owned by the noncontrolling interest. The 20,000 shares multiplied by the active market price of $15 per share results in a total fair value of $300,000 which must be reported as noncontrolling interest. (8982)

50. (d) An acquirer can measure the acquisition-date fair value of a noncontrolling interest on the basis of active market prices for the equity shares not held by the acquirer. If the active market prices for equity shares of the acquiree are not available, the acquirer must use another valuation technique to determine the noncontrolling interest's fair value. One can infer what the fair value must be based upon the percentage acquired by the acquirer and the amount of consideration the acquirer transferred in the business combination. Dividing the consideration transferred by the percentage acquired results in the amount 100% of the acquiree must be worth. Multiplying that total worth by the percentage owned by the noncontrolling interest results in fair value attributable to the noncontrolling interest. Pizza paid $750,000 for 75% of Sausage, thus 25% is considered as noncontrolling interest. $750,000 ÷ .75 = $1,000,000; then $1,000,000 × .25 = $250,000 fair value for the noncontrolling interest. (8981)

51. (c) The amount of goodwill allocated to the controlling interest is the difference between the fair value of the controlling interest and the controlling interest's share in the fair value of the identifiable net assets acquired. Any remaining goodwill is allocated to the noncontrolling interests. (89681)

Other Issues

52. (b) If a parent deconsolidates a subsidiary through a nonreciprocal transfer to owners, such as a spinoff, they shall use nonmonetary transaction accounting guidance in reporting the transaction. Otherwise a parent accounts for the deconsolidation by recognizing a gain or loss in net income attributable to the parent. The gain or loss is measured as the difference between the aggregate of the value of any consideration received plus the fair value of any retained noncontrolling investment in the former subsidiary at the date of deconsolidation plus the carrying amount of any noncontrolling interest in the former subsidiary (including any accumulated OCI attributable to the noncontrolling interest) at the date of deconsolidation versus the carrying amount of the former subsidiary's assets and liabilities. (8986)

53. (a) Historically, where separate incorporation is maintained, the subsidiary's financial records are not affected by either the acquisition or the consolidation. (89686)

54. (d) Combined financial statements may be used to present the financial position and results of operations of commonly controlled companies, such as a group of unconsolidated subsidiaries. They might also be used to combine the financial statements of companies under common management. (4196)

55. (d) There are circumstances where combined financial statements (as distinguished from consolidated financial statements) of commonly controlled companies are likely to be more meaningful than their separate statements. Examples of such circumstances are: (1) where one individual owns a controlling interest in several corporations which are related in their operations, (2) to present the financial position and the results of operations of a group of unconsolidated subsidiaries, and (3) to combine the financial statements of companies under common management. (2516)

56. (c) Where combined financial statements are prepared for a group of related entities, such as a group of commonly controlled entities, noncontrolling interests, foreign operations, different fiscal periods, or income taxes, they should be treated in the same manner as in consolidated financial statements. (2026)

57. (a) Any sale of inventory between a home office and a branch will trigger the individual accounting systems of both units. Revenue is recorded by the seller while the purchase simultaneously is entered into the acquirer's accounts. However, from a combined perspective, neither sale nor purchase has occurred. Thus, only the $250,000 of sales by Branch should be included in the combined income statement; the intracompany billing of $200,000 should be eliminated in preparing the combined financial statements. (3394)

58. (c) Where combined statements are prepared for a group of related companies, such as a group of commonly controlled entities, intercompany transactions and profits or losses shall be eliminated. (1273)

PERFORMANCE BY SUBTOPICS

Each category below parallels a subtopic covered in Chapter 16. Record the number and percentage of questions you correctly answered in each subtopic area.

Cost Method

Question #	Correct √
1	
2	
3	
4	
5	
# Questions	5
# Correct	______
% Correct	______

Equity Method

Question #	Correct √
6	
7	
8	
9	
10	
11	
12	
13	
14	
# Questions	9
# Correct	______
% Correct	______

Business Combinations

Question #	Correct √
15	
16	
17	
18	
19	
20	
21	
22	
23	
24	
25	
26	
27	
28	
# Questions	14
# Correct	______
% Correct	______

Consolidations

Question #	Correct √
29	
30	
31	
32	
33	
34	
35	
# Questions	7
# Correct	______
% Correct	______

Intercompay Transactions

Question #	Correct √
36	
37	
38	
39	
40	
41	
42	
43	
44	
45	
# Questions	10
# Correct	______
% Correct	______

Variable Interest Entities

Question #	Correct √
46	
47	
# Questions	2
# Correct	______
% Correct	______

Noncontrolling Interests

Question #	Correct √
48	
49	
50	
51	
# Questions	4
# Correct	______
% Correct	

Other Issues

Question #	Correct √
52	
53	
54	
55	
56	
57	
58	
# Questions	7
# Correct	______
% Correct	______

Solution 16-2 SIMULATION ANSWER: Costs & Equity Methods

Schedule indicating the amounts Acre should report for the two investments in its December 31 current year balance sheet and statement of income and comprehensive income.

	Amounts
Korn:	
Investment in Korn ($600,000 × 20%)	$120,000
Dividend received ($150,000 × 20%)	$ 30,000
Carrying amount ($900,000 + $120,000 – $30,000)	$990,000
Ward:	
Investment in Ward (Acquisition cost)	$600,000
Divided income ($80,000 × 20%)	$ 16,000
Unrealized gain ($880,000 – $600,000)	$280,000
Korn:	
Balance Sheet	
Acre reported its investment in Korn at a carrying amount of	$990,000
Statement of Income and Comprehensive Income	
Acre's equity in Korn's earnings	$120,000
Ward:	
Balance Sheet	
Acre reported its investment in Ward at a fair value of (40,000 shares × $22)	$880,000
Statement of Income and Comprehensive Income	
Dividend income	$ 16,000
Unrealized gain	$280,000

Solution 16-3: SIMULATION ANSWER: Consolidated Amounts

Item	**Amount**
1. Total current assets	$ 455,000
2. Total assets	$1,460,000
3. Total retained earnings	$ 765,000
4. Net income	$ 210,000

Explanations

1. Because there are no reciprocal or intercompany accounts at year end, the amount of consolidated current assets at that date is the sum of Purl's current assets at carrying amounts ($310,000) and Scott's current assets at fair values ($135,000 + $10,000 inventory adjustment) for a total of $455,000.

2. Purl's *Investment in Subsidiary* account is not included in total consolidated assets because it is eliminated in the consolidation process.

Purchase price		$ 360,000
Fair value of identifiable assets ($410,000 + $10,000 inventory adjustment)	$420,000	
Fair value of liabilities	160,000	
Fair value of identifiable net assets (INA)	260,000	
Percentage acquired	× 100%	
Fair value of INA acquired		(260,000)
Goodwill		$ 100,000

Consolidated current assets	$ 455,000
Purl's plant assets at carrying amounts (net)	625,000
Scott's plant assets at fair values (net)	280,000
Goodwill	100,000
Total consolidated assets	$1,460,000

3. Under the acquisition method, consolidated retained earnings are comprised solely of the *parent's* retained earnings at the balance sheet date since the subsidiary's owners' equity accounts are eliminated in the process of consolidation. Total consolidated stockholders' equity will equal the total stockholders' equity reported by the parent company (assuming no intercompany transactions) of $765,000.

4. The consolidated reported net income will equal the net income reported by the parent company (assuming no intercompany transactions) of $210,000.

Solution 16-4 SIMULATION ANSWER: Consolidated Trial Balance

	Jared, Inc.	Munson Mfg. Co.	Adjustment and Eliminations		Consolidated Balances [B]
	Dr.(Cr.)	Dr.(Cr.)	Debit	Credit	Dr.(Cr.)
Cash	$ 822,000	$ 530,000	0 [A]	0 [A]	$ 1,352,000
Notes receivable	--	85,000	0 [A]	0 [A]	85,000
Accounts receivable, net	2,758,000	1,368,400	0 [A]	56,300 [H]	4,070,100
Inventories	3,204,000	1,182,000	0 [A]	4,200 [7]	4,381,800
Land	4,000,000	1,560,000	$ 540,000 [1]	0 [A]	6,100,000
Machinery and equipment	15,875,000	7,850,000	2,750,000 [1]	0 [A]	26,475,000
Acc. depr.—mach. and equip.	(6,301,000)	(3,838,750)	0 [A]	986,250 [F]	(11,126,000)
Buildings	1,286,000	--	0 [A]	0 [A]	1,286,000
Acc. depr.—buildings	(372,000)	--	0 [A]	0 [A]	(372,000)
Investment in Munson Mfg. Co.	6,000,000	--	0 [A]	6,000,000 [D]	0
Investment in Munson Bonds	1,500,000	--	0 [A]	1,500,000 [5]	0
Other assets	263,000	140,000	0 [A]	90,000 [1]	313,000
Goodwill	--	--	2,300,000 [3]	0 [A]	2,300,000
Notes payable	--	(115,000)	0 [A]	0 [A]	(115,000)
Accounts payable	(1,364,000)	(204,000)	56,300 [H]		(1,511,700)
Long-term debt	(10,000,000)	--	0 A]	0 [A]	(10,000,000)
Subordinated debentures—7%	--	(5,000,000)	1,500,000 [5]	0 [A]	(3,500,000)
Common stock	(2,400,000)	(1,000,000)	1,000,000 [2]	0 [A]	(2,400,000)
Additional paid-in capital	(240,000)	(872,000)	872,000 [2]	0 [A]	(240,000)
Retained earnings	(12,683,500)	(1,006,000)	1,006,000 [2]	0 [A]	(12,683,500)
Noncontrolling interest	--	--	0 [A]	1,500,000 [E]	(1,500,000)
Sales	(18,200,000)	(5,760,000)	388,000 [6]	0 [A]	(23,572,000)
Cost of sales	10,600,000	3,160,000	4,200 [7]	516,000 [G]	13,248,200
Selling, G&A expenses	3,448,500	1,063,900	0 [A]	0 [A]	4,512,400
Depr. exp.—mach. and equip.	976,000	588,750	236,250 [4]	0 [A]	1,801,000
Depr. exp.—buildings	127,000	--	0 [A]	0 [A]	127,000
Interest revenue	(105,000)	(1,700)	78,750 [8]	0 [A]	(27,950)
Interest expense	806,000	269,400	0 [A]	78,750 [8]	996,650
	$ 0	$ 0	$10,731,500 [C]	$10,731,500 [C]	$ 0

Explanations

[A] Zero entry required
[B] Sum for consolidated balances
[C] Column totals (to balance)
[D] $1,857,600 + $2,302,400 + $1,840,000 = $6,000,000; see explanations 1, 2, 3
[E] $464,400 + $575,600 + $460,000 = $1,500,000; see explanations 1, 2, 3
[F] $750,000 + $236,250 = $986,250; see explanations 1 & 4
[G] $128,000 + $388,000 = $516,000; see explanations 1 & 6
[H] $17, 500 + $38,800 = $56,300; see explanations 5 & 6

Note: One of the first things you should do is figure out the fair value of the noncontrolling interest at the acquisition date. If there is no information on the active market prices of equity shares not held by the acquirer and it isn't given, you must infer what the fair value of the noncontrolling interest is based on the consideration paid by the acquirer.

Computation:	
Amount of purchase price by Jared	$6,000,000
Divide by: Percent acquired by Jared (80%)	÷ 0.80
Fair value for total consideration	7,500,000
Times: Noncontrolling interest percentage (100% – 80%)	× 0.20
Noncontrolling interest	$1,500,000

	Debit	Credit
[1] Land	540,000	
Machinery and equipment	2,750,000	
Cost of sales*		128,000
Accumulated depreciation—machinery & equip.		750,000
Other assets		90,000
Investment in Munson Manufacturing Co. (80%)		1,857,600
Noncontrolling interest (20%)		464,400

To adjust Munson's assets acquired and liabilities assumed to fair value at date of acquisition.

* **Editor's Note: As the overvalued inventory was charged to cost of sales (COS) account, the adjustment also is charged to the COS account.**

	Debit	Credit
[2] Common Stock	1,000,000	
Additional Paid-in Capital (Common)	872,000	
Retained Earnings	1,006,000	
Investment in Munson Manufacturing Co. (80%)		2,302,400
Noncontrolling interest (20%)		575,600

To adjust Munson's assets acquired and liabilities assumed to fair value at date of acquisition.

	Debit	Credit
[3] Goodwill	2,300,000	
Investment in Munson Manufacturing Co. (80%)		1,840,000
Noncontrolling interest (any remainder to balance)		460,000

To record excess of cost plus noncontrolling interest over fair value of Munson's net assets at date of acquisition.

Computation:	
Purchase price (common stock)	$ 6,000,000
Plus: Noncontrolling interest fair value	1,500,000
Less: Net of acquisition-date amounts acquired (See J/E No. 1 & J/E No. 2 $2,322,000 + $2,878,000 = $5,200,000)	(5,200,000)
Total goodwill	$ 2,300,000
Fair value of Jared's 80% interest	$ 6,000,000
Less: fair value of Jared's share of net assets ($5,200,000 × 0.80)	(4,160,000)
Jared's share of goodwill	$ 1,840,000

Total goodwill	$ 2,300,000		
Less: Jared's share of goodwill	(1,840,000)		
Noncontrolling interests' share of goodwill	$ 460,000		

[4] Depreciation expense—Machinery and equipment			236,250	
Accumulated Depreciation—Machinery and equip.				236,250
To adjust to fair value at date of purchase.				
Computation:				
Machinery and equipment— $10,600,000 – 4,000,000 / 6 years =	$1,100,000			
Depreciation expense for nine months ($1,100,000 × 9/12)		$ 825,000		
Depreciation expense per books ($3,838,750 – $3,250,000)		(588,750)		
Adjustment		$ 236,250		

[5] Subordinated Debentures 7%	1,500,000	
Accounts Payable	17,500	
Investment in Munson Bonds		1,500,000
Accounts Receivable Net		17,500
To eliminate intercompany bonds and related accrued interest for two months.		
[6] Accounts Payable	38,800	
Sales	388,000	
Accounts Receivable Net		38,800
Cost of Sales		388,000
To eliminate intercompany sales and unpaid balances at December 31.		
[7] Cost of Sales	4,200	
Inventories		4,200
To eliminate intercompany profit (35%) in Jared's inventory at December 31. ($12,000 × 35% = $4,200)		
[8] Interest Revenue	78,750	
Interest Expense		78,750
To eliminate intercompany interest expense and revenue on debentures for nine months. ($105,000 × 9/12 = $78,750)		

Solution 16-5 SIMULATION ANSWER: Research

FASB Accounting Standards Codification

FASB ASC: 810 - 10 - 10 - 1

10-1 The purpose of consolidated statements is to present, primarily for the benefit of the shareholders and creditors of the parent entity, the results of operations and the financial position of a parent entity and all its subsidiaries as if the group were a single entity with one or more branches or divisions. There is a presumption that consolidated statements are more meaningful than separate statements and that they are usually necessary for a fair presentation when one of the entities in the group directly or indirectly has a controlling financial interest in the other entities.

Select Hot•Spot™ Video Description

CPA 2020 Consolidations
This video program provides comprehensive coverage of the cost and equity methods of accounting for investments in subsidiaries and the acquisition method of consolidation. Candidates will learn the accounting rules to know when and how to use each method. Robert Monette details appropriate journal entries for consolidations to include noncontrolling interests, goodwill, a bargain purchase, and the elimination of the effect of intercompany transactions. This lecture is enhanced by 25 multiple-choice questions and 2 simulations based on problems from previous CPA exams. Your confidence will soar as you become comfortable with this complex subject! The approximate duration is 3 hours and 30 minutes.

Call our customer representatives toll-free at 1 (800) 874-7877 for more details about videos.

Subject to Change Without Notice

CHAPTER 17

IFRS & SEC REPORTING

CHAPTER 17

IFRS & SEC REPORTING

I. International Financial Reporting Standards (IFRS)

A. IFRS Foundation Public Accountability

The IFRS Foundation (previously referred to as the IASC Foundation) and its independent standard-setting body, the IASB, provide public accountability through the transparency of their work, consultation with a full range of interested parties in the standard-setting process, and formal accountability links to the public. The leaders of the major economies, through the G20, have confirmed the importance of an independent standard-setter accountable to the public interest.

1. **Trustees' Duty** Public accountability, ensured by the organization's Constitution and governance arrangements, is vital to the organization's success. It is the Trustees' duty to ensure that appropriate governance arrangements are in place and observed by all parts of the organization.

2. **Due Process Oversight Committee** The Trustees' effectiveness in exercising their functions is assessed annually by the Trustees' Due Process Oversight Committee.

3. **The Monitoring Board** The Trustees established a formal public accountability link through a Monitoring Board of public capital market authorities.

4. **The Constitution Review** The Constitution of the IFRS Foundation requires the Trustees to undertake a formal, public, five-year review of the Constitution.

5. **Due Process** A formal due process for the IASB, the IFRS Interpretations Committee and other initiatives ensures extensive outreach, which includes mandatory public consultation. Comment letters received in response to formal proposals are made public on the website.

6. **Public Meetings** All meetings (other than meetings on administrative matters) of the bodies of the IFRS Foundation, including the IASB, the Interpretations Committee and its formal advisory bodies, are held in public and are webcast. Meeting notes are available to the public as observer notes.

B. IASB Formation and Structure

In 2001, the International Accounting Standards Board (IASB) began operations based out of London as an independent accounting standard-setting body. The IASB is comprised of 16 members from nine countries, including four board members from the United States. The IASB may consider initiating studies in the light of its review of IFRS application, changes in the financial reporting environment and regulatory requirements, and comments by the IFRS Advisory Council, the IFRS Interpretations Committee, standard-setters, and constituents about the quality of the IFRS. Those studies may result in items being added to the IASB's agenda. The IASB and related groups is structured similar to the FASB, and includes the following:

1. **International Financial Reporting Interpretations Committee (IFRIC)** is a 12-member group that helps interpret standards.

2. **Standards Advisory Committee (SAC)** is a 40-member group that provides advice concerning priorities, accounting issues, and implications of standards on financial statement users.

3. **Trustees Appointments Advisory Group** is a 22-member group that oversees the operation of the IASB.

C. How IFRS Are Developed

International Financial Reporting Standards (IFRS) are developed through an international consultation due process, which involves interested individuals and organizations from around the world. The development of an IFRS is carried out during public IASB meetings. The due process comprises six stages, with the Trustees having the opportunity to ensure compliance at various points throughout.

Exhibit 1 ▸ IFRS Due Process Stages

1. Setting the agenda
2. Planning the project
3. Developing and publishing the discussion paper
4. Developing and publishing the exposure draft
5. Developing and publishing the standard
6. After the standard is issued

1. **Agenda Decision** The IASB, by developing high-quality accounting standards, seeks to address a demand for better-quality information that is primarily of value to all users of financial statements. As a secondary goal, better-quality information will also be of value to the preparers of financial statements. The IASB evaluates the merits of adding a potential item to its agenda mainly by reference to the needs of investors. The IASB considers the relevance to users of the information and the reliability of information that could be provided, whether existing guidance is already available, the possibility of increasing convergence with other accounting standards, the quality of the standard to be developed, and resource constraints. The IASB's discussions of potential projects, and its decisions to adopt new projects, take place in public IASB meetings.

2. **Discussion Paper** Although a discussion paper is not mandatory, the IASB normally publishes it as a means to more fully explore a major new topic, to explain the issue, and to solicit early comment from constituents. Typically, a discussion paper includes: a comprehensive overview of the issue; possible approaches in addressing the issue; the preliminary views of its authors or the IASB; and an invitation to comment.

3. **Exposure Draft** After resolving initial issues identified through the discussion paper or other means, the IASB instructs the staff to draft the exposure draft. Publication of an exposure draft is a mandatory step in due process.

4. **Final Version Issued** When the IASB is satisfied that it has reached a conclusion on the issues arising from the exposure draft, it instructs the staff to draft the IFRS. Finally, after the due process is completed, all outstanding issues are resolved, and the IASB members have balloted in favor of publication, the IFRS is issued.

II. First-Time Adoption of IFRS

A. Introduction

The International Accounting Standards Board (IASB) published IFRS 1 *First-time Adoption of International Financial Reporting Standards*, in 2003. Since then, significant amendments have been made to the Standard (primarily as a result of changes to other IFRS). It is important to remember that IFRS 1 is not a static standard. It was introduced to address the very real need to ease the burdens (both cost and effort) of transition for first-time adopters. As has been the case in the past, as more entities move towards adopting IFRS, it is possible that additional areas will be identified where the costs of application of IFRS on first-time adoption exceed the benefits, in which case the IASB may introduce additional exemptions. Furthermore, as IFRS continues to evolve, consequential amendments to IFRS 1 will be required.

1. **Purpose** The purpose of IFRS 1 is to establish the rules for an entity's first financial statements prepared in accordance with IFRS, particularly regarding the transition from the accounting principles previously applied by the entity (previous GAAP). Prior to the issuance of IFRS 1, first-time adopters were expected (in most cases) to retrospectively apply all IFRS requirements in their first IFRS-compliant financial statements. Recognizing that this often resulted in costs that exceeded the benefits of the financial information generated, the IASB revised the approach to first-time adoption to include limited exemptions from the principle of retrospective application. As a result, IFRS 1 significantly eases the burden for first-time adopters.

2. **Objective** The objective of IFRS 1 is to ensure that an entity's first IFRS financial statements (and interim financial reports for part of the period covered by those financial statements) contain high quality information that is transparent for users and comparable over all periods presented. It provides a suitable starting point for accounting under IFRS, and attempts to generate financial statements at a cost that does not exceed the benefits to users.

3. **General Principle** The general principle underlying IFRS 1 is that any IFRS effective at the date of an entity's first IFRS financial statements should be applied retrospectively in the opening IFRS statement of financial position, the comparative period, and the first IFRS reporting period. Effectively, this general principle would result in full retrospective application of IFRS as if they had been the framework for an entity's accounting since its inception. However, IFRS 1 adapts this general principle of retrospective application by adding a limited number of very important "exceptions" and "exemptions." The "exceptions" to retrospective application are mandatory. The "exemptions" are optional—a first-time adopter may choose whether and which exemptions to apply.

Exhibit 2 ▸ Mandatory Exceptions

- Accounting estimates
- De-recognition of financial assets and financial liabilities
- Hedge accounting
- Noncontrolling interests

Exhibit 3 ▸ Optional Exemptions

- Business combinations
- Share-based payment transactions
- Insurance contracts
- Fair value or revaluation as deemed cost
- Leases
- Employee benefits
- Cumulative translation differences
- Investments in subsidiaries, jointly controlled entities and associates
- Assets and liabilities of subsidiaries, associates, and joint ventures
- Compound financial instruments
- Designation of previously recognized financial instruments
- Fair value measurement of financial assets or liabilities at initial recognition
- Decommissioning liabilities included in the cost of property, plant, and equipment
- Financial assets or intangible assets accounted for in Service Concession Arrangements
- Borrowing costs
- Transfers of assets from customers

B. First IFRS Financial Statements Defined
An entity may only apply IFRS 1 in its first IFRS financial statements (a term tightly defined in IFRS 1 to mean the first annual financial statements in which the entity adopts IFRS by an explicit and unreserved statement of compliance with IFRS). The Standard provides specific examples of what might or might not qualify as an entity's first IFRS financial statements.

1. **Example of Criteria for First Financial Statements** The Standard notes by way of example that IFRS financial statements would be considered to be an entity's first IFRS financial statements if the entity presented its most recent previous financial statements:

   a. In accordance with national requirements that are not consistent with IFRS in all respects;

   b. In conformity with IFRS in all respects, except that the financial statements did not contain an explicit and unreserved statement that they complied with IFRS;

   c. Containing an explicit statement of compliance with some, but not all, IFRS;

   d. In accordance with national requirements inconsistent with IFRS, using some individual IFRS to account for items for which national requirements did not exist; or

   e. In accordance with national requirements, with a reconciliation of some amounts to the amounts determined under IFRS.

2. **Examples of When Inappropriate to Apply IFRS 1** IFRS 1 is clear that it is inappropriate to apply the standard when an entity:

   a. Stops presenting financial statements in accordance with national requirements, having previously presented them as well as another set of financial statements that contained an explicit and unreserved statement of compliance with IFRS;

   b. Presented financial statements in the previous year in accordance with national requirements and those financial statements contained an explicit and unreserved statement of compliance with IFRS; or

   c. Presented financial statements in the previous year that contained an explicit and unreserved statement of compliance with IFRS, even if the auditors qualified their audit report on those financial statements.

C. Steps for Preparing First IFRS Financial Statements
Entities are required to apply IFRS 1 in their first IFRS financial statements and in each interim financial report, if any, for part of the period covered by those first IFRS financial statements. The following summary provides a reasonable starting point from which to build a more thorough understanding of the steps required in preparing an entity's first IFRS financial statements.

1. **Statement of Financial Position Date of Transition** The starting point in IFRS 1 is an opening IFRS statement of financial position prepared at the date of transition to IFRS. The date of transition to IFRS is defined as "the beginning of the earliest period for which an entity presents full comparative information under IFRS in its first IFRS financial statements." The statement of financial position prepared at the date of transition (which is published in the first IFRS financial statements) is prepared in accordance with IFRS 1, including the general principle of retrospective application, the mandatory exceptions and the optional exemptions. For entities that present one year of comparative information in their financial reports, the date of transition is the first day of the comparative period.

2. **Apply All IFRS, Except Exceptions and Exemptions** In its first IFRS financial statements, an entity applies the version of IFRS effective at the end of its first IFRS reporting period. As a general principle, all IFRS effective at that date are applied retrospectively, subject to certain exceptions and exemptions set out in IFRS 1.

3. **Recognize and Derecognize All Assets and Liabilities, as Appropriate** The entity recognizes all assets and liabilities in accordance with the requirements of IFRS, and derecognizes assets and liabilities that do not qualify for recognition under IFRS. Subject to certain exceptions and exemptions, a first-time adopter is required to:

   a. Recognize all assets and liabilities whose recognition is required by IFRS;

   b. Not recognize items as assets and liabilities if IFRS do not permit such recognition;

   c. Reclassify items recognized under previous GAAP as one type of asset, liability, or component of equity, but which are a different type of asset, liability, or component of equity under IFRS; and

   d. Apply IFRS in measuring all recognized assets and liabilities.

4. **Fair Value or Revaluation as Deemed Cost** Assets carried at cost (e.g., property, plant, and equipment) may be carried at their fair value at the opening IFRS balance sheet date. Fair value becomes the "deemed cost" going forward under the IFRS cost model. Deemed cost is an amount used as a surrogate for cost or depreciated cost at a given date.

5. **Recognize Adjustments to Assets and Liabilities in Retained Earnings or Other Appropriate Category** The transition to IFRS could result in an entity having to change its accounting policies relating to recognition and/or measurement. All adjustments resulting from the application of IFRS to the opening IFRS statement of financial position are recognized in retained earnings (or, if appropriate, another category of equity) at the date of transition, except for reclassifications between goodwill and intangible assets.

6. **Generally Keep Estimates Consistent** With limited exceptions, estimates in accordance with IFRS at the date of transition must be consistent with estimates made for the same date under previous GAAP.

7. **Required Number of Periods to Present** An entity's first IFRS financial statements include at least three statements of financial position (including one at the date of transition—the beginning of the comparative period), two statements of profit or loss and other comprehensive income, two separate statements of profit or loss (if presented), two statements of cash flows and two statements of changes in equity. All of these statements must be in compliance with IFRS. When an entity presents selective information for previous years, or states key figures or ratios for previous years, IFRS 1 does not require such information to be prepared in accordance with IFRS. However, the entity is required to state clearly that the amounts are not calculated in accordance with IFRS and to disclose the nature of the adjustments (not required to be quantified) that would be required to bring them into line with IFRS.

8. **Certain Historical Data Permitted** Entities are permitted to present historical summaries of certain data for periods before the date of transition which do not comply with IFRS, as long as the information is prominently labeled as not being prepared in accordance with IFRS. Where such information is presented, the entity must also explain the nature of the main adjustments that would be required to render the information compliant with IFRS.

9. **Apply the Same Accounting Policies Throughout** Entities are required to apply the same accounting policies in the opening IFRS statement of financial position and throughout all periods presented in the first IFRS financial statements. An entity may not, therefore, apply different versions of IFRS that were effective at earlier dates. However, new IFRS that are not yet mandatory may be applied if those IFRS permit early adoption. Because a first-time adopter is required to comply with all IFRS effective at the reporting date, it is important to note that the specific transitional provisions of the individual standards do not apply to a first-time adopter. Instead, a first-time adopter prepares the opening statement of financial position in accordance with the requirements of IFRS 1.

D. Required Additional Disclosures and Reconciliations

IFRS 1 requires compliance with all of the presentation and disclosure requirements of other standards and interpretations, and imposes additional disclosure requirements specific to the first IFRS financial statements. First-time adopters are required to provide reconciliations clearly explaining how the transition from previous GAAP to IFRS affected their previously reported financial position, financial performance, and cash flows. These reconciliations must clearly identify the correction of any errors in relation to an entity's previous GAAP financial statements.

1. **Equity and Total Comprehensive Income Reconciliation** IFRS 1 requires the presentation of the reconciliations listed below in an entity's first IFRS financial statements.

   a. Reconciliations of equity reported under previous GAAP to equity under IFRS as at the date of transition to IFRS, and the end of the latest period presented in the entity's most recent annual financial statements under previous GAAP.

   b. Reconciliation to total comprehensive income under IFRS for the latest period in the entity's most recent annual financial statements. The starting point for that reconciliation is total comprehensive income under previous GAAP for the same period or, if the entity did not report such a total, profit or loss under previous GAAP.

2. **Recognizing Impairment Losses for the First Time** If an entity recognized or reversed any impairment losses for the first time in preparing its opening IFRS statement of financial position, the entity is required to provide the disclosures that would have been required if the entity had recognized those impairment losses or reversals in the period beginning with the date of transition to IFRS.

3. **Necessary Transition Explanations** Supplementary explanations necessary for understanding the transition to IFRS are also required in the first IFRS financial statements. Explanations provided should be sufficient to enable users to properly understand the material adjustments to the statement of financial position, the statement of comprehensive income and the statement of cash flows (when a statement of cash flows was previously presented). In addition, the reconciliations should clearly distinguish between errors made under previous GAAP (if any) and adjustments arising due to changes in accounting policies.

4. **Interim Financial Reporting** IFRS 1 does not require a first-time adopter to publish interim financial reports in advance of an entity's first IFRS financial statements. When an interim financial report is presented for part of the period covered by an entity's first IFRS financial statements, IFRS 1 requires additional disclosures in that interim report, including reconciliations between previous GAAP and IFRS. Comparative information is required to be restated.

5. **Required Comparative Information** An entity's first IFRS financial statements are required to include at least one year of comparative information under IFRS. As previously noted, the date of transition to IFRS is defined as the beginning of the earliest period for which an entity presents full comparative information under IFRS in its first IFRS financial statements. Some reporting frameworks, stock exchange regulators, or other governing bodies may require an entity to present more than one year of comparative information in accordance with IFRS. If an entity elects (or is required) to present more than one year of full comparative information prepared in accordance with IFRS, the date of transition is the beginning of the earliest period presented. All comparative information subsequent to the date of transition is restated and presented in accordance with IFRS.

6. **Fair Value of Financial Assets or Liabilities** A first-time adopter is required to disclose the fair value of financial assets or financial liabilities designated at the date of transition either as "at fair value through profit or loss" or as "available-for-sale," and the classification and carrying amount of those financial assets and financial liabilities in its previous financial statements.

7. **Fair Value of Nonfinancial Assets** If the election to use fair value as deemed cost is applied to property, plant and equipment, investment property or intangible assets, the following disclosures are required in the entity's first IFRS financial statements for each line item in the opening IFRS statement of financial position: the aggregate of those fair values, and the aggregate adjustment to the carrying amounts reported under previous GAAP.

8. **Deemed Cost for Related Entities** Also, if the first-time adopter uses a deemed cost in its opening IFRS statement of financial position in its separate financial statements for an investment in a subsidiary, associate or jointly controlled entity, those separate financial statements are required to disclose the aggregate deemed cost of those investments for which deemed cost is their previous GAAP carrying amount, the aggregate deemed cost of those investments for which deemed cost is fair value, and the aggregate adjustment to the carrying amounts reported under previous GAAP.

E. Special Considerations

There are some circumstances that should be reviewed for special consideration.

1. **Accounting Estimates** Accounting estimates required under IFRS that were made under previous GAAP may not be adjusted on transition except to reflect differences in accounting policies or unless there is objective evidence that the estimates were in error. The primary objective of this exception is to prevent entities using the benefit of hindsight to adjust estimates based on circumstances and information which were not available when the amounts were originally estimated under previous GAAP.

   a. When restating previous GAAP amounts for the purpose of its opening IFRS statement of financial position, an entity may have information available that was not available at the time the estimate was made. This information is treated as "non-adjusting" (i.e., the amounts recognized are not adjusted). The implementation guidance accompanying IFRS 1 explains that this exception does not override requirements in other IFRS to base classifications or measurements on circumstances existing at a particular date. This means that if an estimate is required at a specific date, the entity is required to adjust those estimates to be in accordance with IFRS.

   b. Examples given in the implementation guidance are: classification of finance leases and operating leases; restrictions that prohibit capitalization of an internally generated intangible asset if that asset did not qualify for recognition when the expenditure was incurred; and classification of financial instruments as equity instruments or financial liabilities.

2. **Hedge** A hedging relationship only qualifies for hedge accounting if a number of restrictive criteria are satisfied, including appropriate designation and documentation of effectiveness at inception of the hedge and subsequently. A hedging relationship will only qualify for hedge accounting at the date of transition if the hedging relationship has been fully designated and documented as effective on or before the date of transition and is of a type that qualifies for hedge accounting. Designation of a hedging relationship cannot be made retrospectively. However, if an entity designated a net position as a hedged item under previous guidance, it may designate an individual item within that net position as a hedged item, provided that the designation is made by the date of transition.

III. Primary Differences Between U.S. GAAP and IFRS

A. Accounting Policies

U.S. GAAP and IFRS are very similar in identifying accounting policies. Under U.S. GAAP, accounting policies are the specific principles an entity considers to be the most appropriate in the circumstances to present fairly its financial statements in accordance with U.S. GAAP. IFRS identifies accounting policies as the "specific principles, bases, conventions, rules and practices applied by an entity in preparing and presenting financial statements."

1. **U.S. GAAP** The FASB Codification is the source of authoritative U.S. GAAP applied by nongovernmental entities. Rules and interpretive releases of the SEC under federal securities laws are also authoritative GAAP for SEC registrants. An entity should first look into the authoritative GAAP for guidance when choosing an accounting policy. If the guidance for a transaction or event is not specified within a source of authoritative GAAP for that entity, the entity shall next consider accounting principles for similar transactions or events within a source of authoritative GAAP and then consider nonauthoritative guidance from other sources.

2. **IFRS GAAP** The first step to selecting an accounting policy in a particular situation is to determine if there is an IFRS that specifically applies to the transaction or event. If none, the consideration should then be given to the following hierarchy of sources for management to use in exercising their judgment:

   a. Requirements and guidance in other IFRS covering similar or related situations and issues.

   b. Definitions, recognition and measurement criteria, and measurement concepts contained in the IFRS conceptual framework.

   c. The most recent pronouncements of other standard-setting bodies that use a similar conceptual framework for developing standards and other accounting literature or industry practice (as long as they don't conflict with IFRS standards and concepts).

B. Financial Statement Presentation

There are many similarities between U.S. GAAP and IFRS relating to financial statement presentation. Under both frameworks, the components of a complete set of financial statements include a balance sheet, income statement, other comprehensive income, cash flows, and accompanying notes to the financial statements; both require that the financial statements be prepared on the accrual basis of accounting (with the exception of the cash flow statement) except for rare circumstances; both standards have similar concepts regarding materiality and consistency that entities have to consider in preparing their financial statements. Accounting for changes in accounting principles and changes in accounting estimates are the same under GAAP and IFRS. Differences between the two tend to arise in the level of specific guidance. For example, IFRS does not prescribe a standard layout on the Income Statement but does include a list of minimum items.

1. **Presentation of Expenses** Under IFRS, entities may present expenses based on either function or nature (for example, salaries, depreciation). However, if function is selected, certain disclosures about the nature of expenses must be included in the notes. Under U.S. GAAP, SEC registrants are required to present by function (e.g., cost of sales, administrative).

2. **Extraordinary Items** IFRS prohibits the presentation of extraordinary items in the income statement.

3. **Balance Sheet/Statement of Financial Position**

- A third balance sheet (and related notes) is required by IFRS as of the beginning of the earliest comparative period presented when an entity restates its financial statements or retrospectively applies a new accounting policy.
- Current assets are generally listed in order of liquidity under U.S. GAAP, but under IFRS current assets are listed in reverse order of liquidity.
- Under IFRS, some companies list liabilities before assets on the Statement of Financial Position, and some list noncurrent before current. Also under IFRS, net current liabilities are offset against net current assets to show working capital on the face of the statement. Under U.S. GAAP, assets precede liabilities; current precedes noncurrent, and working capital is not shown on the face of the balance sheet.
- Discounts and premiums related to bonds payable are shown in separate accounts under U.S. GAAP. Under IFRS, discounts and premiums are netted against the liability.
- Debt issuance costs are recorded in separate accounts and amortized over the life of the bond under U.S. GAAP. They are recorded as a reduction to the carrying amount of the debt under IFRS.

4. **Income Statement** U.S. GAAP requires three years of Income Statements; IFRS only requires two years. Income attributable to a noncontrolling interest does not need to be shown on the Income Statement under U.S. GAAP but does need to be shown under IFRS.

5. **Statement of Cash Flow** IFRS provides entities greater flexibility concerning classifying cash flows as operating, investing, or financing activities. Specifically, interest and dividends received can be either operating or investing, depending on the circumstances. Interest or dividends paid can be either operating or financing. The FASB excludes bank overdrafts from its definition of cash, while the IASB includes them for those countries in which an overdraft is part of normal cash management. The IASB, like the FASB, encourages entities "to report cash flows from operating activities using the direct method." Under U.S. GAAP, noncash investing and financing activities are usually disclosed on bottom of cash flow statement, while under IFRS they are not shown on the Statement of Cash Flows but rather disclosed in the notes to the financial statements.

C. Fair Value

The FASB issued AUS 2011-04, *Fair Value Measurement (Topic 820)*, in conjunction with the IASB's release of IFRS 13, *Fair Value Measurement*, in May 2011. The result is that IFRS and U.S. GAAP have the same definition and meaning of fair value and the same disclosure requirements about fair value measurements. Some of the differences that still remain between U.S. GAAP and IFRS include:

1. **Day One Gains/Losses** U.S. GAAP permits the recognition of day one gains/losses for the difference between transaction price and fair value, if supported by the relevant facts and circumstances, even when the fair value determination includes significant unobservable inputs. IFRS restricts day one gains/losses when the fair value measurement is based on unobservable inputs (i.e., Level 2 or Level 3).

2. **Alternative Investments** ASC Topic 820 includes a practical expedient to measure fair value of certain alternative investments at net asset value; IFRS does not contain a similar practical expedient.

3. **Disclosure Requirements** Quantitative measurement uncertainty analysis is not required under U.S. GAAP but is required under IFRS for financial instruments measured using a Level 3 fair value measurement. Nonpublic entities are exempt from certain disclosure requirements under U.S. GAAP, but IFRS has no exemptions for nonpublic entities.

D. Financial Instruments

The U.S. GAAP guidance for financial instruments is contained in several standards. IFRS guidance for financial instruments, on the other hand, is more limited. Both U.S. GAAP and IFRS require financial instruments to be classified into specific categories to determine the measurement of those instruments, clarify when financial instruments should be recognized or derecognized in financial statements, require the recognition of all derivatives on the balance sheet, and require detailed disclosures in the notes to the financial statements for the financial instruments reported in the balance sheet. Hedge accounting and use of a fair value option is permitted under both.

1. **Debt vs. Equity Classification** Classification requirements under U.S. GAAP specifically identifies certain instruments with characteristics of both debt and equity that must be classified as liabilities. Certain other contracts that are indexed to, and potentially settled in, a company's own stock may be classified as equity if they: (a) require physical settlement or net-share settlement, or (b) give the issuer a choice of net-cash settlement or settlement in its own shares. Under IFRS, classification of certain instruments with characteristics of both debt and equity focuses on the contractual obligation to deliver cash, assets, or an entity's own shares. Economic compulsion does not constitute a contractual obligation. Contracts that are indexed to, and potentially settled in, a company's own stock are classified as equity if settled by delivering a fixed number of shares for a fixed amount of cash.

2. **Compound (Hybrid) Financial Instruments** Under U.S. GAAP, compound (hybrid) financial instruments (e.g., convertible bonds) are not split into debt and equity components unless certain specific conditions are met, but they may be divided into debt and derivative components, with the derivative component subjected to fair value accounting. Under IFRS, compound (hybrid) financial instruments are required to be split into a debt and equity component and, if applicable, a derivative component. The derivative component may be subjected to fair value accounting.

3. **Recognition and Measurement: Impairment Recognition—Available-for-Sale (AFS) Debt Instruments** There are some distinct differences between U.S. GAAP and IFRS pertaining to impairment recognition of AFS debt instruments.

   a. Under U.S. GAAP, declines in fair value below cost may result in an impairment loss being recognized in the income statement on an AFS debt instrument due solely to a change in interest rates if the entity has the intent to sell the debt instrument or it is more likely than not that it will be required to sell the debt instrument before its anticipated recovery. The impairment loss is measured as the difference between the debt instrument's amortized cost basis and its fair value. When a credit loss exists, but the entity does not intend to, nor is it more likely than not that the entity will be required to, sell the debt instrument before the recovery of the remaining cost basis, the impairment is separated into the amount representing the credit loss, and the amount related to all other factors. The amount of the total impairment related to the credit loss is recognized in the income statement and the amount related to all other factors is recognized in other comprehensive income, net of applicable taxes.

   b. Under IFRS, generally, only evidence of credit default results in an impairment being recognized in the income statement for an AFS debt instrument. The impairment loss is measured as the difference between the debt instrument's amortized cost basis and its fair value. Impairment losses for debt instruments classified as available-for-sale may be reversed through the income statement if the fair value of the instrument increases in a subsequent period and the increase can be objectively related to an event occurring after the impairment loss was recognized. When an impairment loss is recognized in the income statement, a new cost basis in the instrument is established equal to the previous cost basis less the impairment recognized in earnings and it cannot be reversed for any future recoveries. Impairment losses may be reversed through the income statement if the fair value of the instrument increases in a subsequent period and the increase can be objectively related to an event occurring after the impairment loss was recognized.

4. **Impairment Recognition—Available-for-Sale (AFS) Equity Instruments** Under U.S. GAAP, for an AFS equity instrument, an impairment is recognized in the income statement if the equity instrument's fair value is not expected to recover sufficiently in the near-term to allow a full recovery of the entity's cost basis. An entity must have the intent and ability to hold an impaired equity instrument until such near-term recovery; otherwise an impairment loss must be recognized in the income statement. The impairment loss is measured as the difference between the equity instrument's cost basis and its fair value. Under IFRS, for an AFS equity instrument, impairment is recognized in the income statement when there is objective evidence that the AFS equity instrument is impaired and the cost of the investment in the equity instrument may not be recovered. The impairment is measured as the difference between the equity instrument's cost basis and its fair value. A significant or prolonged decline in the fair value of an equity instrument below its cost is considered evidence of impairment.

5. **Held-to-Maturity (HTM) Debt Instruments** Under U.S. GAAP, the impairment loss of an HTM instrument is measured as the difference between its fair value and amortized cost basis. Because an entity has asserted its intent and ability to hold an HTM instrument to maturity (i.e., the entity does not intend to sell the debt instrument and it is not more likely than not the entity will be required to sell the debt instrument before recovery of its amortized cost basis), the amount of the total impairment related to the credit loss is recognized in the income statement and the amount related to all other factors is recognized in other comprehensive income. The carrying amount of an HTM investment, after the recognition of an impairment, is the fair value of the debt instrument at the date of the impairment. The new cost basis of the debt instrument is equal to the previous cost basis less the impairment recognized in the income statement. The impairment recognized in other comprehensive income is accreted to the carrying amount of the HTM instrument through other comprehensive income over its remaining life. Under IFRS, the impairment loss of an HTM instrument is measured as the difference between the carrying amount of the instrument and the present value of estimated future cash flows discounted at the instrument's original effective interest rate. The carrying amount of the instrument is reduced either directly or through use of an allowance account. The amount of impairment loss is recognized in the income statement.

6. **Hedging** Under U.S. GAAP, the shortcut method is permitted. Under IFRS, the shortcut method is not permitted. Under U.S. GAAP, the risk components that may be hedged are specifically defined by the literature, with no additional flexibility. Under IFRS, allows entities to hedge components (portions) of risk that give rise to changes in fair value. Under U.S. GAAP, inclusion of option's time value is permitted. Under IFRS, it is not permitted.

7. **Loans and Receivables: Measurement—Effective Interest Method** Under U.S. GAAP, requires catch-up approach, retrospective method or prospective method of calculating the interest for amortized cost-based assets, depending on the type of instrument. IFRS requires the original effective interest rate to be used throughout the life of the instrument for all financial assets and liabilities, except for certain reclassified financial assets, in which case the effect of increases in cash flows are recognized as prospective adjustments to the effective interest rate.

8. **Measurement—Loans and Receivables** Under U.S. GAAP, unless the fair value option is elected, loans and receivables are classified as either (a) held for investment, which are measured at amortized cost, or (b) held for sale, which are measured at the lower of cost or fair value. Under IFRS, loans and receivables are carried at amortized cost unless classified into the "fair value through profit or loss" category or the "available-for-sale" category, both of which are carried at fair value on the balance sheet.

E. **Cash and Receivables**

Accounting and reporting related to cash is essentially the same under GAAP and IFRS. Cash equivalents are defined essentially the same. The basic accounting and reporting issues related to recognition and measurement of receivables (use of allowance accounts; how to record trade and sales discounts, use of percentage-of-sales and receivable methods, pledging and factoring) are essentially the same.

1. **Derecognition of a Receivable** Under U.S. GAAP, loss of control is the primary criteria for derecognition of a receivable; partial derecognition is not allowed. Under IFRS, derecognition of a receivable is based first on a test of risk/reward assessment and considers a test of control second; partial derecognition is permitted.

2. **Impairment of Notes Receivable** U.S. GAAP, if a note receivable is impaired, the loss is measured by the creditor as the difference between the investment in the loan (usually the principle plus accrued interest) and the expected future cash flows discounted at the loan's historical effective interest rate. The uncollectible amount is recognized through an allowance account. U.S. GAAP prohibits the reversal of impairment losses. IFRS specifies that entities should assess whether its financial assets are impaired. If a portion of accounts receivable is impaired, the loss is measured as the difference between the asset's carrying value and the present value of expected future cash flows discounted at the asset's original effective interest rate. Entities can choose to recognize the uncollectible amount either directly or through an allowance account. IFRS refers to the allowance account as a "provision." The amount of the loss is recognized in profit or loss. IFRS allows entities to subsequently reverse impairment losses provided there is objective evidence to warrant reversing the original impairment. Reversal of impairment is recognized in profit and loss.

F. **Inventory**

Under both U.S. GAAP and IFRS, the primary basis of accounting for inventory is cost under either the perpetual or periodic system. Both define inventory as assets held for sale in the ordinary course of business, in the process of production for such sale, or to be consumed in the production of goods or services. The permitted techniques for cost measurement, such as: FIFO, weighted average, specific identification, gross profit method or retail method, are similar under both. Under both the cost of inventory includes all direct expenditures to ready inventory for sale, including allocable overhead, while selling costs are excluded from the cost of inventories, as are most storage costs and general administrative costs. Determination of ownership for goods in transit, under consignment, and special sales arrangements, are essentially the same.

1. **Cost Methods** Under U.S. GAAP, LIFO is an acceptable costing method, and a consistent methodology for similar items is not explicitly required. Under IFRS, LIFO is prohibited, and a consistent costing methodology for inventory items of nature or use is required.

2. **Measurement** Under U.S. GAAP, inventory is carried at the lower-of-cost market. Market is defined as current replacement cost as long as market is not greater than net realizable value (estimated selling price less reasonable costs of completion and sale) and is not less than net realizable value reduced by a normal sales margin. Under IFRS, inventory is carried at the lower of cost or net realizable value (best estimate of the net amounts inventories are expected to realize). This amount may or may not equal fair value.

3. **Impairment Recoveries** Under U.S. GAAP, any write-downs of inventory to the lower of cost or market create a new cost basis that subsequently cannot be reversed. Under IFRS, previously recognized impairment losses are reversed, up to the amount of the original impairment loss when the reasons for the impairment no longer exist.

4. **Biological and Agricultural** Under IFRS, these items are carried at net realizable value at the point of harvest, with changes in value charged to income. U.S. GAAP does not have separate inventory categories for these items.

G. Property, Plant, and Equipment

The U.S. GAAP definition of property, plant, and equipment (PP&E) is similar to IFRS, which addresses tangible assets held for use that are expected to be used for more than one reporting period. If the cost method is used, the asset is carried at cost less accumulated depreciation less impairment. IFRS has several additional classes of PP&E, including: Biological assets and Investment Property. Other important concepts include the following:

1. **Cost** Both accounting models have similar recognition criteria, requiring that amounts be included in the cost of the asset if future economic benefits are probable and can be reliably measured. The costs to be capitalized under both models are similar. Neither model allows the capitalization of start-up costs, general administrative and overhead costs, or regular maintenance. Both U.S. GAAP and IFRS require that the costs of dismantling an asset and restoring its site (i.e., the costs of asset retirement) be included in the cost of the asset. Both models require a provision for asset retirement costs to be recorded when there is a legal obligation, although IFRS requires provision in other circumstances as well.

2. **Depreciation** The depreciation of PP&E is required on a systematic basis under both accounting models. Both treat changes in depreciation method, residual value, and useful economic life as a change in accounting estimate requiring prospective treatment. Under U.S. GAAP, component depreciation is permitted but not common. Under IFRS, component depreciation is required if components of an asset have differing patterns of benefit.

3. **Impairment Recoveries** Under U.S. GAAP, impairment testing uses a two-step process; losses are recognized in current income; subsequent recoveries are not permitted. Under IFRS, if the cost method is used, impairment must be tested and has stricter rules than U.S. GAAP; impairment losses are recognized in income. If the revaluation method is used, impairment gain is treated as a reversal of revaluation unless it exceeds former write-up, in which case excess impairment gain taken to current income.

4. **Assets Held for Sale** Both U.S. GAAP and IFRS have similar held for sale criteria. Under both standards, the asset is measured at the lower of its carrying amount or fair value less costs to sell; the assets are not depreciated and are presented separately on the face of the balance sheet. Exchanges of nonmonetary similar productive assets are also treated similarly in that both allow gain/loss recognition if the exchange has commercial substance and the fair value of the exchange can be reliably measured.

5. **Revaluation** Under U.S. GAAP, revaluation is not permitted. Under IFRS, revaluation is a permitted accounting policy if fair value can be reliably measured (i.e., the revaluation model). Revaluations should be made with sufficient regularity to ensure that the carrying amount of PP&E does not differ materially from the fair value at the balance sheet date. If an item of PP&E is revalued, the entire class to which the asset belongs must also be revalued. If an asset's carrying amount is increased due to revaluation, the increase is credited directly to revaluation surplus in stockholders' equity.

6. **Capitalized Interest** The capitalization of borrowing costs (e.g., interest costs) directly attributable to the acquisition, construction, or production of a qualifying asset are addressed by both U.S. GAAP and IFRS. Qualifying assets are generally defined similarly under both accounting models and both standards require interest costs to be capitalized as part of the cost of a qualifying asset. However, there are differences between U.S. GAAP and IFRS in the measurement of eligible borrowing costs for capitalization.

7. **Measurement of Borrowing Costs** Under U.S. GAAP, eligible borrowing costs do not include exchange rate differences. Interest earned on the investment of borrowed funds generally cannot offset interest costs incurred during the period. For borrowings associated with a specific qualifying asset, borrowing costs equal to the weighted average accumulated expenditures times the borrowing rate are capitalized. Under IFRS, eligible borrowing costs include exchange rate differences from foreign currency borrowings. Borrowing costs are offset by investment income earned on those borrowings. For borrowings associated with a specific qualifying asset, actual borrowing costs are capitalized.

8. **Investment Property** Under U.S. GAAP, investment property is not separately defined and, therefore, is accounted for as held for use or held for sale. Under IFRS, investment property is separately defined as an asset held to earn rent or for capital appreciation (or both) and may include property held by lessees under a finance/operating lease. Investment property may be accounted for on a historical cost basis or on a fair value basis as an accounting policy election. Capitalized operating leases classified as investment property must be accounted for using the fair value model.

H. Intangibles

The definition of intangible assets as identifiable nonmonetary assets without physical substance is the same under both U.S. GAAP and IFRS. The recognition criteria for both accounting models requires that there be probable future economic benefits and that cost can be reliably measured. Cost is the cash equivalent price and includes purchase price, nonrefundable taxes, and direct costs of preparing the intangible asset and bringing it to an appropriate condition for its intended use. Some costs are never capitalized as intangible assets under both models, such as start-up costs. Goodwill is recognized only in a business combination under both U.S. GAAP and IFRS. With the exception of development costs, internally developed intangibles are not recognized as an asset under either U.S. GAAP and IFRS. In addition, internal costs related to the research phase of research and development are expensed as incurred under both accounting models.

1. **Amortization of Intangibles** Amortization of intangible assets over their estimated useful lives is generally required under both U.S. GAAP and IFRS. Both require that if there is no foreseeable limit to the period over which an intangible asset is expected to generate net cash inflows to the entity, the useful life is considered to be indefinite and the asset is not amortized. In addition, goodwill is never amortized.

2. **Development Costs** Under U.S. GAAP, development costs are expensed as incurred unless addressed by a separate standard. Development costs related to computer software developed for external use are capitalized once technological feasibility is established in accordance with specific criteria. In the case of software developed for internal use, only those costs incurred during the application development may be capitalized. Under IFRS, development costs are capitalized when technical and economic feasibility of a project can be demonstrated in accordance with specific criteria. Some of the stated criteria include: demonstrating technical feasibility, intent to complete the asset, and ability to sell the asset in the future. Although application of these principals may be largely consistent with U.S. GAAP, there is no separate guidance addressing computer software development costs.

3. **Advertising Costs** Under U.S. GAAP, advertising and promotional costs are either expensed as incurred or expensed when the advertising takes place for the first time (i.e., a policy choice). Direct response advertising may be capitalized if specific criteria are met. Under IFRS, advertising and promotional costs are expensed as incurred. A prepayment may be recognized as an asset only when payment for the goods or services is made in advance of the entity having access to the goods or receiving the services.

4. **Revaluation** Under U.S. GAAP, revaluation is not permitted. Under IFRS, revaluation to fair value of intangible assets other than goodwill is a permitted accounting policy election for a class of intangible assets. Because revaluation requires reference to an active market for the specific type of intangible, this is relatively uncommon in practice.

I. Impairment of Long-Lived Assets, Goodwill, and Intangible Assets

Both U.S. GAAP and IFRS assess the impairment of long-lived assets in similar manners. Both standards require goodwill and intangible assets with indefinite lives to be reviewed at least annually for impairment and more frequently if impairment indicators are present. Long-lived assets are not tested annually, but rather when there are similar indicators of impairment. In addition, both require that an asset found to be impaired be written down and an impairment loss recognized. Despite the similarity in overall objectives, differences exist in the way in which impairment is reviewed, recognized, and measured.

1. **Method of Determining Impairment—Long-Lived Assets** Under U.S. GAAP, a two-step approach requires a recoverability test be performed first (carrying amount of the asset is compared to the sum of future undiscounted cash flows generated through use and eventual disposition). If it is determined that the asset is not recoverable, impairment testing must be performed. Under IFRS, a one-step approach requires that impairment testing be performed if impairment indicators exist.

2. **Impairment Loss Calculation—Long-Lived Assets** Under U.S. GAAP, the amount by which the carrying amount of the asset exceeds its fair value is considered the impairment loss. Under IFRS, impairment loss is the amount by which the carrying amount of the asset exceeds its recoverable amount. The recoverable amount is the higher of: (a) fair value less costs to sell, and (b) value in use (the present value of future cash flows in use including disposal value). (Note that the definition of fair value in IFRS currently has certain differences from the definition in U.S. GAAP.)

3. **Allocation of Goodwill** Under U.S. GAAP, goodwill is allocated to a reporting unit, which is an operating segment or one level below an operating segment (component). Under IFRS, goodwill is allocated to a cash-generating unit (CGU) or group of CGUs which represents the lowest level within the entity at which the goodwill is monitored for internal management purposes and cannot be larger than an operating segment.

4. **Method of Determining Impairment—Goodwill** Under U.S. GAAP, a two-step approach requires a recoverability test to be performed first at the reporting unit level (carrying amount of the reporting unit is compared to the reporting unit fair value). If the carrying amount of the reporting unit exceeds its fair value, then impairment testing must be performed. Under IFRS, a one-step approach requires that an impairment test be done at the cash-generating unit (CGU) level by comparing the CGU's carrying amount, including goodwill, with its recoverable amount.

5. **Impairment Loss Calculation—Goodwill** Under U.S. GAAP, the amount by which the carrying amount of goodwill exceeds the implied fair value of the goodwill within its reporting unit. Under IFRS, impairment loss on the CGU (amount by which the CGU's carrying amount, including goodwill, exceeds its recoverable amount) is allocated first to reduce goodwill to zero, then, subject to certain limitations, the carrying amount of other assets in the CGU are reduced pro rata, based on the carrying amount of each asset.

6. **Impairment Loss Calculation—Indefinite-Lived Intangible Assets** Under U.S. GAAP, impairment loss is the amount by which the carrying value of the asset exceeds its fair value. Under IFRS, impairment loss is the amount by which the carrying value of the asset exceeds its recoverable amount.

7. **Recoveries** Under U.S. GAAP, reversal of loss is prohibited for all assets to be held and used. Under IFRS, reversal of loss is prohibited for goodwill. Other long-lived assets must be reviewed annually for reversal indicators. If appropriate, loss may be reversed up to the newly estimated recoverable amount, not to exceed the initial carrying amount adjusted for depreciation.

J. Provisions and Contingencies

While the sources of guidance under U.S. GAAP and IFRS differ significantly, the general recognition criteria for provisions (i.e., IFRS term for liabilities of uncertain timing or amount) are similar. IFRS provides the overall guidance for recognition and measurement criteria of provisions and contingencies in a single standard. While there is no equivalent single standard under U.S. GAAP, a number of standards deal with specific types of provisions and contingencies. Both U.S. GAAP and IFRS require recognition of a loss based on the probability of occurrence, although the definition of probability is different under U.S. GAAP (in which probable is interpreted as "likely") and IFRS (in which probable is interpreted as "more likely than not"). Both U.S. GAAP and IFRS prohibit the recognition of provisions for costs associated with future operating activities. Further, both GAAPs require information about a contingent liability, whose occurrence is more than remote but did not meet the recognition criteria, to be disclosed in the notes to the financial statements.

1. **Discounting Provisions** Under U.S. GAAP, provisions may be discounted only when the amount of the liability and the timing of the payments are fixed or reliably determinable, or when the obligation is a fair value obligation (for example, an asset retirement obligation under U.S. GAAP). Discount rate to be used is dependent upon the nature of the provision, and may vary from that used under IFRS. However, when a provision is measured at fair value, the time value of money and the risks specific to the liability should be considered. Under IFRS, provisions should be recorded at the estimated amount to settle or transfer the obligation taking into consideration the time value of money. Discount rate to be used should be a pre-tax rate that reflects current market assessments of the time value of money and the risks specific to the liability.

2. **Measurement of Provisions—Range of Possible Outcomes** Under U.S. GAAP, the most likely outcome within range should be accrued. When no one outcome is more likely than the others, the minimum amount in the range of outcomes should be accrued. Under IFRS, the best estimate of obligation should be accrued. For a large population of items being measured, such as warranty costs, best estimate is typically expected value, although mid-point in the range may also be used when any point in a continuous range is as likely as another. Best estimate for a single obligation may be the most likely outcome, although other possible outcomes should still be considered.

3. **Restructuring Costs** Under U.S. GAAP, once management has committed to a detailed exit plan, each type of cost is examined to determine when recognized. Involuntary employee termination costs are recognized over future service period, or immediately if there is none. Other exit costs are expensed when incurred. Under IFRS, once management has "demonstrably committed" (that is, a legal or constructive obligation has been incurred) to a detailed exit plan, the general provisions of IFRS apply. Costs typically are recognized earlier than under U.S. GAAP because IFRS focuses on the exit plan as a whole, rather than the individual cost components of the plan.

4. **Disclosure of Contingent Liability** Under U.S. GAAP, there is no similar provision to that allowed under IFRS for reduced disclosure requirements. Under IFRS, reduced disclosure is permitted if it would be severely prejudicial to an entity's position in a dispute with other party to a contingent liability.

K. Leases

The overall accounting for leases under U.S. GAAP and IFRS is similar, although U.S. GAAP has more specific application guidance than IFRS. Both focus on classifying leases as either capital (IFRS uses the term "finance") or operating, and both separately discuss lessee and lessor accounting.

1. **Lessee Accounting (Excluding Real Estate)** Both U.S. GAAP and IFRS require the party that bears substantially all the risks and rewards of ownership of the leased property to recognize a lease asset and corresponding obligation, and specify criteria (U.S. GAAP) or indicators (IFRS) to make this determination (that is, whether a lease is capital or operating). The criteria or indicators of a capital lease are similar in that both standards include the transfer of ownership to the lessee at the end of the lease term and a purchase option that, at inception, is reasonably expected to be exercised. Further, U.S. GAAP requires capital lease treatment if the lease term is equal to or greater than 75% of the asset's economic life, while IFRS requires such treatment when the lease term is a "major part" of the asset's economic life. U.S. GAAP specifies capital lease treatment if the present value of the minimum lease payments exceeds 90% of the asset's fair value, while IFRS uses the term "substantially all" of the fair value. IFRS has additional criteria for a finance lease, including: if the asset is of a specialized nature, useful only to the lessee without modification; and if cancellation losses are borne by the lessee. In practice, while U.S. GAAP specifies bright lines in certain instances (for example, 75% of economic life), IFRS's general principles are interpreted similarly to the bright line tests. As a result, lease classification is often the same under U.S. GAAP and IFRS.

2. **Lessor Accounting (Excluding Real Estate)** Lessor accounting under U.S. GAAP and IFRS is similar and uses the above tests to determine whether a lease is a sales-type/direct financing lease or an operating lease. U.S. GAAP specifies two additional criteria (that is, collection of lease payments is reasonably expected and no important uncertainties surround the amount of unreimbursable costs to be incurred by the lessor) for a lessor to qualify for sales-type/direct financing lease accounting that IFRS does not have. Although not specified in IFRS, it is reasonable to expect that if these conditions exist, the same conclusion may be reached under both standards. If a lease is a sales-type/direct financing lease, the leased asset is replaced with a lease receivable. If a lease is classified as operating, rental income is recognized on a straight-line basis over the lease term and the leased asset is depreciated by the lessor over its useful life.

3. **Disclosures** Lease obligation disclosures are more extensive under U.S. GAAP than IFRS.

L. Employee Benefits Other Than Share-Based Payments

Under both U.S. GAAP and IFRS, the periodic postretirement benefit cost under defined contribution plans is based on the contribution due from the employer in each period. The accounting for defined benefit plans has many similarities as well. The defined benefit obligation is the present value of benefits that have accrued to employees through services rendered to that date, based on actuarial methods of calculation. In addition, both U.S. GAAP and IFRS provide for certain smoothing mechanisms in calculating the period pension cost.

1. **Actuarial Method Used for Defined Benefit Plans** Under U.S. GAAP, different actuarial methods are required dependent on the characteristics of the benefit calculation of the plan. Under IFRS, the projected unit credit method is required in all cases.

2. **Valuation of Defined Benefit Plan Assets** Under U.S. GAAP, assets are valued at "market-related" value (which is either fair value or a calculated value that "smooths" the effect of short-term market fluctuations over five years) as of the balance sheet date. Under IFRS, assets are valued at fair value as of the balance sheet date.

3. **Amortization of Prior Service Costs** Under U.S. GAAP, amortization of prior service costs is over the future service lives of employees or, for inactive employees, over the remaining life expectancy of those participants. Under IFRS, it is over the average remaining vesting period; immediate recognition if already vested.

4. **Settlements and Curtailments** Under U.S. GAAP, settlement gain or loss recognized when obligation is settled. Curtailment losses recognized when curtailment is probable of occurring, while curtailment gains are recognized when the curtailment occurs. Under IFRS, gain or loss from settlement or curtailment is recognized when it occurs.

5. **Multi-Employer Pension Plans** Under U.S. GAAP, multi-employer pension plans are accounted for similar to a defined contribution plan. Under IFRS, a multi-employer pension plan is accounted for as either a defined contribution or defined benefit plan based on the terms (contractual and constructive) of the plan. If it's a defined benefit plan, an entity must account for the proportionate share of the plan similar to any other defined benefit plan unless insufficient information is available.

M. Share-Based Payments

The guidance for share-based payments is largely converged. Both U.S. GAAP and IFRS require a fair value-based approach in accounting for share-based payment arrangements whereby an entity (1) acquires goods or services in exchange for issuing share options or other equity instruments (collectively referred to as "shares") or (2) incurs liabilities that are based, at least in part, on the price of its shares or that may require settlement in its shares. Under both GAAPs, this guidance applies to transactions with both employees and nonemployees and is applicable to all companies. Both define the fair value of the transaction to be the amount at which the asset or liability could be bought or sold in a current transaction between willing parties. Further, both U.S. GAAP and IFRS require the fair value of the shares to be measured based on a market price (if available) or estimated using an option-pricing model. The treatment of modifications and settlements of share-based payments is similar in many respects under both U.S. GAAP and IFRS. Finally, both require similar disclosures in the financial statements.

1. **Transactions With Nonemployees** The U.S. GAAP definition of employee focuses mainly on the common law definition of an employee. Either the fair value of (a) the goods or services received, or (b) the equity instruments is used to value the transaction, whichever is more reliable. If using the fair value of the equity instruments, measurement at the earlier of (a) the date at which a "commitment for performance" by the counterparty is reached, or (b) the date at which the counterparty's performance is complete is required. IFRS has a more general definition of an employee that includes individuals who provide services similar to those rendered by employees. Fair value of the transaction should be based on the fair value of the goods or services received, and only on the fair value of the equity instruments if, in the rare circumstance, the fair value of the goods and services cannot be reliably estimated. Measurement date is the date the entity obtains the goods or the counterparty renders the services. No performance commitment concept exists.

2. **Measurement and Recognition of Expense—Awards With Graded Vesting Features** Under U.S. GAAP, entities make an accounting policy election to recognize compensation cost for awards containing only service conditions either on a straight-line basis or on an accelerated basis, regardless of whether the fair value of the award is measured based on the award as a whole or for each individual tranche. Under IFRS, entities must recognize compensation cost on an accelerated basis—each individual tranche must be separately measured.

3. **Equity Repurchase Features at Employee's Selection** U.S. GAAP does not require liability classification if employee bears risks and rewards of equity ownership for at least six months from the date the equity is issued or vests. Under IFRS, liability classification is required (no six-month consideration exists).

4. **Deferred Taxes** Under U.S. GAAP, deferred taxes are calculated based on the cumulative GAAP expense recognized and trued up or down upon realization of the tax benefit. If the tax benefit exceeds the deferred tax asset, the excess ("windfall benefit") is credited directly to shareholder equity. A shortfall of the tax benefit below the deferred tax asset is charged to shareholder equity to the extent of prior windfall benefits, and to tax expense thereafter. Under IFRS, deferred taxes are calculated based on the estimated tax deduction determined at each reporting date (e.g., intrinsic value). If the tax deduction exceeds cumulative compensation cost, deferred tax based on the excess is credited to shareholder equity. If the tax deduction is less than or equal to cumulative compensation cost, deferred taxes are recorded in income.

5. **Modification of Vesting Terms That Are Improbable of Achievement** Under U.S. GAAP, if an award is modified such that the service or performance condition (which was previously improbable of achievement) is probable of achievement as a result of the modification, the compensation cost is based on the fair value of the modified award at the modification date. Grant date fair value of the original award is not recognized. Under IFRS, probability of achieving vesting terms before and after modification is not considered. Compensation cost is the grant-date fair value of the award, together with any incremental fair value at the modification date.

N. Revenue Recognition

Revenue recognition under both U.S. GAAP and IFRS is tied to the completion of the earnings process and the realization of assets from such completion. Under U.S. GAAP, revenues represent actual or expected cash inflows that have occurred or will result from the entity's ongoing major operations. Under IFRS, revenue is defined as "the gross inflow of economic benefits during the period arising in the course of the ordinary activities of an entity when those inflows result in increases in equity other than increases relating to contributions from equity participants." Under both U.S. GAAP and IFRS, revenue is not recognized until it is both realized (or realizable) and earned. Ultimately, both GAAPs base revenue recognition on the transfer of risks and both attempt to determine when the earnings process is complete. Both GAAPs contain revenue recognition criteria that, while not identical, are similar. For example, under IFRS, one recognition criteria is that the amount of revenue can be measured reliably, while U.S. GAAP requires that the consideration to be received from the buyer is fixed or determinable.

1. **Differences in Extent of Guidance** Despite the similarities, differences in revenue recognition may exist as a result of differing levels of specificity between the two GAAPs. There is extensive guidance under U.S. GAAP, which can be very prescriptive and often applies only to specific industries. In addition, the detailed U.S. rules often contain exceptions for particular types of transactions. Further, public companies in the U.S. must follow additional guidance provided by the SEC staff. Conversely, a single standard exists under IFRS, which contains general principles and illustrative examples of specific transactions. Exclusive of the industry-specific differences between the two GAAPs, following are the major differences in revenue recognition.

2. **Sale of Goods** Under U.S. GAAP, revenue recognition requires that delivery has occurred (the risks and rewards of ownership have been transferred), there is persuasive evidence of the sale, the fee is fixed or determinable, and collectibility is reasonably assured. Under IFRS, revenue is recognized only when risks and rewards of ownership have been transferred, the buyer has control of the goods, revenues can be measured reliably, and it is probable that the economic benefits will flow to the company.

3. **Service Revenue** Under U.S. GAAP, certain types of service revenue, primarily relating to services sold with software, have been addressed separately in U.S. GAAP literature. All other service revenue should follow specific industry guidance. Application of long-term contract accounting is not permitted for nonconstruction services. Under IFRS, revenue may be recognized in accordance with long-term contract accounting (i.e., percentage-of-completion), including considering the stage of completion, whenever revenues and costs can be measured reliably, and it is probable that economic benefits will flow to the company.

4. **Construction Contracts** Under U.S. GAAP, construction contracts are accounted for using the percentage-of-completion method if certain criteria are met. Otherwise, completed contract method is used. Construction contracts may be, but are not required to be, combined or segmented if certain criteria are met. Under IFRS, construction contracts are accounted for using the percentage-of-completion method if certain criteria are met. Otherwise, revenue recognition is limited to recoverable costs incurred (i.e., zero-profit method). The completed contract method is not permitted. Construction contracts are combined or segmented if certain criteria are met. Criteria under IFRS differ from those in U.S. GAAP.

5. **Multiple Element Arrangements** Under U.S. GAAP, specific criteria are required in order for each element to be a separate unit of accounting, including delivered elements that must have standalone value. If those criteria are met, revenue for each element of the transaction can be recognized when the element is complete. Under IFRS, recognition of revenue on an element of a transaction is required if that element has commercial substance on its own; otherwise the separate elements must be linked and accounted for as a single transaction. IFRS does not provide specific criteria for making that determination.

6. **Deferred Receipt of Receivables** Under U.S. GAAP, discounting to present value is required only in limited situations. Under IFRS, it is considered to be a financing agreement. Value of revenue to be recognized is determined by discounting all future receipts using an imputed rate of interest.

O. Accounting Changes

U.S. GAAP and IFRS are similar in that the most common reason for an entity to change an accounting principle is that the change is required by a new or revised accounting standard. In U.S. GAAP, an entity can also make a change in accounting principle if the entity can justify the use of an allowable alternative accounting principle on the basis it is preferable. Under IFRS, the only other acceptable reason for a change is that a different policy results in financial statements that provide reliable and more relevant information about the effects of transactions and other events or conditions on the entity's financial position, financial performance, or cash flows. Both U.S. GAAP and IFRS require changes in accounting policy to be accounted for retrospectively unless it is impracticable. Retrospective application for both requires adjustment of the opening balance of retained earnings with the cumulative effect of the change reflected in the carrying amounts of affected assets and liabilities.

P. Interim Financial Reporting

U.S. GAAP and IFRS interim financial reporting are substantially similar with the exception of the treatment of certain costs. Under U.S. GAAP, each interim period is viewed as an integral part of an annual period. As a result, certain costs that benefit more than one interim period may be allocated among those periods, resulting in deferral or accrual of certain costs (e.g., certain inventory cost variances may be deferred on the basis that the interim statements are an integral part of an annual period). Under IFRS, each interim period is viewed as a discrete reporting period. A cost that does not meet the definition of an asset at the end of an interim period is not deferred and a liability recognized at an interim reporting date must represent an existing obligation (e.g., inventory cost variances that do not meet the definition of an asset cannot be deferred). However, income taxes are accounted for based on an annual effective tax rate (similar to U.S. GAAP).

Q. Subsequent Events

Despite differences in terminology, the accounting for subsequent events under U.S. GAAP and IFRS is largely similar. An event that occurs during the subsequent events period that provides additional evidence about conditions existing at the balance sheet date usually results in an adjustment to the financial statements. If the event occurring after the balance sheet date but before the financial statements are issued relates to conditions that arose subsequent to the balance sheet date, the financial statements are not adjusted, but disclosure may be necessary in order to keep the financial statements from being misleading.

1. **Date Through Which Subsequent Events Must Be Evaluated** Under U.S. GAAP, subsequent events are evaluated through the date the financial statements are issued or available to be issued. Financial statements are considered issued when they are widely distributed to shareholders or other users in a form that complies with U.S. GAAP. For SEC registrants, financial statements are issued when the financial statements are filed with the SEC. Financial statements are considered available to be issued when they are in a form that complies with U.S. GAAP and all necessary approvals have been obtained. SEC registrants evaluate subsequent events through the date the financial statements are issued, while all other entities evaluate subsequent events through the date that the financial statements were available to be issued. Under IFRS, subsequent events are evaluated through the date that the financial statements are authorized for issue.

2. **Reissuance of Financial Statements** Under U.S. GAAP, if the financial statements are reissued, events or transactions may have occurred that require disclosure in the reissued financial statements to keep them from being misleading. However, an entity cannot recognize events occurring between the time the financial statements were issued or available to be issued and the time the financial statements were reissued unless the adjustment is required by U.S. GAAP or regulatory requirements (e.g., stock splits, discontinued operations, or the effect of adopting a new accounting standard retrospectively would give rise to an adjustment). Entities must disclose both the date that the financial statements were originally issued and the date that they were reissued if the financial statements were revised due to an error correction or retrospective application of U.S. GAAP. IFRS does not specifically address the reissuance of financial statements and recognizes only one date through which subsequent events are evaluated, that is, the date that the financial statements are authorized for issuance, even if they are being reissued. If financial statements are reissued, the date the reissued statements are authorized for reissuance is disclosed. As a result, only one date will be disclosed with respect to the evaluation of subsequent events, and an entity could have adjusting subsequent events in reissued financial statements.

3. **Short-Term Loans Refinanced With Long-Term Loans After Balance Sheet Date** Under U.S. GAAP, short-term loans are classified as long-term if the entity intends to refinance the loan on a long-term basis *and*, prior to issuing the financial statements, the entity can demonstrate an ability to refinance the loan. Under IFRS, short-term loans refinanced after the balance sheet date may not be reclassified to long-term liabilities.

4. **Stock Dividends Declared After Balance Sheet Date** Under U.S. GAAP, financial statements are adjusted for a stock dividend declared after the balance sheet date. Under IFRS, financial statements are not adjusted for a stock dividend declared after the balance sheet date.

R. Foreign Currency Matters

U.S. GAAP and IFRS are similar in their approach to foreign currency translation. Although the criteria to determine an entity's functional currency are different, both generally result in the same determination (that is, the currency of the entity's primary economic environment). Both require the identification of hyperinflationary economies and generally consider the same economies to be hyperinflationary. Both require foreign currency transactions to be re-measured into an entity's functional currency with amounts resulting from changes in exchange rates being reported in income. Except for the translation of financial statements in hyperinflationary economies, the method used to translate financial statements from the functional currency to the reporting currency is the same. Both require re-measurement into the functional currency before translation into the reporting currency. Assets and liabilities are translated at the period-end rate and income statement amounts generally are translated at the average rate, with the exchange differences reported in equity. Both also require certain foreign exchange effects related to net investments in foreign operations to be accumulated in shareholders' equity (i.e., the cumulative translation adjustment portion of other comprehensive income) instead of recording them in net income as they arise. In general, the cumulative translation adjustments reported in equity are reflected in income when there is a sale, complete liquidation or abandonment of the foreign operation.

1. **Translation/Functional Currency of Foreign Operations in Hyperinflationary Economy** Under U.S. GAAP, local functional currency financial statements are re-measured as if the functional currency was the reporting currency (U.S. dollar in the case of a U.S. parent) with resulting exchange differences recognized in income. IFRS requires that the functional currency be maintained. However, local functional currency financial statements (current and prior period) are indexed using a general price index (i.e., restated in terms of the measuring unit current at the balance sheet date with the resultant effects recognized in income), and then translated to the reporting currency at the current rate.

2. **Consolidation of Foreign Operations** Under U.S. GAAP, a "bottoms-up" approach is required in order to reflect the appropriate foreign currency effects and hedges in place. As such, an entity should be consolidated by the enterprise that controls the entity. Therefore, the "step-by-step" method of consolidation is used whereby each entity is consolidated into its immediate parent until the ultimate parent has consolidated the financial statements of all the entities below it. Under IFRS, the method of consolidation is not specified and, as a result, either the "direct" or the "step-by-step" method of consolidation is used. Under the "direct" method, each entity within the consolidated group is directly translated into the functional currency of the ultimate parent and then consolidated into the ultimate parent (i.e., the reporting entity) without regard to any intermediate parent. The choice of consolidation method used could affect the cumulative translation adjustments deferred within equity at intermediate levels, and, therefore, the recycling of such exchange rate differences upon disposal of an intermediate foreign operation.

3. **Net Investment Denominated in Currencies Other Than Functional Currencies of Entities That Are Parties to Monetary Items** Under U.S. GAAP, intercompany foreign currency transactions between the entities within the consolidated group, for which settlement is neither planned nor likely to occur in the foreseeable future, may be considered a part of the net investment if the monetary items are denominated in the functional currencies of the entities that are parties to the monetary items. IFRS does not require monetary items to be denominated in functional currencies of the entities that are parties to the monetary item in order for it to be accounted for as a part of the reporting entity's net investment in those entities.

S. Income Taxes

U.S. GAAP and IFRS both require entities to account for current tax effects and expected future tax consequences of events that have been recognized (i.e., deferred taxes) using an asset and liability approach. Further, deferred taxes for temporary differences arising from nondeductible goodwill are not recorded under either approach and tax effects of items accounted for directly in equity during the current year also are allocated directly to equity. Finally, neither U.S. GAAP nor IFRS permits the discounting of deferred taxes.

1. **Tax Basis** Under U.S. GAAP, tax basis is a question of fact under the tax law. For most assets and liabilities there is no dispute on this amount; however, when uncertainty exists it is determined in accordance with specific guidance. Under IFRS, tax basis is generally the amount deductible or taxable for tax purposes. The manner in which management intends to settle or recover the carrying amount affects the determination of tax basis.

2. **Taxes on Intercompany Transfers of Assets That Remain Within a Consolidated Group** U.S. GAAP requires taxes paid on intercompany profits to be deferred and prohibits the recognition of deferred taxes on differences between the tax bases of assets transferred between entities/tax jurisdictions that remain within the consolidated group. IFRS requires taxes paid on intercompany profits to be recognized as incurred and requires the recognition of deferred taxes on differences between the tax bases of assets transferred between entities/tax jurisdictions that remain within the consolidated group. Under U.S. GAAP, the tax effect of intercompany transactions are recognized at seller entity's tax rate; under IFRS, the tax effect of intercompany transactions recognized at buyer entity's tax rate.

3. **Uncertain Tax Positions** Under U.S. GAAP, there is a two-step process for separating recognition from measurement. A benefit is recognized when it is "more likely than not" to be sustained based on the technical merits of the position. The amount of benefit to be recognized is based on the largest amount of tax benefit that is greater than 50 percent likely of being realized upon ultimate settlement. Detection risk is precluded from being considered in the analysis. IFRS does not include specific guidance. IFRS indicates that tax assets and liabilities should be measured at the amount expected to be paid. Some adopt a "one-step" approach which recognizes all uncertain tax positions at an expected value. Others adopt a "two-step" approach which recognizes only those uncertain tax positions that are considered more likely than not to result in a cash outflow.

4. **Initial Recognition Exemption** U.S. GAAP does not include an exemption like that under IFRS for nonrecognition of deferred tax effects for certain assets or liabilities. Under IFRS, deferred tax effects arising from the initial recognition of an asset or liability are not recognized when (a) the amounts did not arise from a business combination and (b) upon occurrence the transaction affects neither accounting nor taxable profit.

5. **Recognition of Deferred Tax Assets** Under U.S. GAAP, recognized in full (except for certain outside basis differences), but valuation allowance reduces asset to the amount that is more likely than not to be realized. Under IFRS, amounts are recognized only to the extent it is probable (similar to "more likely than not" under U.S. GAAP) that they will be realized.

6. **Calculation and Classification of Deferred Tax Assets and Liabilities** Under U.S. GAAP, enacted tax rates must be used in the calculation of deferred tax assets and liabilities and either current or noncurrent classification in the balance sheet, based on the nature of the related asset or liability, is required. Report net current and net noncurrent on balance sheet. Under IFRS, enacted or "substantively enacted" tax rates as of the balance sheet date must be used in the calculation of deferred tax assets and liabilities and all amounts are classified as noncurrent in the balance sheet. Report net noncurrent only if it relates to same taxing authority; else do not net.

T. Business Combinations

The first major collaborative convergence project between the IASB and the FASB was on business combinations. Under both U.S. GAAP and IFRS, all business combinations are accounted for using the acquisition method. Under the acquisition method, upon obtaining control of another entity, the underlying transaction should be measured at fair value, and this should be the basis on which the assets, liabilities, and noncontrolling interests of the acquired entity are measured with limited exceptions. Even though the new standards are substantially converged, certain differences still exist.

1. **Measuring the Noncontrolling Interest** Under IFRS, noncontrolling interest is measured either at fair value, including goodwill, or at its proportionate share of the fair value of the acquiree's identifiable net assets, excluding goodwill. Under U.S. GAAP, noncontrolling interest is measured at fair value, which includes the non-controlling interest's share of goodwill.

2. **Intangible Resulting From Acquired Lease Terms** Under U.S. GAAP, if the terms of an acquiree operating lease are favorable or unfavorable relative to market terms, the acquirer recognizes an intangible asset or liability, respectively, regardless of whether the acquiree is the lessor or the lessee. Under IFRS, separate recognition of an intangible asset or liability is required only if the acquiree is a lessee. If the acquiree is the lessor, the terms of the lease are taken into account in estimating the fair value of the asset subject to the lease. Separate recognition of an intangible asset or liability is not required.

U. Consolidated and Combined Statements

Under both U.S. GAAP and IFRS, the determination of whether or not entities are consolidated by a reporting enterprise is based on control, although differences exist in the definition of control. Under IFRS the focus is on the concept of power to govern financial and operating policies. Under U.S. GAAP the focus is on controlling financial interests. Under both, generally, all entities subject to the control of the reporting enterprise must be consolidated (note that there are limited exceptions in U.S. GAAP in certain specialized industries).

1. **Uniform Policies for Consolidated Entities** Uniform accounting policies are used for all of the entities within a consolidated group, with certain exceptions under U.S. GAAP (e.g., a subsidiary within a specialized industry may retain the specialized accounting policies in consolidation). However, under U.S. GAAP, uniform accounting policies are not required between investor and investee for equity method investments, while they are required under IFRS.

2. **Reporting Date of Parent and Subsidiary** Under U.S. GAAP and IFRS, the consolidated financial statements of the parent and its subsidiaries may be based on different reporting dates, as long as the difference is not greater than three months. However, under IFRS, a subsidiary's financial statements should be as of the same date as the financial statements of the parent unless it is impracticable to do so.

3. **Control Definition** The IASB definition of control is as follows: an investor controls an investee when the investor is exposed, or has rights, to variable returns from its involvement with the investee and has the ability to affect those returns through its power over the investee. Power arises from voting rights (either majority or less than a majority), potential voting rights, other contractual arrangements, or a combination thereof. An entity can exercise control with less than 50% of the voting rights. Disclosure requirements were expanded such that investors were able to assess the nature of, and changes in, the risks associated with its interests in consolidated and unconsolidated structured entities.

V. Biological Assets

The term "biological assets" does not exist in U.S. GAAP authoritative literature. In IFRS, the term is defined as a living animal or plant. U.S. GAAP does permit animals available and held for sale and harvested crops to be accounted for at 1) the lower of cost or market or 2) net realizable value. Under IFRS, a biological asset should be measured at fair value less estimated point-of-sale costs. The biological asset may be measured at cost less accumulated depreciation and accumulated impairment losses if upon initial recognition market-determined prices or values are not available and alternative estimates of fair value are unreliable. Then, once the fair value can be determined, the biological asset should be measured at fair value less estimated point-of-sale costs. Agricultural produce is defined as the harvested product of a biological asset. It should be measured at fair value less estimated point-of-sale costs at the point of harvest. Such measurement represents the cost at that date. Examples of these terms would be a vine (the biological asset) and grapes (the agricultural produce from the vine).

IV. IFRS for Small and Medium-Sized Entities (SMEs)

A. Objective of IFRS for SMEs

The IASB created the IFRS for SMEs as a simplified version of IFRS. Companies that do not have public accountability can use these standards. Like the "full" IFRS technical literature, the IFRS for SMEs document is intended to apply when SMEs are preparing general purpose financial statements. These are statements directed to the general financial information needs of a wide range of users who are not in a position to demand reports tailored to meet their particular information needs. General purpose financial statements include those that are presented separately or within another public document (e.g., annual reports).

In 2008, the AICPA recognized the IASB as an accounting body for establishing international financial accounting and reporting principles. As a result, nonpublic U.S. companies could now prepare their financial statements under IFRS for SMEs without having to reconcile to U.S. GAAP.

B. How Smaller Entities Can Benefit From a Single Set of Global Standards

Smaller entities can benefit from a common set of accounting standards comparable across countries in the following ways:

1. Financial institutions make loans across borders, using financial statements in making lending decisions and establishing the terms of loans

2. Vendors want to evaluate the financial health of buyers before selling goods or services on credit

3. Credit rating agencies try to develop uniform ratings across borders

4. Smaller entities may have overseas suppliers, and use financial statements when assessing the viability of long-term business relationships

5. Venture capital firms provide funding across borders

6. Smaller entities may have outside investors who are not involved in the day-to-day management of the entity

C. General Differences Between Full IFRS and *IFRS for SMEs*

Many of the principles for recognizing and measuring financial statement components in full IFRS have been simplified, while topics not relevant to SMEs were omitted or drastically reduced in coverage. The extent of required disclosures has also been significantly reduced, focusing on providing information about short-term cash flows, liquidity, and cash-benefit trade-offs. To further ease the burden of SME reporting, revisions to IFRS for SMEs have been limited to once every three years.

D. Basic Financial Statements

Using the IFRS for SMEs document, a complete set of financial statements includes all of the following:

1. A statement of financial position

2. Either a single statement of comprehensive income for the reporting period that includes display of all items of income and expense recognized during the reporting period, including those items that are recognized in the determination of profit or loss (that would be shown as a subtotal within the statement of comprehensive income) and items that are included in other comprehensive income; or both a separate income statement and a separate statement of comprehensive income.

3. A statement of changes in equity

4. A statement of cash flows

5. Notes to the financial statements, including a summary of significant accounting policies and other explanatory information

When the only changes in equity during the reporting period arise from profit or loss, payment of dividends, corrections of errors, and/or changes in accounting policies, reporting entities may present a single statement of income and retained earnings in lieu of a statement of comprehensive income and statement of changes in equity. Then, when there are no items of other comprehensive income in any period for financial statements presented, it is acceptable to present only an income statement. Alternatively, a statement of comprehensive income can be presented with the bottom line labeled profit or loss.

E. Entities Appropriate for Use of IFRS for SMEs

The IASB holds that the objective of financial statements as set out in IFRS for SMEs is appropriate to a wide range of users in making economic decisions, without regard to the size of the reporting entity itself. Therefore, the existence of IFRS for SMEs does not imply that full IFRS are not appropriate for smaller entities (e.g., those with public accountability). It is left to the jurisdictions to decide that entities that are economically significant in that jurisdiction. IFRS for SMEs is designed for entities, regardless of size, that are required, or elect, to produce general purpose financial statements for external users.

Ultimately, the decision regarding which entities should adopt IFRS for SMEs will rest with national regulatory authorities and standard-setters. However, IFRS for SMEs is intended for entities that do not have public accountability as follows:

1. Debt or equity instruments are not traded in a public market or is not in the process of issuing such instruments for trading in a public market (e.g., domestic stock exchange, foreign stock exchange, over-the-counter market)

2. The entity does not hold assets in a fiduciary capacity for a broad group of outsiders as one its primary businesses (e.g., bank, credit union, insurance company, securities brokers/ dealers, mutual funds, investment banks, etc.)

V. U.S. Securities and Exchange Commission (SEC)

A. SEC Mission

The mission of the U.S. Securities and Exchange Commission (SEC) is to protect investors, maintain fair, orderly, and efficient markets, and facilitate capital formation. The SEC oversees the key participants in the securities world, including securities exchanges, securities brokers and dealers, investment advisors, and mutual funds. The SEC is concerned primarily with promoting the disclosure of important market-related information, maintaining fair dealing, and protecting against fraud.

B. Legal Authority

The U.S. Securities and Exchange Commission (SEC) is a federal agency which folds primary responsibility for enforcing the federal securities laws and regulating the securities industry, the nation's stock and options exchanges, and other electronic securities markets in the United States.

The SEC was established by the U.S. Congress in 1934 as an independent, quasi-judicial regulatory agency during the Great Depression that followed the Crash of 1929. The main reason for the creation of the SEC was to regulate the stock market and prevent corporate abuses relating to the offering and sale of securities and corporate reporting. The SEC was given the power to license and regulate stock exchanges, the companies whose securities traded on them, and the brokers and dealers who conducted the trading.

Currently, the SEC is responsible for administering seven major laws that govern the securities industry. In addition to the 1934 Act that created it, the SEC enforces the Securities Act of 1933, the Trust Indenture Act of 1939, the Investment Company Act of 1940, the Investment Advisers Act of 1940, the Sarbanes-Oxley Act of 2002 and the Credit Rating Agency Reform Act of 2006.

1. ***Securities Act of 1933*** Often referred to as the "truth in securities" law. Issuers of securities making public offerings for sale in interstate commerce or through the mails, directly or by others on their behalf, are required to file with the Commission registration statements containing financial and other pertinent data about the issuer and the offering. A similar requirement is provided with respect to such public offerings on behalf of a controlling person of the issuer.

2. ***Securities Exchange Act of 1934*** This Act requires the filing of registration applications, annual reports, and other reports with national securities exchanges and the Commission by companies whose securities are listed on the exchanges. Annual and other reports must be filed also by certain companies whose securities are traded on the over-the-counter markets. These must contain financial and other data prescribed by the Commission for the information of investors. Material misstatements or omissions are grounds for suspension or withdrawal of the security from exchange trading.

3. ***Public Utility Holding Company Act of 1935*** This Act authorizes the Commission to regulate gas and electric public-utility holding companies under standards prescribed for the protection of the public interest and the interest of investors and consumers. If not exempt, a public-utility holding company must register with the Commission.

4. ***Trust Indenture Act of 1939*** This Act safeguards the interests of purchasers of publicly offered debt securities issued under trust indentures by requiring the inclusion of certain protective provisions in, and the exclusion of certain types of exculpatory clauses from, trust indentures. The Act also requires that an independent indenture trustee represent the debtors by proscribing certain relationships that could conflict with proper exercise of duties.

5. ***Investment Company Act of 1940*** This Act establishes a comprehensive regulatory framework for investment companies and subjects their activities to regulation under standards prescribed for the protection of investors.

6. ***Investment Advisers Act of 1940*** Persons who, for compensation, engage in the business of advising others with respect to their security transactions must register with the Commission. Their activities in the conduct of such business are subject to standards of the Act which make unlawful those practices which constitute fraud or deceit and which require, among other things, disclosure of any interests they may have in transactions executed for clients. The Act grants to the Commission rulemaking power with respect to fraudulent and other activities of investment advisers.

7. ***Securities Investors Protection Act of 1970*** This Act created the Securities Investors Protection Corporation (SIPC), a nonprofit organization composed of all brokers and dealers registered under the 1934 Act and members of national securities exchanges. The SIPC must submit an annual report on its operations to the SEC.

8. ***Public Company Reform and Investor Protection Act of 2002*** This Act, more commonly known as the Sarbanes-Oxley Act, is the most far-reaching legislation to affect public companies since the Depression era. Among other things, this Act requires management (specifically the chief executive and financial officers) to certify as to the accuracy of the financial statements and to evaluate and report on internal controls over financial reporting.

9. ***Chapter 11 of the Bankruptcy Code*** Chapter 11 of the Bankruptcy Code provides for Commission participation as a statutory party in reorganization cases. Under Section 1109(a) of the Bankruptcy Code, which also applies to Chapter 9 cases regarding municipalities, the Commission "may raise and may appear and be heard on any issue in the case."

C. Organizational Structure

The Commission is composed of five members, not more than three of whom may be members of the same political party. The members are appointed by the President, with the advice and consent of the Senate, for 5-year terms, one term ending each year. The Chairman is designated by the President. The Commission is assisted by a staff, which includes lawyers, accountants, engineers, financial security analysts, investigators, and examiners, as well as administrative and clerical employees.

D. The SEC and Auditing Standards

As a general rule, the SEC does not prescribe the procedures to be followed by independent public accountants in their audit of the financial statements. However, under the various acts that it administers, the SEC has broad powers that may extend to prescribing the detailed steps to be followed by accountants in "certifying" statements for filing with the SEC. The SEC has generally relied on the public accounting profession to establish auditing standards. The SEC has, however, commented extensively in Accounting and Auditing Enforcement Releases (AAERs) on audits that were, in its view, deficient.

VI. SEC's Accounting Standard Setting Process

A. The Influence of the SEC in the Development of Accounting Principles

The SEC has the statutory authority to prescribe the accounting principles to be followed in financial statements filed under the 1933 and 1934 Acts. The SEC has broad statutory powers to make, amend, and rescind any rules and regulations that may be necessary to carry out the provisions of the law. The SEC is authorized to define accounting, technical, and trade terms used in the law, and has the power to prescribe the form in which required information shall be set forth and the items or details to be presented in the financial statements.

1. **Specify Detailed Information** The SEC has invoked its authority to specify the detailed information that financial statements should contain. The Commission has indicated an intention to continue its policy of looking to the private sector for leadership in establishing and improving accounting principles and standards through the Financial Accounting Standards Board (FASB) with the expectation that the FASB's conclusions will promote the interests of investors

2. **Assure Adequate Information Available to Investors** In the exercise of its statutory authority with respect to the form and content of filings under the Acts, the Commission has the responsibility to assure that investors are provided with adequate information. A significant portion of the necessary information is provided by a set of basic financial statements (including the notes thereto) which conform to generally accepted accounting principles. Information in addition to that included in financial statements conforming to generally accepted accounting principles is also necessary. Such additional disclosures are required to be made in various fashions, such as in financial statements and schedules reported on by independent public accountants or as textual statements required by items in the applicable forms and reports filed with the Commission.

3. **Interaction With the FASB** The FASB is the primary private sector standard setter. The FASB's standards are designated as the primary level of generally accepted accounting principles (GAAP) which is the framework for accounting. The FASB's standards set forth recognition, measurement, and disclosure principles to be used in preparing financial statements. In light of the SEC's unique role, it is critical that the SEC work closely with the FASB, particularly as it relate to the FASB's agenda. In addition, the SEC has the ultimate responsibility to ensure that the FASB deals with issues referred to it by the SEC.

4. **Identifying Emerging Accounting Issues** The SEC is on the front line of financial reporting and often is among the first to identify emerging issues and areas of accounting that need attention. Issues needing attention often can be attributed to new and unique transactions that arise in the marketplace, but they also may arise from the authoritative literature. The SEC staff frequently learns of these issues when companies engage them in a dialogue as to the appropriate financial reporting answer in advance of an event or transaction, commonly referred to as "pre-clearing" an accounting question. While these pre-clearance questions usually relate to single transactions, trends tend to develop surrounding certain issues. When they do, the staff refers these issues to the FASB and its interpretative bodies for guidance.

5. **Interaction With the EITF** The Emerging Issues Task Force (EITF) was established by the FASB in July 1984. The objective of the EITF is to assist the FASB and its staff in the identification of accounting issues and implementation problems on a timely basis. While the EITF does not have the authority to issue authoritative accounting standards, the Chief Accountant of the SEC attends EITF meetings and takes the position that since an EITF consensus sets the tone for future accounting, a registrant's accounting practice that differs from a consensus position of the EITF is open to challenge. On occasion, the official minutes of an EITF meeting will indicate the view of the Chief Accountant (officially referred to as the SEC observer) on a particular issue, which typically becomes SEC staff policy, until a FASB statement is issued. In addition, the SEC observer is a member of the EITF agenda committee and, therefore, provides input for the items to be discussed by the EITF.

B. Organization of Accounting Rules and Regulations

All registration statements and periodic reports filed with the SEC which contain financial data, primarily in the form of financial statements and related schedules, must be prepared in accordance with the SEC rules and regulations and related financial interpretations. The SEC has codified its accounting rules and financial reporting regulations and related interpretations in five primary areas.

1. **Regulation S-X** Regulation S-X is the principal accounting regulation of the SEC. S-X requirements of the SEC govern the annual report. All financial statements presented in annual reports must conform to the S-X accounting and disclosure rules. Regulation S-X sets forth requirements as to the form and content of financial statements, including what financial statements must be presented and for what periods. The requirements of S-X are for the most part those required by GAAP; however, S-X does add a limited number of significant non-GAAP disclosures to the primary financial statements. In addition, the stockholders' report must include three-year comparative financial statements prepared in conformity with Regulation S-X.

2. **Regulation S-K** Regulation S-K is a regulation under the Securities Act of 1933 that details the reporting requirements for various SEC filings used by public companies. Regulation S-K begins to impact a company with the filing of Form S-1 in conjunction with an Initial Public Offering (IPO). The S-1 contains the basic business and financial information on an issuer with respect to a specific securities offering. Regulation S-K also applies to any other documents required to be filed under the Exchange Act, such as: going-private transaction statements, tender offer statements, annual reports to security holders and proxy and information statements.

3. **Financial Reporting Releases (FRRs)** In 1982, the SEC began issuing separate Financial Reporting Releases (FRRs). The process resulted in the "Codification of Financial Reporting Policies" (FRP). FRP is updated as each new FRR is issued.

4. **Accounting and Auditing Enforcement Releases (AAERs)** Accounting and Auditing Enforcement Releases (AAERs) communicate enforcement actions involving accountants. AAER 1 contains a topical index of accounting, auditing and related enforcement topics together with a listing of all related ASRs.

5. **Staff Accounting Bulletins (SABs**) Staff Accounting Bulletins are intended to achieve dissemination of administrative interpretations and practices of the SEC staff in reviewing financial information in SEC filings. The bulletins are not rules or interpretations of the Commission, nor have they been officially approved. They represent interpretations by the Division of Corporation Finance and the Office of the Chief Accountant in administering the disclosure requirements of the federal securities laws.

6. **Regulation S-B** Regulation S-B is the source of disclosure requirements for "small business issuer" filings. A small business issuer is defined as a company that meets all of the following criteria: has revenues of less than $425,000,000; is a U.S. or Canadian issuer; is not an investment company or an asset-backed issuer; and if a majority owned subsidiary, the parent corporation is also a small business issuer. Provided, however, that an entity is not a small business issuer if it has a public float (the aggregate market value of the issuer's outstanding voting and nonvoting common equity held by nonaffiliates) of $25,000,000 or more.

C. SEC Influencing Accounting Principles Through FRRs and SABs

The professional groups responsible for developing accounting principles (and statements on auditing standards) typically consult with the staff before issuing pronouncements. Suggestions to the FASB by the SEC staff have taken the form of a Financial Reporting Release (FRR) or Staff Accounting Bulletin (SAB) that highlights the problem, requires additional disclosure, or defines the accounting to be followed until the issue is dealt with by the FASB. They often differ from general practice at the time of their issuance. When a new accounting pronouncement dealing with the subject matter is issued, the applicable SEC pronouncement is usually withdrawn. Accordingly, in the preparation of financial statements public companies in the U.S. must consider not only the relevant pronouncements of the professional literature establishing generally accepted accounting principles, but also the applicable published rules and regulations of the SEC.

VII. SEC Financial Statement Filings

A. Filing Size

There are three categories of companies that are required to file documents with the SEC: (1) companies whose stocks are traded on a national stock exchange, (2) companies with assets of over $10 million and have at least 500 shareholders, or (3) companies that have sold securities to the public pursuant to a registration, such as an initial public offering. The SEC not only regulates any companies that sell securities to the public, but also big companies with significant assets.

B. Relevant Documents

To meet the SEC's requirements for disclosure, a company issuing securities, or whose securities are publicly traded, must make available all information, whether it is positive or negative, that might be relevant to an investor's decision to buy, sell, or hold the security. SEC mandates certain content and disclosures in SEC filings, such as audited financial statements and Management's Discussion and Analysis. A company's financial statements form the core of its required SEC filings, and greatly influence the content of the mandated disclosures included elsewhere in the documents.

Exhibit 4 ▸ Relevant Documents

Registration statements for newly offered securities; Proxy materials sent to shareholders before an annual meeting; Annual reports to shareholders Annual and quarterly filings (Forms 10-K and 10-Q); Documents concerning tender offers (a tender offer is an offer to buy a large number of shares of a corporation, usually at a premium above the current market price); and Filings related to mergers and acquisitions.

C. Registration Statements

The Securities Act of 1933 has two basic objectives: (a) require that investors receive financial and other significant information concerning securities being offered for public sale; and (b) prohibit deceit, misrepresentations, and other fraud in the sale of securities. A primary means of accomplishing these goals is the disclosure of important financial information through the registration of securities. This information enables investors to make informed judgments about whether to purchase a company's securities. While the SEC requires the information provided be accurate, it does not guarantee it. Investors who purchase securities and suffer losses have recovery rights if they can prove that there was incomplete or inaccurate disclosure of important information.

1. **Who Must Register** In general, securities sold in the U.S. must be registered. The registration forms provide essential facts about the company, while minimizing the burden and expense of complying with the law. In general, registration forms call for: (a) a description of the company's properties and business; (b) a description of the security to be offered for sale; (c) information about the management of the company; and (d) financial statements certified by independent accountants. Registration statements and prospectuses become public shortly after filing with the SEC. Registration statements are subject to examination for compliance with disclosure requirements.

2. **Registration Exclusions** Not all offerings of securities must be registered with the Commission. Some exemptions from the registration requirement include: (a) private offerings to a limited number of persons or institutions; (b) offerings of limited size; (c) intrastate offerings; and (d) securities of municipal, state, and federal governments. By exempting many small offerings from the registration process, the SEC seeks to foster capital formation by lowering the cost of offering securities to the public.

3. **Management Responsibilities** The responsibility for the accuracy and completeness of factual information contained in the registration statement lies with management. Management cannot just rely on statements made by accountants and attorneys. Management must properly communicate all needed factual information to recipients.

4. **Stop Order** If all material facts regarding a security are not adequately disclosed in the registration statement, or if important information is omitted, the SEC will require that the registration statement be corrected or expanded by means of an amendment. If the amendment does not resolve the deficiencies, the SEC may exercise its "stop-order" or "refusal-order" powers to prevent the registration statement from becoming effective and the securities from being sold until the deficiencies are corrected. If the stop-order is issued after the registration statement has become effective and the securities have been sold the order prevents further sales of the securities by the issuer or underwriter.

5. **No Action Letters** The staff of the SEC frequently furnishes informal advice and assistance to registrants, prospective issuers, lawyers, and others. The staff also issues no-action and interpretive letters. These letters often deal with legal matters. In a no-action letter the SEC staff advises the person soliciting its views that under a described set of facts the staff would not recommend that the SEC take any action, such as enjoining the proposed transaction, if the transaction described were carried out—hence, the term *no-action letter.*

6. **Safe Harbor Rule** Prospective information may be included in SEC registration forms. The safe harbor rule offers protection of the registrant and independent auditor for litigation for a subsequently found incorrect projection as long as the projection was undertaken in good faith and management had a reliable basis for that assessment.

7. **Injured Stockholder Rights** SEC regulations exist to protect stockholder rights in the event a corporate merger or takeover takes place and the affected stockholders have suffered financial damages as a result of misrepresentations or inadequate disclosures. Injured minority stockholders can proceed under federal law when no remedy is available in a state court.

D. Annual and Quarterly Filings

After the registration statement, the primary filings by a company are its annual report, Form 10-K, and Form 10-Q.

1. **Annual Report** The annual report to shareholders is the principal document used by most public companies to disclose corporate information to their shareholders. It is usually a "state-of-the-company" report, including an opening letter from the Chief Executive Officer, financial data, results of continuing operations, market segment information, new product plans, subsidiary activities, and research and development activities on future programs.

   a. Reporting companies must send annual reports to their shareholders when they hold annual meetings to elect directors. Under the proxy rules, reporting companies will be required to post their proxy materials, including their annual reports, on their company websites.

   b. Although similarly named, the annual report on Form 10-K is distinct from the "annual report to shareholders," which a company must send to its shareholders when it holds an annual meeting to elect directors.

2. **Form 10-K** The Form 10-K, which must be filed with the SEC, typically contains more detailed information about the company's financial condition than the annual report. The annual report on Form 10-K provides a comprehensive overview of the company's business and financial condition and includes audited financial statements.

a. Form 10-K (annual report) consists of:

(1) Part I includes the business, properties, litigation, security ownership of beneficial owners and management. Describe the form of organization, when the company was organized and any business combinations, mergers, or acquisitions. If there have been any significant changes in the manner in which business is being conducted, describe those changes here.

(2) Part II contains market information for the registrant's common stock and related security matters, selected financial information, management's discussion and analysis (MD&A), financial statements, and supplementary information.

The SEC has stated that management's most important responsibilities include communicating with investors in a clear and straightforward manner, and that MD&A is a critical component of that communication. The MD&A requirements are intended to satisfy three principal objectives:

- To provide a narrative explanation of a company's financial statements that enables investors to see the company through the eyes of management;
- To enhance the overall financial disclosure and provide the context within which financial information should be analyzed; and
- To provide information about the quality of, and potential variability of, a company's earnings and cash flow, so that investors can ascertain the likelihood that past performance is indicative of future performance.

(3) Part III indicates directors and executive officers, management compensation and management transactions. The information required in Part III is often incorporated by reference into the proxy statement if the proxy statement is filed no later than 120 days after year end.

(4) Part IV presents exhibits, financial schedules and Form 8-K reports (emergency filings such as a sudden lawsuit).

b. If a shareholder requests a company's Form 10-K, the company must provide a copy. In addition, an accelerated filer must disclose on Form 10-K whether the company makes periodic and current reports available, free of charge, on its website.

c. Large companies with an average annual cash flow of more than $700 million are considered to be "large accelerated filers." Large accelerated filers must file their 10-K within 60 days after their fiscal year ends. Companies with an average annual cash flow of more than $75 million are considered to be "accelerated filers." Accelerated filers must file their 10-K or annual report within 75 days after their fiscal year ends. Nonaccelerated filers have 90 days after the end of their fiscal year to file their 10-K. For example, if a company's fiscal year ends when the calendar year ends (December 31), it must file its 10-K by either the end of February if it is a large accelerated filer, or middle of March if it is an accelerated filer. If the company is not an accelerated filer, then it has until the end of March to file its 10-K.

3. **Form 10-Q** Registrants who are required to file annual reports on Form 10-K with the SEC are also required to file quarterly reports on Form 10-Q for each of the first three fiscal quarters of each year. Fourth quarter information is included in the annual report, so a separate quarterly report is not required. In addition to the most recent quarter end, the company is required to present balance sheets for the end of the preceding fiscal year on the Form 10-Q.

   a. The Form 10-Q includes unaudited financial statements and provides a continuing view of the company's financial position during the year. Any updates and changes that have occurred since the company's last filing should be in the most recent quarterly report.

   b. Accelerated and large accelerated filers must file their Form 10-Q's within 40 calendar days of the end of the quarter while non-accelerated filers have 45 days to file.

   c. Similar to the Form 10-K, the requirements for Form 10-Q are divided into several items, although the items are different.

      (1) Part I includes: financial statements; MD&A; quantitative and qualitative disclosures about market risk; and information about controls and procedures.

      (2) Part II includes information about: legal proceedings; risk factors; changes in securities and use of proceeds; defaults on senior securities; submission of matters to a vote of security holders; other information; and exhibits and reports on Form 10-K.

      If there has been a material default in the payment of principal, interest, or any other material default that was not cured within 30 days, identify the indebtedness and describe the nature of the default. If this default was previously reported on Form 8-K, disclosure is not required again in Form 10-Q.

E. Other Required Filings

In addition to filing annual reports on Form 10-K and quarterly reports on Form 10-Q, public companies must report certain material corporate events on a more current basis.

1. **Form 8-K** This form is used to report "current events" so that investors can obtain information in a timely manner about events material to a company's performance rather than waiting until the next quarterly or annual information is filed. Some of the most common events reported on Form 8-K include quarterly earnings releases, notification about entering into material agreements (including merger agreements) and entering into debt or other direct financial obligations.

   a. Companies have four business days to file a Form 8-K for the events specified in Sections 1-6 and 8. However, if the issuer is furnishing a Form 8-K solely to satisfy its obligations under Regulation FD, then the due date might be earlier.

   b. The instructions for Form 8-K describe the types of events that trigger a public company's obligation to file a current report, which include the following (which is not a comprehensive list):

Exhibit 5 ▸ Examples of Triggering Events

Section 1	**Registrant's Business and Operations**
Item 1.03	Bankruptcy or Receivership
Section 2	**Financial Information**
Item 2.01	Completion of Acquisition or Disposition of Assets
Item 2.02	Results of Operations and Financial Condition
Item 2.06	Material Impairments
Section 3	**Securities and Trading Markets**
Item 3.02	Unregistered Sales of Equity Securities
Section 4	**Matters Related to Accountants and Financial Statements**
Item 4.01	Changes in Registrant's Certifying Accountant
Section 5	**Corporate Governance and Management**
Item 5.01	Changes in Control of Registrant
Item 5.02	Departure of Directors or Certain Officers; Election of Directors; Appointment of Certain Officers
Item 5.05	Amendment to Registrant's Code of Ethics, or Waiver of a Provision of the Code of Ethics
Section 6	**Asset-Backed Securities**
Item 6.02	Change of Servicer or Trustee
Item 6.04	Failure to Make a Required Distribution
Section 8	**Other Events**
Item 8.01	Other Events (Can be used to report events that are not specifically called for by Form 8-K that the registrant considers to be of importance to security holders.)

2. **Form 3** Corporate insiders (i.e., meaning a company's officers and directors, and any beneficial owners of more than ten percent of a class of the company's equity securities registered under Section 12 of the Securities Exchange Act of 1934) must file with the SEC a statement of beneficial ownership regarding those securities. The initial filing is on Form 3. An insider of an issuer that is registering equity securities for the first time under Section 12 of the Exchange Act must file this Form no later than the effective date of the registration statement. If the issuer is already registered under Section 12, the insider must file a Form 3 within ten days of becoming an officer, director, or beneficial owner.

3. **Form 4** Changes in beneficial ownership are reported on Form 4 and must be reported to the SEC within two business days.

4. **Form 5** Insiders must file a Form 5 to report any transactions that should have been reported earlier on a Form 4 or were eligible for deferred reporting. If a Form must be filed, it is due 45 days after the end of the company's fiscal year.

5. **Form D** The SEC does not require companies that are raising less than $1 million under Rule 504 of Regulation D to be "registered" with the SEC, but these companies are required to file a Form D with the SEC. The Form D serves as a brief notice that provides information about the company and the offering.

6. **Basic Information Package (BIP)** Financial disclosures for SEC filings are referred to as the Basic Information Package (BIP). BIP requirements are common to 10-K and to the annual report to shareholders. Some differences exist in presenting financial data on the registration forms. The required BIP consists of the following:

   - Management's discussion and analysis of the financial condition and results of operations.
   - Five-year comparative of selected financial information (e.g., net sales, total assets, income/loss from continuing operations, etc.)
   - Description of the registrant's business and particular segmental data.
   - Essential information needed for an informed decision, especially negative facts. A prominent indication should be made in the registration statement and prospectus to significant adverse contingencies.
   - Data explaining the circumstances applicable to a change in the registrant's independent accountant during the prior two years. If the change emanated over a disagreement between the parties regarding accounting policies and disclosures, this should be stated.
   - Information regarding market price of stock and dividends.

F. Electronic Filing and the EDGAR System

In early 1993, the Commission began to mandate electronic filings through its Electronic Data Gathering, Analysis, and Retrieval system (EDGAR). This system is intended to benefit electronic filers, enhance the speed and efficiency of SEC processing, and make corporate and financial information available to investors, the financial community and others in a matter of minutes. Electronic dissemination generates more informed investor participation and more informed securities markets.

The cornerstone of the EDGAR rules is Regulation S-T, a separate regulation containing rules prescribing requirements for filing electronically and the procedures for making such filings. Regulation S-T supersedes a number of the procedural requirements set forth in the Commission's rules and forms (e.g., requirements relating to paper size and number of copies). The Commission amended its rules and forms, as necessary, to make references to specific electronic filing provisions. The Commission will not accept in paper format filings required to be submitted electronically, absent a hardship exemption.

Rule 103 of Regulation S-T provides a safe harbor against liability for errors in, or omissions from, documents filed electronically that result solely from electronic transmission errors beyond the control of the electronic filer. The safe harbor is available where the electronic filer takes corrective action as soon as reasonably practicable after becoming aware of the error or omission.

VIII. SEC Leadership in International Standards

The SEC has long been a strong leader in supporting international efforts to develop a core set of accounting standards that could serve as a conceptual framework for financial reporting in cross-border offerings. It has repeatedly addressed the issue that securities issuers trying to raise capital in more than one country are faced with the increased compliance costs and inefficiencies of preparing multiple sets of financial statements to comply with different jurisdictional accounting requirements.

- In 2007, the SEC unanimously voted to allow foreign private issuers to file financial statements prepared in accordance with IFRS as issued by the IASB without reconciliation to U.S. GAAP.

- In November 2008, the SEC issued a proposed roadmap that included seven milestones for continuing U.S. progress toward acceptance of IFRS.

- In February 2010, the SEC issued Release Nos. 33-9109 and 34-61578, Commission Statement in Support of Convergence and Global Accounting Standards, in which the SEC stated its continued belief that a single set of high-quality globally accepted accounting standards would benefit U.S. investors and expressed encouragement for the continued convergence of U.S. GAAP and IFRS.

- In 2011, assuming completion of the convergence projects and the SEC staff's work plan, the SEC will decide whether to incorporate IFRS into the U.S. financial reporting system for U.S. issuers, and if so, when and how. If the SEC determines to incorporate IFRS into the U.S. financial reporting system, the SEC believes the first time U.S. entities would be required to report under such a system would be no earlier than 2015.

CHAPTER 17—IFRS & SEC REPORTING

Problem 17-1 MULTIPLE-CHOICE QUESTIONS

1. Which of the following is a true statement related to how the IFRS Foundation ensures public accountability for establishing accounting standards?
   a. The Constitution of the IFRS Foundation requires the Trustees to undertake an informal, non-public, annual review of the Constitution.
   b. A formal due process for the IASB and the IFRS Interpretations Committee includes mandatory public consultation.
   c. The Trustees' effectiveness in exercising their functions is assessed every decade by the Trustees' Due Process Oversight Committee.
   d. All meetings of the bodies of the IFRS Foundation, including the IASB, the Interpretations Committee and its formal advisory bodies, are held in private. (07/10, Editors, 9716)

2. Which of the following is not a formal part of the International Accounting Standards Board (IASB) and its supporting structure?
   a. The U.S. Financial Accounting Foundation
   b. The International Financial Reporting Interpretations Committee (IFRIC)
   c. The Standards Advisory Committee (SAC)
   d. The Trustees Appointments Advisory Group (07/10, Editors, 9717)

3. Which of the following is a true statement regarding the use of discussion papers in the International Financial Reporting Standard (IFRS) development due process?
   a. Use of a discussion paper is mandatory in developing new accounting standards.
   b. The IASB normally publishes discussion papers as its first publication on any major new topic to explain the issue and solicit early comment from constituents.
   c. Discussion papers may not include research performed by other accounting standard setters, including the FASB.
   d. Publication of discussion papers requires a unanimous vote of the IASB Trustees.
   (07/10, Editors, 9719)

4. Which of the following is a normal step that occurs prior to the IASB publishing a new International Financial Reporting Standard (IFRS)?
   a. Publication of an exposure draft is a mandatory step in due process.
   b. Similar to a discussion paper, an exposure draft sets out a general proposal that is not yet in the form of a proposed standard (or amendment to an existing standard).
   c. A final IFRS may be issued regardless of whether the IASB members ballot in favor of publication.
   d. After resolving issues arising from an initial exposure draft, the IASB immediately submits the draft to the IASB members for ballot. (07/10, Editors, 9720)

5. On July 1, year 2, a company decided to adopt IFRS. The company's first IFRS reporting period is as of and for the year ended December 31, year 2. The company will present one year of comparative information. What is the company's date of transition to IFRS?
   a. January 1, year 1
   b. January 1, year 2
   c. July 1, year 2
   d. December 31, year 2 (03/10, RCPM, #9, 9725)

6. On August 1, Year 2, Lex Co. decided to adopt IFRS. The company's first IFRS reporting period is for the year ended December 31, Year 2. Lex will present Year 1 statements for comparative purposes. What is Lex's date of transition to IFRS?
   a. January 1, Year 1
   b. January 1, Year 2
   c. August 1, Year 2
   d. August 1, Year 1 (7/11, Editors, 9084)

7. Upon first-time adoption of IFRS, an entity may elect to use fair value as deemed cost for
   a. Biological assets related to agricultural activity for which there is **no** active market.
   b. Intangible assets for which there is **no** active market.
   c. Any individual item of property, plant and equipment.
   d. Financial liabilities that are **not** held for trading. (03/10, RCPM, #6, 9726)

8. Which of the following is a true statement related to the International Accounting Standards Board's (IASB's) IFRS 1, *First-time Adoption of International Financial Reporting Standards*?
   a. IFRS 1 is intended to be a static standard that is not to be amended or altered.
   b. IFRS 1 will not likely not need future amendment, even as IFRS continues to evolve and expand in its broad-based use throughout the world.
   c. In accordance with IFRS 1, first-time adopters are expected to retrospectively apply all IFRS requirements in their first IFRS-compliant financial statements.
   d. IASB revised the approach to first-time adoption to include limited exemptions from the principle of retrospective application within IFRS. (07/10, Editors, 9721)

9. Which of the following is a true statement regarding first-time adopters of International Financial Reporting Standards (IFRS)?
   a. "Exceptions" to retrospective application under IFRS 1 are optional.
   b. "Exemptions" to retrospective application under IFRS 1 are mandatory.
   c. IFRS 1 adapts the general principle of retrospective application by adding a limited number of very important "exceptions" and "exemptions."
   d. IFRS 1 does not take into account cost-benefit considerations, instead focusing solely on the transparency and comparability of financial information. (07/10, Editors, 9722)

10. Which of the following criteria would qualify an entity's IFRS financial statements as their "first set of IFRS financial statements" as defined by IFRS 1? The entity presented its most recent previous financial statements
    a. In accordance with national requirements that are consistent with IFRS in all material respects.
    b. In conformity with IFRS in all respects, including an explicit and unreserved statement that they complied with IFRS.
    c. In accordance with national requirements, including an explicit statement of compliance with all IFRS.
    d. In accordance with national requirements inconsistent with IFRS, using some individual IFRS to account for items for which national requirements did not exist. (07/10, Editors, 9723)

11. How should a first-time adopter of IFRS recognize the adjustments required to present its opening IFRS statement of financial position?
    a. All of the adjustments should be recognized in profit or loss.
    b. Adjustments that are capital in nature should be recognized in retained earnings and adjustments that are revenue in nature should be recognized in profit or loss.
    c. Current adjustments should be recognized in profit or loss and noncurrent adjustments should be recognized in retained earnings.
    d. All of the adjustments should be recognized directly in retained earnings or, if appropriate, in another category of equity. (R/10, FAR, #53, 9353)

12. Which of the following is the minimum reporting requirement for a company that is preparing its first IFRS financial statements?
    a. Three statements of financial position
    b. Two statements of financial position
    c. One statement of comprehensive income
    d. One statement of cash flows (R/10, FAR, #54, 9068)

13. Which of the following statements is NOT required under the IFRS reporting model?
    a. Notes to the Statements
    b. Statement of Cash Flows
    c. Statement of Retained Earnings
    d. Statement of Comprehensive Income (7/11, Editors, 9083)

14. In the year of transition to IFRS, which of the following is not one of the required Statements of Financial Position?
    a. January 1, Year 1
    b. January 1, Year 2
    c. December 31, Year 1
    d. December 31, Year 2 (7/11, Editors, 9085)

15. Which of the following is a required additional disclosure or reconciliation for first-time adopters of International Financial Reporting Standards (IFRS)?
    a. Reconciliation of equity reported under previous GAAP to equity under IFRS as of the date of transition to IFRSs and the end of the latest period presented in the entity's three most recent annual financial statements under previous GAAP
    d. A combined reconciliation of any errors made under previous GAAP consolidated with additional adjustments arising due to changes in accounting policies due to the IFRS transition
    c. Disclosure of an impairment loss recognized or reversed for the first time in preparing the opening statement of financial position
    b. Reconciliation to total comprehensive income under IFRS for the two latest periods in the entity's most recent annual financial statements (07/10, Editors, 9728)

16. Under IFRS, which of the following is the first step within the hierarchy of guidance to which management refers, and whose applicability it considers, when selecting accounting policies?
    a. Consider the most recent pronouncements of other standard-setting bodies to the extent they do **not** conflict with the IFRS or the IASB Framework.
    b. Apply a standard from IFRS if it specifically relates to the transaction, other event, or condition.
    c. Consider the applicability of the definitions, recognition criteria, and measurement concepts in the IASB Framework.
    d. Apply the requirements in IFRS dealing with similar and related issues. (03/10, RCPM, #7, 9729)

17. Which of the following statements appropriately describes the financial statement presentation requirements of IFRS compared to U.S. GAAP?
    a. IFRS has less prescriptive standard financial statement presentation layouts than U.S. GAAP.
    b. Both U.S. GAAP and IFRS allow the financial statements to be prepared on either the accrual basis or cash basis of accounting, at the sole option of the preparer.
    c. Entities must present expenses based on nature under both U.S. GAAP and IFRS.
    d. Both U.S. GAAP and IFRS allow for the presentation of extraordinary items in the income statement. (07/10, Editors, 9730)

18. Which of the following is a true statement regarding the accounting and reporting requirements related to inventory under both IFRS and U.S. GAAP?
    a. Both IFRS and U.S. GAAP are based on the principle that the primary basis of accounting for inventory is fair value.
    b. Under both IFRS and U.S. GAAP the cost of inventory includes all direct expenditures to ready inventory for sale, including selling and storage costs.
    c. Under both IFRS and U.S. GAAP inventory is carried at the lower of cost market, and any write-downs of inventory create a new cost basis that subsequently cannot be reversed.
    d. Under IFRS, LIFO is prohibited. (07/10, Editors, 9731)

19. An entity elects to use the Revaluation model under IFRS. Which of the following items correctly reflects how assets would be adjusted and where the gain/loss would be reported?

	Asset Basis	Gain/loss reported in
a.	fair value	operating income
b.	fair value	retained earnings
c.	book value	operating income
d.	book value	not recognized

(7/11, Editors, 5608)

20. A company determined the following values for its inventory as of the end of its fiscal year:

Historical cost	$100,000
Current replacement cost	70,000
Net realizable value	90,000
Net realizable value less a normal profit margin	85,000
Fair value	95,000

Under IFRS, what amount should the company report as inventory on its balance sheet?

a. $70,000
b. $85,000
c. $90,000
d. $95,000 (03/10, RCPM, #10, 9732)

21. Which of the following is NOT a true statement regarding the accounting and reporting requirements related to property, plant and equipment under both IFRS and U.S. GAAP?

a. Both IFRS and U.S. GAAP require a provision for asset retirement costs to be recorded when there is a legal obligation.
b. Changes in depreciation method, residual value, and useful economic life are treated as a change in accounting estimate requiring prospective treatment under U.S. GAAP and retrospective application under IFRS.
c. Under U.S. GAAP eligible borrowing costs do not include exchange rate differences and under IFRS eligible borrowing costs include exchange rate differences from foreign currency borrowings.
d. Under U.S. GAAP investment property is not separately defined and, therefore, is accounted for as held for use or held for sale where as under IFRS investment property is separately defined. (07/10, Editors, 9733)

22. Under IFRS, when an entity chooses the revaluation model as its accounting policy for measuring property, plant and equipment, which of the following is correct?

a. When an asset is revalued, the entire class of property, plant and equipment to which the asset belongs must be revalued.
b. When an asset is revalued, individual assets within a class of property, plant and equipment to which that asset belongs can be revalued.
c. Revaluations of property, plant and equipment must be made at least every three years.
d. Increases in an asset's carrying value as a result of the first revaluation must be recognized as a component of profit or loss. (03/10, RCPM, #5, 9734)

23. Under IFRS, which of the following is a criterion that must be met in order for an item to be recognized as an intangible asset other than goodwill?

a. The item's fair value can be measured reliably.
b. The item is part of the entity's activities aimed at gaining new scientific or technical knowledge.
c. The item is expected to be used in the production or supply of goods or services.
d. The item is identifiable and lacks physical substance. (03/10, RCPM, #3, 9735)

24. An entity purchases a trademark and incurs the following costs in connection with the trademark:

One-time trademark purchase price	$100,000
Nonrefundable VAT taxes	5,000
Training sales personnel on the use of the new trademark	7,000
Research expenditures associated with the purchase of the new trademark	24,000
Legal costs incurred to register the trademark	10,500
Salaries of the administrative personnel	12,000

Applying IFRS and assuming that the trademark meets all of the applicable initial asset recognition criteria, the entity should recognize an asset in the amount of

a. $100,000.
b. $115,500.
c. $146,500.
d. $158,500. (03/10, RCPM, #4, 9736)

25. Which of the following is a true statement regarding the accounting and reporting requirements related to intangible costs under both IFRS and U.S. GAAP?
    a. Amortization of intangible assets over their estimated useful lives is required under both U.S. GAAP and IFRS, with one minor exception in U.S. GAAP.
    b. Under U.S. GAAP, development costs are capitalized unless addressed by a separate standard.
    c. Under IFRS, advertising and promotional costs are capitalized.
    d. Under both IFRS and U.S. GAAP, revaluation is not permitted. (07/10, Editors, 9737)

26. Under IFRS, an entity that acquires an intangible asset may use the revaluation model for subsequent measurement only if
    a. The useful life of the intangible asset can be readily determined.
    b. An active market exists for the intangible asset.
    c. The cost of the intangible asset can be measured reliably.
    d. The intangible asset is a monetary asset. (03/10, RCPM, #2, 9738)

27. On January 1, Pax Company acquired for $18,000 a new piece of equipment with an estimated useful life of 10 years. The equipment required the addition of a custom-made component, costing $3,000 that must be replaced in 4 years. Pax uses the straight-line method of depreciation. Under IFRS, what is the depreciation expense for the year ended December 31?
    a. none
    b. $1,800
    c. $2,100
    d. $2,550 (7/11, Editors, 2066)

28. Which of the following is **not** an appropriate description of the accounting treatment for impairment of long-lived assets, goodwill and intangibles under U.S. GAAP and IFRS?
    a. Both sets of standards require goodwill and intangible assets with indefinite lives to be reviewed at least annually for impairment, and more frequently if impairment indicators are present.
    b. Both IFRS and U.S. GAAP require that an asset found to be impaired be written down and an impairment loss recognized.
    c. Reversal of loss of long-lived assets held and used is allowed under both sets of standards.
    d. Both IFRS and U.S. GAAP prohibit reversal of impairment of goodwill. (07/10, Editors, 9739)

29. Under IFRS, changes in accounting policies are
    a. Permitted if the change will result in a more reliable and more relevant presentation of the financial statements.
    b. Permitted if the entity encounters new transactions, events, or conditions that are substantively different from existing or previous transactions.
    c. Required on material transactions, if the entity previously accounted for similar, though immaterial, transactions under an unacceptable accounting method.
    d. Required if an alternate accounting policy gives rise to a material change in assets, liabilities, or the current-year net income. (03/10, RCPM, #1, 9740)

30. Which of the following is a true statement related to foreign currency accounting and reporting under U.S. GAAP and IFRS?
    a. Only IFRS requires the identification of hyperinflationary economies.
    b. Both U.S. GAAP and IFRS require foreign currency transactions to be re-measured into an entity's functional currency with amounts resulting from changes in exchange rates being reported in other comprehensive income.
    c. Both U.S. GAAP and IFRS require the "step-by-step" method of consolidation in reporting the consolidation of foreign operations.
    d. Both U.S. GAAP and IFRS require re-measurement into the functional currency before translation into the reporting currency. (07/10, Editors, 9741)

31. Under IFRS, which of the following is not a criteria for a finance lease?
    a. The present value of the lease payments is equal to substantially all of the fair value of the asset
    b. There is a bargain purchase option
    c. Cancellation losses are borne by the lessor
    d. The lessee has the option to continue the lease at lower than market rates (7/11, Editors, 9757)

32. Under IFRS, which of the following is not an allowed method of accounting for long-term construction contracts?
    a. Fair value through profit and loss method
    b. Percentage of completion method
    c. Revenue recognition to the extent of cost incurred
    d. Completed contract method (7/11, Editors, 9824)

33. Under IFRS, which of the following statements is true?
    a. Convertible bonds must have the debt component separated from the equity component
    b. Deferred tax assets and liabilities must be separated into current and noncurrent components
    c. Significant influence over another company must be accounted for using the equity method
    d. Unrealized holding gains/losses on trading securities go to OCI (7/11, Editors, 9825)

34. Under IFRS, which of the following statements is true?
    a. Deferred tax assets and deferred tax liabilities are calculated under the liability method.
    b. Deferred tax assets and liabilities must be separated into current and noncurrent components.
    c. A deferred tax asset from France can be netted against a deferred tax liability from Germany.
    d. Future tax rates cannot be used if they are only substantially enacted. (7/11, Editors, 9826)

35. Under IFRS, which of the following is not a class for long-lived assets?
    a. Inventory
    b. Financial assets
    c. Biological assets
    d. Investment property (7/11, Editors, 9761)

36. According to the IASB framework, qualitative characteristics of reliability include what?
    a. Verifiability, neutrality, and representational faithfulness
    b. Predictive value, feedback value, and timeliness
    c. Substance over form, prudence, and completeness
    d. Materiality, costs and benefits, and timeliness (7/11, Editors, 9082)

37. Under IFRS, noncash investing and financing activities are reported in the
    a. Supplemental Disclosure section of the Statement of Cash Flows
    b. Statement of Financial Position
    c. Notes to the Financial Statements
    d. Noncash investing and financing activities are not reported under IFRS (7/11, Editors, 9823)

38. Under IFRS, which of the following is false concerning the accounting of long-lived assets?
    a. Property, plant and equipment is accounting for under either the cost model or the revaluation model
    b. Reversal of impairment losses is recorded, with the gain going to the Income Statement
    c. Under the revaluation model, PP&E is adjusted to fair value with any gain/loss going to the Income Statement
    d. The revaluation surplus account is transferred to retained earnings when PP&E is sold (7/11, Editors, 9762)

39. Under IFRS, which of the following is not an acceptable method of accounting for inventory?
    a. Gross profit method
    b. Retail method
    c. LIFO
    d. Weighted average (7/11, Editors, 9758)

40. Murray Co. maintains its records under IFRS. During the year, Murray sold a machine that had been accounted for using the revaluation method. Details are presented below:

Sales Price	$150,000
Machine Book Value	80,000
Revaluation Surplus	9,000

Which of the following is correct regarding the sale?

a. The gain of $70,000 should be credited to Other Comprehensive Income (OCI).
b. The gain of $79,000 should be recorded in profit and loss on the Income Statement.
c. The gain of $70,000 should be recorded in profit and loss, and the $9,000 revaluation surplus should be transferred to retained earnings.
d. No gain or loss should be recorded. (7/11, Editors, 9114)

41. Ames Company determined the following values for its inventory as of December 31:

Historical Cost	$200,000
Replacement Cost	160,000
Sales Value	190,000
Cost to Complete and Sell	10,000
Normal Profit Margin	8,000
Fair Value	194,000

Under IFRS, what amount should Ames report for inventory at December 31?

a. $194,000
b. $180,000
c. $172,000
d. $160,000 (7/11, Editors, 9759)

42. Which of the following appropriately describes a difference between full International Financial Reporting Standards (IFRS) and IFRS for Small and Medium-Sized Entities (SMEs)?

a. Most of the complex options in full IFRS are retained in IFRS for Small and Medium-Sized Entities.
b. The use of fair value is pervasively required under both versions of IFRS.
c. The extent of required disclosures is the same under both versions of IFRS.
d. Simplified principles for recognizing and measuring assets, liabilities, income and expense are emphasized in IFRS for Small and Medium-Sized Entities. (7/11, Editors, 9742)

43. Which of the following is provided under the Investment Company Act of 1940?

a. Allows persons guilty of securities fraud to serve as an officer or director of an investment company
b. Allows transactions between investment companies and their officers or directors without approval by the SEC
c. Requires investment companies to register with the SEC
d. Requires investment bankers, underwriters or brokers to constitute a majority of the directors of an investment company (07/10, Editors, 9699)

44. The law that requires issuers of securities making public offerings for sale to register for the SEC is which of the following?

a. The Securities Act of 1933
b. The Securities Exchange Act of 1934
c. The Trust Indenture Act of 1939
d. The Investment Company Act of 1940 (07/10, Editors, 9696)

45. The law that requires companies to file registration applications and annual and other reports with the national security exchange on which they are listed is which of the following?

a. The Securities Act of 1933
b. The Securities Exchange Act of 1934
c. The Trust Indenture Act of 1939
d. The Investment Company Act of 1940 (07/10, Editors, 9697)

46. The law that safeguards the interests of purchasers of publicly traded debt securities issued under trust indentures is which of the following?
    a. The Securities Act of 1933
    b. The Securities Exchange Act of 1934
    c. The Trust Indenture Act of 1939
    d. The Investment Company Act of 1940 (07/10, Editors, 9698)

47. Which of the following is **not** an authoritative role of the SEC?
    a. Oversee securities exchanges
    b. Insure investors against loss
    c. Investigate securities frauds
    d. Supervise the activities of mutual funds (07/10, Editors, 9695)

48. The division of the SEC that reviews documents that publicly held companies are required to file with the SEC is which of the following?
    a. The Chief Accountant
    b. The Division of Corporation Finance
    c. The Division of Internal Affairs
    d. The Division of Accounting (07/10, Editors, 9700)

49. Which of the following is a true statement related to the SECs accounting standard setting process?
    a. The SEC does not have statutory authority to prescribe accounting principles.
    b. The SEC is not authorized to define accounting, technical, and trade terms used in the law.
    c. The SEC may not prescribe methods for appraisal or valuation of assets and liabilities.
    d. The SEC has broad statutory powers to make, amend, and rescind any rules and regulations that may be necessary to carry out the provisions of the law. (07/10, Editors, 9701)

50. Which of the following is a true statement related to setting accounting standards for publicly traded entities?
    a. The SEC is often among the first to identify emerging financial accounting and reporting issues, and may refer those to the FASB for interpretive guidance.
    b. Publicly traded entities rarely clear accounting treatment with the SEC in advance of a transaction or event being recorded in the financial statements.
    c. The SEC Chief Accountant is not allowed to attend or otherwise participate in meetings of the FASB's Emerging Issues Task Force (EITF).
    d. The SEC is not allowed to establish accounting policy prior to FASB interpretive guidance being made available to the general public. (07/10, Editors, 9702)

51. Which of the following is the principal accounting regulation of the SEC that governs an issuer's annual report?
    a. Regulation S-T
    b. Regulation S-X
    c. Regulation 10-K
    d. Regulation 12B (07/10, Editors, 9703)

52. Which of the following comprise the SEC's Codification of Financial Reporting Policies (FRP), which represent the principles of accounting to be followed by registrants?
    a. Financial Reporting Releases (FRRs)
    b. Staff Accounting Bulletins (SAB)
    c. Accounting and Auditing Enforcement Releases (AAERs)
    d. Concept releases (07/10, Editors, 9705)

53. The primary means for disseminating unofficial administrative interpretations and practices of the SECs Division of Corporation Finance in reviewing financial information in SEC filings is which of the following?
    a. Financial Reporting Releases (FRRs)
    b. Staff Accounting Bulletins (SABs)
    c. Accounting and Auditing Enforcement Releases (AAERs)
    d. Concept releases (07/10, Editors, 9706)

54. Which of the following is a true statement related to the responsibility for full and fair disclosure in a SEC registration statement?
    a. It is the SEC's responsibility to ensure full and fair disclosure in a registration statement.
    b. If important information is omitted from a registration statement, the SEC will not request an amendment be made to the registration statement.
    c. Once a registration statement has become effective and securities have been sold, the SEC has no required recourse if the registration statement contains material omissions.
    d. If a registration statement does not adequately disclose all material facts, the SEC may issue a stop-order to prevent the securities from being sold. (07/10, Editors, 9709)

55. Which of the following is true regarding annual reporting and filing requirements in accordance with the SEC regulations?
    a. Reporting companies must send annual reports to their shareholders when holding annual meetings to elect directors, which may not be satisfied by providing the Form 10-K to shareholders.
    b. Form 10-K typically contains less detailed information about the company's financial condition than the traditional annual report to shareholders.
    c. Large accelerated filers must file Form 10-K within 30 days after fiscal year end.
    d. Companies with less than $75 million of average annual cash flow have 90 days after the fiscal year end to file Form 10-K. (07/10, Editors, 9710)

56. A company is an accelerated filer that is required to file Form 10-K with the United States Securities and Exchange Commission (SEC). What is the maximum number of days after the company's fiscal year end that the company has to file Form 10-K with the SEC?
    a. 60 days
    b. 75 days
    c. 90 days
    d. 120 days (R/10, FAR, #51, 9351)

57. The SEC required form used to report extraordinary transactions or major events that shareholders should be made aware of on a current basis (i.e., generally, within 4 business days from the triggering event) is which of the following?
    a. Form 10-Q
    b. Form 8-K
    c. Form 4
    d. Form 10-K (07/10, Editors, 9712)

58. Which of the following is not commonly considered to be a part of the Basic Information Package (BIP) or required financial disclosures for SEC annual filings?
    a. Management's discussion and analysis for financial condition and results of operations
    b. Two-year comparative financial information
    c. Indication of significant adverse contingencies
    d. Data explaining the circumstances applicable to a change in independent accountant during the prior two years (07/10, Editors, 9713)

59. A company is required to file quarterly financial statements with the United States Securities and Exchange Commission on Form 10-Q. The company operates in an industry that is not subject to seasonal fluctuations that could have a significant impact on its financial condition. In addition to the most recent quarter end, for which of the following periods is the company required to present balance sheets on Form 10-Q?
    a. The end of the corresponding fiscal quarter of the preceding fiscal year
    b. The end of the preceding fiscal year and the end of the corresponding fiscal quarter of the preceding fiscal year
    c. The end of the preceding fiscal year
    d. The end of the preceding fiscal year and the end of the prior two fiscal years (R/10, FAR, #52, 9352)

60. Which of the following is an entity that would generally not be required to file documents with the SEC?
    a. Companies whose stocks are traded on a U.S. national stock exchange
    b. Companies with assets of over $10 million and at least 500 shareholders
    c. Companies that have sold securities through an initial public offering
    d. Companies with assets over $5 million and 10 shareholders (07/10, Editors, 9707)

61. Who must generally register with the SEC under The Securities Act of 1933?
    a. Securities sold in the U.S., unless exempt from registration
    b. Securities sold in overseas exchanges, regardless of size of the offering
    c. Private offerings to a very limited number of investors
    d. Securities of municipal, state and federal governments (07/10, Editors, 9708)

Problem 17-2 SIMULATION: U.S. GAAP vs. IFRS

There are various similarities and differences when comparing accounting under U.S. GAAP and IFRS. Listed below are various accounting treatments that may or may not apply under U.S. GAAP and/or IFRS. Indicate whether the accounting treatment is **True** or **False** for each set of accounting standards.

Accounting Treatment	U.S. GAAP	IFRS
1. Compound (hybrid) financial instruments are required to be split into a debt and equity component.		
2. The impairment loss of a held-to-maturity (HTM) instrument is measured as the difference between its fair value and amortized cost basis.		
3. Goodwill and intangible assets with indefinite lives are required to be reviewed at least annually for impairment.		
4. Once management has committed to a detailed exiting plan, each type of individual restructuring cost is examined to determine when recognized.		
5. Under lessee accounting, the party that bears substantially all the risks and rewards of ownership of the leased property recognizes a lease asset and corresponding obligation.		
6. In accounting for defined benefit plans, actuarial gains or losses must be recognized immediately in other comprehensive income.		
7. In accounting for share-based payments, the fair value of the shares to be measured must be based on a market price (if available) or estimated using an option-pricing model.		
8. Construction contracts are accounted for using the percentage-of-completion method if certain criteria are met. Otherwise, the completed contract method may be used.		
9. Regarding interim financial reporting, each interim period is viewed as a discrete reporting period.		
10. Short-term loans are classified as long-term if the entity intends to refinance the loan on a long-term basis and, prior to issuing the financial statements, the entity can demonstrate an ability to refinance the loan.		
11. The discounting of deferred taxes is required when the uncertain tax positions are considered more likely than not to result in a cash outflow.		
12. A noncontrolling interest is measured either at fair value, including goodwill, or at its proportionate share of the fair value of the acquiree's identifiable net assets, excluding goodwill.		

(07/10, Editors, 9744)

Problem 17-3 SIMULATION: SEC Filings

Listed below are items that may or may not require the filing of an SEC form. Choose which form is required for each item, if any, from the list of choices provided. A choice may be used once, more than once, or not at all.

Form Choices						
Form 2	Form 4	Form 8-K	Form 10-K	Form A	Form C	Form S-T
Form 3	Form 5	Form 8-Q	Form 10-Q	Form B	Form D	None

Item Description	Form Choice
1. There is a change in beneficial ownership.	
2. There is a change in control of the company.	
3. The annual report providing a comprehensive overview of a company's business and financial condition.	
4. A brief notice that provides information about a company and offering that is raising less than $1 million and need not be registered with the SEC but is required to file.	
5. To report required disclosures as specified under Rule 504 of Regulation B.	
6. To report insider transactions that should have been reported earlier or were eligible for deferred reporting.	
7. To disclose whether a company that is an accelerated filer makes periodic and current reports available, free of charge, on its website.	
8. A current report to announce major events that shareholders should know about.	
9. The report filed for each of the first three quarters of the company's fiscal year.	
10. The initial filing of a statement of beneficial ownership.	

(07/10, Editors, 9743)

Problem 17-4 SIMULATION: Research

Question: Who's financial statements does the content of SEC Sections of the FASB Codification relate to?

FASB ASC: [ ] - [ ] - [ ] - [ ]

(07/10, Editors, 9745)

Solution 17-1 MULTIPLE-CHOICE ANSWERS

IFRS Introduction

1. (b) The IFRS Foundation ensures public accountability for establishing accounting standards with a formal due process for the IASB, the IFRS Interpretations Committee and other initiatives, via an extensive outreach which includes mandatory public consultation. The Constitution of the IFRS Foundation requires the Trustees to undertake a formal, public, five-year review of the Constitution; not an informal, non-public, annual review. The Trustees' effectiveness in exercising their functions is assessed annually, not every decade, by the Trustees' Due Process Oversight Committee. All meetings of the bodies of the IFRS Foundation, including the IASB, the Interpretations Committee, and its formal advisory bodies, are not private but rather are held in public and are webcast. (9716)

2. (a) The U.S. Financial Accounting Foundation is not a part of the IASB; it is the independent, private sector organization that is responsible for the oversight, administration, and finances of the FASB, the GASB, and their advisory councils FASAC and GASAC. The IASB structure includes: (1) the International Financial Reporting Interpretations Committee (IFRIC), a 12-member group that helps interpret standards; (2) the Standards Advisory Committee (SAC), a 40-member group that provides advice concerning priorities, accounting issues, and implications of standards on financial statement users; and (3) the Trustees Appointments Advisory Group, a 22-member group that oversees the operation of the IASB. (9717)

3. (b) The IASB normally publishes discussion papers as its first publication on any major new topic to explain the issue and solicit early comment from constituents. Use of a discussion paper is not mandatory in developing new accounting standards. Discussion papers may include research performed by other accounting standard setters, including the FASB. Publication of discussion papers requires a simple majority vote by the IASB, it does not need to be unanimous. (9719)

4. (a) Publication of an exposure draft is a mandatory step in due process. Unlike a discussion paper, an exposure draft sets out a specific proposal in the form of a proposed standard (or amendment to an existing standard). A final IFRS is only issued after the due process is completed, all outstanding issues are resolved, and the IASB members have balloted in favor of publication. After resolving issues arising from the exposure draft, the IASB considers whether it should expose its revised proposals for public comment, for example by publishing a second exposure draft. If the IASB decides that re-exposure is necessary, the due process to be followed is the same as for the first exposure draft. (9720)

First-Time Adoption of IFRS

5. (a) The starting point in IFRS 1 is an opening IFRS statement of financial position prepared at the date of transition to IFRS. The date of transition to IFRS is defined as the beginning of the earliest period for which an entity presents full comparative information under IFRS in its first IFRS financial statements. For entities that present one year of comparative information in their financial reports, the date of transition is the first day of the comparative period. In the given situation the company did present one year of comparative information so the transition date to IFRS would be January1, year 1, the first day of the comparative period. (9725)

6. (a) The date of transition is the beginning of the earliest period for which comparative information is presented, which is January 1, Year 1. (9084)

7. (c) Assets carried at cost (e.g., property, plant, and equipment) may be carried at their fair value at the opening IFRS balance sheet date. Fair value becomes the "deemed cost" going forward under the IFRS cost model. The entity could not elect to use fair value for the biological assets and intangible assets because there is no active market for those assets to be able to come up with a fair value. Financial liabilities are not assets that would be carried at cost and could have fair value as their deemed cost. (9726)

8. (d) The IASB revised the approach to first-time adoption to include limited exemptions from the principle of retrospective application within IFRS. IFRS 1 is not a static standard. As IFRS continues to evolve, consequential amendments to IFRS 1 will be required. Prior to the issuance of IFRS 1, first-time adopters were expected (in most cases) to retrospectively apply all IFRS requirements in their first IFRS-compliant financial statements. Recognizing that this often resulted in costs that exceeded the benefits of the financial information generated, the IASB revised the approach to first-time adoption to include limited exemptions. (9721)

9. (c) IFRS 1 adapts the general principle of retrospective application by adding a limited number of very important "exceptions" and "exemptions." The "exceptions" to retrospective application are mandatory. The "exemptions" to retrospective application are optional. Although the objective of IFRS 1 is to ensure that an entity's first IFRS financial statements contain high quality information that is transparent for users and comparable over all periods presented, IFRS 1 does take into account cost-benefit considerations. (9722)

10. (d) The entity presenting its most recent previous financial statements in accordance with national requirements, with a reconciliation of some amounts to the amounts determined under IFRS or using some individual IFRS to account for items for which national requirements do not exist, is one of the criteria that would qualify an entity's financial statements as the entity's "first set" as defined by IFRS 1. Also qualifying an entity's financial statements as the first IFRS set would be the entity presenting its most recent previous financial statements in accordance with national requirements that are not consistent with IFRS in all respects; in conformity with IFRS in all respects, except that the financial statements did not contain an explicit and unreserved statement that they complied with IFRS; or in accordance with national requirements inconsistent with IFRS, using some individual IFRS to account for items for which national requirements did not exist. (9723)

11. (d) For a first-time adopter of IFRS, all the adjustments required to present its opening IFRS statement of financial position should be recognized directly in retained earnings, or, if appropriate, in another category of equity at the date of transition. Adjustments are not recognized in profit or loss regardless if they are current or noncurrent and whether they are capital in nature or revenue in nature. (9353)

12. (a) In preparing its first IFRS financial statements, a company must report a minimum of three statements of financial position (including one at the date of transition—the beginning of the comparative period), two statements of comprehensive income, two income statements (if presented), two statements of cash flows, and two statements of charges in equity. (9068)

13. (c) IFRS reporting model requires 5 statements: Statement of Financial Position, Statement of Comprehensive Income, Statement of Changes in Equity, Statement of Cash Flows, and Notes/Disclosures to the Statements. Statement of Retained Earnings is only a U.S. GAAP statement. (9083)

14. (b) In the year of transition to IFRS, an entity must present three Statements of Financial Position: January 1, Year 1; December 31, Year 1 and December 31, Year 2 (9085)

15. (c) If an entity recognized or reversed any impairment losses for the first time in preparing its opening IFRS statement of financial position, the entity is required to provide the disclosures that IFRS would have required if the entity had recognized those impairment losses or reversals in the period beginning with the date of transition to IFRS. Also required are reconciliations of equity reported under previous GAAP to equity under IFRS as at the date of transition to IFRS, and the end of the latest period presented in the entity's most recent annual financial statements under previous GAAP; reconciliation to total comprehensive income under IFRS for the latest period in the entity's most recent annual financial statements; and that reconciliations need not be combined but should clearly distinguish between errors made under previous GAAP (if any) and adjustments arising due to changes in accounting policies. (9728)

Differences Between U.S. GAAP & IFRS

16. (b) Within the IFRS hierarchy of guidance, the first step to selecting an accounting policy in a particular situation is to determine if there is an IFRS that specifically applies to the transaction or event. If none, the consideration should then be given to the following hierarchy of sources for management to use in exercising their judgment: requirements and guidance in other IFRS covering similar or related situations and issues; definitions, recognition and measurement criteria, and measurement concepts contained in the IFRS conceptual framework; and finally the most recent pronouncements of other standard-setting bodies that use a similar conceptual framework for developing standards and other accounting literature or industry practice (as long as they don't conflict with IFRS standards and concepts). (9729)

17. (a) IFRS has less prescriptive standard financial statement presentation layouts than U.S. GAAP in that it does not prescribe a standard layout, but includes a list of minimum items. Both U.S. GAAP and IFRS require that the financial statements be prepared on the accrual basis of accounting (with the exception of the cash flow statement) except for rare circumstances. Under IFRS, entities may present expenses based on either function

or nature while as under U.S. GAAP, SEC registrants are required to present by function. IFRS prohibits the presentation of extraordinary items in the income statement. (9730)

18. (d) Under IFRS, LIFO is prohibited; under U.S. GAAP, it's an acceptable costing method. Under both U.S. GAAP and IFRS, the primary basis of accounting for inventory is cost. The cost of inventory includes all direct expenditures to ready inventory for sale (excluding selling and storage costs). Inventory is carried at the lower of cost or market with any write-downs of inventory to the lower of cost or market creating a new cost basis. Under IFRS, previously recognized impairment losses can be reversed, up to the amount of the original impairment loss when the reasons for the impairment no longer exists; under GAAP, impairment losses cannot be reversed. (9731)

19. (b) Under the revaluation model, an entity adjusts the asset to fair value on the date of revaluation. The gain/loss would be reflected in retained earnings. Fair value would be the deemed cost going forward. (5608)

20. (c) Under IFRS, inventory is carried at the lower of cost or net realizable value (best estimate of the net amounts inventories are expected to realize). This amount may or may not equal fair value. The net realizable value of $90,000 is lower than the historical cost of $100,000. (9732)

21. (b) Changes in depreciation method, residual value, and useful economic life are treated as a change in accounting estimate requiring prospective treatment under both U.S. GAAP and IFRS. Both IFRS and U.S. GAAP require a provision for asset retirement costs to be recorded when there is a legal obligation. Under U.S. GAAP, eligible borrowing costs do not include exchange rate differences and under IFRS eligible borrowing costs include exchange rate differences from foreign currency borrowings. Under U.S. GAAP, investment property is not separately defined and, therefore, is accounted for as held for use or held for sale where as under IFRS investment property is separately defined. (9733)

22. (a) Under IFRS, revaluation is a permitted accounting policy if fair value can be reliably measured (i.e., the revaluation model). If an item of PP&E is revalued, the entire class to which the asset belongs must also be revalued. Revaluations should be made with sufficient regularity, not at least every three years, to ensure that the carrying amount of PP&E does not differ materially from the fair value at the balance sheet date. If an asset's carrying amount is increased due to revaluation, the increase is credited directly to revaluation surplus in stockholders' equity and not recognized as a component of profit or loss. (9734)

23. (d) Under both IFRS and U.S. GAAP, an intangible asset is defined as identifiable nonmonetary assets without physical substance. The recognition criteria for both accounting models require that there be probable future economic benefits and its cost, not its fair value, can be reliably measured. The item need not be expected to be used in the production or supply of goods or services nor be part of the entity's activities aimed at gaining new scientific or technical knowledge. (9735)

24. (b) A trademark is an intangible asset. The cost of an intangible asset is the cash equivalent price and includes purchase price, nonrefundable taxes, and direct costs of preparing the intangible asset and bringing it to an appropriate condition for its intended use. In this case, the cash equivalent price would include the one-time trademark purchase price, the nonrefundable VAT taxes, and the legal costs incurred to register the trademark ($100,000 + $5,000 + $10,500 = $115,500). The training, research, and salary expenditures would be expensed as incurred. (9736)

25. (a) Amortization of intangible assets over their estimated useful lives is required under both U.S. GAAP and IFRS, with one minor exception in U.S. GAAP. Under U.S. GAAP, development costs are expensed as incurred, not capitalized, unless addressed by a separate standard. Under IFRS, advertising and promotional costs are expensed as incurred. Under U.S. GAAP, revaluation is not permitted. Under IFRS, revaluation to fair value of intangible assets other than goodwill is a permitted accounting policy election for a class of intangible assets. (9737)

26. (b) Under IFRS, revaluation to fair value of intangible assets other than goodwill is a permitted accounting policy election for a class of intangible assets. Revaluation to fair value requires an active market for the specific type of intangible. Though a reliable useful life and cost are used for amortization, they are not elements required for use of the revaluation model. By definition, intangible assets are nonmonetary assets. (9738)

27. (d) Under IFRS, components with a different estimated useful life must be depreciated separately. The equipment would have $1,800 depreciation ($18,000/10 years) and the component would have $750 depreciation ($3,000/4 years), for total depreciation expense of $2,550 annually. (2066)

28. (c) Under U.S. GAAP, reversal of loss is prohibited for all assets to be held and used. Under IFRS, reversal of loss is just prohibited for goodwill. Both sets of standards require goodwill and intangible assets with indefinite lives to be reviewed at least annually for impairment, and more frequently if impairment indicators are present; that an asset found to be impaired be written down and an impairment loss recognized; and prohibit reversal of impairment of goodwill. (9739)

29. (a) A change in accounting principle results from the adoption of a generally accepted accounting principle (GAAP) different from the previous GAAP used for reporting purposes. U.S. GAAP and IFRS are similar in that the most common reason for an entity to change an accounting principle is that the change is required by a new or revised accounting standard. Under IFRS, the only other acceptable reason for a change is that a different policy results in financial statements that provide reliable and more relevant information about the effects of transactions and other events or conditions on the entity's financial position, financial performance, or cash flows. (9740)

30. (d) Both U.S. GAAP and IFRS require re-measurement into the functional currency before translation into the reporting currency. Assets and liabilities are translated at the period-end rate and income statement amounts generally are translated at the average rate, with the exchange differences reported in equity. Both U.S. GAAP and IFRS also require the identification of hyperinflationary economies and foreign currency transactions to be re-measured into an entity's functional currency with amounts resulting from changes in exchange rates being reported in net income, not other comprehensive income. Under U.S. GAAP, the "step-by-step" method of consolidation is used when reporting the consolidation of foreign operations, and under IFRS, either the "direct" or the "step-by-step" method of consolidation may be used. (9741)

31. (c) Cancellation losses are borne by the lessee, not the lessor, for financing leases under IFRS. Under IFRS, the present value only has to equal substantially all of the fair value of the asset, not greater than or equal to 90% as under U.S. GAAP; a bargain purchase option is a finance/capital lease criteria; the option to continue the lease at lower than market rates is a criteria for a finance lease. (9757)

32. (d) The completed contract method is not allowed under IFRS. IFRS requires the percentage of completion method for long-term construction projects. If the percentage cannot be reasonably estimated, then revenue is recognized only to the extent of cost. (9824)

33. (a) Under IFRS: debt and equity components of convertible bonds must be separately reported; all deferred tax assets and deferred tax liabilities are noncurrent only; unrealized holding gains/losses on trading securities are on the Income Statement; and significant influence can be accounted for either under the equity method or fair value through profit and loss. (9825)

34. (a) Under IFRS, deferred tax assets and deferred tax liabilities are calculated under the liability method, same as U.S. GAAP. Under IFRS, all deferred tax assets and deferred tax liabilities are noncurrent; deferred tax amounts can be netted only if they are from the same taxing authority; and unlike U.S. GAAP, under IFRS future tax rates can be used if they are either enacted into law or substantially enacted. Under U.S. GAAP, the future tax rates must be enacted into law prior to use. (9826)

35. (a) IFRS long-lived asset categories include: property, plant and equipment; investment property; intangible assets; financial assets; investments accounted for using the equity method; and biological assets. Inventory is a current asset under both IFRS and U.S. GAAP. (9761)

36. (c) Substance over form, prudence, and completeness are the IFRS ingredients for reliability. Verifiability, neutrality, and representational faithfulness are the U.S. GAAP ingredients for reliability. Predictive value, feedback value, and timeliness are the U.S. GAAP ingredients for relevance. Materiality is an ingredient for relevance. Cost/benefits and timeliness are constraints under IFRS. (9082)

37. (c) IFRS requires that noncash investing and financing activities be disclosed in the Notes to the Financial Statement, one of five required financial statements under the IFRS reporting model. (9823)

38. (c) Gains and losses from the revaluation model are recorded in Other Comprehensive Income in Stockholders' Equity in a revaluation surplus account, not the Income Statement. Under IFRS, either the cost method or the revaluation method is acceptable; impairment losses can be reversed and the gain is recognized; and for PP&E accounted for under the revaluation method, any related revaluation surplus is transferred to retained earnings when the PP&E is sold. (9762)

39. (c) Under IFRS, specific identification is required when the goods are not interchangeable; otherwise, you can use FIFO, the gross profit method (if a physical count is not possible), the retail method (in certain industries), and weighted average. LIFO is prohibited under IFRS. (9758)

40. (c) Two journal entries are required when an asset accounted for under the revaluation model is sold. First, transfer the related revaluation surplus of $9,000 to retained earnings. Second, record the sale and gain/loss as usual. Since the machine's net book value is $80,000, and cash of $150,000 was received, the gain on sale would be $70,000. (9114)

41. (b) Under IFRS, inventory is reported at the lower of cost ($200,000) or market, which is defined as net realizable value (NRV). NRV is the selling price ($190,000) less disposal cost ($10,000), or $180,000. Ames should report inventory of $180,000. (9759)

IFRS for Small & Medium-Sized Entities (SMEs)

42. (d) Simplified principles for recognizing and measuring assets, liabilities, income and expense are emphasized in IFRS for SMEs (e.g., all R&D is expensed, goodwill is amortized, cost method is used for joint ventures, etc.). Most of the complex options in full IFRS are omitted (e.g., only the cost method is permitted for PP&E). For SMEs, the use of fair value is greatly reduced, and the extent of required disclosures was drastically reduced. The emphasis on disclosures is to provide basic information about short-term cash flows, liquidity, and cash-benefit trade-offs. (9742)

SEC Introduction

43. (c) The Investment Company Act of 1940 establishes a comprehensive regulatory framework for investment companies, which subjects their activities to SEC regulation to prescribed for investor protections. This includes a requirement that investment companies register with the SEC. The Act bars persons guilty of securities fraud to serve as an officer or director of an investment company, prohibits transactions between investment companies and their investment companies and their officers or directors without approval by the SEC, and prevents investment bankers, underwriters or brokers to constitute a majority of the directors of an investment company. (9699)

44. (a) The *Securities Act of 1933* is often referred to as the "truth in securities" law. Issuers of securities making public offerings for sale in interstate commerce or through the mails, directly or by others on their behalf, are required to file with the Commission registration statements containing financial and other pertinent data about the issuer and the offering. The *Securities Exchange Act of 1934* requires the filing of registration applications and annual and other reports with national securities exchanges and the SEC, by companies whose securities are listed on the exchanges. The Trust Indenture Act of 1939 safeguards the interests of purchasers of publicly offered debt securities issued under trust indentures by requiring the inclusion of certain protective provisions in, and the exclusion of certain types of exculpatory clauses from, trust indentures. The Investment Company Act of 1940 establishes a comprehensive regulatory framework for investment companies, which subjects their activities to SEC regulation to prescribed for investor protections. (9696)

45. (b) The *Securities Exchange Act of 1934* requires the filing of registration applications and annual and other reports with national securities exchanges and the SEC, by companies whose securities are listed on the exchanges. Annual and other reports must be filed also by certain companies whose securities are traded on the over-the-counter markets. The *Securities Act of 1933* requires issuers of securities making public offerings for sale in interstate commerce or through the mails, directly or by others on their behalf, to file with the Commission registration statements containing financial and other pertinent data about the issuer and the offering. The Trust Indenture Act of 1939 safeguards the interests of purchasers of publicly offered debt securities issued under trust indentures by requiring the inclusion of certain protective provisions in, and the exclusion of certain types of exculpatory clauses from, trust indentures. The Investment Company Act of 1940 establishes a comprehensive regulatory framework for investment companies, which subjects their activities to SEC regulation to prescribed for investor protections. (9697)

46. (c) The Trust Indenture Act of 1939 safeguards the interests of purchasers of publicly offered debt securities issued under trust indentures by requiring the inclusion of certain protective provisions in, and the exclusion of certain types of exculpatory clauses from, trust indentures. The Act also requires that an independent indenture trustee represent the debtors by proscribing certain relationships that could conflict with proper exercise of duties. The *Securities Act of 1933* requires issuers of securities making public offerings for sale in interstate commerce or through the mails, directly or by others on their behalf, to file with the Commission registration statements containing financial and other pertinent data about the issuer and the offering. The *Securities Exchange Act of 1934* requires the filing of registration applications and annual and other reports with national securities exchanges and the SEC, by companies whose securities are listed on the exchanges. The Investment Company Act of 1940 establishes a comprehensive regulatory framework for investment companies, which subjects their activities to SEC regulation to prescribed for investor protections. (9698)

47. (b) Although part of the mission of the SEC is to protect investors, it does **not** insure investors against loss. Registration of securities does not imply approval of the issue by the Commission or insure investors against loss in their purchase, but serves rather to provide information upon which investors may make an informed and realistic evaluation of the worth of the securities. Among other things, the SEC does oversee securities exchanges, investigate securities frauds, and supervise the activities of mutual funds. (9695)

48. (b) The SEC's Division of Corporation Finance reviews documents that publicly held companies are required to file with the SEC. Through the Division's review process, the staff checks to see if publicly held companies meet disclosure requirements. The SEC's Corporation Finance Division also provides administrative interpretations of the Securities Act of 1933, the Securities Exchange Act of 1934, and the Trust Indenture Act of 1939, and recommends regulations to implement these statutes. The Chief Accountant of the Commission is the principal adviser to the Commission on, and is responsible to the Commission for, all accounting and auditing matters arising in the administration of the federal securities laws. There is no known specific Division of Internal Affairs or Division of Accounting. (9700)

SEC Standard Setting

49. (d) The SEC does have broad statutory powers to make, amend, and rescind any rules and regulations that may be necessary to carry out the provisions of the law. The SEC also has the statutory authority to prescribe the accounting principles to be followed in financial statements filed under the 1933 and 1934 Acts, is authorized to define accounting, technical, and trade terms used in the law, and may prescribe the methods to be followed in the preparation in the appraisal or valuation of assets and liabilities. (9701)

50. (a) The SEC is often among the first to identify emerging issues and areas of accounting that need attention. When they do, the staff refers these issues to the FASB and its interpretative bodies for guidance. Publicly traded entities frequently clear accounting treatment with SEC staff in advance of a transaction or event being recorded in the financial statements. The Chief Accountant of the SEC attends the FASB's Emerging Issues Task Force (EITF) meetings and takes the position that since an EITF consensus sets the tone for future accounting, a registrant's accounting practice that differs from a consensus position of the EITF is open to challenge. On occasion, the official minutes of an EITF meeting will indicate the view of the Chief Accountant on a particular issue, which typically becomes SEC staff policy, until a FASB statement is issued. (9702)

51. (b) Regulation S-X is the principle accounting regulation of the SEC, governing the annual report. All financial statements presented in annual reports must conform to the S-X accounting and disclosure rules. Regulation S-T is the cornerstone of the EDGAR rules, prescribing requirements for electronic filing and the procedures for making such filings. There is no regulation 10-K, but there is a form 10-K which typically contains more detailed information about the company's financial condition than the annual report. Regulation 12B governs all registration statements. (9703)

52. (a) Financial Reporting Releases (FRRs) may require an additional disclosure or define accounting to be followed by issuers. The accounting principles are set forth by the SEC in FRRs that are codified in the FRP. Staff Accounting Bulletins are intended to achieve dissemination of administrative interpretations and practices of the SEC staff in reviewing financial information in SEC filings. Accounting and Auditing Enforcement Releases (AAERs) communicate enforcement actions involving accountants. Concept releases are published to solicit the public's views on securities issues so that it can better evaluate the need for future rulemaking. (9705)

53. (b) Staff Accounting Bulletins are intended to achieve dissemination of administrative interpretations and practices of the SEC staff in reviewing financial information in SEC filings. The bulletins are not rules or interpretations of the Commission, nor have they been officially approved. They represent interpretations by the Division of Corporation Finance and the Office of the Chief Accountant in administering the disclosure requirements of the federal securities laws. Financial Reporting Releases (FRRs) may require an additional disclosure or define accounting to be followed by issuers. Accounting and Auditing Enforcement Releases (AAERs) communicate enforcement actions involving accountants. Concept releases are published to solicit the public's views on securities issues so that it can better evaluate the need for future rulemaking. (9706)

SEC Filings

54. (d) If all material facts regarding a security are not adequately disclosed in the registration statement the SEC will require that the registration statement be corrected or expanded by means of an amendment. If the amendment does not resolve the deficiencies, the SEC may exercise its "stop-order" or "refusal-order" powers to prevent the registration statement from becoming effective and the securities from being sold until the deficiencies are corrected. It is the issuer's responsibility, not the SEC's to ensure full and fair disclosure in a registration statement. If important information is omitted from a registration statement the SEC will also request an amendment be made to the registration statement. Once a registration statement has become effective and securities have been sold, if the registration statement contains material omissions the SEC can still issue a stop-order to prevent further sales of the securities. (9709)

55. (d) Non-accelerated filers (i.e., those that have less than $75 million of average annual cash flow) have 90 days after the end of the fiscal year to file the Form 10-K. Companies sometimes elect to send their Form 10-K to their shareholders in lieu of providing shareholders with an annual report. The Form 10-K typically contains more, not less, detailed information about the company's financial condition than the traditional annual report to shareholders. Large companies with an average annual cash flow of more than $700 million are considered to be "large accelerated filers." Large accelerated filers must file their 10-K within 60 days after their fiscal year ends. (9710)

56. (b) The Form 10-K is an annual report that gives a comprehensive summary of a public company's performance. The maximum number of days after the company's fiscal year end that the company has to file the Form 10-K with the SEC depends on the category of the filer. There are three categories of filers: 1) non-accelerated filers, 2) accelerated filers, and 3) large accelerated filers. Non-accelerated filers must file the Form 10-K with the SEC within 90 days after the end of the company's fiscal year. Non-accelerated filers are issuers that have a public float of less than $75 million. Accelerated filers must file the Form 10-K with the SEC within 75 days after the end of the company's fiscal year. Accelerated filers are issuers that have a public float of at least $75 million but less than $700 million. Large accelerated filers must file the Form 10-K with the SEC within 60 days after the end of the company's fiscal year. Large accelerated filers are issuers that have a public float of $700 million or more. (9351)

57. (b) Form 8-K is the "extraordinary transactions or current report" companies must file with the SEC to announce major events that shareholders should know about. The Form 10-Q contains much of the same information as the annual report, with an updates and changes that have occurred since the company's last filing, and must be filed for each of the first three fiscal quarters of the company's fiscal year. The Form 4 identifies changes in ownership and must be reported to the SEC within two business days. The Form 10-K provides an annual report with a comprehensive overview of the company's business and financial condition and includes audited financial statements. (9712)

58. (b) Financial disclosures for SEC filings are referred to as the Basic Information Package (BIP). BIP requirements are common to 10-K and to the annual report to shareholders. Two-year comparative financial information is not commonly considered to be part of the BIP. The BIP does consist of five-year comparative selected financial data, management's discussion and analysis of the financial condition and results of operations, and data explaining the circumstances applicable to a change in the registrant's independent accountant during the prior two years. (9713)

59. (c) The Form 10-Q is a report of a public company's performance that must be filed quarterly with the SEC. It includes unaudited financial statements and provides a continuing view of the company's financial position during the year. In addition to the most recent quarter end balance sheet, a company is required to present the balance sheet for the end of the preceding fiscal year on the Form 10-Q. (9352)

60. (d) Companies with assets over $5 million and 10 shareholders would generally not be required to file documents with the SEC. There are three categories of companies that are required to file documents with the SEC: (1) companies whose stocks are traded on a national stock exchange, (2) companies with assets of over $10 million and have at least 500 shareholders, or (3) companies that have sold securities to the public pursuant to a registration, such as an initial public offering. The SEC not only regulates any companies that sell securities to the public, but also big companies with significant assets. (9707)

61. (a) In general, securities sold in the U.S. must be registered with the SEC. Registration statements and prospectuses become public shorts after filing with the SEC. There are some limited exemptions from the registration requirement. Those exemptions include securities sold in overseas exchanges, private offerings to a very limited number of investors, and securities of municipal, state and federal governments. (9708)

PERFORMANCE BY SUBTOPICS

Each category below parallels a subtopic covered in Chapter 17. Record the number and percentage of questions you correctly answered in each subtopic area.

IFRS Introduction

Question #	Correct √
1	
2	
3	
4	
# Questions	4
# Correct	______
% Correct	______

First-Time Adoption of IFRS

Question #	Correct √
5	
6	
7	
8	
9	
10	
11	
12	
13	
14	
15	
# Questions	11
# Correct	______
% Correct	______

Differences Between U.S. GAAP and IFRS

Question #	Correct √
16	
17	
18	
19	
20	
21	
22	
23	
24	
25	
26	
27	
28	
29	
30	
31	
32	
33	
34	
35	
36	
37	
38	
39	
40	
41	
# Questions	26
# Correct	______
% Correct	______

IFRS for Small & Medium-Sized Entities (SMEs)

Question #	Correct √
42	
# Questions	1
# Correct	______
% Correct	______

SEC Introduction

Question #	Correct √
43	
44	
45	
46	
47	
48	
# Questions	6
# Correct	______
% Correct	______

SEC Standard Setting

Question #	Correct √
49	
50	
51	
52	
53	
# Questions	5
# Correct	______
% Correct	______

SEC Filings

Question #	Correct √
54	
55	
56	
57	
58	
59	
60	
61	
# Questions	8
# Correct	______
% Correct	______

Solution 17-2 SIMULATION: U.S. GAAP vs. IFRS

Accounting Treatment	U.S. GAAP	IFRS
1. Compound (hybrid) financial instruments are required to be split into a debt and equity component.	False	True
2. The impairment loss of a held-to-maturity (HTM) instrument is measured as the difference between its fair value and amortized cost basis.	True	False
3. Goodwill and intangible assets with indefinite lives are required to be reviewed at least annually for impairment.	True	True
4. Once management has committed to a detailed exiting plan, each type of individual restructuring cost is examined to determine when recognized.	True	False
5. Under lessee accounting, the party that bears substantially all the risks and rewards of ownership of the leased property recognizes a lease asset and corresponding obligation.	True	True
6. In accounting for defined benefit plans, actuarial gains or losses must be recognized immediately in other comprehensive income.	False	False
7. In accounting for share-based payments, the fair value of the shares to be measured must be based on a market price (if available) or estimated using an option-pricing model.	True	True
8. Construction contracts are accounted for using the percentage-of-completion method if certain criteria are met. Otherwise, the completed contract method may be used.	True	False
9. Regarding interim financial reporting, each interim period is viewed as a discrete reporting period.	False	True
10. Short-term loans are classified as long-term if the entity intends to refinance the loan on a long-term basis and, prior to issuing the financial statements, the entity can demonstrate an ability to refinance the loan.	True	False
11. The discounting of deferred taxes is required when the uncertain tax positions are considered more likely than not to result in a cash outflow.	False	False
12. A noncontrolling interest is measured either at fair value, including goodwill, or at its proportionate share of the fair value of the acquiree's identifiable net assets, excluding goodwill.	False	True

Explanations are on the next page.

Solution 17-2 SIMULATION: U.S. GAAP vs. IFRS, continued.

Explanations (Provided as needed, only for the False correct answer choices)

1. U.S. GAAP – Under U.S. GAAP, compound (hybrid) financial instruments (e.g., convertible bonds) are not split into debt and equity components unless certain specific conditions are met, but they may be divided into debt and derivative components, with the derivative component subjected to fair value accounting.

2. IFRS – Under IFRS, the impairment loss of an HTM instrument is measured as the difference between the carrying amount of the instrument and the present value of estimated future cash flows discounted at the instrument's original effective interest rate. The carrying amount of the instrument is reduced either directly or through use of an allowance account. The amount of impairment loss is recognized in the income statement.

3. No explanation required.

4. IFRS – Under IFRS, once management has "demonstrably committed" to a detailed exit plan, the general provisions of IFRS apply. Costs typically are recognized earlier than under U.S. GAAP because IFRS focuses on the exit plan as a whole, rather than the individual cost components of the plan.

5. No explanation required.

6. U.S. GAAP and IFRS – Under both U.S. GAAP and IFRS, actuarial gains or losses may be recognized in the income statement as they occur or deferred through a corridor approach or other rational approach applied consistently from period to period. Under IFRS, entities can elect to recognize actuarial gains or losses immediately in other comprehensive income. If immediately recognized in other comprehensive income they are not subsequently recognized in the income statement.

7. No explanation required.

8. IFRS – Under IFRS, construction contracts are accounted for using the percentage-of-completion method if certain criteria are met. Otherwise, revenue recognition is limited to recoverable costs incurred. The completed contract method is not permitted.

9. U.S. GAAP – Under U.S. GAAP, each interim period is viewed as an integral part of an annual period. As a result, certain costs that benefit more than one interim period may be allocated among those periods, resulting in deferral or accrual of certain costs (e.g., certain inventory cost variances may be deferred on the basis that the interim statements are an integral part of an annual period).

10. IFRS – Under IFRS, short-term loans refinanced after the balance sheet date may not be reclassified to long-term liabilities.

11. U.S. GAAP and IFRS – U.S. GAAP and IFRS both require entities to account for both current tax effects and expected future tax consequences of events that have been recognized (i.e., deferred taxes) using an asset and liability approach. Neither U.S. GAAP nor IFRS permits the discounting of deferred taxes.

12. U.S. GAAP– Under U.S. GAAP, noncontrolling interest is measured at fair value, which includes the noncontrolling interest's share of goodwill. There is no option to measure the noncontrolling interest at its proportionate share of the fair value of the acquiree's identifiable net assets, excluding goodwill. (9744)

Solution 17-3 SIMULATION: SEC Filings

Item Description	Form Choice
1. There is a change in beneficial ownership.	Form 4
2. There is a change in control of the company.	Form 8-K
3. The annual report providing a comprehensive overview of a company's business and financial condition.	Form 10-K
4. A brief notice that provides information about a company and offering that is raising less than $1 million and need not be registered with the SEC but is required to file.	Form D
5. To report required disclosures as specified under Rule 504 of Regulation B.	None *
6. To report insider transactions that should have been reported earlier or were eligible for deferred reporting.	Form 5
7. To disclose whether a company that is an accelerated filer makes periodic and current reports available, free of charge, on its website.	Form 10-K
8. A current report to announce major events that shareholders should know about.	Form 8-K
9. The report filed for each of the first three quarters of the company's fiscal year.	Form 10-Q
10. The initial filing of a statement of beneficial ownership.	Form 3

* There is no Regulation B under SEC reporting requirements.

(9743)

Solution 17-4 SIMULATION: Research

FASB Accounting Standards Codification

FASB ASC: 105 - 10 - 15 - 2

15-2 Content in the Securities and Exchange Commission (SEC) Sections of the Codification is provided for convenience and relates only to financial statements of SEC registrants that are presented in conformity with GAAP. (9745)

CHAPTER 18

GOVERNMENT FUNDS & TRANSACTIONS

CHAPTER 18

GOVERNMENT FUNDS & TRANSACTIONS

I. Introduction

A. Funds

A specific governmental unit is not accounted for through a single accounting entity. Instead, the accounts of a government are divided into several funds. A fund is a fiscal and accounting entity with a self-balancing set of accounts recording cash and other financial resources, together with all related liabilities and residual equities and balances, and changes therein, that are segregated for the purpose of carrying on specific activities or attaining certain objectives in accordance with special regulations, restrictions, or limitations. A government should have only one general fund. It may have one, none, or several of the other types of funds, depending on its activities. Governments should use the minimum number of funds consistent with their laws (and contracts) and sound financial management. The fund flow accounting for government funds is one of the truly unique aspects of state and municipal accounting, and it's a heavily tested topic on CPA exams. Comparisons among the types of funds are common questions on the exam.

1. **Governmental Funds** Governmental funds are used to finance general government activities such as police and fire protection, courts, inspection, and general administration. Most of their financial resources are subsequently budgeted (appropriated) for specific general government uses (expenditures) by the legislative body. Governmental funds are essentially working capital funds, and their operations are measured in terms of sources and uses of working capital, that is, changes in working capital. The accounting equation of most governmental funds is: *Current Assets – Current Liabilities = Fund Balance.* Governmental fund types include the general fund, special revenue funds, capital project funds, debt service funds, and permanent funds.

2. **Proprietary Funds** Proprietary funds are used to finance a government's self-supporting business-type activities (for example, utilities). The accounting equation of proprietary funds is identical to that of a business corporation—it includes accounts for all related assets and liabilities, not just for current assets and current liabilities, as well as for contributed capital and retained earnings. Proprietary fund operations are measured in terms of revenues earned, expenses incurred, and net income or loss. Proprietary fund types include enterprise funds and internal service funds.

3. **Fiduciary Funds** Fiduciary funds account for resources (and related liabilities) held by governments in a trustee capacity (trust funds) or as an agent for others (agency funds). Fiduciary fund types include pension trust funds, investment trust funds, private-purpose trust funds, and agency funds.

B. Fundamentals

1. **Basis of Accounting** The basis of accounting used depends on the nature of the fund.

   a. The modified accrual basis is used in the governmental fund type statements (general, special revenue, capital projects, and debt service funds), where revenues and expenditures are recorded.

   b. The accrual basis is used in proprietary fund statements, where revenues and expenses are recorded and net income (loss) is reported. The accrual basis is also used in fiduciary fund statements, except for the recognition of certain liabilities of defined benefit pension plans and certain postemployment healthcare plans.

Exhibit 1 ▸ Basis of Accounting

	Accrual	Modified Accrual
Revenues	Accrued as earned	Accrued when available and measurable
Expenses	Fixed assets are capitalized	Fixed assets are expenditures

2. **Budgets** Annual budgets of estimated revenues and estimated expenditures are prepared for most governmental funds. The approved budgets of such funds are recorded in budgetary accounts in the accounting system to provide control over governmental fund revenues and expenditures. Proprietary and fiduciary funds—and most capital projects funds—are not dependent on annual budgets and legislative appropriations of resources, and thus budgets are not usually incorporated into their accounts. The balances of budget accounts are generally the opposite of the companion accounts. For instance, the *Revenues* account ordinarily has a credit balance, but *Estimated Revenues* is opened with a debit balance.

3. **Encumbrance System** The encumbrance system is used in governmental funds (General, special revenue, and capital projects funds) to prevent over-expenditure and to demonstrate compliance with legal requirements. When a purchase order is issued or a contract is approved, the estimated amount of the planned expenditure is encumbered (committed) by debiting *Encumbrances* (or *Encumbrances Control*) and crediting *Reserve for Encumbrances* (sometimes called *Budgetary Fund Balance—Reserved for Encumbrances*). When the related invoice is received, the encumbrance entry is reversed and the actual expenditure is recorded.

   a. The unencumbered balance of the *Appropriations* account is the amount of uncommitted appropriations funds available for expenditures.

$$\text{Unencumbered Appropriations} = \text{Appropriations} - \left(\text{Outstanding Encumbrances} + \text{Year-to-date Expenditures}\right)$$

   b. If funds are encumbered but not yet expended at the end of the period, the usual accounting treatment is to close the encumbrances account. This is a two step process. First, close out any remaining balance in the *Encumbrance Control* account (i.e., debit *Budgetary Fund Balance-Reserved for Encumbrances* and credit *Encumbrances Control*). Second, adjust the fund balance accounts for the amount of potential obligations.

   If the closing entry is the General Fund, debit *Unassigned Fund Balance* and credit *Committed Fund Balance*. If the closing entry is in one of the other governmental funds (i.e., Capital projects fund), debit *Assigned Fund Balance* and credit *Committed Fund Balance*. The only time you would use *Unassigned Fund Balance* in one of the other governmental funds (i.e., not the General fund), would be if the fund is in deficit; otherwise, use Assigned.

   The *Budgetary Fund Balance-Reserve for Encumbrances account* thus is not a liability, but a reservation of fund balance similar to the appropriated retained earnings of a business enterprise. At the beginning of the subsequent period, the encumbrances closing entry is reversed, returning the *Encumbrances Control and Budgetary Fund Balance-Reserve for Encumbrances* accounts to their usual offsetting relationship.

II. Governmental Funds

A. Overview

The governmental funds are used to account for the general government activities of a state or local government. The measurement focus of governmental funds is on the determination of the flow of financial resources and the financial position.

1. **Accounts** Most governmental fund accounting systems use both budgetary accounts and regular accounts. Budgetary accounts are nominal accounts used to record approved budgetary estimates of revenues and expenditures (appropriations). Regular accounts are used to record the actual revenues, expenditures, and other transactions affecting the fund. Although terminology varies, the following accounts are usually employed in governmental funds:

   a. **Estimated Revenues** Forecasts of asset inflows of estimated sources of fund working capital (except from other financing sources). The *Estimated Revenues Control* account is debited to record the revenue budget (and is closed at the end of the period with a credit).

   b. **Appropriations** Forecasts of (and authorizations of) asset outflows of estimated uses of fund working capital (except for other financing uses). The *Appropriations Control* account is credited to record the budgeted expenditures (and is closed at the end of the period with a debit).

   c. **Revenues** Additions to fund assets or decreases in fund liabilities (except from other financing sources) that increase the residual equity of the fund—inflows (sources) of fund working capital. Governmental fund revenues differ from the commercial concept of revenues in that they often are levied (e.g., taxes) rather than earned per se, and the financial resources must be available working capital to be recognized as revenue.

   d. **Other Financing Sources** Nonrevenue increases in fund net assets and residual equity (e.g., from certain interfund transfers and bond issue proceeds).

   e. **Expenditures** Increases in fund liabilities or decreases in fund assets (except for other financing uses) that decrease the residual equity of the fund—outflows (uses) of fund working capital. Expenditures differ from expenses (as defined in commercial accounting) because expenditures include—in addition to current operating outlays that benefit the current period—capital outlays for general fixed assets and repayment of general long-term debt principal.

   f. **Other Financing Uses** Nonrevenue decreases in fund net assets and residual equity—e.g., for interfund transfers.

   g. **Fund Balance** The fund residual equity account that balances the asset and liability accounts of a governmental fund (and trust funds), thus recording the amount available for expenditures. (The *Fund Balance* account is similar to the owners' equity account of a commercial enterprise only in this balancing feature; however, it does not purport to show any ownership in a fund's assets.). Fund balance should be reported in classifications that comprise a hierarchy based primarily on the extent to which the government is bound to honor constraints on the specific purposes for which amounts in those funds can be spent. The fund balance classifications are nonspendable fund balance, restricted fund balance, committed fund balance, assigned fund balance, and unassigned fund balance. A governmental fund doesn't necessarily use each of these classifications.

2. **Journal Entries** There are three types: (1) those to record (and close) the budget, (2) those to record (and close) encumbrances, and (3) those to record (and close) actual activity.

   a. Budgetary accounting is used by governmental funds.

      (1) The following is typical of the general fund's entry to record the budget at the beginning of the year.

Estimated Revenues Control	700	
Estimated Other Financing Sources	200	
Estimated Other Financing Uses		300
Appropriations		525
Budgetary Fund Balance (DR or CR)		75

      (2) The following is typical of the general fund's entry to close the budget at the end of the year. (Note: Same dollar amounts are used as in the initial entry.)

Estimated Other Financing Uses	300	
Appropriations	525	
Budgetary Fund Balance (DR or CR)	75	
Estimated Revenues Control		700
Estimated Other Financing Sources		200

   b. Encumbrance accounting records obligations to spend (purchase orders) to prevent overspending of appropriations. Encumbrances are not liabilities.

      (1) An encumbrance entry is made when an item is ordered in the amount of the estimated cost. Many amounts are controlled by another means and are frequently not encumbered. For example, salaries and wages are set by contract and controlled by established payroll procedures and are not encumbered.

      (2) The reverse entry is made for the same dollar amount when the invoice arrives.

      (3) Outstanding encumbrances at year end are carried forward as a reserve of fund balance with a corresponding deduction of unassigned fund balance.

      (4) The spending of a prior year's outstanding encumbrances is a use of committed fund balance, not a current year expenditure.

   c. The emphasis on reporting activity is on cash flow, as opposed to profit and loss. The matching principle of accrual accounting is not applicable. The following modified accrual basis guidelines are used.

      (1) Revenues are recorded as received in cash except for revenues susceptible to accrual and revenues of a material amount that have not been received at the normal time of receipt. Revenues are considered susceptible to accrual at the time they become measurable and available for use.

         (a) Available means collected or collectible within the current period or early enough in the next period (e.g., within 60 days or so) to be used to pay for expenditures incurred in the current period (for example, property taxes). If revenue-related assets (e.g., taxes receivable) are **not** available, a *Deferred Revenue* account should be credited initially; when the assets become available, the *Deferred Revenue* account is debited and *Revenue* is credited.

(b) All governmental entities that report using governmental funds should recognize revenues from taxpayer-assessed taxes in the accounting period in which they become susceptible to accrual. This includes personal and realty taxes, taxpayer assessed sales and income taxes, and sales taxes collected and held by one government agency for another at year-end should be accrued if they are remitted in time to be used as a resource for payment of obligations incurred during the preceding year. Remitted in time means collected during the year or within about 60 days after year-end.

(c) Whereas *unrestricted* grants should be recognized immediately as revenue of governmental funds, if available, *restricted* grants should not be recognized as revenue until they are earned. A restricted grant must be expended for the specific purposes to be considered earned. Deferred grant revenue is recorded initially, and the grant revenue is recognized only when qualifying expenditures are incurred.

(d) Significant amounts received before the normal collection time (i.e., early property tax payments) are recorded as deferred revenues.

(2) **Expenditures** Expenditures (not expenses) are recorded when fund liabilities are incurred or assets are expended, except:

(a) Inventory items may be recorded as expenditures either at the time of purchase *or* at the time the items are used.

(b) Expenditures normally are not allocated between years by the recording of prepaids (e.g., a two-year insurance policy). Prepaid expenses may be recorded as expenditures or may be allocated to periods (in funds using accrual accounting).

(c) Interest on general long-term debt, usually accounted for in debt service funds, normally are recorded as an expenditure on its due date rather than being accrued prior to its due date.

(3) **Other Financing Sources/Uses** Transfers in/out or to/from are not netted. Transfers are reported after revenues and expenditures, as they affect operating results.

(4) **Assets** Assets are treated as (capital outlay) expenditures and are not capitalized within the fund. Capital assets are not carried in governmental-type funds, but are included in government-wide financial statements. Fixed assets are rarely expected to contribute to revenues. Depreciation expense is not recorded in the governmental-type funds.

(5) **Debt** Long-term debts are not carried in governmental-type funds, but are included in government-wide financial statements. Money is repaid through the debt service fund.

3. **Transfers** Appropriations constitute maximum expenditure authorization during the fiscal year. Thus, estimated transfers (other financing sources and uses) are merely a specific kind of appropriation. Transfers (either budgeted or actual) are not netted.

B. General Fund

The general fund should be used to account for and report all financial resources not accounted for and reported in another fund. This primary governmental fund is used to account for most routine operations of the governmental entity. General fund revenues primarily consist of taxes (property, sales, income, and excise), licenses, fines, and interest. General fund expenditures are budgeted (and appropriated for) by the legislative body.

1. **Purpose** The general fund finances other funds through capital contributions and operating subsidies. An example is found in the section of the chapter on interfund transactions.

2. **Operation** The general fund uses modified accrual accounting. Budgetary, encumbrance, and actual activity entries usually appear in the general fund.

Exhibit 2 ▸ Sample General Fund Entries

1. To record the budget:

Estimated Revenues Control	1,000	
Estimated Other Financing Sources	100	
Appropriations Control		625
Appropriations: Estimated Other Financing Uses		425
Budgetary Fund Balance [difference]		50

NOTE: Estimated operating transfers are recorded separately as *Estimated Other Financing Sources (Uses);* they are not included with *Estimated Revenues* or *Appropriations.*

NOTE: Some governments use the *Fund Balance* account for both actual and budgetary amounts. Their budgetary entry causes the *Fund Balance* account to be carried during the year at its planned end-of-year balance. Then, the year-end closing entries adjust the *Fund Balance* account from its planned year-end balance to its actual year-end balance. This combination of actual and budget amounts is theoretically less sound than the approach illustrated here.

2. To record actual revenues:

Cash or Receivables	600	
Allowance for Uncollectible Receivables		30
Revenues Control		570

NOTE: Governmental fund revenues are recorded net of estimated bad debts. That is, estimated uncollectible accounts are recorded as direct reductions from revenues rather than as expenditures. If all the revenues are collected in cash, there would not be a credit to the allowance account.

3. To record an encumbrance, in the form of a purchase order issued or contract commitment, for two shipments (one for $120, and one for $10 close to year end):

Encumbrances Control [expected cost]	130	
Budgetary Fund Balance Reserved for Encumbrances		130

4. To record expenditures (for slightly more than the purchase order total) upon receipt of an invoice for the first shipment:

Budgetary Fund Balance Reserved for Encumbrances	120	
Encumbrances Control		120
Expenditures Control [actual cost]	125	
Vouchers Payable		125

5. To record unencumbered expenditures incurred:

Expenditures Control - Salaries	490	
Vouchers Payable		490

6. To record increase in supplies inventory on hand at year-end (supplies purchased were previously recorded as expenditures):

Supplies Inventory	20	
Nonspendable Fund Balance		20

7. To record receipt of a grant from the state government and a bond issue:

Cash (or Receivable)	350	
Grant Revenues		100
Other Financing Sources: Bond Proceeds		250

8. To record payment of a grant to the school district:

Other Financing Uses	245	
Cash (or Payable)		245

9a. Close out the original budget [reverse entry #1]:

Appropriations Control [budgeted]	625	
Appropriations: Estimated Other Financing Uses [budgeted]	425	
Budgetary Fund Balance [difference—debit or credit]	50	
Estimated Revenues Control [budgeted]		1,000
Estimated Other Financing Sources [budgeted]		100

9b. Close out encumbrances:

Budgetary Fund Balance Reserved for Encumbrances	10	
Encumbrances Control		10
Unassigned Fund Balance	10	
Committed Fund Balance		10

9c. Close out actual:

Revenues Control [actual]	670	
Other Financing Sources [actual]	250	
Expenditures Control [actual]		615
Other Financing Uses [actual]		245
Unassigned Fund Balance [difference—debit or credit]		60

NOTE: Since closing the budgetary accounts (i.e., *Estimated Revenues, Appropriations, Estimated Other Financing Sources,* and *Estimated Other Financing Uses*) simply reverses the entry to record the budget, their closing has no effect on fund balance. It is the closing of the activity accounts (i.e., *Revenues, Other Financing Sources, Expenditures, Encumbrances,* and *Other Financing Uses*) that increases or decreases the fund balance.

10. To record encumbrance reversing entry—beginning of next year:

Encumbrances Control	10	
Budgetary Fund Balance Reserved for Encumbrances		10

NOTE: None of the exhibits in this chapter are related to the other exhibits.

C. Special Revenue Funds

Special revenue funds are used to account for and report the proceeds of specific revenue sources that are restricted or committed to expenditure for specified purposes other than debt service or capital projects. The term *proceeds of specific revenue sources* establishes that one or more specific restricted or committed revenues should be the foundation for a special revenue fund.

Exhibit 3 ▸ Sample Special Revenue Fund Entries

1.	To record endowment earnings that are restricted for library purposes:		
	Cash (or Due From Permanent Fund)	45	
	Other Financing Sources: Library Permanent Fund		45
2.	To record expenditures for library purposes:		
	Expenditures—Library Books	40	
	Cash or Payable		40
3.	To close the accounts at year-end:		
	Other Financing Sources: Library Permanent Fund	45	
	Expenditures—Library Books		40
	Fund Balance		5

1. **Source** Those specific restricted or committed revenues may be initially received in another fund and subsequently distributed to a special revenue fund. Those amounts should not be recognized as revenue in the fund initially receiving them; however, those inflows should be recognized as revenue in the special revenue fund in which they will be expended in accordance with specified purposes. The restricted or committed proceeds of specific revenue sources should be expected to continue to comprise a substantial portion of the inflows reported in the fund. Other resources (investment earnings and transfers from other funds, for example) also may be reported in the fund if those resources are restricted, committed, or assigned to the specified purpose of the fund. Governments should discontinue reporting a special revenue fund, and instead report the fund's remaining resources in the general fund, if the government no longer expects that a substantial portion of the inflows will derive from restricted or committed revenue sources.

2. **Use** Special revenue funds should not be used to account for resources held in trust for individuals, private organizations, or other governments. The deciding factor for use of this fund as opposed to an enterprise fund is intent. If the intent is to recover less than 50 percent of expenses from user fees, then the activity is handled in a special revenue fund. The deciding factor for use of this fund as opposed to a private purpose trust fund are the beneficiaries. If the beneficiaries are citizens or the reporting entity, then the activity is handled in a special revenue fund. If the beneficiaries are individuals, private organizations, or other governments, then the activity is handled in a private purpose trust fund.

3. **Operation** The special revenue fund uses modified accrual accounting. Budgetary, encumbrance, and actual activity entries usually appear in special revenue funds. Accounting practices for special revenue funds parallel those for the general fund, so the only sample entries presented are related to a permanent fund endowment.

D. Capital Projects Fund

Capital projects funds are used to account for and report financial resources that are restricted, committed, or assigned to expenditure for capital outlays, including the acquisition or construction of capital facilities and other capital assets. Capital projects funds exclude those types of capital-related outflows financed by proprietary funds or for assets that will be held in trust for individuals, private organizations, or other governments. Most capital project(s) fund entries are similar to those illustrated earlier for the general fund.

1. **Use** Each capital project fund has a life limited to the construction period of the project. Alternatively, several overlapping capital projects may be accounted for in one capital projects fund, which exists as long as any one project is under construction. The acquisition of mobile property (for example, a car) need not be accounted for in a capital projects fund unless required by law or contractual agreement.

2. **Operation** Capital project(s) funds use modified accrual accounting. Encumbrance and actual activity entries usually appear in the capital projects fund. Budget entries are optional, and are usually used when accounting for more than one project in the same fund. Budget and encumbrance entries are similar to those in the general fund.

3. **Financial Resources** Typically are provided by bond issue proceeds, other funds, and interest earnings.

   a. Interfund transfers are classified as operating transfers (other financing sources) or residual equity transfers, as appropriate.

   b. Bond issue proceeds are classified as other financing sources. Premiums and discounts are recorded as other financing sources and uses, respectively. Debt issue costs paid out of proceeds are reported as expenditures. A net premium is usually transferred to the debt service fund.

4. **Interim Financing** Often needed during the early stages of the capital projects to pay for expenditures incurred before the bond issue proceeds or other resources are received. Interim borrowing, if short-term, is a current liability of the capital projects fund and is credited to *Notes Payable or Due To (Fund).* Certain BANs are an exception to the above rule if (a) all legal steps have been taken to refinance the bond anticipation notes and (b) the intent is supported by an ability to consummate refinancing the short-term note on a long-term basis.

Exhibit 4 ▸ Sample Capital Project Fund Entries

1.	To record deferred revenues and other financing received and accrued:		
	Due From Federal Grantor Agency	200	
	Cash	300	
	Deferred Grant Revenues [unearned until expended for project]		225
	Bond Issue Proceeds [a nonrevenue other financing source]		275
2.	To recognize grant revenue earned through expenditures having been incurred (recorded previously) for specified purposes:		
	Deferred Grant Revenues [project expenditures amount earned]	225	
	Grant Revenues		225
	NOTE: Other capital projects fund entries are illustrated in Interfund Transactions (Section IV).		

E. Debt Service Funds

Debt service funds are used to account for and report financial resources that are restricted, committed, or assigned to expenditure for principal and interest. Debt service funds should be used to report resources if legally mandated. Financial resources that are being accumulated for principal and interest maturing in future years also should be reported in debt service funds. The debt service fund uses modified accrual accounting. Budgetary, encumbrance, and actual activity entries usually appear in the debt service fund.

Exhibit 5 ▸ Sample Debt Service Fund Entries

1. Debt service fund budgetary accounts may be used to record the estimated revenues (e.g., from taxes), estimated other financing sources (e.g., from interfund transfer from the general fund for retirement of debt principal and for payment of matured interest), and estimated income (e.g., from investments). To record the budget:

Account	Debit	Credit
Estimated Other Financing Sources [e.g., from interfund transfers]	350	
Required Additions [estimated tax revenues]	250	
Required Earnings [estimated investment income]	150	
Appropriations [for debt service payments		700
Budgetary Fund Balance		50

2. To record actual tax revenues and other financing sources (for example, loans):

Account	Debit	Credit
Cash or Receivables	550	
Allowance for Uncollectible Taxes		10
Tax Revenues		240
Operating Transfer From General Fund		300

3. Debt service payments are recorded by debiting liability accounts (and crediting cash). To record expenditures for debt principal retirement (at maturity date) and interest (at due date):

Account	Debit	Credit
Expenditures	700	
Bonds Payable (or Matured Bonds Payable)		50
Interest Payable (or Matured Interest Payable)		650

4. **Maturing** bond or other long-term debt principal and related interest and fiscal agent charges are recorded as debt service fund expenditures and liabilities when due.
To record payment of matured debt and interest due:

Account	Debit	Credit
Bonds Payable	50	
Interest Payable	650	
Cash		700

NOTE: Payment of matured debt and interest due is generally effected by transferring the required amount of cash to a bank or other fiscal agent, who then pays the creditors.

5. Any matured debt principal and interest that is unpaid at year-end (e.g., because bond interest coupons have not been presented to the fiscal agent for payment) should be recorded, as should the cash with fiscal agent, in the year-end adjusting entry process.
To record unpaid liabilities and cash with fiscal agent at year-end:

Account	Debit	Credit
Cash With Fiscal Agent	50	
Unredeemed Bonds Payable		30
Unredeemed Interest Coupons Payable		20

6. To record closing entries:

Account	Debit	Credit
Appropriations	700	
Required Additions		250
Required Earnings		150
Estimated Other Financing Sources		350
Budgetary Fund Balance [difference]	50	
Tax Revenues	240	
Investment Revenues (entry to record revenue not shown)	210	
Operating Transfer From General Fund	300	
Expenditures		700
Assigned Fund Balance [difference]		50

F. Permanent Funds

Permanent funds should be used to account for and report resources that are restricted to the extent that only earnings, and not principal, may be used for purposes that support the reporting government's programs—that is, for the benefit of the government or its citizenry. Permanent funds do not include private-purpose trust funds, which should be used to report situations in which the government is required to use the principal or earnings for the benefit of individuals, private organizations, or other governments. The name comes from the purpose of the fund; a sum of equity used to permanently generate payments to maintain some financial obligation. A fund can only be classified as a permanent fund if the money is used to report the status of a restricted financial resource. The resource is restricted in that only earnings from the resource are used and not the principal. The permanent funds use modified accrual accounting. Budgetary and encumbrance entries usually aren't made in permanent funds. Accounting practices for permanent funds parallel those for the general fund, so few sample entries are presented.

Exhibit 6 ▸ Sample Permanent Fund Entries

1. To record receipt of a gift of an investment portfolio to establish an endowment; the principal including capital gains and losses, must be maintained intact, but the other earnings are to be transferred to a special revenue fund (SRF) to support the city library operations:

Account	Debit	Credit
Cash	100	
Investments	1,000	
Contribution Revenues		1,100

NOTE: Donations are recorded as revenue at fair value, regardless of their cost to the donor, reported at fair value at statement dates, and closed to *Fund balance—Principal* at year-end.

2. To close revenue and expense accounts to determine earnings to transfer to the SRF:

Account	Debit	Credit
Revenues—Investments	100	
Expenses—Commissions		30
Expenses—Administration		10
Expenses—Other		5
Fund Balance—Earnings		55

NOTE: Revenue and expense accounts, but not investment gains, are closed to *Fund balance—Earnings* to determine the earnings as defined by the donor. (The entries recording revenues, expenses, and gains are not illustrated.)

3. To record transfer of earnings, as defined, to a special revenue fund:

Account	Debit	Credit
Other Financing Uses: Transfer to Library SRF	55	
Cash (or Due to Library SRF)		55

NOTE: A transfer does not necessarily indicate that cash has been disbursed, but may be accrued—and should be accrued if its necessity is indicated in a CPA exam question. Accounting for interfund transfers is discussed further in a later part of this chapter.

4. To close the remaining accounts:

Account	Debit	Credit
Fund Balance—Earnings	55	
Other Financing Uses: Transfer to Library SRF		55
Gain on Sale of Investments	20	
Contribution Revenues	1,100	
Fund Balance—Principal		1,120

NOTE: The gains on sale of investments are closed to principal because the donor's restrictions specified that earnings are to be computed without regard to gains or losses on sale of investments.

III. Proprietary Funds

A. Overview

While the governmental funds account for the general government activities of a state or local government, its business-type activities are accounted for in proprietary funds essentially as if they were private sector profit-seeking business enterprises. The proprietary fund accounting equation is the familiar business accounting equation.

$$\text{Cur. Assets} + \text{Fixed Assets} + \text{Other Assets} = \text{Cur. Liab.} + \text{Long-Term Debt} + \text{Net Assets}$$

1. **Business-Type Accounting** Revenues and expenses (not expenditures) are measured using the accrual basis of accounting, as in business accounting. Fixed assets and long-term debt are recorded in the fund as well as the associated depreciation and interest charges. Contributed capital is no longer separated from retained earnings in the balance sheet; both are labeled *Net Assets.*

2. **Not-for-Profit Accounting and Financial Reporting** GASB 29 allows the use of either the Nonprofit (or AICPA) model or the Governmental model for accounting and reporting by state or local governmental units that have previously applied the principles of SOP 78-10 or *Audits of Voluntary Health and Welfare Organizations.* However, proprietary funds that implement FASB pronouncements released after November 31, 1989, should only apply those pronouncements that are intended for business (as opposed to nonprofit) organizations.

3. **Refundings of Debt Reported by Proprietary Activities** GASB 23 provides standards of accounting and reporting for current refundings and advance refundings resulting in defeasance of debt reported by proprietary activities (proprietary funds and other governmental entities that use proprietary fund accounting). GASB 23 requires that the difference between the reacquisition price and the net carrying amount of the old debt be deferred and amortized as a component of interest expense over the remaining life of the old debt or the life of the new debt, whichever is shorter. The deferred amount is reported on the balance sheet as an addition to or a deduction from the new debt liability. Additionally, current refundings reported by proprietary activities are subject to the disclosure requirements of GASB 7, *Advance Refundings Resulting in Defeasance of Debt.*

   a. Current refundings involve the issuance of new debt, the proceeds of which are to be used immediately.

   b. Advance refundings involve the issuance of new debt that is placed in escrow to be used at a later date to pay principal and interest on the old debt.

B. Internal Service Funds

Internal service funds are used to account for *in-house* business enterprise activities; that is, to account for the financing of goods or services provided by one government department or agency to other departments or agencies of the government (and perhaps also to other governments) on a cost reimbursement basis. Common examples of internal service funds (ISF) are those used to account for government motor pools, central repair shops and garages, data processing departments, and photocopy and printing shops.

1. **Zero Profit** ISFs are supposed to break even annually or over a period of years. The charges to other departments accounted for as ISF revenues are intended to recoup ISF expenses. ISFs are, in essence, cost accounting and cost distribution (to other funds) accounting entities. They are accounted for similarly as enterprise funds.

2. **Establishment** The initial capital to finance an ISF may come from the general fund, the issuance of general obligation bonds, transfers from other funds, or advances from other governments. Permanent capital contributions (i.e., residual equity transfers) must be distinguished from loans and advances that are to be repaid.

3. **Differences Between Enterprise Fund and Internal Service Fund Accounting**

   a. Only the fixed assets that are expected to be replaced through the ISF are recorded therein and depreciated. Thus, the printing equipment for a central printing shop located in the basement of a county courthouse would be recorded in (and depreciated in) the print shop ISF. The courthouse is reported in the government-wide financial statements, a portion of the courthouse cost would not be recorded in the ISF.

   b. An account such as *Billings to Departments* serves as the ISF sales account rather than the usual *Revenues* account.

C. **Enterprise Funds**

Enterprise funds must be used to account for a government's business-type operations that are financed and operated like private businesses—where the government's intent is that all costs (expenses, including depreciation) of providing goods or services to the general public on a continuing basis are to be financed or recovered primarily through user charges (operating revenue). Interest income, interest expense, gain or loss on sales of capital assets, unrestricted grants to or from other governments, and transfers to or from other funds are examples of transactions that are reported as nonoperating revenue. Most government-owned public utilities (e.g., electricity, gas, water, and sewage systems) must be accounted for in enterprise funds under this criteria.

1. **Optional Use** NCGA Statement No. 1 also permits governments to account for virtually any type of self-contained business-type activity in enterprise funds if it prefers to do business-type accounting rather than general government accounting. City bus or other mass transit systems are examples of government activities that are often accounted for through enterprise funds under the NCGA's permissive criteria.

2. **Subfunds** If capital, debt service, trust, or agency funds related to an enterprise activity are required (e.g., by bond indentures, other contractual agreements, grant provisions, or laws), they are accounted for as enterprise fund subfunds rather than as separate funds.

   a. Assets and liabilities of such subfunds are accounted for by using separate asset and liability accounts (e.g., *Cash—Construction*, *Contracts Payable—Construction, Investments—Debt Service, Accrued Interest Payable—Debt Service,* and *Cash—Customer Deposits*) and need not balance, though all except agency subfunds may be balanced by net assets reserve accounts such as *Reserve for Construction* or *Reserve for Debt Service.*

   b. Revenues and expenses related to the subfunds are recorded as enterprise revenues and expenses, not in separate subfund revenue and expense accounts.

   c. Customers' security deposits that cannot be spent for normal operating purposes should be classified in the balance sheet of the enterprise funds as both a restricted asset and a liability.

Exhibit 7 ▸ Sample Enterprise Fund Entries

1. To record operating revenues:

Cash or Receivables	850	
Revenues—Sale of Electricity		725
Revenues—Sale of Appliances		50
Revenues—Other		75

2. To record federal grants for operating and capital purposes:

Cash or Receivables	100	
Cash—Construction	350	
Revenues—Federal Grants [operating grant]		100
Contributed Capital—Federal Grants [capital grant]		350

NOTE: If grants must be expended to be considered earned, they are initially credited to deferred revenues and deferred contributed capital accounts, then credited to revenue and contributed capital accounts when earned by being expended. Also, this entry assumes that a capital projects subfund is required by federal grant and/or bond indenture provisions.

3. To record operating expenses:

Expenses—Cost of Electricity Purchased	400	
Expenses—Depreciation	100	
Expenses—Salaries and Wages	100	
Expenses—Other	50	
Accumulated Depreciation		100
Cash		500
Payables		50

4. To record issuance of enterprise revenue bonds to finance new electricity distribution lines and acquiring transmission equipment under capital lease:

Cash—Construction	450	
Bonds Payable		450
Transmission Equipment	200	
Capital Leases Payable		200

NOTE: This entry assumes that a capital projects subfund is required by federal grant and/or bond indenture provisions.

5. To record use of revenue bond issue proceeds to build new electricity distribution lines:

Transmission Lines	750	
Cash—Construction (or Payables—Construction)		750

6. To record payment of bond and capital lease principal and interest:

Bonds Payable	15	
Expenses—Interest [on bonds]	35	
Cash—Debt Service		50
Capital Leases Payable	10	
Expenses—Interest [on capital lease]	20	
Cash		30

NOTE: This entry assumes that a debt service subfund is used for bond debt service but that the capital lease is serviced from enterprise fund operating cash.

7. To close the accounts at year-end:

Revenues—Sale of Electricity	725	
Revenues—Sale of Appliances	50	
Revenues—Federal Grants [operating grant]	100	
Revenues—Other	75	
Expenses—Cost of Electricity Purchased		400
Expenses—Depreciation		100
Expenses—Salaries and Wages		100
Expenses—Interest ($20 + $35)		55
Expenses—Other		50
Net Assets [debit or credit]		245

NOTE: The revenue and expense accounts may be closed initially to a *Revenue and Expense Summary* account, which is then closed to *Net Assets.*

IV. Fiduciary Funds

A. Overview

GASB Statement No. 34 refined the focus of fiduciary funds to only include resources that are restricted to third parties and cannot be used for any general programs of the primary government. Fiduciary funds are used to account for a government's fiduciary or stewardship responsibilities as an agent (agency funds) or trustee (trust funds) for other governments, funds, organizations, and/or individuals. Fiduciary funds cannot be used for any general programs of the primary government. All fiduciary funds are accounted for on the accrual basis, in essentially the same manner as proprietary funds. Fiduciary funds are included in fund financial statements but not in the government-wide statements.

There is one important criteria for the use of fiduciary funds. Funds cannot be used for any of the government's public purposes. GASB Statement No. 34 segregated fiduciary funds from the governmental and proprietary funds to carve out those activities that solely benefit third parties. This structure allows specific reporting in the fund statements to provide accountability for these fiduciary responsibilities. Readers can assess the government's financial position based solely on the resources that really are available to the government for financing public services and programs. At the same time, the beneficiaries can assess the status of resources that are held for their benefit, separate from the government's funds.

B. Pension Trust Funds

Perhaps the most prevalent fiduciary fund is the pension trust . Used to account for a government's fiduciary responsibilities and activities in managing pension or retirement trust funds for its retired, active, and former employees and their beneficiaries.

1. **Use** Pension trust funds are needed only by governments that manage their own pension plans rather than participate in statewide plans or contract with an insurance or pension management company to manage the plans. (While relatively few businesses manage their own pension plans, many governments do so.)

2. **Basis of Accounting** Pension trust funds are accounted for in essentially the same manner as proprietary funds. All contributions to and earnings of the plan are accounted for as revenues; and all benefit payments, refunds of contributions, and pension plan administrative costs are accounted for as expenses. Depreciation expense is recorded on depreciable fixed assets used in administering the pension plan. A unique series of fund balance reserve accounts is used to account for the equities of the several types of plan participants.

C. Investment Trust Funds

GASB Statement No. 31 created the investment trust fund to account for and report on the *external* portion of an investment pool. This guidance applies to the sponsoring government that administers one or more external investment pools. The external portion includes those resources that belong to legally separate entities that are not part of the sponsoring government's financial reporting entity. The primary government's internal portion is reported as equity (in each fund that participates) in the investment pool.

1. **Basic Reporting** These funds use the accrual basis of accounting and the economic resources measurement focus as other fiduciary fund types. The financial statements will include a statement of net assets and a statement of changes in net assets, but a cash flows statement is not required. There are also specific disclosure requirements that outline significant details about the pool and how it is administered.

2. **Additional Reporting** Additional requirements were included to outline the financial statements and disclosure requirements for the investment fund type. These funds may be reported within the fiduciary section of the sponsoring government or as stand-alone financial reports that may be distributed to the participants. Sponsoring governments will be required to segregate the external portion of the pool to the investment trust fund.

3. **Criteria** There are four elements that are necessary to create an *external* investment pool. They are as follows:

    a. An investment pool provides commingling of assets from more than one source. Individual participants do not have separate ownership of specific investments.

    b. The external component must include at least one legally separate participant from outside the financial reporting entity. Where funds include pooled investments for both internal and external entities, only the external portion is reported in the investment trust fund.

    c. A focus on investment and generating income is the primary purpose for an external investment pool. Asset pooling should not be in conjunction with another purpose, such as investing bond proceeds during construction for a joint venture.

    d. Income generated from the pool should benefit external participants based on their proportional share of the pool. If the income accrues to the benefit of the sponsoring government, it is not an external investment pool.

4. **Segregating Government's Share** The external portion of the investment pool includes those resources that belong to legally separate entities that are not part of the sponsoring government's financial reporting entity. The internal portion is that amount that belongs to the primary government and its component units (the sponsoring primary government). A primary government's internal portion is reported as equity (in each fund that participates) in the investment pool. This will require matching the pool equity for each fund and shifting those balances to the appropriate fund. This is a reporting issue and does not require actual general ledger entries for the reclassification. It will be another item on the worksheet to consolidate the government's funds for the annual financial report.

5. **GASB Statement No. 59, *Financial Instruments Omnibus*** GASB Statement No. 59, issued in June 2010, revised guidance for two issues that will affect external investment pools. First, the guidance was clarified to indicate that a 2a7-like pool is an external investment pool that operates in conformity with the SEC's Rule 2a7. Second, interest rate risk information will only be disclosed for debt investment pools—such as bond mutual funds and external bond investment pools—that do not meet the requirements to be reported as a 2a7-like pool.

D. **Private Purpose Trust Funds**
Private purpose trust funds [PIPPA] are used to account for fiduciary responsibilities and activities in managing all other trust arrangements that benefit individuals, private organizations, or other governments. The important distinction for this fund type is the provision that fund resources "cannot be used to support the government's own programs." If, for instance, state law requires a trust fund for perpetual care in a cemetery, funded with a portion of the sales of cemetery lots, that fund will not be a private-purpose trust fund when the cemetery is owned by the government. In that case, cemetery operations are a "government program" and the trust fund resources are used by the government. There is indirect benefit to private individuals. Private-purpose trust funds must have no public purpose in the distribution of those resources. [Editor's note: Funds that benefit public programs and services delivered by the governmental entity are classified as either special revenue or permanent funds.]

E. **Agency Funds**
Used to account for the custodial activities of a government serving as an agent for other governments, private organizations, or individuals. The government is simply acting as a conduit to collect and disburse funds. These funds will record all transactions as increases or decreases to assets and liabilities. Like other fiduciary funds, agency funds are using the accrual basis of accounting and economic resources measurement focus. In practice, transactions in these accounts will generally only include cash receipts and disbursements, not the types of assets and liabilities subject to accrual. The government has no equity in agency funds. Further, agency funds do not have operating accounts (for instance, *Revenues*). No operating statement is prepared for agency funds.

1. **Accounting Framework** These funds will record all transactions as increases or decreases to assets and liabilities. Like other fiduciary funds, agency funds are using the accrual basis of accounting and economic resources measurement focus. In practice, transactions in these accounts will generally only include cash receipts and disbursements, not the types of assets and liabilities subject to accrual. One of the most common agency funds is the tax collection account that records total payments and distributes funds to variety of taxing entities. The portion of a tax collection fund that is actually receipts of the government should be reclassified to the taxing fund for financial reporting purposes.

2. **Common Types** The most common type of agency fund is the tax agency fund—used when one government collects property (or other) taxes for several governments, usually including the collecting government. Also, some governments use a payroll withholding agency fund to accumulate the payroll taxes, insurance premiums, etc., withheld in its several funds, then remit them to the proper governments, insurance companies, etc.

Exhibit 8 ▸ Sample Property Tax Agency Fund Entries

1. To record property taxes, levied by other governments (in this instance, the city and school district) and for other county funds, which are to be collected through the county's property tax agency fund:

Taxes Receivable—Other Funds and Units	2,000	
Due to City		250
Due to School District		250
Due to General Fund [of county]		1,500

NOTE: The county general fund will be paid the county's share of the property taxes collected plus any collection fees charged the city and school district.

The property tax levies will be recorded also in the county general fund and in the appropriate city and school district governmental funds in the manner illustrated earlier. An allowance for uncollectible taxes is not recorded in the agency fund since the county is responsible for collecting all taxes possible and returning the uncollected tax receivables to the city and school districts (and the county general fund) for further collection effort.

County's General Fund:

Taxes Receivable—Current	1,500	
Allowance for Uncollectible Taxes		75
Revenues—Property Taxes		1,425

2. To record tax collections:

Cash	1,975	
Taxes Receivable—Other Funds and Units		1,975

3. To record payment of tax collections to other units and to the county general fund:

Due to City [collections less any fee] ($245 – $5)	240	
Due to School District [collections less any fee] ($245 – $5)	240	
Due to General Fund [collections **plus** any fees] ($1,485 + $5 + $5)	1,495	
Cash		1,975

NOTE: Entries in the general funds would be the following:

County's General Fund:

Cash	1,495	
Taxes Receivable—Current		1,485
Revenues—Property Tax Collection Fees		10

City's and School District's General Funds:

Cash	240	
Expenditures—Property Tax Collection Fees	5	
Taxes Receivable—Current		245

V. Interfund Transactions & Relationships

A. Overview

The preceding discussions and illustrations focus primarily on accounting for each of the several different types of funds. Interfund transactions and relationships are important aspects of governmental accounting. This part of the chapter focuses on interfund transactions (where one transaction affects two or more funds). These discussions and illustrations also review and expand upon the material covered earlier in this chapter.

B. Interfund Transactions

Interfund transactions simultaneously affect two or more funds of the government. Transfers are **nonreciprocal** shifts of resources among funds and are **not** intended to be repaid. GASB 34 details three types of interfund transactions in the GASB 34 reporting model.

1. **Quasi-External Transactions** These are transactions that would result in recognizing revenues and expenditures or expenses, as appropriate, if they were with organizations apart from the government. These transactions should also result in recognition of revenues and expenditures or expenses, as appropriate, when they occur between or among funds of the government. Examples include routine employer contributions to pension trust funds, enterprise and internal service fund billings to government departments, and enterprise fund payments in lieu of taxes to the general fund or other governmental funds.

Exhibit 9 ▸ Sample Quasi-External Transactions Entries

1. To record billings to departments financed by the general fund for services rendered through enterprise and internal service fund departments:

   a. *General Fund:*

Expenditures—Services	115	
Due to Enterprise Fund		35
Due to Internal Service Fund		80

   b. *Enterprise Fund:*

Due From General Fund	35	
Revenues—Services		35

   c. *Internal Service Fund:*

Due From General Fund	80	
Billings for Services		80

NOTE: An account such as *Billings for Services* is used in internal service fund accounting instead of *Revenues.*

2. To record employer contributions from the general and enterprise funds to the pension trust fund:

   a. *General Fund:*

Expenditures—Pension Contribution	300	
Due to Pension Trust Fund (or Cash)		300

   b. *Enterprise Fund:*

Expenses—Pension Contribution	100	
Due to Pension Trust Fund (or Cash)		100

   c. *Pension Trust Fund:*

Due From General Fund (or Cash)	300	
Due From Enterprise Fund (or Cash)	100	
Revenues—Employer Contributions		400

2. **Reimbursements** These are transactions that reimburse one fund for expenditures or expenses initially recorded there but properly attributable to another fund. Reimbursements are recorded as expenditures or expenses, as appropriate, in the reimbursing fund and as reductions of the recorded expenditures or expenses (not as revenues) in the fund that is reimbursed.

3. **Transfers** The difference between operating transfers and residual equity transfers (RETs) of the previous reporting model is not always easy to distinguish and practice varies widely. GASB 34 eliminated the requirement to distinguish between operating transfers and RETs. (The following illustrations distinguish between the two, as candidates may encounter this terminology.) All transfers must be reported as *Other Financing Sources* or *Other Financing Uses*. [Note that transfers don't include quasi-external transactions and reimbursements.]

Exhibit 10 ▸ Sample Transfer Entries

1. To record transfers made from the general fund to establish a new internal service fund:
   a. *General Fund:*

OFU: Residual Equity Transfer to Internal Service Fund	500	
Cash		500

   b. *Internal Service Fund:*

Cash	500	
Transfer In-RET		500

NOTE: This is a residual equity transfer. In proprietary funds, the RET account(s) will be closed to a *Contribution From Municipality* (or similar contributed capital) account. The general fund RET accounts will be closed to *Fund Balance.*

2. To record routine transfers from the general fund to a debt service fund:
   a. *General Fund:*

OFU: Operating Transfer to Debt Service Fund	350	
Cash		350

   b. *Debt Service Fund:*

Cash	350	
OFS: Operating Transfer From General Fund		350

NOTE: All interfund transfers that are not RETs are operating transfers.

4. **Financial Statement Presentation** Quasi-external transactions and reimbursements are buried in expenditures, expenses, and revenues account detail. In governmental funds, transfers are reported as *Other Financing Sources (Uses).* In proprietary funds, transfers should be reported after nonoperating revenues and expenses as *Transfers In (Out).*

5. **Interfund Loans** Amounts that are expected to be repaid appear in the balance sheets of affected funds; they have no impact on operating statements. Both short-term and noncurrent loans are indicated using *Receivable* and *Payable* accounts, appropriately classified in the balance sheets. Governments are encouraged, but not required, to present assets and liabilities in order of their relative liquidity. Liabilities whose average maturities are greater than one years should be reported in two components (short-term and noncurrent).

Exhibit 11 ▸ Other Sample Interfund Entries

1. To record reimbursement of the general fund for previously recorded operating expenditures that are properly attributable to special revenue and enterprise funds:

   a. *General Fund:*

	Dr.	Cr.
Cash	125	
Expenditures—Operating		125

   b. *Special Revenue Fund:*

	Dr.	Cr.
Expenditures—Operating	40	
Cash		40

   c. *Enterprise Fund:*

	Dr.	Cr.
Expenses—Operating	85	
Cash		85

   NOTE: If cash was not involved, appropriate *Due From* and *Due to* accounts would be debited and credited rather than *Cash.*

2. To record four payments from an enterprise fund to the general fund—(1) a routine payment to subsidize general fund operations, (2) a payment in lieu of taxes, (3) a payment to reimburse the general fund for enterprise fund wages erroneously recorded in the general fund, and (4) a payment reducing the municipality's contributed capital investment in the enterprise fund:

   a. *Enterprise Fund:*

	Dr.	Cr.
Operating Transfer to General Fund	50	
Expenses—Payments in Lieu of Taxes	130	
Expenses—Wages	40	
Transfer Out-RET	350	
Cash		570

   b. *General Fund:*

	Dr.	Cr.
Cash	570	
Operating Transfer From Enterprise Fund		50
Revenues—Payments in Lieu of Taxes		130
Expenditures—Wages		40
Residual Equity Transfer From Enterprise Fund		350

   NOTE: These entries demonstrate and review accounting for quasi-external transactions, reimbursements, residual equity transfers, and operating transfers.

3. To record a short-term loan from the general fund to a special revenue fund:

   a. *General Fund:*

	Dr.	Cr.
Due From Special Revenue Fund	100	
Cash		100

   b. *Special Revenue Fund:*

	Dr.	Cr.
Cash	100	
Due to General Fund		100

   NOTE: In the previous reporting model, the *Due to* and *Due From* accounts indicate a short-term interfund loan that is expected to be repaid during the current year or early the next year. The GASB 34 reporting model uses an account title including the word *payable,* although governments may still use the old account titles internally.

4. To record a long-term loan from the general fund to an enterprise fund:

   a. *General Fund:*

	Dr.	Cr.
Advance to Enterprise Fund	200	
Cash		200
Unassigned Fund Balance	200	
Reserve for Advance to Enterprise Fund		200

   b. *Enterprise Fund:*

	Dr.	Cr.
Cash	200	
Advance From General Fund		200

NOTE: (a) The terms *advance to* and *advance from* denote accounts for noncurrent or long-term interfund loans; and (b) since the amount loaned does not now represent current assets available to finance general fund expenditures, an appropriate fund balance reserve must be established in the general fund. (The general fund reserve will be reduced when the advance becomes an available current asset—in full or in installments.)

5. To record closing of selected operating transfer and RET accounts in governmental (e.g., the general) and proprietary (e.g., enterprise and internal service) funds:

   a. *General Fund:*

	Dr.	Cr.
Operating Transfer From Enterprise Fund	XX	
Transfer In-RET	XX	
Operating Transfer to Enterprise Fund		XX
Transfer Out-RET		XX
Unassigned Fund Balance [difference—debit or credit]		XX

   b. *Enterprise Fund:*

	Dr.	Cr.
Operating Transfer From General Fund	XX	
Retained Earnings [difference—debit or credit]	XX	
Operating Transfer to General Fund		XX
Contributions From Municipality (or Contributed Capital)	XX	
Transfer Out-RET		XX

   c. *Internal Service Fund:*

	Dr.	Cr.
Residual Equity Transfer From General Fund	XX	
Contributions From Municipality (or Contributed Capital)		XX

NOTE: All transfers are closed to *Fund Balance* accounts of governmental funds. In proprietary funds: (a) operating transfers are closed to *Retained Earnings,* since they affect reported operating results, while (b) residual equity transfers are considered capital (not operating) transactions, and thus, are closed to the *Contributions From Municipality* (or similar contributed capital) account.

Select Hot•Spot™ Video Description

CPA 4200 Governmental Accounting
Following previous exam emphasis, this program concentrates on accounting for governmental entities. Governmental, proprietary and fiduciary funds, as well as encumbrances, budgeting, and modified accrual accounting are clarified. Governmental reporting (GASB No. 34) is also discussed, including all six parts of the Comprehensive Annual Financial Report (CAFR). Robert Monette explains 36 multiple-choice questions, and three simulations as well as discussing reconciliations and problem-solving techniques. Approximate time is 3:50.

Call our customer representatives toll-free at 1 (800) 874-7877 for more details about videos.

Subject to Change Without Notice

CHAPTER 18—GOVERNMENT FUNDS & TRANSACTIONS

Problem 19-1 MULTIPLE-CHOICE QUESTIONS

1. Which of the following fund types of a governmental unit has(have) income determination as a measurement focus?

	General funds	Capital project funds	
a.	Yes	Yes	
b.	Yes	No	
c.	No	No	
d.	No	Yes	(11/95, AR, #57, amended, 5800)

2. In governmental accounting, a fund is

    I. The basic accounting unit
    II. Used to assist in ensuring fiscal compliance

    a. I only
    b. II only
    c. Both I and II
    d. Neither I nor II (R/03, FAR, #8, 7610)

3. Fund accounting is used by governmental units with resources that must be

    a. Composed of cash or cash equivalents
    b. Incorporated into combined or combining financial statements
    c. Segregated for the purpose of carrying on specific activities or attaining certain objectives
    d. Segregated physically according to various objectives (11/95, AR, #60, 5803)

4. The measurement focus of governmental-type funds is on the determination of

	Flow of financial resources	Financial position	
a.	Yes	No	
b.	No	Yes	
c.	No	No	
d.	Yes	Yes	(5/96, AR, #4, 6201)

5. Sig City used the following funds for financial reporting purposes:

General fund	Capital projects fund
Internal service fund	Special revenue fund
Airport enterprise fund	Debt service fund
Pension trust fund	

    How many of Sig's funds use the accrual basis of accounting?

    a. Two
    b. Three
    c. Four
    d. Five (R/05, FAR, #12, 7756)

6. The modified accrual basis of accounting should be used for which of the following funds?

    a. Capital projects fund
    b. Enterprise fund
    c. Pension trust fund
    d. Proprietary fund (5/93, PII, #22, 4130)

7. The encumbrance account of a governmental unit is debited when
   a. The budget is recorded
   b. A purchase order is approved
   c. Goods are received
   d. A voucher payable is recorded (11/93, Theory, #51, 4556)

8. Which account should Spring Township credit when it issues a purchase order for supplies?
   a. Appropriations control
   b. Vouchers payable
   c. Reserve for encumbrances
   d. Encumbrance control (11/95, AR, #71, 5814)

9. In the current year, New City issued purchase orders and contracts of $850,000 that were chargeable against current year budgeted appropriations of $1,000,000. The journal entry to record the issuance of the purchase orders and contracts should include a
   a. Credit to vouchers payable of $1,000,000
   b. Credit to reserve for encumbrances of $850,000
   c. Debit to expenditures of $1,000,000
   d. Debit to appropriations of $850,000 (11/94, AR, #18, amended, 4995)

10. Fixed assets donated to a governmental unit should be recorded
    a. At the donor's carrying amount
    b. At estimated fair value when received
    c. At the lower of the donor's carrying amount or estimated fair value when received
    d. As a memorandum entry only (11/95, AR, #58, 5801)

11. Encumbrances would **not** appear in which fund?
    a. Capital projects
    b. Special revenue
    c. General
    d. Enterprise (R/11, FAR, #2, 9852)

12. Which of the following funds of a governmental unit uses the modified accrual basis of accounting?
    a. Internal service funds
    b. Enterprise funds
    c. Special revenue funds
    d. Private-purpose trust funds (R\93, FAR #54, 4559)

13. The budget of a governmental unit, for which the appropriations exceed the estimated revenues, was adopted and recorded in the general ledger at the beginning of the year. During the year, expenditures and encumbrances were less than appropriations; whereas revenues equaled estimated revenues. The budgetary fund balance account is
    a. Credited at the beginning of the year and debited at the end of the year
    b. Credited at the beginning of the year and **not** changed at the end of the year
    c. Debited at the beginning of the year and credited at the end of the year
    d. Debited at the beginning of the year and **not** changed at the end of the year
    (5/91, Theory, #52, 2096)

14. When Rolan County adopted its budget for the current year ending June 30, $20,000,000 was recorded for estimated revenues control. Actual revenues for the fiscal year amounted to $17,000,000. In closing the budgetary accounts at June 30,
    a. Revenues Control should be debited for $3,000,000
    b. Estimated Revenues control should be debited for $3,000,000
    c. Revenues Control should be credited for $20,000,000
    d. Estimated Revenues control should be credited for $20,000,000 (11/90, PII, #57, amended, 1360)

15. Carlson City's fiscal year ends December 31. On August 1, the city issued a purchase order for new vehicles to be delivered at the rate of two per month beginning October 15. Twelve vehicles were delivered as scheduled and payments of $264,000 were made upon delivery. If these were the only transactions made by the city, which of the following balances would appear on the balance sheet as of December 31?

a. Encumbrances	$132,000	
Reserve for encumbrances	132,000	
b. Unassigned fund balance	$132,000	
Reserve for encumbrances	132,000	
c. Reserve for encumbrances	$264,000	
Unassigned fund balance	264,000	
d. Encumbrances	$264,000	
Reserve for encumbrances	264,000	(R/07, FAR, #29, 8350)

16. Elm City issued a purchase order for supplies with an estimated cost of $5,000. When the supplies were received, the accompanying invoice indicated an actual price of $4,950. What amount should Elm debit (credit) to the reserve for encumbrances after the supplies and invoice were received?

a. $ (50)
b. $ 50
c. $4,950
d. $5,000 (11/93, PII, #5, 4434)

17. During its fiscal year ended June 30, Cliff City issued purchase orders totaling $5,000,000 which were properly charged to encumbrances at that time. Cliff received goods and related invoices at the encumbered amounts totaling $4,500,000 before year end. The remaining goods of $500,000 were not received until after year end. Cliff paid $4,200,000 of the invoices received during the year. What amount of Cliff's encumbrances were outstanding at June 30?

a. $0
b. $300,000
c. $500,000
d. $800,000 (11/93, PII, #4, amended, 4433)

18. Which of the following journal entries should a city use to record $250,000 for fire department salaries incurred during May?

	Debit	Credit	
a. Salaries expense	250,000		
Appropriations		250,000	
b. Salaries expense	250,000		
Encumbrances		250,000	
c. Encumbrances	250,000		
Salaries payable		250,000	
d. Expenditures—salaries	250,000		
Salaries payable		250,000	(11/96, AR, #12, amended, 6305)

19. In Soan County's general fund statement of revenues, expenditures, and changes in fund balances, which of the following has an effect on the excess of revenues over expenditures?

a. Purchase of fixed assets
b. Payment to a debt-service fund
c. Special items
d. Proceeds from the sale of capital assets (R/10, FAR, #20, 9320)

20. Expenditures of a governmental unit for insurance extending over more than one accounting period
    a. Must be accounted for as expenditures of the period of acquisition
    b. Must be accounted for as expenditures of the periods subsequent to acquisition
    c. Must be allocated between or among accounting periods
    d. May be allocated between or among accounting periods or may be accounted for as expenditures of the period of acquisition (11/94, AR, #15, amended, 4992)

21. On January 2, City of Walton issued $500,000, 10-year, 7% general obligation bonds. Interest is payable annually, beginning January 2 of the following year. What amount of bond interest is Walton required to report in the statement of revenue, expenditures, and changes in fund balance of its governmental funds at the close of this fiscal year, September 30?
    a. $0
    b. $17,500
    c. $26,250
    d. $35,000 (R/05, FAR, #13, 7757)

Items 22 and 23 are based on the following:

Park City uses encumbrance accounting and formally integrates its budget into the general fund's accounting records. For the current year ending July 31, the following budget was adopted:

Estimated revenues	$30,000,000
Appropriations	27,000,000
Estimated transfer to debt service fund	900,000

22. When Park's budget is adopted and recorded, Park's unassigned fund balance would be a
    a. $3,000,000 credit balance
    b. $3,000,000 debit balance
    c. $2,100,000 credit balance
    d. $2,100,000 debit balance (5/92, PII, #23, amended, 2655)

23. Park should record budgeted appropriations by a
    a. Credit to appropriations control, $27,000,000
    b. Debit to estimated expenditures, $27,000,000
    c. Credit to appropriations control, $27,900,000
    d. Debit to estimated expenditures, $27,900,000 (5/92, PII, #24, amended, 2656)

24. For the budgetary year, Maple City's general fund expects the following inflows of resources:

Property taxes, licenses, and fines	$9,000,000
Proceeds of debt issue	5,000,000
Interfund transfers for debt service	1,000,000

In the budgetary entry, what amount should Maple record for estimated revenues?
    a. $ 9,000,000
    b. $ 10,000,000
    c. $ 14,000,000
    d. $ 15,000,000 (11/93, PI, #3, amended, 4432)

25. When a purchase order is released, a commitment is made by a governmental unit to buy a computer to be manufactured to specifications for use in property tax administration. This commitment should be recorded in the general fund as a (an)

    a. Appropriation
    b. Encumbrance
    c. Expenditure
    d. Fixed asset (R/00, AR, #3, 6908)

26. Which of the following amounts are included in a general fund's encumbrance account?

    I. Outstanding vouchers payable amounts
    II. Outstanding purchase order amounts
    III. Excess of the amount of a purchase order over the actual expenditure for that order

    a. I only
    b. I and III
    c. II only
    d. II and III (5/91, Theory, #53, 2097)

27. Powell City purchased a piece of equipment to be used by a department financed by the general fund. How should Powell report the acquisition in the general fund?

    a. As an expenditure
    b. Capitalize, depreciation is optional
    c. Capitalize, depreciation is required
    d. Capitalize, depreciation is **not** permitted (R/08, FAR, #22, 8577)

28. Dayne County's general fund had the following disbursements during the year.

Payment of principal on long-term debt	$100,000
Payments to vendors	500,000
Purchase of a computer	300,000

    What amount should Dayne County report as expenditures in its governmental funds statement of revenues, expenditures, and changes in fund balances?

    a. $300,000
    b. $500,000
    c. $800,000
    d. $900,000 (R/05, FAR, #22, 7766)

29. A state had general obligation bonds outstanding that required payment of interest on July 1 and January 1 of each year. State law allowed for the general fund to make debt payments without the use of a fiscal agent. The fiscal year ended June 30. Which of the following accounts would have decreased when the state paid the interest due on July 1?

    a. Interest expenditures
    b. Interest payable
    c. Interest expense
    d. Fund balance (R/08, FAR, #46, 8601)

30. Cal City maintains several major fund types. The following were among Cal's cash:

Unrestricted state grant	$1,000,000
Interest on bank accounts held for employees' pension plan	200,000

    What amount of these cash receipts should be accounted for in Cal's general fund?

    a. $1,200,000
    b. $1,000,000
    c. $ 200,000
    d. $0 (11/93, PII, #8, amended, 4437)

31. The following information pertains to Park Township's general fund at December 31:

Total assets, including $200,000 of cash	$1,000,000
Total liabilities	600,000
Reserved for encumbrances	100,000

Appropriations do not lapse at year-end. At December 31, what amount should Park report as unassigned fund balance in its general fund balance sheet?

a. $200,000
b. $300,000
c. $400,000
d. $500,000 (11/93, PII, #20, amended, 4449)

32. A county's balances in the general fund included the following:

Appropriations	$435,000
Encumbrances	18,000
Expenditures	164,000
Vouchers payable	23,000

What is the remaining amount available for use by the county?

a. $230,000
b. $248,000
c. $253,000
d. $271,000 (R/07, FAR, #16, 8337)

33. The following information pertains to certain monies held by Blair County at December 31 that are legally restricted to expenditures for specified purposes:

Proceeds of short-term notes to be used for advances to permanent trust funds	$ 8,000
Proceeds of long-term debt to be used for a major capital project	90,000

What amount of these restricted monies should Blair account for in special revenue funds?

a. $0
b. $ 8,000
c. $90,000
d. $98,000 (11/93, PII, #18, amended, 4447)

34. Lake County received the following proceeds that are legally restricted to expenditure for specified purposes:

Levies on affected property owners to install sidewalks	$500,000
Gasoline taxes to finance road repairs	900,000

What amount should be accounted for in Lake's special revenue funds?

a. $1,400,000
b. $ 900,000
c. $ 500,000
d. $0 (5/92, PII, #27, 2659)

35. The following information pertains to Comb City:

Year 3 real estate property taxes assessed and collected in year 3	$14,000,000
Year 2 real estate property taxes assessed in year 1 and collected in year 3	1,000,000
Year 3 sales taxes collected by merchants in year 3 but not required to be remitted to Comb until January of year 4	2,000,000

For the year ending December 31, year 3, Comb should recognize revenues of:

a. $14,000,000
b. $15,000,000
c. $16,000,000
d. $17,000,000 (R\90, FAR #54, 1357)

36. Grove Township issued $50,000 of bond anticipation notes at face amount in the current year and placed the proceeds into its capital projects fund. All legal steps were taken to refinance the notes, but Grove was unable to consummate refinancing. In the capital projects fund, what account should be credited to record the $50,000 proceeds?

    a. Other Financing Sources Control
    b. Revenues Control
    c. Deferred Revenues
    d. Bond Anticipation Notes Payable (5/90, PII, #10, amended, 1373)

37. A capital projects fund for a new city courthouse recorded a receivable of $300,000 for a state grant and a $450,000 transfer from the general fund. What amount should be reported as revenue by the capital projects fund?

    a. $0
    b. $300,000
    c. $450,000
    d. $750,000 (R/06, FAR, #2, 8069)

38. In the current year, Mentor Town received $4,000,000 of bond proceeds to be used for capital projects. Of this amount, $1,000,000 was expended in this year. Expenditures for the $3,000,000 balance were expected to be incurred in the following year. These bonds proceeds should be recorded in capital projects funds for

    a. $4,000,000 in the current year
    b. $4,000,000 in the following year
    c. $1,000,000 in the current year and $3,000,000 in the following year
    d. $1,000,000 in the current year and $3,000,000 in the general fund the following year (Editors, 9086)

39. Financing for the renovation of Fir City's municipal park, begun and completed during the year, came from the following sources:

Grant from state government	$400,000
Proceeds from general obligation bond issue	500,000
Transfer from Fir's general fund	100,000

In its capital projects fund operating statement, Fir should report these amounts as

	Revenues	Other financing sources
a.	$1,000,000	$0
b.	$ 900,000	$ 100,000
c.	$ 400,000	$ 600,000
d.	$0	$1,000,000

(11/93, PII, #11, amended, 4440)

40. The debt service fund of a governmental unit is used to account for the accumulation of resources for, and the payment of, principal and interest in connection with a

	Private-purpose trust fund	Proprietary funds
a.	No	No
b.	No	Yes
c.	Yes	Yes
d.	Yes	No

(11/94, AR, #12, 4989)

41. A major exception to the general rule of expenditure accrual for governmental units relates to unmatured

	Principal of general long-term debt	Interest on general long-term debt
a.	Yes	Yes
b.	Yes	No
c.	No	Yes
d.	No	No

(11/94, AR, #14, 4991)

42. Tott City's serial bonds are serviced through a debt service fund with cash provided by the general fund. In a debt service fund's statements, how are cash receipts and cash payments reported?

	Cash receipts	Cash payments
a.	Revenues	Expenditures
b.	Revenues	Operating transfers
c.	Operating transfers	Expenditures
d.	Operating transfers	Operating transfers

(5/91, Theory, #54, 2098)

43. Dale City is accumulating financial resources that are legally restricted to payments of general long-term debt principal and interest maturing in future years. At December 31, $5,000,000 has been accumulated for principal payments and $300,000 has been accumulated for interest payments. These restricted funds should be accounted for in the

	Debt service fund	General fund
a.	$0	$5,300,000
b.	$ 300,000	$5,000,000
c.	$5,000,000	$ 300,000
d.	$5,300,000	$0

(5/92, PII, #36, amended, 2668)

44. Oak County incurred the following expenditures in issuing long-term bonds:

Issue cost	$400,000
Debt insurance	90,000

When Oak establishes the accounting for operating debt service, what amount should be deferred and amortized over the life of the bonds?

a. $0
b. $ 90,000
c. $400,000
d. $490,000

(5/92, PII, #28, amended, 2660)

45. Tang City received land from a donor who stipulated that the land must remain intact, but any income generated from the property may be used for general government services. In which fund should Tang City record the donated land?

a. Special revenue
b. Permanent
c. Private-purpose trust
d. Agency

(R/09, FAR, #19, 8769)

46. Arlen City's fiduciary funds contained the following cash balances at December 31:

Under the Forfeiture Act—cash confiscated from illegal activities; principal can be used only for law enforcement activities	$300,000
Sales taxes collected by Arlen to be distributed to other governmental units	500,000

What amount of cash should Arlen report in its permanent funds at December 31?

a. $0
b. $300,000
c. $500,000
d. $800,000

(11/93, PII, #14, amended, 4443)

47. The orientation of accounting and reporting for all proprietary funds of governmental units is

a. Income determination
b. Project
c. Flow of funds
d. Program

(11/94, AR, #3, 4980)

48. The following information for the year ended June 30 pertains to a proprietary fund established by Glen Village in connection with Glen's public parking facilities:

Receipts from users of parking facilities	$600,000
Expenditures—Parking meters	410,000
Expenditures—Salaries and other cash expenses	96,000
Depreciation of parking meters	94,000

For the year ended June 30, this proprietary fund should report net income of

a. $0.
b. $ 94,000.
c. $ 96,000.
d. $410,000. (Editors, 9087)

49. The billings for transportation services provided to other governmental units are recorded by the internal service fund as

a. Transportation appropriations
b. Operating revenues
c. Interfund exchanges
d. Intergovernmental transfers (11/95, AR, #73, 5816)

50. Which of the following does **not** affect an internal service fund's net income?

a. Depreciation expense on its fixed assets
b. Operating transfer sources
c. Residual equity transfers
d. Temporary transfers (11/93, Theory, #55, amended, 4560)

51. Through an internal service fund, New County operates a centralized data processing center to provide services to New's other governmental units. This internal service fund billed New's parks and recreation fund $150,000 for data processing services. What account should New's internal service fund credit to record this $150,000 billing to the parks and recreation fund?

a. Data Processing Department Expenses
b. Intergovernmental Transfers
c. Interfund Exchanges
d. Operating Revenues Control (11/93, PII, #13, amended, 4442)

52. King City Council will be establishing a library fund. Library fees are expected to cover 55% of the library's annual resource requirements. King has decided that an annual determination of net income is desirable in order to maintain management control and accountability over library. What type of fund should King establish in order to meet their measurement objectives?

a. Special revenue fund
b. General fund
c. Internal service fund
d. Enterprise fund (R/10, FAR, #46, 9346)

53. On January 2, Basketville City purchased equipment with a useful life of three years to be used by its water and sewer enterprise fund. Which of the following is the correct treatment for the asset?

a. Record the purchase of the equipment as an expenditure
b. Capitalize; depreciation is optional
c. Capitalize; depreciation is required
d. Capitalize; depreciation is **not** permitted (R/05, FAR, #11, 7755)

54. Cedar City issued $1,000,000, 6% revenue bonds at par on April 1, to build a new water line for the water enterprise fund. Interest is payable every six months. What amount of interest expense should be reported for the year ended December 31?

    a. $0
    b. $30,000
    c. $45,000
    d. $60,000 (R/01, AR, #6, 6991)

55. Which of the following funds of a governmental unit records depreciation?

    a. Capital projects fund
    b. Debt service fund
    c. Internal service fund
    d. Special revenue fund (R/07, FAR, #15, 8336)

56. The town of Hill operates municipal electric and water utilities. In which of the following funds should the operations of the utilities be accounted for?

    a. Enterprise fund
    b. Internal service fund
    c. Agency fund
    d. Special revenue fund (5/93, PII, #28, 4135)

57. The following fund types used by Ridge City had total assets at December 31 as follows:

Special revenue funds	$100,000
Agency funds	200,000
Pension funds	400,000

    Total fiduciary fund assets amounted to

    a. $300,000
    b. $400,000
    c. $600,000
    d. $700,000 (Editors, 1388)

58. Which of the following can be reported in a fiduciary fund?

    a. The managing government's share of investments in a investment pool
    b. Water and sewer operations that provide services to other cities and counties within the region
    c. Special assessment bonds that are supported by general fund contributions for unpaid assessments that are delinquent more than five years
    d. Trusts held specifically for the benefit of third parties (Editor, 89572)

59. Elm City contributes to and administers a single-employer defined benefit pension plan on behalf of its covered employees. The plan is accounted for in a pension trust fund. Actuarially determined employer contribution requirements and contributions actually made for the past three years, along with the percentage of annual covered payroll, were as follows:

	Contribution made		Actuarial requirement	
	Amount	Percent	Amount	Percent
Year 3	$11,000	26	$11,000	26
Year 2	5,000	12	10,000	24
Year 1	None	None	8,000	20

    What account should be credited in the pension trust fund to record the year 3 employer contribution of $11,000?

    a. Revenues Control
    b. Other Financing Sources Control
    c. Due From Special Revenue Fund
    d. Pension Benefit Obligation (5/90, PII, #7, amended, 1370)

60. Which of the following statements are presented for investment trust funds?

a. Cash flows statement
b. Balance sheet and statement of activities
c. Statement of net assets and statement of activities
d. Statements of net assets and changes in net assets (Editor, 89574)

61. Both Curry City and the state have a general sales tax on all merchandise. Curry City's tax rate is 2 percent and the state's rate is 4 percent. Merchants are required by law to remit all sales tax collected each month to the state by the 15th of the following month. By law, the state has 45 days to process the collections and to make disbursements to the various jurisdictions for which it acts as an agent. Sales tax collected by merchants in Curry total $450,000 in May and $600,000 in June. Both merchants and the state make remittances in accordance with statutes. What amount of sales tax revenue for May and June is included in the June 30 year-end financial statements of the state and Curry?

	State	Curry
a.	$1,050,000	$0
b.	$1,050,000	$350,000
c.	$ 700,000	$350,000
d.	$ 300,000	$150,000

(R/00, AR, #2, 6907)

62. Harland County received a $2,000,000 capital grant to be equally distributed among its five municipalities. The grant is to finance the construction of capital assets. Harland had no administrative or direct financial involvement in the construction. In which fund should Harland record the receipt of cash?

a. Agency fund
b. General fund
c. Special revenue fund
d. Private purpose trust fund (R/09, FAR, #2, 8752)

63. In preparing combined financial statements for a governmental entity, interfund receivables and payables should be

a. Reported as reservations of fund balance
b. Reported as additions to or reductions from the unassigned fund balance
c. Reported as amounts due to and due from other funds
d. Eliminated (5/95, AR, #53, 5471)

64. Brandon County's general fund had the following transactions during the year:

Transfer to a debt service fund	$100,000
Payment to a pension trust fund	500,000
Purchase of equipment	300,000

What amount should Brandon County report for the general fund as other financing uses in its governmental funds statement of revenues, expenditures, and changes in fund balances?

a. $100,000
b. $400,000
c. $800,000
d. $900,000 (R/10, FAR, #48, 9348)

65. Which of the following transactions is an expenditure of a governmental unit's general fund?

a. Contribution of enterprise fund capital by the general fund
b. Operating subsidy transfer from the general fund to an enterprise fund
c. Routine employer contributions from the general fund to a pension trust fund
d. Transfer from the general fund to a capital projects fund (R/07, FAR, #13, 8334)

66. For which of the following funds do operating transfers affect the results of operations?

	Governmental funds	Proprietary funds
a.	No	No
b.	No	Yes
c.	Yes	Yes
d.	Yes	No

(11/94, AR, #11, 4988)

Problem 18-2 SIMULATION: Governmental Reporting

The following information relates to Dane City during its fiscal year ended December 31:

- On October 31, to finance the construction of a city hall annex, Dane issued 8% 10-year general obligation bonds at their face value of $600,000. Construction expenditures during the period equaled $364,000.
- Dane reported $109,000 from hotel room taxes, restricted for tourist promotion, in a special revenue fund. The fund paid $81,000 for general promotions and $22,000 for a motor vehicle.
- The general fund revenues of $104,500 were transferred to a debt service fund and used to repay $100,000 of 9% 15-year term bonds, and to pay $4,500 of interest. The bonds were used to acquire a citizens' center.
- At December 31, as a consequence of past services, city firefighters had accumulated entitlements to compensated absences valued at $86,000. General fund resources available at December 31 are expected to be used to settle $17,000 of this amount, and $69,000 is expected to be paid out of future general fund resources.
- At December 31, Dane was responsible for $83,000 of outstanding general fund encumbrances, including the $8,000 for supplies indicated below.
- Dane uses the purchases method to account for supplies. The following information relates to supplies:

Inventory—1/1	$ 39,000
12/31	42,000
Encumbrances outstanding—1/1	6,000
12/31	8,000
Purchase orders during the year	190,000
Amounts credited to vouchers payable during the year	181,000

For Items 1 through 10, determine the amounts based solely on the above information. Enter the amount in the space provided. Round all amounts to the nearest whole dollar.

	Amount
1. What is the amount of general fund operating transfers out?	
2. How much should be reported as general fund liabilities from entitlements for compensated absences?	
3. What is the reserved (nonspendable and committed) amount of the general fund balance?	
4. What is the capital projects fund balance?	
5. What is the fund balance on the special revenue fund for tourist promotion?	
6. What is the amount of debt service fund expenditures?	
7. What amount should be included in the general fund for capital assets acquired in the year?	
8. What amount stemming from transactions and events decreased the long-term liabilities reported in the government activities column of the government-wide statements?	
9. Using the purchases method, what is the amount of supplies expenditures?	
10. What was the total amount of supplies encumbrances?	

(11/95, AR, #117 - 126, amended, 5860)

Problem 18-3 SIMULATION: Governmental-Type Funds

Items 1 through 5 represent transactions by governmental-type funds based on the following selected information taken from Dease City's year-end financial records:

General fund	
Beginning fund balance	$ 700,000
Estimated revenues	10,000,000
Actual revenues	10,500,000
Appropriations	9,000,000
Expenditures	8,200,000
Ending encumbrances	500,000
Ending vouchers payable	300,000
Operating transfers in	100,000
The year's property tax levy	9,500,000
The year's property taxes estimated to be uncollectible when property tax levy for the year is recorded	100,000
The year's property taxes delinquent at end of the year	150,000
Capital projects fund	
Operating transfers in	100,000
Construction of new library wing started and completed in the year	
• Proceeds from bonds issued at 100	2,000,000
• Expenditures	2,100,000

For Items 1 through 5, determine the amounts solely on the above information. Enter the amount in the space provided. Round all amounts to the nearest whole dollar.

	Amount
1. What was the net amount credited to the budgetary fund balance when the budget was approved?	
2. What was the amount of property taxes collected on the property tax levy for the year?	
3. What amount for the new library wing was included in the capital projects fund balance at the end of the year?	
4. What amount for the new library wing was reported in the government-wide statement of net assets in the governmental activities column at the end of the year?	
5. What amount for the new library wing bonds was reported in the government-wide statement of net assets in the governmental activities column at the end of the year?	

(5/97, AR, #2, amended, 6355)

Problem 18-4 SIMULATION: Government Transactions

Items 1 through 10 represent various transactions pertaining to a municipality that uses encumbrance accounting. Select the appropriate recording of the transaction (A through L). A method of recording the transactions may be selected once, more than once, or not at all.

Recording of Transactions Choices
A. Credit appropriations control.
B. Credit budgetary fund balance
C. Credit expenditures control.
D. Credit deferred revenues.
E. Credit interfund revenues.
F. Credit tax anticipation notes payable.
G. Credit other financing sources.
H. Credit other financing uses.
I. Debit appropriations control.
J. Debit deferred revenues.
K. Debit encumbrances control
L. Debit expenditures control.

Event	Choice
1. General obligation bonds were issued at par.	
2. Approved purchase orders were issued for supplies.	
3. The above-mentioned supplies were received and the related invoices were approved.	
4. General fund salaries and wages were incurred.	
5. The internal service fund had interfund billings.	
6. Revenues were earned from a previously awarded grant.	
7. Property taxes were collected in advance.	
8. Appropriations were recorded on adoption of the budget.	
9. Short-term financing was received from a bank, secured by the city's taxing power.	
10. There was an excess of estimated inflows over estimated outflows.	

(11/92, P11, #4 (61 - 80), amended, 3395)

Solution 18-1 MULTIPLE-CHOICE ANSWERS

Fundamentals

1. (c) The general and capital project funds are governmental-type funds. All governmental-type funds have the fund flow measurement focus. The measurement focus of both these funds is on determination of financial position and changes in financial position, rather than on net income determination. (5800)

2. (c) A specific governmental unit is not accounted for through a single accounting entity. Instead, the accounts of a government are divided into several funds. A fund is a fiscal and accounting entity with a self-balancing set of accounts recording cash and other financial resources, together with all related liabilities and residual equities and balances, and changes therein, which are segregated for the purpose of carrying on specific activities or attaining certain objectives in accordance with special regulations, restrictions, or limitations. (7610)

3. (c) Fund accounting is used when there are legal separations between sources and uses of funds. Fund accounting may be used to account for assets aside from cash and cash equivalents. Combined or combining financial statements may be used with or without fund accounting. The resources may be physically in the same account or location. (5803)

4. (d) The governmental fund measurement focus is on determination of financial position and changes in financial position, rather than on net income determination. In governmental funds, the primary emphasis is on the flow of financial resources. (6201)

5. (b) The three funds using the accrual basis of accounting are the (1) internal service fund, (2) airport enterprise fund, and (3) pension trust fund. The modified accrual basis of accounting is used by the general fund, capital projects fund, special revenue fund, and debt service fund. (7756)

6. (a) The modified accrual basis of accounting for a governmental unit recognizes revenues in the period in which they become available and measurable. The modified accrual basis is the appropriate basis of accounting for governmental-type funds, such as the capital projects fund. Proprietary and fiduciary funds use the accrual basis of accounting. The accrual basis of accounting recognizes revenues in the period in which they become earned and measurable. (4130)

7. (b) The following entry is made when a purchase order for $50 is approved:

Encumbrances (estimated cost)	50	
Budgetary Fund Balance Reserved for Encumbrances		50

The following entries would be made to record the receipt of the related goods for $55 and the vouchers payable:

Budgetary Fund Balance Reserved for Encumbrances	50	
Encumbrances (estimated cost)		50
Expenditures (actual cost)	55	
Vouchers Payable		55

(4556)

8. (c) The entry when a purchase order is issued is as follows:

Encumbrances	XX	
Reserve for Encumbrances		XX

When a corresponding invoice is received for $105, the following two entries are made:

Reserve for Encumbrances	XX	
Encumbrances		XX
Expenditures (actual cost)	YY	
Vouchers Payable		YY

(5814)

9. (b) To record purchase orders issued or contract commitments, the *Encumbrances* account is debited and *Reserve for Encumbrances* is credited. (4995)

10. (b) Fixed assets donated to a governmental unit are recorded at fair value when received. (5801)

11. (d) The encumbrance system is used in governmental funds (general, special revenue, and capital projects funds) to prevent over-expenditure and to demonstrate compliance with legal requirements. The enterprise fund is a proprietary fund and does not use the encumbrance system. (9852)

12. (c) The modified accrual basis is the appropriate basis of accounting for governmental funds (i.e., general, special revenue, capital projects, permanent, and debt service). Internal service funds, enterprise funds, and private-purpose funds all use the accrual basis of accounting. (4559)

Governmental Funds

13. (c) The unassigned *fund balance* account of the governmental unit is *debited* at the beginning of the year because appropriations *exceed* estimated revenues, shown in Entry (1). During the year, revenues *equaled* estimated revenues; therefore, the *fund balance* account is *not affected* by the revenue closing entry, as in Entry (2). During the year, expenditures and encumbrances were *less than* appropriations; therefore, the unassigned *fund balance* account is *credited* for the closing entry for the appropriations, expenditures, and encumbrances, as in Entry (3).

		Debit	Credit
(1)	Estimated Revenues Control	XX	
	Unassigned Fund Balance (to balance)	XX	
	Appropriations Control		XX
(2)	Revenues Control	XX	
	Estimated Revenues Control		XX
(3)	Appropriations Control	XX	
	Expenditures Control		XX
	Encumbrances Control		XX
	Unassigned Fund Balance (to balance)		XX

(2096)

14. (d) The *Estimated Revenues Control* account of a governmental fund type is a budgetary account (i.e., it is not used to record actual revenues). Its balance is eliminated when the budgetary accounts are closed. The entry to close the *Estimated Revenues Control* and *Revenues Control* accounts to *Unassigned Fund Balance* is as follows:

	Debit	Credit
Revenues Control	17,000,000	
Unassigned Fund Balance (difference)	3,000,000	
Estimated Revenues Control		20,000,000

(1360)

15. (b) Encumbrances are obligations to spend (purchase orders) to prevent overspending of appropriations. An encumbrance entry is made when an item is ordered in the amount of the estimated cost. The reverse entry is made for the same dollar amount when the invoice arrives. Outstanding encumbrances at year end are carried forward as committed fund balance with a corresponding reduction to unassigned fund balance. The spending of a prior year's outstanding encumbrances is a use of committed fund balance, not a current year expenditure. Only half the new vehicles were delivered by December 31. Thus, there would be half of the $264,000, or $132,000, in outstanding encumbrances at year end carried forward as committed fund balance. (8350)

16. (d) When the purchase order for the supplies was issued, the following entry was made:

	Debit	Credit
Encumbrances Control (estimated cost)	5,000	
Reserve for Encumbrances		5,000

Upon receipt of the supplies and invoice, the following entries were made:

	Debit	Credit
Reserve for Encumbrances (reverse original entry)	5,000	
Encumbrances Control		5,000
Expenditures (actual cost)	4,950	
Vouchers Payable		4,950

(4434)

17. (c) The amount of Cliff's encumbrances that were outstanding at June 30 is $500,000 (i.e., $5,000,000 – $4,500,000). When the purchase orders were issued, the following entry was made:

Encumbrances Control (estimated cost)	5,000,000	
Reserve for Encumbrances		5,000,000

Upon receipt of the goods and related invoices, the following entries were made:

Reserve for Encumbrances	4,500,000		
Encumbrances Control		4,500,000	
Expenditures (actual cost)	4,200,000		
Vouchers Payable		4,200,000	(4433)

18. (d) Fire department salaries are *expenditures* of the general government, not *expenses* of a propriety fund. While goods and services committed for by purchase order or contract are encumbered in governmental funds to avoid overspending appropriations, some expenditures are controlled by other means and need not be encumbered. Salaries are set by contract and controlled by established payroll procedures and are not encumbered. (6305)

19. (a) In governmental funds, revenues are additions to fund assets or decreases in fund liabilities (except from other financing sources) that increase the residual equity of the fund—inflows (sources) of fund working capital. Expenditures are increases in fund liabilities or decreases in fund assets (except for other financing uses) that decrease the residual equity of the fund—outflows (uses) of fund working capital. Expenditures include capital outlays for general fixed assets and repayment of general long-term debt principal. The purchase of fixed assets would have an effect on the excess of revenues over expenditures. The other choices would involve interfund transfers and the use of either other financing sources or other financing uses. (9320)

20. (d) Expenditures are recorded when fund liabilities are incurred or assets expended, except in regard to inventory items, interest on general long-term debt, and prepaids such as insurance. This is due to the emphasis on the flow of financial resources in governmental accounting. (4992)

21. (a) Interest on general long-term debt, usually accounted for in debt service funds, normally are recorded as an expenditure on its due date rather than being accrued prior to its due date. (7757)

22. (c) Although authorized transfers to other fund entities may be viewed as appropriation expenditures from the point of view of the general fund entity, for purposes of financial reporting they are distinguished from expenditures. Control over authorized transfers to other fund entities is achieved by recording them as estimated other financing uses at the beginning of the period for which they are authorized (budgeted), rather than by including them in the budget entry for appropriations. The journal entry to record the adoption of the budget is as follows:

Estimated Revenues Control	30,000,000		
Appropriations Control		27,000,000	
Estimated Other Financing Uses		900,000	
Unassigned Fund Balance (to balance)		2,100,000	(2655)

23. (a) Although authorized transfers to other fund entities may be viewed as appropriation expenditures from the point of view of the general fund entity, for purposes of financial reporting they are distinguished from expenditures. Control over authorized transfers to other fund entities is achieved by recording them as estimated other financing uses at the beginning of the period for which they are authorized (budgeted), rather than by including them in the budget entry for appropriations. The journal entry to record the adoption of the budget is as follows:

Estimated Revenues Control	30,000,000		
Appropriations Control		27,000,000	
Estimated Other Financing Uses		900,000	
Unassigned Fund Balance (to balance)		2,100,000	(2656)

General Fund

24. (a) The general fund records the expected $9,000,000 of inflows of resources for property taxes, licenses, and fines as estimated revenues in the entry to record the adoption of the budget. In this same entry, the expected inflows of resources from the proceeds of the debt issue and the interfund transfers for debt service are recorded as other financing sources. (4432)

25. (b) Commitments made by a government are encumbrances. Appropriations are amounts budgeted to be spent. Expenditures are amounts that have been spent. A fixed assets account is not debited until the property is placed in service. (6908)

26. (c) The encumbrance system is used by governmental funds to prevent overexpenditure and to demonstrate compliance with legal requirements. When a purchase order is issued, the estimated amount of the planned expenditure is **encumbered** by debiting *Encumbrances* and crediting *Budgetary Fund Balance Reserved for Encumbrances.* When the related invoice is received, the encumbrance entry is reversed and the actual expenditure is recorded. Thus, the balance of the *Encumbrance* account will equal the outstanding purchase order amounts until the books are closed at year-end. (2097)

27. (a) The modified accrual basis of accounting is used in the governmental-type fund statements such as the general fund. Under modified accrual, fixed assets are expenditures and not capitalized. (8577)

28. (d) Expenditures differ from expenses (as defined in commercial accounting) because expenditures include—in addition to current operating expenditures that benefit the current period—capital outlays for general fixed assets and repayment of general long-term debt principal.

Payments of principal on long-term debt	$100,000
Payments to vendors	500,000
Purchase of a computer	300,000
Total expenditures	$900,000

(7766)

29. (d) The general fund is used to account for most routine operations of the governmental entity. This fund accounts for all resources that are not required to be accounted for in other funds; in essence, it accounts for all unrestricted resources. The general fund uses modified accrual accounting. A fund balance is the difference between governmental fund assets and liabilities reported on the balance sheet. When the state paid the interest due, it would have reduced the amount of assets (cash) and as such decreased fund balance. (8601)

30. (b) The $1,000,000 unrestricted grant received from the state should be accounted for as revenue in Cal City's general fund. The $200,000 of interest received on bank accounts held for employees' pension plans should be accounted for in Cal City's pension trust fund. (4437)

31. (b) Because Park's appropriations do not lapse at year-end, the *Budgetary Fund Balance Reserved for Encumbrances* account is converted from an offsetting memorandum account in the general ledger to a true commitment of *Fund Balance* at year-end. The amount that Park should report as *Unassigned Fund Balance* in its general fund balance sheet is computed as follows:

Total assets	$1,000,000
Less: Total liabilities	600,000
Total fund balance	400,000
Less: Committed Fund balance	100,000
Unassigned fund balance, December 31	$ 300,000

(4449)

32. (c) Appropriations constitute the maximum expenditure authorization during the fiscal year. Encumbrances are recorded obligations to spend (purchase orders) to prevent overspending of appropriations. Expenditures are normally recorded when fund liabilities are incurred or assets expended. The vouchers payable account has no impact on funds available for use. Taking the appropriations of $435,000 and subtracting both the encumbrances of $18,000 and expenditures of $164,000 nets $253,000 remaining available for use. (8337)

Special Revenue Funds

33. (a) Special revenue funds are used to account for financial resources that are restricted by law or by contractual agreement to specific purposes *other than for permanent funds or major capital projects.* Thus, neither the $8,000 of proceeds of the short-term notes to be used for advances to permanent fund nor the $90,000 of proceeds on long-term debt to be used for a major capital project should be accounted for in a special revenue fund. (4447)

34. (b) The $900,000 of gasoline taxes collected to finance road repairs should be accounted for in a Special Revenue Fund. Special Revenue Funds are used to account for revenues that have been legally restricted as to expenditure. The NCGA provides several examples of revenues which would fall under the heading: (1) a state gasoline tax collected in order to maintain streets, (2) proceeds from parking meters which finance the local traffic court, and (3) state juvenile rehabilitation grants used to operate and maintain juvenile rehabilitation centers. In each of these cases, a service is being provided, but the funding comes from a specific revenue source rather than from property taxes or any other general revenues. (2659)

35. (d) Governmental-type funds use the modified accrual basis of accounting, with revenues recognized when they become measurable and available for use. "Available for use" means that the revenues will be collected within the current period or collected early enough in the next period to be used to pay for expenditures incurred in the current period. (The rule of thumb for available for use is that the revenue is collected within 60 days.) Five classes of revenue that may be accrued if available for use and measurable are: (1) personal property taxes, (2) real estate property taxes, (3) income taxes, (4) sales taxes, and (5) taxes collected by another governmental unit. ($14,000,000 + $1,000,000 + $2,000,000 = $17,000,000) (1357)

Capital Projects Fund

36. (d) A governmental unit would issue bond anticipation notes (BANs) to provide funds to defray costs expected to be incurred before the related bonds are issued. Such notes are treated as long-term debt, even if due within one year, if (1) they are to be repaid with the proceeds of the bond issue, (2) all legal steps have been taken to refinance the notes, and (3) the intent is supported by an ability to refinance the short-term notes on a long-term basis. Since all of these criteria are not met for the bond anticipation notes in question, they are reported as a liability of the capital projects fund. (1373)

37. (b) The capital projects fund reports unrestricted grants received from other governmental units as revenue. Therefore, the $300,000 grant from the state is reported as revenue in the capital projects fund's operating statement. The capital projects fund reports long-term debt proceeds and operating transfers from other funds as other financing sources. Therefore, the $450,000 transfer from the general fund is reported as other financing sources in the capital project fund's operating statement. (8069)

38. (a) Debt proceeds should be recognized by a capital projects fund at the time the debt is incurred, rather than the time the debt is authorized or when the proceeds are expended. Debt proceeds should be reported in the capital projects fund as *Other Financing Sources* rather than as *Revenues.* The entry in the capital projects fund to record the issuance of the bonds is as follows:

Cash	4,000,000	
Other Financing Sources—Bond Proceeds		4,000,000

(9086)

39. (c) The capital projects fund reports unrestricted grants received from other governmental units as revenue. Therefore, the $400,000 grant from the state is reported as revenue in Fir's capital projects fund's operating statement. The capital projects fund reports long-term debt proceeds and operating transfers from other funds as other financing sources. Therefore, the $500,000 proceeds from the general obligation bond issue and the $100,000 transfer from Fir's general fund are reported as other financing sources of $600,000 in the capital project fund's operating statement. (4440)

Debt Service Funds

40. (a) Only general obligation long-term debt should be serviced through debt service funds. Fiduciary and proprietary fund debt are rarely general government obligations. (4989)

41. (a) A major exception to the general rule of expenditure accrual relates to unmatured principal and interest on general long-term debt. This deals with the criterion related to the expenditure recognition on debt known as the "when due" criterion. Entities that budget cash outflows for debt when they legally become due include budget appropriations for debt in the year in which the cash outflow occurs. Because the financial flow of funds to make payment has not been budgeted for, interest and principal payments are not subject to accrual. (4991)

42. (c) The debt service fund of a governmental unit is used to account for accumulation of resources for, and the payment of, general long-term debt principal and interest. The debt service fund reports cash receipts from the general fund as operating transfers. Cash payments for long-term debt principal and related interest are reported as expenditures in the fund. (2098)

43. (d) Debt service funds are used to account for the accumulation of resources for, and the payment of, general long-term debt principal and interest. (2668)

44. (a) Neither the bond issue costs nor the debt insurance are deferred and amortized over the life of the bonds. The bond issue proceeds are recorded at the amount received net of any issue and insurance costs incurred. (2660)

Permanent Funds

45. (b) A permanent fund is used to account for nonexpendable resources that may be used for the government's programs to generate and disperse money, such as the land in this situation, to benefit the reporting entity or its citizens. The name of the fund comes from the purpose of the fund: a sum of equity used to permanently generate payments to maintain some financial obligation. A fund can only be classified as a permanent fund if the money is used to report the status of a restricted financial resource. The resource is restricted in the sense that only earnings from the resource are used and not the principal. A special revenue fund is used to account for revenues that are externally restricted or designated by the legislative body for specific general government purposes other than capital projects. Private-purpose trust funds are used to account for fiduciary responsibilities and activities in managing trust arrangements that benefit individuals, private organizations, or other governments. An agency fund is used to account for the custodial activities of a government serving as an agent for other governments, private organizations, or individuals. Agency funds are purely custodial. (8769)

46. (a) The cash collected under the Forfeiture Act, can only be used for law enforcement activities. It should be accounted for in a special revenue fund because the Act does not require the preservation of fund principal and the principal may be used for Arlen's benefit. An agency fund is established to account for assets received by a government in its capacity as an agent for individuals, businesses, or other governments. Therefore, the sales taxes collected by Arlen to be distributed to other governments are accounted for in an agency fund. (4443)

Proprietary Funds

47. (a) Proprietary funds are accounted for essentially as if they were private sector, profit seeking business enterprises. Therefore, the orientation of these funds is income determination. (4980)

48. (d) Proprietary funds account for their fixed assets in the same manner as commercial enterprises; therefore, the expenditure for the parking meters should be recorded in the fund's fixed asset accounts. Enterprise funds and internal service funds are the two types of proprietary funds. The fund in question is an enterprise fund because it is a self-supporting fund which provides goods and/or services to the general public.

Receipts from users of parking facilities		$600,000
Less: Salaries and other cash expenses	$96,000	
Depreciation of parking meters	94,000	(190,000)
Net income		$410,000

(9087)

49. (b) Internal service funds are accounted for similar to enterprise funds. A *Revenues* or *Billings To Others* account is used for services provided to other departments or governments. Appropriations accounts are budgetary accounts. Interfund exchanges would be between departments in the same government unit. Inter-governmental transfers are used when the same entity is doing the accounting for both governments. (5816)

50. (d) An internal service fund's net income is not affected by temporary transfers. Internal service funds report residual equity transactions as Transfers In or Out. They are reported after nonoperating revenues and expenses as a capital transaction. An internal service fund's net income is affected by operating revenues and expenses, nonoperating revenues and expenses, and operating and residual equity transfers. (4560)

51. (d) Billings for services provided to other governmental units are recorded by the internal service fund as operating revenues. (4442)

52. (d) Enterprise funds must be used to account for a government's business-type operations that are financed and operated like private businesses—where the government's intent is that all costs of providing goods or services to the general public on a continuing basis are to be financed or recovered primarily through users charges. Governments are permitted to account for virtually any type of self-contained business-type activity in enterprise funds if it prefers to do business-type accounting rather than general government accounting. A special revenue fund is used to account for revenues that are externally restricted or designated by the legislative body for specific general government purposes other than capital projects. The general fund is the primary governmental fund used to account for most routine operations of the governmental entity. Internal service funds are used to account for in-house business enterprise activities; that is, to account for the financing of goods and services provided by one government department or agency to other departments or agencies of the government on a cost reimbursement basis. (9346)

53. (c) Depreciation of fixed assets is required and is not optional in an enterprise fund. Enterprise funds must be used to account for a government's business-type operations that are financed and operated like private businesses—where the government's intent is that all costs (expenses, including depreciation) of providing goods or services to the general public on a continuing basis are to be financed or recovered primarily through user charges. Fixed assets are not treated as expenditures in an enterprise fund. (7755)

54. (c) Since this is an enterprise fund, accrual accounting applies. Interest expense for the year includes the $30,000 ($1,000,000 × 6% × 1/2 year) paid on October 1 and the $15,000 ($1,000,000 × 6% × 1/4 year) accrued expense from October 1 through December 31 for a total of $45,000. (6991)

55. (c) Internal service funds are considered a type of proprietary fund. They are used to account for in-house business enterprise activities. Fixed assets that are expected to be replaced through the internal service fund are recorded therein and depreciated. The capital projects fund, debt service fund, and special revenue fund are all governmental-type funds. Governmental-type funds do not maintain fixed assets nor record depreciation. (8336)

56. (a) Enterprise funds are used to account for a government's "business-type" operations that are financed and operated like private businesses (i.e., where the government's intent is that all costs, including depreciation, of providing goods or services to the general public on a continuing basis are to be financed or recovered primarily through user charges). Most government-owned public utilities must be accounted for in the enterprise funds under these criteria. Internal service funds account for the financing of goods or services provided by one department or agency to other departments or agencies of a governmental unit, or to other governmental units, on a cost-reimbursement basis. Agency funds account for resources held by a government as an agent for individuals or other governmental units. Special revenue funds account for general government resources that are restricted by law or contract for specific purposes. (4135)

Fiduciary Funds

57. (c) Fiduciary funds are used to account for assets held by a governmental unit acting as a trustee or agent for individuals, organizations, other governmental units, or other funds of the same government. Four distinct types of fiduciary funds exist: (1) pension trust funds, (2) investment trust funds, (3) private-purpose trust funds, and (4) agency funds. The total fiduciary fund assets amounted to $600,000 ($200,000 of agency fund assets and $400,000 of pension trust fund assets). The special revenue fund is a governmental fund. (1388)

58. (d) GASB Statement No. 34 segregated fiduciary funds from the governmental and proprietary funds to carve out those activities that solely benefit third parties and provide no resources for the government's programs. (89572)

59. (a) All pension trust fund contributions and earnings are accounted for as fund revenues. The pension trust fund makes the following entry to record employer contributions:

Cash	11,000		
Revenues Control—Employer Contribution		11,000	(1370)

60. (d) Investment trust funds only present two statements—statement of net assets and a statement of changes in net assets. A cash flows statement is not required for investment trust funds. Balance sheets are only used for governmental funds. (89574)

61. (c) Under the modified basis of accounting, governments accrue sales tax revenue when it is measurable and available for use. "Available for use" means that the revenues will be collected within the current period or early enough in the next period (i.e., within 60 days or so) to be used to pay for expenditures incurred in the current period. All of these revenues will be collected within 60 days. Curry City's portion of the total is not reported as revenues in the state's financial statements. Curry's portion is reported in the state's books in an agency fund (which does not have operating accounts) in an account such as *Due to City*. [$1,050,000 × (2/3) = $700,000 and $1,050,000 × (1/3) = $350,000] (6907)

62. (a) Harland should record the receipt of cash received from the capital grant in the agency fund. Agency funds are used to account for the custodial activities of a government serving as an agent for other governments, private organizations, or individuals. Harland is serving as an agent for its five municipalities. The general fund is used to account for most routine operations of the governmental entity. The special revenue fund is used to account for revenues that are externally restricted or designated by the legislative body for specific general government purposes other than capital projects. Private purpose trust funds are used to account for fiduciary responsibilities and activities in managing other trust arrangements that benefit individuals, private organizations, or other governments. (8752)

Interfund Transactions

63. (c) Interfund receivables and payables are reported as amounts due to and due from other funds. The option of eliminating the interfund assets and liabilities is allowed, but requires that such eliminations be apparent from the headings, or be disclosed in the notes to the financial statements. (5471)

64. (a) Transfers are nonreciprocal shifts of resources among funds that are not intended to be repaid. All transfers must be reported as either other financing sources or other financing uses. The general fund would report the payment to the pension trust fund and purchase of equipment as expenditures. (9348)

65. (c) Interfund transactions simultaneously affect two or more funds of the government. Quasi-external transactions are those that result in recognizing revenues and expenditures, as appropriate. General fund expenditures relate to external payments of a government and are budgeted (appropriated) by the legislature. Routine employer contributions from the general fund to a pension trust fund is an example of a budgeted expenditure item. Certain types of outlays, including transfers to other agencies or funds of the same government, are excluded from expenditure. Enterprise funds must be operated like private businesses, where the intent is that all costs are to be financed or recovered through user charges. An interfund transfer from the general fund to a capital projects fund would be classified as an operating transfer and thus not an expenditure. (8334)

66. (c) Operating transfers should be reported in *Other Financing Sources (Uses)* or *Other Financing* accounts and reported after revenues and expenditures or expenses, but before determining the results of operations in the operating statements. (4988)

PERFORMANCE BY SUBTOPICS

Each category below parallels a subtopic covered in Chapter 18. Record the number and percentage of questions you correctly answered in each subtopic area.

Fundamentals

Question #	Correct √
1	
2	
3	
4	
5	
6	
7	
8	
9	
10	
11	
12	
# Questions	12
# Correct	________
% Correct	________

Governmental Funds

Question #	Correct √
13	
14	
15	
16	
17	
18	
19	
20	
21	
22	
23	
# Questions	11
# Correct	________
% Correct	________

General Fund

Question #	Correct √
24	
25	
26	
27	
28	
29	
30	
31	
32	
# Questions	9
# Correct	________
% Correct	________

Special Revenue Funds

Question #	Correct √
33	
34	
35	
# Questions	3
# Correct	________
% Correct	________

Capital Projects Fund

Question #	Correct √
36	
37	
38	
39	
# Questions	4
# Correct	________
% Correct	________

Debt Service Funds

Question #	Correct √
40	
41	
42	
43	
44	
# Questions	5
# Correct	________
% Correct	________

Permanent Funds

Question #	Correct √
45	
46	
# Questions	2
# Correct	________
% Correct	________

Proprietary Funds

Question #	Correct √
47	
48	
49	
50	
51	
52	
53	
54	
55	
56	
# Questions	10
# Correct	________
% Correct	________

Fiduciary Funds

Question #	Correct √
57	
58	
59	
60	
61	
62	
# Questions	6
# Correct	________
% Correct	________

Interfund Transactions

Question #	Correct √
63	
64	
65	
66	
# Questions	4
# Correct	________
% Correct	________

Solution 18-2 SIMULATION: Governmental Reporting

		Amount
1.	What is the amount of general fund operating transfers out?	$104,500
2.	How much should be reported as general fund liabilities from entitlements for compensated absences?	$17,000
3.	What is the reserved (nonspendable and committed) amount of the general fund balance?	$125,000
4.	What is the capital projects fund balance?	$236,000
5.	What is the fund balance on the special revenue fund for tourist promotion?	$6,000
6.	What is the amount of debt service fund expenditures?	$104,500
7.	What amount should be included in the general fund for capital assets acquired in the year?	$0
8.	What amount stemming from transactions and events decreased the long-term liabilities reported in the government activities column of the government-wide statements?	$100,000
9.	Using the purchases method, what is the amount of supplies expenditures?	$181,000
10.	What was the total amount of supplies encumbrances?	$190,000

Explanations

1. The general fund operating transfers out (other financing uses) are composed of the $104,500 for bond principal and interest payment.

2. Compensated absences are valued at the salary and wage rates in effect as of the balance sheet date. The liabilities in the general fund are the amounts expected to be settled with resources available at the balance sheet date. The remainder of $69,000 would appear in the government-wide statement of net assets as long-term liability but is not booked in the general fund.

3. The reserved amount is the $83,000 committed fund balance for total encumbrances outstanding at December 31 and the $42,000 nonspendable fund balance for ending supplies inventory. The nonspendable fund balance indicates that a portion of fund balance is not available.

4. Fund balance of the capital projects fund is $600,000 – $364,000 = $236,000.

5. Fund balance of the special revenue fund is $109,000 – $81,000 – $22,000 = $6,000.

6. The debt service fund expenditures for the year are the $100,000 of principal repaid and the $4,500 of interest paid.

7. The cost of capital assets acquired in the year is $22,000 from the special revenue fund's purchase of a motor vehicle plus $364,000 from the capital projects fund. This appears in the government-wide financial statements in the governmental activities column, but is not booked in the general fund.

8. The $100,000 repayment of debt decreased the reported long-term liabilities.

9. Under the encumbrances method, the amount of supplies expenditures is the $181,000 credited to the *Vouchers Payable* account during the year less the $6,000 credited to *Vouchers Payable* account and debited to the *Budgetary Fund Balance Reserved for Encumbrances* account for the encumbrances outstanding as of 1/1. Under the purchases method, the fund balance is not reserved for prior year encumbrances, and thus the amount for expenditures is the full $181,000.

10. The $190,000 of purchase orders issued during the year is the total amount of supplies encumbrances. (5860)

Solution 18-3 SIMULATION: Governmental-Type Funds

		Amount
1.	What was the net amount credited to the budgetary fund balance when the budget was approved?	$1,000,000
2.	What was the amount of property taxes collected on the property tax levy for the year?	$9,350,000
3.	What amount for the new library wing was included in the capital projects fund balance at the end of the year?	-0-
4.	What amount for the new library wing was reported in the government-wide statement of net assets in the governmental activities column at the end of the year?	$2,100,000
5.	What amount for the new library wing bonds was reported in the government-wide statement of net assets in the governmental activities column at the end of the year?	$2,000,000

Explanations

1. The budgetary entry is as follows:

Estimated Revenues	10,000,000	
Appropriations		9,000,000
Budgetary Fund Balance		1,000,000

2. There were no write-offs of current year property taxes. Therefore, the amount collected is the amount of the current year property tax levy ($9,500,000) less the current-year property taxes delinquent at the end of the year ($150,000).

3. $100,000 + $2,000,000 – $2,100,000 = -0- All the current year expenditures are transferred out of the capital projects fund upon completion of the project.

4. The full cost of the library wing is reported.

5. The full amount of the bond debt is reported. (6355)

Solution 18-4 SIMULATION: Government Transactions

	Event	Choice
1.	General obligation bonds were issued at par.	G
2.	Approved purchase orders were issued for supplies.	K
3.	The above-mentioned supplies were received and the related invoices were approved.	L
4.	General fund salaries and wages were incurred.	L
5.	The internal service fund had interfund billings.	E
6.	Revenues were earned from a previously awarded grant.	J
7.	Property taxes were collected in advance.	D
8.	Appropriations were recorded on adoption of the budget.	A
9.	Short-term financing was received from a bank, secured by the city's taxing power.	F
10.	There was an excess of estimated inflows over estimated outflows.	B

Explanations

1. Proceeds of general obligation bonds should not be recorded as a credit to fund liabilities or revenues. Instead they should be recorded as a credit to other financing sources.

Cash	XX	
Other Financing Sources—Bond Proceeds		XX

2. When a purchase order is approved, the following journal entry is made:

Encumbrances Control	XX	
Budgetary Fund Balance—Reserved for Encumbrances		XX

3. When the supplies are received, the original encumbering entry is reversed, and the actual amounts are entered into the accounts as follows:

Budgetary Fund Balance—Reserved for Encumbrances	XX	
Encumbrances Control		XX
Expenditures Control	XX	
Vouchers Payable		XX

4. The general fund salaries and wages incurred should be recorded as follows:

Expenditures Control	XX	
Vouchers Payable		XX

5. The billings of the internal service fund is a "quasi-external" transaction. The internal service fund: (1) debits to receivable for the amount due, and (2) credits interfund revenues.

6. Where revenues are not properly recognized at the time the grant is awarded, Entry (1) is appropriate. When the conditions of the previously awarded grant are met, the deferred revenue is recognized as revenue, as in Entry (2).

Due From Grantor	XX	
Deferred Revenues		XX
Deferred Revenues	XX	
Revenues		XX

7. A deferred revenue account is credited if property taxes are collected prior to the year they apply.

8. The appropriations control account is credited when the following entry is made to record the budget:

Estimated Revenues Control	XX	
Appropriations Control		XX
Budgetary Fund Balance (to balance)		XX

9. Local banks customarily meet the working capital needs of a governmental unit by accepting a "tax anticipation note" from the unit. The journal entry to record the short-term financing received from the bank that is secured by the city's taxing power is as follows:

Cash	XX	
Tax Anticipation Notes Payable		XX

10. If there is an excess of estimated inflows over estimated outflows at the adoption of the budget, the Budgetary Fund Balance increased (i.e., credited). This can be seen from the following journal entry to record the adoption of the budget in question:

Estimated Revenues Control	XX	
Estimated Other Financing Sources	XX	
Appropriations Control		XX
Estimated Other Financing Uses		XX
Budgetary Fund Balance (to balance)		XX

(3395)

How to Pass the CPA Exam

Watching this video program, CPA candidates will gain insight about the CPA exam in general and computer-based testing in particular. Robert Monette discusses why and when to take the exam. Bob introduces the various exam authorities. He discusses the content for the four exam sections and recommends an order in which to take them. Bob finishes with some effective preparation strategies and a successful mindset. Approximately 20 minutes.

Call a Bisk Education customer service representative at 1-800-874-7877 or visit Bisk Education's web-site at www.cpaexam.com. Complimentary copies of this valuable video are available for a limited time to qualified candidates.

CHAPTER 19

GOVERNMENTAL FINANCIAL REPORTING

CHAPTER 19

GOVERNMENTAL FINANCIAL REPORTING

I. Introduction

A. Accounting Standards

1. **Governmental Accounting Standards Board (GASB)** The Governmental Accounting Standards Board (GASB) is the private, nonpartisan, nonprofit organization that works to create and improve the rules U.S. State and local governments follow when accounting for their finances and reporting them to the public. The GASB is responsible for establishing generally accepted accounting principles (GAAP) for state and local governments.

2. **The Hierarchy of Generally Accepted Accounting Principles for State and Local Governments** The GAAP hierarchy governs what constitutes GAAP for all state and local governmental entities. It lists the order of priority of pronouncements that a governmental entity should look to for accounting and financial reporting guidance. The sources of accounting principles that are generally accepted are categorized in descending order of authority as follows.

    a. Officially established accounting principles—Governmental Accounting Standards Board (GASB) Statements and Interpretations. GASB Statements and Interpretations are periodically incorporated in the Codification of Governmental Accounting and Financial Reporting Standards.

    b. GASB Technical Bulletins and, if specifically made applicable to state and local governmental entities by the American Institute of Certified Public Accountants (AICPA) and cleared by the GASB, AICPA Industry Audit and Accounting Guides, and AICPA Statements of Position.

    c. AICPA Practice Bulletins if specifically made applicable to state and local governmental entities and cleared by the GASB, as well as consensus positions of a group of accountants organized by the GASB that attempts to reach consensus positions on accounting issues applicable to state and local governmental entities.

    d. Implementation guides (Q&As) published by the GASB staff, as well as practices that are widely recognized and prevalent in state and local government.

B. Nature of Governmental Entities

1. **Service** Governmental entities are established by the citizenry through the constitutional and charter process. The primary objective of governmental entities is to render services to those citizens.

2. **Lack of Profit Motive** In most cases, governmental entities do not seek to profit from the activities in which they engage. This general absence of profit motive is the primary distinguishing characteristic of governmental entities as compared to commercial enterprises.

3. **Dependence on Legislative Authorities** Governmental entities generally receive their authority to act directly from legislative authorities, which ultimately oversee and circumscribe governmental operations. Although the operation of commercial sector enterprises is also overseen to some extent by public authorities, this type of oversight is regulatory rather than proprietary in nature.

4. **Responsibility to Citizens** In financial reporting matters, governmental entities have the responsibility of demonstrating good stewardship over financial resources provided and entrusted to them by the citizenry. In contrast, commercial sector enterprises have a similar stewardship duty to their debt and equity owners.

5. **Taxes as Source of Revenue** The principal source of revenue for governmental entities is taxes levied on the citizenry. Commercial sector enterprises have no comparable source of revenue.

6. **Restrictions and Controls** In the absence of a profit motive, a net income bottom line, or other performance indicators, governments are subjected to a variety of restrictions and controls. The most important are overall legal restrictions on the use of resources and exercise of financial expenditure control through the annual budget. These lead to the use of fund accounting and budgetary accounting.

C. Governmental Environment

Governmental financial reporting takes into consideration the influence of the governmental environment on reporting both governmental- and business-type activities, and the information needs of users. NCGA and GASB pronouncements primarily address annual financial statements.

1. **Accountability and Interperiod Equity** Governmental accountability requires governments to justify the raising of public resources and to disclose the purposes for which they are used. Accountability means that governments must ultimately answer to the citizenry through financial reporting, part of a government's duty in a democratic society. Accountability is the primary objective. Interperiod equity refers to the concept of paying for current-year services so as not to shift the burden to future-year taxpayers. Interperiod equity is an integral part of accountability. The primary objectives of financial reporting are to

   a. Provide assistance in fulfilling government's duty to be publicly accountable and enable users to assess that accountability.

   b. Assist users in assessing the operating results of the governmental entity for the year, the level of services that can be provided by the governmental entity, and its ability to meet its obligations as they become due.

2. **Users of Governmental Financial Reports**

   a. Citizens include taxpayers, voters, service recipients, the media, advocate groups, and public finance researchers.

   b. Legislative and oversight bodies include members of state legislatures, county commissions, city councils, boards of trustees, school boards, and executive branch officials with oversight responsibilities.

   c. Investors and creditors include individual and institutional investors and creditors, municipal security underwriters, bond rating agencies, bond insurers, and financial institutions.

   d. Internal users are not considered primary users, although they have many uses for external financial reports.

3. **Characteristics of Financial Reporting Information**

   a. **Understandability** To be publicly accountable, financial reports must be understood by those who may not have detailed knowledge of accounting principles.

   b. **Reliability** Information in financial reports should be comprehensive, verifiable, free from bias, and representative of what it purports.

c. **Relevance** Information must be reliable and bear a close logical relationship with the purpose for which it is needed.

d. **Timeliness** Financial reports should be issued soon after the reported events to facilitate timely decisions.

e. **Consistency** Financial reports should be consistent over time in regard to accounting principles, reporting and valuation methods, basis of accounting, and determination of the reporting entity. Changes occurring in these areas should be disclosed.

f. **Comparability** Differences among financial reports should be due to substantive differences in the underlying transactions or structure rather than due to different alternatives in accounting practices or procedures.

g. **Limitations of Financial Reporting** Users must understand limitations of the information to properly assess needs. Limitations are similar to those in commercial accounting.

4. Governmental-Type Activities

a. **Accountability** The need for public accountability in financial reporting arises because of characteristics unique to governmental environments.

(1) Resources are provided by essentially involuntary means, i.e., taxes. Accordingly, difficulties arise when attempting to measure optimal quantity or quality, because consumers cannot choose what or how much to purchase as is the case in the commercial arena.

(2) There is no direct relationship between taxes collected and services rendered except in some instances when fees are charged for specific services. The only relationship that exists in the governmental sector is a timing relationship, i.e., resources provided and services rendered occurring during the fiscal year.

(3) Governments have monopolies on some services provided to the public. It is difficult to measure efficiency without the element of competition.

(4) Because there is no single overall performance measure, the users of governmental financial reports must assess accountability by means of a variety of measures that evaluate performance.

b. **Annual Budget** The annual budget is a plan for the coordination of revenues and expenditures. Legislative approval authorizes expenditures within the limits of the appropriations and any applicable laws. When developing the financial reporting objectives of the budget, the budget is an expression of

(1) The budget is a result of not only the legislative process but also of the direct or indirect participation of the citizenry, or public policy.

(2) A financial plan sets forth the proposed expenditures for the year and the means for financing them. The balanced-budget concept is important to many who expect governments not to exceed their means.

(3) A government should demonstrate that it is accountable from both the authorization and the limitation perspectives, because (a) budgetary allowances and authorizations are the direct result of competition for resources and (b) budget limitations cannot be legally exceeded.

(4) The budget may be a means of evaluating performance by comparing actual results to the legally adopted budget.

c. **Uses of Financial Reports**

(1) Assessing financial condition and the results of operations

(2) Determining compliance with finance-related laws and regulations

(3) Evaluating efficiency and effectiveness

d. **Capital Assets** Commitments to build and maintain infrastructure do not provide a direct return to governments.

5. **Business-Type Activities** Governmental activities resemble private-sector business activities when they provide the same services and/or are self-sufficient, operating as separate, legally constituted organizations.

a. There is often a direct relationship between charges and services rendered; for example, bus fares and tolls. Users of financial reports are able to measure costs and revenues and the differences between them. Further, users may determine the full cost of operating the activity and the financial implications of subsidies or grants. This information is useful for public policy decision-making.

b. The use of the budget and fund accounting is less common in business-type activities. The budget is often merely an internal management process. Similarly, fund accounting is not as common because the business-type activity often represents a single function only.

c. The primary difference in use for business-type activities is the emphasis on financial condition and results of operations, as opposed to the comparison of actual results with budgeted amounts. Uses include assessing reasonableness of user charges and assessing the potential need to subsidize activities with general governmental non-operating revenues.

d. Unlike many governmental-type activities, capital assets of business-type activities have a direct relationship to the entity's revenue-raising capabilities.

6. **Nonprofit Organizations** Some nonprofit organizations have strong ties to governments, making it difficult to determine which guidance applies. Along with public corporations and bodies corporate and politic, the following are governments:

a. Entities that have one or more of the following traits:

(1) Popular election of officers or approval (or appointment) of a controlling majority of the entity's governing board members by state or local government's officials

(2) The possibility of unilateral dissolution by a government with the reversion of the entity's net assets to a government

(3) The ability to enact and enforce a tax levy

b. Entities that have the power to directly issue debt (as opposed to through a state or local authority) that pays interest exempt from federal taxation. Entities having only this trait may refute the presumption that the entity is a government if they provide compelling, relevant evidence.

7. **Governmental Reporting Entity** The governmental reporting entity often coincides with the legal unit (entity) as defined in law or by charter. However, some governments also control other governmental units, quasi-governmental units, or nonprofit corporations (that are in substance its departments or agencies) and must report them in their financial statements.

II. Government-Wide Financial Statements

A. Reporting Model Overview

While legal restrictions generally mandate the continuation of fund segregation in accounting systems, many users want to see the government-wide information to assess the overall financial position of the government. Users are interested in both the short-term and the long-term view.

1. **Objective** The objective for GASB 34, *Basic Financial Statements and Management's Discussion and Analysis for State and Local Governments,* is to establish a basic financial reporting model that will result in greater accountability by state and local governments by providing more useful information to a wider range of users. Operational accountability is important to assess the government's ability to provide services.

2. **Operational Accountability** Operational accountability includes the periodic economic cost of the services provided. It also informs users about whether the government is raising sufficient revenues each period to cover that cost, or whether the government is deferring costs to the future or using up accumulated resources to provide current-period services. The government-wide statements (GWS) are designed to provide an economic long-term view of the government that cannot be seen with the presentation of a collection of funds.

3. **Basis of Accounting** All amounts in the government-wide statements, including from the governmental funds, are determined using the economic resources measurement focus and accrual basis of accounting. Governmental funds presented in the fund financial statements use current financial resources and modified accrual basis. Proprietary and fiduciary funds use the economic resources focus and accrual basis in the fund statements, with limited exceptions for some fiduciary funds.

4. **Basic Financial Statements** Basic financial statements (BFS) include both the government-wide statements and the fund statements, as well as the notes. The only required government-wide statements (GWS) are the Statement of Net Assets and the Statement of Activities. The entity reports net assets, not fund balances or fund equity.

5. **Fiduciary Activities** Fiduciary activities are not included in the GWS because the assets and liabilities cannot be used to support the government's own programs.

6. **Proprietary Activities** Enterprise and internal service funds are proprietary funds. If the sponsoring government is the predominant "customer" for the activity, the activities are reported in an internal service fund. Otherwise, an enterprise fund is used. Internal service fund activities are generally classified as governmental activities in the GWS.

7. **Governmental Activities** This classification includes the amounts from the governmental funds (restated on the accrual basis of accounting) plus, typically, the amounts from the internal service funds. An exception applies if the internal service fund provides services primarily to enterprise funds; such a fund is included in business-type activities in the GWS.

8. **Government-Wide Statements** Government-wide statements (GWS) aggregate information for all governmental and business-type activities. There are four required columns in the GWS, one each for: governmental activities, business-type activities, the primary government (sum of the previous two), and component units. Note that funds do not explicitly appear in GWS; the amounts in governmental fund, proprietary fund, and component unit statements match or are reconciled to GWS amounts. Most component units should be included in the financial reporting entity by discrete presentation (reported in columns separate from primary government).

9. **Fund Statements** Fund statements appear between the GWS and the notes. Fund types are retained by GASB 34, but reporting in the fund financial statements shifts to major fund reporting. The combining statements report funds by type for the fiduciary funds and the combination of nonmajor funds.

   a. A reconciliation to government-wide statements appears on the face of the governmental fund financial statements, in a separate schedule, or in the notes.

   b. Cash flows statements appear only in the fund statements for proprietary funds. (The governmental funds pose significant problems for developing meaningful information for a government-wide cash flow statement.)

   c. Optional combining fund statements (for nonmajor funds) may be presented after the notes to the financial statements.

10. **Terminology**

   a. Special and extraordinary items are nonoperating sources or uses. They are displayed separately on the statement of activities after the calculation of excess revenues. Special items are transactions or other events *within* the control of management that are *both* abnormally large in size and *either* unusual in nature *or* infrequent in occurrence. An event is presumed to be *within* management's control if management normally can influence the occurrence of that event. Extraordinary items are transactions or other events that are *both* unusual in nature *and* infrequent in occurrence.

   b. GASB 34 includes provisions for adjustments, eliminations and reclassifications, of interfund activities in the aggregated data presented in the government-wide statements. Eliminations deduct the duplication resulting from interfund transfers and internal service fund transactions. Interfund receivables and payables are eliminated, except for residual balances between governmental and business-type activities. Internal events that are essentially allocations of overhead expenses are also eliminated from the statement of activities. Interfund services provided and used between functional categories, such as sales of utilities, are not eliminated.

   c. The internal counterpart to exchange and exchange-like transactions, including loans or interfund services provided and used.

   d. Nonreciprocal interfund activity includes internal nonexchange transactions such as transfers or reimbursements.

B. Management's Discussion & Analysis (MD&A)

MD&A is required supplementary information (RSI) in the general purpose external financial report. Although MD&A is classified as RSI, it is presented before the financial statements. The GASB encourages entities not to duplicate information in the MD&A and the more subjective letter of transmittal. The GASB does not require a transmittal letter or provide specific guidance for its contents, although the GASB recommends including a transmittal letter. GASB 37 limits MD&A to eight categories.

1. **Discussion** Brief discussion of the basic financial statements, including the relationship among them and the significant differences in the perspective that they provide.

2. **Comparison** Condensed financial information derived from government-wide statements comparing the current and prior year.

3. **Analysis of Overall Financial Position & Results of Operations** This should include reasons for significant changes from the prior year, including important economic factors.

4. **Analysis of Balances and Transactions of Individual Funds**

5. **Analysis of Significant Budget Changes** Analysis of differences between original and final budget amounts as well as final budget amounts and actual results for the general fund.

6. **Capital Asset & Long-Term Liability Activity Description**

7. **Infrastructure Discussion** (Only by governments using the modified approach.)

8. **Currently Known Facts, Decisions, or Conditions** that are expected to have significant effect on the government's financial condition

C. **Capital Assets & Long-Term Liabilities**
The concept of *fixed assets* generally refers to land, building, and equipment, as well as improvements to those assets. GASB 34 uses the term *capital assets* to include easements, infrastructure, and all other tangible or intangible assets that are used in operations and that have initial useful lives extending beyond a single reporting period. Reporting capital assets and long-term liabilities is required in the GWS.

1. Amounts are presented within the appropriate governmental activities, business-type activities, and component unit classification.

2. Depreciation is not required if governments meet certain criteria for providing alternative information about the condition and financial impact of infrastructure assets and adopt the modified approach for reporting infrastructure. The criteria are:

   a. Have an up-to-date inventory of eligible infrastructure assets

   b. Perform condition assessments of the eligible infrastructure assets and summarize the results using a measurement scale

   c. Estimate each year the annual amount to maintain and preserve the eligible infrastructure assets at the condition level established and disclosed by the government.

3. Infrastructure assets that are part of a network or subsystem of a network are not required to be depreciated as long as two requirements are met: (1) The government manages the eligible infrastructure assets using an asset management system that has the characteristics set forth in the b. criteria above; and (2) the government documents that the eligible infrastructure assets are being preserved approximately at (or above) a condition level established and disclosed by the government.

4. Governments generally should capitalize works of art, historical treasures, and similar assets at their historical cost or fair value at date of donation whether they are held as individual items or in a collection. Capitalized collections or individual items that are exhaustible, such as exhibits whose useful lives are diminished by display or educational or research applications, should be depreciated over their estimated useful lives. Depreciation is not required for collections or individual items that are inexhaustible. Governments are encouraged, but not required, to capitalize a collection (and all additions to it) whether donated or purchased that meets all of the following. The collection is:

   a. Held for public exhibition, education, or research in furtherance of public service, rather than financial gain

   b. Protected, kept unencumbered, cared for, and preserved

   c. Subject to an organizational policy that requires the proceeds from sales of collection items to be used to acquire other items for collections

5. A capital asset generally should be considered impaired if both (a) the decline in service utility of the capital asset is large in magnitude and (b) the event or change in circumstance is outside the normal life cycle of the capital asset.

    a. If not otherwise apparent from the face of the financial statements, the description, amount, and financial statement classification of impairment losses should be disclosed in the notes to the financial statements.

    b. If evidence is available to demonstrate that the impairment will be temporary, the capital asset should not be written down. Impaired capital assets that are idle should be disclosed, regardless of whether the impairment is considered permanent or temporary.

6. An insurance recovery associated with events or changes in circumstances resulting in impairment of a capital asset should be netted with the impairment loss.

    a. Restoration or replacement of the capital asset using the insurance recovery should be reported as a separate transaction.

    b. Insurance recoveries should be disclosed if not apparent from the face of the financial statements. Insurance recoveries for circumstances other than impairment of capital assets should be reported in the same manner.

D. Notes to the Financial Statements

The notes are considered part of the basic financial statements. Some notes presented by governments are identical to notes presented in business financial statements. Notes that are considered essential to the basic financial statements need to be presented and it is acceptable to present them in a very extensive format.

1. GASB 38 highlights the following required disclosures: descriptions of activities within major funds, internal service fund types, and fiduciary fund types; the time period defining "available" for revenue recognition; follow-up on significant finance-related legal or contractual violations; debt service requirements through debt maturity; separate identification of lease obligations, debt principal, and interest for five years subsequent to the financial statement date and in five year increments thereafter; schedule of short-term debt changes and purposes; details on interfund balances and transfers; terms of interest rate changes for variable rate debt; interest requirements using the year-end effective rate for variable rate debt; details about major components of receivables and payables, if obscured by aggregation; identification of long-term receivable balances.

2. GASB 42 requires the following disclosures about the impairment of capital assets: A capital asset generally should be considered impaired if both (a) the decline in service utility of the capital asset is large in magnitude and (b) the event or change in circumstance is outside the normal life cycle of the capital asset. If not otherwise apparent from the face of the financial statements, the description, amount, and financial statement classification of impairment losses should be disclosed in the notes. If evidence is available to demonstrate that the impairment will be temporary, the capital asset should not be written down. Impaired capital assets that are idle should be disclosed, regardless of whether the impairment is considered permanent or temporary.

E. Statement of Activities

Fund statements present the traditional revenue and expenditure format, but the net revenue (expense) format is required for the government-wide statement of activities. The net program cost format provides information about the cost of primary functions of the government and outlines how much each of those programs depends on general revenues of the government. This format also introduces the concept of matching program revenues and costs and allows governments to distribute administrative costs with indirect cost allocations.

F. Fund Financial Statements

GASB 34 shifts to a fund reporting format that presents major fund financial statements to highlight the importance of individual funds and the relationship to the government-wide financial statements. Basic fund financial statements will present a separate column for the General Fund, a separate column for each major fund and a single column to aggregate all nonmajor funds. Governmental and proprietary fund statements are segregated since the basis of accounting for each is different.

1. **Major Funds** Major funds are reported in the governmental and proprietary fund statements to provide users with detailed fund information on significant activities of the government.

   a. The general fund is always a major fund. There are two other criteria for determining major funds. Total assets, liabilities, revenues, or expenditures/expenses of major individual funds are both (1) at least 10% of the corresponding total for the relevant fund category (governmental or proprietary); and (2) at least 5% of the corresponding total for all governmental and proprietary funds combined. In addition to funds that meet the major-fund criteria, any other funds that the government's officials believe are particularly important to financial statement users are reported as major funds.

   b. The fund financial statements for major funds are presented before the notes to the financial statements. Combining statements for nonmajor funds are not required, but may be presented after the notes as supplementary information.

2. **Governmental Fund Reporting** Governmental fund financial statements use the modified accrual basis of accounting and the focus is on fund balance reporting. Two financial statements are required: a Fund Balance Sheet and a Statement of Revenues, Expenditures, and Changes in Fund Balances. Statement of Net assets or Balance Sheet, Long-term debt and capital asset balances are not included in the governmental fund statements. Fund balance for governmental funds should be reported in classifications that comprise a hierarchy based primarily on the extent to which the government is bound to honor constraints on the specific purposes for which amounts in those funds can be spent.

   a. The nonspendable fund balance classification includes amounts that cannot be spent because they are either not in spendable form *or* legally or contractually required to be maintained intact.

      (1) The "not in spendable form" criterion includes items that are not expected to be converted to cash, for example, inventories and prepaid amounts. It also includes the long-term amount of loans and notes receivable, as well as property acquired for resale.

      (2) However, if the use of the proceeds from the collection of those receivables or from the sale of those properties is restricted, committed, or assigned, then they should be included in the appropriate fund balance classification (restricted, committed, or assigned), rather than nonspendable fund balance.

      (3) The principal of a permanent fund is an example of an amount that is legally or contractually required to be maintained intact. These amounts may be classified as "nonexpendable" within the restricted net asset category for purposes of reporting net assets, but for fund balance reporting purposes, those amounts should be classified as nonspendable rather than restricted.

b. The restricted fund balance classification includes amounts restricted to specific purposes, other than those required to be retained in perpetuity as mentioned above.

(1) Fund balance should be reported as restricted when constraints placed on the use of resources are either: (a) externally imposed by creditors, grantors, contributors, or laws or regulations of other governments; or (b) imposed by law through constitutional provisions or enabling legislation.

(2) Enabling legislation authorizes the government to assess, levy, charge, or otherwise mandate payment of resources (from external resource providers) and includes a legally enforceable requirement that those resources be used only for the specific purposes stipulated in the legislation.

(3) Legal enforceability means that a government can be compelled by an external party—such as citizens, public interest groups, or the judiciary—to use resources created by enabling legislation only for the purposes specified.

c. The committed fund balance classification includes amounts that can only be used for specific purposes pursuant to constraints imposed by formal action of the government's highest level of decision-making authority.

(1) Those committed amounts cannot be used for any other purpose unless the government removes or changes the specified use by taking the same type of action (for example, legislation, resolution, ordinance) it employed to previously commit those amounts.

(2) Committed fund balance also should incorporate contractual obligations to the extent that existing resources in the fund have been specifically committed for use in satisfying those contractual requirements.

(3) In contrast to fund balance that is restricted by enabling legislation, amounts in the committed fund balance classification may be redeployed for other purposes with appropriate due process. Constraints imposed on the use of committed amounts are imposed by the government, separate from the authorization to raise the underlying revenue. Therefore, compliance with constraints imposed by the government that commit amounts to specific purposes is not considered to be legally enforceable.

(4) The formal action of the government's highest level of decision-making authority that commits fund balance to a specific purpose should occur prior to the end of the reporting period, but the amount, if any, which will be subject to the constraint, may be determined in the subsequent period.

d. The assigned fund balance classification includes amounts that are constrained by the government's intent to be used for specific purposes, but are neither restricted nor committed and do not include stabilization arrangements. Intent should be expressed by (a) the governing body itself or (b) a body (a budget or finance committee, for example) or official to which the governing body has delegated the authority to assign amounts to be used for specific purposes.

(1) A difference between assigned and committed is that the authority for making an assignment is not required to be the government's highest level of decision-making authority. Furthermore, the actions necessary to remove or modify an assignment is not as prescriptive as it is with regard to the committed fund balance classification. Constraints imposed on the use of assigned amounts are more easily removed or modified than those imposed on amounts that are classified as committed.

(2) Assigned fund balance includes (a) all remaining amounts (except for negative balances) that are reported in governmental funds, other than the general fund, that are not classified as nonspendable and are neither restricted nor committed and (b) amounts in the general fund that are intended to be used for a specific purpose. By reporting particular amounts that are not restricted or committed in a special revenue, capital projects, debt service, or permanent fund, the government has assigned those amounts to the purposes of the respective funds.

(3) Assignment within the general fund conveys that the intended use of those amounts is for a specific purpose that is narrower than the general purposes of the government itself. However, governments should not report an assignment for an amount to a specific purpose if the assignment would result in a deficit in unassigned fund balance.

(4) An appropriation of existing fund balance to eliminate a projected budgetary deficit in the subsequent year's budget in an amount no greater than the projected excess of expected expenditures over expected revenues satisfies the criteria to be classified as an assignment of fund balance. Assignments should not cause a deficit in unassigned fund balance to occur.

e. The unassigned fund balance is the residual classification for the general fund. This classification represents fund balance that has not been assigned to other funds and that has not been restricted, committed, or assigned to specific purposes within the general fund.

(1) The general fund should be the only fund that reports a positive unassigned fund balance amount.

(2) In other governmental funds, if expenditures incurred for specific purposes exceeded the amounts restricted, committed, or assigned to those purposes, it may be necessary to report a negative unassigned fund balance.

f. Fund balance classifications should depict the nature of the net resources that are reported in a governmental fund. An individual governmental fund could include nonspendable resources and amounts that are restricted, committed, or assigned, or any combination of those classifications. Typically, the general fund also would include an unassigned amount.

(1) A government should determine the composition of its ending fund balance by applying its accounting policies regarding whether it considers restricted or unrestricted amounts to have been spent when an expenditure is incurred for purposes for which both restricted and unrestricted (committed, assigned, or unassigned) amounts are available.

(2) Similarly, within unrestricted fund balance, the classification should be based on the government's accounting policies regarding whether it considers committed, assigned, or unassigned amounts to have been spent when an expenditure is incurred for purposes for which amounts in any of those unrestricted fund balance classifications could be used.

(3) If a government does not establish a policy for its use of unrestricted fund balance amounts, it should consider that committed amounts would be reduced first, followed by assigned amounts, and then unassigned amounts when expenditures are incurred for purposes for which amounts in any of those unrestricted fund balance classifications could be used.

(4) The amount that should be reported as nonspendable fund balance should be determined before classifying amounts in the restricted, committed, and assigned fund balance classifications.

(5) In a governmental fund other than the general fund, expenditures incurred for a specific purpose might exceed the amounts in the fund that are restricted, committed, and assigned to that purpose and a negative residual balance for that purpose may result. If that occurs, amounts assigned to other purposes in that fund should be reduced to eliminate the deficit. If the remaining deficit eliminates all other assigned amounts in the fund, or if there are no amounts assigned to other purposes, the negative residual amount should be classified as unassigned fund balance.

(6) In the general fund, a negative residual amount would have been eliminated by reducing unassigned fund. A negative residual amount should not be reported for restricted, committed, or assigned fund balances in any fund.

g. Some governments formally set aside amounts for use in emergency situations or when revenue shortages or budgetary imbalances arise. These stabilization amounts may be expended only when certain specific circumstances exist. For the purposes of reporting fund balance, stabilization is considered a specific purpose.

(1) Stabilization amounts should be reported in the general fund as restricted or committed, if they meet the criteria, based on the source of the constraint on their use.

(2) Stabilization arrangements that do not meet the criteria to be reported within the restricted or committed fund balance classifications should be reported as unassigned in the general fund.

(3) A stabilization arrangement could be reported as a separate special revenue fund only if the resources derive from a specific restricted or committed revenue source associated with special revenue funds.

h. Amounts for the two components of nonspendable fund balance, (1) not in spendable form and (2) legally or contractually required to be maintained intact, may be presented separately or in the aggregate. Restricted fund balance may be displayed in a manner that distinguishes between the major restricted purposes, or it may be displayed in the aggregate. Similarly, specific purposes information for committed and assigned fund balances may be displayed in sufficient detail so that the major commitments and assignments are evident to the financial statement user, or each classification may be displayed in the aggregate.

i. Governments should disclose the following in the notes to the financial statements:

(1) For committed fund balance: (a) the government's highest level of decision-making authority and (b) the formal action that is required to be taken to establish (and modify or rescind) a fund balance commitment.

(2) For assigned fund balance: (a) the body or official authorized to assign amounts to a specific purpose and (b) the policy established by the governing body pursuant to which that authorization is given.

(3) For the classification of fund balances: (a) whether the government considers restricted or unrestricted amounts to have been spent when an expenditure is incurred for purposes for which both restricted and unrestricted fund balance is available and (b) whether committed, assigned, or unassigned amounts are considered to have been spent when an expenditure is incurred for purposes for which amounts in any of those unrestricted fund balance classifications could be used.

(4) If nonspendable fund balance is displayed in the aggregate on the face of the balance sheet, amounts for the two nonspendable components should be disclosed. If restricted, committed, or assigned fund balances are displayed in the aggregate, specific purposes information should be disclosed. Governments may display the specific purpose details for some classifications on the face of the balance sheet and disclose the details for other classifications in the notes to the financial statements.

(5) For governments that use encumbrance accounting, significant encumbrances should be disclosed by major funds and nonmajor funds in the aggregate in conjunction with required disclosures about other significant commitments. Encumbered amounts for specific purposes for which resources already have been restricted, committed, or assigned should not result in separate display of the encumbered amounts within those classifications. Encumbered amounts for specific purposes for which amounts have not been previously restricted, committed, or assigned should not be classified as unassigned but, rather, should be included within committed or assigned fund balance, as appropriate.

(6) For governments that establish stabilization arrangements: (a) the authority for establishing stabilization arrangements (for example, by statute or ordinance), (b) the requirements for additions to the stabilization amount, (c) the conditions under which stabilization amounts may be spent, and (d) the stabilization balance, if not apparent on the face of the financial statements.

(7) If a governing body has formally adopted a minimum fund balance policy (for example, in lieu of separately setting aside stabilization amounts), the government should describe the policy established by the government that sets forth the minimum amount.

j. The link between government-wide and fund statements requires a reconciliation to convert the governmental funds to the economic resources measurement and accrual basis of accounting. Adjustments usually include moving transactions for general capital assets and general long-term liabilities from the operating statements to the balance sheet. Other reconciling items may include adjustments to deferred revenues or internal service fund net assets. If the entity presents summary information on the face of the financial statements, detailed schedules in the notes may be necessary.

3. **Proprietary Fund Reporting** Proprietary fund financial statements should be prepared using the economic resources measurement focus and the accrual basis of accounting. Three financial statements are required: Statement of Net Assets or Balance Sheet, Statement of Revenues, Expenses, and Changes in Fund Net Assets or Fund Equity; and Statement of Cash Flows. Enterprise funds have a separate fund for each major fund and combine nonmajor funds. Internal service funds also should be reported in the aggregate in a separate column after the total of all Enterprise funds. The format use for the fund statements should also be used for the corresponding government-wide statement.

a. Statement of Net Assets or Balance Sheet—net assets should be reported in the same categories required for the government-wide financial statements

b. Statement of Revenues, Expenses, and Changes in Fund Net Assets—distinguish between: (1) current and noncurrent assets and liabilities; (2) operating and nonoperating revenues and expenses; (3) should display restricted assets; and (4) at the bottom of the statement, should report capital contributions, contributions to permanent and term endowments, special and extraordinary items, and transfers separately to arrive at the all-inclusive change in fund net assets.

c. Statement of Cash Flows—should be prepared using the direct method

4. **Fiduciary Fund Reporting** Major fund reporting is not used in the fiduciary fund category. Statements should be prepared using the economic resources measurement focus and the accrual basis of accounting. Required statements for fiduciary funds: (1) Statement of Fiduciary Net Assets; and (2) Statement of Changes in Fiduciary Net Assets. Fiduciary statements include separate columns for each fiduciary fund type used by the governmental entity. Financial statements for individual pension plans and investment trusts are presented in the notes to the financial statements of the primary government if separate, audited financial reports are not issued. The statement of fiduciary net assets and statement of changes in fiduciary net assets are included in the fund statements to report fiduciary activities.

G. Statement of Cash Flows

The major differences between the GASB format and the FASB format are that four categories are used for classifying cash flows instead of three and the operating category is more narrowly focused in that the direct method must be used. This statement classifies cash receipts and payments of all proprietary funds as resulting from operating activities, noncapital financing, capital and related financing, or investing activities. Generally, only investments with a maturity date of three months or less at date of purchase are reported as cash or cash equivalents.

1. **Operating Activities** Cash inflows, receipts, and payments that do not result from transactions defined as capital and related financing, noncapital financing, or investing activities.

a. Cash inflows include receipts from cash and:

(1) Sales of goods or services, including receipts from collection of accounts receivable and both short- and long-term notes receivable from customers arising from those sales.

(2) Quasi-external operating transactions with other funds.

(3) Grants for specific activities that are considered to be operating activities of the grantor government. (A grant arrangement of this type is essentially the same as a contract for services.)

(4) Other funds for reimbursement of operating transactions.

(5) Loan programs that are made and collected as part of a governmental program such as student loans or low-income housing mortgages. Investment type loans would not be included in this category.

b. Cash outflows include cash payments and:

(1) To acquire materials for providing services and manufacturing goods for resale, including principal payments on accounts payable and both short- and long-term notes payable to suppliers for those materials or goods.

(2) To other suppliers for other goods or services, including employees.

(3) For grants to other governments or organizations for specific activities that are considered to be operating activities of the grantor government.

(4) For taxes, duties, fines, and other fees or penalties.

(5) For quasi-external operating transactions with other funds, including payments in lieu of taxes.

2. **Noncapital Financing Activities** Include borrowing for purposes other than to acquire, construct, or improve capital assets, as well as repaying borrowed amounts, including interest. This category includes proceeds from all borrowings (such as revenue anticipation notes) not clearly attributable to capital assets, regardless of the form of the borrowing. Also included are certain other interfund and intergovernmental receipts and payments.

   a. Cash inflows include:

      (1) Proceeds from issuing bonds, notes, and other short- or long-term borrowing not clearly attributable to capital assets.

      (2) Receipts from grants or subsidies except those specifically restricted for capital purposes and those for specific activities that are considered to be operating activities of the grantor government.

      (3) Receipts from other funds except those amounts that are clearly attributable to capital assets, quasi-external operating transactions, and reimbursement for operating transactions.

      (4) Receipts from property and other taxes collected for the governmental enterprise and not specifically restricted for capital purposes.

   b. Cash outflows include:

      (1) Repayments of amounts borrowed for purposes other than acquiring, constructing, or improving capital assets.

      (2) Interest payments to lenders and other creditors on amounts borrowed or credit extended for purposes other than capital assets.

      (3) Payments as grants or subsidies to other governments or organizations, except those for specific activities that are considered to be operating activities of the grantor government.

      (4) Payments to other funds, except for quasi-external operating transactions.

3. **Capital and Related Financing Activities** Include acquiring and disposing of capital assets used in providing services or producing goods; borrowing money for acquiring, constructing, or improving capital assets and repaying the amounts borrowed, including interest; and paying for capital assets obtained from vendors on credit.

   a. Cash inflows include:

      (1) Issuing or refunding bonds, mortgages, notes, and other short- or long-term borrowing clearly attributable to capital assets.

      (2) Capital grants awarded to the governmental enterprise.

      (3) Contributions made by other funds, governments, and organizations or individuals for the specific purpose of defraying the cost of capital assets.

(4) Sales of capital assets; also, proceeds from insurance on capital assets that are stolen or destroyed.

(5) Special assessments or property and other taxes levied specifically to finance capital assets.

b. Cash outflows include:

(1) Payments to acquire, construct, or improve capital assets.

(2) Repayments or refundings of amounts borrowed specifically to acquire, construct, or improve capital assets.

(3) Other principal payments to vendors who have extended credit directly to acquire, construct or improve capital assets.

(4) Payments to creditors for interest directly related to capital assets.

4. Investing Activities Investing activities include making and collecting loans (except program loans) and acquiring and disposing of debt or equity instruments.

a. Cash inflows include: (1) receipts from collections of loans (except program loans) made by the governmental enterprise and sales of other entities' debt instruments (other than cash equivalents) that were purchased by the governmental enterprise; (2) interest and dividends received as returns on loans (except program loans), debt instruments of other entities, equity securities, and cash management or investment pools; and (3) withdrawals from investment pools that the governmental enterprise is not using as demand accounts.

b. Cash outflows include: (1) Loans (except program loans) made by the governmental enterprise and payments to acquire debt instruments of other entities (other than cash equivalents); and (2) deposits into investment pools that the governmental enterprise is not using as demand accounts.

H. Other Required Supplementary Information (RSI)

Required supplementary information is outside the scope of the auditor's opinion. Except for MD&A, RSI is presented after the financial statements.

1. Budgetary Comparison Schedule (BCS) is presented for the general fund and for each major special revenue fund that has a legally adopted annual budget, on the **budgetary** basis of accounting. The BCS presents both the original and final budget as well as actual inflows, outflows, and balances. It uses the same format, terminology, and classifications as either the budget document or a statement of revenues, expenditures, and changes in fund balances. The BCS is accompanied by a reconciliation (in either a separate schedule or RSI notes) of budgetary information to GAAP information. This reconciliation provides the link from the budgetary comparisons to the GAAP statements in the BFS.

2. Infrastructure Schedules (Only for assets reported using the modified approach.) These schedules include (1) information on the assessed condition (assessed at least every 3 years) for at least the 3 most recent assessments (i.e., this information could be from 9 years); and (2) the estimated annual amount to maintain the condition level established and disclosed by the government compared with amounts actually expensed for the past 5 reporting periods. The schedules are accompanied by (1) disclosures on the basis for the condition measurement and the measurement scale; (2) the condition level at which the government intends to preserve assets reported using the modified approach; and (3) factors that could affect trends in these schedules.

I. Comprehensive Annual Financial Report

NCGA Statement 1 requires every governmental entity to prepare and publish, as a matter of public record, a comprehensive annual financial report (CAFR that encompasses all funds of the primary government (including its blended component units). The CAFR should also encompass all discretely presented component units of the reporting entity.

1. Introduction Section

a. Title Page and Table of Contents

b. Report of the Independent Auditor (if an audit has been performed)

c. Letter of Transmittal: Cites legal and policy requirements for report. Governments are encouraged not to duplicate information contained in MD&A in the Letter of Transmittal.

d. Other material deemed appropriate by management

2. Financial Section

a. Management's Discussion & Analysis (MD&A)

b. Basic financial statements

- **(1)** Government-Wide Financial Statements
  - **(a)** Statement of net assets
  - **(b)** Statement of activities
- **(2)** Fund financial statements
  - **(a)** Governmental Funds: Balance sheet; statement of revenues, expenditures, and changes in fund balances
  - **(b)** Proprietary Funds: Statement of net assets; statement of revenues, expenses, and changes in fund net assets; statement of cash flows
  - **(c)** Fiduciary Funds: Statement of fiduciary net assets; statement of changes in fiduciary net assets
- **(3)** Notes to the Financial Statements

c. Required Supplementary Information (RSI)

- **(1)** The budgetary comparison schedule should present both the original and the final appropriated budgets for the reporting period as well as actual inflows, outflows, and balances, stated on the government's budgetary basis.
- **(2)** Governments adopting the modified approach for reporting infrastructure assets should include schedules presenting infrastructure asset condition, required asset preservation amounts, basis for the measurement of asset condition, and the established asset condition level

d. Combining statements for nonmajor funds by fund type of the primary government and the nonmajor discretely presented component units.

e. Individual fund statements & schedules

3. **Statistical Section** The objectives of statistical section information are to provide financial statement users with additional historical perspective, context, and detail to assist in using the information in the financial statements, notes to financial statements, and required supplementary information to understand and assess a government's economic condition (typically for the last ten fiscal years). Statistical section information should be presented in five categories:

   a. Financial trends assist users in understanding and assessing how a government's financial position has changed over time.

   b. Revenue capacity assists users in understanding and assessing the factors affecting a government's ability to generate its own-source revenues.

   c. Debt capacity assists users in understanding and assessing a government's debt burden and its ability to issue additional debt.

   d. Demographic and economic data assists users in understanding the socioeconomic environment within which a government operates and provides information that facilitates comparisons of financial statement information over time and among governments.

   e. Operating data provides contextual information about a government's operations and resources to assist readers in using financial statement information to understand and assess a government's economic condition.

4. **Financial Trends Information** GASB 44, *Economic Condition Reporting: The Statistical Section* requires that governments should present, at a minimum, two types of information in statistical section schedules—net assets and changes in net assets.

   a. The three components of net assets should be shown separately for governmental activities, business-type activities, and the total primary government.

      (1) Net assets invested in capital assets net of related debt

      (2) Net assets restricted

      (3) Net assets unrestricted

   b. At a minimum, governments should present the following information separately for governmental activities and business-type activities:

      (1) Expenses by function, program, or identifiable activity

      (2) Program revenues by category

      (3) Total net (expense) revenue

      (4) General revenues and other changes in net assets by type

      (5) Total change in net assets.

   c. Governments should also present individually their most significant charges for services revenue, categorized by function, program, or identifiable activity.

J. Component Unit Determination

GASB 39, *Determining Whether Certain Organizations Are Component Units—an Amendment of GASB Statement No. 14,* provides additional guidance to determine whether certain entities for which a primary government is not accountable financially must be reported as component units based on the nature and significance of their relationship with the primary government. Generally, it requires reporting, as a component unit, an entity that raises and holds economic resources for the direct benefit of a government.

Legally separate, tax-exempt entities that meet **all** three criteria must be presented discretely as component units.

1. **Direct Benefit** Economic resources received or held by the separate entity are totally (or nearly totally) for the direct benefit of the primary government, its component units, or its constituents.

2. **Majority** The primary government, or its component units, is entitled to (or has the ability to otherwise access) a majority of the economic resources received or held by the separate entity.

3. **Significance** The economic resources received or held by an individual entity that the specific primary government, or its component units, is entitled to, or has the ability to otherwise access, are significant to that primary government.

K. Nonexchange Transactions

In a nonexchange transaction, a government gives (or receives) value without directly receiving (or giving) equal value in return. There are four classes of nonexchange transactions which share characteristics that affect the timing of revenue recognition: derived tax revenues; imposed nonexchange revenues; government-mandated nonexchange transactions; and voluntary nonexchange transactions. The timing of recognition for each class of nonexchange transaction is listed below. The accrual basis of accounting is assumed, except where indicated for revenue recognition.

1. **Derived Tax Revenues** Derived tax revenues are assessments imposed by governments on exchange transactions and generally include sales taxes, income taxes, motor fuel taxes, and similar taxes on earnings or consumption. Assets generally are recognized in the period when the underlying exchange transaction has occurred and the resources are available. Revenues are recognized when the underlying exchange transaction occurs. (If using modified accrual, revenues should be recognized when the underlying exchange transaction has occurred and the resources are available.) Resources received before the underlying exchange transaction has occurred should be reported as deferred revenues.

2. **Imposed Nonexchange Revenues** Imposed nonexchange revenues represent assessments imposed on nongovernmental entities and include property taxes, fines, penalties, or forfeitures. Assets are recognized when the government has an enforceable legal claim to the resources or when the resources are received, whichever occurs first. Revenues are recognized in the period when use of the resources is required or first permitted (e.g., for property taxes, the period for which they are levied), or at the same time as the assets if the government has not established time requirements. For property taxes, the date of enforceable claim is generally specified in the enabling legislation. This is often called the "lien date" or "assessment date."

For property taxes on the modified accrual basis, governments should recognize revenues, net of estimated refunds and estimated uncollectible amounts, in the fiscal year for which the taxes have been levied, provided the "available" criteria has been met. "Available" means collected within the current period or expected to be collected soon enough thereafter to be used to pay liabilities of the current period. Usually, such time shall not exceed 60 days. When property taxes are collected in advance of the year for which they are levied, they should be recorded as deferred revenue and recognized as revenue in the year for which they are levied.

3. **Government-Mandated Nonexchange Transactions** Government-mandated nonexchange transactions occur when a government at one level provides resources to a government at another level and requires that government to use the resources for a specific purpose. Intergovernmental grants fall into this category. There are often eligibility requirements, conditions established by legislation or the provider, that are required to be meet before a transaction (other than cash or other assets in advance) can occur. Until those requirements are met, the recipient does not have a receivable, the provider does not have a liability, and the recognition of revenues or expenses for resources transmitted in advance should be deferred. Recipients recognize assets and revenues when all eligibility requirements have been met and the resources are available. Providers recognize liabilities and expenses using the same criteria. Eligibility requirements include time requirements. Purpose restrictions result in restricted assets until resources are used for the specified purpose.

4. **Voluntary Nonexchange Transactions** Voluntary nonexchange transactions result from legislative or contractual agreements, but do not involve an exchange of equal value. Certain grants, entitlements, and donations are classified as voluntary nonexchange transactions. Both parties may or may not be governmental entities. Specific recognition criteria are the same as those for government-mandated nonexchange transactions.

5. **Continuing Appropriations** If distributions from a provider government are authorized by continuing appropriations (involving no further legislative action), the recipient governments can use any reasonable estimate to accrue revenues.

L. Capital Lease Obligations

The criteria to determine if a lease is a capital lease is the same for governments and businesses.

1. **Capital Leases** If a lease meets any one of the following criteria, it is a capital lease.

   a. Ownership of the property transfers to the lessee by the end of the lease term.

   b. The lease contains an option to purchase the leased property at a bargain price.

   c. The lease term is equal to or greater than 75 percent of the estimated economic life of the leased property.

   d. The present value of the minimum lease payments equals or exceeds 90 percent of the fair value of the leased property at the inception of the lease.

2. **Operating Leases** If none of the criteria for a capital lease is met, the lessee classifies the lease as an operating lease. Payments for assets used by governmental funds are recorded by the using fund as expenditures. Payments for assets used by proprietary funds are recorded by the using fund as expenses.

3. **Governmental Funds**

   a. The governmental fund records an expenditure and an Other Financing Source, just as if the general fixed asset had been constructed or acquired from debt issue proceeds. The amount to be recorded is the lesser of the (1) present value of the minimum lease payments or (2) fair value of the leased property.

b. Commonly, governmental units use the Debt Service Fund (DSF) to record capital lease payments because the annual payments are installments of general long-term debt. Although part of each payment is interest at a constant rate on the unpaid balance of the lease obligation, and part is payment on the principal, the *Expenditures* account is debited in the DSF for the full amount of the lease payment. Only the detail records in the DSF show how much of the expenditure was for interest and how much was for principal.

Exhibit 1 ▸ Leased General Fixed Asset*

1. Lease Inception		
a. Governmental Fund		
Expenditures	XX	
Other Financing Sources—Capital Leases		XX
2. Lease Repayment		
a. Debt Service Fund		
Expenditures (principal and interest)	XX	
Cash		XX

* These entries may be more clear to candidates who are familiar with the material in Chapter 19.

4. Proprietary Funds Assets acquired under capital leases are depreciated by the proprietary fund. Capital leases are generally recorded as an asset and liability at the lesser of (a) the present value of the minimum lease payments or (b) the fair value of the leased property. Lease payments for capital leases are comprised of interest expense and principal reduction.

Exhibit 2 ▸ Leased Proprietary Fixed Asset (in the related proprietary fund)

1. Lease Inception		
Equipment	XX	
Capital Leases Payable		XX
2. Lease Repayment		
Expenses—Interest	XX	
Capital Leases Payable	XX	
Cash		XX

M. Municipal Solid Waste Landfills

Municipal solid waste landfills (MSWLFs) are required by the Environmental Protection Agency (EPA) to follow certain closure functions and postclosure monitoring and maintenance procedures in order to operate. Any state or local government that is required by federal, state, or local laws or regulations to incur MSWLF closure and postclosure care costs is subject to GASB 18.

1. Estimated Total Current Cost The estimated total current costs of closure and postclosure care should include those costs that result in disbursements near the date that the MSWLF stops accepting solid waste and during the postclosure period: equipment expected to be installed and facilities expected to be built; final cover (capping) costs; and monitoring and maintenance costs. These costs are based on laws or regulations enacted or approved as of the balance sheet date, regardless of their effective date. The estimated current cost is reevaluated annually to adjust for the effects of inflation, deflation, or other changes in estimated costs.

2. **Measurement and Recognition** The type of fund employed by the MSWLF determines the recognition method. Estimated total current costs should be based on MSWLF use, not the passage of time. The current year closure and post-closure cost recognition is the difference between the total costs to be recognized to date and the total costs recognized in prior periods. The total costs to be recognized to date are the total estimated costs times the cumulative used percentage of total capacity. (Costs and liabilities are recognized as the MSWLF accepts solid waste.)

   a. For proprietary funds, capital assets should be fully depreciated by the date the MSWLF stops accepting solid waste or, in the case of a single cell, the date that cell is closed.

   b. For governmental-type funds, the MSWLF recognizes expenditures using the modified accrual basis of accounting, with liability reported as with other general long-term debt. Expenditures are disclosed in the notes to the financial statements or appear as a parenthetical display on the statement of operations.

   c. For governmental colleges and universities that use the AICPA College Guide model, expenditures and liabilities should be calculated similarly to other governmental-type funds and be reported in an unrestricted current fund.

3. **Disclosure** The disclosure requirements include the nature of closure and postclosure care estimates, the reported liability at the balance sheet date, the estimated total closure and postclosure care cost remaining to be recognized, the percentage of MSWLF capacity used to date, and the estimated remaining MSWLF life in years. Disclosure of how closure and postclosure care financial assurance requirements are being met is also required.

III. GASB Concepts Statements

A. Objectives

GASB Concepts Statements provide the framework within which the GASB develops standards of financial reporting for governmental entities. However, they do not establish standards of governmental accounting and financial reporting. For this reason, GASB Concepts Statements are not codified but are included in *Appendix B* for the users' information.

B. Concepts Statement No. 1, *Objectives of Financial Reporting*

In May 1987, the GASB issued Concepts Statement No. 1, *Objectives of Financial Reporting.* This Concepts Statement establishes the objectives of general purpose external financial reporting by state and local governmental entities and applies to both governmental-type and business-type activities. The objectives of governmental financial reporting support a paramount responsibility of governmental entities' accountability for public resources. Governments derive their revenues in large part from involuntary payers. Tax assessments, license fees, permits, even many user fees are imposed in accordance with statutory authority rather than the payer's willingness to participate in the transaction. This authority is vested in the governmental entity to protect the public welfare and promote social and economic development.

In this Concepts Statement, accountability was noted as being the cornerstone of all financial reporting in government. Financial reporting objectives include: providing information to users for assessing government accountability, evaluating operating results, and assessing the level of services provided. It was noted that accountability is the paramount objective from which all other objectives must flow.

C. **Concepts Statement No. 2, *Service Efforts and Accomplishments Reporting***

In April 1994, the GASB issued Concepts Statement No. 2, *Service Efforts and Accomplishments Reporting*. The Concepts Statement subsequently was amended by Concepts Statement No. 3, *Communication Methods in General Purpose External Financial Reports That Contain Basic Financial Statements*, in April 2005 and by Concepts Statement No. 5, *Service Efforts and Accomplishments Reporting*, an amendment of GASB Concepts Statement No. 2, in November 2008.

The concepts in this Statement provide a framework that will be used by the Governmental Accounting Standards Board (GASB) in considering guidance for reporting service efforts and accomplishments (SEA) by state and local governmental entities. This Statement provides a rationale for the objective of SEA reporting, and identifies the elements of SEA reporting and the qualitative characteristics that SEA performance information should possess. This Statement also serves as a link between the financial reporting objectives of GASB Concepts Statement No. 1, *Objectives of Financial Reporting*, and future pronouncements or other communications that provide guidance for the reporting of SEA performance information.

D. **Concepts Statement No. 3, *Communication Methods in General Purpose External Financial Reports That Contain Basic Financial Statements***

In April 2005, the GASB issued Concepts Statement No. 3, *Communication Methods in General Purpose External Financial Reports That Contain Basic Financial Statements*. The Concepts Statement subsequently was amended by Concepts Statement No. 4, *Elements of Financial Statements*, in June 2007.

1. **Communication and Financial Reporting** Financial reporting is more than just a summary of the results of operations and the financial position for a governmental entity. At the core of a financial statement, users should find messages about how financial resources were raised, managed, and safeguarded. GASB Concepts Statement No. 3 outlines financial reports in terms of how those communication tools convey messages. Financial reporting includes both the internal and external documents with varying formats to address messages for specific use or general use.

2. **Communication Methods Hierarchy** GASB Concepts Statement No. 3 first identifies a priority for communication methods, based on the level of importance of the information. The GASB will begin their deliberation for a particular issue by considering the definition and criteria for presentation in the financial statements. When an element does not meet these benchmarks, they will move down the list until there is a match. The hierarchy is as follows: basic financial statements; note disclosures; required supplementary information (RSI); and supplementary information.

3. **Communication Methods Criteria** In addition to the definitions for each communication method, GASB Concepts Statement No. 3 also outlines the criteria for using that particular level. If a transaction meets the criteria for a particular level, no other communication method can be used as a substitute. Management uses professional judgment to select supplementary information, so there are no criteria for that level; however, management should follow

E. **Concepts Statement No. 4, *Elements of Financial Statements***

In June 2007, the GASB issued Concepts Statement No. 4, *Elements of Financial Statements*.

GASB Concepts Statement No. 4 focuses on the components of financial statements and outlines the basic definitions for governmental historically based financial statements. All of the definitions focus on resources. Assets, liabilities, deferred outflows, deferred inflows, net position, outflows of resources and inflows of resources are the primary elements of financial statements. All other accounts fit within one of these seven categories. The guidance also separates these elements between the statement of financial position and the resource flows statements.

1. **Assets** Assets are resources with present service capacity that the government presently controls. The GASB definition for "resource," in this context, is "an item that can be used to provide services to the citizenry." These definitions describe the characteristics of each element, but not how the items are measured or when they are recognized. For assets, present service capacity and control are the primary characteristics that distinguish this element. This approach emphasizes the importance of the government's delivery of programs and services as a primary mission.

    a. Present service capacity is the existing capability that allows government to provide services, which in turn enables the government to fulfill its mission. Assets may be tangible or intangible, so physical form is not a characteristic that distinguishes assets.

    b. Control of an asset is the ability of the government to utilize the resource's present service capacity and to determine the nature and manner of use of the present service capacity embodied in the resource. Control implies that a government can choose to directly use the asset, exchange it for another asset, or find other ways to use the asset to support services.

2. **Liabilities** Liabilities are present obligations to sacrifice resources that the government has little or no discretion to avoid. The GASB includes social, legal, or moral requirements in this definition. The guidance further narrows the definition with the characteristics for obligations and present obligations. It is important to understand the difference between a government's mission, which creates a commitment that is not necessarily a liability, and that of a commercial business.

    a. Obligations are something (as a promise or a contract) that binds one to a course of action. Statement No. 4 emphasizes the importance of legal conditions that would lead a court to compel the government to fulfill the obligation (and thus sacrifice resources). Governments engage in both exchange and nonexchange transactions, either of which can give rise to a present obligation.

    b. Like the asset criteria, the creation of a present obligation is based on an event that has already occurred. Commitments that may become a liability in the future are not liabilities with present obligations to sacrifice resources. These commitments require additional actions or events to create the liability, and until those occur, the government may have options to avoid a liability. For instance, the budget is a legal document that outlines the government's intent to provide specific services, but the budget does not create liabilities until the government purchases goods and services.

3. **Outflows of Resources** An "outflow of resources" is a consumption of net assets by the government that is applicable to the reporting period. "Net assets" reflect the difference between assets and liabilities. Consumption may reflect a decrease in assets in excess of any related decrease in liabilities or an increase in liabilities in excess of any related increase in assets—in other words, the bottom line declines, at least the bottom line of a governmental statement of net assets. The measurement focus for a resource flows statement will determine when a resource flow (in or out) is applicable to a particular period. The economic resources measurement uses a different timetable than the current financial resources measurements.

4. **Inflows of Resources** An inflow of resources is just the opposite of an outflow—an acquisition of net assets by the government that is applicable to the reporting period. Acquisition occurs even when those net assets are consumed directly when acquired. Governmental net assets may increase when the underlying taxable event occurs. For instance, a retail purchase by a consumer creates sales tax revenue, even though those collections may take some time to make it to the government's checkbook.

5. **Deferred Inflows and Outflows** Deferred inflows and outflows meet the same definitions (and inherent characteristics) for increases or decreases in net assets, except that these transactions apply to future periods. The applicability may be determined by legal constraints or accounting measurements. Deferred inflows and outflows are reported on the statement of financial position because they apply to future periods.

6. **Net Position** This is the only element that is defined in terms of other elements. "Net position" is the residual of all other elements presented in a statement of financial position. The GASB did not use "net assets" or "fund balance" to avoid confusion. Both of these balances fit the definition of "net position," but are measured differently. Net position is directly related to the net activity on the resource flows statement—net increase or decrease in net position must equal the net amount of inflows and outflows on the resource flows statement. The total balance of net position at any point in time theoretically reflects the cumulative total of all prior resource flows statement.

F. **Concepts Statement No. 5, *Service Efforts and Accomplishments Reporting***

In November 2008, the GASB issued Concepts Statement No. 5, *Service Efforts and Accomplishments Reporting*, an amendment of GASB Concepts Statement No. 2.

Concepts Statement No. 2 was amended to reflect developments that have occurred since it was issued in 1994. Governmental entities are far more complex than just managing financial resources or producing widgets. Governmental services affect the quality of life within that jurisdiction. Elected officials manage public funds to support economic, social and political decisions that merit accountability. Governments must outline far more than just financial position. Constituents will also want to know how effective and efficient public programs are. Service efforts and accomplishments reports complement the financial reporting to provide a more comprehensive assessment of governmental services. Elements of SEA performance measures for reporting purposes focus on the three different types of SEA performance measures: measures of service efforts; measures of service accomplishments; and measures that relate service efforts to service accomplishments.

1. **Measures of Service Efforts** Includes financial as well as nonfinancial information applied to a specific service. Expenditures of financial resources, personnel and equipment, or other capital assets are essential to provide governmental services (i.e., what public resources were "invested" in the delivery of services).

2. **Measures of Service Accomplishments** Focuses on the outputs and outcomes. Outputs consider the quantity of services while outcomes assess results. Outputs may also count the number of units that met certain quality standards. Outcomes become much more useful when trend data provides an analysis of how results are shifting over time.

3. **Measures that Relate Service Efforts to Accomplishments** These items may consider efficiency assessments or cost-outcome evaluations that report costs per unit of outcome or result. Trend data and comparisons with other entities will also add value to these presentations.

4. **Objectives and Characteristics of SEA Information** SEA performance reporting should strive for the same six reporting targets for financial reporting: relevance, understandability, comparability, timeliness, consistency, and reliability. These characteristics are not unique to the governmental environment. External reporting that is deemed essential is generally critical for making informed decisions. Expanding the external reports to provide SEA performance information must also adhere to the basic reporting characteristics.

IV. Appendix: Limited Scope Topics

A. Compensated Absences

GASB 16 establishes accounting standards for compensated absences.

1. **Vacation Leave and Other Compensated Absences with Similar Characteristics** A liability for vacation leave and other compensated absences with similar characteristics (hereinafter referred to as "vacation leave") should be accrued as the benefits are earned by the employees if both of these conditions are met:

   a. The employees' rights to receive compensation are attributable to services already rendered.

   b. It is probable that the employer will compensate the employees for the benefits through paid time off or some other means, such as cash payments at termination or retirement.

   An employer usually would accrue a liability for vacation leave that were earned but not used during the current or prior periods and for which employees can receive compensation in a future period. Benefits that have been earned but that are not yet available for use as paid time off or as some other form of compensation because employees have not met certain conditions (for example, a minimum service period for new employees) should be accrued to the extent it is probable that the employees will meet the conditions for compensation in the future. However, benefits that have been earned but that are expected to lapse and thus not result in compensation to employees should not be accrued as a liability.

2. **Sick Leave and Other Compensated Absences with Similar Characteristics** A liability for sick leave and other compensated absences with similar characteristics (hereinafter referred to as "sick leave") should be accrued using one of the following termination approaches:

   a. A liability should be accrued as the benefits are earned by the employees if it is probable that the employer will compensate the employees for the benefits through cash payments conditioned on the employees' termination or retirement ("termination payments"). Therefore, an accrual for earned sick leave should be made only to the extent it is probable that the benefits will result in termination payments, rather than be taken as absences due to illness or other contingencies, such as medical appointments and funerals. The sick leave liability generally would be an estimate based on a governmental entity's past experience of making termination payments for sick leave. This method is referred to as the termination payment method.

   b. Alternatively, a governmental entity should estimate its accrued sick leave liability based on the sick leave accumulated at the balance sheet date by those employees who currently are eligible to receive termination payments as well as other employees who are expected to become eligible in the future to receive such payments. To calculate the liability, these accumulations should be reduced to the maximum amount allowed as a termination payment. This method is referred to as the vesting method.

3. **Sabbatical Leave** The accounting for sabbatical leave depends on whether the compensation during the sabbatical is for service during the period of the leave or, instead, for past service.

   a. Some employers permit sabbatical leave from normal duties so that employees can perform research or public service or can obtain additional training to enhance the reputation of or otherwise benefit the employer. In this situation, the sabbatical constitutes a change in assigned duties and the salary paid during the leave is compensation for service during the period of the leave. Therefore, the nature of the sabbatical leave is restricted. Accordingly, the sabbatical should be accounted for in the period the service is rendered; a liability should not be reported in advance of the sabbatical.

b. Sometimes, however, sabbatical leave is permitted to provide compensated unrestricted time off. In this situation, the salary paid during the leave is compensation for past service. A liability should be accrued during the period(s) the employees earn the right to the leave if it is probable that the employer will compensate the employees for the benefits through paid time off or some other means.

4. **Liability Calculation** The compensated absences liability should be calculated based on the pay or salary rates in effect at the balance sheet date. However, if the employer pays employees for their compensated absences at other than their pay or salary rates—for example, at a lower amount as established by contract, regulation, or policy—that other rate as of the balance sheet date should be used to calculate the liability.

5. **Additional Accrual** An additional amount should be accrued as a liability for salary-related payments associated with the payment of compensated absences, using the rates in effect at the balance sheet date. The salary-related payments subject to this accrual are those items for which an employer is liable to make a payment directly and incrementally associated with payments made for compensated absences on termination. Such salary-related payments include the employer's share of Social Security and Medicare taxes and also might include, for example, the employer's contributions to pension plans. The accrual should be made based on the entire liability for each type of compensated absence to which the salary-related payments apply. (That is, payments directly and incrementally associated with the payment of sick leave termination payments should be accrued for the entire sick leave liability; salary-related payments associated with termination payments of vacation leave should be accrued for the entire vacation leave liability, including leave that might be taken as paid time off rather than paid as termination payments.)

B. Postemployment Benefits

Editor's Note: As this volume goes to print, the full text of the new standards has not yet been released. The following information will need to be confirmed once the full text becomes available.

1. **GASB 67 and 68** In June 2012, GASB approved two new standards that will substantially improve the accounting and financial reporting with respect to pension plans and the trusts for those plans. Statement No. 67, *Financial Reporting for Pension Plans*, will replace existing guidance under Statement Nos. 25 and 50, while Statement No. 68, *Accounting and Financial Reporting for Pensions*, replaces the requirements of Statement Nos. 27 and 50, as they relate to governments that provide pension plans that are administered as trusts or similar arrangements. The plans are effective for periods beginning after June 15, 2013, and June 15, 2014, respectively. Since earlier application is encouraged, the information is eligible for testing on the exam beginning in January 2013.

   a. Previously, employers disclosed the amount of the unfunded pension liability in the notes to the financial statements. Under GASB 68, governments must now recognize their long-term obligation for pension benefits as a liability on the face of the balance sheet. The net pension obligation to be recognized is the total pension liability (the present value of all projected benefit payments to employees based on their past service) less the amount of plan assets (mostly investments reported at fair value) set aside for payment of benefits as of the reporting date. Annual pension expense will be based on a comprehensive measurement of the annual cost of pension benefits, rather than on required funding amounts.

   b. Employers will be required to present more extensive note disclosures, including descriptive information about the types of benefits provided, how contributions to the pension plan are determined, and assumptions and methods used to calculate the pension liability.

c. A single or agent employer will need to present RSI schedules covering the past 10 years regarding: sources of changes in the components of the net pension liability; ratios that assist in assessing the magnitude of the net pension liability; and comparisons of actual employer contributions to the pension plan with actuarially determined contribution requirements, if an employer has actuarially determined contributions.

d. Cost-sharing employers will have to record a liability and expense equal to their proportionate share of the collective net pension liability and expense for the cost-sharing plan. The proportion approximates the government's long-term expected contributions to the plan divided by those of all governments participating in the plan.

e. GASB 68 calls for immediate recognition of more pension expense than is currently required. This includes immediate recognition of annual service cost and interest on the pension liability and immediate recognition of the effect on the net pension liability of changes in benefit terms. Other components of pension expense will be recognized over a closed period that is determined by the average remaining service period of the plan members (both current and former employees, including retirees). These other components include the effects on the net pension liability of (1) changes in economic and demographic assumptions used to project benefits and (2) differences between those assumptions and actual experience. Lastly, the effects on the net pension liability of differences between expected and actual investment returns will be recognized in pension expense over a closed five-year period.

f. Certain governments are legally responsible for making contributions directly to a pension plan that is used to provide pensions to the employees of another government. For example, a state is legally required to contribute to a pension plan that covers local school districts' teachers. In these special funding situations, GASB 68 requires governments that are nonemployer contributing entities to recognize in their own financial statements their proportionate share of the other governmental employers' net pension liability and pension expense.

g. GASB 68 improves the comparability and consistency of how governments calculate the pension liabilities and expense with the following additional changes:

(1) Projections of benefit payments to employees will be based on the then-existing benefit terms and incorporate projected salary changes and projected service credits (if they are factors in the pension formula), as well as projected automatic postemployment benefit changes (those written into the benefit terms), including automatic cost-of-living-adjustments (COLAs). For the first time, projections also will include ad hoc postemployment benefit changes (those not written into the benefit terms), including ad hoc COLAs, if they are considered to be substantively automatic.

(2) The rate used to discount projected benefit payments to their present value will be based on a single rate that reflects (a) the long-term expected rate of return on plan investments as long as the plan net position is projected under specific conditions to be sufficient to pay pensions of current employees and retirees and the pension plan assets are expected to be invested using a strategy to achieve that return; and (b) a yield or index rate on tax-exempt 20-year, AA-or-higher rated municipal bonds to the extent that the conditions for use of the long-term expected rate of return are not met.

(3) Governments will use a single actuarial cost allocation method—"entry age," with each period's service cost determined as a level percentage of pay.

(4) An RSI schedule of net pension liability, information about contractually required contributions, and related ratios is now required.

h. GASB 67 replaces the requirements of GASB 25 and GASB 50 as they relate to pension plans that are administered through trusts or similar arrangements meeting certain criteria. The Statement builds upon the existing framework for financial reports of defined benefit pension plans, and enhances note disclosures and RSI for both defined benefit and defined contribution pension plans. GASB 67 also requires the presentation of new information about annual money-weighted rates of return in the notes to the financial statements and in 10-year RSI schedules.

2. Current Pension Plan Requirements GASB 25 establishes standards for defined benefit pension plans and defined contribution plans. It does not address healthcare benefits, any plans not providing postretirement income, or the measurement of employer costs. Pension plans are classified by whether the income or other benefits that the employee will receive are defined by the benefit terms (a defined benefit plan) or whether the pensions depend only on the contributions to the employee's account, actual earnings on investments of those contributions, and other factors (a defined contribution plan).

Defined benefit plans are further classified based on the number of governments participating in a particular pension plan and whether assets and obligations are shared among the participating governments. Categories include plans where only one employer participates (single employer); plans in which assets are pooled for investment purposes, but each employer's share of the pooled assets is legally available to pay the benefits of only its employees (agent employer); and plans in which participating employers pool or share obligations to provide pensions to their employees and plan assets can be used to pay the benefits of employees of any participating employer (cost-sharing employer).

a. Disclosures for defined contribution plans must include a brief plan description, a summary of significant accounting policies (including the fair value of plan assets), and information about contributions and investment concentrations. Governments will recognize pension expenses equal to the amount of contributions or credits to employees' accounts, absent forfeited amounts. A pension liability will be recognized for the difference between amounts recognized as expense and actual contributions made to a defined contribution pension plan.

b. Defined benefit pension plans may elect to report one or more years of the required information in an additional financial statement or in the notes to the financial statements. A plan and its participating employer(s) must use the same methods and assumptions for financial reporting.

(1) A statement of plan net assets provides information about the fair value and composition of plan assets, liabilities, and net assets.

(2) A statement of changes in plan net assets provides information about the year-to-year changes in plan net assets, for a minimum of six years.

(3) Notes to the financial statements include a short plan description; a summary of significant accounting policies; and information about contributions, legally required reserves, and investment concentrations.

(4) Required supplementary information includes two schedules of historical trend information for a minimum of six years. Disclosures related to these schedules include the actuarial methods and significant assumptions used for financial reporting. The schedule of funding progress reports the actuarial value of assets, the actuarial accrued liability, and the relationship between the two over time. The schedule of employer contributions provides information about the employer's annual required contributions (ARC) and the percentage of the ARC recognized by the plan as contributed.

3. **Accounting and Reporting** GASB 27 currently addresses accounting and reporting issues related to pension information presented in the financial statements of state and local governments. Limited guidance is provided for defined contribution plans, which do not create the difficult issues raised by a defined benefit pension plan.

   The standards apply to all state and local governmental employers, irrespective of the type of fund (government fund type or proprietary fund type) used to report pension expenditures/ expense. Pension trust funds included in the employer's financial statements are **not** subject to GASB 27. (They are subject to GASB 25.)

   a. For single-employer or agent multiple-employer plans, annual pension costs are equal to the employer's annual required contributions (ARC). The ARC is the employer's periodic required contributions to a defined benefit pension plan, calculated in accordance with sound actuarial parameters. When an employer has more than one plan, all recognition requirements should be applied separately for each plan.

   b. The annual pension cost differs from the pension expenditure/expense reported in the financial statements. The annual pension cost is the period cost of an employer's participation in a defined benefit pension plan. The pension expenditure/expense is the amount recognized by an employer in each accounting period for contributions to a pension plan.

   c. If the contributions are made from more than one fund, the ARC should be allocated on a pro-rata share to the various funds. In addition, the interest and the adjustment to reverse the actuarial amortization should also be allocated on the fund's proportionate share of the beginning balance of the NPO.

   d. Employers participating in multiple-employer plans share costs regardless of individual employer member demographics. The actuary usually calculates a single contribution requirement for all participants. Employers recognize pension expenditures equal to this contractual requirement. The plan description in the employer financial statements should include a reference to any separate issuance of pension plan reports.

   e. Requirements are similar to pension plans' requirements. Single or agent employers have additional requirements to outline the annual pension cost, contributions, and NPOs for the current year and two previous years.

   f. If an insurance company unconditionally undertakes a legal obligation to pay employees' pension benefits, the employer recognizes pension expense equal to the insurance premiums. The notes disclose information about this transfer and describe the benefits provided in the event of the company's default.

   g. The annual expense or expenditure is based on the amounts required by the plan. Benefits are based on accumulated contributions. Differences between required and actual contributions are accumulated as assets or liabilities, and future contributions do not reflect amortization of previous deficiencies. Note disclosures include identification of the plan, description of the plan provisions, contribution requirements, and actual member and employer contributions.

4. **Deferred Compensation Plans** Under GASB 32, as amended by GASB 34, an IRC §457 deferred compensation plan that meets the criteria in NCGA Statement No. 1 for inclusion in the fiduciary funds of a government is reported as a pension trust fund in the financial statements. The government must determine whether it has fiduciary accountability for IRC §457 plans and whether it holds the assets in a trustee capacity. NCGA guidance generally does not require the use of fiduciary funds when the assets are administered by a third party. The likely result of GASB 32 is that many government employers that formerly reported IRC §457 plan assets on their balance sheet will no longer do so.

5. **Other Postemployment Benefit Plans** GASB 43, *Financial Reporting for Postemployment Benefit Plans Other Than Pension Plans,* supersedes GASB 26 and establishes uniform financial reporting standards for other postemployment benefit (OPEB) plans administered by defined benefit pension plans. GASB 45, *Accounting and Financial Reporting by Employers for Postemployment Benefits other Than Pensions,* requires systematic, accrual-based measurement and recognition of OPEB costs (expenses) and requires reporting of information about actuarial accrued liabilities.

   a. OPEB includes postemployment healthcare and other forms of postemployment benefits, such as life insurance, when provided separately from a pension plan.

   b. Plans that administer OPEB plans **must** present:

      (1) A statement of plan net assets

      (2) A statement of changes in plan net assets

      (3) Notes to the financial statements, including: a brief plan description; a summary of significant accounting policies; and information about contributions and legally required reserves

      (4) Two multiyear schedules—required supplementary information (RSI) providing long-term historical trend information immediately following the notes to financial statements showing: the funded status of the plan and sufficiency of assets to pay benefits when due; and employer contributions to the plan

C. Accounting for Termination Benefits

GASB 47 establishes accounting standards for termination benefits.

1. **Recognition in Financial Statements Prepared on the Accrual Basis of Accounting**

   a. Involuntary plan:

      (1) A plan of involuntary termination is defined as a plan that (a) identifies, at a minimum, the number of employees to be terminated, the job classifications or functions that will be affected and their locations, and when the terminations are expected to occur and (b) establishes the terms of the termination benefits in sufficient detail to enable employees to determine the type and amount of benefits they will receive if they are involuntarily terminated.

      (2) Recognize a liability and expense for *involuntary* termination benefits (i.e., severance benefits) when a plan of termination has been approved, communicated to the employees, and the amount can be estimated

      (3) If a plan of involuntary termination requires that employees render future service in order to receive benefits, the employer should recognize a liability and expense for the portion of involuntary termination benefits that will be provided after completion of future service ratably over the employees' future service period, beginning when the plan otherwise meets the recognition criteria.

   b. Voluntary plans recognize a liability and expense for voluntary termination benefits (i.e., early-retirement incentives) when the offer is accepted and the amount can be estimated.

2. **Financial Statements Prepared on the Modified Accrual Basis of Accounting** Liabilities and expenditures for termination benefits should be recognized to the extent the liabilities are normally expected to be liquidated with expendable available financial resources

3. **Measurement Requirements**

   a. Healthcare-related termination benefits that are part of a large-scale, age-related program (i.e., early-retirement incentive program affecting a significant portion of employees) should be measured at their discounted present values based on projected total claims costs (or age-adjusted premiums approximating claims costs) for terminated employees, with consideration given to the expected future healthcare cost trend rate.

   b. Healthcare-related termination benefits that are not part of a large-scale, age-related termination program are permitted, but not required, to measure cost of termination benefits based on projected claims costs for terminated employees (the cost of termination benefits may be based on unadjusted premiums).

   c. The cost of non-healthcare-related termination benefits for which the benefit terms establish an obligation to pay specific amounts on fixed or determinable dates should be measured at the discounted present value of expected future benefit payments (including an assumption regarding changes in future cost levels during the periods covered by the employer's commitment to provide the benefits).

   d. If the benefit terms do not establish an obligation to pay specific amounts on fixed or determinable dates, the cost of non-healthcare-related benefits should be calculated as either (a) the discounted present value of expected future benefit payments or (b) the undiscounted total of estimated future benefit payments at current cost levels.

4. **Exception for Termination Benefits Affecting Defined Benefit Pension or OPEB Obligations** These should be accounted for and reported under the requirements of Statement No. 27 or Statement No. 45, as applicable.

5. **Disclosure Requirements**

   a. Description of the termination benefit arrangement

   b. Cost of the termination benefits

   c. Significant methods and assumptions used to determine termination benefit liabilities

D. Investments

Failures in the governmental sector related to investment performance raised public awareness of investments. GASB 31 requires revenue recognition for changes in the investments' fair value. Internal and external investment pools are required to report, as assets, the equity position of each fund and component unit of the reporting entity that sponsors the pools.

1. **Applicability** GASB 31 establishes standards for all investments held by external investment pools (EIPs). For most other governmental entities, it establishes fair value standards for investments in participating interest-earning investment contracts, external investment pools, open-end mutual funds, debt securities, and equity securities with readily determinable fair values. GASB 31 does **not** apply to securities that are accounted for under the equity method.

2. **Valuation** Fluctuations due to market changes are presented in the financial statements. Non-participating contracts may be valued using a cost-based measure. Participating interest-earning investment contracts include investments whose value is affected by market (interest rate) changes. They participate chiefly because they are negotiable, transferable, or their redemption value considers market rates. GASB 31 states that fair value is, "the amount at which a financial instrument could be exchanged in a current transaction between willing parties, other than in a forced or liquidation sale." Broader than *market value* (associated only with the price for an actively traded security), *fair value* includes active, inactive, primary, and secondary assessments based on negotiations between sellers and buyers.

   a. Entities other than EIPs may use amortized cost for money market investments with a remaining maturity of one year or less at the time of purchase.

   b. EIPs may report short-term debt investments with a remaining maturity of up to 90 days at the financial statement date at amortized cost, provided that the fair value of those investments is not significantly affected by market factors.

   c. Investments in open-end mutual funds and EIPs are valued using the fund's current share price. If the investments are in external pools that are not SEC registered, fair value is determined by the fair value per share of the pool's underlying portfolio.

   d. EIPs that are 2a7-like pools are permitted to report their investments at amortized cost. (This standard parallels an SEC rule that allows money market mutual funds to use amortized cost to report net assets. The pool must operate in a manner consistent with this SEC rule.)

3. **Reporting** The changes in the fair value of investments is included in revenues, captioned *net increase (decrease) in the fair value of investments.* Separate classification for realized and unrealized gains and losses is optional. EIPs can separately display realized gains and losses in their separate reports. Assets are reported in the funds and component units that hold the equity interests. Accounting for the allocations of income based on legal and contractual provisions can be based on those restrictions. For allocations based on management policies, the fund that holds the investment should report the income and record an operating transfer for the amounts transferred to other funds. Notes to the financial statements include:

   a. The methods and significant assumptions used to estimate the fair value of investments, when that fair value is based on other than quoted market prices.

   b. The policy for determining which investments, if any, are reported at amortized costs.

   c. Allocations, if any, of income from investments associated with one fund that is assigned to another fund.

   d. If realized gains and losses are disclosed separately, the notes should also disclose that

      (1) The calculation of realized gains and losses is independent of a calculation of the net change in the fair value of investments.

      (2) Realized gains and losses on investments that had been held in more than one fiscal year and sold in the current year were included as a change in the fair value of investments reported in the prior year(s) and the current year.

4. **External Investment Pools** EIPs are organized to consolidate investment holdings for multiple governmental units and improve performance with the resulting larger holdings. As such, EIPs are likely to be more sensitive to investment performance fluctuations.

   a. An investment trust fund reports the transactions and balances of the EIPs. The investment trust fund reports the external portion of each pool in the financial statements of the sponsoring government, using the accrual basis of accounting. The external portion of the EIP represents the equity interests of legally separate entities that are not part of the sponsoring government. Financial statements for the investment trust fund should include a statement of net assets and a statement of changes in net assets. The difference between EIP assets and liabilities should be captioned *net assets held in trust for pool participants.*

   b. Disclosures in the financial statements of an EIP include: (1) a brief description of any regulatory oversight; (2) the frequency and purpose of determining the fair value of investments; (3) the method used to determine participants shares sold and redeemed and whether that method differs from the method used to report investments; (4) whether the pool sponsor has provided or obtained any legally binding guarantees during the period to support the value of shares; (5) the extent of involuntary participation in the pool, if any; (6) summary of the fair value, the carrying amount (if different from fair value), the number of shares or the principal amount, ranges of interest rates, and maturity dates of each major investment classification; and (7) the accounting policy for defining each of the income components, if the investment income is separated into interest, dividend, and other income versus the net increase or decrease in fair value of investments.

   c. Disclosures for the sponsoring government are expanded if the pool does not issue separate financial statements. These additional disclosures include

      (1) Disclosures required by GASB 31 for separate pool financial statements.

      (2) Disclosures required by GASB 3 and GASB 28 should be presented separately for the external portion of each pool.

      (3) Condensed statements of net assets and changes in net assets, for each pool. Pools with internal and external investors should present net assets in total and distinguish between internal and external portions of assets held in trust for pool participants.

   d. Assets and liabilities arising from reverse repurchase and fixed coupon reverse repurchase agreements should not be netted on the balance sheet. These agreements should be reported as a fund liability and the underlying securities should be reported as investments. Income from these agreements should be shown as interest income. The interest cost of these agreements should be reported as interest expenditure/ expense. The interest cost associated with these agreements should not be netted with interest earned on any related investments.

V. Appendix: Sample Financial Statements

Exhibit 3 ▸ Government-Wide Statement of Net Assets (Balance Sheet)

Sample City
Statement of Net Assets
December 31, Year

	Primary Government			
	Governmental Activities	Business-Type Activities	Total	Component Units
ASSETS				
Cash and cash equivalents	$ 13,597,899	$ 10,279,143	$ 23,877,042	$ 303,935
Investments	27,365,221	—	27,365,221	7,428,952
Receivables (net)	12,833,132	3,609,615	16,442,747	4,042,290
Internal balances	175,000	(175,000)	—	—
Inventories	322,149	126,674	448,823	83,697
Capital assets, net	170,022,760	151,388,751	321,411,511	37,744,786
Total assets	224,316,161	165,229,183	389,545,344	49,603,660
LIABILITIES				
Accounts payable	6,783,310	751,430	7,534,740	1,803,332
Deferred revenue	1,435,599	—	1,435,599	38,911
Noncurrent liabilities:				
Due within one year	9,236,000	4,426,286	13,662,286	1,426,639
Due in more than one year	83,302,378	74,482,273	157,784,651	27,106,151
Total liabilities	100,757,287	79,659,989	180,417,276	30,375,033
NET ASSETS				
Invested in capital assets, net of related debt	103,711,386	73,088,574	176,799,960	15,906,392
Restricted for:				
Capital projects	11,705,864	—	11,705,864	492,445
Debt service	3,020,708	1,451,996	4,472,704	—
Community development projects	4,811,043	—	4,811,043	—
Other purposes	3,214,302	—	3,214,302	—
Unrestricted (deficit)	(2,904,429)	11,028,624	8,124,195	2,829,790
Total net assets	$ 123,558,874	$ 85,569,194	$ 209,128,068	$ 19,228,627

Exhibit 4 ▸ Government-Wide Statement of Activities (Operating Statement)

Sample City
Statement of Activities
For the Year Ended December 31, Year

		Program Revenues			Net (Expense) Revenue and Changes in Net Assets			
					Primary Government			
Functions/Programs	Expenses	Charges for Services	Operating Grants and Contributions	Capital Grants and Contributions	Governmental Activities	Business-Type Activities	Total	Component Units
Primary government:								
Governmental activities:								
General government	$ 9,571,410	$ 3,146,915	$ 843,617	$ —	$ (5,580,878)	$ —	$ (5,580,878)	$ —
Public safety	34,844,749	1,198,855	1,307,693	62,300	(32,275,901)	—	(32,275,901)	—
Public works	10,128,538	850,000	—	2,252,615	(7,025,923)	—	(7,025,923)	—
Engineering services	1,299,645	704,793	—	—	(594,852)	—	(594,852)	—
Health and sanitation	6,738,672	5,612,267	575,000	—	(551,405)	—	(551,405)	—
Cemetery	735,866	212,496	—	—	(523,370)	—	(523,370)	—
Culture and recreation	11,532,350	3,995,199	2,450,000	—	(5,087,151)	—	(5,087,151)	—
Community development	2,994,389	—	—	2,580,000	(414,389)	—	(414,389)	—
Education (payment to school district)	21,893,273	—	—	—	(21,893,273)	—	(21,893,273)	—
Interest on long-term debt	6,068,121	—	—	—	(6,068,121)	—	(6,068,121)	—
Total governmental activities	105,807,013	15,720,525	5,176,310	4,894,915	(80,015,263)	—	(80,015,263)	—
Business-type activities:								
Water	3,595,733	4,159,350	—	1,159,909	—	1,723,526	1,723,526	—
Sewer	4,912,853	7,170,533	—	486,010	—	2,743,690	2,743,690	—
Parking facilities	2,796,283	1,344,087	—	—	—	(1,452,196)	(1,452,196)	—
Total business-type activities	11,304,869	12,673,970	—	1,645,919	—	3,015,020	3,015,020	—
Total primary government	$117,111,882	$28,394,495	$5,175,310	$6,540,834	(80,015,263)	3,015,020	(77,000,243)	—
Component units:								
Landfill	$ 3,382,157	$ 3,857,858	$ —	$ 11,397	—	—	—	$ 487,098
Public school system	31,186,498	705,765	3,937,083	—	—	—	—	(26,543,650)
Total component units	$ 34,568,655	$ 4,563,623	$3,937,083	$ 11,397	—	—	—	$(26,056,552)
General revenues:								
Taxes:								
Property taxes, levied for general purposes					51,693,573	—	51,693,573	—
Property taxes, levied for debt service					4,726,244	—	4,726,244	—
Franchise taxes					4,055,505	—	4,055,505	—
Public service taxes					8,969,887	—	8,969,887	—
Payment from Sample City					—	—	—	21,893,273
Grants and contributions not restricted to specific programs					1,457,820	—	1,457,820	6,461,708
Investment earnings					1,958,144	601,349	2,559,493	881,763
Miscellaneous					884,907	104,925	989,832	22,464
Special item—Gain on sale of park land					2,653,488	—	2,653,488	—
Transfers					501,409	(501,409)	—	—
Total general revenues, special items, and transfers					76,900,977	204,865	77,105,842	29,259,208
Change in net assets					(3,114,286)	3,219,885	105,599	3,202,656
Net assets—beginning					126,673,160	82,349,309	209,022,469	16,025,971
Net assets—ending					$ 123,558,874	$85,569,194	$209,128,068	$ 19,228,627

Exhibit 5 ▸ Governmental Funds Balance Sheet

Sample City
Balance Sheet
Governmental Funds
December 31, Year

	General Fund	Major Special Revenue Funds	Major Debt Service Fund	Major Capital Projects Fund	Other Governmental Funds	Total Governmental Funds
ASSETS						
Cash and cash equivalents	$3,418,485	$1,236,523	—	—	$ 5,606,792	$ 10,261,800
Investments	—	—	$13,262,695	$10,467,037	3,485,252	27,214,984
Receivables, net	3,644,561	2,953,438	33,340	11,000	10,221	6,972,560
Due from other funds	1,370,757	—	—	—	—	1,370,757
Receivables from other governments	—	119,059	—	—	1,596,038	1,715,097
Liens receivable	791,926	3,195,745	—	—	—	3,987,671
Inventories	182,821	—	—	—	—	182,821
Total assets	$9,408,550	$7,504,765	$13,616,035	$10,478,037	$10,689,303	$ 51,705,690
LIABILITIES						
Liabilities:						
Accounts payable	$3,408,680	$ 129,975	$ 190,548	$ 1,104,632	$ 1,074,831	$ 5,908,666
Due to other funds	—	25,369	—	—	—	25,369
Payable to other governments	94,074	—	—	—	—	94,074
Deferred revenue	4,250,430	6,273,045	250,000	11,000	—	10,784,475
Total liabilities	7,753,184	6,428,389	440,548	1,115,632	1,074,831	16,812,584
FUND BALANCES						
Nonspendable:						
Inventory	$ 125,000	$ 224,000	—	—	$ 1,560,000	$ 1,909,000
Permanent fund principal	—	—	—	—	$ 1,164,000	$ 1,164,000
Restricted for:						
Social services	240,000	—	—	—	—	240,000
Parks and recreation	80,000	—	—	—	—	80,000
Education	55,000	—	—	—	—	55,000
Highways	—		—	2,844,000		2,844,000
Road surface repairs	—	74,000	—	—	—	74,000
Debt service reserve	—	—	6,000,000	—	—	6,000,000
School construction	—	—	—	1,301,000		1,301,000
Law enforcement	—	—	—	—	1,214,000	1,214,000
Other capital projects	—	—	—	1,051,000		1,051,000
Other purposes	30,000	—	—	—	3,509,472	3,539,472
Committed to:						
Zoning board	16,000	—	—	—	—	16,000
Economic stabilization	210,000	—	—	—	—	210,000
Homeland security	110,000	—	—	—	—	110,000
Education	50,000	103,000	—	—	—	153,000
Health and welfare	75,000	—	—	—	—	75,000
Assigned to:						
Parks and recreation	50,000	—	—	—	—	50,000
Library acquisitions	50,000	—	—	—	—	50,000
Highway resurfacing	—	358,000	—	—	—	358,000
Debt service	—	—	7,175,487	—	—	7,175,487
Public pool	—	—	—	1,121,000	—	1,121,000
City Hall renovation	—	—	—	1,560,000	—	1,560,000
Other capital projects	50,000	—	—	1,485,405	—	1,535,405
Other purposes	80,000	317,376	—	—	2,176,000	2,573,376
Unassigned:	434,366	—	—	—	—	434,366
Total fund balances	$1,655,366	$1,076,376	$13,175,487	$ 9,362,405	$ 9,623,472	$ 34,893,106
Total liabilities and fund balances	$9,408,550	$7,504,765	$13,616,035	$10,478,037	$10,698,303	

Amounts reported for governmental activities in the statement of net assets (Exhibit 3) are different because:

Capital assets used in governmental activities are not financial resources and therefore are not reported in the funds.	161,082,708
Other long-term assets are not available to pay for current-period expenditures and therefore are deferred in the funds.	9,348,876
Internal service funds are used by management to charge the costs of certain activities, such as insurance and telecommunications, to individual funds. The assets and liabilities of the internal service funds are included in governmental activities in the statement of net assets (Exhibit 3).	2,994,691
Long-term liabilities, including bonds payable, are not due and payable in the current period and therefore are not reported in the funds.	(84,760,507)
Net assets of governmental activities	$123,558,874

Exhibit 6 ▸ Governmental Funds—Statement of Revenues, Expenditures, and Changes in Fund Balances

Sample City
Statement of Revenues, Expenditures, and Changes in Fund Balances
Governmental Funds
For the Year Ended December 31, Year

	General	HUD Programs	Community Redevelopment	Route 7 Construction	Other Governmental Funds	Total Governmental Funds
REVENUES						
Property taxes	$51,173,436	$ —	$ —	$ —	$ 4,680,192	$ 55,853,628
Franchise taxes	4,055,505	—	—	—	—	4,055,505
Public service taxes	8,969,887	—	—	—	—	8,969,887
Fees and fines	606,946	—	—	—	—	606,946
Licenses and permits	2,287,794	—	—	—	—	2,287,794
Intergovernmental	6,119,938	2,578,191	—	—	2,830,916	11,529,045
Charges for services	11,374,460	—	—	—	30,708	11,405,168
Investment earnings	552,325	87,106	549,489	270,161	364,330	1,823,411
Miscellaneous	881,874	66,176	—	2,939	94	951,083
Total revenues	86,022,165	2,731,473	549,489	273,100	7,906,240	97,482,467
EXPENDITURES						
Current						
General government	8,630,835	—	417,814	16,700	121,052	9,186,401
Public safety	33,729,623	—	—	—	—	33,729,623
Public works	497,775	—	—	—	3,721,542	8,697,317
Engineering services	1,299,645	—	—	—	—	1,299,645
Health and sanitation	6,070,032	—	—	—	—	6,070,032
Cemetery	706,305	—	—	—	—	706,305
Culture and recreation	11,411,685	—	—	—	—	11,411,685
Community development	—	2,954,389	—	—	—	2,954,389
Education—payment to school district	21,893,273	—	—	—	—	21,893,273
Debt service:						
Principal	—	—	—	—	3,450,000	3,450,000
Interest and other charges	—	—	—	—	5,215,151	5,215,151
Capital outlay	—	—	2,246,671	11,281,769	3,190,209	16,718,649
Total expenditures	88,717,173	2,954,389	2,664,485	11,298,469	15,697,954	121,332,470
Excess (deficiency) of revenues over expenditures	(2,695,008)	(222,916)	(2,114,996)	(11,025,369)	(7,791,714)	(23,850,003)
OTHER FINANCING SOURCES (USES)						
Proceeds of refunding bonds	—	—	—	—	38,045,000	38,045,000
Proceeds of long-term capital-related debt	—	—	17,529,560	—	1,300,000	18,829,560
Payment to bond refunding escrow agent	—	—	—	—	(37,284,144)	(37,284,144)
Transfers in	129,323	—	—	—	5,551,187	5,680,510
Transfers out	(2,163,759)	(348,046)	(2,273,187)	—	(219,076)	(5,004,068
Total other financing sources and uses	(2,034,436)	(348,046)	15,256,373	—	7,392,967	20,266,858
SPECIAL ITEM						
Proceeds from sale of park land	3,476,488	—	—	—	—	3,476,488
Net change in fund balances	(1,252,956)	(570,962)	13,141,377	(11,025,369)	(398,747)	(106,657)
Fund balances—beginning	2,908,322	1,647,338	34,110	20,387,774	10,022,219	34,999,763
Fund balances—ending	$ 1,655,366	$1,076,376	$13,175,487	$ 9,362,405	$ 9,623,472	$ 34,893,106

Exhibit 7 ▶ Proprietary Funds Balance Sheet

Sample City
Balance Sheet
Proprietary Funds
December 31, Year

	Business-Type Activities—Enterprise Funds			Governmental Activities—Internal Service Funds (Note 4)
	Water and Sewer	Parking Facilities	Totals [2]	
ASSETS [1]				
Current assets:				
Cash and cash equivalents	$ 8,416,653	$ 369,168	$ 8,785,821	$ 3,336,099
Investments	—	—	—	150,237
Receivables, net	3,564,586	3,535	3,568,121	157,804
Due from other governments	41,494	—	41,494	—
Inventories	126,674	—	126,674	139,328
Total current assets	12,149,407	372,703	12,522,110	3,783,468
Noncurrent assets:				
Restricted cash and cash equivalents	—	1,493,322	1,493,322	—
Capital assets:				
Land	813,513	3,021,637	3,835,150	—
Distribution and collection systems	39,504,183	—	39,504,183	—
Buildings and equipment	106,135,666	23,029,166	129,164,832	14,721,786
Less accumulated depreciation	(15,328,911)	(5,786,503)	(21,115,414)	(5,781,734)
Total noncurrent assets	131,124,451	21,757,622	152,882,073	8,940,052
Total assets	143,273,858	22,130,325	165,404,183	12,723,520
LIABILITIES				
Current liabilities:				
Accounts payable	447,427	304,003	751,430	780,570
Due to other funds	175,000	—	175,000	1,170,388
Compensated absences	112,850	8,827	121,677	237,690
Claims and judgments	—	—	—	1,687,975
Bonds, notes, and loans payable	3,944,609	360,000	4,304,609	249,306
Total current liabilities	4,679,886	672,830	5,353,716	4,125,929
Noncurrent liabilities:				
Compensated absences	451,399	35,306	486,705	—
Claims and judgments	—	—	—	5,602,900
Bonds, notes and loans payable	54,451,549	19,544,019	73,995,568	—
Total noncurrent liabilities	54,902,948	19,579,325	74,482,273	5,602,900
Total liabilities	59,582,834	20,252,155	79,834,989	9,728,829
NET ASSETS				
Invested in capital assets, net of related debt	72,728,293	360,281	73,088,574	8,690,746
Restricted for debt service	—	1,451,996	1,451,996	—
Unrestricted	10,962,731	65,893	11,028,624	(5,696,055)
Total net assets	83,691,024	1,878,170	85,569,194	2,994,691
Total liabilities and net assets	$143,273,858	$22,130,325	$165,404,183	$12,723,520

[1] This statement illustrates the "balance sheet" format; the "net assets" format also is permitted. Classification of assets and liabilities is required in either case.

[2] Even though internal service funds (ISF) are classified as proprietary funds, the nature of the activity accounted for in them is generally governmental. By reporting ISFs separately from the proprietary funds that account for business-type activities, the information in the "Totals" column on this statement flows directly to the "Business-Type Activities" column on the statement of net assets, and the need for a reconciliation on this statement is avoided.

Exhibit 8 ▸ Proprietary Funds Operating Statement

Sample City
Statement of Revenues, Expenses, and Changes in Fund Net Assets
Proprietary Funds
For the Year Ended December 31, Year

	Business-Type Activities—Enterprise Funds			Governmental Activities—Internal Service Funds (Note 5)
	Water and Sewer	Parking Facilities	Totals [1]	
Operating revenues:				
Charges for services	$11,329,883	$1,340,261	$12,670,144	$15,256,164
Miscellaneous	—	3,826	3,826	1,066,761
Total operating revenues	11,329,883	1,344,087	12,673,970	16,322,925
Operating expenses:				
Personal services	3,400,559	762,348	4,162,907	4,157,156
Contractual services	344,422	96,032	440,454	584,396
Utilities	754,107	100,726	854,833	214,812
Repairs and maintenance	747,315	64,617	811,932	1,960,490
Other supplies and expenses	498,213	17,119	515,332	234,445
Insurance claims and expenses	—	—	—	800,286
Depreciation	1,163,140	542,049	1,705,189	1,707,872
Total operating expenses	6,907,756	1,582,891	8,490,647	16,863,457
Operating income (loss)	4,422,127	(238,804)	4,183,323	(540,532)
Nonoperating revenues (expenses):				
Interest and investment revenue	454,793	146,556	601,349	134,733
Miscellaneous revenue	—	104,925	104,925	20,855
Interest expense	(1,600,830)	(1,166,546)	(2,767,376)	(41,616)
Miscellaneous expense	—	(46,846)	(46,846)	(176,003)
Total nonoperating revenue (expenses)	(1,146,037)	(961,911)	(2,107,948)	(62,031)
Income (loss) before contributions and transfers	3,276,090	(1,200,715)	2,075,375	(602,563)
Capital contributions	1,645,919	—	1,645,919	18,788
Transfers out	(290,000)	(211,409)	(501,409)	(175,033)
Change in net assets	4,632,009	(1,412,124)	3,219,885	(758,808)
Total net assets—beginning	79,059,015	3,290,294	82,349,309	3,753,499
Total net assets—ending	$83,691,024	$1,878,170	$85,569,194	$ 2,994,691

[1] Even though internal service funds are classified as proprietary funds, the nature of the activity accounted for in them is generally *governmental.* By reporting internal service funds separately from the proprietary funds that account for business-type activities, the information in the "Totals" column on this statement flows directly to the "Business-Type Activities" column on the statement of net assets, and the need for a reconciliation on this statement is avoided.

Exhibit 9 ▸ Proprietary Funds Cash Flows Statement

Sample City
Statement of Cash Flows
Proprietary Funds
For the Year Ended December 31, Year

	Business-Type Activities—Enterprise Funds			Governmental Activities—Internal Service Funds (Note 5)
	Water and Sewer	Parking Facilities	Totals	
CASH FLOWS FROM OPERATING ACTIVITIES				
Receipts from customers	$11,400,200	$ 1,345,292	$12,745,492	$15,356,343
Payments to suppliers	(2,725,349)	(365,137)	(3,090,486)	(2,812,238)
Payments to employees	(3,360,055)	(750,828	(4,110,883)	(4,209,688)
Internal activity—payments to other funds	(1,296,768)	—	(1,296,768)	—
Claims paid	—	—	—	(8,482,451)
Other receipts (payments)	(2,325,483)	—	(2,325,483)	1,061,118
Net cash provided by operating activities	1,692,545	229,327	1,921,872	883,084
CASH FLOWS FROM NONCAPITAL FINANCING ACTIVITIES				
Operating subsidies and transfers to other funds	(290,000)	(211,409)	(501,409)	(175,033)
CASH FLOWS FROM CAPITAL AND RELATED FINANCING ACTIVITIES				
Proceeds from capital debt	4,041,322	8,660,779	12,702,100	—
Capital contributions	1,645,919	—	1,645,919	—
Purchases of capital assets	(4,194,035)	(144,716)	(4,338,751)	(400,086)
Principal paid on capital debt	(2,178,491)	(8,895,000)	(11,073,491)	(954,137)
Interest paid on capital debt	(1,479,708)	(1,166,546)	(2,646,254)	(41,616)
Other receipts (payments)	—	19,174	19,174	131,416
Net cash (used) by capital and related financing activities	(2,164,993)	(1,526,303)	(3,691,303)	(1,264,423)
CASH FLOWS FROM INVESTING ACTIVITIES				
Proceeds from sales and maturities of investments	—	—	—	15,684
Interest and dividends	454,793	143,747	598,540	129,550
Net cash provided by investing activities	454,793	143,747	598,540	145,234
Net (decrease) in cash and cash equivalents	(307,655)	(1,364,645)	(1,672,300)	(411,138)
Balances—beginning of the year	8,724,308	3,227,135	11,951,443	3,747,237
Balances—end of the year	$ 8,416,653	$ 1,862,490	$10,279,143	$ 3,336,099
Reconciliation of operating income (loss) to net cash provided (used) by operating activities				
Operating income (loss)	$ 4,422,127	$ (238,804)	$ 4,183,323	$ (540,532)
Adjustments to reconcile operating income to net cash provided (used) by operating activities:				
Depreciation expense	1,163,140	542,049	1,705,189	1,707,872
Change in assets and liabilities:				
Receivables, net	653,264	1,205	654,469	31,941
Inventories	2,829	—	2,829	39,790
Accounts and other payables	(297,446)	(86,643)	(384,089)	475,212
Accrued expenses	(4,251,369)	11,520	(4,239,849)	(831,199)
Net cash provided by operating activities	$ 1,692,545	$ 229,327	$ 1,921,872	$ 883,084

Note: Required information about noncash investing, capital, and financing activities is not illustrated.

Exhibit 10 ▸ Fiduciary Funds Balance Sheet

Sample City
Statement of Fiduciary Net Assets
Fiduciary Funds
December 31, Year

	Employee Retirement Plan	Private-Purpose Trusts	Agency Funds
ASSETS			
Cash and cash equivalents	$ 1,973	$ 1,250	$ 44,889
Receivables:			
Interest and dividends	508,475	760	—
Other receivables	6,826	—	183,161
Total receivables	515,301	760	183,161
Investments, at fair value:			
U.S. government obligations	13,056,037	80,000	—
Municipal bonds	6,528,019	—	—
Corporate bonds	16,320,047	—	—
Corporate stocks	26,112,075	—	—
Other investments	3,264,009	—	—
Total investments	65,280,187	80,000	—
Total assets	65,797,461	82,010	$228,050
LIABILITIES			
Accounts payable	—	1,234	—
Refunds payable and others	1,358	—	228,050
Total liabilities	1,358	1,234	$228,050
NET ASSETS			
Held in trust for pension benefits and other purposes	$65,796,103	$80,776	

Statements of individual pension plans and external investment pools are required to be presented in the notes to the financial statements if separate GAAP statements for those individual plans or pools are not available.

Exhibit 11 ▸ Fiduciary Funds Operating Statement

Sample City
Statement of Changes in Fiduciary Net Assets
Fiduciary Funds
For the Year Ended December 31, Year

	Employee Retirement Plan	Private-Purpose Trusts
ADDITIONS		
Contributions:		
Employer	$ 2,721,341	$ —
Plan members	1,421,233	—
Total contributions	4,142,574	—
Investment earnings:		
Net (decrease) in fair value of investments	(272,522)	—
Interest	2,460,871	4,560
Dividends	1,445,273	—
Total investment earnings	3,633,622	4,560
Less investment expense	216,428	—
Net investment earnings	3,417,194	4,560
Total additions	7,559,768	4,560
DEDUCTIONS		
Benefits	2,453,047	3,800
Refunds of contributions	464,691	—
Administrative expenses	87,532	678
Total deductions	3,005,270	4,478
Change in net assets	4,554,498	82
Net assets—beginning of the year	61,241,605	$80,694
Net assets—end of the year	$65,796,103	$80,776

Exhibit 12 ▸ Component Units Balance Sheet

Sample City
Statement of Net Assets
Component Units
For the Year Ended December 31, Year

	Sample City School District	Sample City Landfill	Total
ASSETS			
Cash and cash equivalents	$ 303,485	$ 450	$ 303,935
Investments	3,658,520	1,770,432	5,428,952
Receivables, net	3,717,026	325,264	4,042,290
Inventories	83,697	—	83,697
Restricted assets—landfill closure	—	2,000,000	2,000,000
Capital assets, net	34,759,986	2,984,800	37,744,786
Total assets	42,522,714	7,080,946	49,603,660
LIABILITIES			
Accounts payable	1,469,066	334,266	1,803,332
Deposits and deferred revenue	38,911	—	38,911
Long-term liabilities:			
Due within one year	1,426,639	—	1,426,639
Due in more than one year	22,437,349	4,668,802	27,106,151
Total liabilities	25,371,965	5,003,068	30,375,033
NET ASSETS			
Invested in capital assets, net of related debt	12,921,592	2,984,800	15,906,392
Restricted for capital projects	492,445	—	492,445
Unrestricted	3,736,712	(906,922)	2,829,790
Total net assets	$17,150,749	$2,077,878	$19,228,627

Nonmajor component units are aggregated into a single column. Combining statements of nonmajor components have the same status as combining statements for nonmajor funds (supplementary information).

Exhibit 13 ▸ Component Units Operating Statement

Sample City
Statement of Activities
Component Units
For the Year Ended December 31, Year

		Program Revenues			Net (Expense) Revenue and Changes in Net Assets		
	Expenses	Charges for Services	Operating Grants and Contributions	Capital Grants and Contributions	School District	Landfill	Totals
Sample City School District							
Instructional	$16,924,321	$ 147,739	$2,825,109	$ —	$(13,951,473)	$ —	$(13,951,473)
Support services	7,972,559	300	751,711	—	(7,220,548)	—	(7,220,548)
Operation of non-instructional services	1,523,340	557,726	359,092	—	(606,522)	—	(606,522)
Facilities acquisition and construction services	48,136	—	1,171	—	(46,965)	—	(46,965)
Interest on long-term debt	546,382	—	—	—	(546,382)	—	(546,382)
Unallocated depreciation	4,171,760	—	—	—	(4,171,760)	—	(4,171,760)
Total—Sample City School District	31,186,498	705,765	3,937,083	—	(26,543,650)	—	—
Sample City Landfill							
Landfill operations	3,382,157	3,857,858	—	11,397	—	487,098	487,098
Total component units	$34,568,655	$4,563,623	$3,937,083	$11,397			(26,056,552)
General revenues:							
Payment from Sample City					21,893,273	—	21,893,273
Grants, entitlements, and contributions not restricted to specific programs					6,461,708	—	6,461,708
Investment earnings					674,036	207,727	881,763
Miscellaneous					19,950	2,514	22,464
Total general revenues					29,048,967	210,241	29,259,208
Change in net assets					2,505,317	697,339	3,202,656
Net assets—beginning					14,645,432	1,380,539	16,025,971
Net assets—ending					$ 17,150,749	$2,077,878	$ 19,228,627

CHAPTER 19—GOVERNMENTAL FINANCIAL REPORTING

Problem 19-1 MULTIPLE-CHOICE QUESTIONS

1. The primary authoritative body for determining the measurement focus and basis of accounting standards for governmental fund operating statements is the

   a. Governmental Accounting Standards Board (GASB)
   b. Financial Accounting Standards Board (FASB)
   c. Government Accounting and Auditing Committee of the AICPA (GAAC)
   d. National Council on Governmental Accounting (NCGA) (5/91, Theory, #51, amended, 2095)

2. What is the basic criterion used to determine the reporting entity for a governmental unit?

   a. Special financing arrangement
   b. Geographic boundaries
   c. Scope of public services
   d. Financial accountability (11/95, AR, #62, 5805)

3. Which of the following is a unique feature of governmental financial statements?

   a. Demonstrating that the government produces a "bottom line profit"
   b. Highlighting the government's earnings per share for public utilities
   c. The government's relationship with related entities
   d. Identifying how public resources are acquired and used (Editor, 89688)

4. A city taxes merchants for various central district improvements. Which of the following accounting methods assist(s) in assuring that these revenues are expended legally?

	Fund accounting	Budgetary accounting	
a.	Yes	No	
b.	No	Yes	
c.	No	No	
d.	Yes	Yes	(R/03, FAR, #7, 7609)

5. The responsibility for developing goals and objectives for state and local government public policy decisions belongs to which of the following?

   a. Constituents, legislative body, and other regulatory authorities
   b. Federal government
   c. State governments establish goals for local governments, based on federal mandates
   d. Governmental Accounting Standards Board (Editor, 89690)

6. Governmental financial reporting should provide information to assist users in which situation(s)?

   I. Making social and political decisions.
   II. Assessing whether current-year citizens received services but shifted part of the payment burden to future-year citizens.

   a. I only
   b. II only
   c. Both I and II
   d. Neither I nor II (5/95, AR, #52, 5470)

7. What is the measurement focus and the basis of accounting for the government-wide financial statements?

	Measurement focus	Basis of accounting	
a.	Current financial resources	Modified accrual	
b.	Economic resources	Modified accrual	
c.	Current financial resources	Accrual	
d.	Economic resources	Accrual	(R/08, FAR, #21, 8576)

8. South City School District has a separate elected governing body that administers the public school system. The district's budget is subject to the approval of the city council. The district's financial activity should be reported in the City's financial statements by

   a. Blending only
   b. Discrete presentation
   c. Inclusion as a footnote only
   d. Either blending or inclusion as a footnote (11/97, AR, #13, 6541)

9. The statement of activities of the government-wide financial statements is designed primarily to provide information to assess which of the following?

   a. Operational accountability
   b. Financial accountability
   c. Fiscal accountability
   d. Functional accountability (R/01, AR, #8, 6993)

10. All of the following statements regarding notes to the basic financial statements of governmental entities are true **except**

    a. The notes contain disclosures related to required supplementary information.
    b. Some notes presented by governments are identical to notes presented in business financial statements.
    c. Notes that are considered essential to the basic financial statements need to be presented.
    d. It is acceptable to present notes in a very extensive format. (R/08, FAR, #48, 8603)

11. Vale City adopts a cash budget for the current year. What basis should be used in Vale's budgetary comparison schedule?

    a. Accrual
    b. Cash
    c. Modified accrual
    d. Cash or modified accrual (Editors, 6893)

12. Where is the management's discussion and analysis (MD&A) required to be presented?

    a. Before the financial statements
    b. Before the notes to the financial statements, but after the financial statements
    c. In the notes to the financial statements
    d. After the notes to the financial statements, before other required supplementary information (Editors, 6873)

13. Which of the following are governments required to include in the management's discussion and analysis (MD&A)?

    a. Analysis of significant budget variances
    b. Comparisons of current year to prior year, based on government-wide information
    c. Currently known facts, decisions, or conditions that are expected to have a significant effect on financial position or results of operations
    d. All of the above (Editors, 6894)

14. Which of the following funds should be reported as part of local government's governmental activities column in its government-wide statements?

    a. Debt service
    b. Agency
    c. Private-purpose trust
    d. Pension trust (R/09, FAR, #3, 8753)

15. Which of the following would be reported as program revenues on a local government's government-wide statement of activities?

    a. Charges for services
    b. Taxes levied for a specific function
    c. Proceeds from the sale of a capital asset used for a specific function
    d. Interest revenues (R/06, FAR, #44, 8111)

16. Chase City uses an internal service fund for its central motor pool. The assets and liabilities account balances for this fund that are not eliminated normally should be reported in the government-wide statement of net assets as

    a. Governmental activities
    b. Business-type activities
    c. Fiduciary activities
    d. Note disclosures only (R/01, AR, #3, 6988)

17. On March 1, Wag City issued $1,000,000, ten-year, 6% general obligation bonds at par with no bond issue costs. The bonds pay interest September 1 and March 1. What amount of interest expense and bond interest payable should Wag report in its government-wide financial statements at the close of the fiscal year on December 31?

    a. Interest expense, $50,000; interest payable, $20,000
    b. Interest expense, $50,000; interest payable, $0
    c. Interest expense, $60,000; interest payable, $10,000
    d. Interest expense, $30,000; interest payable, $0 (R/08, FAR, #47, 8602)

18. Nox City reported a $25,000 net increase in the fund balances for total governmental funds. Nox also reported an increase in net assets for the following:

Motor pool internal service fund	$ 9,000
Water enterprise fund	12,000
Employee pension fund	7,000

    The motor pool internal service fund provides service to the general fund departments. What amount should Nox report as the change in net assets for governmental activities?

    a. $25,000
    b. $34,000
    c. $41,000
    d. $46,000 (R/02, AR, #7, 7072)

19. During the current year Knoxx County levied property taxes of $2,000,000, of which 1% is expected to be uncollectible. The following amounts were collected during the current year:

Prior year taxes collected within the 60 days of the current year	$ 50,000
Prior year taxes collected between 60 and 90 days into the current year	120,000
Current year taxes collected in the current year	1,800,000
Current year taxes collected within the first 60 days of the subsequent year	80,000

    What amount of property tax revenue should Knoxx County report in its entity-wide statement of activities?

    a. $1,800,000
    b. $1,970,000
    c. $1,980,000
    d. $2,000,000 (R/05, FAR, #19, 7763)

20. It is inappropriate to record depreciation expense in the government-wide financial statements related to the assets in which type of fund?

    a. Agency fund
    b. Enterprise fund
    c. General fund
    d. Special revenue fund (Editors, 6881)

21. Kingwood Town paid $22,000 cash for a flatbed trailer to be used in the general operations of the town. The expected useful life of the trailer is 6 years with an estimated $7,000 salvage value. Which of the following amounts would be reported?

    a. $15,000 increase in equipment in the general fund
    b. $15,000 increase in the governmental activities column for fixed assets
    c. $22,000 increase in the governmental activities column for fixed assets
    d. $22,000 increase in equipment in the general fund (R/99, AR, #16, amended, 6805)

22. Nack City received a donation of a valuable painting. Nack planned to add the painting to its collection and display it in the protected exhibition area of city hall. Nack had a policy that if such donated art works were sold, the proceeds would be used to acquire other items for its collections. Which of the following would be correct regarding the donated painting?

    a. Must be capitalized and depreciated
    b. Must be capitalized but not depreciated
    c. May be capitalized, but it is not required, and it must be depreciated
    d. May be capitalized, but it is not required, and depreciation is not required (R/09, FAR, #32, 8782)

23. During the current year, Wythe County levied $2,000,000 property taxes, 1% of which is expected to be uncollectible. During the year, the county collected $1,800,000 and wrote off $15,000 as uncollectible. What amount should Wythe County report as property tax revenue in its government-wide statement of activities for the current year?

    a. $1,800,000
    b. $1,980,000
    c. $1,985,000
    d. $2,000,000 (R/09, FAR, #35, 8785)

24. In preparing Chase City's reconciliation of the statement of revenues, expenditures, and changes in fund balances to the government-wide statement of activities, which of the following items should be subtracted from changes in fund balances?

    a. Capital assets purchases
    b. Payment of long-term debt principal
    c. Internal service fund increase in net assets
    d. Book value of capital assets sold during the year (R/11, FAR, #32, 9882)

25. Which of the following activities should be **excluded** when governmental fund financial statements are converted to government-wide financial statements?

    a. Proprietary activities
    b. Fiduciary activities
    c. Government activities
    d. Enterprise activities (R/11, FAR, #12, 9862)

26. Which of the following statements are required to be presented for special-purpose governments engaged only in business-type activities (such as utilities)?

    a. Statement of net assets only
    b. Management's Discussion and Analysis (MD&A) and Required Supplementary Information (RSI) only
    c. The financial statements required for governmental funds, including MD&A
    d. The financial statements required for enterprise funds, including MD&A and RSI (R/10, FAR, #47, 9347)

27. Hill City's water utility fund held the following investments in U.S. Treasury securities at June 30, year 5:

Investment	Date purchased	Maturity date	Carrying amount
3-month T-bill	5/31, Yr 5	7/31, Yr 5	$ 30,000
3-year T-note	6/15, Yr 5	8/31, Yr 5	50,000
5-year T-note	10/1, Yr 1	9/30, Yr 6	100,000

In the fund's balance sheet, what amount of these investments should be reported as cash and cash equivalents at June 30, year 5?

a. $0
b. $ 30,000
c. $ 80,000
d. $180,000 (11/93, PII, #19, amended, 4448)

28. For which of the following governmental entities that use proprietary fund accounting should a statement of cash flows be presented?

	Public benefit corporations	Governmental utilities
a.	No	No
b.	No	Yes
c.	Yes	Yes
d.	Yes	No

(5/94, AR, #52, 4657)

29. Which format must an enterprise fund use to report cash flow operating activities in the statement of cash flows?

a. Indirect method, beginning with operating income
b. Indirect method, beginning with change in net assets
c. Direct method
d. Either direct or indirect method (R/09, FAR, #31, 8781)

30. Dogwood City's water enterprise fund received interest of $10,000 on long-term investments. How should this amount be reported on the Statement of Cash Flows?

a. Operating activities
b. Noncapital financing activities
c. Capital and related financing activities
d. Investing activities (R/01, AR, #5, 6990)

31. Cash receipts from grants and subsidies to decrease operating deficits should be classified in which of the following sections of the statement of cash flows for governmental, not-for-profit entities?

a. Operating
b. Noncapital financing
c. Capital and related financing
d. Investing (R/07, FAR, #39, 8360)

32. Which of the following must a budgetary comparison schedule in the required supplementary information include?

I. Actual inflows, outflows, and balances, stated on the basis in the government's budget, with a reconciliation between the budgetary and GAAP information
II. Original budget
III. A separate column to report the variances between the final budget and actual amounts

a. I only
b. I and II only
c. I and III only
d. I, II, and III (Editors, 6895)

33. According to GASB 34, certain budgetary schedules are required supplementary information. What is the minimum budgetary information required to be reported in those schedules?

    a. A schedule of unfavorable variances at the functional level
    b. A schedule showing the final appropriations budget and actual expenditures on a budgetary basis
    c. A schedule showing the original budget, the final appropriations budget, and actual inflows, outflows, and balances on a budgetary basis
    d. A schedule showing the proposed budget, the approved budget, the final amended budget, actual inflows and outflows on a budgetary basis, and variances between budget and actual

(R/02, AR, #10, 7075)

34. If a city government is the primary reporting entity, which of the following is an acceptable method to present component units in its combined financial statements?

    a. Consolidation
    b. Cost method
    c. Discrete presentation
    d. Government-wide presentation (R/11, FAR, #48, 9898)

35. Valley Town's public school system is administered by a separately elected board of education. The board of education is not organized as a separate legal entity and does not have the power to levy taxes or issue bonds. Valley's city council approves the school system's budget. How should Valley report the public school system's annual financial results?

	Discrete presentation	Blended
a.	Yes	Yes
b.	Yes	No
c.	No	Yes
d.	No	No

(R\98, FAR #14, 6687)

36. What is the major difference between an exchange transaction and a nonexchange transaction for governmental units?

    a. The relationship between the amount of value given and received
    b. Time requirements and whether the transaction is required by law
    c. Purpose restrictions placed upon fund balances
    d. Whether resources acquired can be further exchanged (R/10, FAR, #22, 9322)

37. Which of the following items is an example of imposed nonexchange revenue for a governmental entity?

    a. Personal income taxes
    b. Retail sales tax
    c. Federal grant money
    d. Property taxes (R/07, FAR, #38, 8359)

38. Chase City imposes a 2% tax on hotel charges. Revenues from this tax will be used to promote tourism in the city. Chase should record this tax as what type of nonexchange transaction?

    a. Derived tax revenue
    b. Imposed nonexchange revenue
    c. Government-mandated transaction
    d. Voluntary nonexchange transaction (R/02, AR, #4, 7069)

39. When a capital lease of a governmental unit represents the acquisition of a general fixed asset, the acquisition should be reflected as

    a. An expenditure but not as an other financing source
    b. An other financing source but not as an expenditure
    c. Both an expenditure and an other financing source
    d. Neither an expenditure nor an other financing source (11/94, AR, #10, 4987)

40. Jonn City entered into a capital lease for equipment during the year. How should the asset obtained through the lease be reported in Jonn City's government-wide statement of net assets?
    a. General capital asset
    b. Other financing use
    c. Expenditure
    d. Not reported (R/11, FAR, #28, 9878)

41. Polk County's solid waste landfill operation is accounted for in a governmental fund. Polk used available cash to purchase equipment that is included in the estimated current cost of closure and postclosure care of this operation. How would this purchase affect the long-term asset and the long-term liability amounts in Polk's general fund?

	Asset amount	Liability amount
a.	Increase	Decrease
b.	Increase	No effect
c.	No effect	Decrease
d.	No effect	No effect

(11/95, AR, #68, amended, 5811)

42. Which of the following statements meet the measurement and recognition criteria for landfill closure and postclosure costs?
    a. Landfills should only be accounted for in the general fund.
    b. Total landfill liabilities should be recognized in the general long-term debt account group.
    c. Expense recognition should begin when waste is accepted and should continue through the post-closure period.
    d. Equipment and facilities included in estimated total current cost of closure and postclosure care should not be reported as capital assets. (R/99, AR, #19, 6808)

43. Which of the following provide guidance for users trying to understand unique governmental reporting issues?
    a. GASB Interpretations
    b. FASB Statements
    c. GASB Concepts Statements
    d. AICPA Audit Guides (Editor, 89693)

44. Which of the following should be included in financial reports to help users assess the government's operating results?
    a. Cash flow statements
    b. Other supplementary information
    c. Management discussion and analysis
    d. Explanation of the sources and uses of financial resources (Editor, 89695)

45. Which of the following characteristics of service efforts and accomplishments is the most difficult to report for a governmental entity?
    a. Comparability
    b. Timeliness
    c. Consistency
    d. Relevance (R/99, AR, #20, 6809)

46. Which of the following describes GASB's role for improving communications (as described in Concept Statement No. 3) in governmental external financial reporting?
    a. The Board's independence supports governments' credibility and comparability among governments' financial statements.
    b. GASB standards establish performance standards that users can use to evaluate the effectiveness of governmental services.
    c. Developing key financial measures for governmental service performance.
    d. Representing state and local governments at Congressional oversight hearings with the Government Accountability Office. (Editor, 2709)

47. Which of the following is Concept Statement No. 4's definition of assets?
    a. Resources that can be converted to cash in the near-term
    b. Resources that are not encumbered with obligations to provide future benefits
    c. An outflow of resources that will provide services in a future period
    d. Resources with present service capacity that the government presently controls (Editor, 9004)

48. The GASB's primary goal for the SEA Concepts Statements is which of the following?
    a. Provide fundamental reporting characteristics to help preparers develop consistent reporting
    b. Outline specific reporting standards
    c. Identify preferred performance benchmarks
    d. Designate appropriate program data that should be included in SEA reports (Editor, 89696)

49. River City has a defined contribution pension plan. How should River report the pension plan in its financial statements?
    a. Amortize any transition asset over the estimated number of years of current employees' service.
    b. Disclose in the notes to the financial statements the amount of the pension benefit obligation and the net assets available for benefits.
    c. Identify in the notes to financial statements the types of employees covered and the employer's and employees' obligations to contribute to the fund.
    d. Accrue a liability for benefits earned but **not** paid to fund participants. (11/92, Theory, #58, 3491)

50. Which of the following statements is correct concerning disclosure of reverse repurchase and fixed coupon reverse repurchase agreements?
    a. Related assets and liabilities should be netted.
    b. Related interest cost and interest earned should be netted.
    c. Credit risk related to the agreements need **not** be disclosed.
    d. Underlying securities owned should be reported as "Investments." (11/94, AR, #6, 4983)

Problem 19-2 SIMULATION: General Fund Statements

The following selected information is taken from Shar City's general fund operating statement for the year ended December 31, year 2:

Revenues	
Property taxes—year 2	$ 825,000
Expenditures	
Current services	
Public safety	428,000
Capital outlay (police vehicles)	100,000
Debt service	74,000
Expenditures—year 2	$1,349,000
Expenditures—year 1	56,000
Expenditures	$1,405,000
Excess of revenues over expenditures	$ 153,000
Other financing uses	(125,000)
Excess of revenues over expenditures and other financing uses	28,000
Decrease in committed fund balance during year 2	15,000
Residual equity transfers out	(190,000)
Decrease in unassigned fund balance during year 2	(147,000)
Unassigned fund balance January 1, year 2	304,000
Unassigned fund balance December 31, year 2	$ 157,000

The following selected information is taken from Shar's December 31, year 2, general fund balance sheet:

Property taxes receivable—delinquent—year 2	$ 34,000
Less: Allowance for estimated uncollectible taxes—delinquent	20,000
Vouchers payable	89,000
Fund balance—	
Committed fund balance—year 2	43,000
Nonspendable fund balance	38,000
Unassigned fund balance	157,000

Additional Information:

- Debt service was for bonds used to finance a library building and included interest of $22,000.
- $8,000 of year 2 property taxes receivable were written-off; otherwise, the allowance for uncollectible taxes balance is unchanged from the initial entry at the time of the original tax levy at the beginning of the year.
- Shar reported supplies inventory of $21,000 at December 31, year 1.

1. **For items 1 through 7,** indicate the part of Shar's general fund statement of activities affected by the transaction. Any choice may be used once, more than once, or not at all.

Choices
Revenues
Expenditures
Other financing sources
Other financing uses
Statement of activities is **not** affected

	Choice
1. An unrestricted state grant is received.	
2. The general fund paid pension fund contributions that were recoverable from an internal service fund.	
3. The general fund paid $60,000 for electricity supplied by Shar's electric utility enterprise fund.	
4. General fund resources were used to subsidize Shar's swimming pool enterprise fund.	
5. $90,000 of general fund resources were loaned to an internal service fund.	
6. A motor pool internal service fund was established by a transfer of $80,000 from the general fund. This amount will not be repaid unless the motor pool is disbanded.	
7. General fund resources were used to pay amounts due on an operating lease.	

2. **For items 8 through 13**, calculate the numeric amount. Enter the amount in the space provided. Round all amounts to the nearest whole dollar.

	Amount
8. What was the total nonspendable and committed fund balance of the Year 1 general fund?	
9. What amount was collected from Year 2 tax assessments?	
10. What amount is Shar's liability to general fund vendors and contractors at December 31, Year 2?	
11. What amount should be included in the government-wide statement of net assets in the governmental activities column for capital assets acquired in Year 2 through the general fund?	
12. What amount arising from Year 2 transactions decreased long-term liabilities reported in the government-wide statement of net assets in the governmental activities column?	
13. What amount of total actual expenditures should Shar report in its Year 2 general fund statement of activities?	

(5/96, AR, #17 – 35, amended, 6214)

Problem 19-3 SIMULATION: Governmental Revenues & Expenditures

Jey City adopted GASB Statement No. 34. Jey requires its landfill to recover its cost through user fees. The following events affected the financial statements of Jey City during the current year:

Budgetary activities:

- Total general fund estimated revenues $8,000,000
- Total general fund budgeted expenditures 7,500,000
- Planned construction of a courthouse improvement expected to cost $1,500,000, and to be financed in the following manner: $250,000 from the general fund, $450,000 from state entitlements, and $800,000 from the proceeds of 20-year, 8% bonds dated and expected to be issued at par on June 30. Interest on the bonds is payable annually on July 1, together with one-twentieth of the bond principal from general fund revenues of the payment period.
- A budgeted general fund payment of $180,000 to subsidize operations of a solid waste landfill enterprise fund.

Actual results included the following:

- Jey recorded property tax revenues of $5,000,000 and a related allowance for uncollectibles—current of $60,000. On December 31, the remaining $56,000 balance of the allowance for uncollectibles—current was closed, and an adjusted allowance for uncollectibles—delinquent was recorded equal to the property tax receivables balance of $38,000. A police car with an original cost of $25,000 was sold for $7,000.
- Office equipment to be used by the city fire department was acquired through a capital lease. The lease required 10 equal annual payments of $10,000 beginning with the July 1 acquisition date. Using a 6% discount rate, the 10 payments had a present value of $78,000 at the acquisition date.
- The courthouse was improved and financed as budgeted except for a $27,000 cost overrun that was paid for by the general fund. Jey plans to transfer cash to the debt service fund during the following year to service the interest and principal payments called for in the bonds.
- Information related to the solid waste landfill at December 31:

Capacity	1,000,000 cubic yards
Usage prior to the current year	500,000 cubic yards
Usage in the current year	40,000 cubic yards
Estimated total life	20 years
Closure costs incurred to date	$ 300,000
Estimated future costs of closure and postclosure care	1,700,000
Expense for closure and postclosure care recognized prior to current year	973,000

	Amount
1. What was the net effect of the budgetary activities on the general fund balance at January 1 of the current year?	
2. What was the total amount of operating transfers out included in the general fund's budgetary accounts at January 1 of the current year?	
3. What amount of interest payable related to the 20-year bonds should be reported by the general fund at December 31 of the current year?	
4. What lease payment amount should be included in current year general fund expenditures?	
5. What amount was collected from current year property taxes in the current year?	
6. What was the total amount of the capital project fund's current year revenues?	
7. What amount should be reported as long-term liabilities in the government-wide statement of net assets in the governmental activities column at December 31 of the current year?	
8. What net increase in capital assets should be reported in the government-wide statement of net assets in the governmental activities column at December 31 of the current year?	
9. What current year closure and postclosure care expenses should be reported in the solid waste landfill enterprise fund?	
10. What should be the December 31 current year closure and postclosure care liability reported in the solid waste landfill enterprise fund?	

(11/96, AR, #3, amended, 6317)

Problem 19-4 SIMULATION: Governmental Fund Reporting

Bel City, whose first fiscal year ended December 31, has only the long-term debt specified in the information and only the funds necessitated by the information.

General fund:

- The following selected information is taken from Bel's general fund financial records:

	Budget	Actual
Property taxes	$5,000,000	$4,700,000
Other revenues	1,000,000	1,050,000
Total revenues	$6,000,000	$5,750,000
Total expenditures	$5,600,000	$5,700,000
Property taxes receivable—delinquent		$ 420,000
Less: Allowance for estimated uncollectible taxes—delinquent		50,000
		$ 370,000

- There were no amendments to the budget as originally adopted.
- No property taxes receivable have been written off, and the allowance for uncollectibles balance is unchanged from the initial entry at the time of the original tax levy.
- There were no encumbrances outstanding at December 31.

Capital project fund:

- Finances for Bel's new civic center were provided by a combination of general fund transfers, a state grant, and an issue of general obligation bonds. Any bond premium on issuance is to be used for the repayment of the bonds at their $1,200,000 par value. At December 31 the capital project fund for the civic center had the following closing entries:

Revenues	800,000	
Other financing sources—bond proceeds	1,230,000	
Other financing sources—operating transfers in	500,000	
Expenditures		1,080,000
Other financing uses—operating transfers out		30,000
Assigned fund balance		1,420,000

- Also at December 31, capital project fund entries reflected Bel's intention to honor the $1,300,000 purchase orders and commitments outstanding for the center.
- During the year, total capital project fund encumbrances exceeded the corresponding expenditures by $42,000. All expenditures were previously encumbered.
- During the following year the capital project fund received no revenues and no other financing sources. The civic center building was completed early the following year and the capital project fund was closed by a transfer of $27,000 to the general fund.

Water utility enterprise fund:

- Bel issued $4,000,000 revenue bonds at par. These bonds, together with a $700,000 transfer from the general fund, were used to acquire a water utility. Water utility revenues are to be the sole source of funds to retire these bonds beginning in 8 years.

For 1 through 6, enter the appropriate amount in the space provided. Round all amounts to the nearest whole dollar.

Items 1 and 2 relate to Bel's general fund.

	Amount
1. What was the amount recorded in the opening entry for appropriations?	
2. What was the total amount debited to property taxes receivable?	

Items 3 through 6 relate to Bel's funds other than the general fund.

3. What was the completed cost of the civic center?	
4. How much was the state capital grant for the civic center?	
5. In the capital project fund, what was the amount of the total encumbrances recorded during the year?	
6. In the capital project fund, what was the assigned fund balance reported at December 31?	

(5/95, AR, #2 amended, 5479)

Solution 19-1 MULTIPLE-CHOICE ANSWERS

Introduction

1. (a) The GASB sets accounting and financial reporting standards for state and local governments. The FASB sets standards for financial reports published by business and nonprofit enterprises. (2095)

2. (d) A governmental unit must look at its ability to exercise oversight responsibility over an entity when considering that entity's inclusion in a governmental unit. Oversight responsibility includes financial interdependency, selection of governing authority, designation of management, ability to significantly influence operations, and accountability for fiscal matters. (5805)

3. (d) Governmental financial statements provide accountability for public resources. This objective is not addressed in commercial accounting standards. The "bottom line profit" is not a major focus for the governmental operating statement. Governmental entities, even enterprise utility systems, are not financed with public stock offerings, therefore, earnings per share is not a relevant measure for these governmental entities. Financial reporting standards for both governmental and commercial accounting include provisions for reporting related organizations and disclosing the primary entity's responsibilities for these reporting entities. (89688)

4. (d) In the absence of a profit motive, a net income bottom line, or other performance indicators, governments are subjected to a variety of restrictions and controls. The most important are overall legal restrictions on the use of resources and exercise of financial expenditure control through the annual budget. These lead to the use of fund accounting and budgetary accounting. (7609)

5. (a) Goals and objectives for management of state and local public policy decisions are not established without the input and authority of that entity's constituents, legislative body, and other regulatory authorities. While the federal government does play an important role in state and local government programs, the Federal government does not establish specific goals and objectives for local governments. Neither do state governments nor the GASB. (89690)

6. (c) Governmental financial reporting is used in making social and political decisions. Because interperiod equity is important, financial reporting should help users assess whether current-year revenues are sufficient to provide current services or whether future taxpayers are assuming the burden of previously provided services. (5470)

GASB Reporting Model

7. (d) Government-wide financial statements aggregate information for all governmental and business-type activities. GASB 34 requires an economic resources measurement focus and accrual basis of accounting for all amounts in the government-wide financial statements. (8576)

8. (b) Component units should be presented discretely unless either (a) the components unit's governing body is substantively the same as the governing body of the primary government, or (b) the component unit provides services almost entirely to the primary government, or almost exclusively benefits the primary government although it does not provide services directly to it. (6541)

9. (a) Operational accountability is important to assess the government's ability to provide services. Operational accountability includes the periodic economic cost of the services provided. It also informs users about whether the government is raising sufficient revenues each period to cover that cost, or whether the government is deferring costs to the future or using up accumulated resources to provide current-period services. The government-wide statements (GWS) are designed to provide an economic long-term view of the government that cannot be seen with the presentation of a collection of funds. (6993)

10. (a) The notes to the basic financial statements of governmental entities do not contain disclosures related to required supplementary information. The Management's Discussion and Analysis (MD&A) is the required supplementary information in the government's general purpose external report and it is presented before the financial statements. Some notes presented by governments are identical to notes presented in business financial statements. Notes that are considered essential to the basic financial statements need to be presented and it is acceptable to present them in a very extensive format. (8603)

11. (b) Budgetary comparison schedules should be presented as RSI for the general fund and for each major special revenue fund that has a legally adopted annual budget. The budgetary comparison schedule should present both the original budget and the final budget, as well as actual inflows, outflows, and balances, stated on the government's budgetary basis. Governments may present the budgetary comparison schedule using the same format, terminology, and classifications as the budget document, or using the format, terminology, and classifications in a statement of revenues, expenditures, and changes in fund balances. Regardless of the format used, the schedule should be accompanied by information (either in a separate schedule or in notes to RSI) that reconciles budgetary information to GAAP information. This reconciliation provides the link from the budgetary comparisons to the GAAP operating statements in the basic financial statements. (6893)

12. (a) The basic financial statements should be preceded by the MD&A, which is required supplementary information. MD&A should provide an objective and easily readable analysis of the government's financial activities based on currently known facts. (6873)

13. (d) The following are required in the MD&A: a comparison of current to prior year results, based on government-wide information; a brief discussion of the basic financial statements, an analysis of the government's overall financial position and results of operations to assist users in assessing whether financial position has improved or deteriorated as a result of annual operations; an analysis of balances and transactions of individual funds; significant variances between original and final budget amounts, and between final budget and actual results; a description of significant capital asset and long-term debt activity; and currently known facts, decisions, or conditions that are expected to have a significant effect on financial position or results of operations. Governments that use the modified approach to report infrastructure assets must also discuss significant changes in the assessed condition of infrastructure assets from previous assessments; how the current condition compares with the established condition level; and any significant differences from the estimated annual amount to maintain or preserve infrastructure assets compared with actual spending during the current period. (6894)

Government-Wide Statements

14. (a) The debt service fund should be reported as part of local government's governmental activities column in its government-wide statements. Reporting capital assets and long-term liabilities is required in the government-wide statements. Agency, private purpose trust, and pension trust funds are all fiduciary funds. Fiduciary activities are not included in the government-wide statements because the assets and liabilities cannot be used to support the government's own programs. (8753)

15. (a) On the government-wide statement of activities, the net revenue (expense) format and net program cost format are used. Charges for services are one of the program revenues reported on a local government's government-wide statement of activities. Taxes levied, proceeds from the sale of a capital asset, and interest revenues would fall under general revenues. (8111)

16. (a) Although internal service funds are proprietary funds, they appear in the government-wide statements as governmental activities in the new reporting model. (6988)

17. (a) The government-wide financial statements use normal accrual accounting. The bond interest should be the $1,000,000 times 0.03 (because the 6% interest is paid every 6 months) for a total of $30,000 on each due date. The interest expense would be the $30,000 for the period March 1 to September 1 plus $20,000 for the four month period September 1 to December 31 ($30,000 × 4/6 = $20,000) for a total of $50,000. Because the $20,000 for the last four months will not be paid until the next March 1, it would be the interest payable at the close of the fiscal year on December 31. (8602)

18. (b) The GWS governmental activities column includes the governmental funds plus most internal service funds and capital assets not specific to business-type activities or fiduciary funds. $25,000 + $9,000 = $34,000. The water enterprise fund is a business-type activity. The employee pension fund is a fiduciary fund; it doesn't appear in the GWS. (7072)

19. (c) Entity-wide statement, the government-wide statements, are done under normal accrual accounting. Only fund financial statements, done under modified accrual, would take into account any 60-day criteria. Under normal accrual accounting, the amount of property tax revenue reported would be the $2,000,000 property taxes levied less the 1% ($20,000) for estimated uncollectible taxes for a total of $1,980,000. The entry would be:

Taxes receivable—current	2,000,000	
Estimated uncollectible taxes		20,000
Revenues control		1,980,000

To record property tax revenue. (7763)

20. (a) Agency funds should be used to report resources held by the reporting government in a purely custodial capacity (assets equal liabilities). Agency funds typically involve only the receipt, temporary investment, and remittance of fiduciary resources to individuals, private organizations, or other governments. Agency funds generally have neither capital assets nor expenses. (6881)

21. (c) Purchased assets are reported at cost. Long-term capital assets are not recorded in any governmental fund. (6805)

22. (d) Governments are encouraged, but not required, to capitalize a collection of works of art or historical treasures (and all additions to that collection) whether donated or purchased that meets all of the following conditions. The collection is (1) held for public exhibition, education, or research in furtherance of public service rather than financial gain, (2) protected, kept encumbered, cared for, and preserved, and (3) subject to an organizational policy that requires the proceeds from sales of collection items to be used to acquire other items for collections. Capitalized collections or individual items that are exhaustible, such as exhibits whose useful lives are diminished by display or educational or research applications, should be depreciated over their estimated useful lives. Depreciation is not required for collections or individual items that are inexhaustible. (8782)

23. (b) Imposed nonexchange revenues represent assessments imposed on nongovernmental entities and include property taxes and fines or forfeitures. Governments should recognize revenues from property taxes, net of estimated refunds and estimated uncollectible amounts, in the period for which the taxes are levied, even if the enforceable legal claim arises or the due date for payment occurs in a different period. All other imposed nonexchange revenues should be recognized in the same period that the assets are recognized unless the enabling legislation includes time requirements. If so, revenues should be recognized in the period when the resources are required to be used or when use is first permitted. The $1,980,000 is derived by from the total $2,000,000 levied less $20,000 (the 1% of $2,000,000) expected to be uncollectible. The $15,000 written off as uncollectible does not factor anywhere in the equation. (8785)

Other Financial Statements

24. (d) The link between government-wide and fund statements requires a reconciliation to convert the governmental funds to the economic resources measurement and accrual basis of accounting. Capital assets used in governmental activities, internal service funds used by management are not included in funds but are included in the GWS, so they are added to changes in fund balance. Long-term liabilities are also not included in changes in fund balance; any reduction to debt would be added back (increase in long-term debt would be subtracted) to reconcile to GWS. Only book value of capital assets is included in fund balance changes and should be subtracted in the reconciliation to GWS net assets. (9882)

25. (b) Fiduciary activities are not included in the government-wide statements because the assets and liabilities cannot be used to support the government's own programs. Proprietary, governmental and enterprise activities are all included in government-wide statements. (9862)

26. (d) Every government entity is required to prepare and publish, as a matter of record, a comprehensive annual financial report (CAFR) that encompasses all funds of the primary government. The CAFR includes MD&A, basic financial statements, and RSI. Most government-owned public utilities must be accounted for through enterprises funds, so the financial statements for enterprise funds would be required. (9347)

27. (c) For purposes of preparing fund statements, cash equivalents are short-term, highly liquid investments that are both (1) readily convertible into known amounts of cash and (2) so near their maturity that they present insignificant risk of changes in value because of changes in interest rates. Generally, only investments with original maturities to the reporting entity of three months or less qualify as cash equivalents. Both a 3-month bill and a 3-year note purchased three months from maturity qualify as cash equivalents. However, a note purchased three years ago does not become a cash equivalent when its remaining maturity is three months. Therefore, the amount of the investments that Hill should report as cash and cash equivalents at 6/30 of year 5 is the sum of the 3-month bill and the 3-year note purchased less than three months from maturity. The note with an original maturity to Hill of five years (i.e., 10/1 of year 1 to 9/30 of year 6) will never be reported as a cash equivalent by Hill. (4448)

28. (c) A statement of cash flows is required for *all* proprietary funds, including public benefit corporations and governmental utilities. (4657)

29. (c) An enterprise fund is one of the governmental proprietary funds. Governments should present a statement of cash flows for proprietary funds based on the provisions of GASB statements. The GASB states the direct method of presenting cash flows from operating activities (including a reconciliation of operating cash flows to operating income) should be used. (8781)

30. (d) For the statement of cash flows, investing activity cash inflows include interest and dividends received as returns on loans (except program loans), debt of other entities, equity securities, and cash management or investment pools. (6990)

31. (b) Noncapital financing activities include cash receipts from grants and subsidies except (1) those specifically restricted for capital purposes and (2) those for specific activities that are considered to be operating activities of the grantor government. Operating activities include cash inflows, receipts, and payments that do not result from transactions defined as capital and related financing, noncapital financing, or investing activities. Capital and related financing activities include acquiring and disposing of capital assets used in providing services or producing goods; borrowing money for acquiring, constructing, or improving capital assets and repaying the amounts borrowed, including interest; and paying for capital assets obtained from vendors on credit. Investing activities include making or collecting loans and acquiring or disposing of debt or equity instruments. (8360)

32. (b) The budgetary comparison schedule includes the original and final budgets as well as actual inflows, outflows, and balances, stated on the government's budgetary basis of accounting, with a reconciliation between the budgetary and GAAP information. The schedule may have the same format as the budget documents or the statement of revenues, expenditures, and changes in fund balances. A column reporting the variances between the final budget and actual amounts is encouraged, but not required. (6895)

33. (c) Budgetary Comparison Schedule (BCS) is presented for the general fund and for each major special revenue fund that has a legally adopted annual budget, on the budgetary basis of accounting. The BCS presents both the original and final budget as well as actual inflows, outflows, and balances. It uses the same format, terminology, and classifications as either the budget document or a statement of revenues, expenditures, and changes in fund balances. (7075)

34. (c) Government-wide statements (GWS) aggregate information for all governmental and business-type activities. GASB 34 requires an economic resources measurement focus and accrual basis of accounting for all amounts in the GWS. There are four required columns in the GWS, one each for: governmental activities, business-type activities, the primary government (sum of the previous two), and component units. Most component units should be included in the financial reporting entity by discrete presentation (reported in columns separate from primary government). (9898)

35. (c) GASB provides additional guidance to determine whether certain entities for which a primary government is not accountable financially must be reported as component units based on the nature and significance of their relationship with the primary government. Legally separate, tax-exempt entities that meet all three criteria must be presented discretely as component units: (1) economic resources received or held by the separate entity are totally (or nearly totally) for the direct benefit of the primary government, its component units, or its constituents; (2) the primary government, or its component units, is entitled to a majority of the economic resources received or held by the separate entity; and (3) the economic resources received or held by an individual entity that the specific primary government, or its component units, is entitled to, or has the ability to otherwise access, are significant to that primary government. (6687)

Other Recognition Topics

36. (a) There are various types of nonexchange transactions for governmental units; imposed nonexchange transactions, government-mandated nonexchange transactions, and voluntary nonexchange transactions. The difference between an exchange transaction and a nonexchange transaction is the relationship between the amount of value given and received. In an exchange transaction the presumption is the amount of value given and received is the same. A nonexchange transaction does not involve an exchange of equal value. (9322)

37. (d) Imposed nonexchange revenues represent assessments imposed on nongovernmental entities and include property taxes and fines or forfeitures. Taxes on earnings or consumption are classified as derived tax revenues. Certain grants, entitlements, and donations are classified as voluntary nonexchange transactions. Voluntary nonexchange transactions result from legislative or contractual agreements involving parties that may or may not be governmental entities, but do not involve an exchange of equal value. (8359)

38. (a) Derived tax revenues are assessments imposed by governments on exchange transactions and generally include sales taxes, income taxes, motor fuel taxes, and similar taxes on earnings or consumption. Imposed nonexchange revenues represent assessments imposed on nongovernmental entities and include property taxes and fines or forfeitures. Government-mandated nonexchange transactions occur when a government at one level provides resources to a government at another level and requires that government to use the resources for a specific purpose. Voluntary nonexchange transactions result from legislative or contractual agreements, but do not involve an exchange of equal value. (7069)

39. (c) Acquisition of a general fixed asset is an expenditure. A capital lease is an other financing source. (4987)

40. (a) General capital assets are not specifically related to activities reported in proprietary or fiduciary funds. They are associated with, and generally arise from, governmental activities. They should **not** be reported as assets in governmental funds, but should be reported in the governmental activities column in the government-wide statement of net assets. (9878)

41. (d) A MSWLF accounted for in a governmental-type fund should recognize expenditures and fund liabilities on the modified accrual basis of accounting, with the long-term capital assets and liabilities reported in the government-wide financial statements, but not the governmental funds. Equipment, facilities, services, and final cover included in the estimated total current cost of closure and postclosure care should be reported as a reduction of the reported liability for closure and postclosure care when they are acquired. (5811)

42. (d) Proprietary funds may account for landfills. Liabilities are recognized in a proprietary fund when a proprietary fund accounts for the landfill. Expense recognition should be finished when the postclosure period begins. Capital assets should be fully depreciated by the date the MSWLF stops accepting solid waste. (6808)

Concept Statements

43. (c) GASB Concepts Statements provide the basic building blocks for the specific accounting reporting standards. Users can study the Concepts Statements to understand unique reporting issues and how the GASB addresses their needs in financial reporting. GASB Interpretations provide additional explanations of GASB Statements and may assist users, but do not explain unique governmental reporting issues. FASB Statements that are applicable to governmental entities were incorporated into the GASB Codification with Statement No. 62, but do not explain the conceptual framework. AICPA Audit Guides are useful implementation guidance for auditors, but may be too technical for most users of governmental financial statements. (89693)

44. (d) The second reporting objective discussed in Concepts Statement No. 1 suggests that governmental financial reporting should assist users in evaluating the government's operating results by explaining sources and uses of financial resources. Cash flow statements are a specific element in proprietary fund statements and are not discussed in Concepts Statement No. 1. Other supplementary information is useful for enhancing financial statements, but is not necessarily required. The management discussion and analysis is one of the components of required supplementary information, but is not discussed in Concepts Statement No. 1. (89695)

45. (d) Comparability, consistency, and timeliness in SEA reporting are readily accomplished for a single governmental entity. Ensuring that reported performance yardsticks measure goals and desired effects is more complex. (6809)

46. (a) Concepts Statement No. 3 describes the importance of the GASB's independence for establishing communication principles in the reporting standards to support governments' credibility and enhance comparability among external financial statements. (2709)

47. (d) Assets, per Concepts Statement No. 4, must provide present service capacity and be controlled by the government. (9004)

48. (a) The SEA Concepts Statements are focused on a reporting framework, not the specifics to include in a SEA report. The GASB hopes the SEA Concepts Statements and the Voluntary Reporting Guidelines will help preparers develop comparable reports that improve the usefulness of SEA reports. The GASB has not established specific reporting or measurement standards for SEA reports. Identification of the appropriate performance data is a management function, not a role for the GASB. (89696)

Limited Scope Topics

49. (c) Governmental employers identify in the notes to the financial statements the types of employees covered under the defined contribution pension plan and the employer's and employees' obligations to contribute to the fund. (3491)

50. (d) The underlying securities owned with regard to reverse repurchase and fixed coupon reverse repurchase agreements should be reported as "Investments." Related assets and liabilities and interest cost and interest earned should not be netted. Credit risk related to such agreements must be disclosed. (4983)

PERFORMANCE BY SUBTOPICS

Each category below parallels a subtopic covered in Chapter 19. Record the number and percentage of questions you correctly answered in each subtopic area.

Introduction

Question #	Correct √
1	
2	
3	
4	
5	
6	
# Questions	6
# Correct	______
% Correct	______

GASB Reporting Model

Question #	Correct √
7	
8	
9	
10	
11	
12	
13	
# Questions	7
# Correct	______
% Correct	______

Government-Wide Statements

Question #	Correct √
14	
15	
16	
17	
18	
19	
20	
21	
22	
23	
# Questions	10
# Correct	______
% Correct	______

Other Financial Statements

Question #	Correct √
24	
25	
26	
27	
28	
29	
30	
31	
32	
33	
34	
35	
# Questions	12
# Correct	______
% Correct	______

Other Recognition Topics

Question #	Correct √
36	
37	
38	
39	
40	
41	
42	
# Questions	7
# Correct	______
% Correct	______

Concept Statements

Question #	Correct √
43	
44	
45	
46	
47	
48	
# Questions	6
# Correct	______
% Correct	______

Limited Scope Topics

Question #	Correct √
49	
50	
# Questions	2
# Correct	______
% Correct	______

Solution 19-2 SIMULATION: General Fund Statements

1.

	Choice
1. An unrestricted state grant is received.	Revenues
2. The general fund paid pension fund contributions that were recoverable from an internal service fund.	Statement of activities is not affected
3. The general fund paid $60,000 for electricity supplied by Shar's electric utility enterprise fund.	Expenditures
4. General fund resources were used to subsidize Shar's swimming pool enterprise fund.	Other financing uses
5. $90,000 of general fund resources were loaned to an internal service fund.	Statement of activities is not affected
6. A motor pool internal service fund was established by a transfer of $80,000 from the general fund. This amount will not be repaid unless the motor pool is disbanded.	Other financing uses
7. General fund resources were used to pay amounts due on an operating lease.	Expenditures

Explanations

1. Unrestricted grants are reported as revenues.

2. The general fund has a receivable due from the internal service fund (ISF).

3. The purchase of goods or services by a governmental-type fund from a proprietary fund are handled like purchases from other vendors.

4. Operating transfers to internal service or enterprise funds are other financing uses.

5. Loans to an internal service fund would be recorded in the general fund and the statement of activities is not affected.

6. A transfer to establish a proprietary fund is a residual equity transfer, which is reported as an other financing use.

7. General fund payments on operating leases are expenditures.

2.

	Choice
8. What was the total committed and nonspendable fund balance of the Year 1 general fund?	$ 79,000
9. What amount was collected from Year 2 tax assessments?	$ 811,000
10. What amount is Shar's liability to general fund vendors and contractors at December 31, Year 2?	$ 89,000
11. What amount should be included in the government-wide statement of net assets in the governmental activities column for capital assets acquired in Year 2 through the general fund?	$ 100,000
12. What amount arising from Year 2 transactions decreased long-term liabilities reported in the government-wide statement of net assets in the governmental activities column?	$ 52,000
13. What amount of total actual expenditures should Shar report in its Year 2 general fund statement of activities?	$ 1,392,000

Explanations

8. The committed fund balance for year 2 year-end is $43,000. The decrease in committed fund balance is $15,000. Working back to year 1 year-end, the year 1 year-end committed fund balance was $43,000 + $15,000 = $58,000. The nonspendable fund balance at year 1 year-end was $21,000. Total nonspendable and committed fund balance has $79,000. ($58,000 + $21,000 = $79,000)

9. As $8,000 was written-off, $845,000 remained to be collected. Of this, $34,000 was uncollected at year-end, meaning $811,000 was collected during the year. The initial property tax entry was as follows:

Property Taxes Receivable	853,000	
Allowance Property Taxes Uncollectible		28,000
Property Tax Revenues		825,000

10. Vouchers payable is $89,000. Encumbrances are not liabilities until the goods or services are provided. Then they are removed from the encumbrances account and recorded in the payable account.

11. The only capital outlay for governmental activities was the purchase of the police vehicles.

12. The total debt service expenditure was $74,000. This amount included interest of $22,000; the rest reduced debt principal. ($74,000 – $22,000 = $52,000)

13. Total actual expenditures for year 2 are the $1,349,000 made in year 2 and the $43,000 that will be made in year 3 for year 2 encumbrances. (6214)

Solution 19-3 SIMULATION: Governmental Revenues & Expenditures

	Amount
1. What was the net effect of the budgetary activities on the general fund balance at January 1 of the current year?	$ 70,000
2. What was the total amount of operating transfers out included in the general fund's budgetary accounts at January 1 of the current year?	$ 430,000
3. What amount of interest payable related to the 20-year bonds should be reported by the general fund at December 31 of the current year?	-0-
4. What lease payment amount should be included in current year general fund expenditures?	$ 10,000
5. What amount was collected from current year property taxes in the current year?	$5,018,000
6. What was the total amount of the capital project fund's current year revenues?	$ 450,000
7. What amount should be reported as long-term liabilities in the government-wide statement of net assets in the governmental activities column at December 31 of the current year?	$ 868,000
8. What net increase in capital assets should be reported in the government-wide statement of net assets in the governmental activities column at December 31 of the current year?	$1,580,000
9. What current year closure and postclosure care expenses should be reported in the solid waste landfill enterprise fund?	$ 107,000
10. What should be the December 31 current year closure and post closure care liability reported in the solid waste landfill enterprise fund?	$ 780,000

Explanations

1. The general fund budgetary entry is as follows:

Estimated Revenues	8,000,000	
Budgetary Fund Balance		70,000
Appropriations		7,500,000
Est. Other Financing Uses (capital proj.)		250,000
Est. Other Financing Uses (enter. fund)		180,000

2. ($250,000 + $180,000 = $430,000) Also see the explanation to #1.

3. Interest is recorded when due.

4. The full $10,000 lease payment amount should be included in general fund expenditures. In total, $78,000 would be debited in the general fund. The other $68,000 would be credited to Other Financing Sources—Capital Leases in the general fund.

5. Because the December 31 balance of $56,000 was closed and a delinquent receivables account was established for only $38,000, $18,000 must have been collected. (The $4,000 difference between $60,000 and $56,000 was written off during the year.) The estimate for uncollectible taxes was not increased, so apparently the full $5,000,000 of the original entry was collected. ($5,000,000 + $56,000 – $38,000 = $5,018,000) The original entry to record property taxes is:

Property tax receivable	5,060,000	
Allowance for estimated uncollectible taxes		60,000
Property tax revenue		5,000,000

6. The state entitlements are revenues. The general fund money and debt proceeds are Other Financing Source, not revenue.

7. The amount of the principal on the bonds ($800,000) plus the net present value of $68,000 for the capital lease (not counting the $10,000 payment already made) are included.

8. The courthouse improvements ($1,527,000), police car retirement ($25,000), and office equipment acquisition ($78,000) all had an impact on the capital assets amount. The $7,000 paid for the car would not affect the capital assets.

9.

Usage to date (in cubic yards)	540,000
Divided by: Total capacity	÷ 1,000,000
Equals: Capacity used to date (percentage)	54%
Times: Est. closure & postclosure costs	×$2,000,000
Total to be recognized to date	1,080,000
Total previously recognized	973,000
Current year recognition	$ 107,000

10.

Total to be recognized to date	$1,080,000
Total incurred to date	300,000
Closure & postclosure liability	$ 780,000

(6317)

Solution 19-4 SIMULATION: Governmental Fund Reporting

	Amount
1. What was the amount recorded in the opening entry for appropriations?	$5,600,000
2. What was the total amount debited to property taxes receivable?	$4,750,000
3. What was the completed cost of the civic center?	$2,473,000
4. How much was the state capital grant for the civic center?	$ 800,000
5. In the capital project fund, what was the amount of the total encumbrances recorded during the year?	$2,422,000
6. In the capital project fund, what was the assigned fund balance reported at December 31?	$ 120,000

Explanations

1. The appropriations constitute maximum expenditure authorizations during the fiscal year.

2.

2. The total amount debited to property taxes receivable is the actual amount of property taxes. The entry to record property taxes is:

Property taxes receivable	4,750,000	
Allowance for estimated uncollectible taxes		50,000
Property tax revenue		4,700,000

3. The total cost of the project is calculated as follows:

Revenues	$ 800,000
Bond proceeds	1,230,000
Less: Transfer to debt service fund	(30,000)
Operating transfers in	500,000
Less: Transfer to general fund at close	(27,000)
Total cost of project	$2,473,000

4. Grants from another government for a capital project are recorded as deferred revenues in the capital project fund until expended for the project and are then transferred to a revenue account for the remainder of the construction period. Since the state grant is the only grant involved in the project, the amount of the state grant must be the balance in the revenues account at the end of the project life.

5. The total expenditures in the year were $1,080,000, and the related encumbrances were greater by $42,000. To calculate the total encumbrances, add to this sum the unpaid encumbrances of $1,300,000. [($1,080,000 + $42,000) + $1,300,000 = $2,422,000]

6. The fund balance is affected by the opening and closing budget entries and the (actual) closing entries. The illustrated closing entry has a $1,420,000 credit entry to assigned fund balance. Since there is no opening balance and the budget entries are equal in amount and opposite in direction, the combined closing entry amounts are also the ending balance. (**NOTE:** $1,420,000 – $1,300,000 = $120,000) The illustrated closing entry omits the following entry.

Assigned Fund Balance	1,300,000	
Committed Fund Balance		1,300,000

(5479)

CHAPTER 20

NONPROFIT ACCOUNTING

CHAPTER 20

NONPROFIT ACCOUNTING

I. Standard Nonprofit Accounting

A. Concepts

The fundamental presumption used by the FASB in developing financial reporting standards for (non-governmental) nonprofit organizations (NPO) is that the financial reporting practices of non-profit entities should be the same as those for commercial entities.

1. **Standards** There is a parallel hierarchy where non-governmental nonprofit entities are subject to the FASB rather than the GASB standards. The FASB requires nonprofit entities to provide financial statements on an entity-wide basis similar to the concept of consolidated statements for business entities.

2. **Fund Accounting** Use of fund accounting for nonprofit organizations is allowed but not required. Disaggregated financial statements, common with fund accounting, are insufficient by themselves. This relegates fund statements to a supplementary role for external reporting purposes. [Expect the majority of CPA exam points on NPOs to be in areas other than fund accounting.] NPOs generally do not use budgetary and encumbrance accounting.

B. Definitions

1. **Contribution** Contributions are unconditional transfers of cash or other assets to an entity or a settlement or cancellation of its liabilities in a voluntary nonreciprocal transfer by another entity acting other than as an owner. Other assets include, securities, land, buildings, use of facilities or utilities, materials and supplies, intangible assets, services (within certain limited circumstances), and unconditional promises to give those items in the future.

2. **Conditional Promise to Give** Also called a pledge. A written or oral agreement to contribute cash or other assets to another entity that depends on the occurrence of a specified future and uncertain event to bind the promisor. However, to be recognized in financial statements there must be sufficient evidence in the form of verifiable documentation that a promise was made and received. A conditional promise to give is considered unconditional if the possibility that the condition will not be met is remote. Conditional pledges are not recorded until they become unconditional.

3. **Unconditional Promise to Give** A written or oral agreement to make a contribution that depends only on passage of time or demand by the promisee for performance. It may be difficult to determine whether donor stipulations are conditions or restrictions. In cases of ambiguous donor stipulations, a promise containing stipulations that are not clearly unconditional shall be presumed to be a conditional promise. A communication that does not indicate clearly whether it is a promise is considered an unconditional promise to give if it indicates an unconditional intention to give that is legally enforceable.

4. **Donor-Imposed Condition** A donor stipulation on a transfer of assets or promise to give that specifies a future and uncertain event whose occurrence or failure to occur gives the promisor a right of return of the assets transferred or releases the promisor from its obligation to transfer assets promised.

5. **Donor-Imposed Restriction** A donor stipulation that limits the use of contributed assets. It specifies a use for the contributed asset that is more specific than the broad limits of the organization. A restriction on an organization's use of the asset contributed may be temporary or permanent.

6. **Permanent Restriction** A donor-imposed restriction that stipulates that resources be maintained permanently but permits the organization to use up or expend part or all of the income (or other economic benefits) derived from the donated assets.

7. **Temporary Restriction** A donor-imposed restriction that will lapse upon occurrence of conditions specified by the donor. The principal of a temporary endowment or donation may be used after the conditions of the restriction are fulfilled. The allowable use of the income of a temporarily restricted asset may also be restricted by the terms of the donation.

8. **Unrestricted Assets** The assets from donations unrestricted by the donors, and assets formerly temporarily restricted by the donors that have since become unrestricted. Unrestricted assets include board-restricted assets.

9. **Board-Restricted** The governing board of an entity may earmark assets for specific purposes as long as these do not conflict with donor conditions. These assets may be designated board-restricted in the financial statements, but they remain in the unrestricted category.

10. **Endowment Fund** A fund of assets to provide support for the activities of a not-for-profit organization. Endowment funds are typically composed of donor-restricted gifts to provide a permanent source of support. However, use of the fund assets may also be temporarily restricted or unrestricted.

C. Contributions

Accounting for contributions is important because for many NPOs contributions are a significant source of revenue.

1. **Contributions Received** Generally, contributions received are measured at their fair values and recognized as revenues or gains in the period received and as assets, decreases of liabilities, or expenses depending on the form of the benefits received. They shall be reported as restricted support or unrestricted support.

2. **Contributed Services** Contributions of services are measured at their fair values and recognized as revenues for the period only if (a) nonfinancial assets are created or enhanced, or (b) special skills are required, are provided by individuals possessing those skills, and would typically otherwise need to be purchased if not provided by donation. Services requiring specialized skills are provided by accountants, architects, carpenters, doctors, electricians, lawyers, nurses, plumbers, teachers, and other professionals and craftsmen.

3. **Contributed Collection Items** Contributed collection items are recognized as revenues or gains if collections are capitalized and not recognized as revenues or gains if collections are not capitalized. An entity need not recognize contributions of works of art, historical treasures, and similar assets if the donated items are added to collections that meet all of the following conditions:

   a. Are held for public exhibition, education, or research in furtherance of public service rather than financial gain

   b. Are protected, kept unencumbered, cared for, and preserved

   c. Are subject to an organizational policy that requires the proceeds from sales of collection items to be used to acquire other items for collections.

4. **Classification** Contributions are classified as gains when they are peripheral or incidental to the activities of the entity. However, they are classified as revenue in those circumstances in which these sources are deemed to be ongoing major or central activities by which the provider attempts to fulfill its basic function. For example, donor's contributions are revenues if fund-raising is an ongoing major activity by which the provider attempts to fulfill its basic function. The same donations, however, would be a gain to a provider that does not actively seek contributions and receives them only occasionally.

5. **Reporting** NPOs must distinguish between contributions received with permanent restrictions, those received with temporary restrictions, and those received without donor-imposed restrictions. A restriction on the use of the assets contributed results either from a donor's explicit stipulation or from circumstances surrounding the receipt of the contribution that make clear the donor's implicit restriction on use.

   a. Contributions with donor-imposed restrictions are reported as restricted support; however, if those restrictions are met in the same reporting period they may be reported as unrestricted support. Restricted support increases permanently restricted net assets or temporarily restricted net assets.

   b. Contributions without donor-imposed restrictions are reported as unrestricted support that increases unrestricted net assets.

   c. The expiration of a donor-imposed restriction on a contribution must be recognized in the period in which the restriction expires. A restriction expires when the stipulated time has elapsed, when the stipulated purpose for which the resource was restricted has been fulfilled, or both. Expirations of donor-imposed restrictions that simultaneously increase one class of net assets and decrease another (reclassifications) are reported separately from other transactions.

   d. Contributed services are reported as both an expense and a revenue if (1) the services would otherwise be purchased; (2) the value of the services is measurable; and (3) the entity controls the employment and duties of the service donors (i.e., there is the equivalent of an employer-employee relationship).

   e. Receipts of unconditional promises to give, or pledges, are reported as a receivable at their present value in the period in which they are made, net of an allowance for uncollectible amounts. Unrestricted pledges are reported in the statement of revenue and expenses. If part of the pledge is to be applied during some future period, that part is reported as restricted revenue.

   f. Receipts of unconditional promises, or pledges, to give with payments due in future periods shall be reported as restricted support unless explicit donor stipulations or circumstances make clear that the donor intended it to be used to support activities of the current period. A pledge to give in the future has an implied restriction for future use. Receipts of pledges to give cash in future years generally increase temporarily restricted net assets.

   g. An entity that capitalizes its collections prospectively shall report proceeds from sales and insurance recoveries of items not previously capitalized separately from revenues, expenses, gains, and losses.

   h. An entity that does not recognize and capitalize its collections shall report the following on the face of its statement of activities, separately from revenues, expenses, gains, and losses; costs of collection items purchased as a decrease in the appropriate class of net assets, proceeds from sale of collection items as an increase in the appropriate class of net assets, and proceeds from insurance recoveries of lost or destroyed collection items as an increase in the appropriate class of net assets.

6. **Long-Lived Assets** Donations of property and equipment, or of assets to acquire property and equipment, may be initially reported as restricted gain or revenue. A transfer to the unrestricted net assets is reported when the donated property or equipment is placed in service, or when the donated assets are used to acquire property and equipment. If the entity recognizes an implicit restriction in the donation (to be used for the life of the asset, for instance), then the transfer is to the restricted net assets.

   a. Gifts of long-lived assets received without stipulations about how long the donated asset must be used shall be reported as restricted support if it is an organization's accounting policy to imply a time restriction that expires over the useful life of the donated assets. The policy would also imply a time restriction on long-lived assets acquired with gifts of cash or other assets restricted for those acquisitions.

   b. In the absence of a policy to imply a time restriction that expires over the useful life of long-lived donated assets and other donor-imposed restrictions on use of an asset, gifts of long-lived assets shall be reported as unrestricted support.

   c. If unrestricted, report any assets other than long-lived assets as operating gains or revenue or nonoperating gains depending on whether the donations constitute the entity's ongoing major or central operations or are peripheral and incidental to the entity's operations. If restricted, report as restricted gain or revenue.

7. **Contributions Made** Contributions made shall be recognized as expenses in the period made and as decreases of assets or increases of liabilities depending on the form of the benefits given. For example, gifts of items from inventory held for sale are recognized as decreases of inventory and contribution expenses, and unconditional promises to give cash are recognized as payables and contribution expenses. Contributions made shall be measured at the fair values of the assets given or, if made in the form of a settlement or cancellation of a donee's liabilities, at the fair value of the liabilities canceled.

Exhibit 1 ▸ Sample Donation Entries

1.	To record gifts, bequests, and donations received:		
	Cash (or other assets)	XX	
	Nonoperating Gains—(Unrestricted) Contributions		XX
	Liabilities (if any are assumed)		XX
	(Restricted) Revenue		XX
	NOTE: Unrestricted gifts, bequests, and donations are recorded as nonoperating gains, generally. If restricted, they are recorded as permanently or temporarily restricted revenue in the appropriate donor-restricted fund.		
2.	To record donations (to a hospital) of pharmacy supplies and professional services:		
	Inventory of Pharmacy Supplies	XX	
	Operating Expenses (functional expense accounts)	XX	
	Contributions—Donated Pharmacy Supplies		XX
	Contributions—Donated Professional Services		XX
	NOTE: Report the contributions as operating gains or revenue or nonoperating gains depending on whether the donation constitutes the entity's major or central operations or are peripheral and incidental to the entity's operations.		

8. **Disclosures**

   a. Recipients of unconditional promises to give shall disclose the amounts of promises receivable in less than one year, in one to five years, and in more than five years. They shall also disclose the amount of the allowance for uncollectible promises receivable.

   b. Recipients of conditional promises to give shall disclose the total of the amounts promised. They shall also disclose a description and amount for each group of promises having similar characteristics, such as amounts of promises conditioned on establishing new programs, completing a new building, and raising matching gifts by a specified date.

   c. Entities that adopt a policy to imply a time restriction that expires over the useful life of donated long-lived assets must disclose that accounting policy.

   d. An entity that receives contributed services shall describe the programs or activities for which those services were used, including the nature and extent of contributed services received for the period and the amount recognized as revenues for the period. Entities are encouraged to disclose the fair value of contributed services received but not recognized as revenues if that is practicable.

   e. An entity that does not recognize and capitalize its collections, or that capitalizes collections prospectively, shall describe its collections to include their relative significance and its accounting and stewardship policies for collections. If collection items not capitalized are deaccessed during the period, it also shall (1) describe those items given away, damaged, destroyed, lost, or otherwise deaccessed during the period or (2) disclose their fair value. In addition, a line item shall be shown on the face of the statement of financial position that refers to these disclosures.

9. **Intermediary Transactions** When a nonprofit organization (NPO) receives assets in a nonexchange transaction from a resource provider, with the proviso that the assets be redistributed to another specific organization (or ultimate recipient) chosen by the resource provider, the NPO intermediary is functioning as an agent. However, if the NPO has some discretion as the timing, manner, and recipient of the assets, the NPO intermediary may then be either an agent for the resource provider or a donee. The degree of discretion exercised by the NPO intermediary determines the classification of the event as a donation or as an agency transaction.

Exhibit 2 ▸ Some Guidelines for Separating Donations From Agency Transactions

Attribute	Donation Status	Agency Status
NPO's assertions when requesting donations.	Requests assets to provide for own activities.	Requests assets to provide for others or is not much involved in requesting assets.
Composition of assets	Changes while NPO holds assets (Land received, cash redistributed).	Assets redistributed in same composition. (Land received, land redistributed).
Legal title to assets.	NPO holds legal title.	NPO doesn't hold legal title.
Intent of transfer.	NPO commonly has programs that the assets are intended to support.	NPO doesn't commonly have programs that the assets are intended to support.
Donor awareness.	Providers unaware of ultimate recipient.	Providers are aware of ultimate recipient.
Type of NPO operation.	NPO has programs.	NPO exists to collect and redistribute assets.

D. Contributions for Others

The following applies to contributions for others and also to transactions that are not contributions because the transfers are revocable, repayable, or reciprocal.

1. Definitions

a. A not-for profit entity or charitable trust that accepts assets from donors and agrees to use those assets on behalf of, or transfer those assets to, another entity specified by the donor. This transfer of assets includes the assets, the return on investment of those assets, or both.

b. A financially interrelated organization has the ability to influence the operating and financial decisions of another entity, and one entity has an ongoing economic interest in the net assets of the other.

2. **Recipient** A recipient that accepts assets from a donor on behalf of a specified beneficiary recognizes the fair value of those assets as a liability concurrent with the recognition of the assets. If the donor explicitly gives the recipient variance power or if the recipient and the specified beneficiary are financially interrelated entities, the recipient instead recognizes the transaction as a contribution. Four circumstances exist in which a transfer of assets by a donor is recognized by the recipient as a liability and by the donor as an asset.

   a. The transfer is subject to the donor's unilateral right to redirect the use of the assets to another beneficiary.

   b. The transfer is accompanied by the donor's conditional promise to give or is otherwise revocable or repayable.

   c. The donor controls the recipient and specifies an unaffiliated beneficiary.

   d. The donor specifies itself or its affiliate as the beneficiary and the transfer is not an equity transaction.

3. **Beneficiary** A specified beneficiary recognizes rights to assets held by a recipient as an asset (either an interest in the net assets of the recipient, a beneficial interest, or a receivable) unless the donor has explicitly granted variance power to the recipient.

   a. If the beneficiary and the recipient are financially interrelated entities, the beneficiary recognizes an interest in the net assets of the recipient, adjusting that interest for its share of the change in the recipient's net assets.

   b. If the beneficiary has an unconditional right to specified cash flows from a charitable trust or other identifiable pool of assets, the beneficiary is required to recognize that beneficial interest, at fair value as of the transaction date and reporting dates.

   c. If the recipient is explicitly granted variance power, the specified beneficiary doesn't recognize an asset.

   d. In all other circumstances, a beneficiary recognizes its rights as a receivable.

4. **Equity Transaction** If the transfer is an equity transaction and the donor specifies itself as beneficiary, the donor records an interest in the net assets of the recipient. If the donor specifies an affiliate as beneficiary, the donor records an equity transaction as a separate line item in its statement of activities, and the beneficiary records an interest in the net assets of the recipient entity. The recipient entity records an equity transaction as a separate line item in its statement of activities.

5. **Disclosures** If an NPO transfers assets to a recipient and specifies itself or an affiliate as beneficiary or if it includes a ratio of fundraising expenses to amount raised in its financial statements, the NPO must make the following disclosures for each period that it presents a statement of financial position:

   a. Recipient identity.

   b. Whether variance power was granted to the recipient and the terms of any variance power.

   c. The distribution conditions.

   d. The classification (as a beneficial interest or an interest in the net assets of the recipient, etc.) and aggregate amount recognized in the statement of financial position for these transfers.

E. Investments

The following applies to all investments in debt securities and to investments in equity securities that have a readily determinable market value for all nonprofit organizations. It does not apply to investments in equity securities accounted for under the equity method, or that are consolidated.

1. **Applicability** Fair value of equity securities is deemed to be readily determinable if any of the following conditions are met:

   a. Sales prices or bid-and-ask quotations are available on an exchange which is registered with the SEC or where over-the-counter quotations are officially reported.

   b. For securities traded in a foreign market, the market must be of breadth and scope to make it comparable to a U.S. market which meets the condition just mentioned.

   c. For mutual funds, the fair value per share or unit is determined and published, and represents the basis for current transactions.

2. **Valuation** All applicable investments are required to be measured at fair value. Gains and losses on the investments are included in the statement of activities as increases and decreases, respectively, in unrestricted net assets unless the use of the securities is temporarily or permanently restricted.

3. **Investment Income** Any dividends, interest, or other investment income are to be included in the statement of activities as earned. Such amounts would be reported as adjustments to unrestricted net assets unless some restriction exists.

4. **Disclosures**

   a. Composition of the investment return including investment income, net realized gains or losses on investments reported at other than fair value, and net gains or losses on investments reported at fair value.

   b. A reconciliation of investment return to amounts reported in the statement of activities, if investment return is separated into operating and nonoperating amounts, together with a description of the policy used to determine the amount included in the measure of operations and a discussion of circumstances leading to a change in the policy.

   c. Aggregate carrying amount of the investment by major types.

   d. Basis for determining the carrying amount for investments.

   e. Methods and significant assumptions used to estimate the fair values of investments other than financial instruments, if those other investments are reported at fair value.

f. Aggregate amount of the deficiencies for all donor-restricted endowment funds for which the fair value of the assets at the reporting date is less than the level required by donor stipulations or law.

g. The nature and carrying amount of each individual investment group which represents a significant concentration of market risk.

F. Intangibles

Recognized intangible assets need to be amortized over their useful lives unless NPO entities have made the determination that they are indefinite-lived intangible assets. When intangible assets have finite lives, but the precise length of the lives are not determinable, the assets need to be amortized over the best estimate of those lives. Some examples that might be in play for NPO entities are discussed below.

1. **Acquired Lists for Fund-Raising Purposes** An NPO acquires lists of potential donors and expects that it will be able to receive benefits from that information for at least one year, but no more than three years; the best estimate as to how long the list can be used without being updated is 18 months. Since the best estimate is that the fund-raising list will be beneficial without being updated for a period of 18 months, that 18 month period would be the period of time over which the asset would be amortized.

2. **Acquired Patent** An NPO entity acquires a patent that expires in 15 years, and the patented item is expected to be a source of cash flows for at least 15 years. The entity has secured a commitment from a third party to purchase the patent in 5 years for 60% of the value of the patent at the date it was acquired. Further, the entity intends to sell the patent at that point. The acquired patent would need to be amortized over the 5-year useful life of the entity following the pattern that benefits are expected to be consumed or otherwise used. The amount that will be subject to amortization is 40% of the value of the patent at the acquisition date in that there is a commitment to acquire the patent for 60% of that value which would constitute the residual value.

G. Related Organizations

A foundation, auxiliary, or guild is considered to be related to a nonprofit entity if one of the following conditions is met:

1. The nonprofit entity controls the separate organization through contracts or other legal documents that provide the entity with the authority to direct the separate organization's activities, management, and policies.

2. The nonprofit entity is considered to be the sole beneficiary of the organization because one of the three following circumstances exists:

   a. The organization has solicited funds in the name of the nonprofit entity and substantially all of the funds were intended by the contributor to be transferred to or used by the nonprofit entity.

   b. The nonprofit entity has transferred some of the resources to the organization, and substantially all of the organization's resources are held for the benefit of the entity.

   c. The entity has assigned certain of its functions (e.g., the operation of a dormitory) to the organization, which is operating primarily for the benefit of the entity.

3. The nonprofit entity, upon liquidation of the group, is liable for any deficit or due the net assets of the group transfers.

H. Consolidations

Nonprofit entities need to consolidate other nonprofit entities when controlling financial interests exist through direct or indirect ownership of a majority voting interest. Nonprofit entities also need to consolidate other nonprofit entities when the reporting nonprofit entities have both control of the other entities, as evidenced by either majority ownership or majority voting interests in the boards of the other nonprofit entities, and economic interests in the other entities.

Economic interests might include the following:

1. Other entities solicit funds in the name of, and with the expressed or implied approval of, the reporting entity, and substantially all of the funds solicited are intended by contributors or are otherwise required to be transferred to reporting entities or used at their discretion or direction.

2. Reporting entities transfer significant resources to other entities and the resources are held for the benefit of the reporting entities.

3. Reporting entities assign significant functions to other entities.

4. Reporting entities provide, or are committed to provide, funds to other entities, or guarantees of significant debts of those entities

Nonprofit entities may exercise control of other nonprofit entities when economic interests exist by means other than majority ownership or majority voting interests in the boards of the other organizations. In these circumstances, nonprofit entities are permitted, but not required, to consolidate the other entities. If consolidated statements are not presented, nonprofit reporting entities need to incorporate specific financial statement disclosures to address these issues.

I. Mergers and Acquisitions

While all business combinations undertaken by for-profit entities are accounted for using the acquisition method, NPO entities need to address whether the acquisition method is appropriate for use or whether combinations need to be reflected in financial statements as mergers. Many mergers and acquisition by nonprofits do not involve a transfer of consideration; they are not fair value exchanges but rather reciprocal transfers.

An *acquisition* by an NPO entity is a combination where one NPO entity obtains control of one or more activities or businesses. In these circumstances, the acquisition method should be used in reflecting the combination in the financial statements. Conversely, a *merger* is a combination where governing bodies of two or more NPO entities cede control of those entities to create a new NPO entity. To that end, it is important to note that the creation of the new NPO entity results in a new governing body for the entity, but there is no requirement, although it often is the case, for a new legal entity to be formed.

1. **Merger** The nonprofit entity resulting from a merger shall account for the merger by applying the carryover method. Under the carryover method, the combined entity's initial set of financial statements carry forward the assets and liabilities of the combining entities, measured at their carrying amounts in the books of the combining entities at the merger date.

   a. An entity applying the carryover method recognizes neither additional assets or liabilities nor changes in the fair value of recognized assets and liabilities not already recognized in the combining entities' financial statements before the merger under GAAP. If a merging entity's separate financial statements are not prepared in accordance with GAAP, those statements shall be adjusted to GAAP before the new entity recognizes the assets and liabilities.

b. The new entity shall carry forward into the opening balances in its financial statements the merging entities' classifications and designations unless either (1) the merger results in a modification of a contract in a manner that would change those previous classifications or designations or (2) reclassifications are necessary to conform accounting policies.

c. The merging entities may have measured assets and liabilities using different methods of accounting in their separate financial statements. The new entity shall adjust the amounts of those assets and liabilities as necessary to reflect a consistent method of accounting.

d. The new entity shall eliminate the effects of any intraentity transactions on its assets, liabilities, and net assets as of the merger date.

e. The entity resulting from a merger is a new reporting entity, with no activities before the date of the merger. The new entity's initial reporting period begins with the merger date and the merger itself is not reported as activity of the initial reporting period.

f. The new entity shall disclose information that enables users of its financial statements to evaluate the nature and financial effect of the merger that resulted in its formation. It shall include, at a minimum, the following:

   (1) The name and description of each merging entity

   (2) The merger date

   (3) The primary reasons for the merger

   (4) For each merging entity, the amounts recognized as of the merger date for each major class of assets and liabilities and each class of net assets

   (5) For each merging entity, the nature and amounts of any significant assets or liabilities that GAAP does not require to be recognized

   (6) The nature and amount of any significant adjustments made to conform the individual accounting policies of the merging entities or to eliminate intraentity balances

   (7) If the new entity is a public entity, supplemental pro forma information

2. **Acquisition** When the acquisition method is used by NPO entities, the primary difference in the guidance relates to the recognition of goodwill. Additional guidance exists for items unique to nonprofit entities and the elimination of guidance that does not apply to a nonprofit acquirer.

   a. Generally, when NPO entities operate in a business-like fashion, information related to goodwill acquired in a combination is considered to be useful to users of financial statements. Conversely, information about goodwill may be of limited use to donors in making their assessments as to whether to provide resources to NPO entities. As such, guidance requires acquirer entities that operate in a more business-like manner to recognize goodwill when it exists; conversely, those that are solely or predominately supported by contributions would recognize amounts that otherwise would be recorded as goodwill as a separate charge in the statement of activities as of the acquisition date.

While the accounting requirements for goodwill differ significantly depending on the type NPO entity, there is no expectation that the goodwill issue will arise very often in practice in that most acquisitions involving NPO entities are *not* full fair value exchanges. In fact, in most cases, measurements used in NPO acquisitions will relate to measuring the fair values of the underlying net assets acquired so that there is no goodwill that even needs to be considered in the acquisitions.

b. Some nonprofit entities are solely or predominantly supported by contributions and returns on investments. An acquirer that expects to be predominantly supported by contributions and returns on investments shall recognize as a separate charge in its statement of activities the amount that would otherwise be recognized as goodwill at the acquisition date. Also, many acquisitions by nonprofit entities constitute an inherent contribution received because the acquirer receives net assets without transferring consideration. The acquirer recognizes such a contribution received as a separate credit in its statement of activities on the acquisition date.

c. As of the acquisition date, the acquirer shall recognize, separately from goodwill, the identifiable assets acquired, the liabilities assumed, and any noncontrolling interest (whether a business or another nonprofit) in the acquiree.

d. At the acquisition date, the acquirer shall classify or designate the identifiable assets acquired and liabilities assumed as necessary to subsequently apply other GAAP. Those classifications or designations shall be made on the basis of contractual terms, economic conditions, and operating or accounting policies as they exist at the acquisition date.

e. The acquirer shall measure the identifiable assets acquired, the liabilities assumed, and any noncontrolling interest in the acquiree at their acquisition-date fair values.

f. The following are some exceptions particular to nonprofit entities:

(1) The acquirer shall not recognize an acquired donor relationship as an identifiable asset separately from goodwill

(2) An acquirer that has an organizational policy of not capitalizing collections shall not recognize as an asset those items (works of art, historical treasures, or similar assets) that it acquires as part of an acquisition and adds to its collection

(3) An acquirer shall recognize a conditional promise only if the conditions on which it depends are substantially met as of the acquisition date

(4) An acquirer shall recognize a transfer of assets with a conditional promise to contribute them as a refundable advance unless the conditions have been substantially met as of the acquisition date

g. The financial statements of the acquirer, the combined entity, shall report an acquisition as activity of the period in which it occurs.

h. The acquirer shall disclose information that enables users of its financial statements to evaluate the nature and financial effect of an acquisition that occurs either during the current reporting period or after the reporting period but before the financial statements are issued or are available to be issued. It shall include, at a minimum, the following:

(1) The name and a description of the acquiree

(2) The acquisition date

(3) If applicable, the percentage of ownership interests, such as voting equity instruments, acquired

(4) The primary reasons for the acquisition and a description of how the acquirer obtained control of the acquiree

(5) The acquisition-date fair value of the total consideration transferred (or if no consideration was transferred, that fact) and the acquisition-date fair value of each major class of consideration

II. Financial Statements

A. Introduction

Nonprofit organizations are required to present at least three statements; a Statement of Financial Position, a Statement of Activities, and a Statement of Cash Flows. The statements exhibited in this section are similar to those used by a commercial entity. Some entities may choose to also disclose the fund statements. Several formats are acceptable for nonprofit entities, however, *aggregated* statements must be used.

B. Statement of Financial Position

Entities report assets, liabilities, and net assets in this statement. Entities are required to classify net assets based upon the existence or absence of donor-imposed restrictions. Thus, net assets are classified into at least three categories: permanently restricted, temporarily restricted, and unrestricted. Assets are arranged by relative liquidity. Assets restricted to a particular use assume the liquidity of that use. For instance, cash and marketable securities restricted for the purchase of property, plant, and equipment (PPE) are presented below inventories.

Exhibit 3 ▸ Statement of Financial Position

Name of Nonprofit Entity
Statement of Financial Position
December 31, Year 2

Assets:		Liabilities:	
Cash	$ 38	Accounts Payable	$ 1,285
Contributions Receivable	1,512	Grants Payable	438
Accounts Receivable	1,065	Annuity Obligation	842
Marketable Securities	700	Bonds Payable	2,750
Inventory	300	Total Liabilities	$ 5,315
Prepaid Expenses	5	Net Assets	
Assets Restricted to Investment:		Unrestricted	$ 57,614
PPE	2,605	Temporarily Restricted	12,171
Property, Plant, and Equipment	30,850	Permanently Restricted	71,010
Long-Term Investments	109,035	Total Net Assets	140,795
Total Assets	$ 146,110	Total Liabilities and Net Assets	$ 146,110

C. Statement of Activities

This statement is similar to a for-profit entity's income statement. Its primary purpose is to provide relevant information about the effects of transactions and other events that change the amount and nature of net assets, the relationships of those transactions and other events to each other, and how the organization's resources are used in providing various programs or services. It should focus on the organization as a whole and report the amount of the change in net assets for the period.

1. **Sequence** This statement is presented in the following sequence: Revenues and Other Additions; Expenditures and Other Deductions; Transfers Among Funds; Net Increase (Decrease) in Net Assets; Net Assets—Beginning of Year; and Net Assets—End of Year.

2. **Changes in Classes** It reports the amount of change in permanently restricted net assets, temporarily restricted net assets, and unrestricted net assets for the period.

3. **Revenues, Expenses, Gains and Losses** The revenues, gains, and losses are classified into the three classes (unrestricted, temporarily restricted, and permanently restricted). Other events, such as expirations of donor-imposed restrictions, that simultaneously increase one class of net assets and decrease another (reclassifications) shall be reported as separate items. All expenses are reported as decreases in unrestricted net assets.

4. **Gross Amounts** To help explain the relationships of a not-for-profit organization's ongoing major or central operations and activities, a statement of activities shall report the gross amounts of revenues and expenses. However, investment revenues may be reported net of related expenses, such as custodial fees and investment advisory fees, provided that the amount of the expenses is disclosed either on the face of the statement of activities or in notes to financial statements.

5. **Net Amounts** A statement of activities may report gains and losses as net amounts if they result from peripheral or incidental transactions or from other events and circumstances that may be largely beyond the control of the organization and its management. Information about their net amounts, used with statement of cash flows information, generally is adequate enough to understand the organization's activities.

6. **Service Efforts** To help donors, creditors, and others in assessing an organization's service efforts, including the costs of its services and how it uses resources, a statement of activities or notes to financial statements shall provide information about expenses reported by their **functional classification** such as major classes of program services and supporting activities.

7. **Program Services** These are the activities that result in goods and services being distributed to beneficiaries, customers, or members that fulfill the purposes or mission for which the organization exists. For example, a university may have programs for student instruction, research, and patient care, among others. Similarly, a health and welfare organization may have programs.

8. **Supporting Activities** These are the activities of a not-for-profit organization other than program services. Generally, they include management and general, fund-raising, and membership-development activities.

   a. Management and general activities include oversight, business management, general recordkeeping, budgeting, financing, and related administrative activities, and all management and administration except for direct conduct of program services or fund-raising activities.

   b. Fund-raising activities include publicizing and conducting fund-raising campaigns; maintaining donor mailing lists; conducting special fund-raising events; preparing and distributing fund-raising manuals, instructions, and other materials; and conducting other activities involved with soliciting contributions from individuals, foundations, government agencies, and others.

   c. Membership-development activities include soliciting for prospective members and membership dues, membership relations, and similar activities.

Exhibit 4 ▸ Statement of Activities

Name of Nonprofit Entity
Statement of Activities
Year Ending December 31, Year 2

	Total	Unrestricted	Temporarily Restricted	Permanently Restricted
Revenues and Gains:				
Contributions	$ 8,515	$ 4,320	$ 4,055	$ 140
Services Fees	2,700	2,700		
Investment Income	4,575	3,225	1,290	60
Net Unrealized and Realized Gains on Long-Term Investments	7,900	4,114	1,476	2,310
Other	75	75		
Net Assets Released From Restrictions:				
Expiration of Time Requirements		5,995	(5,995)	
Fulfilled Conditions of Equipment Acquisition		750	(750)	
Fulfilled Conditions of Program Services		625	(625)	
Total Revenues, Gains, and Other Support	$ 23,765	$21,804	$ (549)	$ 2,510
Expenses and Losses:				
Program Expenses	$ 13,700	$13,700		
Administration Expenses	1,210	1,210		
Fund-raising Expenses	1,075	1,075		
Loss on Sale of Equipment	40	40		
Actuarial Loss on Annuity Obligations	15		15	
Total Expenses and Losses	$ 16,040	$16,025	$ 15	$ 0
Change in Net Assets (or change in equity)	$ 7,725	$ 5,779	$ (564)	$ 2,510
Net Assets at December 31, Year 1	133,070	51,835	12,735	68,500
Net Assets at December 31, Year 2	$140,795	$57,614	$12,171	$71,010

D. Statement of Activities Alternative Two-Part Format

The statement of activities may be divided into two parts. The statements exhibited in this section are what an entity using optional fund accounting might present. See Exhibits 5 and 6.

1. **Statement of Unrestricted Revenues, Expenses, and Other Changes in Unrestricted Net Assets** The first part of the Statement of Activities is based on the operation of the General Funds. It may also be named Statement of Operations.

Exhibit 5 ▸ Statement of Activities: Part 1

Name of Nonprofit Entity
Statement of Unrestricted Revenue, Expenses, and Other Changes in Unrestricted Net Assets
Year Ending December 31, Year 2

Unrestricted Revenues and Gains:		
Contributions	$ 4,320	
Service Fees	2,700	
Investment Income	3,225	
Net Unrealized and Realized Gains on Long-Term Investments	4,114	
Investment Income	75	
Net Assets Released From Restrictions:		
Expiration of Time Requirements	5,995	
Fulfilled Conditions of Equipment Acquisition	750	
Fulfilled Conditions of Program Services	625	
Total Unrestricted Revenues, Gains, and Other Support		$21,804
Expenses and Losses:		
Program Expenses	13,700	
Administration Expenses	1,210	
Fund-raising Expenses	1,075	
Loss on Sale of Equipment	40	
Total Expenses and Losses		16,025
Change in Unrestricted Net Assets		$ 5,779

2. **Statement of Changes in Net Assets** This part summarizes the first part and reports the changes in restricted assets (increases and decreases in donor-restricted funds).

Exhibit 6 ▸ Statement of Activities: Part 2

Name of Nonprofit Entity Statement of Changes in Net Assets Year Ending December 31, Year 2		
Unrestricted Net Assets		
Total Unrestricted Revenues and Gains	$ 14,434	
Net Assets Released From Restrictions	7,370	
Total Expenses and Losses	(16,025)	
Change in Unrestricted Net Assets		$ 5,779
Temporarily Restricted Net Assets		
Contributions	4,055	
Investment Income	1,290	
Net Unrealized and Realized Gains on Long-Term Investments	1,476	
Actuarial Loss on Annuity Obligations	(15)	
Net Assets Released From Restrictions	(7,370)	
Change in Temporarily Restricted Net Assets		(564)
Permanently Restricted Net Assets (Endowment Funds)		
Contributions	140	
Long-Term Investment Income	60	
Net Unrealized and Realized Gains on Long-Term Investments	2,310	
Change in Permanently Restricted Net Assets		2,510
Change in Net Assets		7,725
Net Assets at December 31, Year 1		133,070
Net Assets at December 31, Year 2		$140,795

E. **Statement of Cash Flows**

The statement reports the change in cash and cash equivalents similar to commercial enterprises. The description of cash flows from financing activities is expanded to include receiving restricted resources that by donor stipulation must be used for long-term purposes. Also, interest and dividend that are donor restricted for these long-term purposes are not part of operating activities.

Exhibit 7 ▸ Statement of Cash Flows

Name of Nonprofit Entity Statement of Cash Flows Year Ending December 31, Year 4	
Cash Flows From Operating Activities:	
Cash Received From Service Recipients	$ 5,220
Cash Received From Contributors	8,030
Collections on Pledges	2,766
Interest and Dividends Received	8,570
Cash Paid to Vendors and Employees	(23,808)
Cash Paid for Interest	(382)
Cash Paid for Grants	(424)
Net Cash Used by Operating Activities	$ (28)
Cash Flows From Investing Activities:	$ (74,900)
Cash Paid for Purchase of Investments	
Cash Received From Sale of Investments	76,100
Cash Paid for Property, Plant, and Equipment	(1,500)
Cash Received From Sale of Property, Plant, and Equipment	250
Net Cash Used by Investing Activities	$ (50)

Cash Flows From Financing Activities:	
Proceeds from Contributions Restricted for:	
Investment in Endowment	$ 200
Investment in Term Endowment	70
Investment in Property, Plant, and Equipment	1,210
Investment Income Restricted for Reinvestment	200
Interest and Dividends Restricted for Reinvestment	300
Less: Payment of Annuity Obligations	(146)
Less: Payment of Notes Payable	(1,140)
Less: Payment on Bonds Payable	(1,000)
Net Cash Used by Financing Activities	$ (306)
Net Increase in Cash and Cash Equivalents	$ (384)
Cash and Cash Equivalents at December 31, Year 3	460
Cash and Cash Equivalents at December 31, Year 4	$ 76
Reconciliation of Change in Net Assets to Net Cash Used by Operating Activities:	
Change in Net Assets	$ 15,450
Reconciling Adjustments:	
Plus: Depreciation	$ 3,200
Plus: Loss on Sale of Equipment	80
Plus: Actuarial Loss on Annuity Obligations	30
Less: Increase in Accounts and Interest Receivable	(460)
Less: Increase in Contributions Receivable	(324)
Plus: Decrease in Inventories and Prepaid Expenses	390
Less: Decrease in Refundable Advance	(650)
Less: Decrease in Grants Payable	(424)
Plus: Increase in Accounts Payable	1,520
Less: Contributions Restricted for Long-Term Investment	(2,740)
Less: Investment Income Restricted for Long-Term Investment	(300)
Less Net Unrealized and Realized Gains on Long-Term Investment	(15,800)
Net Cash Used by Operating Activities	$ (28)
Supplemental Data for Noncash Investing and Financing Activities:	
Gifts of Property, Plant, and Equipment	$ 140
Gifts of Paid-Up Life Insurance, Cash Surrender Value	80

F. Statement of Functional Expenses

The Statement of Functional Expenses is required only for Voluntary Health and Welfare Organizations (VHWO). This details the expenses on the Statement of Activities by functional and natural (or object) classification.

1. **Functional Classification** A method of grouping expenses according to the purpose for which costs are incurred. The primary functional classifications are program services and supporting activities, as described in the Statement of Activities section.

2. **Natural Classification** Regular items such as salaries, rent, electricity, interest expense, depreciation, awards and grants to others, and professional fees.

3. **Presentation** The expenses and classifications must be presented in a matrix format.

Exhibit 8 ▸ VHWO Statement of Functional Expenses

(Heading)

	Program Services				Support Services			
	Research	Education	Community Services	Total	Management and General	Fund Raising	Total	Grand Total
Salaries	XX	XX	XX	XX	XX	XX	XX	XX
Employee Benefits	XX	XX	XX	XX	XX	XX	XX	XX
Payroll Taxes	XX	XX	XX	XX	XX	XX	XX	XX
Professional Fees	XX	XX	XX	XX	XX	XX	XX	XX
Contractual Services	XX	XX	XX	XX	XX	XX	XX	XX
Supplies	XX	XX	XX	XX	XX	XX	XX	XX
Telephone	XX	XX	XX	XX	XX	XX	XX	XX
.	.	.	.	.	.	.	.	.
.	.	.	.	.	.	.	.	.
.	.	.	.	.	.	.	.	.
Miscellaneous	XX	XX	XX	XX	XX	XX	XX	XX
Total	XX	XX	XX	XX	XX	XX	XX	XX
Total Expenses Before Deprec.	XX	XX	XX	XX	XX	XX	XX	XX
Depreciation	XX	XX	XX	XX	XX	XX	XX	XX
Total Expenses	XX	XX	XX	XX	XX	XX	XX	XX

G. General Disclosures

1. **Fundraising** Among other things, the NPO is required to disclose a ratio of fundraising expenses to amounts raised, and also how it computes that ratio, in its financial statements.

2. **Depreciation** An entity shall disclose (a) depreciation expense for the period, (b) depreciable asset balances by nature or function of asset, (c) total accumulated depreciation or accumulated depreciation for the major classes of assets, and (d) the depreciation method or methods used for each major class of assets.

3. **Depreciation Exception** Depreciation should not be recognized on individual pieces of artwork or antiquities. Artwork or antiquities is deemed to have those characteristics only if verifiable evidence exists that the asset has cultural, aesthetic, or historical value that is worth preserving perpetually and the holder has the technological and financial ability to protect and preserve, essentially undiminished, the service potential of the asset and is doing so.

4. **Financial Statement Disclosures** Like their for-profit counterparts, many NPO entities have been facing some significant challenges due to the economic downturn. With diminishing contributions, many NPOs have had to face the reality that funds are not available even to pay normal and recurring operating expenses. Users of financial statements, including lenders, donors, and regulators, have begun to more closely-scrutinize financial information included in financial statements. To that end, many NPO entities found that use of previously-utilized disclosures in current financial statements had the end-result of statements not being transparent and, in certain circumstances, the financial statement disclosures were inadequate.

   Some other areas where disclosures might well need to be expanded include:

   - Liquidity and capital resources.
   - Material impairments.
   - Pension and other postretirement benefit plan assets.
   - Fair value determinations.
   - Critical accounting policies and estimates.

- Subsequent events
- Risk factors.
- Relationships with distressed businesses.

5. **Uncertain Tax Positions** NPO entities might have uncertain tax positions that need to be evaluated for purposes of determining whether those positions do subject the entities to the measurement and/or disclosure requirements within FASB ASC 740. As an example, NPO entities could generate certain types of income that would be subject to income taxes; in those cases, the generally-applicable guidance in GAAP should be considered.

   One of the disclosures that should appear in financial statements of all NPO entities relates to tax years that remain open to examination by taxing authorities. While not onerous, it has been noticed that certain NPO entities inadvertently have not made the disclosure, where the omitted disclosure results from the fact that the conclusion has been reached that no uncertain tax positions are subject to measurement or disclosure provisions.

6. **Net Asset Error Corrections** At times, NPO entities need to make corrections to prior-year financial statements so that net assets are appropriately classified in the financial statements. Errors in previously-issued financial statements include those related to measurement, presentation, or disclosure in the financial statements resulting from mathematical errors; mistakes in the application of accounting principles; and oversight or misuse of facts that existed at the time the financial statements were prepared. A change from an accounting principle that is not considered to be generally accepted to one that is generally accepted would also be considered an error correction.

   NPO entities need to consider individual net asset classes rather than net assets in the aggregate when determining whether correction of classifications in previously-issued statements constitute errors in those statements. The pertinent guidance here actually falls within FASB ASC 958 that contains the clear stipulation that usefulness of information provided in the financial statements is significantly improved if certain basic financial information is classified in a comparable manner from period-to-period.

   Reclassification of net assets (i.e., simultaneously increasing one net asset class and decreasing another asset class) needs to be made when any of the following circumstances exist:

   - NPO entities fulfill purposes for which net assets were restricted.
   - Donor-imposed restrictions expire with the passage of time or with the death of a split-interest agreement beneficiary [if the net assets are not otherwise restricted].
   - Donors withdraw, or court actions remove, previously-imposed restrictions.
   - Donors-imposed restrictions on otherwise unrestricted net assets.

7. **Contributions of Certain Nonfinancial Assets** Not uncommonly, entities other than NPO entities provide, at little or no charge to NPO entities, certain nonfinancial assets that encourage the public to contribute to the NPO entities or help those entities communicate its message or mission. In circumstances where fundraising material, informational material, or advertising used for the benefit of NPO entities (or provided to the entities at no, or a reduced, charge), questions have arisen as to whether NPO entities should report a contribution and, if so, how it should be measured and reported in the financial statements.

   NPO entities need to consider whether they have received a contribution. If they have, the contribution would need to be measured at fair value, and the related expense, at the time the expense is recognized, and should be reported by function based on the nature of the contributed item.

When the fundraising material, informational material, or advertising is used for the benefit of NPO entities through encouraging the public to contribute to those entities or help those entities communicate its message or mission, the NPO entities may have received an unconditional transfer of assets in a voluntary nonreciprocal transfer from another entity acting other than its owner. These type contributions that are received generally should be recognized as revenues or gains in the period received and as assets, decreases of liabilities, or expenses, depending on the form of benefits received.

III. Unique Accounting Features

A. Health Care Entities

All revenues (restricted and unrestricted) and expenses are recognized on the accrual basis. The basis and timing of the recognition of expenses for health care entities are generally the same as for other business organizations. Thus, depreciation and amortization are reported in conformity with commercial GAAP, as is the provision for bad debts.

1. **Unrestricted Revenues and Expenses** Mostly classified as operating because they arise from activities associated with the provision of health care services. Unrestricted revenues are further classified as *patient service revenue* or *other revenue.*

    a. The major classifications of functional expenses include nursing and other professional, general, fiscal, and administrative services; bad debts; depreciation; and interest.

    b. Other revenues include tuition from educational programs, cafeteria revenues, parking fees, fees for copies of medical records, gift shop revenues, and other activities somewhat related to the provision of patient service revenues.

2. **Patient Service Revenue** Patient service revenue (revenue from health care services) is recorded gross, at the provider's regularly established rates, regardless of collectibility.

    a. Charity care is not included in patient service revenues because these services were provided free of charge and, thus, were never expected to result in cash flows. Health care entities must use cost (not revenue) as the measurement basis for charity care disclosure purposes and that cost must be identified as the direct and indirect costs of providing the charity care. Entities must also disclose the method used to identify or determine such costs.

    b. Provisions for *contractual adjustments* (i.e., the difference between established rates and third-party payor payments) and other adjustments are recorded on the accrual basis and deducted from gross patient service revenue to determine *net patient service revenue.* Effective December 2011, health care entities that recognize significant amounts of patient service revenue at the time the service is provided, (even though it does not assess the collectibility of that revenue), should classify the provision for bad debts associated with patient service revenue as a deduction from patient service revenue (net of contractual allowances and discounts).

    Those entities are required to provide enhanced annual and interim disclosures about their policies for recognizing revenue and assessing bad debts. For health care entities affected by this guidance, the provision for bad debts associated with patient service revenue is required to be presented on a separate line that reduces patient service revenue, net of contractual allowances and discounts, in statements of operations.

All other health care entities would continue to present the provision for bad debts, including bad debts associated with patient service revenue, as an operating expense. Bad debts related to receivables from revenue other than patient service revenue will continue to be classified as an operating expense. Additionally, any bad debts related to receivables from patient service revenue where the entity only recognizes revenue to the extent it expects to collect that amount will also continue to be classified as operating expense.

c. Health care entities that recognize significant amounts of patient service revenue at the time the services are rendered without assessing patient ability to pay are required to disclose both of the following in both interim and annual reporting periods:

- Their policies for assessing the timing and amount of uncollectible patient service revenue recognized as bad debts by major payor source of revenue.
- Qualitative and quantitative information about significant changes in the allowance for doubtful accounts related to patient accounts receivable.

Additionally, all of the following should be disclosed as separate line items on the face of the statement of operations: patient service revenue (net of contractual allowances and discounts); the provision for bad debts (the amount related to patient service revenue); and the resulting net patient service revenue less the provision for bad debts.

Exhibit 9 ▸ Hospital Revenue

(Heading)	
Revenues:	
Gross patient service revenue	$ 75,000
Charity care	(5,000)
Patient service revenue	70,000
3rd Party contractuals & discounts	(10,000)
Net patient service revenue	60,000
Provision for bad debt	(6,000)
Net patient service revenue less bad debt provision	54,000
Other operating revenue	14,000
Total Revenues	$ 68,000

3. **Other Revenue** Normally includes revenue from services other than health care provided to patients, as well as sales and services to nonpatients. Depending on the relation to the health care entity's operations, other revenue may include:

a. Revenue from educational programs, including tuition from schools, such as nursing.

b. Revenue from research, gifts, and grants, either unrestricted or for a specific purpose.

c. Revenue such as gifts, grants, or endowment income restricted to finance charity care.

d. Revenue from miscellaneous sources, such as: proceeds from sale of cafeteria meals and guest trays to employees, medical staff, and visitors; proceeds from sales at gifts shops, snack bars, newsstands, parking lots, and vending machines; and fees charged for copies of medical records.

Exhibit 10 ▸ Sample Health Care Entity Journal Entries

1. To record gross charges to patients at established rates:

Accounts Receivable	XX	
Patient Service Revenues		XX

NOTE: Charity care is not included in gross patient service revenues because the services are provided free of charge.

2. To record deductions from gross patient service revenues:

Contractual and Other Adjustments	XX	
Accounts Receivable		XX

NOTE: Contractual and other adjustments are recognized as deductions from patient service revenues rather than as operating expenses.

3. To record hospital operating expenses and other revenues (that is, operating revenues other than patient service revenues):

Operating Expenses (functional expense accounts)	XX	
Depreciation Expense	XX	
Cash or Payable		XX
Inventory		XX
Accumulated Depreciation		XX
Cash or Receivables	XX	
Other Revenues		XX

4. **Gains and Losses** Are generally classified as nonoperating because they generally result from transactions that are peripheral or incidental to the provision of health care services. However, a gain or loss closely related with the provision of health care services may be classified as operating. Therefore, depending on the relation of the transactions to the health care entity's ongoing or major operations, gains (losses) normally include:

   a. Contributions

   b. Returns on investments (i.e., interest, dividends, rents, and gains and losses resulting from increases and decreases in the value of investments). Investment income essential to the provision of health care services is reported as revenue (e.g., a provider with a large endowment that provides funds that are necessary for the provider to operate).

   c. Amounts from Endowment Funds that are available for general operating purposes, which include interest and dividends on Endowment Fund investments. Realized gains or losses on the sale of investments of Endowment Funds are recorded as restricted revenue or gains in the Endowment Fund principal unless such amounts are legally available for other use or are chargeable against other funds.

   d. Miscellaneous gains (losses) such as a gain or loss on the sale of the entity's properties.

5. **Receivables** Receivables for health care services do not include charges related to charity care. They are reported net of valuation allowances for uncollectibles and contractual and other adjustments.

6. **Consolidations** Assessing whether the financial statements of a health care organization reporting entity need to be consolidated to include other for-profit or NPO entities, as well as whether the equity method is appropriate and the extent of disclosure that needs to exist, depends upon the nature of relationships between and among affiliated entities.

   Like the guidance associated with nonprofit entities, health care organizations may be related in a variety of different ways, including ownership, control, and/or economic interests. Also like the generic guidance for nonprofit entities, certain types of control result in the need to consolidate affiliated entities, and other types of control require consolidation only when combined with an economic interest. Additionally, other kinds of control could result in consolidation being permitted, but not required, when combined with an economic interest.

B. Colleges & Universities

1. **Revenue** Where standard established tuition and fee charges are waived, whether partially or entirely, the full amounts of the standard tuition and fees are recognized as revenues and the amounts waived are recorded as expenditures. The amount of *tuition remissions* allowed to faculty members' families and *scholarships* are also recorded as both a revenue and an expenditure. The amount of *class cancellation refunds,* however, are not classified as either a revenue or an expenditure.

2. **Typical Operating Accounts** Revenues, expenditures, and transfers typically are recorded in accounts such as the following, which are adapted from NACUBO's *College and University Business Administration* chart of accounts:

   - Tuition and Fees
   - Appropriations (by source, e.g., state, local)
   - Grants and Contracts (by source, e.g., federal)
   - Private Gifts, Grants, and Contracts
   - Endowment Income
   - Sales and Service of Educational Activities (e.g., testing services)
   - Auxiliary Enterprises (e.g., residence halls, food service, athletic programs, hospitals)
   - Mandatory Transfers
   - Nonmandatory Transfers
   - Educational and General (subclassified)
     - Instruction
     - Research
     - Public Services
     - Academic Support
     - Student Services
     - Institutional Support
     - Operation and Maintenance of Plant
     - Scholarships and Fellowships
   - Auxiliary Enterprises [e.g., as contra to the revenue account]
   - Other

3. **Statement of Activities** The university Statement of Activities is usually presented in a columnar format with one column for each fund group or major subdivision.

Exhibit 11 ▸ University Statement of Changes in Unrestricted Net Assets

(Heading)

	Current Funds			
	Unrestricted	Temporarily restricted	Permanently restricted	Total
Revenues:				
Educational and General [listed by major source]	XX			XX
State Appropriations	XX			XX
Federal Grants and Contracts		XX	XX	XX
Private Gifts, Grants, and Contracts	XX	XX	XX	XX
Endowment Income	XX	XX	XX	XX
Expired Term Endowment	XX	XX		XX
Interest Income	XX			XX
Auxiliary Enterprises	XX	XX	XX	XX
Total Revenues	XX	XX	XX	XX
Net Assets Released From Restrictions:				
Expiration of Time Requirements	XX	XX		
Fulfilled Conditions of Equipment Acquisition	XX	XX		
Fulfilled Conditions of Program Services	XX	XX		
Total Net Assets Released From Restrictions	XX	XX		
Expenditures and Mandatory Transfers:				
Educational and General Expenditures [by type]	XX		XX	XX
Total Educational and General Expenditures	XX		XX	XX
Mandatory Transfers for:				
Debt Service Principal and Interest	XX			XX
Loan Fund Equity	XX		XX	XX
Plant Expansion, Renewal, and Replacement	XX		—	XX
Total Mandatory Transfers	XX		XX	XX
Auxiliary Enterprises:				
Expenditures	XX		XX	XX
Mandatory Transfers	XX		XX	XX
Total Auxiliary Enterprises	XX		XX	XX
Total Expenditures and Mandatory Transfers	XX		XX	XX
Other Transfers and Additions (Deductions):				
Excess of Restricted Receipts and Accruals Over Amounts Reported as Revenues			XX	XX
Nonmandatory Transfers to Plant Funds	XX	—	—	—
Increase (Decrease) in Net Assets	XX	XX	XX	XX

C. Voluntary Health & Welfare Organizations (VHWO)

Voluntary health and welfare organizations (VHWOs) offer free or low cost services to the general public or to certain segments of society, and are supported primarily by public contributions. Examples include the United Way, the American Heart Association, Girl Scouts, Boy Scouts, the YMCA, and the YWCA. Four statements are required for VHWOs: the same statements required for all NPOs, plus a fourth, the Statement of Functional Expenses.

1. **Statement of Activities (or Support, Revenue, and Expenses and Changes in Net Assets)** Many features of typical VHWO accounting and reporting are apparent in the primary VHWO operating statement, which may be presented in the format shown in Exhibit 12. Note that there is a distinct difference between support and revenue.

2. **Statement of Functional Expenses** The "extra" primary VHWO statement is in substance a schedule detailing expenses. One format of this statement is illustrated in Exhibit 8.

Exhibit 12 ▸ VHWO Statement of Activities

(Heading)	Current Funds Unrestricted	Current Funds Restricted	Land, Building, and Equipment Fund	Endowment Fund	Total
PUBLIC SUPPORT AND REVENUE					
Public Support:					
Operating Contributions (net)	XX	XX			XX
Capital Contributions (net)			XX	XX	XX
Legacies and Bequests		XX	XX	XX	XX
Special Events (net of related costs)	XX	XX	XX		XX
United Way [or similar federated or nonfederated support organizations]	XX				XX
Total Public Support	XX	XX	XX	XX	XX
Revenue:					
Membership Dues	XX				XX
Investment Income	XX	XX	XX	XX	XX
Investment Gains	XX	XX	XX	XX	XX
Client Service Fees	XX				XX
Total Revenue	XX	XX	XX	XX	XX
EXPENSES					
Program Services:					
Research	XX	XX	XX		XX
Education	XX	XX	XX		XX
Community Services	XX		XX		XX
Total Program Services	XX	XX	XX		XX
Supporting Services:					
Management and General	XX		XX		XX
Fund-raising	XX		XX		XX
Total Supporting Services	XX	XX	XX		XX
OTHER CHANGES IN NET ASSETS					
Fixed Asset Acquisitions From Unrestricted Funds	(XX)		XX		
Transfer of Realized Endowment Appreciation	XX			(XX)	
Returned to Grantor or Donor		(XX)			(XX)
Net Assets, Beginning	XX	XX	XX	XX	XX
Net Assets, Ending	XX	XX	XX	XX	XX

D. Other Nonprofit Organizations (ONPO)

Other nonprofit organizations include all nonbusiness organizations except (1) those covered by AICPA audit guides, and (2) entities that operate essentially as commercial businesses for the direct economic benefit of stockholders or members (for example, mutual insurance companies or farm cooperatives). ONPOs are required to present the standard three basic financial statements. The ONPO funds are similar to those of VHWOs.

Exhibit 13 ▸ Types of Organizations Classified as ONPO

Civic organizations	Social and country clubs	Performing arts organizations
Labor unions	Cemetery organizations	Private and community foundations
Political parties	Professional organizations	Private elementary and secondary schools
Trade associations	Fraternal organizations	Public broadcasting stations
Libraries	Religious organizations	Research and scientific organizations
Museums	Other cultural institutions	Zoological and botanical societies

IV. Appendix: Health Care Entity Fund Accounting

A. Concepts

All (optional) fund formats are insufficient on their own, without the aggregate information required. Nonprofit health care entities may use fund accounting to account for resources received from donors and grantors and to satisfy their fiduciary responsibilities. The fund accounting model and procedures used are closer to business accounting than to governmental fund accounting. For example, the entity's revenues, expenses, gains, and losses are accounted for and reported in a manner similar to businesses.

1. Except for the aggregate amount reported for revenues and gains in excess of expenses and losses, all other changes in the net assets of the General Fund reported in the Statement of Operations are not reported in the Statement of Revenues and Expenses of General Funds. For example, transfers to the General Fund from the Plant Replacement and Expansion Fund are treated as restricted revenues.

2. Note that investment income restricted for a specific operating purpose by donors and grantors is reported as restricted revenues in the appropriate donor-restricted fund. Unrestricted income of the donor-restricted funds is reported in the Statement of Revenues and Expenses of General Funds.

B. Fund Types

To facilitate reporting on the use of assets available for (the governing board's) use versus assets held under external restrictions, health care entities use two categories of funds—the General Funds and donor-restricted funds—each consisting of a self-balancing group of accounts composed of assets, liabilities, and net assets. All unrestricted resources and obligations are accounted for in the General Funds. Donor-restricted funds are used to account for financial resources that are *externally restricted* for specified operating or research, capital outlay, or endowment purposes. The fund structure of a health care entity is readily apparent in the format of its Statement of Financial Position, shown here in the pancake format with each fund reported separately.

1. **General Funds** Account for all assets and liabilities that are not required to be accounted for in a donor-restricted fund, including assets whose use is limited, Agency Funds, and property and equipment related to the general operations of the entity. Assets and liabilities of General Funds are classified as current or noncurrent in conformity with GAAP.

   a. Assets whose use is limited include assets set aside by the governing board for identified purposes. The board retains control over the board-restricted assets and may, at its discretion, subsequently use them for other purposes.

   b. Agency funds are included in General Funds as both an asset and a liability. Transactions involving receipt and disbursement of agency funds are not included in the results of operations.

   c. Property and equipment used for general operations, and the related liabilities, are reported in General Funds. Property and equipment whose use is restricted (e.g., real estate investments of Endowment Funds) are reported in the appropriate donor-restricted fund.

2. **Donor-Restricted Funds** Account for resources whose use is restricted by donors or grantors and essentially act as holding funds until the resources are used. Donor-restricted funds may be temporarily or permanently restricted and include resources for specific operating purposes, additions to property and equipment, and endowments. Increases and decreases in the donor-restricted fund types are recorded as additions to and deductions from the appropriate fund net assets and are reported in the Statement of Activities (after original recognition as revenue).

   a. Specific-Purpose Funds account for resources restricted by donors and grantors for specific operating purposes (e.g., research or education). These resources are recorded as restricted revenue (or gains) when received. Their expenditure (1) decreases the net assets of the Specific-Purpose Fund and (2) is generally recorded as expenses and net assets released from restrictions in the General Funds.

   b. Plant Replacement and Expansion Funds account for resources restricted by donors and grantors for capital outlay purposes. These resources are recorded as restricted revenues (or gains) when received. Their expenditure (1) decreases the net assets of the Plant Replacement and Expansion Fund, and (2) increases property and equipment and the net assets of the General Funds. Neither the plant assets acquired nor any long-term debt issued for capital outlay purposes is accounted for in the Plant Replacement and Expansion Funds.

   c. Endowment Funds include resources whose principal may not be expended (i.e., an Endowment Fund is generally a permanently restricted fund).

      (1) The receipt of gifts and bequests restricted for endowments are reported as permanently restricted revenues of the Endowment Fund.

      (2) Realized gains or losses on the sale of investments of Endowment Funds are reported as restricted revenues of the Endowment Fund unless such amounts are legally available for other use.

      (3) Investment income is accounted for in accordance with the donor's instructions. If unrestricted, the income is reported as a (unrestricted) nonoperating gain in the General Funds. Investment income temporarily or permanently restricted revenue is reported (a) in the Specific Purpose Fund if restricted for a specified operating purposes (e.g., research or education), or (b) in the Plant Replacement and Expansion Fund if restricted for capital outlay purposes.

   d. Term Endowment Funds account for resources whose principal may be expended after the donor-imposed restrictions are satisfied (e.g., for 15 years or until after the donor's death). Term endowments are accounted for as discussed above during the endowment term. When the term of the endowment ends, the assets are transferred to other funds, as specified by the donor. The transfer increases the net assets of the specific purpose fund or plant replacement and expansion fund, as appropriate, if restricted for specified operating or capital outlay purposes. If the assets are available for general operating purposes, the transfer is generally recorded as an increase in the unrestricted net assets in the general funds.

Exhibit 14 ▸ Hospital Funds

U	**U**nrestricted general
P	**P**lant replacement
S	**S**pecific purpose
E	**E**ndowment
T	**T**erm Endowment

Exhibit 15 ▸ Health Care Entity Statement of Financial Position, Fund Accounting

(Heading)			
GENERAL FUNDS			
Current assets: (e.g., cash, receivables, due from Specific-Purpose Funds)	XX	Current liabilities: (same as business entities)	XX
Assets whose use is limited	XX	Long-term debt: (same as business entities)	XX
Property and equipment, net of accumulated depreciation:	XX	Contingencies:	
Other assets (e.g., investments)	XX	(same as business entities)	XX
	XX	Net assets: Unrestricted	XX
DONOR-RESTRICTED FUNDS			
Specific-Purpose Funds			
Cash	XX	Due to General Funds	XX
Investments	XX	Net Assets: Temp. Restricted	XX
Due From Endowment Funds	XX	Net Assets: Perm. Restricted	XX
	XX		XX
Plant Replacement and Expansion Funds			
Cash	XX	Accounts payable	XX
Investments	XX	Contracts payable	XX
Due From Endowment Funds	XX	Net Assets (Temp. or Perm. Restricted)	XX
	XX		XX
Endowment Funds			
Cash	XX	Due to Specific-Purpose Funds	XX
Investments	XX	Due to Plant Replacemt & Expansion Funds	XX
Pledges receivable, net	XX	Mortgage Assets (related)	XX
Property and Equipment, net	XX	Net Assets (Temp. or Perm. Restricted)	XX
	XX		XX

V. Appendix: University Fund Accounting

A. Concepts

University (and college) fund accounting is both similar and different from that for governments and hospitals. Universities have only a few fund groups, as do hospitals, but divide these into major fund group subdivisions that resemble the municipal funds.

1. **Transfers** Universities account for interfund quasi-external transactions, reimbursements, and transfers similarly to governments.

2. **Number of Fund Groups** Like hospitals, universities may use only one fund of each group for accounting purposes. Alternatively, they may use a separate fund for each major subdivision or may use many separate funds as do municipalities.

B. Restricted vs. Unrestricted Current Funds

Unrestricted Current Funds are used to account for all university financial resources (and related current liabilities) that are expendable for any legal and reasonable institutional purposes and that have **not** been (1) externally restricted by donors or grantors for specified purposes, or (2) designated by the governing board and, thus, accounted for as Net Assets—Unrestricted in another fund. Financial resources (and related current liabilities) that are externally restricted for current operating purposes of the university are accounted for in the *Restricted Current Funds.*

C. Current Fund Unique Accounting Conventions

Current Funds are accounted for on the accrual basis of accounting.

1. Unrestricted Current Funds

a. Where the full amount of specific fees or other revenue sources is legally or contractually restricted for *debt service* or *capital outlay* purposes, the fees are recorded as restricted revenues of the appropriate plant funds rather than as current fund revenues.

b. Where only part of specific fees or other revenue sources is legally or contractually restricted for *debt service* or *capital outlay* purposes, (1) the full amount is reported as unrestricted current fund revenue, and (2) the restricted amount is recorded as a mandatory transfer to the appropriate plant funds.

c. Where the governing board has designated unrestricted resources for purposes usually financed in other funds, the revenues are reported in the unrestricted current fund, as is a *nonmandatory* transfer to the other fund(s). Likewise, returns of such sums are recorded as transfers to the unrestricted current fund rather than as revenues.

d. Residual balances of endowment and similar funds and annuity and life income funds that become unrestricted at the end of their term are recorded in distinctively titled *Net Assets Released From Restrictions* (NARFR) accounts in the unrestricted current fund.

e. Inventory may be accounted for on the consumption or use method whereby (1) inventory purchases are charged to *Expenses,* but (2) the change in inventories during the year is recorded as an adjustment to the *Expenses* account at year-end. (Inventory reserve is not needed unless there is a base stock of inventory not available for use.)

2. Restricted Current Funds

a. Financial resources restricted for operating purposes are recorded as assets and restricted revenues—in the restricted current funds.

b. Restricted current fund expenditures are recorded in expenditures accounts of that fund—not of the unrestricted current funds.

D. Current Fund Budgetary Accounts

Universities may use budgetary accounts—particularly in the current funds—in a manner like that illustrated for a municipal general fund.

1. **Encumbrance Accounting** Generally used in budgeted university funds, parallel to that for municipal general and special revenue funds.

2. **Budgets** The university budgetary account entry usually varies somewhat from that for a municipal general fund. This entry follows a budgetary fund balance approach in that the *Unallocated (or Unassigned) Budget Balance* account is a balancing or offsetting account. The budgetary entry is reversed in the year-end closing entries.

E. Trust & Agency Funds

Accounting for university loan funds, endowment and similar funds, and agency funds parallels that for municipalities and/or hospitals.

F. Annuity & Life Income Funds

Annuity and life income funds are used to account for assets (and related liabilities) given to the university on the condition that the university either (1) make annuity payments of a fixed amount periodically to a named recipient(s) for a fixed or determinable period of time (annuity fund), or (2) pay the income earned by the fund to a named recipient(s) for a fixed or determinable period of time, often the donor's and/or the recipient's lifetime (life income fund).

1. **Fundamental Distinction** The annuity fund guarantees the recipient(s) a fixed dollar payment periodically during its term, while the life income fund involves no guarantees except that whatever income is earned will be paid to the recipient(s) during its term.

   a. No payable to the beneficiary is recorded at the inception of the Life Income Fund because there is no obligation to make fixed payments to the beneficiary. (The beneficiary is entitled only to receive the income from the fund's assets, if any.)

   b. Revenues are not credited for the income generated by the life income fund's assets, since the income is payable to the beneficiary. Therefore, life income fund income is credited to an *Income Payable to Beneficiary* account.

2. **Closing** At the end of their terms, the fund balances of both annuity funds and life income funds become expendable for unrestricted and/or specified restricted purposes and are transferred to the unrestricted current fund or to the appropriate restricted fund.

Exhibit 16 ▸ University Funds

Current Funds [Unrestricted Current Funds, Restricted Current Funds]

Plant Funds
Agency Funds
Loan Funds

Annuity Fund
Life Income Fund
Endowment Fund [Endowment Funds (pure), Term Endowment Funds, Quasi-Endowment Funds (internally designated)]

G. Plant Funds

The plant funds group is used to account for financial resources restricted and/or designated for university capital outlay and debt service, its fixed assets, and its long-term debt. All fixed assets and long-term debt that are not related to the university's trust funds are recorded in the plant funds. This is reasonable since most universities cannot incur long-term debt except for fixed asset acquisitions. The four plant fund subdivisions are closely related, and their accounting procedures are relatively simple.

1. **Unexpended Plant Funds** Used to account for financial resources restricted or designated for acquisition of new fixed assets, the current and long-term liabilities related to such unexpended financial resources, and the net amount available for expenditure for new fixed assets. The new fixed assets acquired consist of both new fixed assets and existing fixed assets newly acquired for university purposes—as opposed to renovating existing university fixed assets. The new fixed assets are capitalized in the *Investment in Plant* accounts.

2. **Plant Funds for Renewals and Replacements** Identical to unexpended plant funds except the financial resources are used to renovate or perhaps replace existing university fixed assets. Long-term debt is not often incurred for such purposes and most renovations, in particular, are not capitalized in the *Investment in Plant* accounts—though major betterment and replacements are capitalized in the *Investment in Plant* accounts.

   NOTE: Both unexpended plant funds and plant funds for renewals and replacements are similar to municipal capital projects funds, except that long-term debt may be accounted for temporarily in these plant fund subdivisions. Because of their similarity, it is acceptable to account for both of these plant fund subdivisions in one plant fund subdivision, provided that separate *Net Assets* accounts distinguish the net assets of the two subfunds.

3. **Plant Funds for Retirement of Indebtedness** Used to account for restricted and designated financial resources to be used for university debt service, related current liabilities for long-term debt principal and interest payable, and the net amount available for future debt service expenditures. The accounting procedures for plant funds for retirement of indebtedness parallel those for municipal debt service funds.

4. **Investment in Plant** An account group in a governmental accounting sense, which is used to record the university's general fixed assets, general long-term debt, and the difference between its fixed assets and long-term debt, referred to as net investment in plant. Thus, the investment in plant fund functions like a combination of the pre-GASB 34 municipal general fixed assets and general long-term debt account groups. Nongovernmental colleges and universities *must* report accumulated depreciation on these assets and the periodic depreciation provision *must* be reported in the Statement of Activities. Colleges and universities that are part of a government had the option of not reporting these amounts (prior to adoption of GASB No. 34) and, historically, have not done so.

Exhibit 17 ▸ Plant Funds

U	**Unexpended** Plant Fund
R	Fund for **Renewals** and **Replacements**
R	Fund for **Retirement** of Indebtedness
I	**Investment** in Plant

H. Statement of Financial Position

The university fund group and major fund subdivisions structure are readily apparent in the format of the university Statement of Financial Position (balance sheet), when presented in the fund pancake format. (See Exhibit 18.)

1. **Unrestricted and Restricted Current Funds** Similar to municipal general and special revenue funds, respectively, and the restricted current fund is like a hospital specific purpose fund.

2. **Trust Funds** The loan fund, endowment funds, and annuity and life income funds are all trust funds. The loan fund is like one of the municipal nonexpendable trust funds. The annuity and life income funds are special types of trust funds.

3. **Agency Fund** Similar to the simpler municipal agency funds.

4. **Plant Funds** Like a combination of municipal (a) capital projects funds—the unexpended funds and fund for renewals and replacements; (b) debt service funds—the funds for retirement of indebtedness; and (c) general fixed assets and general long-term debt account groups—the investment in plant fund. The distinction between the unexpended funds and the fund for renewals and replacements is that (a) the unexpended funds are used to account for resources (and related debt) to be expended for new construction (capitalized in the *Investment in Plant* accounts), while (b) the fund for renewals and replacements are used to account for financial resources to be expended for renovation of existing fixed assets (which are not usually capitalized in *Investment in Plant* accounts).

Exhibit 18 ▸ University Statement of Financial Position, Fund Accounting

(Heading)

Assets		Liabilities and Net Assets	
		CURRENT FUNDS	
Unrestricted		Unrestricted	
Current Assets [list]	XX	Current Liabilities [list]	XX
		Net Assets: Unrestricted	XX
	XX		XX
Restricted		Restricted	
Current Assets [list]	XX	Current Liabilities [list]	XX
		Net Assets: Temporarily Restricted	XX
		Net Assets: Permanently Restricted	XX
Total Current Funds	XX	Total Current Funds	XX
		LOAN FUNDS	
Current Assets [list]	XX	Net Assets:	
Loan Notes Receivable	XX	Unrestricted	XX
Long-Term Investments	XX	Temporarily Restricted	XX
		Permanently Restricted	XX
Total Loan Funds	XX	Total Loan Funds	XX
		ENDOWMENT AND SIMILAR FUNDS	
Current Assets [list]	XX	Current Liabilities [list]	XX
Long-Term Investments [list]	XX	Long-Term Liabilities [list]	XX
Fixed Assets [list, net of accumulated depreciation]	XX		XX
		Net Assets:	
		Perm. Restricted: Endowment	XX
		Temp. Restricted: Term Endowment	XX
		Unrestricted: Quasi-Endowment	XX
Total Endowment and Similar Funds	XX	Total Endowment and Similar Funds	XX
		ANNUITY AND LIFE INCOME FUNDS	
Current Assets [list]	XX	Annuities Payable	XX
Long-Term Investments	XX	Life Income Earnings Payable	XX
		Net Assets: Permanently Restricted	
		Annuity Funds	XX
		Life Income Funds	XX
Total Annuity and Life Income Funds	XX	Total Annuity and Life Income Funds	XX
		PLANT FUNDS	
Unexpended		Unexpended	
Current Assets [list]	XX	Current Liabilities [list]	XX
Long-Term Investments	XX	Notes Payable	XX
Construction in Process	XX		XX
		Net Assets:	
		Unrestricted	XX
		Temporarily Restricted	XX
		Permanently Restricted	XX
Total Unexpended Plant Funds	XX	Total Unexpended Plant Funds	XX
For Renewals and Replacements		For Renewals and Replacements	
Current Assets [list]	XX	Current Liabilities [list]	XX
Long-Term Investments	XX	Net Assets:	
		Unrestricted	XX
		Temporarily Restricted	XX
		Permanently Restricted	XX
Total for Renewals and Replacements	XX	Total for Renewals and Replacements	XX

For Retirement of Indebtedness		For Retirement of Indebtedness	
Current Assets [list]	XX	Net Assets:	
Long-Term Investments	XX	Restricted (Temp. or Perm)	XX
Sinking Fund—Bank Trustee	XX	Unrestricted	XX
Total for Retirement of Indebtedness	XX	Total for Retirement of Indebtedness	XX
Investment in Plant		Investment in Plant	
Fixed Assets [list]	XX	Long-Term Debt [list]	XX
		Net Investment in Plant	XX
Total Investment in Plant	XX	Total Investment in Plant	XX

VI. Appendix: VHWO Fund Accounting

A. Concepts

The VHWO fund structure is similar to that used by universities; furthermore, VHWOs use only one fund of each fund type. Note that fund accounting is not required. Whereas hospital accounting records all revenues and expenses in a single unrestricted fund, VHWOs record revenues and expenses in **each** fund—summarizing them in the total column of a columnar Statement of Activities.

B. Fund Types

1. **Land, Buildings, and Equipment (or Plant) Fund** Used to account for (a) unexpended restricted resources to be used to acquire VHWO fixed assets, (b) the VHWO's general fixed assets, (c) long-term debt related to the VHWO's fixed assets, and (d) the net investment in VHWO general fixed assets. (This fund is identical to the university plant fund—although VHWOs may record debt service in the current unrestricted fund rather than in the plant fund.)

2. **Custodian Fund** Used to account for resources held by the VHWO in an agency capacity for other organizations or individuals. (This fund is identical to the university agency fund and to simple municipal agency funds.)

3. **Restricted Current Fund** Used to account for available financial resources (and related current liabilities) that are expendable only for operating purposes specified by the donor or grantor. (This fund is identical to the university restricted current fund.)

4. **Unrestricted Current Fund** Used to account for all unrestricted resources (and related current liabilities) except those invested in fixed assets, which are accounted for in the land, buildings, and equipment (or plant) fund. (This fund is identical to the university unrestricted current fund.)

5. **Endowment Fund** Used to account for the principal (corpus) of gifts or bequests accepted with donor stipulations that (a) the principal is to be maintained intact—in perpetuity or for a fixed or determinable term of time, and (b) the earnings may be expended for unrestricted purposes and/or specified restricted purposes. (The VHWO endowment fund is identical to those of hospitals and universities and is like some municipal nonexpendable trust funds.)

6. **Loan and Annuity Fund** Used to account for resources restricted to making loans and/or annuity payments to specified recipients for a specified term—after which the VHWO is the remainderman beneficiary of the net assets, which may be unrestricted or restricted to use. (This fund is similar to the university annuity and life income fund.)

International Testing

Qualified candidates may take the exam in Bahrain, Japan, Kuwait, Lebanon, or the United Arab Emirates. For this purpose, qualified candidates are U.S. citizens and citizens and long-term residents of the host country. Qualified citizens and long-term residents of Argentina, Brazil, Colombia, and Venezuela may take the exam in Brazil. Other candidates still must travel to United States, Guam, Puerto Rico, or the Virgin Islands to test.

This exam uses the same bank of questions in English as is used in the United States. Foreign exam administration is limited to the last month of the regular two-month window; other restrictions also may apply.

A candidate testing under the international program must promise to complete credential licensure through one of the United States jurisdictions. Candidates may apply through most (but not all) jurisdictions. Jurisdictions participating in the international program are listed on the AICPA's exam web site.

Additional fees to fund the increased cost of foreign administration are approximately $300 per exam section.

Countries are selected considering the number of candidates, question confidentiality, host country accounting institution attitude, and the local legal environment. The program may expand to additional countries.

Most jurisdictions require candidates with degrees from schools outside of the United States to have their credentials evaluated by a member of the National Association of Credential Evaluation Services (NACES). View the NASBA web site for a list of NACES members.

Consult the NASBA web site for additional details, including information about eligibility requirements and the exam application process for each jurisdiction.

More helpful exam information is included in Appendix B, **Exam Preparation Tips**.

CHAPTER 20—NONPROFIT ACCOUNTING

Problem 20-1 MULTIPLE-CHOICE QUESTIONS

1. Which of the following assets of a nongovernmental not-for-profit charitable organization must be depreciated?

   a. A freezer costing $150,000 for storing food for the soup kitchen
   b. Building costs of $500,000 for construction in progress for senior citizen housing
   c. Land valued at $1 million being used as the site of the new senior citizen home
   d. A bulk purchase of $20,000 of linens for its nursing home (R/06, FAR, #43, 8110)

2. Functional expenses recorded in the general ledger of ABC, a nongovernmental not-for-profit organization, are as follows:

Soliciting prospective members	$45,000
Printing membership benefits brochures	30,000
Soliciting membership dues	25,000
Maintaining donor list	10,000

   What amount should ABC report as fundraising expenses?

   a. $ 10,000
   b. $ 35,000
   c. $ 70,000
   d. $110,000 (R/99, AR, #2, 6811)

3. Settam, a nongovernmental not-for-profit organization, received a donation of stock with donor-stipulated requirements as follows:

   Shares valued at $8,000,000 are to be sold with the proceeds used for renovation.
   Shares valued at $2,000,000 are to be retained with the dividends used to support current operations.

   What amount should Settam include as unrestricted net assets as a result of this donation?

   a. $0
   b. $ 2,000,000
   c. $ 8,000,000
   d. $10,000,000 (R/08, FAR, #25, 8580)

4. A labor union had the following receipts:

Per capita dues	$680,000
Initiation fees	90,000
Sales of organizational supplies	60,000
Nonexpendable gift restricted by donor for loan purposes for 10 years	30,000
Nonexpendable gift restricted by donor for loan purposes in perpetuity	25,000

   The union's constitution provides that 10% of the per capita dues are designated for the Strike Insurance Fund to be distributed for strike relief at the discretion of the union's executive board. In the statement of activity, what amount should be reported as permanently restricted revenues?

   a. $123,000
   b. $ 93,000
   c. $ 55,000
   d. $ 25,000 (Editors, 1361)

5. Janna Association, a nongovernmental not-for-profit organization, received a cash gift with the stipulation that the principal be held for at least 20 years. How should the cash gift be recorded?

   a. A temporarily restricted asset
   b. A permanently restricted asset
   c. An unrestricted asset
   d. A temporary liability (R/06, FAR, #46, 8113)

6. During the current year, Mill Foundation, a nongovernmental not-for-profit organization, received $100,000 in unrestricted contributions from the general public. Mill's board of directors stipulated that $75,000 of these contributions would be used to create an endowment. At the end of the current year, how should Mill report the $75,000 in the net assets section of the statement of financial position?

   a. Permanently restricted
   b. Unrestricted
   c. Temporarily restricted
   d. Donor restricted (R/05, FAR, #18, 7762)

7. Pann, a nongovernmental not-for-profit organization, provides food and shelter to the homeless. Pann received a $15,000 gift with the stipulation that the funds be used to buy beds. In which net asset class should Pann report the contribution?

   a. Endowment
   b. Temporarily restricted
   c. Permanently restricted
   d. Unrestricted (R/11, FAR, #14, 9864)

8. Pica, a nongovernmental not-for-profit organization, received unconditional promises of $100,000 expected to be collected within one year. Pica received $10,000 prior to year end. Pica anticipates collecting 90% of the contributions and has a June 30 fiscal year end. What amount should Pica record as contribution revenue as of June 30?

   a. $ 10,000
   b. $ 80,000
   c. $ 90,000
   d. $100,000 (R/02, AR, #5, 7070)

9. Oz, a nongovernmental not-for-profit organization, received $50,000 from Ame Company to sponsor a play given by Oz at the local theater. Oz gave Ame 25 tickets, which generally cost $100 each. Ame received no other benefits. What amount of ticket sales revenue should Oz record?

   a. $0
   b. $ 2,500
   c. $47,500
   d. $50,000 (R/02, AR, #1, 7066)

10. The Turtle Society, a nongovernmental not-for-profit organization, receives numerous contributed hours from volunteers during its busy season. Chris, a clerk at the local tax collector's office, volunteered ten hours per week for 24 weeks transferring turtle food from the port to the turtle shelter. His rate of pay at the tax office is $10 per hour, and the prevailing wage rate for laborers is $6.50 per hour. What amount of contribution revenue should Turtle Society record for this service?

    a. $0
    b. $ 840
    c. $1,560
    d. $2,400 (R/07, FAR, #31, 8352)

11. The Pel Museum, a nonprofit organization, received a contribution of historical artifacts. It need not recognize the contribution if the artifacts are to be sold and the proceeds used to

    a. Support general museum activities
    b. Acquire other items for collections
    c. Repair existing collections
    d. Purchase buildings to house collections (5/95, AR, #59, amended, 5477)

12. On January 2, the Baker Fund, a nongovernmental not-for-profit corporation, received a $125,000 contribution restricted to youth activity programs. During the year, youth activities generated revenues of $89,000 and had program expenses of $95,000. What amount should Baker report as net assets released from restrictions for the year?

    a. $0
    b. $ 6,000
    c. $ 95,000
    d. $125,000 (R/00, AR, #5, amended, 6910)

13. Gridiron University is a private university. A successful alumnus has recently donated $1,000,000 to Gridiron for the purpose of funding a "center for the study of sports ethics." This donation is conditional upon the university raising matching funds within the next 12 months. The university administrators estimate that they have a 50% chance of raising the additional money. How should this donation be accounted for?

    a. As a temporarily restricted support
    b. As unrestricted support
    c. As a refundable advance
    d. As a memorandum entry reported in the footnotes (R/09, FAR, #37, 8787)

14. How should unconditional pledges received by a nongovernmental not-for-profit organization that will be collected over more than one year be reported?

    a. Long-term pledges receivable, valued at the expected collection amount
    b. Pledges receivable, valued at their present values
    c. Deferred revenue, valued at present value
    d. Pledges receivable, valued at the amount pledged (R/08, FAR, #49, 8604)

15. During the current year, a voluntary health and welfare organization receives $300,000 in unrestricted pledges. Of this amount, $100,000 has been designated by donors for use next year to support operations. If 15% of the unrestricted pledges are expected to be uncollectible, what amount of unrestricted support should the organization recognize in its current-year financial statements?

    a. $300,000
    b. $270,000
    c. $200,000
    d. $170,000 (R/06, FAR, #22, 8089)

16. In the current year, Jones Foundation received the following support:

    - A cash contribution of $875,000 to be used at the board of directors' discretion
    - A promise to contribute $500,000 in the following year from a supporter who has made similar contributions in prior periods
    - Contributed legal services with a value of $100,000, which Jones would have otherwise purchased

    At what amounts would Jones classify and record these transactions as revenue?

	Unrestricted	Temporarily restricted
a.	$1,375,000	$500,000
b.	$0	$875,000
c.	$ 975,000	$0
d.	$ 975,000	$500,000

    (R/00, AR, #4, amended, 6909)

17. A nongovernmental not-for-profit animal shelter receives contributed services from the following individuals valued at their normal billing rate:

Veterinarian provides volunteer animal care	$8,000
Board members volunteer to prepare books for audit	4,500
Registered nurse volunteers as receptionist	3,000
Teacher provides volunteer dog walking	2,000

What amount should the shelter record as contribution revenue?

a. $ 8,000
b. $11,000
c. $12,500
d. $14,500 (R/10, FAR, #23, 9323)

18. Whitestone, a nongovernmental not-for-profit organization, received a contribution in December year 1. The donor restricted use of the contribution until March year 2. How should Whitestone record the contribution?

a. Footnote the contribution in year 1 and record as income when it becomes available in year 2
b. No entry required in year 1 and record as income in year 2 when it becomes available
c. Report as income in year 1
d. Report as deferred income in year 1 (R/10, FAR, #24, 9324)

19. Lori Hospital received a pure endowment grant. The pure endowment grant

a. May be expended by the governing board only to the extent of the principal since the income from this fund must be accumulated
b. Should generally be reported as a nonoperating gain when the full amount of principal is expended
c. Should be recorded as a memorandum entry only
d. Should be recorded as donor-restricted revenue upon receipt (Editors, 1428)

20. A nongovernmental not-for-profit organization received a $2 million gift from a donor who specified it be used to create an endowment fund that would be invested in perpetuity. The income from the fund is to be used to support a specific program in the second year and beyond. An investment purchased with the gift earned $40,000 during the first year. At the end of the first year, the fair value of the investment was $2,010,000. What is the net effect on temporarily restricted net assets at year end?

a. $0
b. $10,000 increase
c. $40,000 increase
d. $50,000 increase (R/11, FAR, #37, 9887)

21. RST Charities received equities securities valued at $100,000 as an unrestricted gift. During the year, RST received $5,000 in dividends from these securities; at year end, the securities had a fair market value of $110,000. By what amount did these transactions increase RST's net assets?

a. $100,000
b. $105,000
c. $110,000
d. $115,000 (R/07, FAR, #30, 8351)

22. A nongovernmental, not-for-profit organization received the following donations of corporate stock during the year:

	Donation 1	Donation 2
Number of shares	2,000	3,000
Adjusted basis	$ 8,000	$5,500
Fair market value at time of donation	8,500	6,000
Fair market value at year end	10,000	4,000

What net value of investments will the organization report at the end of the year?

a. $12,000
b. $13,500
c. $14,000
d. $14,500 (R/10, FAR, #25, 9325)

23. How should a nongovernmental not-for-profit organization report depreciation expense in its statement of activities?

a. It should not be included.
b. It should be included as a decrease in unrestricted net assets.
c. It should be included as an increase in temporarily restricted net assets.
d. It should be reclassified from unrestricted net assets to temporarily restricted net assets, depending on donor-imposed restrictions on the assets. (R/09, FAR, #23, 8773)

24. Hann School, a nongovernmental not-for-profit organization, spent $1 million of temporarily restricted cash to acquire land and building. How should this be reported in the statement of activities?

a. Increase in unrestricted net assets
b. Increase in temporarily restricted net assets
c. Increase in permanently restricted net assets
d. Decrease in permanently restricted net assets (R/08, FAR, #23, 8578)

25. A nongovernmental not-for-profit organization's statement of activities is similar to which of the following for-profit financial statements?

a. Balance sheet
b. Statement of cash flows
c. Statement of retained earnings
d. Income statement (R/09, FAR, #17, 8767)

26. How should operating expenses for a nongovernmental not-for-profit organization be reported?

a. Change in temporarily restricted net assets
b. Change in unrestricted net assets
c. Change in permanently restricted net assets
d. Contra-account to associated revenues (R/10, FAR, #50, 9350)

27. A large not-for-profit organization's statement of activities should report the net change for net assets that are

	Unrestricted	Permanently restricted
a.	Yes	Yes
b.	Yes	No
c.	No	No
d.	No	Yes

(11/95, AR, #74, 5817)

28. In the preparation of the statement of activities for a nongovernmental not-for-profit organization, all expenses are reported as decreases in which of the following net asset classes?

    a. Total net assets
    b. Unrestricted net assets
    c. Temporarily restricted net assets
    d. Permanently restricted net assets (R/07, FAR, #6, 8327)

29. During the year, Public College received the following:

    - An unrestricted $50,000 pledge to be paid the following year
    - A $25,000 cash gift restricted for scholarships
    - A notice that the college is named as a beneficiary of $10,000 in a recent graduate's will

    What amount of contribution revenue should Public College report in its statement of activities?

    a. $25,000
    b. $35,000
    c. $75,000
    d. $85,000 (R/06, FAR, #10, amended, 8077)

30. Which of the following classifications is required for reporting of expenses by all not-for-profit organizations?

    a. Natural classification in the statement of activities or notes to the financial statements
    b. Functional classification in the statement of activities or notes to the financial statements
    c. Functional classification in the statement of activities and natural classification in a matrix format in a separate statement
    d. Functional classification in the statement of activities and natural classification in the notes to the financial statements (11/97, AR, #17, 6545)

31. Nongovernmental not-for-profit organizations are required to provide which of the following external financial statements?

    a. Statement of financial position, statement of activities, statement of cash flows
    b. Statement of financial position, statement of comprehensive income, statement of cash flows
    c. Statement of comprehensive income, statement of cash flows, statement of gains and losses
    d. Statement of cash flows, statement of comprehensive income, statement of unrelated business income (R/11, FAR, #25, 9875)

32. In year 1, Gamma, a not-for-profit organization, deposited at a bank $1,000,000 given by a donor to purchase endowment securities. The securities were purchased January 2, year 2. At December 31, year 1, the bank recorded $2,000 interest on the deposit. In accordance with the bequest, this $2,000 was used to finance ongoing program expenses in March year 2. At December 31, year 1, what amount of the bank balance should be included as current assets in Gamma's classified balance sheet?

    a. $0
    b. $ 2,000
    c. $1,000,000
    d. $1,002,000 (11/96, AR, #11, amended, 6304)

33. On December 30, Leigh Museum, a not-for-profit organization, received a $7,000,000 donation of Day Co. shares with donor stipulated requirements as follows:
    - Shares valued at $5,000,000 are to be sold with the proceeds used to erect a public viewing building.
    - Shares valued at $2,000,000 are to be retained with the dividends used to support current operations.

    As a consequence of the receipt of the Day shares, how much should Leigh report as temporarily restricted net assets on its statement of financial position?

    a. $0
    b. $2,000,000
    c. $5,000,000
    d. $7,000,000 (5/95, AR, #57, amended, 5475)

34. Famous, a nongovernmental not-for-profit art museum, has elected not to capitalize its permanent collections. In the previous year, a bronze statue was stolen. The statue was not recovered and insurance proceeds of $35,000 were paid to Famous in the current year. This transaction would be reported in

    I. The statement of activities as permanently restricted revenues.
    II. The statement of cash flows as cash flows from investing activities.

    a. I only
    b. II only
    c. Both I and II
    d. Neither I nor II (R/99, AR, #23, amended, 6812)

35. How should a nongovernmental, not-for-profit organization report donor-restricted cash contributions for long-term purposes in its statement of cash flows?

    a. Operating activity inflow
    b. Investing activity inflow
    c. Financing activity inflow
    d. As a noncash transaction (R/08, FAR, #50, 8605)

36. A nongovernmental not-for-profit organization borrowed $5,000, which it used to purchase a truck. In which section of the organization's statement of cash flows should the transaction be reported?

    a. In cash inflow and cash outflow from investing activities
    b. In cash inflow and cash outflow from financing activities
    c. In cash inflow from financing activities and cash outflow from investing activities
    d. In cash inflow from operating activities and cash outflow from investing activities

    (R/06, FAR, #45, 8112)

37. Hunt Community Development Agency (HCDA), a financially independent authority, provides loans to commercial businesses operating in Hunt County. This year, HCDA made loans totaling $500,000. How should HCDA classify the disbursements of loans on the cash flow statement?

    a. Operating activities
    b. Noncapital financing activities
    c. Capital and related financing activities
    d. Investing activities (R/01, AR, #2, 6987)

38. Arkin Corp. is a nongovernmental not-for-profit organization involved in research. Arkin's statement of functional expenses should classify which of the following as support services?

    a. Salaries of staff researchers involved in research
    b. Salaries of fundraisers for funds used in research
    c. Costs of equipment involved in research
    d. Costs of laboratory supplies used in research (R/09, FAR, #25, 8775)

39. In a not-for-profit organization, which of the following should be included in total expenses?

	Grants to other organizations	Depreciation
a.	Yes	Yes
b.	Yes	No
c.	No	No
d.	No	Yes

(R/07, FAR, #14, 8335)

40. Under Abbey Hospital's established rate structure, the hospital would have earned patient service revenue of $6,000,000 for the year. However, Abbey did not expect to collect this amount because of charity care of $1,000,000 and discounts of $500,000 to third-party payors. How much should Abbey record as patient service revenue for the year?

a. $6,000,000
b. $5,500,000
c. $5,000,000
d. $4,500,000 (Editors, 1422)

41. Hospital, Inc., a not-for-profit organization with no governmental affiliation, reported the following in its accounts for the current year ended December 31:

Gross patient services revenue from all services provided at the established billing rates of the hospital (note that this figure includes charity care of $25,000)	$775,000
Provisions for bad debts	15,000
Difference between established billing rates and fees negotiated with third-party payors (contractual adjustments)	70,000

What amount would the hospital report as net patient service revenue in its statement of operations for the year ended December 31, 2012?

a. $665,000
b. $680,000
c. $705,000
d. $735,000 (R/05, FAR, #46, 7790)

42. Which of the following normally would be included in Other Revenue of a hospital?

	Revenue from grants, specified by the donor for research	Revenue from a gift shop
a.	No	No
b.	No	Yes
c.	Yes	No
d.	Yes	Yes

(Editors, 2171)

43. In hospital accounting, restricted funds are

a. **Not** available unless the board of directors removes the restrictions
b. Restricted as to use only for board-designated purposes
c. **Not** available for current operating use; however, the income generated by the funds is available for current operating use
d. Restricted as to use by the donor, grantor, or other source of the resources (5/93, PII, #29, 4136)

44. Valley's community hospital normally includes proceeds from sale of cafeteria meals in

a. Deductions from dietary service expenses
b. Ancillary service revenues
c. Patient service revenues
d. Other revenues (5/94, AR, #60, 4665)

45. A not-for-profit hospital issued long-term tax-exempt bonds for the hospital's benefit. The hospital is responsible for the liability. Which fund may the hospital use to account for this liability?

    a. Enterprise
    b. Specific purpose
    c. General
    d. General long-term debt account group (5/94, AR, #58, 4663)

46. Unrestricted earnings on specific purpose fund investments that are part of a hospital's central operations are reported as

    a. Specific purpose fund restricted revenues
    b. Specific purpose fund unrestricted revenues
    c. General fund deferred revenues
    d. General fund unrestricted revenues (5/92, Theory, #60, amended, 2753)

47. For the fall semester, Ames University assessed its students $3,000,000 for tuition and fees. The net amount realized was only $2,500,000 because scholarships of $400,000 were granted to students, and tuition remissions of $100,000 were allowed to faculty members' children attending Ames. What amount should Ames report for the period as unrestricted current fund gross revenues from tuition and fees?

    a. $2,500,000
    b. $2,600,000
    c. $2,900,000
    d. $3,000,000 (5/93, PII, #33, amended, 4140)

48. What describes a private nonprofit university's internally designated asset, the income from which will be used for a specified purpose?

    a. Endowment
    b. Term endowment
    c. Quasi-endowment
    d. Restricted (Editors, 9096)

49. During the year, Smith University's board of trustees established a $100,000 fund to be retained and invested for scholarship grants. The fund earned $6,000 which had not been disbursed at December 31. What amount should Smith report in a quasi-endowment fund's net assets at December 31?

    a. $0
    b. $ 6,000
    c. $100,000
    d. $106,000 (11/93, PII, #17, amended, 4446)

50. During the current year, the Finn Foundation, a nongovernmental not-for-profit organization, received a $1,000,000 permanent endowment from Chris. Chris stipulated that the income must be used to provide recreational activities for the elderly. The endowment reported income of $80,000 in the current year. What amount of permanently restricted contribution revenue should Finn report at the end of the current year?

    a. $1,080,000
    b. $1,000,000
    c. $ 80,000
    d. $0 (R/11, FAR, #5, 9855)

51. Calvin College makes a discretionary transfer of $100,000 to its library fund. This transfer should be recorded by a debit to

    a. Unrestricted current fund net assets.
    b. Restricted current fund net assets.
    c. General fund expenditures.
    d. Library fund expenditures. (5/92, PII, #37, amended, 2669)

52. The current funds group of a not-for-profit private university includes which of the following?

	Loan funds	Plant funds	
a.	No	No	
b.	No	Yes	
c.	Yes	Yes	
d.	Yes	No	(Editors, 2149)

53. Which of the following accounts would appear in the plant fund of a not-for-profit private college?

	Fuel inventory for power plant	Equipment	
a.	Yes	Yes	
b.	No	Yes	
c.	No	No	
d.	Yes	No	(5/93, Theory, #57, 9095)

54. Community College had the following encumbrances at December 31:

Outstanding purchase orders	$12,000
Commitments for services not received	50,000

What amount of these encumbrances should be reported as liabilities in Community's balance sheet at December 31?

a. $62,000
b. $50,000
c. $12,000
d. $0 (5/92, PII, #38, amended, 2670)

55. Which of the following not-for-profit entities is required to prepare a statement of functional expense?

a. An art museum
b. A shelter for the homeless
c. A private foundation
d. A public golf course (R/09, FAR, #33, 8783)

56. Which of the following comprise functional expense categories for a nongovernmental not-for-profit organization?

a. Program services, management and general, and fundraising
b. Membership dues, fundraising, and management and general
c. Grant expenses, program services, and membership development
d. Membership development, professional fees, and program services (R/08, FAR, #24, 8579)

57. Which basis of accounting should a voluntary health and welfare organization use?

a. Accrual basis for some resources and modified accrual basis for resources
b. Modified accrual basis
c. Accrual basis
d. Cash basis (Editors, 9097)

58. In a statement of activities of a voluntary health and welfare organization, contributions to the building fund should

a. Be included as an element of support
b. Be included as an element of revenue
c. Be included as an element of other changes in net assets
d. Not be included (Editors, 9098)

59. During the current year, the local humane society, a nongovernmental not-for-profit organization, received a $100,000 permanent endowment from Cobb. Cobb stipulated that the income must be used to care for older horses that can no longer race. The endowment reported income of $8,000 in the current year. What amount of unrestricted contribution revenue should the humane society report for the current year?

a. $108,000
b. $100,000
c. $ 8,000
d. $0 (R/10, FAR, #49, 9349)

60. A voluntary health and welfare organization received a $700,000 permanent endowment during the year. The donor stipulated that the income and investment appreciation be used to maintain its senior center. The endowment fund reported a net investment appreciation of $80,000 and investment income of $50,000. The organization spent $60,000 to maintain its senior center during the year. What amount of change in temporarily restricted net assets should the organization report?

a. $ 50,000
b. $ 70,000
c. $130,000
d. $770,000 (R/06, FAR, #15, 8082)

Problem 20-2 SIMULATION: Research

Question: What does a complete set of financial statements of a not-for-profit organization include?

FASB ASC: [ ] - [ ] - [ ] - [ ]

(9143)

Problem 20-3 SIMULATION: Nonprofit Promise Transactions

Community Service, Inc. is a nongovernmental not-for-profit voluntary health and welfare calendar-year organization that began operations on January 1, year 1. It performs voluntary services and derives its revenue primarily from voluntary contributions from the general public. Community implies a time restriction on all promises to contribute cash in future periods. However, no such policy exists with respect to gifts of long-lived assets.

Items 1 through 4 are based on the following selected transactions that occurred during Community's year 2 calendar year:

• Unrestricted written promises to contribute cash—year 1 and year 2	
— Year 1 promises (collected in year 2)	$22,000
— Year 2 promises (collected in year 2)	95,000
— Year 2 promises (uncollected)	28,000
• Written promises to contribute cash restricted to use for community college scholarships (year 1 and year 2)	
— Year 1 promises (collected and expended in year 2)	10,000
— Year 2 promises (collected and expended in year 2)	20,000
— Year 2 promises (uncollected)	12,000
• Written promise to contribute $25,000 if matching funds are raised for the capital campaign during year 2	
— Cash received in year 2 from contributor as a good faith advance	25,000
— Matching funds received in year 2	0
• Cash amount of $37,000 received in year 1 with donor's only stipulation that a bus be purchased	
— Expenditure of full amount of donation July 1, year 2	37,000

Items 1 through 4 represent the year 2 amounts that Community reported for selected financial statement elements in its December 31, year 2, statement of financial position and year 2 statement of activities. For each item, indicate whether the amount was Overstated, Understated, or Correctly stated.

Item	Choice
1. Community reported $28,000 as contributions receivable.	
2. Community reported $37,000 as net assets released from restrictions (satisfaction of use restrictions).	
3. Community reported $22,000 as net assets released from restrictions (due to the lapse of time restrictions).	
4. Community reported $97,000 as contributions—temporarily restricted.	

(5/98, AR, #3, amended, 6656)

Problem 20-4 SIMULATION: Nonprofit Statement of Activities

Area Help, Inc. is a nongovernmental not-for-profit voluntary health and welfare calendar-year organization that began operations on January 1, year 1. It performs voluntary services and derives its revenue primarily from voluntary contributions from the general public. Area Help implies a time restriction on all promises to contribute cash in future periods. However, no such policy exists with respect to gifts of long-lived assets.

Items 1 through 7 are based on the following selected transactions that occurred during Area Help's year 2 calendar year:

• Debt security endowment received in year 2 income to be used for community service	
— Face value	$90,000
— Fair value at time of receipt	88,000
— Fair value at December 31, year 2	87,000
— Interest earned in year 2	9,000
• 10 concerned citizens volunteered to serve meals to the homeless	
— 400 hrs. free; fair market value of services $5 per hr.	2000
• Short-term investment in equity securities in year 2	
— Cost	10,000
— Fair value December 31, year 2	12,000
— Dividend income	1,000
• Music festival to raise funds for a local hospital	
— Admission fees	5,000
— Sales of food and drinks	14,000
— Expenses	4,000
• Reading Material donated to Area Help and distributed to the children in year 2	
— Fair market value	8,000
• Federal youth training fee for service grant	
— Cash received during year 2	30,000
— Instructor salaries paid	26,000
• Other cash operating expenses	
— Business manager salary	60,000
— General bookkeeper salary	40,000
— Director of community activities salary	50,000
— Space rental (75% for community activities, 25% for office activities)	20,000
— Printing and mailing costs for pledge cards	2,000
• Short-term bank loan in year 2	
— Interest payment in year 2	1,000
— Principal payment in year 2	20,000

For Items 1 through 7, enter the appropriate amount for each of the following financial statement elements in the year 2 statement of activities. Round all amounts to the nearest whole dollar.

Item	Amounts
1. Contributions—permanently restricted	
2. Revenues—fees	
3. Investment income—debt securities	
4. Program expenses	
5. General fundraising expenses (excludes special events)	
6. Income on long-term investments—unrestricted	
7. Contributed voluntary services	

(5/98, AR, #3, amended, 6674)

Problem 20-5 SIMULATION: Nonprofit Cash Flows

Items 1 through 8 represent a nonprofit organization's transactions reportable in the statement of cash flows. For each of the items listed, determine the section of the cash flows statement where the item would be classified. A section may be selected once, more than once, or not at all.

Sections
Operating Investing Financing

Item	Classification
1. Unrestricted year 1 promises collected	
2. Cash received from a contributor as a good faith advance on a promise to contribute matching funds	
3. Purchase of bus	
4. Principal payment on short-term bank loan	
5. Purchase of equity securities	
6. Dividend income earned on equity securities	
7. Interest payment on short-term bank loan	
8. Interest earned on endowment	

(9154)

Problem 20-6 SIMULATION: Nonprofit Transactions

For Items 1 through 6, indicate the manner in which the transaction affects Association's financial statements. Select the **best** answer for each item.

	Affect
A.	Increase in unrestricted revenues, gains, and other support
B.	Decrease in an expense
C.	Increase in temporarily restricted net assets
D.	Increase in permanently restricted net assets
E.	No required reportable event

Item	Affect
1. Association's board designates $1,000,000 to purchase investments whose income will be used for capital improvements.	
2. Income from investments in item 1, which was not previously accrued, is received.	
3. A benefactor provided funds for building expansion.	
4. The funds in item 3 are used to purchase a building in the fiscal period following the period the funds were received.	
5. An accounting firm prepared Association's annual financial statements without charge to Association.	
6. Association received investments subject to the donor's requirements that investment income be used to pay for outpatient services.	

(11/95, AR, #111-116, amended, 5854)

Solution 20-1 MULTIPLE-CHOICE ANSWERS

Concepts & Definitions

1. (a) All nonprofit organizations are required to recognize depreciation in general purpose financial statements. They would use the same criteria in allocating the depreciable cost of fixed assets over their estimated useful lives as commercial enterprises. The freezer is a fixed asset that the not-for-profit must depreciate. The building is under construction and, thus, is not yet depreciated. Land is never depreciated. The linens may be classified as supplies, not fixed assets, and, thus, need not be depreciated. (8110)

2. (a) Maintaining a donor list is a fundraising activity. Soliciting prospective members, printing membership benefit brochures, and soliciting dues are member development activities. (6811)

3. (a) None of the shares would be included as unrestricted net assets. The shares valued at $8,000,000 would be a temporarily restricted net asset with the allowable use of the income being restricted by the terms of the donation. The shares valued at $2,000,000 would be a permanently restricted net asset. (8580)

4. (d) Only donor restrictions create restricted revenue. Permanently restricted revenue is restricted in perpetuity. Restrictions that lapse are temporary. (1361)

5. (a) The cash gift should be recorded as a temporarily restricted asset because the donor-imposed restriction, that the principal be held, will lapse upon occurrence of conditions specified by the donor, after the 20 years. A permanent restriction is a donor-imposed restriction that doesn't lapse. The gift is not a liability. (8113)

6. (b) The governing board of an entity may earmark assets for specific purposes as long as these do not conflict with donor conditions. Assets may be designated board-restricted in the financial statements, but they remain in the unrestricted category. Donations are reported as unrestricted unless the restrictions are placed by a donor. (7762)

Contributions

7. (b) Entities are required to classify net assets based upon the existence or absence of donor-imposed restrictions. Thus, net assets are classified into at least three categories: permanently restricted, temporarily restricted, and unrestricted. A temporary restriction is a donor-imposed restriction, such as the stipulation that the funds be used to buy beds, that will lapse upon occurrence of conditions specified by the donor. (9864)

8. (c) Pledges are reported in the period in which they are made, net of an allowance for uncollectible amounts. $100,000 × 90% = $90,000. (7070)

9. (b) Contributions are unconditional donations, or gifts of assets, including property and services. By definition, contributions are nonreciprocal and involve no delivery of services or transfer of ownership. Oz gave tickets with a fair market value (FMV) of $2,500 (25 × $100) to the donor, Acme, therefore, Oz should recognize ticket sales revenue for the FMV of the tickets. (7066)

10. (a) Contributions are unconditional donations, or gifts, of assets, including both property (either for general operating purposes or restricted for a specific purpose) and services (under certain limited circumstances). The fair value of donated services (e.g., doctors, nurses) are reported as both an expense and a revenue if (1) the services would otherwise be purchased; (2) the value of the services is measurable; and (3) the entity controls the employment and duties of the service donors (i.e., there is the equivalent of an employer-employee or hired contractor relationship). Contributions of services are recognized as revenues only if nonfinancial assets are created or enhanced, and special skills are required that would otherwise be purchased. There should be no contribution revenue recorded for the turtle food transferring service provided by the clerk. Though the services may have otherwise been purchased and their value is measurable, there is no effective employer-employee relationship, no nonfinancial assets were created or enhanced, and no special skills were required. (8352)

11. (b) There is an exemption to the rule of recognizing donations of collections of historical artifacts if they are held as a collection or are sold and the proceeds used to acquire other items for collections. (5477)

12. (c) The $125,000 contribution is not restricted to the shortfall between youth activity program revenue and expenses; thus, the entire amount of program expenses satisfies the restriction on $95,000 of the contribution. (The youth activity program revenues are not restricted.) (6910)

13. (c) Conditional promises to give, which depend on the occurrence of a specified future and uncertain event to bind the promisor, shall be recognized when the conditions on which they depend are substantially met. A conditional promise to give is considered unconditional if the possibility that the condition will not be met is remote. A transfer of assets with a conditional promise to contribute them shall be accounted for as a refundable advance until the conditions have been substantially met. (8787)

14. (b) Unconditional pledges are reported as a receivable at their present values in the period in which they are made, net of an allowance for uncollectible amounts. They are not recorded as long-term, deferred revenue, or at the full amount pledged. (8604)

15. (d) Pledges are reported in the period in which they are made, net of an allowance for uncollectible amounts. If part of the pledge is to be applied during some future period, that part is reported as restricted revenue. Of the $300,000 in unrestricted pledges, $100,000 would be earmarked as temporarily restricted revenue because it has been designated by donors for use next year. The remaining $200,000 would be earmarked as unrestricted. The $200,000 less 15% allowance for uncollectible amounts would leave $170,000 as the recognizable amount of unrestricted support in the current-year financial statements. (8089)

16. (d) Contributions that may be used at the board of directors' discretion are unrestricted. Pledges are recognized in the period they are made, net of any appropriate allowance for uncollectible amounts. There is an implicit time restriction on the $500,000 donation, because it will not be made until the next year. The fair value of donated services is recognized as both a revenue and expense if the services (1) would otherwise be purchased, (2) the value of the services is measurable, and (3) there is the equivalent of an employer-employee or hired contractor relationship. (6909)

17. (c) Contributed services shall be recognized as revenue if the services received (a) create or enhance nonfinancial assets or (b) required specialized skills, are provided by individuals possessing those skills, and would typically need to be purchased if not provided by donation. Services requiring specialized skills are provided by accountants, architects, carpenters, doctors, electricians, lawyers, nurses, plumbers, teachers, and other professionals and craftsmen. The AICPA gave $12,500 as the unofficial correct answer. While certainly the $8,000 of veterinarian care would be included in the revenue, the $4,500 for board members to prepare books for an audit could be debatable. If the $4,500 was for accountants or a bookkeeper to prepare the books then it would certainly be included in revenue, but here there isn't any definitive evidence that the board members have the skills to prepare books. Certainly a registered nurse volunteering as receptionist and teacher providing dog walking would not qualify as contribution revenue. (9323)

18. (c) Generally, contributions received are measured at their fair values and recognized as revenues or gains in the period received. (9324)

19. (d) Donations are recognized in the period of receipt, not in the period of expenditure for the donor's specified purpose. The principal of a pure endowment may *not* be expended. The receipt of the pure endowment grant is recorded as permanently restricted revenues upon receipt. (1428)

Other Items

20. (d) The receipt of the pure endowment grant is recorded as permanently restricted revenues upon receipt. The principal of a pure endowment may not be expended. Gains and losses on the investments are included in the statement of activities as increases and decreases, respectively, in temporarily restricted net assets as the income is available for use in its intended purpose in year 2. Therefore, the net effect on temporarily restricted net assets is an increase of $50,000 ($40,000 + $10,000). (9887)

21. (d) All applicable investments are required to be measured at fair value. Gains and losses on the investments are included in the statement of activities as increases and decreases, respectively, in unrestricted net assets unless the use of the securities is temporarily or permanently restricted. Any dividends, interest, or other investment income are to be included in the statement of activities as earned. Such amounts would be reported as adjustments to unrestricted net assets unless some restriction exists. The increase in net assets

would be $115,000; the $100,000 equity securities received as an unrestricted gift, $10,000 gain on investment, and $5,000 in dividends received on these securities. (8351)

22. (c) All investments in debt and equity securities that have a readily determinable market value are required to be measured at fair value. Gains and losses on the investments are included in the statement of activities as increases and decreases, respectively, in unrestricted net assets unless the use of the securities is temporarily or permanently restricted. (9325)

Statement of Activities

23. (b) A nongovernmental not-for-profit organization's statement of activities is similar to a for-profit entity's income statement. The change in net assets is reported in the statement of activities. The revenues, gains, and losses are classified into three groups: unrestricted, temporarily restricted, and permanently restricted. All expenses, which would include depreciation expense, are reported as decreases in unrestricted net assets. (8773)

24. (a) Unrestricted assets are assets from donations unrestricted by the donor and assets formerly temporarily restricted by the donors that have since become unrestricted. The $1 million in cash which was temporarily restricted has now been used for its purpose. This results in an increase in unrestricted net assets. There would not be an increase, but instead there would be a decrease, in temporarily restricted net assets. There would be no effect, increase or decrease, in permanently restricted assets. (8578)

25. (d) A nongovernmental not-for-profit organization's statement of activities is similar to a for-profit entity's income statement. The change in net assets is reported in the statement of activities. The revenues, gains, and losses are classified into three groups: unrestricted, temporarily restricted, and permanently restricted. All expenses are reported as decreases in unrestricted net assets. (8767)

26. (b) All expenses for a nongovernmental not-for-profit organization are reported as decreases in unrestricted net assets. Operating expenses would not be associated with any restrictions and are not reported as a contra-account to associated revenues. (9350)

27. (a) The statement of activities reports the net change for all three types of net assets: unrestricted, temporarily restricted, and permanently restricted. (5817)

28. (b) The statement of activities for a nongovernmental not-for-profit is similar to a for-profit entity's income statement. The change in net assets is reported in the statement of activities. All expenses are reported as decreases in unrestricted net assets. Revenues, gains, and losses are classified into the same three groups as in the statement of financial position (unrestricted, temporarily restricted, and permanently restricted). (8327)

29 (c) Contributions are unconditional donations, or gifts, of assets, including both property and services. Donated assets other than property and equipment, are reported as operating gains or revenue if unrestricted and restricted gain or revenue if restricted. Pledges are reported in the period in which they are made, net of an allowance for uncollectible amounts. Conditional pledges are not recorded until they become unconditional. Public College should report $75,000 as contribution revenue in its statement of activities; the total of the $25,000 cash gift restricted for scholarships and the $50,000 unrestricted (unconditional) pledge. The $10,000 is conditional upon the graduate's death. (8077)

30. (b) A statement of activities or notes to financial statements shall provide information about expenses reported by their functional classification such as major classes of program services and supporting activities. VHWOs shall report that information as well as information about expenses by their natural classification...in a separate financial statement. Other NPOs are encouraged, but not required, to provide information about expenses by their natural classification. (6545)

Other Financial Statements

31. (a) Nonprofit organizations are required to present at least three statements; a Statement of Financial Position, a Statement of Activities, and a Statement of Cash Flows. These statements are similar to those used by a commercial entity. Some entities may choose to also disclose the fund statements. Several formats are acceptable for nonprofit entities, however, aggregated statements must be used. (9875)

32. (b) Assets restricted to a particular use assume the liquidity of that use. Endowment funds are typically long-term assets. (Endowment implies a permanent restriction.) Amounts available to spend on ongoing programs are current. The $2,000 was available and spent on programs. (6304)

33. (c) Net assets are allocated among three classifications for nonprofits: unrestricted, temporarily restricted, and permanently restricted. The $2,000,000 is permanently restricted because only the income may be used to support current operations. The $5,000,000 for the public viewing building is temporarily restricted because the terms of the donation will be met when the building is built. (5475)

34. (b) Contributed collection assets are recognized as revenues if collections are capitalized. Revenues are not recognized if collections are not capitalized. Cash flows from operating activities are generally the cash effect of events that enter into the determination of income. Cash flows from financing activities include paying or incurring debt principal, paying dividends, or issuing or acquiring stock. (6812)

35. (c) The statement of cash flows for a nongovernmental not-for-profit organization reports the cash and cash equivalents similar to commercial enterprises. The description of cash flows is expanded to include donor-restricted cash contributions that must be used for long-term purposes. (8605)

36. (c) The statement of cash flows for not-for-profit organizations reports the change in cash and cash equivalents similar to commercial enterprises. The borrowed $5,000 is classified as a cash inflow from financing activities. The purchase of the truck is considered a cash outflow from investing activities. (8112)

37. (a) Hunt Community Development Agency provides loans as its operating activity, not as financing or investing activities. (6987)

38. (b) The statement of functional expenses provides information about expenses reported by their functional classifications, such as major classes of program services and support services, as well as information about expenses by their natural classification, such as salaries, rent, electricity, interest expense, depreciation awards and grants to others, and professional fees, in a matrix format. Program services are the activities that result in goods and services being distributed to beneficiaries, customers, or members that fulfill the purposes or mission for which the organization exists. Those services are the major purpose for and the major output of the organization and often relate to several major programs. Examples include research, education, and community services, among others. Support services are all activities of a not-for-profit organization other than program services. Generally, they include management and general, fundraising, and membership-development activities. The salaries of fundraisers, even though the funds raised may be used in research, are classified as support services. (8775)

39. (a) Contributions are unconditional donations, or gifts, of assets, including both property (either for general operating purposes or restricted for a specific purpose) and services (under certain limited circumstances). Grants to other organizations are considered contributions. Generally, contributions made, including unconditional promises to give, are recognized as expenses in the period made. All nonprofit organizations are required to recognize depreciation in general purpose external financial statements. (8335)

Healthcare Entities

40. (c) Abbey's patient service is determined by subtracting the charity care from the patient service revenue that would have been recorded at Abbey's established rate for all healthcare services provided (i.e., $6,000,000 – $1,000,000 = $5,000,000). Charity care is not included in patient service revenues because these services were provided free of charge and, thus, were never expected to result in cash flows. On the other hand, the discounts to third-party payors are reported as *deductions* from patient service revenues to determine *net* patient service revenue. Note that the amount that would be reported as *net* patient service revenue is $4,500,000 (i.e., $5,000,000 – $500,000). (1422)

41. (a) Patient service revenue (revenue from health care services) is recorded gross, at the provider's regularly established rates, regardless of collectibility. Charity care is not included in patient service revenues because these services were provided free of charge and, thus, were never expected to result in cash flows. Provisions for *contractual adjustments* (i.e., the difference between established rates and third-party payor payments) and *other adjustments* are recorded on the accrual basis and deducted from gross patient service

revenue. Effective December 2011, the provision for bad debt is a deduction from patient service revenue (not an operating expense).

Gross patient services revenue	$775,000
Less: Charity care include in gross revenue	(25,000)
Less: Contractual adjustments	(70,000)
Less: Provision for bad debt	(15,000)
	$665,000

(7790)

42. (d) Other Revenue of a healthcare entity is the usual day-to-day revenue that is not derived from patient care and services, and generally includes (1) revenue from grants for such specific purposes as research and education; (2) revenue from educational programs; and (3) revenues from miscellaneous sources, such as revenue from gift shops and parking lots. Additional sources of Other Revenue include rentals of hospital plant, sales of supplies to physicians, and fees charged for copies of documents. (2171)

43. (d) In hospital accounting, restricted funds account for financial resources that are externally restricted by donors and grantors for specified operating or research, capital outlay, or endowment purposes. The board of directors of a hospital cannot remove restrictions on the use of financial resources imposed by donors and grantors. While unrestricted resources may be appropriated or designated by the governing board of a hospital for special uses, the board nevertheless has the authority to rescind such actions. Therefore, board-designated assets of a hospital are accounted for in the General Fund. The income generated by a restricted fund may or may not be available for current operating use, depending upon the restrictions imposed upon such income by the donor or grantor. (4136)

44. (d) Other Revenue of a healthcare entity is the usual day-to-day revenue that is not derived from patient care and services, and generally includes (1) proceeds from the sale of cafeteria meals, (2) revenue from educational programs, and (3) revenues from miscellaneous sources, such as revenue from gift shops and parking lots. The proceeds from the sale of cafeteria meals do not offset dietary service expenses. Patient service revenues consist of revenue from routine services (e.g., room, board, general nursing, and home health), other nursing services (e.g., operating room, recovery room, and delivery room), and professional services (e.g., physicians' care, laboratories, radiology, and pharmacy). (4665)

45. (c) Healthcare entities have only two categories of funds: (1) the general funds and (2) the donor-restricted funds. The general fund is used to account for all assets and liabilities that are not required to be accounted for in a donor-restricted fund. Since the bonds in question were issued for the hospital's benefit and are unrelated to any donor-restricted assets, they should be accounted for in the general fund. Both enterprise funds and the general long-term debt account group are utilized by state and local governments rather than by nonprofit healthcare entities. Specific-purpose funds are a type of donor-restricted funds that are used to account for resources restricted by donors and grantors for specific operating purposes. (4663)

46. (d) Unrestricted earnings on specific purpose fund investments that are part of a hospital's central operations are reported as general fund unrestricted revenues. If, on the other hand, the investment earnings were restricted by donors or grantors for a specified operating purpose (e.g., research or education), they would be reported as restricted revenues in the specific purpose fund. Deferred revenue is no longer used in nongovernmental nonprofit accounting. (2753)

Colleges and Universities

47. (d) Tuition and fees are recorded as revenue at standard established rates, with amounts waived (such as scholarships or tuition remissions) recorded as expenditures. Therefore, Ames University should report $3,000,000 as unrestricted current fund revenues from tuition and fees. (4140)

48. (c) Assets with *internal* restrictions (i.e., designation by the governing board) are quasi-endowments. Endowment, term-endowment, and restricted current signify resources with *donor* restrictions. (9096)

49. (d) Quasi-Endowment Funds are used by colleges and universities to account for amounts set aside by the governing board to function as endowments. Smith University should report as quasi-endowment fund net assets at December 31, the sum of the $100,000 set aside by the governing board to be invested for scholarship grants and the $6,000 of fund earnings which had not been disbursed at December 31. (4446)

50. (b) The $80,000 income would be held in a restricted current fund which is used for available financial resources and related liabilities that are expendable only for operating purposes specified by the donor, in this case, providing recreational activities for the elderly. An endowment fund would be used to account for the $1,000,000 principal accepted with the donor stipulation. Contributions received are measured at their fair values and recognized as revenues (restricted or unrestricted) in the period received. (9855)

51. (a) The question implies that the library fund is separate from the current fund. Therefore, a discretionary transfer could only be made from the unrestricted portion of the current fund. Consequently, the transfer should be recorded by a debit to the unrestricted current fund net assets. (2669)

52. (a) The fund groups generally used by colleges and universities are (1) current funds, (2) loan funds, (3) endowment and similar funds, (4) annuity and life income funds, (5) plant funds, and (6) agency funds. Loan funds and plant funds are not included in the current funds group as they are separately disclosed. (2149)

53. (b) The asset accounts in the Investment in Plant subgroup of the Plant Funds group of a college contain the carrying amounts of the institution's fixed assets. Therefore, the equipment would be reported in the Investment in Plant subgroup of the Plant Funds group of the college. The fuel inventory for the college's power plant should be reported in the Unrestricted Current Funds under Inventory of Materials and Supplies. (9095)

54. (d) Outstanding encumbrances cannot be reported as liabilities. Any encumbrance outstanding should be reported as part of the equity section of the balance sheet. (2670)

VHWO Accounting

55. (b) A statement of functional expenses is required only for voluntary health and welfare organizations (VHWOs). VHWOs offer free or low cost services to the general public or to certain segments of society, and are supported primarily by public contributions. A shelter for the homeless would be considered a VHWO. A private foundation is not public. An art museum and a public golf course charge fees. (8783)

56. (a) There are two primary functional expense classifications; program services and support services. Program services include research, education, and community services. Support services categories are management and general, and fundraising. Membership dues, grant expenses, membership development, and professional fees are not functional expense categories for a nongovernmental not-for-profit organization. (8579)

57. (c) Nongovernmental nonprofit organizations, including voluntary health and welfare organizations (VHWOs), use the accrual basis of accounting for all external reporting purposes. (9097)

58. (a) The contributions to the building fund are included as support in the statement of activities of a voluntary health and welfare organization. (9098)

59. (d) An endowment fund is used to account for the principal of gifts or bequests accepted with donor stipulations that (a) the principal is to be maintained intact (permanent), and the earnings may be expended for unrestricted purposes and/or specified restricted purposes. Cobb stipulated that the income of $8,000 must be used for older horses that can no longer race so that contribution revenue would be restricted. (9349)

60. (b) The restricted current fund is used for available financial resources and related liabilities that are expendable only for operating purposes specified by the donor. The change in temporarily restricted assets would consist of the $80,000 investment appreciation plus the $50,000 investment income less the $60,000 spent to maintain the center. An endowment fund would be used to account for the $700,000 principal accepted with the donor stipulation that the income and investment appreciation be used to maintain the senior center. (8082)

PERFORMANCE BY SUBTOPICS

Each category below parallels a subtopic covered in Chapter 20. Record the number and percentage of questions you correctly answered in each subtopic area.

Concepts & Definitions

Question #	Correct √
1	
2	
3	
4	
5	
6	
# Questions	6
# Correct	______
% Correct	______

Contributions

Question #	Correct √
7	
8	
9	
10	
11	
12	
13	
14	
15	
16	
17	
18	
19	
# Questions	13
# Correct	______
% Correct	______

Other Items

Question #	Correct √
20	
21	
22	
# Questions	3
# Correct	______
% Correct	______

Statement of Activities

Question #	Correct √
23	
24	
25	
26	
27	
28	
29	
30	
# Questions	8
# Correct	______
% Correct	______

Other Financial Statements

Question #	Correct √
31	
32	
33	
34	
35	
36	
37	
38	
39	
# Questions	9
# Correct	______
% Correct	______

Healthcare Entities

Question #	Correct √
40	
41	
42	
43	
44	
45	
46	
# Questions	7
# Correct	______
% Correct	______

Colleges and Universities

Question #	Correct √
47	
48	
49	
50	
51	
52	
53	
54	
# Questions	8
# Correct	______
% Correct	______

VHWO Accounting

Question #	Correct √
55	
56	
57	
58	
59	
60	
# Questions	6
# Correct	______
% Correct	______

Solution 20-2 SIMULATION: Research

FASB Accounting Standards Codification

FASB ASC:	958	-	205	-	45	-	4

45-4 A complete set of financial statements of an NFP shall include a statement of financial position as of the end of the reporting period, a statement of activities and a statement of cash flows for the reporting period, and accompanying notes to the financial statements. In addition, a voluntary health and welfare entity shall provide a statement of functional expenses.

Solution 20-3 SIMULATION: Nonprofit Promise Transactions

Item	Choice
1. Community reported $28,000 as contributions receivable.	Understated
2. Community reported $37,000 as net assets released from restrictions (satisfaction of use restrictions).	Understated
3. Community reported $22,000 as net assets released from restrictions (due to the lapse of time restrictions).	Correctly Stated
4. Community reported $97,000 as contributions—temporarily restricted.	Overstated

Explanations

1. Contributions receivable should be at least $40,000, to include the unrestricted $28,000 and the restricted $12,000 of year 2 promised contributions that are uncollected.

2. The year 1 promises to contribute cash in year 2 and the bus purchase cash are both assets released from restrictions.

3. The year 1 promises to contribute cash of $22,000 are restricted by time only.

4. Temporarily restricted cash is composed of uncollected year 2 promises to give in future years. At most this is ($28,000 + $12,000) $40,000. The $25,000 matching funds advance is a liability, as the conditions of the potential contributor are apparently not met.

Solution 20-4 SIMULATION: Nonprofit Statement of Activities

Item	Amounts
1. Contributions—permanently restricted	$ 88,000
2. Revenues—fees	$ 5,000
3. Investment income—debt securities	$ 8,000
4. Program expenses	$ 99,000
5. General fundraising expenses (excludes special events)	$ 2,000
6. Income on long-term investments—unrestricted	$0
7. Contributed voluntary services	$0

Explanations

1. Permanently restricted contributions for the year are the debt security endowment, at its fair value at time of receipt.

2. The only revenues that Area Help had during the year are the admission fees to the music festival.

3. Investment income includes interest earned plus the change in fair value from time of receipt to the balance sheet date. ($9,000 – $1,000)

4. Program expenses are those connected with the NPO's mission. These include reading materials distributed to children, instructor salaries, the director of community activities' salary, and a portion of the space rental.

5. The printing and mailing costs for pledge cards are the only general fundraising expenses.

6. There is no unrestricted income from long-term investments.

7. There are no contributed voluntary services that qualify to be included on the statement of activities (i.e., that result from an employer-employee type of relationship).

Solution 20-5 SIMULATION: Nonprofit Cash Flows

Item	Classification
1. Unrestricted year 1 promises collected	Operating
2. Cash received from a contributor as a good faith advance on a promise to contribute matching funds	Operating
3. Purchase of bus	Investing
4. Principal payment on short-term bank loan	Financing
5. Purchase of equity securities	Investing
6. Dividend income earned on equity securities	Operating
7. Interest payment on short-term bank loan	Operating
8. Interest earned on endowment	Operating

Explanations

1. Cash flows from operating activities include most contributions; certain donor-restricted cash that must be used for long-term purposes is included in financing activities.

2. Cash flows from operating activities include most contributions; certain donor-restricted cash that must be used for long-term purposes is included in financing activities.

3. Transactions involving investments as well as property, plant, and equipment generally are classified as investing activities.

4. Principal repayments are cash flows used by financing activities.

5. Cash paid for, and received from, transactions involving investments and property, plant, and equipment generally is classified as investing.

6. Interest and dividends received are cash flows from operating activities.

7. Interest payments are cash flows used by operating activities.

8. Interest and dividends received are cash flows from operating activities.

Solution 20-6 SIMULATION: Nonprofit Transactions

Item	Affect
1. Association's board designates $1,000,000 to purchase investments whose income will be used for capital improvements.	E
2. Income from investments in item 1, which was not previously accrued, is received.	A
3. A benefactor provided funds for building expansion.	C
4. The funds in item 3 are used to purchase a building in the fiscal period following the period the funds were received.	A
5. An accounting firm prepared Association's annual financial statements without charge to Association.	A
6. Association received investments subject to the donor's requirements that investment income be used to pay for outpatient services.	D

Explanations

1. Board designated assets are unrestricted. Only donor restrictions "restrict" assets for external reporting purposes.

2. Income from board-designated assets is unrestricted revenue.

3. The donation is restricted only until the donor's conditions are met.

4. As Association does not have an accounting policy that implies a time restriction on gifts of long-lived assets, the building expansion funds are unrestricted when the building is built.

5. The measurable fair value of donated services that would otherwise be purchased are recorded as both revenue and expense if (1) nonfinancial assets are created or enhanced, (2) the performance of the services is controlled by the NPO, and (3) special skills are required. All of these conditions are met. As the terms of the inherent restriction (to purchase accounting services) is met within the period of donation, this is an unrestricted donation.

6. The donation is subject to the donor's restriction, a requirement that cannot be fulfilled with the passage of time or the accomplishment of a specific objective.

APPENDIX A
PRACTICE EXAMINATION

Editor's Note: There is only one practice (final) examination. Do not take this exam until you are ready for it.

Testlet 1 MULTIPLE-CHOICE QUESTIONS

1. On January 1, year 2, Victor Company purchased for $85,000 a machine having a useful life of ten years and an estimated salvage value of $5,000. The machine was depreciated by the straight-line method. On July 1, year 7, the machine was sold for $45,000. For the year ended December 31, year 7, how much gain should Victor record on the sale?

   a. $0
   b. $1,000
   c. $4,000
   d. $6,750 (8990)

2. Brock Corp.'s transactions for the current year ended December 31 included the following:

   - Acquired 50% of Hoag Corp.'s common stock for $225,000 cash which was borrowed from a bank.
   - Issued 5,000 shares of its preferred stock for land having a fair value of $400,000.
   - Issued 500 of its 11% debenture bonds, due in 3 years, for $490,000 cash.
   - Purchased a patent for $275,000 cash.
   - Paid $150,000 toward a bank loan.
   - Sold investment securities for $995,000.

   Brock's net cash provided by investing activities for the year was

   a. $370,000
   b. $495,000
   c. $595,000
   d. $770,000 (8991)

3. According to the FASB conceptual framework, predictive value is an ingredient of

	Faithful Representation	Relevance
a.	Yes	Yes
b.	No	Yes
c.	No	No
d.	Yes	No

(2695)

4. Roy City received a gift, the principal of which is to be invested in perpetuity with the income to be used to support the local library. In which fund should this gift be recorded?

   a. Permanent fund
   b. Investment trusts fund
   c. Private-purpose trusts fund
   d. Special revenue fund (9853)

5. A company's wages payable increased from the beginning to the end of the year. In the company's statement of cash flows (direct method), the cash paid for wages would be

   a. Salary expense plus wages payable at the beginning of the year
   b. Salary expense plus the increase in wages payable from the beginning to the end of the year
   c. Salary expense less the increase in wages payable from the beginning to the end of the year
   d. The same as salary expense (1935)

6. The following condensed balance sheet is presented for the partnership of Smith and Jones, who share profits and losses in the ratio of 60:40, respectively:

Other assets	$450,000	Accounts payable	$120,000
Smith, loan	20,000	Smith, capital	195,000
	$470,000	Jones, capital	155,000
			$470,000

   The partners have decided to liquidate the partnership. If the other assets are sold for $385,000, what amount of the available cash should be distributed to Smith?

   a. $136,000
   b. $156,000
   c. $159,000
   d. $195,000 (4852)

7. Frey Inc. was organized on January 2 of the current year with the following capital structure:

   - 10% cumulative preferred stock, par value $100 and liquidation value $105; authorized, issued and outstanding 1,000 shares — $100,000
   - Common stock, par value $25; authorized 100,000 shares; issues and outstanding 10,000 shares — 250,000

   Frey's net income for the year ended December 31 was $450,000, but no dividends were declared. How much was Frey's book value per preferred share at December 31?

   a. $100
   b. $105
   c. $110
   d. $115 (1265)

8. In the due process of developing International Financial Reporting Standards (IFRS), which of the following is true in setting the agenda?

   a. The IASB evaluates the merits of adding a potential item to its agenda mainly by reference to the needs of the financial statement preparer over the financial statement user.
   b. The IASB's discussions of potential projects and its decisions to adopt new projects generally takes place in private IASB meetings.
   c. In making decisions regarding its future standard setting agenda priorities, the IASB purposefully excludes consideration of factors related to on-going convergence initiatives with U.S. accounting standard-setters.
   d. The IASB's approval to add agenda items, as well as its decisions on their priority, is by a simple majority vote at a public IASB meeting. (9718)

9. On December 31 of the current year, Jet Co. received two $10,000 notes receivable from customers in exchange for services rendered. On both notes, interest is calculated on the outstanding principal balance at the annual rate of 3% and payable at maturity. The note from Hart Corp., made under customary trade terms, is due in nine months and the note from Maxx Inc. is due in five years. The market interest rate for similar notes on this date was 8%. The compound interest factors to convert future values into present values at 8% follow:

   Present value of $1 due in nine months: .944
   Present value of $1 due in five years: .680

   At what amounts should these two notes receivable be reported in Jet's December 31 balance sheet?

	Hart	Maxx
a.	$ 9,440	$6,800
b.	$ 9,652	$7,820
c.	$10,000	$6,800
d.	$10,000	$7,820

   (2582)

10. Strand Inc., provides an incentive compensation plan under which its president receives a bonus equal to 10% of the corporation's income in excess of $200,000 before income tax but after deduction of the bonus. If income before income tax and bonus is $640,000 and the tax rate is 40%, the amount of the bonus would be

    a. $40,000
    b. $44,000
    c. $58,180
    d. $64,000 (8992)

11. _______________ is (are) classified as current liabilities.

    a. Restricted cash
    b. IOUs from officers
    c. Overdrafts in accounts with no available cash in another account in the same bank to offset
    d. All of the above (9026)

12. According to the FASB conceptual framework, which of the following attributes would **not** be used to measure inventory?

    a. Historical cost
    b. Replacement cost
    c. Net realizable value
    d. Present value of future cash flows (6087)

13. On December 31 of the previous year, Byte Co. had capitalized software costs of $600,000 with an economic life of four years. Sales for the current year were 10% of expected total sales of the software. At December 31 of the current year, the software had a net realizable value of $480,000. In its December 31, current year balance sheet, what amount should Byte report as net capitalized cost of computer software?

    a. $432,000
    b. $450,000
    c. $480,000
    d. $540,000 (6978)

14. Which two of the following statements concerning patents is correct?

    a. Legal costs incurred to successfully defend an internally developed patent should be capitalized and amortized over the patent's remaining economic life.
    b. Legal fees and other direct costs incurred in registering a patent should be capitalized and amortized on a straight-line basis over a five-year period.
    c. Research and development contract services purchased from others and used to develop a patented manufacturing process should be capitalized and amortized over the patent's economic life.
    d. Research and development costs incurred to develop a patented item should be capitalized and amortized on a straight-line basis over 17 years. (9023)

15. DeeCee Co. adjusted its historical cost income statement by applying specific price indexes to its depreciation expense and cost of goods sold. DeeCee's adjusted income statement is prepared according to

    a. Fair value accounting
    b. General purchasing power accounting
    c. Current cost accounting
    d. Current cost/general purchasing power accounting (4507)

16. Which of the following is **not** addressed in an article within Regulation S-X governing SEC accounting regulations?
    a. Definitions of terms used in registration statements and reports
    b. Requirements of qualifications of accountants and accountants' reports in SEC filings
    c. Requirements governing preparation of consolidated, but not combined, financial statements
    d. Requirements for the various financial statements to be included in disclosure documents, and for what periods (9704)

17. Crane Mfg. leases a machine from Frank Leasing. Ownership of the machine returns to Frank after the 15-year lease expires. The machine is expected to have an economic life of 17 years. At this time, Frank is unable to predict the collectibility of the lease payments to be received from Crane. The present value of the minimum lease payments exceeds 90% of the fair value of the machine. What is the appropriate classification of this lease for Crane?
    a. Operating
    b. Leveraged
    c. Capital
    d. Installment (7605)

Items 18 and 19 are based on the following:

Scroll, Inc., a wholly owned subsidiary of Pirn, Inc., began operations on January 1 of the current year. The following information is from the condensed year-end income statements of Pirn and Scroll:

	Pirn	Scroll
Sales to Scroll	$ 100,000	$ --
Sales to others	400,000	300,000
	500,000	300,000
Cost of goods sold:		
Acquired from Pirn	--	(80,000)
Acquired from others	(350,000)	(190,000)
Gross profit	150,000	30,000
Depreciation	(40,000)	(10,000)
Other expenses	(60,000)	(15,000)
Income from operations	50,000	5,000
Gain on sale of equipment to Scroll	(12,000)	--
Income before income taxes	$ 38,000	$ 5,000

- Sales by Pirn to Scroll are made on the same terms as those made to third parties.
- Equipment purchased by Scroll from Pirn for $36,000 on January 1 is depreciated using the straight-line method over four years.

18. In Pirn's December 31 consolidating worksheet, how much intercompany profit should be eliminated from Scroll's inventory?
    a. $30,000
    b. $20,000
    c. $10,000
    d. $ 6,000 (2575)

19. What amount should be reported as depreciation expense in Pirn's year-end consolidated income statement?
    a. $50,000
    b. $47,000
    c. $44,000
    d. $41,000 (2576)

20. Certain balance sheet accounts of a foreign subsidiary of Rowan Inc., at December 31, have been translated into U.S. dollars as follows:

	Translated at	
	Current rates	Historical rates
Note receivable, long-term	$240,000	$200,000
Prepaid rent	85,000	80,000
Patent	150,000	170,000
	$475,000	$450,000

The subsidiary's functional currency is the currency of the country in which it is located. What total amount should be included in Rowan's December 31 consolidated balance sheet for the above accounts?

a. $450,000
b. $455,000
c. $475,000
d. $495,000

(9059)

21. Busy Corp. prepared the following reconciliation between pretax accounting income and taxable income for the year ended December 31:

Pretax accounting income	$ 250,000
Taxable income	(150,000)
Difference	$ 100,000
Analysis of difference:	
Interest on municipal bonds	$ 25,000
Excess of tax over book depreciation	75,000
	$ 100,000

Busy's effective income tax rate for the year is 30%. The depreciation difference will reverse in equal amounts over the next three years at an enacted tax rate of 40%. In Busy's income statement, what amount should be reported as the current portion of its provision for income taxes?

a. $45,000
b. $67,500
c. $75,000
d. $82,500

(2628)

22. Wilson Corp. experienced a $50,000 decline in the market value of its inventory in the first quarter of its fiscal year. Wilson had expected this decline to reverse in the third quarter, and in fact, the third quarter recovery exceeded the previous decline by $10,000. Wilson's inventory did not experience any other declines in market value during the fiscal year. What amounts of loss and/or gain should Wilson report in its interim financial statements for the first and third quarters?

	First quarter	Third quarter
a.	$0	$0
b.	$0	$10,000 gain
c.	$50,000 loss	$50,000 gain
d.	$50,000 loss	$60,000 gain

(6787)

23. On September 1, Brady Corp. entered into a foreign exchange contract for speculative purposes by purchasing 50,000 deutsche marks for delivery in 60 days. The rates to exchange $1 for 1 deutsche mark follow:

	9/1	9/30
Spot rate	$0.75	$0.70
30-day forward rate	$0.73	$0.72
60-day forward rate	$0.74	$0.73

In its September 30 income statement, what amount should Brady report as foreign exchange loss?

a. $2,500
b. $1,500
c. $1,000
d. $500 (4087)

24. Which of the following is used in calculating the income recognized in the fourth and final year of a contract accounted for by the percentage of completion method?

	Actual total costs	Income previously recognized
a.	Yes	Yes
b.	Yes	No
c.	No	Yes
d.	No	No

(5562)

25. How should the effect of a change in accounting principle that is inseparable from the effect of a change in accounting estimate be reported?

a. As a component of income from continuing operations
b. By restating the financial statements of all prior periods presented
c. As a correction of an error
d. By footnote disclosure only (6476)

26. How would the amortization of premium on bonds payable affect each of the following?

	Carrying amount of bond	Net income
a.	Increase	Decrease
b.	Increase	Increase
c.	Decrease	Decrease
d.	Decrease	Increase

(8993)

27. What basis of accounting does Arbor City use to present the general fund in the financial statements?

I. Modified accrual basis in all financial statements
II. Accrual basis in the government-wide statement of activities and statement of net assets
III. Modified accrual basis in the fund financial statements with a reconciliation to the accrual basis

a. I only
b. II only
c. III only
d. Both II and III (6877)

28. Financial statements for which fund type generally report net assets?

a. Capital projects
b. Expendable pension trust
c. Special revenue
d. Enterprise (5812)

29. During the current fiscal year, Foxx, a nongovernmental not-for-profit organization, received unrestricted pledges of $300,000. Of the pledged amount, $200,000 was designated by donors for use during the current year, and $100,000 was designated for next year. Five percent of the pledges are expected to be uncollectible. What amount should Foxx report as restricted support (contributions) in the statement of activities for the current year?

    a. $200,000
    b. $190,000
    c. $100,000
    d. $ 95,000 (8789)

30. Which of the following should normally be considered ongoing or central transactions for a not-for-profit hospital?

    I. Room and board fees from patients
    II. Recovery room fees

    a. Neither I nor II
    b. Both I and II
    c. II only
    d. I only (5818)

Testlet 2 MULTIPLE-CHOICE QUESTIONS

1. In its year 1 income statement, Noll Corp. reported depreciation of $400,000 and interest revenue on municipal obligations of $60,000. Noll reported depreciation of $550,000 on its year 1 income tax return. The difference in depreciation is the only temporary difference, and it will reverse equally over the next three years. Noll's enacted income tax rates are 35% for year 1, 30% for year 2 and 25% for year 3 and year 4. Assuming Noll expects to report taxable income in all future years, what amount should be included in the deferred income tax liability in Noll's December 31, year 1 balance sheet?

    a. $40,000
    b. $52,500
    c. $63,000
    d. $73,500 (3308)

2. On January 1, year 3, Vick Company purchased a trademark for $400,000, having an estimated useful life of 16 years. In January of year 7, Vick paid $60,000 for legal fees in a successful defense of the trademark. Trademark amortization expense for the year ended December 31, year 7, should be

    a. $0
    b. $25,000
    c. $28,750
    d. $30,000 (8994)

3. Pare, Inc. purchased 10% of Tot Co.'s 100,000 outstanding shares of common stock on January 2 of the current year for $50,000. On December 31, Pare purchased an additional 20,000 shares of Tot for $150,000. There was no goodwill as a result of either acquisition, and Tot had not issued any additional stock during the year. Tot reported earnings of $300,000 for the year. What amount should Pare report in its December 31 balance sheet as investment in Tot?

    a. $170,000
    b. $200,000
    c. $230,000
    d. $290,000 (4383)

4. On September 29, Wall Co. paid $860,000 for all the issued and outstanding common stock of Hart Corp. On that date, the carrying amounts of Hart's recorded assets and liabilities were $800,000 and $180,000, respectively. Hart's recorded assets and liabilities had fair values of $840,000 and $140,000, respectively. In Wall's September 30 balance sheet, what amount should be reported as goodwill?

   a. $ 20,000
   b. $160,000
   c. $180,000
   d. $240,000 (6900)

5. What is the underlying concept that supports the immediate recognition of a contingent loss?

   a. Substance over form
   b. Consistency
   c. Matching
   d. Conservatism (5268)

6. On January 2 of the current year, Loch Co. established a noncontributory defined benefit pension plan covering all employees and contributed $400,000 to the plan. At December 31, Loch determined that the service and interest costs on the plan were $720,000 for the year. The expected and the actual rate of return on plan assets for the year was 10%. There are no other components of Loch's pension expense. What amount should Loch report as accrued pension cost in its December 31 year-end balance sheet?

   a. $280,000
   b. $320,000
   c. $360,000
   d. $720,000 (6902)

7. Which of the following is a true statement related to electronic filing of required SEC submissions?

   a. Regulation S-X is the separate regulation that contains the rules prescribing electronic filing and the procedures for such filings.
   b. Regulation S-T requires all SEC filings to be submitted electronically.
   c. Unanticipated technical difficulties can result in a temporary hardship exemption for electronic filing.
   d. Only temporary hardship exemptions are available for electronic filing requirements. (9715)

8. Perk, Inc. issued $500,000, 10% bonds to yield 8%. Bond issuance costs were $10,000. How should Perk calculate the net proceeds to be received from the issuance?

   a. Discount the bonds at the stated rate of interest.
   b. Discount the bonds at the market rate of interest.
   c. Discount the bonds at the stated rate of interest and deduct bond issuance costs.
   d. Discount the bonds at the market rate of interest and deduct bond issuance costs. (6778)

9. The portion of special assessment debt maturing in 5 years, to be repaid from general resources of the government, should be reported in the

   a. General fund column
   b. Governmental activities column
   c. Agency fund column
   d. Capital projects fund column (4990)

10. Rice Co. was incorporated on January 1 of the current year with $500,000 from the issuance of stock and borrowed funds of $75,000. During this first year of operations, net income was $25,000. On December 15, Rice paid a $2,000 cash dividend. No additional activities affected owners' equity in the year. At December 31, Rice's liabilities had increased to $94,000. In Rice's December 31 balance sheet, total assets should be reported at

    a. $598,000
    b. $600,000
    c. $617,000
    d. $692,000 (3239)

11. Bach Co. adopted the dollar-value LIFO inventory method as of January 1, year 1. A single inventory pool and an internally computed price index are used to compute Bach's LIFO inventory layers. Information about Bach's dollar value inventory follows:

	Inventory	
Date	At base year cost	At current year cost
1/1, year 1	$90,000	$90,000
Year 1 layer	20,000	30,000
Year 2 layer	40,000	80,000

What was the price index used to compute Bach's year 2 dollar value LIFO inventory layer?

a. 1.09
b. 1.25
c. 1.33
d. 2.00 (6976)

12. In an exchange with commercial substance, Vey Co. traded equipment with an original cost of $100,000 and accumulated depreciation of $40,000 for similar productive equipment with a fair value of $120,000. In addition, Vey received $30,000 cash in connection with this exchange. What should be Vey's carrying amount for the equipment received on the day of exchange?

a. $ 90,000
b. $ 60,000
c. $ 48,000
d. $ 120,000 (2586)

13. Fish Road property owners in Sea County are responsible for special assessment debt that arose from a storm sewer project. If the property owners default, Sea has no obligation regarding debt service, although it does bill property owners for assessments and uses the monies it collects to pay debt holders. What fund type should Sea use to account for these collection and servicing activities?

a. Agency
b. Debt service
c. Expendable trust funds
d. Capital projects (5807)

14. When the cash proceeds from a bond issued with detachable stock purchase warrants exceeds the sum of the par value of the bonds and the fair value of the warrants, the excess should be credited to

a. Additional paid-in capital
b. Retained earnings
c. Premium on bonds payable
d. Detachable stock warrants outstanding (8995)

15. In financial reporting of segment data, which of the following must be considered in determining if an industry segment is a reportable segment?

	Sales to unaffiliated customers	Intersegment sales
a.	Yes	Yes
b.	Yes	No
c.	No	Yes
d.	No	No

(8354)

16. Theoretically, which of the following costs incurred in connection with a machine purchased for use in a company's manufacturing operations would be capitalized?

	Insurance on machine while in transit	Testing and preparation of machine for use
a.	Yes	Yes
b.	Yes	No
c.	No	Yes
d.	No	No

(5548)

17. Bell Co. is a defendant in a lawsuit that could result in a large payment to the plaintiff. Bell's attorney believes that there is a 90% chance that Bell will lose the suit, and estimates that the loss will be anywhere from $5,000,000 to $20,000,000 and possibly as much as $30,000,000. None of the estimates are better than the others. What amount of liability should Bell report on its balance sheet related to the lawsuit?

    a. $0
    b. $ 5,000,000
    c. $20,000,000
    d. $30,000,000 (7780)

18. Chape Co. had the following information related to common and preferred shares during the year:

Common shares outstanding	1/1	700,000
Common shares repurchased	3/31	20,000
Conversion of preferred shares	6/30	40,000
Common shares repurchased	12/1	36,000

Chape reported net income of $2,000,000 at December 31. What amount of shares should Chape use as the denominator in the computation of basic earnings per share?

    a. 684,000
    b. 700,000
    c. 702,000
    d. 740,000 (9859)

19. Strauch Co. has one class of common stock outstanding and no other securities that are potentially convertible into common stock. During the previous year, 100,000 shares of common stock were outstanding. In the current year, two distributions of additional common shares occurred: On April 1, 20,000 shares of treasury stock were sold, and on July 1, a 2-for-1 stock split was issued. Net income was $410,000 in the current year and $350,000 in the previous year. What amounts should Strauch report as earnings per share in its current and previous year comparative income statements?

	Current Year	Previous Year
a.	$1.78	$3.50
b.	$1.78	$1.75
c.	$2.34	$1.75
d.	$2.34	$3.50

(2448)

20. Whether recognized or unrecognized in an entity's financial statements, disclosure of the fair values of the entity's financial instruments is required when

	It is practicable to estimate those 4.99 values	Aggregated fair values are material to the entity
a.	No	No
b.	No	Yes
c.	Yes	No
d.	Yes	Yes

(8101)

21. Pharm, a nongovernmental not-for-profit organization, is preparing its year-end financial statements. Which of the following statements is required?

    a. Statement of changes in financial position
    b. Statement of cash flows
    c. Statement of changes in fund balance
    d. Statement of revenue, expenses and changes in fund balance (6995)

22. On January 1, year 1, Newport Corp. purchased a machine for $100,000. The machine was depreciated using the straight-line method over a 10-year period with no residual value. Because of a bookkeeping error, no depreciation was recognized in Newport's year 1 financial statements, resulting in a $10,000 overstatement of the book value of the machine on December 31, year 1. The oversight was discovered during the preparation of Newport's year 2 financial statements. What amount should Newport report for depreciation expense on the machine in the year 2 financial statements?

    a. $ 9,000
    b. $10,000
    c. $11,000
    d. $20,000 (9867)

23. A company is an accelerated filer that is required to file Form 10-K with the United States Securities and Exchange Commission (SEC). What is the maximum number of days after the company's fiscal year end that the company has to file Form 10-K with the SEC?

    a. 60 days
    b. 75 days
    c. 90 days
    d. 120 days (9351)

24. Which of the following would be reported in the income statement of a proprietorship?

	Proprietor's draw	Depreciation
a.	Yes	Yes
b.	Yes	No
c.	No	Yes
d.	No	No

(7615)

25. Under current generally accepted accounting principles, which approach is used to determine income tax expense?

    a. Asset and liability approach
    b. "With and without" approach
    c. Net of tax approach
    d. Periodic expense approach (6786)

26. Rose Co. sells one product and uses the last-in, first-out method to determine inventory cost. Information for the month of January follows:

	Total Units	Unit Cost
Beginning inventory, 1/1	8,000	$8.20
Purchases, 1/5	12,000	7.90
Sales	10,000	

Rose has determined that at January 31 the replacement cost of its inventory was $8 per unit and the net realizable value was $8.80 per unit. Rose's normal profit margin is $1 per unit. Rose applies the lower of cost or market rule to total inventory and records any resulting loss. At January 31, what should be the net carrying amount of Rose's inventory?

    a. $79,000
    b. $79,800
    c. $80,000
    d. $81,400 (7612)

27. The following funds were among those held by State College at December 31:

Principal specified by the donor as nonexpendable	$500,000
Principal expendable after 10 years from present	300,000
Principal designated from current funds	100,000

What amount should State College classify as regular endowment funds?

a. $100,000
b. $300,000
c. $500,000
d. $900,000 (2667)

28. On January 2 of the current year, Yardley Co. sold a plant to Ivory Inc. for $1,500,000. On that date, the plant's carrying cost was $1,000,000. Ivory gave Yardley $300,000 cash and a $1,200,000 note, payable in 4 annual installments of $300,000 plus 12% interest. Ivory made the first principal and interest payment of $444,000 on December 31. Yardley uses the installment method of revenue recognition. In its current year income statement, what amount of realized gross profit should Yardley report?

a. $344,000
b. $200,000
c. $148,000
d. $100,000 (4083)

29. On December 31, Pell, Inc., sold a machine to Flax, and simultaneously leased it back for one year. Pertinent information at this date is as follows:

Sales price	$360,000
Carrying amount	315,000
Estimated remaining useful life	12 years
Present value of lease rentals ($3,000 for 12 months @ 12%)	34,100

At December 31, how much should Pell report as deferred revenue from the sale of the machine?

a. $0
b. $10,900
c. $34,100
d. $45,000 (8996)

30. River City has a defined contribution pension plan. How should River City report the pension plan in its financial statements?

a. Within the component units column of its government-wide financial statements
b. Within the fiduciary column of its government-wide financial statements
c. Within its fund financial statements
d. Within the governmental activities column of its government-wide financial statements (6876)

Testlet 3 MULTIPLE-CHOICE QUESTIONS

1. During the current year, Beck Co. purchased equipment for cash of $47,000, and sold equipment with a $10,000 carrying value for a gain of $5,000. How should these transactions be reported in Beck's current year statement of cash flows?

a. Cash outflow of $32,000
b. Cash outflow of $42,000
c. Cash inflow of $5,000 and cash outflow of $47,000
d. Cash inflow of $15,000 and cash outflow of $47,000 (6487)

2. Which of the following appropriately describes a difference between full International Financial Reporting Standards (IFRS) and IFRS for Small and Medium-Sized Entities?
   a. Most of the complex options in full IFRS are retained in IFRS for Small and Medium-Sized Entities.
   b. The use of fair value is pervasively required under both versions of IFRS.
   c. The extent of required disclosures is the same under both versions of IFRS.
   d. Simplified principles for recognizing and measuring assets, liabilities, income and expense are emphasized in IFRS for Small and Medium-Sized Entities. (9742)

3. A company should report the marketable equity securities that it has classified as trading at
   a. Lower of cost or market, with holding gains and losses included in earnings
   b. Lower of cost or market, with holding gains included in earnings only to the extent of previously recognized holding losses
   c. Fair value, with holding gains included in earnings only to the extent of previously recognized holding losses
   d. Fair value, with holding gains and losses included in earnings (5542)

4. Class Corp. maintains its accounting records on the cash basis but restates its financial statements to the accrual method of accounting. Class had $60,000 in cash-basis pretax income for year 2. The following information pertains to Class's operations for the years ended December 31, year 2 and year 1:

	Year 2	Year 1
Accounts receivable	$40,000	$20,000
Accounts payable	15,000	30,000

   Under the accrual method, what amount of income before taxes should Class report in its December 31, year 2, income statement?
   a. $25,000
   b. $55,000
   c. $65,000
   d. $95,000 (4081)

5. Restorations of carrying value for long-lived assets are permitted if an asset's fair value increases subsequent to recording an impairment loss for which of the following?

	Held for use	Held for disposal
a.	Yes	Yes
b.	Yes	No
c.	No	Yes
d.	No	No

(9891)

6. When a parent-subsidiary relationship exists, consolidated financial statements are prepared in recognition of the accounting concept of
   a. Reliability
   b. Materiality
   c. Legal entity
   d. Economic entity (4193)

7. Fenn Museum, a nongovernmental not-for-profit organization, had the following balances in its statement of functional expenses:

Education	$300,000
Fundraising	250,000
Management and general	200,000
Research	50,000

What amount should Fenn report as expenses for support services?

a. $350,000
b. $450,000
c. $500,000
d. $800,000 (9876)

8. Which of the following should be disclosed in a summary of significant accounting policies?

I. Management's intention to maintain or vary the dividend payout ratio
II. Criteria for determining which investments are treated as cash equivalents
III. Composition of the sales order backlog by segment

a. I only
b. I and III
c. II only
d. II and III (3470)

9. According to the FASB conceptual framework, the process of reporting an item in the financial statements of an entity is

a. Allocation
b. Matching
c. Realization
d. Recognition (4816)

10. In its cash flow statement for the current year, Ness Co. reported cash paid for interest of $70,000. Ness did not capitalize any interest during the current year. Changes occurred in several balance sheet accounts as follows:

Accrued interest payable	$17,000 decrease
Prepaid interest	23,000 decrease

In its income statement for the current year, what amount should Ness report as interest expense?

a. $ 30,000
b. $ 64,000
c. $ 76,000
d. $110,000 (7749)

11. On December 31, year 1, Rice Inc., authorized Graf to operate as a franchisee for an initial franchise fee of $150,000. Of this amount, $60,000 was received upon signing the agreement and the balance, represented by a note, is due in three annual payments of $30,000 each beginning December 31, year 2. The present value on December 31, year 1, of the three annual payments appropriately discounted is $72,000. According to the agreement, the nonrefundable down payment represents a fair measure of the services already performed by Rice; however, substantial future services are required of Rice. Collectability of the note is reasonably certain. In Rice's December 31, year 1 balance sheet, unearned franchise fees from Graf's franchise should be reported as

a. $132,000
b. $100,000
c. $ 90,000
d. $ 72,000 (1315)

12. Wood City, which is legally obligated to maintain a debt service fund, issued the following general obligation bonds on July 1:

Term debt	10 years
Face amount	$1,000,000
Issue price	101
Stated interest rate	6%

Interest is payable January 1 and July 1. What amount of bond premium should be amortized in Wood's debt service fund for the year ended December 31?

a. $1,000
b. $ 500
c. $ 250
d. $0

(4435)

13. On July 1, year 1, Cobb Inc. issued 9% bonds in the face amount of $1,000,000, which mature in ten years. The bonds were issued for $939,000 to yield 10%, resulting in a bond discount of $61,000. Cobb uses the interest method of amortizing bond discount. Interest is payable annually on June 30. At June 30, year 3, Cobb's unamortized bond discount should be

a. $52,810
b. $51,000
c. $48,800
d. $43,000

(1064)

14. Which of the following ratios is(are) useful in assessing a company's ability to meet currently maturing or short-term obligations?

	Acid-test ratio	Debt-to-equity ratio
a.	No	No
b.	No	Yes
c.	Yes	Yes
d.	Yes	No

(9038)

15. Rudd Corp. had 700,000 shares of common stock authorized and 300,000 shares outstanding at December 31 of the previous year. The following events occurred during the current year:

January 31	Declared 10% stock dividend
June 30	Purchased 100,000 shares
August 1	Reissued 50,000 shares
November 30	Declared 2-for-1 stock split

At December 31 of the current year, how many shares of common stock did Rudd have outstanding?

a. 560,000
b. 600,000
c. 630,000
d. 660,000

(4110)

16. Super Seniors is a not-for-profit organization that provides services to senior citizens. Super employs a full-time staff of 10 people at an annual cost of $150,000. In addition, two volunteers work as part-time secretaries replacing last years' full-time secretary who earned $10,000. Services performed by other volunteers for special events had an estimated value of $15,000. These volunteers were employees of local businesses and they received small-value items for their participation. What amount should Super report for salary and wage expenses related to the above items?

a. $150,000
b. $160,000
c. $165,000
d. $175,000

(4137)

17. During the year, Fleet Co.'s trademark was licensed to Hitch Corp. for royalties of 10% of net sales of the trademarked items. Returns were estimated to be 1% of gross sales. On signing the agreement, Hitch paid Fleet $75,000 as an advance against future royalty earnings. Gross sales of the trademarked items during the year were $600,000. What amount should Fleet report as royalty income for the year?

    a. $54,000
    b. $59,400
    c. $60,000
    d. $75,000 (8342)

18. On February 2, Flint Corp.'s board of directors voted to discontinue operations of its frozen food division and to sell the division's assets on the open market as soon as possible. The division reported net operating losses of $20,000 in January and $30,000 in February. On February 26, sale of the division's assets resulted in a gain of $90,000. What amount of gain from disposal of a business segment should Flint recognize in its income statement for the three months ended March 31?

    a. $0
    b. $40,000
    c. $60,000
    d. $90,000 (6903)

19. Lema Fund, a voluntary welfare organization funded by contributions from the general public, received unrestricted pledges of $200,000 during the current year. It was estimated that 10% of these pledges would be uncollectible. By the end of the year, $130,000 of the pledges had been collected. It was expected that $50,000 more would be collected in the following year and that the balance of $20,000 would be written off as uncollectible. What amount should Lema include under public support in the current year for net contributions?

    a. $200,000
    b. $180,000
    c. $150,000
    d. $130,000 (4601)

20. The replacement cost of an inventory item is below the net realizable value and above the net realizable value less the normal profit margin. The original cost of the inventory item is above the replacement cost and below the net realizable value. As a result, under the lower-of-cost-or-market method, the inventory item should be valued at the

    a. Replacement cost
    b. Original cost
    c. Net realizable value
    d. Net realizable value less the normal profit margin (8997)

21. A company has outstanding accounts payable of $30,000 and a short-term construction loan in the amount of $100,000 at year end. The loan was refinanced through issuance of long-term bonds after year end but before issuance of financial statements. How should these liabilities be recorded in the balance sheet?

    a. Long-term liabilities of $130,000
    b. Current liabilities of $130,000
    c. Current liabilities of $30,000, long-term liabilities of $100,000
    d. Current liabilities of $130,000, with required footnote disclosure of the refinancing of the loan (8788)

22. Under IFRS, which of the following is not an acceptable method of accounting for inventory?

    a. Gross profit method
    b. Retail method
    c. LIFO
    d. Weighted average (9758)

23. Jan Corp. amended its defined benefit pension plan, granting a total credit of $100,000 to four employees for services rendered prior to the plan's adoption. The employees, A, B, C, and D, are expected to retire from the company as follows:

    "A" will retire after three years.
    "B" and "C" will retire after five years.
    "D" will retire after seven years.

    What is the amount of prior service cost amortization in the first year?

    a. $0
    b. $ 5,000
    c. $20,000
    d. $25,000 (6782)

24. On June 1 of the current year, Ichor Company entered into a ten-year noncancellable lease with Gillie, Inc., for a machine owned by Gillie. The machine had a fair value of $180,000 at inception of the lease. Ownership of the machine is transferred to Ichor upon expiration of the lease. The present value of the ten $30,000 annual lease payments, based on Ichor's incremental borrowing rate of 12%, is $190,000. The lease agreement specifies that all executory costs are assumed by Ichor. How much should Ichor record as an asset and corresponding liability at the inception of the lease?

    a. $0
    b. $180,000
    c. $190,000
    d. $300,000 (8998)

25. On January 1 of the current year, Jambon purchased equipment for use in developing a new product. Jambon uses the straight-line depreciation method. The equipment could provide benefits over a 10-year period. However, the new product development is expected to take five years, and the equipment can be used only for this project. Jambon's current year expense equals

    a. The total cost of the equipment.
    b. One-fifth of the cost of the equipment.
    c. One-tenth of the cost of the equipment.
    d. Zero. (2540)

26. The League, a not-for-profit organization, received the following pledges:

Unrestricted	$200,000
Restricted for capital additions	150,000

    All pledges are legally enforceable; however, the League's experience indicates that 10% of all pledges prove to be uncollectible. What amount should the League report as pledges receivable, net of any required allowance account?

    a. $135,000
    b. $180,000
    c. $315,000
    d. $350,000 (4142)

27. A firm has basic earnings per share of $1.29. If the tax rate is 30%, which of the following securities would be dilutive?

    a. Cumulative 8%, $50 par preferred stock
    b. Ten percent convertible bonds, issued at par, with each $1,000 bond convertible into 20 shares of common stock
    c. Seven percent convertible bonds, issued at par, with each $1,000 bond convertible into 40 shares of common stock
    d. Six percent, $100 par cumulative convertible preferred stock, issued at par, with each preferred share convertible into four shares of common stock (9313)

28. Shared revenues received by an enterprise fund of a local government for operating purposes should be recorded as

    a. Operating revenues
    b. Nonoperating revenues
    c. Other financing sources
    d. Interfund transfers (4661)

29. Fogg Co., a U.S. company, contracted to purchase foreign goods. Payment in foreign currency was due one month after the goods were received at Fogg's warehouse. Between the receipt of goods and the time of payment, the exchange rates changed in Fogg's favor. The resulting gain should be included in Fogg's financial statements as a(an)

    a. Component of income from continuing operations.
    b. Extraordinary item.
    c. Deferred credit.
    d. Item of other comprehensive income. (6114)

30. During year 1, Gum Co. introduced a new product carrying a two-year warranty against defects. The estimated warranty costs related to dollar sales are 2% within 12 months following the sale and 4% in the second 12 months following the sale. Sales and actual warranty expenditures for the prior and current year ended December 31, are as follows:

Year	Sales	Actual warranty expenditures
1	$150,000	$2,250
2	250,000	7,500
	$400,000	$9,750

What amount should Gun report as estimated warranty liability in its December 31, year 2, balance sheet?

    a. $ 2,500
    b. $ 4,250
    c. $11,250
    d. $14,250 (2606)

Testlet 4 SIMULATIONS

Simulation 1 Transaction Classifications

On January 2 of the current year, Quo Inc. hired Reed to be its controller. During the year, Reed, working closely with Quo's president and outside accountants, made changes in accounting policies, corrected several errors dating from the previous year and before, and instituted new accounting policies. Quo's current year financial statements will be presented in comparative form with its previous year financial statements.

Items 1 through 10 represent Quo's transactions. Use List A and B to complete the table on the following page.

List A represents possible classifications of these transactions as:

- A change in accounting principle
- A change in accounting estimate
- A correction of an error in previously presented financial statements
- Neither an accounting change nor an accounting error

List B represents the general accounting treatment required for these transactions. These treatments are:

- Retrospective application—Apply the cumulative effect resulting from the accounting change or error correction to the carrying amounts of assets and liabilities, with an adjustment to opening balance of retained earnings, in the current financial statements. Also apply adjustments to the financial statements for each individual prior period presented.
- Prospective approach—Report current year and future financial statements on the new basis, but do not adjust beginning retained earnings or include the cumulative effect of the change in the current year income statements.

List A—Type of Change
A. Change in accounting principle
B. Change in accounting estimate
C. Correction of an error in previously presented financial statements
D. Neither an accounting change nor an error correction

List B—General Accounting Treatment
Y. Retrospective application
Z. Prospective application

APPENDIX A

Place the letter responses for each question in the spaces provided in front of the questions.

Transactions	Type	Treatment
1. Quo manufactures heavy equipment to customer specifications on a contract basis. On the basis that it is preferable, accounting for these long-term contracts was switched from the completed contract method to the percentage of completion method.		
2. As a result of a production breakthrough, Quo determined that manufacturing equipment previously depreciated over 15 years should be depreciated over 20 years.		
3. The equipment that Quo manufactures is sold with a five-year warranty. Because of a production breakthrough, Quo reduced its computation of warranty costs from 3% of sales to 1% of sales.		
4. Quo changed from LIFO to FIFO to account for its finished goods inventory.		
5. Quo changed from FIFO to average cost to account for its raw materials and work in process inventories.		
6. Quo sells extended service contracts on its products. Because related services are performed over several years, in the current year Quo changed from the cash method to the accrual method of recognizing income from these service contracts.		
7. During the current year, Quo determined that an insurance premium paid and entirely expensed in the previous year was for the period January 1 of the previous year through January 1 of next year.		
8. Quo changed its method of depreciating office equipment from an accelerated method to the straight-line method to more closely reflect costs in later years.		
9. Quo instituted a pension plan for all employees in the current year and adopted FASB Standards. Quo had not previously had a pension plan.		
10. During the current year, Quo increased its investment in Worth Inc. from a 10% interest, purchased in the previous year, to 30%, and acquired a seat on Worth's board of directors. As a result of its increased investment, Quo changed its method of accounting for investment in subsidiary from the cost method to the equity method.		

(4938)

Simulation 2 Equity Accounts

Max Co. is a publicly held company whose shares are traded in the over-the-counter market. The stockholders' equity accounts at December 31, year 3, had the following balances:

Preferred stock, $100 par value, 7% cumulative; 6,000 shares authorized; 3,000 issued and outstanding	$ 300,000
Common stock, $1 par value, 250,000 shares authorized; 200,000 issued and outstanding	200,000
Additional paid-in capital	1,100,000
Retained earnings	1,768,000
Total stockholders' equity	$3,368,000

Transactions during year 4 and other information relating to the stockholders' equity accounts were as follows:

- February 1, year 4—Issued 15,000 shares of common stock to Ewe Co. in exchange for land. On the date issued, the stock had a market price of $12 per share. The land had a carrying value on Ewe's books of $170,000, and an assessed value for property taxes of $115,000.
- March 1, year 4—Purchased 6,000 shares of its own common stock to be held as treasury stock for $13 per share. Max uses the cost method to account for treasury stock. Transactions in treasury stock are legal in Max's state of incorporation.
- May 10, year 4—Declared a property dividend of marketable securities held by Max to common shareholders. The securities had a carrying value of $700,000; fair value on relevant dates were:

Date of declaration 5/10	$840,000
Date of record 5/25	874,000
Date of distribution 6/1	856,000

- October 1, year 4—Reissued 4,000 shares of treasury stock for $15 per share.
- November 4, year 4—Declared a cash dividend of $1.10 per share to all common shareholders of record on November 15, year 4. The dividend was paid on November 25, year 4.
- December 22, year 4—Declared the required annual cash dividend on preferred stock for year 4. The dividend was paid on January 5, year 5.
- Adjusted net income for year 4 was $926,000.

For all items, use the information provided to calculate the amounts requested.

The following represent amounts to be reported on Max's statement of retained earnings and statement of stockholders' equity at December 31, year 4.

Statement of Retained Earnings

1. Preferred dividends	
2. Common dividends—cash	
3. Common dividends—property	

Statement of Stockholder's Equity

4. Treasury stock	
5. Amount of common stock issued	
6. Number of common shares issued at December 31, year 4	
7. Additional paid-in capital, including treasury stock transactions	

(5597t)

Simulation 3 Long-Term Liabilities & Interest Expense

Fato Corporation's liability account balances at December 31, year 6 included the following:

Note payable to bank	$1,200,000
Liability under capital lease	$ 290,205
Deferred income tax liability	$ 140,000

Additional information:

- The note payable, dated October 1, year 6, bears interest at an annual rate of 12% payable quarterly on January 1, April 1, July 1, and October 1. Principal payments are due annually on October 1 in five equal installments.
- The capital lease is for a 5-year period beginning December 31, year 4. Equal annual payments of $125,000 are due on December 31 of each year. The 14% interest rate implicit in the lease is known by Fato. At December 31, year 7, the present value of the three remaining lease payments discounted at 14% was $290,205.
- Deferred income taxes are provided in recognition of temporary differences between financial statement and income tax reporting of depreciation. For the year ended December 31, year 7, depreciation per tax return exceeded book depreciation by $80,000. The enacted tax rate on all types of taxable income for the current and future years is 25%. The alternative minimum tax is less than the regular income tax.
- On September 1, year 7, Fato issued $1,500,000 face amount of 15-year, 8% bonds for $1,269,413, to yield 10%. Interest is payable semi-annually on March 1 and September 1. Bond discount is amortized by the interest method.
- All required principal and interest payments were made on schedule in year 7.

1. Prepare the long-term liabilities section of Fato's balance sheet at December 31, year 7. Round all calculations to the nearest dollar.

Long-Term Liabilities Section of Balance Sheet

Long-term liabilities:	
Bonds payable due September 1, year 22	
Note payable to bank	
Liability under capital lease	
Deferred income tax liability	
Total long-term liabilities	

2. Prepare a schedule showing interest expense that should appear in Fato's income statement for the year ended December 31, year 7. Round all calculations to the nearest dollar.

Interest Expense

Bonds payable	
Note payable to bank	
Liability under capital lease	
Total	

(3417t)

Simulation 4 Consolidation Reporting

Presented below are selected amounts from the separate unconsolidated financial statements of Poe Corp. and its 90%-owned subsidiary, Shaw Co., at December 31 of the current year. Additional information follows.

	Poe	Shaw
Selected income statement amounts		
Sales	$710,000	$ 530,000
Cost of goods sold	490,000	370,000
Gain on sale of equipment	—	21,000
Earnings from investment in subsidiary	63,000	—
Interest expense	—	16,000
Depreciation	25,000	20,000
Selected balance sheet amounts		
Cash	$ 50,000	$ 15,000
Inventories	229,000	150,000
Land	60,000	40,000
Equipment	440,000	360,000
Accumulated depreciation	(200,000)	(120,000)
Investment in Shaw	306,000	—
Investment in bonds	100,000	—
Discount on bonds	(9,000)	—
Bonds payable	—	(200,000)
Common stock	(100,000)	(10,000)
Additional paid-in capital	(250,000)	(40,000)
Retained earnings	(402,000)	(140,000)
Selected statement of retained earnings amounts		
Beginning balance, December 31, previous year	$272,000	$ 100,000
Net income	210,000	70,000
Dividends paid	80,000	30,000

- On January 2, Poe, Inc. purchased 90% of Shaw Co.'s 100,000 outstanding common stock for cash of $270,000. On that date, Shaw's stockholders' equity equaled $150,000 and the fair values of Shaw's assets and liabilities equaled their carrying amounts except for land, for which fair value exceeded the carrying amount by $100,000.
- On September 4, Shaw paid cash dividends of $30,000.
- On December 31, Poe recorded its equity in Shaw's earnings.
- This business combination is being accounted for under the acquisition method.

For Items 1 and 2, using the table of selected information from the consolidated and unconsolidated financial statements, determine the dollar amount to be reported in the December 31 consolidated balance sheet for the following listed accounts. Ignore income tax considerations.

Item	Amount
1. Noncontrolling interest	
2. Goodwill	

Items 3 through 5 represent transactions between Poe and Shaw during the year. Using the table of selected information from the consolidated and unconsolidated financial statements, determine the dollar amount effect of the consolidating adjustment on consolidated income before considering any noncontrolling interest. Ignore income tax considerations. State if the change is an increase, decrease, or not considered.

Item	Amount	Change
3. On January 3, Shaw sold equipment with an original cost of $30,000 and a carrying value of $15,000 to Poe for $36,000. The equipment had a remaining life of three years and was depreciated using the straight-line method by both companies.		
4. During the year, Shaw sold merchandise to Poe for $60,000, which included a profit of $20,000. At December 31, half of this merchandise remained in Poe's inventory.		
5. On December 31, Poe paid $91,000 to purchase 50% of the outstanding bonds issued by Shaw. The bonds mature in six years, on December 31, and were originally issued at par. The bonds pay interest annually on December 31 of each year, and the interest was paid to the prior investor immediately before Poe's purchase of the bonds.		

Items 6 through 17 refer to accounts that may or may not be included in Poe and Shaw's consolidated financial statements. The list of responses refers to the various possibilities of those amounts to be reported in Poe's consolidated financial statements for the current year ended December 31. Consider all transactions stated in items 3 through 5 in determining your answer. Ignore income tax considerations. Any choice may be used once, more than once or not at all.

Item	Choice	Item	Choice
6. Cash		12. Beginning retained earnings	
7. Equipment		13. Dividends paid	
8. Investment in subsidiary		14. Gain on retirement of bonds	
9. Bonds payable		15. Cost of goods sold	
10. Noncontrolling interest		16. Interest expense	
11. Common stock		17. Depreciation expense	

A. Sum of amounts on Poe and Shaw's separate unconsolidated financial statements

B. Less than the sum of amounts on Poe and Shaw's separate unconsolidated financial statements but not the same as the amount on either

C. Same as amount for Poe only

D. Same as amount for Shaw only

E. Eliminated entirely in consolidation

F. Shown in consolidated financial statements but not in separate unconsolidated financial statements

G. Neither in consolidated nor in separate unconsolidated financial statements. (4502)

Statement of Cash Flows

	A	B	C
1	Cash flows from operating activities:		
2	Net income	$	
3	Adjustments to reconcile net income to net cash provided by operating activities:		
4	Depreciation	$	
5	Amortization of patent		
6	Loss on sale of equipment		
7	Equity in income of Word Corp.		
8	Gain on sale of marketable equity securities		
9	Decrease in allowance to reduce marketable equity securities to market		
10	Increase in accounts receivable		
11	Decrease in inventories		
12	Decrease in accounts payable and accrued liabilities		
13	Net cash provided by operating activities		$
14	Cash flows from investing activities:		
15	Sale of marketable equity securities	$	
16	Sale of equipment		
17	Purchase of equipment		
18	Net cash provided by investing activities		$
19	Cash flows from financing activities:		
20	Issuance of common stock	$	
21	Cash dividend paid		
22	Payment on note payable		
23	Net cash used in financing activities		
24	Net increase in cash		$
25	Cash at beginning of year		307,000
26	Cash at end of year		$

(3422)

Simulation 7 Research

Research Question: Whose financial statements does the content of SEC Sections of the FASB Codification relate to?

FASB ASC: ______ - ______ - ______ - ______

(9745)

MULTIPLE-CHOICE ANSWERS

Solution 1

1. (c) The machine had a depreciable basis of $80,000 ($85,000 cost – $5,000 salvage value) and was depreciated at a rate of $8,000 per year ($80,000 / 10-year useful life). At the time of sale, Victor depreciated the machine for 5.5 years and its carrying amount was equal to $41,000, i.e., [$85,000 – (5.5 × $8,000)]. Thus a $4,000 gain ($45,000 – $41,000) should be recognized. (8990)

2. (b) The purchase of the investment securities for cash which was borrowed from a bank is not a non-cash investing and financing transaction because the asset was not acquired by assuming a directly related liability. Examples of acquiring assets by assuming directly related liabilities include purchasing a building by incurring a mortgage to the seller and obtaining an asset by entering into a capital lease. On the other hand, the acquisition of the land by issuing preferred stock is a noncash investing and financing transaction. The proceeds from the issuance of the bonds payable and payment toward the bank loan are to be classified as financing activities.

Purchase of investment securities for cash	$(225,000)
Purchase of a patent for cash	(275,000)
Proceeds from sale of investment securities	995,000
Net cash provided by investing activities	$ 495,000

(8991)

3. (b) The "ingredients" of faithful representation require that the information is: complete, neutral, and free from error. The "ingredients" of relevance are predictive value, confirmatory value, or both. (2695)

4. (a) A permanent fund is used to account for nonexpendable resources that may be used for the government's programs to generate and disperse money, to benefit the reporting entity or its citizens, such as the library in this question. The name of the fund comes from the purpose of the fund: a sum of equity used to permanently generate payments to maintain some financial obligation. A fund can only be classified as a permanent fund if the money is used to report the status of a restricted financial resource. The resource is restricted in the sense that only earnings from the resource are used and not the principal. (9853)

5. (c) Wages payable have increased from the beginning to the end of the year, which means that a portion of the salaries has not been paid. Therefore, wages paid are less than salary expense reported on an accrual basis by the amount of the increase in wages payable from the beginning to the end of the year. (1935)

6. (a) Smith's capital balance of $195,000 is reduced by his $20,000 loan *from* the partnership ($195,000 – $20,000). (in 000's)

	Cash	Other assets	Liabs	Smith (60%)	Jones (40%)
Balances before realization	$ 0	$ 450	$120	$175	$155
Sale of other assets	385	(450)	0	(39)	(26)
Balances after realization	385	$ 0	120	136	129
Pay liabilities	(120)		(120)	0	0
Balances	$ 265		$ 0	$136	$129

(4852)

7. (d) The book value per preferred share is the portion of stockholders' equity distributable to preferred stockholders in the event of liquidation (Liquidation value + Dividends in arrears), divided by the number of preferred shares outstanding. [($105 × 1,000 sh.) + (10% × $100,000)] / 1,000 shares = $115 share. (1265)

8. (d) The IASB's approval to add agenda items, as well as its decisions on their priority, is by a simple majority vote at an IASB meeting. The IASB evaluates the merits of adding a potential item to its agenda mainly by reference to the needs of the financial statement user over the financial statement preparer. The IASB's discussions of potential projects and its decisions to adopt new projects generally takes place in private IASB meetings. In making decisions regarding its future standard setting agenda priorities, the IASB also considers not purposefully excludes, consideration of factors related to on-going convergence initiatives with U.S. accounting standard-setters. (9718)

9. (d) Both notes were received on the balance sheet date. Since the note from Hart arose from a transaction with a customer in the normal course of business and is due in customary trade terms not exceeding one year, it can be reported at its face amount of $10,000 despite the fact that the 3% stated interest rate of the note differs from the prevailing market interest rate of 8% for similar notes at the transaction date. On the other hand, the note from Maxx is due in more than one year. Therefore, the note from Maxx cannot be reported at its face amount because the 3% stated interest rate of the note differs from the prevailing market interest rate of 8% for similar notes at the transaction date. Because neither the fair value of the services performed by Jet nor the fair value of the note received from Maxx is indicated, the note is reported at its present value, determined by discounting all future cash payments of the note at the prevailing (i.e., market) rate of interest for a note of this type.

Principal amount	$10,000	
Interest on outstanding principal balance due on maturity date [($10,000 × 3%) × 5]	1,500	
Amount due on maturity date	11,500	
Present value factor of $1 at 8% for 5 periods	× 0.680	
Present value of note received from Maxx	$ 7,820	(2582)

10. (a) Where B = Bonus:

B = 0.10($640,000 – $200,000 – B)
B = $44,000 – 0.1B; 1.1 B = $44,000
B = $40,000 (8992)

11. (b) Restricted cash is classified as either a current or noncurrent asset, based upon the date of availability or disbursement. IOUs from officers or employees are classified as receivables. Overdrafts in accounts with no available cash in another account at the same bank to offset are classified as current liabilities. Since answers a. and b. are incorrect, answer d., *all of the above*, is also incorrect. (9026)

12. (d) The primary basis for accounting for inventories is cost. The cost of an inventory item is the cash price or fair value of other consideration given in exchange for it. Historical cost, replacement cost, and net realizable value are all appropriate methods for measuring inventory. The present value of future cash flows (which would include profits not yet earned) pertains to the time value of money and is not appropriate for measuring inventory. (6087)

13. (b) The annual amortization of computer software costs is the greater of the amount computed using the percentage of revenue approach and the straight-line method applied over the product's remaining estimated economic life. $600,000 – ($600,000 / 4) = $450,000. Capitalized computer software costs are carried at the lower of unamortized cost or net realizable value, so the answer could not be $480,000. (6978)

14. (a) Legal costs incurred to successfully defend a patent should be capitalized, regardless of whether the patent was externally acquired or internally developed. Legal fees and other direct costs of registering a patent are capitalized and amortized over the lesser of the economic useful life or legal life, if determinable. R&D costs incurred to develop a patent are expensed as incurred. (9023)

15. (c) DeeCee adjusts the depreciation and cost of goods sold reported in the historical cost income statement by applying specific price indexes to these amounts. Therefore, DeeCee's adjusted income statement is prepared using current cost accounting. The income statement is not prepared using fair value accounting because only depreciation expense and cost of goods sold are restated by applying specific price indexes. The income statement is not prepared using general purchasing power accounting because DeeCee's historical costs are not remeasured into units of a currency with the same general purchasing power. The income statement is not prepared using current cost/general purchasing power accounting because amounts are not remeasured into units of a currency with the same general purchasing power. (4507)

16. (c) Requirements governing preparation of consolidated, but not combined, financial statements is not addressed in an article within Regulation S-X. Article 3A sets forth the requirements governing the preparation of consolidated and combined financial statements and the requisite disclosures. Article 1 includes definitions of terms used in registration statements and reports. Article 2 sets forth the requirements as to qualifications of accountants and accountant's reports in filings with the SEC. Article 3 sets forth the various financial statements to be included, and for what periods, in disclosure documents. (9704)

17. (c) The question states that the present value of the minimum lease payments exceeds 90% of the fair value of the machine, and also give information that the lease term is equal to or greater than 75% of the estimated life of the asset (15/17 = 88%). The criteria to classify and account for the lease as a capital lease is that at the date of the lease agreement (date of lease inception), the lease must satisfy at least one of the following four criteria: The lease transfers ownership of the property to the lessee by the end of the lease; the lease contains a bargain purchase option; the lease term is equal to 75% or more of the estimated economic life of the leased property (as determined at the inception of the lease); or the present value of the minimum lease payments (excluding executory costs) equals or exceeds 90% of the fair value of the leased property at lease inception. Even though there is no transfer of ownership, the lease meets two of the four criteria to be classified as a capital lease. (7605)

18. (d) When one company sells merchandise to an affiliate at a price above cost, the ending inventory of the purchasing affiliate contains an element of unrealized gross profit. The gross profit is not realized to the economic entity until the inventory is sold to an unaffiliated company. The unrealized gross profit in inventory must be eliminated in the preparation of consolidated financial statements.

Scroll's ending inventory acquired from Pirn ($100,000 – $80,000)	$20,000	
Times: Pirn's gross profit percentage [100% – ($350,000 / $500,000)]	× 30%	
Unrealized intercompany profit in Scroll's ending inventory	$ 6,000	(2575)

19. (b) The cost of the equipment to the purchasing affiliate exceeds the carrying amount of the equipment to the consolidated entity by the gain recognized on the sale by the selling affiliate. Consolidated depreciation expense must be based upon the cost of the equipment to the consolidated entity. Therefore, consolidated depreciation expense must be reduced by the excess depreciation recorded by the purchasing affiliate [i.e., ($40,000 + $10,000) – ($12,000 / 4) = $47,000]. (2576)

20. (c) Since the subsidiary is using the local currency, the translation method must be used. Under this method, all assets and all liabilities are converted at the current exchange rate. (9059)

21. (a)

Pretax financial income	$250,000	
Permanent difference—interest	(25,000)	
Temporary difference—excess tax depreciation	(75,000)	
Taxable income	150,000	
Tax rate	30%	
Current provision	$ 45,000	(2628)

22. (a) The use of lower of cost or market may result in inventory losses that should not be deferred beyond the interim period in which the decline occurs. Recoveries of these losses in subsequent periods should be recognized as gains, but only to the extent of losses recognized in previous interim periods of the same fiscal year. Temporary market declines, however, need not be recognized at the interim dates since no loss is expected to be incurred in the fiscal year. Because Wilson expected the decline to reverse within the fiscal year, no loss should be recorded for the first quarter. Even though the recovery exceeded the previous decline by $10,000, gains are recognized only to the extent of losses recognized in previous interim periods of the same fiscal year. (6787)

23. (c) A gain or loss on a speculative forward exchange contract is included in determining income from continuing operations in accordance with the requirements for other foreign currency transactions. A gain or loss on a speculative forward contract is computed by multiplying the foreign currency amount of the contract by the difference between the forward rate available for the remaining maturity of the contract and the contracted forward rate (or the forward rate last used to measure a gain or loss on that contract for an earlier period). Thus, the amount that Brady should report as foreign exchange loss for the month ended 9/30 is determined as follows:

Foreign currency units purchased under speculative forward contract	$50,000	
Times excess of contracted forward rate over forward rate available for remaining portion of contract ($0.74 - $0.72)	× 0.02	
Foreign exchange loss recognized September	$ 1,000	(4087)

24. (a) In the final year of a contract accounted for by the percentage of completion method, the final income recognition would take place. The calculation would be the total revenue earned over the entire contract less the actual total costs incurred less the income previously recognized. (5562)

25. (a) When a change in accounting estimate and a change in accounting principle are inseparable, the change should be accounted for as a change in estimate, which is a component of income from continuing operations. A change in estimate does not require the restatement of prior period financial statements. Corrections of errors are reported as prior-period adjustments and prior-period financial statements are restated. Material effects of a change in estimate on income before extraordinary items, net income, and related per share amounts should be disclosed. Footnote disclosure only is not proper accounting treatment of a change in estimate. (6476)

26. (d) The carrying amount of the bonds is the sum of their face amount and the unamortized premium. Therefore, premium amortization will reduce the carrying amount of the bonds. Bond premium amortization will increase income because it will reduce the interest expense associated with the bonds. (8993)

27. (d) Government-wide statements aggregate information for all governmental and business-type activities on the accrual basis of accounting. Fund financial statements use modified accrual and a reconciliation to the government-wide statement must appear on the face of the governmental-type fund financial statements or in a separate schedule. (6877)

28. (d) Enterprise funds generally report net assets. Capital projects and special revenue funds are governmental-type funds, and thus report a fund balance. Expendable trust funds (under the outgoing reporting model) use fund balance accounts also. (5812)

29. (d) Pledges are reported in the period in which they are made, net of an allowance for uncollectible amounts. If part of a pledge is to be applied during some future period, that part is reported as restricted revenue. Although the $300,000 of pledges received during the current year was unrestricted as to its use, there was a time restriction (designated for next year) on $100,000. The $100,000 less $5,000, for the 5% expected to be uncollectible, equals $95,000 to be reported as restricted support. (8789)

30. (b) Room and board for patients and recovery room activities are both central to a hospital's services. (5818)

Solution 2

1. (a) Interest income on municipal obligations is a tax-exempt revenue; therefore, no current or future tax consequences will result and no deferred taxes are recorded for this difference. The $150,000 ($550,000 – $400,000) difference due to depreciation is the only temporary difference existing at the balance sheet date. It will reverse equally over the next three years, resulting in future taxable amounts of $50,000 ($150,000/3). Noll expects to report taxable income in all future periods; therefore, the future taxable amounts are tax effected at the rates scheduled for individual future years.

	Amount	Rate	Def. Tax Liab.	
Depreciation				
Year 2	$ 50,000	30%	$ 15,000	
Years 3-4	100,000	25%	25,000	
Deferred tax liability			$ 40,000	(3308)

2. (d)

Amortization of original cost ($400,000 /16 years)	$ 25,000	
Amortization of legal defense cost, ($60,000 / 12 remaining years)	5,000	
Total amortization expense, year 7	$ 30,000	(8994)

3. (c) When Pare purchased an additional 20,000 shares of Tot at 12/31, it increased its investment in Tot's common stock from 10% to 30%. Thus, at 12/31, Pare gained the ability to exercise significant influence over Tot and should report its investment in Tot using the equity method in its 12/31 balance sheet. The change from the cost method of reporting the investment in Tot to the equity method should be made by retroactively restating all prior periods in which the investment was held as if the equity method were used from inception. Thus, Pare should report the investment in Tot in its 12/31 balance sheet at $230,000, the sum of the amounts paid for Tot's shares (i.e., $50,000 and $150,000) and Pare's equity in Tot's reported earnings for the year (i.e., $300,000 × 10%). (4383)

4. (b) Goodwill is recognized and recorded at an amount equal to the excess of the consideration transferred plus the fair value of any noncontrolling interest over the fair value of the identifiable net assets (INA). Wall paid for all the issued and outstanding common stock of Hart so there is no noncontrolling interest.

Purchase price of 100% of Hart O/S CS	$ 860,000	
Less: Fair value Hart Corp.'s INA	(700,000)	
Goodwill	$ 160,000	(6900)

5. (d) While a contingent loss may be recognized *before* it is realized, a contingent gain cannot be recognized *until* it is realized. Therefore, the underlying concept that supports the immediate recognition of a contingent loss is conservatism. The convention of conservatism urges the accountant to refrain from overstatement of net income or net assets. (5268)

6. (a)

Service and interest costs	$ 720,000	
Less: Contributions	(400,000)	
Less: Actual return on plan assets (10% of $400,000)	(40,000)	
Accrued pension cost	$ 280,000	(6902)

7. (c) Rule 201 of Regulation S-T provides a temporary hardship exemption for electronic filers, generally for unanticipated technical difficulties in submitting an electronic document. The exemption may be appropriate, for example, for a particular document that a filer is unable to file electronically because of problems with the filer's computer equipment that had been used previously to transmit either test or required electronic filings successfully. Regulation S-T, not Regulation S-X, is the separate regulation containing rules prescribing requirements for filing electronically and the procedures for making such filings. Regulation S-T does not require all SEC filings to be submitted electronically, there are certain exceptions. Temporary hardship exemptions are not the only exception available for electronic filing requirements. (9715)

8. (d) The net proceeds of a bond issuance is determined by calculating the present value of the projected cash flows of the bonds at the yield rate (market rate) of interest and then deducting bond issuance costs. The stated rate of interest is used to determine the amount of cash to be paid at each payment date, but the market rate is the rate used to discount the cash flows to present values. (6778)

9. (b) General government fixed assets and long-term debt, are *not* recorded in the governmental funds, but are shown in the governmental activities column of the government-wide financial statements. General long-term debt to be repaid from general resources of the government should not be reported in any fund. (4990)

10. (c) Total assets equal the sum of liabilities and stockholders' equity.

Total liabilities, 12/31 (given)		$ 94,000
Proceeds from stock issue	$500,000	
Net income for current year	25,000	
Cash dividend declared	(2,000)	
Total stockholders' equity, 12/31		523,000
Total liabilities and stockholders' equity (and thus total assets) at 12/31		$617,000

(3239)

11. (c) The price index is computed by dividing the ending inventory at current year cost by its base year cost, $200,000 / $150,000 = 1.33.

Date	Base year cost	Current year cost
1/1, Year 1	$ 90,000	$ 90,000
Year 1 layer	20,000	30,000
12/31 year 1	$110,000	$120,000
Year 2 layer	40,000	80,000
12/31 year 2	$150,000	$200,000

(6976)

12. (d) In an exchange with commercial substance, the exchange is recorded at the fair value of the asset received or the asset given up, whichever is greater (more clearly evident), and a gain or loss is recognized on the exchange.

The journal entry to be recorded in Vey's books is:

Cash	30,000	
New Equipment	120,000	
Accumulated Depreciation	40,000	
Old Equipment		100,000
Gain on Exchange (plug)		90,000

(2586)

13. (a) The agency fund is used to account for the custodial activities of the governmental unit. The debt service fund is used to account for the repayment of the general long-term debt. The capital projects fund accounts for the project itself, not the repayment of debt. (5807)

14. (c) The proceeds from the sale of debt with stock purchase warrants should be allocated between the two instruments based on the relative fair values of the debt security without the warrants and the warrants themselves. The portion of the proceeds so allocated to the warrants is accounted for as paid-in capital. The remainder is allocated to the face amount of the bond, and to the extent remaining, to premium on bonds payable. (8995)

15. (a) There are three tests to determine whether an identified segment of an enterprise should be reported in the enterprise's financial statements. (1) The revenue test: the segment's reported revenue is 10% or more of the combined revenue of all operating segments; (2) The profit (loss) test: the absolute amount of the segment's profit or loss is 10% or more of the greater of the combined reported profit of all operating segments that did not report a loss or the combined reported loss of all operating segments that did report a loss; (3) The assets test: the segment's assets are 10% or more of the combined assets of all operating segments. (8354)

16. (a) The acquisition cost of a machine for use in a company's manufacturing operations includes all costs reasonably necessary to bring the asset to the location where it is to be used and to make it ready for its intended use, including insurance while in-transit and test runs. (5548)

17 (b) Where the likelihood of confirmation of a loss is considered probable and the loss can be reasonably estimated, the estimated loss should be accrued by a charge to income and the nature of the contingency should be disclosed. If, however, only a range of possible loss can be estimated—and no amount in the range is a better estimate than the others—the minimum amount in the range should be accrued. In addition, the nature of the contingency and the additional exposure to loss should be disclosed. (7780)

18. (c) Basic earnings per share (EPS) is computed by dividing income available to common stockholders by the weighted-average number of shares outstanding during the period. Shares issued during the period and shares reacquired during the period are weighted for the portion of the period they were outstanding. Stock dividends, stock splits, and reverse stock splits change the total number of shares outstanding but not the proportionate shares outstanding. For this reason, stock dividends, stock splits, and reverse stock splits are reflected retroactively for all periods presented. The weighted-average number of shares used to calculate basic EPS is 702,000. It's 100% of the 644,000 shares that have been outstanding all year (700,000 – 20,000 – 36,000), plus 3/12 of the 20,000 shares repurchased on March 31 (5,000), plus 11/12 of the shares repurchased on December 1 (33,000), and 50% of the 40,000 preferred shares converted at June 30 (20,000). (9859)

19. (b) Earnings per share for the previous and current year is $1.78 ($410,000 / 230,000 shares) and $1.75 ($350,000 / 200,000 shares), respectively. Stock dividends, stock splits, and reverse splits are given retroactive recognition in the computation of EPS for all periods presented. To compute EPS, the weighted average number of common shares outstanding must be computed for each year.

	Current year	Previous year	
Common shares outstanding at 1/1	100,000	100,000	
Sale of additional shares, 4/1 (20,000 × 9/12)	15,000		
2-for-1 stock split, 7/1			
(Previous year: 100,000 × 100%)		100,000	
(Current year: 115,000 × 100%)	115,000		
Weighted average common shares outstanding	230,000	200,000	(2448)

20. (d) An entity shall disclose, either in the body of the financial statements or in the accompanying notes, the fair value of financial instruments for which it is practicable to estimate that value and the method(s) and significant assumptions used to estimate the fair value of financial instruments. These provisions need not be applied to immaterial items. (8101)

21. (b) Nonprofit organizations are required to present, at a minimum, a statement of financial position, a statement of activities, and a statement of cash flows. (6995)

22. (b) Errors in financial statements result from mathematical mistakes, mistakes in the application of accounting principles, or the oversight or misuse of facts that existed at the time the financial statements were prepared. For an item to be classified as a prior period adjustment, it must be an item of profit or loss related to the correction of an error in the financial statements of a prior period. Any error in the financial statements of a prior period discovered subsequent to their issuance shall be reported as an adjustment to the beginning balance of retained earnings, net of their income tax effect, in the statement of retained earnings. Therefore, Newton would report normal depreciation expense of $10,000 in the year 2 financial statements. (9867)

23. (b) The Form 10-K is an annual report that gives a comprehensive summary of a public company's performance. The maximum number of days after the company's fiscal year end that the company has to file the Form 10-K with the SEC depends on the category of the filer. There are three categories of filers: (1) non-accelerated filers, (2) accelerated filers, and (3) large accelerated filers. Non-accelerated filers must file the Form 10-K with the SEC within 90 days after the end of the company's fiscal year. Non-accelerated filers are issuers that have a public float of less than $75 million. Accelerated filers must file the Form 10-K with the SEC within 75 days after the end of the company's fiscal year. Accelerated filers are issuers that have a public float of at least $75 million but less than $700 million. Large accelerated filers must file the Form 10-K with the SEC within 60 days after the end of the company's fiscal year. Large accelerated filers are issuers that have a public float of $700 million or more. (9351)

24. (c) A sole proprietorship's equity consists of a single proprietor's equity account, *Owner's Equity* or *Net Worth.* This is the sum of the beginning capital balance, plus additional investments during the period, plus net income (or minus net loss) minus withdrawals. The proprietor's draw is not reported separately on the income statement, but rather is included in *Owner's Equity* or *Net Worth.* Depreciation is not included in the *Owner's Equity* or *Net Worth* account. It is reported on the income statement of a proprietorship. (7615)

25. (a) The assets and liability method is required to be used in accounting and reporting for temporary differences between the amount of taxable income and pretax financial income and the tax bases of assets or liabilities and their reported amounts in financial statements. Under this method, a current or deferred tax liability or asset is recognized for the current or deferred tax consequences of all events that have been recognized in the financial statements. (6786)

26. (c) The market *maximum,* or *ceiling,* should not exceed the net realizable value (NRV), which is the estimated selling price in the ordinary course of business less reasonably predictable costs of completion and disposal. Market minimum or floor should not be less than the net realizable value minus normal profit.

Market:	
Ceiling (NRV)	$8.80
Replacement cost	8.00
Floor (NRV minus normal profit)	7.80

LIFO charges Cost of Goods Sold with the latest acquisition costs, while ending inventories are reported at the older costs of the earliest units. The 10,000 units sold reduce the 1/5 purchases, leaving 8,000 units from the beginning inventory and 2,000 units purchased on 1/5.

Cost [(8,000 × $8.20) + (2,000 × $7.90)]	$81,400
Market (10,000 × $8.00)	80,000

$80,000 is the lowest of cost or market. (7612)

27. (c) The $500,000 donated for which a donor or external agency has specified that the principal remains intact in perpetuity should be accounted for in an Endowment Fund. The $300,000 of principal expendable after the year 2010 should be accounted for in a Term Endowment Fund because the principal may be expended after a specified period of time. The $100,000 of principal designated from Current Funds should be accounted for in a Quasi-Endowment Fund because the amount was set aside by the governing board of the institution to function as endowments. (2667)

28. (b) The gross profit on the sale of the plant is $500,000 (i.e., the $1,500,000 sales price minus the $1,000,000 cost). Thus, the gross profit margin ratio to be applied to the annual installment payments is 1/3 (i.e., $500,000 / $1,500,000). During the year, Yardley received (1) $300,000 at the time of sale, (2) the first annual installment on the note of $300,000, and (3) interest of $144,000 (i.e., $1,200,000 × 12%). The amount of realized gross profit that Yardley should recognize from the installment sale is the sum of the down payment and first installment on the note times the gross profit margin ratio [($300,000 + $300,000) × 1/3 = $200,000]. The $144,000 of interest received in the year is recognized separately as interest income. (4083)

29. (a) Gains or losses on sale-leaseback transactions generally are deferred and amortized over the term of the lease. There are two exceptions to this general rule: (1) where the seller-lessee retains only a minor portion of the use of the property, or (2) where the seller-lessee retains more than a minor portion of the use but less than substantially all. For purposes of these tests, a minor portion is defined as 10% or less of the use of the asset; thus, if the present value of lease rentals during the leaseback period is 10% or less than the fair value of the property, the seller-lessee is deemed to have retained only a minor interest in the property. In this case, the sale and leaseback are accounted for as two separate transactions (i.e., the entire gain is recognized upon sale of the property). In this problem, the present value of the lease payments ($34,100) was less than 10% of the fair value of the property (i.e., 10% of $360,000 = $36,000). (8996)

30. (c) The government-wide statements should display information about the reporting government as a whole, except for its fiduciary activities. A pension plan is a fiduciary activity; thus, a pension trust fund is reported in the fund financial statements, but not the government-wide statements. These statements display information about major funds individually and non-major funds in the aggregate for governmental and enterprise funds. Fiduciary statements should include financial information for fiduciary funds and similar component units. Each of the three fund categories should be reported using the measurement focus and basis of accounting required for that category. (6876)

Solution 3

1. (d) The purchase of equipment is reported as a cash outflow of $47,000 and the receipt of $15,000 cash from the sale of equipment ($10,000 carrying value plus the gain of $5,000) is reported as a cash inflow of $15,000 in the investing activities section of the statement of cash flows. Investing cash inflows and outflows should be reported separately in a statement of cash flows. (6487)

2. (d) Simplified principles for recognizing and measuring assets, liabilities, income and expense are emphasized in IFRS for Small- and Medium-Sized Entities (e.g., all R&D is expensed, goodwill is amortized, cost method is used for joint ventures, etc.). Most of the complex options in full IFRS are omitted (e.g., only the cost method is permitted for PP&E) and the use of fair value is greatly reduced. Also, the extent of required disclosures was drastically reduced in IFRS for SMEs. The emphasis on disclosures is to provide basic information about short-term cash flows, liquidity, and cash-benefit trade-offs. (9742)

3. (d) Trading securities are reported at fair value and unrealized holding gains and losses are included in current earnings. (5542)

4. (d) Accrual accounting (1) recognizes revenue in the period it is earned rather than only when the related cash is received and (2) recognizes expenses in the period incurred rather than only when the related cash is paid.

Cash basis pretax income, year 2	$60,000
Add: Increase in accounts receivable—revenues earned but not yet collected in cash ($40,000 – $20,000)	20,000
Add: Decrease in accounts payable—payments made not representing current year expenses ($30,000 – $15,000)	15,000
Accrual basis pretax income, year 2	$95,000

(4081)

5. (c) Impaired assets are divided into three categories: held for use, held for disposal by sale, and held for disposal other than by sale. For assets held for use, any subsequent reversal of a previously recognized impairment loss is prohibited. For assets held for disposal by sale, the asset is measured at the lower of its book or fair value less cost to sell and its depreciation (or amortization) discontinues. Increases in the fair value, up to but not exceeding book value, would be recognized. (9891)

6. (d) Consolidated financial statements are prepared to present the financial position and operating results of the two separate organizations (i.e., parent company and subsidiary) as if only a single entity existed. Although the companies may be legally separate, the control of all decision making is now held by a single party, which indicates that only one economic entity exists. Reliability pertains to whether accounting information represents what it purports to represent, and is coupled with an assurance for the user that it involves the magnitude of an omission or misstatement of accounting information that, in light of the surrounding circumstances, makes it probable that the judgment of a reasonable person relying on the information would have been changed or influenced by the omission or misstatement. (4193)

7. (b) The statement of functional expenses provides information about expenses reported by their functional classifications, such as major classes of program services and support services, as well as information about expenses by their natural classification, such as salaries, rent, electricity, interest expense, depreciation awards and grants to others, and professional fees, in a matrix format. Program services are the activities that result in goods and services being distributed to beneficiaries, customers, or members that fulfill the purposes or mission for which the organization exists. Those services are the major purpose for and the major output of the organization and often relate to several major programs. Examples include research, education, and community services, among others. Support services are all activities of a not-for-profit organization other than program services. Generally, they include management and general, fund-raising, and membership-development activities. The salaries of fundraisers, even though the funds raised may be used in research, are classified as support services. (9876)

8. (c) The summary of significant accounting policies should identify and describe the accounting principles followed by the reporting entity and the methods of applying those principles. Examples of disclosures by a business enterprise commonly required with respect to accounting policies include those relating to basis of consolidation, depreciation methods, amortization of intangibles, inventory pricing, recognition of profit on long-term construction type contracts, and criteria for determining which investments are treated as cash equivalents. Items (I) and (III) are examples of disclosures that are not accounting policies. (3470)

9. (d) Recognition is the process of formally recording or incorporating an item in the financial statements of an entity. Allocation is the accounting process of assigning or distributing an amount according to a plan or formula. Matching is the recognition of revenues and related expenses in the same accounting period. Realization is the process of converting noncash resources into money. (4816)

10. (c) Prepaid expenses are expenses that have been paid, but not yet incurred. A decrease in the Prepaid Interest account indicates that Ness incurred interest expenses of $23,000 during the year. The journal entry would be a debit to Interest Expense $23,000 and a credit to Prepaid Interest $23,000, thus increasing interest expense for the year. It was not included in the $70,000 because no cash was paid out during the year. Accrued Interest Payable is interest that has been incurred (previously Debited to Interest Expense), but has not been paid. A decrease in the Accrued Interest Payable account would indicate that cash was paid out during the year for the accrued interest. The journal entry would be a debit to Accrued Interest Payable and a credit to Cash. In the direct method of reporting cash flows, accrued interest payable was included in the $70,000 because cash was paid out, but should not be included in the current year's interest expense since it was expensed in a prior period. ($70,000 + 23,000 – 17,000 = $76,000) (7749)

11. (d) The $60,000 received in year 1 was for services already performed and is, therefore, recognized as income in year 1. The three payments of $30,000 have not yet been earned as of the signing of the agreement because Rice is required to perform substantial future services. Such payments may not be recognized as revenue until the services are performed. The annual payments should be discounted and reported as unearned franchise fees at their present value of $72,000 at 12/31, year 1. (1315)

12. (d) Governmental-type funds do not defer and amortize a bond premium or discount over the life of the bonds. Bond issue proceeds are recorded in the appropriate governmental fund at the amount received, net of any bond premium or discount. (4435)

13. (a)

Unamortized bond discount, 7/1, year 1		$61,000	
Amortization for 7/1, year 1 - 6/30, year 2:			
Bonds payable carrying amount, 7/1, year 1	$939,000		
Effective interest rate	× 10%		
Interest expense, 7/1, year 1 - 6/30, year 2	93,900		
Interest payment ($1,000,000 × 9%)	(90,000)		
Bond discount amortization, 7/1, year 1 – 6/30, year 3		(3,900)	
Bonds payable carrying amount, 7/1, year 2 ($939,000 + $3,900)	942,900		
Effective interest rate	× 10%		
Interest expense, 7/1, year 2 - 6/30, year 3	94,290		
Interest payment ($1,000,000 × 9%)	(90,000)		
Amortization for 7/1, year 2 - 6/30, year 3		(4,290)	
Unamortized bond discount, 6/30, year 3		$52,810	(1064)

14. (d) The acid-test (quick) ratio is a measure for assessing short-term liquidity risk; it measures a company's ability to meet its currently maturing or short-term obligations. On the other hand, the debt-to-equity ratio is a measure for assessing long-term liquidity risk; it measures the portion of assets being provided by creditors and the portion of assets being provided by the stockholders of a firm. (9038)

15. (a)

Common shares outstanding, previous 12/31	300,000	
10% stock dividend, 1/31 (300,000 × 10%)	30,000	
Treasury shares purchased, 6/30	(100,000)	
Treasury shares reissued, 8/1	50,000	
2-for-1 stock split, 11/30 (300,000 + 30,000 – 100,000 + 50,000)	280,000	
Common shares outstanding, current 12/31	560,000	(4110)

16. (b) Other nonprofit organizations (ONPOs) should report donated services as revenue and expense if the following conditions are met: (1) the services are a normal part of the program or supporting services and would otherwise be performed by salaried personnel, (2) the organization exercises control over the employment and duties of the donors of the services, (3) the ONPO has a clearly measurable basis for the amount, (4) the services are significant, and (5) the services of the ONPO are not primarily for the benefit of its members. Since all of the above conditions are met for the part-time secretaries, Super Seniors should report salary and wages expense of $160,000, comprised of the $150,000 annual cost of its full-time staff and the $10,000 estimated value of the donated secretarial services. (4137)

17. (b) Royalty revenue is recognized in the period(s) the royalties are earned. The $75,000 is an advance and has not yet been earned. There were $600,000 in gross sales with $6,000 (1% of gross sales) estimated for returns leaving a total of net sales at $594,000. With royalties calculated at 10% of net sales there would be $59,400 ($594,000 × 0.10) earned and reported as royalty income for the year. (8342)

18. (b) In the period in which a component of an entity either has been disposed of or is classified as held for sale, the income statement of a business enterprise for current and prior periods shall report the results of operations of the component in discontinued operations in the periods(s) in which they occur.

Gain from sale of division assets on Feb 26	$ 90,000	
Less: Operating loss during the fiscal year	(50,000)	
Gain on disposal of segment, before income taxes	$ 40,000	(6903)

19. (b) Pledges are reported in the period in which they are made, net of an allowance for uncollectible accounts. Assuming there are no restrictions, the following entry would be made the year the pledges were made:

Pledges receivable	200,000		
Unrestricted revenue: contributions		180,000	
Allowance for uncollectible accounts		20,000	(4601)

20. (a) Valuation of inventory items is required at the lower of cost or replacement cost (commonly referred to as market). For purposes of this rule, however, market cannot exceed the net realizable value (ceiling) of the good (i.e., selling price less expected costs to sell), and market should not be less than this net realizable value reduced by an allowance for a normal profit margin (floor). In this problem, the replacement cost is between the ceiling and floor amounts, and so it is compared to cost. Because the original cost is greater than replacement cost, the item will be carried at replacement cost. (8997)

21. (c) The term current liabilities is used primarily to designate obligations whose liquidation is reasonably expected to require the use of existing resources classified as current assets, or the creation of other current liabilities. Accounts payable is a type of current liability. Short-term obligations are those scheduled to mature within one year or operating cycle, whichever is longer, and generally are classified as current liabilities. However, if they are to be refinanced on a long-term basis they will be appropriately classified as long-term liabilities. Exclusion from current liabilities requires two conditions be met; (1) the enterprise must intend to refinance the obligation on a long-term basis, and (2) the enterprise must have the ability to consummate the financing. A refinancing that occurs after the balance sheet date but before the issuance of the balance sheet is evidence of intent and ability. (8788)

22. (c) Under IFRS, specific identification is required when the goods are not interchangeable; otherwise, you can use FIFO, the gross profit method (if a physical count is not possible), the retail method (in certain industries), and weighted average. LIFO is prohibited under IFRS. (9758)

23. (c) The cost of retroactive benefits generated by a plan amendment is amortized by assigning an equal amount to each year of future service for each employee active at the date of the amendment expected to receive benefits under the plan. The use of simplified methods is permitted, including the use of the straight-line method that amortizes the cost over the average remaining service life of the active participants. The average remaining service life is 5 years, calculated by adding the expected remaining years of service of the participants (3 + 5 + 5 + 7 = 20 years) and dividing by the number of participants (4). The total credit of $100,000 would thus be amortized over 5 years, at $20,000 per year. If instead the amortization is calculated by prorating for each year over the next 7 years, during the first year 4 participants remain in active service; 4/20($100,000) = $20,000. In this problem, during each of the first three years the amortization is the same under either method. (6782)

24. (b) Because ownership of the machine is transferred to the lessee upon expiration of the lease, the lessee accounts for the lease as a capital lease. As a result, the lessee, at the inception of the lease, records the asset and the corresponding liability at an amount equal to the lesser of the asset's fair value at the inception date or the present value of the minimum lease payments, or $180,000. (8998)

25. (a) The costs of equipment or facilities that are acquired or constructed for R&D activities and have alternative future uses (in R&D or otherwise) should be capitalized when acquired or constructed. However, the cost of equipment or facilities that are acquired or constructed for a particular R&D project and have no alternative future uses (in other R&D projects or otherwise) are expensed as R&D costs at the time the costs are incurred. (2540)

26. (c) Since the League is an ONPO and all of its pledges are legally enforceable, the League should report $315,000 [i.e., ($200,000 + $150,000) × (100% – 10%)] as pledges receivable, net of the allowance for uncollectible pledges. (4142)

27. (c) A security is dilutive if the inclusion of the security in the computation of earnings per share (EPS) results in a smaller EPS or increases loss per share. Categories of potentially dilutive securities include 1) convertible securities where the if-converted method is used, 2) options, warrants, and their equivalents where the treasury stock method is used, and 3) contingently issuable shares. The cumulative 8%, $50 par preferred stock does not qualify as a potentially dilutive security so it must be one of the other three possible choices. To decide which security would be dilutive you need to look at the per share effect of each. The ten percent convertible bonds would increase the amount of income available to common stockholders by $70 [$1,000 bond × 10% = $100, then – ($100 × 30% tax effect)] and the weighted average number of shares outstanding by 20 shares for each bond converted. The $70 / 20 = a per share effect of $3.50. The seven percent convertible bonds would increase the amount of income available to common stockholders by $49 ($1,000 bond × 10% = $70, then – ($70 × 30% tax effect)]) and the weighted average number of shares outstanding by 40 shares for each bond converted. The $49 / 40 = a per share effect of $1.225. The six percent convertible preferred stock would increase the amount of income available to common stockholders by $6 ($100 bond × 6%) and the weighted average number of shares outstanding by 4 shares for each preferred share converted. The $6 / 4 = a per share effect of $1.50. Convertible preferred stock adjustments do not have tax effects. Only the seven percent convertible bonds have a dilutive effect because their per share effect o $1.225 is less than the basic EPS of $1.29. (9313)

28. (b) Grants, entitlements, and shared revenues received by proprietary funds should be reported as non-operating revenues unless they are externally restricted to capital acquisitions. (4661)

29. (a) A change in exchange rates between the functional currency and the currency in which the transaction is denominated increases or decreases the expected amount of functional currency cash flows upon a settlement of the transaction. That increase or decrease in expected functional currency cash flows is a foreign currency transaction gain or loss that generally should be included as a component of income from continuing operations for the period in which the transaction is settled. (6114)

30. (d) Estimated warranty liability at 12/31, year 2, should be recorded as the excess of the estimated warranty costs for year 1 and year 2 sales over the actual warranty expenditures to date.

Sales (years 1 and 2)	$ 400,000
Estimated warranty cost percentage (2% + 4%)	× 6%
Estimated warranty cost for year 1 and year 2 sales	$ 24,000
Warranty expenditures to date	(9,750)
Estimated warranty liability, 12/31, year 2	$ 14,250

(2606)

PERFORMANCE BY SUBTOPICS

Practice exam Testlet and question numbers corresponding to each chapter of the Financial Accounting & Reporting text are listed below. To assess your preparedness for the CPA exam, record the number and percentage of questions correctly answered in each topic area. Multiple-choice questions are worth one point each.

Chapter 1: U.S. GAAP Concepts & Framework

Question #	Correct √
1:3	
2:5	
3:8	
3:9	
3:14	
# Questions	5
# Correct	______
% Correct	______

Chapter 2: Cash, Receivables & Investments

Question #	Correct √
1:9	
1:11	
2:20	
3:3	
# Questions	4
# Correct	______
% Correct	______

Chapter 3: Inventory

Question #	Correct √
1:12	
2:11	
2:26	
3:20	
# Questions	4
# Correct	______
% Correct	______

Chapter 4: Property, Plant & Equipment

Question #	Correct √
1:1	
2:12	
2:16	
3:5	
# Questions	4
# Correct	______
% Correct	______

Chapter 5: Intangibles, R&D, Software & Other Assets

Question #	Correct √
1:13	
1:14	
2:2	
3:25	
# Questions	4
# Correct	______
% Correct	______

Chapter 6: Bonds

Question #	Correct √
1:26	
2:8	
2:14	
3:13	
# Questions	4
# Correct	______
% Correct	______

Chapter 7: Liabilities

Question #	Correct √
1:10	
2:17	
3:21	
3:30	
# Questions	4
# Correct	______
% Correct	______

Chapter 8: Leases

Question #	Correct √
1:17	
2:29	
3:24	
# Questions	3
# Correct	______
% Correct	______

Chapter 9: Poatemployment Benefits

Question #	Correct √
2:6	
3:23	
# Questions	2
# Correct	______
% Correct	______

Chapter 10: Owners' Equity

Question #	Correct √
1:6	
1:7	
2:10	
2:24	
3:15	
# Questions	5
# Correct	______
% Correct	______

Chapter 11: Revenue & Expense Recognition

Question #	Correct √
1:24	
2:28	
3:4	
3:11	
3:17	
# Questions	5
# Correct	______
% Correct	______

Chapter 12: Reporting the Results of Operations

Question #	Correct √
1:22	
1:25	
2:18	
2:19	
2:22	
3:18	
3:27	
# Questions	7
# Correct	______
% Correct	______

Chapter 13: Reporting: Special Areas

Question #	Correct √
1:15	
1:20	
1:23	
2:15	
3:29	
# Questions	5
# Correct	______
% Correct	______

Chapter 14: Accounting for Income Taxes

Question #	Correct √
1:21	
2:1	
2:25	
# Questions	3
# Correct	______
% Correct	______

Chapter 15: Statement of Cash Flows

Question #	Correct √
1:2	
1:5	
3:1	
3:10	
# Questions	4
# Correct	______
% Correct	______

Chapter 16: Business Combinations and Consolidations

Question #	Correct √
1:18	
1:19	
2:3	
2:4	
3:6	
# Questions	5
# Correct	______
% Correct	______

Chapter 17: IFRS & SEC Reporting

Question #	Correct √
1:8	
1:16	
2:7	
2:23	
3:2	
3:22	
# Questions	6
# Correct	______
% Correct	______

Chapter 18: Government Funds and Transactions

Question #	Correct √
1:4	
2:13	
3:12	
3:28	
# Questions	4
# Correct	______
% Correct	______

Chapter 19: Government Financial Reporting

Question #	Correct √
1:27	
1:28	
2:09	
2:30	
# Questions	4
# Correct	______
% Correct	______

Chapter 20: Nonprofit Accounting

Question #	Correct √
1:29	
1:30	
2:21	
2:27	
3:7	
3:16	
3:19	
3:26	
# Questions	8
# Correct	______
% Correct	______

PERFORMANCE BY AICPA CONTENT SPECIFICATION OUTLINE

Practice exam Testlet and question numbers corresponding to each section of the AICPA Content Specification Outline (CSO) are listed below. To assess your preparedness for the CPA exam, record the number and percentage of questions you correctly answered in each CSO area. The point distribution approximates that of the exam.

CSO I
Conceptual Framework, Standards, Standard Setting, and Presentation of Financil Statements (17% - 23%)

Question #	Correct √
1:2	
1:3	
1:5	
1:8	
1:12	
1:15	
1:16	
2:5	
2:7	
2:10	
2:23	
3:1	
3:2	
3:4	
3:6	
3:8	
3:9	
3:21	
3:22	
# Points	19
# Correct	
% Correct	

CSO II
Financial Statement Accounts: Recognition, Measurement, Valuation, Calculation, Presentation, and Disclosures (27% - 33%)

Question #	Correct √
1:6	
1:7	
1:9	
1:10	
1:11	
1:14	
1:21	
1:24	
1:26	
2:1	
2:2	
2:3	
2:6	
2:8	
2:11	
2:14	
2:16	
2:24	
2:25	
2:26	
2:28	
3:3	
3:10	
3:11	
3:13	
3:14	
3:15	
3:17	
3:20	
3:23	
# Points	30
# Correct	
% Correct	

CSO III
Specific Transactions, Events and Disclosures: Recognition, Measurement, Valuation, Calculation, Presentation, and Disclosures (27% - 33%)

Question #	Correct √
1:1	
1:13	
1:17	
1:18	
1:19	
1:20	
1:22	
1:23	
1:25	
2:4	
2:12	
2:15	
2:17	
2:18	
2:19	
2:20	
2:22	
2:29	
3:05	
3:18	
3:24	
3:25	
3:27	
3:29	
3:30	
# Points	25
# Correct	
% Correct	

CSO IV
Governmental Accounting and Reporting (8% - 12%)

Question #	Correct √
1:4	
1:27	
1:28	
2:9	
2:13	
2:30	
3:12	
3:28	
# Points	8
# Correct	
% Correct	

CSO V
Not-for-Profit (Nongovernmental) Accounting and Reporting (8% - 12%)

Question #	Correct √
1:29	
1:30	
2:21	
2:27	
3:7	
3:16	
3:19	
3:26	
# Points	8
# Correct	
% Correct	

SIMULATION SOLUTIONS

Solution 4

Simulation 1 Transaction Classifications

Transactions	Type	Treatment
1. Quo manufactures heavy equipment to customer specifications on a contract basis. On the basis that it is preferable, accounting for these long-term contracts was switched from the completed contract method to the percentage of completion method.	A	Y
2. As a result of a production breakthrough, Quo determined that manufacturing equipment previously depreciated over 15 years should be depreciated over 20 years.	B	Z
3. The equipment that Quo manufactures is sold with a five-year warranty. Because of a production breakthrough, Quo reduced its computation of warranty costs from 3% of sales to 1% of sales.	B	Z
4. Quo changed from LIFO to FIFO to account for its finished goods inventory.	A	Y
5. Quo changed from FIFO to average cost to account for its raw materials and work in process inventories.	A	Y
6. Quo sells extended service contracts on its products. Because related services are performed over several years, in the current year Quo changed from the cash method to the accrual method of recognizing income from these service contracts.	C	Y
7. During the current year, Quo determined that an insurance premium paid and entirely expensed in the previous year was for the period January 1 of the previous year through January 1 of next year.	C	Y
8. Quo changed its method of depreciating office equipment from an accelerated method to the straight-line method to more closely reflect costs in later years.	B	Z
9. Quo instituted a pension plan for all employees in the current year and adopted Statement of Financial Accounting Standards No. 87, Employers' Accounting for Pensions. Quo had not previously had a pension plan.	D	Z
10. During the current year, Quo increased its investment in Worth Inc. from a 10% interest, purchased in the previous year, to 30%, and acquired a seat on Worth's board of directors. As a result of its increased investment, Quo changed its method of accounting for investment in subsidiary from the cost method to the equity method.	D	Y

Explanations

1. A change from one generally accepted accounting principle to another generally accepted accounting principle when there are two or more generally accepted accounting principles that apply or when the accounting principle formerly used is no longer generally accepted is considered a change in accounting principle. A change in the *method* of applying an accounting principle also is considered a change in accounting principle. An entity shall report a change in accounting principle through retrospective application of the new accounting principle to all prior periods, unless it is impracticable to do so. Retrospective application requires the following: (a) The cumulative effect of the change to the new accounting principle on periods prior to those presented shall be reflected in the carrying amounts of assets and liabilities as of the beginning of the first period presented; (b) an offsetting adjustment, if any, shall be made to the opening balance of retained earnings for that period; and (c) financial statements for each individual prior period presented shall be adjusted to reflect the period-specific effects of applying the new accounting principle.

2. Changes in service lives of depreciable assets are changes in estimate. Changes in estimate are to be reflected prospectively.

3. Warranty costs are also examples of changes in estimate which are to be handled prospectively.

4. A change in the method of inventory pricing is a change in principle. (Also see answer to item 1)

5. A change in the method applying a generally accepted accounting principle is considered a change in principle. (Also see answer to item 1)

6. A change from an accounting principle that is not generally accepted (e.g., the cash method) to one that is generally accepted (the accrual method) is a correction of an error. The cumulative effect of the error on periods prior to those presented shall be reflected in the carrying amounts of assets and liabilities as of the beginning of the first period presented. An offsetting adjustment, if any, shall be made to the opening balance of retained earnings for that period. Financial statements for each individual prior period presented shall be adjusted to reflect correction of the period-specific effects of the error.

7. A change from an accounting principle that is not generally accepted (e.g., the cash method) to one that is generally accepted (the accrual method) is a correction of an error. The cumulative effect of the error on periods prior to those presented shall be reflected in the carrying amounts of assets and liabilities as of the beginning of the first period presented. An offsetting adjustment, if any, shall be made to the opening balance of retained earnings for that period. Financial statements for each individual prior period presented shall be adjusted to reflect correction of the period-specific effects of the error.

8. When a new depreciation method is adopted in partial or complete recognition of a change in the estimated future benefits inherent in the asset, the effect of the change in accounting principle, or the method of applying it, may be inseparable from the effect of the change in accounting estimate. For this reason a change in depreciation methods should be accounted for as a change in estimate, which is reported as part of continuing operations in the period of the change.

9. The initial adoption of an accounting principle in recognition of events or transactions occurring for the first time is not a change in principle.

10. A change in accounting principle is changing from one generally accepted accounting principles to another generally accepted accounting principle for the same events or transactions. Modification of an accounting principle necessitated by transactions or events that are clearly different in substance from those previously occurring is not a change in accounting principles. With a 30% interest in Worth, Inc., and a member on Worth's board of directors, Quo is in a different position than it was before. The cost method may have been appropriate then but would not be acceptable now, assuming Quo has considerable influence over the investee. Therefore, there is no change in accounting principle from one that is acceptable to one that is also acceptable. Only the equity method would be acceptable. Hence D., when an investment qualifies for use of the equity method, the investor should adopt the equity method of accounting. The investment, results of operations (current and prior periods presented), and retained earnings of the investor should be adjusted retroactively in a manner consistent with the accounting for a step-by-step acquisition of a subsidiary. (4938)

Simulation 2 Equity Accounts

Statement of Retained Earnings

1. Preferred dividends	$21,000
2. Common dividends—cash	$234,300
3. Common dividends—property	$840,000

Statement of Stockholder's Equity

4. Treasury stock	$26,000
5. Amount of common stock issued	$215,000
6. Number of common shares issued at December 31, year 4	215,000
7. Additional paid-in capital, including treasury stock transactions	$1,273,000

Explanations

1. The required cash dividend on preferred stock is calculated by multiplying the outstanding preferred stock by the par value and the earnings rate (3,000 shares × $100 par value × 7%). As there are no unpaid amounts from prior years, this is the only amount required to be paid this year.

2. Cash dividends on common stock are calculated by multiplying the declared cash dividends per share times the number of outstanding common shares at the time of declaration (213,000 × $1.10). The outstanding shares on 11/4 are the original 200,000 shares + the 15,000 2/1 issue – the 6,000 treasury shares purchased 3/1 + 4,000 treasury shares reissued 10/1.

3. Property dividends are recorded at the fair value of assets given up, and any difference between fair value and carrying amount of the asset is recorded as a gain or loss as a component of income from continuing operations. Any change in the fair value of the asset to be distributed between the date of declaration and date of payment is ignored.

4. The treasury stock is recorded at cost under the cost method, so the Treasury Stock account is debited for $78,000 (6,000 × $13/shares) when the 6,000 treasury shares are purchased. Since 4,000 shares or 2/3 of the treasury shares are then resold, the Treasury Stock account is only credited for 2/3 of the $78,000, or $52,000. This leaves a balance of $26,000 in the Treasury Stock account at year end.

5. The number of common shares issued at 12/31 year 4, are the original 200,000 shares + the 15,000 2/1 issue. The treasury stock activity is irrelevant as none of these shares were retired. (Treasury stock is issued but not outstanding.) The par value of the stock is $1 per share (215,000 × $1 = $215,000).

6. The number of common shares issued at 12/31 are the original 200,000 shares + the 15,000 2/1 issue. The treasury stock activity is irrelevant as none of these shares were retired. (Treasury stock is issued but not outstanding.)

7. The additional paid-in capital (APIC) balance is the beginning balance of $1,100,000 adjusted for year 4 transactions. In issues of stock for property other than cash, the property received and the amount of contributed capital should be recorded at the fair value of the property received or the market value of the stock, whichever is more objectively determinable. The value of the land purchased on 2/1 is best determinable by the value of stock traded in the over-the-counter market. As the stock has a $1 par value, the remaining $11 per share goes to APIC ($11 × 15,000 = $165,000). Under the cost method of accounting for treasury stock, any reissuance at a price in excess of the acquisition cost, the excess is credited to an appropriate APIC account. [($15 – $13) × 4,000 shares = $8,000]; ($1,100,000 + $165,000 + $8,000 = $1,273,000). (5597t)

Simulation 3 Long-Term Liabilities & Interest Expense

1.

Long-Term Liabilities Section of Balance Sheet

1. Long-term liabilities:	
2. Bonds payable due September 1, year 22	$1,271,727
3. Note payable to bank	$ 720,000
4. Liability under capital lease	$ 109,651
5. Deferred income tax liability	$ 120,000
6. Total long-term liabilities	$2,221,378

Explanations

2	Bonds payable (less unamortized discount of $228,273)		
	Bonds payable issued 9/1, year 7		$1,269,413
	Add amortization of bond discount:		
	Effective interest ($1,269,413 × 10% × 4/12)	$ 42,314	
	Less accrued interest payable 12/31, year 7 ($1,500,000 × 8% × 4/12)	40,000	2,314
	Balance, 12/31, year 7		$1,271,727
3	Note payable to bank (12% note)		
	Note payable, 12/31, year 6		$1,200,000
	Less installment paid 10/1, year 7		240,000
	Balance, 12/31, year 7		960,000
	Less current installment due 10/1, year 8		240,000
	Long-term portion, 12/31, year 7		$ 720,000
4	Liability under capital lease		
	Liability under capital lease, 12/31, year 6		$ 290,205
	Less principal portion of 12/31, year 7 payment:		
	Lease payment	$125,000	
	Less imputed interest ($290,205 × 14%)	40,629	84,371
	Balance 12/31, year 7		205,834
	Less current principal payment due 12/31, year 8:		
	Lease payment	$125,000	
	Less imputed interest ($205,834 × 16%)	28,817	96,183
	Long-term portion, 12/31, year 7		$ 109,651
5	Deferred income tax liability		
	Deferred income tax liability, 12/31, year 6		$ 140,000
	Add temporary difference—excess of tax depreciation over book depreciation of $80,000 × 25%		20,000
	Balance, 12/31, year 7		$ 120,000
6	Total long-term liabilities		
	Calculated sum total of long-term liabilities, year 7 ($1,271,727 + $720,000 + $109,651 + $120,000)		$2,221,378

2.

Interest Expense

7. Bonds payable	$ 42,314
8. Note payable to bank	$136,800
9. Liability under capital lease	$ 40,629
10. Total	$219,743

Explanations

7	Interest expense on bonds payable	
	Bonds payable issued 9/1, year 7	$1,269,413
	Effective interest rate	× 10%
	9/1, year 7 to 12/31, year 7	× 4/12
	Interest, year ended 12/31, year 7	$ 42,314
8	Interest expense on note payable to bank	
	1/1 to 9/30, year 7 ($1,200,000 × 12% × 9/12)	$ 108,000
	10/1 to 12/31, year 7 ($960,000 × 12% × 3/12)	28,800
	Interest, year ended 12/31, year 7	$ 136,800
9	Interest expense on liability under capital lease	
	Liability under capital lease, 12/31, year 6	$ 290,205
	Imputed interest rate	× 14%
	Interest, year ended 12/31, year 7	$ 40,629
10	Total interest expense	
	Calculated sum total of interest expense, year 7 ($42,314 + $136,800 + $40,629)	$ 219,743

(3417t)

Simulation 4 Consolidation Reporting

Item	Amount
1. Noncontrolling interest	$34,000
2. Goodwill	$50,000

Explanations

1. The acquirer, Poe, is to recognize the assets acquired, the liabilities assumed, and any noncontrolling interest in the acquiree, Shaw, at the acquisition, measured at their fair values as of that date. If the fair value of the noncontrolling interest isn't provided you must compute or infer its fair value. As there is no market price of Shaw's stock on the acquisition date given, we can infer that the fair value of the noncontrolling interest is proportionate to the value of consideration transferred by Poe. After calculating the amount of noncontrolling interest on the acquisition date, you must then include the net income or loss for the year and any dividends attributable to the noncontrolling interest.

Amount of purchase price by Poe	$ 270,000
Divided by: Percent acquired by Poe	/ 0.90
Fair value for total consideration	300,000
Times: Portion attributable to the noncontrolling interest (100% – 90%)	× 0.10
Noncontrolling interest, January 2	30,000
Plus: Share of net income (10% × $70,000)	7,000
Less: Share of dividends paid (10% × $30,000)	(3,000)
Noncontrolling interest, December 31	$ 34,000

2. Poe is required to recognize goodwill as of the acquisition date, measured as a residual, as the excess of the consideration transferred plus the fair value of any noncontrolling interest in Shaw over the fair values of the identifiable net assets acquired.

Consideration transferred	$ 270,000
Plus: Noncontrolling interest, Jan. 2	30,000
Aggregate amount	300,000
Less: Fair value of net assets acquired (Shaw's stockholders' equity $150,000 + excess of fair value over carrying amount of the land $100,000)	(250,000)
Total Goodwill	$ 50,000

Item	Amount	Change
3. Sold equipment	$ 14,000	Decrease
4. Sold merchandise	$ 10,000	Decrease
5. Purchased bonds	$ 9,000	Increase

Explanations

3. The intercompany equipment sale resulted in an unrealized gain of $21,000 ($36,000 proceeds received – $15,000 carrying amount) to Shaw, that must be eliminated from consolidated net income. In addition, consolidated net income must be increased by $7,000 [($36,000 cost to Poe / 3) – ($15,000 carrying amount to Shaw / 3)] to eliminate the excess depreciation recorded by Poe, because consolidated depreciation expense must be based upon the equipment cost to the consolidated entity.

Unrealized gain recognized by Shaw from equipment sale	$21,000
Less: Excess depreciation recognized by Poe	(7,000)
Adjustment for intercompany equipment transfer	$14,000

4. When one company sells merchandise to an affiliate at a price above cost, the ending inventory of the purchasing affiliate contains an element of unrealized gross profit. The gross profit is not realized to the economic entity until the inventory is sold to an unaffiliated company, and thus must be eliminated in the preparation of consolidated financial statements.

Poe's 12/31 inventory acquired from Shaw ($60,000 × 50%)	$30,000
Times: Shaw's gross profit percentage ($20,000 / $60,000)	× 1/3
Adjustment for unrealized inter-company profit in Poe's 12/31 inventory	$10,000

5. To the consolidated entity, the acquisition of an affiliate's debt from an outside party is the equivalent of retiring the obligation. Therefore, the consolidated entity must immediately recognize any difference between the price paid and the carrying amount of the bonds retired as a gain or loss.

Carrying amount of Shaw's bonds purchased by Poe	$100,000
Price Poe paid for bonds	(91,000)
Adjustment for gain recognized by consolidated entity on retirement of debt	$ 9,000

Item	Choice	Item	Choice
6. Cash	A	12. Beginning retained earnings	C
7. Equipment	B	13. Dividends paid	C
8. Investment in subsidiary	E	14. Gain on retirement of bonds	F
9. Bonds payable	B	15. Cost of goods sold	B
10. Noncontrolling interest	F	16. Interest expense	D or A
11. Common stock	C	17. Depreciation expense	B

Explanations

6. No consolidating entry affects the *Cash* account. Therefore, the amount to be reported for cash in the consolidated financial statements is the sum of the amounts on Poe's and Shaw's separate unconsolidated financial statements.

7. The amount reported for equipment in consolidated financial statements (CFS) must be based upon the equipment cost to the consolidated entity. Due to the intercompany equipment sale, the amount reported for equipment in the CFS must be decreased by $6,000, the excess of the equipment's $36,000 cost to Poe (the purchasing affiliate) over the equipment's cost of $30,000 to both Shaw and the consolidated entity. Thus, the amount to be reported for equipment in the CFS is $794,000 [($440,000 – $6,000) + $360,000]. This amount is less than the sum of the amounts on Poe's and Shaw's separate unconsolidated financial statements but not the same as the amount on either [$794,000 < ($440,000 + $360,000)].

8. The *Investment in Subsidiary* account is eliminated entirely in the consolidation process so that the subsidiary's individual assets and liabilities can be combined with the parent company accounts.

9. The acquisition of 50% of Shaw's outstanding bonds by Poe from an outside party is the equivalent of retiring the bonds. Thus, the amount to be reported for bonds payable in the consolidated financial statements is $100,000 [$0 + ($200,000 × 50%)]. This amount is less than the sum of the amounts on Poe's and Shaw's separate unconsolidated financial statements but not the same as the amount on either.

10. While no amount is reported for noncontrolling interest in separate unconsolidated financial statements of Poe and Shaw, an amount for noncontrolling interest must be presented in the consolidated balance sheet because Poe did not acquire complete ownership of Shaw.

11. The subsidiary's stockholders' equity accounts are eliminated through consolidation so that only the asset and liability accounts of the subsidiary remain to be combined with the parent company accounts. Therefore, the amount to be reported for common stock in the consolidated financial statements is the same as the amount as reported for Poe in its separate unconsolidated financial statements.

12. The subsidiary's stockholders' equity accounts are eliminated through consolidation so that only the asset and liability accounts of the subsidiary remain to be combined with the parent company accounts. Therefore, the amount to be reported for beginning retained earnings in the consolidated financial statements is the same as the amount as reported for Poe in its separate unconsolidated financial statements.

13. The subsidiary's stockholders' equity accounts are eliminated through consolidation so that only the asset and liability accounts of the subsidiary remain to be combined with the parent company accounts. Therefore, the amount to be reported for dividends paid in the consolidated financial statements is the same as the amount reported for Poe in its separate unconsolidated financial statements.

14. To the consolidated entity, the acquisition of Shaw's bonds by Poe from an outside party is the equivalent of retiring the bonds. The consolidated entity includes the excess of the $100,000 carrying amount of the bonds over the $91,000 price paid by Poe as a $9,000 gain on the early extinguishment of debt in consolidated net income. The gain on the retirement of the bonds is reported in the consolidated financial statements, but not in the separate unconsolidated financial statements of Poe and Shaw.

15. In recording the intercompany sale of the inventory to Poe, Shaw recognized cost of goods sold (CGS) of $40,000 ($60,000 – $20,000). From a consolidated perspective, the sale to Poe (the affiliated company) did not occur. Thus, consolidated cost of goods sold must be decreased by $40,000 as a result of the intercompany sale. In recording the later sale of half of the same inventory to an unaffiliated customer, Shaw recognized CGS of $30,000 ($60,000 × 50%). However, consolidated CGS is based upon the $40,000 cost of the inventory to the consolidated entity. The amount of consolidated CGS that should be recognized from the sale of half of the inventory to the unaffiliated customer is $20,000 ($40,000 × 50%). Thus, consolidated CGS must be decreased by $10,000 ($30,000 – $20,000), the excess of the amount of CGS recognized by Shaw on the sale to the unaffiliated customer over the amount that should be recognized by the consolidated entity. Therefore, consolidated CGS must be decreased by $50,000 ($40,000 + $10,000). The amount to be reported for CGS in the consolidated financial statements is $810,000 ($490,000 + $370,000 – $40,000 – $10,000). This amount is less than the sum of the amounts on Poe's and Shaw's separate unconsolidated financial statements, but not the same as the amount on either.

16. (A is also correct.) Poe purchased bonds issued by Shaw on 12/31. The bonds pay interest annually on December 31 of each year, and the interest was paid to the prior investor immediately before Poe's purchase of the bonds. Thus, no consolidating entry affects the *Interest Expense* account. Since Poe did not report any interest expense, the amount to be reported for interest expense in the consolidated financial statements is the same as the amount Shaw reports in its separate unconsolidated financial statements.

17. Consolidated depreciation expense is based upon the cost of depreciable plant assets to the consolidated entity. Therefore, the expense must be decreased by $7,000 [($36,000 cost to Poe / 3) – ($15,000 carrying amount to Shaw / 3)] to eliminate the excess depreciation recorded by Poe, the purchasing affiliate. Thus, the amount to be reported for depreciation expense in the consolidated financial statements is $38,000 [($25,000 – $7,000) + $20,000]. This amount is less than the sum of the amounts on Poe's and Shaw's separate unconsolidated financial statements but not the same as the amount on either. (4502)

Simulation 5 Government Funds

Fund	Choice
1. Enterprise fund fixed assets.	B
2. Capital projects fund.	F
3. Internal service fund fixed assets.	B
4. Private-purpose trust fund cash.	A
5. Enterprise fund cash.	B
6. General fund.	G
7. Agency fund cash.	A
8. Pension trust fund cash.	A
9. Special revenue fund.	I
10. Debt service fund.	H

Explanations

1. The enterprise fund is a proprietary fund. Therefore, it records its own assets and liabilities, including fixed assets and long-term debt.

2. Capital projects funds are used to account for financial resources that are to be used to construct or otherwise acquire major long-lived "general government" capital facilities—such as buildings, highways, storm sewer systems, and bridges.

3. The internal service fund is a proprietary fund. Therefore, it records its own assets and liabilities, including fixed assets and long-term debt.

4. The private-purpose trust fund is a fiduciary fund. Fiduciary funds are used to account for assets held by a government in a trustee or agency capacity.

5. The enterprise fund is a proprietary fund. Proprietary funds are used to account for a government's continuing business-type activities that are similar to private business enterprises.

6. Property taxes usually are a major revenue source of local governments. Unless the property taxes are restricted for specific purposes or required to be accounted for in another fund, they are accounted for in the general fund.

7. The agency fund is a fiduciary fund. Fiduciary funds are used to account for assets held by a government in a trustee or agency capacity.

8. The pension fund is a fiduciary fund. Fiduciary funds are used to account for assets held by a government in a trustee or agency capacity.

9. Special revenue funds account for proceeds of specific revenue sources that are restricted by law or contract for specified purposes.

10. Debt service funds account for the accumulation of resources for, and the payment of, general long-term debt principal and interest. (9141)

Simulation 6 Statement of Cash Flows

Kern Inc.
Statement of Cash Flows
For the Year Ended December 31, Year 4
Increase (Decrease) in Cash

	A	B	C
1	Cash flows from operating activities:		
2	Net income	$ 305,000	
3	Adjustments to reconcile net income to net cash provided by operating activities:		
4	Depreciation	$ 82,000	
5	Amortization of patent	9,000	
6	Loss on sale of equipment	10,000	
7	Equity in income of Word Corp.	(30,000)	
8	Gain on sale of marketable equity securities	(19,000)	
9	Decrease in allowance to reduce marketable equity securities to market	(15,000)	
10	Increase in accounts receivable	(35,000)	
11	Decrease in inventories	80,000	
12	Decrease in accounts payable and accrued liabilities	(115,000)	
13	Net cash provided by operating activities		$272,000
14	Cash flows from investing activities:		
15	Sale of marketable equity securities	119,000	
16	Sale of equipment	18,000	
17	Purchase of equipment	(120,000)	
18	Net cash provided by investing activities		17,000
19	Cash flows from financing activities:		
20	Issuance of common stock	260,000	
21	Cash dividend paid	(85,000)	
22	Payment on note payable	(300,000)	
23	Net cash used in financing activities		(125,000)
24	Net increase in cash		$164,000
25	Cash at beginning of year		307,000
26	Cash at end of year		$471,000

Explanations

B2 Given in Additional Information.

B4		
	Net increase in accumulated depreciation	$ 65,000
	Accumulated depreciation on equipment sold	17,000
	Depreciation year	$ 82,000

B5 Net change in patent given in scenario.

B6		
	Equipment sold for cash	$ 18,000
	Carrying value of equipment	28,000
	Loss on sale of equipment	$ 10,000

B7		
	Reported net income for Word Corp.	$150,000
	Kern's ownership	× 20%
	Equity in income of Word Corp.	$ 30,000

B8	Marketable equity securities balance 12/31, year 4	$ 150,000
	Marketable equity securities balance 12/31, year 3	250,000
	Change in marketable equity securities	(100,000)
	Cash sale of marketable equity securities	119,000
	Gain on sale of marketable equity securities	$ 19,000

B9 Change in allowance to reduce marketable equity securities to market given in scenario.

B10 Increase in accounts receivable given in scenario.

B11 Decrease in inventories given in scenario.

B12 Decrease in accounts payable and accrued liabilities given in scenario.

C13 Sum of adjustments to reconcile net income to net cash provided by operating activities plus net income.

B15 Sale of marketable equity securities given in additional information.

B16 Sale of equipment given in additional information.

B17 Purchase of equipment given in additional information.

C18 Sum of cash flows from investing activities.

B20 Issuance of common stock, 20,000 shares for cash at $13 per share $260,000

B21 Cash dividend paid given in additional information.

B22 Payment on note payable given in scenario.

C23 Sum of cash used in financing activities.

C24	Net cash provided by operating activities	$ 272,000
	Net cash provided by investing activities	17,000
	Net cash used in financing activities	(125,000)
	Net increase in cash	$ 164,000

C25 Cash at beginning of year given in scenario.

C26	Net increase in cash	$ 164,000	
	Plus cash at beginning of year	307,000	
	Cash at end of years	$ 471,000	(3422)

Simulation 7 Research

FASB ASC:	105	-	10	-	15	-	2

15-2 Content in the Securities and Exchange Commission (SEC) Sections of the Codification is provided for convenience and relates only to financial statements of SEC registrants that are presented in conformity with GAAP. (9745)

APPENDIX B
EXAM PREPARATION TIPS

Your first step toward an effective CPA Review program is to review the material in this appendix. It has been carefully developed to provide you with essential information that will help you succeed on the CPA exam. This material will assist you in organizing an efficient study plan and will demonstrate effective techniques and strategies for taking the CPA exam.

Video Cross-Reference

The video programs are designed to supplement all of our materials. They contain concise, informative lectures, as well as CPA exam tips, tricks, and techniques to help you learn the material needed to pass the exam. The **Hot•Spot**™ videos concentrate on particular topics. Use them to study the areas that are most troubling for you. To round out your review, our Simulation Strategies video programs focus on simulation-answering techniques using questions applicable to one exam section—as opposed to concentrating on content. Please see pages F-3 and F-6 of this volume as well as page iii of any Hot•Spot™ or Simulation Strategies viewer guide for a discussion on integrating videos into your study plan. This information, with approximate times, is accurate as we go to press, but is subject to change without notice.

Hot•Spot™ Video Title	Text Chapter	Time
Cash, Receivables & Marketable Securities	2	2:15
Inventory, Fixed Assets & Intangible Assets	3, 4, 5	2:45
Bonds & Other Liabilities	6, 7	2:50
Leases & Pensions	8, 9	3:00
Owners' Equity & Miscellaneous Topics	10, 13	3:00
Revenue Recognition & Income Statement Presentation	1, 11, 12	3:45
Accounting for Income Taxes	14	2:00
Statement of Cash Flows	15	2:00
Consolidations	16	3:30
IFRS & SEC Reporting*	17	1:40
Governmental Accounting	18, 19	3:50
Nonprofit Accounting	20	1:45
Audit Standards & Planning	1, 2, 9, 10	3:30
Internal Control	3, 7	2:40
Audit Evidence	4, 5	2:30
Statistical Sampling	6	1:30
Standard Audit Reports	8	1:40
Other Reports, Reviews & Compilations	11, 12, 13	2:00
Professional Responsibilities	14	1:40
Contracts	1	3:00
Sales	2	2:20
Commercial Paper & Documents of Title	3	2:05
Secured Transactions	4	1:15
Bankruptcy & Suretyship	5	2:10
Fiduciary Relationships	6, 13	2:00
Business Entities	7	2:25
Government Regulation of Business	8, 9	1:10
Tax Ethics & Legal Duties	10	2:10
Individual Taxation	11	3:00
Gross Income, Tax Liabilities & Credits	11, 14	2:50
Property Taxation	12	2:20
Corporate Taxation	14	3:45
Partnerships & Other Tax Topics	13, 15, 16	1:40
Corporate Governance	1	3:30
Economics	2	3:25
Financial Management	3	3:00
Cost & Managerial Accounting	4, 5, 6	3:20
Information Technology	7	3:00

Simulation Strategies Video	FAR	AUD	REG
Approximate Time	2:30	2:15	2:15

* Available in early 2013

SECTION ONE: GENERAL COMMENTS ON THE CPA EXAM

OVERVIEW

The difficulty and comprehensiveness of the CPA exam is a well-known fact to all candidates. However, success on the CPA exam is a **reasonable, attainable** goal. You should keep this point in mind as you read this appendix and develop your study plan. A positive attitude toward the examination, combined with determination and discipline, will enhance your opportunity to pass.

Purpose of the CPA Exam

The exam is designed as a licensing requirement to measure the technical competence of CPA candidates. Although licensing occurs at the state or territory level, the exam is uniform at all sites and has national acceptance. Passing the CPA exam in one jurisdiction generally allows candidates to obtain a reciprocal certificate or license in another jurisdiction provided they meet that jurisdiction's other requirements.

Boards of accountancy also rely upon other means to ensure that candidates possess the necessary technical and character attributes, including interviews, letters of reference, affidavits of employment, ethics exams, and educational requirements. Each board's contact information is listed on the web site (www.nasba.org) of the National Association of the State Boards of Accountancy (NASBA).

When to Take the Exam

It is advantageous to take the exam as soon as possible after completing the formal education requirements. The CPA exam is essentially an academic exam that tests the breadth of material covered by good accounting curricula. It emphasizes the body of knowledge and skill set required for the practice of public accounting.

We recommend that most candidates sit for no more than two exam sections during one exam window. By taking one exam section at the beginning of a two-month exam window and another exam section at the end, candidates effectively can study for one exam at a time and yet pass two exam sections during an exam window. Candidates with full-time jobs and other extensive time commitments may find that studying for just one exam section in an exam window is best for them.

Exam Partners

The exam is offered jointly by three organizations on behalf of the boards of accountancy. The American Institute of Certified Public Accountants (AICPA) develops and scores the exam. NASBA maintains a national database of candidates. Prometric, a commercial testing center, delivers the exam to eligible candidates in its computer-based test centers. Candidates schedule their exam appointments directly with Prometric after they receive their notice to schedule (NTS).

Exam Sections

The CPA exam is split into four sections of differing length.

1. **Financial Accounting & Reporting**—This section covers generally accepted accounting principles for business enterprises and governmental and nonprofit organizations. This section's name frequently is abbreviated as FAR. (90 multiple-choice questions and 7 task-based simulations, including a research simulation, in four hours)

2. **Auditing & Attestation**—This section covers the generally accepted auditing standards, procedures, and related topics. This section's name often is abbreviated as AUD. (90 multiple-choice questions and 7 task-based simulations, including a research simulation, in four hours)

3. **Regulation**—This section covers federal taxation; tax ethics; accountants' legal responsibilities; and business law. This section's name commonly is abbreviated as REG. (72 multiple-choice questions and 6 task-based simulations, including a research simulation, in three hours)

4. **Business Environment & Concepts**—This section covers corporate governance, economics, financial management, information technology, strategic planning, and operations management. This is the only exam section with written communications. This section's name typically is abbreviated as BEC. (72 multiple-choice questions and 3 written communications in three hours)

Exam Availability—Testing Windows

There are four exam windows each year; the first one starts in January. Generally, a candidate can take any or all sections (in any order) during any testing window, but check your board's requirements. A candidate may **not** take the **same** exam section more than once during any one testing window. Between windows, during the third month of each quarter, the exam is typically not available. Exam sites typically are open Monday through Friday; some also are open on Saturday.

January	February	March
April	May	June
July	August	September
October	November	December

Scores

Generally, boards report scores on a scale of 0-99, with 75 as a passing score. Each exam section is scored separately. All responses except written communications are scored electronically—a combination of human graders and electronic scoring is used to score those responses. Candidates receive credit for correct responses; candidates are **not** penalized for incorrect responses. The FAR, AUD, and REG exam sections have 60% of their point value in the multiple-choice questions and 40% in the simulations and research questions. BEC has 85% of its point value in the multiple-choice questions and 15% in the written communications.

Scores are approved and released to candidates by boards of accountancy. (Prometric, the AICPA, and NASBA do **not** provide score information to candidates.)

Time Limit for Passing All Four Sections

Once a candidate has a passing score for one section, that candidate has a rolling time period (typically 18 months) to pass the remaining exam sections in order to retain that score. Candidates should check with the applicable board of accountancy concerning details on time limits.

Computer-Based Testing (CBT) / Tutorial and Sample Tests

The exam is offered only in English and only in a CBT format. The AICPA provides a tutorial and sample tests for the CBT on their exam web site (www.aicpa.org/BecomeACPA/Pages/BecomeACPA.aspx). Neither is available at the test centers. It is important that you become familiar with the latest version of the AICPA testing software. The AICPA recommends reviewing the tutorial before the sample tests. Exposure to both will allow you to become familiar with how to navigate through the exam and gain exposure to the exam's directions. The time you spend with these materials will prevent you from losing any points on the exam due to unfamiliarity with the CBT system. The test uses both a word processor and a spreadsheet program that are similar, but **not** identical to common commercial applications. Even if you are completely comfortable with commercial applications, you may find it unsettling to encounter a different functionality or interface on your exam day. View the tutorial and take the sample tests at least a month before taking the exam and then again a week before the exam.

Reference Materials

All the content you need to review to pass the CPA exam is in your Bisk Education *CPA Comprehensive Exam Review* texts. However, if you would like more detailed coverage in any area; you can consult the actual authoritative literature. Individual copies of pronouncements are available from the AICPA, FASB, IASB, SEC, etc. To order materials from the FASB or AICPA contact:

AICPA/CPA2Biz Service Center
220 Leigh Farm Road
Durham, NC 27707-8110
Telephone (888) 777-7077
www.aicpa.org
service@cpa2biz.com

FASB Order Department
P.O. Box 5116
Norwalk, CT 06856-5116
Telephone (800) 748-0659
www.fasb.org/public/
fasbpubs@fasb.org

IASC Foundation Publication Dept.
30 Cannon Street
London EC4M6XH, United Kingdom
Telephone +44(0)20 7332 2730
www.iasb.org/
publications@aisb.org

The AICPA offers candidates with their NTS a **free** six-month's subscription to some of the databases of authoritative literature used in some sections of the exam. Visit the AICPA's or NASBA's web site for more information and to subscribe.

If you do not yet have your NTS, the FASB offers free access to a basic view of the FASB Accounting Standards Codification (http://asc.fasb.org). This access has browsing by topic and limited print functionality, but no search features. The AICPA offers a 30% educational discount, which students may claim by submitting proof of their eligibility (e.g., copy of ID card or teacher's letter). AICPA members get a 20% discount and speedier delivery on phone orders.

BOARDS OF ACCOUNTANCY

Certified public accountants are licensed to practice by the individual boards of accountancy of the states and territories (jurisdictions) of the United States. The exam is one component of the licensing process. Application forms to sit for the CPA exam should be requested from your individual board or its designated agent (exam administrator)—some jurisdictions arrange for an exam administrator, such as CPA Examination Services, a division of NASBA, to handle the review of applications, collection of fees, etc. IT IS EXTREMELY IMPORTANT THAT YOU COMPLETE THE APPLICATION FORM CORRECTLY. Errors or omissions may result in the delay of approval or rejection of your application. Be sure to enclose all required materials. For official transcripts and other material that must be sent directly from the issuer, include a notation about any name changes—such as a maiden name—on the application. Requirements vary as to education, experience and other matters. Cutoff dates to apply to receive approval in time to sit for a particular testing window also vary. If you have not already done so, take a moment to call or visit the web site of the appropriate board for specific and current requirements.

PAY SPECIAL ATTENTION TO THE FORM OF YOUR NAME ON YOUR APPLICATION. YOUR APPLICATION INFORMATION WILL BE USED TO GENERATE YOUR NTS AND THE ORDER AND SPELLING OF YOUR NAME ON YOUR NTS MUST EXACTLY MATCH YOUR TWO IDS—THE 3 ITEMS YOU MUST BRING TO THE TEST CENTER IN ORDER TO BE ADMITTED. At least 45 days before you plan to sit for the exam, check to see that your application to sit for the exam has been processed. DON'T ASSUME THAT YOU ARE PROPERLY REGISTERED UNLESS YOU HAVE RECEIVED YOUR NOTICE TO SCHEDULE (NTS). You must present your NTS and proper identification to be admitted to the testing room at an exam site. Contact the applicable board of accountancy if you have any doubts about what constitutes proper ID.

As explained above, your jurisdiction's board will provide you with its specific application requirements. The candidate bulletin provides important general information about the entire process including the requirements for taking the exam. Read it. At the test center you will be required to attest to the fact that you have had the opportunity to read it and that you agree to all its terms and conditions. The candidate bulletin is available on the AICPA's and NASBA's web sites.

Contacting Your Board of Accountancy

The NASBA web site has links (**www.nasba.org**) to all of the board sites. The Bisk Education web site **(www.cpaexam.com)** has links to the AICPA and NASBA web sites.

It may be possible to sit for the exam outside of the jurisdiction where you plan to be certified. Interested candidates should contact the board of accountancy in the jurisdiction where they plan to be certified and also where they want to sit. Candidates wanting to test in foreign countries should consult the NASBA web site.

NATIONAL UNIFORM CPA EXAMINATION PROCESS

The information presented here is intended to give candidates an overall idea of what their exam will be like. It is **not** intended to take the place of the Candidate Bulletin—the Candidate Bulletin contains more detailed instructions and information. In addition to understanding the basic process as described in the Candidate Bulletin, you need to know your board of accountancy's requirements for each step in the exam process.

Candidate Bulletin

The candidate bulletin provides important exam information. At the testing site, candidates must attest that they have had an opportunity to read the bulletin and that they agree to its terms and conditions. The information is presented here as accurate as possible; however, circumstances are subject to change after this text goes to press. Candidates should check the AICPA's or NASBA's web site 45 days before their exam for the most recent candidate bulletin.

Registration Process

To sit for the exam, candidates must apply to the appropriate board of accountancy or its exam administrator. Once a board or its exam administrator determines that a candidate is eligible to sit for the exam, they inform NASBA and NASBA adds the candidate to its database. With a national database, NASBA is able to ensure that no candidate can sit for the same exam section more than once during a single exam window. Within 24 hours, NASBA releases a notice to schedule (NTS).

At that point, a candidate can schedule a date and time to sit for the exam with Prometric. Verify the accuracy of your NTS before making your appointment. Please note that at Prometric's call center, Monday tends to have the longest wait times.

Foreign Test Sites

Eligible candidates may take the exam within select foreign countries; this option involves more restrictions and higher fees than within the United States. Consult the NASBA web site for details.

Notice to Schedule (NTS) & Forms of Identification

Verify that all the information on your NTS is correct. Make sure that your name as it appears on the NTS exactly matches your name on the IDs you will be using to check in at the testing center. If your name on your NTS is different in any way (the order or spelling) from your IDs, you will not be permitted to test. If any information on your NTS is incorrect or your name doesn't match your IDs, immediately contact your board or its exam administrator to request a correction. See the AICPA's candidate bulletin to review a list of examples of acceptable forms of identification. You must have two forms of identification. One ID must contain a recent photograph. Both IDs must bear your signature. Neither can be expired.

Fees

The amount and types of fees as well as the timing for their payment vary by jurisdiction. You may be required to pay all or some the fees when you submit your application. The applicable board or its agent will instruct candidates on applicable fees and whether to pay portions of the fees directly to different entities.

Refunds of fees usually are not available. Generally, if you fail to make an appointment during the exam window(s) for which your NTS is valid or give less than 24 hours notice for a cancellation of your appointment, you will not receive a refund or a credit.

Special Testing Accommodations

Special accommodations must be requested as part of the application process and again when scheduling. Candidates should supply the board or its agent with information about any medical conditions that need to be considered during the exam when scheduling. Approved accommodations are sent to NASBA which ensures that the information is included on your NTS and sent to Prometic. Ordinarily, candidates may not bring anything into the exam room—including insulin and prescription medications. Candidates with special testing accommodations (indicated on the NTS) must call (800) 967-1139 to schedule or change their appointments. If you use a teletypewriter, call (800) 529-3590.

Scheduling

Candidates may select any available date during the open window. Midweek appointments probably will be easiest to schedule. If taking the exam on a certain day is important, **schedule 45 days in advance.** Prometric doesn't overbook like airlines do—that is why there is a rescheduling fee for missed appointments. No appointment can be made fewer than 5 days (10 days, for special testing accommodations) in advance of a desired test date.

Your NTS will have an expiration date set by the applicable board. After the expiration date, you must reapply and pay the fees again.

Candidates may schedule, confirm, reschedule, cancel, or change the location of an exam appointment as well as find their preferred testing location online at www.prometric.com/cpa or by calling (800) 580-9648. Rescheduling fees may apply. The candidate bulletin has instructions for Guam that are different from those for all other locations.

Exam Day

Candidates must arrive **at least** 30 minutes **before** their scheduled appointment to allow enough time for check-in and seating procedures. Late arrivals may be denied permission to test without a refund. Candidates without NTS used to schedule that appointment and two acceptable forms of identification will be denied permission to test without a refund. A digital photograph of your face will be taken. Your ID will be scanned and swiped in a magnetic strip and barcode reader and biometrics will be used to capture your fingerprint. You will be given a key to a small locker for storage of a few belongings such as your wallet and cell phone; you are not allowed to take these items into the testing room. Prometric provides pencils and scratch paper for use in the test room. After the exam, candidates complete a survey to provide feedback.

Prometric

Prometric, a commercial testing center, has facilities at different security levels; the CPA exam is administered only at locations that have the highest restrictions. In other words, not all Prometric facilities may administer the CPA exam. These locations have adjustable chairs, 17-inch monitors, and uninterruptible power supplies (UPS). Prometric generally is closed on Sundays; a few locations are open on Saturdays. Candidates can register either at individual Prometric locations or through Prometric's national call center (800-864-8080). Candidates may schedule, reschedule, cancel, or confirm an exam as well as find the closest testing location online at www.prometric.com. Prometric doesn't score the exam. Candidates do not know their scores when they leave the exam site. Prometric sends a result file to NASBA that includes candidate responses, attendance information, and any incident reports.

Testing Room Regulations

There are strict rules for the testing room. You may not communicate with other candidates when in the testing room. You may not bring paper or pencils (other than that supplied by the test center staff) into the testing room. You will be directed to write your password (from your NTS) on the scratch paper so that it can be accounted for, i.e., you will be required to exchange the original supply for a new supply should you request it, and you must turn it in after the exam.

In the testing room, candidates may not have food, beverages, a watch, a mobile phone, most jewelry, or a container. If you require a sweater or a jacket due to room temperature, it must be worn at all times. See the Candidate Bulletin for a list of prohibited items and other restrictions. After checking in, you will be escorted to your workstation where you must remain seated during the exam except when given permission to leave the testing room for an authorized break. After you log in, proceed to the introductory screens without delay. IF THE TIME LIMIT ON THE INITIAL SCREENS IS EXCEEDED, YOUR TEST SESSION WILL TERMINATE AUTOMATICALLY. One of these screens presents the *Policy Statement Regarding Exam Confidentiality and the Taking of Breaks.* (A copy of this statement is included in the AICPA's candidate bulletin.) If you do not accept it, you will not be allowed to take the exam and your fees will be forfeited.

Breaks

Breaks are allowed only between testlets (see "Exam Format" section). After a break, you **cannot** return to a testlet you were working on prior to your break. Candidates have the option to take a break after each testlet, but break time reduces the amount of time available to answer exam questions. Breaks over 10 minutes may be reported to the board of accountancy. If you choose to take a break, the test center staff will confirm that you have completed a testlet. You must provide a fingerprint prior to leaving and again on your return. Before continuing the exam, you will be required to enter your exam password. If you leave the testing room at any other time, you will not be allowed to return and the incident will be reported to the board of accountancy.

Incident Reports

Prometric prepares an incident report for any unusual circumstances that occur during the exam. If some problem with software or hardware should occur, an incident report is included with the information that Prometric sends to NASBA after the candidate is finished with the exam. An incident report also would be filed for such events as missing scratch sheets or a mid-testlet absence from the testing room. A candidate should inform NASBA independently of any software or hardware malfunction within **five days** of the test date—in addition to Prometric's report.

EXAM FORMAT

The tutorial and sample tests on the AICPA's exam web site provide candidates the opportunity to gain essential exposure to the most recent exam software functionality and question formats. Candidates who fail to use this resource are at a disadvantage.

Testlets

Questions are grouped into testlets. An exam section has three multiple-choice testlets and one simulation or written communication testlet. Candidates may not pick the order in which they answer testlets; within a testlet, questions may be answered in any order. In other words, candidates cannot choose to answer the simulation testlet first and then the multiple-choice question testlets. Within any one testlet, questions cover the entire content specification outline and are presented in random order. Once a testlet is closed, a candidate may not return to it.

Multiple-Choice Question Testlet

Multiple-choice questions comprise a majority of the point value of each section. Because of their objective nature, the correct solution is listed as one of the answer choices. In Bisk Education's printed book, letter answers appear next to each answer option to simplify indicating the correct answer. In the actual exam, a radio button appears instead of this letter. During the exam, candidates indicate their response by clicking the appropriate radio button with a mouse device.

There are three multiple-choice question testlets in each of the four exam sections. FAR and AUD multiple-choice question testlets typically have 30 questions each; REG and BEC multiple-choice question testlets typically have 24 questions each. The multiple-choice questions in each testlet are presented randomly, i.e., they are not in the same order as the content specification outline (CSO). The tutorial on the AICPA's exam web site demonstrates how to select an answer, move to another question, etc. The sample tests allow you to practice answering a few questions.

Adaptive Testing for Multiple-Choice Questions

After a candidate finishes a multiple-choice question testlet, the software selects the next testlet based on the candidate's performance on the previous testlet. The first testlet is always at the "moderate difficultly" level. If a candidate did well on the first testlet, the second testlet will be a little more difficult than average. Conversely, if a candidate did poorly on the first testlet, the second testlet will be of moderate difficulty. The third testlet level is selected based on performance on the first two testlets. Simulations and written communications are not adaptive.

The overall point value of a "moderate difficultly" testlet will be less than the overall point value of a "difficult" testlet. Thus, some candidates may think that they are not doing well because they are finding the questions difficult; when in reality, they are getting difficult questions because of exceptional performance on previous testlets. Other candidates may think that they are doing well because they are finding the questions easy; when in reality, they are getting questions at the "moderate difficultly" level because of average or poor performance on previous testlets.

Simulation Testlet (only FAR, AUD, and REG)

In FAR, AUD, and REG, a simulation typically is a scenario with any of a variety of tasks completed by supplying objective responses. Generally, the FAR and AUD exam sections each have seven task-based simulations; the REG exam section has six.

Simulations may require candidates to select answers from lists or to enter numbers into worksheets or tax forms. Tax forms or schedules may appear on the REG exam section, but not all simulations on tax topics will include tax forms. Candidates don't need to know how to create a spreadsheet from scratch to earn full points on the exam; they do need to know how to categorize, determine value, and expand a previously constructed worksheet.

The exam has a blank **spreadsheet** for use like a piece of electronic scratch paper. Anything in such a spreadsheet generally is not graded. In other words, if a candidate calculates an amount in a spreadsheet, it must be transferred to the appropriate answer location in order to earn points.

There will be at least one **research** simulation in the FAR, AUD, and REG simulation testlet. See the Research Skills appendix in the FAR, AUD, and REG volumes for more details. Research simulations do not appear in the BEC exam section.

Written Communication Testlet (only BEC)

The fourth BEC testlet has three written communication tasks. See the **Writing Skills** appendix in the BEC volume for a discussion of written communications. The exam has a **word processor** tool with limited features (such as cut, paste, copy, spell check, do, and undo features). The word processor intentionally does **not** have many formatting features (such as bold, underline, or bullet features); the examiners don't want candidates spending much time on formatting.

Tutorial & Sample Tests

The AICPA provides a web-based tutorial and sample tests for the CBT. This tutorial has samples of all the different types of questions. The examiners believe that an hour spent with these materials will eliminate any point value loss due merely to unfamiliarity with the software functionality. It is important that you become familiar with the latest version of the AICPA testing software. The examiners may provide a spreadsheet program and a word processor; however, these applications are not Microsoft Excel™ or Word™. It may be unsettling to encounter an unfamiliar interface on your exam day. This tutorial is **not** available at the exam sites.

Pre-Exam Candidate Attestation

Candidates must agree to the nondisclosure statement before starting the exam. The pre-exam attestations are reproduced in the candidate bulletin.

Timing

For a well-prepared candidate, time should not be an issue. Candidates will receive a five or ten minute warning. The software stops accepting exam responses at the end of the exam time automatically. All information entered before that time is scored.

Advice to Candidates

Become familiar with the pre-exam attestations and the exam format. Don't go to the exam without spending at least an hour with the tutorial and the practice exam available on the AICPA exam web-site. The Bisk Education editors recommend viewing this tutorial at least a month before taking the exam and again a second time a week before your exam date.

THE NONDISCLOSED EXAM

The Uniform CPA Examination is nondisclosed. This means that candidates are not allowed to receive a copy of their exam questions after the test. Also, candidates are required to sign a statement of confidentiality in which they promise not to reveal questions or answers. Only the AICPA has access to the test questions and answers. (In the past, the AICPA has released a small number of questions with unofficial answers from each nondisclosed exam; it makes no guarantees that it will continue this practice.) Bisk Education's editors update the questions in Bisk Education materials based upon content changes, items from previously disclosed tests, and their teaching expertise. Due to the nondisclosure requirements, Bisk Education's editors are no longer able to address questions about specific examination questions, although we continue to supply help with similar study problems and questions in our texts.

The AICPA no longer discloses the exam in order to increase consistency, facilitate computer administration, and improve examination quality by pretesting questions. Because the examination is no longer completely changed every year, statistical equating methods are more relevant, and the usefulness of specific questions as indicators of candidates' knowledge can be tested.

Nonscored Pretest Questions

Each exam may include pretest questions. These questions are not included in final scores regardless of whether they were answered correctly; they are presented only so that the Board of Examiners may evaluate them for effectiveness and possible ambiguity. Candidates do not know which questions will not be scored. The examiners do not disclose the percentage of pretest questions.

Time Management

As the extra questions are mixed in among the graded questions, time management becomes crucial. Candidates who are deciding how much time to spend on a difficult multiple-choice question must keep in mind that there is a chance that the answer to the question will not affect them either way. Also, candidates should not allow a question that seems particularly difficult or confusing to shake their confidence or affect their attitude towards the rest of the test; it may not even count. These pretest questions work against candidates who are not sure whether they have answered enough questions to earn a passing score. Candidates should try for a safety margin, so that they will have accumulated enough correct answers to pass, even though some of their correctly answered questions will not be scored.

Post-Exam Diagnostics

The AICPA Board of Examiners' Advisory Grading Service provides boards of accountancy with individual diagnostic reports for candidates. The accountancy boards may mail the diagnostic reports to candidates along with their grades. Candidates should contact the appropriate board to find out its policy on this issue.

Question Re-Evaluation

Candidates who believe that an examination question contains errors that will affect the grading should contact the AICPA Examinations Division, in accordance with the AICPA's *Uniform CPA Examination Candidate Bulletin: Information for Applicants* within **four days** of taking the examination. The examiners ask candidates to be as precise as possible about the question and their reason for believing that it should be re-evaluated, and, if possible, to supply references to support their position. Include your examination section identification number, but not the exact wording or an outline of the question or simulation—simply provide enough information for the examiners to identify the question, such as "question number 12 in the first testlet" or the tab name for a simulation question. The examiners are unable to respond directly to candidates, but review every fax or letter received by the deadline. Since candidates are not able to keep a copy of examination questions, it is important to remember as much detail as possible about a disputed question.

TEN ATTRIBUTES OF EXAMINATION SUCCESS

We believe that successful CPA candidates possess these ten characteristics that contribute to their ability to pass the exam. Because of their importance, we will consider each attribute individually.

1. Positive Mental Attitude

Preparation for the CPA exam is a long, intense process. A positive mental attitude, above all else, can be the difference between passing and failing.

2. Development of a Plan

The significant commitment involved in preparing for the exam requires a plan. We have prepared study plans in the **Getting Started** section of this text. Take time to read this plan. **Amend it to your situation.** Whether you use our study plan or create your own, the importance of this attribute can't be overlooked.

3. Adherence to the Plan

You cannot expect to accomplish a successful and comprehensive review without adherence to your study plan.

4. Time Management

We all lead busy lives and the ability to budget study time is a key to success. We have outlined steps to budgeting time in the **Personalized Training Plan** found in the **Getting Started** section.

5. Knowledge

There is a distinct difference between understanding material and knowing material. A superficial understanding of accounting, auditing, and the business environment is not enough. You must know the material well. Your Bisk Education text is designed to help you acquire the knowledge that is essential to exam success.

6. Exam Strategies

You should be familiar with the CPA exam format and know exactly what you will do in the testing room. In Section Two, we discuss the steps you should take from the time you enter the testing room until you hand in your scratch paper. Advance planning will save you time and confusion on exam day.

7. Exam Grading

Remember that your objective is to score 75 points on each exam section. An understanding of the grading procedures will help you to maximize points. Written communication responses are scored by a combination of electronic and human graders. Objective responses are scored electronically.

8. Solutions Approach™

The Solutions Approach™ is an efficient, systematic method of organizing and solving CPA exam questions. This approach will permit you to organize your thinking and conclusions in a logical manner that will maximize your exam score. Many candidates never have developed an effective problem-solving methodology. Our Solutions Approach™ teaches you to derive solutions independently and will help you avoid drawing "blanks" on the exam; with it, you always know where to begin.

9. Focus on the Ultimate Objective—Passing!

Your primary goal in preparing for the CPA exam is to attain a grade of 75 or better on all sections and, thus, **pass the exam**. Your review should be focused on this goal. Other objectives, such as learning new material or reviewing old material, are important only insofar as they assist you in passing the exam.

10. Exam Confidence

Exam confidence is actually a function of the other nine attributes. If you have acquired a good working knowledge of the material, an understanding of the grading system, a tactic for answering simulations, and a plan for taking the exam; you can go into the testing room **confident** that you are in control.

SECTION TWO: EXAMINATION STRATEGIES

PREPARATION

The CPA exam is more than a test of your knowledge and technical competence. It is also a test of your ability to function under psychological pressure. You easily could be thrown off balance by an unexpected turn of events during the days of the exam. Your objective is to avoid surprises and eliminate hassles and distractions that might shake your confidence. You want to be in complete control so that you can concentrate on the exam material, rather than the exam situation. By taking charge of the exam, you will be able to handle pressure in a constructive manner. The keys to control are adequate preparation and an effective examination strategy.

Overall Preparation

Advance preparation will arm you with the confidence you need to overcome the psychological pressure of the exam. As you complete your comprehensive review, you will cover most of the material that will be tested on the exam; it is unlikely that any question will deal with a topic you have not studied. But if an unfamiliar topic **is** tested or a familiar topic is presented in an unfamiliar manner, you will not be dismayed because you have learned to use the **Solutions Approach™** to derive the best possible answer from the knowledge you possess. Similarly, you will not feel pressured to write "perfect" written communication answers, because you understand the grading process. You recognize that there is a limit to the points you can earn for each answer, no matter how much or how well you write.

The components of your advance preparation program have previously been discussed in this appendix. Briefly summarizing, they include the following.

1. Comprehensive review materials such as your Bisk Education CPA review program.
2. A method for pre-review and ongoing self-evaluation of your level of proficiency.
3. A study plan that enables you to review each subject area methodically and thoroughly.
4. A **Solutions Approach™** for each type of examination question.
5. An understanding of the grading process and grader orientation skills.

CPA Exam Strategies

The second key to controlling the exam is to develop effective strategies for the days you take the exam. Your objective is to avoid surprises and frustrations so that you can focus your full concentration on the questions and your answers.

You should be familiar with the format of the CPA exam and know exactly what you will do when you enter the testing room. Remember to read all instructions carefully, whether general or specific to a particular question. Disregarding the instructions may mean loss of points.

On the following pages, we discuss the steps you should take on exam day. Planning in advance how you will spend your examination time will save you time and confusion.

ANSWERING QUESTIONS

A very effective and efficient manner of answering the multiple-choice questions is to make **two passes** through the testlet. On the first pass, you should answer those questions that you find the easiest. If you encounter a question that you find difficult to solve, note it and proceed to the next one. This will allow you to avoid wasting precious time and will enable your mind to clear and start anew on your **second pass.** On the second pass, you should return and solve those questions you left unanswered on the first pass. Some of these questions you may have skipped over without an attempt, while in others you may have been able to eliminate one or two of the answer choices. Either way, you should come up with an answer on the second pass, even if you have to guess! Once you leave a testlet, you **cannot** return to it. Before leaving a testlet, make sure you have answered all of the questions.

Last Testlet Strategy

Consider spending the first few moments of time on the last testlet planning your work. Do not plunge head-first into answering the questions without a plan of action. You do not want to risk running out of time, becoming frustrated by a difficult question, or missing the opportunity to answer a question that you could have answered well. Your inventory should take no longer than a minute. Classify the topics of the questions and answer the ones in your strongest topics first. Following this plan, if you run out of time, it will be on the question covering your weakest topic, not your strongest topic.

1. Note the question topics displayed in the preview ribbon when mousing over the buttons at the bottom of the screen.

2. Rank the questions according to your strengths and weaknesses.

3. Devise a time schedule on your scratch paper, taking into account the number and type of questions.

Examination Time Budgeting

You must **plan** how you will use your examination time and adhere to your schedule. If you budget your time carefully, you should be able to answer all questions. Your time budgets may be **similar** to these. You may benefit by taking more or less breaks than are included in these schedules. You may benefit by allocating less time to multiple-choice testlets and correspondingly more time to the last testlet or *vice versa*.

	Minutes			
	FAR	AUD	REG	BEC
Answer first multiple-choice question testlet	48	46	36	38
Answer second multiple-choice question testlet	48	46	36	38
Answer third multiple-choice question testlet	48	46	36	38
Break	4	5	0	5
Review simulation or written communication testlet	1	1	1	1
Answer simulation or written communication testlet	91	96	71	60
Total	240	240	180	180

Your objective in time budgeting is to avoid running out of time to answer a question. Work quickly but efficiently (i.e., use the **Solutions Approach™**). Be sure to adjust your time budget to accommodate your individual needs and strengths.

Scratch Paper

Identify and label your scratch paper to avoid confusing yourself during the stress of the exam.

PRACTICAL ADVICE FOR EXAM SUCCESS

As stated previously, the CPA exam is in itself a physical and mental strain. You can minimize this strain by avoiding all unnecessary distractions and inconveniences during your exam week. Consider the following.

- **Use the AICPA's free tutorial and sample examination** at its web site at least a week before your examination. Because the exam interface is subject to change, re-visit the site to be sure that you are familiar with the current interface even if you took an exam in a previous window. The site also has the most current *Uniform CPA Examination Candidate Bulletin,* a publication with useful information for candidates. These are **not** available at the test center.

- **Carefully register for the examination.** You must bring two forms of identification and your notice to schedule to the test center on the day of your exam. The name you use to make the appointment must match **exactly** your name on the identification and your notice to schedule (which also must match each other exactly). The last two weeks of an exam window tend to be the busiest.

- **Stick to your normal eating, sleeping, and exercise habits.** Eat lightly before the exam. Watch your caffeine and alcohol intake. If you are accustomed to regular exercise, continue a regular routine leading up to your exam day.

- **Locate the examination facilities** before your examination day and familiarize yourself with the surroundings and alternate routes.

- **Arrive early for the exam.** Allow plenty of time for unexpected delays. Nothing is more demoralizing than getting caught in a traffic jam ten minutes before your exam is scheduled to begin. Your appointment time is the time that the actual examination process is scheduled to start, **not** the start of the test center pre-exam procedures: identification verification, digital photography, storage locker assignment, etc. The examiners recommend that you arrive **at least** 30 minutes before your scheduled appointment. If your examination doesn't begin within 30 minutes of your scheduled start time, you may have to reschedule. Pre-exam procedures take significant time and are not factored into your scheduled appointment.

- **Avoid possible distractions,** such as friends and pre-exam conversation, immediately before the exam.

- In general, **you should not attempt serious study on the nights before exam sessions.** It's better to relax—watch a movie, exercise, or read a novel. If you feel you must study, spend half an hour or so going over the chapter outlines in the text. Some candidates develop a single page of notes for each chapter (or each exam section) throughout their review process to review for a few minutes during the evening before the exam. This single page includes only those things that are particularly troublesome for that candidate, such as the definition of a capital asset or the economic order quantity formula.

- **Don't discuss exam answers with other candidates.** Not only have you signed a statement of confidentiality, but someone is sure to disagree with your answer, and if you are easily influenced by his or her reasoning, you can become doubtful of your own ability. If you are writing more than one exam section within a two-month exam window, you might not have the reliable feedback that only your score can provide from your first section before you sit for the second section. Wait and analyze your performance by yourself when you are in a relaxed and objective frame of mind.

- **Avoid self-evaluation** of your exam performance until after you receive your official score. Self-evaluation without an official score is unreliable. Not all questions are the same point value. Further, candidates have no reliable way to know which questions are not scored. Instead of speculating, focus on preparing for your next exam section.

GENERAL RULES GOVERNING EXAMINATIONS

1. Read carefully any paperwork assigned to you; make note of numbers for future reference; when it is requested, return it to the examiner. Only the examination number on your card shall be used on your exam for the purpose of identification. If a question calls for an answer involving a signature, **do not** use your own name or initials.

2. Use the exact same name as on your notice to schedule (NTS) when scheduling your appointment. Two current (unexpired) pieces of identification are required; one must have a photo. The name on your identification must match your name on your notice to schedule **exactly**.

3. Seating during the exam is assigned by Prometric.

4. Supplies furnished by the Board remain its property and must be returned whether used or not.

5. Any reference during the examination to books or other matters or the exchange of information with other persons shall be considered misconduct sufficient to bar you from further participation in the examination.

6. The only aids most candidates are permitted to have in the examination room are supplied by the proctors. Wallets, briefcases, files, books, phones, watches, mobile phones, and other material brought to the examination site by candidates must be placed in a designated area before the start of the examination. Candidates must demonstrate that their pockets are empty. Candidates get a key to a **small** storage locker. The test center is not responsible for lost items.

7. Do not leave your workstation during a testlet. Breaks are allowed only before starting and after finishing testlets. Smoking is allowed only in designated areas away from the general examination area.

8. No telephone calls are permitted during the examination session.

9. Answers must be completed in the total time allotted for each exam section. The fixed time for each session must be observed by all candidates. One time warning is given five or ten minutes before the end of the exam. The testing software will end the test at the end of the specified time.

CPA EXAM WEEK CHECKLISTS

What to have on hand for exam week:

1. The CPA exam notice to schedule (NTS) used to register for the exam and **two** forms of identification that exactly match your name on the NTS.

2. Cash and/or a major credit card.

3. An inexpensive watch (will not be allowed in the testing room) to facilitate your timely arrival at the exam site.

4. Comfortable clothing that can be loosened to suit varying temperatures. What is worn into the testing room must be worn throughout the testing period. Once at the testing center, you can remove a coat, for instance, before entering the testing room.

5. Appropriate review materials and tools for final reviews during the last days before the exam.

6. Healthy snack foods (will not be allowed in testing room).

For candidates who travel far to take the exam:

1. Make travel arrangements, including contingency plans, well in advance.

2. If you are traveling, it's best to reserve a room for the preceding night so that you can check in, locate the exam site well before the exam, and get a good night's sleep.

3. Pack travel confirmations and an alarm clock. (Don't rely on a hotel wake-up call.)

4. If crossing time zones, plan to compensate accordingly.

5. International candidates should apply for passports and visas well in advance.

Evenings before exam sections:

1. Briefly review your Bisk Education chapter outlines for the next day's section(s).

2. Eat lightly and monitor your intake of alcohol and caffeine. Get a good night's rest.

3. Do **not** try to cram. A brief review of your notes will help to focus your attention on important points and remind you that you are well prepared, but too much cramming can shatter your self-confidence. If you have reviewed conscientiously, you already are well prepared for the CPA exam.

The hours before each exam section:

1. Eat a satisfying meal before your exam. It will be several hours before your next meal. Eat enough to ward off hunger, but not so much that you feel uncomfortable.

2. Dress appropriately. Wear layers you can loosen to suit varying temperatures in the room.

3. Arrive at the exam center at least 30 minutes early.

What to bring to the exam:

1. Appropriate identification (two forms, one with a picture) and the notice to schedule (NTS) used to schedule for this exam. Your name on the identification must match your name on your NTS **exactly**. (An NTS for a previously taken exam is not acceptable.)

2. An inexpensive watch (to be left outside of the exam room) to ensure that you arrive **at least 30 minutes** early.

3. Take only those articles that you need to get to and from the exam site. Avoid taking any articles that are not allowed in the exam room, especially valuable ones. There are **small** storage lockers outside of the testing room available on a first-come basis to hold wallets, etc. The test center is not responsible for lost items. Watches, phones, pencils, purses, tissues, most jewelry, candy, and gum are not allowed in the exam room. Even medication is not allowed except by previous arrangement.

During the exam:

1. Always read all instructions and follow the directions of the exam administrator. If you don't understand any written or verbal instructions, or if something doesn't seem right, ASK QUESTIONS as allowed. Remember that an error in following directions could invalidate your **entire** exam.

2. Budget your time. Always keep track of the time and avoid getting too involved with one question.

3. **Satisfy the grader.** Remember that the grader cannot read your mind. Tell the grader what you know, don't worry about any points you don't know.

4. Answer every question, even if you must guess.

5. Use **all** the allotted time. If you finish a testlet early, go back and reconsider the more difficult questions.

6. If you feel sluggish, stretch and walk around as allowed between testlets. Breathe deeply; focus your eyes on distant objects to avoid eye strain. Do some exercises at your workstation to relax muscles in the face, neck, fingers, and back.

7. Do not leave your workstation, except between testlets. Leaving your workstation during a testlet may invalidate your score.

8. Take enough time to organize written communications. Well-organized responses will impress the grader.

9. Remember that you are well-prepared for the CPA exam, and that you can **expect to pass!** A confident attitude will help you overcome examination anxiety.

SECTION THREE: EXAMINATION GRADING ORIENTATION

An understanding of the grading procedure will help you maximize grading points on the CPA exam. Remember that your objective is to pass the exam. You cannot afford to spend time on activities that will not affect your grade, or to ignore opportunities to increase your points. The following material summarizes the important substantive aspects of the Uniform CPA Examination itself and the grading procedures used by the AICPA.

The CPA exam is prepared and graded by the AICPA Examinations Division. It is administered by a commercial testing center, Prometric, under tight security measures. The candidates' anonymity is preserved throughout the examination and grading process. Unusual similarities in answers among candidates are reported to the appropriate State Boards of Accountancy through which they registered.

OBJECTIVE QUESTIONS

Objective questions consist of multiple-choice questions and objective format questions in simulations, which include: yes-no, true-false, matching, and questions requiring a numerical response. Objective questions are machine graded. It is important to understand that there is **no grade reduction** for incorrect responses to objective questions—your total objective question grade is determined solely by the number of correct answers. Thus, you **should answer every question.** If you do not know the answer, make an intelligent guess.

The point is to avoid getting "bogged down" on one answer. Move along and answer all the questions. This helps you avoid leaving questions unanswered or panic-answering questions due to poor budgeting of test time.

GRADING IMPLICATIONS FOR CPA CANDIDATES

To summarize this review of the AICPA's grading procedure, we can offer the following conclusions that will help you to **satisfy the grader** and maximize your score:

1. Attempt an answer on every question.
2. Respond directly to the requirements of the questions.
3. Use schedules and formats favored by the AICPA examiners.
4. Answer all requirements.
5. Develop a **Solutions Approach**™ to questions.
6. Allocate your examination time based on AICPA CPA examination scoring weights.

SECTION FOUR: THE SOLUTIONS APPROACH™

The **Bisk Education Solutions Approach™** is an efficient, systematic method of organizing and solving questions found on the CPA exam. Remember that all the knowledge in the world is worthless unless you can communicate it to others. Conversely, a little knowledge can go a long way if you use a proper approach. The **Solutions Approach™** was developed by our Editorial Board in 1971; all subsequently developed copies trace their roots from the original "Approach" that we formulated. Our **Solutions Approach™** and grader orientation skills, when properly developed, can be worth at least 10 to 15 points for most candidates. These 10 to 15 points often make the difference between passing and failing.

We will suggest a number of steps for deriving a solution that will help maximize your grade on the exam. Although you should remember the important steps in our suggested approach, don't be afraid to adapt these steps to your own taste and requirements. When you work the questions at the conclusion of each chapter, make sure you use your variation of the **Solutions Approach™**. Do not consult the unofficial answer until you finish the question. The worst thing you can do is look at an old question and, before answering it, turn to the answer without working the problem. This will build false confidence and provide **no** skills in developing a **Solutions Approach™**.

SOLUTIONS APPROACH™ FOR OBJECTIVE QUESTIONS

We recommend the following framework:

1. Read the "Instructions to Candidates" section on your particular exam to confirm that the AICPA's standard is the same. Generally, your objective portion points will be determined by the number of correct answers with no penalty for incorrect answers.

2. Read the question carefully, noting exactly what the question is asking. Negative requirements are easily missed. Note key words and note when the requirement is an exception (e.g., "except for…," or "which of the following does **not**…"). Perform any intermediate calculations necessary to the determination of the correct answer.

3. Anticipate the answer by covering the possible answers and seeing if you **know** the correct answer.

4. Read the answers given.

5. Select the best alternative. Very often, one or two possible answers will be clearly incorrect. Sometimes, more than one answer is a correct statement, but only one such statement answers the question asked. Of the other alternatives, be sure to select the alternative that **best answers the question asked**. Mark the correct answer.

6. After completing all of the individual questions in a testlet, **go back** and double check your answers—making sure the answer and sequence are correct. READ THE INSTRUCTIONS CAREFULLY.

7. Answer the questions in order. This is a proven, systematic approach to objective test taking. You generally are limited to a maximum of 1½ to 2 minutes per multiple choice question—or even less time. Under no circumstances should you allow yourself to fall behind schedule. If a question is difficult or long, be sure you remain cognizant of the time you are using. If after a minute or so you feel that it is too costly to continue on with a particular question, select the letter answer you tentatively feel is the best answer and go to the next question, flagging the question or noting the question number on your scratch paper. Return to these questions at a later time and attempt to finally answer them when you have time for more consideration. If you cannot find a better answer when you return to the question, use your preliminary answer because your first impressions are often correct. However, as you read other question(s), if something about these subsequent questions or answers jogs your memory, return to the previous tentatively answered question(s) and make a note of the idea for later consideration (time permitting).

A simulation includes a group of objective questions based on one hypothetical situation. A simulation is particularly challenging format for many candidates. In this case, you should consider skimming all the related questions (but not answer possibilities) before you begin answering, since an overall view of the problem will guide you in the work you do.

Note also that many incorrect answer choices are based on the erroneous application of one or more items in scenario of the question. Thus, it is extremely important to **anticipate** the answer before you read the alternatives. Otherwise, you may be easily persuaded by an answer choice that is formulated through the incorrect use of the given data.

Let's consider a multiple-choice question adapted from a past examination.

Sample Multiple-Choice Question

Let's consider the following multiple-choice question adapted from a past examination.

Jel Co., a consignee, paid the freight costs for goods shipped from Dale Co., a consignor. These freight costs are to be deducted from Jel's payment to Dale when the consignment goods are sold. Until Jel sells the goods, the freight costs should be included in Jel's

a. Cost of goods sold.
b. Freight-out costs.
c. Selling expenses.
d. Accounts receivable.

APPLYING THE SOLUTIONS APPROACH™

Let's look at the steps you should go through to arrive at your solution.

In **Step 1**, you must carefully read the "**Instructions**" that precede your particular objective CPA exam portion.

In **Step 2**, you must read the question and its requirements carefully. Look out for questions that require you to provide those options **not** applicable, **not** true, etc…

In **Step 3**, you must anticipate the correct answer **after** reading the question **but before** reading the possible answers.

In **Step 4**, you must read the answer carefully and select the alternative that best answers the question asked. Ideally, the best alternative will immediately present itself because it roughly or exactly corresponds with the answer you anticipated before looking at the other possible choices.

In **Step 5**, you select the best alternative. If there are two close possibilities, make sure you select the **best** one in light of the **facts** and **requirements** of the question.

In **Step 6**, you must make sure you accurately mark the **best answer**.

In **Step 7**, with due regard to time constraints, review the questions previously flagged.

Sample Multiple-Choice Question Solution

The answer is (d).

The consignee will be reimbursed for the freight costs after the sale of the consignment goods by reducing the payment to the consignor. An amount that will be reimbursed in the future represents a receivable.

The other answers are incorrect because an amount that will be reimbursed in the future should not be recorded as an expense.

BENEFITS OF THE SOLUTIONS APPROACH™

The **Solutions Approach™** may seem cumbersome the first time you attempt it, but a haphazard approach often results in a disorganized answer. The Solutions Approach™ will help you recall information under the pressure of the exam. The technique assists you in directing your thoughts toward the information required for the answer. Without the Solutions Approach™, you are apt to become distracted or confused by details that are irrelevant to the answer. Finally, the Solutions Approach™ is a **faster** way to answer exam questions. You will not waste time on false starts. The approach may seem time-consuming at first, but as you become comfortable using it, you will see that it actually saves time and results in a better answer.

We urge you to give the **Solutions Approach™** a good try by using it throughout your review. As you practice, you may adapt or modify it to your own preferences and requirements. The important thing is to develop a system so that you do not approach exam questions with a storehouse of knowledge that you can demonstrate to the examiners.

SECTION FIVE: CONTENT SPECIFICATION OUTLINE

The AICPA Board of Examiners has developed a **Content Specification Outline** of each section of the exam to be tested. These outlines list the areas, groups, and topics to be tested and indicate the approximate percentage of the total test score devoted to each area. The content of the examination is based primarily on the results of two national studies of public accounting practice and the evaluation of CPA practitioners and educators.

FINANCIAL ACCOUNTING & REPORTING

The Financial Accounting and Reporting section tests knowledge and understanding of the financial reporting framework used by business enterprises, not-for-profit organizations, and governmental entities. The financial reporting frameworks that are included in this section are those issued by the standard-setters identified in the references to these CSOs, which include standards issued by the Financial Accounting Standards Board, the International Accounting Standards Board, the U.S. Securities and Exchange Commission, and the Governmental Accounting Standards Board. In addition to demonstrating knowledge and understanding of accounting principles, candidates are required to demonstrate the skills required to apply that knowledge in performing financial reporting and other tasks as certified public accountants. To demonstrate such knowledge and skills, candidates will be expected to perform the following tasks:

- Identify and understand the differences between financial statements prepared on the basis of accounting principles generally accepted in the United States of America (U.S. GAAP) and International Financial Reporting Standards (IFRS).
- Prepare and/or review source documents including account classification, and enter data into subsidiary and general ledgers.
- Calculate amounts for financial statement components.
- Reconcile the general ledger to the subsidiary ledgers or underlying account details.
- Prepare account reconciliation and related schedules; analyze accounts for unusual fluctuations and make necessary adjustments.
- Prepare consolidating and eliminating entries for the period.
- Identify financial accounting and reporting methods and select those that are appropriate.
- Prepare consolidated financial statements, including balance sheets, income statements, and statements of retained earnings, equity, comprehensive income, and cash flows.
- Prepare appropriate notes to the financial statements.
- Analyze financial statements including analysis of accounts, variances, trends, and ratios.
- Exercise judgment in the application of accounting principles.
- Apply judgment to evaluate assumptions and methods underlying estimates, including fair value measures of financial statement components.
- Produce required financial statement filings in order to meet regulatory or reporting requirements (e.g., Form 10-Q, 10-K, Annual Report).
- Determine appropriate accounting treatment for new or unusual transactions and evaluate the economic substance of transactions in making the determinations.
- Research relevant professional literature.

APPENDIX B

The outline below specifies the knowledge in which candidates are required to demonstrate proficiency:

I. Conceptual Framework, Standards, Standard Setting, and Presentation of Financial Statements (17% - 23%)

A. Process by which Accounting Standards are Set and Roles of Accounting Standard-Setting Bodies
   1. U.S. Securities and Exchange Commission (SEC)
   2. Financial Accounting Standards Board (FASB)
   3. International Accounting Standards Board (IASB)
   4. Governmental Accounting Standards Board (GASB)

B. Conceptual Framework
   1. Financial reporting by business entities
   2. Financial reporting by not-for-profit (nongovernmental) entities
   3. Financial reporting by state and local governmental entities

C. Financial Reporting, Presentation and Disclosures in General-Purpose Financial Statements
   1. Balance sheet
   2. Income statement
   3. Statement of comprehensive income
   4. Statement of changes in equity
   5. Statement of cash flows
   6. Notes to financial statements
   7. Consolidated and combined financial statements
   8. First-time adoption of IFRS

D. SEC Reporting Requirements (e.g., Form 10-Q, 10-K)

E. Other Financial Statement Presentations, including Other Comprehensive Bases of Accounting (OCBOA)
   1. Cash basis
   2. Modified cash basis
   3. Income tax basis
   4. Personal financial statements
   5. Financial statements of employee benefit plans/trusts

II. Financial Statement Accounts: Recognition, Measurement, Valuation, Calculation, Presentation, and Disclosures (27% - 33%)

A. Cash and Cash Equivalents

B. Receivables

C. Inventory

D. Property, Plant, and Equipment

E. Investments
   1. Financial assets at fair value through profit or loss
   2. Available for sale financial assets
   3. Held-to-maturity investments
   4. Joint ventures
   5. Equity method investments (investments in associates)
   6. Investment property

F. Intangible Assets – Goodwill and Other

G. Payables and Accrued Liabilities

H. Deferred Revenue

I. Long-Term Debt (Financial Liabilities)
   1. Notes payable
   2. Bonds payable
   3. Debt with conversion features and other options
   4. Modifications and extinguishments
   5. Troubled debt restructurings by debtors
   6. Debt covenant compliance
J. Equity
K. Revenue Recognition
L. Costs and Expenses
M. Compensation and Benefits
   1. Compensated absences
   2. Deferred compensation arrangements
   3. Nonretirement postemployment benefits
   4. Retirement benefits
   5. Stock compensation (share-based payments)
N. Income Taxes

III. Specific Transactions, Events and Disclosures: Recognition, Measurement, Valuation, Calculation, Presentation, and Disclosures (27% - 33%)

A. Accounting Changes and Error Corrections
B. Asset Retirement and Environmental Obligations
C. Business Combinations
D. Consolidation (including Off-Balance Sheet Transactions, Variable-Interest Entities and Noncontrolling Interests)
E. Contingencies, Commitments, and Guarantees (Provisions)
F. Earnings Per Share
G. Exit or Disposal Activities and Discontinued Operations
H. Extraordinary and Unusual Items
I. Fair Value Measurements, Disclosures, and Reporting
J. Derivatives and Hedge Accounting
K. Foreign Currency Transactions and Translation
L. Impairment
M. Interim Financial Reporting
N. Leases
O. Distinguishing Liabilities from Equity
P. Nonmonetary Transactions (Barter Transactions)
Q. Related Parties and Related Party Transactions
R. Research and Development Costs
S. Risks and Uncertainties
T. Segment Reporting
U. Software Costs
V. Subsequent Events
W. Transfers and Servicing of Financial Assets and Derecognition

IV. Governmental Accounting and Reporting (8% - 12%)

A. Governmental Accounting Concepts
   1. Measurement focus and basis of accounting
   2. Fund accounting concepts and application
   3. Budgetary process

B. Format and Content of Comprehensive Annual Financial Report (CAFR)
   1. Government-wide financial statements
   2. Governmental funds financial statements
   3. Proprietary funds financial statements
   4. Fiduciary funds financial statements
   5. Notes to financial statements
   6. Management's discussion and analysis
   7. Required supplementary information (RSI) other than Management's Discussion and Analysis
   8. Combining statements and individual fund statements and schedules
   9. Deriving government-wide financial statements and reconciliation requirements

C. Financial Reporting Entity, Including Blended and Discrete Component Units

D. Typical Items and Specific Types of Transactions and Events: Recognition, Measurement, Valuation, Calculation, and Presentation in Governmental Entity Financial Statements
   1. Net assets and components thereof
   2. Fund balances and components thereof
   3. Capital assets and infrastructure assets
   4. General long-term liabilities
   5. Interfund activity, including transfers
   6. Nonexchange revenue transactions
   7. Expenditures
   8. Special items
   9. Encumbrances

E. Accounting and Reporting for Governmental Not-for-Profit Organizations

V. Not-for-Profit (Nongovernmental) Accounting and Reporting (8% - 12%)

A. Financial Statements
   1. Statement of financial position
   2. Statement of activities
   3. Statement of cash flows
   4. Statement of functional expenses

B. Typical Items and Specific Types of Transactions and Events: Recognition, Measurement, Valuation, Calculation, and Presentation in Financial Statements of Not-for-Profit Organizations
   1. Support, revenues, and contributions
   2. Types of restrictions on resources
   3. Types of net assets
   4. Expenses, including depreciation and functional expenses
   5. Investments

APPENDIX C
RESEARCH SKILLS

For candidates familiar with researching electronic databases, this appendix contains several simulations for practice. If you do not have them already, your first step toward developing research skills is to **study** the material in this appendix.

Editor's Note: This information is as accurate as possible; however, circumstances are subject to change after this text goes to press. Candidates should check the AICPA and NASBA web sites 45 days before their exam for the most recent information.

SECTION ONE: GENERAL RESEARCH SKILLS

OVERVIEW

A research simulation involves a search of an electronic database of authoritative literature for guidance. The examiners devise research questions with references unlikely to be known, requiring candidates to search the material. The research skill evaluation distills down to the ability to structure a search of an electronic database and select the appropriate guidance from the "hits" generated by that search.

Only FAR, AUD, and REG

At least one research simulation will be in the FAR, AUD, and REG exam sections. Research simulations do not appear in the BEC exam section.

Response Nature

In their current form, research simulations merely are objective questions. A research simulation is completed when the candidate narrows the search (to answer the question asked) down to a paragraph reference. No written analysis of the reference is required; the paragraph or its reference is the answer that the examiners seek. Candidates cannot avoid the research merely by answering the question; they must provide the reference to the authoritative literature that provides the guidance.

Interface

The AICPA's testing engine allows candidates to split the screen, so they may view the question/response screen and the professional literature database screen concurrently. Candidates search the professional literature on the database screen and enter the appropriate citation on the question/response screen.

The search can be made either by using the table-of-contents feature or the search engine with Boolean operators. Many candidates find the table-of-contents approach easier to use than a Boolean search, once they become familiar with the authoritative literature.

Additional Research Comments

Research skills are not something you can acquire instantly. If you don't have them already, you must familiarize yourself with the professional literature and practice to become efficient with research skills. The editors strongly recommend that candidates become familiar with the authoritative literature and practice research well before their exam dates.

Candidates should start by using the tutorial and sample test on the examiners' web site to become familiar with the most current research interface. This site is updated as the examiners make changes.

After using the AICPA's tutorial and sample tests, practice research on your own. Along with the research simulations in the chapters, there are additional research simulations in this appendix. The skills that you develop while answering these simulations will assist you in answering whatever research simulation you get on your exam as well as research tasks throughout your career.

Make sure that you meet the requirements of the question in your exam. For most candidates, these are relatively easy points. Don't worry if you get a difficult research question on your exam. Move on after a few minutes. If you are having difficulty with the research simulation, answer another simulation and then return. Often, a simple break helps avoid frustration and allows you to start again with a fresh perspective.

BOOLEAN SEARCH APPROACH

The three Boolean operators are OR, AND, and NOT. Boolean operators can be combined to refine searches. For example, the following parameters would find information on letters to a client's attorney inquiring about litigation, claims, and assessments: (attorney OR lawyer) AND (letter OR inquiry). If you get too many or too few results from a search, refine your search parameters until you find what you need. The exam doesn't limit candidates from repeating searches with refined parameters. A review of Boolean operators is provided here.

OR Operator

A search using "accounting OR auditing" will find all documents containing either the word "accounting" or the word "auditing." OR typically is used to search for terms that are used as synonyms, such as "management" and "client." As more terms are combined in an OR search, more documents are included in the results.

AND Operator

A search using "accounting AND auditing" will find all documents containing both the word "accounting" and the word "auditing." All other things being equal, a search using AND typically will find fewer documents than a search using OR, but more than a search using NOT. As more terms are combined in an AND search, fewer documents are included in the results.

NOT Operator

A search using "accounting NOT auditing" will find all documents containing the word "accounting" except those that also contain the word "auditing." All other things being equal, a search using NOT typically will find the fewest documents. As more terms are combined in a NOT search, fewer documents are included in the results.

Search Phrases

Avoid using a search phrase such as "guidance on materially false and misleading entries in records." Anything that you find in the standards will be guidance; furthermore, the term "guidance" might not be in the reference that you seek. Also, eliminate words such as "on" and "in" unless you are seeking an exact phrase that you are sure includes them.

This leaves "materially false misleading entries records." Typically, search engines default to the Boolean search connector "OR" for all words, which probably would give us many irrelevant hits with this phrase, so modify it to "materially" AND "false" AND "statements."

Why not include "misleading" in this search phrase? If "false" is in the reference, "misleading" probably will be there also. If "misleading" is in the reference without "materially" that reference is likely irrelevant. In other words, the word "misleading" does little to narrow the search. However, if there are too few hits using "materially" AND "false" AND "statements," try ("material" AND "false" AND "statements") OR ("materially" AND "misleading" AND "statements"). The standards are not always consistent with their use of words; the guidance might use both "material" and "materially."

Answer Selection

Once you have narrowed the responses to a few hits (responses to a search) read through the most likely ones to determine which answers the question at hand.

Alternative Approach

If you have difficulty with Boolean searches, consider using the table of contents instead. Research is a very instance-specific activity; search skills are developed with practice. Any particular search will have little value for you when you are confronted with what likely will be a different research question on the exam. Use the process illustrated in this appendix to refine your search process; do not bother to memorize the answer to any particular example.

SECTION TWO: FAR RESEARCH SKILLS

FASB Codification

A new release of authoritative literature—with codified FASB Accounting Standards—was introduced in January 2011. The completely redesigned authoritative literature platform is meant to gain greater stability, facilitate future authoritative literature updates, and improve overall research efficiency. The release requires a task-based format. To maximize familiarity with the exam research interface in use for your particular exam window, the editors strongly encourage candidates to use the AICPA tutorial and practice with authoritative literature databases, as well as the partial databases included with our simulations.

Professional View

The search engine functionality of the authoritative literature database used on the Financial Accounting & Reporting (FAR) section of the CPA examination resembles the functionality of the fee-based *Professional View* of the *FASB Accounting Standards Codification* (FASB Codification) database. CPA exam candidates with a notice to schedule can get a free six-month subscription to professional literature used in the computerized CPA Examination. This online package includes AICPA Professional Standards, FASB Original Pronouncements and FASB Accounting Standards Codification. This online package of literature will familiarize CPA Exam candidates with the use of online accounting resources. Please note that the interface used by the online package is not exactly the same as that used in the operational CPA Examination.

Basic View

If you cannot gain access to fee-based *Professional View*, you can still get access to the FASB Codification using the free *Basic View*. This free access allows browsing by Topic, a utility to identify the location of legacy standards, and limited print functionality. It does **not** allow searching, use of any *Go To* navigation, nor joining sections and combining sections for viewing user-selected excerpts. Even if all you have is the Basic View free access, use it to become familiar with the look and feel of the database. Just browsing by Topic will familiarize you with the database and can lead you to answer references. First time users will have to create a username and password. Once you are registered, simply log in to access the database. For more information, see www.fasb.org/store/subscriptions/fasb/new.

Practice

Whichever resource you use, it's important you become comfortable finding citations with the appropriate authoritative literature requested. It isn't necessary for you to have the most cutting-edge research software available to practice this basic skill. You may even do searches in other databases and on the web to get familiar with simply doing research and this will help increase your skills. The key is to practice and become as familiar as possible with the research methods and database structures. Then you may take these skills and apply them to the authoritative literature database when accomplishing the Research task on the CPA exam.

SECTION THREE: FAR RESEARCH PRACTICE

SIMULATION PROBLEMS

The editors suggest you plan how to do the research for each of the following problems. Think about the Topic areas you would research into first and then the Search criteria you may use to drill down to find an answer.

Problem C-1 Research

What are some of the ways an investor has the ability to exercise significant influence over operating and financial policies of an investee?

FASB ASC: [ ] - [ ] - [ ] - [ ]

(9103)

Problem C-2 Research

Mega Inc. capitalized interest on a new warehouse building constructed during the year. In preparing the annual financial statements, what are the disclosure requirements with respect to capitalized interest costs?

FASB ASC: [ ] - [ ] - [ ] - [ ]

(9108)

Problem C-3 Research

What is the basic principle for the type of basis that should be used when accounting, in general, for nonmonetary transactions?

FASB ASC: [ ] - [ ] - [ ] - [ ]

(9124)

Problem C-4 Research

What conditions must be met for a loss contingency to be accrued?

FASB ASC: [ ] - [ ] - [ ] - [ ]

(9115)

Problem C-5 Research

Lyndhurst Company, Inc. issued convertible bonds in the past and is considering a cash incentive to the bondholders as an inducement to convert the debt into equity shares. How should Lyndhurst Company, Inc. account for these incentive payments to its bondholders?

FASB ASC: [ ] - [ ] - [ ] - [ ]

(9153)

Problem C-6 Research

What forms may termination benefits take?

FASB ASC: [ ] - [ ] - [ ] - [ ]
(9120)

Problem C-7 Research

With respect to a note, what is the interest method?

FASB ASC: [ ] - [ ] - [ ] - [ ]
(9117)

Problem C-8 Research

What is a noncontrolling interest?

FASB ASC: [ ] - [ ] - [ ] - [ ]
(9140)

Problem C-9 Research

What is the exception to the rule that additional paid-in capital (capital surplus) shall not be used to relieve the income account of the current or future years of charges which would otherwise be made to the income account?

FASB ASC: [ ] - [ ] - [ ] - [ ]
(9123)

Problem C-10 Research

In which part of the income statement should deferred tax liabilities and assets that are adjusted for the effect of a change in tax laws or rates be reported?

FASB ASC: [ ] - [ ] - [ ] - [ ]
(9127)

Problem C-11 Research

What is (are) the disclosure requirement(s) concerning a reconciliation of income tax expense?

FASB ASC: [ ] - [ ] - [ ] - [ ]
(9128)

Problem C-12 Research

What are the things the information in a statement of cash flows should help investors, creditors, and others to assess?

FASB ASC: [ ] - [ ] - [ ] - [ ]

(9149)

Problem C-13 Research

When is the acquisition of equipment in the operating section of the statement of cash flows?

FASB ASC: [ ] - [ ] - [ ] - [ ]

(9150)

Problem C-14 Research

When debt securities are issued with detachable stock purchase warrants, how is the portion of the proceeds allocable to the warrants accounted for?

FASB ASC: [ ] - [ ] - [ ] - [ ]

(9148)

Problem C-15 Research

Where and when shall accumulated other comprehensive income be displayed in the financial statements?

FASB ASC: [ ] - [ ] - [ ] - [ ]

(9151)

Problem C-16 Research

How is a corporation's own stock that is acquired for purposes other than retirement presented in the financial statements?

FASB ASC: [ ] - [ ] - [ ] - [ ]

(9152)

SIMULATION SOLUTIONS

Solution C-1

FASB Accounting Standards Codification

FASB ASC:	323	-	10	-	15	-	6

15-6 Ability to exercise significant influence over operating and financial policies of an investee may be indicated in several ways, including the following:

a. Representation on the board of directors

b. Participation in policy-making processes

c. Material intra-entity transactions

d. Interchange of managerial personnel

e. Technology dependency

f. Extent of ownership by an investor in relation to the concentration of other shareholdings (but substantial or majority ownership of the voting stock of an investee by another investor does not necessarily preclude the ability to exercise significant influence by the investor).

Solution C-2

FASB Accounting Standards Codification

FASB ASC:	835	-	20	-	50	-	1

50-1 An entity shall disclose the following information with respect to interest cost in the financial statements or related notes:

a. For an accounting period in which no interest cost is capitalized, the amount of interest cost incurred and charged to expense during the period.

b. For an accounting period in which some interest cost is capitalized, the total amount of interest cost incurred during the period and the amount thereof that has been capitalized.

Solution C-3

FASB Accounting Standards Codification

FASB ASC:	845	-	10	-	30	-	1

30-1 In general, accounting for nonmonetary transactions should be based on the fair values of the assets (or services) involved, which is the same basis as that used in monetary transactions. Thus, the cost of a nonmonetary asset acquired in exchange for another nonmonetary asset is the fair value of the asset surrendered to obtain it, and a gain or loss should be recognized on the exchange. The fair value of the asset received should be used to measure the cost if it is more clearly evident than the fair value of the asset surrendered. Similarly, a nonmonetary asset received in a nonreciprocal transfer should be recorded at the fair value of the asset received. A transfer of a nonmonetary asset to a stockholder or to another entity in a nonreciprocal transfer should be recorded at the fair value of the asset transferred and a gain or loss should be recognized on the disposition of the asset.

Solution C-4

FASB Accounting Standards Codification

FASB ASC:	450	-	20	-	25	-	2

25-2 An estimated loss from a loss contingency shall be accrued by a charge to income if both of the following conditions are met:

a. Information available prior to issuance of the financial statements indicates that it is probable that an asset had been impaired or a liability had been incurred at the date of the financial statements. Date of the financial statements means the end of the most recent accounting period for which financial statements are being presented. It is implicit in this condition that it must be probable that one or more future events will occur confirming the fact of the loss.

b. The amount of loss can be reasonably estimated.

The purpose of those conditions is to require accrual of losses when they are reasonably estimable and relate to the current or a prior period. Paragraphs 450-20-55-1 through 55-17 and Examples 1–2 (see paragraphs 450-20-55-18 through 55-35) illustrate the application of the conditions. As discussed in paragraph 450-20-50-5, disclosure is preferable to accrual when a reasonable estimate of loss cannot be made. Further, even losses that are reasonably estimable shall not be accrued if it is not probable that an asset has been impaired or a liability has been incurred at the date of an entity's financial statements because those losses relate to a future period rather than the current or a prior period. Attribution of a loss to events or activities of the current or prior periods is an element of asset impairment or liability incurrence.

Solution C-5

FASB Accounting Standards Codification

FASB ASC:	470	-	20	-	40	-	16

40-16 If a convertible debt instrument is converted to equity securities of the debtor pursuant to an inducement offer (see paragraph 470-20-40-13), the debtor shall recognize an expense equal to the fair value of all securities and other consideration transferred in the transaction in excess of the fair value of securities issuable pursuant to the original conversion terms. The fair value of the securities or other consideration shall be measured as of the date the inducement offer is accepted by the convertible debt holder. That date normally will be the date the debt holder converts the convertible debt into equity securities or enters into a binding agreement to do so. Until the debt holder accepts the offer, no exchange has been made between the debtor and the debt holder. Example 1 (see paragraph 470-20-55-1) illustrates the application of this guidance.

Solution C-6

FASB Accounting Standards Codification

FASB ASC:	715	-	30	-	25	-	10

25-10 Termination benefits may take various forms including lump-sum payments, periodic future payments, or both. They may be paid directly from an employer's assets, an existing pension plan, a new employee benefit plan, or a combination of those means. An employer that offers special termination benefits to employees shall recognize a liability and a loss when the employees accept the offer and the amount can be reasonably estimated. An employer that provides contractual termination benefits shall recognize a liability and a loss when it is probable that employees will be entitled to benefits and the amount can be reasonably estimated.

Solution C-7

<u>FASB Accounting Standards Codification</u>

FASB ASC:	835	-	30	-	35	-	2

35-2 With respect to a note for which the imputation of interest is required, the difference between the present value and the face amount shall be treated as discount or premium and amortized as interest expense or income over the life of the note in such a way as to result in a constant rate of interest when applied to the amount outstanding at the beginning of any given period. This is the interest method.

Solution C-8

<u>FASB Accounting Standards Codification</u>

FASB ASC:	810	-	10	-	45	-	15

45-15 The ownership interests in the subsidiary that are held by owners other than the parent is a noncontrolling interest. The noncontrolling interest in a subsidiary is part of the equity of the consolidated group.

Solution C-9

<u>FASB Accounting Standards Codification</u>

FASB ASC:	852	-	20	-	25	-	2

25-2 The general requirement is that additional paid-in capital, however created, shall not be used to relieve the income account of the current or future years of charges that would otherwise be made to the income account. As an exception to this requirement, if a reorganized entity would be relieved of charges that would be made against income if the existing corporation were continued, it may be permissible to accomplish the same result without reorganization provided the facts were as fully revealed to and the action as formally approved by the shareholders as in reorganization.

Solution C-10

<u>FASB Accounting Standards Codification</u>

FASB ASC:	740	-	10	-	45	-	15

45-15 When deferred tax accounts are adjusted as required by paragraph 740-10-35-4 for the effect of a change in tax laws or rates, the effect shall be included in income from continuing operations for the period that includes the enactment date.

Solution C-11

FASB Accounting Standards Codification

FASB ASC: | 740 | - | 10 | - | 50 | - | 12 |

50-12 A public entity shall disclose a reconciliation using percentages or dollar amounts of the reported amount of income tax expense attributable to continuing operations for the year to the amount of income tax expense that would result from applying domestic federal statutory tax rates to pretax income from continuing operations. The statutory tax rates shall be the regular tax rates if there are alternative tax systems. The estimated amount and the nature of each significant reconciling item shall be disclosed.

Solution C-12

FASB Accounting Standards Codification

FASB ASC: | 230 | - | 10 | - | 10 | - | 2 |

10-2 The information provided in a statement of cash flows, if used with related disclosures and information in the other financial statements, should help investors, creditors, and others (including donors) to do all of the following:

a. Assess the entity's ability to generate positive future net cash flows.

b. Assess the entity's ability to meet its obligations, its ability to pay dividends, and its needs for external financing.

c. Assess the reasons for differences between net income and associated cash receipts and payments.

d. Assess the effects on an entity's financial position of both its cash and noncash investing and financing transactions during the period.

Solution C-13

FASB Accounting Standards Codification

FASB ASC: | 230 | - | 10 | - | 45 | - | 22 |

45-22 Certain cash receipts and payments may have aspects of more than one class of cash flows. For example, a cash payment may pertain to an item that could be considered either inventory or a productive asset. If so, the appropriate classification shall depend on the activity that is likely to be the predominant source of cash flows for the item. For example, the acquisition and sale of equipment to be used by the entity or rented to others generally are investing activities. However, equipment sometimes is acquired or produced to be used by the entity or rented to others for a short period and then sold. In those circumstances, the acquisition or production and subsequent sale of those assets shall be considered operating activities.

Solution C-14

FASB Accounting Standards Codification

FASB ASC:	470	-	20	-	25	-	2

25-2 Proceeds from the sale of a debt instrument with stock purchase warrants (detachable call options) shall be allocated to the two elements based on the relative fair values of the debt instrument without warrants and of the warrants themselves at time of issuance. The portion of the proceeds so allocated to the warrants shall be accounted for as paid-in capital. The remainder of the proceeds shall be allocated to the debt instrument portion of the transaction. This usually results in a discount (or, occasionally, a reduced premium), which shall be accounted for under Topic 835.

Solution C-15

FASB Accounting Standards Codification

FASB ASC:	220	-	10	-	45	-	14

45-14 The total of other comprehensive income for a period shall be transferred to a component of equity that is displayed separately from retained earnings and additional paid-in capital in a statement of financial position at the end of an accounting period. A descriptive title such as accumulated other comprehensive income shall be used for that component of equity. An enterprise shall disclose accumulated balances for each classification in that separate component of equity on the face of a statement of financial position, in a statement of changes in equity, or in notes to the financial statements. The classifications shall correspond to classifications used elsewhere in the same set of financial statements for components of other comprehensive income.

Solution C-16

FASB Accounting Standards Codification

FASB ASC:	505	-	30	-	45	-	1

45-1 If a corporation's stock is acquired for purposes other than retirement (formal or constructive), or if ultimate disposition has not yet been decided, the cost of acquired stock may be shown separately as a deduction from the total of capital stock, additional paid-in capital, and retained earnings, or may be accorded the accounting treatment appropriate for retired stock specified in paragraphs 505-30-30-7 through 30-10.

APPENDIX D
COMPOUND INTEREST TABLES AND RATIOS

APPENDIX D

I. Compound Interest Tables

A. Table 1—Future Value of $1

$FV = PV(1 + r)^n$

r = interest rate; n = number of periods until valuation; PV = $1

	1%	2%	3%	4%	5%	6%	7%	8%	10%	12%	15%	20%	25%
n = 1	1.010000	1.020000	1.030000	1.040000	1.050000	1.060000	1.070000	1.080000	1.100000	1.120000	1.150000	1.200000	1.250000
2	1.020100	1.040400	1.060900	1.081600	1.102500	1.123600	1.144900	1.166400	1.210000	1.254400	1.322500	1.440000	1.562500
3	1.030301	1.061208	1.092727	1.124864	1.157625	1.191016	1.225043	1.259712	1.331000	1.404928	1.520875	1.728000	1.953125
4	1.040604	1.082432	1.125509	1.169859	1.215506	1.262477	1.310796	1.360489	1.464100	1.573519	1.749006	2.073600	2.441406
5	1.051010	1.104081	1.159274	1.216653	1.276282	1.338226	1.402552	1.469328	1.610510	1.762342	2.011357	2.488320	3.051758
6	1.061520	1.126162	1.194052	1.265319	1.340096	1.418519	1.500730	1.586874	1.771561	1.973823	2.313061	2.985984	3.814697
7	1.072135	1.148686	1.229874	1.315932	1.407100	1.503630	1.605781	1.713824	1.948717	2.210681	2.660020	3.583181	4.768372
8	1.082857	1.171659	1.266770	1.368569	1.477455	1.593848	1.718186	1.850930	2.143589	2.475963	3.059023	4.299817	5.960464
9	1.093685	1.195093	1.304773	1.423312	1.551328	1.689479	1.838459	1.999005	2.357948	2.773079	3.517876	5.159781	7.450581
10	1.104622	1.218994	1.343916	1.480244	1.628895	1.790848	1.967151	2.158925	2.593743	3.105848	4.045558	6.191737	9.313226
11	1.115668	1.243374	1.384234	1.539454	1.710339	1.898299	2.104852	2.331639	2.853117	3.478550	4.652391	7.430084	11.64153
12	1.126825	1.268242	1.425761	1.601032	1.795856	2.012197	2.252192	2.518170	3.138428	3.895976	5.350250	8.916101	14.55192
13	1.138093	1.293607	1.468534	1.665074	1.885649	2.132928	2.409845	2.719624	3.452271	4.363493	6.152788	10.69932	18.18989
14	1.149474	1.319479	1.512590	1.731676	1.979932	2.260904	2.578534	2.937194	3.797498	4.887112	7.075706	12.83918	22.73737
15	1.160969	1.345868	1.557967	1.800943	2.078928	2.396558	2.759032	3.172169	4.177248	5.473566	8.137062	15.40702	28.42171
16	1.172579	1.372786	1.604706	1.872981	2.182875	2.540352	2.952164	3.425943	4.594973	6.130394	9.357621	18.48843	35.52714
17	1.184304	1.400241	1.652848	1.947900	2.292018	2.692773	3.158815	3.700018	5.054471	6.866041	10.76126	22.18611	44.40892
18	1.196147	1.428246	1.702433	2.025816	2.406619	2.854339	3.379932	3.996019	5.559917	7.689965	12.37545	26.62333	55.51115
19	1.208109	1.456811	1.753506	2.106849	2.526950	3.025599	3.616528	4.315701	6.115909	8.612761	14.23177	31.94800	69.38894
20	1.220190	1.485947	1.806111	2.191123	2.653298	3.207135	3.869684	4.660957	6.727500	9.646293	16.36654	38.33760	86.73618
22	1.244716	1.545980	1.916103	2.369919	2.925261	3.603537	4.430402	5.436540	8.140275	12.10031	21.64475	55.20615	135.5253
24	1.269735	1.608437	2.032794	2.563304	3.225100	4.048934	5.072367	6.341180	9.849733	15.17863	28.62518	79.49685	211.7582
26	1.295256	1.673418	2.156591	2.772470	3.555673	4.549383	5.807353	7.396353	11.91818	19.04007	37.85680	114.4755	330.8723
28	1.321291	1.741024	2.287928	2.998703	3.920129	5.111687	6.648839	8.627106	14.42099	23.88387	50.06562	164.8447	516.9879
30	1.347849	1.811362	2.427262	3.243397	4.321942	5.743491	7.612255	10.06266	17.44940	29.95992	66.21178	237.3763	807.7936
32	1.374941	1.884541	2.575083	3.508059	4.764942	6.453386	8.715271	11.73708	21.11378	37.58172	87.56509	341.8219	1262.177
34	1.402577	1.960676	2.731905	3.794316	5.253348	7.251025	9.978113	13.69013	25.54767	47.14251	115.8048	492.2236	1972.152
36	1.430769	2.039887	2.898278	4.103932	5.791816	8.147252	11.42394	15.96817	30.91268	59.13557	153.1519	708.8019	3081.488
38	1.459527	2.122299	3.074783	4.438813	6.385478	9.154252	13.07927	18.62527	37.40435	74.17966	202.5434	1020.675	4814.825
40	1.488864	2.208040	3.262038	4.801021	7.039989	10.28572	14.97446	21.72452	45.25926	93.05096	267.8636	1469.772	7523.164
45	1.564811	2.437854	3.781596	5.841176	8.985008	13.76461	21.00245	31.92045	72.89049	163.9876	538.7694	3657.262	22958.88
50	1.644632	2.691588	4.383906	7.106683	11.46740	18.42015	29.45703	46.90161	117.3909	289.0022	1083.658	9100.439	70064.92
100	2.704814	7.244646	19.21863	50.50494	131.5013	339.3020	867.7164	2199.761	13780.61	83522.24	117×10^4	828×10^5	491×10^7

Example 1 ▸ Future Value of a Single Sum

Required: Find the future value of a $100 certificate of deposit at 8% for three years, (A) compounded annually and (B) compounded quarterly.

Solution A: Let Principal = P = $100, Interest Rate = r = 8%, Period = n = 3 years

Future Value Interest Factor at r Rate for n Periods = FVIF(r, n)

Future Value = FV = P × FVIF(r, n)

FVIF(8%, 3 years) = 1.2597 (from Table 1)

FV = $100 × 1.2597 = $125.97

Solution B: Let Principal = P = $100

Interest Rate = r = 8% / 4 quarters = 2%, Period = n = 12 quarters

Future Value Interest Factor at r Rate for n Periods = FVIF(r, n)

Future Value = FV = P × FVIF(r, n)

FVIF(2%, 12 quarters) = 1.2682 (from Table 1)

FV = $100 × 1.2682 = $126.82

B. Table 2—Present Value of $1

$$PV = \frac{FV}{(1 + r)^n}$$

r = discount rate; n = number of periods until payment; FV = $1

	1%	2%	3%	4%	5%	6%	7%	8%	10%	12%	15%	20%	25%
n = 1	0.990099	0.980392	0.970874	0.961538	0.952381	0.943396	0.934579	0.925926	0.909091	0.892857	0.869565	0.833333	0.800000
2	0.980296	0.961169	0.942596	0.924556	0.907029	0.889996	0.873439	0.857339	0.826446	0.797194	0.756144	0.694444	0.640000
3	0.970590	0.942322	0.915142	0.888996	0.863838	0.839619	0.816298	0.793832	0.751315	0.711780	0.657516	0.578704	0.512000
4	0.960980	0.923845	0.888487	0.854804	0.822702	0.792094	0.762895	0.735030	0.683013	0.635518	0.571753	0.482253	0.409600
5	0.951466	0.905731	0.862609	0.821927	0.783526	0.747258	0.712986	0.680583	0.620921	0.567427	0.497177	0.401878	0.327680
6	0.942045	0.887971	0.837484	0.790315	0.746215	0.704961	0.666342	0.630170	0.564474	0.506631	0.432328	0.334898	0.262144
7	0.932718	0.870560	0.813092	0.759918	0.710681	0.665057	0.622750	0.583490	0.513158	0.452349	0.375937	0.279082	0.209715
8	0.923483	0.853490	0.789409	0.730690	0.676839	0.627412	0.582009	0.540269	0.466507	0.403883	0.326902	0.232568	0.167772
9	0.914340	0.836755	0.766417	0.702587	0.644609	0.591898	0.543934	0.500249	0.424098	0.360610	0.284262	0.193807	0.134218
10	0.905287	0.820348	0.744094	0.675564	0.613913	0.558395	0.508349	0.463194	0.385543	0.321973	0.247185	0.161506	0.107374
11	0.896324	0.804263	0.722421	0.649581	0.584679	0.526788	0.475093	0.428883	0.350494	0.287476	0.214943	0.134588	0.085899
12	0.887449	0.788493	0.701380	0.624597	0.556837	0.496969	0.444012	0.397114	0.318631	0.256675	0.186907	0.112157	0.068719
13	0.878663	0.773033	0.680951	0.600574	0.530321	0.468839	0.414964	0.367698	0.289664	0.229174	0.162528	0.093464	0.054976
14	0.869963	0.757875	0.661118	0.577475	0.505068	0.442301	0.387817	0.340461	0.263331	0.204620	0.141329	0.077887	0.043980
15	0.861349	0.743015	0.641862	0.555265	0.481017	0.417265	0.362446	0.315242	0.239392	0.182696	0.122894	0.064905	0.035184
16	0.852821	0.728446	0.623167	0.533908	0.458112	0.393646	0.338735	0.291890	0.217629	0.163122	0.106865	0.054088	0.028147
17	0.844378	0.714163	0.605016	0.513373	0.436297	0.371364	0.316574	0.270269	0.197845	0.145644	0.092926	0.045073	0.022518
18	0.836017	0.700159	0.587395	0.493628	0.415521	0.350344	0.295864	0.250249	0.179859	0.130040	0.080805	0.037561	0.018014
19	0.827740	0.686431	0.570286	0.474642	0.395734	0.330513	0.276508	0.231712	0.163508	0.116107	0.070265	0.031301	0.014412
20	0.819544	0.672971	0.553676	0.456387	0.376889	0.311805	0.258419	0.214548	0.148644	0.103667	0.061100	0.026084	0.011529
22	0.803396	0.646839	0.521892	0.421955	0.341850	0.277505	0.225713	0.183941	0.122846	0.082643	0.046201	0.018114	0.007379
24	0.787566	0.621722	0.491934	0.390121	0.310068	0.246979	0.197147	0.157699	0.101526	0.065882	0.034934	0.012579	0.004722
26	0.772048	0.597579	0.463695	0.360689	0.281241	0.219810	0.172195	0.135202	0.083905	0.052521	0.026415	0.008735	0.003022
28	0.756836	0.574375	0.437077	0.333477	0.255094	0.195630	0.150402	0.115914	0.069343	0.041869	0.019974	0.006066	0.001934
30	0.741923	0.552071	0.411987	0.308319	0.231377	0.174110	0.131367	0.099377	0.057309	0.033378	0.015103	0.004213	0.001238
32	0.727304	0.530633	0.388337	0.285058	0.209866	0.154957	0.114741	0.085200	0.047362	0.026609	0.011420	0.002926	0.000792
34	0.712973	0.510028	0.366045	0.263552	0.190355	0.137912	0.100219	0.073045	0.039143	0.021212	0.008635	0.002032	0.000507
36	0.698925	0.490223	0.345032	0.243669	0.172657	0.122741	0.087535	0.062625	0.032349	0.016910	0.006529	0.001411	0.000325
38	0.685153	0.471187	0.325226	0.225285	0.156605	0.109239	0.076457	0.053690	0.026735	0.013481	0.004937	0.000980	0.000208
40	0.671653	0.452890	0.306557	0.208289	0.142046	0.097222	0.066780	0.046031	0.022095	0.010747	0.003733	0.000680	0.000133
45	0.639055	0.410197	0.264439	0.171198	0.111297	0.072650	0.047613	0.031328	0.013719	0.006098	0.001856	0.000273	0.000044
50	0.608039	0.371528	0.228107	0.140713	0.087204	0.054288	0.033948	0.021321	0.008519	0.003460	0.000923	0.000110	0.000014
100	0.369711	0.138033	0.052033	0.019800	0.007604	0.002947	0.001152	0.000455	0.000073	0.000012	0.000001	0.000000	0.000000

Note: The future value factor is equal to 1 divided by the present value factor.

Example 2 ▸ Present Value of a Single Sum

Required: Find the present value of $100 paid three years from now if the market rate of interest is 8% (A) compounded annually and (B) compounded quarterly.

Solution A: Let Principal = P = $100, Interest Rate = r = 8%, Period = n = 3 years
Present Value Interest Factor at r Rate for n Periods = PVIF(r, n)
Present Value = PV = P × PVIF(r, n)

PVIF(8%, 3 years) = 0.7938 (from Table 2)

PV = $100 × 0.7938 = $79.38

Solution B: Let Principal = P = $100, Interest Rate = r = 2%, Period = n = 12 quarters
Present Value Interest Factor at r Rate for n Periods = PVIF(r, n)
Present Value = PV = P × PVIF(r, n)

PVIF(2%, 12 quarters) = 0.7885 (from Table 2)

PV = $100 × 0.7885 = $78.85

C. Table 3—Future Value of Annuity of $1 in Arrears

$FV = \frac{(1 + r)^n - 1}{r}$ *r* = interest rate; *n* = number of payments

	1%	2%	3%	4%	5%	6%	7%	8%	10%	12%	15%	20%	25%
***n* = 1**	1.000000	1.000000	1.000000	1.000000	1.000000	1.000000	1.000000	1.000000	1.000000	1.000000	1.000000	1.000000	1.000000
2	2.010000	2.020000	2.030000	2.040000	2.050000	2.060000	2.070000	2.080000	2.100000	2.120000	2.150000	2.200000	2.250000
3	3.030100	3.060400	3.090900	3.121600	3.152500	3.183600	3.214900	3.246400	3.310000	3.374400	3.472500	3.640000	3.812500
4	4.060401	4.121608	4.183627	4.246464	4.310125	4.374616	4.439943	4.506112	4.641000	4.779328	4.993375	5.368000	5.765625
5	5.101005	5.204040	5.309136	5.416323	5.525631	5.637093	5.750739	5.866601	6.105100	6.352847	6.742381	7.441600	8.207031
6	6.152015	6.308121	6.468410	6.632976	6.801913	6.975318	7.153291	7.335929	7.715610	8.115189	8.753738	9.929920	11.25879
7	7.213535	7.434283	7.662462	7.898294	8.142009	8.393838	8.654021	8.922803	9.487171	10.08901	11.06680	12.91590	15.07349
8	8.285670	8.582969	8.892336	9.214226	9.549109	9.897468	10.25980	10.63663	11.43589	12.29969	13.72682	16.49908	19.84186
9	9.368527	9.754628	10.15911	10.58280	11.02656	11.49132	11.97799	12.48756	13.57948	14.77566	16.78584	20.79890	25.80232
10	10.46221	10.94972	11.46388	12.00611	12.57789	13.18079	13.81645	14.48656	15.93742	17.54873	20.30372	25.95868	33.25290
11	11.56683	12.16872	12.80780	13.48635	14.20679	14.97164	15.78360	16.64549	18.53117	20.65458	24.34928	32.15042	42.56613
12	12.68250	13.41209	14.19203	15.02581	15.91713	16.86994	17.88845	18.97713	21.38428	24.13313	29.00167	39.58050	54.20766
13	13.80933	14.68033	15.61779	16.62684	17.71298	18.88214	20.14064	21.49530	24.52271	28.02911	34.35192	48.49660	68.75957
14	14.94742	15.97394	17.08632	18.29191	19.59863	21.01507	22.55049	24.21492	27.97498	32.39260	40.50471	59.19592	86.94947
15	16.09690	17.29342	18.59891	20.02359	21.57856	23.27597	25.12902	27.15211	31.77248	37.27971	47.58041	72.03511	109.6868
16	17.25786	18.63929	20.15688	21.82453	23.65749	25.67253	27.88805	30.32428	35.94973	42.75328	55.71748	87.44213	138.1086
17	18.43044	20.01207	21.76159	23.69751	25.84037	28.21288	30.84022	33.75023	40.54470	48.88367	65.07510	105.9306	173.6357
18	19.61475	21.41231	23.41443	25.64541	28.13239	30.90565	33.99903	37.45024	45.59917	55.74971	75.83636	128.1167	218.0446
19	20.81090	22.84056	25.11687	27.67123	30.53900	33.75999	37.37896	41.44626	51.15909	63.43968	88.21181	154.7400	273.5558
20	22.01900	24.29737	26.87037	29.77808	33.06596	36.78559	40.99549	45.76196	57.27500	72.05244	102.4436	186.6880	342.9447
22	24.47159	27.29898	30.53678	34.24797	38.50521	43.39229	49.00574	55.45675	71.40275	92.50258	137.6317	271.0307	538.1011
24	26.97346	30.42186	34.42647	39.08260	44.50200	50.81557	58.17667	66.76476	88.49733	118.1552	184.1679	392.4843	843.0330
26	29.52563	33.67091	38.55304	44.31174	51.11345	59.15638	68.67647	79.95441	109.1818	150.3339	245.7120	567.3773	1319.489
28	32.12910	37.05121	42.93092	49.96758	58.40258	68.52811	80.69769	95.33883	134.2099	190.6989	327.1041	819.2233	2063.951
30	34.78489	40.56808	47.57542	56.08494	66.43885	79.05818	94.46078	113.2832	164.4940	241.3327	434.7452	1181.882	3227.174
32	37.49407	44.22703	52.50276	62.70147	75.29883	90.88978	110.2182	134.2135	201.1378	304.8477	577.1005	1704.110	5044.710
34	40.25770	48.03380	57.73018	69.85791	85.06696	104.1838	128.2588	158.6267	245.4767	384.5210	765.3655	2456.118	7884.609
36	43.07688	51.99437	63.27594	77.59831	95.83633	119.1209	148.9135	187.1021	299.1268	484.4631	1014.346	3539.010	12321.95
38	45.95272	56.11494	69.15945	85.97034	107.7095	135.9042	172.5610	220.3159	364.0435	609.8305	1343.622	5098.374	19255.30
40	48.88637	60.40198	75.40126	95.02551	120.7998	154.7620	199.6351	259.0565	442.5926	767.0914	1779.091	7343.858	30088.66
45	56.48108	71.89271	92.71986	121.0294	159.7002	212.7435	285.7493	386.5056	718.9048	1358.230	3585.129	18281.31	91831.50
50	64.46318	84.57940	112.7969	152.6671	209.3480	290.3359	406.5289	573.7701	1163.909	2400.018	7217.718	45497.20	280255.7
100	170.4814	312.2323	607.2877	1237.624	2610.025	5638.368	12381.66	27484.51	137796.1	696010.5	783×10^4	414×10^6	196×10^8

Note: To convert from this table to values of an annuity in advance, determine the annuity in arrears factor above for one more period and subtract 1.

Example 3 ▸ Future Value of an Annuity in Arrears

Required: Jones plans to save $300 a year for three years. If Jones deposits money at the end of each period in a savings plan that yields 24%, how much will Jones have at the end of the three years if Jones deposits (A) $75 at the end of each quarter? (B) $25 at the end of every month?

Solution A: Let Payment = P = $75, Interest Rate = r = 6%, Period = n = 12 quarters
Future Value of an Annuity Factor at r Rate for n Periods = FVAF(r, n)
Future Value of the Annuity = FVA = P × FVAF(r, n)

FVAF(6%, 12 quarters) = 16.8699 (from Table 3)

FVA = $75 × 16.8699 = $1,265.24

Solution B: Let Payment = P = $25, Interest Rate = r = 2%, Period = n = 36 months
Future Value of an Annuity Factor at r Rate for n Periods = FVAF(r, n)
Future Value of the Annuity = FVA = P × FVAF(r, n)

FVAF(2%, 36 months) = 51.9944 (from Table 3)

FVA = $25 × 51.9944 = $1,299.86

D. Table 4—Present Value of Annuity of $1 in Arrears

$$PV = \frac{1-(1+r)^{-n}}{r}$$ *r* = discount rate; *n* = number of payments

n	1%	2%	3%	4%	5%	6%	7%	8%	10%	12%	15%	20%	25%
n = 1	0.990099	0.980392	0.970874	0.961538	0.952381	0.943396	0.934579	0.925926	0.909091	0.892857	0.869565	0.833333	0.800000
2	1.970395	1.941561	1.913470	1.886095	1.859410	1.833393	1.808018	1.783265	1.735537	1.690051	1.625709	1.527778	1.440000
3	2.940985	2.883883	2.828611	2.775091	2.723248	2.673012	2.624316	2.577097	2.486852	2.401831	2.283225	2.106482	1.952000
4	3.901966	3.807729	3.717098	3.629895	3.545950	3.465106	3.387211	3.312127	3.169865	3.037349	2.854978	2.588735	2.361600
5	4.853431	4.713459	4.579707	4.451822	4.329477	4.212364	4.100197	3.992710	3.790787	3.604776	3.352155	2.990612	2.689280
6	5.795476	5.601431	5.417192	5.242137	5.075692	4.917325	4.766540	4.622880	4.355261	4.111407	3.784483	3.325510	2.951424
7	6.728195	6.471991	6.230283	6.002055	5.786374	5.582381	5.389289	5.206370	4.868419	4.563756	4.160419	3.604592	3.161139
8	7.651678	7.325481	7.019692	6.732745	6.463213	6.209794	5.971299	5.746639	5.334926	4.967640	4.487321	3.837160	3.328911
9	8.566017	8.162237	7.786109	7.435332	7.107821	6.801692	6.515232	6.246888	5.759024	5.328250	4.771584	4.030966	3.463129
10	9.471305	8.982585	8.530203	8.110896	7.721735	7.360087	7.023582	6.710082	6.144567	5.650223	5.018768	4.192472	3.570503
11	10.36763	9.786848	9.252625	8.760477	8.306415	7.886875	7.498674	7.138964	6.495061	5.937699	5.233712	4.327060	3.656403
12	11.25508	10.57534	9.954004	9.385074	8.863252	8.383844	7.942686	7.536078	6.813692	6.194374	5.420619	4.439217	3.725122
13	12.13374	11.34837	10.63496	9.985648	9.393573	8.852683	8.357651	7.903776	7.103356	6.423549	5.583147	4.532681	3.780098
14	13.00370	12.10625	11.29607	10.56312	9.898641	9.294984	8.745468	8.244237	7.366687	6.628168	5.724475	4.610567	3.824078
15	13.86505	12.84926	11.93793	11.11839	10.37966	9.712249	9.107914	8.559479	7.606080	6.810864	5.847370	4.675473	3.859262
16	14.71787	13.57771	12.56110	11.65230	10.83777	10.10590	9.446649	8.851369	7.823709	6.973986	5.954235	4.729560	3.887410
17	15.56225	14.29187	13.16612	12.16567	11.27407	10.47726	9.763223	9.121638	8.021553	7.119631	6.047161	4.774634	3.909928
18	16.39827	14.99203	13.75351	12.65930	11.68959	10.82760	10.05909	9.371887	8.201412	7.249670	6.127965	4.812195	3.927943
19	17.22601	15.67846	14.32380	13.13394	12.08532	11.15812	10.33560	9.603600	8.364920	7.365777	6.198231	4.843496	3.942354
20	18.04555	16.35143	14.87747	13.59033	12.46221	11.46992	10.59401	9.818148	8.513564	7.469444	6.259331	4.869580	3.953883
22	19.66038	17.65805	15.93692	14.45112	13.16300	12.04158	11.06124	10.20074	8.771541	7.644646	6.358663	4.909431	3.970485
24	21.24339	18.91393	16.93554	15.24696	13.79864	12.55036	11.46933	10.52876	8.984744	7.784316	6.433771	4.937104	3.981111
26	22.79520	20.12104	17.87684	15.98277	14.37519	13.00317	11.82578	10.80998	9.160945	7.895660	6.490564	4.956323	3.987911
28	24.31644	21.28127	18.76411	16.66306	14.89813	13.40616	12.13711	11.05108	9.306566	7.984423	6.533508	4.969668	3.992263
30	25.80771	22.39646	19.60044	17.29203	15.37245	13.76483	12.40904	11.25778	9.426914	8.055184	6.565979	4.978936	3.995048
32	27.26959	23.46833	20.38877	17.87355	15.80268	14.08404	12.64655	11.43500	9.526376	8.111594	6.590533	4.985373	3.996831
34	28.70267	24.49859	21.13184	18.41120	16.19290	14.36814	12.85401	11.58693	9.608575	8.156565	6.609098	4.989842	3.997972
36	30.10751	25.48884	21.83225	18.90828	16.54685	14.62099	13.03521	11.71719	9.676508	8.192414	6.623137	4.992946	3.998702
38	31.48466	26.44064	22.49246	19.36786	16.86789	14.84602	13.19347	11.82887	9.732652	8.220994	6.633752	4.995101	3.999169
40	32.83469	27.35548	23.11477	19.79277	17.15909	15.04630	13.33171	11.92461	9.779051	8.243777	6.641778	4.996598	3.999468
45	36.09451	29.49016	24.51871	20.72004	17.77407	15.45583	13.60552	12.10840	9.862807	8.282516	6.654293	4.998633	3.999826
50	39.19612	31.42361	25.72976	21.48219	18.25593	15.76186	13.80075	12.23349	9.914814	8.304499	6.660514	4.999451	3.999943
100	63.02888	43.09835	31.59891	24.50500	19.84791	16.61755	14.26925	12.49432	9.999274	8.333234	6.666661	5.000000	4.000000

Note: To convert from this table to values of an annuity in advance, determine the annuity in arrears factor above for one less period and add 1.

Example 4 ▶ Present Value of an Annuity in Arrears and Present Value of an Annuity Due

Required: Smith can make annual mortgage payments (not including taxes, etc.) of $4,800. How much can Smith borrow at 8% interest and repay in 20 years: (A) making 20 equal payments at the end of the year? (B) making 20 equal payments at the beginning of the year?

Solution A: Let Payment = P = $4,800, Interest Rate = r = 8%, Period = n = 20 years
Present Value of an Annuity Factor at r Rate for n Periods = PVAF(r, n)
Present Value of the Annuity = PVA = P × PVAF(r, n)

PVAF(8%, 20 years) = 9.8181 (from Table 4)

Loan = PVA = $4,800 × 9.8181 = $47,126.88

Solution B: Let Payment = P = $4,800, Interest Rate = r = 8%, Period = n = 20 years
Present Value of an Annuity Factor at r Rate for n Periods = PVAF(r, n)
Present Value of the Annuity in Advance = PVAA = P × [PVAF(r, n – 1) + 1]

PVAF(8%, 19 years) = 9.6036 (from Table 4)

Loan = PVAA = $4,800 × (9.6036 + 1) = $50,897.28

Example 5 ▸ Capital Lease Obligation

Alpha Company has a 10 year capital lease with an implicit interest rate of 8%. The \$40,000 payments are made at the beginning of each year.

Required: What is the capital lease obligation (the present value of the lease payments)?

Solution: Let Payment = P = \$40,000, Interest Rate = r = 8%, Period = n = 10 years
Present Value of an Annuity Factor at r Rate for n Periods = PVAF(r, n)
Present Value of the Annuity in Advance = PVAA = P × [PVAF(r, n – 1) + 1]

PVAF(8%, 9 years) = 6.246888 (from Table 4)

Capital Lease Obligation = PVAA = \$40,000 × (6.246888 + 1) = \$289,875.52

This is the same as:

Capital Lease Obligation = Initial Payment + PVA (where r = 8%, n = 9)
= Initial Payment + P × PVAF(8%, 9)
= \$40,000 + \$40,000 × 6.246888
= \$289,875.52

Example 6 ▸ Internal Rate of Return

Beta Company is considering the purchase of a machine for \$12,500. Beta expects a net year-end cash inflow of \$5,000 annually over the machine's 3-year life. [The IRR is that rate at which NPV = 0]

Required: What is this project's approximate internal rate of return?

Solution: This example involves a present single sum and an annuity. The present value of the single sum paid today is \$12,500. In this situation, NPV is the present value of the purchase price (P) less the present value of the future annual cash inflow (PVA).

Let Single Payment = P = \$12,500 Interest Rate = r = ?
Annual Cash Inflow = A = \$5,000 Period = n = 3 years
Present Value of an Annuity Factor at r Rate for n Periods = PVAF(r, n)

NPV = P – PVA and NPV = 0 Thus, P – PVA = 0

PVA = A x PVAF(r, n) so P – [A × PVAF(r, n)] = 0 or
P = A × PVAF(r, n) or
P / A = PVAF(r, n) and substituting known values:
\$12,500 / \$5,000 = PVAF(r, 3 years) or
PVAF(r, 3 years) = 2.5

Looking in the 3 period row of Table 4, we find the interest rate that produces the interest factor closest to 2.5 is in the 10% column. (Examiners generally narrow the field somewhat by supplying half a dozen values instead of a whole table, but they frequently also provide values from tables that are misleading. For instance, they may supply future values of annuities or present values of single sums.)

PVAF(8%, 3 years) = 2.577097 rounds to 2.6
PVAF(10%, 3 years) = 2.486852 rounds to 2.5 Thus, r (or IRR) is about 10%.
PVAF(12%, 3 years) = 2.401831 rounds to 2.4

II. Financial Analysis

A. Definition

Financial statement analysis is an attempt to evaluate a business entity for financial and managerial decision-making purposes. In order to draw valid conclusions about the financial health of an entity, it is essential to analyze and compare specific types and sources of financial information. This analysis would include (1) a review of the firm's accounting policies, (2) an examination of recent auditors' reports, (3) analysis of footnotes and other supplemental information accompanying the financial statements, and (4) the examination of various relationships among items presented in financial statements (i.e., ratio analysis).

B. Purpose

Financial ratios measure elements of the firm's operating performance and financial position so that internal as well as industry-wide comparisons can be made on a consistent basis. Ratio analysis provides an indication of the firm's financial strengths and weaknesses and generally should be used in conjunction with other evaluation techniques. Ratio analysis is used primarily to draw conclusions about the solvency, operational efficiency, and profitability of a firm.

III. Ratio Analysis

A. Factors

When computing a ratio, consider the following:

1. Net or gross amounts (e.g., receivables)

2. Average for the period or year-end amounts (e.g., receivables, inventories, common shares outstanding)

3. Adjustments to income (e.g., interest, income taxes, preferred dividends)

B. Evaluation of Solvency

1. **Short-Term Solvency** Short-term solvency is the ability of a firm to meet its current obligations as they mature. The following ratios may be of primary interest to short-term creditors.

Exhibit 1 ▸ Working Capital

Current Assets – Current Liabilities

Comments: Represents the liquid portion of resources or enterprise capital. The greater the amount of working capital, the greater the cushion of protection available to short-term creditors, and the greater assurance that short-term debts will be paid when due.

Exhibit 2 ▸ Current Ratio

$$\frac{\textit{Current Assets}}{\textit{Current Liabilities}}$$

Comments: This is a primary test of the overall solvency of the enterprise and its ability to meet current obligations from current assets. When the current ratio exceeds 1.0 to 1.0, an equal increase in current assets and current liabilities decreases the ratio. When the current ratio is less than 1.0 to 1.0, an equal increase in current assets and current liabilities increases the ratio.

Exhibit 3 ▸ Acid-Test or Quick Ratio

Cash + Marketable Securities + Net Receivables
Current Liabilities

Comments: This ratio provides a more severe test of immediate solvency by eliminating inventories and prepaid expenses (current assets that are not quickly converted into cash).

Exhibit 4 ▸ Defensive-Interval Ratio

Cash + Marketable Securities + Net Receivables
Average Daily Cash Expenditures

Comments: This ratio estimates the number of days that the company can meet its basic operational costs. The average daily cash expenditures can be approximated by reducing total expenses for the year by noncash charges (e.g., depreciation, amortization of intangibles) and dividing this amount by 365.

2. **Long-Term Solvency** Long-term solvency is the ability to meet interest payments, preferred dividends, and other fixed charges. Similarly, long-term solvency is a required precondition for the repayment of principal.

Exhibit 5 ▸ Debt to Equity

Total Liabilities
Owners' Equity

Comments: This ratio provides a measure of the relative amounts of resources provided by creditors and owners.

Exhibit 6 ▸ Times Interest Earned

Income Before Income Taxes and Interest Charges
Interest Charges

Comments: Measures the ability of the firm to meet its interest payments. Income taxes are *added* back to net income because the ability to pay interest is not dependent on the amount of income taxes to be paid, since interest is tax deductible.

Exhibit 7 ▸ Times Preferred Dividends Earned

Net Income
Annual Preferred Dividend Requirement

Comments: Measures the adequacy of current earnings for the payment of preferred dividends.

C. Operational Efficiency

Operational efficiency is the ability of the business entity to generate income as well as its efficiency and effectiveness in using the assets employed.

Exhibit 8 ▸ Total Asset Turnover

Total Sales (Revenue)
Average Total Assets

Comments: This ratio is useful to determine the amount of sales that are generated from each dollar of assets. Average total assets is generally determined by adding the beginning and ending total assets and dividing by two.

Exhibit 9 ▸ Receivables Turnover

$$\frac{\textit{Net Credit Sales}}{\textit{Average Net Receivables}}$$

Comments: This ratio provides an indication of the efficiency of credit policies and collection procedures, and of the quality of the receivables. Average net receivables include trade notes receivable. Average net receivables is generally determined by adding the beginning and ending net receivables balances and dividing by two.

Exhibit 10 ▸ Number of Days' Sales in Average Receivables

$$\frac{360}{\textit{Receivables Turnover}}$$

Comments: Tests the average number of days required to collect receivables. Some analysts prefer to use 365, 300, or 250 as the number of business days in the year.

Exhibit 11 ▸ Inventory Turnover

$$\frac{\textit{Cost of Goods Sold}}{\textit{Average Inventory}}$$

Comments: Indicates the number of times inventory was acquired and sold (or used in production) during the period. It can be used to detect inventory obsolescence or pricing problems. Average inventory is generally determined by adding the beginning and ending inventories and dividing by two.

Exhibit 12 ▸ Number of Days' Supply in Average Inventory

$$\frac{360}{\textit{Inventory Turnover}} \quad \text{or} \quad \frac{\textit{Average (Ending) Inventory}}{\textit{Average Daily Cost of Goods Sold}}$$

Comments: Indicates the number of days inventory is held before it is sold. Some analysts prefer to use 365, 300, or 250 as the number of business days in the year. Average daily cost of goods sold is determined by dividing cost of goods sold by the number of business days.

Exhibit 13 ▸ Length of Operating Cycle

Number of days' sales in average receivables + *Number of days' supply in average inventory*

Comments: Measures the average length of time from the purchase of inventory to the collection of cash from its sale.

D. Profitability & Investment Analysis Ratios

Exhibit 14 ▸ Book Value Per Common Share

$$\frac{\textit{Common Stockholders' Equity}}{\textit{Number of Common Shares Outstanding}}$$

To determine common stockholders' equity, preferred stock is subtracted from total stockholders' equity at the greater of its liquidation, par or stated value. Cumulative preferred stock dividends in *arrears* are also similarly subtracted. Treasury stock affects the denominator as the number of common shares outstanding is *reduced.*

Comments: This ratio measures the amount that common shareholders would receive if all assets were sold at their carrying amounts and if all creditors were paid. When balance sheet valuations do not approximate fair values, the importance of this ratio is diminished.

Exhibit 15 ▸ Book Value Per Preferred Share

$$\frac{\textit{Preferred Stockholders' Equity}}{\textit{Number of Preferred Shares Outstanding}}$$

Preferred stockholders' equity is comprised of (a) preferred stock at the greater of its liquidation, par or stated value and (b) cumulative preferred stock dividends in arrears.

Comments: This ratio measures the amount that preferred shareholders would receive if the company were liquidated on the basis of the amounts reported on the balance sheet.

Exhibit 16 ▸ Return on Total Assets

$$\frac{\textit{Net Income + Interest Expense (Net of Tax)}}{\textit{Average Total Assets}}$$

Comments: This ratio provides a measure of the degree of efficiency with which resources (total assets) are used to generate earnings.

Exhibit 17 ▸ Return on Common Stockholders' Equity

$$\frac{\textit{Net Income – Preferred Dividends}}{\textit{Average Common Stockholders' Equity}}$$

Comments: Measures the rate of earnings on resources provided by common stockholders. Common stockholders' equity is measured as indicated in Exhibit 14. Average common stockholders' equity is generally determined by adding beginning and ending common stockholders' equity and dividing by two.

Successful use of *leverage* is where a company earns more by the use of borrowed money than it costs to use the borrowed funds. When compared to the return on total assets, the return on common stockholders' equity measures the extent to which leverage is being employed for or against the common stockholders. When the return on common stockholders' equity is greater than the return on total assets, leverage is positive and common stockholders benefit.

Exhibit 18 ▸ Return on Stockholders' Equity

$$\frac{\textit{Net Income}}{\textit{Average Stockholders' Equity}}$$

Comments: Measures the rate of earnings on resources provided by all stockholders (i.e., common and preferred). Average stockholders' equity is generally determined by adding beginning and ending stockholders' equity and dividing by two.

Exhibit 19 ▸ Earnings Per Share (EPS)

$$\frac{\textit{Net Income – Preferred Dividends}}{\textit{Average Number of Common Shares Outstanding}}$$

Comments: Measures the ability to pay dividends to common stockholders by measuring profit earned per share of common stock. (EPS is discussed more thoroughly later in this chapter.)

Exhibit 20 ▸ Price Earnings Ratio

$$\frac{\textit{Market Price Per Common Share}}{\textit{Earnings Per Common Share}}$$

Comments: A measure of whether a stock is relatively cheap or relatively expensive based on its present earnings.

Exhibit 21 ▸ Dividend Payout Ratio

$$\frac{\textit{Cash Dividend Per Common Share}}{\textit{Earnings Per Common Share}}$$

Comments: This ratio represents the percentage of earnings per share distributed to common stockholders in cash dividends. A low ratio would probably indicate the reinvestment of profits by a growth-oriented firm.

Exhibit 22 ▸ Yield on Common Stock

$$\frac{\textit{Dividend Per Common Share}}{\textit{Market Price Per Common Share}}$$

Comments: Measures cash flow return on common stock investment.

What are the "minor" topics that I can ignore?

The Bisk Education instructors sometimes mention that some topics are heavily or lightly tested. Bear in mind, these comments do not apply to each specific exam. Rather, when several years' worth of exams are evaluated, some topics average more point value than others. On any one exam, candidates reasonably can expect at least one of the "minor" topics to be heavily tested. In other words, do not read too much into these evaluations; candidates are not tested on an average of several exams, but only one specific exam.

Every now and then so-called "minor" topics show up in a simulation or in several multiple choice questions and so could count for 10 points on the section. What does this mean? You have to know these "minor" topics going into the exam. As a result, successful candidates make a point of studying everything. They concentrate on those topics that are repeatedly tested heavily while bearing in mind that any topic can be tested heavily on any one exam. In other words, any "minor" topic could be uncharacteristically heavily on your particular exam.

Having taken the exam themselves, the editors realize that candidates would like to narrow their studying down to "just what will be on the exam." Unfortunately, the examiners make a point of being unpredictable. As massive as the Bisk CPA review materials may seem, this truly is the "narrowed down" version.

Remember, with the techniques and information in your material,

A passing score is well within reach!

APPENDIX E
RECENTLY RELEASED AICPA QUESTIONS

In April, 2012, the AICPA released fifty multiple-choice questions, two nonresearch simulations and one research simulation relating to the FAR section of the CPA examination. These questions and their unofficial answers are reproduced here, along with the exclusive Bisk Education explanations. The reference to the Content Specification Outline (CSO) at the end of each answer explanation pertains to the current CSO in effect as of January 1, 2011.

The multiple-choice questions in Problems 1 and 2 were labeled *medium* or *hard.* Problem 3 is the simulation that was disclosed.

The AICPA did not state if these questions ever appeared on any exam, whether they were assigned points or merely being pre-tested and earned no points if they did appear on an exam, or if they were now obsolete for some reason. These questions are intended only as a study aid and should not be used to predict the content of future exams. It is extremely unlikely that released questions will ever appear on future examinations. These questions have been reproduced as received from the AICPA examiners. If candidates encounter what they believe are errors or ambiguities in questions during their actual exams, they should bring them to the attention of the examiners in accordance with the procedures outlined on the AICPA's web site.

Problem 1 MULTIPLE-CHOICE QUESTIONS (medium)

1. A company has the following items on its year-end trial balance:

Net sales	$500,000
Common stock	100,000
Insurance expense	75,000
Wages	50,000
Cost of goods sold	100,000
Cash	40,000
Accounts payable	25,000
Interest payable	20,000

What is the company's gross profit?

a. $230,000
b. $275,000
c. $400,000
d. $500,000 (R/12, FAR, #1, 89701)

2. Burns Corp. had the following items:

Sales revenue	$45,000
Loss on early extinguishment of bonds	36,000
Realized gain on sale of available-for-sale securities	28,000
Unrealized holding loss on available-for-sale securities	17,000
Loss on write-down of inventory	3,100

   Which of the following amounts would the statement of comprehensive income report as other comprehensive income or loss?

   a. $11,000 other comprehensive income
   b. $16,900 other comprehensive income
   c. $17,000 other comprehensive loss
   d. $28,100 other comprehensive loss (R/12, FAR, #2, 89702)

3. Baler Co. prepared its statement of cash flows at year-end using the direct method. The following amounts were used in the computation of cash flows from operating activities:

Beginning inventory	$200,000
Ending inventory	150,000
Cost of goods sold	1,200,000
Beginning accounts payable	300,000
Ending accounts payable	200,000

   What amount should Baler report as cash paid to suppliers for inventory purchases?

   a. $1,200,000
   b. $1,250,000
   c. $1,300,000
   d. $1,350,000 (R/12, FAR, #3, 89703)

4. Which of the following transactions is included in the operating activities section of a cash flow statement prepared using the indirect method?

   a. Gain on sale of plant asset
   b. Sale of property, plant and equipment
   c. Payment of cash dividend to the shareholders
   d. Issuance of common stock to the shareholders (R/12, FAR, #4, 89704)

5. Tinsel Co.'s balances in allowance for uncollectible accounts were $70,000 at the beginning of the current year and $55,000 at year end. During the year, receivables of $35,000 were written off as uncollectible. What amount should Tinsel report as uncollectible accounts expense at year end?

   a. $15,000
   b. $20,000
   c. $35,000
   d. $50,000 (R/12, FAR, #5, 89705)

6. Alta Co. spent $400,000 during the current year developing a new idea for a product that was patented during the year. The legal cost of applying for a patent license was $40,000. Also, $50,000 was spent to successfully defend the rights of the patent against a competitor. The patent has a life of 20 years. What amount should Alta capitalize related to the patent?

   a. $ 40,000
   b. $ 50,000
   c. $ 90,000
   d. $490,000 (R/12, FAR, #6, 89706)

7. A retail store sold gift certificates that are redeemable in merchandise. The gift certificates lapse one year after they are issued. How would the deferred revenue account be affected by each of the following?

	Redemption of certificates	Lapse of certificates
a.	Decrease	Decrease
b.	Decrease	No effect
c.	No effect	Decrease
d.	No effect	No effect

(R/12, FAR, #7, 89707)

8. On January 2, Vole Co. issued bonds with a face value of $480,000 at a discount to yield 10%. The bonds pay interest semiannually. On June 30, Vole paid bond interest of $14,400. After Vole recorded amortization of the bond discount of $3,600, the bonds had a carrying amount of $363,600. What amount did Vole receive upon issuing the bonds?

   a. $360,000
   b. $367,200
   c. $476,400
   d. $480,000 (R/12, FAR, #8, 89708)

9. What type of bonds mature in installments?

   a. Debenture
   b. Term
   c. Variable rate
   d. Serial (R/12, FAR, #9, 89709)

10. Balm Co. had 100,000 shares of common stock outstanding as of January 1. The following events occurred during the year:

4/1	Issued 30,000 shares of common stock
6/1	Issued 36,000 shares of common stock
7/1	Declared a 5% stock dividend
9/1	Purchased as treasury stock 35,000 shares of its common stock. Balm used the cost method to account for the treasury stock

What is Balm's weighted average of common stock outstanding at December 31?

   a. 131,000
   b. 139,008
   c. 150,675
   d. 162,342 (R/12, FAR, #10, 89710)

11. The stockholders of Meadow Corp. approved a stock-option plan that grants the company's top three executives options to purchase a maximum of 1,000 shares each of Meadow's $2 par common stock for $19 per share. The options were granted on January 1 when the fair value of the stock was $20 per share. Meadow determined that the fair value of the compensation is $300,000 and the vesting period is three years. What amount of compensation expense from the options should Meadow record in the year the options were granted?

   a. $ 20,000
   b. $ 60,000
   c. $100,000
   d. $300,000 (R/12, FAR, #11, 89711)

12. At the beginning of the year, the carrying value of an asset was $1,000,000 with 20 years of remaining life. The fair value of the liability for the asset retirement obligation was $100,000. At year end, the carrying value of the asset was $950,000. The risk-free interest rate was 5%. The credit-adjusted risk-free interest rate was 10%. What was the amount of accretion expense for the year related to the asset retirement obligation?

    a. $ 10,000
    b. $ 50,000
    c. $ 95,000
    d. $100,000 (R/12, FAR, #12, 89712)

13. Blythe Corp. is a defendant in a lawsuit. Blythe's attorneys believe it is reasonably possible that the suit will require Blythe to pay a substantial amount. What is the proper financial statement treatment for this contingency?

    a. Accrued and disclosed
    b. Accrued but **not** disclosed
    c. Disclosed but **not** accrued
    d. No disclosure or accrual (R/12, FAR, #13, 89713)

14. Jones Co. had 50,000 shares of $5 par value common stock outstanding at January 1. On August 1, Jones declared a 5% stock dividend followed by a two-for-one stock split on September 1. What amount should Jones report as common shares outstanding at December 31?

    a. 105,000
    b. 100,000
    c. 52,500
    d. 50,000 (R/12, FAR, #14, 89714)

15. A transaction that is unusual in nature or infrequent in occurrence should be reported as a(an)

    a. Component of income from continuing operations, net of applicable income taxes
    b. Extraordinary item, net of applicable income taxes
    c. Component of income from continuing operations, but **not** net of applicable income taxes
    d. Extraordinary item, but **not** net of applicable income taxes (R/12, FAR, #15, 89715)

16. Giaconda, Inc. acquires an asset for which it will measure the fair value by discounting future cash flows of the asset. Which of the following terms best describes this fair value measurement approach?

    a. Market
    b. Income
    c. Cost
    d. Observable inputs (R/12, FAR, #16, 89716)

17. A company owns a financial asset that is actively traded on two different exchanges (market A and market B). There is no principal market for the financial asset. The information on the two exchanges is as follows:

	Quoted price of asset	Transaction costs
Market A	$1,000	$ 75
Market B	1,050	150

    What is the fair value of the financial asset?

    a. $ 900
    b. $ 925
    c. $1,000
    d. $1,050 (R/12, FAR, #17, 89717)

18. Brand Co. incurred the following research and development project costs at the beginning of the current year:

Equipment purchased for current and future projects	$100,000
Equipment purchased for current projects only	200,000
Research and development salaries for current project	400,000

Equipment has a five-year life and is depreciated using the straight-line method. What amount should Brand record as depreciation for research and development projects at December 31?

a. $0
b. $ 20,000
c. $ 60,000
d. $140,000 (R/12, FAR, #18, 89718)

19. How should NSB, Inc. report significant research and development costs incurred?

a. Expense all costs in the year incurred
b. Capitalize the costs and amortize over a five-year period
c. Capitalize the costs and amortize over a 40-year period
d. Expense all costs two years before and five years after the year incurred (R/12, FAR, #19, 89719)

20. Kenn City obtained a municipal landfill and passed a local ordinance that required the city to operate the landfill so that the costs of operating the landfill, as well as the capital costs, are to be recovered with charges to customers. Which of the following funds should Kenn City use to report the activities of the landfill?

a. Enterprise
b. Permanent
c. Special revenue
d. Internal service (R/12, FAR, #20, 89720)

21. At the beginning of the current year, Paxx County's enterprise fund had a $125,000 balance for accrued compensated absences. At the end of the year, the balance was $150,000. During the year, Paxx paid $400,000 for compensated absences. What amount of compensated absences expense should Paxx County's enterprise fund report for the year?

a. $375,000
b. $400,000
c. $425,000
d. $550,000 (R/12, FAR, #21, 89721)

22. Which of the following funds would be reported as a fiduciary fund in Pine City's financial statements?

a. Special revenue
b. Permanent
c. Private-purpose trust
d. Internal service (R/12, FAR, #22, 89722)

23. Belle, a nongovernmental not-for-profit organization, received funds during its annual campaign that were specifically pledged by the donor to another nongovernmental not-for-profit health organization. How should Belle record these funds?

a. Increase in assets and increase in liabilities
b. Increase in assets and increase in revenue
c. Increase in assets and increase in deferred revenue
d. Decrease in assets and decrease in fund balance (R/12, FAR, #23, 89723)

24. Ragg Coalition, a nongovernmental not-for-profit organization, received a gift of treasury bills. The cost to the donor was $20,000, with an additional $500 for brokerage fees that were paid by the donor prior to the transfer of the treasury bills. The treasury bills had a fair value of $15,000 at the time of the transfer. At what amount should Ragg report the treasury bills in its statement of financial position?

    a. $15,000
    b. $15,500
    c. $20,000
    d. $20,500 (R/12, FAR, #24, 89724)

25. In year 2, the Nord Association, a nongovernmental not-for-profit organization, received a $100,000 contribution to fund scholarships for medical students. The donor stipulated that only the interest earned on the contribution be used for the scholarships. Interest earned in year 2 of $15,000 was used to award scholarships in year 3. What amount should Nord report as temporarily restricted net assets at the end of year 2?

    a. $115,000
    b. $100,000
    c. $ 15,000
    d. $0 (R/12, FAR, #25, 89725)

Problem 2 MULTIPLE-CHOICE QUESTIONS (hard)

26. Which of the following characteristics of accounting information primarily allows users of financial statements to generate predictions about an organization?

    a. Reliability
    b. Timeliness
    c. Neutrality
    d. Relevance (R/12, FAR, #26, 89726)

27. Polk Co. acquires a forklift from Quest Co. for $30,000. The terms require Polk to pay $3,000 down and finance the remaining $27,000. On March 1, year 1, Polk pays the $3,000 down and accepted delivery of the forklift. Polk signed a note that requires Polk to pay principal payments of $1,000 per month for 27 months beginning July 1, year 1. What amount should Polk report as an investing activity in the statement of cash flows for the year ended December 31, year 1?

    a. $ 3,000
    b. $ 9,000
    c. $12,000
    d. $30,000 (R/12, FAR, #27, 89727)

28. A company that is a large accelerated filer must file its Form 10-Q with the United States Securities and Exchange Commission within how many days after the end of the period?

    a. 30 days
    b. 40 days
    c. 45 days
    d. 60 days (R/12, FAR, #28, 89728)

29. Each of the following is a component of the changes in the net assets available for benefits of a defined benefit pension plan trust, **except**

    a. The net change in fair value of each significant class of investments
    b. The net change in the actuarial present value of accumulated plan benefits
    c. Contributions from the employer and participants
    d. Benefits paid to participants (R/12, FAR, #29, 89729)

30. During the year, Hauser Co. wrote off a customer's account receivable. Hauser used the allowance method for uncollectable accounts. What impact would the write-off have on net income and total assets?

	Net income	Total assets
a.	Decrease	Decrease
b.	Decrease	No effect
c.	No effect	Decrease
d.	No effect	No effect

(R/12, FAR, #30, 89730)

31. The original cost of an inventory item is above the replacement cost. The inventory item's replacement cost is above the net realizable value. Under the lower of cost or market method, the inventory item should be valued at

a. Original cost
b. Replacement cost
c. Net realizable value
d. Net realizable value **less** normal profit margin

(R/12, FAR, #31, 89731)

32. Kauf Co. had the following amounts related to the sale of consignment inventory:

Cost of merchandise shipped to consignee	$72,000
Sales value for two-thirds of inventory sold by consignee	80,000
Freight cost for merchandise shipped	7,500
Advertising paid for by consignee, to be reimbursed	4,500
10% commission due the consignee for the sale	8,000

What amount should Kauf report as net profit(loss) from this transaction for the year?

a. $(12,000)
b. $ 8,000
c. $ 14,500
d. $ 32,000

(R/12, FAR, #32, 89732)

33. A manufacturer has the following per-unit costs and values for its sole product:

Cost	$10.00
Current replacement cost	5.50
Net realizable value	6.00
Net realizable value less normal profit margin	5.20

In accordance with IFRS, what is the per-unit carrying value of inventory in the manufacturer's statement of financial position?

a. $ 5.20
b. $ 5.50
c. $ 6.00
d. $10.00

(R/12, FAR, #33, 89733)

34. At the beginning of the year, Cann Co. started construction on a new $2 million addition to its plant. Total construction expenditures made during the year were $200,000 on January 2, $600,000 on May 1, and $300,000 on December 1. On January 2, the company borrowed $500,000 for the construction at 12%. The only other outstanding debt the company had was a 10% interest rate, long-term mortgage of $800,000, which had been outstanding the entire year. What amount of interest should Cann capitalize as part of the cost of the plant addition?

a. $140,000
b. $132,000
c. $ 72,500
d. $ 60,000

(R/12, FAR, #34, 89734)

35. Bondholders of Balm Co. converted their bonds into 90,000 shares of $5 par value common stock. In Balm's accounting records, the bonds had a par value of $775,000 and unamortized discount of $23,000 at the time of conversion. What amount of additional paid-in capital from the conversion should Balm record?

    a. $302,000
    b. $325,000
    c. $348,000
    d. $798,000 (R/12, FAR, #35, 89735)

36. On January 1 of the current year, Barton Co. paid $900,000 to purchase two-year, 8%, $1,000,000 face value bonds that were issued by another publicly traded corporation. Barton plans to sell the bonds in the first quarter of the following year. The fair value of the bonds at the end of the current year was $1,020,000. At what amount should Barton report the bonds in its balance sheet at the end of the current year?

    a. $ 900,000
    b. $ 950,000
    c. $1,000,000
    d. $1,020,000 (R/12, FAR, #36, 89736)

37. The funded status of a defined benefit pension plan for a company should be reported in

    a. The income statement
    b. The statement of cash flows
    c. The statement of financial position
    d. The notes to the financial statements only (R/12, FAR, #37, 89737)

38. Martin Pharmaceutical Co. is currently involved in two lawsuits. One is a class-action suit in which consumers claim that one of Martin's best selling drugs caused severe health problems. It is reasonably possible that Martin will lose the suit and have to pay $20 million in damages. Martin is suing another company for false advertising and false claims against Martin. It is probable that Martin will win the suit and be awarded $5 million in damages. What amount should Martin report on its financial statements as a result of these two lawsuits?

    a. $0
    b. $ 5 million income
    c. $15 million expense
    d. $20 million expense (R/12, FAR, #38, 89738)

39. Wood Co.'s dividends on noncumulative preferred stock have been declared but not paid. Wood has not declared or paid dividends on its cumulative preferred stock in the current or the prior year and has reported a net loss in the current year. For the purpose of computing basic earnings per share, how should the income available to common stockholders be calculated?

    a. The current-year dividends and the dividends in arrears on the cumulative preferred stock should be added to the net loss, but the dividends on the noncumulative preferred stock should **not** be included in the calculation.
    b. The dividends on the noncumulative preferred stock should be added to the net loss, but the current-year dividends and the dividends in arrears on the cumulative preferred stock should **not** be included in the calculation.
    c. The dividends on the noncumulative preferred stock and the current-year dividends on the cumulative preferred stock should be added to the net loss.
    d. Neither the dividends on the noncumulative preferred stock nor the current-year dividends and the dividends in arrears on cumulative preferred stock should be included in the calculation. (R/12, FAR, #39, 89739)

40. The fair value for an asset or liability is measured as
    a. The appraised value of the asset or liability
    b. The price that would be paid to acquire the asset or received to assume the liability in an orderly transaction between market participants
    c. The price that would be received when selling an asset or paid when transferring a liability in an orderly transaction between market participants
    d. The cost of the asset **less** any accumulated depreciation or the carrying value of the liability on the date of the sale (R/12, FAR, #40, 89740)

41. Hudson Corp. operates several factories that manufacture medical equipment. The factories have a historical cost of $200 million. Near the end of the company's fiscal year, a change in business climate related to a competitor's innovative products indicated to Hudson's management that the $170 million carrying amount of the assets of one of Hudson's factories may not be recoverable. Management identified cash flows from this factory and estimated that the undiscounted future cash flows over the remaining useful life of the factory would be $150 million. The fair value of the factory's assets is reliably estimated to be $135 million. The change in business climate requires investigation of possible impairment. Which of the following amounts is the impairment loss?
    a. $15 million
    b. $20 million
    c. $35 million
    d. $65 million (R/12, FAR, #41, 89741)

42. On January 1, year 1, Peabody Co. purchased an investment for $400,000 that represented 30% of Newman Corp.'s outstanding voting stock. For year 1, Newman reported net income of $60,000 and paid dividends of $20,000. At year end, the fair value of Peabody's investment in Newman was $410,000. Peabody elected the fair value option for this investment. What amount should Peabody recognize in net income for year 1 attributable to the investment?
    a. $ 6,000
    b. $10,000
    c. $16,000
    d. $18,000 (R/12, FAR, #42, 89742)

43. On June 19, Don Co., a U.S. company, sold and delivered merchandise on a 30-day account to Cologne GmbH, a German corporation, for 200,000 euros. On July 19, Cologne paid Don in full. Relevant currency exchange rates were:

	June 19	July 19
Spot rate	$988	$ 995
30-day forward rate	990	1,000

    What amount should Don record on June 19 as an account receivable for its sale to Cologne?
    a. $197,600
    b. $198,000
    c. $199,000
    d. $200,000 (R/12, FAR, #43, 89743)

44. On June 1 of the current year, a company entered into a real estate lease agreement for a new building. The lease is an operating lease and is fully executed on that day. According to the terms of the lease, payments of $28,900 per month are scheduled to begin on October 1 of the current year and to continue each month thereafter for 56 months. The lease term spans five years. The company has a calendar year end. What amount is the company's lease expense for the current calendar year?

    a. $ 86,700
    b. $161,838
    c. $188,813
    d. $202,300 (R/12, FAR, #44, 89744)

45. On March 21, year 2, a company with a calendar year end issued its year 1 financial statements. On February 28, year 2, the company's only manufacturing plant was severely damaged by a storm and had to be shut down. Total property losses were $10 million and determined to be material. The amount of business disruption losses is unknown. How should the impact of the storm be reflected in the company's year 1 financial statements?

    a. Provide **no** information related to the storm losses in the financial statements until losses and expenses become fully known
    b. Accrue and disclose the property loss with **no** accrual or disclosure of the business disruption loss
    c. Do **not** accrue the property loss or the business disruption loss, but disclose them in the notes to the financial statements
    d. Accrue and disclose the property loss and additional business disruption losses in the financial statements (R/12, FAR, #45, 89745)

46. On January 1, Fonk City approved the following general fund resources for the new fiscal period:

Property taxes	$5,000,000
Licenses and permits	400,000
Intergovernmental revenues	150,000
Transfers in from other funds	350,000

    What amount should Fonk record as estimated revenues for the new fiscal year?

    a. $5,400,000
    b. $5,550,000
    c. $5,750,000
    d. $5,900,000 (R/12, FAR, #46, 89746)

47. Which of the following is one of the three standard sections of a governmental comprehensive annual financial report?

    a. Investment
    b. Actuarial
    c. Statistical
    d. Single audit (R/12, FAR, #47, 89747)

48. A government makes a contribution to its pension plan in the amount of $10,000 for year 1. The actuarially determined annual required contribution for year 1 was $13,500. The pension plan paid benefits of $8,200 and refunded employee contributions of $800 for year 1. What is the pension expenditure for the general fund for year 1?

    a. $ 8,200
    b. $ 9,000
    c. $10,000
    d. $13,500 (R/12, FAR, #48, 89748)

49. On January 1, Read, a nongovernmental not-for-profit organization, received $20,000 and an unconditional pledge of $20,000 for each of the next four calendar years to be paid on the first day of each year. The present value of an ordinary annuity for four years at a constant interest rate of 8% is 3.312. What amount of restricted net assets is reported in the year the pledge was received?

    a. $ 66,240
    b. $ 80,000
    c. $ 86,240
    d. $100,000 (R/12, FAR, #49, 89749)

50. Which of the following financial categories are used in a nongovernmental not-for-profit organization's statement of financial position?

    a. Net assets, income, and expenses
    b. Income, expenses, and unrestricted net assets
    c. Assets, liabilities, and net assets
    d. Changes in unrestricted, temporarily restricted, and permanently restricted net assets

    (R/12, FAR, #50, 89750)

Problem 3 Simulation 1

JRM Co. is in the process of closing its books for the year ended December 31, year 2.

The following business events are not properly reflected in JRM's December 31, year 2, unadjusted trial balance:

1. The controller determined that half of the recorded rent expense is attributable to year 3.
2. JRM depreciates its property, plant and equipment using the straight-line method over 10 years. The property, plant and equipment had an original cost of $20,000 and a salvage value of $5,000.
3. JRM uses the percentage-of-sales method to determine the addition to bad debt expense. Uncollectible accounts receivable for year 2 was estimated to be 0.25%.
4. On December 31, year 2, a customer declared bankruptcy and its account receivable of $855 is uncollectible.
5. Life insurance premiums for the period ended December 31, year 2, of $650 for key members of management are included in prepaid expense.
6. Interest of $300 was earned and outstanding on notes receivable during year 2. The note receivable is due at the end of year 5.
7. Income taxes for year 2 are estimated to be $3,000.

Based on the business events on the previous page, calculate the adjustments necessary to JRM's unadjusted trial balance by entering the appropriate debit and credit amounts in columns D and E, respectively. Enter the debit adjustments as positive values and credit adjustments as negative values.

	A	B	C	D	E	F
1	**Account name**	**Trial balance debit**	**Trial balance (credit)**	**Adjustment debit**	**Adjustment (credit)**	**Adjusted trial balance debit/(credit) balance**
2	Cash	1,000	0			
3	Interest receivable	0	0			
4	Accounts receivable	25,000	0			
5	Allowance for doubtful accounts	0	(2,500)			
6	Prepaid expenses	1,000	0			
7	Property, plant and equipment	20,000	0			
8	Accumulated depreciation —property, plant and equipment	0	(10,000)			
9	Notes receivable	20,000	0			
10	Accounts payable	0	(33,000)			
11	Taxes payable	0	(1,000)			
12	Equity	0	(1,500)			
13	Sales	0	(300,000)			
14	Cost of goods sold	195,000	0			
15	Salaries, office, and general expenses	75,000	0			
16	Rent expense	10,000	0			
17	Tax expense	1,000	0			
18	Bad debt expense	0	0			
19	Depreciation expense	0	0			
20	Insurance expense	0	0			
21	Interest income	0	0			
22		**348,000**	**(348,000)**			

(R/12, FAR, 9088)

Problem 3 SIMULATION 2

For each situation below, record the appropriate journal entry for Richter Corp.

Assume the company uses the straight-line method for amortization and depreciation and that all amortization and depreciation is recorded on December 31 of each year. Richter uses separate general ledger accounts to record accumulated amortization for each intangible asset.

To prepare each entry:

- Select from the list provided the appropriate account name. If no entry is needed, select "No entry required."
- An account may be used once or not at all for each entry.
- Enter the corresponding debit or credit amount in the appropriate column.
- Round all amounts to the nearest dollar.
- All rows may not be required to complete each entry.

Account Title Choices	
Accumulated amortization-patent	Investment
Accumulated depreciation	Legal expense
Amortization expense	Patents
Cash	Prepaid patent expense
Depreciation expense	Research & Development expense
Equipment	Trademark
Goodwill	No entry required
Goodwill impairment loss	

	A	B	C
1	April 1, year 1: Richter purchased a patent with a 10-year life for $50,000 from DD Co. DD incurred costs of $35,000 developing the patent. Prepare the journal entry, if any, to record the patent.		
2	**Account name**	**Debit**	**Credit**
3			
4			
5			
6			

7	July 1, year 1: Richter purchased scientific equipment used in product development studies having potential alternative uses for future products. The equipment cost $75,000 and the company paid an additional $4,000 for delivery. The equipment has an estimated useful life of 5 years. Prepare the journal entry, if any, to record the purchase of the equipment.		
8	**Account name**	**Debit**	**Credit**
9			
10			
11			
12			

13	October 1, year 1: Richter received an unfavorable judgment in defense of a trademark and paid $25,000 in fees to their law firm. Prepare the journal entry, if any, to record the legal fees.		
14	**Account name**	**Debit**	**Credit**
15			
16			
17			
18			

19	December 31, year 1: Prepare the journal entry, if any, to account for the patent purchased on April 1, year 1.		
20	**Account name**	**Debit**	**Credit**
21			
22			
23			
24			

25	December 31, year 1: Prepare the journal entry, if any, to account for the scientific equipment purchased on July 1, year 1.		
26	**Account name**	**Debit**	**Credit**
27			
28			
29			
30			

31	December 31, year 1: Richter had previously recorded $300,000 of goodwill related to an acquisition. At December 31, year 1, the carrying value of the identifiable net assets acquired exceeded their fair value by $50,000. The implied fair value of the goodwill was $310,000. Prepare the journal entry, if any, to adjust the carrying value of goodwill.		
32	**Account name**	**Debit**	**Credit**
33			
34			
35			
36			

(R/12, FAR, 9089)

Problem 3 SIMULATION 3: RESEARCH

ABC Corp., an issuer, is planning to implement an employee share purchase plan. Substantially all employees that meet the limited employment qualifications may participate on an equitable basis. Which section of the authoritative guidance best outlines the criteria that allow a company to provide a share purchase plan that does not require compensation cost to be recognized?

Enter your response in the answer fields below. Unless specifically requested, your response should not cite implementation guidance. Guidance on correctly structuring your response appears above and below the answer fields.

FASB ASC: [ ] - [ ] - [ ] - [ ]

(R/12, FAR, 9090)

Solution 1 MULTIPLE-CHOICE ANSWERS (medium)

1. (c) Gross profit is the excess of sales over cost of goods sold. It does not consider all operating expenses. ($500,000 – $100,000 = $400,000) (Chapter 1-3-3, CSO: 1.3.2)

2. (c) Items that previously were included in the equity section as a separate component of owners' equity are required to be reported in other comprehensive income. OCI must be classified by their nature, in one of these categories: foreign currency items, pension adjustments, unrealized gains and losses on certain investments in debt and equity securities, and gains and losses on cash flow hedging derivative instruments. Only the unrealized holding loss on AFS securities of $17,000 qualifies as an item of OCI. (Chapter 11-3-2, CSO: 1.3.3)

3. (b) Accounts Payable decreased by $100,000 (from $300,000 to $200,000). That means Baler paid $100,000 **more** for goods than it actually purchased. Since Baler purchased $1,150,000 ($150,000 + $1,200,000 – $200,000), total cash paid to suppliers for inventory purchases must have been $1,250,000 ($1,150,000 + $100,000). (Chapter 14-1-3, CSO: 1.3.5)

4. (a) Cash flows from operating activities include the cash effects of transactions and other events that enter into the determination of net income, including the gain on sale of plant assets. The sale of fixed assets is an investing activity. The payment of dividends and the issuance of common stock are financing activities. (Chapter 14-2-1, CSO: 1.3.5)

5. (b) The allowance account has an ending balance of $55,000. Prior to the bad debt adjustment, the allowance balance is $35,000 [$70,000 – $35,000 in write offs], so an adjustment to bad debt expense and the allowance account for $20,000 is required. (Chapter 2-2-2, CSO: 2.2.0)

6. (c) Future economic benefits deriving from R&D activities are uncertain in their amount and timing; therefore, most R&D costs are expensed in the year incurred. Legal fees for both the license application and successful defense of the patent are capitalized because they offer probable future benefits. They are amortized over the remaining useful life of the patent. Atla should capitalize $90,000 ($40,000 + $50,000). (Chapter 5-1-2, CSO: 2.6.0)

7. (a) When the redeemable gift certificates are sold, the sales price collected represents unearned revenue and an unearned revenue account is credited (i.e., increased). As the certificates are redeemed, the earned revenue is recognized, decreasing the unearned portion. Lapsed certificates would also decrease unearned revenue, but would increase *Gain on Lapsed Certificates* rather than *Revenue* account. In either case, the *Deferred Revenue* account is decreased. (Chapter 7-1-6, CSO: 2.8.0)

8. (a) The effect of the amortization entry is to increase the carrying value of the bonds. Since the carrying amount is $363,600, the amount that Vole received upon issuing the bonds would be less the amortized discount of $3,600, or $360,000. (Chapter 6-2-3, CSO: 2.9.2)

9. (d) Serial bonds are bonds issued at the same time but having different maturity dates. These are also called installment bonds because they provide a series of installments for repayment of principal. Debenture bonds are unsecured bonds; they are not supported by a lien or mortgage on specific assets, but they mature at the same time. Term bonds all mature on a specified date. Variable rate bonds have a fluctuating interest rate, but mature at the same time. (Chapter 6-4-1, CSO: 2.9.2)

10. (b) For basic EPS, weighted average common stock outstanding includes shares outstanding the entire period, shares issued during the period, and shares where all of the conditions of issuance have been met. Issuance of stock and reacquisition of stock during the period are prorated for the period outstanding. Stock dividends, stock splits, and reverse stock splits change the total number of shares outstanding but not the proportionate shares outstanding. Therefore, stock dividends, stock splits, and reverse stock splits are reflected retroactively for all periods presented. (Chapter 16-3-2, CSO: 3.6.0)

Total Shares Outstanding		Months Outstanding		Stock Dividend		Weighted Average
100,000	×	3/12	×	1.05	=	26,250
130,000	×	2/12	×	1.05	=	22,750
166,000	×	1/12	×	1.05	=	14,525
174,300	×	2/12			=	29,050
139,300	×	4/12			=	46,433
						139,008

11. (c) The cost of services received from employees in exchange for awards of share-based compensation generally shall be measured based on the grant-date fair value of the options. The account Stock Options Outstanding is increased on the grant date. The subsequent exercising, forfeiture, or lapsing of the stock options reduces this account. (Chapter 9-5-3 CSO: 2.13.5)

January 1, Year 1		
Deferred Compensation Cost (option/compensation value at grant date)	300,000	
Stock Options Outstanding		300,000
December 31, Year 1, 2, 3		
Wages and Compensation Expense	100,000	
Deferred Compensation Cost		100,000

12. (a) An asset retirement obligations (ARO) must be recorded at fair value in the accounting period in which it occurs and in which its amount can be reasonably measured. AROs incur depreciation and accretion expenses each year. Accretion expense is offset with an increase to the liability account, and, at the end of the asset's life, the liability account will have a balance equal to the amount needed to settle the retirement obligation. Accretion expense is calculated by multiplying the balance of the recorded liability by the company's credit-adjusted discount rate each year, so the amount of accretion expense for the year is $10,000 ($100,000 × 15%). (Chapter 7-2-5, CSO: 3.2.0)

13. (c) Where the loss is considered reasonably possible, no charge should be made to income but the nature of the contingency should be disclosed. This treatment also applies to probable losses that cannot be reasonably estimated. (Chapter 7-1-5, CSO: 3.5.0)

14. (a) Jones should report 105,000 shares outstanding (50,000 shares × 1.05 × 2). (Chapter 9-4-6, CSO: 2.10.0)

15. (c) A transaction that is unusual in nature or infrequent in occurrence, but not both, is reported as a component of income from continuing operations. A transaction must be both unusual in nature and infrequent in occurrence to be classified as an extraordinary item. The nature and financial effects of an unusual item or an infrequently occurring item should be disclosed on the face of the income statement, or alternatively, in the notes to the financial statements. (Chapter 11-2-2, CSO: 3.8.0)

16. (b) The income approach uses valuation techniques to convert/discount future amounts to a single present amount. The measurement is based on the value indicated by current market expectations about those future amounts. The market approach uses prices and other relevant information generated by market transactions involving identical or comparable assets or liabilities. The cost approach is based on the amount that currently would be required to replace the service capacity of an asset, often referred to as the current replacement cost. Observable inputs are inputs for the valuation technique; they are not a technique in and of themselves. (Chapter 1-2-4, CSO: 3.9.0)

17. (c) Fair value is the price that would be received to sell an asset or paid to transfer a liability in an orderly transaction between market participants at the measurement date. It is assumed that the transaction would occur in the principle market for the asset or liability, or in the absence of such, the most advantageous market for the asset or liability. The most advantageous market is the market with the price that maximizes the amount that would be received for the asset or minimizes the amount that would be paid to transfer the liability. In determining the most advantageous market, transaction costs must be netted against the price of the asset. The fair value price is **not** adjusted for incremental direct transaction costs. Market A would yield a net $925 ($1,000-$75) while Market B would yield $900 ($1,050-$150), so Market A is the most advantageous, and the fair value of the asset would be $1,000. (Chapter 1-2-4, CSO: 3.9.0)

18. (b) Materials, equipment, facilities, or intangibles that are acquired for a current R&D project and have no alternative future use in other R&D projects should be expensed in the period in which acquired. If alternative future uses are expected, whether in other R&D activities or in normal operations, these items should be recorded as assets and the cost should be amortized over their useful lives by periodic charges to R&D expense. If, at any point, these assets are no longer deemed to have alternative future uses, the remaining unamortized cost is charged to R&D expense for the period. Depreciation expense would be $20,000 ($100,000 / 5 years). (Chapter 5-2-2, CSO: 3.18.0)

19. (a) *Research* activities are those aimed at the discovery of knowledge that will be useful in developing or significantly improving products or processes. *Development* activities are those concerned with translating research findings and other knowledge into plans or designs for new or significantly improved products or processes. Since future economic benefits deriving from R&D activities are uncertain in their amount and timing, most R&D costs are required to be charged to expense the year in which incurred. (Chapter 5-2-3, CSO: 3.18.0)

20. (a) Enterprise funds are used to account for a government's business-type operations that are financed and operated like private businesses—where the government's intent is that all costs of providing goods or services to the general public are to be recovered primarily through user charges (operating revenue). Permanent funds are used to account for and report resources that are restricted to the extent that only earnings, and not principal, may be used for purposes that support the reporting government's programs. Internal service funds are used to account for in-house business enterprise activities; that is, to account for the financing of goods or services provided by one government department or agency to other departments or agencies of the government. Special revenue funds are used to account for and report the proceeds of specific revenue sources that are restricted or committed to expenditure for specified purposes other than debt service or capital projects. (Chapter 19-3-3, CSO: 4.1.2)

21. (c) Enterprise funds must be used to account for a government's business-type operations that are financed and operated like private businesses—where the government's intent is that all costs of providing goods or services to the general public on a continuing basis are to be recovered primarily through user charges (operating revenue). Enterprise funds use normal accrual accounting. Compensated absence expense is $425,000 ($400,000 + $150,000 – $125,000). (Chapter 18-3-3, CSO: 4.2.3)

22. (c) Fiduciary funds are used to account for a government's fiduciary or stewardship responsibilities as an agent (agency funds) or trustee (trust funds) for other governments, funds, organizations, and/or individuals. Fiduciary funds cannot be used for any general programs of the primary government. Fiduciary funds are included in fund financial statements but not in the government-wide statements, and include: pension trust funds; investment trust funds; private purpose trust funds; and agency funds. Special revenue and permanent funds are governmental funds. Internal service funds are proprietary funds. (Chapter 18-4-4, CSO: 4.2.4)

23. (a) A recipient that accepts assets from a donor on behalf of a specified beneficiary recognizes the fair value of those assets as a *liability* concurrent with the recognition of the *assets*. Therefore, both assets and liabilities will increase as a result of the pledged funds. (Chapter 20-1-4, CSO: 5-2-1)

24. (a) Generally, contributions received are measured at their fair values and recognized as revenues or gains in the period received and as assets, decreases of liabilities, or expenses depending on the form of the benefits received. They shall be reported as restricted support or unrestricted support. Ragg should report $15,000 in its statement of financial position. (Chapter 20-1-5, CSO: 5-2-1)

25. (c) Entities are required to classify net assets based upon the existence or absence of donor-imposed restrictions. Net assets are classified into three categories: permanently restricted, temporarily restricted, and unrestricted. Contributions with donor-imposed restrictions are reported as restricted support. Restricted support increases permanently restricted net assets or temporarily restricted net assets. Since the restrictions will be met in year 3, the $15,000 is considered temporarily restricted. (Chapter 20-1-3, CSO: 5-2-2)

Solution 2 MULTIPLE-CHOICE ANSWERS (hard)

26. (d) Fundamental qualitative characteristics of information are relevance and faithful representation. Information is relevant if it is capable of making a difference in a decision by helping users to form predictions about the outcomes of past, present, and future events or to confirm or correct prior expectations. Components of relevance are predictive value, confirmatory value, or both. Information is faithfully represented if it represents what it purports to represent. Components of faithful representation are that it is complete, neutral, and free from error. Reliability exists when information represents what it purports to represent, coupled with an assurance for the user that it has representational faithfulness. Timeliness is an enhancing qualitative characteristic. Neutrality is free from bias. (Chapter 1-6-5, CSO: 1.2.1)

27. (a) Cash flows from investing activities include 1) making and collecting loans (excluding those acquired specifically for resale), 2) acquiring and disposing of property, plant and equipment, and other productive assets, and 3) purchases, sales, and maturities of debt and equity securities (excluding those acquired specifically for resale. Borrowing money and repaying amounts borrowed, or otherwise settling the obligation represents cash flows from financing activities. Polk should report $3,000 in investing activities, and $27,000 in financing activities. (Chapter 14-2-2, CSO: 1.3.5)

28. (b) There are three categories of filers: 1) non-accelerated filers, 2) accelerated filers, and 3) large accelerated filers. Non-accelerated filers are issuers that have a public float of less than $75 million. Accelerated filers are issuers that have a public float of at least $75 million but less than $700 million. Large accelerated filers must file the Form 10-Q with the SEC within 40 days after the end of the company's fiscal year. Large accelerated filers are issuers that have a public float of $700 million or more. (Chapter 17-7-4, CSO: 1.4.0)

29. (b) Net plan assets include amounts contributed by the employer (and by employees for a contributory plan) and amounts earned from investing the contributions, less benefits paid. The net change in the actuarial present value of accumulated plan benefits is not part of net plan assets. (Chapter 8-8-1, CSO: 1.5.5)

30. (d) The journal entry to record the write-off of an account is as follows:

Allowance for Uncollectible Accounts	XX	
Accounts Receivable—Joe Doe		XX

This entry would decrease both accounts receivable and allowance for uncollectible accounts; however, it would have no impact on net income or total assets. (Chapter 2-2-2, CSO: 2.2.0)

31. (c) Valuation of inventory items is required at the lower of cost or replacement cost (commonly referred to as market). Market cannot exceed the net realizable value (ceiling) of the good (i.e., selling price less expected costs to sell), and market should not be less than this net realizable value reduced by an allowance for a normal profit margin (floor). In this problem, the replacement cost exceeds net realizable value, so market is defined as NRV. Since the original cost is greater than defined market, the item will be carried at the lower of market/NRV amount. (Chapter 3-2-4, CSO: 2.3.0)

32. (c) Cost of goods sold will be two-thirds of the goods shipped (including two-thirds of the freight), but all of the advertising and commission will be deducted from gross profit to determine net profit. (Chapter 3-2-2, CSO: 2.3.0)

Revenue		$ 80,000
Less: Cost of consigned goods	$72,000	
Plus Freight for consigned goods	7,500	
Total cost of consigned goods	$79,500	
Percentage sold	67%	
Cost of Goods Sold (rounded)		(53,000)
Gross Profit		$ 27,000
Less advertising		(4,500)
Less commission		(8,000)
Net Profit		$ 14,500

33. (c) Under IFRS, inventory is carried at the lower of cost or net realizable value (best estimate of the net amounts inventories are expected to realize). This amount may or may not equal fair value. The net realizable value of $6.00 is lower than the historical cost of $10.00. (Chapter 17-3-6, CSO: 2.3.0)

34. (c) The cost of assets constructed for the use of the business should include all directly related costs; cost of direct materials, cost of direct labor, additional overhead incurred, and interest costs incurred during the construction period. If the average accumulated expenditures of an asset exceed the amount of any specific borrowings associated with the asset, the excess should be capitalized at the weighted average of interest rates applicable to other borrowings of the business. (Chapter 4-2-1, CSO: 2.4.0)

Average expenditure during year)	
$200,000 × 2/12	$200,000
600,000 × 8/12	400,000
300,000 × 1/12	25,000
Average expenditures	$625,000

Specific borrowings	500,000 × 12%	$60,000
Excess expenditures	125,000 × 10%	12,500
Total capitalized interest		$72,500

35. (a) Convertible bonds provide the bondholder the option of converting the bond to capital stock, typically common stock. Using the book value method, the conversion of the bonds into common stock is generally recorded by crediting the paid-in capital accounts for the carrying amount of the debt at the date of the conversion, less any cost associated with the conversion. The carrying amount of the bonds on the date of conversion is the $775,000 face value less the $23,000 unamortized discount. The journal entry would be: (Chapter 6-4-3, CSO: 2.9.3)

Bonds Payable	775,000	
Bond Discount		23,000
Common Stock (90,000 × $5 par)		450,000
APIC (to balance)		302,000

36. (d) Trading securities are debt and equity securities that are bought and held principally for the purpose of selling them in the near term to generate profits on short-term differences in price. They are reported at fair value. Unrealized holding gains and losses are included in current earnings for trading securities. Barton should report the investment at the fair value of $1,020,000. (Chapter 2-5-3, CSO: 2.5.1)

37. (c) The funded-status amount is measured as the difference between the fair value of plan assets and the benefit obligation, with the benefit obligation including all actuarial gains and losses, prior service cost, and any remaining transition amounts. If the benefit obligation is larger than the fair value of plan assets, the plan is underfunded, and a net liability is reported. Conversely, if the fair value of the plan assets is larger, the plan is overfunded, and a net asset is reported on the statement of financial position (i.e., balance sheet). (Chapter 8-8-2, CSO: 2.13.4)

38. (a) Reasonably possible means more than remote, but less than probable. Where the loss is considered reasonably possible, no charge should be made to income but the nature of the contingency should be disclosed. This treatment also applies to probable losses that cannot be reasonably estimated. Gain contingencies should be disclosed but not recognized as income. Care should be taken to avoid misleading implications as to the likelihood of realization. Therefore, Martin should report $0 on its financial statements, but disclose both events in the notes. (Chapter 7-1-5, CSO: 3.5.0)

39. (c) The numerator for basic EPS is fairly simple to determine. The income number used for basic EPS is income from continuing operations adjusted for the claims by senior securities. Senior security claims generally refer to preferred stock and are adjusted in the period earned. All preferred stock dividends declared reduce income to arrive at IAC. Cumulative preferred stock dividends of the current period, even though not declared, also reduce income to arrive at IAC. Both the dividends on the noncumulative preferred stock and the current-year dividends on the cumulative preferred stock should be added to the net loss. (Chapter 16-3-2, CSO: 3.6.0)

40. (c) Fair value is the price that would be received to sell an asset or paid to transfer a liability in an orderly transaction between market participants at the measurement date, conceptually an exit price. (Chapter 5-2-4, CSO: 3.9.0)

41. (c) A long-lived asset shall be tested for recoverability whenever events or changes in circumstances indicate that its carrying amount may not be recoverable. Impairment is the condition that exists when the carrying amount of a long-lived asset, or asset group, exceeds its fair value. An impairment loss shall be recognized only if the carrying amount of a long-lived asset is not recoverable and exceeds its fair value. The carrying amount (book value) is not recoverable if it exceeds the sum of the undiscounted cash flows expected to result from the use and eventual disposition of the asset. The amount of an impairment loss is the difference between an asset's book and fair value. The new book value is used as a basis for depreciation. Since the carrying amount of $170,000 exceeds the undiscounted cash flows of $150,000 an impairment loss must be recognized. The $35,000 impairment loss is the difference between the book value of $170,000 and the fair value of $135,000. (Chapter 4-4-1, CSO 3.12.0)

42. (c) Entities may choose to measure eligible items at fair value (the "fair value option") that are not currently required to be measured at fair value. The decision to elect the fair value option is applied instrument by instrument, is irrevocable, and is applied only to an entire instrument. A business entity shall report unrealized gains and losses on items for which the fair value option has been elected in earnings at each subsequent reporting date. The Investment in Newman would be increased by 30% of the net income and decreased by 30% of the dividends, resulting in a year end carrying amount of $412,000 ($400,000 + 18,000 – 6,000). Since the fair value was $410,000, Peabody had an unrealized loss of $2,000. This loss is netted against the investment income previously recognized of $18,000 for a $16,000 net income impact. Dividends do not affect net income (they reduce the Investment account). (Chapter 1-2-5, CSO: 3.9.0)

43. (a) At the date a transaction is recognized, each asset, liability, revenue, expense, gain, or loss arising from a foreign currency transaction should be measured and recorded in the functional currency of the recording entity by use of the exchange rate (i.e., spot rate) in effect at that date. Don Co should record an account receivable of $197,600 on June 19 (200,000 × .988). (Chapter 12-5-4, CSO: 3.11.0)

44. (c) Under operating leases, lessees recognize rent as expense over the lease term in a systematic and rational. The lease term is five years, or 60 months. Total lease payments are $1,618,400 ($28,900 × 56 months). This expense is allocated on a straight line basis over the 60-month term. Seven months expense should be recognized, or $188,813 ($26,973.33 × 7). (Chapter 8-3-2, CSO: 3.14.0)

45. (c) An entity shall not recognize subsequent events that provide evidence about conditions that did not exist at the date of the balance sheet but arose after the balance sheet date but before financial statements are issued or are available to be issued. Some nonrecognized subsequent events may be of such a nature that they must be disclosed to keep the financial statements from being misleading. Since property losses were of a material nature, the entity should disclose the nature of the event and an estimate of its financial effect or a statement that such an estimate cannot be made. (Chapter 12-1-3, CSO: 3.22.0).

46. (b) Revenues are recorded as received in cash except for revenues susceptible to accrual and revenues of a material amount that have not been received at the normal time of receipt. Revenues are considered susceptible to accrual at the time they become measurable and available for use (e.g., when the tax is levied). Available means collected or collectible within the current period or early enough in the next period (e.g., within 60 days or so) to be used to pay for expenditures incurred in the current period (for example, property taxes). General fund revenues primarily consist of taxes (property, sales, income, and excise), licenses, fines, and interest. Transfers are nonreciprocal shifts of resources among funds and are not intended to be repaid. Transfers are reported after revenues and expenditures, as they affect operating results, but they are recorded separately and are not part of estimated revenues. Therefore, Fonk should record estimated revenues of $5,550,000 ($5,000,000 + 400,000 + 150,000). (Chapter 18-2-1, CSO: 4.1.3)

47. (c) The comprehensive annual financial report contains the following sections: Introduction Section; Financial Section; and the Statistical Section. (Chapter 19-2-9, CSO: 4.2.8)

48. (c) The annual pension cost differs from the pension expenditure/expense reported in the financial statements. The annual pension cost is the period cost of an employer's participation in a defined benefit pension plan. The pension expenditure/expense is the amount recognized by an employer in each accounting period for contributions to a pension plan. Therefore, the $10,000 contribution represents the pension expenditure for year 1. (Chapter 19-4-2, CSO: 4.4.7)

49. (a) Contributions received are measured at their fair values and recognized as revenues or gains in the period received. Receipts of unconditional promises to give, or pledges, are reported as a receivable at their present value in the period in which they are made, net of an allowance for uncollectible amounts. If part of the pledge is to be applied during some future period, that part is reported as restricted revenue. Therefore, Read should report $66,240 (3.312 × $20,000) of restricted net assets. (Chapter 20-1-3, CSO: 5.2.1)

50. (c) Entities report assets, liabilities, and net assets in the statement of financial position. Entities are required to classify net assets based upon the existence or absence of donor-imposed restrictions. Thus, net assets are classified into at least three categories: permanently restricted, temporarily restricted, and unrestricted. (Chapter 20-2-2, CSO: 5.1.1)

Solution 3 SIMULATION 1 ANSWER

	A	B	C	D	E	F
1	**Account name**	**Trial balance debit**	**Trial balance (credit)**	**Adjustment debit**	**Adjustment (credit)**	**Adjusted trial balance debit/(credit) balance**
2	Cash	1,000	0			1,000
3	Interest receivable	0	0	300		300
4	Accounts receivable	25,000	0		(855)	24,145
5	Allowance for doubtful accounts	0	(2,500)	855	(750)	(2,395)
6	Prepaid expenses	1,000	0	5,000	(650)	5,350
7	Property, plant and equipment	20,000	0			20,000
8	Accumulated depreciation—property, plant and equipment	0	(10,000)		(1,500)	(11,500)
9	Notes receivable	20,000	0			20,000
10	Accounts payable	0	(33,000)			(33,000)
11	Taxes payable	0	(1,000)		(2,000)	(3,000)
12	Equity	0	(1,500)			(1,500)
13	Sales	0	(300,000)			(300,000)
14	Cost of goods sold	195,000	0			195,000
15	Salaries, office, and general expenses	75,000	0			75,000
16	Rent expense	10,000	0		(5,000)	5,000
17	Tax expense	1,000	0	2,000		3,000
18	Bad debt expense	0	0	750		750
19	Depreciation expense	0	0	1,500		1,500
20	Insurance expense	0	0	650		650
21	Interest income	0	0		(300)	(300)
22		**348,000**	**(348,000)**	**11,055**	**(11,055)**	0

Explanations:

1. Half the rent expense is attributable to next year. Therefore, $5,000 ($10,000 × 50%) prepaid rent should be recorded.

Prepaid Expenses	5,000	
Rent Expense		5,000

2. Straight line depreciation is cost less salvage value, if any. Depreciation expense of $1,500 [($20,000 – 5,000) / 10 years] should be posted to the trial balance:

Depreciation Expense	1,500	
Accumulated Depreciation-PPE		1,500

3. Under the percentage-of-sales method, bad debt expense is computed as a percentage of net credit Sales, regardless of any balance in Allowance for Doubtful Accounts. Bad debt expense of $750 ($300,000 × .0025) should be recognized.

Bad Debt Expense	750	
Allowance for Doubtful Accounts		750

4. Regardless of the allowance method used to estimate uncollectible receivables, the following journal entry should be made to record accounts written off during the period. This entry has no effect on net income, net accounts receivable, current assets, or working capital.

Allowance for Uncollectible Accounts	855	
Accounts Receivable		855

5. Companies frequently insure the lives of key executives. The amount to be reported as life insurance expense for a year is the annual premium paid, less (1) the increase in cash surrender value (CSV) and (2) any dividends received. Since no information was provided regarding CSV or dividends, life insurance expense is $650.

Insurance Expense	650	
Prepaid Expenses		650

6. Interest receivable is recognized in the year earned.

Interest Receivable	300	
Interest Income		300

7. Ending tax expense is $1,000 prior to any adjustments. Since total tax expense for the period should be $3,000, an additional $2,000 in expense should be recognized.

Tax Expense	2,000	
Taxes Payable		2,000

Solution 3 SIMULATION 2 ANSWER

Editor's Note: The AICPA's released solutions do not enter the phrase "No entry required" into unused rows as required by the AICPA directions. Therefore, these rows, if any, have been left blank as well.

	A	B	C
1	April 1, year 1: Richter purchased a patent with a 10-year life for $50,000 from DD Co. DD incurred costs of $35,000 developing the patent. Prepare the journal entry, if any, to record the patent.		
2	**Account name**	**Debit**	**Credit**
3	Patents	50,000	
4	Cash		50,000
5			
6			

Explanation:

A patent represents a special right to a particular product or process that has value to the holder of the right. Only the external acquisition costs, including items such as legal costs associated with obtaining a patent on a new product, are capitalized. DD would expense any development costs on their books, not on Richter's books.

7	July 1, year 1: Richter purchased scientific equipment used in product development studies having potential alternative uses for future products. The equipment cost $75,000 and the company paid an additional $4,000 for delivery. The equipment has an estimated useful life of 5 years. Prepare the journal entry, if any, to record the purchase of the equipment.		
8	**Account name**	**Debit**	**Credit**
9	Equipment	79,000	
10	Cash		79,000
11			
12			

Explanation:

Materials, equipment, facilities, or intangibles purchased from others that are acquired for a particular R&D project and have no alternative use in other R&D projects or in normal operations should be expensed in the period in which acquired. However, these items should be recorded as assets if **alternative future uses** are expected, whether in other R&D activities or in normal operations. Acquisition cost is defined as the cash price, plus all other costs reasonably necessary to bring it to the location and to make it ready for its intended use. Machinery and equipment charges typically include: transportation, insurance while in transit, special foundations, installation, and test runs.

13	October 1, year 1: Richter received an unfavorable judgment in defense of a trademark and paid $25,000 in fees to their law firm. Prepare the journal entry, if any, to record the legal fees.		
14	**Account name**	**Debit**	**Credit**
15	Legal expense	25,000	
16	Cash		25,000
17			
18			

Explanation:

The cost of a successful legal defense of a trade mark is capitalized. The cost of an **unsuccessful defense** is expensed in the period in which an unfavorable court decision is rendered.

19	December 31, year 1: Prepare the journal entry, if any, to account for the patent purchased on April 1, year 1.		
20	**Account name**	**Debit**	**Credit**
21	Amortization expense	3,750	
22	Accumulated amortization-patent		3,750
23			
24			

Explanation:

An intangible asset with a finite useful life is amortized; an intangible with an indefinite useful life is not amortized. The useful life of an intangible asset to an entity is the period over which the asset is expected to contribute directly or indirectly to the future cash flows of that entity. Amortization expense would be prorated over the first year: $50,000 / 10 years × 9/12 = $3,750.

25	December 31, year 1: Prepare the journal entry, if any, to account for the scientific equipment purchased on July 1, year 1.		
26	**Account name**	**Debit**	**Credit**
27	Research and development expense	7,900	
28	Accumulated depreciation		7,900
29			
30			

Explanation:

Depreciation is the process of allocating the depreciable cost of fixed assets over their estimated useful lives in a systematic and rational manner. This process matches the depreciable cost of the asset with revenues generated from its use. Depreciable cost is the capitalized cost less its estimated residual (salvage) value, if any. Depreciation is prorated over the first year: $79,000 / 5 years × 6/12 = $7,900.

31	December 31, year 1: Richter had previously recorded $300,000 of goodwill related to an acquisition. At December 31, year 1, the carrying value of the identifiable net assets acquired exceeded their fair value by $50,000. The implied fair value of the goodwill was $310,000. Prepare the journal entry, if any, to adjust the carrying value of goodwill.		
32	**Account name**	**Debit**	**Credit**
33	No entry required		
34			
35			
36			

Explanation:

Goodwill impairment testing consists of two steps. The first step used to identify potential goodwill impairment compares a reporting unit's fair value with its carrying amount, including goodwill. If the carrying amount exceeds its fair value, as it does in the above item, the second step is performed. The second step compares the implied fair value of reporting unit's goodwill (i.e., $310,000) with its carrying amount (i.e., $300,000). Since the implied fair value exceeds the carrying amount, no impairment loss is recognized, and no journal entry is required.

Solution 3 SIMULATION 3 ANSWER

FASB ASC:	718	-	50	-	25	-	1

Explanation:

25-1 An employee share purchase plan that satisfies all of the following criteria does not give rise to recognizable compensation cost (that is, the plan is noncompensatory):

a. The plan satisfies either of the following conditions:

   1. The terms of the plan are no more favorable than those available to all holders of the same class of shares. Note that a transaction subject to an employee share purchase plan that involves a class of equity shares designed exclusively for and held only by current or former employees or their beneficiaries may be compensatory depending on the terms of the arrangement.

   2. Any purchase discount from the market price does not exceed the per-share amount of share issuance costs that would have been incurred to raise a significant amount of capital by a public offering. A purchase discount of 5 percent or less from the market price shall be considered to comply with this condition without further justification. A purchase discount greater than 5 percent that cannot be justified under this condition results in compensation cost for the entire amount of the discount. Note that an entity that justifies a purchase discount in excess of 5 percent shall reassess at least annually, and no later than the first share purchase offer during the fiscal year, whether it can continue to justify that discount pursuant to this paragraph.

b. Substantially all employees that meet limited employment qualifications may participate on an equitable basis.

c. The plan incorporates no option features, other than the following:

   1. Employees are permitted a short period of time—not exceeding 31 days—after the purchase price has been fixed to enroll in the plan.

   2. The purchase price is based solely on the market price of the shares at the date of purchase, and employees are permitted to cancel participation before the purchase date and obtain a refund of amounts previously paid (such as those paid by payroll withholdings).

APPENDIX F
SELECT SEC FORMS

Editor's Note: Instructional pages and some signature pages have been omitted from the samples in this appendix. SEC forms/instructions may be downloaded from www.sec.gov/about/forms/secforms.htm.

OMB APPROVAL	
OMB Number:	3235-0063
Expires:	December 31, 2014
Estimated average burden hours per response	. . 1,998.65

UNITED STATES
SECURITIES AND EXCHANGE COMMISSION
Washington, D.C. 20549

(Mark One)

FORM 10-K

[ ] ANNUAL REPORT PURSUANT TO SECTION 13 OR 15(d) OF THE SECURITIES EXCHANGE ACT OF 1934

For the fiscal year ended______________________________

or

[ ] TRANSITION REPORT PURSUANT TO SECTION 13 OR 15(d) OF THE SECURITIES EXCHANGE ACT OF 1934

For the transition period from ________________ to ________________

Commission file number ______________________________

(Exact name of registrant as specified in its charter)

State or other jurisdiction of incorporation or organization	(I.R.S. Employer Identification No.)

(Address of principal executive offices) (Zip Code)

Registrant's telephone number, including area code ________________________

Securities registered pursuant to Section 12(b) of the Act:

Title of each class	Name of each exchange on which registered

Securities registered pursuant to section 12(g) of the Act:

(Title of class)

(Title of class)

Indicate by check mark if the registrant is a well-known seasoned issuer, as defined in Rule 405 of the Securities Act.
☐ Yes ☐ No

Indicate by check mark if the registrant is not required to file reports pursuant to Section 13 or Section 15(d) of the Act.
☐ Yes ☐ No

Note – Checking the box above will not relieve any registrant required to file reports pursuant to Section 13 or 15(d) of the Exchange Act from their obligations under those Sections.

Persons who respond to the collection of information contained in this form are not required to respond unless the form displays a currently valid OMB control number.

SEC 1673 (01-12)

6

Indicate by check mark whether the registrant (1) has filed all reports required to be filed by Section 13 or 15(d) of the Securities Exchange Act of 1934 during the preceding 12 months (or for such shorter period that the registrant was required to file such reports), and (2) has been subject to such filing requirements for the past 90 days. ☐ Yes ☐ No

Indicate by check mark whether the registrant has submitted electronically and posted on its corporate Web site, if any, every Interactive Data File required to be submitted and posted pursuant to Rule 405 of Regulation S-T (§232.405 of this chapter) during the preceding 12 months (or for such shorter period that the registrant was required to submit and post such files).

☐ Yes ☐ No

Indicate by check mark if disclosure of delinquent filers pursuant to Item 405 of Regulation S-K (§229.405 of this chapter) is not contained herein, and will not be contained, to the best of registrant's knowledge, in definitive proxy or information statements incorporated by reference in Part III of this Form 10-K or any amendment to this Form 10-K. ☐

Indicate by check mark whether the registrant is a large accelerated filer, an accelerated filer, a non-accelerated filer, or a smaller reporting company. See the definitions of "large accelerated filer," "accelerated filer" and "smaller reporting company" in Rule 12b-2 of the Exchange Act.

Large accelerated filer ☐ Accelerated filer ☐

Non-accelerated filer ☐ (Do not check if a smaller reporting company) Smaller reporting company ☐

Indicate by check mark whether the registrant is a shell company (as defined in Rule 12b-2 of the Act). ☐ Yes ☐ No

State the aggregate market value of the voting and non-voting common equity held by non-affiliates computed by reference to the price at which the common equity was last sold, or the average bid and asked price of such common equity, as of the last business day of the registrant's most recently completed second fiscal quarter.

Note.—If a determination as to whether a particular person or entity is an affiliate cannot be made without involving unreasonable effort and expense, the aggregate market value of the common stock held by non-affiliates may be calculated on the basis of assumptions reasonable under the circumstances, provided that the assumptions are set forth in this Form.

APPLICABLE ONLY TO REGISTRANTS INVOLVED IN BANKRUPTCY

PROCEEDINGS DURING THE PRECEDING FIVE YEARS:

Indicate by check mark whether the registrant has filed all documents and reports required to be filed by Section 12, 13 or 15(d) of the Securities Exchange Act of 1934 subsequent to the distribution of securities under a plan confirmed by a court. ☐ Yes ☐ No

(APPLICABLE ONLY TO CORPORATE REGISTRANTS)

Indicate the number of shares outstanding of each of the registrant's classes of common stock, as of the latest practicable date.

DOCUMENTS INCORPORATED BY REFERENCE

List hereunder the following documents if incorporated by reference and the Part of the Form 10-K (e.g., Part I, Part II, etc.) into which the document is incorporated: (1) Any annual report to security holders; (2) Any proxy or information statement; and (3) Any prospectus filed pursuant to Rule 424(b) or (c) under the Securities Act of 1933. The listed documents should be clearly described for identification purposes (e.g., annual report to security holders for fiscal year ended December 24, 1980).

OMB APPROVAL	
OMB Number:	3235-0070
Expires:	January 31, 2013
Estimated average burden hours per response	.187.2

UNITED STATES
SECURITIES AND EXCHANGE COMMISSION
Washington, D.C. 20549

FORM 10-Q

(Mark One)

[ ] **QUARTERLY REPORT PURSUANT TO SECTION 13 OR 15(d) OF THE SECURITIES EXCHANGE ACT OF 1934**

For the quarterly period ended ______________________________

or

[ ] **TRANSITION REPORT PURSUANT TO SECTION 13 OR 15(d) OF THE SECURITIES EXCHANGE ACT OF 1934**

For the transition period from ______________________ to ______________________

Commission File Number: ______________________________

____

(Exact name of registrant as specified in its charter)

____

(State or other jurisdiction of incorporation or organization) (I.R.S. Employer Identification No.)

____

(Address of principal executive offices) (Zip Code)

____

(Registrant's telephone number, including area code)

____

(Former name, former address and former fiscal year, if changed since last report)

Indicate by check mark whether the registrant (1) has filed all reports required to be filed by Section 13 or 15(d) of the Securities Exchange Act of 1934 during the preceding 12 months (or for such shorter period that the registrant was required to file such reports), and (2) has been subject to such filing requirements for the past 90 days. ☐ Yes ☐ No

Indicate by check mark whether the registrant has submitted electronically and posted on its corporate Web site, if any, every Interactive Data File required to be submitted and posted pursuant to Rule 405 of Regulation S-T (§232.405 of this chapter) during the preceding 12 months (or for such shorter period that the registrant was required to submit and post such files).
☐ Yes ☐ No

Indicate by check mark whether the registrant is a large accelerated filer, an accelerated filer, a non-accelerated filer, or a smaller reporting company. See the definitions of "large accelerated filer," "accelerated filer" and "smaller reporting company" in Rule 12b-2 of the Exchange Act.

Large accelerated filer ☐ Accelerated filer ☐

Non-accelerated filer ☐ (Do not check if a smaller reporting company) Smaller reporting company ☐

SEC 1296 (01-12) **Potential persons who are to respond to the collection of information contained in this form are not required to respond unless the form displays a currently valid OMB control number.**

4

OMB APPROVAL
OMB Number: 3235-0060 Expires: December 31, 2014 Estimated average burden hours per response........5.00

UNITED STATES
SECURITIES AND EXCHANGE COMMISSION
Washington, D.C. 20549

FORM 8-K

CURRENT REPORT
Pursuant to Section 13 OR 15(d) of The Securities Exchange Act of 1934

Date of Report (Date of earliest event reported) ____________________

____
(Exact name of registrant as specified in its charter)

____

(State or other jurisdiction of incorporation)	(Commission File Number)	(IRS Employer Identification No.)

____

(Address of principal executive offices) (Zip Code)

Registrant's telephone number, including area code ____________________

____
(Former name or former address, if changed since last report.)

Check the appropriate box below if the Form 8-K filing is intended to simultaneously satisfy the filing obligation of the registrant under any of the following provisions (see General Instruction A.2. below):

[ ] Written communications pursuant to Rule 425 under the Securities Act (17 CFR 230.425)

[ ] Soliciting material pursuant to Rule 14a-12 under the Exchange Act (17 CFR 240.14a-12)

[ ] Pre-commencement communications pursuant to Rule 14d-2(b) under the Exchange Act (17 CFR 240.14d-2(b))

[ ] Pre-commencement communications pursuant to Rule 13e-4(c) under the Exchange Act (17 CFR 240.13e-4(c))

GENERAL INSTRUCTIONS

A. Rule as to Use of Form 8-K.

1. Form 8-K shall be used for current reports under Section 13 or 15(d) of the Securities Exchange Act of 1934, filed pursuant to Rule 13a-11 or Rule 15d-11 and for reports of nonpublic information required to be disclosed by Regulation FD (17 CFR 243.100 and243.101).

2. Form 8-K may be used by a registrant to satisfy its filing obligations pursuant to Rule 425 under the Securities Act, regarding written communications related to business combination transactions, or Rules 14a-12(b) or Rule 14d-2(b) under the Exchange Act, relating to soliciting materials and pre-commencement communications pursuant to tender offers, respectively, provided that the Form 8-K filing satisfies all the substantive requirements of those rules (other than the Rule 425(c) requirement to include certain specified information in any prospectus filed pursuant to such rule). Such filing is also deemed to be filed pursuant to any rule for which the box is checked. A registrant is not required to check the box in connection with Rule 14a-12(b) or Rule 14d-2(b) if the communication is filed pursuant to Rule 425. Communications filed pursuant to Rule 425 are deemed filed under the other applicable sections. See Note 2 to Rule 425, Rule 14a-12(b) and Instruction 2 to Rule 14d-2(b)(2).

FORM 3

UNITED STATES SECURITIES AND EXCHANGE COMMISSION
Washington, D.C. 20549
Form 3

INITIAL STATEMENT OF BENEFICIAL OWNERSHIP OF SECURITIES

OMB APPROVAL	
OMB Number:	3235-0104
Expires:	December 31, 2014
Estimated average burden hours per response.	0.5

(Print or Type Responses)

1. Name and Address of Reporting Person*

(Last) (First) (Middle)

(Street)

(City) (State) (Zip)

2. Date of Event Requiring Statement (Month/Day/Year)

3. Issuer Name **and** Ticker or Trading Symbol

4. Relationship of Reporting Person(s) to Issuer (Check all applicable)
_____ Director _____ 10% Owner
_____ Officer (give title below) _____ Other (specify below)
____

5. If Amendment, Date Original Filed (Month/Day/Year)

6. Individual or Joint/Group Filing (Check Applicable Line)
_Form filed by One Reporting Person
_Form filed by More than One Reporting Person

Table I — Non-Derivative Securities Beneficially Owned

1. Title of Security (Instr. 4)	2. Amount of Securities Beneficially Owned (Instr. 4)	3. Ownership Form: Direct (D) or Indirect (I) (Instr. 5)	4. Nature of Indirect Beneficial Ownership (Instr. 5)

Reminder: Report on a separate line for each class of securities beneficially owned directly or indirectly.
* If the form is filed by more than one reporting person, *see* Instruction 5(b)(v).

Potential persons who are to respond to the collection of information contained in this form are not required to respond unless the form displays a currently valid OMB control number.

(Over)
SEC 1473 (11-11)

FORM 3 (continued)

Table II — Derivative Securities Beneficially Owned (*e.g.*, puts, calls, warrants, options, convertible securities)

1. Title of Derivative Security (Instr. 4)	2. Date Exercisable and Expiration Date (Month/Day/Year)		3. Title and Amount of Securities Underlying Derivative Security (Instr. 4)		4. Conversion or Exercise Price of Derivative Security	5. Ownership Form of Derivative Security: Direct (D) or Indirect (I) (Instr. 5)	6. Nature of Indirect Beneficial Ownership (Instr. 5)
	Date Exercisable	Expiration Date	Title	Amount or Number of Shares			

Explanation of Responses:

** Intentional misstatements or omissions of facts constitute Federal Criminal Violations. *See* 18 U.S.C. 1001 and 15 U.S.C. 78ff(a).

Note: File three copies of this Form, one of which must be manually signed. If space is insufficient, *See* Instruction 6 for procedure.

Potential persons who are to respond to the collection of information contained in this form are not required to respond unless the form displays a currently valid OMB Number.

______________________ **Signature of Reporting Person

______________ Date

FORM 4

☐ **Check this box if no longer subject to Section 16. Form 4 or Form 5 obligations may continue. *See* Instruction 1(b).**

(Print or Type Responses)

UNITED STATES SECURITIES AND EXCHANGE COMMISSION
Washington, D.C. 20549

STATEMENT OF CHANGES IN BENEFICIAL OWNERSHIP

OMB APPROVAL	
OMB Number:	3235-0287
Expires:	December 31, 2014
Estimated average burden hours per response.	0.5

1. Name and Address of Reporting Person*	2. Issuer Name and Ticker or Trading Symbol		5. Relationship of Reporting Person(s) to Issuer (Check all applicable) _____ Director _____ 10% Owner _____ Officer (give title below) _____ Other (specify below) ________________
(Last) (First) (Middle)	3. Date of Earliest Transcaction Required to be Reported (Month/Day/Year)	4. If Amendment, Date Original Filed(Month/Day/Year)	
(Street)			6. Individual or Joint/Group Filing (Check Applicable Line) _Form filed by One Reporting Person _Form filed by More than One Reporting Person
(City) (State) (Zip)	**Table I — Non-Derivative Securities Acquired, Disposed of, or Beneficially Owned**		

1. Title of Security (Instr. 3)	2. Trans-action Date (Month/ Day/ Year)	2A. Deemed Execution Date, if any (Month/ Day/Year)	3. Trans-action Code (Instr. 8)		4. Securities Acquired (A) or Disposed of (D) (Instr. 3, 4 and 5)			5. Amount of Securities Beneficially Owned Following Reported Transaction (s) (Instr. 3 and 4)	6. Owner-ship Form: Direct (D) or Indirect (I) (Instr. 4)	7. Nature of Indirect Beneficial Owner-ship (Instr. 4)
			Code	V	Amount	(A) or (D)	Price			

Reminder: Report on a separate line for each class of securities beneficially owned directly or indirectly.
* If the form is filed by more than one reporting person, *see* Instruction 4(b)(v).

Potential persons who are to respond to the collection of information contained in this form are not required to respond unless the form displays a currently valid OMB control number.

(Over)
SEC 1474 (11-11)

FORM 4 (continued)

Table II — Derivative Securities Acquired, Disposed of, or Beneficially Owned
(*e.g.*, puts, calls, warrants, options, convertible securities)

1. Title of Derivative Security (Instr. 3)	2. Conversion or Exercise Price of Derivative Security	3. Transaction Date (Month/ Day/ Year)	3A. Deemed Execution Date, if any (Month/ Day/ Year)	4. Transaction Code (Instr. 8)		5. Number of Derivative Securities Acquired (A) or Disposed of (D) (Instr. 3, 4, and 5)		6. Date Exercisable and Expiration Date (Month/Day/ Year)		7. Title and Amount of Underlying Securities (Instr. 3 and 4)		8. Price of Derivative Security (Instr. 5)	9. Number of derivative Securities Beneficially Owned following Reported Transaction (s)(Instr. 4)	10. Ownership Form of Derivative Security: Direct (D) or Indirect (I) (Instr. 4)	11. Nature of Indirect Beneficial Ownership (Instr. 4)
				Code	V	(A)	(D)	Date Exercisable	Expiration Date	Title	Amount or Number of Shares				

Explanation of Responses:

** Intentional misstatements or omissions of facts constitute Federal Criminal Violations. *See* 18 U.S.C. 1001 and 15 U.S.C. 78ff(a).

____________________ **Signature of Reporting Person

____________ Date

Note: File three copies of this Form, one of which must be manually signed. If space is insufficient, *see* Instruction 6 for procedure.

Potential persons who are to respond to the collection of information contained in this form are not required to respond unless the form displays a currently valid OMB Number.

Page 2

FORM 5

☐ Check box if no longer subject to Section 16. Form 4 or Form 5 obligations may continue. *See* Instruction 1(b).
☐ Form 3 Holdings Reported
☐ Form 4 Transactions Reported

UNITED STATES SECURITIES AND EXCHANGE COMMISSION
Washington, D.C. 20549

ANNUAL STATEMENT OF CHANGES IN BENEFICIAL OWNERSHIP OF SECURITIES

OMB APPROVAL	
OMB Number:	3235-0362
Expires:	January 31,2014
Estimated average burden hours per response.	1.0

1. Name and Address of Reporting Person*	2. Issuer Name **and** Ticker or Trading Symbol		5. Relationship of Reporting Person(s) to Issuer (Check all applicable) ____ Director ____ 10% Owner ____ Officer (give title below) ____ Other (specify below) ________
(Last) (First) (Middle)	3. Statement for Issuer's Fiscal Year Ended (Month//Day/Year)	4. If Amendment, Date Original Filed (Month/Day/Year)	
(Street)			6. Individual or Joint/Group Reporting (check applicable line) ____ Form Filed by One Reporting Person ____ Form Filed by More than One Reporting Person
(City) (State) (Zip)	**Table I — Non-Derivative Securities Acquired, Disposed of, or Beneficially Owned**		

1. Title of Security (Instr. 3)	2. Transaction Date (Month/Day/Year)	2A. Deemed Execution Date, if any (Month/Day/Year)	3. Transaction Code (Instr. 8)	4. Securities Acquired (A) or Disposed of (D) (Instr. 3, 4 and 5)			5. Amount of Securities Beneficially Owned at end of Issuer's Fiscal Year (Instr. 3 and 4)	6. Ownership Form: Direct (D) or Indirect (I) (Instr. 4)	7. Nature of Indirect Beneficial Ownership (Instr. 4)
				Amount	(A) or (D)	Price			

Reminder: Report on a separate line for each class of securities beneficially owned directly or indirectly.
* If the form is filed by more than one reporting person, see instruction 4(b)(v).

Potential persons who are to respond to the collection of information contained in this form are not required to respond unless the form displays a currently valid OMB control number.

(Over)
SEC2270(11-11)

FORM 5 (continued)

Table II — Derivative Securities Acquired, Disposed of, or Beneficially Owned
(*e.g.*, puts, calls, warrants, options, convertible securities)

1. Title of Derivative Security (Instr. 3)	2. Conversion or Exercise Price of Derivative Security	3. Transaction Date (Month/Day/Year)	3A. Deemed Execution Date, if any (Month/Day/Year)	4. Transaction Code (Instr. 8)	5. Number of Derivative Securities Acquired (A) or Disposed of (D) (Instr. 3, 4, and 5)		6. Date Exercisable and Expiration Date (Month/Day/Year)		7. Title and Amount of Underlying Securities (Instr. 3 and 4)		8. Price of Derivative Security (Instr. 5)	9. Number of Derivative Securities Beneficially Owned at End of Issuer's Fiscal Year (Instr. 4)	10. Ownership Form of Derivative Securities: Direct (D) or Indirect (I) (Instr. 4)	11. Nature of Indirect Beneficial Ownership (Instr. 4)
					(A)	(D)	Date Exercisable	Expiration Date	Title	Amount or Number of Shares				

Explanation of Responses:

________________________ ________________
** Signature of Reporting Person Date

** Intentional misstatements or omissions of facts constitute Federal Criminal Violations.
See 18 U.S.C. 1001 and 15 U.S.C. 78ff(a).

Note: File three copies of this Form, one of which must be manually signed.
If space provided is insufficient, *see* Instruction 6 for procedure.

Potential persons who are to respond to the collection of information contained in this form are not required to respond unless the form displays a currently valid OMB number.

Page 2

You may not send a completed printout of this form to the SEC to satisfy a filing obligation. You can only satisfy an SEC filing obligation by submitting the information required by this form to the SEC in electronic format online at https://www.onlineforms.edgarfiling.sec.gov.

FORM D

Notice of Exempt Offering of Securities

U.S. Securities and Exchange Commission

Washington, DC 20549

(See instructions beginning on page 5)

Intentional misstatements or omissions of fact constitute federal criminal violations. See 18 U.S.C. 1001.

OMB APPROVAL	
OMB Number:	3235-0076
Expires:	June 30, 2012
Estimated average burden hours per response:	4.00

Item 1. Issuer's Identity

Name of Issuer

Jurisdiction of Incorporation/Organization

Previous Name(s) ☐ None

Entity Type (Select one)

- ☐ Corporation
- ☐ Limited Partnership
- ☐ Limited Liability Company
- ☐ General Partnership
- ☐ Business Trust
- ☐ Other (Specify)

Year of Incorporation/Organization (Select one)

◯ Over Five Years Ago ◯ Within Last Five Years (specify year) ◯ Yet to Be Formed

(If more than one issuer is filing this notice, check this box ☐ and identify additional issuer(s) by attaching Items 1 and 2 Continuation Page(s).)

Item 2. Principal Place of Business and Contact Information

Street Address 1

Street Address 2

City

State/Province/Country

ZIP/Postal Code

Phone No.

Item 3. Related Persons

Last Name

First Name

Middle Name

Street Address 1

Street Address 2

City

State/Province/Country

ZIP/Postal Code

Relationship(s): ☐ Executive Officer ☐ Director ☐ Promoter

Clarification of Response (if Necessary)

(Identify additional related persons by checking this box ☐ and attaching Item 3 Continuation Page(s).)

Item 4. Industry Group (Select one)

◯ **Agriculture**

Banking and Financial Services

- ◯ Commercial Banking
- ◯ Insurance
- ◯ Investing
- ◯ Investment Banking
- ◯ Pooled Investment Fund

If selecting this industry group, also select one fund type below and answer the question below:

- ◯ Hedge Fund
- ◯ Private Equity Fund
- ◯ Venture Capital Fund
- ◯ Other Investment Fund

Is the issuer registered as an investment company under the Investment Company Act of 1940? ◯ Yes ◯ No

◯ Other Banking & Financial Services

◯ **Business Services**

Energy

- ◯ Electric Utilities
- ◯ Energy Conservation
- ◯ Coal Mining
- ◯ Environmental Services
- ◯ Oil & Gas
- ◯ Other Energy

Health Care

- ◯ Biotechnology
- ◯ Health Insurance
- ◯ Hospitals & Physcians
- ◯ Pharmaceuticals
- ◯ Other Health Care

◯ **Manufacturing**

Real Estate

- ◯ Commercial
- ◯ Construction
- ◯ REITS & Finance
- ◯ Residential
- ◯ Other Real Estate

◯ **Retailing**

◯ **Restaurants**

Technology

- ◯ Computers
- ◯ Telecommunications
- ◯ Other Technology

Travel

- ◯ Airlines & Airports
- ◯ Lodging & Conventions
- ◯ Tourism & Travel Services
- ◯ Other Travel

◯ **Other**

FORM D

U.S. Securities and Exchange Commission
Washington, DC 20549

Item 5. Issuer Size (Select one)

Revenue Range (for issuer not specifying "hedge" or "other investment" fund in Item 4 above)

- ◯ No Revenues
- ◯ $1 - $1,000,000
- ◯ $1,000,001 - $5,000,000
- ◯ $5,000,001 - $25,000,000
- ◯ $25,000,001 - $100,000,000
- ◯ Over $100,000,000
- ◯ Decline to Disclose
- ◯ Not Applicable

OR

Aggregate Net Asset Value Range (for issuer specifying "hedge" or "other investment" fund in Item 4 above)

- ◯ No Aggregate Net Asset Value
- ◯ $1 - $5,000,000
- ◯ $5,000,001 - $25,000,000
- ◯ $25,000,001 - $50,000,000
- ◯ $50,000,001 - $100,000,000
- ◯ Over $100,000,000
- ◯ Decline to Disclose
- ◯ Not Applicable

Item 6. Federal Exemptions and Exclusions Claimed (Select all that apply)

- ☐ Rule 504(b)(1) (not (i), (ii) or (iii))
- ☐ Rule 504(b)(1)(i)
- ☐ Rule 504(b)(1)(ii)
- ☐ Rule 504(b)(1)(iii)
- ☐ Rule 505
- ☐ Rule 506
- ☐ Securities Act Section 4(6)

Investment Company Act Section 3(c)

- ☐ Section 3(c)(1)
- ☐ Section 3(c)(2)
- ☐ Section 3(c)(3)
- ☐ Section 3(c)(4)
- ☐ Section 3(c)(5)
- ☐ Section 3(c)(6)
- ☐ Section 3(c)(7)
- ☐ Section 3(c)(9)
- ☐ Section 3(c)(10)
- ☐ Section 3(c)(11)
- ☐ Section 3(c)(12)
- ☐ Section 3(c)(13)
- ☐ Section 3(c)(14)

Item 7. Type of Filing

◯ New Notice **OR** ◯ Amendment

Date of First Sale in this Offering: ________ **OR** ☐ First Sale Yet to Occur

Item 8. Duration of Offering

Does the issuer intend this offering to last more than one year? ☐ Yes ☐ No

Item 9. Type(s) of Securities Offered (Select all that apply)

- ☐ Equity
- ☐ Debt
- ☐ Option, Warrant or Other Right to Acquire Another Security
- ☐ Security to be Acquired Upon Exercise of Option, Warrant or Other Right to Acquire Security
- ☐ Pooled Investment Fund Interests
- ☐ Tenant-in-Common Securities
- ☐ Mineral Property Securities
- ☐ Other (Describe)

Item 10. Business Combination Transaction

Is this offering being made in connection with a business combination transaction, such as a merger, acquisition or exchange offer? ☐ Yes ☐ No

Clarification of Response (if Necessary)

Form D 2

FORM D U.S. Securities and Exchange Commission
Washington, DC 20549

Item 11. Minimum Investment

Minimum investment accepted from any outside investor $ [ ]

Item 12. Sales Compensation

Recipient [ ]

Recipient CRD Number [ ] ☐ No CRD Number

(Associated) Broker or Dealer ☐ None [ ]

(Associated) Broker or Dealer CRD Number [ ] ☐ No CRD Number

Street Address 1 [ ]

Street Address 2 [ ]

City [ ]

State/Province/Country [ ]

ZIP/Postal Code [ ]

States of Solicitation ☐ All States

☐ AL	☐ AK	☐ AZ	☐ AR	☐ CA	☐ CO	☐ CT	☐ DE	☐ DC	☐ FL	☐ GA	☐ HI	☐ ID
☐ IL	☐ IN	☐ IA	☐ KS	☐ KY	☐ LA	☐ ME	☐ MD	☐ MA	☐ MI	☐ MN	☐ MS	☐ MO
☐ MT	☐ NE	☐ NV	☐ NH	☐ NJ	☐ NM	☐ NY	☐ NC	☐ ND	☐ OH	☐ OK	☐ OR	☐ PA
☐ RI	☐ SC	☐ SD	☐ TN	☐ TX	☐ UT	☐ VT	☐ VA	☐ WA	☐ WV	☐ WI	☐ WY	☐ PR

(Identify additional person(s) being paid compensation by checking this box ☐ and attaching Item 12 Continuation Page(s).)

Item 13. Offering and Sales Amounts

(a) Total Offering Amount $ [ ] **OR** ☐ Indefinite

(b) Total Amount Sold $ [ ]

(c) Total Remaining to be Sold (Subtract (a) from (b)) $ [ ] **OR** ☐ Indefinite

Clarification of Response (if Necessary)

[ ]

Item 14. Investors

Check this box ☐ if securities in the offering have been or may be sold to persons who do not qualify as accredited investors, and enter the number of such non-accredited investors who already have invested in the offering: [ ]

Enter the total number of investors who already have invested in the offering: [ ]

Item 15. Sales Commissions and Finders' Fees Expenses

Provide separately the amounts of sales commissions and finders' fees expenses, if any. If an amount is not known, provide an estimate and check the box next to the amount.

Sales Commissions $ [ ] ☐ Estimate

Finders' Fees $ [ ] ☐ Estimate

Clarification of Response (if Necessary)

[ ]

Form D 3

INDEX

A

B

C

D

E

F

G

H

I

J

L

M

N

O

P

Q

R

S

T

U

V

W

Y

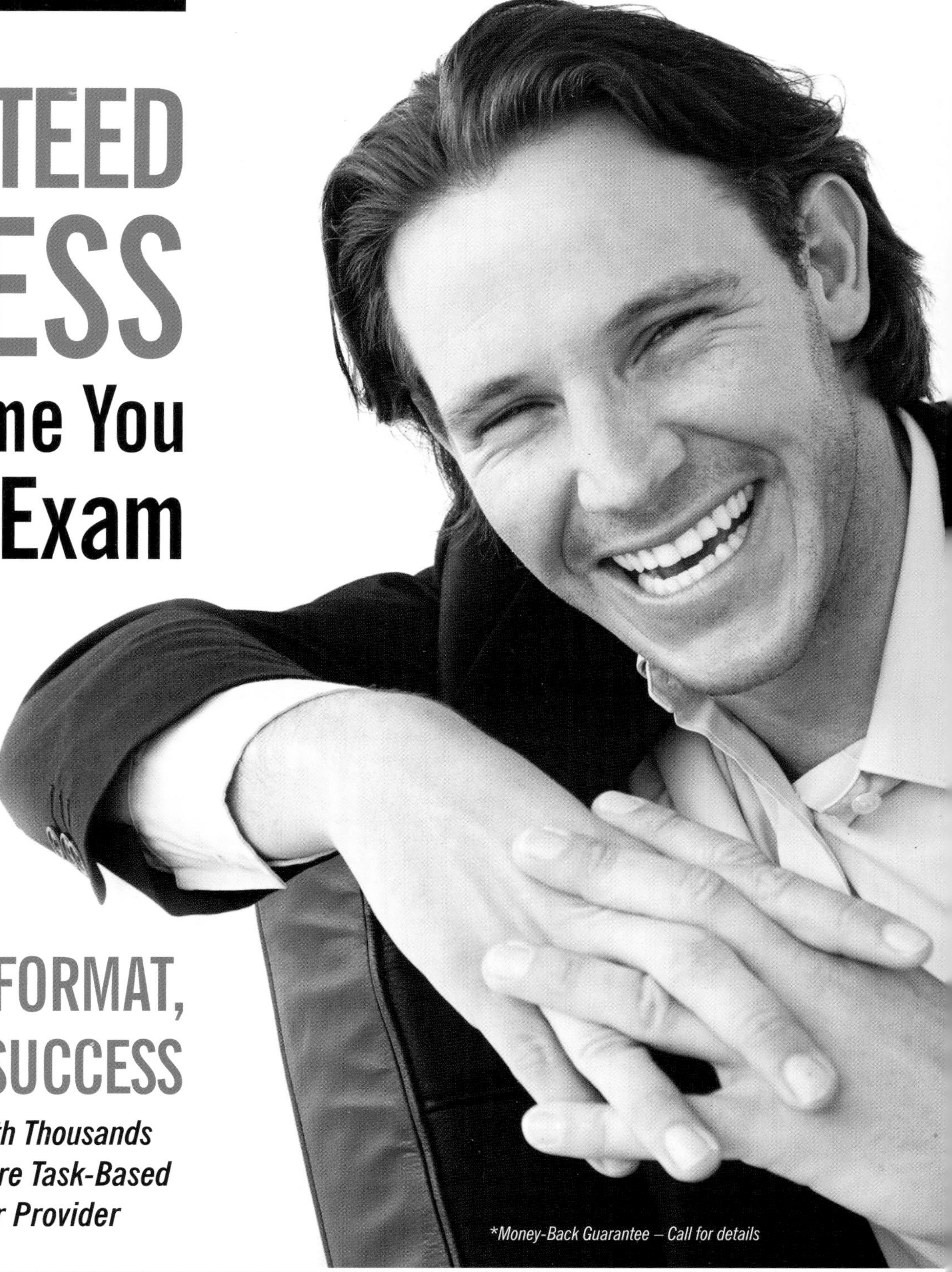

2

HOT • SPOT™ DVDs

Weak in a specific area? Master it with your choice of topic-specific videos ... they're perfect for rounding out those rough spots before you sit for the exam!

These videos provide extensive coverage of the toughest, most challenging and most frequently tested topics within each of the four sections of the computer-based CPA exam – Financial Accounting & Reporting, Auditing & Attestation, Business Environment & Concepts, and Regulation.

Featuring America's best CPA review instructor – Bob Monette, JD, CPA, who uses humor to help you remember his problem-solving tips – each video is packed with valuable exam strategies and comes with a comprehensive viewer's guide for easy reference.

- Order just the titles you need (topic-specific videos available)
- Each video provides extensive coverage of a specific topic area
- Each video focuses on the toughest, most challenging and most frequently tested topics on the computer-based CPA exam
- Each video comes with a comprehensive viewer's guide

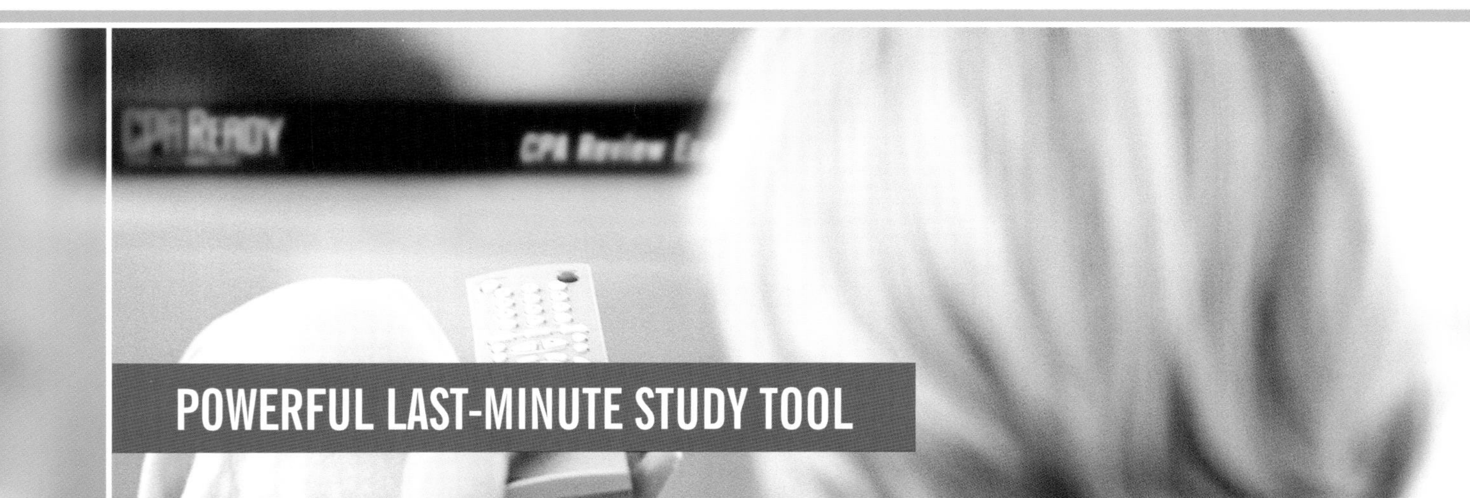

CALL NOW 888-CPA-BISK